THE NEW
AMERICAN
COMMENTARY

An Exegetical and Theological
Exposition of Holy Scripture

THE NEW
AMERICAN
COMMENTARY

Volume
24

LUKE

Robert H. Stein

PUBLISHING GROUP

Nashville, Tennessee

© Copyright 1992 • B&H Publishing Group
All rights reserved
ISBN: 978-08054-0124-0
Dewey Decimal Classification: 226.4
Subject Heading: BIBLE. N.T. LUKE
Library of Congress Catalog Card Number: 92-30024
Printed in the United States of America
16 15 14 13 12   15 14 13 12 11

Library of Congress Cataloging-in-Publication Data
Stein, Robert H., 1935–
  Luke / Robert H. Stein.
    p.   cm.—(The New American commentary; v. 24)
  Includes indexes.
  ISBN 0-8054-0124-5
  1. Bible. N.T. Luke—Commentaries. I. Bible. N.T. Luke. English. New International. 1992.
II. Title. III. Series.
BS2595.3.S74   1992
226.407—dc20

To

JOAN

O Lord . . . Grant that she and I may find mercy
and grow old together

Tobit 8:7b

Editors' Preface

God's Word does not change. God's world, however, changes in every generation. These changes, in addition to new findings by scholars and a new variety of challenges to the gospel message, call for the church in each generation to interpret and apply God's Word for God's people. Thus, THE NEW AMERICAN COMMENTARY is introduced to bridge the twentieth and twenty-first centuries. This new series has been designed primarily to enable pastors, teachers, and students to read the Bible with clarity and proclaim it with power.

In one sense THE NEW AMERICAN COMMENTARY is not new, for it represents the continuation of a heritage rich in biblical and theological exposition. The title of this forty-volume set points to the continuity of this series with an important commentary project published at the end of the nineteenth century called AN AMERICAN COMMENTARY, edited by Alvah Hovey. The older series included, among other significant contributions, the outstanding volume on Matthew by John A. Broadus, from whom the publisher of the new series, Broadman Press, partly derives its name. The former series was authored and edited by scholars committed to the infallibility of Scripture, making it a solid foundation for the present project. In line with this heritage, all NAC authors affirm the divine inspiration, inerrancy, complete truthfulness, and full authority of the Bible. The perspective of the NAC is unapologetically confessional and rooted in the evangelical tradition.

Since a commentary is a fundamental tool for the expositor or teacher who seeks to interpret and apply Scripture in the church or classroom, the NAC focuses on communicating the theological structure and content of each biblical book. The writers seek to illuminate both the historical meaning and contemporary significance of Holy Scripture.

In its attempt to make a unique contribution to the Christian community, the NAC focuses on two concerns. First, the commentary emphasizes how each section of a book fits together so that the reader becomes aware of the theological unity of each book and of Scripture as a whole. The writers, however, remain aware of the Bible's inherently rich variety. Second, the NAC is produced with the conviction that the Bible primarily belongs to the church.

We believe that scholarship and the academy provide an indispensable foundation for biblical understanding and the service of Christ, but the editors and authors of this series have attempted to communicate the findings of their research in a manner that will build up the whole body of Christ. Thus, the commentary concentrates on theological exegesis, while providing practical, applicable exposition.

THE NEW AMERICAN COMMENTARY's theological focus enables the reader to see the parts as well as the whole of Scripture. The biblical books vary in content, context, literary type, and style. In addition to this rich variety, the editors and authors recognize that the doctrinal emphasis and use of the biblical books differs in various places, contexts, and cultures among God's people. These factors, as well as other concerns, have led the editors to give freedom to the writers to wrestle with the issues raised by the scholarly community surrounding each book and to determine the appropriate shape and length of the introductory materials. Moreover, each writer has developed the structure of the commentary in a way best suited for expounding the basic structure and the meaning of the biblical books for our day. Generally, discussions relating to contemporary scholarship and technical points of grammar and syntax appear in the footnotes and not in the text of the commentary. This format allows pastors and interested laypersons, scholars and teachers, and serious college and seminary students to profit from the commentary at various levels. This approach has been employed because we believe that all Christians have the privilege and responsibility to read and seek to understand the Bible for themselves.

Consistent with the desire to produce a readable, up-to-date commentary, the editors selected the *New International Version* as the standard translation for the commentary series. The selection was made primarily because of the NIV's faithfulness to the original languages and its beautiful and readable style. The authors, however, have been given the liberty to differ at places from the NIV as they develop their own translations from the Greek and Hebrew texts.

The NAC reflects the vision and leadership of those who provide oversight for Broadman Press, who in 1987 called for a new commentary series that would evidence a commitment to the inerrancy of Scripture and a faithfulness to the classic Christian tradition. While the commentary adopts an "American" name, it should be noted some writers represent countries outside the United States, giving the commentary an international perspective. The diverse group of writers includes scholars, teachers, and administrators from almost twenty different colleges and seminaries, as well as pastors, missionaries, and a layperson.

The editors and writers hope that THE NEW AMERICAN COMMENTARY will be helpful and instructive for pastors and teachers, scholars and students, for men and women in the churches who study and teach God's Word in various settings. We trust that for editors, authors, and readers alike, the commentary will be used to build up the church, encourage obedience, and bring renewal to God's people. Above all, we pray that the NAC will bring glory and honor to our Lord who has graciously redeemed us and faithfully revealed himself to us in his Holy Word.

SOLI DEO GLORIA
The Editors

Author's Preface

In this commentary the author of the Third Gospel is viewed as an authoritative spokesman of the Gospel tradition. It is unnecessary to choose between whether he is a "historian" or a "theologian," for such a disjunction is neither necessary nor accurate. He is both! Luke's interest in history is shown by his tying the Jesus events to the events of his day (2:1-2; 3:1-2) and his desire to help his readers know the certainty of the traditions which they had been taught (1:4). Yet the Evangelist, led by the Spirit, not only recounts these historical traditions but interprets them as well. Thus he presents to Theophilus not just a collection of *brute facts* but something even more valuable—the *meaning* of those facts.

The primary goal of the commentary is to assist the readers in understanding what Luke seeks to teach by the traditions found in his Gospel. One can study a Gospel in order to learn about the life and teachings of Jesus, the early church which preserved those traditions, the sources used by the Evangelist, the history of the traditions found in those sources, etc. In the present commentary, however, the study of each passage focuses on the question of what Luke is seeking to teach Theophilus by the passage. Thus after introducing the readers each time to the "Context" surrounding a passage and providing various exegetical "Comments" on the material, the final section of each passage is entitled "The Lukan Message." In this section the commentary seeks to complete the following paradigm: "I, Luke, have told you, Theophilus, how that . . . [the passage being discussed], *because . . ."* In *"The Lukan Message" the focus of attention is upon the because.* In so doing the object of investigation is not so much on what happened but rather on how Luke interpreted what happened, i.e., on the meaning of what is being reported.

Numerous references are cited within the commentary which cast light on the passages being discussed. These are usually found in parentheses such as (2:22-24), (contrast Mark 15:15; Matt 27:26), (cf. Lev 5:7; 6:23; Ezek 43:21), (cf. 9:22; 24:46; Acts 1:3; 3:18; etc.), etc. At times the reader will also come across "See comments on 4:15; 6:47" and "See Introduction 7 (2)," and so forth. The reader is encouraged to look up these passages or sections in the commentary because at these locations there is a more detailed discussion of this or a related subject that will be of value for understanding the present passage.

I would like to thank my teaching assistants Jeannine Brown, Alison Bucklin, and Luiz Gustavo da Silva Goncalves, along with my colleague Dr. Tom Schreiner, for their help in reading the earlier manuscripts of the commentary. Their suggestions and criticisms have made this a much more readable and useful work. I also want to thank Gloria Metz, the faculty secretary, for her invaluable assistance. I never cease admiring her skills. Her help in rescuing me on numerous occasions from confrontations with my word processor is most appreciated, as is her editorial work in preparing the final draft submitted to the publisher. Finally, I want to express my thanks to and for my wife, Joan, without whom this work could not have been written.

Abbreviations

Bible Books

Gen	Isa	Luke
Exod	Jer	John
Lev	Lam	Acts
Num	Ezek	Rom
Deut	Dan	1,2 Cor
Josh	Hos	Gal
Judg	Joel	Eph
Ruth	Amos	Phil
1,2 Sam	Obad	Col
1,2 Kgs	Jonah	1,2 Thess
1,2 Chr	Mic	1,2 Tim
Ezra	Nah	Titus
Neh	Hab	Phlm
Esth	Zeph	Heb
Job	Hag	Jas
Ps (*pl.* Pss)	Zech	1,2 Pet
Prov	Mal	1,2,3 John
Eccl	Matt	Jude
Song of Songs	Mark	Rev

Apocrypha

Add Esth	Additions to the Book of Esther
Bar	Baruch
Bel	Bel and the Dragon
1,2 Esdr	1,2 Esdras
4 Ezra	4 Ezra
Jdt	Judith
Ep Jer	Epistle of Jeremiah
1,2,3,4 Macc	1,2,3,4 Maccabees
Pr Azar	Prayer of Azariah and the Song of the Three Jews
Pr Man	Prayer of Manasseh
Sir	Sirach, Ecclesiasticus
Sus	Susannah
Tob	Tobit
Wis	Wisdom of Solomon

Commonly Used Sources

AB	Anchor Bible
ACNT	Augsburg Commentary on the New Testament
AnBib	Analecta biblica
B. Bat.	*Baba Batra*
Ber.	*Berakot*
Bib	*Biblica*
B. Meş	*Baba Meşi'a*
CBQ	*Catholic Biblical Quarterly*
CD	*Cairo* (Genizah text of the) *Damascus Document*
Did.	*Didache*
EBC	Expositor's Bible Commentary
EvQ	*Evangelical Quarterly*
GNS	Good News Studies
HTR	*Harvard Theological Review*
ICC	International Critical Commentary
it	Itala, or Old Latin
JBL	*Journal of Biblical Literature*
JSNTSup	*Journal for the Study of the New Testament—Supplement Series*
JTS	*Journal of Theological Studies*
NAC	The New American Commentary
NCB	New Century Bible
NIGTC	The New International Greek Testament Commentary
NovT	*Novum Testamentum*
NTS	*New Testament Studies*
1QM	*War Scroll* from Qumran Cave 1
1QpHab	*Pesher on Habakkuk* from Qumran Cave 1
1QS	*Rule of the Community, Manual of Discipline* from Qumran Cave 1
SBT	Studies in Biblical Theology
SBLDS	SBL Dissertation Series
SNTSMS	Society for New Testament Studies Monograph Series
TPINTC	Trinity Press International New Testament Commentaries
TDNT	G. Kittel and G. Friedrich, eds., *Theological Dictionary of the New Testament*
Tg. Onq.	*Targum Onqelos* (also *Onkelos*)
Tg. Ps-J.	*Targum Pseudo-Jonathan*
WBC	Word Biblical Commentary
WUNT	Wissenschaftliche Untersuchungen zum Neuen Testament
Vg	Vulgate
ZNW	*Zeitschrift für die neutestamentliche Wissenschaft*

Contents

Introduction 19
   I. The Prologue (1:1–4) 62
  II. The Infancy Narrative (1:5–2:52) 69
 III. The Preparation of Jesus' Ministry (3:1–4:15) 125
 IV. Jesus' Ministry in Galilee (4:16–9:50) 151
  V. Jesus' Journey to Jerusalem (9:51–19:27). 295
 VI. Jesus' Ministry in Jerusalem (19:28–21:38). 476
 VII. Jesus' Passion (22:1–23:56) 533
VIII. The Resurrection and Ascension of Jesus (24:1–53) 602

Selected Subject Index 626
Person Index 628
Selected Scripture Index 630
Selected Bibliography. 653

Luke

─────────────── *INTRODUCTION OUTLINE* ───────────────

1. Authorship
   (1) Internal Evidence
   (2) Church Tradition
   (3) The "We" Sections
   (4) Conclusion
2. The Date of Luke
3. The Audience of Luke
4. The Place of Origin
5. The Sources of Luke
6. An Outline of Luke
7. The Purpose of Luke
   (1) To Help Convince His Readers of the Truthfulness of What They Had Been Taught
   (2) To Clarify the Christian Self-understanding of His Readers
   (3) To Clarify Jesus' Teachings concerning the End Times
   (4) To Assure Readers That Rome Was Not a Threat to Them
8. The Lukan Theological Emphases
   (1) The Sovereign Rule of God over History
   (2) The Kingdom of God
   (3) The Holy Spirit
   (4) Christology
   (5) The Last Shall Be First—The Great Reversal
   (6) The Call to Salvation
   (7) The Christian Life
   (8) The Atonement
9. The Goal of This Commentary

─────────────── **INTRODUCTION** ───────────────

1. Authorship

The authorship of the Gospel of Luke was never disputed until the second half of the nineteenth century. Yet it should be observed that Luke and Acts are two of the nine books in the NT canon that are anonymous.[1]

---

[1] The others are Matthew; Mark; John; Hebrews; 1, 2, 3 John.

19

Evidence for the authorship of Luke comes essentially from three main areas: internal evidence, church tradition, and the "we" sections of Acts.

(1) Internal Evidence

Several clues about the author of Luke-Acts can be found within the works themselves. One such clue is found in Luke 1:2, where the author relates how he ("us") received ("was handed down") information for his Gospel from those who were "eyewitnesses and ministers of the word." From this it is clear that the author of Luke-Acts was not an apostle or follower of Jesus during his ministry. The same prologue shows the author was a well-educated person who intended his writings to be understood as a serious literary and historical work. The author apparently was a Gentile Christian, since he avoided Semitic words (cf. 6:14; 8:54; 22:42; 23:45) and omitted various traditions dealing with intra-Jewish controversies.[2] The strongest evidence of Gentile authorship is his reference to Jews, which suggests he was not part of this group.[3] This is also supported by Col 4:10-14, if this Luke was the actual author of Luke-Acts.

In the nineteenth century W. K. Hobart sought to demonstrate that the author of Luke-Acts was a physician and thus to support the tradition that the author was Luke, the "beloved physician" (Col 4:14).[4] Evidence for this was found in the medical interests and language of Luke-Acts.[5] Luke's interest in healing is evident from the fact that he recorded all the Markan healing accounts, shared with Matthew the healing of the centurion's slave in Luke 7:1-10, and had five healings unique to his Gospel (7:11-17; 13:10-17; 14:1-6; 17:11-19; 22:51). Furthermore the terminology Luke used in these accounts has close parallels with the ancient Greek medical writers such as Hippocrates, Galen, and Dioscorides. Hobart's reasoning, however, was refuted by H. J. Cadbury in his doctoral thesis. Cadbury demonstrated that the language of Luke-Acts was no more "medical" than that of educated nonmedical writers such as Josephus, Lucian, or Plutarch. Thus the medical language of Luke-Acts does not prove that the author was in fact a physician, although such terminology and interests fit well the view that the author of this two-part work was Luke, the physician.[6]

---

[2]Cf. Mark 7:1-23; 10:1-12; Matt 5:33-42; 6:1-6,16-18; 17:24-27.

[3]Cf. Luke 4:44; 23:51; Acts 10:39; 13:5; 14:1; 17:1; 21:11.

[4]See W. K. Hobart, *The Medical Language of St. Luke* (Dublin: Hodges, Figgis, & Co., 1882).

[5]Cf. such passages as Luke 4:38; 5:12,18,24,31; 6:18; 8:44; 10:34-35; 13:11,32; Acts 3:7; 5:5,10; 9:33; 12:23; 28:8. Cf. also Luke 8:43, which omits the negative comment about doctors found in Mark 5:26.

[6]See H. J. Cadbury, *The Style and Literary Method of Luke* (Cambridge: Harvard University Press, 1920), 39-72.

(2) Church Tradition

The church tradition for the Lukan authorship of Luke-Acts is early and unanimous. Possibly the earliest references to Luke as the author of Luke-Acts are to be found in the Bodmer Papyrus (𝔓75) and the Muratorian Canon. The oldest Greek manuscript of Luke (𝔓75) dates at the end of the second century and contains the title "Gospel according to Luke" at the end of the Gospel. The Muratorian Canon (ca. 170–180) reads: "The third book of the Gospel: According to Luke. This Luke was a physician." About the same time (ca. 185) Irenaeus (*Against Heresies* 3.1.1; 3.14.1) referred to Luke, the companion of Paul, as the author. The so-called Anti-Marcionite Prologue also refers to Luke as a physician and a Syrian from Antioch.[7] About 208 Tertullian (*Against Marcion* 4.2.2; 4.2.5; 4.5.3) mentioned Luke, a follower of Paul, as the author of the Third Gospel. Lukan authorship was also attested by Clement of Alexandria, Origen, Eusebius, Jerome, and other early church fathers.

Such unanimity in the tradition is impressive. Although care must be taken not to equate tradition with truth, readers should also be careful not to be so cynical as to reject such testimony simply because of dislike for anything traditional. In general such uncontested and ancient tradition should be accepted unless there is good reason to the contrary. This is especially so when it names a minor figure in the early church and a non-apostle as the author of over one quarter of the entire NT.[8]

(3) The "We" Sections

The third major area involved in the discussion of authorship is the "we" sections found in Acts 16:10-17; 20:5–21:18; 27:1–28:16. The common authorship of Luke-Acts is accepted by almost all.[9] The Gospel

---

[7] Some scholars find support for this in Luke's knowledge of the Antiochian church community in Acts 11:19-20; 13:1-4; 14:26-28; 15:1-3,13-40; 18:22-23.

[8] Contrast how many of the later apocryphal gospels, such as the gospels of Philip, Thomas, Judas, Bartholomew, or the Twelve Apostles, claim apostolic authorship.

[9] The reason for this is clear when one compares the two works:

a. Both begin with a similar preface (Luke 1:1-4; Acts 1:1-5).

b. Both are addressed to the same person, Theophilus (Luke 1:3; Acts 1:1).

c. Acts 1:1 serves as a recapitulation of the material found in Luke.

d. Acts begins where Luke leaves off temporally, i.e., at Jesus' ascension (Luke 24:50-51; Acts 1:9-10).

e. Acts begins where Luke leaves off geographically, i.e., in Jerusalem (Luke 24:52-53; Acts 1:9-10).

f. Acts begins with the same situation with which Luke ends, i.e., the disciples waiting for the coming of the Spirit (Luke 24:49; Acts 1:4-5,8).

g. There is a clear parallelism between the arrangement of Luke and that of Acts: an introductory period typified by prayer (Luke 1:5–2:32; Acts 1:6-26) followed by the coming

of Luke was written with Acts in mind, for without Acts the plan of the Gospel would be incomplete. And Acts was plainly written in light of and to complete the Gospel of Luke. The author of Luke-Acts claimed in the "we" passages to have been a companion of Paul during certain periods in the apostle's ministry. Traditionally the "we" sections have been understood as eyewitness accounts stemming from the author's own experience. Recently an attempt has been made to see in these "we" sections a sea-voyage genre used by the author, who was not an actual participant of the events recorded in these sections.[10] Yet more careful investigation of the passages that supposedly demonstrate the use of "we" passages in such a genre has revealed no such documented use.[11] Many of the "we" passages furthermore have nothing to do with a sea voyage (cf. Acts 16:13-17; 20:7-12,18-38; 28:2-10a), and numerous sea passages in Acts have no "we" style (cf. 13:4-5,13; 14:25-26; 17:14-15; 18:18,21; 20:1-2).

Other interpretations that deny the author's participation in the events of the "we" sections assert that the author used another's eyewitness source or that this was simply a fraudulent claim on the author's part to have been a participant in certain events. These interpretations, however, do not arise out of an exegesis of the text itself but are imposed upon the text because of the interpreter's presupposition that the author of Acts could not have known Paul or been an eyewitness to these events. Yet such a fictitious "we" is almost without parallel in the literature of its day and would have contradicted the author's intention in Luke 1:1-4 that his work be taken seriously. This is especially true if Theophilus knew Luke personally. Since the "we" sections appear incidentally in Acts and without any literary pretense, it is most difficult to think of them as a contrived deception or ploy by the author. The author clearly wanted his readers to believe he was a participant in the events of the "we" sections.

The main objection for taking the "we" sections at face value is a historical-critical one. For one, certain historical discrepancies between Acts and the Pauline Letters are said to exist, such as the accounts of the Jerusalem Council (cf. Acts 15:1-29 and Gal 2:1-10). It is also believed that

---

of the Spirit in fulfillment of prophecy (Luke 3; Acts 2), followed by a thematic sermon (Luke 4:14-30; Acts 2:14-40).

h. Both share a common vocabulary, style, structure, and theological concern.

[10] See V. K. Robbins, "By Land and By Sea: The We-Passages and Ancient Sea Voyages" in *Perspectives on Luke-Acts*, ed. C. H. Talbert (Danville: Association of Baptist Professors of Religion, 1978), 215-42; and E. Plümacher, "Wirklichkeitserfahrung und Geschichtsschreibung bei Lukas," *ZNW* 68 (1977): 2-22.

[11] See C. J. Hemer, *The Book of Acts in the Setting of Hellenistic History* (Tübingen: J. C. B. Mohr, 1989), 308-64; C. K. Barrett, "Paul Shipwrecked" in *Scripture: Meaning and Method*, ed. B. P. Thompson (Hull, England: University Press, 1987), 52-56; J. A. Fitzmyer, *Luke the Theologian* (New York: Paulist, 1989), 17-32.

the theology of Paul and Luke-Acts is so different and that the theology attributed to Paul in Acts is so different from that of the Pauline Letters that the writer of Luke-Acts could not have known, and still less been a companion of, the apostle Paul. Supposedly the differences in such areas as Christology, eschatology, soteriology, the law, Paul's apostleship, and natural theology are simply too diverse.

In response to these objections, significant differences between the theology of these two writers cannot be denied. Clearly the author of Luke-Acts was not the protégé of Paul. Yet the author of the "we" sections is not portrayed in Acts as a protégé or disciple of Paul but as one of several companions of the apostle. He was furthermore not a companion of Paul during the major debates on justification by faith. His actual time with Paul also may have been considerably less than sometimes imagined. In addition the author probably did not write his works until perhaps two decades after events narrated in the last "we" section, so that one would expect various differences to exist. One must also allow that personal differences in emphasis and situation might play an important role in how each author formulated his works. Differences of emphasis do exist between the author of Luke-Acts and Paul, but one should not overlook the broader unity underlying both sets of writings. The writer of Luke, like Paul, knew that justification is by grace (Luke 18:13-14) and that Jesus has been exalted as Lord (24:25-26). And Paul knew that the baptism of the Spirit (1 Cor 12:13) is the distinguishing mark of the believer (Rom 8:9-11).

If the author of Acts was Paul's companion, he quite likely was one of those Paul listed in his letters, especially in the letters written during the "we" periods of his ministry. Eliminating those companions of Paul mentioned in the third person in the "we" sections of Acts (and thus distinguished from the author, cf. Acts 20:4-5), we arrive at a number of possibilities. Among these is Luke (cf. Col 4:14; Phil 24; 2 Tim 4:11).

(4) Conclusion

In light of the universal voice of tradition and the author's claim to be Paul's companion, the case for Lukan authorship of Luke-Acts is quite strong. It is furthermore quite probable that this Luke is identical with Luke, the beloved physician and Paul's companion in Col 4:14. To what other Luke would the tradition be referring? Other traditions, such as Luke's being a resident of Syrian Antioch, that he was unmarried, or that he died in Boeotia, are much more questionable.[12]

How valuable or important is the establishment of Lukan authorship for the understanding of the Third Gospel? It may seem strange after our discussion of authorship to realize that whether the author of Luke-Acts

---

[12] For further discussion see J. Wenham, "The Identification of Luke," *EvQ* 63 (1991): 3-44.

was Luke or someone else, the meaning of Luke-Acts remains the same. The Third Gospel means what its author intended it to mean. Whoever the author was, he meant to share with his readers his understanding of the life and teaching of Jesus Christ. That meaning can only be obtained from the text he has given us. If knowing his name were essential for understanding his work, he would have included it. Yet no Gospel writer believed that knowing his name was essential for understanding his work since all the Gospels are anonymous. The Third Gospel has the same meaning whether the author's name was Luke or Julius! Thus the meaning of this Gospel is obtained by knowing the range of meanings of the words used, the possibilities of the grammar, and how the grammatical context used limits these possibilities to the author's intended meaning. All we know about the vocabulary, style, and theology of the author comes from within his twofold work itself.

In the past there was a great concern for authorship questions because of apologetic considerations. Apostolic authorship, i.e., the authorship of the eyewitnesses, was assumed to guarantee the truthfulness of their accounts. Whereas the Gospels of Matthew and John were associated with two of the apostles, Mark and Luke were not written by eyewitnesses. However, Mark was associated with Peter and thus was the recording of Peter's eyewitness testimony by his disciple. Similarly, the Third Gospel's truthfulness was assured since its author (Luke) was Paul's disciple. Though the author of the Third Gospel did seek to impress his readers that his account ultimately was due to eyewitness testimony (1:2), he also added that he had "carefully investigated everything from the beginning" (1:3), so that his readers "may know the certainty of the things ... [they] have been taught" (1:4). Such certainty does not ultimately come from knowing that Luke, the beloved physician, wrote Luke-Acts. Rather, only the Spirit, working in and through this work, is fully able to persuade us that this orderly account is in fact the Word of God.

2. The Date of Luke

The earliest and latest possible dates for the writing of the Third Gospel are quite clear. The earliest would be immediately after the events of Acts 28, i.e., after Paul's arrest and two-year stay in Rome. This would give a date in the early sixties. The latest possible date would be shortly before the earliest reference to the Gospel in early Christian literature. However, it is far from certain about where the earliest "clear" reference to Luke is to be found.[13] Within the period of 60–170, two main factors are determinative.

---

[13] Is it I Clement 13:2 (ca. 95–96); Ignatius, *Smyrna* 3:1-2 (ca. 110); Polycarp 2:3 (ca. 135)? Second Clement 5:2-4; 13:4 certainly knows the Gospel of Luke, but its date is uncertain, lying probably between 120 and 170.

The first involves the ending of Acts. Why did Luke not tell his readers what happened to Paul? It seems strange not to share that information if the author wrote after, perhaps decades after, Paul's trial and ultimate martyrdom. The simplest explanation about why Acts ends where it does is that Luke could not write anything more. He had brought his readers completely up to date. If this is so, then Luke wrote his first work before 60–62. (The possibility that Luke wrote Acts before his Gospel is refuted by Acts 1:1.)

The second main factor affecting the dating of Luke-Acts involves the relationship of the Gospel of Luke to the Gospel of Mark. If one of the accounts Luke investigated and used was the Gospel of Mark, then we must, of course, date Luke after Mark. Despite some objections to the priority of Mark, it seems reasonably certain that Luke used Mark in the writing of his Gospel,[14] and this will be demonstrated repeatedly in this commentary. The tradition concerning the authorship and date of Mark is particularly strong. The attribution of authorship to a nonapostle is so contrary to the tendency of the early church, as witnessed to by the apocryphal gospels, that this tradition must be taken seriously. The tradition attributes the work to John Mark and dates it with Peter's death (usually after, although in one instance before). There is little reason to doubt the tradition that Peter was martyred ca. 65–67, near the end of Nero's reign. If Luke used Mark, then Luke-Acts would have been written after 65–67 and thus after the events of Acts 28. The Lukan use of Mark would suggest a date of 70–90 for the Gospel.

Such a date fits well three additional pieces of evidence found within the Gospel. The first involves the "many" accounts Luke referred to in 1:1. A later date would fit the existence of many accounts of Jesus' life more easily than an earlier one. The second involves certain prophecies concerning Jerusalem's destruction in Luke which seem to look back at the events of A.D. 70. This in no way requires that these prophecies must be *vaticinia ex eventu*, or prophecies after the events; but it does appear that Jesus' prophecies concerning Jerusalem's destruction were written in light of the knowledge of that destruction. Passages such as 13:35a; 19:43-44; 21:20; 23:28-31, while not requiring a post-70 date, probably are best understood as having been written after the event. The third piece of evidence involves the positive light in which the Roman government is portrayed. See Introduction 7 (4). This would suggest a date some years after the Neronian persecution in the mid-sixties and before the persecution under Domitian in 95–96.

As to the lack of information concerning Paul's trial, we must remind ourselves of the purpose of Acts. Acts was not meant to be Paul's biography any more than it was to be Peter's. Luke's interest in Peter ended when

---

[14]For a detailed argument in favor of the priority of Mark, see R. H. Stein, *The Synoptic Problem* (Grand Rapids: Baker, 1987), 45-88.

his function in the spread of the gospel in the world had been told. Peter's value in Acts is that he was a vital instrument in the fulfillment of Acts 1:8—the spread of the gospel in Jerusalem, Judea, Samaria, and to the first Gentile convert. (Compare how Barnabas also was forgotten after Acts 15:39.) The references to Paul function similarly. His role in the spread of the gospel among the Gentiles and before the emperor is recorded. To write about Paul's trial in Rome and its outcome would be to change Acts from a primarily theological-historical work to a biographical one. Luke intended Acts to serve as the former, not the latter.

Acts fulfills Luke's purpose of showing how the gospel message, rejected by Judaism, had found fruit among the Gentiles. Within Acts are three events, each recorded three times, and all relate to the spread of the gospel to the Gentiles. These are Paul's conversion (chaps. 9; 22; 26), Cornelius's conversion (chaps. 10; 11; 15), and the rejection of the gospel by Judaism and its offer to the Gentiles (13:46-47; 18:5-6; 28:25-28). Thus Luke ended his two-volume work quite appropriately for his purpose and demonstrated that the breach between Judaism and Christianity was the fault of Jewish unbelief.

3. The Audience of Luke

Both Luke and Acts are addressed to someone named "Theophilus" (Luke 1:3; Acts 1:1). Someone has suggested that since *Theo-philus* means *friend of God*, the name does not refer to an actual person but to a metaphorical or fictional one. It is far more likely, however, that Theophilus was a real person. The adjective "most excellent" (Luke 1:3) used to describe him is found three other times in the NT and is used in addressing the Roman governors Felix (Acts 23:26; 24:2) and Festus (26:25). As a result some have suggested that Theophilus also may have been a provincial governor or Roman official, perhaps even the official who was to hear Paul's case in Rome. However, this is unlikely if, as we will see, the readership addressed in Luke-Acts was Christian. Theophilus probably was a Gentile Christian of some means and social position, and the description "most excellent" was a polite form of address. Identifying him specifically with any known historical person is not possible.

That the audience envisioned in Luke was Gentile is evident for a number of reasons. These involve (1) Luke's avoidance of Semitic expressions (6:14; 8:54; 22:42; 23:45); (2) the substitution of non-Palestinian architecture (5:19; 8:16), weather, or geography (6:48-49) for Palestinian; (3) the substitution of the term "lawyer" for the more Jewish "scribe" (10:25; 11:52); (4) the use of Judea to describe Palestine in general (1:5; 4:44; 6:17; 7:17; etc.); (5) the explanation of Jewish customs (22:1,7). Other reasons include (6) the omission of accounts dealing with specifically Jewish traditions or customs;[15] (7) the extension of Jesus' genealogy back past Abraham to Adam (3:38); (8) the references to the Jews in the third person (7:3; 23:51; Acts 10:39; 13:5; 14:1; 17:1; 21:11); and (9) the concern for the Gentile mission (Acts 10–11; 13:46-48; 18:6; 28:24-28). None of these reasons by itself is absolutely convincing (Matthew, for instance, also omitted Semitic expressions and had a similar concern for the Gentile mission), but together they suggest that Luke was writing to a primarily Gentile audience. The Hellenistic style of the prologue (Luke 1:1-4) also supports such an interpretation. It is also probable that this was a Gentile audience unfamiliar with Palestinian geography (1:26; 4:31).

The Gentile audience for which Luke wrote can be further described as a Christian audience. There are several reasons for this. It is clear that Luke expected his readers to be familiar with the Gospel traditions. They had been taught them (1:4), and he expected them to understand such expressions as the "Son of Man" and the "Kingdom of God," which he never explained. At times he even omitted parts of the tradition he assumed his audience would "fill in" by their previous knowledge.[16] There are also present various teachings (12:35-48; 16:1-9 [esp. vv. 8-9]; 17:7-10) and worship materials (the Lord's Prayer and Lord's Supper) that apply specifically to Christians. In general the Third Gospel does not appear to be an evangelistic tract addressed to unbelievers, for Luke did not seek to explain difficult or confusing issues as he would have done if writing to non-Christians.

If Luke's readers were Gentile-Christians, there are some clear implications about the purpose of his writing. Various suggestions that Luke wrote Luke-Acts for the purpose of evangelism or to defend Paul at his trial or to defend Christians in the eyes of Rome must be rejected. The purpose of Luke-Acts must be understood in some way as ministering to the needs of a specifically Christian audience.

4. The Place of Origin

The place of origin of Luke-Acts is uncertain. Numerous suggestions include Antioch, Achaia, Rome, Caesarea, the Decapolis, and Asia Minor. All such suggestions, however, are quite speculative and ultimately of little, if any, importance and value for understanding Luke-Acts.

5. The Sources of Luke

In his prologue (1:1-4) Luke stated that he was not an eyewitness with regard to the Gospel materials but that his information came from those

---

[15] Cf. Mark 10:1-12; Matt 5:33-37; 38-42; 6:1-6,16-18; 17:24-27.

[16] Cf. for instance his omission of Pilate's custom of releasing a prisoner in the Barabbas episode in 23:18-20.

who were "eyewitnesses and servants of the word" (1:2). He also revealed that other written accounts existed (1:1) and that he had followed all these things for some time. In writing his account, Luke made use of certain written sources. This is evident from the close verbal agreements we find in the Synoptic Gospels. Such close verbal agreements, as we find in 18:15-17; 20:27-40; 21:7-11 and the parallel accounts in Mark and Matthew (and in Luke 10:21-22; 11:9-13; 13:34-35; 16:13 and the parallels in Matthew) reveal that some sort of literary source lies behind these agreements. Along with these verbal agreements we also find agreements in the order of the material (cf. Luke 4:31–6:19; 9:18-50; 18:15-43 with the parallel accounts in Mark and Matthew) and even in the presence of common parenthetical material (cf. Luke 5:24; 8:29 and parallels). From all this it is clear that Luke in writing his Gospel made use of various written sources.

The attempt to explain the sources used by Matthew, Mark, and Luke that caused them to "look alike" is called the Synoptic Problem. The majority of NT scholars see some form of what is called the two-document (or four-document) hypothesis as the best explanation of this common look-alike character. According to this explanation, Mark was the first Gospel written and was used by both Matthew and Luke in the writing of their Gospels. In addition to Mark, Matthew and Luke also used at least one other source, which has been called "Q." (Q is a symbol for the German word *Quelle*, which means *source*.) Along with these two sources Matthew and Luke also had other sources available to them that are represented by the symbols "M" (Matthew's unique source or sources) and "L" (Luke's unique source or sources). Whether Q and L were written sources is uncertain. Probably Q, or at least part of what is called Q, was; but the nature of the L material is uncertain. Of Luke's 1,149 verses, approximately 350 come from Mark, 230 from Q, and the rest from L or Luke's own editorial work. The exact number of verses he obtained from Q is uncertain, for by definition the Q material consists of the material common to Matthew and Luke, but not Mark. If, as is almost certain, Luke at times used material from their common source which Matthew chose to omit, this material by definition will appear as L material. (The same would also be true of the Q material in Matthew, which would appear as M material.)[17]

---

[17]This solution to the Synoptic Problem has been challenged of late by a revival of the Griesbach Hypothesis. Those who hold this view argue that Matthew was the first Gospel written, that Luke used Matthew, and that Mark used Matthew and Luke. There are serious problems with this view, however. For one, it would require Mark to have used Matthew and Luke in a most incomprehensible way. Why would Mark omit the birth accounts, the resurrection accounts, the Sermon on the Mount, and the Lord's Prayer? If it is suggested that he sought to compose an abbreviated Gospel, this solution is confounded by the fact that within Mark the individual stories and accounts are usually longer than in Matthew and Luke. Luke's use of Matthew is also difficult to imagine. Given Luke's emphasis on the fulfillment

Along with written sources, various oral traditions no doubt also played a part in the Third Gospel's composition. Some of these oral traditions were of the kind that circulated throughout the church in the form of parables, pronouncement stories, stories about Jesus, and so forth. Some, however, may have been oral recollections shared with Luke during his time in Judea (Acts 21:7-27:1). Perhaps during this period many of the traditions contained in Luke 1-2 and Acts 1-8 were obtained.

Although Luke tends to follow the Markan outline quite closely, there is one section of Mark (6:45-8:26) not found in Luke. There have been a number of suggested explanations for this. One is that Luke may have used a defective copy of Mark (or of an Urmarkus, i.e., an early edition of Mark) that lacked these verses. This explanation, however, faces the difficulty that the Gospel of Matthew contains this material and elsewhere the copy of Mark that Matthew used appears to be very much like the copy Luke used. Probably the best explanation for the "great omission" is that Luke did this intentionally. Perhaps he omitted this section because he wanted to de-emphasize a Gentile mission of Jesus during his earthly ministry. Since Mark 6:45-8:26 might have been considered by Luke as occurring in Gentile territory (cf. 6:45,53; 7:24,31; 8:22), and since Luke would deal systematically with the spread of the gospel to the Gentile world not in his Gospel but in Acts, he may have omitted this material to preserve the "orderly" (1:3) flow of his Gospel. It has been suggested that the omission may be due to Luke's desire to connect the confession at Caesarea Philippi with the miracle of the feeding of the five thousand (9:10-17). Others have sought to explain Luke's omission of this section pericope by pericope.[18] In writing his Gospel, Luke was also confronted with a scroll of limited length. The Gospels of Matthew, Luke, and John, as well as the Book of Acts are roughly the same size; and each would

---

of the OT, why would he omit Matthew's fulfillment quotations (cf. Matt 4:14-16; 8:17; 13:35; 21:4-5; 27:9)? Given his emphasis on the Spirit, why would he omit Matt 12:28? An even more weighty reason, however, for assuming that Luke used Mark and not Matthew is that it leads to a better understanding of Lukan theology. Luke's use of Mark is both understandable and consistent. Seeking to understand Luke's theological emphasis by assuming that he used Matthew results in chaos. Therefore it is difficult to think of the Third Gospel as the product of Luke's use of Matthew. For a full discussion of the literary relationship of the Synoptic Gospels, see Stein, *The Synoptic Problem*, 29-157.

[18]Thus Mark 6:45-52 was omitted due to its similarity to Luke 8:22-25; the summary in Mark 6:53-56 was omitted due to Luke's use of the name "Gennesaret" for the Sea of Galilee rather than for a region (cf. 5:1 with Mark 6:53 and Matt 14:34); Mark 7:1-23 was omitted due to Luke's tendency to omit intra-Jewish controversies (cf. his omission of Mark 10:1-12); Mark 7:24-37 was omitted to provide for a more "orderly" approach to the Gentile mission that takes place after the resurrection; the feeding of the four thousand in Mark 8:1-21 was omitted due to Luke's previous recording of the feeding of the five thousand in 9:12-17; his omission of the blind man in Mark 8:22-26 was due to the possible implication that Jesus was unable to heal the blind man instantaneously.

have taken up all the thirty feet that made up the average scroll. In his desire to include not just the material in Mark but also the Q and L material, Luke had to select what he would include and also what he would exclude from his Gospel. As a result such material as Mark 6:45–8:26 was omitted because it did not serve his purpose as well as other material (e.g., Luke 1–2; 24).

Some have suggested that in the construction of his Gospel, Luke may have used or composed an earlier draft he later incorporated into his Gospel. This earlier draft, or Proto-Luke as it is called, supposedly began at 3:1 and consisted of Q and L material. Later Luke in composing his Gospel added material from Mark.[19] There are a number of difficulties with the proto-Luke hypothesis. Most important is that our present Gospel possesses a clear overall unity. Chapters 1–2, for instance, are not simply tacked onto the rest of the Gospel but are carefully integrated into and foreshadow what appears later. It also seems that Luke inserted his Q and L material into Mark rather than inserting the Markan material into an earlier proto-Luke.[20] For the purpose of this commentary, whether Luke used or wrote a proto-Luke is of no major importance because we will not concern ourselves with a history of the traditions that led up to our present Gospel of Luke, i.e., the discipline called *Traditionsgeschichte*. Rather, we will concern ourselves with what the Evangelist was seeking to teach his readers by our present Gospel of Luke. In other words, this commentary will concern itself with the meaning of Luke 1:1–24:53.

6. An Outline of Luke

Any outline of the Gospel of Luke is to a certain extent arbitrary. Whereas there are certain clear divisions in the Gospel (1:5; 3:1; 9:51), elsewhere we face considerable uncertainty. Where does the central section beginning at 9:51 end? At 19:10; 19:17; or 19:44? Should Jesus' ministry in Jerusalem (19:28–21:38) be included with the passion narrative (22:1–23:56) and the resurrection account (24:1-53), or should these be considered two or three separate divisions? Or should these be broken

---

[19] Support for this is seen in the following: the sequence of events in the Lukan passion narrative is quite different at times from that in Mark even though elsewhere he followed the Markan order quite closely; the passion narrative also contains a number of incidents not found in Mark which are woven into the account and do not simply appear to be L additions to the Markan narrative; the vocabulary of the Lukan passion narrative is less Markan than in other places where he has a parallel to Mark; Luke 3:1-2 would make a plausible beginning for such a Gospel in that 1:5–2:52, whose vocabulary and style are somewhat different from the rest of Luke, can be omitted quite easily; the genealogy in 3:23-38 seems to be out of place since one would expect it to appear earlier in chaps. 1 or 2.

[20] See J. A. Fitzmyer, *The Gospel according to Luke*, AB (Garden City: Doubleday, 1979), 89-91.

down into even smaller divisions? If we have too many divisions in our outline, the value of the outline will be diminished, and we would be less able to grasp how Luke organized his Gospel. Therefore we will divide Luke into the following eight sections:

OUTLINE OF THE BOOK

I. The Prologue (1:1-4)
II. The Infancy Narrative (1:5–2:52)
  1. John the Baptist's Birth Announced (1:5-25)
  2. Jesus' Birth Announced (1:26-38)
  3. The Meeting of John the Baptist and Jesus (1:39-56)
  4. The Birth of John the Baptist (1:57-80)
  5. The Birth of Jesus (2:1-52)
    (1) The Birth Proper (2:1-20)
    (2) The Circumcision and the Prophets, Simeon and Anna (2:21-40)
    (3) The Boy Jesus in the Temple (2:41-52)
III. The Preparation of Jesus' Ministry (3:1–4:15)
  1. John the Baptist (3:1-20)
    (1) The Person of John the Baptist—The Eschatological Prophet (3:1-6)
    (2) The Mission of John the Baptist (3:7-20)
  2. Jesus (3:21–4:15)
    (1) The Person of Jesus—The Son of God (3:21-38)
    (2) The Prelude to Jesus' Mission (4:1-15)
IV. Jesus' Ministry in Galilee (4:16–9:50)
  1. The Beginning of Jesus' Ministry (4:16–5:16)
    (1) Jesus' Sermon in Nazareth—A Thematic Explanation of Jesus' Ministry (4:16-30)
    (2) Jesus' Healings in Capernaum (4:31-44)
    (3) The Call of the First Disciples (5:1-11)
    (4) Jesus' Healing of a Leper (5:12-16)
  2. The Beginning of Controversy (5:17–6:11)
    (1) Conflict over Jesus' Forgiveness of Sins (5:17-26)
    (2) Conflict over Jesus' Association with Tax Collectors and Sinners (5:27-32)
    (3) Conflict over Jesus' Disciples' Not Fasting (5:33-39)
    (4) Conflict over Jesus' Attitude Toward the Sabbath (6:1-11)
  3. The Teaching of the Disciples: The Sermon on the Plain (6:12-49)
    (1) Choosing the Twelve Disciples (6:12-16)
    (2) Ministry to the Crowds (6:17-19)
    (3) Beatitudes and Woes (6:20-26)

(4) Love of One's Enemies (6:27-36)

(5) Judging Others (6:37-42)

(6) Two Foundations (6:43-49)

4. Who Is This Jesus? (7:1-50)

    (1) Jesus Heals the Centurion's Servant (7:1-10)

    (2) Jesus Raises the Widow of Nain's Son (7:11-17)

    (3) Jesus Reveals Himself to John the Baptist (7:18-23)

    (4) Jesus Bears Witness to John the Baptist as His Forerunner (7:24-30)

    (5) Jesus Experiences Rejection (7:31-35)

    (6) Jesus Forgives Sins (7:36-50)

5. Jesus Teaches in Parables (8:1-21)

    (1) A Summary of Jesus' Ministry (8:1-3)

    (2) The Parable of the Soils (8:4-15)

    (3) The Parable of the Lamp (8:16-18)

    (4) Jesus' True Family (8:19-21)

6. Jesus Reveals His Mastery over the World, the Devil, and the Flesh (8:22-56)

    (1) Jesus Calms the Sea (8:22-25)

    (2) Jesus Casts Out a Demon (8:26-39)

    (3) Jesus Heals the Hemorrhaging Woman and Raises Jairus's Daughter (8:40-56)

7. Jesus and the Twelve (9:1-50)

    (1) The Mission of the Twelve (9:1-6)

    (2) Herod's Question about Jesus (9:7-9)

    (3) Feeding the Five Thousand (9:10-17)

    (4) Peter's Confession and Teachings on the Passion and Discipleship (9:18-27)

    (5) The Transfiguration (9:28-36)

    (6) The Healing of the Boy with an Unclean Spirit (9:37-43a)

    (7) The Second Passion Announcement (9:43b-45)

    (8) Humility and Openness (9:46-50)

V. Jesus' Journey to Jerusalem (9:51–19:27)

1. The First Mention of the Journey to Jerusalem (9:51–13:21)

    (1) The Mission to Samaria (9:51-56)

    (2) Teachings on Discipleship (9:57-62)

    (3) The Mission of the Seventy(-two) (10:1-16)

    (4) The Return of the Seventy(-two) (10:17-20)

    (5) The Blessedness of the Disciples (10:21-24)

    (6) The Parable of the Good Samaritan (10:25-37)

    (7) Martha and Mary (10:38-42)

    (8) Jesus' Teaching on Prayer (11:1-13)

    (9) The Beelzebub Controversy (11:14-23)

    (10) The Return of the Unclean Spirit and True Blessedness (11:24-28)
    (11) The Sign of Jonah (11:29-32)
    (12) Sayings about Light (11:33-36)
    (13) A Denunciation of the Pharisees and Scribes (11:37-54)
    (14) Warnings and Exhortations (12:1-12)
    (15) The Parable of the Rich Fool (12:13-21)
    (16) Care and Anxiety (12:22-34)
    (17) The Watchful Servants (12:35-48)
    (18) Jesus—The Great Divider (12:49-53)
    (19) Signs of the Time and Settling with One's Opponents (12:54-59)
    (20) The Need to Repent (13:1-9)
    (21) The Healing of the Crippled Woman on the Sabbath (13:10-17)
    (22) The Parables of the Mustard Seed and Leaven (13:18-21)
  2. The Second Mention of the Journey to Jerusalem (13:22–17:10)
    (1) The Narrow Door (13:22-30)
    (2) Warning concerning Herod and the Lament over Jerusalem (13:31-35)
    (3) Healing of the Man with Dropsy (14:1-6)
    (4) Sayings concerning Banquet Behavior (14:7-14)
    (5) The Parable of the Great Banquet (14:15-24)
    (6) Conditions of Discipleship (14:25-35)
    (7) The Parables of the Lost Sheep, Lost Coin, and Gracious Father (15:1-32)
    (8) The Parable of the Dishonest Manager (16:1-8)
    (9) Sayings on Stewardship (16:9-18)
    (10) The Parable of the Rich Man and Lazarus (16:19-31)
    (11) Teachings Addressed to the Disciples (17:1-10)
  3. The Third Mention of the Journey to Jerusalem (17:11–19:27)
    (1) The Grateful Samaritan (17:11-19)
    (2) The Coming of the Kingdom of God (17:20-37)
    (3) The Parable of the Unjust Judge (18:1-8)
    (4) The Parable of the Pharisee and the Tax Collector (18:9-14)
    (5) Jesus' Blessing the Children (18:15-17)
    (6) The Rich Ruler (18:18-30)
    (7) The Third Passion Announcement (18:31-34)
    (8) The Healing of the Blind Man at Jericho (18:35-43)
    (9) Zacchaeus, the Tax Collector (19:1-10)
    (10) The Parable of the Ten Minas (19:11-27)
VI. Jesus' Ministry in Jerusalem (19:28–21:38)
  1. The Messianic Entry into Jerusalem (19:28-40)

2. Lament over Jerusalem and the Cleansing of the Temple (19:41-48)
3. A Question of Jesus' Authority (20:1-8)
4. The Parable of the Wicked Tenants (20:9-19)
5. A Question about Tribute to Caesar (20:20-26)
6. A Question about the Resurrection (20:27-40)
7. A Question about the Son of David (20:41-44)
8. Warnings concerning the Scribes (20:45-47)
9. The Widow's Offering (21:1-4)
10. The Destruction of the Temple (21:5-6)
11. Signs before the End (21:7-11)
12. The Coming Persecution of the Disciples (21:12-19)
13. The Desolation Coming upon Jerusalem (21:20-24)
14. The Coming of the Son of Man (21:25-28)
15. The Parable of the Fig Tree (21:29-33)
16. Exhortation to Vigilance (21:34-36)
17. The Ministry of Jesus in the Temple (21:37-38)
VII. Jesus' Passion (22:1–23:56)
   1. The Last Supper (22:1-38)
     (1) The Plot to Kill Jesus (22:1-6)
     (2) Preparation of the Passover Meal (22:7-13)
     (3) The Passover—Lord's Supper (22:14-20)
     (4) Jesus' Betrayal Foretold (22:21-23)
     (5) Greatness in the Kingdom of God (22:24-30)
     (6) Peter's Denial Foretold (22:31-34)
     (7) Two Swords (22:35-38)
   2. Arrest and Trial (22:39–23:56)
     (1) The Prayer of Jesus (22:39-46)
     (2) The Arrest of Jesus (22:47-53)
     (3) Peter's Denial (22:54-62)
     (4) The Mocking of Jesus (22:63-65)
     (5) Jesus before the Sanhedrin (22:66-71)
     (6) Jesus before Pilate (23:1-5)
     (7) Jesus before Herod (23:6-12)
     (8) Pilate's Sentence (23:13-16)
     (9) Jesus Delivered to Be Crucified (23:18-25)
     (10) The Way to the Cross (23:26-32)
     (11) The Crucifixion (23:33-38)
     (12) The Two Criminals (23:39-43)
     (13) The Death of Jesus 23:44-49)
     (14) The Burial of Jesus (23:50-56)
VIII. The Resurrection and Ascension of Jesus (24:1-53)
   1. The Women at the Empty Tomb (24:1-12)

2. Jesus' Appearance on the Road to Emmaus (24:13-35)
3. Jesus' Appearance to the Disciples in Jerusalem (24:36-43)
4. Jesus' Commission to the Disciples (24:44-49)
5. The Ascension (24:50-53)

7. The Purpose of Luke

Rather than speak of a single purpose,[21] it may be more accurate to speak of the various purposes Luke had in writing Luke-Acts.[22] There does not appear to be a single theme that is able to explain why the Evangelist wrote his entire two-volume work. The wealth of material found in Luke-Acts seems to indicate that whereas Luke clearly had some specific aims in mind, there also exists lesser themes he sought to share with his readers as he related to them the Gospel traditions and the traditions he had either learned or shared in concerning the early church. It has also become clear that one cannot treat the Gospel or the Book of Acts in isolation from each other, for they are both parts of one work which the author had planned from the beginning. Therefore to understand why Luke wrote his Gospel we must seek an answer not from the Gospel alone but from Luke-Acts.

Luke was not writing a work of fiction. On the contrary, in his prologue (1:1-4) he asserted that he was writing as a *historian*. As a historian there were restraints placed upon Luke by his sources. Since his readers already were familiar with these traditions, Luke was under even greater restraint, for how could he convince his readers of the certainty of the traditions they had been taught if he were to change them radically? It is unlikely that everything in the fifty-two chapters of Luke-Acts is directly applicable to the particular purposes for which he was writing. Although Luke would not have knowingly included materials that would contradict his purposes and goals, he might well have included traditional materials not directly related to them. As a result some traditional material in Luke-Acts may have no specific bearing on the immediate situation of Luke's readers.

The "mirror reading" of Luke-Acts, i.e., seeing behind every command and teaching a specific application for the situation of Luke's readers, is

---

[21] For a more detailed discussion see I. H. Marshall, *Luke: Historian and Theologian* (Grand Rapids: Zondervan, 1989); M. A. Powell, *What Are They Saying about Luke?* (New York: Paulist, 1989); F. Bovon, *Luke the Theologian: Thirty-Three Years of Research (1950-1983)*, Princeton Theological Monograph Series, no. 12 (Allison Park: Pickwick, 1987).

[22] Cf. S. G. Wilson, *The Gentiles and the Gentile Mission in Luke-Acts* (Cambridge: University Press, 1973), 265-66, who states: "Recent studies of Acts have shown that it is almost always unsatisfactory to isolate any one theme as representing Luke's total purpose, because to do so fails to do justice to the whole book." The same can be said for the Gospel of Luke. For the contrary view, see R. F. O'Toole, *The Unity of Luke's Theology: An Analysis of Luke-Acts*, GNS 9 (Wilmington: Glazier, 1984).

clearly an error. Some teaching may be preventative (Acts 20:28-31 does not require that there was a problem of false teachers troubling Luke's readers) or historical (the references to and warnings about persecution for the gospel may refer to a past situation, not to a present one) in nature. Various stories and teachings of Jesus may have been included because Luke wanted his readers to know the acts and teachings of the Lord, not because he saw a specific need in his readers' situation that a certain account met. Was the Lord's Prayer in 11:2-4 given because of a particular need? Not necessarily. Having said this, it should not be denied that the selection of material in Luke-Acts will generally reveal something concerning the Lukan purpose(s).

(1) To Help Convince His Readers of the Truthfulness of What They Had Been Taught

LUKE'S CREDENTIALS AS A HISTORIAN.   One major purpose of Luke was to assure his readers of the truthfulness of that which they had been taught about Jesus' life and teachings. This is clear from the prologue, where Luke stated that "it seemed good also to me to write an orderly account for you, most excellent Theophilus, so that you may know the certainty of the things you have been taught" (1:3-4). He sought to do this in several ways. One was by emphasizing the care with which he had researched his work. In the prologue he listed his credentials as a historian. He had investigated (1) "everything," i.e., all things, (2) "from the beginning" (3) "carefully" (4) in order to write "an orderly account" (1:3). Throughout his work Luke sought to demonstrate the truthfulness of what he recorded by tying the events to universal history.[23] He even appealed to the well-known nature of this material (24:18). Luke emphasized to his readers what Paul confessed to Festus, namely, that this "was not done in a corner" (Acts 26:26).

Luke expected that his readers would accept his account as a faithful interpretation "of the things that have been fulfilled among us" (Luke 1:1). Since Luke also expected that his account would agree with what his readers had been taught, he anticipated that as they read his "orderly account" (1:4) they would come to a greater assurance of the truthfulness of this material. Luke did not expect to have his work treated with skepticism. On the contrary, since it corresponded with what his Christian readers already had been taught, he expected that it would be received warmly and with faith. Whether a non-Christian reader in Luke's day would have come to believe the "truthfulness" of what Luke wrote is another question. Luke, however, was not writing to skeptics or to a hostile audience. Rather he was writing to believers whose hearts he expected would "burn within them"

---

[23] E.g., Luke 1:5; 2:1-3; 3:1-3; Acts 5:36; 11:28; 18:2,12: 25:1.

(24:32) as he recounted in a more organized way the things they already had been taught. Of course, this does not mean that everything in the Gospel was already known to his readers. Much, however, was familiar to them, and Luke built on this prior knowledge and understanding.

EYEWITNESS TRADITIONS. A second reason Luke's readers could know the certainty of what they had been taught was that this teaching, which is now written down in his Gospel, came from those who were eyewitnesses from the beginning (1:2). The Gospel of Luke begins with a reference to these eyewitnesses and concludes with a similar reference to them (24:48). Acts then begins with Jesus commissioning his disciples to be his witnesses (Acts 1:8). The first task of the disciples in Acts was to replace the apostate Judas, and the only mentioned requirement to becoming one of the Twelve is that he must "have been with us the whole time the Lord Jesus went in and out among us, beginning from John's baptism to the time when Jesus was taken up from us. For one of these must become a witness with us of his resurrection" (1:21-22). Time and time again in Acts the disciples mentioned that they were witnesses, i.e., eyewitnesses, of what they were proclaiming: "God has raised this Jesus to life, and we are all witnesses of the fact" (2:32). "We are witnesses of this" (3:15), Peter stated as he proclaimed the resurrection of Jesus from the dead. (Cf. also 5:32; 10:39-41; 13:31.) The apostolic preaching in Acts seeks to persuade its listeners, in part at least, by the claim that this preaching comes from eyewitnesses who were proclaiming what they themselves had seen. (Cf. 1 John 1:1-3.) Luke also anticipated that the eyewitness testimony that lies behind his twofold work would provide additional assurance to his readers about the truthfulness of the Christian teachings they received. This eyewitness testimony along with the Spirit's witness (Acts 5:32) would enable them to know that what they had been taught was divine truth.

THE PROOF FROM PROPHECY. A third means by which Luke sought to bring assurance to his readers was through demonstrating that the things that had taken place in the experiences of Jesus (and the church in Acts) were the fulfillment of prophecy. Luke in fact referred to these things in his prologue as "the things that have been fulfilled among us" (Luke 1:1). In no other Gospel, not even in Matthew, do we find so many references and allusions to how the life, death, and resurrection of Jesus fulfilled the Scriptures. This same emphasis is continued in Acts, where the experiences of the church are also understood as the fulfillment of prophecy. The extent to which the many allusions to and quotations of the OT fit a "proof from prophecy" scheme in Luke-Acts is debated, but that such a scheme is present cannot be denied. Luke sought to assure his readers of the truthfulness of the Christian message by showing how all that took place in Jesus' ministry, passion, and resurrection, as well as in the Jewish rejection and Gentile acceptance of the church's preaching, was prophe-sied beforehand in the Scriptures.

This proof from prophecy is seen in several areas. The most evident is in the fulfillment of the OT Scriptures.[24] To these can be added general references to the OT.[25] Luke anticipated that such references to the Scrip-tures would help his readers understand why the crucifixion took place and why Judaism had not accepted the Christian message. In particular he sought to demonstrate that since Jesus' sufferings and resurrection corre-spond to numerous prophecies concerning the Messiah, Jesus must be the Messiah. Jesus' hearers (24:32; cf. Acts 8:27-40) came to this conclusion, and Luke expected that his readers would also. Since what Luke's readers had been taught and now read in his Gospel was in accord with this pro-phetic material, they should have had a greater certainty of the truthful-ness of the Christian message.

Two other areas of prophetic fulfillment also play a role in Luke-Acts. One involves the prophecies of Jesus concerning various future events. These include prophecies of his rejection by Israel (9:22; 13:32-34; 17:25; 18:31; 24:7), his delivery to and death by the Gentiles (9:44; 18:32), his res-urrection (9:22; 11:29-30; 18:33; 24:7), the Spirit's coming (24:49; Acts 1:4-5,8; 11:16), and Jerusalem's destruction (11:49-51; 13:5,35a; 19:27,43-44; 21:5-24; 23:28-31).[26] The second area of fulfillment involves prophe-cies from angels,[27] from prophets,[28] and from God.[29] Just as later in the history of the Christian church the proof from prophecy argument was used both apologetically and even evangelistically to convince people of the truthfulness of the Christian faith, so in a similar although less developed way Luke sought to help his readers come to a greater assurance of the truthfulness of what they had been taught. He did this by showing that the

---

[24]Some of the clearest examples are Luke 3:4-6 (Isa 40:3-5); Luke 4:17-21 (Isa 61:1-2; 58:6); Luke 7:22-23 (Isa 29:18; 35:5-6; 42:18; 26:19; 61:1); Luke 7:27 (Mal 3:1); Luke 20:17 (Ps 118:22; Isa 28:16); Luke 22:37 (Isa 53:12); Acts 2:16-21 (Joel 2:28-32); Acts 2:25-28,31 (Ps 16:8-11); Acts 2:34-35 (Ps 110:1); Acts 3:22-23 (Deut 18:15-19); Acts 3:25 (Gen 12:3; 18:18; 22:18; 26:4); Acts 4:25-26 (Ps 2:1-2); Acts 13:33 (Ps 2:7); Acts 13:34 (Isa 55:3); Acts 13:35 (Ps 16:10); Acts 15:16-17 (Jer 12:15; Amos 9:11-12); Acts 28:26-27 (Isa 6:9-10).

[25]E.g., Acts 1:16-21; 3:18; 10:43; 13:27; 17:2; 26:22-23.

[26]To these we can add Luke 4:24 (4:28-30); 5:4 (5:5-7), 10 (Acts 2:1ff.); 8:50 (8:54-56); 9:27 (9:28-36); 12:11-12 (Acts 4:5-22; 7:2-60; 22; 23:1-10; 24:10-23; 26:1-32); 16:31 (Acts 13:46-47; 18:6; 28:25-28); 19:29-31 (19:32-34); 21:15 (Acts 6:10); 22:10-12 (22:13), 21-22 (22:3-6,47-48), 31-34 (22:54-62).

[27]Luke 1:14-17 (1:24-25,57-80); 1:20 (1:22,63-64); 1:31-33 (1:41-45; 2:1-7); 2:11-12 (2:15-18); Acts 27:23-24 (27:44).

[28]Luke 2:35b (22:63–23:38); 3:16 (Acts 2); Acts 11:27-28a (11:28b-30); 21:10-11 (21:33f.).

[29]Luke 2:26 (2:27-32); Acts 9:15-16 (9:20-25; 22:21; 26:16-18); 18:9-10 (18:11-18).

events experienced by Jesus and the early church fit God's plan and were foretold by the prophets.[30]

THE PROOF FROM MIRACLES. A fourth way in which Luke sought to assure his readers is through the proof of miracles.[31] For Luke the truth that Jesus is the Christ, the Son of God, was "attested to you by God with mighty works and wonders and signs which God did through him in your midst" (Acts 2:22, RSV). Jesus himself used his miracles as an explanation and proof that he is the expected Messiah (7:18-23). The apostles in Acts referred to their working miracles as proof that Jesus is the Christ (3:12-16; 4:30), and Luke emphasized this in editorial work in Acts (2:43; 5:12; 6:8; 8:13; 14:3; 15:12). The life of Jesus is clearly bathed in miracles. For those with eyes to see, the miraculous birth (1:31-35), the baptism (3:21-22), the numerous healings (4:40-41), the nature miracles (8:22-25; 9:10-17), and the miracles of Acts are all signs and proofs of the truth of the Christian message, not only to the original audience but now also to Luke's readers. Yet there is one supreme miracle that serves as a proof of Jesus' claims and the Christian message in general. It is the sign of Jonah (11:29-30). Although this is not enough to convince the hard of heart (16:31; cf. John 12:9-11), it is enough for those open to the divine message. The greatest miracle and proof is the resurrection. This is evident by the amount of space devoted to the resurrection in Peter's Pentecostal address (Acts 2:24-36; cf. also 13:33-38). Luke sought to bring assurance to his readers concerning their Christian faith by recalling to their minds the miracles associated with the life of Jesus, his resurrection, and also those that occurred in the life of the early church.

THE PROOF FROM THE GROWTH OF THE CHURCH. A final proof of the truth of the Christian message is found in the growth of the Christian church. Luke was fond of reporting how the church increased. Starting with 120 (Acts 1:15), it increased on the day of Pentecost to over three thousand (2:41). Following Pentecost God added to this number daily (2:47). Shortly thereafter we read of five thousand (4:4), of the number of disciples in Jerusalem increasing rapidly (6:7; cf. 5:14; 6:1). We read of a church throughout Judea, Galilee, and Samaria (9:31), of a great number in Antioch believing and turning to the Lord (11:21,24), and of the increase and spread of the word of God (12:24). We further read of a great number believing in such places as Iconium (14:1), of the winning of a larger number of disciples in Derbe (14:21), of churches in the Greek

---

[30]For a comprehensive discussion of this subject, see D. L. Bock, *Proclamation from Prophecy and Pattern: Lucan Old Testament Christology*, JSNTSup 12 (Sheffield: Sheffield Academic Press, 1987); cf. also B. S. Childs, *The New Testament as Canon: An Introduction* (Philadelphia: Fortress, 1984), 113-16.

[31]The use of miracles as a proof of the truthfulness of the Christian faith is not limited to Luke (cf. Heb 2:4; 2 Cor 12:12; and also the contested passage in Mark 16:20).

world growing daily (16:5), and of the word of God spreading widely and growing in power (19:20). For Luke all this must be understood in light of the advice given by Gamaliel in Acts 5:33-39. Concerning the Christian movement he told the Sanhedrin: "Therefore in the present case I advise you: Leave these men alone! Let them go! For if their purpose or activity is of human origin, it will fail. But if it is from God, you will not be able to stop these men; you will only find yourselves fighting against God" (5:38-39). Luke, through Gamaliel's speech, told his readers that if the Christian movement and message were not true, it would have failed. But since it has grown mightily, it is evident that Christianity is not "of human origin" but "from God." The growth of the Christian church reveals that what Theophilus had been taught came from God, for God had witnessed and was still witnessing to its truth by providing growth.

From the above it seems clear that one of the purposes of Luke in writing his twofold work was that his Christian readers would come to a greater assurance of the certainty of their faith (cf. Luke 1:4). We cannot know whether he was successful in accomplishing this purpose, but we must remember that Luke was not seeking to convince atheists, agnostics, or skeptics of the truth of the Christian faith. Rather he was seeking to help Christian readers come to a deeper assurance of this truth. The preservation of Luke-Acts suggests that this work obtained a favorable reception from its original audience.

(2) To Clarify the Christian Self-understanding of His Readers

In Luke-Acts the author sought to resolve two related problems. The first was the rejection of Christ and Christian preaching by the majority of Israel. Why had Israel rejected the fulfillment of God's promises in Jesus Christ? Luke assumed that his readers were aware of this rejection by the Jews. This is clear in the way Jesus (4:23-30) and Paul (Acts 13:45-47) presupposed and anticipated the Jewish rejection of the divine message. That this rejection by the Jews was also a problem for Paul is evident in Rom 9–11. The second problem was how Gentile believers related to the promises God made to Israel. Or to state this somewhat differently: How were ethnic Israel and the Christian church related? (Cf. Acts 10–11; 15.) Again we find that Paul wrestled with this problem as well. (Cf. Rom 9–11 and Gal 3–4.)

For Luke Christianity was not a new religion. It was not even a revised form of Judaism resulting in a new Israel. On the contrary the Christian church is the present-day expression of the religion of Abraham, Moses, and the prophets. It is the religion of the patriarchs and prophets now fulfilled. Ethnic Israel, as in OT times, consists of both a believing Israel, i.e., the Israel that follows in the faith of the OT saints, and an unbelieving Israel. The former are the sons of the prophets (Acts 3:25-26) and thus believe in Jesus; the latter are the sons of those who killed the prophets (Luke 6:23; 11:47-48,50; 13:34) and thus do not believe in Jesus. The church thus consists of faithful Israel and those Gentiles who in faith have joined faithful Israel in following Jesus and live in the fulfillment of the OT promises now realized in the coming of Jesus as Messiah/Christ. This is clearly seen in the early preaching of Acts. The apostolic message is weighted on the side of continuity with the OT. In essence the early Christian proclamation was that "the promises made to Abraham, Isaac, Jacob and the Prophets have been fulfilled." [32] It was not, Do you want to join a new religion? Thus in Luke we do not find a dichotomy of law, i.e., Judaism and the OT, versus grace, i.e. Christianity and the NT. Rather we see a complementary scheme of promise and fulfillment, a looking forward and an already realized, an expectation and the dawning of the new age.

The promises God made to Israel had now come to pass. The kingdom of God had come. God's reign had begun. The salvation promised to Israel had been realized through Jesus' birth, life, passion, and resurrection. The rejection of their Messiah by most of Israel did not negate this. Their unbelief caused them to reject and crucify God's Son. Nevertheless believing Israel faithfully accepted this message and carried it to the Gentiles as the Scriptures foretold, and there it brought forth much fruit. Judgment would therefore come upon unbelieving Israel and blessing upon believing Israel. The church was not in any way to be blamed for what had happened. Its relationship with Israel had been without fault. The strong apologetic concerning Paul's innocence in Acts 21–28 was directed less to Roman authorities than to demonstrate to Luke's readers that the Jewish rejection of the apostolic message and their subsequent persecution of the church were due solely to hardness of heart.

Luke's entire geographical scheme serves to illustrate this theme. The Gospel begins in Jerusalem (1:5ff.; 2:22,41-45); the temptations end in Jerusalem (4:9-13); the transfiguration points to Jerusalem (9:31); the large travel section has as its goal Jerusalem;[33] and the Gospel concludes in Jerusalem (19:29–24:53; esp. 24:49-53), where all the resurrection appearances take place (contrast Matthew and John). Acts then begins in Jerusalem (1:4ff.) and gradually reaches outward to Judea, Samaria, and the Gentile world (1:8; 8:1,5; 9:2,31; 10:1ff.; 11:19ff.; 13:1ff.) until it ends with the gospel being proclaimed in Rome (28:16-31). For Luke, Jerusalem and the temple represented the Jewish people and demonstrated how God visited his people in fulfillment of the OT promises. The movement away from Jerusalem in Acts reveals how these promises were now

---

[32] Cf. Acts 2:16-21; 3:13,24-26; 7:2-53; 13:16-41 [esp. 32-33]; 26:6; 28:20.
[33] Luke 9:51–19:27; esp. 9:51,53; 13:22,33; 17:11; 18:31; 19:11.

also offered to the Gentiles and how the majority of Israel rejected the fulfillment of the hopes of their fathers as accomplished in Jesus, the Christ.

Luke revealed the importance of this also by his threefold repetition of Israel's rejection of the gospel and the subsequent mission to the Gentiles in Acts 13:46; 18:6; 28:28. As has been mentioned, only two other incidents in Acts are repeated three times, and both relate to this one. These are Paul's conversion and call to preach to the Gentile world (9:3-19; 22:6-16; 26:12-18) and the conversion of the "first" Gentile—Cornelius (10:34-48; 11:1-18; 15:7-11,13-21). The importance of this theme can also be seen in the fact that the two longest OT quotations in Acts are found in 2:17-21 and 28:26-27. Whereas the former reference is less explicit ("all people" and "everyone"), the latter is explicit in referring to the unbelief of Israel and is followed by Paul's words that now the gospel would be offered instead to the Gentiles. Clearly for Luke what had happened to Israel was due solely to their unbelief.[34]

(3) To Clarify Jesus' Teachings concerning the End Times

The importance of this theme for Luke is debated. For some it is *the* purpose of Luke-Acts. For others this is of lesser importance. What is clear is that the discussion of Luke's view of the end times has played a major role in all discussions of Luke-Acts in the last forty years. This is due primarily to the work of Hans Conzelmann.[35] Conzelmann argued that during the earliest days of the church there was present a dominating eschatological expectation of the parousia. The early church possessed a hope in the imminent return of the Son of Man within their own lifetime. As the fulfillment of this hope was frustrated, this eschatological expectation came to naught. Luke in his work therefore sought to allay this disappointment by replacing this hope in the imminent return of Jesus with an understanding of salvation history in which the parousia was pushed back into the distant future[36] and the missing Son of Man was replaced by the presence of the Holy Spirit. This history of salvation was divided into three distinct periods. The first was the Period of Israel, which consisted of the time of the OT through the ministry of John the Baptist. The second was the Period of Jesus, i.e., the middle of time (in German *Die Mitte der Zeit*), which included the time between Jesus' ministry and his ascension. The third period, in which Luke and his readers found themselves, was the Period of the Church, in which the parousia has been pushed into

---

[34] See R. Maddox, *The Purpose of Luke-Acts* (Edinburgh: T & T Clark, 1982), 183-87.

[35] Conzelmann's work first appeared as *Die Mitte der Zeit* (Tübingen: Mohr, 1953) and later appeared in English as *The Theology of St. Luke* (New York: Harper, 1960).

[36] Luke 9:27; 17:22; 19:11,41-44; 21:20-24; 22:69; Acts 1:6-8.

the distant future. Because he found himself in this latter period, Luke emphasized a realized eschatology.

This schematization of Luke-Acts has undergone a great deal of examination, and its various weaknesses have been recognized.[37] For Conzelmann the key verse for his thesis was Luke 16:16. Yet this verse does not speak of three periods but only two, and John the Baptist is best understood as being part of the second period, not the first. Since Conzelmann rejected the first two chapters of Luke from consideration, this led him to place John the Baptist with the old period rather than the new. Yet in Luke 1–2 it is clear that he belongs to the new period. It is also clear in Luke 1–2, as well as in the speeches of Acts, that Luke sought to emphasize the continuity of the new period with the old, not its disjunction. The new period is the fulfillment of the old, not a rejection of it. Luke recognized two developmental stages in salvation history: The Period of Promise (the OT period), and the Period of Fulfillment (the NT period inaugurated by Jesus) which continues into the time of the church. John the Baptist belonged to the latter. (Cf. how in 3:1-2 Luke introduced the beginning of Jesus' ministry with the dating of the coming of John the Baptist.) Again, Luke did not understand these as two different and isolated periods or dispensations but as two stages in the covenantal dealings of God with his people. See comments on 16:16.

It is furthermore incorrect from the Lukan point of view to speak of a "delay" of the parousia. Luke's emphasis upon God as the Lord of history, upon the necessary fulfillment of the Scriptures, and his understanding of the divine will as controlling events (see Introduction 8 [1]) clearly reveal that there could be no such "delay" in God's plans. God, who controls history, does not determine something and then "delay." On the contrary God's plan by definition has to be on time, for God is clearly in control of history rather than controlled by it. What Luke sought to correct was the misunderstanding of certain Christians who thought that Jesus taught the parousia would come immediately.[38] Yet this was a misunderstanding of the early Christians, not a delay on God's part. Luke did not demythologize the parousia (Acts 1:11) or push it into the far distant future.[39] He still possessed an imminent expectation.[40] In Luke-Acts

[37] For a detailed critique of Conzelmann's thesis, see I. H. Marshall, *Historian and Theologian*, 77-88, 107-15.

[38] Luke 9:27 (cf. Mark 9:1); 19:11,41-44; 20:20-24; 22:69 (cf. Mark 14:62); Acts 1:6-9.

[39] See A. J. Mattill, Jr., *Luke and the Last Things* (Dillsboro: Western N.C. University Press, 1979) and R. H. Hiers ("The Problem of the Delay of the Parousia in Luke-Acts," *NTS* 20 [1974]: 152), who states: "There is no evidence that Luke meant his contemporaries to understand that the Parousia would occur only in the remote future. There is considerable evidence that he intended them to understand that it could come at any time."

[40] Luke 3:9,17; 12:38-48; 18:8; 21:32.

realized eschatology[41] has not displaced consistent eschatology.[42] For Luke the believer lives in the joy of the already now and the hope of the final consummation. In part the joy of the already now keeps alive and fuels the hope of the final consummation. The length of the interval until the parousia was of less importance to Luke.[43]

(4) To Assure His Readers That Rome Was Not a Threat to Them

Throughout his two-volume work Luke sought to portray Rome in a positive light. If Rome had been left to itself, it would have released Jesus; for both Herod (Luke 23:15) and Pilate (23:4,14-16,22) pronounced him innocent. (Cf. also the Roman centurion [23:47].) It was due to Jewish pressure alone that Jesus was crucified. In Acts, Paul also would have been released except for Jewish pressure; for Festus (25:18-19) and Agrippa (26:32) acknowledged his innocence, as did Felix (24:23,26-27) and the Roman tribune (23:29). Time and time again, for example in Corinth (18:12-17) and Ephesus (19:35-37,40), Rome protected the believer. When persecution arose, it usually was due to opposition from the Jewish leadership (Acts 4:1-22; 5:17-40; 9:1-2) or a mob stirred up or led by the Jewish leadership (7:1-8:3). When persecution came from Rome, it was due to error and ceased, as in Philippi, when this error was recognized (Acts 16:22-39). Isolated instances such as Herod's persecution of the church (Acts 12:1-5) were exceptions, as were isolated attacks from Gentiles (Acts 19:23-41). Sometimes, however, Jews were portrayed as taking part in such incidents although no mention was made of the Jewish leadership (Acts 9:23-25; 13:50; 14:19).

How should this positive portrayal of the Roman authorities be understood? If Luke-Acts was written to non-Christians, this might indicate that Luke was seeking to write an apologetic for the Christian faith in order to show that Christians posed no threat to the empire. On the contrary, the portrayal of the church's behavior in Acts would indicate that they were living out the teachings of Jesus in Luke 20:20-26 and thus were not a threat but an asset to the empire. If on the other hand Luke wrote to Christians, and this seems more likely, then his purpose was not to defend Christianity before unbelievers but rather to assure Christians that as they followed Jesus they did not need to fear Rome. They should have prepared for persecution, but such persecution was seen as coming from Jewish or family opposition.[44] Ultimately, however, they needed to fear no one but God himself (12:4-5).

[41]Cf. Luke 1–2; 4:16-30; 9:27; 10:9,11,18,23-24; 11:20; 16:16; 17:20-21; Acts 2:16-21.
[42]Cf. Luke 12:35-48; 17:22–18:8; 21:25-36; Acts 1:11; 3:21.
[43]For a helpful discussion see R. J. Bauckham, "The Delay of the Parousia," *TynBul* 31 (1980): 3-36.
[44]Luke 6:22,27; 9:23; 12:50-53; 14:26-27; 21:16-17.

8. The Lukan Theological Emphases

The distinction between Luke's theological emphases[45] and his purposes for writing (see Introduction 7) is somewhat arbitrary. The relationship between the two is further confused in that a number of theological emphases are closely related to and involved in the Lukan purposes for writing. The latter, however, deal more with why Luke wrote. They tend to be broad in scope and deal with possible problems or needs of the community to which Luke wrote. Luke's theological emphases on the other hand tend to be more specific in nature and need not involve an explicit reason for his writing. While writing Luke-Acts, the Evangelist emphasized certain theological truths that he thought were important, irrespective of the particular situation of his readers. The selection of which theological emphases were seen as important is somewhat arbitrary. The majority of the following, however, do appear to have legitimate claims to be Lukan emphases.

(1) The Sovereign Rule of God over History

In this area more than any other Luke's purpose for writing and his theological emphases come together. For Luke all history is salvation history, for God clearly controls and directs history's course.[46] Luke especially sought to demonstrate how the crucifixion of Jesus, the rejection of the gospel by the majority of Jews, and the extension of the divine promises to the Gentile world followed the divine plan exactly. He did so in various ways. We have referred earlier to Luke's use of the "proof from prophecy." See Introduction 7 (1). One way in which Luke demonstrated God's sovereign control of history was by showing that these events, which cause the most questions with regard to God's control of history, had been prophesied beforehand. As a result their occurrence in history must coincide with the divine plan.

Concerning these events Luke stated that Jesus "was handed over ... by God's set purpose and foreknowledge" (Acts 2:23) and that Herod, Pilate, the Gentiles, and the Jewish people "did what ... [God's] power and will had decided beforehand should happen" (Acts 4:28). What took place was according to the divine will (boulē), for God was in control of all this.[47] Luke firmly believed in the sovereign will of God controlling

[45] For a more detailed discussion, see Fitzmyer, *Luke*, 143-270.

[46] Perhaps the clearest example of how Luke understood God's control and rule over events is found in Acts 13:17-23. There we read: "God ... chose"; "he made"; "with mighty power he led them out" (13:17); "he endured" (13:18); "he overthrew" (13:19); "he ... gave" (13:19); "[God] gave" (13:20); "God gave" (13:21); "after removing" (13:22); "he made [raised up]" (13:22); "God has brought ... as he promised" (13:23).

[47] Cf. Luke 7:30; Acts 2:22-25; 5:38; 13:36; 20:27 for further examples of the divine *boulē* and Luke 22:22,42; Acts 22:14 for similar expressions.

history.[48] Because of God's sovereign will, there lies over history a divine necessity for God's purposes to be fulfilled. Luke referred repeatedly to this divine "must" (*dei*): "The Son of Man *must* suffer many things and be rejected by the elders, chief priests and teachers of the law, and he *must* be killed and on the third day be raised to life" (9:22, author's italics).[49] To these can also be added those passages in which God is seen as controlling history and the course of events both specifically and in general.[50] Since God is in sovereign control of history, believers can rest secure that even those events of history that seem confusing, such as the rejection and crucifixion of God's Son and Israel's rejection of the gospel message, are not simply acts of cruel fate but are under God's sovereign control and rule.

(2) The Kingdom of God

The importance of this theme is evident both by its frequency of occurrence (some forty times in Luke and thirty-two specifically as the "kingdom of God") and its centrality in the Gospel. It occurs in the birth narratives (1:33) and is the main theme of Jesus' (4:43) and the disciples' preaching (9:2).[51] The kingdom is the inheritance of the righteous (6:20), the most important petition of the prayer Jesus taught his disciples (11:20), and the future hope of the believer (13:28-29). In Acts this theme also plays an important role.[52] At times salvation is portrayed as entering the kingdom.[53]

According to Luke the kingdom of God has come, i.e., it has been "realized" in history with Jesus' coming. When Jesus announced that the OT prophecies were fulfilled in his coming (4:16-21), he announced that God's kingdom had come (4:43; 8:1; Acts 28:31). His overcoming of Satan (11:20) witnesses to this. Thus Jesus did not announce simply the nearness of the kingdom but its arrival. It was in their midst, i.e., in their presence (17:20-21). Salvation history consists of two stages: the period of promise and the period of fulfillment when the kingdom comes. With John the Baptist the period of fulfillment began (16:16; Acts 13:32-33). God's kingdom has come, for in Jesus' coming God "has come and has redeemed his people" (Luke 1:68; cf. 7:16; 19:44; Acts 15:14).

---

[48] Cf. R. C. Tannehill (*The Narrative Unity of Luke-Acts* [Philadelphia: Fortress, 1986], 2), who states, "Luke-Acts has a unified plot because there is a unifying purpose of God behind the events which are narrated."

[49] Cf. also Luke 13:33; 17:25; 22:37; 24:7,26-27,44; Acts 17:3; cf. also Luke 2:49; 4:43; 19:5; Acts 1:16.

[50] E.g., Luke 1:32-33,51-55,68-75; 3:1-6; 21:9; Acts 1:16; 3:18; 14:16; 17:26-27,31; 26:22-23.

[51] Cf. Luke 9:60; Acts 8:12; 20:25; 28:23,31.

[52] Acts 1:3; 8:12; 14:22; 19:8; 20:25; 28:23,31.

[53] Cf. Luke 18:24-25 with 18:19-20; 13:28-29 with 13:23; Acts 28:23,31 with 28:28.

The kingdom's presence is seen in Luke's Gospel primarily in Jesus' ministry. Prophecies are fulfilled (4:16-21; 7:22-23; 10:23-24); the oppressed are delivered from demons (10:17; 11:20); Satan is defeated (10:18; 11:21-22); the poor and outcast have the gospel preached to them (1:52-53; 7:22). Salvation has come upon God's people (1:68-71,77; 2:30; 3:6; 19:9-10). Yet it is above all in the Spirit's coming that this realized eschatological dimension of God's kingdom is seen. He who anointed the Son of God at his baptism (3:21-22) is promised to every believer as well. This baptism of the Spirit, which distinguishes the members of the kingdom from the OT devout as represented by John the Baptist's followers, is prophesied by John as coming upon Jesus' followers (3:16), is promised by Jesus at the end of Luke (24:49) and the beginning of Acts (1:5,8), and comes upon every believer at Pentecost (Acts 2:1-2). See Introduction 8 (3). To use Pauline terminology, the Spirit was for Luke the "firstfruits" (Rom 8:23) and "guarantee" (2 Cor 1:22; 5:5; Eph 1:14, RSV), or better yet the "earnest," of God's kingdom.

Whereas for Luke God's kingdom already was realized, it also possessed a future, not-yet-realized dimension. The consummation of the kingdom in all its fullness is still future. The general resurrection of the believer has not yet begun (20:27-38). Sin, death, and disease are still present. The final judgment has not yet occurred (Acts 17:31). Faith has not yet turned to sight. Thus believers pray for the kingdom to come (Luke 11:2) and look for the time when they will sit at table and eat in God's kingdom (13:28-29; 22:18), when the hungry will be fed and the weeping will laugh (6:21). The church therefore lives in the joy of the already now but still awaits our Lord's coming with anticipation and hope (18:1-8; 21:27-28; Acts 1:11).[54]

(3) The Holy Spirit

The Holy Spirit's importance in Luke's theology is widely acknowledged. In comparison to Mark (six times) and Matthew (twelve times), Luke referred to the Spirit at least seventeen times in his Gospel; and to this we can add such references that refer to the Spirit as "power" or "promise." It is above all in Acts, however, where we encounter most strongly this Lukan emphasis. Here the Spirit is referred to approximately seventy times, and specific reference is made to the "Holy Spirit" over forty times. This Lukan theological emphasis is present from Luke 1 through Acts 28.

We find reference to the Spirit's being active in Jesus' conception (Luke 1:35) and birth (2:25-27) as well as in John the Baptist's birth (1:15,17). He was present in Jesus' baptism, in which Jesus was anointed

---

[54] For further reading, see R. H. Stein, *The Method and Message of Jesus' Teachings* (Philadelphia: Westminster, 1978), 60-79.

and empowered for his ministry (3:22). He was present at the temptation (4:1), in Jesus' earliest ministry (4:14; 5:17), and was referred to by Jesus in his first sermon (4:18). He was prophesied by John the Baptist as coming upon Jesus' disciples (3:16) and promised to them by Jesus (24:49; Acts 1:4-5,8). This "baptism of the Spirit" comes upon every believer at Pentecost in fulfillment of Joel 2:28-32 (Acts 2:1ff.) and is promised to all who will become Christians (Acts 2:38-39).

The Spirit's presence is the single most distinctive mark of the Christian. Cornelius's possession of the Spirit was proof that God had accepted him and other Gentile believers into full membership in the church despite their uncircumcised status (Acts 10–11). Thus circumcision could not be required of Gentile believers because the gift of the Spirit witnesses to God's acceptance of them in their uncircumcised state. As a result Peter baptized Cornelius (10:44-48), the church recognized that God had granted repentance to the Gentiles (i.e., that God had accepted believing Gentiles apart from circumcision [11:17-18]), and the church concluded that nothing more was needed of Gentiles but to live in faith and to be sensitive with respect to various Jewish traditions (15:12-21). If the question arose about whether someone was a Christian, this could be addressed by a simple but definitive question, "Did you receive the Holy Spirit when you believed?" (19:2).

(4) Christology

Because of the central role Jesus played in all four Gospels, it is evident that each Gospel has a Christological emphasis. Luke's Gospel is no exception since Jesus Christ lies at the center of Luke's twofold work. This is not only evident in the Gospel, where Jesus is the main theme from chap. 1 through chap. 24, but also in the early sermons in Acts. If we omit Stephen's sermon in chap. 7, we find the Christological content dominates the earliest sermons.[55] Clearly the early sermons of Acts are Christologically oriented. Throughout the Gospel the reader encounters the crucial and decisive question, "Who is this?"[56] Luke even reported that the name given to early believers was "Christians" (Acts 11:26).

The Christology of Luke-Acts is rich and varied. Numerous titles and attributes are given Jesus, and these are not to be isolated from one another. Jesus is Prophet,[57] Christ/Messiah,[58] Son of God/Son,[59] Lord,[60]

---

[55] Acts 2:22-36 (out of 2:14-36); 3:13-23 (out of 3:12-26); 4:10-12 (out of 4:8-12); 10:36-43 (out of 10:34-43); 13:23-40 (out of 13:16-41).

[56] Luke 5:21; 7:49; 8:25; 9:9; cf. also 9:18-20; 19:3.

[57] Luke 4:24; 7:16,39; 9:8,19; 13:33; 24:19.

[58] Luke 2:11,26; 3:15; 4:41; 9:20; 22:67; 23:2,35,39; 24:26,46, etc.

[59] Luke 1:32,35; 3:22; 4:3,9,41; 8:28; 9:35; 20:13; 22:70, etc.

[60] Luke 2:11,26; 5:8,12; 6:46; 9:54, etc.

Son of Man,[61] Servant (Acts 3:13,26; 4:30), King of the Jews,[62] Son of
David,[63] Holy and/or Righteous One,[64] Author of Life (Acts 3:15),
Leader (Acts 3:15; 5:31), Savior,[65] and Judge (Acts 10:42; 17:31). Luke
made no specific reference to preexistence in his Christological descrip-
tion of Jesus. It may be, however, that the designation "God" is applied to
Jesus in Luke 8:39; 9:43; Acts 20:28, although this is uncertain.

Since all these titles apply to Jesus, it is not surprising that they are at
times used interchangeably. We can note Luke 2:11 (Savior-Christ-Lord; cf.
also the implications of his birth in the City of David); 1:32-33 (Son-King
of the Jews [cf. "the throne of his father David"]); 4:34,41 (Holy One of
God-Son of God-Christ); 22:67-70 (Christ-Son of Man-Son of God); 23:35-
37 (Christ-Chosen One-King of the Jews). All these titles, of course, refer to
the same person—Jesus. Because the same person possesses all these titles,
it is not surprising that some titles, whose full realization lay in the future,
are proleptically attributed to Jesus during his ministry. Thus, whereas Jesus
was "made both Lord and Christ" in the fullest sense after the resurrection
(Acts 2:36; cf. Rom 1:4; Phil 2:9-11), at his birth he already was Christ and
Lord (Luke 2:11), and he was crucified as the Christ (Acts 23:3; 24:26;
3:18). Since for Luke the early Jesus and the risen Lord are one and the same
person, all the above mentioned titles can be used of Jesus of Nazareth from
the very beginning even if their full significance lies in the future.

The Lukan Christology involves far more than just the titles applied to
Jesus in Luke-Acts. We must also include the unique way he acted and
spoke. Jesus claimed and manifested a unique authority (Luke 20:1-8;
6:1-5) over nature (8:25; 9:10-16), over disease (4:38-40; 7:22), and over
Satan (4:36,41; 10:17-20). Jesus also spoke with a unique authority and
made what can only be called ultimate claims (12:8-9; 7:23; 9:23-26).
Luke's overall Christology, like that of the other Gospel writers, was of
one who was not only greater than all other men (i.e., he was not only
quantitatively different) but was also qualitatively different in that he
claimed divine prerogatives (5:20-26; 7:48-49; 24:52).

(5) The Last Shall Be First—The Great Reversal

A strong theological emphasis that continually appears in Luke-Acts
involves God's concern for the downtrodden and outcasts:[66] the poor,[67] tax

---

[61] Luke 5:24; 6:5,22; 7:34; 9:22,26; 12:40; 17:26,30; 18:8, etc.
[62] Luke 19:38; 23:2-3,37-38; Acts 17:7.
[63] Luke 1:32; 2:4,6-7; 3:31; 18:38-39; Acts 2:30-31. Cf. Luke 1:27,69; 2:11.
[64] Luke 4:34; Acts 3:14; 4:27; 22:14.
[65] Luke 2:11; Acts 5:31; 13:23. Cf. Luke 19:10; 23:35,39.
[66] See R. F. O'Toole, *The Unity of Luke's Theology: An Analysis of Luke-Acts*, GNS
(Wilmington: Glazier, 1984), 109-48.
[67] Luke 1:48,51-53; 2:7-14; 4:18; 6:20,24-26; 7:22; 14:13,21; 16:19-31; 18:22; 19:8. Cf.
Acts 3:1-10; 4:34-35; 6:1.

collectors,[68] sinners,[69] Samaritans,[70] Gentiles,[71] and women.[72] The Gospel opens with a hymn of praise, for God was about to lift up the humble (1:52) and fill the hungry with good things (1:53). It was to the barren (1:7) and humble (1:48) that God would manifest himself. It was to those reckoned last (13:30) that the kingdom would come. In the Gospel's opening thematic sermon (4:16-30) Jesus announced that the Spirit had anointed him to bring the gospel to the poor, freedom for prisoners, sight for the blind, and release for the oppressed (4:18). Thus Jesus' ministry to the hated tax collectors was not simply an accident but intentional. (Note the "I must" of 19:5 and the explanations in 5:32; 19:10.) It furthermore was understood by his opponents as intentional (5:32; 19:7). One of the signs that the kingdom had come was that God was now visiting the outcasts. When Jesus was asked by John the Baptist whether he was the one the people expected (7:20), he answered that the blind, the lame, the lepers, the deaf, the dead, and the poor were receiving the divine salvation (7:22). For Luke this proved that Jesus was the Expected One.

(6) The Call to Salvation

In Luke-Acts a number of different expressions are used to describe the salvation God offers in Jesus Christ.[73] One can describe this as "entering the kingdom of God" (18:17,24-25), being "saved" (Acts 16:30), inheriting "eternal life" (Luke 10:25; 18:18), or receiving "the forgiveness of sins" (1:77; 24:47). That these are essentially synonymous is evident from the fact that these various expressions are frequently used interchangeably. In the account of the rich ruler "salvation" (18:26), "eternal life" (18:18), and the "kingdom of God" (18:25-26) are freely interchanged. This is also clear in that repentance is the requirement for forgiveness (3:3; 24:47), entering the kingdom of God (Acts 20:21,25), being saved (2:21,38), and inheriting eternal life (11:18).

How does one share in God's gracious offer of salvation? What response is demanded by God's initiative in offering salvation to humanity? In Luke-Acts this also is expressed in various ways. One of the most frequent descriptions of the necessary response is "to believe." This is clearly seen in Acts 16:31, where the question "What must I do to be saved?" in 16:30 is answered, "Believe in the Lord Jesus, and you will be

---

[68] Luke 3:12-13; 5:27-32; 7:29,34; 15:1-32; 18:9-14; 19:1-10.

[69] Luke 5:29-32; 7:34-50; 15:1-32; 19:1-10; 23:40-43.

[70] Luke 9:52-55; 10:25-37; 17:11-19. Cf. Acts 1:8; 8:1,4-25; 9:31; 15:3.

[71] Luke 2:32; 7:1-10; 24:47. Cf. Acts 1:8; 2:5; 8:26-40; 10:1-2.

[72] Luke 1:7,25,27; 4:38-39; 7:11-17,36-50; 8:1-3,40-56; 10:38-42; 13:10-17; 18:1-8; 21:1-4; 23:55-56; 24:1-11. Cf. Acts 1:14; 6:1-2.

[73] See Marshall (*Luke: Historian and Theologian*), who argues that "salvation" is the main theme of Luke-Acts.

saved." The offer of salvation requires the human response of faith.[74] A second response frequently emphasized is the need for repentance. One receives salvation by repenting.[75] This repentance can be expressed in specific ways, such as selling one's possessions and giving to the poor (16:9; 18:22; 19:8-10) or bearing fruit befitting repentance (3:8; Acts 26:20). The need for baptism is also frequently associated with the human response, which results in salvation.[76] Sometimes the needed response is said to be confessing Christ (9:26; 12:8-9; Acts 22:16; cf. Rom 10:9), taking up a cross (Luke 9:23; 14:27), following Jesus (9:23,57-62), keeping the commandments (10:25-28; 18:18-20), hearing and keeping God's word (11:28), or being obedient to God (Acts 5:31-32; 10:35).[77]

Clearly these are not to be understood as different ways of acquiring salvation. Rather they are various ways of expressing *the* needed human response to God's offer of salvation. All the above are part of *the* response God demands. Disciples do not pick and choose which aspects of the response they "like." They enter into God's kingdom through *one* response that involves faith, repentance, baptism, confessing Christ, following Jesus, and keeping the commandments. This does not mean that entrance into salvation is a process. Rather entrance into salvation involves that indivisible act in which all these responses are contained; for true faith includes repentance, the willingness to be baptized, and obedience.

(7) The Christian Life

Several distinct Lukan emphases exist concerning Christian living. Only two will be mentioned here. The first involves the importance of prayer for the believer. Whereas the terms "prayer" and "pray" are found thirteen times in Mark and seventeen times in Matthew, they are found twenty-one times in Luke and twenty-five times in Acts.[78] More significant, however, than the frequency of this concept in Luke-Acts is that it occurs at key times and places. The Gospel begins with prayer in the temple (1:9-10). After its brief summary of the Gospel's contents, Acts begins with the disciples' praying (1:14) and maintains this emphasis.[79]

---

[74]Luke 7:50; 8:12,48; 17:19; 18:42; Acts 3:16; 4:4; 10:43; 15:9,11; 26:18.

[75]Luke 3:3; 5:32; 15:7,10; 16:30-31; 24:47; Acts 2:38; 3:19; 11:18; 17:30; 20:21.

[76]Acts 2:38; 8:12,36-37; 9:18; 10:47-48; 22:16.

[77]For further discussion see Fitzmyer, *Luke*, 235-41; O'Toole, *Unity of Luke's Theology*, 191-224.

[78]To these can be added ask-pray [*deomai*] in Luke 10:2; 21:36; 22:32; Acts 4:31; 8:22,24; 10:2.

[79]The selection of Judas's replacement takes place after prayer (1:24-26 and so is understood by Luke as a good procedure and choice). Life in the early church can be described as attending to the apostles' teaching, breaking bread, and prayer (2:42); and the role of prayer in the church is emphasized (1:14; 3:1). The selection of the seven deacons is followed by

Luke alone recorded that Jesus was praying at his baptism when he was anointed by the Spirit (see comments on 3:21) and that Jesus chose the Twelve after he had prayed all night (Luke 6:12). Only Luke recorded that Jesus prayed before he asked his disciples, "Who do the crowds say I am?" (9:18). Again only Luke mentioned that at his transfiguration Jesus went up on the mountain to pray and that while he was praying he was transfigured (9:28-29). In the context of his own praying, Jesus taught the Lord's Prayer (11:1-4). Through prayer believers are able to persist and not lose heart (18:1) and to keep from falling into temptation (22:40,46). And because of Jesus' prayer, Peter's denial did not turn into apostasy (22:32). Clearly for Luke prayer was seen as a vital and necessary part of the Christian life both individually and corporately.[80]

A second area of concern in Luke-Acts involves possessions. No other books in the NT are as concerned about the Christian's relationship to material possessions. Within Luke's writings are several passages that appear to teach the need for Christians to renounce all personal possessions. For example we read, "Sell your possessions" (12:33), or, "Any of you who does not give up everything he has cannot be my disciple" (14:33). Luke quoted Jesus' words to the rich ruler found in Mark but intensified the demands by adding "everything": "You still lack one thing. Sell everything you have and give to the poor, and you will have treasure in heaven. And come, follow me" (18:22).[81] Elsewhere we find in Luke an emphasis on generosity and the giving of alms.[82] The danger of possessions is emphasized (12:13-21; 16:10-13,19-31) because a primary reason for the choking of God's word is riches (8:14). Disciples should use possessions to obtain treasure in heaven (12:33-34; 16:9; 18:22). "It is more blessed to give than to receive" (Acts 20:35); and the generosity of Tabitha (Acts 9:36), Cornelius (Acts 10:2,4,31), the centurion (Luke 7:5), the good Samaritan (10:34-35), and the women who followed Jesus (8:3) are held up to the reader as exemplary.[83]

---

prayer (6:6), and the work of the Twelve is summarized as a ministry of preaching the word and prayer (6:4). Prayer is mentioned in the Samaritans' receiving the Spirit (8:15), in Ananias's going to baptize Saul (9:11), and in Dorcas's being restored to life (9:40). The conversion of the first Gentile is directed by God through prayer (10:4,9,30-31; 11:5), and Peter's rescue from prison was due to prayer (12:12). The first missionaries, Barnabas and Saul, were commissioned with prayer (13:3) as were the elders they appointed (14:23). Prayer is associated with the conversion of the Philippian jailor (16:26), in Paul's going to Jerusalem (21:5), and in the healing of Publius's father (28:8).

[80] For further discussion see A. A. Trites, "The Prayer Motif in Luke-Acts" in *Perspectives on Luke-Acts*, 168-86.

[81] Cf. Mark 10:21. Cf. also Luke 5:11; Acts 2:44-45; 4:32; 5:1-11.

[82] Luke 3:11; 6:34-35,38; 11:41; 12:33; 14:12-14; 19:8.

[83] For further discussion see W. Pilgrim, *Good News to the Poor: Wealth and Poverty in Luke-Acts* (Minneapolis: Augsburg, 1981); D. P. Seccombe, *Possessions and the Poor in*

Perhaps the earliest attempt to bring together this radical demand for selling all one's possessions and the more moderate call to generosity and charity is the early church interpretation of a two-level Christian ethic. On the one level were those demands that every believer had to keep: the Ten Commandments; the Golden Rule; the love commandment; and, in the case of one's possessions, generosity. These were the "requirements" the gospel placed upon every Christian. On the other hand, there was also a higher "evangelical counsel" for those seeking a greater righteousness; and this involved such things as the renunciation of family (14:26), marriage (Matt 19:3-12), and possessions. One can readily see how such an understanding would lead to a two-level Christianity. On the one level stood the laity and on the other the clergy.[84]

Luke's teaching in this area, however, does not divide neatly into this two-level system. What the rich ruler lacked because he did not sell all that he had was not a higher righteousness but membership in the kingdom of God (18:24-25), i.e., salvation (18:26). What Jesus was giving to the rich ruler was not "evangelical counsel" but rather an answer to the question "What must I do to inherit eternal life?" (18:18). We must also note that the demand to "sell your possessions" in 12:33 is followed by "provide purses for yourselves that will not wear out." This latter command assumes that one will continue to have the means to give alms, i.e., that one will still have purses out of which to give alms.[85]

It may be that 12:33 provides the needed clue for resolving this tension between the radical demand to sell and the more moderate teaching concerning the need for generosity. As is often found in the Gospels, various teachings of Jesus are presented hyperbolically and without qualification. The context of 12:33a clearly indicates that the total renunciation of all personal possessions is not the intent of this saying since disciples are expected to have the means to practice a continual generosity (12:33b). At times believers may be called on to sell all their possessions, as in the case of the rich ruler (18:22), but this is not a universal demand. Luke strongly emphasized the danger that possessions involve (8:14; 12:13-21; 16:10-13,19-31). He, more than any other Evangelist, saw how riches can keep one from God's kingdom. He perceived clearly that the possession of wealth tends to lead to arrogance and self-sufficiency and so warned, "Woe to you that are rich, for you have already received your comfort"

Luke-Acts, Studien zum Neuen Testament und seiner Umwelt; (Freistadt: Plöchl, 1982); L. T. Johnson, *The Literary Function of Possessions in Luke-Acts*, SBLDS 39 (Missoula: Scholars, 1977).

[84]For further discussion see Stein, *Method and Message*, 88-111.

[85]Cf. also 6:34-35,38; 11:41; 14:12-14. As for Acts 2:44-45; 4:32; and 5:1-11, selling all one's possessions is not seen as a requirement but as an option (note Acts 5:4), and it did not bring about a higher status.

(6:24). Here Luke stood in close agreement with such OT teachings as Jer 5:26-29; Amos 8:4-6; Mic 2:1-5. But to the humble poor who share what they have with those who are even more needy, he shared the beatitude, "Blessed are you who are poor, for yours is the kingdom of God" (6:20). One cannot serve God and mammon (16:13). One must use mammon in order to serve God, not God in order to serve a lust for mammon.

(8) The Atonement

Luke did not emphasize the atoning significance of Jesus' death in his two-volume work. Some have even argued that he in fact rejected a soteriological significance for the cross. This is seen primarily in two editorial changes made to his sources. The first involves his omission of Mark 10:45, where Jesus' death is described as a "ransom for many." That Luke omitted Mark 10:45 from his Gospel is obvious. But it must be pointed out that Luke omitted the entire pericope, Mark 10:35-45, from his Gospel and replaced it with another tradition at a different place—Luke 22:24-27.[86] Furthermore Luke was following a different source in 22:24-27. As a result we cannot say that his omission of Mark 10:45 proves his rejection of the atoning significance of Jesus' death. For some reason Luke chose to omit Mark 10:35-45, but to say that he omitted this entire account because he disagreed with Mark 10:45 is not permissible. If this were true, he could have included Mark 10:35-44 and simply omitted v. 45. More likely Luke omitted Mark 10:35-45 because of his inclusion of similar material in 22:24-27 and his desire to avoid a doublet (two similar accounts). It may also be that Luke omitted Mark 10:35-45 due to his desire to portray the disciples in an exemplary light.[87] It could even be that Luke omitted the Markan account in order to bring the travel journey to a close.[88]

A second reason Luke has been seen as opposing an atoning significance for Jesus' death is his modification of "poured out for many" in his account of the last supper to "poured out for you" (cf. Luke 22:20 with Mark 14:24). Yet this entire expression is missing in the Pauline version of the last supper, and it certainly would be incorrect to argue that the lack of this expression in Paul's version of the last supper indicates that he saw no atoning significance in the death of Jesus. Actually the Lukan change is due less to theological grounds than to literary ones. After the reference to the bread in Luke 22:19, Luke used the expression "given for you," which is paralleled in 1 Corinthians but not found in Matthew or Mark. As a result it was quite natural for Luke in 22:28 to change "poured out for many" in his

---

[86] Mark 10:35-45, if included by Luke, would have appeared after Luke 18:34.

[87] Cf. Luke 8:11 with Mark 4:13; Luke 8:25 with Mark 4:40; Luke 9:43a with Mark 9:28-29.

[88] Cf. Luke 18:31—Jerusalem; 18:35 and 19:1—Jericho; 19:11,28—Jerusalem.

Markan source to "poured out for you" in order to give the same rhythmic balance after each element of the last supper. Thus we have, "This ... given *for you*" and "This ... poured out *for you*."

There are several additional reasons why one should hesitate in saying that Luke saw no soteriological significance in the cross. For one, we find in Acts 20:28 the statement that God has "bought" the church "with his own blood." The fact that in the Lukan crucifixion account "blood" is not mentioned supports the view that Acts 20:28 is not simply referring to the fact that Jesus died on a cross but rather that his death was sacrificial. To this we can also add the reference in Luke 22:20 where Jesus referred to the cup as "the new covenant in my blood." The interpretation most available to Luke and his readers was that Jesus' death was like the sacrificial offering in Exod 24:5-8. Here the sacrificial blood of the Passover lamb is covenantal blood "poured out" for the people. It is blood that makes atonement and brings forgiveness of sins. That this was the normal understanding of Exod 24:8 is evident from the Targums Onkelos and Pseudo-Jonathan, where this aspect of the blood of the covenant is made explicit by the addition of the phrase "to atone for the people," and by Matt 26:28, where the Evangelist likewise made explicit this implicit dimension of the blood of the (new) covenant by adding "for the forgiveness of sins." (Cf. also Heb 9:20-22.) It is difficult to imagine that Luke and his readers would not have interpreted these references to Jesus' blood and death in light of the OT passages dealing with sacrifice and in particular with respect to the Passover sacrifice.

Along with these specific references are also several possible allusions to the atoning significance of Jesus' death in Luke-Acts. In the account of the last supper we read, "This is my body given for you" (Luke 22:19). The term "given" can have sacrificial implications as 2:24; Mark 10:45; Gal 1:4; 1 Tim 2:6; and Titus 2:14 indicate. In the context of the reference to "blood" in Luke 22:20, *given* may well mean *given in sacrifice for you.* It should be observed that *give* is used with reference to sacrifice in Exod 30:14 and Lev 22:14. The references to Jesus "hanging on a tree" (Acts 5:30; 10:39; cf. 13:29) probably should be interpreted in light of Deut 21:23 (cf. Gal 3:13), where such a person is "cursed." Luke did not develop this thought, but an understanding such as we find in Gal 3:13 is not impossible. The references to the divine necessity of Jesus' having to suffer[89] naturally raise the question of why. To claim that Jesus had to die because this was the plight of all the prophets (13:33) loses sight of the fact that Jesus was much more than a prophet and that no prophet's death was portrayed as providing the "blood of a covenant." For Luke salvation did not come despite Jesus' death on a cross. Rather it came because of

---

[89]Luke 9:22; 17:25; 24:7; cf. also 9:44; 18:32; 24:26,46; Acts 3:18.

Jesus' death on a cross. (Cf. how the cross and forgiveness are associated in 24:46-47.)[90]

Jesus' death as the Righteous One (Acts 3:14; 7:52; 22:14; cf. Luke 23:47) does not emphasize primarily that he was innocent. Paul also was innocent in his trial, but he was not described as "the" or even "a" righteous one. Rather he was described as undeserving of death or imprisonment.[91] Even if one refrains from reading into this the theology of 2 Cor 5:21 or 1 Pet 3:18, the source of this title is most likely the Righteous Servant of Isa 53:11.[92] Luke's references to Jesus as "servant" (*pais*, Acts 3:13,26; 4:27,30) make it difficult to imagine that Luke expected these references to the Suffering Servant of Isaiah to be interpreted in an altogether different manner from the other NT writers in Rom 4:25; 1 Pet 2:24; 1 John 3:5.

Finally, even though Mark in contrast to Luke is understood to have portrayed Jesus' death as having soteriological significance, only two explicit references to this are in his Gospel—Mark 10:45 and 14:22-25. If one interprets the various allusions listed above as suggested, the Lukan emphasis may in fact be greater.

Luke in his portrayal of Jesus' death usually went no further than to explain it as due to divine necessity. In those instances, however, where Luke did address himself to *why* there was this divine necessity (Luke 22:20; Acts 20:28), he made use of the sacrificial terminology "new covenant in my blood" and "bought with his own blood." Most probably Jesus' death can be referred to as the shedding of blood because Luke, like the other NT writers, understood that "the life of a creature is in the blood, and I have given it to you to make atonement for yourselves on the altar; it is the blood that makes atonement for one's life" (Lev 17:11).

9. The Goal of This Commentary

The task of writing a commentary is not a self-explanatory one, for what one does in a commentary is not specifically defined by the term *commentary*. There is furthermore no definition of a commentary on

---

[90]Cf. Fitzmyer (*Luke the Theologian*, 212), who states: "The real question about the Lucan story is whether God is portrayed in it bringing to realization his salvific plan *despite* the suffering and death of Jesus or *through* that suffering and death. In my opinion, it is the latter."

[91]Acts 23:29; 25:25; 26:31; cf. 25:11.

[92]Other references to the Suffering Servant of Isaiah can be found in Luke 22:37 (Isa 53:12); Luke 23:4,14-15,22 (Isa 53:11); Luke 23:9 (Isa 53:7); Luke 23:35 (Isa 42:1); Acts 3:13-14 (Isa 52:13–53:12); Acts 8:32-33 (Isa 53:7-8); Acts 13:47 (Isa 49:6); cf. also Luke 2:28-32.

which all commentators have agreed.[93] Generally the commentator and/or publisher determine what the goal of the commentary will be.[94] This commentary *on Luke* is not primarily concerned with cutting trenches or "balks" in this Gospel "tell" in order to discover the various layers of Hebrew, Aramaic, or Greek traditions. As a commentary *on Luke* it focuses on the message Luke himself sought to convey to his readers. This approach (sometimes called *composition criticism*) has more in common with redaction criticism than with any of the other historical-critical disciplines.[95] Nevertheless, it differs from redaction criticism in that it seeks to understand not just the unique Lukan emphases but his complete message, i.e., it seeks to understand Luke's total message, not just that part of his message that is unique in content or emphasis to him. In this commentary we will seek to answer the question, What was Luke seeking to teach his readers through the stories and teachings of Jesus that make up his Gospel?

In this commentary we will seek in the investigation of each pericope to answer the following: "I have told you, Theophilus, this account/teaching of Jesus because ..." It is the conviction of the present writer that the most important task of a commentary is not to reconstruct the process by which the work came into being or to reconstruct the historical situation being reported. Even less important is the idolatrous desire to arrive

---

[93] See R. A. Culpepper, "Commentary on Biblical Narratives: Changing Paradigms," *Forum* 5.3 (1989): 87-102.

[94] As a result, for some the goal of writing a commentary on a Gospel is to reconstruct from the account as far as possible the exact historical circumstances in Jesus' life and the exact words he spoke. Such *historical criticism* may involve the reconstruction of an exact chronology of Jesus' life, as found in the older "harmonies" of the Gospels, or it may involve an attempt to establish the *ipsissima verba* of Jesus, i.e., the exact words he spoke. If one is theologically conservative, this approach often has the apologetic aim of proving that Luke's Gospel is an accurate report of the events and words of Jesus. On the other hand, if one is a rationalist and allows no room for the supernatural, this approach usually results in a radical reconstruction of Jesus' life and teachings that not unexpectedly reflects the author's own presuppositions and beliefs. The clearest example of this is the *Quest for the Historical Jesus*. A commentary *on Luke*, however, should not have as its primary goal the mining of the Lukan Gospel in order to discover the gems of Jesus' *ipsissima verba* or the jewels of *wie es eigentlich war*, i.e., exactly what happened. For other scholars the goal of writing a commentary on Luke might be to reconstruct the written sources available to Luke as he wrote his work (*source criticism*), or to analyze the oral sources that underlie these written sources (*form criticism*), or to seek to understand the unique contribution Luke made to the Jesus tradition (*redaction criticism*), or to do all of these (*tradition criticism*). Each of these disciplines is a legitimate and interesting way of investigating the material found in Luke.

[95] For a detailed definition of redaction criticism, see R. H. Stein, "What Is Redaktionsgeschichte?" *JBL* 88 (1969): 45-56 or *Gospels and Tradition* (Grand Rapids: Baker, 1991), 21-34.

at one's own self-understanding. Rather the primary task is to understand the author's message. With regard to Luke's Gospel this means that the goal of a commentary on Luke above everything else should be to seek to understand what the author of Luke 1:1–24:53 wanted to tell Theophilus. Whatever the difficulties facing such a task, this goal must be clearly understood and pursued.

In this commentary we will seek to avoid the so-called intentional fallacy by concentrating on what Luke consciously willed to express in his work and not by seeking such inaccessible matters as the subconscious state and desires of the author while writing. If we grant to Luke anywhere near the intelligence and literary skill that present-day scholarship does, we should have no problem attributing to him the linguistic ability to express in his writings what he consciously intended to say through them. Furthermore if one attributes to Luke a divine enabling by the Holy Spirit, such an ability should be even more readily granted. In concentrating our attention on the Evangelist's conscious meaning, we hope to avoid both the so-called intentional fallacy and the error of concentrating on the various subject matters discussed in the text instead of on the meaning of the text itself.

We will also avoid seeking to interpret the Gospel in light of a particular hypothetical situation in the early church (*Sitz im Leben Kirche*), such as defending Paul at his trial, resolving a crisis of faith due to the delay of the parousia, defending Christianity against Gnosticism, or defending Paul against Jewish Christians. The *why* of what the Evangelist was saying is far less accessible to the reader than the *what*. We frequently can and do know *what* Luke was telling his readers even if we do not know *why*. Furthermore we must understand the *what* before we can posit a hypothetical *why*. It is therefore foolish to seek to ascertain the more accessible *what* of the Gospel on the basis of the much more hypothetical *why*.

The methodology to be used in seeking Luke's meaning presupposes that Luke wanted his readers to understand him and that he possessed the ability to express his meaning adequately. In writing his Gospel, Luke submitted himself to the vocabulary and grammatical norms of the Greek language of his readers. This as well as the context he provided his readers in Luke-Acts is the main source for understanding his Gospel. Some helpful contexts for understanding the vocabulary and grammar of Luke can be found in the other Synoptic Gospels, John, the rest of the NT, and the Septuagint; but it is Luke-Acts itself that provides the most helpful and definitive context for understanding the meaning of the author, Luke.

The use of historical and traditional materials by Luke limited the extent and method by which the Evangelist could shape his Gospel. If Luke were composing a pure work of fiction, his freedom and creativity would have been unlimited. However, since he was working with known pieces of tradition and historical events, this placed considerable restraint on his "creativity." This was especially true because his readers were already familiar with the Gospel traditions he used (Luke 1:4) and because of the historical pretensions he made in writing his work (1:1-4; 2:1-2; 3:1-2). Luke worked within a particular historical-traditional context. (This is also true with regard to Acts, although to a lesser extent since the Acts traditions were not nearly as well known to his readers as the Gospel traditions.) It should not be surprising therefore to find in the Gospel various emphases of Jesus and the early church that are not especially Lukan. That these are not opposed to Luke's theology is evident, for Luke could have omitted such traditions from his Gospel. Clearly for Luke the traditions he included in his Gospel do not conflict with his overall purpose and meaning. They may at times be tangential to his purpose, but in Luke's mind they were not contradictory to it. It is inconceivable that Luke could at any point be thought to have said, "Theophilus, I have included this tradition in my orderly account because it is well-known even though it clearly contradicts my purpose and I do not believe it!" Unless we accuse the Evangelist of deceit or incompetence, we can assume that he believed in the truthfulness (1:4) of what he was writing and that the traditions he repeated fit, or at least did not contradict, his overall purpose in writing.

How then did Luke draw out his own particular theological emphases from these traditions? One way was by his selection of material. What Luke chose to include in his Gospel is clearly indicative of what he sought to teach. The same is true of what he chose to omit, although this is less accessible. (It may be that the "great omission" of Mark 6:45–8:26 is best explained as intentional since those verses do not fit well Luke's overall geographical plan and scheme.) We are also better able to understand his purpose in writing by carefully observing his editorial reworking of the traditions. This is most clearly seen in his introductory, summary, and interpretative comments as well as in the modifications of his sources. These are most evident in the material of the triple tradition, i.e., those accounts for which Luke (and Matthew) used Mark or the traditions best represented by Mark. It can also be seen reasonably well in his use of the Q traditions, for here one can compare Luke with the form of the tradition in Matthew. It is less clearly seen in the L traditions. Yet one must be careful not to limit one's investigation of the Lukan purpose and theology to his editing of Mark, Q, and L; for this would reveal primarily what is "unique" to Luke, but not the emphasis of his entire Gospel. The redaction critic who focuses attention only on the unique emphases of Luke will understand "Lukan theology" less well than the individual who simply reads Luke 1:1–24:55 and seeks to understand the meaning of the entire work. Redaction criticism provides helpful clues to various Lukan emphases, but to understand the meaning of the Gospel of Luke we must not pay attention simply to what is unique to Luke but to all that Luke sought to teach in his Gospel.[96]

---

[96]For a comprehensive bibliography of the Lukan literature, see Fitzmyer, *Luke*, 29-34, 59-62, 97-106, 125-27 and J. Nolland, *Luke 1:1–9:20*, WBC (Waco: Word, 1989), xlix-lxvi and the bibliography associated with each exegetical section of their commentaries.

—————————————— SECTION OUTLINE ——————————————

—————————————— **I. THE PROLOGUE (1:1-4)** ——————————————

[1]Many have undertaken to draw up an account of the things that have been
fulfilled among us, [2]just as they were handed down to us by those who from the
first were eyewitnesses and servants of the word. [3]Therefore, since I myself
have carefully investigated everything from the beginning, it seemed good also
to me to write an orderly account for you, most excellent Theophilus, [4]so that
you may know the certainty of the things you have been taught.

Context

Luke's Gospel begins with a literary prologue or "period" that ranks
among the best Greek literature of the first century. Numerous parallels of
such a prologue exist in the Jewish and Hellenistic literature of that day.[1]
In this period Luke manifested his skill as a writer (cf. also 3:1-2 and Acts
1:1-2) and his conscious intention to follow the conventional introductory
form of contemporary literature. In so doing he clearly revealed literary as
well as historical pretensions.

Whether the prologue introduces both Luke and Acts is debated.
Although all accept that the third and fifth books of the NT were not
designed as two independent works (i.e., Luke and Acts) but rather as two
parts of a single work (i.e., Luke-Acts), the prologue introduces primarily
the first part. Support for this conclusion is found in Acts 1:1-2, which
introduces anew the second part of Luke-Acts. Also the description of the
handing down of "the things . . . fulfilled among us" in Luke 1:1-2 fits
better the handing down of Gospel traditions (found in Luke) than the
handing down of church traditions (found in Acts). Finally, the prologue
refers to others' having also written accounts of these things (1:1).
Although we know of Gospels or gospel-like accounts similar to Luke, we
do not have any knowledge of works similar to Acts. As a result the prologue serves primarily as an introduction to Luke's Gospel.[2] Nevertheless
when Luke penned his Gospel, he already had in mind the second part of
his work—Acts.

Luke artistically crafted the prologue. It consists of a single sentence
with two relatively equal parts. The first (vv. 1-2) is a dependent clause

---

[1]See for example Acts 15:24-26, the prologues that begin Ecclesiasticus, Josephus's
Against Apion 1.1-18 and *Jewish War* 1.1-30, and the numerous examples given by H. J.
Cadbury in "Commentary on the Preface of Luke" in *The Beginnings of Christianity*, ed.
F. J. Foakes-Jackson and K. Lake (London: Macmillan, 1922), 2:489-510.

[2]For the contrary view see I. H. Marshall, "Luke and His 'Gospel' " in *The Gospel and
the Gospels*, ed. P. Stuhlmacher (Grand Rapids: Eerdmans, 1991), 278-80.

(the *protasis*) informing Theophilus of Luke's predecessors and the prior transmission of the Gospel traditions. The protasis consists of v. 1, to which Luke added the parenthetical comment of v. 2. The second part of the prologue (vv. 3-4) is an independent clause (the *apodosis*) in which Luke presented his credentials (1:3) and his purpose in writing (1:4). There is a carefully constructed parallelism between these two parts. Compare the balance between "many" in v. 1 and "also to me" in v. 3, "draw up an account" in v. 1 and "to write an orderly account" in v. 3, and "eyewitnesses" in v. 2 and "certainty" in v. 4.

Comments

1:1 Luke began his prologue with an opening conjunction not translated by the NIV that can be either causal (*because*) or concessive (*even though*). This is the only time "forasmuch" (KJV, Greek *epeidēper*) occurs in the NT or in the LXX. Certainty as to its meaning is impossible, but in other literature the meaning tends to be causal.

Many. The number implied by this term is unclear. Some have suggested that it refers to two or three.[3] Others have suggested it may refer to dozens. We should not simply read into this term an implied number in order to fit our solution to the Synoptic Problem. Since "many" and its related expressions are frequently found in rhetorical prefaces, the term should not be taken as an exact reference to a specific number. It probably is best to understand it as meaning *others*. What is clear is that before Luke wrote his Gospel, others had written accounts concerning Jesus. The reference to "many" does focus on the importance of what Luke was reporting. These "things" were so important that "many" have written about them.

Have undertaken. This word is frequently used to describe the literary effort of authors. It can be used in a pejorative sense (cf. Acts 9:29; 19:13; and esp. Josephus, *Life* 9 [40]; 65 [338]). This does not seem to be the case here, however, because (1) it is frequently used in literary introductions in a positive sense; (2) Luke made positive use of his other sources (Mark, Q, L); (3) the statement in v. 3 "it seemed good also to me" identifies itself with the other works rather than criticizes them; and above all (4) the positive attitude of Luke in Acts toward the witnesses and ministers of the word (Acts 1:8,22; 2:32; 3:15; 26:16; etc.) requires that Luke 1:1 be understood positively as well. The lack of any clearly critical comments about his predecessors sets Luke apart from most authors of other prologues and suggests that this word should not be interpreted pejoratively.[4]

An account. This term was frequently used by Greek writers to describe historical works. Thus Luke related his own work to that of the historians, and such passages as 2:1-2 and 3:1-2 clearly reflect historical pretensions.

Of the things that have been fulfilled. This does not refer primarily to specific OT prophecies fulfilled in Jesus' life, for Luke did not understand all the

[3] See R. J. Dillon, "Previewing Luke's Project from His Prologue (Luke 1:1-4)," *CBQ* 43 (1981): 207.
[4] C. H. Talbert, *Reading Luke* (New York: Crossroad, 1982), 7; cf. also Marshall, "If Luke had any quarrel with his predecessors, it was not because what they wrote was faulty but because it was incomplete" ("Luke," 291).

various teachings of Jesus as fulfilling specific prophecies. Not even all the events in Jesus' life had specific OT prophecies associated with them. Therefore it is best to interpret this as referring to how Jesus' life and teachings fulfilled the OT. Jesus is the awaited Messiah who by his life and death fulfilled the promises of the OT. The fulfillment of prophecy is a clear Lukan theme. See Introduction 7 (1).

Us. This does not refer exclusively to Luke and his readers but broadly to the Christian church at large. This includes the characters of Luke 1–2, the eyewitnesses and servants of the word, Luke, Luke's Christian readers, and others.

1:2 Handed down. This is a technical term used to describe the passing on of authoritative tradition.[5]

Us. The pronoun at this point has been narrowed down to a smaller group within the church, i.e., those like Luke and his readers who were neither eyewitnesses (1:2) nor writers of the Gospel traditions mentioned in 1:1.

From the first. This, according to Acts 1:21-22, refers to the beginning of Jesus' ministry, i.e., his baptism by John. This does not mean, however, that the events occurring before the baptism, as found in Luke 1–2, do not ultimately come from eyewitness testimony. The eyewitnesses of these earlier events were not, however, the eyewitnesses referred to in 1:2.

Eyewitnesses and servants of the word. The use of a single Greek article before "eyewitnesses and servants" indicates that Luke was referring to a single group, i.e., the eyewitnesses and servants of the word" rather than "the eyewitnesses plus also the servants of the word." (Note how *servant* and *witness* refer to the same person in Acts 26:16.) The term "were" (*genomenoi*) was frequently used with "eyewitnesses" among Greek writers and thus should be interpreted as describing both nouns, i.e., "were eyewitnesses and ministers of the word" rather than "eyewitnesses who became ministers of the word."[6] For Luke the leading element of this group was the Twelve (Luke 6:13-16; Acts 1:21-26; 13:31), even if others (such as the seventy, Luke 10:1-12) could be included.

Word. This term and the expression "word of God" are technical terms in Luke-Acts for the gospel message. In Luke-Acts they are used over forty times in this sense.[7]

1:3 Customarily ancient authors gave some statement concerning their qualifications for writing. Luke in this verse set forth his credentials.

Have investigated. The three primary ways of understanding this verb involve Luke's (1) having studied the various narratives referred to in v. 1, (2) having become acquainted with the things that had been fulfilled (1:1), and (3) having participated in the events.[8] Although the latter interpretation is possible in Acts with regard to the "we" sections, Luke was not interested at this point in establishing his qualifications for writing the second part of his work (Acts) by showing his participation in those events. This interpretation is also refuted by 1:2, where the author implied that he was not an eyewitness, i.e., he did not participate

---

[5]Cf. Mark 7:13; Acts 6:14; 1 Cor 11:2,23; 15:3; 2 Pet 2:21; Jude 3.

[6]See R. H. Stein, "Luke 1:1-4 and *Traditionsgeschichte*," *JETS* 26 (1983): 425.

[7]Cf. Luke 5:1; 8:11,12,13,15; 10:39; 11:28; Acts 4:4,29,31; 6:4.

[8]J. A. Fitzmyer, *The Gospel according to Luke*, AB (Garden City: Doubleday, 1981), 296-97.

in the things referred to in his Gospel. It seems best to understand this term (a participle in Greek) in the first sense. Luke, in describing his credentials for writing his Gospel, claimed that he had investigated the various narratives and eyewitness accounts which tell of "the things fulfilled."

Carefully. Luke added that his investigation was carefully/accurately done. This adverb modifies the participle "having investigated" rather than the verb "write."

Everything. Luke's careful investigation involves all the things that have been fulfilled among us (1:1).

From the beginning. The adverb *anōthen* goes with "have investigated" and can be translated either "for some time past," indicating the length or duration of his research, or "from the beginning," which would designate the extent of Luke's research. It is best to interpret this as a synonym for "from the first [beginning, *ap' archēs*]" in 1:2 and thus as a designation of the extent of his research, i.e., he had investigated the things he was reporting from start to finish. The starting point therefore for Luke was not the baptism of Jesus but rather the conception of Jesus' forerunner (cf. 1:5ff.). This interpretation is supported by the only other appearance of the same term in Acts 26:4-5, where *anōthen* is once again preceded by its synonym *ap' arches*.

Also to me. A few Old Latin manuscripts add "and the Holy Spirit" (cf. Acts 15:28). This, however, is clearly a later scribal addition to the text.

To write an orderly account. The exact meaning of "orderly" is uncertain. It can refer to a temporal (Acts 3:24), geographical (18:23), or literary-logical sequence (11:4). The fact that Peter in 11:15 stated that the Spirit came upon Cornelius as he began to speak, whereas in 10:44-45 the Spirit came after Peter had spoken for some time, indicates that the "order" Luke was referring to was a logical rather than a chronological one. Several examples of Luke's concern for logical order can be mentioned. In Luke 3:19-20 the arrest of John the Baptist is placed next to the baptism account due to topical considerations, whereas chronological considerations would place it later (cf. Mark 6:17-18), after Jesus' baptism (Luke 3:21-22). In 4:16-30 Luke recorded Jesus' "first" sermon even though earlier he had preached/healed in Capernaum (4:23). In 6:12-16 Jesus' calling of the twelve disciples is placed before his withdrawal with them in 6:17-19, whereas the order in Mark is reversed (3:13-19 and 3:7-12). In Luke 8:23 Jesus' sleeping is mentioned before the storm (cf. Mark 4:37-38). In Luke 8:42 the daughter's age is given at her first mention rather than as a parenthetical comment at the end (cf. Mark 5:42). In 9:14 Luke placed the number of people present next to the amount of bread needed (cf. Mark 6:44), and in 22:56-62 he placed Peter's denial next to the mention of Peter in 22:54-55 rather than reintroducing him later as Matthew and Mark did (cf. Matt 26:57-58 and 26:69-75; Mark 14:53-54 and 14:66-72).

The term *orderly* was used throughout Greek literature by writers who sought to convince their hearers of the meticulous research and careful organization of their material. By his use of this term Luke was stating that he had written his Gospel in a logical fashion. In the next verse he gives the purpose of this meticulous research and orderly writing.

Most excellent. This polite form of address used of lofty persons is found in the NT only here and in Acts 23:26; 24:3; and 26:25. In the latter instances it is used to address Roman governors. This address unfortunately does not allow us to conclude what kind of person Theophilus was. See Introduction (3).

Theophilus. This name means *friend (philys) of God (theos).* This probably was the name of a real person rather than a symbolic metaphor or a pseudonym to obscure the real identity of the letter's recipient. Numerous suggestions about Theophilus's identity have been made; they include a Roman governor, the official who was to hear Paul's case in Rome, and Luke's literary patron. Nevertheless who this person was remains unknown. Compare Acts 1:1.

1:4 So that. Along with the presentation of the writer's credentials, some comment concerning the work's purpose was an integral part of an ancient prologue.

May know the certainty. If "orderly" is understood to mean "chronological," then Luke's purpose would have been to convince Theophilus that the things he had been taught were chronologically correct. However, since it is best to understand "orderly" as designating a logical order, the certainty being sought involves the truthful quality of the material. In using this phrase Luke did not mean that he was seeking to demonstrate that the church traditions go back to the historical Jesus. This concern belongs primarily to the eighteenth to twentieth centuries. Rather Luke hoped that through his Gospel the Christian faith of his readers would be strengthened and encouraged as they saw how Jesus' life and death truly fulfilled what the prophets had earlier proclaimed, how God confirmed the life and teachings of Jesus by numerous miracles, and so forth. For a fuller discussion of how Luke hoped Theophilus would come to this certainty, see Introduction 7 (1).

You have been taught. The term "taught" can be understood in the sense that Theophilus had been "informed" (Acts 21:21,24) or taught/instructed in (18:25-26; cf. Gal 6:6) the Gospel traditions. The Greek term is *katēchēthēs*, from which the word "catechism" comes. It later became a technical term for the prebaptismal teaching or catechizing of new converts. This later meaning, however, should not be read into the present context. The meaning of this term is intimately connected with the issue of whether Theophilus was a Christian. If we knew for certain how this verb should be translated, we would know whether Theophilus was a Christian. Similarly, if we knew for certain whether or not Theophilus was a Christian, then we would know how to translate this verb. In Introduction 3 we have argued that the readers of Luke-Acts probably were Christians. As a result it appears best to translate *katēchēthēs* as *taught* rather than as *informed.*

The Lukan Message

Although Luke in his prologue sought primarily to establish his credentials as a writer and historian, he revealed a great deal about how the Gospel traditions proceeded from the historical Jesus to the writing of the Gospels. Of all the Gospel writers, Luke alone discussed the methodology used in the composition of his Gospel, and his prologue is the most explicit statement available about how the Gospel traditions were transmitted and incorporated into a Gospel.[9] Luke informed us that three separate situations

---

[9]M. O. Tolbert ("Luke," BBC, vol. 9 [Nashville: Broadman, 1970], 17) rightly points out that "any adequate concept of inspiration of the biblical record must come to grips with this the sole autobiographical statement of a Gospel writer about his method."

in life (*Sitz[e]* *im Leben*) were involved. (1) The situation of the events themselves, i.e., the time of "the things that have been fulfilled among us" (1:1). This refers to the life and teachings of the historical Jesus. (2) The time and situation in which the eyewitnesses and ministers of the word handed down these materials (1:2). This is the period in which the Gospel materials were being passed on orally under the supervision of the eyewitnesses. (3) Finally, there is the period in which the Gospel traditions were being written down and in which our present Gospels came to be formed. Luke placed himself in this last situation. For Luke these latter two periods overlapped somewhat, for the traditions his readers received according to 1:2 were being circulated while he and others undertook to write them down. The study of the first situation, or *Sitz im Leben*, involves various historical interests such as the quest for the historical Jesus and the pursuit for Jesus' actual words. The investigation of the second situation involves primarily the discipline of form criticism, and the investigation of the third situation involves primarily the disciplines of literary and redaction criticism. These three situations together form the provenance of the discipline of tradition history or *Traditionsgeschichte*.[10]

For Luke this process was not chaotic but controlled by the apostolic eyewitnesses and by writers like himself. He believed that his orderly presentation of the Gospel traditions would reinforce his readers' present understanding of these traditions because his Gospel was in accord with what they had already been taught, and what they had been taught came from those who were themselves eyewitnesses of Jesus' acts and sayings. It has been the conviction of the church through the centuries that the God who sent his Son as Savior of the world by the divine superintendence of his Spirit also guided in the writing, preservation, and recognition of this material. This, of course, is a theological confession and not capable of demonstration, but it is a confession that has served the church well over the centuries.

For Luke the main purpose of the prologue was to establish his credibility as a historian. He sought to do this in 1:3 by compounding terms that reveal his care and expertise in writing. Such terms as "carefully," "everything," "from the beginning," and "orderly account" describe qualities that any historian would be proud to have included in an assessment of his or her work. Luke further argued the case for the accuracy of what he wrote by pointing to a direct tie between his Gospel and the testimony of the eyewitnesses in 1:2 and by mentioning his investigation of various written accounts (1:1). Finally he stated that his goal in writing was to help his readers come to a certainty of the truthfulness of the gospel teachings the readers had been taught. Was Luke successful in this? We

---

[10]For further discussion see R. H. Stein, *The Synoptic Problem* (Grand Rapids: Baker, 1987).

cannot be certain, but the very fact that his works were preserved indicates that his earliest readers thought sufficiently of them to preserve them. As for later readers they quickly included Luke-Acts among the *Homologoumena* or books that everyone in the church confessed and acknowledged as authoritative. The church has reserved a place in its canon for this Gospel, and commentaries, like this one, continue to be written on it because throughout the centuries people have come to recognize the truthfulness of what it says and to encounter in and through it the Lord of whom it speaks.

─────────────── *SECTION OUTLINE* ───────────────

II. THE INFANCY NARRATIVE (1:5–2:52)
1. John the Baptist's Birth Announced (1:5-25)
2. Jesus' Birth Announced (1:26-38)
3. The Meeting of John the Baptist and Jesus (1:39-56)
4. The Birth of John the Baptist (1:57-80)
5. The Birth of Jesus (2:1-52)
  (1) The Birth Proper (2:1-20)
  (2) The Circumcision and the Prophets, Simeon and Anna (2:21-40)
  (3) The Boy Jesus in the Temple (2:41-52)

──────── **II. THE INFANCY NARRATIVE (1:5–2:52)** ────────

After stating in his prologue that he sought to write an orderly account that started at the beginning, Luke commenced his narrative by providing his readers a carefully organized account of "the things that have been fulfilled among us" (1:1). He began with God visiting his people (1:68) in the miraculous birth of the Messiah's forerunner, John the Baptist, and in the Messiah's even more miraculous birth. Unlike Mark, who started his Gospel at the baptism, Luke began his with the fulfillment of the covenantal promises God made to his people. This divine fulfillment commences with the miraculous conceptions and births of the Messiah and his forerunner.

The orderly nature of the Lukan account involves a careful paralleling of the events associated with the birth and coming of John the Baptist and the birth and coming of Jesus. Through this parallelism Luke emphasized both the common unity of their task and the differences between John as the forerunner and Jesus as the Messiah. John is not seen as a rival of Jesus (regardless of how one explains Acts 19:1ff.); rather in these parallels Jesus is always displayed as the superior. The Lukan parallelism reflected in the outline above extends to specific elements in the accounts: the same angel, Gabriel, appeared to Zechariah and Mary; both were troubled by the angelic visit; both were told not to be afraid; both were told of the future birth of a son; both births were associated with the work of the Holy Spirit; in both passages the angel gave the name for the son; in both the angel stated that the son would be great; in both the sons' future roles in God's plan were announced; and in both we are told of the birth, circumcision, and naming of the sons. Both the opening (1:8-23) and concluding (2:22-38,41-51) accounts of this section (1:5–2:52) took place in the temple. By this inclusio Luke bracketed the unit and gave it an overall unity.[1]

In this section Luke revealed his meaning to Theophilus in several different ways. One way was through the hymns and prophecies of various authoritative spokespersons, including angels (1:13-17,30-37; 2:10-12), the "upright" priest Zechariah (1:67-79), the "upright" Elizabeth (1:41-45), the "highly favored" Mary (1:46-55), and the "righteous and devout" prophet Simeon (2:29-32,34). Their hymnic and prophetic pronouncements declare to the reader the divinely ordained coming of the Messiah and his forerunner and their future roles and work. They even allude to the future passion of which the readers are already aware. The reliability of these pronouncements is evident in the Lukan description of their character and in their subsequent fulfillment.

Another means by which Luke shared his meaning with the readers was through the numerous allusions and analogies to the OT Scriptures. Some of the more evident are barrenness followed by a miraculous birth and a special divine mission for the child (Gen 18; 25; 30; Judg 13; 1 Sam 1), a birth announcement (Gen 25; Judg 13), reference to the angel Gabriel (Dan 8-9; cf. 1 Enoch 9; 40; 2 Enoch 21:24), the appearance of a prophet and a divine revelation, and various other allusions to the OT.[2] Finally Luke helped his readers to a proper understanding by means of his editorial work throughout the narrative[3] and his repetition of important themes, such as the divine promises having been fulfilled;[4] God's having sent his Son, the Messiah, to Israel;[5] the Messiah's being born of a virgin (1:27,34,37); the Spirit's being active once again in Israel;[6] God's seeking the downtrodden;[7] and the presence of the joy of salvation (1:14,46; 2:10).

The infancy narratives of Matthew and Luke are frequently compared and contrasted. The differences between them are well known.[8] Numerous common elements exist between them, however, and should not be overlooked.[9] Thus although there are some serious differences between the

[1] For further discussion see R. E. Brown, *The Birth of the Messiah* (Garden City: Doubleday, 1979), 248-53, 292-98, 408-10; J. A. Fitzmyer, *The Gospel according to Luke*, AB (Garden City: Doubleday, 1981), 309-16.

[2] Luke 1:7,14-17,24-25,31-33,52-55,68-75; 2:11,22-24.

[3] Luke 1:41,80; 2:25-27,38,40,52.

[4] Luke 1:16-17,32-33,54-55,68-75; 2:11,26-32,38.

[5] Luke 1:17,32-33,35,42-45,68-75; 2:4,11,26,40,49-50,52.

[6] Luke 1:15,17,35,41; 2:25-27.

[7] Luke 1:24,47-48,53,68-70,72-74; 2:8-20.

[8] These include the difference in their genealogies; the lack of any mention of wise men, the massacre of the innocents, or the flight to Egypt in Luke; the lack of reference to Zechariah and Elizabeth, the census, the shepherds, Jesus' circumcision, or Simeon and Anna in Matthew; and the lack of a single common narrative between the two Gospels.

[9] We find a common reference to Jesus' birth during the reign of Herod the Great (Luke 1:5; Matt 2:1); Mary's and Joseph's being engaged (Luke 1:27,34; 2:5; Matt 1:18); Mary's

two accounts, we must also observe the broad agreement that exists between them.

The Semitic character of Luke 1–2 has been recognized for a long time. In the past this was seen as an indication of an Aramaic source or sources lying behind these chapters. More recently scholars have stressed Luke's conscious decision to imitate Jewish Septuagintal Greek in order to explain why this was the most Jewish section of his Gospel. Still others have suggested that the Semitic character of this section arises from the fact that Luke was using Hebrew sources.[10] While the investigation of this issue is a legitimate exegetical task, it has surprisingly little value for understanding the meaning of Luke 1:1–24:53. Our task is to understand the meaning of our present Gospel, not to investigate the individual pre-Lukan sources. As a result we will not seek to resolve this present issue, which may in fact be unsolvable.

At times the rest of the Gospel has been treated in almost total isolation from these first two chapters.[11] Conzelmann has argued that there is present in Luke a threefold scheme of salvation history. The first is the Period of Israel, the second is the Period of Jesus, and the third is the Period of the Church.[12] However, once one seeks to interpret Luke 3:1–Acts 28:31 in light of these two chapters, it appears that John the Baptist cannot be relegated to the OT Period of Israel. He clearly is part of the good news (1:19,77) and belongs with Jesus. It is best therefore in light of 1:1–2:52 to see in Luke-Acts a twofold scheme of salvation history. The first is the Period of Promise, which is the time of the law and the prophets, i.e., the OT. The second is the Period of Fulfillment, which consists of the transition period to which John the Baptist and Jesus belong and which is followed by the arrival of the new age at Pentecost.

1. John the Baptist's Birth Announced (1:5-25)

[5]In the time of Herod king of Judea there was a priest named Zechariah, who belonged to the priestly division of Abijah; his wife Elizabeth was also a

being a virgin (Luke 1:27,34; Matt 1:18,23,25); Joseph's being of Davidic descent (Luke 1:27; 2:4; Matt 1:16,20); Matt 1:20-21); Jesus' being a descendant of David (Luke 1:32; Matt 1:1); the conception as the work of the Holy Spirit (Luke 1:35; Matt 1:18,20); the angel's directing the naming of the child (Luke 1:31; Matt 1:21); the angel's stating that Jesus would be a Savior (Luke 2:11; Matt 1:21); Jesus' being born after Mary came to live with Joseph (Luke 2:4-7; Matt 1:24-25); Jesus' being born in Bethlehem (Luke 2:4-7; Matt 2:1); and Jesus' being raised in Nazareth (Luke 2:39,51; Matt 2:22-23).

[10]For further discussion see S. Farris, *The Hymns of Luke's Infancy Narratives, JSNTSup* (Sheffield: JSOT, 1985), 14-98; J. Nolland, *Luke 1–9:20*, WBC (Waco: Word, 1989), 17-23.

[11]See P. S. Minear ("Luke's Use of the Birth Stories," in *Studies in Luke-Acts*, ed. L. E. Keck and J. L. Martyn [New York: Abingdon, 1966], 111-30), who demonstrates the integral relationship of these chapters to the rest of Luke-Acts.

[12]See H. Conzelmann, *The Theology of St. Luke* (New York: Harper, 1960), 16-17.

descendant of Aaron. [6]Both of them were upright in the sight of God, observing all the Lord's commandments and regulations blamelessly. [7]But they had no children, because Elizabeth was barren; and they were both well along in years.

[8]Once when Zechariah's division was on duty and he was serving as priest before God, [9]he was chosen by lot, according to the custom of the priesthood, to go into the temple of the Lord and burn incense. [10]And when the time for the burning of incense came, all the assembled worshipers were praying outside.

[11]Then an angel of the Lord appeared to him, standing at the right side of the altar of incense. [12]When Zechariah saw him, he was startled and was gripped with fear. [13]But the angel said to him: "Do not be afraid, Zechariah; your prayer has been heard. Your wife Elizabeth will bear you a son, and you are to give him the name John. [14]He will be a joy and delight to you, and many will rejoice because of his birth, [15]for he will be great in the sight of the Lord. He is never to take wine or other fermented drink, and he will be filled with the Holy Spirit even from birth. [16]Many of the people of Israel will he bring back to the Lord their God. [17]And he will go on before the Lord, in the spirit and power of Elijah, to turn the hearts of the fathers to their children and the disobedient to the wisdom of the righteous—to make ready a people prepared for the Lord."

[18]Zechariah asked the angel, "How can I be sure of this? I am an old man and my wife is well along in years."

[19]The angel answered, "I am Gabriel. I stand in the presence of God, and I have been sent to speak to you and to tell you this good news. [20]And now you will be silent and not able to speak until the day this happens, because you did not believe my words, which will come true at their proper time."

[21]Meanwhile, the people were waiting for Zechariah and wondering why he stayed so long in the temple. [22]When he came out, he could not speak to them. They realized he had seen a vision in the temple, for he kept making signs to them but remained unable to speak.

[23]When his time of service was completed, he returned home. [24]After this his wife Elizabeth became pregnant and for five months remained in seclusion. [25]"The Lord has done this for me," she said. "In these days he has shown his favor and taken away my disgrace among the people."

Context

In this section Luke recorded how God after four hundred years once again visited Israel and raised up a prophet who would prepare the people for the coming of the Messiah. Although the Qumran community believed that God was active and revealed himself through their movement and that their Teacher of Righteousness was a prophet, for the majority of Israel the prophets had fallen asleep (2 Bar 85:1-3; 1 Macc 4:46; 9:27; 14:41) and the Holy Spirit had ceased in Israel (*Tosefta Sota* 13:3). As a result most people tended to look back to the period of the law and the prophets when God was active among his people or forward to the time of the messianic age when God would once again be active and fulfill his covenantal promises. Thus God's visit to Zechariah marks for Luke the breaking in of the messianic age, i.e., the beginning of the things that God has fulfilled among his people.

The announcement of the birth of John the Baptist can be subdivided into the following units: the setting (1:5-7), the announcement (1:8-20), the people's amazement (1:21-23), and the fulfillment of the announced promise (1:24-25).

Comments

1:5 In the time of Herod king of Judea. Literally, *And it came to pass in the days of.* This is a common literary form in Luke-Acts.[13] The expression "in the/ those days" also occurs frequently.[14] Luke at the very beginning of his Gospel revealed his historical and chronological interests (cf. also 2:1-2; 3:1-2). Jesus' birth is also tied to Herod the Great in Matt 2:1. Unfortunately Herod's reign was long (ca. 40 B.C. [granted kingship by Rome] or 37 B.C. [established his rule] to 4 B.C.), so that this temporal designation does not satisfy the desire for greater specificity.

Judea. The term is used broadly here for the land of the Jews[15] and not in the narrower sense for the Roman province of Judah.[16]

Priestly division of Abijah. The service of the temple was divided into twenty-four divisions, and each provided for the needs of the temple service for a week at a time, twice a year.[17] During the major religious festivals (Passover, Pentecost, and the Feast of Tabernacles) all the divisions served.

1:6 Both of them were upright [righteous] in the sight of God. Righteousness is an important characteristic of God's people in Luke-Acts.[18] Their righteousness was in the sight of God and not just in appearance as in the case of some Pharisees.

Observing . . . commandments and regulations blamelessly. "Commandments and regulations" is a frequent OT combination.[19] Other synonyms are laws, ordinances, and judgments. For Luke, as for the psalmist in Ps 119:1, keeping the commandments and regulations results in being upright and blameless before God. This is true for the Christian as well.[20] A correct understanding of the law includes recognizing God's gracious provision of mercy for the sinner and the law as the ethical embodiment of God's will for his children. To keep God's commandments and regulations means to believe in and follow God's Son and by his grace to observe the "commandments and regulations" that embody his will. Zechariah and Elizabeth

---

[13]Luke 2:1; 6:12; Acts 9:37; cf. also Luke 8:22; 9:37; 17:26; 20:1; Acts 9:43; 28:17; cf. Jer 1:2-3; Amos 1:1.

[14]Luke 1:39; 2:1; 4:25; 5:35; 6:12; 9:36; etc.

[15]As in 4:44; 6:17; 7:17; 23:5; Acts 10:37; 15:1.

[16]As in 1:65; 2:4; 3:1; 5:17; 21:21; 23:5-7.

[17]See J. Jeremias, *Jerusalem in the Time of Jesus* (Philadelphia: Fortress, 1969), 198-207.

[18]Luke 1:17; 2:25; 23:47,50; Acts 10:22; cf. also 14:14; 20:20; Acts 3:14; 7:52; 22:14; 24:15.

[19]E.g., Gen 26:5; Exod 15:26; Deut 4:40; 6:1-2; 1 Kgs 8:61.

[20]Luke 10:25-28; 16:17; 18:18-20; 23:56b; Acts 21:20,24; 22:12.

represent the best of OT piety and as the faithful remnant received the good news of
the gospel (Luke 1:19). They are an indication that the good news Jesus brings does
not conflict with the faith of Israel in the OT. If some in Israel opposed Jesus, it was
not because there was a conflict between the religion of the OT and the Christian
faith. Rather it was due to their being unfaithful to the teachings of the law and the
prophets. See Introduction 7 (2). The term "blamelessly" does not mean that they
possessed a sinless perfection as 1:18-20 reveals. Luke used this verse to explain to
his readers that Zechariah and Elizabeth's childlessness, as mentioned in the next
verse, was not due to sin.[21]

1:7   No children ... both well along in years.   The Greek term "no children" (*steira*) is used of Sarah (Gen 11:30), Rebekah (25:21), Rachel (29:31), and
Samson's mother (Judg 13:2-3; cf. also 1 Sam 1:5). "Well advanced in years" is
used in Gen 18:11 of Sarah. The mention of Zechariah and Elizabeth's childlessness and their being past childbearing age points to the human impossibility of the
coming events and heightens the miraculous character of God's intervention in
their son's birth. Luke assumed that his readers would recall similar situations in
the OT in which God blessed the barren with a son who was uniquely called to
fulfill a divine task.

1:8   Luke began and closed his Gospel with a scene taking place in the temple
(cf. 24:53). In Acts we also find a temple scene in the beginning (2:1f.), and the
temple remains central from Acts 2 through 26.

1:9   He was chosen by lot.   This indicates that God's providential leading
caused Zechariah to be chosen.[22] For Luke this was not the result of "chance" or
"fate." God was clearly in control of this event. See Introduction 8 (1).

Since so many priests served the temple (about eighteen thousand), entering
the holy place to clean the altar of incense and to offer fresh incense usually occurred only once in the lifetime of a priest.

To go ... and burn incense.   Compare Exod 30:7-8.

Temple.   Temple (*naos*) here refers to the sanctuary proper and not the entire
temple complex (*hieron*) as in Luke 2:27,37,46.

1:10   Time for the burning of incense.   We are not told whether this was
the morning or evening time.

Were praying.   It is a Lukan characteristic to point out that major events are
associated with prayer. See Introduction 8 (7). By his reference to worshipers being assembled outside for prayer, Luke prepared his readers for 1:21ff.

1:11   Appeared.   This term (*ōphthē*) frequently denotes divine epiphanies.[23]

Angel of the Lord.   This refers to God's messenger who in OT times was at
times indistinguishable from God himself.[24] In 1:19 he is named Gabriel.

---

[21] For childlessness as a disgrace and punishment for sin, see comments on 1:25; cf. Gen
16:4,11; 29:32; 30:1,22-23; Lev 20:20-21; 1 Sam 1:5-6,11; 2:5-8; 2 Sam 6:23; Jer 22:30; 36:30.

[22] This example and the fact that the selection of Matthias (Acts 1:26) was preceded by
prayer (vv. 24-25) make clear that that act should also be understood as taking place according to God's providential will.

[23] Luke 24:34; Acts 2:3; 7:2,30,35; 9:17; 13:31; 16:9; 26:16.

[24] Gen 16:7-13; 21:17-18; 22:10-18; 31:11-13; Exod 3:2-4; 14:19-20; Judg 2:1-5; cf. also
2:9; Acts 5:19-20; 8:26; 12:7-11,23.

Right side. This favored side indicates that the visit was not ominous but one of favor and blessing (cf. Acts 7:55). For a similar incident outside of Scripture, see Josephus, *Antiquities* 13.10.3 (13.282-83).

1:12 Startled and was gripped with fear. This is a standard reaction even for the upright (see comments on 1:65; 23:40) when experiencing the presence of God.

1:13 Do not be afraid. This is a standard word of reassurance.[25]

Your prayer is heard. Does this refer to a prayer Zechariah was currently praying, i.e., was Zechariah still hoping that God would bless them with a child? In light of 1:7 this seems doubtful. More likely this refers to the prayer for a son made previously. Another possibility is that this refers to Zechariah's prayer for God to send the Messiah and deliver Israel. Verses 13b-17, however, speak more of John the Baptist as forerunner than to the Messiah's coming. It appears in light of 1:7 and the latter part of this verse that Luke expected his readers to assume the content of this prayer involves the birth of a child.[26] This prayer will be answered but in a richer sense than Zechariah and Elizabeth ever dreamed. No doubt Zechariah and Elizabeth, as devout Israelites, also prayed for the coming of the redemption of Israel. Both these prayers were to be answered in the same event because their son would prepare the way for the Messiah.

John. The name means *Yahweh has been gracious*, but the significance of the name was not explained. The name was not given because of its etymology (contrast Matt 1:21). It was noted because Luke's readers already knew of John the Baptist and his role in salvation history and because Luke wanted to point out John's miraculous birth and divine calling to prepare for the coming of the Messiah. John is referred to again in Luke 3:1-20; 5:33; 7:18-35; 9:7-9; 11:1; 16:16; 20:4-6.

1:13b-20 The angelic announcement follows a typical pattern found in OT birth announcements.[27] The pattern usually involves (1) the appearance of the angel, 1:11; (2) a response of fear on the part of the one contacted, 1:12; (3) a word of reassurance, 1:13a; (4) the divine message, 1:13b-17; (5) an objection and request for a sign, 1:18; (6) the giving of a sign of assurance, 1:19-20.[28] The importance of this announcement is evident by its coming from an authoritative messenger (the angel Gabriel), by its allusions to Scripture, and by its later fulfillment.

1:14 Joy and delight. Just as Jesus' birth would bring joy, so did John's. This joy was not just a personal feeling but the eschatological joy brought by the arrival of the messianic age (2:10; 10:17; 24:41,52).

Many will rejoice because of his birth. "Birth" here means *the coming on the scene [of the Messiah's forerunner].* Clearly Luke did not see John the Baptist as bringing a negative message that stands in contrast to Jesus' "good news." On the contrary, he brought the joyous announcement of the awaited eschatological hope of Israel!

---

[25] Luke 1:30; 2:10; 8:50; Gen 15:1; Judg 6:23; Dan 10:12,19.

[26] For OT examples of such prayer, see Gen 25:21; 30:22; 1 Sam 1:10-17; and for examples of God hearing prayer, see 2 Kgs 20:5; Dan 10:12; cf. Sir 51:11; Sus 44.

[27] Cf. Gen 16:7-13; 17:1-21; 18:1-15; Judg 13:3-20; Luke 1:26-38.

[28] See Fitzmyer, *Luke*, 318-21.

1:15 He will be great in the sight of the Lord. Luke 1:15-17 gives the reason for the joy and delight mentioned in 1:14. In the subsequent description in 1:32, Jesus' superiority over John is evident in that there is no qualification of the designation "great." Luke in his comparison of John the Baptist and Jesus did not minimize John's greatness (7:28). Instead he maximized Jesus' greatness.

Lord. "Lord" refers here to God, as 1:16 indicates.

He is never to take wine or other fermented drink. This could refer to John's being a Nazirite (Num 6:2-5; Judg 13:4-5; 1 Sam 1:11) or to a requirement to abstain from strong drink since he was to live an ascetic life (7:33) and serve God in a special way (Lev 10:9). The latter is more likely, for other things required of a Nazirite, such as not cutting the hair, are not mentioned.[29]

He will be filled with the Holy Spirit. Compare Luke 1:41,67, where this same expression is used.[30] The work of the Holy Spirit is a favorite Lukan emphasis. See Introduction 8 (3). The expression "filled with the Spirit" probably is traditional.[31] Once again God was about to send a prophet to his people. Although the Spirit came upon John and made him "a prophet of the Most High" (1:76), his followers would not share in the promised baptism of the Spirit, whereas the followers of the One he announced would (3:16; cf. Acts 1:5; 2:1ff.; 11:15-16).

Even from birth. This expression can mean "from birth" as in Ps 22:10; Isa 48:8; or "while still in the womb" as in Judg 13:3-5; 16:17; Isa 44:2. The latter is undoubtedly the meaning here due to Luke 1:41. In the OT the Holy Spirit usually came upon a prophet later in life, although certain prophets were also called while still in the womb or from birth (Samson, Judg 16:17; Jeremiah, Jer 1:5; the Servant of the Lord, Isa 49:1,5; Paul, Gal 1:15).

1:16 Will . . . bring back. "Bring back" is a technical term for conversion in the NT.[32]

1:17 Go on before the Lord. "Lord" (literally *him*) can refer to God as in Luke 1:15-16 or to Jesus, but of the twenty-six times it is used in chaps. 1–2, it is used of Jesus at most only three other times (1:43,76; 2:11). Nevertheless, since this describes the role of John in preceding and preparing the way for Jesus (1:76-77; cf. 3:4 and 7:26-27 with the quotation from Isa 40:3-5), it is best to see "Lord" (or "him") as a reference to the Lord Jesus Christ. Luke no doubt built on his readers' understanding (Luke 1:4) of John's role, which was to go before the Lord and prepare the people. As a result it would have been quite natural for them, as for the present-day reader who knows the story, to interpret "Lord" in light of John's specific role as the Lord's forerunner. See comments on 1:43.

In the spirit and power of Elijah. Like Elijah (2 Kgs 2:9-10) John was endowed with the Spirit. There is a close tie between "spirit" and "power" in Luke-

---

[29] For a discussion of the meaning of "wine" in the time of Jesus, see R. H. Stein, *Difficult Passages in the New Testament* (Grand Rapids: Baker, 1990), 233-38.

[30] Luke could refer to the Holy Spirit without an article, with a double article, or with a single article. These are simply stylistic differences, however, and no theological implications should be deduced from this, as a comparison of the Greek text of 2:25 and 2:26 indicates.

[31] Cf. 1:41,67; Acts 4:8,31; 6:5; 7:55; 9:17; 11:24; 13:9,52; Eph 5:18.

[32] Acts 9:35; 11:21; 14:15; 2 Cor 3:16; 1 Thess 1:9; 1 Pet 2:25; cf. also 22:32; Acts 3:19; 15:19; 26:18,20; 28:27.

Acts,[33] and when "power" is mentioned, one can usually assume that it is the
Spirit who is empowering (5:17). This role of John will be described in 3:1-22.
John never exhibited this "power" by way of miracles in Luke (or the other Gospels; cf. John 10:41), but there was clearly present in his ministry and preaching
the power of the Spirit.

To turn the hearts . . . of the righteous. The meaning of these words is uncertain. One of the problems involves to whom "disobedient" and "righteous" refer. Is
this best interpreted as an example of synonymous parallelism in which "disobedient" parallels "fathers" and "righteous" parallels "children," i.e., fathers are to children as disobedient are to righteous? Or should this be interpreted as an example of
chiastic parallelism in which "disobedient" parallels "children" and "righteous" parallels "fathers," i.e., fathers (A) to children (B) and disobedient (b) to righteous (a)?

Some suggest it refers to the restoration of family relationships. Others suggest
it means that disobedient fathers will receive children's hearts. It may be that seeing this as an example of chiasmic parallelism is the best interpretation of these
verses. Because of John's ministry, fathers will turn compassionately and lovingly
toward their children (cf. Mal 4:6), and disobedient people will turn and accept the
wisdom of the righteous.[34]

1:18 Zechariah demanded proof by means of some sign. Compare Luke
11:16,29; 16:27-31. Also compare the disbelief of Abraham in Gen 15:8 as well as
the parallels in Exod 4:1-17; Judg 6:36-40; 1 Sam 10:2-7; 2 Kgs 20:8-9; Isa 7:11.

1:19 I am Gabriel. By revealing himself as Gabriel, the angel of Dan 8:16;
9:21ff. (cf. 1 Enoch 9:1; 10:9-10; 40:9) and one of only three angels named in the
OT, he lent reliability to what he was saying. He thus was qualified to speak for
God to Zechariah and also to reveal Luke's meaning to his readers.

I stand in the presence of God. This statement gives additional weight and
a sense of truthfulness to what the angel was saying.

To tell you this good news. This verb (*euangelisasthai*) was a favorite term
of Luke even though he avoided the related noun totally in the Gospel and used it
only twice in Acts.[35] Because of his role in introducing Jesus the Christ to Israel,
the conception of John the Baptist is part of the "good news" of Jesus Christ.

1:20 You will be silent. Zechariah graciously was given a sign as an aid to
faith even though the sign also was a rebuke for lack of faith. The sign was a punitive miracle but contained the promise "until the day this happens." Muteness is
a sign in Ezek 3:26; 24:27 and a judgment in 2 Macc 3:29.

Because you did not believe my words. This was the punitive reason for the
sign.

1:21 A delay in the priest's leaving the sanctuary would cause alarm and concern (cf. *Yoma* 5.1 and *Yoma* 52b).

1:22 He could not speak to them. According to *Tamid* 7.2 priests coming
out of the holy place were expected to pronounce a customary blessing, such as
Num 6:24-26, upon the people. Whether Luke's readers would have known this is
uncertain. Luke 1:62 implies that Zechariah also could not hear.

---

[33] Luke 1:35; 4:14; Acts 1:8; 10:38; cf. also Luke 5:17; 24:49; 1 Cor 2:4.

[34] See I. H. Marshall, *The Gospel of Luke*, NIGTC (Grand Rapids: Eerdmans, 1978), 60.

[35] Luke 2:10; 3:18; 4:18,43; 7:22; 8:1; 9:6; 16:16; 20:1; Acts 5:42; 8:35; 11:20; 17:18; etc.

They realized he had seen a vision. Luke did not say how they came to this conclusion, but the implication is that they noted the delay and the muteness of Zechariah and assumed that something must have happened in the sanctuary where God dwelt.

1:23 This transition verse explains the return of Zechariah and Elizabeth to their home somewhere in Judah (1:39).

1:24 For five months remained in seclusion. We know of no custom that would have required Elizabeth to do this. During this period her pregnancy apparently was unknown (cf. 1:36). Some have suggested that Elizabeth went into seclusion in order to avoid reproach from incredulous neighbors during the time when her pregnancy was not obvious. Luke, however, did not explain why Elizabeth remained in seclusion, but this explains Mary's ignorance of Elizabeth's pregnancy in 1:36.

1:25 The Lord has done this for me. In typical Jewish piety praise is addressed to God for what he has done. Attention was focused by Elizabeth for her neighbors and by Luke for his readers on the "Blessor" rather than the blessing. Compare Gen 21:6; 30:23—"God has."

He has . . . taken away my disgrace. Compare Gen 30:23. For childlessness as a disgrace, see comments on 1:6. (The *hoti* that begins this sentence should be left untranslated. It is best understood as introducing a quotation rather than a causal clause.)

The Lukan Message

In the opening account of his Gospel, Luke introduced his readers to several important theological emphases. This is not surprising since good writers seek to prepare readers for what is to come by foreshadowing numerous themes and events. Luke therefore used the infancy narratives to establish a theological foundation for understanding what he was planning to write in the rest of his work. We find several important themes in this section.

One such theme is that the OT promises have been fulfilled in Jesus.[36] Luke showed his readers that the hopes of the upright/righteous (1:6) have been fulfilled in the coming of Jesus and his forerunner, John the Baptist. God has come to redeem his people (cf. 1:68). Zechariah's prayer had been heard; and while this involves primarily the birth of a son (1:13), it also includes every devout Israelite's prayer that God would establish his kingdom. The angelic announcement also points out that Zechariah's son would play a major role in this by preparing a people for the Lord's coming (1:17).

Another emphasis involves the Spirit's coming. Closely related to the previous theme is the Spirit's activity among his people. In this account he is portrayed as active in John the Baptist's birth and ministry (1:15,17; cf. 1:36 with vv. 35,37). This foreshadows the Spirit's even greater activity in

---

[36]This emphasis on fulfillment of OT prophecy is seen most clearly in the early sermons of Acts (2:16-21,25-36; 3:12-18,22-26; 7:2-53; 13:16-37; etc.). Cf. also Luke 4:16-21.

the Messiah's birth to a virgin (1:35). The Spirit is portrayed as active in Jesus' ministry (see Introduction 8 [3]), but the ultimate fulfillment of the Spirit's coming involved the promised baptism of the Spirit (3:16; Acts 1:4-5) which came upon Jesus' followers at Pentecost (Acts 2:1ff.; 11:15-16). Three times within the first chapter of Luke (1:15,41,67) we find a reference to being filled with the Holy Spirit (cf. also Acts 4:8,31; 9:17; 13:9,52).

Luke in this opening account also painted a portrait of what an ideal believer should be. Zechariah and Elizabeth possessed a righteousness or uprightness not simply before others but more importantly before the Lord (Luke 1:6). Like these ideal believers Luke's readers should keep blamelessly the ethical teachings found in God's revelation. For Luke and his readers this meant, of course, the commandments and regulations found in the OT.[37] Jesus' teachings, which are not mentioned here due to the orderly nature of Luke's presentation, would also be included in the thinking of the Evangelist and his readers, but they in no way negate the OT ethical teachings. Rather, Jesus' teachings help interpret the OT teachings more clearly and fully. There is no legalism here, for people come to salvation by grace through faith (Acts 16:31), but saving faith seeks to know how a person can live to the glory of the God who by grace has granted the sinner salvation. This knowledge is found in the commandments and regulations of Scripture. It is clear that Luke in no way disparaged the ethical teachings of the OT.

We also find in this account a Christological foreshadowing of future events. Although Jesus' name does not yet appear, the Gospel readers know that the role of Zechariah and Elizabeth's son was to make ready a people prepared for Jesus, the Lord (1:17). As they read this story, they thus already know how John's birth related to Jesus, the chief actor, in "the things that have been fulfilled among us" (1:1) and "the things [they] have been taught" (1:4). Furthermore the various aspects of John the Baptist's conception and birth invite comparison with what the reader already knows about Jesus.

Several other emphases of Luke are alluded to in this passage and will be mentioned briefly. There is a reference to God's people praying together (1:10, see Introduction 8 [7]), as well as an emphasis upon the eschatological joy that has come to God's people (1:14).[38] Also present is an obvious concern on Luke's part to place his orderly account within the framework of history (1:5; cf. 2:1-2; 3:1-2). Thus it is evident that Luke

---

[37] For a more detailed discussion from different perspectives, see J. Jervell, "The Law in Luke-Acts" in *Luke and the People of God* (Minneapolis: Augsburg, 1972), 133-51 and C. L. Blomberg, "The Law in Luke-Acts" *JSNT* 22 (1984): 53-80.

[38] Cf. Luke 1:44,47,58; 6:23; 10:17,20-21; 13:17; 15:6-7,9-10,32; 19:6,37; 24:41; Acts 5:41; 8:8,39; 13:52; 16:34.

was writing Theophilus a historical narrative. Luke 1:5-25 is not written in the literary genre of myth. There is no "Once upon a time" but rather "In the time of Herod king of Judea." Readers may deny the historicity of the events Luke described, but they cannot deny he was asserting that these events were a part of universal history. To describe them as myth is to confuse a critical evaluation of a historical account—which takes place at a specific time in history (the time of Herod the Great), at a historical place (the temple in Jerusalem), involves specific people (a priest named Zechariah and his wife Elizabeth), and concerns the birth of a historical person (John the Baptist)—with a literary genre called myth. What we have in Luke 1:5-25 is not the literary form one finds in an ancient myth. Nor is it the form found in a midrash, for we do not have in 1:5-25 OT texts explained and interpreted by historical events, but on the contrary we have historical events interpreted and explained by OT texts. In other words the starting point of 1:5-25 is not Luke's exegesis of OT texts but the historical events he was reporting, which are then seen as the fulfillment of the OT texts. In a midrash the OT texts are primary and rule the events. Here the events are clearly primary and rule the OT texts.

2. Jesus' Birth Announced (1:26-38)

[26]In the sixth month, God sent the angel Gabriel to Nazareth, a town in Galilee, [27]to a virgin pledged to be married to a man named Joseph, a descendant of David. The virgin's name was Mary. [28]The angel went to her and said, "Greetings, you who are highly favored! The Lord is with you."

[29]Mary was greatly troubled at his words and wondered what kind of greeting this might be. [30]But the angel said to her, "Do not be afraid, Mary, you have found favor with God. [31]You will be with child and give birth to a son, and you are to give him the name Jesus. [32]He will be great and will be called the Son of the Most High. The Lord God will give him the throne of his father David, [33]and he will reign over the house of Jacob forever; his kingdom will never end."

[34]"How will this be," Mary asked the angel, "since I am a virgin?"

[35]The angel answered, "The Holy Spirit will come upon you, and the power of the Most High will overshadow you. So the holy one to be born will be called the Son of God. [36]Even Elizabeth your relative is going to have a child in her old age, and she who was said to be barren is in her sixth month. [37]For nothing is impossible with God."

[38]"I am the Lord's servant," Mary answered. "May it be to me as you have said." Then the angel left her.

Context

Having just described the announcement of John the Baptist's birth, Luke proceeded with a description of the announcement of Jesus' birth. This account is tied to the first not only by the parallelism between the two accounts but also by the mention of the sixth month (1:26) and of two of the main characters from the previous account: the angel Gabriel (1:26ff.) and Elizabeth (1:36-37). An even more important tie between the accounts is that the whole significance of John the Baptist's ministry, as pointed out in 1:17, is found in his preparation for the One coming after him who was more powerful than he (3:16). The parallels between the two accounts are found both in content and form.[39]

This passage assumes and builds upon the previous one. The mighty work God has done in John the Baptist's conception would be surpassed by an even greater miracle in the virginal conception of Jesus, God's Son. The mighty work God foretold he would do through John the Baptist's ministry would be surpassed by an even greater work through his Son's ministry. Whereas John would be "great in the sight of the Lord" (1:15), Jesus would be great without qualification (1:32) and would be called the Son of God (1:35).

Much research has been expended in an attempt to explain the origin of the story Luke reported here. It is clear from the first chapter of Matthew as well as the traditional nature of the material in Luke 1–2 that Luke did not create all this material. In the past attempts have been made to explain the origin of the virgin birth story by proposing that the early church borrowed mythical material from pagan sources. Yet it is clear today that one cannot explain the virgin birth traditions as originating from pagan sources. There are simply no clear pagan parallels.[40] The Jewish nature of the virgin birth traditions also make this theory most improbable.[41] Attempts have also been made to see the virgin birth traditions as originating from Jewish myths. Yet we find no evidence anywhere of a Jewish expectation that the

---

[39]Cf. the following: the setting, 1:5-7 and 26-27; the angelic greeting, confusion, and reassurance, 1:11-13a and 28-30; the angelic message, 1:13b-17 and 31-33b; the problem, 1:18 and 34; reassurance through a sign, 1:19-20 and 35-37; and the miraculous conception, 1:21-24 and 38. For further discussion see Brown, *Birth of the Messiah*, 292-98; C. H. Talbert, *Reading Luke* (New York: Crossroad, 1988), 18-21.

[40]In fact the vast majority of alleged parallels involve a sexual relationship between a "god" and a human woman. The virgin birth traditions, on the other hand, are completely asexual. Furthermore, the early church's antagonism toward paganism makes a direct dependence most unlikely.

[41]For comparative materials to the virgin birth, see T. D. Boslooper, *The Virgin Birth* (Philadelphia: Westminster, 1962), 135-86. R. E. Brown (*The Virginal Conception and Bodily Resurrection of Jesus* [New York: Paulist, 1973], 62) gives a helpful summary of these comparisons when he states that "the story of Jesus' conception has, in fact, taken a form for which, to the best of our knowledge, there is no exact parallel or antecedent in the material available to the Christians of the first century who told of this conception" and that the alleged parallels "are not really similar to the nonsexual virginal conception that is at the core of the infancy narratives, a conception where there is no male deity or element to impregnate Mary." Although dated, J. G. Machen's *The Virgin Birth of Christ* (New York: Harper, 1930) is still useful in this area.

Messiah would be born of a virgin.[42] If one is open to the possibility of
God entering into history and being able to transcend the "laws of nature,"
it is not difficult to believe that the God who raised his Son from the dead
and empowered him to do many mighty miracles could have sent him into
the world by the miracle of the virgin birth.

Comments

1:26 In the sixth month. This refers not to the sixth month of the year but
to the sixth month of Elizabeth's pregnancy as indicated by 1:36.

Nazareth, a town in Galilee. The qualifying phrase was to help Luke's intended readers, who were non-Palestinian, understand Nazareth's location.

1:27 To a virgin. Luke clearly emphasized that Mary was a virgin (not just
a "girl" as in the NEB) both before and after conception (1:34-35). For Luke's tendency to pair men and women, see comments on 13:19.

Pledged to be married. Marriage consisted of two distinct stages: engagement
followed by the marriage itself. Engagement involved a formal agreement initiated
by a father seeking a wife for his son. The next most important person involved was
the father of the bride. A son's opinion would be sought more often in the process
than a daughter's. Upon payment of a purchase price to the bride's father (for he lost
a daughter and helper whereas the son's family gained one) and a written agreement
and/or oath by the son, the couple was engaged. Although during this stage the couple in some instances cohabited, this was the exception. An engagement was legally
binding, and any sexual contact by the daughter with another person was considered
adultery. The engagement could not be broken save through divorce (Matt 1:19), and
the parties during this period were considered husband and wife (Matt 1:19-20,24).
At this time Mary likely was no more than fifteen years old, probably closer to thirteen, which was the normal age for betrothal.

A descendant of David. This describes Joseph, not the virgin as is evident
from Luke's reintroduction of Mary ("the virgin's name") immediately following
this description. If it referred to Mary, Luke could simply have said "a descendant
of David whose name was Mary." By this comment Luke was preparing his readers for what he would say in 1:32-33. The importance of the Davidic descent of
Jesus is evident from 2:4; 3:23-38 (cf. Matt 1:1-17; Rom 1:3; 2 Tim 2:8). Compare
2 Esdr 12:32, where the Messiah is equated with the Son of David.

Mary. Luke made nothing of the etymology of this name ("exalted one").

1:28 Greetings. "Hail" (RSV) was a normal form of address in the NT and
the Greek world. Some have sought to see in this greeting a special emphasis to
"rejoice" (*chaire*, cf. Luke 1:14), but Luke's readers would not have understood
this as anything more than a normal greeting.

You who are highly favored. Mary had been "graced" by God in that she
had been chosen to bear God's Son (1:31,35). She had not been chosen for this
task because she possessed a particular piety or holiness of life that merited this

---

[42]Isaiah 7:14 was not interpreted in the intertestamental period as teaching a messianic
virgin birth. It is much more likely that after the origination of the virgin birth traditions, Isa
7:14 began to be used to support the traditions rather than that it created this tradition.

privilege. The text suggests no special worthiness on Mary's part.[43] Some scholars have argued that behind the Greek term for "highly favored" lies a Hebrew word that translates into the name "Hannah" and that there may therefore be an echo here of Samuel's miraculous birth to Hannah. Luke, however, made nothing of this, and Theophilus would never have picked up a subtle play on words in Hebrew. The Latin Vulgate translated this "full of grace" (*gratia plena*).

The Lord is with you. Compare Judg 6:12; Ruth 2:4. This is not a wish ("may the Lord be with you") but a statement and refers to God's mighty power being present and upon Mary.[44]

1:29 Mary was greatly troubled. Compare 1:12. Mary's surprise was not primarily because it was not customary for a man to greet a woman but because it was not customary for an *angel* to greet a woman.

1:30 Do not be afraid. This parallels 1:13.

You have found favor with God.[45] Here as in Judg 6:17; 2 Sam 15:25 (cf. 1 Sam 1:18) the issue is God's gracious choice, not Mary's particular piety (cf. Gen 6:8); for unlike Luke 1:6, nothing is made of Mary's personal piety either before or after this verse. The emphasis is on God's sovereign choice, not on human acceptability.

1:31 You will be with child. For the combination of *conceive, bear*, and *call*, which we find in this verse, see Gen 16:11; Judg 13:3,5; Isa 7:14; Matt 1:21. For other instances in which women "name" their child or are told the name of their child, see Gen 16:11; 30:13; Judg 13:24; 1 Sam 1:20.

You are to give him the name Jesus. This means "He shall be called Jesus." (Cf. Matt 1:25, where Joseph named him "Jesus" as a sign of his legal adoption.) This is fulfilled in Luke 2:21.

Jesus. Although heaven-given names usually have etymological significance, nothing is made of this by Luke. Contrast, however, Matt 1:21.

1:32 Here Luke began a fivefold description about "who" Jesus is.

He will be great. This greatness contrasts with the rest of humanity, which is not great, and also with the greatness of John the Baptist, whose greatness was not "absolute" but qualified with "in the sight of the Lord" (Luke 1:15). Thus Jesus and John were both alike ("great") and different (Jesus' greatness is an unqualified greatness). This adjective functions not as a name but rather indicates his being and nature.[46]

He . . . will be called the Son of the Most High. This means "will be the Son of God." This is evident from Matt 5:9 and Luke 6:35, where "will be called" in Matthew has the same meaning as "will be" in Luke (cf. also Rom 9:7; Heb 11:18; Gen 21:12). "Most High" is a circumlocution for God (Luke 1:35,76; 6:35; Acts 7:48). Once again Jesus is shown to be greater than John the Baptist, for John is described as a "prophet" of the Most High (Luke 1:76) whereas Jesus is

---

[43] Some manuscripts add "blessed are you among women," which is found in 1:42; but it is not to be read as original here.

[44] See W. C. van Unnik *"Dominus Vobiscum*: The Background of a Liturgical Formula" in *New Testament Essays*, ed. A. J. B. Higgins (Manchester: University Press, 1959), 270-305.

[45] Cf. Gen 6:8; 18:3; Judg 6:17; 1 Sam 1:18; 2 Sam 15:25.

[46] Marshall, *Luke*, 67.

described as "Son" of the Most High. The mention of Jesus' divine sonship before mention of his Davidic messiahship in the next part of the verse indicates that the latter is grounded in the former and that Jesus' messiahship should be interpreted in terms of his sonship.

The Lord God will give him the throne of his father David. Clearly 2 Sam 7:12-13,16 and Jesus' role as Israel's Messiah are in view here. Compare Luke 1:69; 2:4,11; Acts 2:30 for this same emphasis. Jesus' Davidic descent already has been alluded to in Luke 1:27, where Joseph is described as "a descendant of David."

1:33   He will reign over the house of Jacob. Like the previous description, this description depicts Jesus as the awaited Messiah. Thus, like David, he is the King of Israel.[47] The "house of Jacob" was a traditional term to describe Israel (Exod 19:3; Isa 2:5-6; 8:17; 48:1).

Forever. The eternal rule of the Davidic kingship is taught in 2 Sam 7:13,16; Pss 89:4,29; 132:12; Isa 9:7, but in this verse it is the final Davidic King, the Messiah, who will reign forever. Compare also Dan 7:13-14, where one "like a son of man" is given an everlasting kingdom.

His kingdom will never end. This may be an allusion to Isa 9:6 (LXX) or to Dan 7:14. The kingdom of God that is realized in the coming of Jesus and is to be consummated at the parousia will continue forever.

1:34   How . . . since I am a virgin? Literally *since I know no man.* Although technically Joseph was Mary's husband (see comments on 1:27), no sexual consummation had as yet taken place (cf. Matt 1:25). The word "know" is used to describe the sexual act.[48] Attempts to interpret the Lukan account as portraying a normal birth by a virgin who will give birth in a normal way, i.e., by later sexual intercourse with her husband, are impossible since the angelic message had not mentioned Joseph or the normal marital relationship. Furthermore, since it would be natural to assume that a young woman would in the marital relationship bear children, the angelic message is interpreted by Mary as meaning that she, as she was then, i.e., as a virgin, was to bear a son; and she asked, "How?" That this was to be a virgin birth[49] is also confirmed by the fact that, since Jesus is greater than John the Baptist, his birth must also be greater. If John's birth was miraculous but Jesus' birth was the result of a normal sexual relationship, then the whole parallel between 1:5-25 and 1:26-38 breaks down at this point. Jesus' birth had to be greater than that of John the Baptist, and this requires us to understand his birth as a virgin birth. Luke told his readers this to prepare them for 1:35.

Attempts to interpret Mary's words in this verse as expressing a vow of perpetual virginity (several early church fathers)[50] are incorrect. (Such explanations clash with

---

[47]Cf. Luke 19:14,27; 19:38 (Luke alone of the Synoptic Gospels uses the title "King" here); 23:2 (this is unique to Luke); 23:3; 23:37 (unique to Luke); 23:38; Acts 17:7.

[48]Cf. Gen 4:1,17,25; 19:8; Judg 11:39; 21:12; 1 Sam 1:19; Matt 1:25.

[49]Technically it is more correct to talk about the virginal conception than the virgin birth. Technically speaking, *virgin birth* refers to the Gnostic doctrine that Mary remained physically a virgin after Jesus' birth, i.e., that her physical organs (the hymen) remained intact. The dangerous corollary of this doctrine is a docetic Christology. A Christ "born" in this fashion would have passed through the birth canal and hymen as a spirit would rather than as a flesh-and-blood baby would.

[50]Fitzmyer, *Luke*, 348-49.

Matt 1:25, which implies that after the birth of Jesus, Joseph and Mary had a normal husband-wife relationship.) Although Luke and Matthew both clearly affirmed that Jesus' conception was miraculous in that Mary was a virgin when she conceived, what is most important in the NT teaching of the virgin birth (or virginal conception) is not the manner in which God sent his Son but the fact that he sent him. To use later terminology we might say that what is of primary importance is not the virgin birth but the incarnation. In other words it is not the "how" but the "what" of Christmas that is most important.

Mary's question should not be understood as reflecting the same kind of doubt Zechariah possessed (Luke 1:18), since there is present no rebuke as in 1:19-23.

1:35 The Holy Spirit will come upon you. For similar wording see Acts 1:8. Whereas John the Baptist was filled with the Spirit from his mother's womb (Luke 1:15), Jesus was conceived by the Spirit, and this witnesses to his being greater than John.

And the power of the Most High will overshadow you. This sentence stands in synonymous parallelism with the preceding one. Luke was fond of referring to the Spirit's influence as "power" (see comments on 1:17). For "overshadow" cf. 9:34. There is no allusion here to the shekinah glory "overshadowing" Mary.

So. "So" (literally *Therefore*) is causal and has been explained in two ways: (1) Jesus is God's Son because of the Spirit's activity in causing the virgin birth,[51] and (2) Jesus is holy because of the Spirit's activity.[52] According to John's Gospel, Jesus was God's Son before creation (John 1:1-3), so that the manner of his birth would have nothing to do with his nature or being. Yet it is dangerous to read into our passage John's teaching on preexistence, since Luke did not explicitly teach this theological concept in Luke-Acts. A determining factor in this issue involves how the rest of this verse should be translated.

The holy one to be born shall be called the Son of God. The other possible way of translating this sentence is "the child to be born will be called holy, the Son of God" (footnote in NIV; RSV). Both are grammatically possible; but in light of Luke 2:23, where there is a similar construction,[53] "holy" is the object of the verb. Thus the marginal translation of the NIV and the RSV is better. If we have "holy" and "Son of God" here, we have a better parallel to the twofold description in 1:32, where we have "great" and "Son of the Most High." It is better therefore to understand the Spirit's activity as resulting in the Son of God's being called, i.e., being (see comments on 1:32) "holy." In light of 2:23 the term "holy" is best interpreted as designating not a particular ethical quality (as in Acts 3:14) so much as indicating that the Son of God was to be dedicated or set aside for a unique, divine purpose. Each firstborn male (Luke 2:23) was consecrated to God. This does not mean that the firstborn possessed a moral or ethical quality over his brothers at birth. Rather he was dedicated to God in a unique way because God had a special claim on the firstborn (cf. 2:23). In a similar way the Son of God through his conception by the Spirit was set apart by God for a divine task. In this sense "holy" is related to "anointed," which also points out that God set apart

---

[51] So Fitzmyer, *Luke*, 351.

[52] Talbert, *Reading Luke*, 19.

[53] A nominative participle and the term *holy* preceding the verb *shall be called.*

(and equipped) his Son for a particular task (cf. how "anointed" and "holy servant" are closely related in Acts 4:27). For Jesus as "holy," cf. Luke 4:34; Acts 3:14; 4:27,30.

One should not read into this verse the thought that since Jesus was not conceived through sexual intercourse he was as a result "uncontaminated" by such a natural birth. Rather, Luke sought to teach that since Jesus' birth was entirely due to the "overshadowing" of the Holy Spirit, Jesus would be uniquely set aside for God's service, i.e., he would be "holy."

Son of God. At times this title is a synonym for Messiah/Christ (4:41; Acts 9:20,22). We find a similar paralleling of the title "Son of God" and of the Davidic Messiah in Rom 1:3-4. Yet Jesus cannot be described simply in messianic terms such as the Son of David. He is more than this, and the title "Son of God" carries with it other implications as well.[54] The title does not demand an ontological sense of preexistence, but it allows for this.[55]

1:36 Sixth month. Compare 1:26. Elizabeth's conception of John the Baptist when she was past childbearing age reveals God's miraculous power and confirms the angelic message to Mary. God already had done the impossible in Elizabeth's case so that the problem Mary raised in 1:34 is insignificant.

1:37 For with God nothing will be impossible. Compare Gen 18:14 (LXX), where the same expression is found; cf. also Matt 19:26; Job 42:2; Zech 8:6 for the same thought. This refers primarily to Mary's conceiving as a virgin, but it also alludes to Elizabeth's conceiving referred to in the previous verse.

1:38 I am the Lord's servant. . . . May it be to me as you have said. Compare 1 Sam 1:18. Whereas Zechariah and Elizabeth provide an example for the reader of true discipleship in their obedience to the commandments and regulations of the OT (1:6), Mary is exemplary because of her submission to God's will.

Then the angel left her. Luke frequently concluded an account with such a departure (cf. 1:23,56; 2:20; 5:25; 8:39; 24:12).

The Lukan Message

Although the present account involves a conversation between the angel Gabriel and the virgin Mary, the key figure in this section is clearly Mary's future offspring, Jesus, just as the key figure of the previous sec-

---

[54] This title will be affirmed by Jesus in Luke 2:49; 10:22; 22:70; by God in 3:22; 9:35; by demons in 4:41; 8:28; indirectly by Satan in 4:3,9; and by Paul in Acts 9:20; 13:33.

[55] Some scholars have argued that 1:34-35 is a later insertion into this account. Yet without these two verses the parallelism between 1:26-38 and 1:5-25 would be destroyed. The announcement pattern would clearly be broken, for the objection (cf. 1:34 and 1:18) and reassurance (cf. 1:35 and 1:19-20) that are integral to such a scene would be lacking. It would also destroy the great-greater parallelism established between John the Baptist and Jesus, for without a virginal conception Jesus' birth would not have been greater than John's. On the contrary it would have been inferior! It should also be noted that we find in 1:35 the same names for God ("Most High" and "God") that we find in 1:32. When we also realize that the title "Son of God" found in 1:34-35 does not have Greek mythological connotations but is essentially a synonym for the Messiah of 1:32-33, any alleged conflict between these two passages disappears. In our present text 1:34-35 is an integral part of the account and not simply an insertion.

tion was Zechariah and Elizabeth's future offspring, John the Baptist. As might be expected, Luke used this section dealing with Jesus' conception to reveal Christological insights to his readers. He did this through the same reliable messenger from God which the reader already met in 1:5-25. The angel Gabriel, coming from God's presence (1:19), informs us of what we should know about Jesus of Nazareth. Luke in no way minimized John the Baptist's greatness in describing Jesus. Rather he showed that whereas John was great, Jesus is greater still. This is shown in several ways. John was "great in the sight of the Lord" (1:15), but Jesus is "great" (1:32), and his greatness is unqualified. Whereas John is later described as "a prophet of the Most High" (1:76), Jesus is the "Son of the Most High" (1:32). Whereas John's birth was miraculous and had OT parallels, Jesus' birth was even more miraculous. John's conception, like that of Isaac, Samson, and Samuel, was miraculous; but Jesus' conception was absolutely unique. It was not just quantitatively greater; it was qualitatively different. Whereas John's task was to prepare for the Coming One (1:17,76-79), Jesus is the Coming One who will reign forever (1:33); and whereas John was filled with the Spirit while still in the womb (1:15), Jesus' very conception would be due to the Spirit's miraculous activity in a virgin (1:35-37).

Various aspects of the Lukan Christology that appear in this passage are Jesus as the Son of God (1:32,35), Jesus as the Davidic Messiah (1:32-33) and King whose reign is eternal (1:33), and Jesus as the Holy One (1:35). Jesus' greatness described in our text is not due to any human achievement on his part. The greatness of Mary's son is not a result of his human striving. In light of this account no adoptionist Christology can be found in Luke. Jesus is the Messiah and Son of God from birth. In fact he was this before birth as 1:41-45 indicates. Luke sought to show his readers that Jesus, who was already well known to them, was born in a unique way and was already Son of God, Christ, and King before his birth.

Several other Lukan emphases also appear in this account. These involve the Holy Spirit once again acting in history and his association with the power of God (1:35). We also have present a model of Christian obedience in Mary's acquiescence to the divine will (1:38). Finally, as in 1:5-25, we are not dealing with the literary genre of myth here. On the contrary Luke was using the literary form of historical narrative and expected his readers to understand that he was recalling history. (See comments on 1:5-25, "The Lukan Message.")

3. The Meeting of John the Baptist and Jesus (1:39-56)

[39]**At that time Mary got ready and hurried to a town in the hill country of Judea,** [40]**where she entered Zechariah's home and greeted Elizabeth.** [41]**When Elizabeth heard Mary's greeting, the baby leaped in her womb, and Elizabeth**

was filled with the Holy Spirit. [42]In a loud voice she exclaimed: "Blessed are you among women, and blessed is the child you will bear! [43]But why am I so favored, that the mother of my Lord should come to me? [44]As soon as the sound of your greeting reached my ears, the baby in my womb leaped for joy. [45]Blessed is she who has believed that what the Lord has said to her will be accomplished!"
      [46]And Mary said:
      "My soul glorifies the Lord
      [47]and my spirit rejoices in God my Savior,
      [48]for he has been mindful
            of the humble state of his servant.
      From now on all generations will call me blessed,
      [49]for the Mighty One has done great things for me—
            holy is his name.
      [50]His mercy extends to those who fear him,
            from generation to generation.
      [51]He has performed mighty deeds with his arm;
            he has scattered those who are proud in their inmost thoughts.
      [52]He has brought down rulers from their thrones
            but has lifted up the humble.
      [53]He has filled the hungry with good things
            but has sent the rich away empty.
      [54]He has helped his servant Israel,
            remembering to be merciful
      [55]to Abraham and his descendants forever,
            even as he said to our fathers."
      [56]Mary stayed with Elizabeth for about three months and then returned home.

Context

This section complements the previous two accounts and is built upon them. At this point the two miraculously conceived children encounter each other. Luke prepared the reader for this episode by means of 1:24-25,36-37. The account consists of an introductory narrative (1:39-41) followed by two hymns (1:42-55) and a conclusion (1:56). The hymnic section divides naturally into two parts: 1:42-45, in which Elizabeth uttered praise toward Mary and her child, and 1:46-55, in which Mary uttered her praise to God in the famous "Magnificat." (The name "Magnificat" comes from the opening word in the Latin Vulgate's translation of Mary's hymn.) Although the former lacks a clear literary structure, the Magnificat is carefully formed and structured and contains several examples of parallelism.[56] The phraseology of Mary's hymn of praise shows clear similarities

---

[56]There has been much debate about whether 1:46-55 existed as a pre-Lukan hymn and whether that hymn may have had as its object John the Baptist rather than Jesus. Some of the reasons for this are that much of the Magnificat does not seem to fit Mary specifically; the

to Hannah's hymn of praise in 1 Sam 2:1-10 as well as other OT passages (cf. also Jdt 16:1-17).[57]

Comments

1:39   At that time.   The time notice (literally *In these days*) serves primarily as a literary link tying what follows to the previous account (cf. 6:12; Acts 1:15).

Got ready and hurried.   This should not be interpreted as an attempt to prevent Mary's neighbors in Nazareth from knowing that she was pregnant. Rather Luke here described Mary as a model believer eagerly responding in obedience to the heavenly message of Luke 1:36.

A town in the hill country of Judea.   Compare 1:23. Judea refers here to the Roman province in contrast to 1:5, where it refers to Palestine. The name of the city is not given. Perhaps Luke did not know it or thought it unimportant. Or he may have sought to use terminology that would be parallel to Samuel's miraculous birth. Compare 1 Sam 1:1, where Samuel's parents are described as being from the "hill country" of Ephraim.

1:40   Greeted Elizabeth.   Nothing is said concerning the content of this greeting, for this is not important. Luke reported only what is theologically significant.

1:41   Leaped in her womb.   Just as John the Baptist in his ministry was to be Jesus' precursor and prepare his way (1:17,76), so even here he prepared the way, i.e., he announced the Messiah's presence by leaping in his mother's womb. Compare Gen 25:22 for an OT parallel. (For leaping for joy, see 2 Sam 6:16; Mal 4:2.) Attempts to see this as a technical medical term and thus identify Luke as a physician are unconvincing due to the appearance of this expression in Gen 25:22. This prenatal cognition is meant to attest to the truth and fulfillment of Gabriel's prophecy in Luke 1:31-33,35. In 1:44 Elizabeth would explain the significance of her child's action.

Filled with the Holy Spirit.   What was promised to Zechariah (1:15) was now fulfilled. John and Elizabeth were filled with the Holy Spirit even before John's birth. Thus they were the first persons to realize that Mary's child is the Messiah. That the hymn that follows conveys a correct Christological understanding is evident from

---

childless Elizabeth seems to fit these verses better (cf. 1:48); the mention of Mary in 1:56 seems to introduce a new subject; and there are a few textual variants that name Elizabeth rather than Mary in 1:46. (See Farris, *Hymns of Luke's Infancy Narratives*, 108-13; Brown, *Birth of the Messiah*, 334-36.)

On the other hand we should note that the reference to the "servant" or "handmaid" (RSV) in 1:48 ties the hymn to 1:38, where the same expression is used of Mary. In addition nothing in this hymn applies specifically to John the Baptist. Clearly the best textual support favors the reading "Mary" in 1:46. It would also be incredible if, contrary to the "Jesus greater than John" scenario in 1:5-38 and the "Mary greater than Elizabeth" scene in 1:39-45, Elizabeth would occupy the center of attention in 1:46-56. In the present text this hymn is Mary's. As a result we will seek to understand what Luke was trying to teach his readers by means of this hymn of Mary. We will not seek to formulate a hypothetical reconstruction of the pre-Lukan form of this hymn or comment on the meaning of that hypothetical reconstruction.

[57] See Brown, *Birth of the Messiah*, 358-60.

the character description of Elizabeth in 1:6 and from the fact that she was filled with the Holy Spirit as she spoke. **1:42 In a loud voice.** This expression is frequently used to describe an inspired utterance (cf. Mark 9:24; John 1:15; 7:28,37; Rom 8:15; 9:27; Gal 4:6). The first two lines of Elizabeth's blessing found in this verse possess poetic parallelism, but the rest do not. **Blessed are you among women.** Compare Judg 5:24; Jdt 13:18. This is a Semitic way of saying "most blessed." "Since according to contemporary Jewish ideas a woman's greatness was measured by the greatness of the children that she bore," Fitzmyer notes, "the mother of the *Kyrios* (1:43) would naturally be said to surpass all others."[58] (Note, however, that Jael's and Judith's blessedness was not due to their children.) What God had done in Mary outshone even what God had done in Elizabeth. Mary was blessed here not because of her faith, as in Luke 1:45; rather her blessedness depended entirely on her son and his greatness. A similar beatitude is repeated in 11:27. This blessing is not to be interpreted as a call to praise/bless Mary but as an affirmation that Mary stood in a state of blessedness.

Blessed is the child you will bear. "The child you will bear" is literally *the fruit of your womb* (cf. Gen 30:2; Lam 2:20; cf. also Deut 7:13; 28:4). The Lord had already been conceived.

Although the two blessings stand essentially parallel, i.e., they are in parataxis, the first stands logically in subordination to the second. Mary's blessedness was based on the blessedness of the child she would bear. This fits an OT pattern in which the second blessing gives the cause of the first (cf. Gen 14:19-20; Deut 7:14; Ruth 2:20; cf. also Jdt 13:18).[59]

1:43 My Lord. This indicates that the focus in this account is upon Mary's child more than Mary herself. Here "Lord" is clearly a Christological title and refers to Jesus. The title is used in our account (and in Luke 1–2 in general) both for God (1:46) and Jesus (1:43; cf. Acts 2:36), and it reveals the greatness of Mary's child already before his birth. Whereas the title "Lord" is used for Jesus only six times in Mark,[60] it is used over twenty times in Luke.[61] To these can be added the nineteen times Jesus is addressed in the vocative as Lord.[62] It is above all by the resurrection that Mary's child is recognized as Lord (Acts 2:36), although this verse indicates that from his conception he was already Lord. The use of the title "Lord" indicates that Luke understood Jesus as standing on a different level from others. He, like God, is deserving of the title "Lord."

1:44 For joy. This is a partial fulfillment of Luke 1:14. For a similar expression of joy on Mary's part, cf. 1:47. Even as Elizabeth rejoiced in her subservient role to Mary, so later John would also rejoice in his subservient role in preparing for Jesus (John 3:29).

---

[58] Fitzmyer, *Luke*, 364.

[59] J. Nolland, *Luke 1–9:20*, WBC (Waco: Word, 1989), 66-67.

[60] Mark 1:3; 2:28; 7:28; 11:3; 12:36-37.

[61] Luke 1:76; 2:11; 3:4; 6:5; 7:13,19; 10:1,39,41; 11:39; 12:42; 13:15; 17:5-6; 18:6; 19:8,31,34; 20:42-44; 22:61 [twice]; 24:3,34.

[62] Luke 5:8,12; 6:46 (twice); 7:6; 9:54,59,61; 10:17,40; 11:1; 12:41; 13:23,25; 17:37; 18:41; 22:33,38,49 (see comments on 6:46).

1:45 Blessed. Although the word used here is different (*makaria*) from that used in Luke 1:42 (*eulogēmenē/os*), no theological significance should be read into this since the words have essentially the same meaning.

Blessed is she who has believed. Elizabeth's praise both begins and now ends with a reference to Mary's blessedness. The blessedness of Mary's faith stands in contrast to Zechariah's lack of faith in 1:20. Her blessedness is a present state (cf. 6:20-22). Again Mary serves as an example for the believer. Indeed Luke sought to maximize Mary's role as a model believer. For example, in 8:19 he omitted the "outside" (*heksō*) of Mark 3:31; in 4:24 Luke omitted "in his own house" (cf. Mark 6:4); and in Acts 1:14 he mentioned that Mary and her other children were among the inner core of disciples. Mary is "blessed" here for her faith but is "most blessed" in Luke 1:42 for the privilege of being the mother of God's Son.

That. "That" (*hoti*) could be causal (cf. 6:20-21; 14:14) and would refer to Mary's being blessed "because" of believing that what God had promised would come true. On the other hand it could refer to the content, i.e., the "that" which Mary believed as in the parallel construction in Acts 27:25.

1:46 And Mary said. The best textual reading by far, which is found in all the ancient Greek manuscripts and in almost all the ancient translations, is "Mary" rather than "Elizabeth."

The Magnificat which follows is named from the opening verb of the Latin Vulgate's translation of Mary's hymn in 1:46.[63] As Hannah did in 1 Sam 2:1-10, Mary praised God for what he was about to do and for the part she was privileged to play in his plan.

My soul glorifies the Lord. Compare Ps 69:30. The use of "my soul" for "I" is found in Gen 27:4 (LXX); 27:25 (LXX); Ps 34:2. The verb "glorifies" also appears in Luke 1:58; Acts 5:13; 10:46; 19:17. "Lord" refers here to Yahweh as the parallelism with the next verse indicates.

1:47 My spirit. This is another synonym for "I" as shown by Gen 6:3; Ps 143:4. We find a similar parallelism between "soul" and "spirit" in Ps 77:2-3; Job 12:10 (LXX); Isa 26:9; cf. Wis 15:11. This verse stands in synonymous parallelism with Luke 1:46 and thus emphasizes the praiseworthiness of God by repetition.

God my Savior. Compare Pss 24:5; 25:5; 95:1; Mic 7:7; Hab 3:18; cf. also Sir 51:1. (In the OT "Savior" is used thirty-five times with respect to God and five times with respect to persons.) This verse anticipates the thought of Luke 1:69,71,77; 2:11,30. The use of alternative names for God in parallel statements is common in the OT (cf. 1 Sam 2:2; Pss 62:11-12; 69:6; 70:1).

1:48 For. What follows will be the grounds for Mary's praise of God.

He has been mindful of the humble state of his servant. This is the first ground for Mary's praise and has as its background Hannah's prayer and vow (1 Sam 1:11).[64] In the coming of God's Son into the world, the poor and downtrodden have been visited with salvation. See Introduction 8 (5).

---

[63] This hymn consists of either three parts: the introduction proper, 1:46b-47; two strophes, 1:48-50 and 1:51-53; and a conclusion, 1:54-55 or else two parts: the introduction proper, 1:46b-47 and three strophes, 1:48-50; 1:51-53; and 1:54-55. It probably is best to see 1:54-55 as a conclusion since its content essentially repeats the material found in 1:51-53.

[64] Cf. Gen 29:32; Deut 26:7; 1 Sam 9:16; Ps 31:7; cf. also 2 Esdr 9:45.

Humble state. This humble state or lowliness is referred to again in 1:52. It need not refer to childlessness as in 1 Sam 1:11 (or to a hypothetical vow of perpetual virginity and thus childlessness on Mary's part). Rather it refers to such a low estate as described in Acts 8:33; Phil 3:21; Jas 1:10. In this verse it may refer to the low state or status in which Mary was held by the standards of this world. Her child would also share this low estate, being born in a manger and of poor, insignificant parent(s). Yet the salvation of which Mary rejoiced also looks beyond her to the nation of Israel, as Luke 1:50-55 makes clear.

Servant. This self-designation has already been used by Mary in 1:38.

[For] from now on. This does not stand in parallelism with the first part of the verse but gives the result of God's having been mindful of his servant in her humble state. "From now on" in Luke frequently refers to an important event in salvation history. Compare 12:52; 22:18,69; Acts 18:6.

All generations will call me blessed. Mary would not be called blessed because of any intrinsic personal worth or holiness on her part but because of the child she was bearing. Compare Gen 30:13 for an example of synonymous parallelism in which Leah's blessedness was due not to her own piety but to God's goodness toward her in granting her a child. For a parallel to the proclamation of Mary's blessedness to all generations, see Jdt 13:18; 14:7.

1:49 For he who is mighty has done great things for me. This is best seen not as a second ground for Mary's praise but as a synonymous parallel with Luke 1:48a much like 1:42c stands in parallel with (and gives the cause of) 1:42b.[65] God is described as "mighty" in Ps 24:8; Zeph 3:17, and Luke used this word to describe God's mighty power (Luke 18:27; 24:19). As affirmed in Deut 10:21, God does "great things." Whereas in Deuteronomy this refers to God's having worked his wonders for Israel in leading them out of Egypt, here the "great things" refers to the virginal conception of Jesus, who in his ministry would bring about the events described in Luke 1:51-55. Since this involves not only Mary but is for all believers, perhaps we should understand "for me" as meaning "to me," although the parallel with 1:48 favors "for me."

Holy is his name. Compare Ps 111:9. This is simply another way of saying, "He [i.e., God] is holy." God's holiness here refers not simply to his moral perfection but even more to his acts of righteousness and justice by which he fulfills his covenantal promises to the humble and lowly (Luke 1:48-50,53-55) and brings judgment upon the unrighteous and haughty (1:51-52). In 11:2 the believer prayed that this holiness would soon be manifested, and in Matt 6:10 this is further clarified by the words "on earth as it is in heaven." Luke's statement probably is best taken with what follows rather than with what precedes.

1:50 The hymn now moves from Mary to believing Israel as the change of pronouns from the first person singular to the third person plural indicates. This statement of God's positive behavior toward the humble stands roughly parallel to Luke 1:48. It parallels closely Ps 103:17. God's gracious mercy comes upon the humble devout (such as Mary) who "fear," i.e., reverently obey, him. See comments on 23:40.

---

[65] R. C. Tannehill, "The Magnificat as Poem," *JBL* 93 (1974): 266-67.

1:51 Whereas the first strophe of the Magnificat refers to the great things the Mighty one had done to Mary, the second strophe is a prophetic forward look at the results of the ministry of Mary's child for believing Israel (Luke 1:54). For a hymn or psalm to begin with an individual's situation and conclude with a reference to Israel's situation is not unusual (cf. Pss 25; 69; 128; 130; 131).

He has performed mighty deeds with his arm. This is the second ground for Mary's praise in Luke 1:46b-47. God's "arm" is a frequent anthropomorphism and symbol for God's might[66] and the thought of the verse finds a close parallel in Ps 89:10b. The tense of the verb (and the following verbs) is best understood as a futuristic aorist or the equivalent of the prophetic perfect in Hebrew. It describes the future work of God's Son with the certainty of a past event. Mary saw as already accomplished what God would do through her son.

He has scattered those who are proud in their inmost thoughts. The proud are those who do not fear God (Luke 1:50), who are not hungry (1:53) or afflicted (1:48,52). The salvation Jesus brings to the humble also works judgment for the arrogant (cf. 6:20-26). Compare Num 10:35; Pss 68:1; 89:10; 146:7-9.

Inmost thoughts. "Inmost thoughts" are literally *hearts*. The heart serves as the center of a person's reasoning power (cf. 1 Chr 29:18).

Whatever the original meaning of Luke 1:51-53, for Luke the rich/poor contrast was not primarily a political one, i.e., the rich, ruling Gentiles versus the poor Israelites. Luke understood the contrast in its religious sense as a contrast between the humble poor and the haughty rich (cf. 6:20-26). This does not mean that there are not sociopolitical implications in this contrast. The proud are frequently the ruling rich; and the humble, the oppressed poor.

1:52 In 1:52-53 we find an example of chiasmic parallelism.[67] Whereas each verse alone is an example of antithetical parallelism, together they are an example of chiasmic parallelism—*A* (rulers) *B* (humble) *b* (hungry) *a* (rich).

He has brought down the rulers from their thrones. The rulers are identified in this verse with the proud of 1:51 and the rich of 1:53. There are several OT allusions here (cf. Job 12:19; 1 Sam 2:7; cf. also Sir 10:14; 1 QM 14:11), but how did Luke understand these words? Such passages as Luke 10:13-15; 14:11; 16:19-31; 18:14 reveal that Luke interpreted this primarily in a metaphorical sense as indicating the reversal of fortune Jesus brought. See Introduction 8 (5).

Exalted the lowly. This is demonstrated in the immediate context by the divine selection of Mary to be the mother of Jesus, but it is found elsewhere in that "the Son of Man came to seek and to save what was lost" (19:10; cf. 15:7,10).

1:53 He has filled the hungry with good things. This reflects such OT passages as 1 Sam 2:5; Pss 72:11-12; 107:9 but foreshadows such future teachings of Jesus as Luke 6:21; 11:5-13; and 16:19-31 and such events as the feeding of the five thousand (9:10-17) and the breaking of bread at the Lord's Supper (22:14-20; 24:13-35; Acts 2:42,46; 20:7,11).

---

[66]Cf. Exod 6:6; 15:16; Deut 3:24; 4:34; Isa 40:10; 51:5,9; 53:1.
[67]*A* "He has brought down rulers from their thrones"
   B "but has lifted up the humble."
   b "He has filled the hungry with good things"
   a "but has sent the rich away empty."

But has sent the rich away empty. Compare 6:24-26; 12:13-21; 16:25; 21:1-4.

1:54 He has helped his servant Israel. For Israel as the Lord's servant, cf. Isa 41:8-9; 42:1,19; 44:1,21; 45:4.

Remembering. This is an infinitive in Greek, but its exact relationship to the verb "helped" is uncertain. It may function here to express the cause of his helping Israel and should then be translated "because of remembering [his] mercy." This thought is repeated in Luke 1:72 (cf. Gen 19:29; Exod 2:24; Pss 98:3; 105:42).

1:55 To Abraham and his descendants. By referring to Abraham, Luke emphasized the continuation of salvation history in Jesus' coming rather than its disruption. It is probably best to see this phrase as being in apposition to "our fathers," thereby avoiding having a parenthetical comment within the hymn.[68] For God remembering Abraham, see Exod 2:24; 32:13; Deut 9:27; Ps 105:7-11,42.

1:56 Mary stayed with Elizabeth for about three months. It is uncertain why Luke mentioned this. It is not, however, to indicate that Mary assisted in the birth of John the Baptist, for no mention is made of her being present at his birth (1:57-58).

And then returned home. Luke did not specify whether "home" referred to her mother's home or Joseph's. For Luke this was unimportant.

The Lukan Message

Within this account we find several important Lukan theological emphases. One that is dealt with at length is the theme of reversal. The humble are exalted, and the arrogant are brought low. We find the coming of God's mercy and salvation to the lowly especially in 1:48-49,52b,53a. The corresponding judgment and bringing low of the haughty is found in 1:51b,52a,53b. Whereas this teaching has OT precedents,[69] we find this theme frequently in Jesus' teaching (6:20-26; 13:30; 16:25). Clearly Luke saw in Jesus' coming a great reversal of the world's value system. Indeed with Jesus' coming the humble poor and outcasts become first, i.e., they are receiving salvation, whereas the proud and arrogant become last, i.e., they are rejecting salvation and receiving divine judgment.

A second Lukan emphasis found within our passage involves the fulfillment of prophecy and the divine promises. This is already seen in Elizabeth's and the virgin Mary's pregnancies (1:41-44); but it is also evident in Mary's hymn, which speaks of God's visiting his people (1:51-54), remembering God's mercy, and helping his servant Israel just as he said, i.e., promised, to the fathers (1:54-55). Although the term "fulfilled" is not found in the

---

[68]There is some confusion about whether these words serve as indirect objects to the infinitive "remembering" in Luke 1:54 (which would make the expression "even as he said to our fathers" parenthetical), stand in apposition to "our fathers" in 1:55, or are a dative of interest with the verb "said" in 1:55.

[69]Cf. 1 Sam 2:4-5,7-8; Pss 75:7; 107:40-41; 113:7-9; 147:6; Job 12:19; cf. also Jdt 9:3; Wis 10:14 in the LXX.

account, the entire context and vocabulary come from the OT and speak of God's keeping his covenantal promises and visiting his people in his Son's coming. This theme is again picked up in 1:67-80 and in the next chapter in 2:11,25-26,29-32,38. For further discussion see Introduction 7 (1).

A third emphasis found in our text involves the Christological understanding of Mary's offspring. The child born by Mary was clearly greater than the child born by Elizabeth. Thus Jesus received homage from John the Baptist in 1:41,44 and from Elizabeth's prophetic utterance (1:42) that Mary was the most blessed among women. Since Mary's blessedness came from the child she bore (1:43), her child must be greater than all other children born of women. The Christological emphasis takes on an even nobler significance when Elizabeth called Mary the "mother of my Lord" (1:43). Even though unborn, Mary's son was Elizabeth's Lord. Those familiar with the Greek OT, as Luke's readers were, would be aware that the name Yahweh in the OT was translated in Greek by the title "Lord" (*kyrios*). Jesus' ministry would be the means by which God's promises were fulfilled to his people (1:54-55). Jesus is *the* mediator of God's salvation and judgment (1:48-55).

Two other Lukan themes appear in this account. The first involves Mary's role as an ideal believer who believed God's promises (1:45) and who praised God (1:46-55), and the second is the Holy Spirit's active role once again in Israel's history (1:41). See Introduction 8 (3) and (5).

4. The Birth of John the Baptist (1:57-80)

[57]When it was time for Elizabeth to have her baby, she gave birth to a son. [58]Her neighbors and relatives heard that the Lord had shown her great mercy, and they shared her joy.

[59]On the eighth day they came to circumcise the child, and they were going to name him after his father Zechariah, [60]but his mother spoke up and said, "No! He is to be called John."

[61]They said to her, "There is no one among your relatives who has that name."

[62]Then they made signs to his father, to find out what he would like to name the child. [63]He asked for a writing tablet, and to everyone's astonishment he wrote, "His name is John." [64]Immediately his mouth was opened and his tongue was loosed, and he began to speak, praising God. [65]The neighbors were all filled with awe, and throughout the hill country of Judea people were talking about all these things. [66]Everyone who heard this wondered about it, asking, "What then is this child going to be?" For the Lord's hand was with him.

[67]His father Zechariah was filled with the Holy Spirit and prophesied:

[68]"Praise be to the Lord, the God of Israel,
    because he has come and has redeemed his people.
[69]He has raised up a horn
    of salvation for us
    in the house of his servant David

[70](as he said through his holy prophets of long ago),
[71]salvation from our enemies
   and from the hand of all who hate us—
[72]to show mercy to our fathers
   and to remember his holy covenant,
[73]the oath he swore to our father Abraham:
[74]to rescue us from the hand of our enemies,
   and to enable us to serve him without fear
[75]in holiness and righteousness before him all our days.
[76]And you, my child, will be called a prophet of the Most High;
   for you will go on before the Lord to prepare the way for him,
[77]to give his people the knowledge of salvation
   through the forgiveness of their sins,
[78]because of the tender mercy of our God,
   by which the rising sun will come to us from heaven
[79]to shine on those living in darkness
   and in the shadow of death,
   to guide our feet into the path of peace."
[80]And the child grew and became strong in spirit; and he lived in the desert until he appeared publicly to Israel.

Context

At this point Luke recorded the fulfillment of the birth announcement concerning John the Baptist (1:5-25). In the following account he continued the Jesus—John the Baptist parallelism by recording Jesus' birth. The present passage falls into three parts: 1:57-58 (the birth); 1:59-66 (the circumcision and naming); and 1:67-80 (Zechariah's hymn of praise). The latter part, which is called the Benedictus because in Latin Vulgate the hymn begins in 1:68 with the word "Benedictus" (like the Magnificat), is heavily dependent on the OT both for its terminology and content and can be divided into four parts: 1:67 (the narrative introduction); 1:68a (the opening statement of praise); 1:68b-79 (the hymn itself, which can be subdivided into 1:68b-75,76-79); and 1:80 (the narrative conclusion).[70]

The Benedictus has been the object of much research. The views concerning its prehistory vary.[71] In its present form the function of the Bene-

---

[70]Brown, *Birth of the Messiah*, 380-92.

[71]Some see it as a Jewish, perhaps Maccabean or messianic, hymn; a Jewish-Christian hymn; a hymn concerning John the Baptist developed by the later followers of John; or a Jewish-Christian hymn reworked by Luke. Along with such theories are additional theories about how the present hymn was composed: 1:76-79 as a Christian addition to a Jewish or Baptist hymn (1:68-75); 1:76 or 1:76f. as a Lukan addition to an early Christian hymn; 1:67,76-79 as the original core of the hymn, having been expanded by the addition of 1:68-75, which was a Christian hymn; 1:76f.,79b as originally part of a hymn about John the Baptist with 1:68-75, which was a messianic hymn, having been added. For a further discussion see Brown, *Birth of the Messiah*, 346-55; Farris, *Hymns of Luke's Infancy Narratives*, 127-42.

dictus is clear. Luke wanted his readers to understand this as Zechariah's divinely inspired hymn praising God for fulfilling his promises to his people and describing the roles of John the Baptist and especially the Messiah.

Comments

1:57 When it was time for Elizabeth to have her baby. Compare 2:6 (Gen 25:24) for a similar miracle and vocabulary.

1:58 Her neighbors and relatives heard. Apparently Elizabeth remained in seclusion throughout her pregnancy.

The Lord has shown her great mercy. Compare Luke 1:25 and Gen 19:19 for similar terminology. One should not seek to find here a play on the Hebrew name for John (*Yohanan*, meaning *Yahweh has given grace*), for this would have been much too subtle for Luke's Greek readers who would not have been able to understand a Hebrew pun such as this.

And they shared her joy. This joy is a partial fulfillment of Luke 1:14. Later in the description of Jesus' birth, Luke would parallel this with the shepherds' joy (2:10).

1:59 On the eighth day they came to circumcise the child. Here Luke pointed out John the Baptist's Jewish origin. This will be paralleled in 2:21 with Jesus' circumcision and naming. Note also how Paul in Phil 3:5 pointed out his Jewishness in a similar manner. Circumcision was the covenant mark (cf. Gen 17:12-14; 21:4; Lev 12:3). It is irrational for a Gentile believer to be anti-Semitic when the leading heroes of the faith (John the Baptist, Paul, Peter, the apostles, the OT saints, and above all the Savior of the world) were Jewish.

And they were going to name him. We find a parallel to this naming of John the Baptist at his circumcision in the following account about Jesus (Luke 2:21), but it was more common to name a child at birth (cf. Gen 4:1; 21:3; 25:25-26). It was unusual to name a son after his father, since a man tended to be identified as (*John*) son of (*Zechariah*), i.e., (*John*), Bar-(*Zechariah*); and Zechariah Bar-Zechariah would have been strange.

1:60 How Elizabeth knew that the name to be given was John is not stated. Zechariah probably revealed this to her along with what happened to him in the temple (cf. Luke 1:13).

John. The etymological meaning of the name is not stated, and it is doubtful that Luke's readers knew it. Nothing therefore should be made of it. For Luke what was important for his readers was to know that the birth and role of the one they knew as John the Baptist were divinely foreordained.

1:62 Zechariah was both deaf and mute (cf. 1:22,64), so they appealed to him by means of signs. He responded by means of writing (1:63). These two infirmities are often associated with each other (cf. Mark 7:32,37; 9:25).

1:63 He asked for a writing tablet. The writing tablet consisted of a wood tablet (a *pinakidion*) covered with wax.

To everyone's astonishment he wrote, "His name is John." Why the astonishment? Probably this was because "John" was not a name used in their family and because Zechariah was not able to hear Elizabeth's choice of this name.

Since Zechariah was mute, he could not "say" anything.[72] The NIV translation recognizes this.

1:64 Immediately his mouth was opened and his tongue was loosed. Zechariah's speaking further heightens the miraculous nature of this event, and thus its importance. It also fulfills the angel Gabriel's word in 1:20. The neighbors (and the readers) realized that God would work great things through this child. **And he began to speak, praising God.** Zechariah is a model of an ideal believer. His first words were used in praise of God. These words are found in the Benedictus of 1:68f., which begins, "Praise be to the Lord, the God of Israel." The importance of the praising or blessing (*eulogōn*) for Luke is evident.[73]

1:65 The neighbors were all filled with awe. "All" here, later in this verse, and in 1:66 should not be pressed. It probably means "many."[74] "Awe" is literally *fear (phobos*, Compare 1:12 and 1:30). Awe, or fear, is the proper reverent attitude which those who witness a heavenly intervention or manifestation of divine power should express. It may begin as a terrifying fear of judgment or wrath,[75] but it progresses to a holy awe of God and a recognition of his otherness, which leads to "glorifying and praising God" (cf. 2:10,20; 5:26; 7:16). This experience at John's birth is paralleled at Jesus' birth (2:17-18). See comments on 23:40.

And throughout the hill country of Judea people were talking about all these things. This comment by Luke enhances John the Baptist's importance and role as well as the magnitude of this event. Clearly Luke in no way sought to minimize John's importance.

1:66 Everyone . . . wondered. Compare 2:19,51; 3:15; 5:22 (cf. also 1 Sam 21:13-14; Mal 2:2 [LXX]). This again heightens the importance of these events. **What then is this child going to be?** The use of *what* instead of *who* emphasizes John the Baptist's *role* as the one who will go before his superior, i.e., the Messiah, and prepare his way. John was important not in himself but because he assisted in preparing for Jesus. Luke sought to help his readers, who knew of John the Baptist's importance, to understand that his importance was due to his role in preparing the way for the One greater than he. **For the Lord's hand was with him.** This is better understood as an editorial comment than as part of the preceding quotation due to the change in the tense of the verb (an imperfect instead of a future). "Hand of the Lord," is a common OT expression for God's powerful presence.[76]

1:67 His father Zechariah was filled with the Holy Spirit and prophesied. Just as Elizabeth was filled with the Spirit (Luke 1:41), so was Zechariah.

---

[72]The term "wrote" in Greek is literally, He wrote saying. Cf. 2 Sam 11:15; 2 Kgs 10:6; 1 Macc 8:31; 11:57 in the LXX. This is a good example of the idiomatic use of a verb and participle in which the literal meaning of the words should not be pressed. An even more common idiom is "answering said" where frequently, as in Luke 1:60, what is said is not at all related to a question.

[73]Luke 1:68; 2:28; 9:16; 13:35; 19:38; 24:30,53; cf. also 1:42; 2:34; 6:28; 24:50-51 (see comments on 5:25-26).

[74]As in 1:63; 2:18-20; 4:22,40; 6:19; 7:16; 8:40; 9:43; 18:43; 19:37; 21:38.

[75]Cf. Luke 1:12,30; 2:10; cf. also 5:26; 8:25,37; Acts 2:43; 5:5,11; 19:17.

[76]Cf. 1 Kgs 18:46; Ps 80:17; Isa 66:14; Ezek 1:3; 3:14,22.

See comments on 1:15. Since Zechariah was a reliable witness due to his character (1:6) and his being filled by the Spirit, the hymn that follows reveals the divine understanding of the relationship of John the Baptist to Jesus and their respective roles.
1:68 What follows in 1:68-75 consists of a single sentence in Greek. **Praise be to the Lord, the God of Israel.** The verb "be" (rather than "is"), although not in the text, is assumed. Even as Mary in the Magnificat (1:46-47) began with a word of praise, so Zechariah in the Benedictus began similarly.[77]
Because he has come and has redeemed his people. The "because" indicates that what follows is understood to be the cause of the preceding praise. The past tenses (aorists) witness to the fact that the promised time of salvation has already come. God has already in the events recorded in 1:5-67 visited his people, and although the "redemption" awaits the future work of the Son of God, its certainty is such that a past tense corresponding to a prophetic perfect can be used to describe this future event (cf. 1:50). In this hymn Luke understood the work of John the Baptist and Jesus as two parts of the same divine visitation.[78] The term "came" or "visited" appears in 1:78; 7:16; Acts 15:14 (cf. Gen 21:1; Exod 4:31; Ruth 1:6; Jer 15:15), and "redeemed" is found in Luke 2:38; 21:28; 24:21 and is a synonym for "salvation" found in 1:69,77. The Dead Sea Scrolls (CD 1:5-12) also refer to God's having visited his people and having raised up the teacher of righteousness.
1:69 He has raised up a horn of salvation for us. The image of a horn symbolized the strength of the animal.[79] Since John the Baptist is not linked to the house of David (Luke 1:69b; cf. Ps 132:17), the "horn" refers not to him but to the Messiah he was announcing. The fifteenth benediction of the *Shemonah Ezreh*, a Jewish prayer dating from the first century, states, "Blessed be Thou, O God, who causeth the horn of salvation to sprout forth." The salvation Jesus brought is a strong Lukan theme. The term "Savior" found in Luke 1:47; 2:11; Acts 5:31; 13:23 appears only once in the other Gospels (John 4:42); "salvation" is found ten times in Luke-Acts[80] but only once in the other Gospels (John 4:22); and the verb "to save" is found seventeen times in Luke (more than any other Gospel) and thirteen times in Acts. This salvation is not primarily concerned with political matters but with the individual's relationship to God. It involves the individual's "life" (Luke 9:24) and is for those who recognize that they are "lost" (19:10). It comes through faith[81] and involves the forgiveness of sins (1:77).[82] See comments on 7:50.

---

[77] For similar OT blessings see 1 Sam 25:32; 1 Kgs 1:48; 8:15; Pss 41:13; 72:18; 106:48; for NT parallels cf. Eph 1:3-10; 2 Cor 1:3-4; 1 Pet 1:3-5. One also finds parallels in 1 QH 5:20; 10:14.

[78] It is impossible therefore in light of the Benedictus to assign John to the OT period and Jesus to the period of the kingdom of God as Conzelmann does.

[79] For OT parallels see Deut 33:17; Pss 18:2; 132:17; 1 Sam 2:10; 2 Sam 22:3; Ezek 29:21.

[80] Luke 1:69,71,77; 19:9; Acts 4:12; 7:25; 13:26,47; 16:17; 27:34 (cf. also Luke 2:30; 3:6; Acts 28:28).

[81] Luke 7:50; 8:12,48,50; 17:19; 18:42; Acts 14:9; 15:11; 16:31.

[82] Cf. Acts 5:31. Also cf. Luke 9:24; 19:10; Acts 2:21; 4:12; 15:1,11.

In the house of his servant David. See comments on 1:27. Compare 2 Sam 7:12-16.

1:70 As he said through his holy prophets of long ago. This parenthetical comment, probably from Luke, emphasizes the theme of prophetic fulfillment. See Introduction 7 (1). The Greek text uses the expression "through the mouth of his holy prophets."[83]

1:71 Salvation from our enemies. This terminology comes from such OT passages as Pss 18:17; 106:10; 2 Sam 22:18. The "enemies" are further described in this verse as those who "hate us." Luke understood this less as a political and nationalistic deliverance from enemies than as an OT metaphorical description of personal salvation from sin (Luke 1:77) and judgment. See comments on 1:69. In the case of physical healings, the healing usually serves as a type of the individual's spiritual salvation. This is how, according to Luke, John the Baptist understood the salvation the Coming One brings as witnessed in John's message (3:7-14). Nevertheless there is a sense in which believers will be saved from their enemies at the parousia (18:7-8; 21:27-28).

1:72 To show mercy to our fathers and to remember his holy covenant. This begins the second major part of the hymn.[84] The two parts of this verse stand in synonymous parallelism with each other and describe two aspects of the same idea. For Luke the coming of Christ clearly did not bring the creation of a new religion but the fulfillment of the covenantal promises God made to the saints of the OT. See comments on 1:5-25—"The Lukan Message."

1:73 The oath he swore to our father Abraham. Compare Gen 17:4; 22:16-17. For "father Abraham" see Josh 24:3; Isa 51:2.

1:74 To rescue us from the hand of our enemies. Compare Ps 97:10. This clause and the next verse give the oath's content. Again Luke understood this rescue figuratively. It involves the kind of salvation that we read of in the rest of Luke-Acts and that is exemplified by such passages as Acts 2:37-41.

Without fear. This expression appears emphatically as the first word of this verse in Greek. It could go with the participle "rescue" but fits better with the infinitive "serve."

1:75 The Benedictus, begun in Luke 1:68, ends at this point.

1:76 This verse begins the second major part of the hymn honoring the miraculously born child whom God has appointed for his service. There is a change of tense at this point, from the past tense, which describes what God had already begun to do, to the future tense, which speaks specifically of John's future mission.

Will be called a prophet of the Most High. As in 1:35 this is not simply a prediction of what John would be called but primarily of what he would be. God would make John his prophet. John is called a prophet in 7:26 and 16:16. The one whom John announced, however, would be called "the Son of God" (1:35).

For you will go before the Lord to prepare the way for him. This clause provides the reason for John's prophetic status. John's preparatory role already has been

---

[83]This same expression is found in Acts 1:16; 3:18,21; 4:25 (cf. 2 Chr 36:22). The expression "holy prophets of long ago" is also found in Acts 3:21.

[84]For the thought and wording of 1:72, cf. Exod 2:24; Lev 26:42; Pss 105:8; 106:45 (cf. also 1 QM 14:4-5).

stated in 1:15,17 and prepares the reader for its fulfillment in 3:4 and 7:27. "Lord" (and "him") is best understood in light of 3:4; 7:27 and John's preparatory role, namely, as a reference to Jesus (cf. 1:43) rather than to God (Yahweh) as in 1:15-16.

1:77 To give his people the knowledge of salvation through the forgiveness of sins. This verse explains how John prepared Jesus' way. The expression "through the forgiveness of sins" defines salvation and reveals that Luke understood the Benedictus to refer to a spiritual rather than a political salvation. John's role is not being contrasted here with that of Jesus, for repentance and baptism leading to forgiveness and salvation are intimately associated with the preaching of both. The main difference is that the eschatological gift of the Spirit would be given to Jesus' disciples, but not to John's. This, however, must wait until after Jesus' glorification. Here "knowledge" is not theoretical but rather the experiencing of this salvation by means of the forgiveness of sins.

Forgiveness of sins. This important Lukan theological emphasis is found in key places throughout Luke-Acts. It is mentioned in the overall summary of John the Baptist's message in 3:3 and is mentioned in both Jesus' sermonic summary of his mission (4:18) and his great commission to the disciples after his resurrection (24:47). It is also found in the conclusion of the introductory sermon of Acts (2:38), in the explanation of God's having accepted the Gentiles apart from circumcision (Acts 10:43), in Paul's defense before Agrippa (26:18), and in two other sermons in Acts (5:31; 13:38). The redemption with which God visits his people is not a political liberation but rather a salvation that involves the forgiveness of sins.[85]

1:78 Because of the tender mercy of our God. The reason this salvation is possible, i.e., its cause, picks up the thought of Luke 1:72.

The rising sun. This is an enigmatic and most difficult phrase. In 1:76-77 Luke clearly referred to John the Baptist, since in 1:76 the allusions to Mal 3:1 and Isa 40:3 are used of his mission elsewhere (cf. Luke 3:4) and 1:77 contains terminology used of John's baptism (cf. 3:3). Nevertheless it is most unlikely that the phrase "the rising sun" refers to John the Baptist, for the present context (1:78-79) refers to Jesus' works. (Note how the terminology of 1:79 is used for Jesus in Matt 4:16.) Suggestions about what "rising sun" (*anatolē*) means include the rising of a star or sun, a metaphor for Yahweh (but 1:78a seems to distinguish God from *anatolē*), the shoot or offspring of David (Jer 23:5; 33:15; Zech 3:8; 6:12), and the star from Jacob (Num 24:17). At the present time it is impossible to be certain about the exact meaning Luke intended. It seems best to assume he was in some way referring to the coming of the Messiah—Son of God—and leave it at that.[86]

1:79 To shine on those living in darkness and in the shadow of death. This picks up the image of "the rising sun" in the previous verse. Compare Ps 106:10 (LXX) for this terminology (cf. also Isa 9:2; 42:7; 49:9).

To guide our feet into the path [way] of peace. John prepared the way of the Messiah (Luke 1:76), which is the way of peace. Compare Acts 10:36.

1:80 And the child grew and became strong in spirit. We find parallel statements describing Jesus' growth in Luke 2:40 (the first seven words [six words

[85]Cf. Jer 31:34; Isa 38:17; cf. also 1 QH 4:35f.; 7:30; 11:9-10.
[86]See Fitzmyer, *Luke*, 387.

in Greek] are identical) and 2:52. (Cf. Gen 21:8; Judg 13:24-25; 1 Sam 2:21,26.) In light of Luke 1:15,41,67 "spirit" here may refer to the Holy Spirit. **And he lived in the desert [wilderness] until he appeared publicly to Israel.** With this conclusion to the narrative Luke prepared the reader for 3:2, where John once again appeared "in the desert [wilderness]." Since the discovery of the Dead Sea Scrolls, there has been much speculation about whether John the Baptist was a member of the Qumran community, which produced these scrolls.[87] While parallels between John and the Essenes permit all sorts of speculation, at the present time no definitive decision can be made. Even if John were once a member of the Qumran community, this would have no real bearing on understanding the Lukan portrait of John since Luke made no reference to this.

The Lukan Message

The present passage is a rich source for understanding the Lukan message. Several important Lukan themes appear, including Lukan Christology. The Evangelist continued his comparison of the mission of John the Baptist and Jesus, and time and time again Jesus' superiority is shown. This is even seen in the amount of space given to John's birth (1:57-58) in comparison to the amount devoted to Jesus' birth (2:1-20). Whereas John is described as "a prophet of the Most High" (1:76), Jesus is "the Son of God" (1:35), "a horn of salvation" (1:69), and "the Lord" (1:76), who through his life and death will "redeem" God's people (1:68). John is described by the question "What?" (1:66), for his greatness is seen in how he served the Greater One. On the other hand Jesus will be described by the question "Who?" (5:21; 7:49; 9:9; cf. also 4:34; 19:3).

Another Lukan emphasis involves the dawn of a new stage in salvation history (1:68-79) and John the Baptist's role in it. Clearly John's conception, birth, and ministry (1:76-77) are part of the coming of God's kingdom in fulfillment of God's covenantal promises (1:68-75). The coming of the kingdom in fulfillment of the OT begins with John's conception and includes his birth and ministry; Jesus' conception, birth, and ministry; and it reaches its climax in Acts 2:1f. with the Spirit's coming. It cannot be narrowed to a single moment of time such as the resurrection or Pentecost but involves God's visitation of his people begun at 1:5f.[88]

Some other important themes found in our passage involve (1) God's sovereign rule over creation as revealed in his raising up the horn of sal-

---

[87] Both used Isa 40:3 as their theme verse (Luke 3:4; 1 QS 8:12-14); their ministries were both located "in the wilderness"; they possessed a similar initiation rite—baptism (Luke 3:3; 1 QS 3:4-9; 5:13-14), although at Qumran this was repeated; both criticized the Pharisees, were ascetic, were priestly in descent, and saw their time as the eschatological turning of the ages.

[88] The attempt by Conzelmann to relegate John the Baptist to the period of Israel is clearly flawed and does not take seriously Luke 1:5-80. See Introduction 7 (3).

vation for his people (1:69); one can compare this with Dan 2:21;
4:15,25,34-35; 5:21; (2) the continuity between Christianity and the religion of Israel; God has visited his people not to start a new religion but
rather to fulfill the holy covenant he made with Abraham and the fathers
(Luke 1:72-73); (3) the close association between salvation and the forgiveness of sins (1:77); (4) the coming of the Spirit to Israel (1:67); and
(5) Zechariah as a typical Lukan model of piety.[89]

5. The Birth of Jesus (2:1-52)

At this point Luke continued the parallel presentation of the coming of
John the Baptist and Jesus by recounting Jesus' birth. In contrast to John
the Baptist's birth, which is told in only two verses (1:57-58), Jesus' birth
occupies twenty verses (2:1-20). This is in keeping with the superiority of
Jesus over John. The birth narrative is followed by Jesus' circumcision
and Simeon's and Anna's prophetic pronouncements (2:21-40; cf. 1:59-
79) and the boy Jesus' visit to the temple (2:41-52; cf. 1:80).

(1) The Birth Proper (2:1-20)

[1]In those days Caesar Augustus issued a decree that a census should be
taken of the entire Roman world. [2](This was the first census that took place
while Quirinius was governor of Syria.) [3]And everyone went to his own town to
register.
[4]So Joseph also went up from the town of Nazareth in Galilee to Judea, to
Bethlehem the town of David, because he belonged to the house and line of
David. [5]He went there to register with Mary, who was pledged to be married to
him and was expecting a child. [6]While they were there, the time came for the
baby to be born, [7]and she gave birth to her firstborn, a son. She wrapped him
in cloths and placed him in a manger, because there was no room for them in
the inn.
[8]And there were shepherds living out in the fields nearby, keeping watch
over their flocks at night. [9]An angel of the Lord appeared to them, and the
glory of the Lord shone around them, and they were terrified. [10]But the angel
said to them, "Do not be afraid. I bring you good news of great joy that will be
for all the people. [11]Today in the town of David a Savior has been born to you;
he is Christ the Lord. [12]This will be a sign to you: You will find a baby wrapped
in cloths and lying in a manger."
[13]Suddenly a great company of the heavenly host appeared with the angel,
praising God and saying,
    [14]"Glory to God in the highest,
        and on earth peace to men on whom his favor rests."

---

[89]Cf. W. Carter ("Zechariah and the Benedictus [Luke 1,68-79]: Practicing What He
Preaches," *Bib* 69 [1988]: 247), who states: "Presented by Luke as a worshiper and as a
dikaios one, he [Zechariah] thus models in his own living the goal of God's saving act—a
life of service to God marked by righteousness."

[15]When the angels had left them and gone into heaven, the shepherds said to one another, "Let's go to Bethlehem and see this thing that has happened, which the Lord has told us about." [16]So they hurried off and found Mary and Joseph, and the baby, who was lying in the manger. [17]When they had seen him, they spread the word concerning what had been told them about this child, [18]and all who heard it were amazed at what the shepherds said to them. [19]But Mary treasured up all these things and pondered them in her heart. [20]The shepherds returned, glorifying and praising God for all the things they had heard and seen, which were just as they had been told.

Context

This present passage consists of three distinct parts: (1) the historical setting, which explains how Mary, whose home was Nazareth (1:26), gave birth to God's Son in Bethlehem (2:1-5);[90] (2) the birth itself (2:6-7); and (3) the angelic announcement to the shepherds (2:8-20).[91] Just as the pronouncement to Mary of Jesus' birth was superior to that given to Zechariah about John the Baptist's birth, and just as Jesus' conception was more wonderful, so was his birth. John's birth was marked by his father Zechariah's prophecy. Jesus' birth was marked by a theophany and angelic chorus, a historical dating, and the use of several Christological titles.

Comments

2:1   In those days.   According to Luke, all that follows must be understood as falling under God's sovereign rule. The date is imprecise (contrast 3:1-2)[92] and probably is due to Luke's ignorance of the exact date. Note the "about thirty years old" in 3:23.

---

[90]Numerous theories have been put forth that attempt to explain the origin of this story. Some have suggested it arose out of a midrashic reflection of the OT accounts concerning the birth of the Messiah. Micah 5:2 is especially pointed out in this regard, but the lack of reference to specific prophecies being fulfilled, above all the lack of reference to Mic 5:2, argues against this account being the product of midrashic reflection.

[91]Some have suggested that the story of the shepherds arose due to the association of the Messiah's birth with Bethlehem, the city of David; for David had been a shepherd there. Others have suggested that behind the reference to the shepherds lies a Hellenistic idea of shepherds representing the ideal, paradisaical world; but this was certainly not the way shepherds were thought of in Israel. Others have suggested that it may have arisen due to the reference in Mic 4:8 to the "watchtower of the flock," which in the Targum Pseudo-Jonathan is the place where the Messiah was to reveal himself. This, however, appears too subtle. Luke wanted his readers to see this account as an accurate description of what actually took place at the birth of Jesus, and he anticipated that his readers would accept it as such. For further discussion see Brown, *Birth of the Messiah*, 412-24; Fitzmyer, *Luke*, 392-98.

[92]For "in those days" cf. 1:5,39; 4:2; 5:35; 9:36; 21:23; Acts 2:18; 7:41; 9:37.

Caesar Augustus. Born Gaius Octavius, the Roman senate bestowed upon him the title Augustus in 27 B.C. He ruled until A.D. 14 and was succeeded by Tiberius (3:1). Like Nebuchadnezzar and Cyrus, Caesar Augustus is seen as a divine agent bringing about God's purpose and plan. In mentioning this Roman emperor, Luke revealed his historical interests and indicated that salvation history is both particular (Jewish) and universal in its implications (the Roman world). "Augustus," which is both a title and a name, is the transliteration of the Latin term into Greek and functions primarily as a name here. The Greek translation of the term would have been *Sebastos*, which we find in Acts 25:21,25, where it is used as a title.

Issued a decree. A "decree" is an "imperial edict" as in Acts 17:7.

That a census should be taken of the entire Roman world. This census was for taxes and not military service, since Jews were exempted from the latter. "The entire Roman world" (*oikoumenēn*; the Greek text has no qualifying "Roman"), as in Acts 11:28, is hyperbolic. "Entire" or "all" is used twenty-three times in chaps. 1–2.

2:2 This was the first census that took place while Quirinius was governor of Syria. This statement is a *crux interpretum* due to the historical problems incurred in this text. These problems include the lack of an extrabiblical reference to a universal census of the whole Roman Empire and the unusual nature of Joseph's returning to his birthplace for the census and Mary's normally unnecessary presence at the census. The date of the census causes the most difficulty. The dating of the governors of Syria appears to have been as follows: 10 B.C., M. Titius; 9–6 B.C., C. Sentius Saturnius; 6–4 B.C., P. Quintilius Varus. The birth cannot be later than this because Herod the Great died in 4 B.C., and he was alive when Jesus was born (cf. Matt 2:1-18). We also know that P. Sulpicius Quirinius (Cyrenius, KJV) was governor of Syria from A.D. 6 to 7.

Numerous attempts have been made to explain these difficulties. Although no record exists of a single census involving all the Roman Empire, under Augustus a tax assessment of all the Roman Empire did take place, even if this was not the result of a single census. In addition at times it was important for persons to return to their hometowns for a census. (Such a census took place in Egypt under G. Vibius Maximus in A.D. 104.) We also know of a poll tax in Syria in which women of twelve years or older were required to appear personally for the tax. And, of course, Mary could simply have wished to be with Joseph during the time of her delivery, and this required her to go with him to Bethlehem for his required enrollment.

The heart of the problem, as has already been stated, is the dating of the census within the rule of Quirinius. It is the date, not the existence of the census, that is problematic. Several attempts have been made to reconcile this biblical statement with the historical materials. Some of these involve the discrediting of Josephus, who stated that the census under Quirinius took place in A.D. 6–7. Another attempt is to argue that the appearance of the name "Quirinius" in 2:2 is a textual error and that the name C. Sentius Saturnius should be read instead. There is, however, no textual evidence that the name "Quirinius" is a scribal error. Another attempt is to divide the census into two parts. The first part, or ordering of a census, took place during the time of Caesar Augustus; and the second part, the census itself, was completed under Quirinius in A.D. 6–7 (cf. Acts 5:37). But why then would Joseph and Mary go to Bethlehem during the ordering of the census in the time of Herod when the actual census did not take place until later? Another attempt is to understand Quirinius, who was placed in charge of putting down the Homodensian revolt in northwestern Syria, i.e., southeastern Turkey today (see Strabo, *Geography* 12.6.5), as being a kind of second governor at the time. He was the governor of external affairs, whereas Saturnius was governor of internal affairs. Still another explanation is that the term "first," or "first census," should be understood not as "first" but should be translated, "This was the census 'before' Quirinius was governor." The genitive absolute "while Quirinius was governor of Syria," however, makes this unlikely. It must be confessed that there is no easy explanation at the present time for this historical problem of the census date, but some new evidence might in the future vindicate the historical accuracy of Luke on this point.[93]

Governor. The rulers of imperial provinces such as Syria were technically called "legates" or "prefects." (The latter were also called "procurators.") The more established senatorial provinces had "proconsuls." The term "governor" is not used in a technical sense here and means *ruler.*

2:3   And everyone went to his own town to register. "Own town" means one's ancestral home. In 2:39 Joseph's hometown is called Nazareth and is described as where he and Mary lived. Luke, as a result, did not see any conflict in calling both Bethlehem and Nazareth the hometown of Joseph. "Everyone" is another example of Lukan hyperbole.

2:4   So Joseph. Joseph is introduced as one already known (cf. 1:27), and this reveals that chap. 2 builds upon chap. 1.

Went up. Due to the height of Bethlehem (2,564 feet above sea level), travelers would go up from Nazareth (1,830 feet above sea level) to Bethlehem even though proceeding south.[94]

Because he belonged to the house and line of David. Joseph's Davidic lineage, and thus Jesus' Davidic (and messianic) lineage, is pointed out. The redundancy "house and line" probably is a result of Luke's fondness for doublets (see comments on 2:25) and does not imply that Joseph owned a house in Bethlehem. If the latter were true, then his search for a room in an inn (2:7) makes no sense.

From . . . Nazareth . . . to Bethlehem. This would entail a trip of eighty-five to ninety miles if one went through Samaria. Although Jerusalem is called the city of David,[95] Bethlehem could also be called the city of David since it was his ancestral home (1 Sam 16:1ff.; 17:12,15,58; Ps 78:70). Compare also Luke 2:11.

2:5   To register with Mary. It is uncertain why Mary went to Bethlehem. Was it to register along with Joseph? Usually women were not required to register,

[93] For further discussion see G. Ogg, "The Quirinius Question Today," *ExpTim* 79 (1968): 231-36; H. W. Hoehner, *Chronological Aspects of the Life of Christ* (Grand Rapids: Zondervan, 1977), 11-27; Nolland, *Luke 1–9:20*, 99-102.
[94] A traveler always "goes up" to Jerusalem (2:22; 18:31; 19:28; Acts 11:2; 13:31; 15:2; 21:12,15; 25:1,9) and "goes down" from Jerusalem (10:30; Acts 11:27; 25:7) because Jerusalem lies 2,500 feet above sea level.
[95] Cf. 2 Sam 5:7,9; 6:10,12,16; 2 Kgs 9:28; 12:21.

although in Syria women had to register for a poll tax. If Mary did not personally have to register, did she go to be with Joseph? Was it because of a conscious desire on her part to have her son born in David's city and thus fulfill Mic 5:2? Was it to avoid scandal? Luke did not tell us the immediate reason for this, but ultimately he would say that it was due to God's providence, for God's Son had to be born in David's city. As for Mary's own thinking, we are not able to know her thoughts.

Who was pledged to be married to him. This is an unusual way of expressing a journey made by a husband and wife. Luke may have been suggesting here what Matt 1:25 states explicitly, that the marriage had not yet been consummated, although Mary was living as a wife with Joseph (as her going to Bethlehem with him suggests).

And was expecting a child. This is not a causal clause but an adjectival one, i.e., "being with child," not "because she was with child."

2:6 The time came for the baby to be born. Compare Luke 1:57 and Gen 25:24. Whether Luke placed Jesus' birth sometime after Joseph and Mary arrived in Bethlehem (cf. *Prot. Jas.* 17.3) or immediately upon their arrival is uncertain.

2:7 And she gave birth to her firstborn. The reference to Jesus as the "firstborn" does not preclude Mary's and Joseph's later having had children as "only" (*monogenēs*) would, but it need not require the birth of other children either. An ancient grave inscription that speaks of the deceased as having died while giving birth to her "firstborn" son proves this (cf. also 2 Esdr 6:58; *Pss. Sol.* 13:9; 18:4).[96] In light of the later references to the "brothers and sisters of Jesus" (Luke 8:19-21; Acts 1:14; cf. Mark 6:3; etc.), Luke probably used "firstborn" instead of *monogenēs* because he knew of other sons. Luke clearly did not want to indicate that Jesus was Mary's only son, or else he would have used *monogenes*. In addition Matt 1:25 strongly implies that Joseph and Mary lived in a normal marital relationship after Jesus' birth. This reference to Mary's firstborn son prepares the reader for Luke 2:22-24.

She wrapped him in clothes. "Wrapped . . . in clothes" is literally *swaddled him.* This normal child care of the time sought to keep the limbs of a child straight (Ezek 16:4; cf. Wis 7:4). The irony of the most important event in history taking place in a manger should not be lost sight of; it reveals how God elevates the lowly and humble and rejects the proud and mighty of this world. Compare Phil 2:6-7. For Luke this theme of reversal was of major importance. See Introduction 8 (5).

And placed him in a manger. The manger was no doubt a feeding trough for animals. One should probably not see here any allusion to Isa 1:3; Jer 14:8; Wis 7:4-5.

Because there was no room for them in the inn. This does not refer to a lack of a "hotel room" but lack of a suitable "place" for Mary to give birth to her son. It does not imply any rejection on the part of the much maligned innkeeper. The "inn" probably refers to a public caravansary (a crude overnight lodging place for caravans), which was the one lodging place in Bethlehem. Note that Luke made no mention of either animals or wise men being present.[97]

---

[96] See Fitzmyer, *Luke,* 407-8.

[97] For further discussion see R. Laurentim, *The Truth of Christmas* (Petersham: St. Bede's, 1986), 180-82.

2:8   And there were shepherds. The scene changes, and the "humble" of Luke 1:52 are visited (cf. 7:22). One should not romanticize the occupation of shepherds. In general shepherds were dishonest (*Sanh.* 25b) and unclean according to the standards of the law. They represent the outcasts and sinners for whom Jesus came. Such outcasts were the first recipients of the good news.

Out in the fields. Shepherds were out in the fields with their flocks usually during the months of March to November. Nothing in the two birth accounts ties Jesus' birth to any specific date.

Keeping watch. "Keeping watch" is literally *watching watches*—a Semitic literary form.

2:9 The subsequent material follows the same announcement form we have encountered in 1:13-20,28-37. Here we again have (1) the angel's appearance (2:9a), (2) a response of fear (2:9b), (3) a word of reassurance (2:10), (4) the divine message (2:11), and (5) the giving of a sign (2:12). What is lacking is the objection and request for a sign. See comments on 1:13-20.

An angel of the Lord appeared to them. Unlike 1:11,19,26 the angel is not identified. For "appeared" cf. also 24:4; Acts 12:7; 23:11.

Glory of the Lord. This is the manifestation of God's presence among his people. Compare Exod 16:7,10; 24:17; 40:34; Ps 63:2.

2:10   Do not be afraid. See comments on 1:13.

I bring you good news. This translates the Greek verb *euangelizō*, which means *to preach the good news*. The noun (*euangelion*) is translated by the word "gospel." This verb is found eleven times in the Gospels, and ten of these are found in Luke. See comments on 1:19.

Of great joy. See comments on 1:14.

That will be for all the people. Are Gentiles included here, or is this a reference only to the Jewish people? Luke envisioned the gospel as being for all people, including the Gentiles (Acts 15:1-29; 18:10); but here, as in 3:21; 7:29; 8:47, the people of Israel were primarily in Luke's mind. The singular "people" refers everywhere else in Luke to the people of Israel.[98]

2:11   Today. This term designates the beginning of the time of messianic salvation.[99]

A Savior . . . Christ the Lord. Jesus' role as Savior is qualified by the title "Christ" and "Lord." For the pairing of these last two titles, cf. Lam 4:20; *Pss. Sol.* 17:36 (32). For the use of multiple titles for Jesus, see Introduction 8 (4). This verse gives a brief summary of the gospel message and provides the reason for the statement found in the previous verse. It tells of the birth of a Savior. This title is applied to God in Luke 1:47, but its use here of Jesus is prepared for by 1:69 (cf. Acts 5:31; 13:23). There is a sense in which this statement is not only Christological in nature (in what it says about Mary's child) but also anthropological, for it says that the Gospel's readers, both past and present, are the kind of people who need a Savior! This verse also states that the child's name is Christ, for Christ functions here primarily as an identifying name. Although "Christ" is actually a title (Acts 5:42; cf. also Acts 17:3), this verse reveals that the title was

---

[98]Cf. 3:21; 7:29; 8:47; 18:43; 19:47-48; 21:38; 24:19.
[99]Cf. Luke 4:21; 5:26; 13:32-33; 19:9; 23:43.

so closely identified with Jesus of Nazareth that it soon became part of his name—Jesus Christ. The reader has been prepared for the use of this title by 1:32-33,69; 2:4. This Savior is also the Lord. See comments on 1:43; cf. also 1:17,76. (In 2:26 we have the expression "Lord's Christ," but here in 2:11 the title "Lord" clearly refers to Jesus rather than God.) Although the realization of the authority of the titles "Christ" and "Lord" would await the resurrection (Acts 2:36), Jesus at his birth was already both Christ and Lord, for the one born to Mary in Bethlehem is the same person who is raised in glory and given the authority to be Lord and Christ. See Introduction 8 (4). No doubt for Luke's readers this description of the child would have far greater theological meaning than for its original hearers. These three titles also appear together in Phil 3:20.

In the town of David. By this phrase Luke was drawing attention to the messianic role of Mary's child (cf. 1:27).

2:12 This shall be a sign. Since the odds of finding another newborn baby boy lying in a manger would be extremely small, this would function as a sign of identity for the shepherds.

2:13 Suddenly a great company of the heavenly host appeared. Compare 1 Kgs 22:19; Jer 19:13; Dan 8:10; Hos 13:4 (LXX); 2 Chr 33:3,5; cf. Rev 19:1-2,6-8; also Neh 9:6.

Praising God. "Praising God" is the proper response not only of the believer (Luke 2:20; 19:37; 24:53; Acts 2:47; 3:8-9) but all of God's creation (cf. Ps 148:1-4). The term "praising" was a favorite of Luke and is found eight times in the NT, six of which appear in Luke-Acts. See comments on 1:64; 5:25-26.

2:14 We find a parallelism in the following two lines consisting of glory-peace; in the highest-on earth; to God-to men.

Glory to God in the highest. The verb "be" is understood. Here the "highest" refers to the highest heavens (cf. 19:38), not to the highest degree. For the glory of Jesus, cf. 9:26,32; 21:27; 24:26; for his receiving glory from people, cf. 4:15.

And on earth peace to men on whom his favor rests. "Peace" refers here to the fullness of blessing which the Savior/Christ/Lord brings and is essentially a synonym for salvation (cf. Acts 10:36). The latter part of the hymn has been interpreted in several ways: goodwill to men (KJV); to men of good will (Douay); among men with whom he is pleased (RSV). The favor/goodwill referred to in the verse does not belong to men but to God. This is clear from Luke 10:21 (cf. also 1 QH 4:32-33; 11:9), where the Father's good pleasure or favor is referred to, so that it is best to translate this sentence as it is found in the NIV, RSV, NRSV, REB.

2:15 Let's go to Bethlehem and see this thing that has happened. "This thing" is literally *this word* as in Luke 2:17,19, but "this word" can refer to an event as it does here.

Which the Lord has told us about. The angelic intermediary is left unmentioned, and only the ultimate source of the revelation is mentioned.

2:16 So they hurried off. This refers more to the obedience of the shepherds than to the actual speed of their travel (cf. 1:39).

No mention is made here of the child's virginal conception, and Joseph appears to be the father. Some scholars have claimed that this account once existed independently of chap. 1 and did not know of a virginal conception. But for Luke the mention of the virginal conception at this point was totally unnecessary. His readers before reading chap. 2 would have read chap. 1 and assumed that Luke intended for them to read the present account in light of the previous chapter. In fact, this is the way Christians have always read this account. Joseph's mention here is quite natural since the trip to Bethlehem was made due to his need to enroll in the census. The shepherds' visit at Jesus' birth corresponds to the neighbors' visit at John the Baptist's birth (1:58). See comments on 2:27.

Lying in the manger. The child was found just as the angel had prophesied in 2:12.

2:17 Child. A different word is used here from the one in 2:12,16, but there does not seem to be any theological significance in this.

Spread the word. Compare 1:65-66.

2:18 And all who heard it were amazed. "Amazed" is a favorite term of Luke and is found thirteen times in Luke and five times in Acts, whereas it is found only four times in Mark and seven times in Matthew.[100]

2:19 But Mary treasured up . . . and pondered. This along with Luke 2:51 indicates that Mary did not fully understand the implications of all that happened to her. Compare Dan 4:28 (LXX) and Gen 37:11, where this word or a similar one is used to describe a person who is puzzled by what they have heard but keeps it in mind in order to understand, often with divine help, its meaning. Luke did not specify exactly what the object of this pondering was. Was it the titles Savior-Christ-Lord? Was it the nature of what had taken place in her life? Probably Luke intended his readers to think of all that had happened in Luke 1:5ff., i.e., how God had visited his people through the miraculous conceptions of John the Baptist and Jesus and the significance of all this. It has been argued that the Lukan portrayal of these events cannot be historical because of the lack of understanding portrayed in Mark 3:21, but it would have been remarkable indeed for Mary not to have been confused about the significance of all that had happened to her. No doubt she recognized her child's divine calling and destiny; but exactly what that entailed was not known to her, and she may at times have had the same kinds of questions that John the Baptist had in Luke 7:18-23. Earlier commentators held that this reference to Mary's inner thoughts (cf. also 2:51) indicated that Mary was the source for this account.

All these things. This includes not just the immediate encounter with the shepherds but all that preceded from 1:5ff.

In her heart. This can go with either "treasure up" or "pondered," but its location suggests that it goes with "pondered."

2:20 The shepherds returned glorifying and praising God. What the angelic host had done in 2:13-14 was now carried on by the shepherds.

For all the things they had heard and seen. This is the ground for the shepherds' glorifying and praising God.

Just as they had been told. This refers to the fulfillment of divine prophecy given by the angel.

---

[100]Cf. Luke 1:21,63; 2:33; 4:22; 7:9; 8:25; 9:43; 11:14,38; 20:26; 24:12,41; Acts 2:7; 3:12; 4:13; 7:31; 13:41.

The Lukan Message

Several Lukan themes are found in our passage. The Christological description of Mary's firstborn son is clearly one. Luke taught his readers that Jesus is the fulfillment of the Jewish messianic hopes by showing that he was born in David's town (2:4,11). Although he did not quote Mic 5:2 as Matt 2:6 does, the account of the birth in Bethlehem is clearly meant to demonstrate that Jesus is David's legitimate offspring and the promised Davidic King/Messiah. Thus Luke 2:4,11 picks up the theme of 1:27,32-33,69. Mary's child is also referred to as a Savior, is called the Christ in a way that indicates that Luke's readers were already aware that this title had become a name for Jesus, and is called the Lord (2:11). Although the child's work as Savior and full authorization as Lord was still future, he was proleptically referred to as such. Later the church would proclaim that Jesus is the only Savior, for salvation is found in no one else (Acts 4:12). Luke also continued the John the Baptist—Jesus parallelism in this account. Once again the greater nature of Jesus is evident, for whereas John the Baptist was the prophet of the Most High (1:16,17,76; 7:26), Jesus is Savior, Christ, and Lord. And whereas at John the Baptist's birth Zechariah uttered a prophetic pronouncement, at Jesus' birth an angelic host sang a doxology to God.

Another theme that appears in this passage involves God's sovereignty over history. The historical description in 2:1-3 is to be understood not simply as an accidental quirk but rather as showing how God, who rules over nations, directed Caesar Augustus to issue the census decree in order to bring about the fulfillment of what God had decreed centuries earlier. Thus in God's providence while they were there (2:6) David's greatest Son was born. God's sovereign rule is also emphasized in 2:20, where Luke remarked that all took place "just as they had been told."

A final Lukan theme is the divine visitation to the poor and humble of Israel. God's visitation of salvation comes to the humble (1:48,52) and hungry (1:53), not the proud (1:51-52) and rich (1:53). Thus those present at the birth of God's Son were not this world's rulers or its religious leaders. Rather the angelic invitation was extended to shepherds on the fringe of society, and they were present to see the birth of the Lord Christ.

(2) The Circumcision and the Prophets, Simeon and Anna (2:21-40)

[21]On the eighth day, when it was time to circumcise him, he was named Jesus, the name the angel had given him before he had been conceived.

[22]When the time of their purification according to the Law of Moses had been completed, Joseph and Mary took him to Jerusalem to present him to the Lord [23](as it is written in the Law of the Lord, "Every firstborn male is to be consecrated to the Lord"), [24]and to offer a sacrifice in keeping with what is said in the Law of the Lord: "a pair of doves or two young pigeons."

²⁵Now there was a man in Jerusalem called Simeon, who was righteous and devout. He was waiting for the consolation of Israel, and the Holy Spirit was upon him. ²⁶It had been revealed to him by the Holy Spirit that he would not die before he had seen the Lord's Christ. ²⁷Moved by the Spirit, he went into the temple courts. When the parents brought in the child Jesus to do for him what the custom of the Law required, ²⁸Simeon took him in his arms and praised God, saying:

²⁹"Sovereign Lord, as you have promised,
  you now dismiss your servant in peace.
³⁰For my eyes have seen your salvation,
³¹which you have prepared in the sight of all people,
³²a light for revelation to the Gentiles
  and for glory to your people Israel."

³³The child's father and mother marveled at what was said about him. ³⁴Then Simeon blessed them and said to Mary, his mother: "This child is destined to cause the falling and rising of many in Israel, and to be a sign that will be spoken against, ³⁵so that the thoughts of many hearts will be revealed. And a sword will pierce your own soul too."

³⁶There was also a prophetess, Anna, the daughter of Phanuel, of the tribe of Asher. She was very old; she had lived with her husband seven years after her marriage, ³⁷and then was a widow until she was eighty-four. She never left the temple but worshiped night and day, fasting and praying. ³⁸Coming up to them at that very moment, she gave thanks to God and spoke about the child to all who were looking forward to the redemption of Jerusalem.

³⁹When Joseph and Mary had done everything required by the Law of the Lord, they returned to Galilee to their own town of Nazareth. ⁴⁰And the child grew and became strong; he was filled with wisdom, and the grace of God was upon him.

Context

This section continues the Jesus-John the Baptist parallelism and corresponds to 1:59-80. We have Jesus' circumcision and naming, 2:21 (2:22-24 are also best included here; cf. 1:59-66); Simeon's and Anna's prophetic encounter and pronouncements, 2:25-38 (cf. the Benedictus of Zechariah in 1:67-79); and a summary of Jesus' growth, 2:39-40 (cf. 1:80). As with its parallel, so here also we find in this passage a good example of first-century Jewish piety. It is better to include 2:21 with this section than to place it with 2:1-20 in order to retain the Jesus—John parallelism. Thus even as 1:56 concludes 1:39-55 with a reference to Mary's returning home and 1:57 introduces a new account (1:58-80), so 2:20 concludes 2:1-19 with a reference to the shepherds' returning (to the fields), and 2:21 is linked to what follows. Both the opening (1:9-23) and concluding (2:22-38,41-51) accounts of this section (1:5-2:52) take place in the temple. By this inclusio Luke bracketed this unit and gave it an overall unity. The literary influence of 1 Sam 1:24-28; 2:20,21,26 on this section is quite evident.[101]

Comments

2:21 On the eighth day, when it was time to circumcise him. For the "eighth day" see comments on 1:59; for similar chronological references, cf. 1:23,57; 2:6,22. Even though it is not emphasized, Jesus' circumcision reveals the solidarity of God's Son with his people, namely, that he was born under the law (Gal 4:4).

He was named Jesus. As in the case of John, the emphasis falls not on the child's circumcision but rather on his naming. Unlike Matt 1:21, however, no interpretation or etymology of the name (*Jesus* means *Yahweh saves*) is given, although Acts 4:12 suggests that Luke may have been aware of the etymology due to the play on the words "salvation" and "name." Luke did not specify who named the child (cf. Luke 1:31).

The name the angel gave him. Compare 1:31.

2:22-24 The "purification" contained three elements: Mary's purification (Lev 12:6-8), which involved a sacrifice being offered at the Nicanor Gate in the court of the women; the redemption of the firstborn son (Exod 13:1-2), which involved five shekels (Num 3:47-48) and which Luke did not mention; and the consecration of the firstborn son (cf. 1 Sam 1:11,22,28). We find in 2:22-24 a chiasmus.[102]

2:22 When the time of their purification according to the Law of Moses had been completed. This would have been forty days after Jesus' birth (seven days after birth, circumcision; thirty-three days after circumcision, purification; cf. Lev 12:3-4). The law is mentioned five times in this account (Luke 2:22,23,24,27,29 [cf. RSV]), and thus its value as a moral guide is revealed. The reference to "their purification" is difficult in that only Mary needed the purification rite. Also does "their" refer to Jesus and Mary or to Joseph and Mary? The clearest antecedent of "their" appears to be subject of the verb "took," i.e., they. (The names Joseph and Mary are not found in the Greek text.) If it refers to Joseph and Mary, the pronoun "their" gives a sense of family solidarity in which Mary's need of purification is seen as a need for this "one flesh" (Gen 2:24) unit. Since a child did not need to experience any such purification, if the "their" refers to Mary and Jesus this would indicate that Luke simply used the term "purification," which was one element of the ritual, to describe the entire ritual that Mary and her son needed to experience. Compare 1 Sam 1:22-24.

Took him. "Took him" is literally *took him up*. One always goes up to Jerusalem, even though in this instance Bethlehem is slightly higher than Jerusalem. Since Nazareth is not mentioned in Luke 2:1-39, Luke expected his readers to think of this trip as originating in Bethlehem, which is five miles south of Jerusalem. It

---

[101] For further discussion see Brown, *Birth of the Messiah*, 443-47.
[102] *A* Mary's purification (2:22a);
    B Jesus' consecration (2:22b);
    b Jesus' consecration (2:23);
    a Mary's purification (2:24).

is uncertain about whether the purification-redemption-consecration had to be done in the temple in Jerusalem, although Neh 10:35-36 at least portrayed this as the ideal. Since Bethlehem lay so close to Jerusalem, there is good reason to think that Joseph and Mary would have sought to perform these rites in the temple. For Luke this scene is crafted after such passages as Exod 13:2,12,15; Lev 12:6,8; 1 Sam 1–2 (esp. 1:24-28).

To present him to the Lord. This was seen by Luke as the main reason for going to Jerusalem. One should not interpret the verb "present" as the offering of Jesus as a sacrifice to God along the lines of Rom 12:1. This goes beyond the Lukan teaching.

2:23 (As it is written). The tense of this verb is an "intensive perfect" and indicates that what has been written in the past has an abiding value, i.e., what has been written in the Scriptures remains written. This verse demonstrates that the main element in this account for Luke was the Savior's consecration rather than his redemption or Mary's purification.[103] One should not read into this a Nazirite dedication, for Luke made no mention of this.

2:24 And to offer . . . "a pair of doves or two young pigeons." Why did Luke describe the sacrifice? Was it purely for historical reasons? Was it to demonstrate that Joseph and Mary obeyed the law? Or was it because he expected his readers to know that according to Lev 12:8 the normal sacrifice involved a lamb and a dove or pigeon and thus to understand that Joseph and Mary were of a "humble state" (Luke 1:48), i.e., too poor to be able to afford a lamb? Certainty is impossible, but the latter explanation fits well the Lukan emphasis in 1:48,52-53; 2:8. That Mary offered a dove as a sin offering (Lev 12:6) for her purification indicates that the mother of God's Son also needed the forgiveness and redemption that her son brought. (The description of Mary's offering also suggests that Joseph and Mary were not yet in possession of the rich gifts of the wise men mentioned in Matt 2:11, i.e., the wise men had not yet come. Cf. also Matt 2:7,16.)

2:25-38 Even as John the Baptist's circumcision and naming was followed by prophetic statements praising God and indicating John's future destiny, so Jesus' naming and consecration was followed by praise to God and the foretelling of Jesus' destiny. Jesus' destiny, however, involved a surpassing greatness.

2:25 Simeon. Apart from this incident Simeon is unknown. Who he was was unimportant for Luke. Only the role he played in Jesus' story is important.

A man . . . who was righteous and devout. Compare 1:6; 23:50-51; Acts 10:22. Luke had a love for pairs.[104]

He was waiting for the consolation of Israel. This refers to the consolation that would be brought about by the inauguration of the messianic age.[105] Compare Luke 2:26, where this consolation is described as "seeing the Lord's Christ" (cf.

---

[103] Cf. Exod 13:2,12,15; Num 3:13; 18:15-16; Deut 21:15-17.

[104] Cf. commandments and regulations (1:6); his pairing of Simeon and Anna (2:25-38); night and day (2:37); relatives and friends (2:44); listening . . . and asking (2:46); understanding and answers (2:47); blessings and woes (6:20-26); disasters in Galilee and Siloam (13:1-5); parables of lost sheep and coin (15:4-10); Herod and Pilate (23:1-12); Theudas and James (Acts 5:36-37).

[105] Cf. Gen 49:10; Ps 119:166; Isa 25:9; 40:1f.; 66:13.

also 1:54,68-75). For Luke this referred not to the fulfillment of Jewish political hopes involving deliverance from their enemies and restoration of David's throne but rather to the salvation Jesus brought. This is clear when one compares 2:30 with such verses as 19:10. See the discussion at 1:69. Like other devout model believers (Anna, 2:38; Joseph of Arimathea, 23:51; cf. also 12:36; Acts 24:15), Simeon was looking forward to Israel's consolation (2:25), i.e., Jerusalem's redemption (2:38); the coming of God's kingdom (23:51); the Master's return (12:36); the resurrection of the just and the unjust (Acts 24:15).

And the Holy Spirit was upon him. See Introduction 8 (3). Luke wanted his readers to understand that Simeon was providing reliable testimony to the person and work of God's Son.[106]

2:26 It had been revealed to him by the Holy Spirit. Here there is an article before "Holy Spirit."

Should not die. "Should not die" is literally "to see death," an OT expression for dying.[107]

The Lord's Christ. Perhaps this can better be translated "the 'Anointed' of the Lord" or "the Lord's Messiah" (NRSV; REB).[108]

2:27 Moved by the Spirit. This does not refer to an ecstatic experience such as Rev 1:10 but rather to the Spirit's guidance such as referred to in Luke 4:1.

He went into the temple. Here "temple" refers to the temple court, not the temple sanctuary. Luke knew the difference between *hieron* (temple court or temple in general, 2:37,46; 4:9; etc.) and *naos* (temple sanctuary or holy place, 1:9,21-22; 23:45).

When the parents brought in the child Jesus to do for him what the custom of the Law required. Luke omitted the details of the carrying out of Mary's purification, since the readers already knew what was involved due to 2:24. Luke described Joseph and Mary as Jesus' "parents" (cf. also 2:33,41,43,48). He, of course, intended his readers to understand his use of this term here in light of the virginal conception discussed in chap. 1. Joseph was the adopted and legal father of Jesus. Attempts to say that this designation was part of a pre-Lukan source that either denied or was unaware of a virginal conception tradition are both highly speculative and unprovable. Luke at least saw no contradiction between this term and a virgin birth. As a result he avoided any awkward circumlocution for "parents," such as "virgin-mother of Jesus and his adopted, but not physical, father."

2:29 Sovereign Lord. "Sovereign Lord" (Greek *despota*, cf. Acts 4:24) is an appropriate title in light of the use of the term "servant" (*doulos*) in the latter part of the verse.

Now. It is unfortunate that the NIV places this word in the middle of the sentence. It is the first word in the Greek text and thus in an emphatic position: "*Now* [that salvation, God's Kingdom, the Messiah has come] dismiss your servant in peace because."

---

[106]Nothing should be made of the fact that the Greek text lacks an article before "Holy Spirit." The article is also missing in 1:15,35,41,67.

[107]Ps 89:48; John 8:51; Acts 2:27; Heb 11:5.

[108]Cf. Luke 9:20; 23:35; Acts 3:18; 4:26; cf. also 1 Sam 24:6,10; 26:9,11,16,23; *Pss. Sol.* 18:7.

Dismiss your servant in peace.   A Semitic way of saying, "Let me die."[109]
For "in peace" see Gen 15:15. The verb "dismiss" is a present indicative ("you are
dismissing") and introduces some difficulties in translating. Perhaps it should be
understood as indicating that now that Simeon had seen the Lord's Christ, God
was beginning to fulfill Luke 2:26, and Simeon was already in the process of experiencing his "peaceful dismissal." This verse and 2:26 suggest that Simeon died
shortly after 2:35.

2:30   For my eyes have seen your salvation.   This does not imply that Simeon had been physically blind up to this point. "Salvation" here further describes
the "consolation" of 2:25. For "salvation" see comments on 1:69. In the child
Jesus, Simeon saw the Savior who would bring about Israel's salvation. There is a
clear allusion here to Isa 40:5 (LXX).

**2:31   Which you have prepared in the sight of all people [Greek
"peoples"].**   Does "people" refer to the Jews alone (cf. Acts 4:25,27) or to Jews
and Gentiles together (cf. Acts 26:17,23, where the singular is used for Israel and
is contrasted with the Gentiles)? It is best understood as referring to both Jews and
Gentiles due to the reference to Gentiles and Israel in the next verse and the use of
"people" (singular) there for Israel. Luke probably changed the quotation in Isa
52:10 (LXX) from nations to peoples in order to include both Jews and Gentiles.
For other prophecies referring to salvation coming to the Gentiles, cf. Luke 3:6;
Acts 2:21; 28:28.

2:32   A light for revelation to the Gentiles.   "Light" stands in apposition to
"salvation" in Luke 2:30 (cf. Isa 49:6). For "light" as a metaphor to describe Jesus
see John 1:4-5,9; 8:12; 9:5; 12:46; etc.

And for glory to your people Israel.   "Glory" can be understood as standing
in apposition to "revelation" (NIV, RSV) or to "light." All three nouns are accusa-
tives in the Greek text. The latter possibility is better due to the parallels in Isa
60:1,19; 58:8 so that our text should be translated "light for revelation to the Gentiles and glory to your people Israel." Thus the salvation Jesus brings is light (to
give revelation) to the Gentiles and glory to Israel. (The Jews already had the divine revelation but awaited the manifestation of the glory God had promised.) This
verse goes a step further than the angelic song found in Luke 2:14 and is the clearest indication so far of the universal dimension of Jesus' redemptive work.

2:33   The child's father and mother.   This is the most natural way of referring to Joseph's and Mary's relationship to Jesus apart from a cumbersome circumlocution. See comments on 2:27.

Marveled at what was said about him.   Did Joseph and Mary marvel because
Simeon's prophecy in 2:31-32 revealed a new dimension to Jesus' ministry not previously revealed to them? Or was this simply a normal reaction in the experiencing
of a divine revelation or the witnessing of a miracle?[110] The latter is more likely.

2:34   Then Simeon blessed them and said to Mary.   Simeon addressed his
words to Mary rather than to Mary and Joseph. This may be because of Mary's
unique relationship to Jesus due to the virginal conception or due to Joseph's death
pre-dating the crucifixion, so that a sword could not pierce his soul. Whether Luke

---

[109]Cf. Gen 15:2; Num 20:29; and in the LXX Tob 3:6,13; 2 Macc 7:9.
[110]Cf. 1:21,63; 2:18; 4:22; 8:25; 9:43.

intended this to be understood as a priestly blessing (cf. 1 Sam 2:20; Num 6:23ff.) is uncertain. Luke must not have thought the latter was an important issue, however, because he did not indicate whether or not Simeon was a priest.

This child is destined to cause the falling and rising of many in Israel. The prophecies concerning John the Baptist given at his birth (1:68-79) are now paralleled by prophecies concerning Jesus at his presentation in the temple. Luke may have been referring here to one group that falls (humbles itself) and rises (is lifted up by God). If so, this saying is to be interpreted positively and stands in contrast to the sign being "spoken against," which is negative. On the other hand Luke may have been referring to two separate groups, one of which falls (negative) and the other of which rises (positive). The latter appears more likely and indicates that there is a double significance to Jesus' ministry. For the humble and poor it is positive, salvation; for the haughty and rich it is negative, judgment. This twofold aspect of the coming Messiah is found both in the OT (Isa 8:14; 28:16-17) and the NT (Rom 9:33; 1 Pet 2:6-8).

Jesus' rejection by his people (cf. John 1:11), which was already known to Luke's readers, was announced early in his infancy. This verse foreshadows such passages as Luke 4:29; 13:33-35; 19:41-44,47-48; 20:14,17-19. "Many" here and in 2:35 should be understood in the Semitic sense of "all" (cf. Isa 53:12).

And to be a sign that will be spoken against. Just as in the case of Isaiah and his children (cf. Isa 8:18; 7:14), so Jesus would be a sign from God rejected by Israel (cf. Luke 11:30).

2:35 So that the thoughts of many hearts will be revealed. This indicates one of the purposes for Jesus' coming. "The thoughts of many hearts" (*dialogismoi*, the innermost thoughts) should be understood negatively here because in its other uses in Luke (five times) and in the rest of the NT (eight times) it is always used pejoratively.

And [in addition] a sword will pierce your own soul too. The meaning of this parenthetical comment is not certain. The most common interpretation is that it refers to the sorrow Mary would experience in seeing her son rejected and crucified. It has also been suggested, however, that this should be interpreted in light of 8:19-21, and this refers to the fact that Mary would also stumble and experience difficulty in her son's mission.[111] Such passages as 8:21; 11:27-28; 12:51-53 and the fact that Mary was not stated as being present at the crucifixion tend to support this interpretation. However, Luke knew that Theophilus was well aware of Jesus' rejection and death and possibly even of Mary's presence at the crucifixion (cf. John 19:25, although Luke did not mention this). It is difficult to be dogmatic about which is the more likely interpretation, although the context favors the second.

2:36 There was also a prophetess. Being a prophetess,[112] Anna recognized the child and Jesus' salvific role. Just as Simeon's righteous and devout character qualified him to give reliable information concerning Jesus, so Anna's prophetic role and piety (2:37) qualified her in a similar way. She clearly was a reliable spokesperson for the reader. Why Luke made mention of her coming from

---

[111] So Marshall, *Luke*, 429-30.

[112] We read of prophetesses also in Acts 21:9 (cf. 1 Cor 11:5; Exod 15:20; Judg 4:4; 2 Kgs 22:14).

the tribe of Asher is unclear, but it does lend credence to the story. See comments on 13:19.

She had lived with her husband seven years after her marriage and then was a widow until she was eighty-four. Whether "eighty-four" is meant to signify Anna's age or the years of her widowhood is uncertain. Judith was devout (Jdt 8:4-8) and lived to be 105 years old (Jdt 16:23). While of historical interest, this question is of no exegetical importance. Whether Luke sought to portray Anna here as a prototype of the Christian widow is also uncertain.[113]

2:37 She had never left the temple but worshiped night and day, fasting and praying. The reference to Anna's age indicates her long and single-minded devotion to God. Like Zechariah and Elizabeth (1:6) and Simeon (2:25), Anna was devout and righteous and a model for the believer. "Night and day" corresponds well to the Jewish reckoning of time since a day began at sunset (cf. Acts 20:31; 26:7). This expression should probably not be pressed to mean twenty-four hours a day, i.e., she lived in the temple, because women were not normally allowed to stay in the temple during the night. It is best therefore to interpret it in the popular sense of *all the time*, i.e., she was "in church" all day long (cf. 24:53).

2:38 She gave thanks to God. This serves as an example of model Christian behavior.

Looking forward to the redemption of Jerusalem. The "redemption of Jerusalem" (cf. 1:68, "redeemed his people") serves as a synonym for the "consolation of Israel" in 2:25 (see discussion there) and "salvation" in 2:30. The references in 2:25 and here serve as an inclusio and bracket the Simeon and Anna accounts.

2:39 When Joseph and Mary had done everything required by the Law of the Lord. Luke portrayed Joseph and Mary as models for his readers. They, like Zechariah and Elizabeth (1:6), kept the law blamelessly. This is not a simple historical anecdote that has no value for the reader. Rather Luke sought to show that this was how Theophilus and the other readers should live.[114]

They returned to Galilee to their own town of Nazareth. With this comment Luke prepared his readers for the following account in 2:41-52. Luke did not mention a visit to Egypt as we find in Matt 2:13-22, but such a visit would have to be placed between Luke 2:38 and 2:39.

2:40 In comparison to the account of John the Baptist's growth in 1:80, which contains a twofold description ("grew and became strong in spirit"), this verse gives a fourfold description of Jesus ("grew and became strong; he was filled with wisdom, and the grace of God was upon him"). This again shows that Jesus was greater than John. Instead of a reference to Jesus' becoming strong in spirit, Luke made mention of Jesus as full of "wisdom." This prepares us for the following account, where Jesus' wisdom is displayed (cf. 2:46-47,52; cf. also 4:22; Acts 6:3) and perhaps highlights the Spirit's coming upon Jesus at his baptism (Luke 3:21-22). Compare 1 Sam 2:21,26; 3:19.

---

[113]Luke's concern for widows is evident from 4:25-26; 7:11-17; 18:2-5; 20:47; 21:1-4; Acts 6:1; 9:39-43.
[114]Cf. 10:25-28; 16:17; 18:18-30; 23:56; cf. Acts 22:12; 25:8.

The Lukan Message

Within this passage two major Lukan theological emphases can be seen. The first involves the ethical behavior Luke was commending to his readers. We find several ethical models in this passage, and they were all commended by Luke because they keep God's law. Joseph and Mary, whose behavior hitherto has been portrayed most positively, kept the ritual law by submitting their son to the circumcision rite (2:21) and by having Mary and Jesus fulfill the rites of purification and redemption (2:22-24). They did what the law required (2:27). In fact, they did "everything" the law required (2:39). Likewise Simeon is described as righteous and devout (2:25), and the reader at this point assumes that he was so because he observed "all the Lord's commandments and regulations blamelessly" (1:6). Anna also portrays the best in OT piety, for she was always worshiping in the temple, fasting, praying, and giving thanks (2:37-38). Significantly Luke referred to the law four times in this passage (2:22,23,24,27, cf. also 2:29 [*rhēma*, "thy word," RSV]). He clearly believed that the OT is still operative as a guide for Christian behavior. True piety in the kingdom is basically no different from true piety in the OT period. The God of Abraham is the God of Jesus Christ and the God of Peter and Paul as well. The behavior God sought from Abraham is the same behavior he was seeking from Theophilus.[115]

There is also an emphasis in this passage on Mary's child. Even as the circumcision and naming of John the Baptist is followed by a revelation of what he would do (1:76-79), so Jesus' circumcision, naming, and consecration is followed by a revelation of what this one who is greater than John would do. Jesus is clearly portrayed as the object of Israel's fondest hopes and dreams (2:25-26,29-32,34,38). Mary's child is the long-awaited Christ (2:26) who would bring about the fulfillment of Israel's dreams, i.e., their consolation (2:25), salvation (2:30), glory (2:32), and redemption (2:38).

A number of other Lukan themes are also alluded to in this passage. These include the activity of the Holy Spirit (2:25-27); the fulfillment of various prophetic hopes (2:26,29,38); perhaps a reference to God's visitation of the poor as evidenced by the sacrifice offered by Mary and Joseph (2:24); and a brief comment about the universal offer of the gospel (2:32).

The Boy Jesus in the Temple (2:41-52)

[41]Every year his parents went to Jerusalem for the Feast of the Passover. [42]When he was twelve years old, they went up to the Feast, according to the

---

[115]For further discussion and a somewhat different point of view, see Blomberg, "The Law in Luke-Acts," 53-80.

custom. [43]After the Feast was over, while his parents were returning home, the boy Jesus stayed behind in Jerusalem, but they were unaware of it. [44]Thinking he was in their company, they traveled on for a day. Then they began looking for him among their relatives and friends. [45]When they did not find him, they went back to Jerusalem to look for him. [46]After three days they found him in the temple courts, sitting among the teachers, listening to them and asking them questions. [47]Everyone who heard him was amazed at his understanding and his answers. [48]When his parents saw him, they were astonished. His mother said to him, "Son, why have you treated us like this? Your father and I have been anxiously searching for you."

[49]"Why were you searching for me?" he asked. "Didn't you know I had to be in my Father's house?" [50]But they did not understand what he was saying to them.

[51]Then he went down to Nazareth with them and was obedient to them. But his mother treasured all these things in her heart. [52]And Jesus grew in wisdom and stature, and in favor with God and men.

Context

With this account Luke ended the infancy narrative (1:5–2:52) in the temple where it began (1:5-23). Just as the previous account portrayed Jesus as having fulfilled the Jewish law by his circumcision and redemption (2:21-40), so here he is portrayed as trained in the law (2:46-47). There has been a great deal of speculation about whether 2:40 may have been the original conclusion to the infancy narrative and whether this passage was a later insertion into the account by Luke.[116] As it now stands, however, the account concludes the infancy narrative, and in it Luke portrayed Jesus' awareness of his unique relationship to the Father. Because of that relationship, Jesus must be in his Father's house. Later in 9:51–19:28 Jesus would again go to Jerusalem, and again it would be at a Passover. The form of this account is that of a pronouncement story in that its goal and culmination come in the concluding statement or pronouncement by Jesus in 2:49. This is the first such story in the Gospel.

The existence of other stories concerning the unusual abilities of great men in their youth says nothing about the historicity of such stories but only of the fact that there exists a natural interest in information concerning the childhood and youth of famous people. Today historians are often interested in the early years of famous people in order to understand how and why they developed into the people they became. What were the childhood experiences that caused them to become the kind of people they were? Luke had no such purpose in mind. He sought rather to show that Jesus Christ, the risen Lord, was already aware of his being Christ and Lord, or better yet the Son of God, when he was twelve.

[116]See Brown, *Birth of the Messiah*, 479-84.

The setting of our story is Jewish and the history-like quality of the account becomes immediately apparent when one compares it to the stories found in the Infancy Gospel of Thomas or the Protevangelium of James.[117] The present account foreshadows Jesus' future greatness as well as his future teaching mission and reveals an awareness of his unique relationship with God. It forms a fitting transition to Jesus' ministry in 3:1ff.

Comments

2:41 Every year his parents went to Jerusalem for the Feast of the Passover. "Went" is an example of the iterative imperfect which indicates that Jesus' family habitually went to Jerusalem to celebrate Passover. "Every year" further emphasizes this. Passover was one of the three annual festivals Jewish men were required to celebrate in Jerusalem (Deut 16:16). Passover itself was the opening feast of the seven-day (or eight-day by another reckoning) festival called the Feast of Unleavened Bread and was celebrated on the fifteenth day of Nisan. The entire feast, however, was popularly called the Feast of Passover (cf. Luke 22:1; John 13:1). Passover commemorates God's deliverance or exodus of his people out of Egypt and the death angel's passing over Israel's firstborn. In this last plague the death angel visited Egypt's firstborn. However, when he came upon the households of Israel, he observed the blood of the Passover lamb smeared on the door lintels and "passed over" those homes. Passover could not be observed annually by Jews living in the Diaspora since it had to be observed in Jerusalem. This verse and the next indicate that Joseph and Mary, as devout Jews, sought to celebrate the festival yearly in Jerusalem (cf. 1 Sam 1:3,7,21; 2:19).

2:42 When he was twelve years old. At the age of thirteen a Jewish boy became obligated to observe the law (*Nid.* 5:6; *Nazir* 29b) and in more recent years has begun to be called a "son of the covenant—*Bar-Mitzvah*."

According to the custom. Compare Luke 1:9; 22:39.

2:43 After the Feast was over. That is, after seven days (cf. Lev 23:5-6).

While his parents were returning home. For "parents" see comments on 2:27.

Jesus stayed behind in Jerusalem. Luke did not tell us whether this was intentional or unintentional on Jesus' part, and this was ultimately irrelevant for his purpose.

But they were unaware of it. Since Joseph and Mary were traveling in a caravan of pilgrims, they assumed that Jesus was with the other children (cf. 2:44) and did not notice that he was missing until evening when the people in the caravan would come together again as family units. Although later interpreters speculated about where they stopped that night, how large the group was, and so forth, Luke showed no interest in such details.

2:44 They traveled for a day. A day's journey was about twenty to twenty-five miles.

---

[117] See W. Schneemelcher, *New Testament Apocrypha* (Philadelphia: Westminster, 1963), 1:370-401.

2:46   After three days.   We probably should not see in this temporal designation a reference to the resurrection because when Luke referred to the resurrection, he used the expression "on the third day" (9:22; 18:33; 24:7,21,46; Acts
10:40). This expression probably is to be understood (as in 25:1; 28:7) as simply a
temporal designation, i.e., after the first day of travel from Jerusalem, they returned back on the second day to Jerusalem; and they found Jesus on the third day.
Luke was not interested in such details about where Jesus spent the first and second nights, for this was irrelevant to his purpose.

In the temple courts.   The temple plays a central role in Luke's Gospel. See
Introduction 7 (2).

Sitting among the teachers.   Luke did not use the term "teachers of the law"
("scribes" in the RSV) here, since this has a negative connotation in his Gospel.
This scene may foreshadow Jesus' future teaching ministry (Luke 19:47; 21:37-
38) as well as the ministry of the early church (Acts 4:2; 5:25).

2:47   Everyone who heard him was amazed.   Jesus' wisdom (cf. 2:52)
caused Israel's leading teachers to be amazed. No doubt Luke wanted his readers
to see in this incident the unique wisdom of God's Son. This amazement is caused
by the wisdom of his understanding as revealed by both his questions (2:46) and
answers (2:47). We have already seen the response of "amazement" in 2:18,33,
and this was a favorite word of Luke's (see comments on 2:18). Since this amazement is frequently the result of an encounter with the supernatural (cf. 8:56;
24:22; Acts 2:7,12), Luke may have intended his readers to see in this incident a
supernatural display of wisdom. (Cf. Acts 9:21 for the same reaction to the witness of Saul of Tarsus.)

2:48   When his parents saw him, they were astonished.   The object of
their astonishment is uncertain. Their astonishment may have been due to their
seeing Jesus' wisdom as manifested in the scene described in Luke 2:46-47.

Your father and I.   For Luke this did not contradict the account of the virginal conception in chap. 1. "Your adopted father and I" would be most awkward,
and it would be unnecessary since his readers would interpret this saying in light
of chap. 1. See comments on 2:27. Luke actually chose the wording carefully, for
he was preparing his readers for Jesus' saying in the next verse.

2:49   The culminating verse of this account lies not in the comment concerning Jesus' wisdom in 2:46-47 but rather here in Jesus' pronouncement. This pronouncement shows Luke's readers that Jesus possessed a unique relationship with
God and confirms the angelic message that Jesus is God's Son (1:32,35).

Why . . . ? Didn't you know?   Some have sought to see in these words an accusation by Jesus' parents of deception or betrayal on the basis of such passages
as Gen 12:18; 20:9; 26:10, but this seems too subtle and would not have been perceived by Luke's readers. Why were Joseph and Mary surprised by this incident in
light of the miraculous announcement of Jesus' birth (1:26-38), the angelic message (2:1-20), and the prophetic pronouncements (2:21-40)? Mary, despite all
these indicators, seems to have been uncomprehending of just who her son really
was. Such a failure to understand is also found in the disciples (cf. 9:44-45; 18:31-
34; 24:25-26). We should remember, however, that some twelve years had transpired between this event and what had preceded. In the meantime the lack of
other stories like this suggests that Jesus' "silent years" were quite normal. After

over a decade of normalcy the supernatural nature of their son and his destiny broke in on them again. As a result they were surprised and once more needed to reflect on these things (2:19,51). Also possible is that the confusion of Jesus' parents here involved not so much the identity of their son, i.e., his divine sonship, but rather how his sonship was manifesting itself.

Why were you searching for me? This can be understood in two ways: (1) Why were you searching all over for me? Didn't you know I would be in the temple? (2) Why were you looking for me? Didn't you know I must be in my Father's house? The latter (which focuses on the why) is more probable than the first (which focuses on the where), since it better fits the thought of the rest of this verse. It is unnecessary to see in this a rebuke or accusation on Jesus' part. Rather it is better to see this as an expression of surprise. It assumes that Joseph and Mary, due to their previous experiences as recorded in chaps. 1–2, had a basis for understanding Jesus' unique behavior and relationship to God. The "me" and the "I" in the next phrase are emphatic.

I had to be. There is a strong sense of divine causality present here in this verb (*dei*). See Introduction 8 (1).

In my Father's house. Literally *in the* ____ *of my Father*. This can also refer to the "things/affairs" or "people" of my Father, but it is best understood as "house of my Father" due to the parallels in 6:4 and 19:46, where the temple is referred to as God's house. (Cf. also John 2:16, where in the temple cleansing Jesus called the temple "my Father's house.") The fact that Jesus was found in the temple (Luke 2:46) also supports this interpretation. Compare 10:22; 22:29; 24:49, where Jesus referred to God as "my Father."

2:50 But they did not understand. In the past attempts have been made to preserve Mary, the mother of God's Son, from this lack of understanding; but such attempts do violence to the text and lose sight of the contrast between Jesus' wisdom and understanding as God's Son (2:40,47,52) and his parents' lack of understanding. Similar misunderstandings occurred throughout Jesus' ministry (cf. 4:22; 9:45; 18:34; 24:5-7,25-26,45) and would only be remedied by the resurrection.

2:51 Then he went down to Nazareth with them. This is the reverse of "went up" in 2:4.

And was obedient to them. Luke probably emphasized this in order to avoid the misconception that Jesus was disobedient to his parents in this incident. The use of a paraphrastic ("was being obedient") adds emphasis to the assertion.

But his mother treasured all these things in her heart. Compare 2:19 and also 1:66.

2:52 Jesus grew in wisdom and stature, and in favor with God. Luke provided his readers with a concluding summary of the years between this event and Jesus' baptism. Compare 1:80 and 1 Sam 2:21,26 for similar statements concerning John the Baptist and Samuel, and cf. Luke 2:40 concerning Jesus' earlier years. Some scholars have seen a reference to this commendation in 3:22. For a similar statement concerning the development of Jesus' character, see Heb 5:8-9; 2:14-18.[118]

---

[118]Brown (*Birth of the Messiah*, 483) correctly points out that "whether one is liberal or conservative, one must desist from using the present scene to establish a historical development (or lack of development) in Jesus' self-awareness."

And man. In Luke the majority of the Jewish people are portrayed as responding favorably to Jesus. See comments on 4:15.

The Lukan Message

The main theological emphasis of this passage is Christological. Long before Jesus began his public ministry, Luke revealed that he was aware of his unique relationship to God. Already at the age of twelve he knew that he was God's Son and that he possessed a unique calling. He demonstrated a higher allegiance to his divine sonship than to Mary and Joseph (Luke 2:49), although because he kept the law he would be obedient to them (2:51). This is no adoptionist Christology from below but one from above. Before his birth Mary's child was already Lord (1:43) and Son of God (1:35), and this was affirmed by the twelve-year-old Jesus (2:49) and would soon be affirmed by God (3:22).

Along with the "person" of Mary's son, Jesus' role as teacher (cf. 2:46; 4:20-27; 5:3) and the centrality of Jerusalem and the temple may also be alluded to in this account. See Introduction 7 (2). One other possible emphasis found in this passage is the equating of true piety with the keeping of the law. We find this in Jesus' parents' yearly celebration of the Passover Feast of Unleavened Bread in Jerusalem (2:41), in Jesus' training in the law (2:46-47), and in his obedience to his parents (2:52).

———————————————— *SECTION OUTLINE* ————————————

III. THE PREPARATION OF JESUS' MINISTRY (3:1–4:15)
  1. John the Baptist (3:1-20)
     (1) The Person of John the Baptist—The Eschatological Prophet
        (3:1-6)
     (2) The Mission of John the Baptist (3:7-20)
  2. Jesus (3:21–4:15)
     (1) The Person of Jesus—The Son of God (3:21-38)
     (2) The Prelude to Jesus' Mission (4:1-15)

—— **III. THE PREPARATION OF JESUS' MINISTRY (3:1–4:15)** ——

In 3:1 Luke began the second major section of his Gospel. This section consists of two balanced parts. The first involves John the Baptist (3:1-20), and the second involves Jesus (3:21–4:15). We can subdivide these sections as indicated in the outline above. Because of the parallelism in this section, it is best to see 4:14-15 as a concluding summary to 3:1–4:13 rather than an introduction to 4:16–9:50.

From the parallelism between Jesus and John the Baptist in this section it would appear that rather than separating John the Baptist and his message from Jesus, as Conzelmann has tried to do (see Introduction 7 [3]), we should see John as a bridge who belongs both to the OT and the NT eras. In preparing the way for the Son of God, he both marked the end of the old era and introduced the new (16:16). Furthermore John's message is understood as identical to that of Jesus and the early church, for Jesus also would preach a repentance for the forgiveness of sins.[1] And even as Jesus preached the "good news" (4:18), John did as well (3:18). If Luke had wanted to separate John's ministry from that of Jesus, as Conzelmann argues, then he would have used something like 3:1-2 to introduce Jesus' ministry rather than John the Baptist's.

It has frequently been suggested that 3:1f. was the original beginning of Luke's Gospel and that chaps. 1–2 were added later.[2] (Cf. how Jeremiah, Hosea, Joel, Amos, Micah, Zephaniah, Haggai, and Zechariah begin.) There are, however, serious difficulties in seeing chaps. 1–2 as

---

[1]Luke 5:32; 11:32; 15:7,10; 24:47; Acts 2:38; 3:19; 5:31; 11:18; esp. 13:24; 26:20.
[2]See W. G. Kümmel, *Introduction to the New Testament* (Nashville: Abingdon, 1975), 130-38.

being a simple addendum inserted into the Gospel after chaps. 3–24 had already been completed.[3]

1. John the Baptist (3:1-20)

(1) The Person of John the Baptist—The Eschatological Prophet (3:1-6)

[1]In the fifteenth year of the reign of Tiberius Caesar—when Pontius Pilate was governor of Judea, Herod tetrarch of Galilee, his brother Philip tetrarch of Iturea and Traconitis, and Lysanias tetrarch of Abilene— [2]during the high priesthood of Annas and Caiaphas, the word of God came to John son of Zechariah in the desert. [3]He went into all the country around the Jordan, preaching a baptism of repentance for the forgiveness of sins. [4]As is written in the book of the words of Isaiah the prophet:

"A voice of one calling in the desert,
'Prepare the way for the Lord,
   make straight paths for him.
[5]Every valley shall be filled in,
   every mountain and hill made low.
The crooked roads shall become straight,
   the rough ways smooth.
[6]And all mankind will see God's salvation.' "

Context

As in 2:1 Luke opened this account by tying the opening events of Jesus' ministry to contemporary history. For Luke the beginning of Jesus' ministry started at a particular time in history (the fifteenth year of Tiberius Caesar's reign) with John the Baptist's ministry. That Jesus' ministry began with, rather than after, John the Baptist's is evident not only from the present text but also from Acts 1:22; 10:37; 13:24-25. The good news of the gospel (Acts 10:36) began with God's word coming to John (Luke 3:2). Mark had a similar understanding of the gospel's beginning, for John's appearance is the first account found in his Gospel (Mark 1:2-11). Those who maintain that Q was a written source used by Matthew and Luke believe that it also contained at its beginning a similar account concerning John the Baptist's ministry. This may explain some of the unique Matthew-Luke agreements against Mark in this account.

---

[3]Luke 3–24 was written with chaps. 1–2 clearly in mind and not vice versa. Support for this is found in numerous ties between chaps. 1–2 and the rest of the Gospel. John (3:2) is introduced as someone already known from 1:13-17,57-80, and Zechariah is likewise introduced without comment in 3:2 because of 1:5-25,57-80. The locus of John's ministry, i.e., the "desert" (3:4), has been carefully prepared for by 1:80. That the use of "word" (rhēma) in 3:2 caused its heavy usage in 1:37-38,65; 2:15,17,19,29,50-51 is unlikely. Rather Luke in 3:2 picked up the earlier use of this term from chaps. 1–2. The reference to the "one more powerful than I" in 3:16 also refers to someone who is already known due to Luke 1–2.

Comments

3:1 In the fifteenth year of the reign of Tiberius Caesar. Although at first glance this appears to give us a specific date for the beginning of John's ministry, upon closer examination several problems arise. (1) Did the first year of Tiberius's reign begin in A.D. 11/12 when he became co-regent with Augustus Caesar, or did the first year begin on August 19, A.D. 14 when Augustus died? (2) Did Luke distinguish between the accession year and the regnal year and count the period between August 19 and New Year's Day as a year? (3) Did he include this period between August 19 and New Year's Day with the first regnal year? (4) Which calendar was Luke using for the regnal years of Tiberius? Was it the Julian (1 January), the Jewish (1 Nisan), the Syrian-Macedonian (1 October), or the Egyptian (29 August)? If, as seems more likely, Luke reckoned these years from Augustus's death, the fifteenth year probably would be A.D. 28 plus or minus a year. Unfortunately the references to the other rulers are not very helpful, for there were several years when their rules overlapped. Luke mentioned them less to add chronological precision than to relate the decisive event of salvation history to the context of world history.

When Pontius Pilate was governor of Judea. The term "governor" could be used to describe a procurator or prefect, of which Pilate was the latter, as a famous inscription discovered at Caesarea in 1961 reveals.[4] We encounter Pilate again in 13:1; 23:1-56. Pilate ruled Judea from A.D. 26–36.

Herod tetrarch of Galilee. Herod Antipas[5] was the son of Herod the Great and step-brother of Philip the tetrarch, who was also a son of Herod the Great. Herod Antipas ruled Galilee as tetrarch from 4 B.C. to A.D. 39. His step-brother Philip reigned until A.D. 34.

Lysanias tetrarch of Abilene. It is uncertain why Luke mentioned Lysanias. Some have speculated that it may have been because Luke came (supposedly) from Syria, and Abilene bordered Syria.

3:2 During the high priesthood of Annas and Caiaphas. Caiaphas was the actual high priest at this time, but Annas was the high priest from A.D. 6–15; and it was customary to attribute the title to former living high priests since the high priesthood was a "life office." (A contemporary practice can be found in addressing former presidents of the United States as "Mr. President.") Annas continued to exert a strong influence in Israel's religious life after A.D. 15.[6] The plural "high priests" is found throughout the Gospels, and Annas is called the high priest in Acts 4:6 and John 18:19 (cf. 18:13,24).

The word of God came to John son of Zechariah. Luke reintroduced John here by the phrase "son of Zechariah." The lack of this phrase in the parallel accounts in Matthew and Mark indicates that its presence here is due to Luke's hand and that he was writing this account in light of what had preceded in chap. 1. Thus chaps. 1–2 are not a later appendage to 3:1f., but, on the contrary, Luke wrote 3:2

---

[4]See J. A. Fitzmyer, *The Gospel according to St. Luke*, AB (Garden City: Doubleday, 1981), 456.

[5]Luke 3:19; 8:3; 9:7,9; 13:31; 23:7-12; Acts 4:27; 12:1-23; 13:1; 23:35.

[6]His son Eleazar was high priest from A.D. 16–17, four other sons were high priests (Josephus, *Antiquities* 20.9.1 [20.198]), and Caiaphas, who reigned from A.D. 18–36, was his son-in-law.

in light of chaps. 1–2. The similarity in wording to Jer 1:2; Hos 1:1; Mic 1:1; and Hag 1:1 indicates that Luke sought to portray John the Baptist as a God-sent prophet. As one filled with the Spirit from his birth (Luke 1:15,44), he now fulfilled his role as a prophet (1:76).

In the desert. Mark 1:4 and Matt 3:1 place John "in the desert," indicating that this was part of the tradition; but Luke prepared us for this by Luke 1:80, and he picked it up again in 7:24-28. Although this is a geographical designation, its main function is not to designate a physical place but to indicate that John was the promised prophet of Isa 40:3, i.e., the one who was the voice calling "in the desert" (Luke 3:4).

3:3 Preaching a baptism of repentance for the forgiveness of sins. John "preached" (cf. Acts 10:37) just like Jesus (4:18-19,44) and the early church (Acts 8:5; 15:21), and his message was essentially the same "gospel" (3:18)[7] Jesus and the early church proclaimed.

"Repentance" here literally means *a change of mind* but refers more broadly to the human dimension involved in the experience of conversion in contrast to the divine element (regeneration).

"The forgiveness of sins" is a present realization of the future eschatological forgiveness at the final judgment. The message of repentance for the forgiveness of sins is a central theme in Luke-Acts[8] and must always be a central part of the gospel message.

This forgiveness, which already has been mentioned as part of John's ministry in 1:77, is seen as intimately associated with repentance (24:47; Acts 5:31) and is the desired result of John's baptism. See Introduction 8 (6). This does not mean that baptism is understood as a rite that automatically brings forgiveness, i.e., that baptism brings forgiveness *ex opere operato.*

Baptism is not to be isolated from the repentance mentioned here.[9] Nor is it to be isolated from faith.[10] Josephus (*Antiquities* 18.5.2; 18.116-19) also stated that John's baptism required a "cleansed soul," and the baptism-washing at Qumran [1 QS 3:3-12; 5:13-14] was likewise understood as doing nothing by itself.[11]

3:4 As is written in the book of the words of Isaiah the prophet. See comments on 2:23. John the Baptist's ministry, i.e., his preaching of a baptism of repentance to the people, is the fulfillment of Isaiah's prophecy and witnesses to the fulfillment theme in Luke. See Introduction 7 (1). Whereas the Isaianic quotation that follows is preceded by a quotation from Mal 3:1 in Mark 1:2-3, both Matthew (11:10) and Luke (7:27) placed this quote from Malachi later in their Gospels due most probably to the influence of their Q source.

---

[7] Note how in Luke 4:18-19 preaching the gospel and preaching the good news are used synonymously.

[8] Cf. Luke 4:18; 5:17-32; 24:47; Acts 5:31; 8:22.

[9] Cf. Acts 2:38; 13:24; 19:4; 22:16.

[10] Cf. Acts 8:12-13; 16:31-33; 18:8; 19:4-5.

[11] The relationship of John's baptism to Jewish proselyte baptism, which required Gentile converts to Judaism to be baptized, is unclear since the dating of such proselyte baptism is uncertain.

A voice of one calling in the desert. This picks up Luke 1:80. All four Gospels locate John's ministry in the desert, which biblical (Ezek 20:33-38; Hos 2:14-23) and contemporary literature (1 QS 8:12-15; 9:18-20) portrayed as the likely sight for the renewal of the people of Israel. Both the location of John's ministry and his theme verse (Isa 40:3), which was the theme verse of the Qumran community (1 QS 8:12-15), have caused a great deal of speculation about whether John was once a member of this community.[12] If John had once been a member of the Qumran community, the "word of the Lord" coming to him probably would refer to his break with the community and his new understanding that the way to prepare for the Lord's coming was not through a monasticlike attempt to keep the law perfectly but to preach to the masses and prepare them for Messiah's coming. All this is highly speculative, however, and at the present time there is not sufficient evidence to tie them together in this way.

Prepare the way for the Lord. "Lord" refers here to the Savior of Luke 2:11 who is "Christ the Lord." John's preparation for the Lord can be seen in such passages as 7:29-30,31-35; 20:1-8 and because several of Jesus' disciples were originally John's (cf. John 1:35ff.).

Make straight paths for him. "Paths for him" is literally "his paths." Matthew, Mark, and Luke all refer to "his" paths, whereas the LXX, following the Hebrew, has "paths of our God." This agreement of the Gospels against the OT texts indicates some literary relationship between the Synoptic Gospels. To "make straight" is a poetic way of saying "make easier."

3:5 Every mountain and hill made low. This and the other pictures in this verse should be seen as metaphors or images of repentance. To be "made low" (literally *humbled*) refers to the humbling of the proud mentioned earlier in Luke 1:52; 14:11; 18:14.

The crooked roads shall become straight. This may be an allusion to the "corrupt generation" (literally *crooked*) of Acts 2:40 (cf. also Luke 13:11-13). That Luke alone added Isa 40:4 to the Isa 40:3 quotation indicates that in his understanding repentance is part of the central core of the gospel message.

3:6 And all mankind will see God's salvation. The Lukan emphasis on the universal nature of the gospel, i.e., that God's grace is offered to all (cf. Luke 2:32), is seen here by his addition of this part of the Isaiah quotation (Isa 40:5b) to his source. This is not found in the parallel accounts in Matthew or Mark. That Luke added to Isa 40:3 (which was found in the tradition), Isa 40:4, skipped 40:5a[13] and then included 40:5b indicates that this latter statement was important for his theological emphasis. The universalism found here has been alluded to

---

[12] Several other similarities exist between the two: Qumran was a priestly community, and John was the son of a priest; Qumran and John both bitterly criticized the Pharisees; both were located in the desert where the Jordan River enters the Dead Sea; Qumran also had an introductory baptism or washing ceremony (but it was apparently repeated yearly). For further discussion see L. F. Badia, *The Qumran Baptism and John the Baptist's Baptism* (Lanham, Md.: University Press of America, 1980).

[13] Why did Luke omit Isa 40:5a? Did he want to abbreviate the quotation, or did he think this had not yet been realized and would only be fulfilled at the parousia (Luke 21:27)? We cannot be certain.

already in Luke 2:30-31. The term "salvation" is found in the LXX translation of Isa 40:5 and indicates that this, rather than the Masoretic text, was the OT text Luke was using.

The Lukan Message

This opening account of Jesus' ministry serves as an introductory summary for numerous Lukan themes. One of these involves the coming of divine salvation and the human response needed. That Luke wanted to emphasize the coming of salvation is evident by his preparation of this theme in 1:47,69,71; 2:11,30 and above all by his unique addition of Isa 40:5b to the traditional quotation of Isa 40:3. (For a fuller discussion of this theme, see comments on 1:69.) The human response called for by this offer of salvation is also emphasized. It involves a *baptism* of *repentance* for the *forgiveness of sins*. The latter two expressions are tied together in 24:47; Acts 2:38; 5:31 (cf. also 26:18-20). The use of the expression "forgiveness of sins" to describe salvation is already found in Luke 1:77 and is also seen in 24:47.[14] The material itself comes from several of Luke's sources: 3:7-9 (Q); 3:10-14 (L, or perhaps Q material not found in Matthew); 3:15-17 (Mark and Q). Luke 3:18-20 is a Lukan summary based on such historical information as found in Mark 6:17-18. "Repentance" is found eleven times as a noun and fourteen times as a verb in Luke-Acts compared to a total of seven and three times in Matthew and Mark, respectively.

We also find in 3:1-2 the Lukan desire to place the coming of Jesus and John within the framework of secular and divine history. The former has already been seen and noted in 2:1-2. The latter is seen in the Lukan emphasis on the fulfillment of prophecy. Luke introduced John the Baptist's mission with an OT quotation and thus placed his ministry within the divine plan. Consequently his ministry was the fulfillment of prophecy. Luke would also introduce the ministries of Jesus, Peter, and Paul with OT prophesies (cf. 4:18-20; Acts 2:17-21; 13:47). Luke wanted Theophilus to understand that the things he had been taught were not done in a corner (Acts 26:26) but in fact occurred in accordance with the divine purpose for history. See Introduction 8 (1).

Several other Lukan themes are found in this passage. One theme is the demand for humility before God and is evident from Luke 3:5, which is a Lukan addition to the tradition and picks up such thoughts as found in 1:48,51-52; 2:24. This theme will be repeated in 6:20-26. Another theme is that the gospel is for all. This will become clearer in 24:47 and above all in Acts, but it already has been alluded to in 2:30-32 and is quite clear in our passage from Luke's addition of Isa 40:5b.

---

[14]Cf. Acts 2:38; 5:31; 10:43; 13:38; 26:18.

(2) The Mission of John the Baptist (3:7-20)

[7]John said to the crowds coming out to be baptized by him, "You brood of vipers! Who warned you to flee from the coming wrath? [8]Produce fruit in keeping with repentance. And do not begin to say to yourselves, 'We have Abraham as our father.' For I tell you that out of these stones God can raise up children for Abraham. [9]The ax is already at the root of the trees, and every tree that does not produce good fruit will be cut down and thrown into the fire."

[10]"What should we do then?" the crowd asked.

[11]John answered, "The man with two tunics should share with him who has none, and the one who has food should do the same."

[12]Tax collectors also came to be baptized. "Teacher," they asked, "what should we do?"

[13]"Don't collect any more than you are required to," he told them.

[14]Then some soldiers asked him, "And what should we do?"

He replied, "Don't extort money and don't accuse people falsely—be content with your pay."

[15]The people were waiting expectantly and were all wondering in their hearts if John might possibly be the Christ. [16]John answered them all, "I baptize you with water. But one more powerful than I will come, the thongs of whose sandals I am not worthy to untie. He will baptize you with the Holy Spirit and with fire. [17]His winnowing fork is in his hand to clear his threshing floor and to gather the wheat into his barn, but he will burn up the chaff with unquenchable fire." [18]And with many other words John exhorted the people and preached the good news to them.

[19]But when John rebuked Herod the tetrarch because of Herodias, his brother's wife, and all the other evil things he had done, [20]Herod added this to them all: He locked John up in prison.

Context

In this section Luke gave three examples of John the Baptist's preaching. The first (3:7-9) is eschatological in nature and proclaims that God's kingdom has come. Because of this the need to repent in light of the times is reinforced. The second (3:10-14) involves various ethical instructions describing the fruits that must accompany the repentance called for in 3:7-9. These two passages indicate that baptism by itself cannot save a person from the coming judgment if unaccompanied by a changed life. The third passage (3:15-17) deals with John's announcement of the coming Messiah. This is followed by a concluding summary of his ministry (3:18) and a historical summary (3:19-20) unique to Luke. The summaries serve to bring to a conclusion the story about John the Baptist before proceeding to the next one. This also serves to prepare for the only other account involving John found in Luke, which takes place during this imprisonment (7:18-28).

The close tie between the preaching of John the Baptist and of Jesus (and the early church) is clearly seen in this material. John in fact served as an example for Christian preaching in Luke's day. Because this passage reflects so well the church's early teachings, some have suggested that these teachings did not originate with John but are later Christian teachings read back on his lips. Yet if the Qumran community warned against a merely formal ritual of washing (see comments on 3:3), why should it be difficult to assume that John taught similarly? There is no convincing reason these teachings could not have originated with John the Baptist.[15]

Comments

3:7   John said to the crowds.   With this transitional verse Luke introduced his readers to John's teachings.

Brood of vipers!   Like Jesus, John did not avoid harsh metaphors. For the same expression cf. Matt 12:34; 23:33; cf. also John 8:44. "Viper" probably refers to any of over twenty different kinds of poisonous snakes in Israel. The poison of true "vipers" affects the respiratory systems and destroys the red blood cells, whereas the poison of cobras affects the nervous systems.

Who warned you to flee from the coming wrath?   This question can be translated in a number of ways: (1) Who warned *you* to flee from the coming wrath? (2) Who has shown you how to flee from the coming wrath? (3) Who has shown you how to flee from the coming wrath (by merely submitting to a rite of baptism)? The implied answer is, I certainly have not! The following verse favors the third alternative, i.e., it is addressed to insincere potential converts. "Wrath" here, as in Luke 21:23, refers to a future manifestation of God's wrath (cf. Isa 30:27-28; Zeph 2:2). John's message appears to conflict with E. P. Sanders's "covenantal nomism," which argues that Jews in general were not concerned with "getting into" God's kingdom (i.e., in being saved) but with "staying in."[16]

John's preaching was clearly concerned with the means of getting into the messianic community and experiencing its salvation, and thus he preached a universal call to repentance.

3:8   Produce fruit in keeping with repentance.   John (and of course Luke) emphasized that baptism and holy living go hand in hand, i.e., one cannot separate the objective aspects of conversion, such as the forgiveness of sins and justification, and the subjective aspects, such as regeneration and sanctification. John was aware of the danger of a "sacramentalistic" way of thinking that assumes salvation can be acquired by means of a rite (baptism, Luke 3:8a) or a privileged relationship (having Abraham as father, 3:8b). True repentance will produce fruit (6:43-45). The term "fruit" is frequently used to designate a life of deeds whether

---

[15]The material itself comes from several of Luke's sources: 3:7-9 (Q); 3:10-14 (L or perhaps Q material that Matthew omitted); 3:15-17 (Mark and Q). Luke 3:18-20 is a Lukan summary based on such historical information as found in Mark 6:17-18.

[16]See E. P. Sanders, *Paul and Palestinian Judaism* (Philadelphia: Fortress, 1977).

good or bad (Ps 1:3; Jer 17:8; cf. also Acts 26:20). The plural ("fruits") is used
due to the details of Luke 3:10-14.

Do not begin to say. This is a Semiticism for "do not even begin to think."

Abraham as our father. That is, as our forefather. Compare John 8:39,53
(note 8:37). The issue here is not "staying in" the kingdom but "getting in."

Out of these stones God can raise up children for Abraham. Several attempts have been made to see in this expression a pun of some sort (stones and sons,
i.e., children, sound alike in Aramaic), but the meaning of this picturesque language
is clear without resorting to such literary explanations. From lifeless stones God the
Creator can create children for Abraham. He does not need physical offspring. Apart
from repentance, one's physical descent from Abraham is valueless.

3:9 The ax is already at the root. The imagery here is clearly one of judgment (cf. Isa 10:33-34; Ezek 31:12; Dan 4:14), but this refers not to the final judgment but rather to the judgment occurring due to the arrival of God's kingdom.
Already now the messianic banquet has begun (Luke 14:15-24), and the judgment is
taking place. The invited guests are being excluded, and the outcasts are now invited
in their place. Indeed the last are becoming first, and the first are becoming last
(13:30). The barren fig tree is now experiencing its final hour (13:6-9). Unless there
is repentance, it will be cut down (13:9). Compare Rom 11:17f. for a Pauline parallel.

3:10 In this and the following verses we find practical examples of the kind
of fruit that is in keeping with true repentance. A living eschatological hope does
not ignore social concerns but provides the ground for such concerns as well as its
motivation. John did not require his hearers to follow his particular "desert life-
style" or still less the monastic life-style of the Qumran community. Rather the
life of one awaiting the kingdom of God is to be lived out in the world.

What should we do? Such a question does not suggest that the individual is
seeking to achieve a relationship with God based upon his or her works but is an
appropriate and sincere response to the divine message.[17] Luke understood what
followed as applicable to his Christian readers since it came from an authoritative
spokesman, John the Baptist.

3:11 The man with two tunics. The tunic was the inner garment worn under a cloak. Compare Luke 6:29. What we find in this verse has clear OT roots
(Job 31:16-20; Isa 58:7; Ezek 18:7) and is a theological emphasis found throughout the Judeo-Christian tradition. Any proper faith must involve a social concern
for the poor and unfortunate, and of all the Evangelists, Luke particularly sought
to stress this point (Luke 6:30; 12:33; 14:12-14; 16:9; 18:22).

3:12 Tax collectors also came to be baptized. This is understood better as
"toll collectors" who were located at commercial centers, such as Capernaum and
Jericho, to collect tolls, customs, and tariffs.[18] Such people had bid and won the
right to collect such tolls for the Romans. The fact that their profit was determined
by how much they collected and that their bid had been paid for in advance led to
great abuse. They were hated and despised by their fellow Jews. Dishonesty
among tax collectors was the rule (*Sanh* 25b), and their witness was not accepted
in a court of law. Thus they were often associated with sinners and prostitutes.

---

[17]Cf. Luke 3:12,14; 10:25; Acts 2:37; 22:10; cf. also Luke 18:18; Acts 16:30.

[18]For other references to tax collectors, cf. 5:27,29-30; 7:29,34; 15:1; 18:10-13; 19:2.

Teacher. Like Jesus, John the Baptist was recognized as a teacher and an authoritative spokesman for God.

3:13 Tax collectors were not required to resign but to become honest. John's statement confirms the view that most tax collectors tended to be dishonest (cf. 19:8).

3:14 These soldiers probably were not Romans but Jews whom Herod Antipas employed (cf. Josephus, *Antiquities* 18.5.1 [18.113]) perhaps to assist tax collectors in their duties.[19] Soldiers were also not required to resign but to avoid the sins of their profession, i.e., violent intimidation ("extort"), robbing by false accusation, and dissatisfaction with "wages" (or perhaps "rations").

3:15 The people were waiting expectantly and were all wondering . . . if John might be the Christ. Did Luke add the following account because of the existence of followers of John the Baptist in his day who were rivals to the Christian church?[20] John's Gospel suggests that in some circles John the Baptist was the object of great veneration (cf. John 1:20). Whatever the reason, in the present context the following verses serve mainly to point to the one who is greater than John—the Messiah.

3:16 In this and the next verse Matthew and Luke possess several agreements against Mark, including (1) the order of the two clauses about baptism and the Coming One ("I baptize" then "the more powerful one"), (2) the addition of "and with fire," and (3) the addition of the saying concerning the winnowing fork. This probably indicates that the material common to Matthew and Luke also contained an introductory account concerning John the Baptist which at these points Matthew and Luke preferred over their Markan source.

With water. This is in an emphatic position to show the contrast between John's baptism with water only and Jesus' baptism, which also involved the Holy Spirit. This contrast is seen clearly in Acts 19:1-7.

But one more powerful than I will come. Most translations tend to ignore the article associated with the one more powerful. It would be better to read, "But *the* one more powerful than I will come." This indicates that the reader already knows about this more powerful one, who was introduced in the first two chapters.

This same expression is also used in Luke 11:22, where Jesus is described as "stronger," i.e., more powerful, than Satan. The expression "will come" appears first in this sentence and is thus emphatic—"He is coming, the one more powerful than I."

He will baptize you with the Holy Spirit and with fire. Like Matthew's, Luke's description of the baptism of the Messiah involves the Spirit and fire. (Cf. however, Acts 1:5; 11:16, which omit the reference to "fire.") The main question about this statement involves whether the reference to "fire" is to be understood positively or negatively, i.e., does it refer to a blessing (the flaming, purifying work of the Spirit) the Messiah brings for the believer or to a fiery judgment that will fall upon the unbeliever. In favor of the former is the parallelism between the "you" who received John's baptism and the "you" who receive the Messiah's baptism. This suggests that the same group receives both the Spirit and fire. This

---

[19]C. F. Evans, *Saint Luke, TPI New Testament Commentaries* (London: SCM, 1990), 241.
[20]Cf. Luke 5:33; 7:18-24; 11:1; Acts 18:25; 19:1-7.

would then mean that the baptism of the Spirit Jesus promised (Acts 1:5) was fulfilled at Pentecost when the Spirit came with tongues of fire (2:3). Yet if Luke
wanted his readers to see the reference to "fire" in Luke 3:16 as being fulfilled in
Acts 2:3, one would have expected him to include "and with fire" in 1:5, but he
did not. On the other hand, the reference to fire in Luke 3:9 involves divine judgment, and the immediate context of the following verse that refers to "burning
fire" is clearly one of judgment. In fact, "fire" appears throughout Luke as a metaphor for divine judgment (cf. 9:54; 12:49; 17:29). In the other two instances in
which Luke mentioned the baptism of the Spirit (Acts 1:5; 11:16), there is no
mention of a baptism of "fire." Perhaps this is because the audience addressed in
these two instances consists of believers and thus "fire" does not fit their situation.
In Luke 3:16, however, the audience is mixed, and "fire" describes well what happens to those who do not believe in Jesus. For Luke the baptism with the Holy
Spirit and fire is thus best understood as involving two separate groups. For the
"wheat" there is the blessing of the Spirit, whereas for the "chaff" there is the
judgment of burning. The messianic age therefore is seen as twofold in nature. It
brings the blessing of the Spirit to the repentant[21] but the fires of judgment to the
unrepentant.[22]

According to CD 2:12 the Messiah, who is anointed by the Spirit (Isa 11:2;
42:1; 61:1), would be the bringer of the Holy Spirit. This promise, however, is not
fulfilled until Pentecost (Luke 24:49; Acts 1:4-5,8; 2:1ff.). This "baptism of the
Spirit"[23] is best understood as referring to a water baptism (as in John's case) but
associated with messianic benefits that John's mission lacked (the gift of the
Spirit). In other words as the response to John's preaching brought repentance,
faith, and forgiveness and was marked by baptism, so the response to Jesus'
preaching would bring repentance, faith, and forgiveness but also the blessing of
the messianic age (the coming of the Spirit) and was likewise marked by baptism.
Thus the "baptism of the Spirit" involves a baptism in water by immersion that is
the result of repentance and faith on the believer's part and renewal on the Holy
Spirit's part. That the baptism of the Spirit is the experience of every true believer
is evident from the parallelism with John's baptism; for all, not just part, of John's
followers experienced his baptism (cf. also 1 Cor 12:13).[24]

The thongs of whose sandals I am not worthy to untie. The Messiah is so
much greater than John that the great prophet was not worthy to perform a task
that only non-Jewish slaves had to do for their Jewish masters, for Jewish slaves
were exempt from this demeaning act.

3:17 The imagery of this verse is that of a winnowing fork, a forklike shovel
used to throw the grain and chaff (husk and straw) into the air so that the wind
would blow the lighter chaff away from the heavier grain as they fell to the earth.

---

[21] Cf. Isa 32:15; 44:3; Ezek 36:27; 37:14; 39:29; Joel 2:28.

[22] For the opposing view, which sees "fire" as positive, see J. Nolland, *Luke 1–9:20*,
WBC (Waco: Word, 1989), 152-53.

[23] Cf. Matt 3:11; Mark 1:8; John 1:33; Acts 1:5; 11:16; 1 Cor 12:13.

[24] For further discussion of the relationship of faith, confession, repentance, regeneration, and baptism in the early church, see R. H. Stein, *Difficult Passages in the New Testament* (Grand Rapids: Baker, 1990), 328-38.

Since burnable materials were in short supply, the chaff would be gathered to burn in the oven for cooking (cf. Matt 6:30). For Luke this winnowing already was realized in Jesus' ministry rather than in the distant future. Already for Luke and his readers there was a fulfillment of this in Israel's exclusion from God's kingdom, Jerusalem's destruction in A.D. 70, and the gathering of the outcasts into the kingdom. See comments on 3:9.

With unquenchable fire. This portrays the eternal finality and irreversible nature of the final judgment. It fits well the description of Gehenna as a metaphor for the place of eternal judgment, for there Jerusalem's garbage was burned, and its fires never went out. (*Gehenna* is Hebrew for *the Valley of Hinom*, which was the valley marking Jerusalem's southern boundary.)[25]

3:18 And with many other words John exhorted the people and preached the good news to them. Luke concluded this section by a summary statement in which John is portrayed as preaching the "good news," i.e., the gospel. The message of repentance is "good news," for it means that forgiveness is possible. Persons can still pass from death to life and become part of God's kingdom if they repent. The tragedy and consequences of sin are not irreversible, and this is "good news." Thus Luke saw John the Baptist in preaching the "good news" as part of the kingdom age and not simply the last prophet of the old age. By his preaching John was preparing the Lord's way (3:4).

3:19 But when John rebuked Herod. Whereas Josephus's *Antiquities* 18.5.2 (18.116-19) deals with the political reason Herod imprisoned John, Luke and the other Gospel accounts provide the religious reason.

Herod the tetrarch. See comments on 3:1. Herod is described accurately here as a "tetrarch" whereas Mark 6:14 describes him more popularly as a "king."

Because of Herodias, his brother's wife. Luke did not go into as much detail as the other Synoptics (Mark 6:17-19; Matt 14:3-4) in describing John's rebuke, but it clearly involved marrying a woman who had been married to his brother. John was scandalized by Herod having married a divorced woman and entering into what OT law regarded as an incestuous relationship. We are not told who this brother was (though see Mark 6:17 and Josephus, *Antiquities* 18.5.1 [18.109-10]).

3:20 Herod added this to them all. The epitome of Herod Antipas's evil career for Luke, and that for which he is known in history, was the arrest and death of John the Baptist (Luke 9:7-9). Luke could think of no greater evil than to reject and persecute God's messenger. John, however, was not the only one who would be persecuted for rebuking sin (cf. 4:28; 20:19; Acts 7:54).

He locked John up in prison. Josephus (*Antiquities* 18.5.2 [118.119]) states that John was imprisoned in the fortress of Machaerus on the eastern side of the Dead Sea. According to John 3:22-23; 4:1-2, the ministries of Jesus and John the Baptist overlapped for a time. Luke, however, in presenting his orderly account told of John's imprisonment at this point in order to complete John's story, so that he now could concentrate on Jesus' story (cf. also Mark 1:14 but note 6:17-18).

---

[25]Cf. Matt 3:12; 18:8; 25:41; Mark 9:43,48; Jude 7; Rev 14:10-11.

The Lukan Message

Within this account Luke sought to demonstrate to Theophilus that participation in God's kingdom involves not just a rite of baptism and a profession of repentance but a life that manifests a true conversion. Baptism in itself is insufficient for salvation. Luke clearly rejected a sacramentalist interpretation that thinks the rite of baptism in and of itself brings about the forgiveness of sins. One dare not depend for salvation upon a rite (such as baptism), a family relationship (whether involving a claim to be the offspring of Abraham or of devout, godly parents), or a confession of repentance. One must bear evidence of good fruit. "Each tree is recognized by its own fruit" (Luke 6:44). Thus a good Christian will bear good fruit (6:43-45; 8:15; cf. Jas 3:11-12). This fruit in the Lukan context involves both acts of mercy (Luke 12:33) and the keeping of the commandments (1:6; 2:22-24, 27,39), which must be lived out in the world.

An eschatological and a Christological emphasis is present as well. The coming of the messianic age with a twofold dimension of blessing and judgment is evident. Judgment was about to come. The divine axe was about to strike (3:9). God's wrath was about to fall upon unrepentant Israel (3:7). Those who did not respond to the preaching of John and the coming Messiah would be consumed with the divine fire just as chaff was burned up. For Luke and his readers this can now be seen in part by what happened to Israel. Judgment indeed came upon Israel (19:41-44; 21:5-24), for they were excluded from the banquet (14:24), and the vineyard was given to others (20:16; Acts 13:46; 18:6; 28:25-28). Also involved in this eschatological emphasis was the coming of the Spirit for expectant Israel. Although this coming was future for John the Baptist and even for those who followed Jesus during his ministry, it was a present reality for Luke and his readers. For them the events of Pentecost and its meaning for the church had already taken place.

The Christological element in our account is also clear. Jesus is the one "greater" than the prophet, John the Baptist. He is in fact so much greater that John was not worthy to perform the most menial task of untying his sandals. He is the "coming one" upon whom the hopes and longings of Israel focused. He is the one who brings the awaited Spirit. Jesus is the Christ; John was not. John the Baptist's imprisonment may also have foreshadowed Jesus' fate, for this was the fate of all the prophets (Luke 13:33; cf. also 4:24; 11:49-51; Acts 7:52).

2. Jesus (3:21–4:15)

(1) The Person of Jesus—The Son of God (3:21-38)

[21]When all the people were being baptized, Jesus was baptized too. And as he was praying, heaven was opened [22]and the Holy Spirit descended on him in

bodily form like a dove. And a voice came from heaven: "You are my Son, whom I love; with you I am well pleased."
[23]Now Jesus himself was about thirty years old when he began his ministry. He was the son, so it was thought, of Joseph, the son of Heli, [24]the son of Matthat, the son of Levi, the son of Melki, the son of Jannai, the son of Joseph, [25]the son of Mattathias, the son of Amos, the son of Nahum, the son of Esli, the son of Naggai, [26]the son of Maath, the son of Mattathias, the son of Semein, the son of Josech, the son of Joda, [27]the son of Joanan, the son of Rhesa, the son of Zerubbabel, the son of Shealtiel, the son of Neri, [28]the son of Melki, the son of Addi, the son of Cosam, the son of Elmadam, the son of Er, [29]the son of Joshua, the son of Eliezer, the son of Jorim, the son of Matthat, the son of Levi, [30]the son of Simeon, the son of Judah, the son of Joseph, the son of Jonam, the son of Eliakim, [31]the son of Melea, the son of Menna, the son of Mattatha, the son of Nathan, the son of David, [32]the son of Jesse, the son of Obed, the son of Boaz, the son of Salmon, the son of Nahshon, [33]the son of Amminadab, the son of Ram, the son of Hezron, the son of Perez, the son of Judah, [34]the son of Jacob, the son of Isaac, the son of Abraham, the son of Terah, the son of Nahor, [35]the son of Serug, the son of Reu, the son of Peleg, the son of Eber, the son of Shelah, [36]the son of Cainan, the son of Arphaxad, the son of Shem, the son of Noah, the son of Lamech, [37]the son of Methuselah, the son of Enoch, the son of Jared, the son of Mahalalel, the son of Kenan, [38]the son of Enosh, the son of Seth, the son of Adam, the son of God.

Context

In this section Luke reaffirmed the description of Jesus given in 1:31-35; 2:11. He did this in two ways. The first involved Jesus' baptism. In 3:21-22 Jesus' divine sonship was affirmed by a voice from heaven; and his role as the Christ, or Anointed One, is seen by the Spirit's descent upon him. In the following genealogy Luke demonstrated that Jesus' lineage stemmed not only from David, from whom the Christ was to come, but also from Abraham and from Adam. Thus Jesus is the fulfillment not only of Jewish hopes and aspirations but of the hopes of the entire world. Like Adam, who was described as the son of God because of his unique relationship to God, so Jesus also is understood as possessing a unique relationship to God. The theme of Jesus' sonship unites these two parts of this section (3:22,38) with the following one (4:3,9) as do the references to the Spirit (3:22; 4:1; cf. also 4:18). The section is united to what precedes it by the references to baptism (3:3,7,12,16,21).

Comments

3:21 This verse and the next one consist of a single sentence in Greek, and in these two verses we encounter a classical problem that has plagued interpreters. Why did Jesus submit to a baptism of "repentance"? This problem is evident not only in Matt 3:14-15 but in a number of early church writings (cf. *The Gospel of the Nazareans* 2 quoted in Jerome, *Against Pelagius* 3.2). In *The Gospel of the Naza-*

reans Jesus, upon being asked by his mother and brothers about going with them to be baptized by John the Baptist, replied: "Wherein have I sinned that I should go and be baptized by him? Unless what I have said is ignorance?" (a sin of ignorance).[26] Various answers have been given about why Jesus was baptized by John the Baptist. (1) Jesus was repenting (cf., however, John 8:46; 2 Cor 5:21; Heb 4:15; 7:26; 9:14). (2) Jesus was affirming John the Baptist's ministry as being from God (cf. Luke 20:4-7). (3) Jesus was fulfilling all righteousness (cf. Matt 3:15; what this means, however, is far from clear). (4) Jesus was originally a disciple of John the Baptist and was baptized by him, and this fact remained part of the Jesus tradition (apart from the issue of whether this was true, this was certainly not Luke's understanding). (5) Jesus submitted to baptism as a symbolic anticipation of his passion and death (cf. Luke 12:50; Isa 53:12; Mark 10:38-39). (6) We simply do not know. This very difficulty of explaining why Jesus experienced a baptism of repentance is a guarantee of its historicity. In our present account Luke did not tell us why Jesus submitted to a baptism of "repentance." Nevertheless the announcement of the voice from heaven that God was well pleased with Jesus probably indicates that the theory that Jesus was here experiencing repentance was far removed from Luke's thinking. Jesus' baptism was important for Luke, even more important than for the other Evangelists, but that Jesus' baptism was a baptism of "repentance" seems not to have entered into his mind.

When all the people were being baptized. That is, the people of 3:7. "Were being baptized" is literally *had been baptized*.

Jesus was baptized too. Luke saw Jesus' baptism as the climax and culmination of John's ministry of baptism. Luke (cf. John 1:31-33) did not directly state that Jesus was baptized by John the Baptist (cf. Mark 1:9; Matt 3:13). It is unclear why Luke omitted this. Perhaps it is that a reference to John baptizing Jesus might seem anachronistic in light of Luke 3:19-20.

And as he was praying. For Luke prayer was frequently a time of revelation and direction from God.[27] Indeed Luke often added to narratives references to Jesus at prayer (6:12; 9:18,28-29; 11:1; cf. 22:40-41). The Holy Spirit, furthermore, often comes in response to prayer.[28] Jesus serves here as a model for Christians in their prayer lives. See Introduction 8 (7).

Heaven was opened. The opening of heaven is a frequent apocalyptic motif found in the giving of revelation[29] as is a voice from heaven.[30]

3:22 The Holy Spirit descended on him. Before Jesus began his ministry, he was anointed by the Spirit. The importance of this for Luke is evident from 4:1,14 and especially vv. 18-21 (cf. also Acts 4:26-27; 10:37-38). For Luke, Jesus then was "anointed" for his ministry as the "Anointed-Messiah-Christ."[31] There is a clear

---

[26]E. Hennecke, *New Testament Apocrypha* (Philadelphia: Westminster, 1963), 1:146-47. Cf. C. L. Blomberg, *Matthew*, NAC (Nashville: Broadman, 1992), 81-82.

[27]Cf. Luke 1:9-11 (Zechariah); 2:37-38 (Anna); Acts 9:11-12 and 22:17-21 (Paul); 10:2-6 (Cornelius); 10:9-16 (Peter); 13:2-3 (prophets and teachers of the church).

[28]Cf. Luke 11:13; Acts 1:14; 2:1-4; 21 (note 38-39); 4:23-31; 8:15-17.

[29]Cf. Ezek 1:1; John 1:51; Acts 7:56; 10:11; Rev 19:11.

[30]Cf. Isa 6:4,8; Ezek 1:25,28; Rev 4:1; 10:4,8; 11:12; 14:13.

[31]Cf. how the Spirit came upon the servant of the Lord (Isa 42:1; 61:1); prophets (Luke 1:15; 2:25-38; 2 Chr 15:1; 20:14; Neh 9:30); judges (Judg 3:10; 6:34; 11:29); and the Messiah (Isa 11:2; *Pss. Sol.* 17:37,42) to prepare them for their missions.

allusion here to Isa 61:1, which Luke would develop in 4:18-19 (cf. Acts 10:38). Even as Jesus received this divine equipping for his ministry, so the disciples also would be equipped in the future (Luke 24:49; Acts 1:4-8). Luke, unlike the other Gospel writers, added the term "Holy" due probably to Luke 3:16 and the fact that in Luke "spirit" can be used to describe an evil spirit (cf. 4:33; 8:29; 9:39,42; 11:24; 13:11). The Spirit's descent upon Jesus should not be confused with the "baptism of the Spirit" spoken of by John the Baptist (3:16), for the baptism of the Spirit was something Jesus himself did for his followers, whereas the descent of the Spirit was something that happened to Jesus.

Descended on him in bodily form like a dove. The analogy of the Spirit's descent "like a dove" is found also in Mark 1:10, but Luke alone added "in bodily form" and thus intensified the reality of the Spirit's coming upon Jesus. This indicates that, for Luke, Jesus' sonship and anointing go hand in hand (cf. 4:41; 22:67, 70; Acts 9:20,22). Like Matthew, Luke also had the Spirit coming "upon" Jesus rather than "into" him (cf. 4:18). "Like a dove" is a simile and does not mean that the Spirit actually took the form of a dove to descend upon Jesus.

And a voice came from heaven. This *bath qol* (divine voice) was clearly God's voice.

You are my Son, whom I love. It is unclear whether this is an allusion to Ps 2:7, although a few Western manuscripts (Codex Beza and the Itala) make this explicit by adding "this day I have begotten you." The latter, however, is a scribal addition. The voice from heaven clearly reveals a unique relationship between Jesus and God and refers to Jesus' past as well as present status with God. The voice did not confer upon Jesus a new status, so we should not see here some kind of adoptionist Christology. Rather, the voice confirmed what the readers read already in Luke 1:32-35 and 2:49, i.e., that Jesus was the Son of God before his baptism.

In light of 20:13 "whom I love," i.e., *beloved*, may mean *only*.

With you I am well pleased. This is a possible allusion to Isa 42:1.

3:23 Unlike Matthew, who placed his genealogy at the very beginning of his Gospel (1:1-17), Luke placed his genealogy between the accounts of Jesus' baptism and temptation. There is OT precedent for this in Moses' genealogy (Exod 6:14-25), which is not recorded at the beginning of his life but just before he started his ministry.[32]

The genealogy contains seventy-seven ancestors.[33] The exact arrangement of generations, in contrast to Matt 1:1-17, is uncertain. The intended pattern may be: Jesus to exile (3 x 7 generations); exile to David (3 x 7 generations); David to Abraham (2 x 7 generations); Abraham to Adam, son of God (3 x 7 generations).[34]

---

[32] Thus the presence of the genealogy at this point need not suggest that the original form of this Gospel began at 3:1.

[33] Many of the names are obtained from Gen 5:1-32; 11:10-26; and 1 Chr 1-3. Yet thirty-six names are unknown. None of the names from Jesus to Rhesa (3:23-27) are found in the OT. Nor are the names Neri, Melki, Addi, Cosam, Elmadam, and Er (3:27-28). The names Admin [or Ram] and Arni [or Hezron] (3:33)—the textual evidence is uncertain here—are not found in the OT either.

[34] There are also seven generations between Adam, son of God and Enoch.

With this genealogy of Jesus we encounter a classic problem involving the differences between the Matthean and Lukan genealogies. There are several minor differences in form[35] and in content. For example, Matthew's genealogy stopped at Abraham, whereas Luke's went back to "Adam, the Son of God"; Matthew added occasional descriptions (cf. 1:3,5-6,11-12,16-17); Luke listed sixty names not found in Matthew.[36]

The key issue, however, involves the differences in names between David and Jesus in the two genealogies. Thirty-eight names are different, and most important is the difference in the name of the alleged grandfather of Jesus. According to Matt 1:16 it was Jacob, but according to Luke 3:23 it was Heli. Numerous attempts have been made to explain this. Most scholars think that at present the two lists resist any and all attempts at harmonization.[37] Others seeking to harmonize the two accounts have offered various explanations.[38]

The existence of such extensive genealogies in Jesus' day is well established. The rabbi Hillel was able to trace his genealogy back to David, and Josephus (*Life* 1.3) also gave his own extensive genealogy. Yet at the present time with the material available, no truly satisfying solution has been brought forward to resolve this difficulty.[39]

---

[35] E.g., Matthew used "*x* begat *y*," whereas Luke used "[son] of *y*"; Matthew worked forward to Jesus, whereas Luke worked backward from Jesus; and Matthew arranged his list into three groups of fourteen names each (cf. 1:17).

[36] The twenty names from David to Shealtiel are different; eighteen from Zerubbabel to Jesus are different.

[37] In fact, the textual problem involved in Admin/Ram and Arni/Hezron may reflect an early scribal attempt to harmonize the Lukan account with Matthew.

[38] E.g., Luke followed the Davidic line through Nathan (cf. Zech 12:12-13), whereas Matthew (cf. 1 Chr 1–3) followed the line through Solomon. The Matthean genealogy thus gives the legal line of descent from David, whereas the Lukan genealogy gives the actual physical line of descent.

Or both Jacob and Heli were in some sense Jesus' grandfathers. Variations of this explanation include: (a) Jacob (Matt 1:16) and Heli (Luke 3:23) were brothers, and upon Jacob's death Heli assumed the role of husband via a Levirate marriage (cf. Deut 25:5-10) and fathered Joseph. Heli was thus Joseph's natural father, whereas Jacob was the legal father. According to Eusebius (*Eccl. Hist.* 1.7.1-15), Julius Africanus (ca. 225) claimed that he knew this from information that came from the descendants of James, the brother of Jesus. However, whereas the father of Joseph and Heli for both Matthew and Luke was Matthat/Matthan, the father of Matthan in Matthew is Eleazar, while in Luke, it was Levi. (See R. E. Brown, *The Birth of the Messiah* [Garden City: Doubleday, 1979], 503-04.) (b) Matthew's genealogy was that of Joseph, whereas Luke's genealogy was that of Mary. This depends upon how one reads "so it was thought, of Joseph" (Luke 3:23). The phrase can be interpreted in two ways: "Jesus was the son (supposedly) of Joseph, who was the son of Matthat" or "Jesus was the son (supposedly of Joseph but really) of Matthat," who is then identified as the father of Mary. The major problem with this explanation is that in 1:27 Jesus' Davidic descent via *Joseph* is stressed. (c) Heli was Mary's father, but due to lack of a male heir, he adopted Joseph as his son in order to maintain the family line. Thus the Matthean genealogy was Joseph's actual lineage, whereas the Lukan genealogy was his adopted lineage. This latter explanation lacks any evidence and can neither be proven nor disproven.

[39] For a more detailed discussion, see Fitzmyer, *Luke*, 488-98; and R. Laurentin, *The Truth of Christmas: Beyond the Myths* (Petersham: St. Bede's, 1986), 354-57.

Now Jesus himself was about thirty years old. If Jesus was born during the reign of Herod (1:5; Matt 2:1-19) who died in 4 B.C., and if Jesus was born ca. 6 B.C. and began his ministry ca. 28 (see comments on 3:1), Jesus would indeed have been in his early thirties. There does not seem to be here any reference or allusion to David's age when he began his reign ("thirty years old," 2 Sam 5:4), and there is even less likely an allusion to Gen 41:46 or Num 4:3. Luke may simply not have been able to be more specific about Jesus' age.

He began his ministry. Compare Luke 23:5; Acts 1:22; 10:37. Jesus' ministry began with his anointing by the Spirit.

So it was thought. This assumes that the reader has read Luke 1-2 and knows of the virginal conception. Luke 3:23 was therefore written after Luke 1-2. The best translation seems to be, "Jesus was the son (supposedly) of Joseph, the son of Heli," although "Jesus was the son (supposedly of Joseph), of Heli" is possible.

3:24 Matthat. This is the Matthan of Matt 1:15. A major agreement in both genealogies is that Matthat/Matthan was the great-grandfather of Jesus.

3:27 Rhesa. No available records indicate that Zerubbabel had a son by this name.

Neri. Although Matt 1:12 and 1 Chr 3:17-19 name Jeconiah as Zerubbabel's grandfather, Jer 22:30 may suggest that Jeconiah was childless and that he adopted Neri as son and heir.

3:28-31 The names (up to David) are all different from Matt 1:7-12.

3:32-34 The names in these verses are the same as in Matt 1:2-6 except for Admin [or Ram] and Arni [or Hezron]. The textual variants in Codex Beza, the Itala, and various church fathers probably are due to an attempt to harmonize the Lukan list with that of Matthew.

3:38 The son of Adam. Clearly Luke's universalistic perspective must be seen here. Jesus is the fulfillment not just of Jewish hopes but of the hopes of all people, both Jew and Gentile. For out of Adam the whole human family has come (cf. Acts 17:26), and Jesus is the son of Adam. Luke (like Paul in Rom 5:12-21; 1 Cor 15:22,45-49) obviously thought of Adam as a historical person.

The son of God. For a parallel to this, see Philo, *On the Virtues*, 204-5. There is a sense in which Adam was a type of Jesus in that he did not have a human father, for the one who gave him life was God himself. Similarly God through his Spirit was the creative power who gave life to his Son, Jesus.

The Lukan Message

The main Lukan message in this account is Christological. Yet there are at least three other Lukan emphases as well. One involves the importance of prayer. Only in Luke is Jesus described as praying at his baptism. Although it would be an exaggeration to say that Luke turned the entire narrative about Jesus' baptism into an episode of prayer, he wanted to show his readers that Jesus entered into this crucial experience, as he did all important experiences, in an attitude of prayer. See comments on 3:21 and Introduction 8 (7). Another Lukan emphasis is present in the genealogical record. By tracing Jesus' line back to Adam, Luke stressed the universal nature of the gospel and significance of Jesus, which we have already observed in 2:32.

In addition the Spirit's central role in the new age is once again evident. Like the other Gospel writers, Luke recorded the Spirit's coming upon Jesus like a dove, but he emphasized this anointing in two ways. One was by adding "in bodily form," and the other was by highlighting the Spirit's role in the events that follow (cf. 4:1,14,18-19; 5:17). For Luke Jesus began his ministry as the Anointed, i.e., the Messiah/Christ. This has been prepared for in 1:27,32-33,69-70; 2:4,11,26,38, and at this point Jesus assumed the messianic calling (cf. 4:18-19; Acts 4:26-27; 10:37-38).

The Christological emphasis found in this account involves the designation of Jesus as God's Son. The voice from heaven announcing that Jesus is God's Son was already part of the tradition Luke drew upon. This is evident from Matt 3:17 and Mark 1:11 (cf. John 1:34). But to this Luke added his genealogy, which traces Jesus' lineage back to Adam and ultimately to God (Luke 3:38). Even if Luke's exact reasoning is unclear, in some way Adam's unique sonship with God was being compared to Jesus' unique sonship.

(2) The Prelude to Jesus' Mission (4:1-15)

[1]Jesus, full of the Holy Spirit, returned from the Jordan and was led by the Spirit in the desert, [2]where for forty days he was tempted by the devil. He ate nothing during those days, and at the end of them he was hungry.

[3]The devil said to him, "If you are the Son of God, tell this stone to become bread."

[4]Jesus answered, "It is written: 'Man does not live on bread alone.' "

[5]The devil led him up to a high place and showed him in an instant all the kingdoms of the world. [6]And he said to him, "I will give you all their authority and splendor, for it has been given to me, and I can give it to anyone I want to. [7]So if you worship me, it will all be yours."

[8]Jesus answered, "It is written: 'Worship the Lord your God and serve him only.' "

[9]The devil led him to Jerusalem and had him stand on the highest point of the temple. "If you are the Son of God," he said, "throw yourself down from here. [10]For it is written:

" 'He will command his angels concerning you
    to guard you carefully;
[11]they will lift you up in their hands,
    so that you will not strike your foot against a stone.' "

[12]Jesus answered, "It says: 'Do not put the Lord your God to the test.' "

[13]When the devil had finished all this tempting, he left him until an opportune time.

[14]Jesus returned to Galilee in the power of the Spirit, and news about him
spread through the whole countryside. [15]He taught in their synagogues, and
everyone praised him.

Context

In all the Synoptic Gospels the baptism account is followed by the
account of Jesus' temptation.[40] In Luke it functions as the last preparatory
episode that introduces the public ministry of Jesus.[41] Having been
affirmed as God's Son by the voice from heaven and having been anointed
by the Spirit, Jesus was led out by the Spirit into the desert to do battle
with the devil. The temptations draw upon the divine pronouncement of
Jesus' sonship at the baptism ("You are my Son") and are Satanic temptations directed at this sonship ("If you are the Son of God"). There is no
developmental view of Jesus' sonship portrayed in the temptation. On the
contrary, he who was led by the Spirit to do battle and defeat the devil
was God's Son long before this (1:32,35; 3:22). Although Luke did
emphasize the physical and spiritual development of God's Son (2:40,52;
cf. Heb 5:8), it was not a development in which Jesus became progres-
sively more divine. Rather, it was as God's Son that Jesus was baptized
and tempted.

The temptations themselves came from external sources, and in all
three Jesus was obedient to God's will. The temptations were all messianic in nature and thus should not be seen as a parallel to 1 John 2:16.
Jesus was specifically tempted as God's Son. This is most clearly seen in
the second and third temptations, but the fact that the temptations were
introduced and concluded by "If you are the Son of God" indicates that
all three were messianic in nature. The account consists of three scenes,

---

[40]The source of this account is unclear since no one was present other than Jesus and the
devil. Some have suggested that the account originated out of temptations early Christians
faced that were then read back into Jesus' life. But were Jesus' temptations Christian-like temptations? They do not appear to have been, for no Christian is tempted to worship Satan in order
to be ruler of the world. Others have suggested that this account may have originated out of
parabolic stories Jesus told the disciples in which he expressed the temptations he faced with
regard to false messianic conceptions of his ministry. Still others have seen this as Jesus'
autobiographical sharing with his disciples of his messianic temptation in order to clarify for
them his own understanding of the messianic task. It is unlikely that the temptations simply
arose out of midrashic reflections on various OT passages, such as Deut 6:10-16; 8:1–9:22.

[41]Whether these experiences were mental, i.e., visionary in some way, or whether we
should think here of an actual experience in the desert and on the pinnacle of the temple is
also debated. Whereas the second temptation does seem to be visionary in some sense (Jesus
was shown all the world's kingdoms in an instant), the natural reading of the other two
temptations appears to portray a real experience, and most probably Luke understood them
this way. (If one denies the existence of the devil and the miraculous, these temptations
must, of course, be seen as either mythical or at best visionary in nature.)

and each scene contains a temptation from the devil and a reply from Jesus. They are also tied together by Jesus' use of Scripture in each of his replies and by the fact that all three scriptural quotations come from Deuteronomy. Apart from these quotations, no other words of Jesus are recorded.

The order of the three temptations differs from the order in Matt 4:1-11. In Matthew the final temptation took place on a high mountain and involved worshiping the devil, whereas in Luke the last temptation took place on the pinnacle of the temple in Jerusalem. This fits well with each of their theological interests, for Matthew preferred the mountain motif (5:1; 28:16-20), whereas Luke was deeply concerned with Jerusalem.[42] Which order is the original is uncertain.

Even as Luke concluded the account of the mission of John the Baptist with a summary (3:18-20), so also he concluded the prelude to Jesus' mission with a summary (4:14-15).[43] Unlike the parallels in Matt 4:13-17 and Mark 1:14-15, Luke did not at this point give a specific summary of Jesus' preaching concerning God's kingdom. This will be dealt with in Luke 4:14-15 in general terms but will be more specific in 4:43. Luke focused his attention in this concluding summary (4:16-30) less on the message, i.e., the coming of God's kingdom, than on the Messenger and thus heightened the Christological and pneumatical emphases. The general context found in 4:14-44 is Israel's synagogues (4:15-16,20,28,[31], 33,38,44).

Comments

4:1 Jesus, full of the Holy Spirit. Jesus would be victorious over the devil because he was full of the Spirit. This was a favorite expression of Luke.[44]

Returned from the Jordan. This links the present account to the baptism.

Was led by the Spirit. Luke linked both Jesus' being equipped by God and his encounter with the devil as the result of the Spirit's having come upon him. The conflict was not initiated by the devil but by the Spirit. Thus Jesus was not portrayed as passively being dragged out by the Evil One to endure temptation, for the initiator of this event was not the devil but God. The picture is that of the Anointed of the Lord on the offensive and led by the Spirit to confront the devil.

In the desert. Probably the geographical place designated here by Luke was the wilderness of Judah, but the "desert" is also frequently understood as a place where one contacts God (Hos 2:14-15) or the abode of demons and wild beasts (cf. Isa 13:21; 34:14; Tob 8:3; also cf. Mark 1:13). It was also seen by some as a

---

[42] This we see both in his Gospel (2:49; 9:51; 13:32-35; 19:45-46; 24:53) and in Acts (1:4).

[43] This parallelism indicates that 4:14-15 serves better as a summary for 3:21-4:13 than as an introduction for 4:16ff. The term "returned" (4:14) furthermore is often found in the conclusions to accounts or sections in Luke (cf. 1:56; 2:20; 7:10; 9:10; 24:33,52).

[44] Cf. Luke 1:15,41,67; Acts 2:4; 4:8,31; 6:3,5 (6:8); 7:55; 9:17; 11:24; 13:9.

place where a messianic-like deliverance of Israel would take place (cf. Acts 21:38; Josephus, *War* 2.13.4 [2.258-60]).

4:2   For forty days.   This probably is a round number.[45] Although it brings to mind the forty years the people of Israel wandered in the wilderness (Num 14:34) and the forty-day fasts of Moses (Exod 34:28; Deut 9:9) and Elijah (1 Kgs 19:8), the Evangelists did not dwell on or develop any of these allusions.

Tempted by the devil.   The present participle (literally *being tempted*) indicates that Jesus was tempted throughout the forty days and that the three temptations were the culmination of this time of temptation. The term "devil" (seven times in Luke-Acts) is the Greek term used to translate the Hebrew "Satan," which is also found in Luke (seven times in Luke-Acts). Luke assumed the existence of this supernatural adversary of God and saw no need to convince his readers of the devil's existence.

He ate nothing during those days.   Did Luke intend us to interpret this literally, or was this his equivalent of Matthew's "fasting" (4:2)? The latter commonly involved abstinence from certain foods or from all food for certain parts of the day.

4:3   If you are the Son of God.   This temptation was intimately tied to the divine affirmation at the baptism and appealed to Jesus' status as God's Son (3:22, 38). A similar challenge appears in 23:35-39, and the latter probably indicates that the titles Son of God, Christ of God, Chosen One, and King of the Jews are mutually interchangeable, i.e., when Luke used one of them to describe Jesus, he assumed the applicability of the others as well.

Tell this stone to become bread.   Was this temptation a challenge to provide a sign (such as when God gave manna in the wilderness) in order for Jesus to gain a following? This is unlikely since no audience was present and the miracle was not to provide manna (loaves of bread, plural) for the people but a single loaf for Jesus' own hunger. Or was this a temptation to cause Jesus to doubt that he really is the Son of God? This also is unlikely since Jesus' answer did not deal with such a thought. More likely Jesus was tempted to use his power as God's Son for his own ends. Jesus clearly rejected such a view of his messianic role since it would indicate a lack of trust on his part in the provision and care of his Heavenly Father. He also had to trust and pray, "Give us each day our daily bread" (11:3) and seek first the kingdom of God (12:31), just as he would soon teach his disciples. Later Luke recorded a miracle of Jesus' multiplying bread (9:10-17), but that was to satisfy the needs of others. Jesus would not, however, use his messianic anointing to satisfy his own needs but rather would submit himself to his Father.

4:4   Jesus answered, "It is written."   Throughout his temptations Jesus found his answers in the Scriptures. He was armed with the "sword of the Spirit" (Eph 6:17) for his battle with the devil. See comments on 2:23.

Man does not live on bread alone.   This, as well as the other two temptations, was messianic in nature in that Jesus understood the messianic role as requiring that he too must humble himself and trust himself to God (cf. Phil 2:7-8). Israel in the wilderness needed to trust God for their sustenance; so must God's Son (Deut 8:1-3).

4:5   The devil led him up to a high place.   How was this done? Was it by walking? By some sort of levitation? We are not told because for Luke what was important was not the *how* but the *what* that took place.

---

[45] Cf. Deut 8:2,4; 9:9; Exod 16:35; 24:18; 34:28; 1 Kgs 19:8.

Showed him in an instant all the kingdoms of the world. Luke in his wording (esp. "in an instant") suggested that he understood this temptation at least in part as a visionary experience. "World" (*oikoumenēs*) is a favorite term in Luke[46] and refers to the inhabited world, whereas "world" (*kosmos*) refers more frequently to the geographical world.

4:6 I will give you. The "you" is emphatic.

Authority. This favorite Lukan word[47] is not found in the Matthean parallel. It is better understood as describing *oikoumenēs* than *kosmos*.

Splendor. Another favorite word in Luke, "splendor," can also be translated "glory." [48] It refers to the glory that comes to the ruler who possesses such authority. This word is missing from the Matthean parallel.

For it has been given to me. "Has been given" is a divine passive, i.e., *God* has placed this world's kingdoms under the devil's temporary rule.[49] God is clearly sovereign, but within his permissive will the devil is temporarily given this authority. This statement explains why the next one is true.

And I can give it to anyone I want to. That God's Son would one day reign over the world's kingdoms was clear for Luke.[50] The issue is *how* he would achieve this. Would it be through the shortcut the devil offered or by submitting to God's will, which involved suffering and death? The devil offered Jesus a crossless path of messiahship, and Luke assumed that the devil had in fact the authority to offer the world's kingdoms to Jesus.

4:7 So if you worship me, it will all be yours. God's Son was asked to give to the devil what belonged to God alone and thus to assume a different kind of messiahship from that to which God had called him. Like every believer, Jesus too was faced with the need and choice to take up the cross (9:23).

4:8 Jesus answered, "It is written." Again Jesus appealed to the Scriptures. See comments on 2:23.

Worship the Lord your God and serve him only. Both Matthew and Luke differ from the LXX translation of Deut 6:13 (and the Hebrew) in their use of the term "worship" instead of "fear." This suggests their use of a common source. See Introduction 5.

4:9 The devil led him to Jerusalem. The climax of the temptations for Luke took place in Jerusalem. Matthew, writing to a Jewish audience, could simply say "to the holy city" (cf. Matt 4:5; 27:53). For Jerusalem's importance in Luke-Acts, see Introduction 7 (2).

On the highest point of the temple. We do not know exactly what part of the temple is meant. The term is used of the temple only here and in the Matthean parallel in 4:5. The Greek term means "extremity" or "tip." Traditionally the site thought to be described here is the southeastern corner of the temple area overlooking the

---

[46]Cf. Luke 2:1; 21:26; Acts 11:28; 17:6,31; 19:27; 24:5.

[47]Cf. Luke 4:32,36; 5:24; 7:8; 9:1; 10:19; 12:5,11; 19:17; 20:2,8,20; 22:53; 23:7; Acts 1:7; 5:4; 8:19; 9:14; 26:10,12,18.

[48]Luke 2:9,14,32; 9:26,31-32; 12:27; 14:10; 17:18; 19:38; 21:27; 24:26; Acts 7:2,55; 12:23; 22:11.

[49]Cf. John 12:31; 14:30; 16:11; 1 Cor 2:6; 2 Cor 4:4; Eph 2:2.

[50]Cf. Luke 19:12,15; 21:27; 22:69; 23:42; Acts 1:6; 2:32-36; 17:31; cf. Phil 2:10-11.

Kidron Valley, but again Luke was less concerned with identifying the exact geographical location as in telling what happened.

If you are the Son of God. Like the first temptation, the third was introduced by this conditional phrase.

4:10 For it is written. Even the devil can quote Scripture, and here he sought to support his challenge to Jesus from the Scripture itself. Defeated by Jesus' use of the Word of God in the previous two temptations, the devil sought to use the Scriptures for his own purposes. There is no evidence that Ps 91:11-12, which the devil quoted, was interpreted messianically in Judaism; but if the psalm states a truth concerning any believer, how much more (*a fortiori*) is this true of the Messiah. Yet knowing Scripture is not enough; one must interpret it correctly.

He will command his angels concerning you. Was Jesus being tempted here to perform a great sign before the people and thus prove that he is the Messiah? The weakness of this interpretation is that Luke did not mention an audience for whom such a sign could be performed.[51] Furthermore Jesus' answer was not directed at such an interpretation. The temptation appears to have been to tempt God by putting him to the test by forcing him to fulfill his promise of protection.[52] True worship does not seek to dictate to God how he must fulfill his covenantal promises.

4:12 Luke understood the OT quotation from Deut 6:16 as a command for Jesus to obey rather than as a command for the devil to refrain from tempting Jesus, who is the "Lord your God."

4:13 When the devil had finished all this tempting. Luke understood the three temptations as representative of the kinds of temptations Jesus confronted during the forty days in the desert.

He left him until an opportune time. Someone has suggested that Jesus was free from temptation from here on until Satan entered Judas Iscariot (22:3) and Peter (22:31) and his time came once more (22:53).[53] Yet Satan was active during all of Jesus' ministry as well (8:12; 10:17-18; 11:14-22; 13:11-17; 22:28). This statement rather indicates that a direct confrontation with the devil (such as we read of here) does not occur again until the arrest, trial, and crucifixion.[54]

4:14 Jesus returned to Galilee. Galilee, which has been proleptically alluded to in 1:26; 2:4,39; cf. also 3:1, is described as where the opening scene of Jesus' ministry took place. Compare also 23:5; Acts 10:37; 13:31.

In the power of the Spirit. Having been anointed at his baptism by the Spirit "in bodily form" (3:22, only Luke), being "full of the Spirit" (4:1, only Luke),

---

[51] A rabbinic tradition found in *Pesiqta rabbati* 36 states that when the Messiah would reveal himself to Israel he would come and stand on the roof of the temple, but this does not seem to play any role in the present account because the tradition says nothing about jumping off. See H. L. Strack and P. Billerbeck, *Kommentar zum Neuen Testament* (München: C. H. Beck'sche, 1956), 1:151.

[52] One cannot help thinking of those who handle poisonous snakes and drink poison on the basis of the scribal addition found in Mark 16:18!

[53] So H. Conzelmann, *The Theology of St. Luke* (New York: Harper, 1960), 28, 124, 170.

[54] See S. Brown, *Apostasy and Perseverance in the Theology of Luke*, AnBib (Rome: Pontifical Biblical Institute, 1969), 5-19.

and having been led by the Spirit to do battle and defeat Satan, Jesus "in the power of the Spirit" (4:14, only Luke) returned to Galilee to begin his ministry. His ministry, like the church's later ministry, was marked by the Spirit's power.[55] For the tie between the "Spirit" and "power," see comments on 1:17.

And news about him spread through the whole countryside. This summary of Jesus' actions and fame was known to Luke's readers even though Luke had not yet given any examples, for these things were "not done in a corner" (Acts 26:26). No doubt they knew "how God anointed Jesus of Nazareth . . . and how he went around doing good and healing" (Acts 10:38). Another such proleptic reference to Jesus' ministry is found in Luke 4:23.

4:15   He taught in their synagogues. What Jesus taught was not mentioned at this point, but Luke emphasized his role as a teacher.[56] As a result of Jesus' teaching ministry, Theophilus could assume that the ultimate source of what he had been taught (1:4) was Jesus himself. All of 4:14-44 is set in the context of Jesus' preaching in the synagogues of Galilee. "Their" suggests that Luke was a Gentile writing to Gentiles.

And everyone praised him. The universal, positive response of the common people to Jesus was a strong Lukan emphasis.[57] See Introduction 7 (1). The term "praise" (literally *glorified*) was usually used for God (Mark 2:12; Matt 9:8).

The Lukan Message

We already have noted the importance Luke placed on the Spirit's coming at Jesus' baptism. This theme is picked up in 4:1,14,18-19,36. Luke retained the reference in the tradition to Jesus' being led by the Spirit into the wilderness (cf. Matt 4:1), but he added the statement that Jesus was "full of the Spirit" (Luke 4:1). We have noted already the frequency and thus the importance of this expression in Luke-Acts. Jesus' victory over the devil thus resulted not simply because of his knowledge and use of the Scriptures (as in Matthew) but also because he was "full of the Spirit." Thus unlike Israel, which failed in its wilderness experience, God's Son was victorious. The Spirit's importance in this is evident, and Jesus' experience became a model of how Theophilus was to live out his life. Even as Jesus, "full of the Spirit," was victorious over the devil, so in Acts, Peter (4:8), Stephen (6:5,8; 7:55), Barnabas (11:24), and Paul (13:9) were also filled with the Spirit and followed in their Lord's footsteps. Luke's readers are exhorted by their example to be filled with the Spirit as well. The concluding summary again emphasizes that Jesus' entire future ministry is to be understood as taking place "in the power of the Spirit."

[55]Luke 4:36; 5:17; 6:19; 8:46; 10:13; Acts 10:38; cf. Luke 9:1; 10:19; 24:49; Acts 1:8; 4:7,33; 6:8; 19:11.
[56]Luke 4:31; 5:3,17; 6:6; 11:1; 13:10,22,26; 19:47; 20:1,21; 21:37; 23:5.
[57]Luke 5:26; 6:17; 7:16; 9:43; 18:43; 19:37,48; 20:6,19,26; 21:38; 22:2; 24:19; Acts 2:47; 3:9; 4:21.

The passage's primary function, however, is to demonstrate to Luke's readers why Jesus was the kind of Messiah he was. At the temptation Jesus' messianic role is made clear for the reader. The temptation did not serve to clarify this role for Jesus himself, for there was no struggle and introspection for him about which path to take. God's Son clearly knew what the messianic role called for. The temptations involved a willingness to do what he already knew God wanted him to do. For the reader, however, this account makes clear why Jesus was not a political messiah. Such a view of the messianic task comes from the devil. Jesus would have nothing to do with it. Thus he would not fit the Jewish portrait of the messiah. He was called to a messiahship that in our passage is described negatively (i.e., what he would not do). In the next account it would be described positively (cf. 4:18-19).

An additional Lukan emphasis found in this passage involves the central importance of the Scriptures in the life of the church. Jesus' knowledge and understanding of the Scriptures helped enable him to defeat the devil. Like the church in Berea (Acts 17:11), Jesus' attitude was shaped by the Scriptures. Like Zechariah and Elizabeth (Luke 1:6), Jesus observed the commandments and regulations of Scripture blamelessly. He had been raised this way by his parents (2:39,41). He saw his mission in light of the fulfillment of Scripture (4:18-19) and taught that the way to eternal life lies in the obedience to the scriptural teaching (10:25-28; 18:18-22). As for Luke's readers, obedience to that scriptural teaching centers on faith in and obedience to the one who is the focus of the Scriptures—Jesus Christ, God's Son. It would be difficult for Luke's readers not to understand how central and important the Scriptures are for their Christian life. Here as in his being "full of the Spirit," Jesus is a model for the believer.

Finally we find in the concluding summary the Lukan emphasis that points out that the people ("everyone") had a positive attitude and response toward Jesus.

———————————— *SECTION OUTLINE* ————————————

IV. JESUS' MINISTRY IN GALILEE (4:16–9:50)
  1. The Beginning of Jesus' Ministry (4:16–5:16)
    (1) Jesus' Sermon in Nazareth—A Thematic Explanation of Jesus' Ministry (4:16-30)
    (2) Jesus' Healings in Capernaum (4:31-44)
    (3) The Call of the First Disciples (5:1-11)
    (4) Jesus' Healing of a Leper (5:12-16)
  2. The Beginning of Controversy (5:17–6:11)
    (1) Conflict over Jesus' Forgiveness of Sins (5:17-26)
    (2) Conflict over Jesus' Association with Tax Collectors and Sinners (5:27-32)
    (3) Conflict over Jesus' Disciples' not Fasting (5:33-39)
    (4) Conflict over Jesus' Attitude toward the Sabbath (6:1-11)
  3. The Teaching of the Disciples—The Sermon on the Plain (6:12-49)
    (1) Choosing the Twelve Disciples (6:12-16)
    (2) Ministry to the Crowds (6:17-19)
    (3) Beatitudes and Woes (6:20-26)
    (4) Love of One's Enemies (6:27-36)
    (5) Judging Others (6:37-42)
    (6) Two Foundations (6:43-49)
  4. Who Is This Jesus? (7:1-50)
    (1) Jesus Heals the Centurion's Servant (7:1-10)
    (2) Jesus Raises the Widow of Nain's Son (7:11-17)
    (3) Jesus Reveals Himself to John the Baptist (7:18-23)
    (4) Jesus Bears Witness to John the Baptist as His Forerunner (7:24-30)
    (5) Jesus Experiences Rejection (7:31-35)
    (6) Jesus Forgives Sins (7:36-50)
  5. Jesus Teaches in Parables (8:1-21)
    (1) A Summary of Jesus' Ministry (8:1-3)
    (2) The Parable of the Soils (8:4-15)
    (3) The Parable of the Lamp (8:16-18)
    (4) Jesus' True Family (8:19-21)
  6. Jesus Reveals His Mastery over the World, the Devil, and the Flesh (8:22-56)
    (1) Jesus Calms the Sea (8:22-25)
    (2) Jesus Casts Out a Demon (8:26-39)
    (3) Jesus Heals the Hemorrhaging Woman and Raises Jairus's Daughter (8:40-56)

7. Jesus and the Twelve (9:1-50)
   (1) The Mission of the Twelve (9:1-6)
   (2) Herod's Question about Jesus (9:7-9)
   (3) The Feeding of the Five Thousand (9:10-17)
   (4) Peter's Confession and Teachings on the Passion and
       Discipleship (9:18-27)
   (5) The Transfiguration (9:28-36)
   (6) The Healing of the Boy with an Unclean Spirit (9:37-43a)
   (7) The Second Passion Announcement (9:43b-45)
   (8) Humility and Openness (9:46-50)

──────── **IV. JESUS' MINISTRY IN GALILEE (4:16–9:50)** ────────

The fourth major section of Luke centers in Galilee and is held
together primarily by this geographical orientation. As in Mark and Matthew, Luke portrayed the beginning of Jesus' ministry as taking place in
Galilee.[1] In "orderly" fashion (1:3) Luke prepared his readers for this section by beginning with Jesus' sermon at Nazareth, which serves as a programmatic explanation of Jesus' ministry.[2]

In this major section "the Evangelist spoke about one stage of Jesus'
way. In this phase of his career Jesus was the one who was anointed-
empowered by the Holy Spirit, and his activity demonstrated God's kingly
power. The accent is on power."[3]

1. The Beginning of Jesus' Ministry (4:16–5:16)

Jesus' programmatic sermon is meant to assist Luke's readers in understanding the nature of Jesus' messiahship and the response it would elicit
from the Jewish leadership. Thereupon Luke followed Mark 1:21-45
closely and provided his readers with examples of Jesus' healing power
and teaching ministry.

───────────────────

[1] The one exception to this is found in 8:22-39, which takes place on the eastern side of
the Sea of Galilee in "the region of the Gerasenes" (8:26,37), but here Luke simply was following his Markan source (cf. Mark 4:35–5:20).
[2] After this sermon Luke followed closely the material in Mark from 4:31–6:16 (cf. Mark
1:21–3:19). The main difference is his insertion of 5:1-11 (the call of the first disciples) into
the material. At 6:11 Luke then added the Sermon on the Plain (6:12-49), which came from
his other major source, the Q material. To this Luke added other material that he shared in
common with Matthew (Q material) in 7:1-10,18-35 or that is unique to his Gospel (the L
material) in 7:11-17,36-50; 8:1-3 before returning again to his Markan source in 8:4–9:50
(cf. Mark 4:1–9:41). Here he again tended to follow the material in Mark except for his
insertion of 8:19-21 and the omission of Mark 4:26-34; 6:1-6a; and 6:45–8:26, i.e., "the
Great Markan Omission."
[3] C. H. Talbert, *Reading Luke* (New York: Crossroad, 1982), 52-53.

(1) Jesus' Sermon in Nazareth—A Thematic Explanation of Jesus' Ministry (4:16-30)

[16]He went to Nazareth, where he had been brought up, and on the Sabbath day he went into the synagogue, as was his custom. And he stood up to read. [17]The scroll of the prophet Isaiah was handed to him. Unrolling it, he found the place where it is written:
[18]"The Spirit of the Lord is on me,
   because he has anointed me
   to preach good news to the poor.
He has sent me to proclaim freedom for the prisoners
   and recovery of sight for the blind,
   to release the oppressed,
[19]to proclaim the year of the Lord's favor."
[20]Then he rolled up the scroll, gave it back to the attendant and sat down. The eyes of everyone in the synagogue were fastened on him, [21]and he began by saying to them, "Today this scripture is fulfilled in your hearing."
[22]All spoke well of him and were amazed at the gracious words that came from his lips. "Isn't this Joseph's son?" they asked.
[23]Jesus said to them, "Surely you will quote this proverb to me: 'Physician, heal yourself! Do here in your hometown what we have heard that you did in Capernaum.' "
[24]"I tell you the truth," he continued, "no prophet is accepted in his hometown. [25]I assure you that there were many widows in Israel in Elijah's time, when the sky was shut for three and a half years and there was a severe famine throughout the land. [26]Yet Elijah was not sent to any of them, but to a widow in Zarephath in the region of Sidon. [27]And there were many in Israel with leprosy in the time of Elisha the prophet, yet not one of them was cleansed—only Naaman the Syrian."
[28]All the people in the synagogue were furious when they heard this. [29]They got up, drove him out of the town, and took him to the brow of the hill on which the town was built, in order to throw him down the cliff. [30]But he walked right through the crowd and went on his way.

Context

Luke began his portrayal of Jesus' ministry with the account of Jesus' first sermon.[4] This sermon is quite important, for it is programmatic, and

---

[4]The relationship between this account and Mark 6:1-6a is uncertain. There are certain similarities. Both take place in the synagogue in Nazareth (Mark 6:2; Luke 4:16); both begin with a positive reaction that becomes negative (Mark 6:2/3-6; Luke 4:22/23-30); both refer to Jesus' parentage (Mark 6:3; Luke 4:22); both contain the same proverb (Mark 6:4; Luke 4:24); and in both there is a reference to a lack of signs being performed in Nazareth (Mark 6:5; Luke 4:23-27). Yet there are numerous differences as well. Some have suggested that Luke added to his Markan source (Luke 4:16,22,24) an account from another source (4:17-21,23,25-30). This is supported by the use of the Aramaic form of "Nazareth" in 4:16, which

in it Luke provided his readers with Jesus' own description of his mission and ministry.[5] Luke placed this first description of what Jesus taught at the very beginning of his ministry, even though he knew that Jesus already had a successful ministry in Capernaum (4:23), for his orderly presentation of the things Jesus said and did was more important than chronological exactness. In a similar way he began his portrayal of the ministry of the early church in Acts with Peter's sermon (cf. Acts 2:14-40). The programmatic nature of Jesus' sermon is evident from the summary in Luke 4:43-44 in which the "good news" refers back to the contents of this sermon (4:18). The importance of Jesus' sermon is also highlighted by Luke's statement that "the eyes of everyone in the synagogue were fastened on him" (4:20) as well as by Luke's recording that Jesus intentionally "found the place where it is written" (4:17). The importance of the sermon is further heightened by the fact that it involves the fulfillment of the Scriptures. Finally, the central role of this account is witnessed to by the fact that when John the Baptist raised the question of whether Jesus was the expected one (7:20), Jesus in His reply repeated this text (cf. 7:21-22 with 4:18-21).

The main problem within this account involves the relationship of 4:16-22 with 4:23-30. In the former Jesus appears to have been accepted and praised, but in the latter there is a surprising reversal, and he was rejected.[6] Yet this apparent conflict clearly fits Luke's purpose, for the account reveals not only the heart and content of Jesus' message to Luke's readers (4:18-21) and the favor Jesus found in general among the common people (4:22), but it also foresees his rejection (4:23-30); the shadow of the cross hung over Jesus' ministry from the very beginning.

Comments

4:16 He went to Nazareth. No doubt Luke's readers knew about Jesus of "Nazareth,"[7] and Luke prepared them for this by his statements in 1:26; 2:4,39,51. The parallel in Mark 6:1 states "to his hometown," but from Mark 1:24 and 6:4 it is evident that Nazareth was meant.

Where he had been brought up. This recalls Luke 2:39-51 and prepares us for 4:24.

---

stands in contrast to Luke's use of the Greek form everywhere else, by the use of *biblion* ("scroll") in 4:20 instead of the more expected *biblos* and the awkward flow of various verses in the account.

[5] J. A. Fitzmyer (*The Gospel according to St. Luke*, AB [Garden City: Doubleday, 1981], 529) states: "Luke has deliberately put this story at the beginning of the public ministry to encapsulate the entire ministry of Jesus and the reaction to it."

[6] Some have suggested that Luke combined two separate incidents. However, this is difficult to determine.

[7] Cf. Mark 1:24; 10:47; Acts 10:38; John 1:45.

As was his custom. Even as Jesus attended the synagogue and the temple, so would the early church.[8]

And he stood up to read. Luke implied that the ruler of the synagogue (*archisynagogos*; cf. Acts 13:15) invited Jesus to read and comment on the Scriptures.[9] This is the oldest account we possess of a synagogue service, which apparently contained the following: the singing a psalm; the reading of the Shema (Deut 6:4-9; 11:13-21); the repetition of the Eighteen Blessings (the *Shemoneh Esreh*); a reading of the Law in Hebrew, followed by a translation in Aramaic from the targum since Hebrew was no longer used and understood by the average person; a reading from the Prophets in Hebrew, followed by a translation in Aramaic from the targum; a sermon on the Scripture; and a concluding blessing by the ruler of the synagogue.

4:17   The scroll of the prophet Isaiah was handed to him. There was perhaps in Jesus' day a fixed three-year pattern of readings from the Law, and the present text may suggest that there was a cycle of assigned readings in the Prophets as well. As the Dead Sea Scrolls have shown, the entire text of Isaiah could be contained in a single scroll.

Unrolling it. Some manuscripts (A,B,L,W) read "opened," perhaps because the word used for scroll here is *biblion*, which later came to mean a *codex* or *book*. "Unrolling," however, is the better reading and a more appropriate expression for the opening of a scroll.

He found the place where it is written. Luke indicated that Jesus deliberately chose the following passage to read and thus emphasized Jesus' messianic consciousness as he began his ministry. See comments on 2:23.

4:18   The following scriptural quotation comes from Isa 61:1a,b,d [c is omitted]; 58:6d; and 61:2a.[10] Most significant in this quotation is the omission of Isa 61:2b,

---

[8]Cf. Acts 2:46; 3:1; 4:1; 5:12,42; 6:9; 9:2,20; 13:5,14,43; 21:26. In Acts 17:2 this same expression is used, but here it refers more to Paul's regularly teaching in the synagogues than to his regularly attending the synagogue.

[9]Talbert (*Reading Luke*, 54-55) points out in 4:16-20 an extended chiasmus as follows:

A (stood up, 4:16c);
  B (was handed, 4:17a);
    C (unrolling, 4:17b);
      D (4:18-19);
    c (rolled up, 4:20a);
  b (gave back, 4:20b);
a (sat down, 4:20c).

[10]The exact form of the passage is uncertain. It is appealing to see in it six parallel lines: (1) the Spirit of the Lord is upon *me*, (2) because he has anointed *me* (3) to preach good news to the poor. He has sent *me* (There is a grammatical question about whether "to preach the good news" goes with "he anointed me" or "he sent me." The latter seems more likely.) (4) *to proclaim* freedom for the prisoners and recovery of sight for the blind, (5) *to release* the oppressed, (6) *to proclaim* the year of the Lord's favor. This would involve three lines ending with "me" (*eme, me, me*) and three lines beginning with infinitives describing what it means to preach good news to the poor. Yet since Luke was following the wording of the LXX almost exactly, it is questionable whether we should see in the quotation a unique Lukan literary arrangement.

"And the day of vengeance of our God." For Luke the present day, i.e., the "today" of Luke 4:21, was a day of salvation, the time of opportunity (cf. 2 Cor 6:2). Most scholars have argued that the insertion of Isa 58:6d into the quotation is from Luke's hand. If this is so, Luke was then adding another part of the description of the suffering servant of Isaiah to help explain Jesus' mission more clearly for his readers. The importance of this Isaianic quotation for Luke is evident for a number of reasons. First, he did not have to include this quotation in the account, as the parallel in Mark 6:1-6a reveals. Second, this is Scripture and thus for Luke and his readers infallibly reveals the purpose of Jesus' ministry. Finally, Luke pointed out that Jesus himself chose this passage and described his ministry as aimed at its fulfillment.

The Spirit of the Lord . . . anointed me. This anointing refers to Luke 3:22 (cf. Acts 10:38) and the divine commissioning for Jesus' ministry. This anointing was not just a prophetic anointing (Luke 4:24) but a messianic one as well (3:22; Acts 4:26-27; 10:38), for Jesus is the bringer, not just the herald, of salvation. Although only Jesus was said by Luke to have been anointed by the Spirit (cf. Acts 4:26; 10:38), he serves here as a model for Spirit-filled teachers and healers in Acts.

To preach good news. For Luke "to preach the good news" meant *to preach the gospel.* In Luke the terms to "preach" (*kērussō*) and "preach the gospel" (*euangelizō*) are essentially synonyms.[11]

Poor. The "poor" is a strong Lukan concern. See Introduction 8 (5). In Luke the term "poor"[12] does refer to an economic condition, but not merely to economic status, for the poor and humble hope in God.[13]

To proclaim freedom for the prisoners. This is to be understood metaphorically. Whereas it may include healings and exorcisms, "freedom" (*aphesin*) always refers to the forgiveness of sins elsewhere in Luke-Acts.[14]

Recovery of sight for the blind. This may be a reference to the blind that Jesus healed. Only one specific example is given in Luke (18:35-43), but others are clearly referred to in 7:21-22. There is another sense, however, in which "blind" refers metaphorically to those who are "spiritually blind."[15]

To release the oppressed. The same word translated "release" here is translated "freedom" earlier in this verse. It probably is best to understand this metaphorically as standing in synonymous parallelism with the preceding statements (cf. esp. Acts 26:18, where forgiveness of sins parallels release for the oppressed in Luke 4:18), although there is a literal dimension in it as well (cf. 4:31-37; 13:16; Acts 10:38). This statement from Isa 58:6 is not meant to serve as a substitute for Luke's omission of 61:2b in the next verse because it appears before rather than after 61:2a.

---

[11] As Luke 4:43-44; 8:1; 9:2,6; Acts 8:4-5; and 10:36-37 reveal. Note the continuity here with John the Baptist's preaching in 3:18.

[12] Cf. also Luke 6:20; 7:22; 14:13,21; 16:20,22; 18:22; 19:8; 21:3.

[13] Cf. Luke 1:52-53; 3:10-11; 5:11,28, 12:33; 16:20-22; 18:28-30. See the comments on 6:20.

[14] Cf. Luke 1:77; 3:3; 24:47; Acts 2:38; 5:31; 10:43; 13:38; 26:18.

[15] Cf. Luke 1:78-79; 2:30-32; 3:6; 6:39; Acts 9:8-18; 13:47; 22:11-13; 26:17-18. The latter example is especially interesting because of the close parallels: sent—Luke 4:18 and Acts 26:17; sight—Luke 4:18 and Acts 26:18; release/forgiveness—Luke 4:18 and Acts 26:18. Cf. also Isa 42:7; 49:6; 58:8,10.

4:19   The year of the Lord's favor.   This is basically a synonym for the "good news of the kingdom of God," as Luke 4:43 shows. Jesus claimed here that God's kingdom had come. In fulfillment of the OT promises, salvation was now being offered to all. Even though the Lord purposely omitted the reference to the "day of God's vengeance" from his quotation of Isa 61:2 to emphasize the present time and opportunity for salvation, there is nevertheless present here the implication that this period of God's favor would not last forever. Although Isa 61:1-2 develops certain themes from the concept of the Jubilee Year (cf. Lev 25:8-55), Luke did not seem to have been thinking of this here.[16]

4:20   Then he rolled up the scroll, gave it back to the attendant and sat down.   The three verbs *rolled* (c), *gave back* (b), *sat down* (a) form a chiasmus with *stood up* (A), *was handed* (B), *unrolling* (C) in Luke 4:16-17. Whereas the reading of Scripture was done standing (4:16), the exposition was performed sitting (cf. Matt 23:2; 26:55). In Acts 13:16 Paul is portrayed as standing in the synagogue while preaching. This may indicate a different practice in the Diaspora. Luke made no mention of the reading of the targumic translation of the Hebrew text, since it was irrelevant to his purpose.

The eyes of everyone . . . were fastened.   "Everyone" is in emphatic position. The fixture of the eyes upon someone is used positively in Acts 1:10; 6:15. This serves as a literary device to focus the attention of Luke's readers upon the importance of what Jesus is about to say.

4:21   This verse is best understood as a summary of Jesus' sermon.

Today.   Luke gave special emphasis to this word by placing it first in Jesus' saying. "Now" the messianic age is already realized in Jesus' coming. See Introduction 8 (2). This period continues into the time of the church (cf. Acts 13:32-33), i.e., the time of Luke's readers, as the Spirit who anointed Jesus then comes upon the church (Acts 2:16-21). "Today" does not mean literally *in these last twenty-four hours* but *since the events of Luke 3:1ff.*

This scripture is fulfilled.   For the importance of this theme, see Introduction 7 (1).

4:22   All spoke well of him.   Literally, *All were witnessing to him.* This can be understood positively as "witnessed to" (cf. Acts 13:22; 14:3; 15:8; 22:5) or negatively as "witnessed against" (cf. Matt. 23:31; John 7:7; 18:23) with the pronoun "him" being either a dative of advantage ("to him") or disadvantage ("against him"). Most commentators understand this as a positive statement, although a negative interpretation would fit better with the next verses. The following verb, "were amazed," can also be understood positively (Luke 7:9) or negatively (John 7:15,21). It seems best to understand both these two verbs positively because Luke tended to use these terms positively elsewhere in Luke-Acts and because the object of the latter verb is "the gracious words that came from his lips." As a result (although it will make the transition to Luke 4:23-30 more difficult) it is best to understand this verse as a positive response toward Jesus' teaching up to this point. As in Acts 4:13-16; 6:15, Jesus' opponents witnessed to the truth of his claims (and to the church's proclamation).

---

[16] See R. C. Tannehill, *The Narrative Unity of Luke-Acts* (Philadelphia: Fortress, 1986), 68.

Gracious words. Whereas the Greek expression "words of grace" may be understood as a descriptive genitive (i.e., "grace" describes the kind of words—gracious words), it is better to understand the expression as an objective genitive describing the content of his words, i.e., words concerning God's grace, as in Acts 14:3; 20:32.

Isn't this Joseph's son? This can be understood positively as a pleasant surprise or negatively as in Mark 6:3 (cf. John 7:15). In light of what follows, it is best to interpret it as a negative statement.

4:23   This proverb. The Greek term is *parabolē*, which has a broad range of meaning from story and example parables, allegories, similitudes, and metaphors to proverbs. This particular proverb has numerous parallels both in form and in context. For the latter cf. Luke 23:35. For the former we find in Greek literature (Euripides, *Incertarum Fabularum Fragmenta* 1086) the following proverb, "A physician for others, but himself teeming with sores"; and in Jewish literature (*Genesis Rabbah* 23:4) we find, "Physician, physician heal thine own limp!" Here as elsewhere (Luke 5:22; 6:8; 7:40; 9:47; 11:17) Jesus possessed a unique awareness of others' thoughts.

What we have heard that you did in Capernaum. In the setting of Jesus this expresses a skepticism about the factuality of these reports and a demand that Jesus perform the alleged miracles before them.[17] This incident in Nazareth, although placed first in Jesus' ministry by Luke, was not first chronologically. Rather its placement served Luke's "orderly" purpose. Only in the following account in 4:31-37 and in 7:1-10 (cf. also 10:15) do we read of Jesus' miracles in Capernaum. The invitation to read and comment on the Scriptures would also have been more likely after Jesus had already become engaged in a ministry of preaching and healing. This is therefore another proof that "orderly" in 1:3 does not mean chronologically.

4:24   I tell you the truth. "The truth" is literally *Amen*, which can be translated "verily/truly." This expression is found singularly or doubly over seventy times in the Gospels and only on Jesus' lips. It was used traditionally in Judaism at the end of a statement in order to confirm what had been said, but Jesus used it to introduce and stress what follows.

No prophet is accepted. Mark 6:4 has "a prophet [is not] without honor." Luke perhaps used the word "accepted" (*dektos*) in order to better parallel the "acceptable [*dekton*] year of the Lord" in Luke 4:18. No mention is made in this saying of Jesus' rejection by his family as in the parallel in Mark 6:4. In general Luke tended to minimize the negative descriptions of Jesus' family found in Mark. This proverb is also found in John 4:44 and the GT 31. Even as the prophets were rejected by Israel,[18] so too Jesus was rejected in Nazareth and later rejected in Jerusalem.[19]

In his hometown. This picks up "in your hometown" of the previous verse.

---

[17] "In Capernaum" is literally *into* (*eis*) *Capernaum* and is a good example of how the use of *eis* was beginning to encroach on the preposition *en* in first-century Greek.

[18] Cf. Luke 6:23; 11:47,49-50; 13:33-34; 20:9-19; Acts 7:52.

[19] For Jesus as a prophet cf. Luke 7:16,39; 9:8,19; 13:33; 24:19.

4:25 I assure you. "I assure you" is literally, *I say to you in truth.* Like "truly," this emphasizes the truthfulness of what is to follow.

In Elijah's time. Besides this passage we find clear allusions to Elijah/Elisha in 7:11-17; 9:52-55,61-62. Luke may have had a special interest in Elijah/Elisha because of their ministry to Gentiles.[20] In both this and the next example, Gentiles were dealt with graciously by God over Israelites. In 2:30-32; 3:6 God's purpose included Gentiles, and in Acts the Gentile mission evoked a positive response whereas the Jewish mission for the most part did not (cf. 10:34-35; 13:46-47; 18:5-6; 28:25-28).

Three and a half years. As in Jas 5:17, Luke used three and a half years instead of the three years stated in 1 Kgs 18:1. Three and a half may function more as a stereotyped number of a period of distress (cf. Dan 7:25; 12:7; Rev 11:2; 12:6,14) than an exact period of time.

4:26 Yet Elijah was not sent. This is an example of the "divine passive" and means *God did not send.* It avoids using God's name out of reverence for that name in keeping with the Third Commandment. "The sky was shut" of the previous verse is another example.

To any of them. This can be understood: Elijah was sent "to none of them except this one of them" or "to none of them but instead to someone else." The latter alternative is more likely.

4:27 The story of Naaman provides a second example of God's grace to Gentiles. Luke 4:25-27 supplies the key for understanding this account. For Jesus these examples demonstrated that Nazareth could not make exclusivistic claims on him; and since Nazareth had in fact rejected him, he would go elsewhere. Nazareth may have rejected him, but others would receive him gladly. For Luke these examples showed that the Jewish people had no exclusivistic claims on Jesus, and since they rejected him, the gospel of 4:18-21 has been offered to the Gentiles. And just as Elijah and Elisha were better received outside of Israel, so the gospel message would receive a better hearing among the Gentiles.

4:28 All the people. An example of Luke's use of overstatement (cf. 4:15). The furious response finds parallels in Acts.[21]

4:29 They got up. Compare Acts 6:9.

Drove him out of the town. Compare Luke 20:15; Acts 7:58.

Took him to the brow of the hill. It is difficult to know exactly what Luke meant in that Nazareth is built on a slope and no clear "brow" or cliff is nearby. He may have been less concerned here with the topography than with a desire to allude specifically to the martyrdoms of Stephen (Acts 7:58) and possibly James (cf. Eusebius, *Eccl. Hist.* 2.23.11-18) or in general to the customary practice of throwing a person down from a height before stoning (cf. John 8:59; Acts 7:54-60; *Sanh* 43a, 45a).

To throw him down. The degree in which the preceding statements foreshadow the coming crucifixion is unclear, but at the very beginning of Jesus' Galilean ministry, the cross was casting its shadow over Jesus' life.

---

[20] See C. A. Evans, "Luke's Use of the Elijah/Elisha Narratives and the Ethic of Election," *JBL* 106 (1987): 75-83.

[21] Cf. Acts 7:54-60; 18:4-6; 19:28-30; 22:14-24; cf. 13:44-48.

4:30   But he walked right through the crowd. Luke may or may not have
been implying a miraculous escape here. Regardless, Luke's point was that Jesus'
hour would not come until he arrived in Jerusalem (cf. Luke 22:53; John 7:30;
8:59).

The Lukan Message

The importance of this account for understanding Luke's theology is
clearly evident by its programmatic nature. We already have had such reliable witnesses as a devout priest and his wife, the angel Gabriel, an angel
of the Lord, the righteous Simeon, and prophets such as Anna and John
the Baptist witness to Jesus' person and role. Now, however, *Jesus himself*
answered the question, "Who is this one?" (5:21; 7:49; 8:25; 9:9). Its
importance is further heightened by the fact that whereas Luke's source
introduces Jesus' ministry with his proclamation concerning God's kingdom (Mark 1:14-15; cf. Matt 4:12-17), Luke's Gospel begins Jesus' ministry with this incident involving Jesus' self-description.

Luke's Jesus is the promised Christ, i.e., the Anointed One (Luke 4:18;
Acts 10:38). He already has been described as the Christ, the Son of
David in Luke 1:32-33,69; 2:4,11; 3:31. His anointing by the Spirit at his
baptism (3:22), his being led by the Spirit (4:1) in a victorious confrontation with Satan, and his returning in the power of the Spirit to Galilee
(4:13) have all prepared us for this. But now *Jesus himself* confessed that
he is the awaited Messiah (4:18-21). In 4:41 this emphasis appears again
when Luke added to the demons' confession of Jesus as God's Son the
title "the Christ" (cf. Mark 1:34). The Spirit's role in all of this is, of
course, quite obvious.

We also find in this account a Lukan emphasis on the realization of
God's kingdom. The OT promises, with their messianic hopes, are fulfilled. God's kingdom has come (cf. Luke 11:20; 16:16; 17:20-21). Today
(4:21) is the promised time. The omission of Isa 61:2b ("the day of vengeance") from the OT quotation is intentional. The present time is one of
grace and opportunity (cf. 2 Cor 6:2). Yet by its very nature the "today" of
grace implies a "tomorrow" when that grace will be withdrawn and judgment will come (Luke 20:47; 22:30; Acts 17:31).

One other favorite Lukan theme in our passage is the offer of salvation
to the oppressed. See Introduction 8 (5). Christ came for the "poor," "prisoners," the "blind," and the "oppressed" (Luke 4:18; cf. 19:10). It was
"their" day. The rejection in Nazareth was not by them. Rather, for them
this was a time of salvation.

Two final Lukan themes foreshadow Jesus' future rejection by Israel
which would result in the mission to the Gentiles. The former is clearly
seen in the rejection of the people of Nazareth. From the beginning Jesus
was aware that he, like the prophets, would be rejected by his own (4:24),

and the rejection in Nazareth is programmatic of the future rejection in Jerusalem. Yet this very rejection would confirm his prophetic and messianic identity, for this was the fate of all true prophets. The incident also foreshadows the future mission to the Gentiles, for even as Gentiles were the recipients of God's grace in the ministry of Elijah and Elisha (4:25-27), so it would be Gentiles who would be the primary recipients of the gospel's words of grace.

(2) Jesus' Healings at Capernaum (4:31-44)

[31]Then he went down to Capernaum, a town in Galilee, and on the Sabbath began to teach the people. [32]They were amazed at his teaching, because his message had authority.

[33]In the synagogue there was a man possessed by a demon, an evil spirit. He cried out at the top of his voice, [34]"Ha! What do you want with us, Jesus of Nazareth? Have you come to destroy us? I know who you are—the Holy One of God!"

[35]"Be quiet!" Jesus said sternly. "Come out of him!" Then the demon threw the man down before them all and came out without injuring him.

[36]All the people were amazed and said to each other, "What is this teaching? With authority and power he gives orders to evil spirits and they come out!" [37]And the news about him spread throughout the surrounding area.

[38]Jesus left the synagogue and went to the home of Simon. Now Simon's mother-in-law was suffering from a high fever, and they asked Jesus to help her. [39]So he bent over her and rebuked the fever, and it left her. She got up at once and began to wait on them.

[40]When the sun was setting, the people brought to Jesus all who had various kinds of sickness, and laying his hands on each one, he healed them. [41]Moreover, demons came out of many people, shouting, "You are the Son of God!" But he rebuked them and would not allow them to speak, because they knew he was the Christ.

[42]At daybreak Jesus went out to a solitary place. The people were looking for him and when they came to where he was, they tried to keep him from leaving them. [43]But he said, "I must preach the good news of the kingdom of God to the other towns also, because that is why I was sent." [44]And he kept on preaching in the synagogues of Judea.

Context

The four incidents recorded in this section come from Mark 1:21-39.[22] They summarize Jesus' Capernaum ministry alluded to in 4:23. It is best

---

[22]The four incidents follow the same order as Mark: Luke 4:31-37 (Mark 1:21-28); Luke 4:38-39 (Mark 1:29-31); Luke 4:40-41 (Mark 1:32-34); Luke 4:42-44 (Mark 1:35-39). Luke tied these first three accounts together literarily by the use of the term "rebuke" (cf. 4:35,39, 41, RSV). Luke reproduced all the healing miracles found in Mark except for those in Mark 6:45–8:26 (Luke's great omission).

therefore to see this section as a continuation of the Galilean ministry begun at 4:16 rather than as beginning a new section.[23] Since these events precede the calling of the disciples (cf. 5:1-11 and esp. 6:12-16), they play no role in these events.

Luke 4:31-37 is the first of twenty-one miracle stories in Luke, which serve either a Christological function as in 4:36 or an eschatological one as in 11:20 (cf. 4:43). Even in the latter instances, however, the miracles that reveal the coming of God's kingdom also reveal that the kingdom is here because its King (1:32-33) has come. This first miracle was an exorcism.[24] In telling the story anything that might detract from a Christological emphasis was omitted.

The second ministry story (4:38-39) is another example of Jesus' "authority and power" (4:36), and whereas the first miracle benefited a man, this one benefited a woman. The third account is a summary of Jesus' healings and exorcisms and culminates in the demons' confession that Jesus is the Son of God, which Luke equated with the title Christ (4:41). The final account records Jesus' leaving Capernaum in order to continue his ministry of preaching the gospel of the kingdom.[25] For Luke the account functioned primarily as a summary of Jesus' preaching ministry.[26]

Comments

4:31 Then he went down to Capernaum. Since Nazareth is 1,300 feet above sea level and Capernaum, lying on the Sea of Galilee, is 695 feet below sea level, this is an accurate description of the geographical situation.

A town in Galilee. Again Luke described for his readers the location of Capernaum, as he did earlier with regard to Nazareth (1:26); thus he indicated that his audience was almost certainly non-Judean Gentiles.

On the Sabbath began to teach the people. This shows the habitual character of Jesus' synagogue teaching ministry. Although the term "Sabbath" is plural, Luke usually, if not always, meant by this the singular "Sabbath."

4:32 They were amazed. Compare 9:43; 2:48; 4:22. This reaction is external in nature and does not imply a change of heart.

His message had authority. This refers not so much to the manner of Jesus' teaching, i.e., to his ability to elicit conviction and decision, but to his divine power to heal (4:39) and cast out demons (4:35-36,41). (The term "authority" is

---

[23] For the opposing view see Talbert, *Reading Luke*, 58-61.

[24] There is no set form in the description of exorcisms in Luke. We do not have here a description of the man's condition as in 8:27; 9:39,42; 11:14, nor is attention paid to the healed condition of the man as in 8:35; 9:42. We do have, however, a reference to the amazement caused by the exorcism as in 8:35; 9:43; 11:14.

[25] It is difficult to classify this account. Some call it a story about Jesus and others, due to the saying of Jesus in 4:43, a pronouncement story. For Luke such classification was irrelevant.

[26] Similar summaries or summary-like statements can be found in 4:14-15; 6:17-19; 7:21; 8:1-3; 9:1-2; 11:53-54; 19:47-48; 21:37-38.

used over twenty times in Luke-Acts and is not associated with teaching in any other instance.) Luke lacks the statement "not as the teachers of the law" found in the parallel in Mark 1:22 perhaps because Luke's Gentile audience had no contact with the rabbis or their influence in their teaching of the OT, or perhaps he simply shortened the account. The latter probably is the main reason.

4:33 There was a man possessed by a demon, an evil spirit. Due to the positive way Luke used "spirit" in 2:27; 4:1,14, he qualified Mark's "evil spirit" (1:23) by adding the term "demon."[27]

He cried out at the top of his voice. Compare Luke 9:39.

4:34 What do you want with us? Compare 8:28; John 2:4; Judg 11:12; 2 Sam 16:10; 19:22; 1 Kgs 17:18; 2 Kgs 3:13.

Have you come to destroy us? This may be a question or a statement. There is little difference, if any, in meaning. The demon recognized the "today" of Luke 4:21. God's kingdom had come; thus the demons were being driven out (11:20; 10:17-18), and they knew that the abyss awaited them (8:31; cf. Rev 20:3,9-10).

I know who you are. The demon recognized Jesus as "the Holy One of God," recalling Luke 1:35 (cf. Acts 3:14; John 6:69). That Luke took this to be essentially a synonym for *Christ, Lord, Son, and Son of Man* is evident from Luke 4:41, where the demons were able to say this because they knew that Jesus was the Christ. In 1:35 it is a synonym for "Son of God." We are not told how the demon knew Jesus' identity, but the assumption is that they possessed supernatural knowledge and thus recognized him. Thus they provided a reliable witness to Jesus' identity as Luke pointed out in 4:41.

4:35 Be quiet! This must be understood in light of 4:41 and the secrecy motif. Jesus did not want to be publicly espoused as the Christ due to the political misconceptions associated with that title.

Jesus said sternly. "Said sternly" is literally *rebuked*. This involves not simply a moral censure or rebuke but rather an act of authority and power in which Jesus controlled and judged the demon.

Came out without injuring him. Luke added this statement to the account in order to enhance the miracle and to emphasize that despite the demon's throwing the man down, Jesus' healing was positive in nature.

4:36 All the people were amazed. See comments on 4:32. Compare 5:9; Acts 3:10.

What is this teaching? Literally *word* (*logos*) in the sense of the Hebrew *debar* or "thing." Compare Acts 15:6; 8:21.

With authority and power he gives orders. Luke added "and power," which fits well Jesus' having received "power" through the Spirit (4:14). Luke apparently joined these two terms together, since the summaries in vv. 14,32 use "power" and "authority." In so doing we have a chiasmus: power (4:14); authority

---

[27]This is literally "the spirit of an unclean demon" (RSV) in which "of an unclean demon" is an epexegetical genitive or genitive of apposition. (Cf. Luke 4:35 with Mark 1:26; Luke 8:27 with Mark 5:2; Luke 8:33 with Mark 5:13; Luke 9:1 with Mark 6:7; Luke 9:42a with Mark 9:20, where Luke replaced Mark's "evil [unclean] spirit" with "demon"; but cf. also Luke 8:29 with Mark 5:8; Luke 9:42b with Mark 9:25, where Luke did not.)

(4:32); authority (4:36); power (4:36). Whether this was intentional on Luke's part is impossible to say.

4:37 The spread of Jesus' fame is reported; this fame would spread even more (5:15), and a greater audience is described in 5:17. This audience in turn would be surpassed in 6:17-18 and reach its climax in 7:17.

4:38 Luke in abbreviating his account did not include Mark's "as soon as" (Mark 1:29) as well as the references to Andrew, James, and John, since the disciples had not yet been introduced to the readers.

Simon's mother-in-law. That Peter was married is evident not only from this account in the Synoptic tradition but also from 1 Cor 9:5. Luke switched from the name "Simon" to "Peter" in Luke 6:14.

High fever. Luke intensified the miracle by referring to her fever as "high." He also made clearer than Mark ("told," 1:30) that faith in Jesus' ability to heal is present through an implicit request—"asked [to heal]."

4:39 So he . . . rebuked the fever. This is the only account in Luke where Jesus addressed his healing words to the disease rather than the person. The fever was rebuked as the demon was in Luke 4:35,41. Does this imply that Luke associated this illness with Satan (cf. 13:16)? Although Satan is often associated with illness (Acts 10:38; cf. *Testament of Solomon* 18:20,23), we will see in the next two verses that Luke did differentiate between illness and demon possession. See comments on 7:21.

She got up at once and began to wait on them. This indicates that the healing was instantaneous ("at once" is found in Luke) and complete (see comments on 18:43), and it also serves to emphasize that God's grace is to be followed by gratitude and service (cf. Luke 17:11-19). Luke was fond of pointing out the role of women in service to Jesus,[28] although her service was not directed just to Jesus, as in Matt 8:15, but to the entire group. The term "serve" (*diēkonei*), although not a technical term, is used elsewhere for service for Christ.[29]

4:40 When the sun was setting. Luke omitted the redundant "that evening" of Mark 1:32.

All who had various kinds of sickness. In this and the next verse Luke seems to have distinguished between sickness and demon possession,[30] even if at times they may be connected (13:16; cf. 9:1 with 9:2). The wording of this statement emphasizes the extensiveness of Jesus' healing work."[31]

And laying his hands on each one, he healed them. Although this physical gesture is unknown in the OT healings (though see Deut 34:9), it is common in the NT.[32]

4:41 Moreover, demons came out of many people. Luke 4:40-41 formed a chiasmus with 4:31-39: demon cast out (4:31-37); fever healed (4:38-39); healings (4:40); demons cast out (4:41).

---

[28] Cf. Luke 1:5-80; 2:36-38; 8:1-3; 23:49,55; Acts 9:36-42; 12:12-17; 18:24-28; 21:9.
[29] Luke 8:3; 17:8; Acts 6:2-4; 19:22 (cf. also the noun in Acts 1:17,25; 6:4; 12:25; 20:24; 21:19).
[30] E.g., Luke 6:17-18; 7:21; 8:2; Acts 5:16.
[31] See Tannehill, *Narrative Unity*, 83.
[32] Cf. Luke 5:13; 13:13. Cf. Acts 3:7; 4:30; 5:12; 9:12,17; 28:8.

You are the Son of God! Neither Mark (1:34) nor Matthew (8:16-17) in their parallels to this account mentioned "what" the demons said. Later Mark in 3:11 did reveal that the demons knew that Jesus was the Son of God. Some have suggested this may have been an attempt by the demon to demonstrate superiority over Jesus by showing that he knew Jesus' name. Luke, however, did not allude to anything like this but simply interpreted this as a confession of the true identity of Jesus by an evil but supernatural being.

Because they knew he was the Christ. Since Luke added the statement that the demons knew Jesus was the Christ (cf. Mark 1:34 and Matt 8:16-17), the titles "Son of God" and "Christ" were interchangeable for Luke. This is also true of "Holy One of God" in Luke 4:34. Compare in 1:35 how the "Son of God" is referred to as "Savior . . . Christ the Lord" in 2:11. Because Luke said the demons knew Jesus to be the Christ, this means that the demonic witness to Jesus must be understood as trustworthy.

4:43 I must preach. There was a divine imperative controlling Jesus' ministry. Of all the Evangelists, Luke was most fond of the divine "must" (*dei*).[33]

The good news of the kingdom of God. This is the first occurrence of the expression "kingdom of God" in Luke. It occurs earlier in Mark (1:15) and in Matthew (4:17). Luke, however, chose to introduce it at this point. The expression occurs thirty-one times in Luke, and "kingdom" occurs another six times. Luke made no attempt to define this expression here, for he anticipated that his readers already possessed some understanding of its meaning. Furthermore the preceding material in Luke 1:1–4:42 should help further clarify what his message of God's kingdom entails.

The expression "kingdom of God" should be interpreted dynamically rather than statically, for it involves the dynamic of God's reign rather than a territory with static borders. The term "kingdom" in the Bible usually refers to the *rule* of someone rather than the *territory* controlled (cf. 19:12,15; 23:42). Understood this way, God's kingdom was proclaimed by Jesus and Luke as a present reality (11:14-22; 16:16; 17:20-21) as well as a future hope (11:2; 13:22-30; 22:16-18). The alternatives of either a "realized" understanding of God's kingdom (the kingdom already has come) or a "consistent" understanding (the kingdom is still entirely in the future) are therefore unnecessary. God's kingdom is both present and future. It already has been realized in fulfillment of the OT promises but awaits the final consummation when Jesus returns. In this verse the "good news of the kingdom of God refers to its present realized manifestation.[34] See Introduction 8 (2).

To the other towns also. From 5:12 it is evident that in 5:1f. Luke further explained what this preaching entails.

I was sent. This divine passive meaning *God has sent me* reveals that Jesus possessed a divine calling from birth as the earlier chapters have revealed. Although it does not exclude the idea of an incarnation, it does not expressly teach it.

---

[33] Cf. Luke 2:49; 9:22; 12:12; 13:14,16,33; 17:25; 18:1; 19:5; 21:9; 22:7,37; 24:7,26,44; and the twenty-two times *dei* is found in Acts.

[34] For further discussion see R. H. Stein, *The Method and Message of Jesus' Teachings* (Philadelphia: Westminster, 1978), 60-79.

Two important differences exist between the Lukan and Markan accounts of this summary. Luke added the expression "preach the good news" and the reference to being "sent." In so doing he tied this summary closely to the Isaiah quotation in Luke 4:18. Thus we know that the way Luke understood how 4:18-19 were to be fulfilled was along the lines of 4:31-43.

4:44 He kept on preaching in the synagogues of Judea. Some manuscripts read "Galilee" instead of Judea, but this is no doubt due to attempts by scribes to be more exact. Jesus was not in Judea proper but in Galilee. The term "Judea," however, can be interpreted as referring to the country of the Jews in a comprehensive sense (see comments on 1:5). As in 4:18-19 "preaching" is a synonym here for "preaching the good news" in 4:43 and probably also for "teaching" in 4:31 (cf. also 13:22). All three terms are used interchangeably in Luke-Acts (cf. 8:1; 9:2,6). In Acts the early church's preaching is often described as "preaching the good news" and "teaching" (cf. Acts 5:42; 15:35; 28:31; cf. also Luke 20:1). As a result the popular distinction between the early church's *kerygma* (preaching) and *didache* (teaching) made so popular by C. H. Dodd has no basis in Luke-Acts because for Luke they were essentially synonyms.

The Lukan Message

Within this passage we encounter two major Lukan emphases. The main emphasis is clearly Christological. This is evident by comments that draw the readers' attention to Jesus such as: "They were amazed at his teaching" (4:32); "What is this teaching?" (4:36); "The news about him spread throughout the surrounding area" (4:37). This is further witnessed to by Jesus' unique authority: "his message had authority" (4:32); Jesus had authority over the demons (4:33-36,41); Jesus has authority over the disease (4:38-40). We also find the demons confessing Jesus as "the Holy One of God" and "Son of God" (4:34,41), which are synonyms for Christ (4:41). These confessions are clearly trustworthy in that Luke said the demons truly knew who Jesus was (4:41). Luke also heightened the miracles by enhancing them ("without injuring him," 4:35) and by focusing our attention upon Jesus by omitting a description of the demonic man's healing and references to the disciples. Jesus is described in our account by three titles that are essentially synonyms in Luke: Holy One of God (4:34), Son of God (4:41), and Christ (4:41).

A second major emphasis of Luke was to clarify for his readers what the programmatic sermon of 4:18-19 meant. Luke 4:31-44 is Luke's commentary on how Jesus' self-proclaimed messianic mission is to be interpreted. This is most clear from 4:43, where Jesus' words recall 4:18-19 (preach the good news, sent). This proclamation of the good news can also be described as the proclamation of the good news of God's kingdom. Jesus' message in 4:18-19 is the announcement of the fulfillment of the messianic promises, i.e., of the coming of God's kingdom. The manifestation of the realization of God's kingdom is revealed in Jesus' healings and especially in his mastery of the demons. The implications of the latter will become even clearer in 11:20.

(3) The Call of the First Disciples (5:1-11)

[1]One day as Jesus was standing by the Lake of Gennesaret, with the people crowding around him and listening to the word of God, [2]he saw at the water's edge two boats, left there by the fishermen, who were washing their nets. [3]He got into one of the boats, the one belonging to Simon, and asked him to put out a little from shore. Then he sat down and taught the people from the boat. [4]When he had finished speaking, he said to Simon, "Put out into deep water, and let down the nets for a catch." [5]Simon answered, "Master, we've worked hard all night and haven't caught anything. But because you say so, I will let down the nets." [6]When they had done so, they caught such a large number of fish that their nets began to break. [7]So they signaled their partners in the other boat to come and help them, and they came and filled both boats so full that they began to sink. [8]When Simon Peter saw this, he fell at Jesus' knees and said, "Go away from me, Lord; I am a sinful man!" [9]For he and all his companions were astonished at the catch of fish they had taken, [10]and so were James and John, the sons of Zebedee, Simon's partners.

Then Jesus said to Simon, "Don't be afraid; from now on you will catch men." [11]So they pulled their boats up on shore, left everything and followed him.

Context

Having given a brief summary and overview of Jesus' mission in 4:16-44, Luke began to describe the appropriate response to Jesus' preaching in 5:1-11.[35] Since he had already mentioned Simon in 4:38-39, and since

---

[35]The origin of Luke 5:1-11 has been much discussed. There are several parallels between it and other Gospel accounts. These include 5:1-3 and Mark 4:1-2; Luke 5:3-9 and John 21:1-11; and Luke 5:10-11 and Mark 1:16-20. The first parallel is less significant than the other two. With regard to the second, involving the miraculous haul of fish, R. E. Brown lists ten specific points of similarity (*The Gospel according to John*, AB [Garden City: Doubleday, 1970], 1090. See also J. A. Bailey, *The Traditions Common to the Gospels of Luke and John*, NovTSup 7 [Leiden: Brill, 1963]: 12-17), but A. Plummer points out seven points of dissimilarity (*A Critical and Exegetical Commentary on the Gospel according to St. Luke*, ICC [Edinburgh: T & T Clark, 1896], 147). There is also much debate about whether we are dealing here with two separate incidents or two versions of the same account.

With regard to the third, the similarity between Luke 5:10-11 and Mark 1:16-20 is obvious. In both we encounter Simon, James, and John; in both we have a call to "catch men," although the wording is slightly different; and in both the disciples left "everything" and followed Jesus. Apparently Luke 5:10-11 is the Lukan version of Mark 1:16-20. The omission of Mark 1:16-20 in Luke's Gospel suggests that this account served for Luke as a substitute for that material. (Luke 5:1-3 may also be the reason there is no parallel to Mark

Simon would become the apostles' leader, Luke told the story of the calling of the first disciples. Luke also used 5:1-11 as an introductory paradigm for what is to follow in 5:12–6:16. After 5:1-11 Luke followed the
Markan order.[36] The only difference between Luke and Mark involves the
reversal of the last two accounts. Luke did this in order to have 6:17-19
serve as a summary conclusion for what precedes and as an introduction
for what follows. Literarily, these passages are tied together by the term
egeneto in 5:1,12,17; 6:1,6,12.

Some commentators have expressed surprise at Peter's response. Readers tend to expect a sense of awe and appreciation for the catch of fish
rather than a confession of sinfulness. Yet if we understand this account
not so much as a miracle or pronouncement story but rather as a theophany involving a call to service, the response is very appropriate. In a
theophany a confession of one's sinfulness and the title "Lord" (5:8) are
most fitting.[37] Such a theophany often occurs before a divine call to service, and here it foreshadows 6:12-16 and Peter's future role in the
church. There is no need to see in this account a postresurrection appearance of Jesus read back into Jesus' life.

Comments

5:1   By the Lake of Gennesaret.   The term "Gennesaret" refers to a fertile,
heavily populated area at the northwestern corner of the Sea of Galilee. Capernaum
lies at the lake's northern tip. The district's name was at times extended to the lake
so that it could be called the Lake of Gennesaret. In light of the setting, this description serves primarily a geographical purpose rather than a theological one.

Word of God.   This is the first appearance of the expression in the Gospel. It
should be interpreted as a subjective genitive, i.e., as the word that comes from
God. We also find this expression in 8:11,21 (where it is not found in the Markan
parallels) and in 11:28, which is unique to Luke.[38] In contrast it appears only once
in Mark (7:13) and John (10:35) and possibly once in Matthew (15:6). The "word
of God" refers to the gospel message as Acts 8:12,14 reveals.

5:2   Two boats.   This prepares us for the miracle in 5:6-7.

By the fishermen.   Luke did not mention Andrew (cf. Mark 1:16), but the
plural leaves room for him. He may have omitted mentioning Andrew in order to
focus the readers' attention on the central figure—Simon Peter.

4:1-2 in Luke's Gospel.) It also appears that Luke had access to tradition concerning a
miraculous haul of fish, not found in Mark, which he added to the account. It is uncertain,
however, whether Luke 5:3-9 and John 21:1-11 are two versions of the same incident or two
traditions of different incidents whose wordings have mutually influenced each other.

[36]Luke 5:12-16 (Mark 1:40-45); Luke 5:17-26 (Mark 2:1-12); Luke 5:27-32 (Mark 2:13-
17); Luke 5:33-39 (Mark 2:18-22); Luke 6:1-5 (Mark 2:23-28); Luke 6:6-11 (Mark 3:1-6);
Luke 6:12-16 (Mark 3:13-19); Luke 6:17-19 (Mark 3:7-12).

[37]Cf. Isa 6:5; Exod 3:4-6; Judg 6:22-23; 13:22-23; Ezek 1:28-2:2; Rev 1:17.

[38]"Word of God" also appears fourteen times in Acts (4:31; 6:2,7; 8:14; 11:1; 12:24;
13:5,7,44,46,48; 16:32; 17:13; 18:11).

5:3 **And asked him to put out a little from shore.** Even though more disciples than Simon Peter would be involved in this (for the command to "let down [5:4]" is plural as is "the nets"—literally *your* [plural] *nets*), Jesus' conversation was directed to Simon, who was the leader. One should not see in the expression "put out [into the deep]" any allegorical nuances.[39]

The one belonging to Simon. Luke did not mention any of the other men, such as James and John (5:10), in order to focus the readers' attention on the calling of the most famous and important disciple. The following references to Simon in 5:4-5,8-10 continue to emphasize his importance.

5:5 **Simon answered, "Master."** This title (Greek *epistatēs*) was a favorite of Luke and was used only by him in the NT (cf. 8:24,45; 9:33,49; 17:13). Whereas the title "teacher" in Luke was used of Jesus only by strangers, "Master" was used only by Jesus' followers and reveals better his authority and might. Luke also avoided completely the use of the title "Rabbi" for Jesus.

We've worked hard all night and haven't caught anything. This is not to be understood as a reply of disobedience, for the use of the title "Master" and the next statement in this verse reveal Simon's obedience. In light of his previous experience in 4:38-41, Simon agreed to do something that at face value appears foolish. This statement and the next heighten the following miracle.

5:6 **Such a large number of fish . . . nets began to break.** These two statements stress the size of the catch. Is this "great multitude" of fish a symbol of the "great multitude" who would come to Jesus due to the preaching of Peter and the other disciples? Luke gave evidence that he might have been thinking this way.[40]

5:7 This verse further heightens the miraculous nature of the catch by mentioning the need for another boat and the fact that both boats were about to sink. The latter statement probably is hyperbolic since the remaining verses show no concern about the possibility of sinking. Where the other boat was at the time (nearby on the lake, on shore) is not stated. It was unimportant for Luke's purpose.

5:8 **Simon Peter . . . fell at Jesus' knees.** This was an appropriate posture in a theophany when one encountered the Lord. Objections have been raised that this would not have been physically possible to do in a boat, but the recent discovery in the Sea of Galilee of a boat twenty-six and a half feet long and seven and a half feet wide dating from Jesus' day has refuted this.[41] Luke provided at this point the full name by which Simon is known to the readers of his Gospel because this event marks the call of the great apostolic leader.

Go away from me, Lord; I am a sinful man. In the presence of this theophany Peter responded much like Isaiah did (cf. Isa 6:5). The request is not to be taken literally, for where would Peter have expected Jesus to go? Rather it is idiomatic for "Lord, be merciful to me a sinner" or "Forgive me" or something like, "What is a Holy One like you doing with a sinner like me?" Peter's sense of his own sinfulness was not due to disobedience in Luke 5:5a but to a general unworthiness (cf. 7:6; Job 42:5-6) as he confronted the Lord's might and majesty.

---

[39] See J. Nolland, *Luke 1–9:20*, WBC (Waco: Word, 1989), 222.

[40] Cf. Luke 6:17; 23:27; Acts 14:1; 17:4; also 4:32; 5:14; 6:2,5; 15:12,30.

[41] See S. Wachsmann, "The Galilee Boat—2,000-Year-Old Hull Recovered Intact," *BAR* 14.5 (1988): 18-33.

5:9-10 That Luke intended his readers to see the catch of fish as miraculous is evident by Peter's response and now by that of his companions.

5:10 And so were James and John. These two are encountered again in 9:54 and Acts 12:2. They appear together with Peter in Luke 8:51; 9:28, and Peter and John appear together in 22:8; Acts 3:1,3-4,11; 4:13,19; 8:14.

Then Jesus said to Simon, "Don't be afraid." Fear is a normal reaction to the experience of God's glory. These words of reassurance were frequently part of a theophany.[42] They brought the assurance of the forgiveness of sins.

From now on. A Lukan expression (cf. 1:48; 12:52; 22:18,69).

You will catch men. Some argue that the fishing metaphor is a poor one because of what fishermen do to the fish they catch, whereas a shepherd metaphor would be much more positive (cf. Mark 6:34). The fishing analogy can be used negatively as Jer 16:16; Amos 4:2; 1 QH 5:7-9 indicate. However, this metaphor should not be pressed beyond the one basic point of analogy, namely, that just as fishermen catch fish, so Peter would catch people for his Lord. The shepherd metaphor is not without its own problems, for shepherds raise sheep not just for their wool but also for their meat.

Is this metaphor of fishing for disciples directed only to Peter in this passage? In Mark 1:17 it is addressed to Simon and Andrew, and the implication is that when James and John left their nets (1:19-20), they did so to follow Jesus and to be fishers of men as well (cf. Matt 4:18-22). That Luke spoke of "their" leaving everything and following Jesus in the next verse implies that James and John also were included in the call to be fishers of men. If Luke had sought to apply this metaphor to Peter alone, he would have had to make this clearer to his readers, for they would have interpreted this passage in light of their knowledge of the tradition (cf. Luke 1:4) such as found in Mark.

5:11 So they . . . left everything and followed him. Whereas Mark 1:20 has "left their father Zebedee in the boat with the hired men and followed him" and Matt 4:22 has "immediately they left the boat and their father and followed him," Luke pointed out that they left "everything."[43] The term "followed" is frequently used to denote Christian discipleship in Luke.[44] For Luke everyone who is a Christian is called to "follow Jesus," both apostles and nonapostles. The particular kind of calling may vary, but all are called to the same commitment. The ability to follow Jesus assumes the forgiveness that enables one to follow. This is evident from Luke 5:27-32, where Levi followed Jesus (5:27-28), for 5:32 implies that Levi was one of the tax collectors and sinners who repented and thus received the forgiveness of sins (1:77; 3:3).

The Lukan Message

In this account Luke sought once again to demonstrate to his readers Jesus' greatness. Like God the Father, Jesus possesses omniscience. Although experienced fishermen with all their wisdom and skill knew that

---

[42]Cf. Luke 1:13,30; 2:10; 8:50; 12:32; Acts 18:9; 27:24.
[43]Cf. Luke 5:28; 14:33; 18:22,28; 21:4; as well as 9:57-62; Acts 2:45; 4:32,34.
[44]Cf. Luke 5:27-28; 9:23,49,57,59,61; 18:22,28,43.

there should be no fish present, Jesus without any such experience knew
that there were in fact fish there. Peter recognized through this experience
that he was in the presence of the divine. As a result the title of respect
and authority, "Master" (5:5), now gave way to the title "Lord" (5:8) and
to the acknowledgment of human frailty and sinfulness.

Along with this theophany is also a call to service much like we find in
Isa 6:1-13. The Lord in his glory appeared to Peter (cf. Luke 5:5-7 with
Isa 6:1-4), and this is followed by a sense of sinfulness and unworthiness
(cf. Luke 5:8-9 with Isa 6:5-7) and then by a divine commissioning (cf.
Luke 5:10-11 with Isa 6:8-13). Peter's call to follow Jesus in this account
serves a twofold purpose for Luke. First, it satisfies the historical interest
of Luke's readers by telling them about the experiences and calling of the
greatest and most famous apostle, the apostle Peter. Even as Christians
today are interested in learning about the early apostles, so Luke's readers
were as well. Second, Luke used this incident as a paradigm to show what
it means to be a Christian. Being a Christian involves following Jesus and
leaving everything (Luke 5:11).

(4) Jesus' Healing of a Leper (5:12-16)

[12]**While Jesus was in one of the towns, a man came along who was covered
with leprosy. When he saw Jesus, he fell with his face to the ground and begged
him, "Lord, if you are willing, you can make me clean."**

[13]**Jesus reached out his hand and touched the man. "I am willing," he said.
"Be clean!" And immediately the leprosy left him.**

[14]**Then Jesus ordered him, "Don't tell anyone, but go, show yourself to the
priest and offer the sacrifices that Moses commanded for your cleansing, as a
testimony to them."**

[15]**Yet the news about him spread all the more, so that crowds of people came
to hear him and to be healed of their sicknesses. [16]But Jesus often withdrew to
lonely places and prayed.**

Context

With this account Luke returned to the sequence of Markan stories he
had been following in 4:31-44 (Mark 1:21-39). He continued this
sequence from Luke 5:12 to 6:19 (Mark 1:40–3:12).[45] Thus the Lukan
theological emphasis is seen primarily in the content of these accounts
rather than in their order.

The present account may have been placed next to Luke 5:1-11 due to
the similarity between Peter's response in 5:8 and the leper's in 5:12. In
his abbreviation of the Markan account Luke produced a more rounded

---

[45]The rationale for the order of events in 5:12–6:19 is due less to a particular theological
or literary purpose on Luke's part than to the fact that this order is found in his source (Mark
1:40–3:12).

miracle story. This and 17:11-19 are the only accounts in his Gospel involving the healing of lepers.

Comments

5:12 While Jesus was in one of the towns. This picks up 4:43. "One of" is a common Lukan expression and ties this account with the following (5:17; cf. also 8:22; 13:10; 20:1).

A man came along who was covered with leprosy. This almost certainly does not refer to Hansen's disease or what most people today understand as leprosy. It most probably was some sort of skin disease, such as psoriasis, which caused inflammation and scaly, splotchy skin. The OT background for understanding the incident comes from Lev 13–14 (cf. Num 5:2-3; 12:9-15; 2 Kgs 7:3-9; 15:5). Victims of leprosy in biblical times were ostracized from cities and towns and from interaction with others. This continued into NT times as Luke 17:12 reveals. It is uncertain whether Luke intended to heighten the miracle by his description of the man as "covered with leprosy" (cf. 4:38).

He fell with his face to the ground and begged him. The posture of the man is an expression of reverence or respect.[46] It is also found in 17:16 (cf. also 8:41; Acts 5:10; 9:4; 10:25). Luke apparently changed the Markan expression in order to better fit the LXX terminology.

Lord. This is an interesting Matthew-Luke agreement against Mark that is fairly natural since it makes Mark's statement, which can be either indirect or direct discourse, into a clear direct discourse. In the original setting this title probably was one of respect such as "Sir," but for Luke and his readers the more pregnant meaning and significance of the term "Lord" would have been understood. See comments on 6:46.

If you are willing, you can make me clean. As in the previous account, there is a recognition here of Jesus' divine ability. In the previous account his omniscience was highlighted; here his omnipotence was the emphasis.

5:13 Luke omitted "filled with compassion" (Mark 1:41) in his abbreviation of the account. This corresponds well with his tendency to eliminate references to Jesus' emotions.[47] He also eliminated Mark's "strong warning" in Luke 5:14 (cf. Mark 1:43). In so doing he focused the reader's attention more on the power and will of Jesus than on his emotions.[48]

Be clean! Jesus uttered only one word (the Greek consists of only one word), and the leprosy left.

And immediately the leprosy left him. All three parallel accounts contain the term "immediately" and thus heighten the miracle and emphasize Jesus' power.

5:14 Don't tell anyone. Luke in his abbreviation of the account did not describe the young man's disobedience of the command (cf. Mark 1:45). The command is understandable in its historical setting if Jesus wanted to avoid the crowds coming to him simply to seek healing without regard to the message that this healing symbolized.

---

[46] Of reverence (Gen 17:3,17; Lev 9:24; Num 16:22; Jos 5:14; 7:6,10); of respect (Ruth 2:10; Num 14:5; 16:4).

[47] Cf. Luke 6:10; 9:11,48; 18:16-17,22; 22:40; 23:46.

[48] So Fitzmyer, *Luke*, 95, 574.

But go, show yourself to the priest. Compare Luke 17:14. The reason for this instruction is found in Lev 14:2-32. Priests alone could legally readmit into the community those who had contracted leprosy.

That Moses commanded. This fits well the Lukan emphasis that the OT law continues to function as a guide for the believer (see comments on 1:6).[49]

As a testimony to them. This can be understood in several ways. The "to them" can refer to the "priest(s)" or to the "people." If it refers to the former, it is for a testimony to show that he was healed. If it refers to the latter, it is for a testimony to Jesus' power. In the original setting Jesus probably meant the former due to what had been said earlier in the verse, but in Luke's setting the latter aspect clearly played a role. For Luke the healing was a testimony to Jesus' authority and power (4:36), but in light of his concern for keeping the law, the former meaning was also important to the Evangelist. The expression can also be understood positively as a testimony "for" them or negatively as "against" them. We have an example of the latter in 9:5, but the Greek wording there is different. "For" them probably is best understood both in the original situation and in Luke.

5:15 **Yet the news spread all the more.** See comments on 4:15.

Crowds of people came to hear him and to be healed of their sicknesses. Luke placed Jesus' preaching ministry before his healing ministry.

5:16 **But Jesus often withdrew to lonely places.** The tense of this verb and the next (both imperfect periphrastics) emphasizes that this was a regular practice of Jesus. Since Luke continued to speak of Jesus' ministry in the cities (7:11-17,36-50; 8:1), he omitted Mark 1:45b.

And pray. Luke omitted the Markan reference to Jesus' prayer in Luke 4:42 (Mark 1:35). Instead he introduced this strong Lukan emphasis here.[50]

The Lukan Message

The major differences between this and the Markan account can be explained by Luke's abbreviation of the story. The changes that are theologically important involve Luke's recording of the crowd's reaction (5:15), his mention of Jesus' praying (5:16), and the address "Lord" (5:12). The crowd's positive reaction toward Jesus and his ministry is a frequent Lukan emphasis (see comments on 4:15) and stands in sharp contrast with the attitude of the Pharisees and teachers of the law in the following accounts (5:17,21,30,33; 6:2,7). Concerning prayer, Luke had on a number of occasions pointed out its importance (see comments on 3:21 and Introduction 8 [7]). The believer's need to keep the law is seen again in 5:14. Although this is found in his source (Mark 1:44; cf. Matt 8:4), it is an especially important emphasis for Luke.

Christologically our passage once again portrays Jesus' great authority and might (4:32,36). Whereas his divine power was manifested in his unique knowledge in the previous account, here it is manifested in his healing ability. Luke heightened this power and authority by omitting the

---

[49] J. A. Fitzmyer, *Luke the Theologian* (Mahweh, N.J.: Paulist, 1989), 176-87.
[50] Cf. Luke 3:21; 6:12; 9:18; 11:1; 22:41; 23:46. See Introduction 8 (7).

Markan reference to Jesus' being "filled with compassion" (1:41) and perhaps by pointing out that the man was "covered with leprosy" (5:12). The former causes the account to focus more pointedly on the Lord's (5:12) ability to heal (5:13). In light of 5:8, the use of the vocative "Lord" is more than just a polite form of address. The Jesus revealed in the previous account is the "Lord," possessing the divine ability to know what human experts cannot (5:5-10) and to heal whomever he wills. There is no limitation to his "can" (5:12) other than how he "wills" to exercise his power.

2. The Beginning of Controversy (5:17–6:11)

Having shown in 4:16–5:16 how Jesus' ministry involved preaching the good news (4:31-32,43-44), healing (4:33-36,38-41), and enlisting disciples to carry on Jesus' ministry, Luke then illustrated the hostility Jesus encountered (cf. 4:28-30). He did so by including the five controversy stories found in his source (cf. Mark 2:1–3:6).

(1) Conflict over Jesus' Forgiveness of Sins (5:17-26)

[17]One day as he was teaching, Pharisees and teachers of the law, who had come from every village of Galilee and from Judea and Jerusalem, were sitting there. And the power of the Lord was present for him to heal the sick. [18]Some men came carrying a paralytic on a mat and tried to take him into the house to lay him before Jesus. [19]When they could not find a way to do this because of the crowd, they went up on the roof and lowered him on his mat through the tiles into the middle of the crowd, right in front of Jesus.

[20]When Jesus saw their faith, he said, "Friend, your sins are forgiven."

[21]The Pharisees and the teachers of the law began thinking to themselves, "Who is this fellow who speaks blasphemy? Who can forgive sins but God alone?"

[22]Jesus knew what they were thinking and asked, "Why are you thinking these things in your hearts? [23]Which is easier: to say, 'Your sins are forgiven,' or to say, 'Get up and walk'? [24]But that you may know that the Son of Man has authority on earth to forgive sins. ... " He said to the paralyzed man, "I tell you, get up, take your mat and go home." [25]Immediately he stood up in front of them, took what he had been lying on and went home praising God. [26]Everyone was amazed and gave praise to God. They were filled with awe and said, "We have seen remarkable things today."

Context

In 5:17–6:11 we have five controversy stories that contrast the people's enthusiastic reaction toward Jesus here and earlier (4:31–5:15) with the negative reaction of the Pharisees and teachers of the law. The culmination of these controversy stories is found in 6:7,11. The source for these four accounts is Mark 2:1–3:6, but the setting is enlarged by Luke from

Capernaum (Mark 2:1) to "every village of Galilee and . . . Judea and Jerusalem" (Luke 5:17) in order to explain the presence of the Pharisees and scribes who had come to see Jesus.

Hitherto Jesus had been portrayed as healing (4:38-39,40-41; 5:12-16), exorcizing (4:31-37), and performing a nature miracle (5:4-9), but now in this and the next account attention is focused upon Jesus' divine prerogative to forgive sins. Luke heightened this aspect of Jesus' authority by his addition of the word "alone" (5:21). The divine ability to forgive sins is again portrayed in 7:36-50. The reader has been prepared for the present account by Jesus' paradigmatic sermon in 4:18 that includes Jesus' mission "to proclaim freedom for the prisoners" (see comments on 4:18).

As the early church proclaimed and lived out the implications of these incidents from Jesus' life, various controversies arose between the early church and its antagonists.[51]

Comments

5:17 Pharisees. Whereas Mark noted later (cf. Mark 2:6) the presence of teachers of the law (who were primarily Pharisaic in orientation), Luke referred to them at the beginning of the account. This is the first mention of this group in his Gospel. The Pharisees were the most influential of the three major Jewish sects (the other two being the Sadducees and the Essenes). We first read of them in the second century B.C. (see Josephus, *Antiquities* 13.10.5-6 [13.288-98]). In contrast to the Sadducees, the Pharisees believed in the resurrection, the existence of angels and demons (20:27; Acts 23:6-9), predestination as well as free will, and the validity of both the written and the oral law. Politically they were more conservative than the Sadducees, but religiously they were more liberal due to their acceptance of the oral law.

And teachers of the law. This term (*nomodidaskaloi*) occurs only here in the Gospels and may be a synonym for "teachers of the law" (*grammateis*) in Luke 5:21. Although one could be a "teacher of the law" or scribe and not a Pharisee, most scribes were in fact Pharisees and leaders in this sect.

From every village of Galilee and from Judea and Jerusalem. Whereas Mark (2:1) mentioned Capernaum as the specific scene (cf. also Matt 9:1 with 4:13), Luke, who already had mentioned Jesus' activity in that city in Luke 4:23,31, enlarged the scene by designating the areas from which the Pharisees and teachers of the law came. Judea and Jerusalem were used here in the narrow, more restricted sense (see comments on 1:5). Luke may have referred to Judea and Jerusalem at this point to

---

[51] Some have sought to explain the present account as the result of an early conflation of two different stories: a miracle story (5:17-20b,24c-26) and a pronouncement story (5:20c-24b). Bultmann claims that 5:20c-24 (cf. Mark 2:5b-10) was a secondary edition to the miracle story (*The History of the Synoptic Tradition* [New York: Harper, 1968], 14-16, 66). Such views, however, are based on the arbitrary, form-critical assumption that stories that do not possess a "pure" form cannot be original. With regard to Luke, clearly this account always was considered a unity. As to the claim that later controversies in the early church gave rise to this and the following controversy stories, the reverse more likely is true.

alert his readers that what happened here in the controversy stories foreshadowed what would happen later in Jerusalem.

And the power of the Lord was present for him[52] **to heal the sick.** This comment clearly reveals Luke's theological emphasis of the Spirit's coming upon Jesus (cf. 3:21-22; 4:1,14,18-21,36). It prepares the reader for the miracle of healing that is to follow. The term "Lord" here refers to God/YHWH as in 1:6,9,11,15, 16. The Spirit and "power" are intimately connected in Luke (see comments on 1:17). Power is associated with healing in 4:36; 6:19; 8:46; 9:1; Acts 3:12; 4:7.

5:18 Luke omitted Mark's description of the crowded house and doorway that necessitated lowering the man through the roof. He may have assumed that his readers, like modern readers who read the present account in light of the Markan account, were familiar enough with the story (cf. 1:4) to supply this detail. Or Luke may have thought it sufficient simply to tell about a large crowd in 5:17,19.

5:19   Lowered him on his mat through the tiles. Luke here "contextualized" the tradition for Theophilus and provided a thought-for-thought translation, whereas Mark in his description (cf. Mark 2:4) provided a word-for-word translation. Both conveyed accurately what they wanted to say, i.e., that the paralytic was lowered into Jesus' presence through the roof. Mark, however, portrayed a typical Galilean home with a mud-thatch roof that must be dug through, whereas Luke portrayed a home such as that in which Theophilus lived, which had a tile roof.[53]

5:20   When Jesus saw their faith. This included the faith both of the paralytic and his companions. This faith[54] in the original setting would have been a faith in Jesus as one come from God who could heal. For Luke and his readers this would have involved a greater understanding of who Jesus is and would have involved faith in him as the risen Lord. The faith of the paralytic and the men was manifested by their "works," i.e., their removal of the tiles to lower the paralytic. A favorite expression of Luke was "your faith has 'saved' you" (cf. 7:50; 8:48; 17:19; 18:42). For the tie between faith and miracles, cf. 7:9,50; 8:25,40,50; 17:5, 6,19; 18:42.

Friend, your sins are forgiven. This is not to be understood as a "divine passive" or circumlocution for "God forgives you."[55] This is evident from the following verses (esp. 5:24) where Jesus' words are understood to be an implicit claim of equality with God (5:21; 7:49; cf. John 5:18; 10:33), i.e., Jesus himself is understood as having forgiven the man his sins. The Greek perfect tense of "are forgiven" emphasizes the abiding state of this forgiveness.

---

[52]There are several variants for him/αὐτόν due to scribes' having interpreted "Lord" as referring to Jesus rather than God/YHWH and due to their seeing the pronoun as the object rather than the subject of the infinitive "to heal." The NIV text correctly translates the better reading.

[53]I. H. Marshall (*The Gospel of Luke*, NIGTC [Grand Rapids: Eerdmans, 1978], 213) suggests that we may have other examples of such contextualization in 6:48; 12:57-59; and 21:29.

[54]The noun "faith" is also found in Luke 7:9,50; 8:25,48; 17:5,6,19; 18:42; 22:32, whereas the verb is found in 1:20,45; 8:12,13,50; 20:5; 24:25 (cf. also 16:11; 22:67).

[55]For the view that this is a divine passive, see J. Jeremias, *New Testament Theology* (New York: Scribner's, 1971), 10-11, and Nolland, *Luke 1–9:20*, 235.

5:21 The Pharisees and the teachers of the law. The word translated "teachers of the law" is not the one so translated in Luke 5:17. Probably this word (*grammateis*) would better be translated here as "scribes" to show the difference. The pairing of the scribes and Pharisees is also found in 5:30; 6:7; 11:53; 15:2 (cf. Acts 23:9). We find, in addition, a strong criticism of the Pharisees in Luke 7:30; 11:39-44; 12:1; and 16:14.

Who is this fellow? This unspoken thought, reported by the "omniscient" Gospel writer, is the key to understanding this passage. This crucial question will be answered in the following verses. Jesus is the Son of Man who possesses the divine prerogative to forgive sin and the divine power to heal. Luke's wording of this and the next phrase emphasizes the Christological nature of this question more than Mark 2:7 does. Compare Luke 7:49; 8:25; and 9:9 (cf. also 4:36) for this same question.

Who speaks blasphemy? This is a frequent charge leveled against Jesus (cf. Mark 14:64; John 5:18; 10:33,36). There are no OT analogies to Jesus' actions here. Traditional Protestant practice has, on the basis of this passage, made a clear distinction between a pastor's "pronouncement" of God's forgiveness of sins and the direct forgiving of sins by the pastor/priest. The latter is not acknowledged. Consequently, passages such as Matt 16:19; 18:18; and John 20:23 are interpreted in light of this.

Who can forgive sins but God alone? Luke by his addition of "alone" indicates that Jesus' actions put him on a par with God! Luke believed that God alone can forgive sins just as the scribes and Pharisees did. But Luke also believed that Jesus can forgive sins. The Christological implications are not stated but are clear.

5:22 Jesus knew what they were thinking. Jesus' awareness of the scribes thoughts need not imply a "divine omniscience," particularly since none of the Evangelists made anything of it. However, in Luke 7:36-50 such knowledge serves to show that Jesus is indeed a prophet, and this probably is the sense here. Compare 2:35; 6:8; 9:47; 24:38.

5:23 Which is easier? To make sense of this counterquestion[56] and the next verses we must distinguish between what is easier to say and what is easier to do. It is easier to say, "Your sins are forgiven" than, "Get up and walk" because the legitimacy of the former cannot be disproven whereas the latter can if no healing takes place. However, since God alone can forgive sins and since numerous people, both in and out of the Bible, have performed healings, the former is more difficult to do. Luke understood that if God granted Jesus power to work this miracle, then God himself supported Jesus' claim that he can forgive sins.[57]

5:24 Traditionally 5:24a and 5:24c are interpreted as said by Jesus to the Pharisees and 5:24b as directed by the Evangelist to the reader.[58] The fact that elsewhere the title Son of Man appears almost exclusively on the lips of Jesus argues against it

---

[56]For other examples of Jesus' use of a counterquestion in Luke, cf. 5:34; 6:3-4,9; 7:40-42; 10:26; 11:18-19; 13:15-16; 14:3-5; 20:3-4,24.

[57]See Stein, *Method and Message of Jesus' Teachings*, 23-25.

[58]More recently it has been suggested that the entire verse should be seen as an editorial comment directed to the reader (C. P. Cerokee, "Is Mark 2,10 a Saying of Jesus?" *CBQ* 22 [1960]: 369-90, and Nolland, *Luke 1–9:20*, 237).

as an editorial comment here. In its present location Luke (and Mark) certainly did not think of this as an editorial comment, for he was not addressing his reader, Theophilus, in 5:24a but only in 5:24b. Usually such editorial comments addressed to the readers are clearly delineated (cf. Mark 13:14; John 19:35; 20:30-31).

Son of Man. In verses where this title is used[59] it is not an additional comment by the Evangelist, so it is unlikely that its appearance here is editorial in nature. By introducing "Son of Man" without explanation, Luke indicated that this title was known to his readers. That the Son of Man refers to Jesus in our passage is clear. Whether it was a circumlocution for "I" or a specific title in the original context is debated. Nevertheless for all four Gospel writers it was clearly understood as a title. And as a title the setting given to it[60] indicates that the Evangelist interpreted this title in light of the reference to "one like a son of man" in Dan 7:13-14. Of the sixty-nine times this title is found in the Gospels, it is always found on the lips of Jesus or in Luke 24:7 and John 12:34 in reference to Jesus' earlier use of the title as a self-designation. Such usage argues strongly in favor of its authenticity.[61]

Has authority on earth to forgive sins. Luke referred earlier to Jesus' authority and power to heal and exorcize (Luke 4:14,32,36), but here that authority was extended to the divine prerogative of forgiving sins.

Get up, take . . . and go home. This is paralleled by "stood up . . . took . . . and went home" in the next verse.

5:25 Immediately he stood up. Luke, by adding "immediately" to his description of the healing, sought to emphasize the instantaneous nature of Jesus' healing. See comments on 18:43. Thus Jesus' claim to be able to forgive sins was immediately verified.

In front of them. This stresses the certainty and proof of the healing.

And went home praising God. The term "praise" can also mean *to glorify.* Only Luke had this further description of the paralytic's activity,[62] for Luke wanted to tell his readers that this is the proper response of those who experience God's grace.

5:26 Everyone was amazed and gave praise to God. Luke reiterated that praise is the proper response to this manifestation of God's grace.

They were filled with awe. "Awe" or fear is a common response to witnessing God's power.[63]

We have seen remarkable things today. This indicates that the "today" of 4:21 means *since the events of 3:1f.* and refers to the present period of salvation history in which God's kingdom has now come.[64]

---

[59] Luke 6:5,22; 7:34; 9:22,26,44,58; 11:30; 12:8,10,40; 17:22,24,26,30; 18:8,31; 19:10; 21:27,36; 22:22,48,69; 24:7.

[60] Luke 9:26; 12:8,40; 17:22,24,26,30; 18:8; 21:27,36; 22:69.

[61] See Stein, *Method and Message of Jesus' Teachings,* 133-48.

[62] The Lukan nature of this emphasis on praise is evident from Luke 2:20; 5:26; 7:16; 13:13; 17:15; 18:43; 23:47; Acts 4:21; 11:18; 21:20, which are (except for Luke 5:26) all unique to Luke (cf. also 4:15; 13:17; Acts 3:9; 13:48).

[63] Cf. Luke 2:9; 8:25,35,37; 9:34; cf. also 1:13,30; 2:10; 5:10; 8:50.

[64] For other instances where Luke alone used "today," cf. Luke 2:11; 4:21; 13:32-33; 19:5,9; 22:61; 23:43.

The Lukan Message

Although we find several Lukan emphases in this passage, the main emphasis is clearly Christological. Whereas Jesus' authority and power to heal and exorcize demons have already been shown, now Luke revealed Jesus' unique authority to forgive sins (5:21; cf. 7:48-49). Jesus' ability to forgive sins is verified by the healing miracle in 5:24-25. This miracle, performed by the Lord's power (5:17), is divine proof that Jesus indeed has power to forgive sins. The implication of this ability to forgive sins is raised by the question, "Who can forgive sins but God?" which Luke intensified by adding the term "alone." If no human being can forgive sins, if God alone can forgive sins, and if Jesus is able to forgive sins, what does this imply? It would be wrong at this point to read into Luke's mind a complete Trinitarian formulation of Jesus' deity such as found in the later creeds of Nicea (325) or Chalcedon (451). Nevertheless, Luke certainly saw Jesus as possessing an exclusive "divine right" in this area. Jesus, the Son of Man, can forgive sins. As in 7:49; 8:25; and 9:9, Luke wanted his readers to reflect on the question, "Who is this" who possesses such authority? In this same respect the use of the title Son of Man in this passage indicates that Jesus possessed another divine prerogative, that of passing judgment upon the world.[65] Clearly Luke had a high Christology.

There is soteriological teaching in this passage that fits well the Lukan emphasis elsewhere. One aspect involves the importance of the forgiveness of sins which we find in 5:23-24.[66] The importance of forgiveness has been shown also in Jesus' first sermon in 4:18. Along with this we also find an emphasis in the account on the need for faith (5:20). Faith is one way in which the required human response to God leading to forgiveness/salvation can be described. In the next account the required response will be described as repentance (5:32). These are not different ways by which salvation is achieved but rather different ways the one necessary response of repentance-faith can be expressed. Whereas each emphasizes a different aspect of that basic response, both must be understood as assuming the other response as well.

Several other Lukan themes that are also present in this passage can be mentioned. One is the Spirit's role in Jesus' ministry. Luke introduced the account with his editorial comment that "the power of the Lord was present for him to heal the sick" (5:17). The Spirit's role in the present period of salvation history is emphasized in the births of John the Baptist and Jesus,

---

[65] Cf. Dan 7:13-14 with Luke 9:26; 12:8; 17:22-30; 22:69; and esp. 21:36.

[66] This emphasis is also found in Luke 1:77; 3:3; 5:20; 24:47 in which preaching of the forgiveness of sins is part of the Great Commission; in Acts 2:38, where it is part of the first sermon; and in 5:31; 10:43; 13:38; 26:18. Cf. also Luke 5:8,10, where forgiveness is implied.

in Jesus' baptism and temptation, in his first sermon, and now in his ministry. Another theme alluded to in our text is the present realization of God's kingdom in Jesus' ministry. The ministry of Jesus is the "today" realization of God's promises. The kingdom of God has come. "Today" in Jesus' ministry (and for Luke's readers in the gospel proclamation), God is visiting his people in fulfillment of the Scriptures. Still another emphasis is the need to glorify God (5:25). Negatively, the presence of the Pharisees and teachers of the law and their hostility here and in the following accounts (5:27–6:11) serve to foreshadow the opposition that would ultimately lead to Jesus' crucifixion.

(2) Conflict over Jesus' Association with Tax Collectors and Sinners (5:27-32)

[27]After this, Jesus went out and saw a tax collector by the name of Levi sitting at his tax booth. "Follow me," Jesus said to him, [28]and Levi got up, left everything and followed him.
[29]Then Levi held a great banquet for Jesus at his house, and a large crowd of tax collectors and others were eating with them. [30]But the Pharisees and the teachers of the law who belonged to their sect complained to his disciples, "Why do you eat and drink with tax collectors and 'sinners'?"
[31]Jesus answered them, "It is not the healthy who need a doctor, but the sick. [32]I have not come to call the righteous, but sinners to repentance."

Context

The present account has been placed next to the preceding one because both Pharisees and scribes were opposing Jesus and because Jesus' ability to forgive sins in 5:17-26 was now illustrated in his calling and forgiveness of Levi, the tax collector. Verses 27 ("Follow me") and 32 ("I have come to call . . . to repentance") form an inclusio in which the call to discipleship is emphasized. Luke made several important editorial modifications in this account, apart from various literary refinements and abbreviations. One is his addition of "left everything" (5:28). Another is his clarification that the call of Jesus is a call "to repentance" (5:32).

That Luke sought to defend the church's practice of ministering to the outcasts is evident from his work, for he alone pointed out that the complaint of the Pharisees and scribes was directed to the disciples (5:30). As a result the significance of this passage for the church in Luke's day is all the more apparent. Yet it is much more likely that the church's practice of fellowshiping with repentant sinners was the result of Jesus' teachings and such incidents as this than that the church's practice created this account.[67]

---

[67]Some scholars have suggested that the present account arose out of the early church's desire to justify their practice of consorting with the undesirables of society. The difficulty of

Comments

5:27 Jesus went out and saw a tax collector by the name of Levi. In Matt 9:9 the name given to the tax collector was Matthew, and in all four lists of the twelve disciples the name Matthew appears. Although Mark and Luke did not equate Levi with Matthew, Matthew clearly did. Since first-century Jews often had two names (usually one in Hebrew or Aramaic and the other in Greek or Latin), there is no reason why this tax collector could not have been called Levi Matthew. For "tax collector" see comments on 3:12-13.

At his tax booth. Levi was not the chief toll collector but an agent working at a toll post, quite possibly in Capernaum.

Follow me. In Luke this phrase is used frequently to describe Christian discipleship (cf. 5:11; 9:23,49,57,59,61; 18:22,28). This expression is not used here to describe a deeper Christian commitment to Jesus, i.e., entering some sort of second-level of discipleship, but rather the commitment to become a Christian, as is clear from 5:32.

5:28 Left everything. This is not found in the Markan and Matthean parallels. Luke added this to the narrative to clarify for his readers what it means to follow Jesus. This also ties the present account to the call of Simon, James, and John, who also "left everything and followed" (5:11). In 14:33 Jesus stated that one must "give up everything" to become a disciple, and there also this refers to becoming a Christian since it is addressed to the "crowds" and "anyone" (14:25-26). Elsewhere following Jesus involves denying oneself and taking up one's cross daily (9:23) and leaving one's house and family (9:57-62; 18:28). To such "poor" belong the kingdom of God (6:20).

And followed him. This is an inceptive imperfect and should be translated "and he began to follow him." It emphasizes the commencement and continuation of Levi's discipleship. Thus the subsequent banquet should be understood as one of the ways Levi was following Jesus.

5:29 Then Levi held a great banquet for Jesus. Luke alone designated this meal[68] as a great banquet. This expression may come from Gen 21:8 (cf. also 26:30; Esth 1:3; 5:4,8). Later Luke gave a parable of a great banquet (Luke 14:15-24) that was likewise filled with outcasts.

At his house. Luke clarified that the banquet was held in Levi's house.

5:30 The Pharisees and the teachers of the law who belonged to their sect. The phrase is literally *the Pharisees and their scribes.* "Their" is somewhat strange, but it may be due to Mark's unusual "and the scribes of the Pharisees" (Mark 2:16, RSV).

Complained. In Luke 15:1-2 we find a similar murmuring among the Pharisees and scribes, and in 19:7 they murmured because Jesus was eating with a sinner who was a chief tax collector.

---

classifying whether this is more properly defined as a controversy story or a pronouncement story has also raised doubts in the minds of some about the historicity of the account. Yet this difficulty has less to say about its historicity than about the arbitrariness of such form-critical classifications.

[68] We find other meal scenes in Luke 7:36-50; 9:10-17; 10:38-42; 11:37-54; 14:1-24; 19:1-10; 22:14-38; 24:29-32,41-43.

To his disciples. This is the first use of "disciples" in the Gospel. The story may well have been remembered and preserved in the early church because of the criticism leveled against early Christians who were associating and ministering to the outcasts of society. In addition Luke's designating the disciples as the object of this complaint may seek to demonstrate that the present church situation of his readers has parallels to what happened to the disciples. The reason for this Christian behavior arose from incidents such as this in Jesus' life, not vice versa, i.e., the stories were not created by the early church to defend such behavior, but such behavior arose from Jesus' behavior and teachings. True Christianity has always broken down economic, social, ethnic, and racial barriers; for where Christ is truly present, "people will come from east and west and north and south, and will take their places at the feast in the kingdom of God" (13:29).

Why do you eat and drink? This shared activity implied acceptance of such people as one's "brothers and sisters" (cf. Acts 11:3 and the explanation in 11:4-18, esp. 11:18; cf. also Gal 2:12-13). To "break bread" with someone had important consequences. Even as contact with lepers (Luke 5:12-16) brought ritual uncleanness, so in the minds of the Pharisees contact with tax collectors and sinners brought moral (as well as ritual) uncleanness.

With tax collectors and "sinners"? This association is also found in 7:34; 15:1-2. Gentiles could also be included under the latter term (Gal 2:15), but in the setting of Jesus "sinners" probably referred to those Jews who did not keep the Mosaic law's ceremonial details or its moral precepts, as interpreted by the Pharisees. "Tax collectors" are grouped with "sinners" not so much because they were "traitors" who collected taxes for the Roman oppressors but because they were dishonest and practiced distortion (cf. Luke 5:32). Note the advice of John the Baptist to them in 3:12-13, which assumes their dishonesty, and Zacchaeus's behavior in 19:8-9. The use of a single article, "the tax collectors and sinners," rather than "the tax collectors and the sinners" indicates that Luke saw them as making up a single group.

5:31 It is not the healthy. Luke used a more "medical" term here than we find in Mark and Matthew, although the NIV translates both terms identically. Compare 4:23. The metaphorical contrast between healthy and sick prepares the reader for the synonymous parallelism of righteous and sinners in the next verse.

5:32 This verse serves as the culmination of the account and as a clarification of 4:18-19.

I have . . . come. Even as a doctor has a duty and calling to care for the sick, so Jesus has a calling to care for sinners.

Not . . . to call the righteous. In light of the biblical teaching that there is none righteous (Rom 3:10-23) and that the call to repentance is universal (Luke 3:3; 13:3,5; 24:47; Acts 2:38; 17:30), "righteous" here should be understood as *those who falsely think themselves righteous*, i.e., the Pharisees. Luke did not raise the question here about whether the Pharisees were truly righteous, but later in Luke 16:15 he described them as "ones who justify [themselves] in the eyes of men" and in 18:9 as "confident of their own righteousness and look[ing] down on everyone else," i.e., as falsely assuming that they were righteous. Luke 15:7 should be interpreted similarly.

Sinners to repentance. Luke added this phrase to clarify what response sinners are to make to Jesus' gracious call. Repentance[69] here corresponds to and is thus another way of expressing *leaving all and following Jesus* (5:28). Compare 15:7.

The Lukan Message

In this passage Luke emphasized an aspect of the human response to the gospel which, while not unique to him, is clearly a strong Lukan emphasis. He did this by adding "to repentance" in 5:32, which is lacking in the parallel accounts. Jesus' mission was to call sinners to repentance. The Great Commission is a call to preach in Jesus' name "repentance and forgiveness of sins" to all the world (24:47). When asked what one must do to be saved, Peter would later respond, "Repent and be baptized" (cf. Acts 2:38,40). At times the appropriate response is described as "believe" (cf. 16:31), but faith and repentance were for Luke essentially two sides of the same coin.

Another aspect of the response to God's call is to follow Jesus. This was not thought of as a once-for-all event never to be repeated, as is evidenced by Luke's use of the imperfect tense in Luke 5:28, where Levi "begins to follow" Jesus. (Mark and Matthew used the simple aorist, "followed.") This same emphasis appears in 9:23, where taking up the cross is something done "daily" and where one is called "to continually follow" Jesus. In describing this "following," Luke alone of the Gospel writers added that Levi "left everything." We have encountered this thought in 5:11 and find it also in 9:57-62; 14:33; 18:22 (where Luke added "all"); 18:28. The call to follow Jesus was not understood by Luke as a call to halfhearted loyalty but as involving a continual following of Jesus.

Finally Luke reminded us that the call of Jesus was addressed to the outcasts. Jesus came for sinners (5:32) and for the lost (19:10; 15:7). The gospel is for the poor, for prisoners, for the blind, and for the oppressed (4:18). Those who falsely think they are healthy and righteous will reject Jesus' message, but since his message openly challenges and refutes this false assumption of well-being, the gospel cannot be ignored. It will meet hostile resistance, as our account shows. C. S. Lewis once wrote: "Christianity tells people to repent and promises them forgiveness. It has nothing (as far as I know) to say to people who do not know they have done anything to repent of and who do not feel that they need any forgiveness."[70] Yet to those who see and acknowledge their own unrighteousness before God, the gospel offers forgiveness (5:20) and blessing (6:20).

---

[69]This term is also found in Luke 3:3,8; 15:7; 24:47; Acts 5:31; 11:18; 13:24; 19:4; 20:21; 26:20. The verb is also found in Luke 10:13; 11:32; 13:3,5; 15:7,10; 16:30; 17:3,4; Acts 2:38; 3:19; 8:22; 17:30; 26:20.

[70]C. S. Lewis, *Mere Christianity* (London: Collins, 1956), 37.

(3) Conflict over Jesus' Disciples' not Fasting (5:33-39)

[33]They said to him, "John's disciples often fast and pray, and so do the disciples of the Pharisees, but yours go on eating and drinking."

[34]Jesus answered, "Can you make the guests of the bridegroom fast while he is with them? [35]But the time will come when the bridegroom will be taken from them; in those days they will fast."

[36]He told them this parable: "No one tears a patch from a new garment and sews it on an old one. If he does, he will have torn the new garment, and the patch from the new will not match the old. [37]And no one pours new wine into old wineskins. If he does, the new wine will burst the skins, the wine will run out and the wineskins will be ruined. [38]No, new wine must be poured into new wineskins. [39]And no one after drinking old wine wants the new, for he says, 'The old is better.' "

Context

The third controversy story in the present series involves a contrast between Jesus' disciples who were not fasting and the practice of fasting of both the disciples of John the Baptist and of the Pharisees.[71] The culmination of the present story is found in the two similitudes and the proverb at the end, which are dominated by the catchwords "new" and "old." The scarcity of discussion of fasting in the NT makes it difficult to believe that this account was created by the early church or that it was preserved in order to justify the Christian practice of fasting. Because of the joy of living in the victory of their Lord's resurrection, fasting appears to have been an exception in the early church and was limited to special occasions (cf. Acts 13:2-3; 14:23; 27:1-38). Even when the church fasted, sorrow was not present, and the examples of fasting in Acts have nothing to do with mourning (cf. Matt 6:17-18). Furthermore the early church did not seek to explain its practice of fasting on the basis of this passage.

This account demonstrates the contrast that exists between the new and the old, i.e., between the coming of God's kingdom inaugurated by Jesus (Luke 16:16) and the old Judaism of the Pharisees. Luke made a number of changes to the Markan account. Several are merely literary or stylistic, but by his changes in 5:36-39 Luke sought to heighten the eschatological realization of the new age inaugurated by Jesus.

Comments

5:33 John's disciples often fast and pray. That John had disciples is evident here and in 7:18-19; 11:1.[72] The reference to John's disciples praying was added

---

[71]Whatever the original reason for the connection between this and the previous account (literary similarity, Levi's feast and eating; similar kind of controversy, violation of Pharisaic ceremonial regulations), Luke found them already together in his source (cf. Mark 2:13-17 and 18-22).

[72]That they continued as a group long after his death is evident from Acts 18:25-26; 19:1-7 and is suggested by Mark 6:29 and the polemic found in John 1:6-8,15,19-23,35,37; 3:25-26; 4:1-2.

by Luke, who also pointed out in 11:1 that they had a specific prayer or way of praying that identified them as a group. The combination of "fast and pray" is also found in 2:37; Acts 13:3; 14:23.

Eating and drinking. Luke changed Mark's "not fasting" to "eating and drinking," which was a favorite expression.[73] In so doing he tied this account more closely with the preceding one in which Jesus' disciples were accused of eating and drinking with tax collectors and sinners (5:30). In 7:34 these two criticisms are brought together when Jesus is described as a friend of tax collectors and sinners and as a glutton and drunkard.

5:34 Jesus' reply assumes that the expression of sadness and sorrow through fasting is inappropriate in the present context.[74] The bridegroom's presence and the joy of the kingdom inaugurated by Jesus makes such behavior highly inappropriate. There is a time for everything. But this was not a time for weeping or mourning; it was rather a time for laughing and dancing (Eccl 3:4).[75] Since the question is introduced with the Greek particle *mē*, it anticipates a negative answer from the reader. Even though Jesus' message is one of repentance (Luke 5:32), such repentance leads not to sorrow and mourning but rather to the joyous celebration of forgiveness and membership in the kingdom. Compare 15:17-24.

Guests of the bridegroom. There is no OT or rabbinic example in which the term, bridegroom, is used as a messianic title. As a result Jesus appears to have been using this term as a simple metaphor and not making a specific messianic claim by applying a well-known messianic title to himself.

5:35 The time will come. "The time" is literally *days*. (By translating the text in this manner we better observe the tie with the same expression used again later in this verse.)[76]

The bridegroom will be taken. This is a reference to the violent end of the banquet time brought about by the crucifixion. Although in the setting of Jesus this saying would have possessed a riddlelike quality, for Luke and his readers the once-veiled reference to the crucifixion would have been transparent.

In those days. The contrast is not between the time of Jesus' ministry and the time of the church after the resurrection, as in 22:35-36, but between the period of Jesus' ministry and the time between his arrest and resurrection (24:17-20; cf. also John 16:20; 20:11-13). The period after the resurrection was not characterized by sorrowful fasting but rather by joy (Luke 24:41,52; Acts 8:8; 13:52).

5:36 He told them this parable. Luke added the term "parable" to the account.[77] The term *parabole* has a large semantic range and can include proverbs (4:23), metaphorical or figurative sayings (Mark 7:14-17), similitudes (Luke 13:18-19), story parables (14:16-24), example parables (12:16-21), and allegory (20:9-19). Here it describes a metaphorical or figurative saying.

---

[73] Cf. Luke 5:30; 7:33-34; 10:7; 12:19,29,45; 13:26; 17:8,27-28; 22:30.

[74] Matthew 9:15 uses the word "mourn" instead of "fast," which reveals his understanding of the mood represented in fasting.

[75] The *Megillat Ta'anit* (literally *scroll of fasting*) lists thirty-six days on which fasting is not only inappropriate but forbidden.

[76] This expression also appears in Luke 17:22; 21:6; cf. also 19:43; 23:29.

[77] Cf. also Luke 6:39; 12:16; 13:6; 18:1; 21:29.

The analogy that follows is heightened by Luke's modification of Mark 2:21: "unshrunk cloth" (Mark) to "new garment" (Luke); "the new piece will pull away from the old" (Mark) to "he will have torn the new garment" (Luke); and "making the tear worse" (Mark) to "the patch from the new will not match the old" (Luke). Since a patch is not destroyed in the same way as wine, Luke used the illustration of a new garment from which a patch is taken in order to create better parallelism between the two figurative sayings. Luke's emphasis in the analogy lies with the new garment and new wine, for the term "new" appears seven times in Luke 5:36-38 compared to only four times in the Markan parallel. Thus in Luke the emphasis falls on the "newness" of the kingdom brought by Jesus, whereas in Mark it falls on the tearing of the old garment. For Luke, to patch the old with the new not only did not help the old but, more importantly, tore apart the new.[78]

5:37 The incompatibility of the new and the old is demonstrated by another analogy. New wine if placed in old wineskins will destroy both skins and wine because as the new wine ferments, the old wineskin is not sufficiently pliable and thus will burst, spilling out the wine. One cannot place the new wine of the gospel in the old wineskins of Pharisaic Judaism, for what will result is neither the gospel nor Judaism. Later history has shown that attempts to syncretize Christianity with another religious movement lead to an offspring inferior to both.

Wineskins. These were dehaired skins of small animals, such as goats, which were sewn together to hold water (Gen 21:15), milk (Judg 4:19), and wine (Josh 9:4,13).

5:38 This saying emphasizes the need for compatibility in both the metaphorical picture (new wine cannot be placed in old wineskins) and the reality (the "new" gospel cannot be placed within the "old" Pharisaic Judaism).

5:39 No one after drinking old wine wants the new. An attempt has been made to interpret this verse, so that Jesus is portrayed as the one who preserves rather than abolishes the old,[79] but the concern of the two similitudes is with the "new," not the "old." In order to maintain consistency with the meaning of the previous statements, this verse should be interpreted as an ironical condemnation of those who cling so closely and dearly to the past that they are not open to the present realization of God's kingdom. In particular we should see here the preference of the Pharisees in Jesus' time (and the circumcision party in Acts 11:2-3; 15:1-2,5 in Luke's time) for the "old" over the "new."

The Lukan Message

The main Lukan emphasis in this passage is eschatological. Jesus brought with him the "new" (cf. Jer 31:31-33). God's kingdom has been realized. The Anointed One has brought with him the fulfillment of the OT promises (Luke 4:18), and the joy of the awaited age has come. As a

---

[78] Tannehill (*Narrative Unity of Luke-Acts*, 174) suggests that in this account as well as in 5:17–6:11 Luke portrayed "Jesus . . . resisting his critics' attempt to destroy the new garment for the sake of the old one and to store the new wine in old wineskins." Thus the saying associated with fasting also applies to Jesus' eating with tax collectors and sinners.

[79] See R. S. Good, "Jesus, Protagonist of the Old, in Luke 5:33-39," *NovT* 25 (1983): 19-36.

result there is no room for fasting or mourning. There would come a brief period (Good Friday to Easter Sunday) where such fasting would be appropriate. This, however, would pass quickly and then, even more than before, fasting would be inappropriate as the church lives in the joy of the resurrection and the exaltation of our Lord. What fasting there will be has nothing to do with sorrow or mourning (cf. Acts 13:3; 14:23). This "newness" is later described as the inauguration of a "new covenant" (Luke 22:20). The new covenant is not contrary to the "old covenant" but is instead its realization and fulfillment. See Introduction 7 (2). Yet it cannot simply be absorbed into the "old," and some of the implications of this truth can be seen in Acts 11:2-3; 15:1-5.

The exact relationship of John the Baptist to the new covenant is not clear. In this passage it seems that he was understood as part of the old since his disciples fasted whereas Jesus' disciples did not (cf. Luke 7:28). Yet it seems best to see John as a transitional figure who in one sense belonged both to the "old" and the "new." See comments on 16:16. A foreshadowing of the passion is again seen in the forceful "taking away" (5:35) of the bridegroom.

(4) Conflict over Jesus' Attitude toward the Sabbath (6:1-11)

[1]One Sabbath Jesus was going through the grainfields, and his disciples began to pick some heads of grain, rub them in their hands and eat the kernels. [2]Some of the Pharisees asked, "Why are you doing what is unlawful on the Sabbath?"

[3]Jesus answered them, "Have you never read what David did when he and his companions were hungry? [4]He entered the house of God, and taking the consecrated bread, he ate what is lawful only for priests to eat. And he also gave some to his companions." [5]Then Jesus said to them, "The Son of Man is Lord of the Sabbath."

[6]On another Sabbath he went into the synagogue and was teaching, and a man was there whose right hand was shriveled. [7]The Pharisees and the teachers of the law were looking for a reason to accuse Jesus, so they watched him closely to see if he would heal on the Sabbath. [8]But Jesus knew what they were thinking and said to the man with the shriveled hand, "Get up and stand in front of everyone." So he got up and stood there.

[9]Then Jesus said to them, "I ask you, which is lawful on the Sabbath: to do good or to do evil, to save life or to destroy it?"

[10]He looked around at them all, and then said to the man, "Stretch out your hand." He did so, and his hand was completely restored. [11]But they were furious and began to discuss with one another what they might do to Jesus.

Context

In the first pericope (6:1-5), Jesus claimed that he, as the Son of Man, is Lord of the Sabbath. In the second (6:6-11) he manifested this authority by healing a man on the Sabbath.[80] Jesus' attitude toward the Sabbath must have been a continual issue of contention as seen by these two accounts.[81]

Comments
6:1 Began to pick some heads of grain. The picking of grain from someone else's field was permissible according to Deut 23:24-25, so that the issue was not picking the grain but doing so on the Sabbath, as the next verse makes clear.
Rub them in their hands and eat the kernels. Luke added this to explain that the disciples were picking grain on the Sabbath because of their hunger.
6:2 Some of the Pharisees asked. Luke qualified his source by adding "some." He may have done this in order to avoid condemning all the Pharisees. He knew of some good (Luke 13:31; Acts 5:34-39) and even Christian Pharisees (Acts 15:5). For the same Lukan qualification, see comments on 13:31 and 19:39.
Why are you doing what is unlawful on the Sabbath? In Matthew and Mark, Jesus was attacked indirectly through the actions of his disciples. Luke, however, sought to show that the attack was ultimately directed against Jesus, for a teacher could be called into account for the behavior of his disciples. Thus the "you," which is plural, included Jesus along with his disciples. The reverence for the Sabbath among Jews can be seen in such writings as 1 Macc 2:32-41; 2 Macc 15:1-5; Jubilees 2:19ff; Fragments of a Zadokite Work 13:22-27; CD 11:13ff. The Pharisaic interpretation of plucking grain as work may be reflected in *Šabbat* 7:2. Whether or not this was a valid interpretation of the OT teachings is not pursued in the account (although note Matt 12:5-7) because the issue for Luke was not hermeneutical but Christological.
6:3 Jesus answered them. Luke's use of the verbal form "answering said" indicates that Jesus assumed the responsibility of his disciples' behavior in answering the criticism of the previous verse.
Have you never read? Jesus used a counterquestion in his answer. See comments on 5:23.
What David did? Jesus recalled an event in David's life when due to hunger he and his men ate the consecrated sanctuary bread, i.e., the bread of the presence. The account in 1 Sam 21:1-6 does not mention that this took place on a Sabbath, but the issue was not so much the day or the need but Jesus' authority, which extends over even the Sabbath. If David was free of the restraints of the law on that occasion, how much more is the Son of Man.
6:4 He entered the house of God. This is not the Solomonic temple but rather the tabernacle. Luke, as Matthew did, omitted the reference to Abiathar's

---

[80]The following two accounts were combined in Luke's source and may have been associated together in the pre-Markan tradition because of their similar theme. Marshall (*Luke*, 229) argues for the historicity of the first account by stating: "The trivial nature of the illegality committed by the disciples suggests that an actual incident forms the basis of the tradition rather than that the church chose this particular example to serve as the basis of a conflict story." Once again we encounter a problem of classification with regard to whether the second account is a miracle or a conflict story. The account does not fit either category neatly, for the account is clearly a miracle-conflict story.

[81]As well as Luke 4:31-41; 13:10-19; 14:1-6; John 5:1-18; 7:23-24; 9:13-16.

being high priest. He may have done this to shorten his account, but he may also have done it because of the difficulty associated with this reference.[82]

He ate what is lawful only for priests to eat. Compare Lev 24:5-9. Luke added "only" to his account in order to emphasize David's violation of the commandment. This ultimately then heightens the authority of the One greater than David, i.e., the Lord of the Sabbath.

6:5 The Son of Man. See comments on 5:24. Clearly this is a title in our present passage and not a statement about Jesus' humanity in general. Luke and Matthew differ from Mark 2:27a, which heightens the Christological sense of this passage. If David could in certain instances of overriding need dispense with this OT regulation, then how much more can the Son of Man who is greater than David do so.

Is Lord of the Sabbath. It is thus the Son of Man, not the Pharisees by means of their regulations, who ruled and properly interpreted the Sabbath. Whereas there might be some ground for arguing that this statement in Mark 2:28 is an editorial comment by the Evangelist, both here and in the Matthean parallel this is not possible. Matthew and Luke understood Mark 2:28 as a saying of Jesus.[83]

6:6 On another Sabbath. Luke, by adding this to the account, tied the present incident even more closely to the preceding one than in Mark.

He went into the synagogue and was teaching. Luke pointed out that Jesus' purpose for being in the synagogue was to teach. No doubt he deduced this from Jesus' normal synagogue activity (cf. Luke 4:15,16-30,31-38).

And a man was there whose right hand was shriveled. Luke accentuated the man's physical woes by pointing out that the hand affected was the most important one, i.e., the right hand. In 22:50 Luke also became more specific and added "right," but in 6:29 he omitted "right." "Shriveled" refers here either to paralysis or atrophy.

6:7 The Pharisees and the teachers of the law were looking for a reason to accuse Jesus. Jesus' opponents did not doubt Jesus' ability to heal. This is granted. The issue for them was whether Jesus' healing power was divine or demonic (11:14-20). Although the Pharisaic tradition knew of exceptions when the Sabbath could be broken, e.g., for life-threatening situations (*Yoma* 8:6), the healing of a shriveled hand did not qualify as such an exception (cf. Luke 13:14). By now, due to 4:31-41; 6:1-5, Jesus' attitude toward the Sabbath was well-known, so that his opponents were observing his Sabbath behavior to see if they could catch him profaning the Sabbath. The term "to accuse" refers to finding a legal accusation that could be used in court against Jesus.

6:8 But Jesus knew what they were thinking. Luke was not seeking here to indicate that Jesus possessed a great understanding of human nature. Rather he

---

[82] See J. A. Brooks, *Mark*, NAC (Nashville: Broadman, 1991), 66.

[83] The Codex Beza (D) at this point places Luke 6:5 after 6:10 and replaces it with the following saying, "On the same day he saw a man working on the sabbath and said to him, 'Man, if you know what you are doing, you are blessed; but if you do not know, you are accursed and a transgressor of the law.'" While interesting, this is clearly a later scribal addition and not part of the canonical text of Luke.

indicated Jesus possessed a prophetic awareness of human thoughts.[84]

Get up and stand in front of everyone. Jesus was in charge of the situation and confronted his opponents.

6:9 Jesus challenged the thought of his opponents. The ultimate issue for him was not doing good versus doing nothing but rather doing good versus doing evil, for failure to do good in such instances is in effect to do evil (cf. Jas 4:17).[85]

6:10 Jesus' opponents were not able to respond. Compare Luke 13:17; 14:6. Luke in abbreviating the Markan account did not include the statement that Jesus looked around in anger and was deeply distressed (Mark 3:5).

He did so, and his hand was completely restored. Jesus' healing on the Sabbath is evidence that he is indeed Lord of the Sabbath (Luke 6:5).

6:11   But they were furious. "Were furious" is literally *filled with madness* or *folly.*

What they might do to Jesus. This serves as the conclusion of both 6:1-5 and 6:6-11.

The Lukan Message

Although both passages center around Jesus' activity on the Sabbath and the conflict this brought with "some" Pharisees, the main Lukan emphasis does not focus on hermeneutics or seek to defend Christian behavior with respect to the Sabbath. Whatever value these accounts had apologetically to explain the Christian attitude toward the Sabbath is overshadowed by the Evangelist's desire to continue his Christological teaching. Building on what had already been said about Jesus' "power" in 4:14,36; 5:17 and his "authority" in 4:32,36; 5:24, Luke then revealed that Jesus, as the Son of Man, is also Lord of the Sabbath. All the commandments and veneration centering on this day are subject to Jesus' teaching, for he is Master of the Sabbath. One greater than David has come who is not controlled by Sabbath regulations but instead controls the Sabbath itself. This authority is demonstrated by his healing on the Sabbath. Jesus' knowledge of his opponents thoughts (6:8) is also best understood as supporting his prophetic-divine authority. This passage had apologetical significance with regard to the life-style of the early church, for it pointed out that the Christian attitude toward the Sabbath was determined by the example and teachings of Jesus, the Lord. The basic Lukan teaching in this passage, however, involves Jesus' lordship over the Sabbath.

---

[84]Cf. Luke 5:22; 11:17; and both 9:47 and 11:17, which Luke added to his Markan source; cf. also 2:35.

[85]First Maccabees 2:32-41 may serve as a background for this saying. There in order to avoid being annihilated in battle, Mattathias and the Hasidim decided that, although they would not initiate a battle on the Sabbath, if attacked they would fight. Thus it was acceptable to "destroy life" on the Sabbath.

3. The Teaching of the Disciples—The Sermon on the Plain (6:12-49)

The following section is organized around Jesus' teaching the disciples on a "level place" (6:17). The exact arrangement of this material is debated, as a look at various commentaries reveals.[86] We have separated 6:27-36 and 6:37-42, but because the latter is essentially a commentary of 6:36, one could combine them almost equally as well.

(1) Choosing the Twelve Disciples (6:12-16)

[12]One of those days Jesus went out to a mountainside to pray, and spent the night praying to God. [13]When morning came, he called his disciples to him and chose twelve of them, whom he also designated apostles: [14]Simon (whom he named Peter), his brother Andrew, James, John, Philip, Bartholomew, [15]Matthew, Thomas, James son of Alphaeus, Simon who was called the Zealot, [16]Judas son of James, and Judas Iscariot, who became a traitor.

Context

This and the next account occur in reverse order in Mark. This may be due to Luke's desire to use the summary of the crowd's following Jesus (6:17-19) as both a summation of what preceded and as an introduction to what followed (6:20-49).[87] Luke again was less interested in the chronological order of certain events than in their logical order (see comments on 1:3). The present account by its placement serves to contrast the negative behavior of Jesus' opponents in 6:1-11 (esp. v. 11) with that of the disciples. The choosing of the twelve also prepares the reader for their mission in 9:1-6 and their later role in Acts 1:2,8,26; and 2:14. The main Lukan contribution to this account is found in his additions "to pray, and spent the night praying to God" in Luke 6:12 and "whom he also designated apostles" in 6:13.[88]

There are four lists of the disciples in the NT: Matt 10:2-4; Mark 3:16-19; Acts 1:13; and the present passage. No two lists are identical, not even the two in Luke-Acts. The four lists each consist of three groups of four, and in each list the same names introduce each group: Peter (group one), Philip (group two), and James the son of Alphaeus (group three).

---

[86]This involves not only the sermon itself but also the question of whether 6:12-16 goes better with what precedes or follows. It seems best, however, to include 6:12-16 with what follows since 6:17 refers to "them" and 6:20 refers to the "disciples" (6:13). Thus "6:12-16 . . . functions to establish an apostolic guarantee [cf. 1:2] for the tradition which follows [6:20-49]" (Talbert, *Reading Luke*, 68).

[87]Cf. how the summary in Matt 4:23-25 precedes the Sermon on the Mount in 5:1-7:29. See Nolland (*Luke 1-9:20*, 264), however, for the view that Luke 6:12-16 goes better with 5:1-6:11.

[88]The latter comment is also found in certain manuscripts of the Markan parallel (Mark 3:14), but its presence in Mark is most probably due to later scribal insertion.

This and the fact that the first four disciples are always Peter, Andrew, James, and John (or Peter, James, John, and Andrew); that the second group always consists of Philip, Bartholomew, Thomas, and Matthew; and that the last group always ends with Judas Iscariot (except in Acts, where he is omitted) suggests that there was a general order in the lists of the disciples. The minor variations within the list, however, indicate that this order was not set in stone.

Comments

6:12   Jesus went out to a mountainside to pray.   The parallel in Mark 3:13 also mentions a mountain. Luke alone mentioned that before the selection of the Twelve Jesus prayed (cf. Luke 6:12 with Mark 3:13 and Matt 10:1), for in Luke-Acts prayer preceded every major decision or crisis in the life of Jesus and the early church. See comments on 3:21 and Introduction 8 (7). In Acts 1:2 Jesus' prayer and choice of the twelve is described in *The Jerusalem Bible* as having occurred "through the Holy Spirit." It is uncertain, however, whether the phrase "through the Holy Spirit" goes better with the participle "giving instructions" (NIV) or the verb "chosen."

Spent the night praying.   This places even greater emphasis on Jesus' prayer and heightens the importance of the forthcoming decision.

6:13   He called his disciples.   "His disciples" refers to a larger group of Jesus' followers, who already have been mentioned in 6:1. From this group the Twelve were chosen.[89] This distinction between the Twelve and Jesus' disciples is clearly seen in the mission of the Twelve (9:1-6) and the mission of the seventy (10:1-12,17-20).

Chose twelve of them.   The grammar of this phrase is unclear. The participle "having chosen" does not appear to modify the main verb "called," so that it probably is best to understand it as a circumstantial or coordinate participle and to translate it as a finite verb as the NIV has done. Compare Matt 19:28 for another example.

The historicity of this group sometimes has been challenged; but the early reference to the Twelve in a pre-Pauline hymn (1 Cor 15:5), the importance of this group in Acts 1:21-26, and above all the fact that one of the Twelve was a traitor witness strongly to the historicity of this group. This also finds support in that references to the Twelve are found in several Gospel strata.[90]

Whom he also designated apostles.   Mark's Gospel lacks this statement but mentions that Jesus chose the Twelve in order that "he might *send them out* (*apostellē*) to preach" (Mark 3:14; cf. 6:7). Thus even as he was sent from God (Luke

---

[89] Jeremias (*New Testament Theology*, 235) points out that in Jesus' day only two and a half tribes (Judah, Benjamin, and half of Levi) remained. Only in the messianic age would the twelve tribes be restored. Thus Jesus' selection of the Twelve "announces the establishment of the *eschatological* people of God."

[90] In Mark (3:14,16; 4:10; 6:7; 9:35; 10:32; 11:11; 14:10,17,20,43), in John (6:67,70-71; 20:24), in the Q material (cf. Luke 22:30), and perhaps in the L material (8:1) and M material (Matt 11:1).

4:18,43; 9:48; 10:16), so both during his earthly ministry (9:2,10; 10:1,3; cf.
22:35) and as the risen Christ (24:47) Jesus sent out his disciples to preach. The
reference to the "apostleship" of the Twelve in Mark 3:14 is less developed theologically than the more technical term "apostles" in the present verse.[91] For Luke
the apostles were more than "sent ones."

The term "apostles" has a range of meanings, and Luke's meaning was somewhat narrower than Paul's. For Paul the criteria for being an apostle consisted of
(1) being an eyewitness of the risen Christ (1 Cor 9:1) and (2) being commissioned to proclaim the gospel (Gal 1:15-16). Thus the term was broad enough to
include Paul himself, and at times Paul even understood it to include others who
had not seen the risen Christ.[92] Luke seemed to accept (1) and (2) in Acts 1:22
when the replacement for Judas was chosen. Yet he added another requirement as
well. The apostolic replacement for Judas must have been present during Jesus'
entire ministry (Acts 1:22). Thus the "apostles" Jesus chose during his ministry
were the apostles par excellence of the risen Christ (1:2,26; 2:37,42,43; 4:33; cf.
also Luke 1:2). By this criterion Paul would be excluded. Yet there is a sense in
which Luke could refer to Paul, and even Barnabas, as apostles (Acts 14:4,14).
For Luke, however, the term "apostle" was almost a technical term for the
"Twelve," with Matthias taking the place of Judas Iscariot (cf. 1:26 "the Eleven
apostles"). Unlike the other Evangelists, Luke frequently called the Twelve "apostles,"[93] and he alone stated that Jesus referred to the Twelve as apostles (Luke
6:13). No doubt Jesus' usage of this term, which means *one who is sent*, took on
an even fuller sense as the Twelve sought to be witnesses unto the ends of the
earth (Acts 1:8).

6:14 Simon (whom he named Peter). The first person called by Jesus
(Luke 5:1-11) and the most famous of the disciples heads the list. Unlike Matt
16:16-19 no reason is given for the name "Peter." Whereas Luke used "Simon"
(*God has heard*) up to this point, he henceforth would use "Peter" (*Stone*) except
in 22:31; 24:34.

His brother Andrew. As in Matt 10:2, Andrew is placed next to his brother,
Simon. From Mark 1:16 we learn that he was a fisherman like his brother.

James, John. These were the second set of brothers and were also Galilean
fishermen (Luke 5:10-11). James, sometimes called "the Great" to distinguish him
from the James of Mark 15:40, was martyred in the early forties by Herod Agrippa
(Acts 12:1-2). Since Luke already had pointed out in Luke 5:10 that these were
the sons of Zebedee, he omitted this designation here (contrast Mark 3:17; Matt
10:2).

Philip. According to John 1:44, Philip came from Bethsaida, the same city as
Peter and Andrew.

Bartholomew. There is no other reference to Bartholomew in the NT other
than his appearance in the four lists of the disciples. Some have speculated that

---

[91] This assumes that "designating them apostles" is not part of the Markan text but a later
scribal addition.
[92] Cf. 2 Cor 8:23 for emissaries of Paul's churches; 2 Cor 11:5; 12:11-12 for Paul's
"superapostle" opponents; Phil 2:25 for Epaphroditus; 1 Cor 4:6,9 for Apollos.
[93] Luke 9:1,10; 11:49 (?); 17:1,5; 22:3,14; 24:10; Acts 1:2,13,26; etc.

Bartholomew was another name for the Nathanael of John 1:45-51; 21:2, but there is no real evidence for this.

6:15 Matthew. In Matt 10:3, Matthew is identified as a tax collector. See comments on 5:27.

Thomas. Thomas is called "Didymus" or "The Twin" in John 11:16; 20:24; 21:2.

James son of Alphaeus. This James is not to be confused with James the brother of John, the James of Mark 15:40, or James the brother of Jesus (Mark 6:3; Gal 1:19; 1 Cor 15:7).

Simon who was called the Zealot. In Mark 3:18 and Matt 10:4 Simon is referred to as Simon the Cananaean. "Cananaean" is simply a transliteration of the Aramaic word for "Zealot," for which Luke gave the Greek translation. The "Zealot" movement, which led to the Jewish revolt from A.D. 67–70, probably did not exist as a distinct political entity in Jesus' day. Simon was a "Zealot" in the sense that he was a follower of the revolutionary movement(s) that later developed into a unified nationalistic party of Zealots.[94]

6:16 Judas son of James. In Mark 3:18 and Matt 10:3 this name does not appear, but instead we find the name "Thaddaeus." It is not impossible that these are two names for the same person. Double names were not at all rare (cf. Simon Peter; Saul-Paul). Furthermore, the other apostles whose names are qualified (Simon Peter and Simon the Zealot; James [the son of Zebedee] and James the son of Alphaeus) share names with others in the list. These shared names are qualified to distinguish them. Had there been only one Judas, why qualify his name with Iscariot here, in Mark 3:19, and in Matt 10:4? There would be no need to do so. If, however, as the Lukan account states, there were two disciples named Judas, then such a qualification would have been needed. Matthew and Mark may have preferred the other name "Thaddaeus" to Judas because of the connotations associated with the name Judas. (What Christians today name their son "Judas"?)

Judas Iscariot. The latter designation probably means *man (Is[h]) from [the town of] Karioth (cariot).* This would make Judas a Judean and the only non-Galilean of the group.

Who became a traitor. The name of Judas has forever become associated with and even a synonym for "traitor."

The Lukan Message

Within this passage we find two important theological emphases of Luke. The importance of prayer is clearly seen in his adding to the parallel account that Jesus went to a mountainside "to pray" and his intensifying this by stating that Jesus "spent the night praying to God." Within this one verse (6:12) Luke made two references to Jesus' having prayed before choosing the twelve apostles. This prayer, furthermore, lasted through the whole night. We already have noted the general importance prayer played in the life of Jesus and the early church (see comments on 3:21 and Intro-

---

[94] See M. Smith, "Zealots and Sicarii, Their Origins and Relation," *HTR* 64 (1971): 1-19.

duction 8 [7]), but prayer by Jesus before his selection of the church leaders was being portrayed consciously as the normative pattern for the later selection of church leaders. This is evident from Acts 1:24; 6:6; 13:2-3; 14:23. Luke was seeking to teach his Christian readers that prayer should be made before church decisions concerning leadership.

Another emphasis of Luke found in our passage involves Jesus' selection of the early church leaders, the apostles. Jesus chose these twelve from a larger group of disciples. That this decision was made after a night of prayer heightens the Twelve's authoritative position in the church. In Acts 1 the first action of the early church was to make sure this leadership was maintained. There had to be "twelve." The Twelve's role was not simply their having been "sent out" as missionaries. This seems to be more the emphasis of Mark 3:14. For Luke the Twelve apostles' leadership role was multiple. They indeed were the evangelists, preachers, and missionaries of the early church (Luke 9:1-2; 24:46-49; Acts 2:14-42; 4:33; 5:12), but they also were the church's leaders.[95] In times of crisis the church turned to the apostles in Jerusalem (8:14; 15:2). The apostles also were the authorized conveyers of the tradition, for through these eyewitnesses and ministers of the word the Jesus tradition has been handed down to the church (Luke 1:2; Acts 2:42; 10:34-39).

(2) Ministry to the Crowds (6:17-19)

[17]**He went down with them and stood on a level place. A large crowd of his disciples was there and a great number of people from all over Judea, from Jerusalem, and from the coast of Tyre and Sidon, [18]who had come to hear him and to be healed of their diseases. Those troubled by evil spirits were cured, [19]and the people all tried to touch him, because power was coming from him and healing them all.**

Context

At this point Luke introduces Jesus' Sermon on the Plain with a summary of Jesus' activity taken from Mark 3:7-12. A comparison of the two accounts helps reveal Luke's theological emphases. The addition "went down" (6:17) and the setting on a mountain (6:12) tie the preceding account geographically and chronologically to the following sermon "on a level place" (6:17). Luke also emphasizes the presence of "power" (6:19) and Jesus' healing ministry (6:17-19). The addition of "had come to hear him" (6:18) also places greater emphasis on Jesus' message than we find in Mark's account.

---

[95] Acts 4:37; 5:2,18; 6:6; 8:14; 15:2,22-23; 16:4.

Comments

6:17 He went down with them. This is due to the mention of the "mountainside" in 6:12. One should not read into this a parallel to Moses' descent from the mountain (Exod 32), since Luke's Sermon on the Plain does not possess any allusions or echoes of Moses' having received the law on a mountain and going down to give it to the people.

And stood on a level place. The KJV reads "in the plain," and the Lukan material that follows (Luke 6:17-49) has been entitled the "Sermon on the Plain," whereas the related Matthean material has been called the "Sermon on the Mount" (Matt 5:1). As Sabourin notes, "Even an elevated plateau, quite above the sea of Galilee, could be described as 'a level place,' so that a contrast in location . . . does not have to be stressed."[96]

A large crowd of his disciples. Luke added this comment (cf. Luke 19:37) to show that Jesus' teachings received a positive response from the people. This positive response continues in Acts. See Introduction 7 (1). Three groups are mentioned in this verse: them (the Twelve apostles), a large crowd of disciples, and a great number of people. This may reflect an understanding of society as consisting of the apostles, the church, and the world.

From all over Judea. This also emphasizes the positive response Jesus elicited. "Judea" is best understood broadly as the land of the Jews rather than the province of Judea (see comments on 1:5). The mention of Tyre and Sidon, coastal cities in the province of Syria, prepare for 10:13-14.

6:18 Who had come to hear him. This prepares the reader for the following sermon and is picked up in 6:27,47 (cf. also 8:4-15). Although Mark 3:8 states that the crowd came because they heard about what Jesus did (a casual participle), Luke commented that the purpose of their coming was to hear Jesus (an infinitive of purpose). Thus he placed greater emphasis on Jesus' message.

And to be healed of their diseases. This gives the second reason for their coming. By placing "to hear" before "to be healed," Luke stressed the importance of Jesus' preaching ministry over his healing ministry (cf. 5:15).

6:19 And the people all tried to touch him. Compare 8:44-47; 18:15; cf. also 5:13; 7:14; 22:51.

Because power was coming from him and healing them all. Compare 5:17. Jesus' power is a clear Lukan emphasis. See comments on 1:17 and 4:36.

The Lukan Message

We find in this brief introduction to the Sermon on the Plain two important Lukan emphases. The reference to Jesus' "power" to heal is most clear and fits well with Jesus' being empowered by the Spirit's anointing.[97] The tie between the Spirit and power has already been emphasized in 1:17,35; 4:14 (cf. also 4:36; 5:17) and prepares for the extension of the Spirit's power to the church in 24:49; Acts 1:8. See Introduction 8 (3).

---

[96] L. Sabourin, *The Gospel according to St. Luke* (Bandra, Bombay: St. Paul Publications, 1984), 162.

[97] The connection between power and healing is seen in Luke 4:36; 5:17; 6:19; 8:46; 9:1 as well as in Acts 2:22; 3:12; 4:7,33; 6:8.

A second emphasis in this passage involves the importance of hearing Jesus' message. Even more important than seeking healing, the importance of which need not be minimized, is the need to "hear" the word of God (6:17-18).[98]

(3) Beatitudes and Woes (6:20-26)

[20]Looking at his disciples, he said:
"Blessed are you who are poor,
  for yours is the kingdom of God.
[21]Blessed are you who hunger now,
  for you will be satisfied.
Blessed are you who weep now,
  for you will laugh.
[22]Blessed are you when men hate you,
  when they exclude you and insult you
  and reject your name as evil,
    because of the Son of Man.
[23]"Rejoice in that day and leap for joy, because great is your reward in
  heaven. For that is how their fathers treated the prophets.
[24]"But woe to you who are rich,
  for you have already received your comfort.
[25]Woe to you who are well fed now,
  for you will go hungry.
Woe to you who laugh now,
  for you will mourn and weep.
[26]Woe to you when all men speak well of you,
  for that is how their fathers treated the false prophets.

Context

At this point Luke introduced a second sermon of Jesus. The first was recorded in 4:16-30 and was addressed to the "crowds." Here in 6:20-49 he addressed his disciples (6:20). The parallel to Luke's Sermon on the Plain (6:17) is Matthew's Sermon on the Mount (5:1-7:29).[99] Luke interestingly enough also mentioned a mountain in 6:17. The Lukan sermon (30 verses) is much shorter than the sermon in Matthew (107 verses), and much of the material in Matthew's sermon is found elsewhere in Luke.

The beatitudes in Luke 6:20-23 possess both similarities and dissimilarities with those found in Matt 5:3-12. The similarities involve: the same audience—disciples; the same basic form—"Blessed are . . . poor, for" (the

---

[98]Cf. Luke 5:1,15 (note the order of hearing and being healed); 8:8,18; 10:16,39; 11:28; 14:35; 15:1.

[99]The Sermon on the Mount is the first of five Matthean discourses, all of which end in a similar manner; cf. 5:1–7:27 (7:28); 10:1-42 (11:1); 13:1-52 (13:53); 18:1-35 (19:1); and 23:1–25:46 (26:1).

first three words in Greek are identical); a reference to the kingdom of God/ heaven in the first beatitude of each; the use of the divine passive ("you will be satisfied") in each; shared material—three of the four Lukan beatitudes are found in Matthew; and the same concluding beatitude in Luke (6:22) and in Matthew (5:11) using the second person plural. Finally each list of beatitudes ends with the same entreaty to "Rejoice" because the disciples stood in the company of the OT prophets.

On the other hand there are dissimilarities. The most striking is the difference in number. Luke has four beatitudes; Matthew, eight. The order of the beatitudes is also somewhat different. Luke's four beatitudes appear as numbers one, four, two, and nine in Matthew. Matthew's beatitudes are also more developed. Finally Luke's beatitudes are followed by four corresponding woes, whereas Matthew's are not.

Several attempts have been made to explain why these differences (and the difference in scene—mountainside versus level place) exist. Augustine suggested that the differences are due to their being two different sermons uttered by Jesus at two different times and places. Others, like Calvin, have argued that they are two versions of the same basic sermon of Jesus. The Sermon on the Mount (Matt 5:1–7:29) and the Sermon on the Plain (Luke 6:20-49) are literary creations of Matthew and Luke in the sense that they are collections of Jesus' sayings that were uttered at various times and places and have been brought together primarily due to topical considerations, i.e., in order to have an orderly account (1:3). There is no need, however, to deny that a historical event lies behind the scene. Jesus' teaching on a mountain/plain has been used as an opportunity by the Evangelists (or the tradition) to bring other related teachings of Jesus in at this point.

Today most commentators see the sermons as two versions of the same teachings of Jesus, so that the beatitudes in Matthew and Luke are two forms of the same beatitudes of Jesus. Much debate has arisen about which of the two sermons (and beatitudes) is more like Jesus' actual words, i.e., which is more "authentic." Since Jesus taught in Aramaic, each of the sermons is a translation into Greek; and the process of translation, of course, requires interpretation. In the comments it will be suggested that the beatitudes in Luke are more of a word-for-word translation (like such translations of the Bible as the KJV, RSV, and NASB) whereas the beatitudes in Matthew are more of a thought-for-thought translation (like such translations as the NIV and NEB) of Jesus' teachings.

Other beatitudes can be found in Luke.[100] They frequently are found in wisdom literature.[101] The eschatological dimension of our present beati-

---

[100] Luke 1:45; 7:23; 10:23; 11:27-28; 12:37-38,43; 14:14-15; 23:29.
[101] Cf. Pss 1:1; 40:4; 41:1; 106:3; 127:5; Eccl 10:17; Prov 3:13; Sir 26:1.

tudes, however, is quite striking. The pairing of blessing and woe has already been seen in the chiasmic parallelism of 1:52-53, where we find woe (1:52a), blessing (1:52b), blessing (1:53a), and woe (1:53b). It has also been argued that Jesus' baptism of the Holy Spirit and fire (see comments on 3:16) should be interpreted as referring to blessing (Holy Spirit) and woe (fire). The combining of blessing and woe is found in the OT (Deut 27:15–28:6; Isa 3:10ff.; 65:13ff.; Eccl 10:16ff.) as well as the intertestamental (Tob 13:12; 1 Enoch 5:7) and rabbinic literature (*Ber.* 61b; *Yoma* 87a; *Sukk.* 56b).

The key hermeneutical issue encountered in our passage involves how to interpret the beatitudes. Are the beatitudes to be interpreted as requirements for entering God's kingdom or as eschatological pronouncements of blessing upon believers? In other words, are the beatitudes an evangelistic exhortation for salvation or pastoral words of comfort and encouragement, a kind of congratulation, to those who already possess faith? For several reasons they should be understood as the latter. For one, both in Matthew (5:1) and Luke (6:20) the audience to whom they are addressed is not the crowds but the disciples. Second, the concluding beatitude refers to those who are persecuted for the Son of Man (Luke 6:22; Matt 5:11). Third, the beatitudes end (Luke 6:23; Matt 5:12) with the statement that those to whom these beatitudes are addressed have a great reward in heaven. Matthew 5:12 also places the people to whom the beatitudes are addressed in the same category with the OT prophets ("the prophets who were before you"). Finally, the nearest OT parallel to these beatitudes are the words of comfort addressed to God's people in such passages as Isa 29:19; 49:13; 61:1-2. The four beatitudes should not be interpreted as referring to four separate groups but to one group, God's people who are the poor-hungry-weeping-hated. This is true of the four woes as well, although a different group is envisioned.

Therefore the beatitudes should not be read as words of condemnation—"You are not blessed unless you perfectly fulfill these beatitudes in your life"—but rather as words of encouragement: You who believe in Jesus—i.e., you who are the poor, the hungry, the weeping, the hated—blessed are you. God's kingdom belongs to you. God will indeed comfort you and wipe away every tear. This, of course, does not mean that the beatitudes possess no hortatory significance. Words of comfort and encouragement do challenge believers to greater zeal and commitment, for they know that their labor in the Lord is not in vain (1 Cor 15:58). Yet the primary goal of the beatitudes is to encourage the disciples by telling them of the blessedness of the eschatological consummation that awaits them. Luke's readers were not to be deceived by the present appearance of things. The "now" may at times have been discouraging, but the "then" would more than make up for this.

Comments

6:20 Looking at his disciples, he said. Both here and in Matt 5:1-2 the beatitudes are addressed to the disciples, not to the crowds, i.e., to believers and not humanity in general. The beatitudes therefore are not addressed to the poor and hungry of the world but to the believing poor and hungry.

Blessed are you. Some translations use the term "happy" to express the Greek *makarioi*, but happiness tends to be associated more with feelings, and what is being referred to here is not the feelings of believers but their status and situation. (The difficulty of translating *makarioi* as "happy" is evident from The Jerusalem Bible—"Happy are you who weep now.") Perhaps "favored" is a better thought-for-thought translation. The poor of this beatitude possess the blessedness of being the object of God's favor. They may weep now, but theirs is a blessed state, for God's kingdom belongs to them.

Who are poor. The term "poor" has more of a theological than an economic sense here. In the OT the term is used in Pss 40:17; 86:1; 109:22, where the psalmist stated, "I am poor and needy." These psalms are all psalms of "David." Clearly no reader of these psalms thought that King David was referring to his economic status, for, as a king, David was not economically poor. They would have interpreted this metaphorically along the lines of Matt 5:3, "poor in spirit." (Whether or not these psalms were originally Davidic is immaterial, since the first-century reader thought they were Davidic.)[102] The term "poor" is also used in Prov 3:34; 16:19 antithetically to those who are proud, not to those who are rich. The religious nature of this term is also revealed by the fact that the members of the Qumran community referred to themselves as "poor."[103] The term "poor" furthermore was "a traditional characterization of Israel understood in terms of its suffering and humiliation at the hands of the nations.[104] The fact that "poor" is not qualified by "now," as hungry and weep are in the next beatitudes, also indicates that "poor" does not refer to an economic status that will change but to a permanent religious character. The believer will always be "poor" in that he or she will always be humble. It is clear that Matthew understood "poor" in this religious sense, for he qualified the term by adding "in spirit." Thus Luke provided his readers with a word-for-word translation of Jesus' beatitude and Matthew a thought-for-thought one, but for both this term was understood as referring not to the economic poor of the world but to believers who are poor, i.e., the humble/poor in spirit.

Having said this, it is also clear that Luke in his Gospel had a special concern for the economic poor. See Introduction 8 (5). He stated earlier that Jesus came "to preach good news to the poor" (4:16; cf. 1:52-53). He also pointed out that the disciples left everything to follow Jesus (5:11,28; cf. also 18:28), and in their mission they would be dependent on the hospitality of others (9:3-5,57-58; 10:8-11).

---

[102]Cf. also *Pss. Sol* 15:1, where the author, supposedly King Solomon, referred to himself as "poor." In 10:6 of the same work the terms "poor" and "devout" stand in synonymous parallelism.

[103]Cf. 1QH 5:13-22; 1QpHab 12:3,6,10; 4QpPs37 1:9; 2:10; 1QM 11:9.

[104]D. P. Seccombe, *Possessions and the Poor in Luke-Acts*, Studien zum Neuen Testament and seiner Umwelt (Freistadt: Plochl, 1982), 94.

Furthermore such teachings as those found in 6:30,35, if heeded, certainly do not lead to earthly riches. Nevertheless Luke was aware both that there are "blessed" disciples who are not economically poor[105] and that the term refers primarily to the believing poor (cf. Jas 2:5). As a result, whereas this beatitude fits especially well the believing poor, it also is a pronouncement of blessing on all those who, like David, have humbled themselves before the Lord. The latter are also the poor of this beatitude.[106]

For yours is the kingdom of God. Already now and therefore in the future when the kingdom will be consummated (see Introduction 8 [2]), God's kingdom belongs to the "poor." The tie between the poor and God's kingdom has already been alluded to in Luke 4:18,43, where the good news preached to the poor is the good news of God's kingdom. Thus the kingdom is given (12:31-32; 18:16-17) to the poor, i.e., to those who in humility accept the gospel.

6:21 Blessed are you who hunger now. Unlike Matthew, Luke did not have "and thirst for righteousness."[107] The Lukan beatitude deals more with physical hunger than Matthew's,[108] the main emphasis of which is on spiritual hunger.[109] Unlike "poor," which describes a positive religious characteristic that will continue, the "now" of this "hunger" refers to an undesirable condition that will one day be forever changed when the kingdom is consummated.[110] Although not all Luke's readers hungered now, they nonetheless could identify with those who did; and, while seeking to alleviate this problem as much as their means permitted,[111] they longed with them for the consummation when God would fill his people with good things.

You will be satisfied. This is an example of the "divine passive," i.e., a means by which the devout Jew avoided the name of God in order to protect himself from breaking the Third Commandment (Exod 20:7).[112] If the passive is not used, one would have to say, "God will satisfy you." Another way in which the devout Jew avoided using the name of God was by circumlocution, or substituting another word for God. See comments on 15:18.

The portrayal of the age to come as a great messianic banquet where the redeemed would sit and feast with the Messiah was a common one in Judaism (Isa 25:6-7; 49:10-13; Ps 107:3-9) and occurs frequently in Luke.[113] This banquet already is anticipated and realized in part, as Luke 9:15-17; Acts 2:42-47; 20:7-11 suggest; but the fulfillment of the beatitude is primarily future, as the divine passive and the future tense indicate.

---

[105]Cf. Luke 7:1-10; 8:3; 19:1-10; 23:50-56; Acts 28:30.

[106]See R. A. Guelich, *The Sermon on the Mount: A Foundation for Understanding* (Waco: Word, 1982), 67-76.

[107]The combination of hunger and thirst is found quite frequently. Cf. Matt 25:35,37,42, 44; John 6:35; Rom 12:20; 1 Cor 4:11; Rev 7:16.

[108]See L. Goppelt, in *TDNT* (Grand Rapids: Eerdmans, 1968), 6:17-20.

[109]Matthew's emphasis finds a parallel in John 6:35 (cf. Isa 55:1; Amos 8:11; Sir 24:21).

[110]For the view that this term in Luke refers primarily to a spiritual condition, see Talbert, *Reading Luke*, 71-72.

[111]Cf. Luke 6:30a,38; 14:12-14; 16:9-13; 19:8; Acts 2:43-47; 4:34; etc.

[112]Other examples of the divine passive in Luke can be found in 6:37; 8:18; 11:9-10; 12:7.

[113]Luke 12:37; 13:29; 14:12-24; 22:16,30.

Blessed are you who weep now.   This corresponds to the second beatitude in Matthew, which speaks of those who "mourn." The terms "mourn" and "weep" are used together in 6:25; Jas 4:9; Rev 18:11,15,19. This may refer to the weeping caused by the kind of oppression mentioned in the next beatitude. This is more likely than the view that this refers to the sorrow that comes from repentance of sin (Jas 4:9-10). The "now" fits the former better and alludes to the time when there will be no more weeping, for God will wipe away every tear from the believers' eyes (Rev 7:17; 21:4).

You will laugh.   Although this verb is not a passive, it functions like a divine passive for "God will cause you to laugh" and refers to the coming consolation of God's people (2:25; 16:25).[114] Although laughter is usually portrayed negatively as a sign of derision or joy over one's enemies, in Ps 126:1-2 it is a positive expression of joy for God's having brought his people back to Zion (cf. Gen 21:6; Job 8:21).

6:22 Blessed are you when men hate you.   This is the ninth beatitude in Matthew and, like Matthew's, is different in form from the other beatitudes. It is the one beatitude in Matthew that uses the second person rather than the third person plural. This suggests that the original form of the other beatitudes also used the second person plural. In a series of parallel sayings, such as we find in Luke 6:20-23, the last member of the series is frequently longer (cf. the fourth command of 6:37-38).[115] *Hatred* is commonly used to describe the attitude of those who are opposed to God's people.[116] In contrast to the state or condition described in the first three beatitudes, this beatitude refers to those instances "when" or "whenever" believers are hated. The tense of this and the following three verbs (aorist subjunctives) implies that such hatred is viewed as occasional. Luke has four elements in this beatitude in contrast with Matthew's three. The love for groups of four is a Lukan stylistic feature. We see this throughout the Sermon on the Plain and elsewhere in Luke-Acts.[117]

When they exclude you.   When Luke wrote his Gospel, Jewish Christians had already been expelled from the synagogue, and he may have been alluding to this here.[118]

And insult you.   This situation of exclusion, insults, and rejection seems to contradict what we read concerning the church in Acts 2:47, where the church is described as enjoying the "favor of all the people" (cf. also 4:21; 5:13). However, for Luke both the believers' rejection and their acceptance by outsiders points to God's favor on them.[119]

---

[114]The idea of sorrow (weeping) turning to joy (laughter) is also found in John 16:20; Isa 60:20; 61:3; 65:19; 66:10; Jer 31:13.

[115]See D. Daube, *The New Testament and Rabbinic Judaism* (London: Athlone, 1956), 196-201.

[116]Luke 1:71; 21:17; Mark 13:13; John 15:18ff.; 17:14; 1 John 3:13; Isa 66:5.

[117]In the sermon (Luke 6:20-22,24-26,27-28,29-30,37-38); elsewhere in Luke (10:27; 12:19; 13:29; 14:12-13,21; 17:27; 21:16; 22:19); in Acts (2:42; 11:6; 15:20,29; 21:25). See M. D. Goulder, *Luke: A New Paradigm* (Sheffield: JSOT, 1989), 1:113-15.

[118]For this use of the term "exclude," cf. Isa 66:5; Ezra 10:8; 1 QS 5:18; 6:25; 7:1-5; 8:24.

[119]Cf. 1 Pet 4:14; Rom 15:3; Heb 11:26; Ps 69:7.

And reject your name as evil. This may refer to Jesus' followers' having been called "Christians,"[120] or it may allude to the expulsion of Jewish Christians from the synagogue as reflected in the twelfth benediction in the Jewish prayer called the *Shemoneh 'Esreh*. Dated around A.D. 85,[121] it reads: "For the renegades let there be no hope, and may the arrogant kingdom soon be rooted out in our days, and the Nazarenes [Christians] and the *minim* [heretics] perish as in a moment and be blotted out from the book of life and with the righteous may they not be inscribed. Blessed art thou, O Lord, who humblest the arrogant."[122]

Because of the Son of Man. Matthew has "because of me." The interchange of a title for a pronoun or phrase such as "because of me" is not unusual, nor should it be unexpected since such titles describe the same person as the pronoun, i.e., Jesus.[123] This clause clearly indicates that the beatitudes are addressed to believers.

6:23 Rejoice in that day. "In that day" refers to the times or occasions spoken of in the previous verse. It is not a reference to "the" day of tribulation coming at the end of history. Immediately after the beatitude-woe parallelism, Luke shared further with his readers how they should behave at such times (Luke 6:27-28).

And leap for joy. The same verb is used to express the joy of John the Baptist as he met Jesus (1:41-44). Even amid persecution Christians can rejoice, and Luke gave illustrations of this in Acts 5:41; 16:25; 21:13f.[124]

Because great is your reward in heaven. This explains why in the midst of persecution believers are able to rejoice. There is no idea of merit in this statement, for even after perfect obedience and service to God, believers will only be able to say, "We are unworthy servants; we have only done our duty" (Luke 17:10). It is pure grace that causes God to reward his servants; but reward there will be, and this is not an uncommon theme in the NT.[125] "In heaven" designates not a present geographical location but is a metaphor for God's presence.

For that is how their fathers treated the prophets. Those persecuted for Jesus' sake stand in good company. Matthew made this tie with the OT prophets even closer by adding "the prophets who were before you" (Matt 5:12). There is here an unstated but nevertheless clear understanding that Christianity stands in continuity with OT religion. There are two ways of interpreting this verse. Believers should rejoice (1) because they will share God's kingdom with the prophets or (2) because their persecution assures them that they are indeed God's people; for

---

[120] Acts 11:26; 26:28; 1 Pet 4:14; cf. also Rom 15:3; Heb 11:26.

[121] See W. D. Davies, *The Setting of the Sermon on the Mount* (Cambridge: University Press, 1964), 275-77, and W. Horbury, "The Benediction of the *Minim* and Early Jewish-Christian Controversy," *JTS* 33 (1982): 19-61.

[122] C. K. Barrett, *The New Testament Background: Selected Documents* (New York: Harper, 1961), 167.

[123] With regard to the Son of Man, compare Luke 12:8 with Matt 10:32; Mark 8:31 with Matt 16:21; Matt 16:13 with Mark 8:27 and Luke 9:18; and Matt 19:28 with Luke 22:30. With regard to the title "Christ," compare Matt 16:20 with Mark 8:30 and Luke 9:21; Mark 9:41 with Matt 10:42; Matt 24:5 with Mark 13:6 and Luke 21:8; Matt 27:17 with Mark 15:9; Matt 27:22 with Mark 15:12 and Luke 23:20; and Luke 4:41 with Mark 1:34.

[124] Cf. also Rom 5:3-5; Jas 1:2; 1 Pet 1:6; 4:13.

[125] Luke 6:35; 12:33; 18:22; Matt 6:1-6,18; 10:41-42; Mark 9:41; 1 Cor 3:14.

God's people, the prophets, have suffered similarly. The latter interpretation is to be preferred due to the parallel in Luke 6:26. Luke often emphasized this persecution of the prophets.[126]

6:24   Luke, unlike Matthew, followed his list of beatitudes with a parallel list of woes. Although a different audience is envisioned by the very nature of the material, Luke placed this material here because of its parallelism to the four beatitudes. We find a similar parallelism in Isa 65:13-14. Even as the blessings of the beatitudes reverse the present negative circumstance of the second, third, and fourth beatitudes, so the woes reverse the present positive circumstances of the corresponding woes.

But woe to you who are rich.   Such "woes" are found elsewhere in the Gospels (esp. in Luke), as well as in the rest of the Bible.[127] The meaning of "woe" and "rich" must be understood in light of the meaning of "blessed" and "poor" in Luke 6:20. Thus rich should not simply be equated with an economic status. It denotes the arrogant, haughty (Prov 28:11; Sir 13:20), and dishonest (Prov 28:6) who oppress the poor (Sir 13:19) and who were the object of the prophets' criticism (Isa 32:9-14; and esp. Amos 6:1f.). The kind of "rich" Luke had in mind is clear from Luke 12:13-21; 16:14,19-31; 18:18-30.[128] The woes refer to the experiencing of God's wrath instead of his blessing. The strong adversative "but" indicates that what awaits the rich is not the blessedness of the beatitudes but terrible torment (16:19-31).

For you have already received your comfort.   The rich now have all the consolation that their wealth will ever bring. At best it may last them their lifetime, but for some even that lifetime may be considerably shorter than they expected, as the rich fool discovered (12:16-21).

6:25   **Woe to you who are well fed now, for you will go hungry.**   This reversal proclaimed by Jesus already had been announced by Mary (1:53). This is an example of synecdoche in which a part of the judgment upon the satiated, namely, hunger, serves as a metaphor for the whole of the judgment that will come upon them.

Woe to you who laugh now.   The present temporary state of happiness, laughter, and gluttony of the haughty rich will one day end and will be followed by an eternal state of mourning and weeping. (Cf. Jas 4:9 for the contrasting of weeping, mourning, and laughing.)

6:26   Even as the reader encounters in the fourth beatitude a style change, so in the fourth woe there is also a style change. This woe again speaks to those arrogant, oppressive, unbelieving rich about whom "all" speak well. When all people praise someone, he or she best beware, for those prophets in the OT who received universal praise were in fact false prophets (Isa 30:9-11; Jer 5:31; 23:16-22; Mic 2:11).

---

[126]Cf. Luke 4:24; 11:47-51; 13:33-34; Acts 7:52; cf. also 2 Chr 36:15-16; Jer 2:30.

[127]Mark 13:17; 14:21; Matt 18:7; 23:13-29. Besides Luke's parallels to the Mark-Matthew references, cf. Luke 11:42-44,46-47,52; 17:1; 21:23; 22:22. Elsewhere, cf. Isa 1:4ff.; 5:8-23; Amos 5:18; 6:1; 1 Cor 9:16; Jude 11; Rev 8:13.

[128]Cf. Jas 5:1; 1 Enoch 94:8-9.

The Lukan Message

We find in this section a major Lukan emphasis on the great reversal the kingdom brings. See Introduction 8 (5). Blessings await the poor, who hunger, weep, and are hated; for God's kingdom belongs to them, and God will one day wipe away each tear. This momentary ("now") affliction will soon give way to glory (2 Cor 4:17). On the other hand for the arrogant rich, who are now satiated, there is a fourfold woe. For Luke's readers this should encourage them not to lose heart (cf. 2 Cor 4:16) but to continue with greater resolve to live with eternity's values in view. Whereas the coming of God's kingdom brings with it a partial realization of these blessings, believers understand that the ultimate filling and laughter spoken of in the beatitudes is "not yet" and awaits the consummation of the kingdom that belongs to them. In these verses Luke also sought to warn of the dangers of riches and to exhort his readers to make judicious use of their possessions. See Introduction 8 (7).

Two other Lukan themes appear in this passage. One involves the persecution that comes upon God's people. God's people must prepare themselves for persecution. This was the lot of the prophets (Luke 11:47-51; 13:33-34; Acts 7:52), the lot of Jesus (Luke 4:24: Acts 7:52), and would on occasion be theirs as well. Such persecution, however, affirms that they are indeed God's people. A second involves teachings given to the disciples that recall what Luke stated concerning the traditions being passed down by the "eyewitnesses and servants of the word" (Luke 1:2). Having chosen the twelve who would be his apostles (6:13), Jesus now was teaching them the traditions they would pass on to the church (6:20f.). Thus Luke's readers could be assured of the certainty of what they had been taught (1:4). See Introduction 7 (1).

(4) Love of One's Enemies (6:27-36)

[27]"But I tell you who hear me: Love your enemies, do good to those who hate you, [28]bless those who curse you, pray for those who mistreat you. [29]If someone strikes you on one cheek, turn to him the other also. If someone takes your cloak, do not stop him from taking your tunic. [30]Give to everyone who asks you, and if anyone takes what belongs to you, do not demand it back. [31]Do to others as you would have them do to you.

[32]"If you love those who love you, what credit is that to you? Even 'sinners' love those who love them. [33]And if you do good to those who are good to you, what credit is that to you? Even 'sinners' do that. [34]And if you lend to those from whom you expect repayment, what credit is that to you? Even 'sinners' lend to 'sinners,' expecting to be repaid in full. [35]But love your enemies, do good to them, and lend to them without expecting to get anything back. Then your reward will be great, and you will be sons of the Most High, because he is kind to the ungrateful and wicked. [36]Be merciful, just as your Father is merciful.

Context

Having completed the parallelism of the beatitudes and the woes, Luke now turned his attention back to the last beatitude, which speaks of the times "when men hate you . . . because of the Son of Man" (6:22). The entire section is devoted to this theme and contains the following subdivisions: 6:27-28—four commands concerning love of one's enemies; 6:29-30—four examples of the commands; 6:31—a summary; 6:32-34—three further examples of the commands; 6:35a—three commands concerning love of enemies; 6:35b—a divine promise; 6:36—a concluding summary. Much of this material is paralleled in Matt 5:38-48.[129] A Lukan emphasis in this section can be seen in the additional commands to love one's enemies found in 6:28,34-35a.

Comments

6:27 But I tell you who hear me. "You" is emphatic: *But to you I say who hear.* Because the woes of 6:24-26 were not directed to the disciples (see comments on 6:24), Luke included these words to help his readers recognize that what follows is not a set of conditions needing to be met in order to become disciples but rather directions to those who are already disciples.

In 6:27-28 we find four commands in synonymous parallelism, in which the same thought is repeated in poetic rhythm. The importance of these commands is evident in that they are Jesus' first direct commands in the Gospel. Luke may have included four commands concerning enemy love in order to match the four reproaches in 6:22. (For Luke's love of "fours," see comments on 6:22.) We find a sharp contrast in the four commands to normal attitudes toward enemies. At Qumran one was to love all the sons of light (fellow members of the sect) and hate the sons of darkness (those outside the sect—1 QS 1:9-11). We find a more positive remark toward enemies in the *Testament of Joseph* 18:2, "If anyone wishes to do you harm, you should pray for him, along with doing good" (cf. also Exod 23:4-5).[130] But Jesus' positive emphasis on loving your enemies is unique in its clarity as well as in the numerous examples given to explain what this love entails.

Love . . . do good . . . bless . . . pray. The synonymous parallelism that follows the first command helps to explain and clarify what loving one's enemies means. The last three commands reveal that the command to love one's enemies does not appeal to the emotions but to the will. Jesus did not command his followers "to feel" in a certain way but to act in a certain way. Emotions can be elicited but not commanded. Actions and the will can be commanded. Thus the command to love one's enemies is not directed to how believers are to feel but how they are to act. Often loving feelings follow loving actions much like a caboose follows an

---

[129] Luke 6:27 (Matt 5:43); Luke 6:29 (Matt 5:39-40); Luke 6:30 (Matt 5:42); Luke 6:31 (Matt 7:12); Luke 6:32-33 (Matt 5:46-47); Luke 6:36 (Matt 5:48). (Luke 6:28,34-35 has no Matthean parallel.) It would appear from this comparison that some of this material already existed together in the tradition used by Luke and Matthew.

[130] For additional examples, see Nolland, *Luke 1–9:20*, 294-95.

engine. Jesus' commands, however, are addressed to the engine of the will and not the caboose of feelings. Love involves doing good. (Cf. how the centurion's love for Israel resulted in his building a synagogue, i.e., his doing good [7:5], even as the good Samaritan's love of his neighbor [10:27-37] resulted in his doing good to the needy man, who as a Jew was his enemy.)

Do good to those who hate you. Although the Greek wording is different, this is essentially a synonym for "do good" in 6:33,35. The expressions "enemies" and "those who hate you" are used interchangeably in 1:71.[131] We find two good examples of the fulfillment of this command in Acts 7:54-60 and 16:28-32. This command, for Luke, did not mean that Christians were prohibited from defending themselves by legal means against non-Christians (cf. Acts 16:37-39; 22:25-29; 25:10-11).

6:28 Bless those who curse you. There are numerous examples of blessing only those who bless you and cursing those who curse you (Gen 12:3; 27:29; Judg 17:2; cf. 1 QS 2:2-17), so that this command represents a sharp contrast. The contrast between Jesus' words and the common way of thinking is heightened in Matthew by his "You have heard that it was said. . . . But I tell you" (5:43-48). Romans 12:14 may indicate that Paul knew of this command (cf. 1 Cor 4:12; Rom 12:19-20; and also 1 Pet 3:9). Justin Martyr used the word *curse* seven times in his *Dialogue with Trypho* (16, 93, 95, 96, 108, 123, 133) to describe the treatment of Christians by Jews in his day.

6:29 At this point Luke gave four examples about how the four commands of enemy love should be carried out (6:29-30). The literary symmetry in these two verses involves the following: "to the one ____, turn/give; and from the one ____, do not stop/demand." The four examples, however, do not correspond exactly in content with the four commands in 6:27-28.[132]

If someone strikes you on one cheek. Whereas the "you" of 6:27-28 is plural, here and in the next verse it is singular due to the specific nature of the examples. (The use of the plural here would also be more clumsy.) What is being referred to involves insult more than injury (cf. Isa 50:6, esp. in the LXX) and should be understood as occurring "because of the Son of Man" (Luke 6:22).

If someone takes your cloak. The parallel in Matthew envisioned a legal situation in which the believer is sued for his inner garment (the tunic) and also gives up the outer garment (the cloak), which was exempt from legal suits because it was a basic essential for life (Exod 22:26-27). Luke in contrast envisioned a situation in which a thief takes the outer garment (the cloak) and is also given the inner garment (the tunic). The former example no doubt would have been more meaningful for Matthew's Jewish audience, whereas for Theophilus, Luke's example would have been more relevant. The reader is urged to give up his or her possessions in such instances as willingly as Peter (Luke 5:11) and Levi (5:28) did.

---

[131] Cf. also Pss 18:17; 21:8; 25:19; 69:4; 106:41-42.

[132] In Matthew we find a fifth, additional example: "If someone forces you to go one mile, go with him two miles" (Matt 5:41). Luke may have omitted this from his source since it was less applicable to his readers than it was for Jesus' original hearers and in order to have four examples in parallel to the four commands (Luke 6:27-28), the four beatitudes (6:20-23), and the four woes (6:24-26).

6:30   Give to everyone who asks you. No exceptions are stated. Luke's "everyone" is not found in Matt 5:42 and intensifies the command.[133] It is best to understand this as an overstatement for effect, for we do find an exception in other NT examples (cf. 2 Thess 3:6-13). Nevertheless the use of overstatement in this command serves to heighten its importance, and this issue will come up again in Luke 6:34-35.

If anyone takes what belongs to you. Here as in 6:29 theft is in mind.

6:31 By this conclusion Luke indicated that the Golden Rule is a summary of what it means to love your enemies and, *a fortiori*, your friends. We find several examples of the Golden Rule in extrabiblical literature. Negative examples are found in Tob 4:15 ("What you hate, do not do to anyone"); *Did.* 1:2 ("Whatever you would not like done to you, do not do to another"); *Sabb.* 31a ("What is hateful to you, do not to your neighbor").[134] A positive example is found in Lev 19:18, which is being alluded to here. Despite these parallels, Jesus' teaching on enemy love is unique in its clarity and positive emphasis as well as in the numerous examples given to explain what this command means. The command furthermore is not simply seen as a prudent rule but as corresponding to God's character of mercy (Luke 6:36; cf. Rom 5:8-10). The Golden Rule is essentially another way of saying, "Love your neighbor"; and, as the following verses clearly show, this love of one's neighbor, which involves doing not feeling, goes beyond simple reciprocity toward one's friends. Whereas the lawyer of Luke 10:29 sought to restrict the command to love one's neighbor, the Golden Rule permits no such restriction, for Christian love is not dependent on others' behavior.

6:32 In each of the next three verses we find three examples of the Golden Rule that show that reciprocity is not enough (cf. 14:12-14). Christian love must go beyond the kind of love sinners have toward one another, for like the first command in 6:27-28 believers must love even their enemies. The parallel in Matt 5:46-47 involves "tax collectors and pagans" (Gentiles), but Luke contextualized the categories for his readers.

What credit is that to you? The word "credit" was "regularly employed by Hellenistic ethicists to designate the return for his good deeds a moral man might properly expect."[135] The Golden Rule, however, goes far beyond this, for it seeks nothing in return for its love. (For a similar use of the term "credit, cf. 1 Pet 2:19-20.)

6:33 The second example is patterned after the second command in Luke 6:27-28. It again demonstrates that reciprocity is not enough.

6:34   And if you lend to those from whom you expect repayment. The third example follows the same pattern as the first example in 6:32.[136] The kind of

---

[133]Cf. Luke 5:28 with Mark 2:14 and Luke 11:4 with Matt 6:12 for other examples of such Lukan intensification.

[134]It is interesting to note that both Matthew and the Talmud have similar comments after their "Golden Rule." Matthew 7:12 adds "for this sums up the Law and the Prophets," whereas *Sabb.* 31a adds "that is the whole Torah, while the rest is the commentary thereof."

[135]V. P. Furnish, *The Love Command in the New Testament* (Nashville: Abingdon, 1972), 58.

[136]The only major difference between the three examples is that the first example uses

repayment being referred to is unclear. Does it refer to return of the principle that was loaned or return of the principle with interest (which technically was forbidden by Exod 22:25; Lev 25:35-37; Deut 23:20), or does it refer to the opportunity of being offered future loans in return? The reciprocity of the previous two verses favors the latter interpretation.

6:35 The three commands in this verse build upon Luke 6:32-34: love (6:32), do good (6:33), and lend (6:34). They are present imperatives and emphasize the need for the believer to continually love, do good, and lend. Even as God has been gracious to believers "while we were still sinners" (Rom 5:8; cf. "ungrateful and wicked" in this verse), so we are to give freely in return. For the command to lend, compare Lev 25:35-37.

Then your reward will be great. Whereas in Luke 6:32-34 Jesus commanded believers to do good and not to base their behavior on the hope of receiving reciprocal treatment, now he promised that in so doing God would reward them. Believers are to focus not on the kinds of things this world provides but on the treasure that cannot be exhausted (12:33-34). For the idea of reward, see comments on 6:23.

And you will be the sons of the Most High. Matthew (5:45) used a typical Matthean phrase, "sons of your Father in heaven," but Luke used the same terminology ("son[s] of the Most High") that he used in Luke 1:32 with respect to Jesus.[137] Like the beatitudes, this whole section (6:27-36) is addressed to believers who already have God as their Father, as the next verse clearly states (cf. also 11:2,13; 12:30,32).[138] Therefore the verb "will be" should not be understood as "will become" but rather "will show yourselves to be." An interesting parallel to this promise is found in Sir 4:10.

Because he is kind to the ungrateful and wicked. The commands given above are not based on the shortness of time remaining before the kingdom's consummation, i.e., as an interim ethic, but upon God's character. It is not an eschatological urgency that serves as the basis for these commands but God's character ("he is kind"—cf. Rom 2:4) and the fact that the believer while ungrateful and wicked has been the recipient of God's mercy.

6:36 Be merciful, just as your Father is merciful. This concluding summary follows the form found in Lev 19:2. The Matthean parallel (Matt 5:48) reads, "Be perfect, therefore, as your heavenly Father is perfect." The main difference involves the terms "merciful" and "perfect." "Merciful" suits the immediate context better in that it matches "kind" in Luke 6:35. (Matthew's "be perfect," on the other hand, fits well his emphasis in chap. 6 concerning the need for a righteousness that surpasses that of the Pharisees and teachers of the law, i.e., a perfect righteousness.) We also find reference to God's mercy in Luke 1:50,54,58,72, 78 (cf. also 10:37; Ps 145:8-9).

---

the indicative mood (a first class condition) and the last two use the subjunctive mood (third class conditions), but there is no significant difference in meaning between them.

[137]"Most High" is also used for God in 1:32,35,76; Acts 7:48 (cf. also Luke 8:28; Acts 16:17).

[138]For Paul's understanding of Christian sonship, cf. Gal 4:4-7 and Rom 8:14-15.

The Lukan Message

The Lukan emphasis on love for enemy is seen most clearly when one compares his expanded account with the parallel in Matthew.[139] Luke's stress on the command to love one's enemies is also seen in the following account (6:37-42), which deals with the need to forgive and not condemn others. His addition of "everyone" to the example in 6:30 also reveals his emphasis. Luke wanted his readers to recognize the need to love their enemies.

Jesus, the early church, and all the Evangelists of course emphasized that the command to love lies at the heart of Jesus' ethical teaching. Luke nevertheless went out of his way to stress this. The believer is to love the outcasts, sinners, and Samaritans. See Introduction 8 (5). Only in Luke do we read that at his crucifixion Jesus said, "Father, forgive them, for they do not know what they are doing" (23:34). This prayer is then paralleled in Acts 7:59-60, where "while they were stoning him, Stephen prayed . . . 'Lord, do not hold this sin against them.' " Luke's readers, just as Jesus' disciples, are to love their neighbors regardless of whether they are friends or enemies. Whereas feeling positively toward one's enemies and "liking" them are indeed impossible at times, Luke helps us to understand that we can love our enemies by willing good toward them, by doing good in return for evil, by blessing instead of cursing, and by praying for them. Often even the ability to will good for one's enemies may seem impossible, but Luke believed that the same Spirit who empowered Jesus (Luke 4:14) dwells in believers and can empower them to choose love for enemies. Thus Pentecost keeps this from being simply an impossible ideal.

(5) Judging Others (6:37-42)

[37]"Do not judge, and you will not be judged. Do not condemn, and you will not be condemned. Forgive, and you will be forgiven. [38]Give, and it will be given to you. A good measure, pressed down, shaken together and running over, will be poured into your lap. For with the measure you use, it will be measured to you."

[39]He also told them this parable: "Can a blind man lead a blind man? Will they not both fall into a pit? [40]A student is not above his teacher, but everyone who is fully trained will be like his teacher.

[41]"Why do you look at the speck of sawdust in your brother's eye and pay no attention to the plank in your own eye? [42]How can you say to your brother,

---

[139]Luke 6:27-28 has four commands concerning love for enemies, whereas Matt 5:43 has two; Luke 6:32-34 has three examples of how this love is to be lived out, whereas Matt 5:46-47 has two; Luke 6:35 has three commands, whereas Matthew has none. Only in Luke 6:29-30 do we find that Matthew is greater in length than Luke in having a fifth example. Yet, as mentioned in our comments under 6:29, Luke's omission in this instance is quite understandable.

'Brother, let me take the speck out of your eye,' when you yourself fail to see the plank in your own eye? You hypocrite, first take the plank out of your eye, and then you will see clearly to remove the speck from your brother's eye.

Context

This third section of the Sermon on the Plain picks up the principle of 6:36, which involves being "merciful." God's mercy is frequently associated with his lack of condemnation (cf. 6:37ab) and his gracious forgiveness (6:37c,38; cf. Pss 103:8-12; 111:4). As a result the mention of God's mercy and the command to be merciful leads quite naturally to the specific application of that mercy in not judging or condemning others and in being forgiving. This section begins with a twofold prohibition followed by a twofold positive command and reveals once again Luke's love for "fours" (see comments on 6:22).

Comments

6:37 Do not judge. What is being forbidden here is not the legitimate exercise of judgment in lawcourts or in church discipline but the tendency to criticize and find fault with others. Marshall aptly observes, "It is not the use of discernment and discrimination which is forbidden but the attitude of censoriousness."[140] It forbids a Christian from finding "status by negation," i.e., looking better by criticizing others as worse. The use of the present imperative in this and the next prohibition can better be translated "stop judging" and suggests that readers stop what they are presently doing, rather than that they should guard themselves against ever doing this sometime in the future.

And you will not be judged. Luke concluded this command with an emphatic promise by using the subjunctive of emphatic negation—the strongest negation possible in Greek, i.e., you shall not in any way be judged. Matthew has this as a purpose clause, "[so] that you be not judged" (Matt 7:1, RSV). In both we have the use of the "divine passive" in order to avoid using God's name, i.e., instead of "and God will not judge you." (See comments on 6:21.) In keeping this commandment one will not entirely escape God's final judgment (cf. 2 Cor 5:10), but rather in the day of judgment one will be judged mercifully (Luke 6:38c; Matt 7:2).

Do not condemn. The second command stands in synonymous parallelism with the first, for "condemn" is essentially a synonym for "judge." This command both clarifies the meaning of "Do not judge" and, by repeating the same thought, adds emphasis to this teaching. Note that the rhythmic balance of this parallelism is quite evident even in the English translation.

And you will not be condemned. Again there is a corresponding promise made emphatic by the use of the subjunctive of emphatic negation.

Forgive ... Give. These two commands are also present imperatives and thus emphasize that forgiving and giving are seen as actions that are to be done continually. Both these commands have positive promises after them as well, so

---

[140]Marshall, *Luke*, 266.

that all four commands in Luke 6:37-38 stand in synonymous parallelism with one another. All four also possess a promise in the form of a divine passive. This command does not require that the believer ignore the guilt of those who have sinned against them or to proclaim the guilty as innocent. It means instead to forgive the guilty. Compare 11:4, where the believer forgives people who are indeed guilty of sinning against him.

6:38   Give, and it will be given to you. This command goes beyond not judging, not condemning, and forgiving personal injuries and injustices. Like the Golden Rule (6:31), it seeks the positive good of others. As in the Beatitudes, the last member of the four-part series is expanded. It is best to see 6:38b as modifying only the last command and describing how "it will be given," using a scene from the world of Jesus.

A good measure. The scene is the purchasing of a commodity of some sort where the amount measured out is not short, skimpy, or even fair but a "good" measurement.

Pressed down. The grain in the measuring container is pressed down, so that all the spaces are filled and the container holds as much as possible.

Shaken together. The measuring container is shaken, so that the grain can fill every empty space.

Running over. The container is filled and on top is a rounded heap so great that it overflows the container. God will bless believers not just in equal proportion to how they give to others but far, far more—superabundantly!

Will be poured into your lap. The picture is of this measure now being poured in the individual's "container," which is the fold of his outer garment. Between the shoulders and the belt, this outer cloak would be loose and could form a kind of pocket into which this measurement could be poured. The third person plural (literally *they will pour*) is a circumlocution for "God will pour." See comments on 6:19.

For with the measure you use. This concluding proverb, which is also found in Matt 7:2 and Mark 4:24 (cf. also *Soṭa* 1:7), points out that the believer's behavior toward others will determine God's behavior toward him or her. The issue is not that human generosity is accorded the same generosity (no more or no less) from God but that human generosity is rewarded with divine generosity, which is far greater, as the early part of this verse shows. Of course, showing little generosity will result in little receiving (cf. 8:18; 19:25-26).

6:39   He also told them this parable. The following parable is a proverb (cf. 4:23).[141] The parable is in the form of two rhetorical questions and expects a negative answer for the first (due to the use of *mēti*) and a positive answer for the second (due to the use of *ouchi*). How this parable relates to what has preceded is unclear. This might be a polemic addressed against false teachers, but Luke implied in the next verse (cf. also 6:20) that the disciples were the main audience to whom these teachings were addressed. Or the parable might describe the kind of inward character that causes one to keep the commands of 6:37-38, but this is far from evident. More probably, in light of the subject of 6:37-38,41-42 (judging others), Luke understood the parable as referring to the danger of being blind to

---

[141] The parable is also found in Matt 15:14 (cf. GT 34), where it is addressed to the Pharisees.

one's own faults and at the same time judging others. If a disciple has not learned enough to see his or her own faults and yet judges others, how can such a person truly teach or correct others? Both teacher and pupil will be blind and fall into a pit. For a similar parallel in Paul, cf. Rom 2:19. (There is no reason to assume that Luke had in mind the practice of some Christians establishing rules going beyond the actual teachings of Jesus.)

6:40   A student is not above his teacher. We find parallels to this verse in Matt 10:24-25 and John 13:16. The major issue in interpreting this verse involves whether the two parts are to be understood as antithetical or synonymous. It appears that the former is more likely, so that we have a contrast between a "student" (literally a "disciple" as in Luke 6:20) and his teacher, who is Jesus.

But everyone who is fully trained will be like his teacher. Since the disciples are not greater than Jesus, they must therefore train themselves fully in order to be like Jesus. How is this "training" to be accomplished? Jesus was gracious, forgiving, and did good; so the disciples should be gracious, forgiving, and good.

6:41-42   These verses (cf. also Matt 7:3-5; GT 26) are loosely linked with what has preceded in that if a blind man leads a blind man he is like a person having a beam in his eye while trying to correct another's faults. This is also an example of hyperbolic language found quite often in Jesus' teachings.[142] It powerfully illustrates why one should not judge and condemn (Luke 6:37-38). The judgment of others always exposes the reality that the "judger" is imperfect. At times the one judging may be blatantly imperfect and unaware of this. One who is unable to see his or her own imperfections while seeing so vividly the imperfections of others is clearly a hypocrite.[143] This parable may be aimed at Pharisaic Christians picking out specks in the eyes of Gentile Christians, but there is no way of demonstrating this.

The Lukan Message

This passage continues Luke's emphasis on the necessity of love for enemy. This Lukan emphasis stands in continuity with the teachings of Jesus and the other Evangelists, as the parallels in the other Gospels reveal (Matt 7:1-5; 10:24-25; Mark 4:24-25; John 13:16). Nevertheless the importance of this teaching in Luke is most clearly seen in his greater parallelism (note again his love of "fours") and his collecting of so much related material together in this one section (6:27-42).

(6) Two Foundations (6:43-49)

[43]"No good tree bears bad fruit, nor does a bad tree bear good fruit. [44]Each tree is recognized by its own fruit. People do not pick figs from thornbushes, or

---

[142]Cf. Matt 6:2-4; 7:3-5; 23:23-24; Mark 10:24-25. For Jesus' use of hyperbolic language, see R. H. Stein, *Difficult Passages in the New Testament* (Grand Rapids: Baker, 1990), 133-220.

[143]Luke 11:42 provides a good example. The term "hypocrite" is also used in 12:56 and 13:15. Matthew used this term thirteen times.

grapes from briers. [45]The good man brings good things out of the good stored up in his heart, and the evil man brings evil things out of the evil stored up in his heart. For out of the overflow of his heart his mouth speaks. [46]"Why do you call me, 'Lord, Lord,' and do not do what I say? [47]I will show you what he is like who comes to me and hears my words and puts them into practice. [48]He is like a man building a house, who dug down deep and laid the foundation on rock. When a flood came, the torrent struck that house but could not shake it, because it was well built. [49]But the one who hears my words and does not put them into practice is like a man who built a house on the ground without a foundation. The moment the torrent struck that house, it collapsed and its destruction was complete."

Context

Luke included two additional sets of teachings at this point involving being known by one's fruit and the two foundations. They are connected with what has preceded in that the love of enemies (6:27-32) and the non-judgmental attitude (6:37-42) prescribed by Jesus only stem from an inner character that can produce such good fruit (6:43-45). Only out of a good heart (6:45) can flow the good fruit described in 6:27-42. The Sermon on the Plain then ends with a concluding exhortation that stresses the need to build one's life on a sure foundation (6:46-49), i.e., the unshakable foundation of Jesus' teachings (6:47) in the sermon begun at 6:20.

Some have suggested that these sayings are meant to combat "false prophets" (cf. the parallels in Matt 7:16-18; 12:33-37). Luke, and probably Jesus as well, was more concerned, however, with the application of these truths by believers (Luke 6:20,27).

Comments

6:43 No good tree bears bad fruit. Although the terms *kalon* ("good") here and *agathos* ("good") in 6:45 are different, no major distinction should be made between them. (Cf. 8:15, where they are used together.) Most probably this is due to the former term fitting trees better and the latter fitting persons better.[144] "Bad" is to be understood in the sense of "unfit" and thus uneatable rather than "rotten," for the next verse describes good fruit as edible, not decaying. This proverb simply states that a tree is known by the fruit it produces. A bad tree produces hate and judgment of others, whereas a good tree produces a love even of enemies and a noncondemning attitude.

6:44 Several other sayings use this imagery of bearing fruit.[145] In Sir 27:6 we read, "The fruit discloses the cultivation of a tree; so the expression of a thought discloses the cultivation of a man's mind."

---

[144]For *kalos* applied to things, cf. Luke 3:9; 6:38; 8:15; 14:34; 21:5; and for *agathos* applied to persons cf. 10:42; 18:18-19; 19:17; 23:50; Acts 11:24.
[145]Cf. Luke 8:8,15; 13:6-9; Matt 3:8-10; cf. also Luke 20:10; GT 45.

6:45 The good man brings good things out of the good stored up in his heart. This verse applies the analogies of the previous two verses to people and in particular to the human heart. The expression "heart" is commonly used by Luke to refer to the inner being of an individual out of which attitudes (Luke 2:35; 16:15) and values come (12:34). An evil heart produces critical and judgmental attitudes (5:22; 9:47), doubts (24:38), and wickedness (Acts 8:22); but a good heart produces good fruit (Luke 8:8; note especially 8:15, which is a Lukan addition to the parable). As a result one should guard his or her heart (21:34). What makes a heart "good" is not explicitly stated in this verse, but Luke no doubt intended his readers to interpret this verse in light of such passages as 3:7-9, which calls people to repent and bear good fruit, and especially 6:27-42, in which Jesus instructed the repentant, i.e., believers, about how to bear good fruit. In the next account Luke gave an example of a centurion who out of the good treasure of his heart loved Israel and built a synagogue for them in Capernaum (7:5).

6:46 Why do you call me, "Lord, Lord"? Some have questioned the authenticity of this saying since the title "Lord" was used in the early church to describe the risen Christ (Acts 2:36; Phil 2:9-11). No doubt the meaning of the title "Lord" was greater and richer for Luke's audience than for Jesus', but the Aramaic equivalent *Mar* ("Sir" or "Master") was no doubt used as a title of respect for Jesus during his ministry, as the prayer "*marana tha*" in 1 Cor 16:22 (cf. Rev 22:20 in the NEB) reveals. See comments on 1:43.

And do not do what I say? The contrast between hearing and doing corresponds to the contrast between confession and obedience in the parallel in Matt 7:21. The importance of obeying what Jesus said is also found in Luke 8:21; 11:28 (cf. Jas 1:21-25; Rom 2:13). "What I say" in the present context refers to Luke 6:20-45.

6:47 Who comes to me. Compare 6:18.

6:48-49 If we compare the analogy found here with the parallel in Matt 7:25-27, it is evident that Luke "contextualized" the message of Jesus in order to fit better the situation of Theophilus and his other readers. The account in Matthew envisions a storm in Palestine that produces rising streams, i.e., wadis swollen with rainwater descending down from the hills. In contrast Luke envisioned a storm that causes a river to rise and the torrent or flood to hit a house. Luke also may have been describing a house with a basement ("dug down deep") that fits well Hellenistic houses that typically had basements.[146] The reality to which this analogy points is clear. The foundation corresponds to what a person does with Jesus' claims and his teachings, and the flood refers to divine judgment. Thus the exhortation warns the reader not only to hear Jesus' words but to put them into practice (6:47), in order that he or she may escape the divine judgment. Jesus' Christological claim should be noted. The issue at the divine judgment is ultimately dependent upon whether people become his followers. For those who follow Jesus and bear good fruit, there will be blessing and reward in heaven (6:20-23), but for those who reject him and his teachings there will be woes (6:24-26) and complete destruction (6:49).

---

[146] See J. Jeremias, *The Parables of Jesus* (New York: Scribner's, 1963), 194, n. 4.

The Lukan Message

Blessedness in God's kingdom (6:20) and escape from the divine judgment (6:48-49) are dependent upon how people respond to Jesus. This Christological emphasis is also evident in 6:22 ("because of the Son of Man") and in 6:47. The person who hears Jesus' words and does them will escape judgment. Although it may seem that judgment is based upon doing Jesus' commandments, it is not the actions themselves that bring about the final verdict but rather the reason one is committed to those actions. Believers keep Jesus' commandments because they are committed to him. Thus disciples' behavior is ultimately determined by their Christological commitment. Because they are committed to Jesus, who is the Son of Man (6:22) and Lord (6:46), they behave in a particular way. Even as the beatitudes are directed to the followers of Jesus, so the behavior that stems from keeping Jesus' teachings, described as building on a rock, is due to a prior Christological decision to follow Jesus, the Son of Man-Lord-Christ-Son of God. For Luke the final judgment, either heaven or hell, is dependent on what a person does with Jesus' claims (cf. 9:23-27; 12:8-9; 14:26; etc.).

A second emphasis found in this passage that is related to the first involves the importance of being "doers of the word and not hearers only" (Jas 1:22, RSV). That this is not a theme unique to Luke is evident from its frequent appearance throughout the NT (cf. John 15:14; Jas 1:22-25; Rom 2:13). Yet this is a Lukan emphasis and is found not only in our present text but also in Luke 8:21 (cf. the parallel in Mark 3:35) and Luke 11:28, which is found only in Luke (cf. also 14:35c, which is found only in Luke). It is important to hear the message of Jesus (5:1,15; 6:17,27), and others would have been delighted to have had the opportunity to hear what the disciples heard (10:23-24), but hearing is not enough. Some hear but do not heed and as a result come to grief (18:23). Luke's readers have also heard and been taught (1:4), and Luke exhorted them by means of these teachings of Jesus to make sure they put into practice what they have been taught (6:47-49).

4. Who Is This Jesus? (7:1-50)

After dealing with Jesus' teaching of his disciples in the Sermon on the Plain (6:12-49), Luke recorded a series of incidents that reveal that Jesus is indeed the Promised One John the Baptist announced. This is shown by Jesus' healing (7:1-10) and raising the dead (7:11-17) and the following interpretation of these events given to John the Baptist (7:18-23). The fact that this healing and raising of the dead was performed among the outcasts of society (a Gentile who was a member of the army of occupation [7:1-10], a helpless widow [7:11-17], and later a woman who was a sinner [7:36-50]) further explains who Jesus is (7:19-20). Luke prepared the reader for this ministry to the outcasts of society by Jesus' programmatic sermon given in 4:16-30. Already associated in the tradition with 7:18-23 was Jesus' testimony to John the Baptist and a prediction of his rejection (7:24-35; cf. Matt 11:7-19). Thus its placement at this point by Luke (and Matthew) is due to the fact that these two accounts were already connected. For Luke, Jesus' prediction of his rejection in 7:24-35 also clarifies who he is. It does this by describing John the Baptist's role and how he served as the Messiah's precursor in preparing the people for God's kingdom (7:27-28) and by showing that the Son of Man will be rejected (7:34). The section reaches its culmination in Jesus' forgiving a woman of her sins (7:36-50), which looks back to 7:22-23. The section concludes with the question, "Who is this who even forgives sin?" (7:49).

In this section Luke is telling Theophilus that Jesus is indeed "the one who was to come" (7:19), the one with authority to raise the dead (7:14-15) and even with the divine authority to forgive sins (7:49; cf. 5:21). Who is this one? Luke and the reader know. He is "the Son of the Most High" (1:32), "the Son of God" (1:35; 3:22), the "Lord" (1:43; 2:11; 3:4), the "Christ" (2:11,26; 4:18,41), and the "Savior" (2:11).

(1) Jesus Heals the Centurion's Servant (7:1-10)

[1]When Jesus had finished saying all this in the hearing of the people, he entered Capernaum. [2]There a centurion's servant, whom his master valued highly, was sick and about to die. [3]The centurion heard of Jesus and sent some elders of the Jews to him, asking him to come and heal his servant. [4]When they came to Jesus, they pleaded earnestly with him, "This man deserves to have you do this, [5]because he loves our nation and has built our synagogue." [6]So Jesus went with them.

He was not far from the house when the centurion sent friends to say to him: "Lord, don't trouble yourself, for I do not deserve to have you come under my roof. [7]That is why I did not even consider myself worthy to come to you. But say the word, and my servant will be healed. [8]For I myself am a man under authority, with soldiers under me. I tell this one, 'Go,' and he goes; and that one, 'Come,' and he comes. I say to my servant, 'Do this,' and he does it."

[9]When Jesus heard this, he was amazed at him, and turning to the crowd following him, he said, "I tell you, I have not found such great faith even in Israel." [10]Then the men who had been sent returned to the house and found the servant well.

Context

The story of the healing of the centurion's servant is also found in Matt 8:5-13, and we find a similar account in John 4:46-53.[147] The main differences

---

[147]The relationship between these three accounts is much debated. The Johannine account contains several similarities to the Lukan/Matthean story (Capernaum, an official, Jesus healing

in the Matthean and Lukan accounts are due to Matthew's abbreviation of the incident.[148] Again we find the classification of the account difficult.[149] What is clear is the stress on Jesus' commendation of the centurion's faith (7:9).

Comments

7:1   When Jesus had finished saying all this in the hearing of the people. This serves as a transition from the Sermon on the Plain to the present account (cf. Matt 7:28a).

He entered Capernaum. Capernaum already has been mentioned in Luke 4:23, and this incident may have been one of those referred to in 4:23 but, because of Luke's "orderly" arrangement of material, comes at this point. See comments on 4:23.

7:2   There a centurion's servant. A centurion in the Roman army was an officer in charge of one hundred men. Six centurions and their men served under a tribune. In this instance the centurion was not serving in a direct Roman military capacity because Roman soldiers were not stationed in Capernaum. (Apparently no Roman forces resided in Galilee until A.D. 44.) As a result he may have been in the service of Herod Antipas, who used non-Jewish soldiers. It is clear from 7:5-6,9 that this centurion was a Gentile. The term for "servant" here is *doulos*. In 7:7 *pais* is used. They are essentially synonymous in this account.

Whom his master valued highly. Luke probably added this to heighten the centurion's concern for his servant.

Was sick and about to die. Matthew 8:6 describes the servant as "paralyzed and in terrible suffering."

7:3   The centurion heard of Jesus. Even as the centurion had heard of Jesus, so Theophilus also had heard (Luke 1:4); and just as the centurion learned certainty and truth from what he heard, Luke hoped that Theophilus would also recognize the certainty and truth of what he had heard and now was reading.

Sent some elders of the Jews. The term "elder" refers not to the age of those sent (as in 15:25; Acts 2:17) but to their being Jewish officials (as in Luke 9:22; 20:1; 22:52; Acts 4:5,8,23). Here they refer to leaders of the local Jewish community, not to members of the Jerusalem Sanhedrin. The use of the expression "of the Jews" suggests that the author of this Gospel and its readers were Gentiles. In

---

from a distance, etc.). However, some significant differences exist (the official was not a centurion; there is no clear reference to his being a Gentile; the sick person was a son, not a servant; and no reference is made to the great/unique faith of the official). It is not impossible that two different incidents lie behind our three accounts (Luke/Matthew and John).

[148] In so doing he has omitted the role of the elders since they function much like translators do in meetings between international leaders, who for the sake of space are simply omitted from reports of such meetings. For a fuller discussion of this, see Stein, *Difficult Passages*, 34-38. One finds other examples of Matthean abbreviations in Matt 8:14-15 (cf. Mark 1:29-31); Matt 9:1-8 (cf. Mark 2:1-12); Matt 9:18-26 (cf. Mark 5:21-43); and Matt 11:2-6 (cf. Luke 7:18-23).

[149] Miracle or pronouncement story is inadequate to describe this incident, for the present account has aspects of a pronouncement story (7:9) and a miracle story (7:10). The emphasis of this story, however, falls more on Jesus' pronouncement; for although a healing took place, the act of healing was not mentioned.

the abbreviated Matthean account the centurion is portrayed as approaching Jesus and talking to him directly.[150]
Asking him to come and heal his servant. Luke also believed that the "asking" of Luke 7:3 and the "saying" of 7:6-8 came from the centurion, for these participles are both in the singular and have as their antecedent the centurion and not the elders. In other words if asked, "Who spoke to Jesus?" Luke would answer as Matthew would, "The centurion did."

7:4 The man deserves to have you do this. The term "deserves" should not be interpreted to mean *earned* or *merited*, as the replies of the centurion in 7:6 ("I do not deserve to have you come under my roof") and 7:7 ("I did not even consider myself worthy to come to you") reveal. That Jesus commented on the centurion's faith rather than his good works indicates that "deserves" is not understood meritoriously. In essence this expression means something like, *He is a kind man who has been good to our people.* The centurion may have been a "god-fearer," i.e., a Gentile who believed in the teachings of Judaism and kept the moral law but who had not become a Jewish proselyte (cf. Acts 10:2,22; 13:16,26).

7:5 Because he loves our nation. "Nation" here refers to the Jewish people, not a Jewish political entity since at the time of Jesus and Luke no independent Jewish nation existed.

And has built our synagogue. This probably was the synagogue mentioned in Luke 4:33. The giving of contributions by Gentiles to support Jewish synagogues is well attested. The building of a synagogue by a Gentile would have been quite unusual, although we do possess an inscription that tells of a Gentile building a Jewish place of prayer.[151] It has been suggested that what was meant was that the centurion was a large (or the largest) contributor for the building of the synagogue.

7:6 So Jesus went with them. Compare Acts 10:20,23 for a parallel in which Peter proceeded to the house of the Gentile, Cornelius.

When the centurion sent friends to say to him. "To say" or "saying" (RSV) is again a singular participle indicating that Luke envisioned the following conversation as taking place between Jesus and the centurion.

Lord. The Aramaic equivalent of "Lord" (*Mar*) was a title of respect in the setting of Jesus, but the title took on greater meaning after the resurrection. See the comments on 6:46.

Don't trouble yourself. Compare Luke 8:49.

I do not deserve. This could involve either a sense of "unworthiness" or "uncleanness."

Under my roof. For a Jew to enter a Gentile's home would defile him ceremonially. The centurion knew this and did not want to subject Jesus to ritual

---

[150]Matthew used 124 words to tell this incident compared to Luke's 186. He therefore eliminated the role played by the elders as "translators" between Jesus and the centurion. This should no more disturb the reader than the fact that when the newspaper speaks of the president of the United States talking with leaders from Russia or China it never mentions the translators who were present. In seeking to abbreviate the story, Matthew simply ignored these "translators," i.e., the elders, and dealt with the two main parties of the conversation— Jesus and the centurion.

[151]See Fitzmyer, *Luke*, 652, and Marshall, *Luke*, 280.

impurity (cf. Acts 10:28; 11:2,12). This passage is a good example of the social and religious gap that existed between Jew and Greek in the first century and with which the early church struggled.

7:7 That is why I did not even consider myself worthy to come to you. This favors the view that "unworthiness" rather than "uncleanness" is the greater issue (cf. 3:16; 5:8). No reason is given for this sense of unworthiness. To claim that this feeling of unworthiness was due to a sense of depravity, a sense of immorality, being a Gentile, a recognition of the contrast between himself and Jesus, or a sense of defilement is purely speculative. Whereas both Luke and Matthew emphasized the faith of the centurion, Luke emphasized his humility as well.

But say the word. True faith realizes that God can heal apart from rituals, special ointments, touch, or monetary gifts to the healer. The centurion recognized that all Jesus needed to say was a single word. His faith in Jesus was absolute and unlimited. Even a single word from the Lord (cf. Matt 8:16; Ps 107:20) spoken at a distance could heal his servant, for the Spirit of the Lord was present with Jesus to heal (Luke 5:17). No doubt Luke would long for his readers, as well as for the church today, to have such faith.

7:8 The centurion explained his faith in Jesus by giving an illustration of authority. If the centurion with his authority could simply order certain things done, how much more (*a fortiori*) could Jesus as "Lord" do the same.

For I myself am a man under authority. This can be interpreted to mean that just as the centurion was under authority and thus could do things because of that authority, so Jesus, being under divine authority, had greater power and could give orders to heal his servant in God's name (cf. 5:17). It can also be interpreted in a concessive sense as, "Even though I am a man under authority, I can still give orders, but you Jesus have even more power since you are not under authority." However we interpret this phrase, Luke was not seeking to downplay Jesus' authority but to emphasize it.

7:9 I have not found such great faith even in Israel. In Luke's context the centurion became a symbol of believing Gentiles who stood in contrast to unbelieving Jews, so that what was true in Jesus' situation became even more true in the Evangelist's. By adding 8:11-12 at this point (in Luke this appears later in 13:28-29), Matthew heightened this contrast between unbelieving Israel and believing Gentiles. Yet for both Matthew and Luke, this affirmation of the centurion's faith served as support and encouragement for the acceptance of Gentiles into the church.

7:10 As in all miracle stories, proof of the healing is given.

The Lukan Message

It is difficult to read this story without thinking of how Luke in Acts described the spread of the gospel to the Gentile world. This story clearly foreshadows the later Gentile mission. We find some obvious parallels between this story and Cornelius's conversion in Acts 10.[152] Luke no

---

[152]Cf. Luke 7:2 with Acts 10:1; Luke 7:3 with Acts 10:5; Luke 7:4-5 with Acts 10:2; Luke 7:6 with Acts 10:23,28.

doubt sought to help the church of his day understand how the inclusion of the Gentiles into the church was foreshadowed and envisioned by Jesus during his earthly ministry. He may even have hoped that this account would help Christian Jews and Gentiles in his day to welcome each other in the fellowship of the church. Nolland observes, "In the later church the existence of such a Gentile who had manifested such an outstanding spiritual perception and responsiveness would have served as a strong argument against the exclusion of Gentiles on principle from Christian fellowship."[153]

In the present context, however, this account serves an even more important Christological function. In 7:1-50 Luke answered the question, "Who is this Jesus?" and showed how the programmatic sermon of 4:16-30 was being fulfilled. Jesus had been anointed (4:18) and the power of the Lord was present with him (5:17), so that he could bring the blessings of God's kingdom (4:18-19). Shortly, John the Baptist would raise the question, "Are you the one who was to come, or should we expect someone else?" (7:20). Jesus would respond affirmatively by pointing out that the promises of the messianic age were being fulfilled (7:22-23). Luke wanted his readers to see in the present miracle a proof that Jesus is indeed the awaited Messiah. He possesses a unique authority. Even at a distance a single word brings instant healing. "Who is this one who possesses such authority?" The answer is clear. Jesus of Nazareth is the Christ, the Son of God, the Lord!

(2) Jesus Raises the Widow of Nain's Son (7:11-17)

[11]Soon afterward, Jesus went to a town called Nain, and his disciples and a large crowd went along with him. [12]As he approached the town gate, a dead person was being carried out—the only son of his mother, and she was a widow. And a large crowd from the town was with her. [13]When the Lord saw her, his heart went out to her and he said, "Don't cry."

[14]Then he went up and touched the coffin, and those carrying it stood still. He said, "Young man, I say to you, get up!" [15]The dead man sat up and began to talk, and Jesus gave him back to his mother.

[16]They were all filled with awe and praised God. "A great prophet has appeared among us," they said. "God has come to help his people." [17]This news about Jesus spread throughout Judea and the surrounding country.

Context

In the previous account Luke demonstrated Jesus' divine authority and power to heal someone near death. Here Luke revealed the even greater power of Jesus to raise someone from the dead. This is the first of three or

---

[153]Nolland, *Luke 1–9:20*, 318.

perhaps four such raisings in Luke-Acts (Luke 8:40-48; Acts 9:36-43; cf. also Acts 20:7-12). It is evident from Luke 7:22 that this account functions as a Christological explanation of who Jesus is because Jesus answered the question, "Are you the one who was to come, or should we expect someone else?" (7:20) with, "Go back and report to John what you have seen and heard." In the present account Jesus is described as a "great prophet" (7:16) who has power even over life and death. Clearly Luke sought to demonstrate that the power of God was present in Jesus of Nazareth in a unique way; and even if this one account does not in itself contain a complete Christological affirmation that Jesus is the Christ, the Lord, the Son of God, Luke wanted his readers to understand this incident in conjunction with and in support of such a Christology. It was after all the "Lord" (7:13) who was referred to as the "great prophet."

We find an important parallel to this story in 1 Kgs 17:17-24, where Elijah raised the son of a widow of Zarephath (cf. also 2 Kgs 4:8-37). The close similarity between these two accounts suggests that Luke wrote 7:11-17 with 1 Kgs 17:17-24 in mind.

Comments

7:11   Jesus went to a town called Nain.   Nain is located six miles south southeast of Nazareth and is about twenty-five miles from Capernaum.

7:12   A dead person was being carried out.   Luke used a technical term here for carrying out a corpse for burial.

The only son of his mother.   Luke provided this description to reveal not only the emotional loss of the woman but also the desperate economic straits she was now in. With neither a husband nor a son to care for her, she would have had no means of support. The term "only" also is found in Luke 8:42 and in 9:38, where Luke added it to the Markan parallels (cf. Mark 5:23; 9:17).

And she was a widow.   This recalls Luke 4:25-26 and 1 Kgs 17:10.

And a large crowd from the town was with her.   Attendance at a funeral was considered a work of love,[154] and the mourning for an only child would have been especially bitter. By his mention of the large crowd, Luke further heightened the tragedy and revealed that the things he recorded in Luke-Acts were "not done in a corner" (Acts 26:26).

7:13   When the Lord.   Luke in narrating this account picked up the term "Lord" from the previous account (Luke 7:6) and used this favorite postresurrection title to describe Jesus. This is not surprising because for Luke and his readers the Jesus of this story and the church's risen Lord were one and the same. See comments on 1:43.

His heart went out to her.   The woman's dire situation caused Jesus to have compassion on her. This compassion, however, was no condescending pity but rather a loving concern.

---

[154]See H. L. Strack and P. Billerbeck, *Kommentar zum Neuen Testament* (Munchen: C. H. Beck'sche, 1965), 4:578-92.

Don't cry. This command anticipates that Jesus would do something.

7:14 Then he went up and touched the coffin. Touching a dead body made one ceremonially unclean (Num. 19:11,16), but Jesus ignored this convention. This was not a closed coffin but a bier or litter used to carry the body outside the city to its burial place.

He said, "Young man, I say to you, get up!" In this healing, unlike the preceding one, no mention is made of anyone's faith. This shows that Jesus' healings ultimately were not dependent on the faith of the person being healed but on his own power and might. By his word alone the sick were healed and the dead raised.

7:15 The dead man sat up. Jesus' purpose in performing this miracle was not to witness to who he was but rather to show compassion toward this woman. However, even though this was not Jesus' purpose, the miracle does in fact function as a sign of who he is both in the original situation and for Luke. This is evident from 7:22. For "sat up," compare Acts 9:40. For Luke the healing serves as a "sign" of the arrival of God's kingdom and its Messiah. In Acts such implicit signs of the arrival of the kingdom and of the Messiah give way to a more direct proclamation of their presence.

And began to talk. This and the man's sitting up are proof of the miracle.

Jesus gave him back to his mother. Compare 1 Kgs 17:23 (LXX), where we have the exact wording (cf. also 2 Kgs 4:36).

7:16 They were all filled with awe. Literally, *Fear took [possession of] all.* This fear was not terror but holy awe. See comments on 1:65.

And praised God. For a similar tie between an experience of reverential awe and the consequent glorifying of God, cf. Luke 2:13,20; 5:26.

"A great prophet has appeared among us," they said. Luke did not understood this title as an inadequate confession but as indicating that Jesus, as Elijah in 1 Kgs 17:17-24, possesses God's unique authority and power. Whether this is an allusion to *the* prophet of Deut 18:15-18 is uncertain. For the comparison of Jesus to Elijah, cf. 4:24-26.[155] For the description of Jesus as a prophet, cf. 4:23-24; 7:39; 9:8,19; 13:33; 22:64; 24:19; Acts 3:22; 7:37. Like the OT prophets, Jesus was concerned for the poor, and he would later be put to death as the OT prophets were (Luke 4:24; 6:22-23; 11:47-51; 13:33-34). The title "Lord" in 7:13 shows Luke's belief that Jesus was more than a great prophet.

God has come to help his people. This is a common OT expression describing God's actions on behalf of his people (Exod 4:31; Ruth 1:6; Ps 106:4; cf. Luke 1:48). Compare Luke 1:68,79; 19:44; Acts 15:14, which reveal that the theological emphasis of Luke 1–2 stands in close continuity with that of Luke 3–24.

7:17 This news about Jesus spread throughout Judea and the surrounding country. For "Judea" see comments on 1:5. Compare 4:14,37.

The Lukan Message

Within this passage Luke continues the description of Jesus of Nazareth begun in 7:1. Jesus is described positively as a great prophet in 7:16.

---

[155] See Nolland, *Luke 1–9:20*, 322.

He was not just "a" prophet but "a great" prophet. For Luke this was a correct description as far as it went, but it clearly was inadequate by itself. Even within this passage it is evident that Jesus' prophetic ministry must be understood in the context of his being "Lord." While it is true that in the original setting of Jesus this form of address (Aramaic *Mar*) lacked the fuller understanding that came after the resurrection, for Luke the address "Lord" would have been understood in its richest sense. See Introduction 8 (4). Who is this Jesus of Nazareth? He is the great prophet and the Lord (7:13) who is "exalted to the right hand of God" (Acts 2:33-35). He who raised the widow's son would one day himself be raised from the dead. Through this account Luke also wanted his readers to understand that Jesus is the one whom the Scriptures said would come and is the fulfillment of the hopes and longings of God's people (Luke 7:20-23).

Two other themes appear in this account: an emphasis on God's sovereign rule of history (see Introduction 8 [1]) and an emphasis on glorifying God. God has visited his people (7:16) in order to bring about the fulfillment of the promises he has made to them. In visiting his people, he has inaugurated the kingdom of God. See Introduction 8 (2). The emphasis on glorifying God (7:16) also appears frequently in Luke.[156]

(3) Jesus Reveals Himself to John the Baptist (7:18-23)

[18]John's disciples told him about all these things. Calling two of them, [19]he sent them to the Lord to ask, "Are you the one who was to come, or should we expect someone else?"

[20]When the men came to Jesus, they said, "John the Baptist sent us to you to ask, 'Are you the one who was to come, or should we expect someone else?' "

[21]At that very time Jesus cured many who had diseases, sicknesses and evil spirits, and gave sight to many who were blind. [22]So he replied to the messengers, "Go back and report to John what you have seen and heard: The blind receive sight, the lame walk, those who have leprosy are cured, the deaf hear, the dead are raised, and the good news is preached to the poor. [23]Blessed is the man who does not fall away on account of me."

Context

After Jesus' miracles of healing (7:1-10) and raising the dead (7:11-17), Luke placed a trilogy of passages concerning Jesus and John the Baptist. The first involves John's question to Jesus (7:18-23), the second involves Jesus' testimony to John (7:24-30), and the third involves the judgment of Israel for their rejection of John and Jesus (7:31-35).[157]

---

[156]Cf. Luke 2:20; 4:15; 5:25-26; 13:13; 17:15; 18:43; 23:47; Acts 4:21; 11:18; 21:20.

[157]In Matt 11:2-19 we find the same three accounts in the identical order; and although the Matthean parallel to the first passage is shorter due to his omission of 7:20-21, he added to this trilogy 11:12-14, which occurs later in Luke (cf. 16:16).

The historicity of this episode is supported by a number of factors. For one, John does not appear in this account as a witness to Jesus but as someone uncertain and questioning—hardly what one would expect if the church had created this account. John 1 clearly shows that the early church saw John the Baptist as an unequivocable witness to Jesus. Second, the description of Jesus is too vague to be attributed to the early church, which had at its disposal such titles as Christ, Messiah, Lord, or Son of Man. Finally, John's role as the "messenger who would prepare the way" (Mal 3:1) for the Coming One is not only attested here (Luke 7:9; cf. Matt 11:3) but also in Luke 7:27 (cf. Matt 11:10) and Luke 3:4 (cf. Mark 1:2).[158]

Various attempts have been made to explain the question of John the Baptist in Luke 7:19. These include: (1) John used the question as a fictive device to help his own disciples better understand who Jesus was, but he himself had no such doubts. The problem with this explanation is that not only does the question come from John (7:19) but Jesus' answer is also directed to him (7:22-23). The fact that the beatitude in 7:23 is singular, even though the plural form is more normal in beatitudes (cf. 6:20-22), also indicates that Jesus' answer is directed to John. (2) John was now for the first time thinking that Jesus possibly was the "coming one" whom he and Israel had been awaiting. But this interpretation completely ignores 3:15-22 and that the question in this passage was, at least in Luke's mind (due to 3:16), one of doubt and not rising faith. (3) John experienced real doubt and questioning about whether Jesus, in whom he had originally believed, truly was the Christ because Jesus was so unlike what he had expected. This is the best interpretation and is in fact quite understandable. John, as well as the Twelve, had difficulty adjusting their preconceptions of what the Messiah was to be like with what they saw in Jesus' ministry. Thus he experienced a period of real doubt. Jesus' reply in 7:22-23, however, erases these doubts. As we will see (see "The Lukan Message"), Luke used this doubt to address his own situation.

Comments

7:18 John's disciples told him about all these things. "These things" refer to Jesus' activity in general but especially to such things as the previous two miracles. In Matthew 11:2 John heard "what Christ was doing" (literally *the works of Christ*).

Calling two of them, he sent them. Luke may have mentioned the presence of "two" of John's disciples in order to provide, according to Deut 19:15 (cf. 1 Tim 5:19; Heb 10:28), a sure testimony for John of "all these things" that witness to Jesus' messiahship. The sending out of disciples in pairs corresponds to Jewish and Christian practice.[159]

---

[158] See W. G. Kümmel, *Promise and Fulfillment* (London: SCM, 1961), 110-11.
[159] Cf. Luke 10:1; 19:29; 22:8; 24:4; Acts 3:1; 11:30; 13:2; 15:39-40.

Luke did not tell us where John was at this time, but Matt 11:2 states that he was in prison. Luke had alluded to John's imprisonment in 3:20 so that another reference to this fact was unnecessary. According to Josephus, John was imprisoned and later executed by Herod at the fortress of Machaerus, which was at the southern border of Perea near the Dead Sea. (See *Antiquities* 18.5.2 [18.116-19].)

7:19 To the Lord. As in 7:13 Luke used this title in the fullest sense in his narrative. Marshall rightly observes, "Although John may have his doubts about Jesus, Luke . . . has none."[160]

Are you the one who was to come? This echoes 3:16, where John spoke of one more powerful than he who was coming (cf. 19:38). The phrase "the coming one" has a range of referents in the OT. It could refer to the religious pilgrim coming to Jerusalem (Ps 118:26), to Yahweh (Zech 14:5), to the coming prophet (Deut 18:15-18; cf. John 6:14), to Elijah (Mal 4:5), or to the Messiah (cf. Luke 3:15). Evidence for the future coming of a messianic figure includes Hab 2:3; Mal 3:1; Dan 7:13. While Jesus' contemporaries shared an expectation of the coming of a messianic figure, they were confused and uncertain about what this one would be like, and Jesus did not fit the common expectations well. Thus John's question is understandable. For Luke and his readers, however, there was little question about whom John was referring to in his question. John was asking if Jesus was the Christ-Lord-Son of God-Son of Man. The question refers to Christ's coming in John's day, not the future parousia of the Son of Man.

7:20 John the Baptist sent us. The full name appears here as in Luke 7:33; 9:19.

Are you the one who was to come? Luke emphasized the importance of this question by repeating it a second time (cf. 7:19).

7:21 This verse appears to be a Lukan summary.[161] In this verse the "all these things" of 7:18 is explained. The answer to John's question is to be found in Jesus' miracles, which the two men would witness and which Luke told about in 7:1-17.

Diseases, sicknesses and evil spirits. Although it is argued by some that no distinction was made between these categories in ancient times,[162] Luke was able to distinguish between illness and possession,[163] for in 13:32 evil spirits are "cast out" and cures are "performed" (RSV). Compare 6:18-19; 8:2; Acts 5:16; cf. also Mark 1:32-34; Matt 8:16.

And gave sight to many who were blind. This clause is literally *has graced many blind to see.* This verb is also used in Luke 7:42-43; Acts 3:14; 25:11,16; 27:24 but is not found in any other Gospel. Whereas in Luke 4:18 the quotation from Isa 61:1 is interpreted metaphorically and thus more broadly, the present reference and the healing of blindness found in Luke 18:35-43 indicate that physical blindness is also included in Luke's understanding of this prophecy. See comments on 4:18.

7:22 Go back and report to John what you have seen and heard. This refers back to 7:21. Jesus did not answer John's question directly but told the two

---

[160] Marshall, *Luke*, 289.

[161] Cf. Luke 4:40-41; 5:15; 6:18-19. If so, this explains why it is not found in Matthew.

[162] See Fitzmyer, *Luke*, 667, 544-45.

[163] See Nolland, *Luke 1–9:20*, 329, 211-12 and L. Sabourin, *The Divine Miracles Discussed and Defended* (Rome: Catholic Book Agency, 1977), 95-97.

witnesses to report what they had seen him do. Both Jesus and Luke believed this would be sufficient to demonstrate that Jesus is the Christ who was to come. If these things were taking place in Jesus' ministry, then God's kingdom, i.e., the messianic age, has already begun; and the one who has inaugurated that age must be "the one who was to come."

Even as the two disciples of John returned reporting what they had seen and heard, so Luke in writing Luke-Acts was reporting what he had seen (the "we" sections) and heard (1:2-3). Christians throughout the centuries have continued to witness to what they have heard, seen with their eyes, and experienced concerning the Word of life (cf. 1 John 1:1-4).

In both this account and the Matthean parallel six works of Jesus are mentioned.

Blind receive sight.   Compare Luke 4:18; 18:35-43; Isa 61:1 (LXX); 29:18; 35:5; 42:18.

The lame walk.   Compare Luke 5:17-26; Acts 3:1-10; 8:7; 14:8-10; Isa 35:6.

Those who have leprosy are cured.   Compare Luke 5:12-16; 17:11-19; 2 Kgs 5:1-19.

The deaf hear.   Compare Luke 1:22,64; 11:14; Isa 29:18; 35:5; 42:18.

The dead are raised.   Compare Luke 7:11-17; 8:40-56; Acts 9:36-43; and possibly 20:7-12; 1 Kgs 17:17-24; Isa 26:19 (cf. also 2 Baruch 30:1-2).

And the good news is preached to the poor.   Compare Luke 4:18; Isa 61:1; cf. also 6:20; 14:13,21. This is the climax of the six works and witnesses to the importance of this theme for Luke. The six works mentioned above divide neatly into two groups of three members each and possess a distinct rhythm: each work consists of two Greek words; the first word in all six examples consists of two syllables; the second word (each a verb) ends in either an *ousin* or *ontai*. Since the first and last members of the six works are mentioned in Isa 61:1, they also form a kind of inclusio indicating that all these works should be interpreted in light of Isa 61:1 and the programmatic sermon found in Luke 4:18-21.

7:23   Blessed is the man who does not fall away on account of me.   This beatitude is unusual in that it involves not so much a proclamation of blessing (as in 6:20-22) but a challenge as in 11:28. Those who are not scandalized (cf. 17:1-2) by preconceived ideas of the messianic task but instead judge by what they see happening will know that Jesus is indeed the Promised One and will as a result be blessed. Those, however, who are offended because of their preconceived notions and by what they do not see happening (such as the judgment of the nations, or the restoration of political independence and greatness for Israel) will miss out on this blessing.

Although the beatitude is addressed in the original setting to John the Baptist (note the singular tense of the verbs—see "Context"), it is so worded that it also is applicable for Luke's original readers and present-day readers as well. As in Jesus' day, Luke's time, and today, the final eschatological verdict is dependent upon people's attitude toward Jesus. In the final judgment they will stand or fall based upon whether they are his followers (cf. 6:47-49; 9:23-26,48; 12:8-9; 14:26).

The Lukan Message

Some argue that Jesus in this incident was rejecting the role John the Baptist ascribed to him in 3:15-18. This was the role of *Elijah redivivus,* i.e., the role that the returning Elijah was to fulfill.[164] Luke, however, did not suggest in any way that John the Baptist was incorrect in 3:15-18 in his assessment of Jesus' ministry. On the contrary he affirmed that Jesus is indeed the one "who is to come" (7:19-20) spoken of in 3:16. See comments on 3:15-18. In this passage Luke used John the Baptist as a foil for those in his own day who argued that Jesus could not be the one promised in the OT because he did not fulfill their particular conception of what the Messiah/Christ would be like. Yet to those willing to look at the evidence (7:22), Jesus fulfilled the OT messianic promises. God has indeed visited his people (1:68,78; 7:16); for the blind saw, the lame walked, the lepers were cured, the deaf heard, the dead were raised, and the poor were hearing the good news. In these works John's questions, and the questions of Luke's readers, find their answer. Luke ended the account (as did Matthew in 11:6) with a challenge to his readers to accept the witness of Luke 7:22 as proof that Jesus is the Coming One of whom the OT spoke. Later other evidence, such as the resurrection and the miraculous growth of the church, added additional support to this. Luke hoped that through this account his readers would be strengthened and would become even more certain concerning what they had been taught (1:4). See Introduction 7 (1).

Another Lukan theme found in this passage involves God's visitation of the outcasts and needy. The healing and proclamation of the gospel to the blind, lame, leprous, deaf, dead, and poor show the fulfillment of 1:50, 52-53,79; 4:18. Still another theme found in this passage involves Jesus' central role in salvation. Blessing (or woe) depends totally upon what people will do with Jesus. See comments on 6:47-49.

(4) Jesus Bears Witness to John the Baptist as His Forerunner (7:24-30)

24After John's messengers left, Jesus began to speak to the crowd about John: "What did you go out into the desert to see? A reed swayed by the wind? 25If not, what did you go out to see? A man dressed in fine clothes? No, those who wear expensive clothes and indulge in luxury are in palaces. 26But what did you go out to see? A prophet? Yes, I tell you, and more than a prophet. 27This is the one about whom it is written:

" 'I will send my messenger ahead of you,
   who will prepare your way before you.'
28I tell you, among those born of women there is no one greater than John; yet the one who is least in the kingdom of God is greater than he."
   29(All the people, even the tax collectors, when they heard Jesus' words, acknowledged that God's way was right, because they had been baptized by John. 30But the Pharisees and experts in the law rejected God's purpose for themselves, because they had not been baptized by John.)

---

[164] See Fitzmyer, *Luke*, 664.

Context

As in the Matthean parallel (11:2-19), Jesus' testimony to John the Baptist is attached to the preceding account. Having described how Jesus fulfilled the OT promises of Isaiah (see comments on 7:22), the present account now describes how John fulfilled the OT promises of Mal 3:1. There is no reason why the connection between these events cannot be historical, unless one assumes *a priori* that a chronological link between such accounts is impossible[165] or that Jesus could not have quoted the OT. We treat Luke 7:29-30 as the conclusion of the present pericope rather than the beginning of the next.

Comments

7:24 What did you go out into the desert to see? The "desert" refers less to a particular geographical location than to the "desert" of Isa 40:3. See comments on 3:2. There are several ways of translating this passage. The two main ones are: (1) "What did you go out into the desert to see? A reed swayed?" This is found in most translations. (2) "Why did you go out into the desert? To see a reed shaken?" The latter is found in GT 78, but the former is more likely. There is little, if any, difference in meaning between the two. It is assumed that people did indeed go out into the wilderness to see John (cf. Mark 1:5).

A reed swayed by the wind? This can be interpreted by either (1) "such an insignificant thing as a reed being swayed by the wind?" The implication then is that they of course did not go out to see such a commonplace and trivial thing as one of the many reeds that exist in the wilderness being moved by the wind. (2) "A weak and wavering person?" Here the implication is that they of course did not go out to see such an insignificant person. The former interpretation is to be preferred.

7:25 The first part of this verse stands in synonymous parallelism with the latter part of Luke 7:24.

A man dressed in fine clothes? This can also be interpreted in two ways. (1) Did the crowds go out to see a finely dressed person? This might have been worth the trip, but such finely dressed people are not located in the desert. (2) Did the crowds go out to see a timid, frail ruler? The former interpretation is more likely. Whether Luke intended to contrast the fine clothes of such a person with the dress of John the Baptist (cf. Mark 1:6) is uncertain, for he did not mention John's dress in his Gospel. However, Jesus could have been alluding to such a contrast.

No, those . . . are in palaces. Whereas the question of Luke 7:24 is not directly answered, this one is. The people did not go into the desert to see a finely dressed person, for such people do not live in the desert but in palaces.

7:26 What did you go out to see? The people did indeed go out to the desert. If they did not go to see a common desert sight (a reed swayed by the wind) or an unusual sight (a finely dressed man), what did they go out to see? The answer was clear both to Jesus' hearers and to Luke's readers.

---

[165] For a discussion of this, see R. H. Stein, *The Synoptic Problem* (Grand Rapids: Baker, 1987), 165-68.

A prophet? This is why the people proceeded out into the desert. Jesus' audience would readily have agreed with this answer (7:29). Yet although this answer is correct, it is not entirely adequate, for John was not just "a" prophet.
Yes, I tell you, and more than a prophet. The assessment of John by both Jesus and Luke was that he was far more than "a" prophet, and this is explained in the next two verses.

7:27 The first reason John was more than a prophet is that he was the one who fulfilled the prophecy of Mal 3:1. John was "the" prophet who was awaited, "the" prophet and messenger who would precede the Messiah's coming. See comments on 1:76.

I will send my messenger ahead of you, who will prepare your way before you. The "you" referred to is understood by Luke as referring to Jesus. We should therefore interpret the "Lord" of 1:17,76; 3:4 as Jesus. There is no evidence that pre-Christian Judaism believed that Elijah would return as the Messiah's forerunner. Elijah's coming was associated with the consummation and with judgment (Mal 3:1), and for many this consummation was associated with the Messiah's coming. As a result it is not unlikely that for some Elijah's and the Messiah's comings were connected (cf. Mark 9:9-13).

7:28 I tell you. This highlights the following statement.
Among those born of women there is no one greater than John. The second reason John was more than just "a" prophet is that he was the greatest of all men. The expression "born of women" is a synonym for being human.[166] Luke assumed that Jesus was excluded from this comparison. The greater quality of Jesus over John the Baptist has been a recurring theme in Luke 1–2 (see 1:26-38, "The Lukan Message"), and Luke's readers know that Jesus was greater than John. The comparison here was between John and other humans.

Yet the one who is least.—The term "least" (literally *lesser*) can be understood as (1) the least person in God's kingdom. The use of the comparative pronoun (*lesser, mikroteros*) for the superlative ("least") was common in koine Greek (cf. 9:48). (2) The "lesser" in the sense of "younger." This then refers to Jesus, who although younger was greater than John the Baptist in God's kingdom. The first interpretation is more likely.

In the kingdom of God is greater than he. The expression "in the kingdom of God" is better understood as modifying the verb "is" than the adjective "least." (Cf. 13:28-29; 14:15; 22:16; and possibly 22:30.) Although in the thinking of the world this is not true, in God's kingdom the "least" is greater than the greatest prophet. This should not be interpreted as a denigration of John the Baptist. The main contrast in this verse involves the contrast between human greatness and membership in the kingdom of God. Even being the greatest prophet is less important than being a lowly member in God's kingdom (cf. 11:27-28). Membership in the kingdom is more wonderful than being the greatest of human beings.

This interpretation understands 7:28a,b as an example of step parallelism, in which the second line or thought is advanced a step higher than the first, rather than an example of antithetical parallelism, in which the second line stands in opposition to the first. (That John the Baptist would share in the final consummation of the kingdom is evident from 13:28.) There may also be a sense that although

---

[166]Cf. Job 14:1; 15:14; 25:4; Gal 4:4.

John was both a bridge crossing the ages and part of the inauguration of God's kingdom (note he too preached the "gospel" in 3:18), yet he lived before the greater realization of the kingdom at Pentecost. Thus, although John marked the beginning of God's kingdom and overlapped it, he may be viewed here as the last great figure of the old era. See comments on 16:16.

7:29 All the people. Compare 1:10; 2:10; 18:43. See comments on 4:15.

When they heard. In light of 7:22,24 this is best understood as referring to Jesus' testimony to John rather than John's preaching.

Acknowledged that God's way was right. Literally *justified God* (cf. RSV). "Justified" is used here in its forensic sense of *declaring right*. Compare also 7:35; 10:29; 16:15; 18:14; Acts 13:39.

Because they had been baptized by John. The means by which the people "justified" God was by their submission to the baptism of God's prophet.

7:30 But the Pharisees and experts in the law. The "experts in the law" (literally *lawyers*) are also referred to in Luke 10:25; 11:45-46,52; and 14:3. This is essentially a synonym for "scribe" (cf. 11:52-53). For "Pharisees" see comments on 5:17.

Rejected God's purpose for themselves. How they did this is shown in the last part of this verse. By not submitting (an instrumental participle) to John's baptism (and, of course, the repentance it demanded), the Pharisees and lawyers rejected God's purpose for them.

The Lukan Message

The main emphasis in this passage involves understanding the role of John the Baptist in salvation history. John was truly a prophet (3:2; 7:26), but he was more than a prophet. He was humanly speaking the greatest of all human beings, Jesus excepted. He furthermore was that prophet spoken of in Mal 3:1 whose task it was to go before the Lord Christ. He was the one who would bridge the two eras and announce the coming of God's kingdom. He, not Jesus, was *Elijah redivivus* (Mal 3:1; 4:5). This is evident from Luke 7:27, even if it is not as clear as in Mark 9:9-13 and Matt 11:14. With John the Baptist's coming, God's kingdom was announced as at hand, and with Jesus' coming it was inaugurated.

Another theme we find in the Lukan comment of 7:29-30 involves the great reversal. This is most clearly seen in the Lukan reference to the tax collectors in 7:29. The religious leadership, represented by the Pharisees and experts of the law, rejected the coming of the kingdom because they rejected John's baptism and the one he announced. The tax collectors and the people, however, responded positively. As a result those who were last became first, and the first became last (13:30; cf. 1:48-53; 6:20-26; 16:25).

(5) Jesus Experiences Rejection (7:31-35)

[31] "To what, then, can I compare the people of this generation? What are they like? [32]They are like children sitting in the marketplace and calling out to each other:

" 'We played the flute for you,
  and you did not dance;
we sang a dirge,
  and you did not cry.'
[33]For John the Baptist came neither eating bread nor drinking wine, and you say, 'He has a demon.' [34]The Son of Man came eating and drinking, and you say, 'Here is a glutton and a drunkard, a friend of tax collectors and "sinners." ' [35]But wisdom is proved right by all her children."

Context

This third account concerning John the Baptist builds upon 7:29-30 and forms a chiasmus with it (A—7:39; B—7:30; b—7:31-34; a—7:35). This material is part of the common tradition (Q) which Matthew and Luke used in writing their Gospels, and in both Gospels these three accounts occur together in the same order. The two accounts contain some minor differences (Luke added "bread" and "wine" in 7:33 and used "children" instead of "works" in 7:35), but these differences possess no theological significance. The key issue of interpretation involves the relationship of the parable (7:31-32) to the sayings (7:33-35).

Comments

7:31   To what, then?   This indicates that 7:29-30 serves as a bridge connecting 7:24-28 with 7:31-35.

Can I compare?   Compare 13:18,20.

This generation?   This refers to all those who in this age oppose Jesus and the gospel and who stand in contrast to the sons of light (16:8). For a similar pejorative use of this expression, cf. 9:41; 11:29-32,50-51; 16:8; 17:25; Acts 2:40.

What are they like?   A more complete translation of this thought would be, "The situation (not just 'the people of this generation') about which we are talking can be compared to the following analogy/parable."

7:32   The parable involves the following components: (1) children, who represent Jesus' contemporaries, sitting in a marketplace and (2) other children, who represent Jesus and John the Baptist, inviting the first group of children to play. The first group, however, finds neither the ascetic John nor the nonascetic Jesus to their liking.

We played the flute for you, and you did not dance.   The flute was frequently played at a wedding dance.

We sang a dirge, and you did not cry.   This involved taking part in the mourning associated with a funeral. Compare 8:52; Matt 2:18; John 11:31-33. The picture is that of children inviting other children to play "wedding" or "funeral" and being turned down.

7:33   The rejection of the gospel message is not due to the form of its presentation. John preached the gospel while living an ascetic life-style (Luke 5:33a). Jesus preached the gospel in the joy of the kingdom's arrival, but both were rejected (5:33b-35). Neither satisfied the wishes of this generation because their message was the same. Both preached a message of repentance (cf. 3:3,8 and 5:32; 13:3,5), and both offered salvation to the outcasts (cf. 3:12-14 with 4:18; 5:27-32; 7:22).

Neither eating bread. Compare Mark 1:6.

Nor drinking wine. See comments on 1:15.

He has a demon. That is, he was mad (cf. John 7:20; 8:48-49,52; 10:20).

7:34 The Son of Man. For Luke this served as a title paralleling "John the Baptist" in the previous verse. Whether in the original setting it was used by Jesus as a circumlocution for "I"[167] is uncertain, but for Luke the title "Son of Man" refers to the person described in Dan 7:13.

Came eating and drinking. Compare Luke 7:36-50; 11:37; 14:1. The difference between the form of Jesus' message and of John's message was striking. John understood the coming of God's kingdom as requiring repentance and portrayed this via his fasting; Jesus saw the coming of God's kingdom as a time of great celebration and portrayed this by the analogy of a wedding feast (5:33-34). Both are valid expressions of different aspects of God's kingdom, and if either is totally ignored, an unbalanced portrayal will result.

A friend of tax collectors and "sinners." Compare 5:30; 15:1. For "tax collectors" see comments on 3:12.

7:35 But wisdom is proved right by all her children. Matthew's "actions" (11:19) is probably less authentic than Luke's "children." Wisdom, which is personified and corresponds to "God's way" in Luke 7:29, is justified (declared right) by her offspring. The "children" do not refer to John the Baptist and Jesus but rather to those who follow them. They have seen and heard Jesus' deeds (7:22) and "do not fall away" (7:23); on the contrary they see these deeds as signs of the messianic age (12:56) and prove the wisdom of Jesus' and John's preaching by putting it into practice (8:21). The children in the parable who did not respond represent the Pharisees and experts of the law (7:30).

The Lukan Message

We find in this account a clear emphasis both on the unity of the message of Jesus and John the Baptist as well as the rejection of that message by the Jewish leadership. Despite its different appearance, the message of Jesus and John was the same. It was not therefore the form of the message that caused its rejection but rather its content. The message was rejected because it demanded repentance. For the Pharisees and law experts such a message was received with hostility (7:30). Others might need to repent, but they were confident in their own righteousness (18:9-14). But for those who knew they were sinners and needed to repent, for tax collectors and sinners (7:29,34), the good news of John and Jesus offered hope and forgiveness, and it was gladly accepted. They saw the ministries of Jesus and John as evidence of the arrival of the messianic age (12:56). Thus once again we see the great reversal.

---

[167] Fitzmyer, *Luke*, 681.

Along with the description of the rejection of John's and Jesus' message, we have a hint of future problems. If their message was not accepted by the leaders of the nation, what would happen? Luke's readers, of course, know. As a result this passage foreshadows the ultimate rejection and martyrdom of John and Jesus.

(6) Jesus Forgives Sins (7:36-50)

[36]Now one of the Pharisees invited Jesus to have dinner with him, so he went to the Pharisee's house and reclined at the table. [37]When a woman who had lived a sinful life in that town learned that Jesus was eating at the Pharisee's house, she brought an alabaster jar of perfume, [38]and as she stood behind him at his feet weeping, she began to wet his feet with her tears. Then she wiped them with her hair, kissed them and poured perfume on them.

[39]When the Pharisee who had invited him saw this, he said to himself, "If this man were a prophet, he would know who is touching him and what kind of woman she is—that she is a sinner."

[40]Jesus answered him, "Simon, I have something to tell you."

"Tell me, teacher," he said.

[41]"Two men owed money to a certain moneylender. One owed him five hundred denarii, and the other fifty. [42]Neither of them had the money to pay him back, so he canceled the debts of both. Now which of them will love him more?"

[43]Simon replied, "I suppose the one who had the bigger debt canceled."

"You have judged correctly," Jesus said.

[44]Then he turned toward the woman and said to Simon, "Do you see this woman? I came into your house. You did not give me any water for my feet, but she wet my feet with her tears and wiped them with her hair. [45]You did not give me a kiss, but this woman, from the time I entered, has not stopped kissing my feet. [46]You did not put oil on my head, but she has poured perfume on my feet. [47]Therefore, I tell you, her many sins have been forgiven—for she loved much. But he who has been forgiven little loves little."

[48]Then Jesus said to her, "Your sins are forgiven."

[49]The other guests began to say among themselves, "Who is this who even forgives sins?"

[50]Jesus said to the woman, "Your faith has saved you; go in peace."

Context

The exact relationship of this account to the preceding material is uncertain. Some suggest Luke placed it here as an example of Jesus' friendship with tax collectors and sinners (7:34). Others suggest he placed it here as an example of Jesus' prophetic role (cf. 7:16 and 39). Still others suggest this account exemplifies how wisdom is proven correct by its children. In the context of chap. 7, Luke included this passage primarily due to its Christological content, so that it too seeks to help Theophilus understand "Who is this Jesus?" Earlier in the chapter Jesus is portrayed as a healer (7:1-10), one who raised the dead (7:11-17), and the Coming One promised in the Scriptures, who like John the Baptist would meet with rejection (7:18-35). In this account the question of "Who is this?" is again raised, and the answer from the present account and what has preceded is clear. Jesus of Nazareth, prophet-Coming One-Christ-Lord, is the one who has divine authority to forgive sins. Thus this account serves as a Christological conclusion for the chapter.

The existence of two close parallels to this account in Mark 14:3-9 (Matt 26:6-13) and John 12:1-8 raises the difficult issue of how these three accounts are related. The similarities between Mark and Luke are quite striking.[168] Note that, whereas Luke used Mark as a source in writing his Gospel, he did not include the account in Mark 14:3-9. Probably he did this to avoid two very similar accounts. There are also some significant differences between the Markan and Lukan accounts.[169] The Johannine account has similarities with both these accounts.[170] It is quite possible that these accounts go back to two separate incidents in Jesus' life (Luke and Mark/John). As they were told and retold during the oral period, a certain standardization of terminology might have taken place between the stories, and this might explain some of the similarities and differences between the accounts. This seems more likely than the explanation that these are three different accounts of the same incident.[171]

Comments
7:36 Now one of the Pharisees invited Jesus to have dinner. For "Pharisees" see comments on 5:17. For Jesus eating with Pharisees, note also 11:37; 14:1.

And reclined at the table. That they reclined at the meal indicates that it was a banquet or Sabbath meal. Concerning the latter, it was quite common to

---

[168]They include (1) an anointing by an unnamed woman (Luke 7:37; Mark 14:3); (2) Jesus' reclining at a meal (Luke 7:36; Mark 14:3); (3) the woman anointing Jesus from an alabaster jar (*alabastron myrou*; Luke 7:37; Mark 14:3); (4) a host named Simon (Luke 7:40; Mark 14:3); (5) the presence of objections over the action (Luke 7:39; Mark 14:4-5); and (6) Jesus' defense of the woman (Luke 7:40-48; Mark 14:6-9).

[169]In Luke (1) the scene was Galilee, whereas in Mark it was Bethany in Judea; (2) the event took place early in Jesus' ministry, whereas in Mark it was at the end; (3) Jesus' head was anointed, whereas in Mark his feet were anointed; (4) the objections came from Simon, whereas in Mark they came from the disciples; (5) Simon is described as a Pharisee, whereas in Mark he is described as a leper; and (6) the reason for the objection was the woman's character, whereas in Mark the objection was due to the wasting of money.

[170]Like Mark (1) the scene was Bethany (John 12:1; Mark 14:3); (2) a disciple raised the objection (John 12:4-6; Mark 14:4-5); (3) Jesus defended the woman (John 12:7-8; Mark 14:6-8); (4) there was a word concerning the poor (John 12:8; Mark 14:7); and (5) the ointment's value was said to have been three hundred denarii (John 12:5; Mark 14:5). Like Luke (1) Jesus' feet were anointed (Luke 7:38; John 12:3), and (2) the woman used her hair to wipe Jesus' feet (Luke 7:38; John 12:3).

[171]For a fuller discussion see Fitzmyer, *Luke*, 684-88.

invite a visiting rabbi or teacher to the Sabbath meal after he had taught in the synagogue (cf. Mark 1:29-31). If it was a banquet meal, Jesus may have been invited because of his reputation as a prophet.

7:37 When a woman. She is unnamed as in Mark 14:3, but compare John 12:3. **Who had lived a sinful life.** Literally *who was a sinner.* The character of the woman is important due to 7:39,47 (cf. 7:34; 19:10). This woman could have been a sinner because of her occupation. Tax collectors, tanners, camel drivers, custom collectors, among others were considered ceremonially impure because of their occupations and could be labeled "sinners." In this instance, however, this woman's sinfulness involved moral not ceremonial matters (note 7:47-50).

An alabaster jar of perfume. In Mark 14:5 and John 12:5 the cost of the jar of perfume is given—three hundred denarii. (A denarius was the equivalent of a day's wages.) Alabaster is soft stone that frequently was used to make perfume containers (so Pliny the Elder, 13.4.), and thousands of such containers have been found.

7:38 And as she stood behind him at his feet weeping. We are not told why she was weeping. It could have been due to her remorse over and repentance for sin or to the joy over the forgiveness of her sins. The interpretation of 7:47-48 will determine this. Since the guests were reclining at the meal and facing a short table upon which the food was placed, the woman had easy access to Jesus' feet.

Then she wiped them with her hair. Letting down one's hair in public was shameful and even a ground for divorce, but in her deep gratitude toward Jesus the woman forgot social propriety and used what was available to wipe Jesus' feet—her hair.

7:39 If this man were a prophet. This is a contrary-to-fact condition, which assumes that Jesus was not a prophet. Whether Simon was repeating a popular view among the people or his own previous view is uncertain. The Pharisee assumed that Jesus was not a prophet because of two false presuppositions: (1) a true prophet would not allow a sinful woman to do this (note the scandal of Jesus' behavior in 7:34), or (2) Jesus did not know that this was a sinful woman and thus was not a prophet. Luke would show in 7:44-47 that both presuppositions are wrong. It is uncertain whether we should read "a prophet" or "the prophet," but "a prophet" is more likely.[172]

7:40 Jesus sought to disarm Simon's prejudice by drawing him into the parable (cf. 10:36). The implicit Christological teachings in this incident should be noted: (1) Jesus knew Simon's thoughts (cf. 5:22; 6:8); (2) he knew that the woman was a sinner as the parable shows and thus refuted Simon's second presupposition (see previous verse); (3) Jesus is able to forgive sins—something God alone can do (cf. 5:21; 7:49); and (4) Simon's and the woman's standing before God was revealed and determined by their attitude toward Jesus.

Tell me, Teacher. This is the first use of this particular title for Jesus in the Gospel (cf. 8:49; 9:38; 10:25; etc.). It was used of John the Baptist in 3:12. See comments on 5:5.

7:41 Two men owed money to a certain moneylender. For the use of "a certain . . . " for introducing parables, see comments on 10:30.

---

[172]The major support for reading "the prophet" comes from the Codex Vaticanus.

One owed him five hundred denarii. This sum would be approximately one and a half years' wages. See comments on 10:35; 20:24. Fifty denarii would be about two months' wages.

7:42 So he canceled the debts of both. Sin is frequently referred to as a "debt," so this analogy in the parable would easily be understood as parallel to the forgiveness of sins (cf. Matt 6:12 with Luke 11:4). Compare also the interchange of "sinners" and "more guilty" (literally *debtors*) in 13:2,4.

Now which of them will love him more? Since there is no specific word for *to show gratitude* or *to thank* in Hebrew or Aramaic, such words as *love, praise, bless, glorify* were used to express thanks or gratitude. Thus "love him more" probably means *was more grateful/thankful.* Jesus sought to further disarm Simon by having him answer the parable.

7:43 Simon answered correctly. The one forgiven most will be most grateful.

7:44 You did not . . . but she. Jesus now applied the parable. In the parable the behavior of the two debtors toward the moneylender is analogous to the behavior of Simon and the sinful woman's behavior toward him.

You did not give me any water for my feet. While not mandatory, it would have been a kind gesture for Simon as the host to have had his servants wash the feet of his guest.[173] Simon was not necessarily being rude in neglecting to do this,[174] but he certainly did not go out of his way to show hospitality to Jesus.

7:45 You did not give me a kiss. A kiss was a common form of greeting, although not necessarily an expected act of courtesy. There are, however, worse things than not greeting someone with a kiss, as 22:47-48 clearly reveals.

7:46 You did not put oil on my head. It was also a kind gesture to anoint the head of one's guest with olive oil. Whether this, the washing of feet, or giving a kiss were required acts of courtesy is uncertain, but it is evident that Simon in no way expressed any affection toward Jesus when he came to his home. On the other hand the woman did all three. It is unlikely that the actions of the woman were consciously done to redress Simon's lack of affection.

7:47 Therefore, I tell you, her many sins have been forgiven. This statement about her forgiveness can be understood in one of two ways. (1) Because of what she had done, her sins were now forgiven. That is, because the woman loved much, her sins were as a result forgiven. (2) Because of what she had done, I can now conclude that her sins had in fact been forgiven. That is, the woman's attitude (as revealed in her loving much) was evidence that she had experienced forgiveness. The second explanation fits better the last statement in this verse and the context provided by 7:29-30. Thus "therefore" is best understood as going with "I tell you" rather than the statement about her sins being forgiven.

For she loved much. The "for" should not be understood in a causal sense. Her love was not the basis or ground for her forgiveness. It is better understood in the sense of "as evidenced by the fact that" or "thus we know." Therefore "for she loved much" provides the evidence (not the cause) by which Jesus was able to conclude that the woman's sins were forgiven. (Cf. 8:25 for a similar use of "for [*hoti*].") As in 1 John 4:19, love was the result of forgiveness.

---

[173] Cf. Gen 18:4; 19:2; 24:32; 43:24; 1 Sam 25:41; John 13:13-14.
[174] See Marshall, *Luke*, 311-12.

We are not told when or how the woman experienced forgiveness, and speculation on this (e.g., in Jesus' synagogue preaching just before this or in Jesus' preaching to the multitudes) is of little value.

But he who has been forgiven little loves little. As in the parable in which love (or gratitude) was the response to having one's debt canceled, so here love is the result of having been forgiven. The tense of the verb "forgiven" also favors this since the perfect tense speaks of a past forgiveness the results of which extend into the present time. Some suggest that "has been forgiven" is a divine passive for "God has forgiven," but Luke certainly did not understand it this way in 7:49. This last statement is the theoretical completion of Jesus' parable. It completes the parable's interpretation, but it should not be pressed to assume that Simon had also been forgiven but that his sins were less than the woman's, so that he did not need as much gratitude.

7:48   Your sins are forgiven. Since the woman had, according to 7:47, already been forgiven of her sins, this statement serves as a word of assurance to her, namely, "Your sins have indeed been forgiven."

7:49   Who is this who even forgives sins? From this verse it is clear that Jesus' hearers (and Luke) did not understand the statements about forgiveness in 7:47-48 as divine passives, i.e., they were not an attempt to avoid God's name by using the passive "you are forgiven" instead of "God forgives you." On the contrary, Jesus is understood as exercising a divine prerogative and personally announcing, as in 5:20-21, that the woman's sins were forgiven. See comments on 5:20.

7:50   Your faith has saved you. Through faith salvation came to the woman. Not because of her love but through faith the woman experienced the forgiveness of sins. Her love was a subsequent witness to her faith and forgiveness. The same statement is also found in 8:48; 17:19; 18:42.

Go in peace. Compare 8:48; Acts 16:36.[175]

Several metaphors are used in our passage to describe the experience of salvation. One such metaphor is the "forgiveness of sins" (Luke 7:49).[176] Another is the use of the verb "saved" (7:50),[177] which is used some thirty times in Luke-Acts. Another metaphor found in this passage is the term "peace" (7:50).[178]

The Lukan Message

Since this passage concludes the section entitled "Who Is This Jesus?" it should not be surprising that its central teaching is Christological. The emphasis in the passage falls upon the question in Luke 7:49, "Who is this who even forgives sins?" Luke intended that his readers would answer this question in light of what preceded in this and the previous chapters. This Jesus is one who has unusual power, for he can heal the

---

[175]Cf. also Judg 18:6; 1 Sam 1:17; 20:42; 1 Kgs 22:17; Jas 2:16.

[176]Cf. also 1:77; 3:3; 24:47; Acts 2:38; 5:31; 10:43; 13:38; 26:18.

[177]Cf. also 1:69,77; 2:11,30; 3:6; Acts 16:31.

[178]Cf. also Luke 1:79; 2:14; 8:48; Acts 10:36. All three of these metaphors (forgiveness, salvation, peace) are also found together in Luke 1:77-79. (Cf. also Acts 10:36,43, where peace and forgiveness occur together.)

sick (7:1-10) and even raise the dead (7:11-17). He is the Coming One for whom Israel awaited and hoped (7:18-35). He is indeed a prophet but more than a prophet, for he has the authority to forgive sins (7:36-50). To this can be added earlier statements about his being the Son of the Most High, Lord, Christ, Son of David, Son of Man, and Savior of the world. Theophilus and Luke's other readers could know the certainty of this because of the things Jesus did (7:18,22) and because of what this account reveals concerning Jesus' unusual knowledge (of Simon's thoughts and the woman's status) and authority (to forgive sins). As elsewhere (see comments on 7:23) an individual's attitude toward Jesus revealed her or his relationship with God.

Several other Lukan themes also appear in this account. One involves the need for forgiveness and how this forgiveness (7:48-49), which is a synonym for salvation (7:50), comes through faith (7:50). We find a frequent tie between salvation and faith in Luke. See Introduction 8 (6). A final theme that will be mentioned involves the great reversal. Once again the one expected to have the inside track to forgiveness and salvation is found outside of God's kingdom. Simon knew nothing of love and gratitude toward Jesus. The reason is clear. He knew nothing of the forgiveness and salvation Jesus brings. On the other hand, the outcast, a woman who was a sinner and despised by religious leaders such as Simon, found forgiveness. Again the last have become first and the first last. See Introduction 8 (5).

5. Jesus Teaches in Parables (8:1-21)

A summary (8:1-3) that resembles the one in 4:40-44 concludes the "little interpolation," the first major Q section in Luke (6:20–8:3).[179] Luke then returned to the Markan source he followed in Luke 4:14–6:16 (Mark 1:14–3:19). From Luke 8:4–9:17 he followed essentially the material found in Mark 4:1–6:44.[180]

(1) A Summary of Jesus' Ministry (8:1-3)

[1]After this, Jesus traveled about from one town and village to another, proclaiming the good news of the kingdom of God. The Twelve were with him, [2]and also some women who had been cured of evil spirits and diseases: Mary (called Magdalene) from whom seven demons had come out; [3]Joanna the wife of Cuza, the manager of Herod's household; Susanna; and many others. These women were helping to support them out of their own means.

---

[179]Some of Luke 6:20–8:3 may be L material.

[180]Luke omitted Mark 3:20-21 due to the negative statement concerning Jesus and his family's misunderstanding and Mark 3:22-30 due to the inclusion of a variant form of the account later in Luke 11:14-23.

Context

At this point Luke briefly summarized Jesus' ministry of proclaiming the good news of God's kingdom and ministry of healing. This summary is similar to that in 4:40-44, but here Luke mentioned the Twelve and "some women" and even named three of the latter. Since Luke had just referred to Jesus' forgiveness of a woman in the previous account, it may have seemed natural to mention Jesus' ministry to other women in this summary. In introducing the women, Luke also prepared the reader for the role they would play at the crucifixion (23:49), the empty tomb (24:1-11), and perhaps also in the early church (Acts 1:14).

Comments

8:1 Proclaiming the good news of the kingdom of God. For "kingdom of God" see comments on 4:43. The reference to God's kingdom indicates that the message that brings forgiveness, salvation, and peace (7:48-50) is the message concerning God's kingdom. This is what Jesus had been preaching to the "people of this generation" (7:31). The phrase "proclaiming the good news" in Greek consists of the two verbs "preaching [*keryssōn*] and proclaiming the good news" (*euangelizomenos*). The expression "proclaiming the good news of the kingdom of God" is also found in 4:43; 16:16. Earlier portrayals of Jesus' preaching and teaching ministry are found in 4:43-44; 5:1,17; 7:1,24.

The Twelve were with him. The Twelve were mentioned earlier (see comments on 6:13), and they will appear more often from this point on.

8:2 And also some women. Only one cure of a woman (4:38-39) has been mentioned up to this point, but Luke assumed that his readers knew of Jesus' ministry to women and that they were to be included in the summaries of 4:40-41 and 6:17-19. Of all the Gospels, Luke records the most prominent appearances by women.[181] That certain women followed Jesus indicates that his attitude toward women was quite different from the attitude of most first-century rabbis (cf. John 4:27; *'Abot* 1:5). In a sense these women modeled Jesus' words in Luke 14:26; 18:28-30. Luke frequently paired men and women in his Gospel.[182]

Mary (called Magdalene). Magdala, the home of Mary, is not mentioned in ancient sources outside of the NT, and its location is also unknown. The way Luke introduced Mary Magdalene indicates that she was not the same woman mentioned in 7:36-50. She probably was mentioned before the other women because of her being better known.[183]

[181] For other examples involving women note 1:26-56; 2:36-38; 4:38-39; 7:11-17,36-50; 8:40-48; 10:38-42; 11:27-28; 13:10-17; 23:27,49,55; 24:1-11. See B. Witherington III, *Women in the Earliest Churches*, SNTSMS (Cambridge: University Press, 1988), 138-57, and *Women and the Genesis of Christianity* (Cambridge: University Press, 1990), 201-24.

[182] Cf. Zechariah and Mary in Luke 1–2; the widow of Zarephath and Naaman (4:25-27); the centurion and the widow of Nain (7:1-17); the shepherd and the woman in the parables of the lost sheep and coin (15:3-10). See Nolland, *Luke 1–9:20*, 365-66.

[183] Mary Magdalene is also referred to in 24:10; Mark 15:40,47; 16:1; John 19:25; 20:1, 18; cf. also Luke 23:49,55; and the noncanonical Mark 16:9.

From whom seven demons had come out. Luke mentioned this in order to show the severity of her problem (cf. 11:26) and the greatness of Jesus' miracle of healing.

8:3 Joanna. The only other time Joanna appears in the NT is in 24:10.

The wife of Cuza, the manager of Herod's household. Although Jesus' preaching found a favorable audience primarily among the poor, some of the wealthy and powerful also welcomed it.[184] Luke seems to have had good information concerning the household of Herod Antipas[185] which may have come to Luke via Joanna.

Susanna. This is the only reference to her in the NT.

These women were helping to support them out of their own means. These women apparently were well-to-do. The verb "were helping" is the Greek term *diēkonoun* from which we get the word "deacon" (cf. Mark 15:41; Acts 6:1-6). The way the women are introduced in these verses may indicate they were known to the Gospel's readers.

The Lukan Message

Within this summary Luke alluded to several theological emphases. These include the coming of God's kingdom (8:1), a Christological allusion to Jesus' power to heal and cast out demons (8:2), the visitation of God's grace to the outcast, for women who were discriminated against (8:3), and the proper use of possessions (8:3). See Introduction 8 (2), (4), (5), and (7).

One other issue is Jesus' encouraging women to listen to his teaching (cf. 10:42) and become part of his ministry, in contrast to common rabbinic practice.[186] In a day when some argue that biblical teaching demeans women, note that women are treated in a most positive manner in Luke-Acts.

(2) The Parable of the Soils (8:4-15)

⁴While a large crowd was gathering and people were coming to Jesus from town after town, he told this parable: ⁵"A farmer went out to sow his seed. As he was scattering the seed, some fell along the path; it was trampled on, and the birds of the air ate it up. ⁶Some fell on rock, and when it came up, the plants withered because they had no moisture. ⁷Other seed fell among thorns, which grew up with it and choked the plants. ⁸Still other seed fell on good soil. It came up and yielded a crop, a hundred times more than was sown."

When he said this, he called out, "He who has ears to hear, let him hear."

⁹His disciples asked him what this parable meant. ¹⁰He said, "The knowledge of the secrets of the kingdom of God has been given to you, but to others I speak

---

[184] Cf. Luke 19:8; 23:50-53; Acts 6:7; 9:36-39; 10:1-48; 13:1,7,12; 18:8; 19:31.

[185] Cf. Luke 3:1,19-20; 9:7-9; 13:31; 23:7-15; Acts 12:20-23; 13:1.

[186] For rabbinic attitude toward women, see A. Oelke, γυνή, *TDNT* (Grand Rapids: Eerdmans, 1964), 1:781-82.

in parables, so that,
"'though seeing, they may not see;
though hearing, they may not understand.'
[11]"This is the meaning of the parable: The seed is the word of God. [12]Those along the path are the ones who hear, and then the devil comes and takes away the word from their hearts, so that they may not believe and be saved. [13]Those on the rock are the ones who receive the word with joy when they hear it, but they have no root. They believe for a while, but in the time of testing they fall away. [14]The seed that fell among thorns stands for those who hear, but as they go on their way they are choked by life's worries, riches and pleasures, and they do not mature. [15]But the seed on good soil stands for those with a noble and good heart, who hear the word, retain it, and by persevering produce a crop.

Context

At this point Luke returned to his Markan source. The parable of the soils (cf. Mark 4:1-20) serves as an example of the preaching mentioned in Luke 8:1. Since Luke already included a similar incident in which Jesus taught at the seaside from a boat, he omitted Mark 4:1 (cf. Luke 5:1-3). Within the parable we find several variations from the parallel account in Mark. Luke added that the seed is "trampled on" and gave the immediate cause of the seed on rock withering (no moisture) rather than the ultimate cause (no root to reach down into the subsoil for moisture). He also omitted the description of its withering, that the seed among thorns bore no grain, and the terms "thirty" and "sixty." These editorial changes are due primarily to Luke's desire to abbreviate the account. The more important Lukan changes are found in the interpretation of the parable and include the omission of the negative statement about the disciples in Mark 4:13; equating the seed with the "word of God"; associating the lack of belief and salvation to the devil's work rather than the form of the teaching (Luke 8:12); and stating that the second type of hearers "believe" and that the fourth hold the word "with a noble and good heart" and "persevere."

The parable of the sower is one of four major parables found in all three Synoptic Gospels (cf. 13:18-19; 20:9-17; 21:29-31; cf. also 5:34-35,37-38). This parable is unique in that it contains an extended explanation of why Jesus taught in parables. Unlike the Markan and Matthean parallels, Luke's explanation (8:9-10) does not involve the reason Jesus taught in parables (cf. Mark 4:10-12; Matt 13:10-17) but is simply an explanation of this parable. This is made even more obvious by Luke's omission of Mark 4:33-34. The passage is notoriously difficult, although it is less difficult in Luke than in Mark. Whereas the disciples, and of course those to whom the disciples hand down their interpretations (Luke 1:2), are given the secrets of God's kingdom, others find the parables little more than riddles.

This section concludes with an allegorical interpretation of the parable (8:11-15). Whereas the authenticity of the parable is seldom questioned, critical orthodoxy rejects the authenticity of the interpretation.[187] There are several reasons usually given for this: (1) the unqualified use of the term "word" for "gospel" is not found elsewhere on Jesus' lips. On the other hand this expression is found frequently in the Evangelists' editorial work (cf. 1:2; Acts 4:4; 8:4; Mark 1:45; 2:2; 4:33). (2) A number of words in the interpretation ("to sow" for *to preach* [Mark 4:14], "root" to denote inward stability [Luke 8:13], "for a while" [8:13], "do not mature," i.e., are unfruitful [8:14], "produce a crop," i.e., bear fruit [8:15]) are not found elsewhere in the Synoptic Gospels. (3) The Gospel of Thomas 9 lacks the interpretation and may witness to an earlier tradition of the parable. (4) The interpretation does not fit the reconstructed original meaning of the parable, which stresses that despite all obstacles God's kingdom will ultimately meet with success, for Jesus' message will be heard and bear abundant fruit. The present interpretation loses this sense of the eschatological harvest found in the unusual harvest numbers.[188] (5) The interpretation implies a situation in the early church where there was a real danger of falling away from one's allegiance to Christ rather than a situation in Jesus' life.

If the interpretation is not authentic, then what we possess is an inspired interpretation of the parable by Jesus' authoritative spokesmen—the apostles and Evangelists. It need not be denied that the interpretation of the parable reflects the situation and vocabulary of the early church. After all, the Evangelists were interpreters of Jesus' words, not mere stenographers. Luke in particular interpreted this parable in light of his own theological interests. Yet the interpretation does fit the parable well, and the reconstructed interpretation given above under (4) does not really do justice to the parable. Four different soils are mentioned in all three Synoptic accounts, and the amount of space and detail devoted to the first three soils is too great simply to relegate them to storylike embellishments or "local coloring." It also is obvious that in all three accounts the space devoted to the good soil is far less than that devoted to the other soils. As a result, even if there were no interpretation of this parable given in the Gospels, the reader might well raise the question of what the

---

[187]It has been a tenet on the part of some commentators that Jesus *never* interpreted any of his parables, so that every interpretation of a parable found in the Gospels must be unauthentic. But in Luke alone we find that the following parables possess interpretations: 4:23b (23c); 7:31-32 (33-34); 7:41-43 (44-47); 10:30-35 (36-37); 11:5-7 (8); 12:16-20 (21); 12:35-38 (39-40); 13:25-27 (28-30); 14:8-10 (11); 14:28-32 (33); 15:4-6 (7); 15:8-9 (10); 16:1-8a (8b-13); 17:7-9 (10); 18:2-6 (1 and 7-8); 18:9-14a (14b); 19:12-27 (11); 20:9-16 (17); 21:29-30 (31). Before one labels everyone of these interpretations as secondary, it would be wise to reconsider the thesis that Jesus could not have given interpretations to some of his parables.

[188]So Jeremias, *Parables of Jesus*, 77-79.

different soils represent; for in the process of interpreting this parable, one tends naturally to ask, What is the reality to which Jesus was comparing the sower, the seed, and the four soils? Each of the Evangelists thought this way, and there is no reason why Jesus could not have thought similarly. As a result there is no necessity for seeing the interpretation of the parable as a pure creation of the early church.[189]

Comments

8:4   While a large crowd was gathering and people were coming. Just as the church in Acts would continually increase, the multitudes who eagerly came to hear Jesus also continued to increase. See comments on 4:15.

From town after town. This picks up Luke 8:1 and links the account closely with the preceding one.

He told this parable. Whereas Mark 4:2 has the plural "parables," Luke concentrated his readers' attention on this particular parable and the need to pay attention to how they heard Jesus' teachings (Luke 8:8,18).

8:5   A farmer went out. In Luke's setting it is unlikely that this is to be interpreted as a reference to Jesus and his preaching ministry, for the sowers of God's word for Luke's readers are the apostles and their disciples.

To sow his seed. By the addition of "his seed" Luke may have been placing greater emphasis upon the seed and thus to the gospel message in 8:1. To understand this parable we must recognize that seeding in Palestine generally preceded plowing, so that the path through the field would eventually be plowed (cf. Jubilees 11:11; *Sabb* 73b; *Sabb* 7.2.).

It was trampled on. This Lukan comment perhaps refers to "contempt which the word suffers in the world (Heb 10:29)."[190] No reference, however, is made in Luke 8:11-15 to this comment, so that it may be best to see this as an example of "local coloring."

And the birds of the air ate it up. The expression "birds of the air" is also found in 9:58; 13:19; Acts 10:12; 11:6. Here they represent the devil (Luke 8:12; cf. also Jubilees 11:11; 1 Enoch 90:8-13; *Apoc. Abraham* 13:3-7).

8:6   Some fell on rock. This rock was under a thin layer of soil.

The plants withered because they had no moisture. Luke gave the immediate cause of the withering ("they had no moisture"), and Mark gave the ultimate cause (they "did not have much soil," i.e., they had no deep roots to draw moisture from the subsoil when a dry period came).

8:8   A hundred times more. Luke abbreviated Mark's "thirty, sixty, or even a hundred times." The number is not so large and unrealistic as to require an eschatological interpretation of the parable.[191] The elimination of the thirty and sixty probably is due to Luke's desire to abbreviate the account.

---

[189]For a detailed attempt to defend the authenticity of the interpretation of the parable, see P. B. Payne, "The Authenticity of the Parable of the Sower and Its Interpretation," in *Gospel Perspectives* (Sheffield: JSOT, 1980), 1:163-207.

[190]Marshall, *Luke*, 319.

[191]See Payne, "Authenticity of the Parable of the Sower," 1:181-86.

He who has ears to hear, let him hear. Both for Jesus and the Evangelists the statement emphasizes the importance of paying heed to how a person responds to the gospel message.[192]

8:9 His disciples asked him. This replaces Mark's more awkward "the Twelve and the others around him." Although Luke, due to his abbreviation of the account, omitted a change of scene such as we find in Mark ("when he was alone," 4:10), he envisioned a private conversation between Jesus and the disciples.

8:10 The knowledge of the secrets of the kingdom of God has been given to you. Luke, like Matthew, used the more common "secret(s)" (*mysteria*) in contrast to Mark's singular "secret." These secrets refer to different aspects of the arrival of God's kingdom, which Jesus has shared with the disciples. (For other references to the disciples' unique accessibility to the divine revelation, cf. 10:21-22; 12:32; 22:29; cf. also Matt 16:17.) "Has been given to you" probably is a divine passive for "God has given to you." The words "to you" are the first words in the sentence and are thus emphasized. Perhaps this can be revealed better by translating this verse, "*To you* the knowledge has been given." The disciples chose not only to hear but also to know these "secrets" concerning God's kingdom. This, however, was not simply for their own benefit but in order that they might be able to make this known to others (Luke 1:3; 24:45-49; Acts 1:8; cf. the condemnation of the Pharisees in Luke 11:52 for not doing this).

But to others. The "others" are "those on the outside" (Mark 4:11).

In parables. It may be best to translate this adverbially as "enigmatically" or "in riddles" (cf. John 16:25,29).

So that. The key issue in this passage involves the understanding of the Greek term (*hina*) translated "so that." Does the *hina* clause that follows indicate the "result" of Jesus' teaching in parables or the "cause." (In more technical terminology, does the *hina* introduce a consecutive/result clause or a final/purpose clause?) If it is the latter, then Jesus taught in parables for the purpose of hardening the hearts of his hearers. Thus they would not have been able to believe. If this is the correct interpretation, perhaps Luke was thinking somewhat along the lines of Paul when he said, "Israel has experienced a hardening in part until the full number of the Gentiles has come in" (Rom 11:25). If, however, *hina* indicates the result of Jesus' preaching in parables (cf. Luke 9:45; 11:50), the lack of an obedient response to Jesus' preaching results in the fulfillment of the Scriptures. Thus what Isa 6:9 said would happen has resulted. For Luke this was more likely because of his emphasis on fulfillment and his omission of Mark 4:12c, which supports the former interpretation. That Luke understood the *hina* as indicating the result of Jesus' preaching receives additional support from Acts 28:26-28, where Luke quoted Isa 6:9 once again. Here the responsibility for what happens lies clearly upon those who willingly reject the gospel message.[193]

8:11 Luke omitted Mark 4:13 in his abbreviated account. This may have been due to his desire to omit the negative comment about the disciples.

---

[192]The same statement is found in 14:35; Mark 7:16; cf. also Luke 4:23; 8:18; Matt 11:15; 13:43; Rev 2:7,11,17,29; 3:6,13,22; 13:9.

[193]For a fuller discussion of the problems associated with this difficult saying, see R. H. Stein, *An Introduction to the Parables of Jesus* (Philadelphia: Westminster, 1981), 27-35.

The seed is the word of God. In Mark the seed is "the word," which Luke qualified with "of God" (cf. Luke 5:1; 8:21), because this expression had not yet been used absolutely, i.e., without qualification. (Contrast Mark 1:45; 2:2.) In so doing Luke emphasized that the gospel message the disciples proclaimed and which he was writing has God as its source, not human beings (cf. 1 Thess 2:13). Later "the word" will be used without qualification throughout Acts (cf. 4:4; 6:4; 8:4; 10:36). Luke did not mention the sower in the interpretation. Because the seed that was sown was God's word, Luke probably understood the sower as representing every preacher of God's word. See comments on 8:5.

8:12 Then the devil comes. Luke substituted the Greek name translated "devil" for the Semitic "Satan" found in Mark 4:15. In the interpretation the birds' actions represent the devil's removal of the word of God.

And takes away the word from their hearts. The devil does this "so that they may not believe and be saved." For Luke "faith" was clearly the means by which salvation comes to the individual.[194] For "heart" see comments on 1:51 and 6:45.

So that they may not believe and be saved. Luke associated this with the work of the devil. In Mark 4:12 the inability to believe is more directly associated with Jesus' teaching in parables.

8:13 Although the four soils represent various kinds of people, there is a certain looseness in the metaphor, and at times the plants produced by the soils represent the various kinds of people rather than the soils. This does not cause any major confusion, however, for each kind of soil produces its own particular kind of plant. The second kind of soil hears and joyfully receives the word. The term "receive" is a Lukan expression for responding positively toward Jesus, the gospel, or the gospel messengers.[195] These hearers even receive the word with the proper attitude of "joy" (cf. 1:14; 2:10; 24:41,52).

They have no root. They believe for a while. Criticism is not directed to the quality or kind of faith these hearers possess. The problem is rather that they only hold this faith "for a while"; but as the rest of this text and the full canonical message suggest, this faith is not saving faith.

But in the time of testing they fall away. Whereas Mark and Matthew emphasized the temporary nature of their faith as being due to tribulation and persecution, Luke emphasized a particular aspect of this danger. This is the danger of succumbing to such testing in times of tribulation. The term "testing" or "temptation" can refer to temptation toward immoral conduct, but it is used by Luke in the context of persecution in 22:40,46; Acts 20:19 (cf. Luke 11:4), and so the testing referred to here probably refers to the temptation to fall away during times of persecution. "Falling away" frequently is used in the Bible to denote falling away from God (1 Tim 4:1; Heb 3:12; Jer 3:14; cf. Wis 3:10).

8:14 The third kind of hearers hear the word; but as life goes on, worries (cf. Luke 12:22-34; cf. also 21:34), riches (cf. 6:24; 16:1-13; cf. also 12:15), and pleasure (found only here in Luke-Acts) choke out the gospel message. Like the second soil, there is a start in faith but no perseverance. Such hearers do not continue

---

[194]Cf. Luke 7:50; 8:48,50; 17:19; 18:42; Acts 16:31.
[195]Cf. Luke 9:5,48,53; 10:8,10; 18:17; Acts 8:14; 11:1; 17:11.

overcoming until the end (Rev 2:26). The expression "life's" modifies all three of the dangers listed.

8:15 The fourth kind of soil represents those who hear the word of God "with a noble and good heart" (cf. Tob 5:14, LXX; 2 Macc 15:12). This qualification is in an emphatic position and denotes what is different about this group. The other soils also hear the word of God, but this soil hears it *with a noble and good heart*.

By persevering produce a crop. Like the woman in Luke 7:36-50 who produced the fruit of love, so they also produce a crop. The term *hypomone* is better translated "with perseverance" (cf. 21:19; 22:28; Acts 11:23; 14:22) than "with patience."[196] Luke omitted the *thirty, sixty, one hundred times* found in Mark 4:20. He may have omitted this to show that there are no degrees of success or levels of status in the Christian life (cf. Luke 9:46-48; 22:24-27). Or perhaps he simply omitted this material due to his desire to abbreviate the Markan account. Exactly what this "crop" consists of is not described, but Luke no doubt expected his readers to understand this as involving a life of heeding God's word.

The Lukan Message

In its present form the parable of the soils is an allegory. There has been a lengthy debate concerning the original meaning of the parable, and almost always the presuppositions of the interpreter have predetermined what Jesus originally meant. If it is predetermined that Jesus never gave interpretations to his parables, that Jesus never included any allegorical details in his parables, then the authenticity of the interpretation found in 8:11-15 must be rejected. Yet it would be strange if, as claimed, it seemed perfectly in order for the disciples and Evangelists to add allegorical details and interpretations to a parable, that Jesus absolutely could not have done so himself. Our task in this commentary is limited in that we have focused our goals on the investigation of Luke's understanding of the material in his Gospel.

For Luke the meaning of the parable is fairly clear. The picture part of the parable involves a sower, seed, and soils. Of all the versions of the parable, in Luke the sower is least important (cf. 8:11 with Mark 4:14; Matt 13:18). The key picture parts of the parable in Luke are the seed and the soils. Luke tells us what the reality part represented by the seed is in Luke 8:11, where the seed in the parable is said to represent God's word. The soils represent different responses of those who hear (8:12,14-15) or receive (8:13) God's word.

Thus the Lukan version of the parable is best named "the parable of the soils." The parable deals with various responses of people toward God's word. Luke was warning his readers that they need to take heed as to how they respond to God's word. "He who has ears to hear, let him hear" (8:8).

---

[196] See S. Brown, *Apostasy and Perseverance in the Theology of Luke*, AnBib (Rome: Pontifical Biblical Institute, 1969), 50.

Several unique Lukan emphases are in this parable. Luke warned against a faith that believes for a while but eventually falls away in time of testing (8:13). For Luke it was important not only how one begins the Christian experience, but it was even more important to persevere until the end (8:15). One must be aware of the danger of riches and pleasures (8:14). As a result Luke's readers should take note that they have not believed in vain but that they have believed with a noble and good heart and persevere (8:15). Then they will indeed be fruitful. Since Luke did not specifically designate whom the fruitless soils represent, it would be speculative to assume that we are to see in the parable the lack of response to the gospel from Jews in contrast to the positive response from Gentiles. Luke probably left the soils undesignated in order for his readers to wrestle with what kind of soil they themselves are.

The question is often raised about which of these soils represent true Christians. Who of these will be saved (8:12; Acts 16:30)? There is general agreement that the first hearers were not true Christians (Luke 8:12c) and that the last hearers were. Despite such phrases as "receive the word with joy" and "believe," the second and even more so the third kind of hearers should be grouped with the first. For Luke "faith" and "hearing" were valuable only if those who believe also endure and bring forth fruit (3:8-9; 6:43-44; 13:6-9; 20:10). The faith that leads to salvation is a faith that does not fall away or endure only for a time (8:13). It is on the contrary a faith that perseveres until the end (8:15). Luke's emphasis in the parable is not on "eternal security" but rather on "the persevering of the saints."

(3) Parable of the Lamp (8:16-18)

[16]"No one lights a lamp and hides it in a jar or puts it under a bed. Instead, he puts it on a stand, so that those who come in can see the light. [17]For there is nothing hidden that will not be disclosed, and nothing concealed that will not be known or brought out into the open. [18]Therefore consider carefully how you listen. Whoever has will be given more; whoever does not have, even what he thinks he has will be taken from him."

Context

These three sayings, which also follow the parable of the soils in Mark, emphasize the importance of how listeners are to hear God's word. The disciples are to "consider carefully how you listen" (8:18a; cf. 8:8a) and hear God's word with "a noble and good heart" and with perseverance (8:15). Then they will be good soil and bear fruit (8:15) by speaking this good news throughout the world (24:48; Acts 1:8). Although Luke 8:17 is closely tied grammatically to 8:16, the exact relationship between them is unclear. Most probably these two verses refer to the secrets of

God's kingdom, which the disciples had been privileged to learn (8:10) and which they would proclaim after the resurrection (9:36). Luke 8:18a ties the concluding promise/warning closely with 8:16-17 and with the preceding parable and thus serves as a closing saying to Jesus' teachings in 8:4-17. All three verses are found as doublets in 11:33; 12:2; and 19:26.

Comments

8:16   This verse, like its parallel in 11:33, consists of a common similitude from everyday life. An oil lamp is not lit in order to be covered by a jar or vessel, for this probably would extinguish it; nor is it lit in order to be placed under a bed, for this would hide its light. The purpose of the lamp would be thwarted by such actions. Rather a lamp is to be placed on a stand in order for its purpose of giving light to be aided. Since 8:18 is directed to Jesus' followers, it is incorrect to understand this verse as referring to Jesus as the light and his teaching ministry as representing the shining of the light. It refers rather to those who hear God's word (8:8,15,21) and let their light shine.

Those who come in can see the light.   The purpose of the light is that those, i.e., the "others" of 8:10, may share in the light of the gospel. The disciples, who know the secrets of God's kingdom (8:9-10), are to provide that light in order that others might believe and be saved (8:12). Luke may have been envisioning here a large Greco-Roman house (cf. 11:33) rather than a typical Palestinian single-room house in which a lamp would provide light throughout the entire room (cf. Matt 5:15). See comments on 5:19.

8:17   For.   This ties Luke 8:17 closely to 8:16, but the exact relationship between these two verses is debated. This verse is associated with the preceding by similar contrasts (light/darkness; disclosed/hidden; brought out into the open/ concealed), so that Luke probably used it as a commentary on 8:16.[197] As the disciples (and the believers of Luke's day) witness and proclaim the good news, the secrets of God's kingdom which are hidden to the others (8:10) will become known and understood (cf. Matt 10:26-27).

8:18   Therefore consider carefully how you listen.   Whereas the parallel in Mark 4:24 emphasizes "what" one is to hear, Luke emphasized more "how" one is to hear (cf. Luke 8:15).

Whoever has will be given more.   Compare the modern proverb, "The rich get richer and the poor get poorer." In the present context, however, the concern is not wealth or possessions but rather the revelation of God. The person who has listened carefully to God's word will understand it even more clearly, but the person who does not pay heed to how he or she hears God's word will lose even that which they think they know. Careful hearing, i.e., heeding, results in greater understanding of God's revealed word; careless hearing, i.e., a lack of heeding, results in the loss of what has been heard. How Luke understood this latter negative result is not clear, but perhaps he may have had such passages in mind as 20:16-18; Acts 13:46; 18:6; 28:25-28. The parallelism found in this saying makes the

---

[197]Cf. also the similar contrasts in 8:10: know/secrets; see/not see; hear/not understand.

exact correspondence between the picture part of the saying (having and not having possessions) and the reality part to which the picture points (hearing and not hearing God's word) somewhat awkward.

The Lukan Message

The theological message found in our passage focuses on the hearing (8:18) and proclamation of God's word (8:16-17). Having emphasized through the preceding parable the importance of both hearing and heeding God's word, Luke stressed the importance of the church's proclamation of that word. The gospel light is not meant to be hidden. Even before the missionary commissions of 24:48 and Acts 1:8, the reader is aware of the need to spread the good news. How will people turn from "darkness to light, and from the power of Satan to God, so that they may receive forgiveness of sins" (Acts 26:18) unless those who know the secrets of God's kingdom (Luke 8:10) let their light shine?

There is also present a concluding emphasis on the necessity of heeding God's word. It is not enough to hear the word. It is not enough to hear correct doctrine and theology. One must pay careful attention to how one hears God's message. The word must be heard with a "noble and good heart" (8:15), so that a faith results that will be "persevering" (8:15).

(4) Jesus' True Family (8:19-21)

[19]Now Jesus' mother and brothers came to see him, but they were not able to get near him because of the crowd. [20]Someone told him, "Your mother and brothers are standing outside, wanting to see you."

[21]He replied, "My mother and brothers are those who hear God's word and put it into practice."

Context

Luke used the following story to conclude this section (8:1-21) on Jesus' teaching in parables. It is found earlier in Mark, but Luke chose to include it here because it forms an excellent conclusion to his teaching concerning the hearing of God's word and in particular hearing God's word in Jesus' parables. In our passage Luke seeks to inform his readers that belonging to Jesus' family is not a matter of physical kinship (cf. John 1:13 "of natural descent") but of hearing and doing God's word.

Comments

8:19   Now Jesus' mother and brothers came to see him.   In the history of the church there have been three main explanations about who the "brothers" of Jesus were. (1) The Helvidian view argues that they were the subsequent sons (and daughters, cf. Mark 6:3) of Joseph and Mary. (2) The Epiphanian view argues that they were the sons (and daughters) of Joseph via an earlier marriage in which the wife died, i.e., Jesus' older step-brothers and step-sisters. (3) The Hieronymian view (the view of Jerome) argues that they were the cousins of Jesus, i.e., the term "brothers" is being used figuratively. The first view best explains the biblical data.[198]

8:20   Your mother and brothers are standing outside. This should not be interpreted metaphorically, as designating that they were outside the believing community, but literally.

Wanting to see you. They wanted to visit with Jesus (cf. "met" in Acts 16:40, which is the same Greek word).

8:21   My mother and brothers. This can be interpreted in two ways: (1) "Do you see my mother and brothers out there? They are the ones who hear . . . "[199]; (2) "My real mother and brothers are not my physical kin but those who . . . "[200] In the context of Luke 8:15,18, where Luke emphasized how one should hear God's word and that those who heed the word are the good soil, it seems that (2), which is addressed to the hearers in general, is the best translation. This would also agree with the interpretation of this saying found in Mark 3:35; Matt 12:50; and GT 99; and with Luke 11:28 (cf. also 14:26; 18:29-30). The lack of the Greek article, i.e., a *the* before "mother and brothers," also favors (2), for this indicates that the group being referred to was a less specific group than "the mother and the brothers of Jesus."[201]

Those who hear God's word and put it into practice. Compare Luke 6:47; 11:28. This is the climax of 8:1-21. For Luke, as well as James, "faith by itself, if it is not accompanied by action, is dead" (Jas 2:17).

The Lukan Message

The main point of our passage is found in Luke 8:21, which serves as a summary for the entire section that began in 8:1. Even as Luke through the preaching of John the Baptist in 3:7-14 pointed out that salvation does not come through a sacramental act, so here he pointed out that it does not come through birth or the circumstance of having heard the gospel. To have heard God's word is of no value (8:4-7,11-14) unless accompanied by "faith." Yet that "faith" is of no value, as 8:13 reveals, unless it is a faith that puts God's word into practice (8:21). Earlier Luke described this kind of faith as a faith "with a noble and good heart" which perseveres (8:15). The gospel must be responded to in faith, but saving faith is more than mere intellectual assent. True faith endures. It perseveres. It puts into practice the teachings of that faith. Luke believed that we are indeed saved by faith alone, but the faith that saves is never alone. This

---

[198]Cf. Mark 6:3; Acts 1:14; John 2:12; 7:3,5; 1 Cor 9:5; Gal 1:19; cf. also Matt 1:25, which assumes that a normal husband-wife relationship existed between Joseph and Mary after the birth of Jesus.

[199]So Fitzmyer, *Luke*, 341.

[200]So C. F. Evans, *Saint Luke*, TPI New Testament Commentaries (London: SCM, 1990), 378.

[201]For a similar grammatical example that favors the second interpretation, see Acts 2:7.

faith is accompanied by action (Jas 2:17), expresses itself through love
(cf. Gal 5:6), and puts God's word into practice (Luke 8:21).

6. Jesus Reveals His Mastery over the World, the Devil, and the Flesh (8:22-56)

Whereas the preceding section (8:1-21) focused upon Jesus' teaching
and preaching, this new section will focus on his power. The four miracle
stories that follow in 8:22-25,26-39,40-48,49-56 demonstrate Jesus' power
and might over nature, demons, physical disease, and death respectively.[202]
They answer the Christological question, "Who is this?" (8:25). This question, although not repeated in the last three accounts, is to be asked with
regard to all four miracle stories. It appears again in 9:9, where Herod asks,
"Who, then, is this I hear such things about?" (Cf. also 9:18-19.) It will be
answered in part by the confessions we find in 8:28; 9:20,35.

(1) Jesus Calms the Sea (8:22-25)

**22One day Jesus said to his disciples, "Let's go over to the other side of the
lake." So they got into a boat and set out. 23As they sailed, he fell asleep. A
squall came down on the lake, so that the boat was being swamped, and they
were in great danger.**

**24The disciples went and woke him, saying, "Master, Master, we're going to
drown!"**

**He got up and rebuked the wind and the raging waters; the storm subsided,
and all was calm. 25"Where is your faith?" he asked his disciples.**

**In fear and amazement they asked one another, "Who is this? He commands
even the winds and the water, and they obey him."**

Context

This account is a typical miracle story and contains (1) a description of
the need (8:23), (2) the miracle itself (8:24), and (3) the reaction to the
miracle (8:25). It even possesses a reference to faith, or in this instance
lack of faith (8:25). To Luke's readers, who were familiar with the OT,
Jesus' miracle would have reminded them of Yahweh's mastery of wind
and water.[203]

Comments

8:22 One day Jesus said to his disciples. Whether this refers to the
"Twelve" or the Twelve plus the women and others of 8:1-3,10 is uncertain. The

---

[202]The four accounts follow the same order found in Mark 4:35–5:43. The differences
between Mark and Luke are due, for the most part, either to Luke's desire to abbreviate the
Markan account or to improve his grammar.

[203]Cf. Pss 29:3-4; 65:7; 89:9; 104:6-7; 106:9; 107:23-32.

former was more likely in Luke's mind since they all seem to have been present in the boat. Contrast, however, Mark 4:36b.

So they got into a boat and set out. Since Luke did not mention the presence of a boat in 8:4 (contrast Mark 4:1,35), he needed to do so at this point. "Set out" is used some thirteen times in Acts and is a technical term for embarking or setting sail.

8:23 He fell asleep. A squall came down on the lake. Luke in reciting the story made it more "orderly" (Luke 1:3) by telling about Jesus' falling asleep before telling of the storm. Contrast Mark 4:37-38 and Matt 8:24. Although for Luke Jesus' falling asleep served a different purpose, it aptly portrays Jesus' humanity. For a similar incident compare Jonah 1:4-5.

The boat was being swamped, and they were in great danger. Luke was telling the story from the perspective of the participants. Contrast Mark 4:37 and Matt 8:24, which tells the story with respect to the boat itself.

8:24 Master, Master. For Luke's preference of this title to "Teacher," see comments on 5:5. Luke seems to have used this title in situations in which the disciples did not understand Jesus' power or purpose (cf. Luke 5:5; 8:45; 9:33,49).[204]

He got up and rebuked the wind and the raging waters. Jesus rebuked the elements in the sense of commanding them to stop. There is no need to assume that demonic powers stood behind the wind and the waters and that Jesus' command was directed to them.

8:25 Where is your faith? Luke's wording lessens the harshness of Mark's, "Do you still have no faith?" (4:40). The disciples were not rebuked for having no faith at all but for lacking sufficient faith. They lacked sufficient faith to realize that if they were in the Lord's presence, they need not have feared. No harm could come upon them when they were in the presence of the Master of nature. Luke may have been suggesting that his readers presently lacked the kind of faith that would help them persevere in time of testing (8:13,15).[205]

In fear and amazement. Such a reaction is natural and appropriate before such a person. See comments on 5:26.

Who is this? Luke intended that his readers would ask themselves this question. Who is this Jesus of Nazareth that even the storms and raging waters obey him?

The Lukan Message

In the present context the major theme of this account is Christological and seeks to describe who Jesus is (8:25). Luke wanted Theophilus and his other readers to reflect on the questions: Who is this Jesus of the Christian proclamation in whom we believe? How is it that he has the power to control the wild fury of nature like God? (Cf. Pss 65:7; 104:7; 107:29.) Truly he must be someone unique. Truly this one is the Son of the Most High (Luke 1:32), the Lord's Christ (2:26), and the Lord (2:11).

[204] See Tannehill, *Narrative Unity of Luke-Acts*, 213.
[205] For a Lukan example of how faith functions in such circumstances, cf. Acts 27:13-44.

Like Yahweh he controls the winds and the waves, and before such a person fear and awe are highly appropriate.

Luke perhaps also wanted his readers to understand how Jesus' power and might relate to their own situation. This does not mean that he intended them to allegorize this passage as the early church did and see the boat as representing the church but rather that he wanted his readers to recognize that because of their Lord's power there is no need to fear. Jesus' power is greater than their needs. Therefore they should not doubt or fear but only believe (cf. also 8:50), for their Lord can and will calm the storms that rage against them (cf. Ps 18:16-19). Such a theme, although not the main purpose of the passage, is a natural implication.

(2) Jesus Casts Out a Demon (8:26-39)

[26]They sailed to the region of the Gerasenes, which is across the lake from Galilee. [27]When Jesus stepped ashore, he was met by a demon-possessed man from the town. For a long time this man had not worn clothes or lived in a house, but had lived in the tombs. [28]When he saw Jesus, he cried out and fell at his feet, shouting at the top of his voice, "What do you want with me, Jesus, Son of the Most High God? I beg you, don't torture me!" [29]For Jesus had commanded the evil spirit to come out of the man. Many times it had seized him, and though he was chained hand and foot and kept under guard, he had broken his chains and had been driven by the demon into solitary places.

[30]Jesus asked him, "What is your name?"

"Legion," he replied, because many demons had gone into him. [31]And they begged him repeatedly not to order them to go into the Abyss.

[32]A large herd of pigs was feeding there on the hillside. The demons begged Jesus to let them go into them, and he gave them permission. [33]When the demons came out of the man, they went into the pigs, and the herd rushed down the steep bank into the lake and was drowned.

[34]When those tending the pigs saw what had happened, they ran off and reported this in the town and countryside, [35]and the people went out to see what had happened. When they came to Jesus, they found the man from whom the demons had gone out, sitting at Jesus' feet, dressed and in his right mind; and they were afraid. [36]Those who had seen it told the people how the demon-possessed man had been cured. [37]Then all the people of the region of the Gerasenes asked Jesus to leave them, because they were overcome with fear. So he got into the boat and left.

[38]The man from whom the demons had gone out begged to go with him, but Jesus sent him away, saying, [39]"Return home and tell how much God has done for you." So the man went away and told all over town how much Jesus had done for him.

Context

The second example describing Jesus' might and power involves his casting out a demon. The account consists of seven parts: (1) Jesus' arrival, 8:26-27a; (2) a description of the demoniac's condition, 8:27b,29; (3) the demoniac's recognition of Jesus, 8:28; (4) the exorcism itself, 8:30-32; (5) the proof of the exorcism, 8:33; (6) the people's reaction, 8:34-37; and (7) the conclusion, 8:38-39.[206] The majority of differences between the accounts in Mark and Luke are due to literary considerations rather than theological ones.[207] The changes that bear theological significance are found in 8:26,28,31,39 and will be discussed under "Comments."

Numerous criticisms have been leveled against the historicity of this account. Some argue that since Jesus' action toward the swine is cruel— and he would not have done anything cruel—the story is not historical. Similarly, some argue that Jesus would never have caused so great an economic loss to the swine's owners by having them drown. Others argue against there being swine raised in the area, since Jews could not eat pork. The problem of the city's name is a classical one and goes back at least to Origen's time. The city of Gerasa lies approximately thirty miles southeast of the Sea of Galilee, and as one commentator somewhat sarcastically states, "The stampede of the pigs from Gerasa to the Lake would have made them the most energetic herd in history!"[208] In the heyday of theological liberalism it was also objected that Jesus could not have been so superstitious as to believe in demons, so that the account could not be historical on that basis. The latter objection was sometimes answered by a theory of accommodation, i.e., Jesus himself did not believe in demons, but in speaking to people who did, he shaped his healings and teachings to accommodate the naive beliefs of the people to whom he was ministering. Others have explained the story "mythically," i.e., such stories are due to the early church's expressing its religious ideas and ideals in the concrete forms of myths. We will deal with other objections under "Comments."

Comments

8:26 They sailed to the region of the Gerasenes. There is a major textual problem involving this geographical designation. The three main readings are: (1) Gerasenes—Gerasa (modern Jerash), which lies thirty miles southeast of the Sea of Galilee; (2) Gergesenes—Gergese (modern Kersa), which lies on the Sea of Galilee; (3) Gadarenes—Gadara (modern Umm Qeis), which lies five miles southeast of the Sea of Galilee and possessed lands extending to the lake; but Gadara has no steep slope leading to the lake.[209] There are serious geographical and

---

[206] See Fitzmyer, *Luke*, 733-34.

[207] They involve such things as Luke's abbreviating the account, his describing the demoniac's behavior later in the story, and his making the command and request of 8:29,32 into indirect discourse (cf. Mark 5:8,12).

[208] Fitzmyer, *Luke*, 736.

[209] Gerasenes is favored by 𝔓[75], B, D, it, vg, sa; Gergesenes is favored by ℵ, L, X, θ; Gadarenes is favored by A, K, W, *f*[13] and the majority of the Byzantine manuscripts. This problem is aggravated further in that some manuscripts, such as ℵ, B, X, K, Ω have different readings in the parallel passages.

historical implications involved in this issue that cannot be ignored. Already in the first half of the third century Origen in his commentary on John wrestled with this problem. It is impossible, however, even to be certain about which word Luke actually used when he wrote his text. As a result we cannot be sure that the first alternative (Gerasenes) is the correct one. As for the other two, they do not create as significant a geographical-historical problem. For Luke the key issue was not the question of "where" this took place but "what" took place and its significance for understanding who Jesus is.

Which is across the lake from Galilee. Since this account takes place during Jesus' Galilean ministry, Luke integrated the account into his scheme.

8:27 A demon-possessed man. "A demon-possessed man" is literally *a certain man having demons.*[210] Luke used the plural (demons) in light of the later reference to their number. Contrast Mark 5:2, where the singular is used. Luke again sought to avoid Mark's "unclean spirit" by using the term "demon." See comments on 4:33.

For a long time. This phrase goes better with what follows (so NIV, RSV) than with what precedes.

But had lived in the tombs. For a Jew this description might have overtones of ceremonial uncleanness, but for Luke and his readers it described the demoniac's terrible condition of alienation from other people and perhaps even his and the demons' association with death.

8:28 When he saw Jesus, he cried out and fell at his feet, shouting. At this point the demons acted in unity, so that singular pronouns and nouns are used—*he, me, I, demon.*

What do you want with me? This phrase is literally, "What [is it] to me and you?" Compare 1 Kgs 17:18 (LXX).

Jesus, Son of the Most High God? The demons provide a partial answer to the question of Luke 8:25. Because of the supernatural sphere from which the demons came, the man possessed preternatural knowledge of who Jesus truly was (cf. 4:41). For "Son(s) of the Most High," "Most High God," cf. 1:32; 6:35; Acts 16:17.

I beg you. Luke changed "swear to God that you won't torture me" (NIV) or "I adjure you by God, do not torment me" (RSV) in Mark 5:7 because it seemed ludicrous for a demon to "adjure" Jesus by God. Luke's wording accurately discloses the impotency of the demon(s) before Jesus.

Don't torture me! We are not told what this torture consisted of until 8:31. Matthew 8:29 adds "before the appointed time" and indicates that what the demons feared was that Jesus would enact the torture of 8:31 immediately rather than on the final day of judgment.

8:29 For Jesus had commanded the evil spirit. The verb is best understood as an inceptive aorist and translated, "For Jesus had begun to command the evil spirit."

Many times it had seized him. The terrible condition of the man existed over a period of time. This is revealed by "for a long time" (8:27); "many times" (8:29); and the tenses of the verbs "had seized," "was chained," and "had been

---

[210]Frequently we find that Luke introduced a parable by "a certain man" (see comments on 10:30; 16:19), but in such cases we find τις ἄνθρωπος whereas in this verse we find τις ἀνήρ.

driven" (iterative imperfects, which emphasize the continual repetition of these past actions). Luke gave a flashback and incorporated these details to describe the demoniac's condition. The comment about the demoniac's frequent breaking of his chains serves to emphasize the demon's power and thus Jesus' greater power.

8:30   What is your name?   This is the only incident in the Gospels in which Jesus conversed with a demon. Luke did not indicate that Jesus' power over the demon was somehow linked to his knowing the demon's name, even if this was a popular belief.[211]

"Legion," he replied.   The demon gave to Jesus a name that also was a number. Multiple possession has already been mentioned in 8:2, but this man's condition was far worse than that of Mary Magdalene, who possessed seven demons. A legion in the Roman army consisted of six thousand men.

Because many demons had gone into him.   Luke directed this explanatory statement to his readers, whereas in Mark 5:9 it is addressed to Jesus.

8:31   And they begged him . . . into the Abyss.   This is the "torment" the demons were seeking to avoid in 8:28. The abyss is the final destiny of the devil and his angels (Matt 25:41; 2 Pet 2:4; Rev 20:3).[212] See comments on 4:34.

8:32   A large herd of pigs was feeding. . . . The demons begged Jesus to let them go into them.   Pigs are forbidden and unclean for Jews since they do not "chew the cud" (Lev 11:7; Deut 14:8). For a Jew therefore pigs would be a very appropriate home for the demons.

And he gave them permission.   This permission allows the man's healing to be verified in the story when the swine were destroyed.

8:33-34   And the herd rushed down the steep bank into the lake and was drowned.   The demons were conquered, not converted! The swine's destruction proves that the demons truly left the man as does the description of the man's condition in 8:35. For the reference to the steep slope and the lake as a historical-geographical problem, see comments on 8:26. Although Luke omitted the number of the swine (Mark 5:13 states that there were two thousand), he still mentioned that it was a large herd (Luke 8:32). None of the Gospel writers seemed to be troubled by the economic loss that the drowning of the swine would have caused their owners. For the Evangelists the spiritual issues involved in the story are far more important than financial considerations (cf. 12:31). Various commentators' concern for the owners' economic loss may be due to a greater sensitivity for the property of others than the Evangelists had, but it may also reveal a lesser concern for the spiritual issues involved. The Gospel writers saw the story as involving a man's deliverance from enslavement to the demonic. The demoniac's deliverance and the demons' judgment were their primary concerns.[213]

8:35   The demoniac's conversion is now described. Instead of being driven by the demon (8:29), he was "sitting" (8:35); instead of being without clothes (8:27), he was "dressed" (8:35); instead of being among the tombs (8:27), he was "at Jesus' feet" (8:35; cf. 10:39 and Acts 22:3); and instead of being "chained hand

---

[211] See Nolland, *Luke 1–9:20*, 409.

[212] The term is also found in Rom 10:7; Rev 9:1-2,11; 11:7; 17:8; 20:1,3; cf. also 1 Enoch 10:13-14; 18:11; 21:7-10; 90:24.

[213] For a concise discussion of this issue, see Plummer, *Luke*, 228-29.

and foot and kept under guard" (Luke 8:29), he was "in his right mind" (8:35). This, even more than the drowning of the swine, demonstrates that the demons had left him. The demons' prisoner had been freed from their oppression (cf. 4:18).

8:36   The demon-possessed man had been cured. Luke added the word "cured" to his account. The Greek word *esōthē*, or "saved," is a favorite Lukan word to describe the healing-salvation Jesus brings. The man had not simply been cured of his demon possession but of everything that separated him from God. Thus he sat at Jesus' feet as a disciple (cf. 10:39; Acts 22:3).

8:37   Then all the people . . . asked Jesus to leave them. Much of the seed had fallen upon unfertile soil and bore no fruit (Luke 8:4-15). Despite the healing they saw, the people of Gerasa did not want Jesus to remain.

Because they were overcome with fear. The people's fear is mentioned again (cf. 8:35). Luke added this comment (cf. 7:16; Acts 2:43; 5:5,11). The cause of this fear is not given, and it is of little value to speculate about what caused this fear in Jesus' situation. For Luke, however, it was clear that just as hearing God's word is not enough (8:12-14), so seeing God at work is also not enough. Even a greater miracle (16:31) cannot compel faith. Apart from a noble and good heart, God's presence produces only fear. For the believer such fear turns to a holy awe, but to the unbelieving it is only a fearsome dread from which they seek to rid themselves. God can be rejected, as the people of Gerasa in fact did. Peace, however, came to the demoniac. He who was last became first.

So he got into the boat and left. In "orderly" (1:3) fashion Luke finished the people's encounter with Jesus before he completed the demoniac's story.

8:38   The man . . . begged to go with him. The man wanted to join Jesus and his disciples, but Jesus commanded him to a life of discipleship in his own village. The request to join Jesus was not rejected but refocused in that he was to join in the proclamation of the good news to his own village.

8:39   Return home. The man, who previously was unable to live at home but instead lived in the tombs, was directed to "return home."

Jesus' command to "return . . . tell . . . what God has done" is paralleled by "went away . . . told how much Jesus had done." Did Luke mean here that the man told what God, i.e., Jesus, had done for him and that he was thus calling Jesus God? We find parallels in 9:43 and Acts 20:28 that may support such an understanding, but there is a textual problem associated with the latter verse. More likely Luke here tied Jesus' works and ministry so close to that of God the Father that what Jesus does and what God does are one. We find the same idea in chap. 15, where Jesus' association with publicans and sinners (15:1-2) is likened in the three parables (15:3-32) to God's love for the outcasts. Even if Jesus is not directly referred to as God in this verse, he uniquely possesses rights and honor that in Luke belong only to God. Compare 5:24.

Told all over town. Mark 5:20 has "in the Decapolis," but for Luke the mission to the Gentile world would begin in earnest only after the resurrection. Marshall notes, "The story is a paradigm of what conversion involves: the responsibility to evangelize."[214]

---

[214]Marshall, *Luke*, 341.

The Lukan Message

The story of the demoniac in its present context serves primarily a Christological function. Jesus' greatness is shown in his mastery of the demonic. Jesus defeated the demons, a legion in number (8:30) and with superhuman power to break chains (8:29). The supernaturally powerful demons, however, could only "beg" (8:28) Jesus, for they had no ability to counter the power of the "Son of the Most High God." The attempt to see in this story a "duped demon" who sought to circumvent Jesus' power by not giving their name but only their number and by asking to enter swine rather than the abyss (only to be "fooled" by Jesus, who caused them to drown) is highly imaginative. Luke, however, did not in any way suggest such an interpretation. Jesus did not outwit the demons. He dominated and defeated them. Jesus' mighty works are such that to proclaim them is to proclaim what God has done. "Who is this" (8:25)? He is the Son of God, the Lord of all creation, whether the physical world (wind and waves [8:25; cf. Ps 65:7]) or the spiritual world of demons.

For Luke this story also prefigured the future mission to the Gentiles. Already in Jesus' ministry a Gentile was converted, for this took place across the Lake of Galilee among people who raised swine. Even though Luke wanted to maintain his geographical scheme and thus omitted mention of the Decapolis (cf. Mark 5:20), the scene nevertheless foreshadows what we find in Acts. Already in his ministry Jesus had a concern for Gentiles and ministered to their needs (cf. also Luke 7:1-10).

(3) Jesus Heals the Hemorrhaging Woman and Raises Jairus's Daughter (8:40-56)

[40]Now when Jesus returned, a crowd welcomed him, for they were all expecting him. [41]Then a man named Jairus, a ruler of the synagogue, came and fell at Jesus' feet, pleading with him to come to his house [42]because his only daughter, a girl of about twelve, was dying.

As Jesus was on his way, the crowds almost crushed him. [43]And a woman was there who had been subject to bleeding for twelve years, but no one could heal her. [44]She came up behind him and touched the edge of his cloak, and immediately her bleeding stopped.

[45]"Who touched me?" Jesus asked.

When they all denied it, Peter said, "Master, the people are crowding and pressing against you."

[46]But Jesus said, "Someone touched me; I know that power has gone out from me."

[47]Then the woman, seeing that she could not go unnoticed, came trembling and fell at his feet. In the presence of all the people, she told why she had touched him and how she had been instantly healed. [48]Then he said to her, "Daughter, your faith has healed you. Go in peace."

⁴⁹While Jesus was still speaking, someone came from the house of Jairus, the synagogue ruler. "Your daughter is dead," he said. "Don't bother the teacher any more."
⁵⁰Hearing this, Jesus said to Jairus, "Don't be afraid; just believe, and she will be healed."
⁵¹When he arrived at the house of Jairus, he did not let anyone go in with him except Peter, John and James, and the child's father and mother. ⁵²Meanwhile, all the people were wailing and mourning for her. "Stop wailing," Jesus said. "She is not dead but asleep."
⁵³They laughed at him, knowing that she was dead. ⁵⁴But he took her by the hand and said, "My child, get up!" ⁵⁵Her spirit returned, and at once she stood up. Then Jesus told them to give her something to eat. ⁵⁶Her parents were astonished, but he ordered them not to tell anyone what had happened.

Context

The present account contains two miracle stories that reveal Jesus' power over sickness and death. This completes the portrayal of Jesus' power in 8:22-56. He is Lord over nature, demons, sickness, and even death. The present two stories are intimately associated, with the story of the woman with a hemorrhage (8:43-48) inserted into the story of Jairus's daughter (8:40-42,49-56).[215] The resuscitation of Jairus's "only" daughter parallels the resuscitation of the widow of Nain's "only" son in 7:11-17. See comments on 13:19.

The Lukan version of this incident differs from that of Mark in a number of ways. First, Luke stated that this was Jairus's "only" daughter (8:42), whereas in Mark 5:23 the daughter's condition is described by Jairus himself. Second, Luke mitigated the criticism of the doctors who treated the hemorrhaging woman. (Cf. Luke 8:43 with Mark 5:26. Some have suggested that this may have been due to Luke's desire to defend his profession. See Introduction 1.) Third, Luke changed the statement about power proceeding from Jesus from indirect to direct discourse (Luke 8:46). Finally, even though Luke's abbreviated version (280 words from the 374 in Mark) eliminates the reason the woman sought to touch Jesus (cf. 8:44 and Mark 5:28), it explains why the people laughed at Jesus (Luke 8:53) and describes the resuscitation (8:55).

Comments
8:40 Now when Jesus returned, a crowd welcomed him. This picks up the references to the "crowd" of 8:4,19. Their positive response contrasts with that of

---

[215]Whether these two stories originally happened in this order or were brought together, due to topical considerations, word association ("daughter," 8:42,48; "twelve years," 8:42-43), or to provide time for the daughter to die is debated. For Luke, however, the stories were already joined when he found them (cf. Mark 5:21-43).

the people of Gerasa (8:34-37). In general crowds reacted favorably toward Jesus. Attempts to find reasons for the crowd's positive reaction toward Jesus (because of having witnessed the previous miracles or because of a desire to see additional miracles) are purely speculative. In the Lukan setting the Evangelist sought to underline the crowd's positive attitude toward Jesus.

8:41 Then a man named Jairus. "Jairus" is the Greek form of the name "Jair" (Num 32:41; Deut 3:14; Josh 13:30; 1 Chr 20:5). Some scholars have sought to find symbolism in this name because *Jair* means *he [God] will awaken*, which fits Luke 8:52 nicely, but none of the Evangelists made any allusion to this. If Luke wanted Theophilus to see such a symbolism based on this Hebrew meaning, he would have needed to do something similar to what we find Matt 1:21.

A ruler of the synagogue. There is a slightly different wording in Luke 8:49. Jairus most probably was the official in charge of arrangements for synagogue services or a synagogue board member (cf. Acts 13:15; 18:8,17). If Jairus's specific position is unclear, his general status as a synagogue official and a representative of the Jewish establishment is not.

Came and fell at Jesus' feet, pleading with him. Like the hemorrhaging woman, Jairus revealed his faith by coming to Jesus. Earlier a centurion (a Gentile) manifested his faith by *not* coming directly to him (7:1-10). Jairus's action showed his desperation as well as his faith in Jesus.

8:42 Because his only daughter. The term "only" is found three times in the Synoptic Gospels and all are in Luke (cf. also 7:12; 9:38). Here and in 9:38 Luke added it to the parallel material in Mark. As in the other two examples, Luke emphasized the tragedy of the situation by this comment.

8:43 The scene switches now to a woman who had been bleeding for twelve years.[216] The exact nature of this bleeding is uncertain, but it may have been some sort of uterine hemorrhaging. The woman's plight is highlighted by the length of her illness (twelve years) and the hopelessness of her situation (no one could heal her).

8:44 She came up . . . and touched the edge of his cloak. Luke's abbreviated account omits what the woman was thinking as she sought to touch Jesus' garment (cf. Mark 5:28). The "edge" of the cloak (Matt 14:36; Mark 6:56) may refer to either the hem or a tassel on the corner of his garment (Num 15:38-39; Deut 22:12).

And immediately her bleeding stopped. The "immediately" heightens Jesus' miracle-working power (see comments on 18:43). His power and might is such that a twelve-year sickness, which no one else could heal, was instantaneously healed.

8:45 Who touched me? Was this an actual question or a device Jesus used to bring the woman before him? The question and what follows in 8:45b-46 suggest that Jesus did not know who touched him (cf. Mark 5:32). Luke in his orderly

---

[216]There is a textual problem in this verse in that some manuscripts (א, A, K, L, W, f^1, f^{13}) add "and she had spent all she had on doctors." This fits well the tendency of scribes to harmonize the various accounts. Here it is most likely that a scribe added this statement to make Luke more like Mark 5:26. The manuscript evidence for its omission includes $\mathfrak{P}^{75}$, B, D and various ancient translations; and although it is far from certain, it probably is best, as the NIV has done, not to include it in the text.

fashion (Luke 1:3) placed Jesus' question before the explanation of why he knew he had been touched (cf. Mark 5:30). **Peter said.** Peter spoke for the disciples (cf. Mark 5:31). **Master, the people are crowding and pressing against you.** For "Master" see comments on 5:5. Peter assumed that Jesus' question was somewhat foolish because Jesus was being jostled by the crowd around him, but he also assumed that Jesus was seeking an answer.

8:46 Someone touched me; I know that power has gone out from me. For the tie between the Spirit and power, see comments on 1:17. For the tie between power and healing, see comments on 5:17.

8:47 Seeing that she could not go unnoticed. Luke did not explain how she came to this conclusion. Perhaps she saw that Jesus would not rest until what had happened to him had been explained.

Came trembling and fell at his feet. No reason is given for her fear. In the original situation it may have been because in touching Jesus she caused him to become ceremonially unclean (cf. Lev 15:19-27; Ezek 36:17) or because the experience of God's power and might in her healing caused her to have a reverent fear or awe. Perhaps she feared rebuke for her presumption of touching Jesus. Luke was not interested in pursuing this. For him fear was an appropriate response to the experience of God's presence.[217]

She told why she had touched him. Luke referred here to why the woman touched Jesus, even though he omitted the explanation earlier (cf. 8:44 and Mark 5:28).[218] Did Luke assume that his readers knew the story well enough to supply the reason in such instances?

8:48 Daughter. By the affectionate term "Daughter," Jesus immediately reassured the woman and assuaged her fears.

Your faith has healed you. "Healed you" is literally *saved you*. It was not simply the woman's touching of Jesus' garment that healed her, for others pressed against Jesus as well; it was the faith that caused her to touch Jesus that brought healing.[219] Yet something more happened than the cessation of her bleeding. She experienced physical healing but even more. If Jesus' concern for her involved physical healing only, what occurred in Luke 8:45-48 could have been omitted. Luke reported that Jesus sought out the woman because something greater than physical healing was taking place. Through faith the woman also received spiritual healing. See comments on 5:20.

Go in peace. This was a common formula for dismissal, as 7:50 and Acts 16:36 reveal (cf. Judg 18:6; 1 Sam 1:17; 20:42; 29:7). But these words from Jesus contain a blessing as well.

8:49 While Jesus was still speaking. The scene now changes back to Jairus. **Your daughter is dead.** Luke wanted his readers to believe that the daughter was dead, not ill and sleeping (cf. also Luke 8:53). As a result what Jesus said in 8:52 should be interpreted in light of this statement, not vice versa. The rationalist

[217]Cf. Luke 1:12,65; 2:9; 5:26; 7:16; 8:37; Acts 2:43; 5:5,11; 16:29; 19:17.
[218]He would do the same in Luke 23:18 (cf. Mark 15:7).
[219]This is even clearer in the parallel accounts. See V. K. Robbins, "The Woman Who Touched Jesus' Garment," *NTS* 33 (1987): 506-7.

attempts of the past to reinterpret this story as a healing rather than a raising of the dead are contrary to the Lukan intention.

Don't bother the teacher any more. This must be understood as a further indication that the daughter had died. The messenger had a limited view of Jesus' power. He thought: *If the daughter were still alive, Jesus might be able to help, but no one can bring the dead back to life. Therefore it makes no sense to trouble Jesus about this.*

8:50 Don't be afraid. As with the woman in 8:48, Jesus gave a word of reassurance and sought to allay Jairus's doubts and to strengthen his faith.[220] What happened to the woman could happen to his daughter.

Just believe. The object of this faith is not described, but Luke expected his readers to know and to add "in the Lord Jesus" (Acts 16:31). Luke used the aorist imperative, in contrast to the present imperative in Mark 5:36, to emphasize the act by which persons place their faith in Jesus (cf. Acts 4:4,32; 8:12; esp. 16:31).

And she will be healed. "Healed" is literally *saved*. Luke added this. As elsewhere such healing or resuscitation from the dead represents the greater salvation that faith brings. See comments on 8:48.

8:51 He did not let anyone go in with him except Peter, John and James. This great miracle of God's grace was to be observed by his chosen witnesses only (cf. Acts 10:39-41). The inner group of the disciples is mentioned here in Luke for the first time.[221]

8:52 All the people were wailing and mourning for her. "Mourning" literally refers to the beating of one's breast in mourning. Among this group would have been relatives, friends, and official mourners.

She is not dead but asleep. This should be interpreted in light of the comments made in 8:49,53. It was not a denial that the girl was dead but a recognition that the girl's death was, like sleep, of limited duration. Jesus' statement "is prognosis, not diagnosis."[222]

8:53 They laughed at him, knowing that she was dead. Again Luke made clear that the girl was dead. The mourners knew the girl was dead and thus laughed at Jesus because they believed he was using the term "asleep" in ignorance rather than as a metaphor.

8:54 Get up! The same term is used in the raising of the widow's son in 7:14 and of Jesus' resurrection from the dead in 24:6. Luke omitted the Aramaic *Talitha koum!* of Mark 5:41, for his readers would not have understood it.[223]

8:55 Her spirit returned. Compare 1 Kgs 17:21-22. The girl returned to her former earthly life, not to the final resurrection state. The girl's "spirit," not the Holy Spirit, is seen as distinct from and surviving the death of the physical body (cf. Luke 23:46; Acts 7:59). Questions such as where the girl's spirit was during the time of death or what she experienced were of no interest to Luke. His primary goal was to teach about Jesus, not about death.

---

[220] Cf. Luke 1:13,30; 2:10; 5:10; 12:7,32; Acts 18:9; 27:24.

[221] The order is somewhat unusual, but note Luke 9:28 and Acts 1:13. Luke may have placed Peter and John together because of their association in Acts 3:1,3-4,11; 4:13; 8:14.

[222] Nolland, *Luke 1–9:20*, 421.

[223] Luke 6:14; 19:38; 22:42; 23:33 also omit Mark's Aramaic phrases.

And at once she stood up. This immediate response and her subsequent eating underline the reality of the miracle.

8:56   Her parents were astonished. This verb is also found in Luke 2:47 and 24:22.

But he ordered them not to tell anyone what had happened. This command stands in sharp contrast with the command to the healed demoniac in 8:39, but the people's scorn in 8:53 may reveal they were unfit recipients for the gospel message. Or perhaps Jesus did not want the little girl to become a public curiosity. For Luke, however, this might have exemplified the secret of God's kingdom (8:10). Yet how could such a fact be concealed? As Marshall observes, "The command itself should not be regarded as historically impossible: so long as the parents said nothing, the scornful Jews could . . . [believe] that the girl had been merely asleep."[224]

The Lukan Message

The section of Luke in which this account is found (8:22-56) focuses on Jesus' mastery over the world. Luke demonstrated Jesus' authority over nature (8:22-25) and over the demonic world (8:26-39). The external world, both physical and spiritual, is subject to him. Luke showed that two of the effects of the fall, disease and death, are subject to Jesus. Who is this before whom nature, the spirit world, disease, and death prostrate themselves? The Christological emphasis of this section cannot be missed. Later in the Apocalypse, Jesus is described as the First and the Last, the one who has the keys of death and Hades (Rev 1:17-18). Luke's purpose in this section is to reveal to Theophilus that the Jesus in whom he believed possesses all power and authority and can save from all things those who call upon his name.

A second theme found in this passage is the importance of faith. Through faith the woman with the hemorrhage was healed (saved) and could go away in peace (8:48). Jairus was also informed that if he believed, healing (salvation) would come to his daughter (8:50). The use of the term "saved" to describe the woman's healing and the girl's resuscitation clearly would remind Luke's readers of such preaching as found in Acts 16:31, which they themselves had heard and to which they themselves had responded. Salvation comes through faith, and the woman and Jairus revealed the kind of faith that Jesus seeks.

7. Jesus and the Twelve (9:1-50)

At this point in his Gospel, Luke omitted the account found in Mark 6:1-6a because he had included a similar account in Luke 4:16-30. In 9:1-9 he continued to follow the material in Mark 6:6b-16, omitting the account of

---

[224] Marshall, *Luke*, 342.

the death of John the Baptist with which he dealt in "orderly" fashion in Luke 3:19-20. Luke followed the progression of events found in Mark 6:30-44 by including the feeding of the five thousand (Luke 9:10-17). At this point, however, we encounter what has been called the "great Lukan omission," for the material found in Mark 6:45–8:26 is completely missing from Luke. In Luke the feeding of the five thousand is immediately followed by Peter's confession in 9:18-21, which is found in Mark 8:27-30. Parallel material for Luke 9:18-50 is found in Mark 8:27–9:41.

Numerous attempts have been made to explain why the material in Mark 6:45–8:26 is not found in Luke. Some of these are:

1. Luke abbreviated the material in Mark to allow room for his other material (Q and L) due to the limited size of his scroll. (The average scroll was about thirty to thirty-five feet long, and the Gospel of Luke would have required a whole scroll.) A number of healing miracles in the great omission, however, would seem to have served the Lukan purpose well.

2. Upon coming to Mark 6:45-52, which refers to Bethsaida, Luke decided for one reason or another to omit it. Looking away or being distracted when he came back to the scroll, he accidentally focused on Mark 8:22, where Bethsaida is again mentioned. Thinking that he was looking at the earlier reference to Bethsaida, he began to use the material in Mark once again. Later scribes frequently made such an error, which is called haplography, in their copying of the NT manuscripts. The great omission was, therefore, quite unintentional.

3. Luke omitted this material to avoid having repetitive incidents. Compare Mark 6:32-44 (the feeding of the five thousand) and Mark 8:1-10 (the feeding of the four thousand). Much of the material in the great omission, however, has no parallel elsewhere in Luke.

4. Luke was using a defective copy of Mark that lacked 6:45–8:26. Most defective copies, however, tend to be defective either at the beginning or at the end rather than in the middle; for when a scroll is rolled up, these are the most vulnerable parts.

5. Luke wanted to limit Jesus' ministry to Galilee due to his geographical scheme and thus omitted Jesus' contact with Gentiles outside of Galilee (cf. Mark 7:24-37). Much of the great omission, however, takes place or could be thought to have taken place among Jews in Galilee.

6. Luke proceeded directly from the feeding miracle in 9:10-17 and Herod's question about Jesus in 9:7-9 to highlight the explicit Christology found in Peter's confession. Therefore he omitted Mark 6:45–8:26.

That we have so many attempts to explain the great omission suggests that there is no convincing solution. Luke 9:1-50 does, however, form a cohesive unit centering around Jesus and the twelve disciples. The disciples are expressly mentioned in each episode except one (9:7-9), and even here the disciples' mission (9:1-6) seems to be the reason Herod "heard about all that was going on" (9:7). The result is that this is a rather homogeneous section, and this suggests that the great omission probably was more intentional than accidental.

(1) Mission of the Twelve (9:1-6)

[1]When Jesus had called the Twelve together, he gave them power and authority to drive out all demons and to cure diseases, [2]and he sent them out to preach the kingdom of God and to heal the sick. [3]He told them: "Take nothing for the journey—no staff, no bag, no bread, no money, no extra tunic. [4]Whatever house you enter, stay there until you leave that town. [5]If people do not welcome you, shake the dust off your feet when you leave their town, as a testimony against them." [6]So they set out and went from village to village, preaching the gospel and healing people everywhere.

Context

Jesus' selection of the twelve apostles (6:13, *apostoloi*) was partially fulfilled when he sent them out (*apostellо*μ) to preach and heal. Having been taught by Jesus, armed with their knowledge of the "secrets" of God's kingdom, they went out to proclaim the message of the kingdom and its Lord. The Twelve's mission served as an apprenticeship for their ultimate mission (24:45-49). As they proclaimed the acts ("miracle stories" and "stories about Jesus") and teachings of Jesus, these oral traditions became firmly rooted in the apostles' minds, solidifying into memorable units their hearers could more readily "receive." These would then be the traditions delivered to them by the "eyewitnesses and servants of the word" (1:2). The importance of this mission for the later transmission of the Gospel traditions cannot be overestimated. During this period they recounted time and time again "the things that have been fulfilled among us" (1:1), things they had seen Jesus do and heard him say and which he had explained to them (8:10).[225] The mission also provided time for the disciples to reflect and discuss, "Who is this" (8:25) who teaches and does such things? Such questions would naturally have arisen not just among themselves but from their audiences as well. No doubt they would frequently be asked, "Just who exactly is this Jesus of whom you speak?" Jesus may in fact have intended for these experiences to assist his disciples in answering the question he asks in 9:18.

The Twelve were to proceed unencumbered by possessions (9:3), depending instead upon God's providence and their fellow Jews' hospitality (9:4). This would enable them to concentrate on their appointed task without being distracted by a concern for provisions or other baggage.

---

[225]See Stein, *Synoptic Problem*, 203-5.

These instructions, in contrast to those found in 22:35-38, appear to have been meant for a particular place and time in Jesus' ministry, and they rely heavily upon the practice of Jewish hospitality. The rest of Jesus' instructions would apply both to this mission and to the greater one that awaited them. The relationship between this account and its parallel in 10:1-12 will be discussed at that point. Luke omitted several things from the parallel account in Mark 6:6b-13. He did not refer to sandals or going out by twos. Whereas Mark's account permitted carrying a staff, Luke forbade it. The most important theological comments found in the Lukan account, however, involve the additions of "power" and "to heal the sick" in Luke 9:1 and "preach[ing] the kingdom of God and . . . heal[ing] the sick" in 9:2.

This passage can be broken down into the following subdivisions: (1) the disciples were given power and authority over demons and sickness; (2) they were told to preach God's kingdom and to heal; (3) the rules of travel were given that prohibit taking provisions; (4) the rules of lodging were given requiring that they be satisfied with the first offer of hospitality; (5) the disciples were instructed to sever symbolically all relations with those who rejected their message; and (6) they are described as having fulfilled their commission.[226]

Comments

9:1 When Jesus called the Twelve together. See comments on 6:13; cf. also 8:1.

He gave them power and authority. "Authority" (see comments on 5:24) is found in Mark, but "power" is not. Both terms are found in Luke 4:36, where again Mark has only "authority." Luke typically emphasized Jesus' "power." See comments on 4:14; cf. also Acts 1:8; 10:38. The use of the aorist tense for the verb "gave" should not be pressed to mean "once for all." On the contrary, Luke 9:40 suggests that this endowment of power and authority was only for the duration of this particular mission, as suggested by 24:49 and Acts 1:8.

To drive out all demons. As elsewhere, Luke preferred this term to "evil spirits" (literally *unclean spirits*) found in Mark 6:7. See comments on 4:33.

And to cure diseases. This Lukan addition places the healing aspect of the disciples' ministry on an equal footing with exorcism and preaching. Here he clearly distinguished between demon possession and illness. See comments on 4:40.

9:2 And he sent them out. The verb is *apostellō*, from which "apostle" comes (see comments on 6:13). In his abbreviated account Luke omitted "two by two" (Mark 6:7). This fact may have been so well known that he did not think it needed to be stated, but its omission also gives a greater sense of the Twelve as a unified body.

To preach the kingdom of God and to heal the sick. The disciples had a threefold task: preaching, healing, and exorcising. The first two are mentioned in

---

[226] So Fitzmyer, *Luke*, 752.

Luke 9:11, but not the third. Jesus' healing and preaching ministry was even more important for Luke than the exorcising of demons.[227] For "kingdom of God" see comments on 4:43; Introduction 8 (2).

Take nothing for the journey. The Twelve were to travel without equipment. This may have been due to the brevity of their mission or to Jesus' desire to have them avoid the appearance of preaching for profit. It may also have been in order to require them to trust in God alone to supply their needs (cf. 12:22-31).

No staff. Such a staff could be used either as a walking stick or for protection against bandits. It was also a characteristic trademark of the "wandering" Cynic preachers of that day. Luke may have been thinking that the disciples should consciously avoid resembling them. This differs from "except a staff " in Mark 6:8. No satisfactory solution of this apparent conflict has been forthcoming as of yet.

No bag. This refers to a "knapsack" for carrying provisions.

No extra tunic. The "tunic" was the garment worn under the outer "cloak" (cf. Luke 6:29). The idea is of carrying a spare tunic, not of wearing two.

9:4 Whatever house you enter, stay. Those ministering in Jesus' name should not use their ministry for personal gain and seek better housing if it becomes available later (cf. 10:7). The implications of this, while clear and forever applicable, are all too often ignored.

9:5 If people do not welcome you. The verb "welcome" is also used in 8:13, which speaks of those who "receive" or welcome God's word, as well as in the parallel passage in 10:8,10. Elsewhere it is used of receiving Jesus himself (9:48,53) or receiving God's kingdom (18:17). Here it refers to the acceptance or rejection of the apostles as the equivalent of receiving or rejecting the good news they preached and, by implication, the Bringer of that good news, Jesus.

Shake the dust off your feet. Compare 10:11; Acts 13:51. This symbolic act severs all relationship with the town, leaving it in a state of condemnation to await the final judgment (cf. Luke 10:12-15).

As a testimony against them. This condemnation is directed not against individuals and families but against villages (9:6). Compare 10:10-11.

9:6 Preaching the gospel and healing people everywhere. Mark 6:12 reads "preached that people should repent," which is another aspect of the gospel message. See comments on 3:18 and 5:27-32—"The Lukan Message." Luke omitted the reference to exorcisms found in his source (Mark 6:13), indicating that for him preaching and healing were more important. The term "everywhere" should not be pressed to include the surrounding Gentile area. The mission to the Gentiles would take place in Luke-Acts only after the resurrection. Nonetheless, this mission during Jesus' ministry foreshadows the future Gentile mission.

The Lukan Message

The historicity of this episode and the role that it plays in the future transmission of the Gospel materials are extremely important for any dis-

---

[227] "The sick" is not found in B, and there is a minor variation among the manuscripts about whether "sick" is a noun or a participle. The NIV translation follows the most likely reading.

cussion of the history of tradition (*Traditionsgeschichte*). Since our purpose is to focus on what Luke sought to convey to his readers, however, this other important issue must be set aside. For Luke the Twelve's "first missionary journey" was a rehearsal for their future mission as witnesses to Jesus throughout the world (Luke 24:46-48; Acts 1:8). That mission would involve preaching (1) the word (Acts 8:4; 15:35—the word of the Lord); (2) Jesus as the Christ (5:42); (3) the kingdom of God (8:12); (4) the good news (Acts 8:25,40; 14:7,21; 16:10); (5) Jesus (8:35); (6) peace (10:36); (7) the Lord Jesus (11:20); (8) the promise (13:32); and (9) Jesus and the resurrection (17:18). It also would involve healing (3:1-10; 5:16; 9:17-19, 36-41 [a resuscitation from the dead]; 14:8-10; 19:12-16; 28:3-6) and exorcisms (5:16; 8:7; 16:16-18; 19:12). The first two (preaching and healing) were more important for Luke than the last (exorcisms).

Not all the specifics given in Luke 9:3-5 would apply directly to the situation after Pentecost, where lengthier missions would be the rule (Acts 13:1f.). This is evident from Luke 22:35-36. Much of what is said in these verses, however, will be applicable later. In Acts the disciples also would experience both acceptance and rejection of their preaching (Luke 9:5), and there too their preaching was not to be for personal gain (cf. Acts 8:18-23). They would go out depending upon God's grace and the hospitality of others (Acts 16:15,34; 17:5; 18:3).

Still another Lukan emphasis is found in his addition of the term "power" in 9:1. See comments on 1:17 and 4:14. Luke understood the "authority" to drive out demons and heal as due to the Spirit's empowering. This clearly foreshadows that future empowerment the Father (24:49) and the Son promised (Acts 1:8), which would come at Pentecost and equip the Twelve and the entire church to be Jesus' witnesses.

(2) Herod's Question about Jesus (9:7-9)

[7]Now Herod the tetrarch heard about all that was going on. And he was perplexed, because some were saying that John had been raised from the dead, [8]others that Elijah had appeared, and still others that one of the prophets of long ago had come back to life. [9]But Herod said, "I beheaded John. Who, then, is this I hear such things about?" And he tried to see him.

Context

This section reintroduces the question raised in 8:25 (cf. also 5:21; 7:20, 49) concerning Jesus' identification and begins a section in which this is the main theme. It also provides an interlude for the Twelve's mission to take place. This "story about Jesus" focuses the readers' attention on the question, "Who is Jesus?" That it was a ruler, the tetrarch of Galilee (3:1), who raised the question lends it even greater importance. Later it would be asked again by the high priest (22:67) and the Roman governor (23:3).

Luke modified the tradition about John the Baptist, recounting it in more "orderly" fashion in 3:19-20 and omitting the story of his imprisonment and martyrdom (cf. Mark 6:17-29). The significant changes include (1) Luke's reference to Herod as tetrarch rather than as king (cf. Mark 6:14); (2) "all that was going on" instead of Mark's "miraculous powers are at work in him" (6:14); (3) the formulation of Herod's puzzlement with the question, "Who, then, is this I hear such things about?"; and (4) mentioning that Herod was anxious to meet Jesus.

Comments

9:7 Herod the tetrarch. See comments on 3:1,19. Luke used Herod's correct title of tetrarch, whereas both Mark 6:25 and Matt 14:9 refer to him less precisely as a "king."[228]

Heard. This was due in part to the Twelve's preaching (Luke 9:6).

All that was going on. Luke is more comprehensive than Mark, including the exorcisms, preaching, and healing referred to in the previous section. Compare 24:18.

John the Baptist had been raised from the dead. In the Markan account Herod's treatment of John the Baptist is dealt with at considerable length (6:17-29). Luke had already reported (3:19-20) that Herod had imprisoned him and now succinctly informed his readers of John's death by referring to the rumor of his resurrection (9:9). Yet since Jesus and John the Baptist were contemporaries (cf. 7:18-35), how could such a belief arise? No clear analogy exists in which a person was thought to have been resurrected and reincarnated into another person. Possibly what is envisioned here is that the "spirit" of John the Baptist had passed on to Jesus in much the same way as Elijah's spirit came to rest upon Elisha in 2 Kgs 2:1-15.

9:8 Others that Elijah had appeared. For the popular view that Elijah would return in the last days, compare Luke 1:17; Mal 4:5; Mark 9:11-13. Whether an actual reappearance of the historical Elijah was meant or the assumption of Elijah's role in fulfillment of Mal 4:5 is uncertain. In Mark 9:11-13 Jesus interpreted Elijah's coming in the latter way.

One of the prophets of long ago. Does this refer to a prophet like Moses (Deut 18:15) or like Jeremiah (Matt 16:14)? The reference is ambiguous (cf. John 6:14).

Had come back to life. The term "come back to life" (*anistanai*) is used to describe Jesus' resurrection in Luke 16:31; 18:33; 24:7,46; Acts 2:24, so that it is best understood as a reference to resurrection than metaphorically as "appearing in the scene."[229]

9:9 Who, then, is this? Compare 5:21; 7:20,49; 9:18-20; 20:2; 22:67-71; 23:3,9.

I beheaded John. The implication is that in Herod's mind John the Baptist could not have risen from the dead and that Jesus was somewhat different.

And he tried to see him. This foreshadows 13:31 and 23:6-12 and is not due to Herod's "faith." At best this may reflect Herod's curiosity and desire to see a miracle (23:8), but perhaps it refers more ominously to a desire to get rid of Jesus (13:31).

---

[228]Cf., however, Matt 14:1, where the title "tetrarch" is used to describe Herod.

[229]Contra Fitzmyer, *Luke*, 759 and C. F. Evans, *Luke*, 398.

The Lukan Message

Whereas the literary function of this passage is to provide an interlude for the disciples' mission and to foreshadow the future meeting of Jesus and Herod (23:6-12), its theological emphasis is Christological. Once again the question is raised, this time by Herod the tetrarch, of who Jesus is. He is explicitly linked with the great: John the Baptist, Elijah, one of the OT prophets. The same possibilities will be raised again shortly in 9:19, and there the answer will at last be given. Jesus is greater still! He is "The Christ of God."[230]

(3) The Feeding of the Five Thousand (9:10-17)

[10]When the apostles returned, they reported to Jesus what they had done. Then he took them with him and they withdrew by themselves to a town called Bethsaida, [11]but the crowds learned about it and followed him. He welcomed them and spoke to them about the kingdom of God, and healed those who needed healing.

[12]Late in the afternoon the Twelve came to him and said, "Send the crowd away so they can go to the surrounding villages and countryside and find food and lodging, because we are in a remote place here."

[13]He replied, "You give them something to eat."

They answered, "We have only five loaves of bread and two fish—unless we go and buy food for all this crowd." [14](About five thousand men were there.)

But he said to his disciples, "Have them sit down in groups of about fifty each." [15]The disciples did so, and everybody sat down. [16]Taking the five loaves and the two fish and looking up to heaven, he gave thanks and broke them. Then he gave them to the disciples to set before the people. [17]They all ate and were satisfied, and the disciples picked up twelve basketfuls of broken pieces that were left over.

Context

After Herod's question about Jesus (9:7-9), Luke recorded the disciple's return and the feeding of the five thousand. This miracle is the only one found in all four Gospels that occurs in Galilee.[231] This nature miracle, like

---

[230]For the Christological dimension of this chapter, see J. A. Fitzmyer, "The Composition of Luke, Chapter 9," in *Perspectives on Luke-Acts*, ed. C. H. Talbert (Danville: Association of Baptist Professors of Religion, 1978), 139-52.

[231]Several historical questions are raised by this account. A number center around whether there were originally two separate feeding accounts (Mark 6:30-44 and 8:1-10) or whether these are two variants of the same tradition. Mark 8:19-20 and Matt 16:9-12 clearly understand them as two separate accounts. A number of Matthew-Luke agreements against Mark in the account suggest that, even if these are two separate accounts, the traditions may have been mutually influenced during the period of oral proclamation (see R. H. Stein, "The Matthew-Luke Agreements against Mark: Insight from John," *CBQ* 54 [1972]: 496-97), as well as by the account of the Lord's Supper. If one precludes the possibility of miracle, one would of course argue that these are two variants of the same myth. It is possible that Luke omitted

the stilling of the storm (8:22-25), deals with the question, "Who is this one?" (8:25 and 9:9). In this story Jesus clearly is "a man accredited by God to you by miracles and wonders and signs, which God did among you through him" (Acts 2:22). Even as the storms of sea posed no problem for Jesus, neither would a shortage of food. Unlike most miracle stories there is no description of the people's reaction. This miracle was meant primarily for the disciples and would enable them to answer the question Jesus asked in Luke 9:20. In Luke a meal setting is especially appropriate for understanding who Jesus is (cf. 24:30-31).

Comments
9:10   When the apostles returned. The term "apostles" is used here for the Twelve (9:1,12) who were "sent out" (*apostellō*) in 9:2. They also are called "disciples" in 9:14,16. Therefore, although "apostles" and "disciples" are more inclusive terms than the Twelve, the Twelve nevertheless were the apostles and disciples par excellence, even as they were the "eyewitnesses and servants of the word" (1:2) par excellence.

They reported to Jesus what they had done. Luke abbreviated Mark's "done and taught" (Mark 6:30), but no doubt he meant both. When the apostles reported what they had done—i.e., their ministry of exorcisms, preaching, and healing (9:1-2)—we assume they received Jesus' approval, although this was not explicitly stated.

Then he took them . . . and they withdrew. Jesus' purpose, to get away from the crowd, is more clearly stated in Mark 6:31.

To a town called Bethsaida. Mark and Matthew have "a solitary place." Bethsaida lies just north of the Sea of Galilee on the eastern side of the Jordan River. Although it was technically part of Gaulanitis, it was usually associated with Galilee (cf. John 12:21). In Mark, Bethsaida is mentioned right after this account (Mark 6:45) and just before the account of Peter's confession (cf. Mark 8:22,27-30), and Luke also followed this account with Peter's confession (Luke 9:18-21). See the discussion in 9:1-50. This miracle in the neighborhood of Bethsaida will be referred to in 10:13-14.

9:11   But the crowds . . . followed. Compare Matt 14:13 and John 6:2.

He welcomed them. The term "welcome" or "receive" was a favorite with Luke.[232]

And spoke to them about the kingdom of God. The Twelve's preaching ministry (9:1-2) continued Jesus' preaching (cf. 4:43; 8:1; Acts 1:8). For "kingdom of God" see comments on 4:43; Introduction 8 (2).

And healed. The healing ministry of the Twelve (Luke 9:1-2) was a continuation of Jesus' healing. Luke's failure to mention exorcisms indicates that this aspect

---

the feeding of the four thousand due to his tendency to avoid duplication of similar accounts. Another problem involves whether the area around Bethsaida can be thought of as a "remote place," i.e., a desert place (9:12).

[232] Sixteen times in Luke (also Acts 2:41; 18:27; 21:17; 24:3; 28:30) compared to Mark's six times and Matthew's ten times.

of their ministry was less significant for him than preaching and healing. See comments on 9:6.

9:12 Late in the afternoon. Late in the afternoon, around sunset, was when the main meal was eaten. It is doubtful that we should see in this statement an allusion to the time of day when the Lord's Supper was celebrated because each Evangelist used different terminology to state this, and their wording does not resemble 1 Cor 11:23.

The Twelve came. The switch from Twelve to apostles and again to Twelve indicates that for Luke these terms were interchangeable.

Send the crowd away. The singular "crowd" agrees with John 6:2, but not with Luke 9:11 (Cf. Matt 14:15 and Mark 6:36). Although the Twelve had the practical needs of the people in mind, they had forgotten both Jesus' miracles (Luke 8:22-56), which they witnessed, and their own mission.

Because we are in a remote place here. "Remote place" is literally *desert place*, but it need not imply a vast desert region like Sinai. Here it refers to an uninhabited area in the vicinity of Bethsaida. The disciples' suggestion to dismiss the crowds so they could acquire food in the neighboring villages indicates that the location envisioned was not remote desert but simply an uninhabited place near villages and towns such as Bethsaida.

9:13 You give them something to eat. Some have seen here a possible allusion to 2 Kgs 4:42-44, but Luke made no clear reference to this, and the Greek is far from exact.

Five loaves of bread and two fish. The number is the same in all the parallel accounts. The miracle of the feeding of the four thousand, however, speaks of seven loaves and a few small fish, which reinforces the conclusion that it was a separate event.

Unless we go and buy food. The disciples were thinking quite logically in terms of the natural order of things, but they were forgetting the presence of the one who is Lord over the natural order. Luke and his readers knew that the Lord of the wind and the water (8:22-25) is also Lord over bread and fish.

9:14 About five thousand men were there. Luke introduced the number earlier than Mark and Matthew to make this a more orderly account.

In groups of about fifty each. Nothing should be read into this number, for passages such as Exod 18:21,25 are not close parallels.

9:15 The disciples followed Jesus' command, even though they still thought that the crowds should have been dismissed (cf. Luke 5:5). Sometimes obedience must precede understanding.

9:16 "Gave thanks" (*eulogeō*) is better translated *blessed*. All five verbs occur in the parallels in Mark 6:41 and Matt 14:19. In the account of the Lord's Supper all but "looking up" are found in Mark 14:22 and Matt 26:26. Luke 22:19 also has four verbs but "gave thanks" (*eucharisteō*).[233] There are four verbs in 1 Cor 11:23-24 as well, but they are "took . . . gave thanks (*eucharisteō*) . . . broke . . . said." The feeding of the five thousand was seen by the early church to prefigure the Lord's Supper and the coming messianic banquet (cf. Luke 12:37; 13:28-29;

---

[233] Why the NIV translates the verb *eulogeō* as "gave thanks" in Luke 9:16 is hard to understand.

22:15-16,18,30). They are, of course, distinct from one another, but this account does remind the reader of the Lord's Supper (see comments on 24:30) even though the latter does not have a miraculous multiplication of food. No doubt the wording of the Lord's Supper would have been sufficiently familiar to Theophilus and Luke's other readers that this sequence of verbs would have triggered an automatic association with the Supper.

Gave thanks. This "blessing" in Luke is associated with the bread and the fish because the pronoun "them" follows the verb (*eulogeō*). Mark and Matthew, which lack the pronoun, focus the blessing on God. It has been suggested that "them" may be an accusative of respect and that the text should thus be translated "blessed [be God] with respect to the bread and fish." This, however, would be a more appropriate action and interpretation after, rather than before, the multiplication of the loaves and fish.

Broke. This aspect of the meal would especially call the Lord's Supper to the minds of Luke's readers since it was often called the "breaking of bread" (Acts 2:42,46; 20:7,11; cf. also Luke 24:29-30).

Gave. "Gave" is literally *was giving*. Whereas the previous verbs indicate punctiliar action (aorists), the passing out of the food is durative (imperfect). One should not read into the text that this "giving" symbolizes how the early church leaders would be able to "feed" and meet the needs of the church. By omitting any reference to the distribution of the fish, Luke heightened the analogy to the Lord's Supper (cf. Mark 6:41).

9:17 They all ate and were satisfied. The word "satisfied" is the same word used in the beatitude of Luke 6:21. There is more than enough in the kingdom.

Twelve basketfuls. This involves a basket for each of the Twelve, but the main emphasis is on the great abundance.

Broken pieces. This term (*klasmatōn*) is used to describe the bread of the Lord's Supper in *Didache* 9:3-4, which indicates that the feeding of the five thousand was very early seen to prefigure the Lord's Supper.

That were left over. The description of the collection of the leftovers is not meant to teach stewardship or to show that Jesus did not litter but to display the surpassing greatness of Jesus. He does "immeasurably more than all we ask or imagine, according to his power" (Eph 3:20). The abundance witnesses both to Jesus' power and to his grace.

The miracle proper ("how" Jesus actually did this) is not explained. The tradition and the Gospel writers all understood this to be a miracle and thus beyond rational explanation. All rationalistic attempts to explain the event (behind Jesus hidden from the crowd was a cave full of supplies that provided the bread and fish; or the generosity of a small boy [John 6:9] who, sharing his food, caused others who had more than enough to share their food as well, so that all had enough) violate the clear meaning of the text. Luke and the other Evangelists clearly intended to demonstrate Jesus' supernatural, miracle-working power.

The Lukan Message

This story, like most miracle stories in the Gospels, serves a Christological function. This is made evident not only by the miracle itself but by Luke's placement of the account. It follows and answers Herod's question, "Who, then, is this I hear such things about?" (Luke 9:9). It is itself followed by Jesus' own question, "Who do you say I am?" in the next account (9:20). The feeding of the five thousand is a somewhat atypical miracle story because it does not describe the crowd's reaction.[234] The miracle was meant for the disciples, and it would enable them to answer the coming question in 9:20. (This also suggests that the great omission of Mark 6:45–8:26 is not accidental.) He who can provide a "messianic banquet" (cf. Isa 25:6; 65:13-14; Pss 78:24; 81:16) must be the Messiah. The disciples had thus been given the answer to the question, "Who is this Jesus?" He is the Christ of God (9:20)!

There is an eschatological teaching in this passage as well. If the miraculous feeding is understood as a partial fulfillment of the messianic banquet, then in some way the messianic age must have begun. This fits well with the concept of God's kingdom as a present reality, which is explicitly taught elsewhere in Luke (see comments on 4:43). As already seen, the feeding of the five thousand foreshadows the Lord's Supper, which in turn prefigures the coming messianic banquet when the Son of Man returns. The firstfruits of the kingdom already were present, however, and being experienced in this miracle.

(4) Peter's Confession and Teachings on the Passion and Discipleship (9:18-27)

[18]Once when Jesus was praying in private and his disciples were with him, he asked them, "Who do the crowds say I am?"

[19]They replied, "Some say John the Baptist; others say Elijah; and still others, that one of the prophets of long ago has come back to life."

[20]"But what about you?" he asked. "Who do you say I am?"

Peter answered, "The Christ of God."

[21]Jesus strictly warned them not to tell this to anyone. [22]And he said, "The Son of Man must suffer many things and be rejected by the elders, chief priests and teachers of the law, and he must be killed and on the third day be raised to life."

[23]Then he said to them all: "If anyone would come after me, he must deny himself and take up his cross daily and follow me. [24]For whoever wants to save his life will lose it, but whoever loses his life for me will save it. [25]What good is it for a man to gain the whole world, and yet lose or forfeit his very self? [26]If anyone is ashamed of me and my words, the Son of Man will be ashamed of him when he comes in his glory and in the glory of the Father and of the holy angels. [27]I tell you the truth, some who are standing here will not taste death before they see the kingdom of God."

---

[234]Cf. Luke 4:36; 5:15,26; 6:11; 7:17; 8:37,56.

Context

Whereas in Luke this account is located immediately after the miracle of the feeding of the five thousand, in Mark these two accounts are separated by Mark 6:45–8:26. By his "great omission" Luke tied these two events together. Mark and Matthew used the account of Peter's confession as the turning point in Jesus' ministry, after which he began to teach his disciples about the necessity of his death (cf. Mark 8:31; Matt 16:21). Luke again revealed that he was more concerned with logical rather than chronological order because for him Peter's confession served primarily as the answer to Herod's question concerning Jesus (Luke 9:7-9), even though it also served as a turning point. The location of the confession (cf. Mark 8:27; Matt 16:13) and Jesus' rebuke of Peter (cf. Mark 8:32-33; Matt 16:22-23) are both unimportant and contrary to Luke's interests. (Luke's Gospel minimizes both Jesus' ministry in "Gentile" territory [cf. Acts 10:39; 13:31] and some of Mark's negative descriptions of the disciples.) Additional clarification of Herod's musing will be provided in Luke 9:28-36.

The present account consists of three distinct parts: (1) Peter's confession, 9:18-21; (2) Jesus' passion prediction, 9:22; and (3) Jesus' teachings on discipleship, 9:23-27.[235] In favor of the historicity of the confession is the fact that it is tied to a relatively unknown place, Caesarea Philippi (Mark 8:27). Numerous places would better serve as a location for such a confession if this were simply a creative piece of fiction. (Think of how well this account would function after Luke 19:38.) The negative portrayal of Peter (Mark 8:32-33) is frequently pointed to as supportive of its historicity. As to the passion prediction, it must be admitted that Luke and the early church did word such predictions in light of their knowledge of subsequent events. Yet this is no reason to assume that the passion prediction is unauthentic, a creation of the early church. Even if one discounts the possibility of genuine foreknowledge, surely Jesus must have been aware of the possibility of a violent death; for John the Baptist and many OT prophets had been martyred. Given the hostility his preaching frequently aroused, it would be incredible for Jesus not to have contemplated the possibility of a like fate. There is also no reason Jesus could not have used the "cross" as a symbol of commitment, since the sight of people carrying a cross to execution was all too familiar.

The Lukan redaction is seen in several areas in addition to his omission of Mark 6:45–8:26, the place of Caesarea Philippi, and the rebuke of Peter. Luke also: omitted "and he began to teach" (Mark 8:31); enlarged

---

[235] For a contrary view see Nolland (*Luke 1–9:20*, 448), who divides his two-volume work into Luke 1:1–9:20 and 9:21–24:53.

the call to discipleship to "all" (Luke 9:23); added "daily" (9:23); omitted "the gospel" (Mark 8:35) and all of Mark 8:37; and changed Mark's "in his Father's glory" (8:38) to "in his glory and in the glory of the Father and of the holy angels" (9:26).

Comments

9:18   Once when Jesus was praying.   Again Luke portrayed Jesus at prayer before a significant event. See comments on 3:21 and Introduction 8 (7).

Who do the crowds say I am?   Matthew 16:13 uses "Son of Man" instead of "I." See Introduction 8 (4).

9:19   The possibilities given in Luke 9:7-8 are repeated here, so that this account forms its climax. Luke had no objection to portraying Jesus as a prophet (see comments on 4:24). It is not an incorrect description but an inadequate one by itself: Jesus is a prophet and more. Tannehill aptly notes, "Those who speak of Jesus as a prophet in Luke may not understand him completely, but this title does not represent a distortion to be rejected."[236]

9:20   But what about you?   The "you" is emphatic. This question of Jesus clearly implies that Jesus wanted more from the disciples than a repetition of the current speculation found in 9:7-8,19. Jesus expected more insight from the disciples. Having experienced the preceding miracles, they should have had a better understanding than the crowds.

Peter answered.   Peter replied as spokesman for the disciples.

The Christ.   For the meaning of this term, see comments on 2:11 and 3:22. Jesus already had been so designated by the angels (2:11), the narrator (2:26), the demons (4:41), and indirectly by Jesus himself (4:18); but this is the first time the disciples had recognized him as such. It thus marks an important step in their training. (The importance of this event is heightened in the parallels in Mark 8:31 and Matt 16:21.) Peter and the disciples had witnessed Jesus' miracles of healing, his rule over nature, his raising of the dead, and had heard his teachings. They now acknowledged that God has, indeed, visited his people. The promised Messiah has come. He who brings God's kingdom is the King, David's Son, the Anointed! Luke's readers have been prepared for this by 1:32-33,69; 2:11.

Of God.   By this qualification Luke emphasized that Jesus is the Anointed One whom God had promised to send.[237] It is thus an allusion here to the fulfillment of Scripture.

9:21   Not to tell this.   The command for silence was given not because Peter's confession was false but precisely because it was true. The confession was not inappropriate, but its proclamation was dangerous. Such a proclamation would have had disastrous consequences; for to Jesus, "Christ/Messiah" meant suffering and death as God's Anointed, whereas among the people it signified the Anointed King who would throw off the Roman yoke, smite the Gentiles, and bring political independence and greatness to Israel. Jesus had rejected such a nationalistic

---

[236]Tannehill, *Narrative Unity of Luke-Acts*, 97.

[237]Cf. Luke 2:26—"Lord's Christ"; 23:35—"Christ of God"; and Acts 3:18; 4:26—"his Christ."

conception of messiahship at the beginning of his ministry (see 4:1-15, "Context"). Because of this popular misconception, the public proclamation of Jesus as the Christ would have brought about an immediate confrontation between Jesus and Rome. Even the disciples failed to comprehend what Jesus' role as the Christ entailed. What was lacking in Peter's confession was the realization that Christ's role included the suffering of 9:22.[238]

9:22 Jesus' first passion prediction follows immediately upon Peter's confession. This close association underlines the fact that for Jesus and the church, God's Anointed was a suffering Messiah (cf. also Luke 9:43b-45; 18:31-34; cf. also 24:7).[239]

The Son of Man. See comments on 5:24. Here it is the Son of Man who suffered, whereas elsewhere it is the Christ (24:26,46; Acts 3:18; 17:3; 26:23). Since these two titles, as well as such titles as Prophet and Lord, were used to describe Jesus, it is not surprising that his suffering could be described variously as the suffering of a prophet (Luke 13:33-34), of the Son of Man, of the Christ, and of the Lord (Acts 2:36). The titles most commonly associated with the passion, however, are the Son of Man and Christ.

Must. The death of Jesus is not to be seen as a mistake or tragedy. It was a divine necessity and took place in accordance with the divine plan.[240] This will be confirmed in 9:31. See Introduction 8 (1).

Suffer. This is not a synonym for "to die" in Greek, but in the context of Jesus' passion it does refer to his death.[241] For its use with "many things and be rejected," cf. Luke 17:25.

By the elders, chief priests and teachers of the law. The use of a single "the" indicates the unity of these three groups in their plan and purpose.[242] "Chief priests" does not refer to the high priests but to those priests who held leading positions in the temple hierarchy.

On the third day. Both Luke and Matthew (Matt 16:21) preferred "on the third day" to Mark's "after three days" (Mark 8:31). (Cf. Mark 9:31 and 10:34 with Matt 17:23 and 20:19/Luke 18:33.) This may be due to a concern that "after three days" could be misunderstood and not allow for a Friday crucifixion and a Sunday resurrection. "After three days," however, can simply mean on the third day (cf. 1 Sam 30:12 "for three days and nights" with 1 Sam 30:13 "the third day today" in the LXX). It is more likely that Luke and Matthew chose "on the third day" because it was the more traditional designation.[243]

---

[238]This lack of understanding on the part of Peter and the disciples in the *Sitz im Leben Jesu*, or situation in the life of Jesus, is shown in Mark 8:32-33.

[239]For other more veiled references to Jesus' passion, cf. Luke 5:33-35; 11:29-32; 13:31-35; 20:9-18; 22:19-20,28; cf. also 12:50; 17:25; 22:22.

[240]For the divine necessity, cf. Luke 13:33; 17:25; 22:37; 24:7,26,44; Acts 17:3. For God's plan cf. Acts 2:23; 4:28; 13:32-33.

[241]Luke 13:33; 17:25; 22:37; 24:7,26,46; Acts 1:3; 3:18; 17:3.

[242]Cf. Matt 16:21 but contrast Mark 8:31 in the Greek text, which would be better translated "the elders, the chief priests and the teachers of the law."

[243]Cf. Luke 13:32; 18:33; 24:7,21,46; Acts 10:40; 1 Cor 15:4.

Be raised to life. Here God's raising of Jesus from the dead is emphasized by the use of the passive. The active tense can also be used (cf. 16:31; 24:46; Acts 10:41; 17:3).

9:23 Then he said to them all. The audience of disciples in Luke 9:18 is enlarged.

If anyone would come after me. This metaphor describes what it means to become a disciple (in the sense of a follower) of Jesus as 14:27 shows.

Three conditions of discipleship are laid out. The first involves a need to deny oneself. This is much more radical than simply a denial of certain things. This mandates a rejection of a life based on self-interest and self-fulfillment. Instead a disciple is to be one who seeks to fulfill the will and the teachings of Christ. Another metaphor to express this act of commitment is to hate one's own life (14:26). The opposite response can be seen in 12:9; Acts 3:13-14; 7:35.

The second condition involves the need to take up one's cross. This need not be a *vaticinia ex eventu*, or a prophecy after the fact, but Jesus' own crucifixion reveals more fully to Luke's readers that this call is for a commitment unto death. There needs to be willingness to suffer martyrdom if need be. (Cf. Luke 14:27 and 23:26, where Simon of Cyrene takes up the cross and follows Jesus.) Luke added the need to do this "daily." Whereas Mark emphasized the initial act of denying oneself once and for all (Mark 8:34), in Luke there is an emphasis on the need to make such a commitment each day.

The final condition is the need to follow Jesus. In contrast to the other conditions this verb is a present imperative, indicating that following Jesus must be continual. For this metaphor see comments on 5:11.

9:24 This saying is an example of both antithetical and chiasmic parallelism: A = save; B = lose; b = lose; a = save. There is also a pun, in that the first use of "save" means *a failure to deny oneself*, but the second means *to receive eternal life* (cf. John 12:25). Conversely, to "lose" in the first instance means *to suffer the judgment of hell*, but in the second it means *to deny oneself*. This verse is also an example of paradox.

For whoever wants to save his life. This is the opposite of Luke 9:23. Compare 17:33.

Loses his life. To lose one's life is to be equated not with Christian martyrdom but with the fulfillment of the three conditions given in 9:23. On rare occasions this may lead to martyrdom, but one can fulfill the conditions of 9:23 without suffering martyrdom.

For me. In Mark's parallel "and the gospel" (Mark 8:35) is added, emphasizing that commitment to Jesus involves a commitment to his teachings as well. By not including this statement, Luke focused attention more upon Jesus' person. Nevertheless, being ashamed of Jesus' teachings is equivalent to being ashamed of Jesus himself (Luke 9:26). Once again Jesus was claiming that the eternal state of humanity depends on a relationship to him. See comments on 7:23.

9:25 This verse is essentially a proverb stating that one should live in light of ultimate values. The loss of one's soul, i.e., experiencing God's judgment (cf. 10:14), is far too great a price to pay for possessing the whole world.

9:26 If anyone is ashamed of me. This is another way of saying "to disown me," and the opposite is "to acknowledge me" as 12:8-9 points out (cf. 22:54-61). The loyalty to ultimate values demanded in 9:24 becomes more focused on Jesus.

And my words. The person and message of Jesus cannot be separated. (Cf. how Paul combined being ashamed and the gospel in Rom 1:16.)

The Son of Man. Attempts have been made to distinguish between Jesus and the Son of Man in this verse because the Son of Man is referred to in the third person (cf. also Luke 12:8; 22:69; Matt 19:28), but no Evangelist interpreted these sayings in this way. It is better to interpret the Son of Man sayings in the third person as referring not to two different persons but rather to two different states: Jesus' present lowly condition and his future glory and exaltation. See comments on 5:24.

When he comes in his glory and in the glory of the Father. The parallels in Mark 8:38 and Matt 16:27 have only "his Father's glory." Luke heightened the Christological nature of this saying by attributing personal glory to Jesus (Luke 21:27; 24:26). The coming of the Son of Man is also referred to in 12:40; 17:22, 24,26,30; 18:8; 21:27,36.

9:27 Some who are standing here will not taste death before they see the kingdom of God. Grammatically this is a subjunctive of emphatic negation used to indicate strong denial. This statement has caused a great deal of confusion. It does not say that the disciples would not die but rather that they would not die before they saw "the kingdom of God." Some of the various interpretations suggested include: (1) the coming of God's kingdom in Jesus' resurrection; (2) the coming of God's kingdom in the Spirit's coming at Pentecost (this is weakened by Luke's omission of "come with power" from the parallel in Mark 9:1); (3) the spread of the church throughout the world; (4) the recognition that God's kingdom is already realized; (5) Jerusalem's destruction in A.D. 70; (6) the transfiguration, which follows this saying in each Synoptic Gospel; and (7) the parousia, or second coming. The last interpretation has as a corollary that this saying is, of course, in error since the Lord has not returned. It is most unlikely that Luke understood this as a reference to the parousia; for by the time he wrote, the disciples were for the most part, if not entirely, deceased. If Luke wrote his Gospel in part in order to correct a disappointment caused by a misunderstanding concerning Jesus' return, it is even more unlikely that this saying refers to the parousia. See Introduction 7 (3). Although Luke's omission of the expression "come with power" (Mark 9:1) was quite intentional, it appears that he understood this promise (Luke 9:27) as having been fulfilled in the next event—the transfiguration. The form of this saying in Luke is less troublesome than in the Matthean counterpart (Matt 16:28). The expression "taste death" is also found in John 8:52 and Heb 2:9 and refers to "death as a bitter experience."[244]

The Lukan Message

This section contains several Lukan theological emphases, and it is difficult to do justice to all of them. One clear theme found in the passage involves Christology. Peter's confession is perhaps the Christological high point of the entire Gospel. Here is the authoritative confession of the

---

[244]Sabourin, *Luke*, 215.

"eyewitnesses and servants of the word" (Luke 1:2) about the identity of Jesus of Nazareth. Who is this man? He is the Christ of God (9:20). Peter thus provided a definitive answer to Herod's question in 9:9. Additional titles may be attributed to him in Luke-Acts, but none are more important or more basic than this. Jesus is God's Anointed, the Messiah, the Christ. Along with the description of who Jesus is, this passage also contains the clear teaching that the destiny of all humanity is based upon one's relationship to him. Salvation consists of following him (9:23), of losing or surrendering one's life to him (9:24), of not being ashamed of him or his teachings (9:26). The "totalitarian" nature of this claim must not be overlooked. For Luke (as for all the NT writers) life, death, heaven, hell, salvation, judgment, justification, and damnation are all determined by one's attitude toward Jesus. Jesus is unlike all others in that the destiny of this world and the ultimate fate of all humanity revolves around him.

A second Lukan theme in this passage is Jesus' future death. This is the clearest reference found so far in the Gospel. The necessity of this death is clearly taught (9:22). The "must" (*dei*) reveals the divine imperative, but Luke did not give a clear explanation of why this death was a divine necessity. We cannot obtain any doctrine of the atonement from this passage. See Introduction 8 (8).

This passage also contains a description of the human response necessary for participation in the divine plan of salvation. Whereas elsewhere the required response has been described primarily as the need to "believe" and "repent," here a different set of metaphors are introduced. One needs to "come after" or "follow" Jesus, "deny oneself," "take up the cross daily," "lose one's life," and not be "ashamed" of Jesus or his words. These are not additional requirements on top of "believing and repenting." Nor are they to be seen as a challenge urging Christians to a deeper commitment, for what is at stake is saving one's life (9:24), forfeiting one's life (9:25), and being denied (access to God's presence) at the final judgment (9:26). These new metaphors are best understood as different aspects of faith and repentance. To deny oneself is to have a radical change of mind (to repent) regarding one's priorities in life. These metaphors help to focus attention on what is involved in true faith and repentance. If one were to look at the human response in conversion as a kind of prism, the faith, repentance, denying oneself, and not being ashamed would all be different refractions of that prism, viewed from different angles.

(5) The Transfiguration (9:28-36)

[28]About eight days after Jesus said this, he took Peter, John and James with him and went up onto a mountain to pray. [29]As he was praying, the appearance of his face changed, and his clothes became as bright as a flash of lightning. [30]Two men, Moses and Elijah, [31]appeared in glorious splendor, talking with

Jesus. They spoke about his departure, which he was about to bring to fulfillment at Jerusalem. [32]Peter and his companions were very sleepy, but when they became fully awake, they saw his glory and the two men standing with him. [33]As the men were leaving Jesus, Peter said to him, "Master, it is good for us to be here. Let us put up three shelters—one for you, one for Moses and one for Elijah." (He did not know what he was saying.) [34]While he was speaking, a cloud appeared and enveloped them, and they were afraid as they entered the cloud. [35]A voice came from the cloud, saying, "This is my Son, whom I have chosen; listen to him." [36]When the voice had spoken, they found that Jesus was alone. The disciples kept this to themselves, and told no one at that time what they had seen.

Context

In Luke as in the parallel accounts in Matthew and Mark, the transfiguration follows Peter's confession (9:18-21), Jesus' passion prediction (9:22), and the sayings on discipleship (9:23-27). The temporal designation that introduces the transfiguration account (9:28; Mark 9:2; Matt 17:1) probably is traditional, indicating that these accounts were already associated in the oral period. The imagery draws heavily from the OT, in particular from the theophany to Moses on Mount Sinai in Exodus. Some of the OT images that parallel Luke's account are a mountain on which revelation takes place (Exod 19:3; 24:15; cf. also 1 Kgs 19:7-18), the alteration of Jesus' face (Exod 34:29), the glory of the Lord (Exod 24:16), a cloud (Exod 24:16; 33:10); lightninglike appearance (Dan 10:6), and fear (Exod 34:30; Dan 10:7). Parallels between this account and Jesus' baptism include the common voice from heaven, "You/This is my Son" (Luke 3:22; 9:35); the use of *eidos* to refer to "bodily form" (3:22) and "appearance of his face" (9:29); and the reference to Jesus' praying (3:21; 9:28-29).

The differences between Luke and the other accounts may be due to his use of a special source, but they are more probably due to his own editorial work in that most of the differences express Lukan theological motifs. The oral traditions of this incident with which Luke was familiar may have influenced him as well. Some of the more evident differences are: "about eight days" (9:28) instead of "after six days" (Mark 9:2); the addition of references to Jesus' praying in Luke 9:28-29; the omission of Jesus' "transfiguration" (Mark 9:2); the reference to Jesus' "glory" (Luke 9:32); the explanation of the disciples' foolish comment as due to their being "very sleepy" (9:32); the change of "Rabbi" (Mark 9:5) to "Master" (Luke 9:33); and reference to Jesus as God's "chosen" (9:35).[245]

[245]For a more detailed discussion of the Lukan editorial features in this account, see A. A. Trites, "The Transfiguration in the Theology of Luke: Some Redactional Links" in *The Glory of Christ in the New Testament*, ed. L. D. Hurst and N. T. Wright (Oxford: Clarendon, 1987), 71-81.

The historicity of this account is often denied. If one's world view does not allow for the supernatural, then naturalistic or mythical explanations must be found. Some have sought to explain the incident as a vision (cf. Matt 17:9), but *horama* can also be used to describe historical events (Deut 28:34,67, LXX). All three Gospel writers, as well as 2 Pet 1:16-18, however, understand this to be a real event. There is also no evidence that this account was originally a resurrection experience read back into the life of the historical Jesus because "Rabbi" and even "Master" are not completely adequate forms of address for the risen Lord. Furthermore the error of placing Jesus on the same level as Moses and Elijah ("let us put up three shelters") is most unlikely after the resurrection.[246]

If one accepts the historicity of this account, the question of what actually happened still must be raised. There are three main explanations. (1) The preexistent glory of the preincarnate Son temporarily broke through the limitations of his humanity (cf. Phil 2:6-9; John 1:14b). (2) A glimpse of the future glory of the risen Christ is given to the disciples. Even as the first passion prediction (Luke 9:22) does not end in an announcement of death but in the promise of resurrection, so the discussion of Jesus' departure is followed by a glimpse of the glory awaiting him at the resurrection (24:26; cf. also Heb 2:9; 1 Pet 1:21). (3) A glimpse of the glory of the Son of Man at the time of the parousia is given to the disciples. In support of the last explanation is the fact that the glory of the Son of Man at his parousia has just been mentioned (Luke 9:26; cf. also 21:27, where Luke referred to "cloud," as in 9:34-35, rather than "clouds" as found in Mark and Matthew). Also 2 Pet 1:16-18 clearly understands it in this manner. Although the last explanation is the primary understanding of the event for Luke, elements of the second may also be present.

Comments

9:28 About eight days. There is no totally convincing explanation of why Luke changed this temporal designation. It has been suggested that he may have sought to translate the Jewish week ("after six days") into a Hellenistic reckoning of an eight-day week. Others have sought to explain this as a reference to the eighth day in the Feast of Tabernacles/Booths in Lev 23:36 (cf. Luke 9:33). The use of "about" eliminates any idea of chronological discrepancy. The chronological tie to the preceding event indicates that one should interpret what is happening in the transfiguration account in light of Peter's confession.

After Jesus said this. By this addition (literally *after these words*) Luke tied this account even more closely to the preceding one.

He took Peter, John and James. See comments on 8:51.

---

[246]For further discussion see R. H. Stein, "Is the Transfiguration (Mark 9:2-8) a Misplaced Resurrection-Account?" *JBL* 95 (1976): 79-96.

And went up onto a mountain. Speculation about which mountain (Mount Tabor, Hermon, or Carmel) was of no interest to the Evangelists. For them it was not where this happened that was most important but what happened. Luke was even less interested than the other Evangelists in the geographical designation. This is evident by his dropping of the term "high" (cf. Mark 9:2; Matt 17:1), even as he dropped the designation Caesarea Philippi from the preceding account. This may be due to his desire not to place Jesus outside of Galilee and in Gentile territory (Caesarea Philippi; "high" mountain, perhaps designating Mount Hermon on the border with Lebanon).

To pray. It has frequently been noted that this is a strong emphasis in Luke. See comments on 6:12. Luke added this statement of Jesus' purpose in going to the mountain. Did Luke have special information about Jesus on this occasion? Or did he know that Jesus' life was so characterized by prayer that his desire to be "alone" (Mark 9:2) would naturally mean "alone to pray"?

9:29 As he was praying. This second reference to Jesus' praying adds even more emphasis to this theme.

At this point Luke omitted the reference to Jesus' being "transfigured" (Mark 9:2; Matt 17:2) or "metamorphosed." Luke may have done this to avoid any similarity with pagan religious myths. (Cf. Acts 14:11, "The gods have come down to us in human form!")[247]

The appearance of his face changed. The transfiguration was not from the outside in but from the inside out. Jesus' "person" was transfigured before his clothing. Both Matthew and Luke referred to Jesus' face shining "like the sun" (Matt 17:2). It is difficult not to see in this some allusion to Exod 34:29-35 (cf. also 2 Cor 3:7-13). Moses' glory, however, came from the outside.

His clothes became as bright as a flash of lightning. Compare Luke 24:4; Acts 1:10 (cf. also Luke 17:24). This description shows the heavenly character of the event and may be understood by Luke as a foreshadowing of the glory of the Son of Man when he returns (cf. 17:24).

9:30 Two men, Moses and Elijah. Luke placed the two men in chronological order in contrast to Mark 9:4. Do these men represent (1) the law (Moses) and the prophets (Elijah)—cf. Luke 16:29,31; 24:27; (2) heavenly figures who were expected to return at the end time; or (3) two OT prophetic figures who had not experienced death? The first possibility seems best. The reference to "two men" ties together the transfiguration, resurrection (24:4), and ascension (Acts 1:10). The presence of Moses and Elijah refutes the incorrect guesses about Jesus' identity given in Luke 9:8,19.

9:31 In glorious splendor. By this addition Luke emphasized that Moses and Elijah brought them the glorious splendor that came from their presence with God.

They spoke about his departure. The term "departure" is *exodos*. This can refer to (1) Jesus' death. This interpretation is supported by the following statement "which he was about to bring to fulfillment at Jerusalem" (cf. 13:33; 2 Pet 1:15; cf. also Wis 3:2; 7:6). (2) His death and resurrection. This is supported by the passion prediction in Luke 9:22, which mentions both Jesus' death and resurrection. (3) His

---

[247] See J. Behm, μορφή, *TDNT* (Grand Rapids: Eerdmans, 1967), 4:746-48.

death, resurrection, and ascension. Luke 9:51 and perhaps also 24:26 favor this, although the latter may also be understood in light of the second interpretation. It seems probable that the most inclusive interpretation (3) is the correct one. Moses and Elijah did not "inform" Jesus of the details of his "exodus," for by 9:22 he already knew them. They were present rather to illustrate Jesus' fulfillment of the divine plan in the OT, i.e., he fulfilled the law and the prophets. This verse prepares the reader for 9:51f. There may be present a chiasmas in 9:30-31 in which A = Moses; B = Elijah; b = glorious splendor; a = departure [exodos].

Bring to fulfillment. This can refer to the fulfillment of the OT (cf. 24:25-27, 44) or the fulfillment of what God has ordained. The latter, which includes the former, is more comprehensive and fits better the thought of 13:33 (cf. also Acts 12:25; 13:25,27).

At Jerusalem. Luke purposefully mentioned Jerusalem, for it was in this city that the redemptive acts of salvation history took place. These acts included the announcement in the temple to Zechariah (Luke 1:5-23); the dedication of Jesus (2:22-38); the yearly pilgrimage to Jerusalem (2:41); Jesus' final journey to Jerusalem (9:51f.); the crucifixion, resurrection, postresurrection appearances, ascension, and the coming of the Spirit. Jerusalem also would be significant as the center of world evangelism and the site of the Jerusalem Council.

9:32 Were very sleepy. Compare Mark 14:40. Only in Luke do we find this explanation of Peter's unconsidered offer to build three shelters. Luke sought to explain the disciples' sleeping at Gethsemane as having been due to their being "exhausted from sorrow" (Luke 22:45), and in 9:22-23 he omitted Mark 8:32-33. Luke clearly painted a sympathetic portrait of the disciples.

They saw his glory. That is, they saw Jesus transfigured. Compare also Luke 9:26.

And the two men standing with him. This should not be interpreted as the fulfillment of 9:27 because the men standing were not the disciples of 9:27 but Moses and Elijah.

9:33 As the men were leaving Jesus. This refers to Moses and Elijah, not the three disciples. Only Luke recorded the departure of Moses and Elijah.

Master. See comments on 5:5.

It is good for us to be here. Peter's appreciation was for the opportunity to share in this experience, not for being able to serve Jesus and build shelters.

Let us put up three shelters. Such huts were constructed at the festival of tabernacles/booths (cf. Lev 23:33-43; Exod 23:16; 34:22; Deut 16:13-16). In Luke 16:9 the same Greek term is used in referring to the final state of the righteous as "eternal dwellings."

He did not know what he was saying. Luke explained this in the previous verse by stating that Peter's offer was due to his being sleepy. Clearly Peter's suggestion was out of order. But what exactly was wrong with it? Was Peter wrong for suggesting that this experience should be prolonged? The previous statement about Moses and Elijah leaving gives some support to this view. A better explanation, however, is that Peter erred in equating Jesus with Moses and Elijah. They were not equals. The Voice from heaven explains Peter's error. In contrast to Moses and Elijah, who were God's servants, Jesus is God's Son, the Chosen One. He is unique. He cannot be classed with anyone else, even two of God's greatest servants. He is not only greater but other. It is hard not to see in the Voice from heaven at least a hint of an ontological Christology in which Jesus' essential nature is sharply distinguished from that of Moses and Elijah.

9:34 A cloud appeared. The divine presence comes upon the scene in the form of a cloud, a common symbol of the presence of God.[248] Clouds are also a means of taking people up to heaven (Acts 1:9; 1 Thess 4:17; Rev 11:12) and are associated with the parousia (Mark 13:26; Matt 24:30). In Luke 21:27 Luke used the singular "cloud" rather than the plural found in Mark 13:26 and Matt 24:30, tying the parousia more closely to the transfiguration. He also used the singular "cloud" in Acts 1:9.

And enveloped them. Compare Exod 24:15-18; 40:34-38. "Them" most probably refers to Jesus, Moses and Elijah, and the disciples.

And they were afraid as they entered the cloud. Both "theys" refer to the disciples and are an appropriate response to a theophany. See comments on 5:10.

9:35 A voice came. See comments on 3:22 and cf. 2 Pet 1:18.

This is my Son. Whereas these words were spoken to Jesus at the baptism (Luke 3:22), here they are addressed to the disciples. This title is also found in the temptation (4:3,9) and trial (22:70). See comments on 3:22.

Whom I have chosen. This is the only place where this title is used in the NT, although a related term is found in 23:35 (cf. also John 1:34, which is textually questionable, and 1 Pet 2:4,6). It is used in the LXX of Aaron (Ps 105:26), the Suffering Servant (Isa 42:1; 44:1f.; 49:7), Moses (Ps 106:23), and David (Ps 88:20-21, LXX).

Listen to him. In Mark this refers back to Peter's refusal to accept Jesus' teaching concerning his death (cf. Mark 9:7 and 8:32-33), for Jesus had not spoken anything in the account itself. The "after Jesus said this" of Luke 9:28 reveals that Luke wanted to tie this injunction more broadly to the need to obey Jesus' teachings/commands on discipleship in general. The Voice affirmed Jesus' teachings, especially those in 9:22-27. Theophilus and the other readers needed to realize that the words of the Son of God have even greater authority than those of Moses and Elijah and therefore need to be heeded all the more.

9:36 Jesus was alone. The account centers on Jesus, not on Moses and Elijah and not even on Moses, Elijah, and Jesus. The law and the prophets pointed to Jesus. He is the essence and the heart of God's revelation. Anything that detracts from Jesus "alone," such as Peter's suggestion in 9:33, loses sight of the fact that believers in the early church were called "Christians" (Acts 11:26) because Jesus "alone" was the ground of their faith. Therefore when anyone seeks to add something, making the Christian faith "Jesus + _____ ," a basic misunderstanding of the Christian faith has occurred.

The disciples kept this to themselves. Luke did not refer to Jesus' command (Mark 9:9) but only to its observance. Compare Luke 9:21.

At that time. This contrasts the situation of Jesus' day with that in Luke's day. Luke clearly viewed his situation as different from "that time."[249]

---

[248]Cf. Exod 16:10; 19:9; 24:15-18; 33:9-11; 40:34; 2 Sam 22:12; 1 Kgs 8:10-11; Ezek 10:3-4; Ps 18:11.

[249]Cf. Luke 2:1; 4:2; 5:35; 9:36; 21:23; Acts 2:18; 7:41; 9:37.

What they had seen. The verb is an intensive perfect, which indicates that this scene produced lasting effects on the disciples.

The Lukan Message

Once again we come across an account that reveals several Lukan theological emphases. As in Matthew and Mark, the account serves a clear Christological purpose. The answer to the question of "Who is this?" in Luke 8:25 and 9:9, which was answered by Peter's confession on behalf of the disciples in 9:20, is now confirmed by God himself. The heavenly confession addressed to Jesus at the baptism (3:22) was now shared with the disciples. Jesus is indeed the Christ, God's Chosen. He is not just Moses or Elijah risen from the dead. He is God's Son.

While Luke was not reporting this confession in order to affirm the later Christological understanding of Nicea, it is clear that he wanted his readers to know that Jesus is unique. No one is like him. He does not fit any human category available.

A second major Lukan theme involves the understanding of Jesus' death. Jesus' forthcoming death in Jerusalem was not a tragedy or mistake. It was an *exodos* known beforehand by the OT prophets (9:31). It was furthermore an event that would be a "fulfillment" of the divine plan. The divine "must" (*dei*) of which Jesus had just spoken (9:22) was now affirmed by the prophets (9:31) and by the Voice from heaven (9:35). (The latter is not as emphatic in Luke as it is in Mark, but one cannot eliminate from the command to heed Jesus' words what Jesus had just taught the disciples in 9:22.) See Introduction 8 (1).

Another Lukan theological emphasis also merits attention. Luke probably wanted his readers to see a partial fulfillment of 9:27 in Jesus' transfiguration. This is seen in the twofold reference to glory found in 9:31-32. The glory of the returning Son of Man (9:26) is in part foreshadowed in the transfiguration as the three disciples "saw his glory" (9:32). This understanding is supported by the use of the term "bright as a flash of lightning" (*exastraptō*) in 9:29 and the use of a related term to describe the returning of the Son of Man (*astraptō*) in 17:24.

(6) The Healing of the Boy with an Unclean Spirit (9:37-43a)

[37]The next day, when they came down from the mountain, a large crowd met him. [38]A man in the crowd called out, "Teacher, I beg you to look at my son, for he is my only child. [39]A spirit seizes him and he suddenly screams; it throws him into convulsions so that he foams at the mouth. It scarcely ever leaves him and is destroying him. [40]I begged your disciples to drive it out, but they could not."

[41]"O unbelieving and perverse generation," Jesus replied, "how long shall I stay with you and put up with you? Bring your son here."

⁴²Even while the boy was coming, the demon threw him to the ground in a
convulsion. But Jesus rebuked the evil spirit, healed the boy and gave him back
to his father. ⁴³And they were all amazed at the greatness of God.

Context

At this point Luke omitted the passage about Elijah's return in Mark
9:11-13. This may have been because he already had alluded to how John
the Baptist fulfilled Mal 3:1 (Luke 1:17,76; 7:24-30 [esp. v. 27]). As a
result Luke tied the present account more closely to the transfiguration so
that the healing provides an illustration of Jesus' glory seen in 9:32 (cf.
9:43). The Lukan editorial work consists primarily of abbreviation. The
Markan account, consisting of sixteen verses, is condensed to only seven
in Luke.[250] However, Luke also added a few comments, such as "the next
day" (9:37), "only" (9:38), and "and they were all amazed at the greatness
of God" (9:43).

Comments

9:37 The next day. While Mark 9:14 does give the impression that this incident took place on the same day as the transfiguration, only Luke made an explicit
temporal link between the two accounts, resulting in an ever closer tie between them.

Down from the mountain. The mountain was mentioned in Luke 9:28. Just
as Luke said that after the Sermon on the Plain Jesus descended to minister to the
crowds (6:17), so after the transfiguration he reported that Jesus came down from
the mountain to heal a boy.

9:38 Teacher. Mark also used "teacher," but Matt 17:15 has "Lord."

I beg you. Compare Luke 8:28.

Only child. See comments on 7:12. By mentioning that this was an "only
child," Luke heightened the pathos of the situation.

9:39 A spirit seizes. Matthew 17:15 refers to the child as being "epileptic"
(RSV, NEB) or having "seizures" (NIV). In Luke 13:11,16 a demon is associated
with a disease. The description of the child's situation appears to correspond to
epilepsy.[251]

It scarcely ever leaves him. The demon plagued the child continuously.

9:40 Your disciples. The historicity of the disciples receives support from
the indirect nature of this statement. See comments on 6:13.

They could not. Whether this implies that the "power" given in 9:1 was limited to that mission only is uncertain, but in the present account this statement
serves primarily to demonstrate that Jesus' power is still greater.[252] Both Matthew
(17:16, "could not heal him") and Luke (literally *were not able*) clarified Mark
9:18, "could not" (literally *were not strong enough*).

---

[250]Luke omitted Mark 9:14b-16,20c-25a,25c-27a, a reduction of over 50 percent of the
material in Mark.

[251]So Fitzmyer, *Luke*, 808; Marshall, *Luke*, 391.

[252]Cf. 2 Kgs 4:31-37, where Elisha was able to do what his servant, Gehazi, could not do.

9:41 O unbelieving and perverse generation. Matthew and Luke both added "perverse" to this saying. For parallels to this saying, see Deut 32:5,20; Matt 12:39; 16:4; Phil 2:15. This is the first explicit reference to the perverse character of Jesus' contemporaries, who represent humanity in general. Compare also Luke 11:30-32,50-51; 17:25. In the present context this pejorative description seems to refer to the disciples who were not able to heal the child. Despite what they had seen and done, the disciples were still unbelieving (cf. 8:25). Yet it probably is best to see this description as applicable to everyone covered by the "all" of 9:43a, i.e., the disciples and the crowd. All these are members of the present unbelieving and perverse generation. The use of the singular "generation" almost always has negative connotations in Luke-Acts.[253]

Put up with you? Compare Isa 46:4 (LXX). This prepares for Luke 9:43b-45.

Bring your son. Although Jesus' action and subsequent healing in his own time and situation were due to his compassion, Luke's purpose in recounting the event was to demonstrate Jesus' glory and might.

9:42 The demon threw him to the ground in a convulsion. Compare 8:28 for a similar last-minute action by the demon.

Jesus rebuked the evil spirit. The demon was exorcised. Compare 4:39, where a fever was rebuked.

Healed the boy. This term "healed" (*iaomai*) is used of healing diseases.[254] The term can also be used broadly to describe exorcising and healing (9:2) and to describe exorcising alone (Acts 10:38). The term "cure" (*therapeuō*) used in reference to diseases in Luke 9:1 can be used for "curing" evil spirits (6:18). Thus, although Luke did see a difference between exorcisms and healing (see comments on 4:39 and 7:21), they are not mutually exclusive.

Gave him back to his father. Compare 7:15.

9:43 They were all amazed. Fitzmyer notes this "typically Lukan reaction to the miracle."[255] Compare 4:32; 8:25; 11:14.

At the greatness of God. Some have suggested that this is a reference to Jesus' greatness as "God" (cf. 8:39; Acts 20:28). Luke more likely saw in Jesus' healing the greatness of God working through his Anointed, his Son. Compare Luke 5:26, which is similar to this verse but which clearly refers to God (cf. also 7:16). For Luke this Christological statement, which points to God's greatness and majesty in Jesus' activity, was so overriding that he omitted Mark's reference to prayer (9:29), another strong Lukan emphasis.

The Lukan Message

Luke once again pointed out Jesus' greatness and uniqueness.

Faced with a plight the disciples could not remedy, Jesus healed with no difficulty even though the child had been continually plagued by the evil spirit. The demon had to obey him. Jesus' authority is such that all

---

[253]Cf. Luke 7:31; 11:29-32,50-51; 16:8; 17:25; Acts 2:40; cf. also Phil 2:15. In Luke 21:32; Acts 8:33; 13:36 it is used in a more neutral sense.

[254]Luke 5:17; 6:18-19; 7:7; 8:47; 9:2,11; 14:4; 17:15; 22:51; Acts 9:34; 28:8.

[255]Fitzmyer, *Luke*, 810.

were amazed at his manifestation of God's greatness. There is also an allusion to humanity's sinfulness and depravity in 9:41. In its unbelief and perversity this "generation" was not able to heal. It was powerless against the demonic. This generation's unbelief and perversity (9:44) were such that the Son of Man would soon be delivered into their hands.

(7) The Second Passion Announcement (9:43b-45)

While everyone was marveling at all that Jesus did, he said to his disciples, ⁴⁴"Listen carefully to what I am about to tell you: The Son of Man is going to be betrayed into the hands of men." ⁴⁵But they did not understand what this meant. It was hidden from them, so that they did not grasp it, and they were afraid to ask him about it.

Context

Jesus' second passion announcement recalls not only the first such announcement (9:21-22) but also the uniquely Lukan statement in the transfiguration account where Moses and Elijah spoke of Jesus' "departure" (9:31). Luke's editorial work is seen primarily in his reference to the people's "marveling" at what Jesus did (9:43b), his omission of the resurrection prediction (9:44), and the addition of the fact that the meaning was hidden from the disciples so that they were not able to understand it (9:45b).

Comments

9:43b While everyone was marveling. Such wonder and amazement was not faith. Although this "unbelieving and perverse generation" (9:41) marveled at Jesus' ministry, its perversity and lack of faith resulted in unbelief and incomprehension (9:45).

At all that Jesus did. This refers backward, not just to the preceding incident but to Jesus' entire ministry up to this point.

9:44 Listen carefully to what I am about to tell you. This addition (literally *You [emphatic] set into your ears these words*) is not found in the parallels in Mark 9:31 and Matt 17:22. It highlights the following passion saying and makes this passion announcement more emphatic in Luke. The NIV correctly understands "these words" as referring forward to the passion announcement rather than as looking backward either to what Jesus already had said in his public ministry or to the crowd's superficial response in Luke 9:43b. The imperative suggests that Jesus intended his disciples to understand the following passion announcement.

The Son of Man. The "for" (*gar*) that begins this statement is epexegetical and best left untranslated. For Son of Man, see comments on 5:24.

Is going to be betrayed. The verb *paradidōmi* can mean "betray" (NIV, NRSV) or "deliver up/over" (RSV, KJV, cf. NEB). Since God is the subject (not Judas, for Judas is not mentioned), "deliver up/over" is the better choice. This translation also fits well Luke's emphasis on the divine necessity of Jesus' death. The verb should be understood as a "divine passive." It is a circumlocution for

"God is about to deliver." God's providence is clearly intended to be seen here as in 9:22, although no mention is made here of the resurrection. See comments on 9:22 and Introduction 8 (1). The passion was Luke's primary focus at this point, and the disciples' incomprehension in the next verse involved their failure to understand the divine necessity of Jesus' death.

Into the hands of men. There is a play on words, "Son of *Man* . . . hands of *men*," in all three Synoptic accounts.

9:45 But they did not understand what this meant. The "this" (literally *this thing*) refers to the passion announcement in the preceding verse.

It was hidden from them. Compare 18:34, which is almost a duplicate of this verse. Is this to be understood as a divine passive ("God hid it from them") or as a simple passive ("They did not understand it")? The answer is determined primarily by how the following "so that" is interpreted. Jesus' command in 9:44a suggests that he wanted his disciples to understand the passion announcement. Furthermore, a related word is used in 19:42, and 19:44d makes clear that the lack of knowledge or "hiddenness" is clearly culpable. In 18:34, a Lukan editorial comment, there is no suggestion that the "hiddenness" was God's doing. The "it" is not defined with a doctrine of the atonement (see Introduction 8 [8]) but is simply a reference to Jesus' forthcoming death and, according to 9:22, resurrection.

So that [hina]. Is what follows to be interpreted as the purpose or the result of "It was hidden from them"? If it is purpose, then it means that it was God's will that the disciples not understand Jesus' passion announcement at this time. In favor of this interpretation is the fact that *hina* indicates *purpose* more often than *result*. On the other hand, if "so that" should be read as indicating result, then the disciples did not grasp Jesus' meaning simply because they were slow to catch on. The latter interpretation is favored by the fact that the disciples were afraid to ask Jesus what he meant. They could have asked but chose not to. This weakens the idea that God did not intend them to understand. Also the inability of this "unbelieving and perverse generation" to heal should perhaps logically be extended to an inability to understand. This also favors interpreting "so that" as signaling result rather than purpose. A final argument in favor of result is 9:22. Nothing is said after this more complex passion announcement about the disciples' inability to understand. The reader assumes, since there is no reference to such a difficulty of understanding, that this was clear to the disciples. Luke, furthermore, eliminated the reference in the parallel account (Mark 8:33) that reveals Peter's lack of understanding. It is therefore best to interpret this verse as indicating that the disciples were not able to understand this passion prediction at that time due to unbelief and perversity.

And they were afraid to ask him about it. There is a similar statement in Mark (9:32). The disciples' fear may have been due to their having witnessed God's greatness (Luke 9:43; cf. 8:25).

The Lukan Message

More than either Matthew or Mark, Luke emphasized the disciples' inability to understand Jesus' teaching concerning his future passion. This is evident by his addition of 9:45b,c. He added the same material to 18:34. According to Luke, only after the resurrection were the disciples able to understand the divine necessity of their Lord's passion (cf. 24:6-7, 13-35,44-47). There is much speculation about why Luke emphasized this ignorance. Since Luke tended to eliminate negative portrayals of the disciples (see comments on 9:32), we may assume that he was not seeking to demean them. For Luke they were revered "eyewitnesses and servants of the word" (1:2). Luke's intention may have been to alleviate some confusion among his readers about the necessity of Jesus' death by pointing out that even the apostles could not understand at first. After the resurrection, however, the plan of God and the fulfillment of the Scriptures has been made plain. See Introduction 8 (1).

(8) Humility and Openness (9:46-50)

[46]An argument started among the disciples as to which of them would be the greatest. [47]Jesus, knowing their thoughts, took a little child and had him stand beside him. [48]Then he said to them, "Whoever welcomes this little child in my name welcomes me; and whoever welcomes me welcomes the one who sent me. For he who is least among you all—he is the greatest."

[49]"Master," said John, "we saw a man driving out demons in your name and we tried to stop him, because he is not one of us."

[50]"Do not stop him," Jesus said, "for whoever is not against you is for you."

Context

The last two accounts of Jesus' Galilean ministry are found in this section. They were already tied together by the expression "in my name" (9:48-49) before Luke wrote his Gospel.[256] It is impossible to say whether or not the first incident was triggered by Jesus' taking only three disciples to pray with him on the mount of transfiguration and excluding the others. The first account involved only disciples, while the second arose from an encounter between the disciples and someone outside their circle (cf. Num 11:26-30 and Acts 19:13-16). Both witness to the disciples' failure to understand Jesus' passion announcement in Luke 9:45. In Luke the two incidents are more closely associated with the passion prediction because he omitted the scene change in Mark 9:30,33. Tellingly, the disciples' failure to understand that the Son of Man's greatness (9:43) would lead to his sacrificial death (9:44; 19:10; 22:27) leads directly into their speculations on human greatness (9:46-48). Their inability to understand this same teaching at the Lord's Supper (22:15-23) is followed by similar speculations (22:24-30). The present scene is followed by a second failure in the disciples' understanding, that the work of God's kingdom was also going on outside their immediate circle.

---

[256]The major differences in Luke's version of these two accounts are due to his abbreviation. He omitted Mark 9:33a,b,34a,35,39b, and 41. In typical Lukan fashion he changed "Teacher" to "Master" (9:49). He also omitted "taking him [the child] in his arms" (9:47), added 9:48c, and changed "against us . . . for us" to "against you . . . for you" (9:50).

Comments

9:46 As to which of them would be the greatest. The term "greatest" can be understood in several ways: having the most authority, receiving the most preferable treatment, being the most valuable, or being most favored by God. Matthew 18:1 reads "greatest in the kingdom of heaven." What is clear is that a comparison was being made among the disciples, i.e., "them."[257]

9:47 Jesus, knowing their thoughts. This Lukan addition to the narrative reveals Jesus' prophetic insight. See comments on 5:22.

9:48 Whoever welcomes this little child. In the first century a child was an insignificant, weak member of society and so exemplified one who is "least."

In my name. This can be understood to modify either the verb "welcome" or the noun "child." If it is an adjective modifying "child," it would mean *because of the child's being a Christian.* If it is an adverb modifying "welcomes," it would mean *welcomes because of being a Christian such a child.* In the other examples where Luke used this phrase or a related one, it appears to be adverbial[258] rather than adjectival.

Welcomes me. Insight into the meaning of this comes from a rabbinic saying in *Berakot* 5:5, "A man's representative is like the man himself." If we assume that the child was a follower of Jesus, this would fit Acts 9:4-5 and the Pauline idea of the church as the "body of Christ" (cf. 1 Cor 12:12-31). Compare also Matt 25:31-46 (esp. vv. 40,45). The hospitality believers receive reveals the attitude people have toward Jesus (cf. Acts 16:33-34).

And whoever welcomes me welcomes the one who sent me. This verse is a good example of step parallelism in which the first thought (child—me) is raised a step higher in the second thought (me—him who sent me). Even as a child is received as a representative of Jesus, so Jesus is received as the representative of God (cf. Luke 10:16). There is a strong emphasis here on the idea that Jesus' mission originated with God (cf. 4:18,43).

For he who is least. Again a comparative adjective is used in a superlative sense (see 9:46 footnote). The term "least" has nothing to do with rank, talent, or importance but refers instead to the one most willing to humble himself in order to serve others (cf. Mark 9:35).

He is the greatest. "Greatest" is literally *great,* but due to the context it means *the greatest.* Something like "in God's eyes" must be added to this sentence, for to be greatest in the sense of Luke 9:46 would contradict the saying. Compare 14:11; 18:14; 22:26.

9:49 Master. As elsewhere Luke preferred "Master" to Mark's "Teacher." See comments on 5:5.

Said John. As one of the "inner three," John assumed authority and exercised it by forbidding those outside of the immediate fellowship of disciples to minister in Jesus' name.

Driving out demons in your name. Compare 10:17; Acts 3:6; 4:7,10,30; 16:18; 19:13-16.

---

[257] Although the comparative form is used here μείζων, the superlative is meant. This is an example of how the comparative was being used for the superlative in koine Greek. See F. Blass and A. Debrunner, *A Greek Grammar of the New Testament* (Chicago: University Press, 1961), 32-33.

[258] As in Luke 9:49; 21:8; 24:47; Acts 4:17-18; 5:28,40.

We tried to stop him. John's condemnatory attitude is manifest again in Luke 9:54.

Because he is not one of us. This is given as the reason for forbidding the exorcist to continue. Luke did not specify whether this person was a non-Christian exorcist using Jesus' name (cf. Acts 8:18-19; 19:13-16) or a believer who was simply outside the circle of the disciples. In light of the unhappy fate of the non-Christian exorcists in Acts 19:13-16, however, it is unlikely that Luke was referring to them here. If Luke really was thinking broadly enough to include non-Christian exorcists, he would not have omitted the passage most supportive of such an interpretation, "No one who does a miracle in my name can in the next moment say anything bad about me" (Mark 9:39).[259]

9:50 Whoever is not against you is for you. The reverse of this proverb appears in Luke 11:23a, "He who is not with me is against me." These complement, rather than contradict, each other and reveal that one cannot be neutral with respect to Jesus. Luke changed the saying in Mark from "us" to "you." In so doing he may have been applying Jesus' saying to the current situation in which the attitude of people toward Jesus in Luke's day was revealed by their attitude toward his disciples, the church ("you").

The Lukan Message

Luke addressed two kinds of misunderstandings surrounding the Lord's mission and ministry. The Son of God's greatness (9:43) is only understood properly in light of the passion (9:44). True greatness comes from serving (22:27). The first misunderstanding involves the nature of greatness. Greatness lies not in receiving preferential treatment from others or in having more authority than others. On the contrary it involves serving others, especially the outcasts of society as represented by a little child. Greatness ministers to the poor, crippled, lame, and blind who can never repay (14:12-14).

The second error is to think that God is only working exclusively in one's immediate circle. Other followers of Christ were also exorcising demons in Jesus' name. It has been suggested that Luke may have been referring to a narrow sectarianism that excluded other servants of Christ, particularly thinking of the unwillingness of some in the Jerusalem church to accept the ministry of the apostle Paul "because he is not one of us" (9:49). Such speculation can never be demonstrated, but the practice of excluding others who minister in Christ's name because "they are not one of us" has been all too frequent within the Christian church. One need only think of the "established church" and the dissident or "nonconformist church." The church must guard itself against excluding outsiders who believe the cardinal tenets of historic Christianity simply because they are not associated "with us."

---

[259] See M. D. Goulder, *Luke: A New Paradigm*, 450.

---------------------- SECTION OUTLINE ----------------------

V. JESUS' JOURNEY TO JERUSALEM (9:51–19:27)
  1. The First Mention of the Journey to Jerusalem (9:51–13:21)
     (1) The Mission to Samaria (9:51-56)
     (2) Teachings on Discipleship (9:57-62)
     (3) The Mission of the Seventy(-two) (10:1-16)
     (4) The Return of the Seventy(-two) (10:17-20)
     (5) The Blessedness of the Disciples (10:21-24)
     (6) The Parable of the Good Samaritan (10:25-37)
     (7) Martha and Mary (10:38-42)
     (8) Jesus' Teaching on Prayer (11:1-13)
     (9) The Beelzebub Controversy (11:14-23)
     (10) The Return of the Unclean Spirit and True Blessedness
          (11:24-28)
     (11) The Sign of Jonah (11:29-32)
     (12) Sayings about Light (11:33-36)
     (13) A Denunciation of the Pharisees and Scribes (11:37-54)
     (14) Warnings and Exhortations (12:1-12)
     (15) The Parable of the Rich Fool (12:13-21)
     (16) Care and Anxiety (12:22-34)
     (17) The Watchful Servants (12:35-48)
     (18) Jesus—The Great Divider (12:49-53)
     (19) Signs of the Time and Settling with One's Opponents
          (12:54-59)
     (20) The Need to Repent (13:1-9)
     (21) The Healing of the Crippled Woman on the Sabbath
          (13:10-17)
     (22) The Parables of the Mustard Seed and Leaven (13:18-21)
  2. The Second Mention of the Journey to Jerusalem (13:22–17:10)
     (1) The Narrow Door (13:22-30)
     (2) Warning concerning Herod and the Lament over Jerusalem
          (13:31-35)
     (3) Healing of the Man with Dropsy (14:1-6)
     (4) Sayings concerning Banquet Behavior (14:7-14)
     (5) The Parable of the Great Banquet (14:15-24)
     (6) Conditions of Discipleship (14:25-35)
     (7) The Parables of the Lost Sheep, Lost Coin, and Gracious
          Father (15:1-32)

(8) The Parable of the Dishonest Manager (16:1-8)
(9) Sayings on Stewardship (16:9-18)
(10) The Parable of the Rich Man and Lazarus (16:19-31)
(11) Teachings Addressed to the Disciples (17:1-10)
3. The Third Mention of the Journey to Jerusalem (17:11–19:27)
   (1) The Grateful Samaritan (17:11-19)
   (2) The Coming of the Kingdom of God (17:20-37)
   (3) The Parable of the Unjust Judge (18:1-8)
   (4) The Parable of the Pharisee and the Tax Collector (18:9-14)
   (5) Jesus' Blessing the Children (18:15-17)
   (6) The Rich Ruler (18:18-30)
   (7) The Third Passion Announcement (18:31-34)
   (8) The Healing of the Blind Man at Jericho (18:35-43)
   (9) Zacchaeus, the Tax Collector (19:1-10)
   (10) The Parable of the Ten Minas (19:11-27)

——— V. JESUS' JOURNEY TO JERUSALEM (9:51–19:27) ———

Luke 9:51 begins a new section in the Gospel. This "travel section" consists for the most part of material not found in Mark and continues into either chap. 18 or 19. There is considerable debate about where this section ends. The decision ultimately depends on whether Luke's structure is controlled by geography and the travel motif (going to Jerusalem) or by his use of sources. If it is the latter, then the section begins at 9:51, where Luke left his Markan source, and ends at 18:14, where he picked it up again. Narratives on children (9:46-48; 18:15-17) would then both conclude the previous section (4:16–9:50) and begin the following one (18:15–21:38).[1] In favor of the first view are the numerous references to Jerusalem[2] and the central role Jerusalem plays in Luke (cf. 9:31) and Acts. The travel idea of "going" to Jerusalem is also found throughout this section.[3]

Even if Luke was dependent on a different source in 9:51–18:14, and this seems reasonably certain, it does not mean that the arrangement of his Gospel was completely governed by his sources. If one grants that

---

[1] J. Kodell ("Luke and the Children: The Beginning and End of the Great Interpolation [Luke 9:46-56; 18:9-23]," *CBQ* 49 [1987]: 430) finds "the key to a major unifying theme of the interpolation [9:51–18:14] is found in the use of the two children passages (9:46-48; 18:15-17), i.e., in those interlocking frames that form a thematic inclusion for the entire section: a disciple must 'receive the kingdom of God like a child' (18:17), i.e, with lowliness characterized by availability for God's action and dependence on God."

[2] Luke 9:53; 13:22,33-34; 17:11; 18:31; 19:11; cf. 19:28.

[3] Luke 9:51-53,56-57; 10:38; 13:33; 17:11; 19:28; cf. also 10:1; 11:53; 13:22; 18:31,35; 19:1; cf. 19:11.

Luke was master of his materials, although Jesus' journey to Jerusalem
was dominated by non-Markan material, by adding Markan material at
18:15f. Luke produced a larger literary unit that is a thematic whole. It
makes better sense to consider this unit as ending at either 19:10 or 19:27.
We have chosen the latter because 19:28 functions better as a beginning
for the next section (19:28–21:38), which involves Jesus' ministry in
Jerusalem. We have divided the travel section into three somewhat arbitrary subdivisions (9:51–13:21; 13:22–17:10; 17:11–19:27), which center
around three major references to Jerusalem.

It is hard to find a definitive pattern and plan within the material in
9:51f. Attempts to find a chiasmic structure[4] or some other carefully organized framework in this section tend to do violence to the material. It may
be that Luke followed the order of his source here and that his editorial
work was limited to his choice of terms, various editorial comments, and
the design of individual pericopes rather than in rearranging the sequence
in order to create a specific overarching pattern. Fitzmyer has summarized
Luke's purpose in this section: "The travel account, therefore, becomes a
special device used by Luke for the further training of these Galilean
witnesses. . . . The travel account becomes, then, a collection of teachings
for the young missionary church, in which instruction of disciples alter-
nates with debates with opponents."[5]

1. The First Mention of the Journey to Jerusalem (9:51–13:21)

(1) The Mission to Samaria (9:51-56)

[51]As the time approached for him to be taken up to heaven, Jesus resolutely
set out for Jerusalem. [52]And he sent messengers on ahead, who went into a
Samaritan village to get things ready for him; [53]but the people there did not
welcome him, because he was heading for Jerusalem. [54]When the disciples
James and John saw this, they asked, "Lord, do you want us to call fire down
from heaven to destroy them?" [55]But Jesus turned and rebuked them, [56]and
they went to another village.

Context

In the opening account of this section Jesus is rejected by Samaritans,
just as in the opening account of the last section (4:16-30) he was rejected
by citizens of Nazareth. In this passage, which is unique to Luke, Jesus
purposes to go to Jerusalem to fulfill the "departure" spoken of in 9:31.
The divine "must" of 9:22,44 is about to take place. As he and his followers proceed south from Galilee to Jerusalem, they enter into Samaria.

[4]C. H. Talbert, Reading Luke (New York: Crossroad, 1982), 111-12.
[5]J. A. Fitzmyer, The Gospel according to Luke, AB (Garden City: Doubleday, 1981), 1:826.

Comments

9:51 As the time approached. This term (*symplērousthai*) is also found in Acts 2:1, and a related term lies behind varied English expressions in Luke 1:23; 2:6,21-22; 21:22. It refers here to God's purpose soon to be realized.

For him to be taken up to heaven. In Acts 1:2,11,22 the verbal form of this noun (*analēmpseōs*), here translated as a verb, refers to the ascension. The NIV makes the meaning clear by adding "to heaven." The ascension marks the culmination of the Christ event, which embraces Jesus' conception, birth, ministry, death, burial, and resurrection.

Jesus resolutely set out. Knowing the divine plan, Jesus (literally) "set his face to go to Jerusalem" (cf. Isa 50:7) in order to fulfill God's purpose for his life. He was determined to follow God's plan and deliberately initiated the precipitating events, showing that he was in control of what was about to happen.

Jerusalem. This is the city of Jesus' destiny (Luke 9:22). It is central to Luke's view of God's plan in that his Gospel also begins (1:9) and ends there (24:53). Furthermore, Acts also begins in Jerusalem (Acts 1:4), and it soon becomes the center of the church (8:1,14; 15:1-2) with Paul returning to Jerusalem after every missionary journey.

9:52 And he sent messengers on ahead. It has been suggested that this is an allusion to Mal 3:1, and this is supported by Luke's use of *angelous*, or "messengers," and by "on ahead" (literally *before his face*). Both are found in Luke 7:27 and Mal 3:1.

Into a Samaritan village. For the Jewish attitude toward Samaritans see comments on 10:33. Only Luke, of the Synoptic writers, referred to Jesus' ministry to the Samaritans.[6] A journey through Samaria would normally take about three days.

To get things ready for him. That is, to arrange for lodging.

9:53 But the people there did not welcome him. Josephus (*Antiquities* 20.6.1 [20.118-24]) gave an example of the animosity of Samaritans toward Galilean pilgrims proceeding to Jerusalem to celebrate the various religious festivals. The term "receive" is the same one used in Luke 9:48, making this experience an illustration of that verse. The rejection of the messengers was, in fact, a rejection of Jesus.

Because he was heading for Jerusalem. The NIV unfortunately loses the play on words found in the original. In 9:51 Luke spoke of Jesus' setting his face toward Jerusalem. Here the same expression is used: "because his face" was set for Jerusalem. This play on words is clearer in the RSV. In Jesus' day the reason behind the Samaritan's lack of welcome was simply the general Samaritan hostility toward Jewish pilgrims heading toward Jerusalem. In Luke's retelling, the explanation became more pointed. The Samaritans rejected Jesus because they too lacked an understanding of the coming passion and its necessity.[7]

9:54 When the disciples James and John. Although Luke did not refer to them as "Boanerges . . . Sons of Thunder" (cf. 6:14 and Mark 3:17), their attitude here merits such a description. Their request went far beyond what Jesus taught in Luke 9:5.

---

[6] Cf. Luke 10:25-37; 17:11-19; Acts 1:8; 8:1,4-25; 9:31; 15:3. Note, however, John 4:4-42.

[7] So R. C. Tannehill, *The Narrative Unity of Luke-Acts* (Philadelphia: Fortress, 1986), 230.

Fire down from heaven to destroy them. The idea of fire coming down from heaven is an allusion to 2 Kgs 1:10,12. It is unlikely that Luke intended to combat the equation of the Messiah with Elijah, for that was not the lesson drawn from the incident.[8] Ethics, not Christology, was the object of Luke's reciting this account. It is unclear whether the disciples were praying an imprecation ("Should we ask that God would send down fire to destroy them?") or whether they thought that they themselves had such power. See comments on 9:1,40 (cf. also 10:17).

9:55 Jesus turned and rebuked them. The disciples had not only failed to understand Jesus' teaching concerning his passion (9:45) but also much of his ethical teaching as well (cf. 6:27-31). Jesus once again had to censure the disciples' misconception about authority and power (9:46-50). Although what Jesus said was not recorded, scribes later inserted various comments into several Greek manuscripts (see NIV footnote).

9:56 And they went to another village. Luke did not give the name of either village. Such information, although interesting to us, was irrelevant for his purpose.

The Lukan Message

We see once again that Jesus' fate in Jerusalem was completely under control. It was divine necessity that caused Jesus to head resolutely for the holy city. The time had come to accomplish his mission and to fulfill the divine plan (9:31). Along with the emphasis on God's providential control of Jesus' fate, and thus of history (see Introduction 8 [1]), Jerusalem's importance is also underlined. Here and here alone Jesus was to complete his departure. Along the way Luke told of the Samaritans' negative response, but later they would respond positively to the gospel message. He gave a glimpse of this in 17:11-19, and the present account foreshadows the future mission to the Samaritans, which would come to fruition after Jesus' departure. When Jesus next visited the Samaritans, through the apostles' preaching, the word would bear good fruit (Acts 8:1, 4-25; 9:31; 15:3).

The ethical teaching should also be noted. Jesus firmly rebuked the disciples' desire to bring judgment and wrath upon the Samaritan village. This was the "year of the Lord's favor" (Luke 4:19). It was a time when the disciples were to love their enemies and bless those who cursed them (6:27-36). James and John went far beyond Jesus' directions on how to treat the unreceptive (9:5). There will be a "day of vengeance of our God" (Isa 61:2), but that day lies in the future and in any case is God's prerogative. If a village did not receive Jesus, the disciples were to go elsewhere. For Theophilus and the other readers the message was clear. Their attitude was to be one of "Father, forgive them, for they do not know what they are doing" (Luke 23:34; cf. Acts 7:60).

---

[8]For the contrary view, see E. E. Ellis, *The Gospel of Luke*, NCB (Grand Rapids: Eerdmans, 1981), 151-52.

(2) Teachings on Discipleship (9:57-62)

[57]As they were walking along the road, a man said to him, "I will follow you wherever you go."
[58]Jesus replied, "Foxes have holes and birds of the air have nests, but the Son of Man has no place to lay his head."
[59]He said to another man, "Follow me." But the man replied, "Lord, first let me go and bury my father."
[60]Jesus said to him, "Let the dead bury their own dead, but you go and proclaim the kingdom of God."
[61]Still another said, "I will follow you, Lord; but first let me go back and say good-by to my family."
[62]Jesus replied, "No one who puts his hand to the plow and looks back is fit for service in the kingdom of God."

Context

In these verses three sayings of Jesus are addressed to potential followers, and all three center around the term "follow" (9:57,59,61). The first two are found together in Matt 8:19-22, but the last is unique to Luke. Luke placed these sayings in the travel narrative by the words "as they were walking along the road" (Luke 9:57). Luke differed from Matthew in not directing the first two sayings to a specific audience (a teacher of the law in Matt 8:19 and a disciple in 8:21). Instead he referred to "a man, "another man," and "still another." By so doing, these sayings become applicable to anyone who might consider being Jesus' follower.[9]

The three sayings remind Luke's Christian readers of the stringent nature of discipleship. They are absolute in nature, for Jesus demands unqualified commitment, far beyond what a rabbi might require of his disciples. The first saying shows that Jesus seeks no flippant, frivolous decision to follow him. Following Jesus means becoming a stranger and exile on earth (Heb 11:13). Those who volunteer to be disciples must first count the cost.

The next two sayings concern legitimate requests for temporary delay.

The first man wanted to bury his father and the other to bid his parents farewell. Both requests were denied; for discipleship involves the sacrifice of comfort and security, family ties, and family affection (Luke 9:58, 60,62).

Comments

9:57   As they were walking.   Luke reminded his readers that these teachings of Jesus took place on the way to Jerusalem. Thus Jesus' absolute demands of disciples are accompanied by his own unconditional sacrifice for disciples.

---

[9]Some of the other editorial work in this passages includes: the omitting of the titles "Teacher" and "Lord" (Matt 8:19,21); adding "proclaim the kingdom of God" (9:60); placing "follow me" in 9:59 instead of 9:60; and adding the third saying.

Along the road. "Road" is literally *way* (*hodos*). Luke may have been presenting Jesus' teachings along the "way" to Jerusalem as a metaphor for the ethical demands of the Christian "way." [10]

9:58   Son of Man. This refers to Jesus as the Son of Man, not to humanity in general. For Son of Man see comments on 5:24.

Has no place to lay his head. The preceding account (9:51-56), which Luke intentionally placed before this one, has just illustrated this point. Jesus' followers must be prepared for the same conditions (6:40). The main emphasis here is less on the loss of creaturely comfort (a place to sleep) than with rejection (9:22,44; 17:25; 20:17).

9:59   First, let me go and bury my father. For a Jew this was a religious duty having precedence over everything else. Only in the case of a temporary Nazirite vow (Num 6:6-7) or if one were the high priest (Lev 21:10-11) could one be absolved from this duty. The seriousness of this responsibility is seen in Tobit's first two deathbed requests of his son, "My son, when I die, bury me, and do not neglect your mother" (Tob 4:3, RSV), and in one of the son's greatest fears in dying—that his parents would have no one to bury them (6:14, RSV; cf. Gen 50:5). Jesus demands an allegiance transcending even this greatest of filial obligations. Some interpreters have sought to relieve the hardness of this saying by assuming that the father was not yet dead and that the son was saying, "Wait until my father dies, and then I will follow you." There is, however, no hint of this in the text.

9:60   Let the dead bury their own dead. This saying contains a play on the word *dead.* "Let the [spiritually] dead bury their own [physical] dead." In this pun the spiritually dead are those who do not follow Jesus (Luke 15:24,32; cf. also John 5:24-25; Rom 6:13; Eph 2:1; 5:14). The meaning of 14:26 (cf. 12:53; 18:29-30) becomes acutely real when placed alongside a saying such as this.

Go and proclaim the kingdom of God. That is, become my follower and proclaim my message. Luke added this (cf. Matt 8:22) to help his readers understand that Jesus' uncompromising command is uttered in light of the supreme good of proclaiming the good news. It also prepares the reader for the next account in which the seventy were sent out to proclaim God's kingdom (10:11).

9:61 The third man's request was similar to that of Elisha in 1 Kgs 19:19-21. Yet although Elijah granted the young man's request, Jesus did not. God's kingdom has come, and the summons to follow Jesus takes precedence over everything else. The old family relationships are part of what one must leave behind to follow him (Luke 5:11,28).

9:62   No one who . . . looks back. "Looks back" is literally *looks unto the things behind.* The imagery comes from 1 Kgs 19:19-21. It refers here to gazing back on the things abandoned in order to follow Jesus (cf. Phil 3:13). In this instance the reference is to family relationships (Luke 9:61), but the saying has broader implications as well (cf. 2 Tim 2:4).

---

[10]Cf. Acts 9:2; 19:9,23; 22:4; 24:14,22; cf. also 16:17; 18:25-26.

The Lukan Message

The extreme harshness of these sayings is the best proof of their authenticity. At the same time, they create a serious problem, for how can Jesus command his followers to love their neighbors (10:25-37) and even their enemies (6:27-35; 14:26) and yet prohibit so fundamental an act of love as burying one's parents? Does not such a command conflict with 1 Tim 5:8? What did Luke intend by this section? Was he suggesting that Jesus' followers are uniquely devoted to the service of God like Nazirites or the high priest (cf. Num 6:6-7; Lev 21:10-11) and thus may not defile themselves by touching the dead? The present account does not exhibit any concern with respect to such ritual defilement. The issue in our text, and other passages such as Luke 12:53; 14:26; 18:29-30, involves priorities. In both the second and third sayings the individual's "first" priority was clearly something other than following Jesus. For Luke allegiance to Jesus required loving one's parents and honoring them in the ways described in 9:59,61. He did not mean that his readers should refrain from performing such duties. Rather he chose a particularly forceful way to demonstrate that discipleship requires a radical shift in priorities. Jesus must be "first." He will not accept second place to anyone or anything. Even a good thing, such as honoring one's parents by seeing that they receive proper burial, cannot usurp the place of the best thing, which is to love Jesus with all one's heart, strength, and mind. Luke's readers are thus prompted to examine themselves to see if, having begun to follow Jesus, they are now "looking back."

(3) The Mission of the Seventy(-two) (10:1-16)

[1]After this the Lord appointed seventy-two others and sent them two by two ahead of him to every town and place where he was about to go. [2]He told them, "The harvest is plentiful, but the workers are few. Ask the Lord of the harvest, therefore, to send out workers into his harvest field. [3]Go! I am sending you out like lambs among wolves. [4]Do not take a purse or bag or sandals; and do not greet anyone on the road.

[5]"When you enter a house, first say, 'Peace to this house.' [6]If a man of peace is there, your peace will rest on him; if not, it will return to you. [7]Stay in that house, eating and drinking whatever they give you, for the worker deserves his wages. Do not move around from house to house.

[8]"When you enter a town and are welcomed, eat what is set before you. [9]Heal the sick who are there and tell them, 'The kingdom of God is near you.' [10]But when you enter a town and are not welcomed, go into its streets and say, [11]'Even the dust of your town that sticks to our feet we wipe off against you. Yet be sure of this: The kingdom of God is near.' [12]I tell you, it will be more bearable on that day for Sodom than for that town.

[13]"Woe to you, Korazin! Woe to you, Bethsaida! For if the miracles that were performed in you had been performed in Tyre and Sidon, they would

have repented long ago, sitting in sackcloth and ashes. [14]But it will be more bearable for Tyre and Sidon at the judgment than for you. [15]And you, Capernaum, will you be lifted up to the skies? No, you will go down to the depths.

[16]"He who listens to you listens to me; he who rejects you rejects me; but he who rejects me rejects him who sent me."

Context

At this point Luke recorded the mission of the seventy(-two), which is similar to the mission of the Twelve told earlier (9:1-6). As in the earlier account he made no specific mention of the location or length of the mission. In his "orderly account" (1:3) Luke was more interested in what Jesus said than in where the disciples went, when they returned, or their personal experiences. The mission charge to the seventy(-two) is closely tied to the preceding passage by "he sent . . . ahead of him" (10:1; cf. "resolutely set out" [9:51] and "ahead of him" [9:52]) and references to the kingdom (10:9,11; cf. the Lukan addition of "proclaim the kingdom of God" in 9:60).

Luke also added various "woes," or judgments, to the account (10:13-15) as well as a concluding summary (10:16). Luke's editorial work shows up most clearly in his arrangement of the material, in the introduction (10:1), in 10:7a,c, and 10:10-11.

The exact relationship of the mission of the seventy(-two) and the mission of the Twelve is greatly debated. For one, the charge to the seventy(-two) is found nowhere else in the Gospels. Second, the similarity between the two mission charges is striking.[11] Third, Matthew's mission of the Twelve includes material found in Luke's mission charge to the seventy(-two).[12] Finally, in 22:35 when Jesus addressed the Twelve, referring to his mission charge to them, he mentioned instructions involving a purse and sandals that do not appear in the charge to the Twelve but only in that to the seventy(-two). Compare 10:4, noting the same order of purse, bag, sandals as in 22:35.

Scholars have debated the origin of this mission narrative.[13] That Jesus sent his disciples on a preaching mission during his ministry, however, is too well attested in the tradition to be denied. Some of the regulations found in 10:10-11, which depend upon Jewish hospitality, seem better suited to a mission in Israel than a postresurrection mission in Gentile territory. What

[11]Cf. Luke 9:3 with 10:4; 9:4 with 10:5,7; 9:5 with 10:10-11.
[12]Cf. Matt 10:13 with Luke 10:6; Matt 10:15 with Luke 10:12; Matt 10:16 with Luke 10:3.
[13]Some have suggested therefore that Luke created this entire account out of various traditional materials (so Fitzmyer, *Luke*, AB [Garden City: Doubleday, 1985], 2:843). Others suggest that perhaps Matthew combined two originally separate missions into one in order to conserve space. Others have argued that community regulations for missionary work in the early church have been read back into the life of Jesus (so R. Bultmann, *The History of the Synoptic Tradition* [New York: Harper, 1968], 145).

is certain is that Luke wanted to demonstrate to his readers that the work of missions was not restricted to the Twelve. He used this account to point forward to the church's universal mission after the resurrection.

Comments

10:1 After this. This is a common Lukan expression.[14]
The Lord appointed. For "Lord" see comments on 7:13.
Seventy-two others. This seems to imply that the twelve remained with Jesus and did not take part in this mission. There is a textual problem with respect to the number. "Seventy" is found in א, A, W, f^1, f^{13}, whereas "seventy-two" is found in $\mathfrak{P}^{75}$, B, D. Internal evidence favors seventy-two in that the frequency with which seventy appears in Scripture[15] makes it easier to understand why a scribe would want to change seventy-two to seventy. On the other hand, seventy-two appears less frequently.[16] It is difficult to choose between these two readings. Whichever one is chosen, however, the number suggests one for each nation of the world (Gen 10).

Sent them two by two. On a practical level the sending out "two by two" provided mutual support for the disciples,[17] but the theological reason is more important. Two witnesses were needed (Deut 19:15; Num 35:30) in order to bring the condemnation we read of in Luke 10:11-15.

Ahead of him. Literally *before his face*. This literary tie with the preceding materials (9:52-53) is also the exact expression used in 7:27 (cf. Acts 13:24) for John the Baptist's mission. After the death of John the Baptist, the Twelve (Luke 9:52) and the seventy(-two) (10:1) took up the task of preparing the way for the Lord.[18]

Where he was about to go. The seventy(-two) were to go before Jesus and prepare the way. That Luke wanted his readers to think that Jesus was to visit thirty-six separate towns on the way to Jerusalem is unlikely. To do so would have entailed a most circuitous route. It probably is better to understand this as preparing these villages for Jesus' spiritual coming after the resurrection. Luke 10:16 gives support to such an interpretation (cf. Matt 10:40-42).

10:2 The harvest is plentiful. Compare Matt 9:37-38; John 4:35-38. This harvest has been referred to in Luke 8:15. It would have been understood as being much larger by Luke and his readers than by the seventy(-two) who actually went on the mission because Luke and his readers would have understood this as involving a mission to the whole world (cf. 24:47; Acts 1:8). This harvest is not to be confused with the final harvest "on that day" (Luke 10:12-15; cf. Matt 13:24-

[14]Luke 5:27; 12:4; 17:8; 18:4; Acts 7:7; 13:20; 15:16; 18:1.
[15]Exod 24:1; Num 11:16,24—seventy elders; Exod 1:5; Deut 10:22—seventy offspring of Jacob; Gen 10:2-31—seventy nations [cf. 1 Enoch 89:59f.]; cf. also Exod 15:27; Judg 9:2; 2 Kgs 10:1; and the seventy members that made up the Sanhedrin.
[16]Gen 10:2-31 (LXX)—seventy-two nations; cf. also Letter of Aristeas 46-50; 3 Enoch 17:8; 18:2f.; 30:2.
[17]Cf. Mark 6:7 and Acts 8:14 (Peter and John); 13:2 (Barnabas and Saul); 15:32 (Judas and Silas); 15:40 (Paul and Silas; Barnabas and Mark).
[18]See Tannehill, *Narrative Unity of Luke-Acts*, 232-35.

30,36-43; Rev 14:15-16) but refers to the present harvest of believers in the "now" time (John 4:35).

Ask the Lord of the harvest.   Since the mission involves carrying out God's orders, it is appropriate to pray to him for the tools necessary to accomplish the work.

10:3 I am sending you.   The verb (*apostellō*) indicates that apostleship in Luke entails mission. Although the Twelve were the apostles par excellence (cf. Luke 9:10; 22:14; Acts 1:26), others like the seventy(-two) can be "sent ones" who proclaim the gospel message. This "apostolic" mission clearly foreshadows Luke 24:46-48; Acts 1:8.

Like lambs among wolves.   Compare Matt 10:16; John 10:12.

10:4 Do not take a purse or bag or sandals.   Only the command concerning a bag is mentioned at Luke 9:3, but in 22:35 the same three are found in the same order. The "purse" is essentially a money bag as is evident from 12:33. It is uncertain about whether "take" no sandals means that they could wear sandals but not carry an extra pair or whether they could not even wear them. Like the Twelve, the seventy(-two) were to go out in faith.

Do not greet anyone.   Compare 2 Kgs 4:29. This is not to be interpreted as a discourtesy, but since Oriental greetings were long and time-consuming, such greetings were best avoided. The urgency of the mission did not permit such lengthy niceties. On the other hand, the greeting found in the next verse was part of the mission.

10:5 Peace to this house.   Compare Luke 24:36 (cf. also John 20:19,21,26; Judg 6:23; 19:20). This is a typical OT greeting. The more "Christianized" forms are "Grace and peace" and "Grace, mercy and peace." [19] This proclamation of peace, however, serves more as a benediction than a greeting. "House" refers to the household, not to the building.

10:6 A man of peace.   That is, a believer (cf. Luke 2:14).

Your peace will rest upon him.   This peace is God's peace brought through the mission and ministry of the seventy(-two) as they proclaimed the good news. This "peace" is not a feeling of ease or contentment but an objective reality. It is a synonym for the messianic salvation and its attendant blessings, referred to in 1:79; 2:14; 7:50; 8:48; Acts 10:36. Paul spoke of such peace as being the result of justification (Rom 5:1). Compare the term "sons of the kingdom" in Matt 13:38.

If not, it will return to you.   The benediction or prayer of peace will not be effective if faith is not present.

10:7 Stay in that house.   Compare 9:4.

Eating and drinking whatever they give you.   The issue for the seventy(-two) was not whether the food had been offered to idols (1 Cor 10:25-31) or whether it was clean or unclean (Rom 14:13-23). It involved rather the quality of the food (steak or hamburger), for Samaritans kept the same food laws as Jews.[20] For Luke

---

[19]"Grace and peace," Rom 1:7; 1 Cor 1:3; 2 Cor 1:2; Gal 1:3; Eph 1:2; Phil 1:2; Col 1:2; 1 Thess 1:1; 2 Thess 1:2; Titus 1:4; Phlm 3; cf. 1 Pet 1:2; 2 Pet 1:2; "grace, mercy, and peace," 1 Tim 1:2; 2 Tim 1:2. A more secular salutation, "Greetings," is found in Acts 15:23; 23:26.

[20]There may also be a "purity" question here since Jews "do not use dishes Samaritans have used," John 4:9, NIV marg.). The NIV text reading, "Jews do not associate with

and his readers, however, this saying might very well have had implications for these other areas. Table fellowship had great symbolic significance in the first century, for such fellowship signified acceptance into God's people (cf. Acts 11:3; Gal 2:12).

For the worker deserves his wages. The parallel in Matt 10:10 reads "keep" or, more literally, *food*.[21] As in Gal 6:6 the messengers of the gospel are entitled to their keep. This involves sustenance, however, not luxury.

Do not move around from house to house. Jesus' messengers merit provisions from believers in return for their ministry, but this injunction warns against manipulation of ministry to gain better housing and food.

10:8 The missionary instruction is now enlarged from the setting of individual homes to that of a town. Matthew 10:11-14 combines the charge concerning the house (Luke 10:5-7) and the town (Luke 10:10-15).

Eat what is set before you. Again the messenger is to be content rather than self-seeking.

10:9 Heal the sick . . . and tell them. In 9:2 preaching God's kingdom is placed before healing, but here the order is reversed. Luke may have placed healing first because such healings are to be understood as signs that God's kingdom has come (cf. 11:20). In Matt 10:8 there is a more comprehensive description of the mission.

The kingdom of God is near you. Although elsewhere God's kingdom is said to have arrived (Luke 11:20; 16:16; 17:21), here its nearness is emphasized. This may be due to the fact that Jesus is about to come (see comments on 10:1).

10:10 Go into its streets. These were wide streets. This rejection was to be highly visible and public.

10:11 Even the dust. See comments on 9:5.

Against you. This dative of disadvantage is a shortened form for "as a testimony against you" (cf. 9:5).

Yet be sure of this: The kingdom of God is near. Luke underlined this theological truth by referring to it once again (cf. 10:9).

10:12 Sodom. The judgment of Sodom (Gen 19:24-28), which was proverbial (Isa 1:9-10), would be less severe than the judgment that would come upon those cities who reject the missionary preaching of the seventy(-two). The ignorant, even though culpable, would be judged less severely than those who are given the opportunity to hear the gospel and reject it (cf. 12:48).

On that day. In light of Luke 10:14, this designates the final day of judgment (cf. Matt 10:15).

10:13 The woes that follow envision a different audience from the seventy(-two) and illustrate the harsher judgment of Luke 10:12.[22] For "woe" see comments on 6:24.

Samaritans," also would preclude table fellowship, a more intimate association than a simple conversation.

[21]This saying is alluded to in 1 Cor 9:14 and quoted in 1 Tim 5:18 ("wages") and in *Didache* 13:1 ("food").

[22]They are given a different setting in Matt 11:21-23. The repetition of "it will be more bearable" (Luke 10:12,14) probably caused Luke to attach 10:13-15 to the mission charge of 10:1-12.

Korazim. The exact location of this town is uncertain, and this verse is the only indication that Jesus visited it.

Bethsaida! For if the miracles performed in you. The miracle of the feeding of the five thousand was located near Bethsaida (9:10-17).

Tyre and Sidon. These well-known cities represented the pagan world. The point was not that pagan cities would be excused but rather that the cities of Galilee would experience an even greater condemnation.

Sitting in sackcloth and ashes. This was an ancient form of expressing mourning and repentance.[23] Sackcloth was a rough cloth made from goat's hair, and the ashes were either placed on the head (Matt 6:16) or sat on (Job 2:8; Jonah 3:6).

10:15 Capernaum. This was one of the first towns in which Jesus worked a miracle (Luke 4:23; 7:1-10).

Will you be lifted up to the skies? The idea may have been that because Jesus visited Capernaum or performed miracles there (or both) that it expected to be exalted above other cities.

Go down to the depths. Literally *go down to Hades.* "Hades" is the Greek term used to translate *Sheol* in the LXX. It can refer to the place of the dead (Ps 89:48), the opposite of heaven (Ps 139:8; Amos 9:2), or the place of the unrighteous dead (1 Enoch 22:3-13; 63:10; 99:11; 2 Esdr 7:36). It is used in the latter sense in Luke 16:22-26 and probably should be understood in the same way here. Whether in Jesus' day there was a clear distinction between "Hades" and hell (*Gehenna*) is much debated but still uncertain. What is clear is that it designates a place of punishment for the unrighteous. The imagery comes from Isa 14:13,15.

10:16 He who listens to you. Although not stated, a change of audience from the residents of Korazin and Bethsaida to the seventy(-two) is envisioned. To "listen" or "hear" the disciples means to "receive" them, as the parallel in Matt 10:14 (cf. John 5:24) and the antithetical parallel in Luke 10:16b make clear.

Listens to me. The corporate solidarity of the messenger and the Lord is clear in this verse. See comments on 9:48.

But he who rejects you. To "reject" is the opposite of to "listen."

Rejects him who sent me. This and the previous statement, 10:16b,c, are an example of step parallelism. See comments on 9:48. This saying envisions only two possible responses to the preaching of the seventy(-two). People would either receive/listen or not receive/not listen. No distinction is made between receiving the messengers (10:8,10; 9:5) and receiving/hearing the message (10:16).

The Lukan Message

Luke's main emphasis in this passage centers around the church's evangelical mission. Although this theme became more explicit after the resurrection when specific charges were given (24:47-49; Acts 1:8), and although Luke devoted the second part of his work (Acts) to the subject, in this passage he emphasized Jesus' concern for such missions during his own ministry. The mission of the historical Jesus to the Samaritans as

---

[23]Jonah 3:6; Isa 58:5; Esth 4:2-3; Dan 9:3; Matt 11:21.

presented by Luke became symbolic, foreshadowing the church's later role in worldwide ministry extending far beyond ethnic Israel. This can be seen in part by his omission of the injunction in the Matthean parallel (Matt 10:5), in which Jesus told the disciples not to go to the Gentiles or the Samaritans during their mission. It is true that Matt 10:5f. is a closer parallel to the mission of the Twelve in Luke 9:1-6 than to the present account, but it is significant that Luke omitted this saying from 9:1-6 and 10:1-16. As Ellis observes, "For Luke, the mission of the Seventy is the continuing task of the Church." [24]

The instructions given in this account would also serve, with several important qualifications, as instructions for the church's mission in Luke's day. Luke reinforced the missionary movement of the church in his day by emphasizing its urgency (10:2,4), the need for commitment (cf. 9:57-62) and endurance in time of persecution (10:3,6,10), the means by which the mission was to be sustained (10:4a,7-8), the message to be proclaimed (10:9,11), and the eternal significance of the mission (10:5-6,11-15). He did this by recounting Jesus' own words and ministry, although some modifications would be necessary after the resurrection (22:35-36; 24:49; Acts 1:8).

Another emphasis that must not be ignored is the final judgment. Luke's conviction that such a judgment will take place goes without saying.[25] Luke made clear that the harshness of judgment is based to a great extent upon whether or not one has been given the opportunity to repent. Hearing the good news, if not followed by faith, has terrible implications. The explicit rejection of the gospel carries tragic and inescapable consequences (Luke 10:12,14).

Luke touched upon other themes as well: the need for prayer for mission workers (10:2; cf. Acts 13:1-3); the repeated admonition not to use the ministry for personal gain (Luke 10:7-8 and 9:4); the arrival of God's kingdom (see Introduction 8 [2]); and the need for repentance (see Introduction 8 [6]).

(4) The Return of the Seventy(-two) (10:17-20)

[17]The seventy-two returned with joy and said, "Lord, even the demons submit to us in your name."

[18]He replied, "I saw Satan fall like lightning from heaven.

[19]I have given you authority to trample on snakes and scorpions and to overcome all the power of the enemy; nothing will harm you. [20]However, do not rejoice that the spirits submit to you, but rejoice that your names are written in heaven."

---

[24]Ellis, *Luke*, 155.

[25]The references are numerous: Luke 10:14; 11:31-32; 16:19-28 (the whole parable would be meaningless if there were no final judgment); 22:30; Acts 10:42; 17:30-31.

Context

In contrast to the mission of the Twelve (9:1-6), the return of the sev-enty(-two) follows immediately. The joy of the returning disciples (10:17) and Jesus' teaching on rejoicing (10:20) form an inclusio, between which are sandwiched two sayings concerning the fall of Satan (10:18-19).[26] In Luke they become a commentary on the mission of the seventy(-two) and, like the mission, also point forward to the later ministry of the early church in Acts.

Comments

10:17   With joy. Joy is a characteristic of salvation (1:14; 2:10; 8:13; 15:7, 10; 24:41,52). Both the noun and the verb occur more frequently in Luke than in Mark and Matthew.[27]

Even the demons submit. The power to cast out demons is not specifically mentioned in 10:1-16, but it can be assumed that 9:1-2 was true of the mission of the seventy(-two) as well. Luke probably excluded it simply for the sake of abbre-viation. Note how the themes of the coming of God's kingdom (10:9) and the de-feat of Satan/demons (10:17-18) are brought together in 11:20.

In your name. This phrase should be understood not as a magical incantation but as another way of saying "by the power of Jesus" (Acts 19:13), "for Jesus' sake" (21:13), or "the Christian message" (Acts 4:17-20). Here the emphasis is on Jesus' power.[28]

10:18   The difficulty of this verse argues in favor of its authenticity.

I saw. The verb "saw" can mean an ordinary physical experience (14:29; 21:6; 23:35,48; 24:37), a gift of foresight or insight (Acts 27:10; John 4:19; 12:19), or have a symbolic meaning. Here it could refer to the fall of Satan seen by the pre-existent Son (Isa 14:12). It is more likely, however, that it refers symbolically to what the ex-orcisms performed by the seventy(-two) meant. Their casting out of demons demon-strated the defeat of Satan (cf. Luke 11:20-22). The tense of this verb, an inceptive aorist, is better captured by translating it "I was seeing." Luke understood each ex-orcism by the seventy(-two) as demonstrating the defeat of Satan.[29]

Satan fall. "Satan" is the Greek transliteration of the Hebrew term used to describe the archenemy of God and humanity (Job 1:6-12; 2:1-7). It is usually translated into Greek by the term "devil," though in Luke-Acts "Satan" is also used.[30] Although Isa 14:12 may refer to the original fall of Satan, most references tend to refer to his future fall or defeat.[31]

---

[26]These may have existed in the tradition as isolated sayings of Jesus.

[27]The noun occurs eight times in Luke, four times in Acts, only once in Mark, and six times in Matthew. The verb occurs eleven times in Luke, seven times in Acts, but only twice in Mark, and six times in Matthew.

[28]Cf. Luke 9:49; Acts 3:6; 4:10,17-18,30; 9:27-28.

[29]For further discussion see W. G. Kümmel, *Promise and Fulfillment*, SBT (London: SCM, 1961), 113-14.

[30]Luke 11:18; 13:16; 22:3,31; Acts 5:3; 26:18.

[31]John 12:31; Rom 16:20; Rev 12:7-10,13; 20:1-3,10; cf. also *Jub.* 23:29; *T. Levi* 18:12; *T. Judah* 25:3; *T. Asher* 27:3; *T. Dan* 5:10-11; *As. Mos.* 10:1.

Fall like lightning from heaven. There are two ways of translating "from heaven": adjectivally ("fall as lightning-from-heaven") or adverbially ("fall from heaven like lightning"). The second is more likely. "Lightning" indicates not brightness but the suddenness of the fall. In the exorcisms of the seventy(-two), Jesus saw Satan's defeat resulting from his coming.

10:19 I have given you authority to trample on snakes and scorpions. These were both well-known symbols for evil.[32] The snake is a symbol for Satan in Gen 3:1-15; 2 Cor 11:3; Rev 12:9,14-15; 20:2. For a parallel to Luke's statement, cf. Ps 91:13; *T. Levi* 18:12—"Beliar shall be bound by him [the Messiah], and he shall give power to his children to tread upon the evil spirits" (cf. also *T. Simeon* 6:6; *T. Zebulon* 9:8). The perfect tense of the verb ("have given you authority") refers to the authority already given to the disciples (cf. 9:1), not to some future authority such as in Acts 1:8. It is likely, however, that Luke's readers would include Acts 1:8 as well.

Power of the enemy. Satan's power is described in Luke 11:21-22.

Nothing will harm you. Compare 21:18; Acts 28:3-6 (and Mark 16:18 for those who accept the longer ending of Mark). This can also be translated "he will hurt you [in] nothing," but the NIV translation captures better the original flavor. The Greek form, a subjunctive of emphatic negation, indicates in the strongest possible way that the enemy will not harm Jesus' messengers in any way whatsoever.

10:20 However, do not rejoice. This picks up the "joy" of Luke 10:17 and points out that their true joy should arise not from missionary accomplishments but from their eternal salvation.

That your names are written in heaven. This metaphor for eternal salvation is found in the OT, the intertestamental literature, and the NT.[33] "Are written" is a divine passive meaning *God has written your names in heaven.*

The Lukan Message

This passage continues the theme of the mission of the seventy(-two) and thus, by extension, the future mission of the church. But there is also a strong witness to the realization of the OT promises concerning Satan's defeat in the messianic age. The Satanic power is broken. Because of his exorcisms, Jesus can assure his audience that God's kingdom has come (11:20). The exorcism of demons by Jesus' messengers is another witness to the realization of God's kingdom. Jesus saw in each one Satan's overthrow. Luke understood, as did Paul, that Jesus disarmed and conquered the powers and authorities of Satan's domain (11:21-22; cf. Col 2:15). Satan's defeat brings joy, the eschatological joy of God's triumphant kingdom.

A warning against self-exaltation is also present in this passage. Even as earlier the disciples were warned against thinking that greatness lies in

---

[32]For the snake as a symbol of evil, cf. Num 21:6-9; Pss 58:4; 140:3; cf. Sir 21:2; 39:30; for scorpion cf. 1 Kgs 12:11,14; 2 Chr 10:11,14; cf. Sir 39:30; for the pair cf. Deut 8:15; Luke 11:11-12; cf. Sir 39:30.

[33]Exod 32:32-33; Ps 69:28; Isa 4:3; 34:16; Dan 12:1; Mal 3:16-17; Jub. 19:9; 23:32; 30:19-23; 36:10; 1 Enoch 47:3; 104:1; 108:3,7; 1QS 7:2; 1QM 12:2; Phil 4:3; Heb 12:23; Rev 3:5; 13:8; 17:8; 20:12,15; 21:27.

being served by others (Luke 9:46-48), so here Jesus gave another warning against the kind of attitude that boasts in what one has done for God, or, more piously, "in what God has done through me." An example of this can be found in 2 Cor 11, where Paul denounced the boasting of his opponents. To Paul it was preferable to "boast of the things that show [his] weakness" (2 Cor 11:30). In a similar way Luke reminded Theophilus not to boast in his accomplishments for God. Rather he was to "boast in the Lord" (1 Cor 1:31), who has written his name in the book of life.

(5) The Blessedness of the Disciples (10:21-24)

[21]**At that time Jesus, full of joy through the Holy Spirit, said, "I praise you, Father, Lord of heaven and earth, because you have hidden these things from the wise and learned, and revealed them to little children. Yes, Father, for this was your good pleasure.**

[22]**"All things have been committed to me by my Father. No one knows who the Son is except the Father, and no one knows who the Father is except the Son and those to whom the Son chooses to reveal him."**

[23]**Then he turned to his disciples and said privately, "Blessed are the eyes that see what you see.** [24]**For I tell you that many prophets and kings wanted to see what you see but did not see it, and to hear what you hear but did not hear it."**

Context

These verses, along with the preceding, cast additional illumination on the relationship between Jesus and his disciples. They not only were his representatives (Luke 10:16), with their names written in the book of life (10:20), but they had been uniquely blessed (10:23-24) by the gift of the Father's revelation (10:21-22). The present passage completes the description of the responsibilities and privileges of discipleship begun in 9:51. The disciples' elevation to a position of privilege, over their contemporaries (10:21-22), and even to one surpassing their predecessors (10:23-24) is described. The present passage is tied to the preceding one by the time designation "at that time" (10:21), the reference to "joy" in the same verse (cf. 10:20), and the mention of the disciples in 10:23. Parallels to these verses are found in Matt 11:25-27; 13:16-17.

Comments

10:21 At that time. Compare 2:38; 12:12; 13:31; 20:19; 24:33; Acts 16:18; 22:13.

Full of joy through the Holy Spirit. Compare Luke 1:47, where the same verb is used. This expression displays again the connection between Jesus' mission and his anointing by the Spirit.[34]

---

[34]There is a textual problem in the Greek text about whether the pronoun "in" should or should not be included before "the Holy Spirit." The meaning, however, is not seriously affected by this.

I praise you. Jesus rejoiced in God's actions, which are now described. The focus of his praise may be on the hiding itself, the revealing, or both. Probably, in light of the emphasis of Luke 10:22, it is on the revealing.[35]

Father. The Greek here is *patēr*, but the Aramaic behind this is *Abba*. While the Hellenistic Jewish literature of Jesus' day did use *Abba* as a form of address for God (cf. 3 Macc 6:4,8; Sir 23:1,4), it was unusual, and it is not found at all in the OT. Its frequent use by Jesus as a favorite term of address for God is unique. It was once popular to think that the best English equivalent was "Daddy" because children used it to address their fathers. It is now evident, however, that *Abba* was also the way adults addressed their fathers. As a result *Abba* is best translated "Father." [36]

Whereas *Abba* was certainly not a formal expression of address, neither was it a childlike one. See comments on 11:2.

Lord of heaven and earth. Compare Acts 17:24; cf. also Tob 7:18; Jdt 9:12.

You have hidden these things. "These things" can refer either to the following material, i.e., Jesus' unique status as the only Son (Luke 10:22) and the disciples' privileged relationship to God through Jesus (10:23-24) or to what has preceded, i.e., the presence of God's kingdom and Satan's fall (10:17-18). The latter is more likely. The verb "have hidden" can have an active meaning, as in the case of Pharaoh (Exod 7:3; cf. Mark 4:10-12), or a passive or concessive sense, in which God has permitted the arrogant to remain in their sin-induced blindness.

From the wise and learned. The exact meaning is unclear. Suggestions include: the arrogant; the intelligentsia (cf. 1 Cor 1:19-25); the Pharisees, Sadducees, and scribes; Jesus' opponents (Luke 19:47); or the objects of the woes in 6:24-26. The phrase is found only once in Luke-Acts, so certainty about its meaning is not possible. Probably it refers to the "wise and learned" of this world who have rejected the gospel. Like Jesus before him, Luke observed their rejection of the good news of God's kingdom and exulted in the reversal now taking place (cf. 1:51-52). God permitted the sin of arrogance to blind them so that these things remained hidden. God was beginning to destroy the wisdom of the wise and frustrate the intelligence of the intelligent (1 Cor 1:19).

And revealed them to little children. In the Matthean parallel the term "little children" refers primarily to believers in general, such as tax collectors and sinners (Matt 11:19; cf. also 18:2-6,10-14), but in Luke it refers to the seventy(-two) (Luke 10:17,19-20). Neither Matthew nor Luke used it to refer to immature Christians, as Paul did in 1 Cor 3:1.

10:22 All things. This includes not only "these things" of Luke 10:21 but also Jesus' authority and power[37] and his authority to judge the world.[38]

Have been committed to me by my Father. The Father, as "Lord of heaven and earth" (10:21), has placed all things under Jesus' command.

---

[35]Cf. 2 Sam 22:50; Pss 6:5; 9:1; 35:18; and 1QH 2:20,31; 3:19,37 but especially 7:26-27—"I [praise Thee, O Lord,] for Thou hast enlightened me through Thy truth. And Thy marvelous mysteries Thou hast made known to me."

[36]See J. Barr, "'Abbā Isn't Daddy," *JTS* 39 (1988): 28-47.

[37]Luke 9:1; 10:17; 24:49; Acts 1:8; cf. Matt 28:18; Phil 2:9-11; Eph 1:20-22; Col 1:17-18.

[38]Luke 9:26; 12:8; 21:27,36; Acts 10:42; 17:31; cf. John 3:35; 13:3.

No one knows who the Son is except the Father. The only other place in the Synoptic Gospels where the term "Son" is used in this absolute sense is Mark 13:32. Jesus' sonship is qualitatively different from ours, not just quantitatively. This is made clear by Luke's use of "no one." Jesus' status is unique. The Father's knowledge of the Son should not be interpreted as referring to a divine election of him (cf. Amos 3:2; Jer 1:5) because the Son "knows" the Father in the same way.

And no one knows who the Father is except the Son. This forms a chiasmus with the preceding verse: Son-Father-Father-Son.

And those to whom the Son chooses to reveal him. The only way to a saving knowledge of God is through Jesus. Compare Acts 4:12; John 14:6.

10:23 To his disciples . . . privately. This qualification is somewhat unexpected because no crowds have been mentioned, but Luke may have added it in order to indicate that the beatitude that follows is for believers only. See comments on 6:20.

Blessed. Compare Luke 1:45; 6:20-22; 7:23; 11:28.

Are the eyes that see what you see. The parallel in Matt 13:16 reads "your eyes" and refers to the disciples' privilege of being eyewitnesses. Luke may have intended to broaden the group to include his readers. If so, the term "see" means not so much physical seeing as understanding that God's kingdom has arrived (10:17-18), that Jesus possesses a unique relationship to the Father, and that he alone is the way to salvation (10:22). Compare 8:10; 9:27.

10:24 For I tell you. Compare Matt 13:17 in which "the truth" (literally *Amen*) is added.

Many prophets and kings. The saying underscores both the disciples' privilege and the importance of the events taking place. A new era in redemptive history has dawned. God's kingdom has come! Matthew 13:17 reads "many prophets and righteous men." By his choice of expressions, Luke may have been alluding to Isa 60:3 and 52:15 (cf. 1 Pet 1:10-12).

See what you see . . . hear what you hear. Luke's readers, and the reader today, share in this experience of God's saving rule when they hear the gospel message.

The Lukan Message

The elevated Christology in this passage is evident. While Jesus' unique sonship is taught elsewhere in the Synoptic Gospels (Mark 13:32; Matt 24:36; 28:19), Luke's emphasis here on the "nature" of the Son of God is reminiscent of Johannine Christology (John 3:35-36; 5:19-30; 10:15; 17:1-5). This passage has in fact been called "a Johannine thunderbolt." Like John, Luke taught that Jesus is uniquely the Son of God, with an exclusive relationship with God. John described this more fully in his teaching concerning the incarnation.

There is also a strong emphasis on the realization of God's kingdom. The disciples had witnessed a unique event. They lived in the time of fulfillment. What prophets and kings of past generations had longed and yearned for had come to fruition. The new age had begun. The law and the prophets were until John, but now the kingdom had come. Furthermore, this was revealed to the disciples by the Messiah, God's Son. There was also a great upheaval, for the kingdom was not coming to the wise and powerful but to babes who received the kingdom like little children (Luke 18:17). What Mary proclaimed in the Magnificat was now being accomplished. God brought down the proud and exalted the humble (1:51-53).

(6) The Parable of the Good Samaritan (10:25-37)

[25]On one occasion an expert in the law stood up to test Jesus. "Teacher," he asked, "what must I do to inherit eternal life?"

[26]"What is written in the Law?" he replied. "How do you read it?"

[27]He answered: " 'Love the Lord your God with all your heart and with all your soul and with all your strength and with all your mind'; and, 'Love your neighbor as yourself.' "

[28]"You have answered correctly," Jesus replied. "Do this and you will live."

[29]But he wanted to justify himself, so he asked Jesus, "And who is my neighbor?"

[30]In reply Jesus said: "A man was going down from Jerusalem to Jericho, when he fell into the hands of robbers. They stripped him of his clothes, beat him and went away, leaving him half dead. [31]A priest happened to be going down the same road, and when he saw the man, he passed by on the other side. [32]So too, a Levite, when he came to the place and saw him, passed by on the other side. [33]But a Samaritan, as he traveled, came where the man was; and when he saw him, he took pity on him. [34]He went to him and bandaged his wounds, pouring on oil and wine. Then he put the man on his own donkey, took him to an inn and took care of him. [35]The next day he took out two silver coins and gave them to the innkeeper. 'Look after him,' he said, 'and when I return, I will reimburse you for any extra expense you may have.'

[36]"Which of these three do you think was a neighbor to the man who fell into the hands of robbers?"

[37]The expert in the law replied, "The one who had mercy on him."

Jesus told him, "Go and do likewise."

Context

Following the assertion that the so-called wise lack true understanding (10:21), Luke gave an illustration of just such a lack of understanding. One of the wise, an expert in the law, came to Jesus to ask the most basic of all religious questions, "What must I do to inherit eternal life?" Although the question was not sincere, it nevertheless revealed ignorance. This question and the parable that follows form a unified whole. This is evident in that the questions introducing and concluding the parable (10:29,36) refer back to the commandment (10:27). While there is considerable debate about whether the question and the parable originally formed a unified event in Jesus' ministry, they fit well together.[39]

---

[39]The relationship between the question and the parable is complicated by the issue of how 10:25-28 is related to Mark 12:28-34/Matt 22:34-40. The similarities are apparent: (1) Both

These two commandments (Deut 6:5; Lev 19:18) were no doubt a basic element in Jesus' teachings, and "great teachers constantly repeat themselves." [40] Furthermore the question of the great commandment frequently arose in rabbinic discussion. It may even be that the lawyer in Luke 10:27 was repeating what Jesus himself had been teaching for the purpose of presenting his counterquestion, "And who is my neighbor?" (10:29).

Comments

10:25 On one occasion. Luke did not give a setting for this incident.

An expert in the law stood up to test Jesus. Both Luke and Matthew (Matt 22:35) saw this question as a hostile one and agreed against Mark in calling the person an expert in the law (see comments on 7:30) rather than a teacher of the law (Mark 12:28).

What must I do to inherit eternal life? For "eternal life" cf. Luke 18:18, 30; Acts 13:46,48. This is a good question, not to be confused with an attempt to earn salvation. It is repeated in 18:18 and with some variation in Acts 2:37 and 16:30.[41] All four passages express the same basic question and reveal that "eternal life" is a synonym for being "saved," or entering God's kingdom (cf. 18:18

accounts are introduced by a question from an expert in the law (Matthew; Luke) or a teacher of the law (Mark). (2) Both accounts quote Deut 6:5 and Lev 19:18 and quote them in the same order. (3) Luke omitted the Markan parallel in chap. 20, although he included the material that surrounds it (Mark 12:18-27 = Luke 20:27-40; Mark 12:35-37 = Luke 20:41-44). On the other hand, there are a number of differences as well. (1) In Mark and Matthew it is the expert/teacher who quoted the OT, whereas in Luke it was Jesus. (2) In Mark and Matthew the question was about the most important/greatest commandment, whereas in Luke it was how to have eternal life. (3) In Mark the question addressed to Jesus was neutral, but in Matthew and Luke it was hostile. (4) Only in Luke is the incident followed by the parable of the good Samaritan. (5) In Mark and Matthew the incident took place after Jesus arrived in Jerusalem, whereas in Luke it took place before.

Several attempts to explain this have been made. One is that the same incident in Jesus' ministry lies behind all of the accounts and that Luke simply inserted it at a different place in his Gospel. Yet if this were so, it is strange for Luke to have changed Mark's "teacher of the law" to "expert in the law," for he never did this elsewhere. In the other instances where Luke used this term, it is in non-Markan material (Luke 7:30; 11:45-46,52; 14:3). Furthermore, this would be the only Markan material that Luke placed in all of 9:51–18:15. Another suggestion is that Luke found the same incident in another tradition (L or Q) in a different form. Some of the Matthew/Luke agreements suggest that this is possible. It may also be, however, that these are two different incidents in Jesus' ministry.

Another issue involved in this account is whether the question (10:25-28) and the parable (10:29-37) were originally connected. Two reasons are generally given for denying this. (1) If only one incident in Jesus' life lay behind these two traditions, then why is the parable missing from Mark and Matthew? (2) The parable does not answer the question of 10:29, for it deals with giving neighborly love, not receiving it, and it is argued that it is unlikely that Jesus would have answered the question with an inappropriate illustration. Yet if Jesus' question in 10:36 is a correction of the lawyer's, then the latter objection is not valid.

[40] T. W. Manson, *The Sayings of Jesus* (London: SCM, 1954), 260.
[41] Cf. Luke 3:10,12,14.

with 18:24). The four responses should be understood as variant ways of giving the same answer.

10:26   What is written in the Law?   See comments on 2:22. Jesus' question revealed that the answer to the lawyer's question is found in the OT. What "is written" is decisive. Compare 10:28. As in the case of the rich ruler (18:18-23), Jesus affirmed the law. The teaching of the law is definitive. The way to eternal life is the same in both the OT and the NT. It is by grace through a faith that works in love (Gal 5:6). At times the word "faith" may need to be emphasized; at other times, "love." The answer given in Luke 10:27 involves a faith consisting of love for God and one's neighbor, for it is inconceivable to love God apart from faith. Furthermore, a faith that does not produce love of one's neighbor is dead (Jas 2:17). It is no faith; it never was faith.

10:27   He answered.   In both Mark and Matthew, Jesus gave the following answer. In Luke the expert in the law answered.

Love the Lord your God . . . and love your neighbor.   The expert's answer consisted of two OT passages. The first (Deut 6:5) was called the *Shema* because it begins *"Hear, O Israel."* A devout Jew would repeat it twice each day (*Ber.* 1:1-4). In the *Shema* three prepositional phrases describe the total response of love toward God. These involve the heart (emotions), the soul (consciousness), and strength (motivation). The Synoptic Gospels all have "heart" and "soul," Matthew omits strength, and all add "mind" (intelligence). The second OT passage in the lawyer's answer is Lev 19:18. It is found also in Rom 13:9; Gal 5:14; and Jas 2:8. In Luke the two OT passages are combined into a single command, whereas in Mark 12:31; Matt 22:39 they are left separate.[42] Whether these two OT passages were linked before Jesus' time is uncertain.[43] They appear together in the early Christian literature.[44] That this two-fold summary was basic to Jesus' teaching is evident by its appearance in his parables (Luke 15:18,21; 18:2; cf. also 11:42, where "justice" equals "love your neighbor"). For a similar but indirect connection, see Mic 6:8.

Neighbor.   For most Jews a neighbor was another Jew, not a Samaritan or a Gentile. The Pharisees (John 7:49) and the Essenes did not even include all Jews (1QS 1:9-10). The teaching of the latter stands in sharp contrast with that of Jesus. The Essenes taught that one was to love all the children of light who are part of the community but to hate the children of darkness who stand outside the community.

There appears to be a chiasmus between this verse and what follows: God—neighbor—man/neighbor (Luke 10:29-37)—Jesus/God (10:38-42).

10:28   You have answered correctly.   Jesus' affirmation reveals to Luke's readers that 10:27 is indeed the way to eternal life (cf. 18:20).

Do this and you will live.   Another way of phrasing this idea is found in Acts 2:38 and 16:31 (cf. Lev 18:5). The verb "do this" is in a present imperative, and Luke emphasized by this the continual nature of the Christian commitment (cf. Luke 9:23).

---

[42] For further discussion see V. P. Furnish, *The Love Command in the New Testament* (New York: Abingdon, 1972), 22-45.

[43] They are found together in *T. Issachar* 5:2; 7:6; *T. Dan* 5:3, but these may be later Christian interpolations. Philo, *De Specialibus Legibus* 2.63 is definitely post-Jesus.

[44] *Didache* 1:2; Barn. 19:2-5; Justin, *Dialogue with Trypho* 93:2-3.

10:29 But he wanted to justify himself. This indicates a less than sincere response on the part of the lawyer, reinforcing his negative attitude in 10:25.
And who is my neighbor? This is not the same question as the one asked by Jesus in 10:36. Luke almost certainly was aware of this. It is quite possible that he saw Jesus in the parable twisting this improper question, "Who is my neighbor?" (i.e., what must a person do to qualify that I should love him as a neighbor?) into a proper one ("What must I do to be a loving neighbor?"). See comments on 10:36.
10:30 A man. Luke used this expression (literally *a certain man*) only when introducing a parable.[45] See comments on 16:19.
Was going down from Jerusalem to Jericho. Because Jerusalem sits on a mountain twenty-five hundred feet above sea level, one always goes down from Jerusalem no matter which direction one takes.[46] Jericho was seventeen miles east of Jerusalem and approximately eight hundred feet below sea level.
When he fell into the hands of robbers. Robbers hid in the mountains, rocks, and desert along the road between Jerusalem and Jericho.
10:31 A priest. As descendant of Aaron involved in the sacrifices and maintenance of the temple, as well as in various purification rites, a priest could not defile himself by contact with the dead, except in the case of a close relative. Some have suggested that this was why the priest refused any contact with the presumably dead man. Others have suggested that he feared stopping because he might then be attacked by robbers. Still others hypothesize that he had just finished his service in the temple. Luke did not imply anything like this, and attempts to ascertain the inner thoughts and motives of the priest are irrelevant because he is a fictional character. This particular priest never existed. It is pointless to discuss what the priest and Levite were thinking as they came upon this man.[47] If an author wants to place particular thoughts in the mind of his fictional character, he may certainly do so, but he must then share them with his readers.
Happened to be going. This may have been intended to show that it was a lonely road.
Passed by on the other side. This is a colorful way of describing the priest's unwillingness to love his neighbor as himself.
10:32 So, too, a Levite. The Levite was a descendant of Levi who assisted the priests in various sacrificial duties and policing the temple but could not perform the sacrificial acts. Luke was not suggesting that since the Levite's duties were inferior to those of a priest he might have been more open to help because the problem of becoming defiled was less acute. Rather he was emphasizing that neither the wise and understanding (10:21) nor the proud and ruling (1:51-52) practice being loving neighbors.
Passed by on the other side. The Levite behaved just like the priest.
10:33 But a Samaritan. The term "Samaritan" is in an emphatic position in the sentence. Jesus deliberately chose an outsider, and a hated one at that, for his hero in order to indicate that being a neighbor is not a matter of nationality or

[45]Cf. Luke 14:16; 15:11; 16:1,19; 19:12; 20:9 (cf. 12:16; 18:2).
[46]East (Luke 10:30-31), north (Mark 3:22; John 4:47; Acts 8:15; 18:22), south (Acts 8:26), or west (Acts 24:1,22; 25:6-7).
[47]Cf. P. R. Jones, *The Teaching of the Parables* (Nashville: Broadman, 1982), 224-25.

race. The mutual hatred of the Jews and the Samaritans is evident in such passages as John 4:9; 8:48. The united kingdom was divided after Solomon's death due to the foolishness of his son, Rehoboam (1 Kgs 12). The ten northern tribes formed a nation known variously as Israel, Ephraim, or (after the capital city built by Omri) Samaria. In 722 B.C. Samaria fell to the Assyrians, and the leading citizens were exiled and dispersed throughout the Assyrian Empire. Non-Jewish peoples were then brought into Samaria. Intermarriage resulted, and the "rebels" became "half-breeds" in the eyes of the Southern Kingdom of Judea. (*Jews* comes from the term *Judea*.) After the Jews returned from exile in Babylon, the Samaritans sought at first to participate in the rebuilding of the temple. When their offer of assistance was rejected, they sought to impede its building (Ezra 4–6; Neh 2–4). The Samaritans later built their own temple on Mount Gerizim, but led by John Hyrcanus the Jews destroyed it in 128 B.C. (cf. John 4:20-21). So great was Jewish and Samaritan hostility that Jesus' opponents could think of nothing worse to say of him than, "Aren't we right in saying that you are a Samaritan and demon-possessed?" (John 8:48; cf. also 4:9).[48]

Took pity on him. This action is like that of Jesus in Luke 7:13 and the gracious father in 15:20.

10:34 He bandaged his wounds, pouring on oil and wine. The lovingkindness of the Samaritan is shown in his applying basic first aid and "medicines" to his neighbor (cf. *Sabb.* 19:2; Isa 1:6).

Put the man on his own donkey. This shows the desperate condition of the man.

Took him to an inn. That this "inn" had an "innkeeper" (Luke 10:35) indicates that it was much closer to a present-day inn than the inn in 2:7.

10:35 Two silver coins. An attempt to translate the value of "two silver coins" (literally *two denarii*) into a present-day monetary unit has little meaning. A denarius was the equivalent of a day's wages for a working man (cf. Matt 20:2, 9,13). This indicates that sufficient money was given to take care of the penniless man. The Samaritan made wise use of his possessions (oil, wine, donkey, money) and thus provides the reader with an example of appropriate use of material goods demanded at Luke 6:32-36 (cf. also 16:9-12), for he gave expecting nothing in return. See comments on 20:24.

10:36 In his counterquestion to 10:29 (cf. 7:40-42), Jesus indicated that one should worry less about who a neighbor is than about being a good neighbor. See comments on 10:29. Jesus' counterquestion reversed the roles, so that just as Jesus answered the lawyer's question (10:29), the lawyer had to answer Jesus.

10:37 The expert . . . replied, "The one who had mercy on him." Note the lawyer's avoidance of the term "Samaritan," which would have been the more natural way of answering the question.

The Lukan Message

Probably no parable has been allegorized more often than this one. The most famous allegory is that of Augustine.[49] The irony of Augustine's

---

[48] See J. Jeremias, *Jerusalem in the Time of Jesus* (Philadelphia: Fortress, 1969), 352-58.

[49] Here the man represents Adam; Jerusalem represents the city of heavenly peace; Jericho represents the moon, which signifies mortality; the robbers represent the devil and his

and similar allegorical interpretations is that the parable is introduced (10:29) and concludes with (10:36) questions about what it means to be a neighbor, whereas the allegorical interpretations do not deal with this issue at all. Clearly, Luke's main point in retelling the parable must have been what it means to be a neighbor. Jesus and Luke sought to illustrate that the love of one's neighbor must transcend all natural or human boundaries such as race, nationality, religion, and economic or educational status.

Another Lukan emphasis in this passage centers around the lawyer's question, "What must I do to inherit eternal life?" (10:25). Luke made the importance of this question apparent by his frequent repetition of it and related questions in 18:18; Acts 2:37 and 16:30. Ultimately it profits a person nothing "to gain the whole world, and yet lose or forfeit his very self" (Luke 9:25). Whereas the answer given to this question in Acts 16:31 is what most Christians expect and whereas the answer in Acts 2:38 is only a little more uncomfortable, Jesus' two answers in Luke 10:27-28 and 18:22 are disconcerting for many Christians. Yet they need not be. To love God means to accept what God in his grace has done and to trust in him. Faith involves more than mental assent to theological doctrines. Similarly, love is not just an emotion. Both entail an obedient trust in the God of grace and mercy. The response of love to God and of faith in God are very much the same. This intimate association between love and faith is seen most clearly in 7:47,50.[50] For Luke, as for Paul, salvation was by grace (Acts 13:38-39) through faith (Luke 7:50; 8:48; 17:19; 18:42), but this faith works through love (see Gal 5:6). At times the aspect of faith may need to be emphasized and at other times love.

A third Lukan emphasis in our passage involves his understanding of the OT. In this passage Luke made clear that the OT is the final authority in matters of faith.[51] The answer to the most basic of all religious questions is to be sought in the law (Luke 10:26), and what it teaches is correct (10:28). Luke's view of the law was not unlike that of Matt 5:17-20.

---

angels; the stripping of the man represents the loss of immortality; the beating of the man represents persuasion to sin; leaving the man half-dead represents humanity as half-dead spiritually due to sin but half-alive due to knowledge of God; the priest represents the law; the Levite represents the prophets; the good Samaritan represents Christ; the binding of wounds represents the restraint of sin; the oil represents the comfort of a good hope; the wine represents exhortation to spirited work; the beast represents the body of Christ; the inn represents the church; the two denarii represent the two commandments of love; the innkeeper represents the apostle Paul; the return of the good Samaritan represents the resurrection of Christ. For a survey of how this parable has been interpreted in the history of the church and further discussion, see R. H. Stein, *An Introduction to the Parables of Jesus* (Philadelphia: Westminster, 1981), 42-71.

[50] Cf. also 11:42, where Luke has "the love of God" and Matt 23:23 has "faith" (RSV).

[51] For Luke's readers the teachings of Jesus no doubt also possessed canonical authority, but at that time the NT canon was still in the process of being written.

Another theme is the wise use of possessions. The Samaritan provides an appropriate example of how one should use material goods. His oil, wine, money, and mount were all used wisely (cf. 6:32-36), for he gave expecting nothing in return.

Finally, we should note the recurrent theme of the great reversal. Those who are fulfilling the scriptural injunctions and entering the kingdom are not the expected ones, for the priest and the Levite demonstrated that they loved neither God nor their neighbor. Strangely enough the outcast, a cursed Samaritan, satisfied the requirements of the law. Once again the last became first and the first last.

(7) Martha and Mary (10:38-42)

[38]As Jesus and his disciples were on their way, he came to a village where a woman named Martha opened her home to him. [39]She had a sister called Mary, who sat at the Lord's feet listening to what he said. [40]But Martha was distracted by all the preparations that had to be made. She came to him and asked, "Lord, don't you care that my sister has left me to do the work by myself? Tell her to help me!"

[41]"Martha, Martha," the Lord answered, "you are worried and upset about many things, [42]but only one thing is needed. Mary has chosen what is better, and it will not be taken away from her."

Context

It is uncertain how this passage relates to the preceding material.[52] Some have suggested that it is an example of how to seek eternal life (cf. 10:25 and 10:42). Others argue that it is a continuation of contrasts: priest/Levite—Samaritan; Martha—Mary. Others see a literary relationship and the completion of a chiasmus in which in 10:27 we have (A) Love of God—(B) Love of Neighbor followed by—(b) Samaritan's Love of Neighbor in 10:29-37—(a) Mary's Love of Jesus in 10:38-42. Thus the love of the injured man (10:29) by his Samaritan "neighbor" (10:36) is now complemented by Mary's love/reverence for God and his Son. If the tradition found in John 11–12 correctly associated Mary and Martha with Bethany, this last interpretation is quite possible because Luke then intentionally placed this incident after the preceding materials.

Comments
10:38 Were on their way. Compare 9:51-56.

---

[52]There is also a debate about whether this account is more properly classified as a pronouncement story or a story about Jesus. The decision of which classification best fits is dependent upon whether one thinks that the main point involves a Christological truth or the teaching of 10:42.

He came to a village. According to John 11–12, Mary and Martha lived in Bethany, which lies on the eastern slope of the Mount of Olives. The city is mentioned in Luke 19:29.

A woman named Martha opened her home. The term "opened" or "welcomed" is also found in 19:6 and Acts 17:7 (Jas 2:25). The name "Martha" is the feminine form of the Aramaic term *Mar* and means *mistress.* Martha appears to have been the mistress in charge of the house, but Luke did not expect his Greek readers to see a pun in this and use of the title "Lord" in Luke 10:40. Such a pun is possible in Aramaic, where Lord is translated *Mar,* but not in Greek, where it is translated *Kyrios.*

10:39 She had a sister called Mary. John 11:1 also mentions that she was the sister of Martha.

Who sat at the Lord's feet. This was a disciple's proper place (Acts 22:3; *Aboṭ* 1.4; cf. also 8:35).

Lord. Luke again used his favorite designation for Jesus. Compare 7:13.

Listening to what he said. "Listening" is a durative imperfect and emphasizes a continual listening. She was listening to "what he said" (literally *his word*). For the importance of the term *word,* see comments on 1:2.

10:40 But Martha was distracted. Martha also wanted to hear Jesus, but the tyranny of the urgent prevented her from doing this.

By all the preparations that had to be made. The Greek is literally *with much serving.* The same term, "serving," is used in 8:3; 4:39. Martha's "service" for Jesus got in the way of her sitting lovingly at his feet.

Lord. This title would have been more pregnant with meaning for Luke and his readers than for Martha.

10:41 Martha, Martha. Compare 22:31; Acts 9:4; 22:7; 26:14; and also Luke 6:46; 8:24; 13:34; 23:21.

You are worried and upset about many things. Martha was too easily distracted by less important things. Compare John 6:25; 1 Cor 7:32-35. Ultimately such worries choke out the word of God (Luke 8:14).

10:42 But only one thing is needed. This is the more probable reading and translation.[53] There is a need to focus on what is most important, for although serving is good, sitting at Jesus' feet is best.

What is better. "Better" is literally *good,* but in koine Greek the positive adjective (good) could be used for the comparative (better) or even the superlative (best; cf. Matt 5:19; 22:36). Although there is a comparison between two things here, the superlative is to be preferred, for nothing is better than what Mary chose. It is best to sit at Jesus' feet and hear God's word. What feeds the soul is more important than what feeds the body. (Sometimes church suppers become an end in themselves, losing sight of the best thing—hearing God's word.)

It will not be taken away from her. The "it" has been interpreted several ways: she will not be forced to stop listening; the blessings of the kingdom of God or her heavenly reward will not be lost; she will be remembered in history for this. Clearly the first interpretation is true, but it is possible that more may be intended as well.

---

[53] For a discussion of textual problems involved here, see I. H. Marshall, *The Gospel of Luke,* TNIGTC (Grand Rapids: Eerdmans, 1978), 452-53.

The Lukan Message

Within this short passage is a clear emphasis on the importance of hearing Jesus' word (Luke 10:39). The centrality of this theme is evident from the use of the term "word," in the sense of the divine proclamation, over forty times in Luke-Acts. The one thing needed above all else is hearing the proclamation of how one can inherit eternal life/be saved. For only by hearing the word, retaining it, and persevering can one be fruitful (8:15,21). To listen to Jesus as Mary did is the best thing one can do, even better than serving. One should not press this account into advocating a life of contemplation over a life of service, or of celibacy over marriage (à la 1 Cor 7:28-35). Nor should one see here a disparagement of the command to love one's neighbor relative to the command to love God. One serves a neighbor best when one loves God, and one loves God in part by serving one's neighbor.

One other issue that should be mentioned involves again the great reversal. In contrast to common rabbinic practice, Jesus encouraged women to listen to his teaching and become part of his ministry (8:3).[54]

(8) Jesus' Teaching on Prayer (11:1-13)

[1]One day Jesus was praying in a certain place. When he finished, one of his disciples said to him, "Lord, teach us to pray, just as John taught his disciples."
[2]He said to them, "When you pray, say:
" 'Father,
hallowed be your name,
your kingdom come.
[3]Give us each day our daily bread.
[4]Forgive us our sins,
for we also forgive everyone who sins against us.
And lead us not into temptation.' "
[5]Then he said to them, "Suppose one of you has a friend, and he goes to him at midnight and says, 'Friend, lend me three loaves of bread, [6]because a friend of mine on a journey has come to me, and I have nothing to set before him.'
[7]"Then the one inside answers, 'Don't bother me. The door is already locked, and my children are with me in bed. I can't get up and give you anything.' [8]I tell you, though he will not get up and give him the bread because he is his friend, yet because of the man's boldness he will get up and give him as much as he needs.
[9]"So I say to you: Ask and it will be given to you; seek and you will find; knock and the door will be opened to you. [10]For everyone who asks receives; he who seeks finds; and to him who knocks, the door will be opened.

---

[54]This is seen most clearly when one notes the rabbinic attitude toward women. See A. Oelke, γυνή, *TDNT* (Grand Rapids: Eerdmans, 1964), 1:781-84.

[11]"Which of you fathers, if your son asks for a fish, will give him a snake instead? [12]Or if he asks for an egg, will give him a scorpion? [13]If you then, though you are evil, know how to give good gifts to your children, how much more will your Father in heaven give the Holy Spirit to those who ask him!"

Context

At this point in his Gospel, Luke inserted three accounts that deal with one of his favorite themes—prayer.[55] It is difficult to see a connection between this passage and what has preceded, despite Fitzmyer's claim that this material "fits well into this context of the Gospel."[56] The prayer Jesus taught his disciples (11:1-4) is followed by a parable (11:5-8) that serves as an encouragement to pray. This has been interpreted as teaching the contrast between the householder's unwillingness to assist his neighbor and God's great desire to assist his children. Others have interpreted the parable as teaching that persistence in prayer will be rewarded. Both emphases are found elsewhere in the Gospel. The former is clearly taught in 11:13 and the latter in the parable of the unjust judge (18:1-8). There is no need, however, to choose between these interpretations. Both meanings are contained in the parable and in the concluding sayings in 11:9-13, which are connected to 11:5-8 by the words "ask" and "give." The believer is encouraged to pray because of the Father's gracious character. If inhospitable neighbors and unjust judges will eventually grant the requests of those entreating them, how much more will a loving Heavenly Father. As a result the believers are to persist in prayer not in order to overcome God's reluctance but because they know God will hear and answer (11:9-13). When one wonders if it is really worthwhile to pray when it seems the prayer goes unanswered, when the believer walks through the valley of the shadow and heaven seems deaf, the believer nonetheless persists in prayer due to the character and the promises of the one they call "Abba"—Father.

Comments

11:1 One day Jesus was praying. The same wording is found in 9:18. Once again before a major event, such as teaching his disciples "the prayer," Jesus is shown praying. See Introduction 8 (7).

---

[55] Much discussion has taken place about which version, the Lukan or the Matthean one, more closely resembles Jesus' original words. The tendency in recent scholarship is to see as more authentic the form in Luke but the wording in Matthew. As in the Jewish prayer called the *Qaddish* has only two "Thou petitions." On the other hand Matthew's use of "give us" (an aorist tense) rather than "[continually] give us," "today" rather than "each day," "debts" rather than "sins," "have forgiven" rather than "forgive," and "debtors" rather than "everyone who sins against us" are generally viewed as more authentic.

[56] Fitzmyer, *Luke* 2:896.

Teach us to pray, just as John taught his disciples. The following prayer is to be considered a mark of identification. Even as the followers of John the Baptist had a distinctive prayer, so Jesus' disciples requested such a prayer. Far from being a prayer for all people everywhere, Luke understood the Lord's Prayer to be exclusively a believer's prayer, i.e., the "Disciples' Prayer." This was also the understanding of the early church. In practice an individual would first pray this prayer immediately after baptism and their first participation in the Lord's Supper. In the *Didache* the Lord's Prayer is taught after the section on Christian baptism. The prayer assumes that those who pray it have been born into God's family and may therefore call God, "Father" (cf. Rom 8:14-17 and esp. Gal 4:4-7).

11:2 When you pray. Literally *whenever you are praying.* Luke saw the Lord's Prayer as the pattern for all Christian prayer. All occasions of prayer should be approached in this manner. The "you" is plural, indicating that both Matthew and Luke understood this to be a corporate prayer (cf. *us, our, us, we, us, us*).

The Lord's Prayer is organized into three parts: the invocation, the "Thou" petitions, and the "we" petitions.

Father. It is not surprising to find that various Greek manuscripts read "Our Father in heaven" since scribes tended to make parallel accounts conform to the best known and most esteemed Synoptic Gospel, Matthew. As a title for God, "Father" is found only fifteen times in the entire OT, and in none of these instances is God being addressed in prayer. No doubt this in part was because "father" was a frequent title for God in ancient Near Eastern religions and therefore carried the sexual overtones of fertility religions. The title is used sixty-five times in the Synoptic Gospels and over one hundred times in John. The importance of this title is also witnessed to in that we still possess three instances in the NT of the original word "Abba" (Mark 14:36; Rom 8:15-16; Gal 4:6). The presence of the Aramaic word, in letters written in Greek to the Roman and Galatian Christians, indicates that Jesus' use of this title and the early repetition of the Lord's Prayer were so meaningful that the Gentile church continued to call God "Abba" even though it was a foreign word. In all the more than 165 examples found in the Gospels, Jesus is always engaged in teaching the disciples, except in Matt 23:9, where Jesus is teaching both the disciples and the multitudes. The use of this title as an address for God was thus reserved by Jesus exclusively for himself and for his followers. Far from being a title that all people may use for God, the Gospels teach that only the believer has the right and privilege to address God in this manner.

It was once popular to say that "Abba" or "Father" was the equivalent of "Daddy." The reason for this is that small children called their father by this term. In the Jewish Talmud (*Sanh.* 70b) we read, "An infant cannot say 'father' [Abba] and 'mother' until it has tasted wheat [i.e., until it is weaned]." However, adults also called their fathers "Abba," which indicates that "Daddy" is a less appropriate translation of "Abba" than "Father." See comments on 10:21. This does not, however, diminish the importance of the fact that through his ministry Jesus has enabled those who believe in him to call God their "Father." Nowhere, however, did Jesus refer to God as *"our* Father." Jesus' relationship with God was unique (10:21-23), as is most clearly seen in John 20:17. Matthew 6:9 is no exception because Jesus was teaching the disciples to say "Our Father" when they prayed.

Hallowed be your name. The first petition asks God to cause his name to be hallowed.[57] The "name" refers to God's reputation and thus to his honor. For God's name to be "hallowed" or glorified, God must receive the honor and praise he deserves. The prayer does not seek a continual reverencing of God and his name or in the next petition a continual coming of God's kingdom. It does not refer to a gradual or evolutionary improvement but rather looks for the day when God will once and for all receive the honor due him when the kingdom will be consummated. Although the believer continually prays "hallowed by your name," the fulfillment of the prayer involves that event in which history as we know it will come to an end and God's name will be hallowed in the consummated kingdom. Matthew 6:10 points out that the scene is "on earth," not in the human heart, and that its extent is "as . . . in heaven."

The substance of this prayer is found elsewhere as *"Maranatha"* (1 Cor 16:22, NEB) or "Come, Lord Jesus" (Rev 22:20). This petition and the next look longingly far beyond anything that can take place in the life of an individual, church, denomination, or even in the church universal to that great day when God will receive on earth the same honor he receives in heaven. The *Qaddish*, a Jewish prayer that probably dates before A.D. 70 due to its failure to request Jerusalem's rebuilding, confirms this interpretation. The *Qaddish*, prayed at the end of the synagogue service, contains the following petitions: "Exalted and hallowed be his great name in the world which he created according to his will. May he rule his kingdom in your lifetime and in your days and in the lifetime of the whole house of Israel, speedily and soon." Here the two similar petitions in the same order and dating from the same time are clearly eschatological in nature.

Your kingdom come. For Jesus' and Luke's understanding of God's kingdom, see comments on 4:43. Although the kingdom has already come in Jesus' ministry (11:20), its final consummation awaits the future. It is for this final form of the kingdom that the believer longs and prays (cf. Rom 8:23). Like the preceding one, this verb is a divine passive. These two petitions will not be fulfilled by human effort but by God. One day God will hallow his name and bring about his kingdom. The focus is not on the believer in this prayer but on God. Many wonderful things will take place for the believer at the parousia, and focusing on these wonders is often appropriate (1 Thess 4:13-18); the desire of the church in this prayer, however, is for God to receive the glory that is due him (cf. Phil 2:10-11). The anthropomorphic dimension is pushed aside, and the theocentric dimension is brought to the fore.

These two petitions form an example of synonymous parallelism in that the same basic prayer is being repeated in rhythmic balance.

11:3 The third part of the prayer, the "we petitions," begins here.

Give us this day our daily bread. There is great confusion about what the word "daily" (*epiousion*) means, for it is found only three times in all of Greek literature: here, in the Matthean parallel, and in the *Didache's* version of the Lord's Prayer. (Another instance was allegedly found in a fifth-century papyrus, but that papyrus is now lost.) Even the early church fathers remarked about the obscurity of this word. The following meanings have been suggested: (1) bread

---

[57] Cf. John 12:28; 2 Sam 6:2; Jer 7:11; Amos 9:12; Ezek 36:22-28.

that is essential for existence; (2) bread of the coming day, i.e., tomorrow's bread (the bread of the Great Tomorrow, i.e., the eschatological bread of the coming messianic banquet [as in Luke 14:15; 22:30] or the bread we need to eat tomorrow for nourishment); or (3) bread for the present day. Luke made clear that it could not mean the bread of the messianic age because the tense of the verb (an iterative present) means "to continually give us" and because "this day" means "each day." Luke may have tried to help his readers understand "daily" by adding "each day." It is impossible to be certain what this petition means in the parallel in Matthew, but in Luke it is clear that the petition asks for God to provide his church with the bread necessary for living. "Bread" is an example of synecdoche, in which a part (bread) represents the whole (food). Compare 7:33; John 13:18 (Ps 41:9); 2 Thess 3:8 ("food" is literally "bread"). It is a request for the basic necessities of life, not for luxuries.

11:4 Forgive us our sins. The Matthean parallel has a more rhythmic "Forgive us our debts." "Debt" was a well-known metaphor among Jews for sin, but since this religious sense may not have been understood by Gentiles, Luke used the actuality ("sins") rather than the metaphor ("debts").[58] The prayer assumes the regular need for confession of sin, even as 1 John 1:9 does. The issue is not one of entrance into God's people, i.e., salvation, but the regular cleansing from sin that each believer needs. The scene is not a courtroom where the final judgment is being pronounced (as in Rom 8:31-34) but a family setting in which a son or daughter confesses his or her sins (Luke 11:2), not to become or to remain part of the family but in order that nothing should spoil the relationship.

For. There is a condition attached, or more accurately an attitude required, for receiving divine forgiveness. The believer is forgiven not "because" of forgiving others but because of God's grace in Christ. Humanity is forgiven by the death of Christ (22:20; Acts 20:28) for the lost (Luke 19:10), but the appropriation of that forgiveness is through faith. That faith, however, is not merely intellectual assent to certain doctrines but a combination of faith, repentance, confession, baptism, following Jesus, and as our text states, the willingness to forgive others. The hand that reaches out to God for forgiveness cannot withhold forgiveness to others (cf. Matt 6:14-15; 18:23-35; Mark 11:25).

We also forgive everyone. The present tense of this verb indicates that the believer is always to be ready and willing to forgive others.

Who sins against us. Literally *indebted to us*. Here it becomes evident that Luke used "sins" and "debts" interchangeably.

Lead us not into temptation. Compare 22:40 and especially 22:46. "Temptation" should not be interpreted as a reference to the Great Temptation (or tribulation) of the end time but to the ordinary temptations that every believer encounters in life. This is made clear by the lack of the article, i.e., "into temptation," not "into *the* temptation." The meaning of this phrase has been debated from earliest times. On several occasions in the OT, God put his people to a test,[59] and the term "temptation" is used elsewhere in the NT to refer to a trial that is expected to have a positive outcome (Jas 1:12; 1 Pet 4:12-13; Rev 2:10). What

---

[58] He still retained the metaphor "debt" in Luke 7:41-43; 13:4.

[59] Exod 16:4; 20:20; Deut 8:2,16; 13:3; 33:8; Judg 2:22.

Luke meant by temptation here, however, is something that might lead an unwary believer to sin and apostasy: "Do not allow us to enter into temptation that could destroy us" or perhaps, "Keep us from yielding to temptation." It is also better to see the verb not as causative ("Do not cause us to enter into temptation") but as permissive ("Do not permit us to enter into temptation").

11:5 Suppose one of you. Elsewhere the NIV translates this phrase "which of you."[60] In that case we have a rhetorical question Jesus himself answered.[61]

Three loaves. There is no allegorical significance in the number; it was simply the amount needed for a meal.

Bread. This ties the following parable neatly to the first "We petition" of the Lord's Prayer (11:3).

11:6 This verse gives the reason for the request.

11:7 Don't bother me. The neighbor did not return the salutation "Friend" (11:5), indicating his aggravation.

My children are with me in bed. All the family was sleeping (on mats) in the same room, and an attempt to open the bolted door would have awakened the whole family.[62]

11:8 Because of the man's boldness. This refers to the petitioner's refusal to give up until his neighbor met his need.[63] The term *anaideian* is best translated "persistence." In 18:1-8 the emphasis is also on persistence, and a dishonorable character also contrasts with God. As Sabourin observes, "Luke ... may be responsible for a shift in emphasis, not a change in meaning."[64]

11:9 The third section of this passage serves as an encouragement to continue in prayer.

Ask. "Ask" is commonly used for prayer.[65] This is best understood not as an imperative of command ("You must ask in order to receive") but as an imperative of condition ("If you ask, you will indeed receive"; cf. 6:37-38), for the saying is an invitation to prayer, not an order to do so.

Seek. "Seek" is frequently used to describe seeking after/for God (Deut 4:29; Isa 55:6; 65:1). To "seek God's face" is to pray.[66]

Knock. Compare *Megilla* 12b, which speaks of the one praying as having "knocked at the gates of mercy and [finding that] they were opened to him."

This verse is an example of synonymous parallelism, in which the same essential thought is repeated rhythmically. It is also an example of the divine passive ("it will be given to you" means *God will give it to you*; "it will be opened to you"

---

[60] The same introduction is found in 11:11; 12:25; 14:28; 15:4; 17:7; cf. 14:5.

[61] For other examples of rhetorical questions answered by Jesus, cf. 15:7,10; 16:9; 18:8,14.

[62] So J. Jeremias, *The Parables of Jesus* (New York: Scribner's, 1963), 157; but contrast M. D. Goulder, *Luke: A New Paradigm* (Sheffield: JSOT, 1989), 499.

[63] It is preferable to translate the two uses of αὐτοῦ (his) as referring to the same person, the petitioner. One can also make the second αὐτοῦ refer to the neighbor and translate this clause "because of his [the neighbor's] ἀναίδειαν, i.e., his desire not to be shamed"; but this is a less likely interpretation.

[64] L. Sabourin, *The Gospel according to St. Luke* (Bombay: St Paul, 1984), 241.

[65] Matt 18:19; Mark 11:24; John 11:22; Eph 3:20; Jas 1:5-6; 4:3.

[66] See 2 Sam 21:1; Pss 24:6; 27:8; Hos 5:15; cf. Acts 17:27; Jer 29:13.

means *God will open it to you*) and of Jesus' use of exaggeration,[67] for not all prayers are answered (Jas 4:3). Jesus assumed that such prayer would be in accordance with God's will and would include an implied "yet not my will, but yours be done" (Luke 22:42). To qualify the saying, however, would displace the focus from God's gracious response to believers' prayers to the qualifications, which would defeat Jesus' purpose. See comments on 6:41.

11:10 The corresponding promise is also in the form of synonymous parallelism.

11:11-12 The following is an example of what the rabbis called a *Qal waḥomer* argument. This is also called an *a fortiori* or *a minori ad maius* argument, which reasons from the "lesser" to the "greater." Here it is based on the assumption that if *A* (11:11-12) is true, how much more must *B* (11:13) be true. The argument begins with the fact that even sinful fathers answer their children's requests, providing them with basic needs such as food (fish/eggs). If this is true of sinful parents, how much more certain can the believer be that their gracious and loving Heavenly Father will answer the asking, seeking, and knocking described in 11:9.

Fish . . . snake. These are similar in appearance, as are the egg-scorpion, for a scorpion with its claws and tail rolled up resembles an egg. For the combination of snake and scorpion, see comments on 10:19.

11:13 If you then, though you are evil. Human sinfulness was a given among Jesus' audience (11:29; 13:1-5) in light of Gen 3 (cf. 2 Esdr 7:48-56).

Will give the Holy Spirit. The parallel in Matt 7:11 ("good gifts") probably is closer to Jesus' exact words, but Luke's theological emphasis is revealed here. The good gift par excellence that God can give his children was for Luke clearly the Holy Spirit, who brings with him a partial realization of God's kingdom (Luke 11:2; cf. Acts 2:17). For this Lukan emphasis see Introduction 8 (3). Luke's readers, living in the post-Pentecost situation, would readily have understood the gift of the Spirit. For an unbeliever it would have involved the Spirit's coming in the experience of salvation (Acts 2:38; 11:15-18), and for Christians it would involve experiences such as are found in Acts 4:8-13,31; 6:3-5,8-10; 7:54-60.

The Lukan Message

The importance of prayer in this passage is self-evident, for it is entirely dedicated to this theme. That this is also a Lukan theme is evident. See Introduction 8 (7). In this passage Luke shared with Theophilus *the* prayer of the believing community, which Jesus gave both as a pattern for prayer and as a mark of identification. Within this prayer (and also in the rest of the account) two additional Lukan theological emphases are manifest. One involves the church's eschatological hope. For Luke, God's kingdom was already realized both in Jesus' coming (Luke 11:20; 16:16; 17:20-21) and in the Spirit's presence (11:13; 24:49; Acts 1:8; 2:1f.). Yet as the "Thou petitions" reveal, the church also longs for the consumma-

---

[67] For additional examples of exaggeration, cf. 6:30,36; 10:19; 14:26; 16:17; 18:25. For further discussion of Jesus' use of this literary form, see R. H. Stein, *Difficult Passages in the New Testament* (Grand Rapids: Baker, 1990), 135-220.

tion of the kingdom, for only then will the divine plan be completed. See Introduction 7 (3). Within this short passage Luke acknowledged the present reality of God's kingdom while at the same time recognizing that a not-yet dimension still remains. Having tasted of the "already now," the believing community prays fervently for God's name to be hallowed and his kingdom to come. When this desire is no longer present in the heart of the believing community, when the church no longer prays *Maranatha*, then it no longer loves God with all its heart, soul, strength, and mind.

This passages also emphasizes the need for forgiveness (see comments on 1:77; 3:3). While this is most often associated with admission into God's kingdom,[68] here forgiveness is asked by those who are already forgiven. The privilege of calling God Father does not eliminate the need for continual forgiveness. In the life of obedience, as the believer follows after God, confession of sin plays an important role. The repetition of the Lord's Prayer is a continual "day of atonement" for the believer, where sins committed in the life of faith are removed and the Father-child relationship is restored (cf. 1 John 1:9).

(9) The Beelzebub Controversy (11:14-23)

[14]Jesus was driving out a demon that was mute. When the demon left, the man who had been mute spoke, and the crowd was amazed. [15]But some of them said, "By Beelzebub, the prince of demons, he is driving out demons." [16]Others tested him by asking for a sign from heaven.

[17]Jesus knew their thoughts and said to them: "Any kingdom divided against itself will be ruined, and a house divided against itself will fall. [18]If Satan is divided against himself, how can his kingdom stand? I say this because you claim that I drive out demons by Beelzebub. [19]Now if I drive out demons by Beelzebub, by whom do your followers drive them out? So then, they will be your judges. [20]But if I drive out demons by the finger of God, then the kingdom of God has come to you.

[21]"When a strong man, fully armed, guards his own house, his possessions are safe. [22]But when someone stronger attacks and overpowers him, he takes away the armor in which the man trusted and divides up the spoils.

[23]"He who is not with me is against me, and he who does not gather with me, scatters.

Context

The preceding passage, which deals with instructions to the disciples on prayer, gives no indication that other people were present. This pericope does not therefore follow neatly upon the preceding material.[69] This

---

[68]Luke 1:77; 3:3; 5:20; 24:47; Acts 2:38; 5:31.

[69]The exact relationship between this account and the parallels in Mark 3:22-27; Matt 12:22-30; and 9:32-34 is much debated. It is unlikely, however, that Luke depended on Matthew; for in 11:20 he would have had to change Matt 12:28, "by the Spirit of God," to "by

is also true with regard to its content, for there is an abrupt change in theme. It is uncertain whether the key uniting the following pericopes is one of controversy, extending from 11:14-36[70] or 11:14-54,[71] or whether the uniting theme is the desire for signs from heaven and extends from 11:14-32.[72]

In this pericope Jesus defended himself against the attacks of opponents who accused him of working exorcisms and miracles in collusion with Satan. Jesus advanced two arguments in his defense. The first consists of two metaphors, one of a kingdom divided against itself and the other a divided household. Together they show how absurd it is to argue that Jesus was casting out demons by the power of the prince of demons, for this would cause Satan's kingdom to self-destruct. Second, he used an *ad hominem* argument, which shows that the same charge also could have been leveled against the Pharisees. In contrast with the exorcisms performed by the Pharisees and their disciples, Jesus argued that his exorcisms (11:20) revealed that the kingdom of God, whose coming they prayed for (see comments on 11:2), was here already and was attested to by Jesus' liberation of Satan's captives (11:21-22). There is a similar pattern of Jesus' acting, followed by an attack on Jesus, and Jesus' ensuing defense in 7:36-50; 13:10-17; 15:1-32; cf. also Acts 11:1-17.

Comments

11:14   Jesus was driving out a demon. The transition from the preceding account is abrupt. The tense of the verb (an imperfect periphrastic) throws us immediately into the present story.

Demon. The demon is distinguished from the chief demon, Beelzebub, which is another name for Satan (Luke 11:18).

That was mute. This particular demon was mute, i.e., it caused "muteness" (cf. Matt 9:33, but in 12:22 the demon also caused blindness).

The man who had been mute spoke. This was proof of the exorcism.

And the crowd was amazed. See comments on 2:18; 5:26. The miracle was acknowledged.

11:15   Some of them said. Luke left Jesus' opponents unnamed, but in Matt 12:24 they are Pharisees, and in Mark 3:22 they are teachers of the law.

Beelzebub. The majority of Greek witnesses reads *Beelzeboul.* "Beelzebub" in the KJV tradition comes from the Latin and Syriac translations. For a similar

---

the finger of God" (11:20), which is improbable in light of his strong emphasis on the Spirit. See Introduction 8 (3) and cf. 11:13 with Matt 7:11. (The omission of the reference to the Spirit in Luke 21:15 is understandable due to its having been included in 12:12, and his omission in 20:42 may be due to discomfort with Mark's "in/by the Holy Spirit" and a preference for "in the Book of Psalms"; Acts 1:20; cf. also 7:42.) Luke probably was dependent on Q material.

[70] So Tannehill, *Narrative Unity of Luke-Acts*, 149.
[71] So Marshall, *Luke*, 470.
[72] So Fitzmyer, *Luke* 2:917.

charge in which Jesus' miraculous powers were acknowledged but attributed to sorcery, cf. *Sanhedrin* 43a.

11:16 Others tested him by asking for a more spectacular sign from heaven. Only Luke referred to the temptation/test for a sign. Some opponents did not see the exorcism as sufficient evidence. They wanted a clearer sign, i.e., a sign from heaven. With this statement Luke tied this pericope to Luke 11:29-32 by foreshadowing it. Luke wanted his readers to understand that to ask for signs, both in Jesus' day and possibly their own (cf. 1 Cor 1:22), was to tempt the Lord (Luke 4:12). There was sufficient proof for faith in the Scriptures (cf. 16:31).

11:17 Jesus knew their thoughts. See comments on 6:8.

The first of the next two analogies portrays a war. In the parallel accounts (Mark 3:25; Matt 12:25) the second analogy involves strife within the family, i.e., a "house" (cf. Luke 10:5; 19:9; Acts 16:15,31). Here, however, the meaning is less certain and may refer to one household attacking another at a time of civil strife.[73] Most translations (NIV, RSV, NEB, NASB) imply division and strife within a family.

11:18 This verse applies these two analogies. That Satan's kingdom would be divided against itself because Jesus, as a servant of the prince of demons, was undermining Satan's work by liberating the demon possessed makes no sense. It is illogical.

11:19 This verse reveals the inconsistency of his opponents' argument. Why should only Jesus' exorcisms be attributed to Beelzebub?

Your followers. "Followers" is literally *sons* but is used in the sense of disciples.

So then . . . your judges. This points up the culpability of the opponents' arguments, for they attributed God's work to Satan (cf. 12:10; Mark 3:28-30).

11:20 Another explanation is therefore necessary. The most obvious one is that Jesus has been sent from God and that the destruction of Satan's authority as ruler of this world (cf. John 12:31; 14:30; 16:11; Eph 2:2) means that God's kingdom has now come (Luke 11:20).

Finger of God. "Finger" is more authentic than Matthew's "Spirit of God" (Matt 12:28; cf. also Exod 8:19; 31:18; Deut 9:10). Both refer to God's power.

The kingdom of God has come. The tense of the verb (an ingressive aorist) should be taken at face value, i.e., as something that has already taken place. God's kingdom has arrived in Jesus' coming. The verb itself means to "arrive" as in Rom 9:31; 2 Cor 10:14; Phil 3:16; 1 Thess 2:16. See Introduction 8 (2). This argument creates a difficulty. If Jewish exorcists were casting out demons by God's power (cf. Luke 9:49; Mark 9:38; Acts 19:13-14; Josephus, *Antiquities* 8.2.5 [8.42-49]), how did Jesus' doing so indicate that God's kingdom has come? Two things may be said in response. First, the degree of Jesus' authority and the number of his exorcisms was notably greater and indicated that something unusual was indeed taking place. Second, the exorcisms Jesus performed must be understood in light of his overall teachings and claims. His actions confirm his message concerning the kingdom's arrival.

11:21 Another analogy involving battle is given.

---

[73] Marshall, *Luke*, 474.

11:22   Someone stronger.   This refers not to God but to Jesus, who in Luke 3:16 is referred to as "one more powerful." The terms "someone stronger" and "one more powerful" translate the same Greek term (cf. *T. Levi* 18:12). Luke may have intended for his readers to interpret Luke 11:21-22 in light of 10:18.

11:23   This is an example of synonymous parallelism, which links metaphors of fighting and farming. For the combination of gathering-scattering, see Matt 25:24-26; John 11:52. At first this verse seems to conflict with Luke 9:50, but both are true. One is either pro-Jesus or con-Jesus, for or against, yes or no, heaven bound or hell bound, righteous or unrighteous, gatherers or scatterers. This verse applies the truth of the pericope both to Jesus' listeners and to Luke's readers. Neutrality with respect to Jesus is impossible.

The Lukan Message

This text contains important Christological and eschatological principles. The first involves Jesus' greatness. He is the "more powerful one" of whom John the Baptist spoke (3:16), for he is stronger than Satan himself (11:22; cf. also 4:1-13). He is truly the Lord, the One for whom Israel had waited and longed. The master of nature (8:22-25), disease, and death (8:40-56) is also master of demons (8:26-39), even of the prince of demons. He is therefore truly able to do immeasurably more than all Theophilus and Luke's other readers could ask or imagine (Eph 3:20).

Through this account Theophilus had also been made aware that God's kingdom had already come and that the ruler of this age had been vanquished. Luke clearly teaches a truly realized eschatology in this passage. Although God's kingdom still has a future dimension that is to be prayed for (Luke 11:2), it is in part already realized. In this passage Satan's defeat is the aspect of the kingdom already realized. In other passages the fulfillment of the Scriptures or the coming of the Spirit may be emphasized. God's kingdom has come in all of these. See Introduction 8 (2).

(10)   The Return of the Unclean Spirit and True Blessedness (11:24-28)

[24]"When an evil spirit comes out of a man, it goes through arid places seeking rest and does not find it. Then it says, 'I will return to the house I left.' [25]When it arrives, it finds the house swept clean and put in order. [26]Then it goes and takes seven other spirits more wicked than itself, and they go in and live there. And the final condition of that man is worse than the first."

[27]As Jesus was saying these things, a woman in the crowd called out, "Blessed is the mother who gave you birth and nursed you."

[28]He replied, "Blessed rather are those who hear the word of God and obey it."

Context

Attached to the exhortation in 11:23 is another involving the return of the unclean spirit. This is also associated with the Beelzebub account in

Matt 12:43-45 and is almost identical in form, but in Matthew the sign of Jonah precedes it (Matt 12:38-42), whereas in Luke it follows (Luke 11:29-32). It is clear that in the pre-Lukan tradition these three accounts were associated. The major difference between the two accounts is that Matthew concluded with "That is how it will be with this wicked generation" (Matt 12:45), while Luke added in 11:27-28 an incident found in GT 79 but not in Matthew or Mark. Its connection to Luke 11:24-26 is unclear. It may serve as a positive contrast to the warning found in 11:26 (cf. 8:19-21).

Comments

11:24 Evil spirit. "Evil spirit" is a synonym for "demon" (11:14).

It goes through arid places seeking rest. The desert was often thought to be inhabited by demons (8:29; Lev 16:10; Isa 34:13-14).

11:25 Swept clean. The "house" has been made clean through Jesus' exorcism and the accompanying forgiveness of sins.

11:26 Seven other spirits. "Seven" demons represent a totality of evil (cf. 8:2).

Final condition . . . worse than the first. Compare 2 Pet 2:20; Heb 6:4-8; 10:26-27; John 5:14.

11:27 Blessed. See comments on 6:20.

Is the mother. Literally *the womb*, which is an idiomatic expression (a synecdoche) for "your mother" (cf. Gen 49:25). Compare "Blessed is my mother among those that bear, and praised among women is she that bore me" (2 Baruch 54:10).

11:28 Blessed rather. The meaning of the Greek term "rather" (*menoun*) is unclear. It is used only four times in the NT, but it has three possible meanings: (1) adversative—"on the contrary," or "no, but rather," as in Rom 9:20; 10:18. This would repudiate the blessing of Jesus' mother by the woman in the crowd. (2) Affirmative—"indeed," as in Phil 3:8. This would agree with the woman's blessing and identify Jesus' mother as an example of one who hears God's word and obeys it. (3) Corrective—"yes, but rather." This would show that although the blessing is correct, there is a greater blessing available to those who believe. Usually if Luke wanted to express the adversative meaning (1), he used *ouchi* and *legō hymin* (cf. Luke 12:51; 13:3,5), and if he wanted to express the affirmative meaning (2), he used *nai* (cf. 7:26; 10:21; 11:51; 12:5). The third meaning is therefore more likely. An expanded translation of this sentence would read: "What you have said is true as far as it goes. But Mary's blessedness does not consist simply in her relationship with me, but in the fact that she heard the word of God and kept it, which is where true blessedness lies."[74]

Those who hear the word of God and obey it. Compare 6:47; 8:15,21. This explains what it means to gather with Jesus (11:23) and stands in contrast to the failure to persevere in faith illustrated in 11:24-26.

---

[74]M. E. Thrall, *Greek Particles in the New Testament* (Grand Rapids: Eerdmans, 1962), 35.

The Lukan Message

The first saying (11:24-26) warns against complacency about God's redemptive work. The experience of salvation, which brings cleansing and forgiveness, creates a vacuum that must be filled. The Christian must fill the void created by the expulsion of the demonic, worldliness, or immorality lest these evils be replaced by hypocrisy, self-righteousness, pride, or relapse, which would be worse still. Christian perseverance (8:15) entails devotion to God's word (11:28), to prayer, and to the breaking of bread (Acts 2:42). Otherwise, like the nine lepers, they may experience healing but not salvation (Luke 17:11-19). Some have argued that this parable is aimed at Jewish exorcists, who by failing to teach Jesus' message left those who had been exorcised open to worse trouble.[75] Luke left open the question of who performed the exorcisms, whether Jewish exorcists (11:19) or Jesus. His readers are expected to apply the teaching to their own situation, i.e., to their own need to follow their salvation in Christ with obedience to God's word (11:28).

The second saying (11:27-28) is a parallel to 8:19-21, where a reference to Jesus' mother and brothers occasions a similar teaching that physical relationship is less important than hearing and obeying God's word. Luke did not write this saying in response to a later veneration of Mary. For him Mary was blessed among women (1:42,45). Yet she was blessed not because she bore the Son of God but because she believed God's word (1:45; 11:28). She was blessed just as all who hear and keep God's word are blessed (11:28; 8:21).

(11) The Sign of Jonah (11:29-32)

[29]As the crowds increased, Jesus said, "This is a wicked generation. It asks for a miraculous sign, but none will be given it except the sign of Jonah. [30]For as Jonah was a sign to the Ninevites, so also will the Son of Man be to this generation. [31]The Queen of the South will rise at the judgment with the men of this generation and condemn them; for she came from the ends of the earth to listen to Solomon's wisdom, and now one greater than Solomon is here. [32]The men of Nineveh will stand up at the judgment with this generation and condemn it; for they repented at the preaching of Jonah, and now one greater than Jonah is here.

Context

At this point Luke answered the request for a sign in 11:16 by linking it to the tradition concerning the present generation's desire for a sign (11:29).[76]

---

[75] So Marshall, *Luke*, 479.

[76] It comes from the Q material and, as the Matthean parallel reveals, was already connected to the material found in Luke 11:14-28.

There are parallels in Mark 8:11-12 and Matt 12:39; 16:1, and the reference to the sign of Jonah (Luke 11:30-32) also appears in Matt 12:40-42. This passage provides a negative example of Luke 11:28, for "this evil generation" does not hear and heed Jesus' words.

Comments
11:29 As the crowds increased. This picks up the crowd mentioned in 11:14.[77]
Jesus said. The answer to 11:16 is now forthcoming.
This is a wicked generation. "This generation" was characterized as basically evil, in dire need of repentance.[78] That it was an evil generation is revealed partly by its demand for a sign (11:16).
It asks for a miraculous sign. Literally *seeks a sign*. What was demanded was divine authentication of Jesus' message and work.
But none will be given. Jesus' opponents, having dismissed the "sign" of his healings and exorcisms, wanted something more spectacular, but Jesus rejected this approach at the very beginning of his ministry as Satanic in nature (4:9-12). Would even such a sign, however, lead to faith? Not according to 16:31 (cf. John 12:9-11).
Except the sign of Jonah. This has been interpreted as (1) the preaching of Jonah to the Ninevites and their subsequent repentance.[79] But how could Jesus' *present* preaching have been interpreted as a *future* sign or, indeed, as a sign at all since a "sign" in the present context refers to a miracle (11:16,29,30); (2) the parousia, which would come too late to confirm Jesus' person and work to this generation; and (3) the miracle of Jonah's being swallowed by a fish and later being spit out. Matthew 12:40 clearly interprets it as the latter. Although Jonah's deliverance was not witnessed by the Ninevites, Luke's readers probably would associate Jesus' resurrection with Jonah's rescue from his fishy grave, for unlike his preaching that was truly a miraculous sign.[80] The third interpretation also agrees better with the future tense of the verb "will be given" and fits well Luke 16:30-31.
11:30 As Jonah was a sign . . . so also will the Son of Man. Even as Jonah's experience was a sign, so the resurrection of the Son of Man would be a sign, and the core of the early church's preaching would be Jesus' death *and resurrection* (Acts 1:22; 2:31; 3:15; 4:33; 5:30-32).
11:31 The Queen of the South. That is, the Queen of Sheba (1 Kgs 10:1-13; 2 Chr 9:1-12).
Will rise. This is a reference to the general resurrection of the dead at the final judgment. Jesus (and Luke) clearly sided with the Pharisees against the Sadducees on this important doctrine (Luke 20:27-40; Acts 23:6-10).
At the judgment. This refers to *the* judgment (note the article), i.e., the final judgment, which was associated with the resurrection of the dead (Rev 20:11-15).
The men of this generation. "Men" is generic for "people" (cf. NRSV).

[77]Cf. Luke 4:42; 5:1; 6:17; 8:4; 9:37; 12:1; 14:25; 18:36.
[78]Cf. Luke 7:31; 9:41; 11:50-51; 17:25; cf. also 21:32.
[79]R. A. Edwards, *The Sign of Jonah in the Theology of the Evangelists and Q*, SBT (Naperville: Allenson, 1971), 89-95; Fitzmyer, *Luke*, 2:933.
[80]D. Gooding, *According to Luke* (Grand Rapids: Eerdmans, 1987), 227-28.

She came from the ends of the earth. This part of the tradition no doubt would have been understood by Luke and Theophilus as an example of Gentile participation in the OT salvation. The same would be true of the following reference to the Ninevites, for they too were Gentiles whom God had included in the divine salvation.

To listen to Solomon's wisdom. Compare 1 Kgs 10:1-4,7.

One greater than Solomon is here. Literally *something greater than Solomon.* The use of "something" instead of "someone" indicates that the comparison was more than just between Solomon and Jesus but between Solomon and his wisdom and Jesus and his wisdom. Jesus is the ultimate "wise man," and his wisdom has no equal.

11:32 The men of Nineveh will stand up. As wicked as the Ninevites were, they nevertheless were qualified to judge this generation, for they repented when Jonah preached. This generation, however, refused to repent, even though it was Jonah's Lord who was preaching. Compare Luke 10:12-15 for a similar comparison.

Now one greater than Jonah is here. Literally *something greater than Jonah.* See comments on 11:31. Jesus is not only the ultimate "prophet" but the Lord of the prophets.

The Lukan Message

Luke explained to Theophilus and his readers that the desire for a sign, which was prevalent among the Jews (23:8; John 2:18; 4:48; 1 Cor 1:22), was actually a rejection of God's revelation in Christ. Signs do not produce faith (Luke 16:31). If one's heart is not open to the truth, signs may be interpreted as demonic (11:15). Even the greatest sign, the resurrection, will not produce faith in an unwilling heart. This is powerfully demonstrated in John 11:1–12:11 (esp. 12:9-11). Luke's readers are to understand that the Scriptures and Luke's orderly account of Jesus' life, death, resurrection, and ascension are sufficient for faith. Read in the fellowship of the believing community, this is all that is necessary for the heart that is warm toward God. (See the discussion of 24:30-32.)

A second emphasis of this account centers around the "greater" character of Jesus. Proclaimed by John the Baptist as the "one more powerful" (3:16), shown to be "someone stronger" than Satan (11:22), Jesus is now presented as greater/wiser than the wisest man of all, Solomon (11:31), and as a greater prophet than Jonah (11:32). Although this evil generation was unable to recognize him, the Queen of Sheba and the Ninevites would have. Another motif is also present although not emphasized: the certainty of a future judgment when the resurrection of both just and unjust takes place (cf. 11:32; Acts 24:15).

(12) Sayings about Light (11:33-36)

[33] "No one lights a lamp and puts it in a place where it will be hidden, or under a bowl. Instead he puts it on its stand, so that those who come in may see

the light. [34]Your eye is the lamp of your body. When your eyes are good, your whole body also is full of light. But when they are bad, your body also is full of darkness. [35]See to it, then, that the light within you is not darkness. [36]Therefore, if your whole body is full of light, and no part of it dark, it will be completely lighted, as when the light of a lamp shines on you."

Context

It is difficult to relate these verses to the preceding ones. Luke may have been using them to explain that if one's spiritual sight is not damaged there is no need for a spectacular sign from heaven,[81] or perhaps Luke's source had already connected them, and he was simply following it. The sayings are linked by the word "light" and function essentially as three independent proverbs. The Matthean parallels to the first two (Luke 11:33-35) are quite similar in wording and order (Matt 5:15; 6:22-23), but the third (Luke 11:36) is found only in Luke. The first saying likens Jesus' ministry to light (cf. 2:32; 8:16), which is not to be hidden but made available to all (cf. Isa 48:6). The light of Jesus himself, which shines for all to see, makes any other sign pale by comparison. The second proverb is a comment on the recipients of the light. Where in Luke 11:33 the lamp is a metaphor for Jesus, who shines on those who accept him, here it becomes a metaphor for one's reaction to Jesus. How one responds to Jesus and his ministry determines one's ultimate spiritual condition. Those who react to Jesus' works and words as those in 11:15 do will remain in darkness. In contrast the third proverb points out that accepting Jesus as the Christ, the Son of God, illuminates one's understanding and thus the whole of life.

Comments

11:33   In a place where it will be hidden.   This is a lengthy but correct way of translating the Greek term *kryptēn*.

Or under a bowl.   There is a textual problem here. Two important papyri ($\mathfrak{P}^{45}$, $\mathfrak{P}^{75}$) lack this expression. The meaning of the proverb, however, is not greatly affected. Its inclusion simply adds a second example of hiding a lamp.

Those who come in.   The same expression appears in 8:16, and a similar one in 18:24, to describe entrance into God's kingdom.

May see the light.   This analogy likens Jesus' preaching to the provision of light in order that people might see how to become part of God's kingdom. See comments on 8:16.

11:34   Your eye.   This refers to one's spiritual vision or openness to God's word, i.e., Jesus' teaching.

Of your body.   This encompasses the whole person (cf. Rom 12:1; Eph 5:28; Phil 1:20).

---

[81] Talbert, *Reading Luke*, 139.

When your eyes are good. "Good" means *morally healthy*.
When they are bad. "Bad" is literally *evil* or *wicked*. The same word is used in "wicked generation" (11:29).
Your body also is full of darkness. Even as the whole person becomes filled with light upon acceptance of Jesus and his teaching, so does darkness fall upon those who reject him.

11:35 This oxymoron or paradox is intensified by the imperative "see to it." Make sure that what directs your thoughts/life is in fact the true light.

11:36 Although the general sense of this verse is clear, the exact meaning is not. It may mean, "If you are truly receptive to Christ (v. 36a) and there is no hardness of heart in you toward him and his message (v. 36b), then you will truly shine with the light of Christ and his gospel (v. 36c); just like when a shining light illuminates you with its rays, so will Christ illumine you" (v. 36d).

The Lukan Message

Jesus and his words were light to Theophilus and the other readers of this Gospel, and Luke taught that they must respond with "good eyes," i.e., with true faith and obedience. It was their responsibility to rid themselves of any possible obstruction and to receive the word with a noble and good heart. Only thus could they persevere and produce fruit (8:15). Then their light, a reflection of the light of their Lord, would shine out to others. Compare how Matt 5:15-16 makes this thought clearer and more explicit.

(13) A Denunciation of the Pharisees and Scribes (11:37-54)

[37]When Jesus had finished speaking, a Pharisee invited him to eat with him; so he went in and reclined at the table. [38]But the Pharisee, noticing that Jesus did not first wash before the meal, was surprised.

[39]Then the Lord said to him, "Now then, you Pharisees clean the outside of the cup and dish, but inside you are full of greed and wickedness. [40]You foolish people! Did not the one who made the outside make the inside also? [41]But give what is inside [the dish] to the poor, and everything will be clean for you.

[42]"Woe to you Pharisees, because you give God a tenth of your mint, rue and all other kinds of garden herbs, but you neglect justice and the love of God. You should have practiced the latter without leaving the former undone.

[43]"Woe to you Pharisees, because you love the most important seats in the synagogues and greetings in the marketplaces.

[44]"Woe to you, because you are like unmarked graves, which men walk over without knowing it."

[45]One of the experts in the law answered him, "Teacher, when you say these things, you insult us also."

[46]Jesus replied, "And you experts in the law, woe to you, because you load people down with burdens they can hardly carry, and you yourselves will not lift one finger to help them.

[47]"Woe to you, because you build tombs for the prophets, and it was your forefathers who killed them. [48]So you testify that you approve of what your

forefathers did; they killed the prophets, and you build their tombs. [49]Because of this, God in his wisdom said, 'I will send them prophets and apostles, some of whom they will kill and others they will persecute.' [50]Therefore this generation will be held responsible for the blood of all the prophets that has been shed since the beginning of the world, [51]from the blood of Abel to the blood of Zechariah, who was killed between the altar and the sanctuary. Yes, I tell you, this generation will be held responsible for it all.

[52]"Woe to you experts in the law, because you have taken away the key to knowledge. You yourselves have not entered, and you have hindered those who were entering."

[53]When Jesus left there, the Pharisees and the teachers of the law began to oppose him fiercely and to besiege him with questions, [54]waiting to catch him in something he might say.

Context

At this point Luke introduced an incident that Matthew placed in a different location (Matt 15:1-9). Luke's placement of the account emphasizes the need to keep one's eyes "good" (Luke 11:34). The setting, Jesus' dining at a Pharisee's home, provides a context for a series of judgmental woes on the Pharisees and the experts in the law. After being criticized again, this time for neglecting the ceremonial washing before a meal (11:37-38), instead of defending himself Jesus attacked his opponents by proclaiming the need for an inner purity of heart as the basis for one's external behavior (11:39-40). Luke then added a saying concerning almsgiving, a favorite Lukan theme, followed by two sets of three woes each (11:42-44,46-52).[82] Luke concluded the passage with a summary displaying the hostility of the Pharisees and experts of the law toward Jesus (11:53-54). In comparing the woes in Luke with those in Matthew, it is apparent that Luke modified the tradition to facilitate his Gentile audience's understanding of it.[83]

Comments

11:37 When Jesus had finished speaking. This ties the present account closely to the preceding one.

A Pharisee. See comments on 5:17. This Pharisee was a person who kept both the oral and written law "perfectly" in regard to its external commandments but lost sight of the more important internal or spiritual requirements of the law.

---

[82]These six woes are also found in Matthew but at a different place (23:13-36) and in a different order.

[83]Some examples of this include: "all other kinds of garden herbs" (Luke 11:42; cf. Matt 23:23—"cummin"); omitting "more important matters of the law" (Luke 11:42; cf. Matt 23:23); omitting "to be called 'Rabbi'" (Luke 11:43; cf. Matt 23:7-8); omitting "whitewashed tombs" (Luke 11:44; cf. Matt 23:29); omitting "flog in your synagogues" (Luke 11:49; cf. Matt 23:34); and omitting "son of Berakiah" (Luke 11:51; cf. Matt 23:35).

Reclined at the table.　Reclining was the usual posture for a Sabbath meal. Compare Luke 14:10; 17:7 and see comments on 22:14.

11:38　Wash before the meal.　This practice was due to the oral tradition (cf. Mark 7:2-4); the OT has no such requirement. The purpose of such washing was ceremonial, not hygienic. Whether or not Jesus omitted it intentionally was irrelevant to Luke's purpose. In Matt 15:1-2 Jesus is criticized because his disciples did not wash, but here Jesus is attacked directly.

Was surprised.　"Surprised" is literally *amazed*. See comments on 2:18; 9:43.

11:39　Then the Lord said to him.　See comments on 7:13.

Clean the outside of the cup and dish.　Jesus was not accusing the Pharisees of washing the outside of cups but not the inside but that the Pharisaic traditions were equivalent to this because their entire concern was focused on external actions rather than on the more important internal condition.

Greed and wickedness.　The Pharisees are described elsewhere as lovers of money (cf. 16:14) and unscrupulous in their pursuit of it (20:47). Compare *Assumption of Moses* 7:6-9.

11:40　You foolish people!　Compare Luke 12:20.

The one who made?　This is a circumlocution for God. This rhetorical question implies that since God made both, both the inside and outside should be cleaned. How to cleanse the inside from greed and wickedness is the subject of the next verse. God is the ultimate Maker, even of cups made by humans.

11:41　This verse has no parallel in the other Gospels. Here, as in 16:9, Luke argued the need for a correct attitude toward and use of possessions. In the context of greed an appropriate cleansing of the inner heart is through repentance leading to generosity/alms for the poor (cf. 19:8).

Give what is inside [the dish].　This can be translated as an accusative of respect, "as far as what is inside the dish is concerned," [84] or as an accusative of direct object, "give the things inside the cup" as alms.[85] The latter is preferable.

11:42　The first woe refers to their concern for minutiae, even to the tithing of herbs lest something "titheable" be overlooked. The oral traditions were much more explicit and extensive than the OT with regard to what one was supposed to tithe. Compare Deut 14:22-29; Lev 27:30-33; 2 Chr 31:5-12.

Woe.　See comments on 6:24.

To you Pharisees.　Jesus was neither condemning all Pharisees nor the Pharisaic movement in toto. Condemnation of hypocritical Pharisees can be found even within the Talmudic literature. In Ṣoṭa 22b seven types of Pharisees are described. The first five are hypocritical: (1) the "shoulder" Pharisee, who wears his good actions on his shoulder for all to see; (2) the "wait-a-little" Pharisee, who finds excuses for putting off a good deed; (3) the "bruised" Pharisee, who to avoid looking at a woman runs into walls; (4) the "pestle" or hunched-over Pharisee, who walks bent over in pretended humility; and (5) the "ever-reckoning" Pharisee, who is always weighing his good deeds against his bad. But also mentioned are (6) the

---

[84] Marshall, *Luke*, 495.
[85] Fitzmyer, *Luke* 2:947.

"God-fearing" Pharisee, who lives in holy awe and the fear of God, and (7) the "God-loving" Pharisee, who loves God from his heart. The kind of commitment that leads to the finest piety is also frequently accompanied by hypocrisy. Neither Pharisaism nor Christianity is exempt from this unfortunate tendency.

All other kinds of garden herbs. This is an overstatement for, according to the Pharisaic tradition, not every herb needed be tithed. See *Šeb.* 9.1.

You neglect justice. This refers to human/social justice, not the divine judgment. The Pharisees were indifferent to the poor.

The love of God. "Love of God" means love *for* God (an objective genitive). The Matthean parallel has "mercy and faith" (Matt 23:23, RSV). For the close tie between the love of God and faith, see 10:25-37, "The Lukan Message."

You should have practiced the latter. This statement is somewhat surprising. Jesus probably meant that tithing in general was commendable and not that they should follow all the oral traditions on tithing. Tithing herbs was not condemned; neglecting more important issues was. A visible preoccupation with the trivial while neglecting the most important is hypocrisy.

Without leaving the former undone. The Pharisaic concern for tithing was hypocritical because it was not accompanied by the much more important commandments to love God and to love one's neighbor (i.e., not to neglect justice). Not only does Luke 11:42d echo Mic 6:8 but, more importantly, it summarizes the two commandments in Luke 10:27. See comments on 10:27.

11:43 The second woe involves the pursuit of public recognition and self-aggrandizement. Compare 14:7-11 for a commentary on this verse.

You love the most important seats in the synagogues. This tendency toward social prominence is repeated in 20:46 (cf. Mark 12:38-40). Such a desire is condemned in Luke (cf. 9:46-48; 14:7-11; 18:14; 22:24-27).

And greetings in the marketplaces. This too is repeated in 20:46.

11:44 The meaning of the third woe is not as clear as the first two. The parallel in Matt 23:27-28 is much easier to understand. Luke may have omitted the reference to "whitewashed tombs" in order avoid having to explain this Jewish practice meant to protect people from accidentally becoming ceremonially unclean by contact with a tomb (*Šeqal.* 5.1). The picture part of the analogy is clear. People were unknowingly walking over unmarked graves. But it is uncertain to what this refers. It may mean that the Pharisees were like walking dead and that those in contact with them (their followers) became unclean just as they would by contact with a dead body (Num 9:6-10; Lev 21:1-4,11). Another possibility is that their followers were unconscious that contact with the Pharisees' teachings was death-giving.

11:45 This verse has no parallel in Matthew and marks a change in the scene from the Pharisees to lawyers.

One of the experts in the law. See comments on 7:30.

You insult us also. Those in the Pharisaic community who were most responsible for the Pharisaic teaching were the experts in the law. They recognized that Jesus' woes were particularly directed at them.

11:46 The second set of woes begins with the condemnation of the lawyers for creating innumerable laws and traditions (cf. Mark 7:2-5; Gal 1:14).

You load people down with burdens. By their interpretation of the law and the addition of their traditions, they made serving God impossible for the average believer. The preoccupation with the details of the Pharisaic tradition often resulted in the neglect of God's commandments found in the OT (cf. Mark 7:2-8). The concern for ceremonial aspects of the Jewish law was also seen by the early church as a "yoke that neither we nor our fathers have been able to bear" (Acts 15:10).

You yourselves will not lift one finger to help them. This can be interpreted in two ways: (1) you make no attempt to help the average person keep all these laws or (2) not even you, yourselves, through your casuistry keep the obligations of the law which you impose on others (cf. Matt 23:3). The first interpretation, which complements the preceding criticism in the verse, is to be preferred.

11:47-48 The fifth woe involves the hypocrisy of building monuments (literally *tombs*) to honor the prophets while not honoring their message (cf. Luke 11:42; Mic 6:8) or the message of the present-day prophets, John the Baptist and Jesus (Luke 9:22; 11:49; 13:33-34), and such leaders of the early church as Stephen (Acts 7), the apostle James (12:2-3), and Jesus' brother, James (Josephus, *Antiquities* 20.9.1 [20.200]). James's martyrdom is not mentioned in Acts, but it was almost certainly known to Luke and his readers. This teaching is repeated in Acts 7:51-52.

Build tombs for the prophets. On one hand the Pharisees acknowledged the truth of the prophets' message while on the other they endorsed what their fathers did. The latter is shown by their concentration on externals rather than on the inner condition of the heart (which is a rejection of the prophets' message) and also by their refusal to heed the present-day prophetic message. While the lawyers were called the sons of those who killed the prophets (cf. also Acts 7:52), Peter's Jewish audience in Acts 3:25 was called the sons of the prophets because they responded favorably to the prophetic message (4:4).

11:49 Because of this. That is, because of the behavior described in 11:39-48.

God in his wisdom said. This is literally *The wisdom of God said.* It is not known what exactly is meant by "wisdom." The following have been suggested: a saying recorded neither in the OT nor in the surviving intertestamental literature; a lost book called "The Wisdom of God"; Jesus himself prophesying regarding the early church (cf. Matt 23:34); or wisdom personified (Prov 1:20-33; 8:1-36). Selecting among these conflicting interpretations is also influenced by how one interprets the tense (past, aorist) of the verb "said" (Luke 11:49), "this generation" (11:50), and the reference to "Zechariah" in 11:51. If this Zechariah is the Zechariah of 2 Chr 24:20-22, how could the present generation be held responsible for martyrdoms occurring centuries before?

I will send. This could refer to an event fulfilled in OT times or, more probably, to one about to take place. It is best to understand the tense as a prophetic perfect, in which the following prophecy about the future is spoken of with the certainty of a past event.

Prophets and apostles. Although the reference to prophets could refer to the OT prophets, Luke's readers would undoubtedly have understood "apostles" to refer specifically to the Christian apostles (Acts 1:2). Therefore "prophets" should also be interpreted "Christian prophets" (11:27; 13:1; 15:32; 21:9-10). This interpretation receives additional support from the future tense of "I will send."

Some ... kill and others ... persecute. The fulfillment of this prophecy will be described by Luke in the second volume of his work (cf. 1 Thess 2:15). It appears best to interpret the expression "the wisdom of God" as referring to Jesus, now speaking a prophetic word about how this generation would confirm the actions of their forefathers by killing the prophets and apostles of the new age.

11:50 Will be held responsible. Compare Gen 9:5; 42:22; 2 Sam 4:11; Ps 9:13; Ezek 3:18,20; 33:6. Compare 1 Thess 2:16.

The blood of all the prophets. This generation, repeating the past evil deeds of their fathers by martyring God's servants in the present, will be held guilty of all such crimes from the beginning of creation until the end (cf. Matt 23:32; 1 Thess 2:16). This refers primarily to the final judgment (cf. Luke 11:31-32), but it might also contain a reference to Jerusalem's destruction in A.D. 70. "Blood" is a metaphor for the death/murder of the prophets and apostles (11:47-49).

11:51 Abel. The term "prophet" is used broadly enough to cover the first martyr, Abel, who was killed for his righteousness. Abel is described as a prophet because Luke regarded the entire OT as prophecy.

Zechariah. It is best to interpret this as a reference to the high priest whose death is recorded in 2 Chr 24:20-22 rather than to a later Zechariah slain by the Zealots in the temple in A.D. 67 (Josephus, *Wars* 4.5.4 [4.334-44]), for it is doubtful that Luke's readers would have been familiar enough with the events of A.D. 66–70 to have known of this other Zechariah. If the order of the OT books was the same in Jesus' day as in the present Hebrew OT, Abel to Zechariah would represent the entire OT canon, from the first book (Genesis, Abel) to the last book (2 Chronicles, Zechariah). Since the murder of God's prophets is attested to from the beginning to the end of the Scriptures, Theophilus should not have been surprised that Jesus of Nazareth, the Prophet, Christ, and Son of God, also died at the hands of wicked men (Acts 2:23).

11:52 You have taken away the key to knowledge. The sixth and final woe condemns the leading expositors of the law, for their false interpretation of Scripture and their many traditions had deprived the people of the key to knowledge, i.e., God's plan of salvation. The phrase "key of knowledge" can be understood as the key that is knowledge (a genitive of apposition) or as a key that leads to knowledge (an objective genitive). The latter is more likely.

You yourselves have not entered. This is evident by their rejection of John the Baptist and Jesus (Luke 7:30). What they had not entered, according to Matt 23:13, was God's kingdom.

Have hindered those who were entering. The religious teaching of the experts of the law was not simply unhelpful; it was in fact an obstacle to seekers and caused them to oppose God's messengers.[86] Their "religion" was worse than neutral; it was hostile.

---

[86]Cf. Luke 5:21; 6:2; 7:39; 10:25; 15:2; 19:39; Acts 4:17-18; 8:1; 9:1-3; 13:45,50; 14:2, 19; 17:5,13; 21:21,27; 25:2,7; cf. 1 Thess 2:16.

11:53   The Pharisees and the teachers of the law. The term "teachers of
the law" (*grammateis*) serves as a synonym for "experts of the law" (*nomikōn*) of
Luke 11:45.

Began to oppose him fiercely. Luke indicated by his use of "oppose" and
"besiege" (two present infinitives) that a new level of antagonism toward Jesus began at this point.[87]

11:54   Waiting to catch him in something. This expression is used in Acts
23:21 of people waiting in ambush to kill the apostle Paul. The pericope ends
ironically; those who possess the key to knowledge, who build tombs to honor the
prophets and even tithe all kinds of herbs, follow their fathers by seeking to trap
Jesus in order to kill the greatest of the prophets. "To catch him in something" refers not to overcoming Jesus in debate but to finding an accusation against him
that would hold up in a trial and foreshadows the events of Luke 22:66–23:25.

The Lukan Message

Each of the six woes is a variation on the central theme of the passage,
which essentially addresses the concentration on external religious perfor-
mance to the neglect of one's inner spiritual character. In the end, however, God judges the heart (16:15; Acts 1:24; 15:8). This same
concentration on externals and outer appearances is encountered in the
early church as well (Acts 11:1-18; 15:1-29). The passage also touches
upon several Lukan ethical concerns. The narrow concentration on tithing
herbs allowed the Pharisees to ignore their responsibility for justice to the
poor and the outcast, thus permitting greed and wickedness to flourish
unchecked (Luke 11:39-42). The love for money (16:14) caused the Pharisees to "devour" the homes of widows (20:47). An earlier woe against the
rich is also appropriate here (6:24). Luke's reaction to greed is clear from
his addition in 11:41—Sell and give alms to the poor. The importance of
this theme is also stressed in 16:9-12; 19:8. To follow Jesus means leaving everything (see comments on 5:11). One way to guard against the sin
of greed is to use of one's possessions wisely. Another is to love one's
neighbor. This theme is described in 11:42 as the pursuit of justice. The
pairing of the love of God with the love of justice cannot help but recall
the two commandments that summarize the law (see comments on 10:27).
Another way to avoid enslavement to externals is by remembering Jesus'
teaching on true greatness. One should refrain from seeking one's own
glory or exaltation. The woe against such pursuits in 11:43 is echoed
throughout the Gospel.[88]

In this passage Luke also revealed the culpability of the Jewish leadership in rejecting the preaching of John the Baptist and Jesus (11:47-51).

---

[87] Tannehill, *Narrative Unity of Luke-Acts*, 180.

[88] Luke 9:46-48; 14:7-11 (L material); 16:14-15 (L material); 18:9-14 (L material);
22:24-30; cf. Acts 12:20-23.

This rejection both corresponds to their fathers' killing of the prophets and exceeds it. Although they claimed to honor the prophets by building tombs for them, they rejected both their message and the present prophets and apostles (11:49). There is a clear reference to Jesus' coming death in Luke's editorial comment in 11:53-54. See comments on 9:22 and Introduction 8 (1). The judgment that was to come upon Israel (see Introduction 7 [2]) is also foreshadowed in 11:50-51 and has been prepared for by 11:31-32.

(14) Warnings and Exhortations (12:1-12)

[1]Meanwhile, when a crowd of many thousands had gathered, so that they were trampling on one another, Jesus began to speak first to his disciples, saying: "Be on your guard against the yeast of the Pharisees, which is hypocrisy. [2]There is nothing concealed that will not be disclosed, or hidden that will not be made known. [3]What you have said in the dark will be heard in the daylight, and what you have whispered in the ear in the inner rooms will be proclaimed from the roofs.

[4]"I tell you, my friends, do not be afraid of those who kill the body and after that can do no more. [5]But I will show you whom you should fear: Fear him who, after the killing of the body, has power to throw you into hell. Yes, I tell you, fear him. [6]Are not five sparrows sold for two pennies? Yet not one of them is forgotten by God. [7]Indeed, the very hairs of your head are all numbered. Don't be afraid; you are worth more than many sparrows.

[8]"I tell you, whoever acknowledges me before men, the Son of Man will also acknowledge him before the angels of God. [9]But he who disowns me before men will be disowned before the angels of God. [10]And everyone who speaks a word against the Son of Man will be forgiven, but anyone who blasphemes against the Holy Spirit will not be forgiven.

[11]"When you are brought before synagogues, rulers and authorities, do not worry about how you will defend yourselves or what you will say, [12]for the Holy Spirit will teach you at that time what you should say."

Context

The opening verse of this section both concludes the preceding section and introduces what follows. The discourse continues to 13:21.[89] Having denounced the glaring inconsistency of the Pharisees' behavior, Jesus' warning against imitating their hypocrisy (12:1) makes a fitting conclusion. The sayings that follow are a loose collection of Jesus' teachings directed to his disciples.[90]

---

[89]So Talbert, *Reading Luke*, 140-46.

[90]A similar set of teachings, directed more pointedly to the early church, is found in 21:12-19. The first group of sayings (12:2-9) were already associated together in the tradition (cf. Matt 10:26-33). Luke may have placed them at this point because of the similarity of 12:2-3 to 11:37-54. It is unclear if the placement of 12:10-12 at this point is due to Luke or the tradition because the parallels in Matthew are found in a different place.

After a warning to beware of the Pharisees' hypocrisy, two proverbs assure the readers that such hypocrisy will be revealed and judged (12:2-3). Next comes a warning to the disciples about whom they should truly fear (12:4-5) followed by an encouragement that although God is to be feared, they need not be afraid, for this omniscient and omnipotent God values and cares for them (12:6-7). These verses are tied together themat-ically by the word "fear" (12:4-5,7). Two additional warnings follow con-cerning Christian confession and the unpardonable sin (12:8-10). They too are accompanied by words of encouragement, assuring Jesus' follow-ers of God's presence and the Spirit's guidance in times of persecution (12:11-12).

Comments

12:1 Meanwhile. Compare Acts 26:12. The following material is closely tied to the preceding woes.

A crowd of many thousands. Luke wanted to show Theophilus that in con-trast to the Pharisees and law experts, Jesus was popular among the masses.[91] As Marshall notes: "The implication is that the crowds have increased in size since 11:29. . . . The situation is similar to that in the Sermon on the Plain and else-where (cf. 20:45) where teaching intended primarily for the disciples is given in the presence of the crowds who are thus taught what is involved in discipleship."[92] See comments on 6:17; Introduction 7 (1).

Began to speak first to his disciples. The adverb "first" can be taken as modifying the verb "speak" or "Be on your guard." It goes best with "speak." (Cf. 21:9; Acts 7:12.)

Be on your guard. Compare Luke 17:3; 20:46; 21:34; Acts 5:35; 20:28.

The yeast of the Pharisees. The picture involves not yeast as we think of it today but sourdough (cf. Luke 13:21; 1 Cor 5:6). The reality part of this metaphor is the Pharisees' pervasive religious influence. The parallel in Mark 8:15 reads, "Pharisees and that of Herod," and Matt 16:6 has, "Pharisees and Sadducees." Luke tied this passage more closely to the preceding one by mentioning only the Pharisees.

Which is hypocrisy. The parallels in Mark and Matthew do not spell out what the yeast represents. By his explanatory comment Luke made an explicit connection with the material in 11:37-54, which describes this hypocrisy. For Jewish criticism of the Pharisees ("the seekers after smooth things") by the Essenes, see 1QH 2:15,32; CD 1:18; cf. also 1QH 2:34; 4:10. For a self-criticism, see *Soṭa* 22b.

12:2 This verse and the next are examples of synonymous parallelism. They are proverbs of judgment directed against the Pharisees' hypocrisy.

Nothing concealed that will not be disclosed. Compare Luke 8:17. The sec-ond verb is a divine passive for "God will disclose." What is on the inside of the cup cannot remain concealed. Hypocrisy is folly, for the true inner self will one day be revealed. The Pharisees' hypocrisy, greed, and wickedness will be dis-

---

[91] Luke 3:7; 11:29; cf. Acts 2:41,47; 4:4; 5:13-14; 6:1,7; 21:20.
[92] Marshall, *Luke*, 511.

played (11:39), and they will be seen as graves full of corruption (11:44). Both in Jesus' situation and Luke's, this proverb would be a truism, for a future divine judgment was part of the people's worldview (cf. Acts 17:31).[93]

12:3 Because 12:2 is true, the events described in 12:3 will also take place.

12:4 **My friends.** Here and in John 15:13-15 only is this expression used for the disciples. This designation assured them that the preceding words of judgment were directed not toward them but toward the Pharisees. Now Jesus addressed his disciples' concerns.

Do not be afraid of those who kill the body. Others can bring the believers' human existence to an end. The prophets experienced this (Luke 11:47), and the church was experiencing it now (11:49). Whether persecution unto death was a present reality for Theophilus and Luke's readers is not known.

After that can do no more. Since opponents can only bring about physical death, there is no need to fear them, for they cannot affect the believer's ultimate destiny. The believer's "real" life is an eternal one to be spent in God's presence, and no outside power can affect this (cf. Rom 8:35-39).

12:5 **But I will show you.** Compare Luke 6:47; Acts 9:16; 20:35.

Fear. This refers not to a hopeless terror but to a kind of reverential awe that leads to obedience.[94]

Him who. This refers to God rather than the Son of Man. As for Satan the believer is not to "fear" him but to resist him (cf. Jas 4:7; 1 Pet 5:9).

Has power to throw you into hell. "Hell" is literally *Gehenna*, the Hebrew for the Valley of Hinnom. This valley to the south of Jerusalem became a symbol for the place where the unrighteous were forever punished because it was used as a refuse dump where fires were always burning (cf. Mark 9:47-48; cf. also 1QH 3:19-36). This was Luke's only use of this term.

Yes, I tell you, fear him. The repetition of the command gives added emphasis and weight to this saying.

12:6 **Sparrows.** These were considered good, cheap food and were sought after by the poor.[95]

Pennies. The *assarion* (NIV penny) was a Roman copper coin worth one-sixteenth of a denarius.

Yet not one of them is forgotten by God. In God's providential rule of creation, not even something as inconsequential as the fall of a sparrow occurs apart from his omniscience and will.

12:7 **Hairs . . . are all numbered.** This is a second example of God's omniscience.[96] The divine passive means *God has numbered all your hairs.*

You are worth more than many sparrows. This example of *a fortiori* reasoning assures believers that as God's children they are far more important to God than sparrows. As a result believers can be assured that God knows and rules over every aspect of their lives.

---

[93] In Rom 3:4 Paul "proves" God's righteous character from the accepted fact that he will one day judge the world.

[94] Cf. Acts 9:31; Rom 11:20; 2 Cor 7:1; Phil 2:12; 1 Pet 1:17; 2:17.

[95] So Fitzmyer, *Luke* 2:960.

[96] Cf. Luke 21:18; Acts 27:34; cf. also 1 Sam 14:45; 2 Sam 14:11; 1 Kgs 1:52.

12:8 I tell you. Compare 12:4. This verse introduces the second warning and encouragement in this section. The warnings in this and the next verse are examples of antithetical parallelism.

Acknowledges me before men. This "acknowledgment" involves more than simply a verbal confession. It involves a witness of both word and deed, i.e., this public confession is to be accompanied by a life of obedience to God's commandments. The Pharisees were criticized because their inner selves did not correspond to their outer profession. In contrast believers are challenged to integrate their outer and inner selves.

The Son of Man. The parallel in Matt 10:32 has "I," revealing the freedom the Evangelists felt to interchange Jesus' titles (Son of Man, Christ, Lord) and the personal pronoun. See Introduction 8 (4). For the attempt to distinguish Jesus and the Son of Man in this verse, see comments on 9:26.

Angels of God. This is a circumlocution for "God," as is evidenced by Matthew's "my Father in heaven" (Matt 10:33). Compare Luke 15:10; cf. also Acts 10:3. This verse, though a warning, is also a promise. To acknowledge Jesus as Savior is to be acknowledged as his follower (cf. Acts 7:55-56).

12:9 But he who disowns me before men. The same word is used in Luke 22:34,57,61; Acts 3:13; 7:35. To be ashamed of Jesus and his words (9:26) is a synonym. Jesus in 9:23 spoke of denying oneself to follow him. To refuse to deny oneself is to disown Jesus. Both put self before God and bring about the loss of life. Whereas 9:23 is an invitation to follow Jesus, 12:9 is addressed to the believing community (cf. Rev 2:13).

12:10 The first half of this verse seems to contradict the previous verse. Luke, however, did not see them as contradictory, for if he had, he would not have placed them side by side. Luke 12:10a may refer to something like what happens in Acts 3:17-21, where a non-Christian speaks against Jesus in ignorance. Luke 12:9, however, is a clear instance of apostasy by a member of the Christian community (cf. 12:4).

Will be forgiven. This is a divine passive, i.e., *God will forgive.* Although unstated, subsequent repentance is assumed. As Marshall notes: "It would not need to be pointed out to a Jewish audience that the forgiveness promised here is not granted automatically but is conditional on the repentance of the person seeking it."[97]

Blasphemes against the Holy Spirit. Blasphemy is not limited to speaking evil of the Holy Spirit.[98] It can also mean a hardened attitude toward God and unrelenting opposition to what he is doing through his Spirit in leading individuals to faith.

Will not be forgiven. This is another divine passive, i.e., *God will not forgive.* Compare GT 44.

The second part of this verse is a warning about the unforgivable sin of speaking against the Holy Spirit. What exactly this sin consists of is far from clear. The suggested interpretations include:[99] (1) claiming that Jesus possessed an unclean

---

[97] Marshall, *Luke*, 517.

[98] The verb is also found in Luke 22:65; 23:39; Acts 13:45; 18:6; 19:37; 26:11.

[99] Fitzmyer, *Luke* 2:964-65.

spirit (cf. Mark 3:28-30); (2) apostasy by a Christian (Luke 12:8-9), as opposed to a nonbeliever speaking against Jesus (as in 12:10a); (3) rejecting Christ after his resurrection, in contrast to doing so before the resurrection; (4) rejection of the disciples' testimony, which (after Pentecost) was inspired by the Holy Spirit; (5) persistent and unremitting resistance to the Spirit's work as he brings conviction of sin and reveals the need for repentance and faith. The last probably is the best interpretation, for rejection of the Spirit's work renders faith impossible and salvation unattainable (cf. Acts 7:51). One thing is clear. Anyone concerned about this sin has nothing to fear, for such a concern witnesses to a sensitivity and openness to the Spirit's work, which those who have sinned in this way do not possess.

12:11 Both the first (Luke 12:4-5) and the last set of warnings (12:8-10) are followed by encouraging words (12:6-7,11-12).

Brought before synagogues. Compare 21:12. This refers to Jewish persecution.[100]

Rulers and authorities. Compare 21:12. This refers to appearing in Gentile courts.[101]

Do not worry. This encouraging word was not addressed to Christian ministers and teachers who had been negligent in handling God's word (cf. 2 Tim 2:15) but to Christians facing possible martyrdom.

12:12 For the Holy Spirit will teach you. Jesus gave the reason his followers do not have to worry (Luke 21:14-15). Luke gave examples of this in Acts 4:8-13; 6:10; 7:2-60. John 14:26 and 1 Cor 2:13 mention a similar kind of teaching by the Holy Spirit under different circumstances.

At that time. Compare Luke 7:21; 10:21; 13:31; 20:19; cf. also 2:38; Acts 16:18; 22:13.

The Lukan Message

Luke's key concern in this passage centers around the requirements and assurances of Christian discipleship. Luke shared this theme with his readers already and would deal with it again.[102] His unique contribution to the account involves a clear warning to beware of religious hypocrisy (12:1). This emphasis is heightened by the extensive description of such hypocrisy given in 11:37-54. The Christian's inner self and outer demeanor are to be the same. The reader should realize that ultimately nothing will remain hidden, for a day is coming in which everything hidden will be made known. Believers are also admonished concerning the need for fearless confession. They need fear no one but God, for he alone controls their ultimate fate. Therefore, even under persecution, they dare not deny their Lord and become like the seed planted on rocky soil, which believed for a while but in time of testing fell away (8:13). Yet Luke's readers are also given words of encouragement to help them follow the

---

[100] Luke gave examples of this in Acts 4–5; 6:8-10; 9:1-3; 22:19; 26:11. Cf. 2 Cor 11:24.
[101] Luke gave examples of this in Acts 12:1-5; 16:22-40; 17:6-8; 18:12-16; 24–26.
[102] Luke 5:1-11; 9:1-6,23-27,57-62; 10:1-24; 14:25-35; 17:1-10; 18:18-30; etc.

Lord. They are reminded of God's omniscience and omnipotence as well as his providential care for them (12:6-8). They need not fear, for their names are written in heaven (10:20), and God has promised to provide for their needs. Even in times of persecution, God will direct and provide for his children through his Spirit (12:11-12).

Two other brief references to important Lukan themes should be noted. One is that despite the animosity of the Jewish leadership, the people still favored Jesus and sought to hear his teaching (see comments on 12:1). The second is the Spirit's role in the believer's life. In times of persecution and trial the believer need not fear, for God's Spirit will be present. Should Luke's readers find themselves in such a situation, they need not worry about what to say. The Spirit will give them the right words. This does not mean that they should not think about what to say or fail to prepare. It means rather that they can be at peace knowing that the Spirit will guide in the preparation of their defense.

(15) The Parable of the Rich Fool (12:13-21)

[13]Someone in the crowd said to him, "Teacher, tell my brother to divide the inheritance with me."

[14]Jesus replied, "Man, who appointed me a judge or an arbiter between you?" [15]Then he said to them, "Watch out! Be on your guard against all kinds of greed; a man's life does not consist in the abundance of his possessions."

[16]And he told them this parable: "The ground of a certain rich man produced a good crop. [17]He thought to himself, 'What shall I do? I have no place to store my crops.'

[18]"Then he said, 'This is what I'll do. I will tear down my barns and build bigger ones, and there I will store all my grain and my goods. [19]And I'll say to myself, "You have plenty of good things laid up for many years. Take life easy; eat, drink and be merry." '

[20]"But God said to him, 'You fool! This very night your life will be demanded from you. Then who will get what you have prepared for yourself?'

[21]"This is how it will be with anyone who stores up things for himself but is not rich toward God."

Context

Luke next introduced an account unique to his Gospel (cf. however GT 63,72). A question from the crowd (Luke 12:13) ties this passage to the preceding one and leads to Jesus' teaching regarding possessions, and in particular on inheritance rights. Jesus rejected the role of arbiter between brothers. He did not come to reconcile such family disputes. On the contrary, his coming would at times divide families (12:51-53). What this individual needed was not some casuistic legal ruling by a religious teacher but a basic understanding of how possessions relate to the purpose of life. Who one is is far more important than what one possesses.

The latter is outside a person; the former is within (11:37-54). Jesus also opposed the request because it arose from greed (11:39). Greed is to be rejected, for the meaning and purpose of life is not found in the accumulation of wealth and possessions (12:15; cf. 1 Tim 6:6-10).

Jesus illustrated the principle, stated as a proverb, with an example parable.[103] In the parable a rich and greedy man, failing to guard himself against covetousness, thinks that success is measured in terms of the abundance of possessions. Although he already possesses more than enough, he can think only of himself (note the frequent "I" in Luke 12:17-19) and his accumulation of more possessions for his personal enjoyment (12:19). But they are not permanent possessions, as he tragically discovers, for what is "invested" with God is permanent, not economic circumstances. When God takes his life, his temporary possessions are all left behind. Instead of being rich toward God, who never entered his thoughts, he lost all he ever worked for and far more besides (cf. 9:25). The parable concludes with an admonition addressed to the brother (12:21) but which Luke hoped Theophilus and his other readers would apply to themselves.

Comments

12:13 **Someone in the crowd.** Compare 12:1.

Teacher. See comments on 7:40.

Tell my brother to divide the inheritance with me. The OT regulations regarding the inheritance of property are found in Deut 21:15-17; Num 27:1-11; 36:7-9. In the Talmudic literature see *B. Bat.* 8:1–9:10. Luke did not state what the specific problem was, but this is ultimately irrelevant. What is clear is that the motive behind the question was greed (Luke 11:39), not the fulfillment of Ps 133:1.

12:14 **Who appointed me a judge or an arbiter between you?** This may imply that Jesus did not have the legal standing to make such a decision, but it more likely means that he had not come to deal with such temporary trivia but to offer the world eternal salvation. In light of the arrival of God's kingdom, issues such as inheritance rights are of little consequence. Better to suffer loss and follow Jesus (cf. Luke 9:57-62).

12:15 **Be on your guard.** The Greek verb here is different from the one used in 12:1.

All kinds of greed. Greed is an insatiable desire and lust for more and more.[104] It is all-consuming, so that all of life becomes focused on the accumulation of wealth. There is no room for anything else, not even God. This is why it is so hard for a rich person to enter God's kingdom (18:25).

Life does not consist in the abundance of his possessions. Compare 4:4; 9:24-25; 12:22-34.

---

[103]Despite Goulder (*Luke: A New Paradigm*, 535-37), there is no reason to doubt the authenticity of this parable.

[104]Cf. Rom 1:29; Eph 4:19; 5:3; Col 3:5; 2 Pet 2:3,14.

12:16 An example parable follows. Like the parable of the good Samaritan (10:30-36), "Go and do likewise" (10:37) can be added, although since this one is a negative example we should add, "Do not go and do likewise." Compare 1 Enoch 97:8-10.

The ground of a certain rich man. Literally *the land of a certain rich man.* Compare 10:30; 16:19-31, "Context." The man already was rich at the beginning of the story.

12:17 He thought to himself. Compare 12:45; 15:17-19; 16:3-4; 18:4-5; 20:13. **What shall I do?** Compare 16:3; 20:13. The thought itself was in order. His answer, however, was not. The verb (*poiēsō*) can be translated either as future tense ("shall") or as an aorist subjective ("should"—a deliberative subjunctive). There is no significant difference in meaning.

12:18 I will tear down . . . and build bigger ones. A first-century way of "building his investment portfolio."

Store all my grain and my goods. "Goods" may indicate that he possessed more than just farm produce.

12:19 At this point the man's greedy character is clearly seen. If he had been aware of 10:25-37, he would have said, "And I shall be even more able to serve God and those less fortunate than I!"

Take life easy; eat, drink and be merry. This capsulizes the hedonistic life-style he planned to follow.[105]

12:20 Now for the first time God abruptly intruded into the man's thinking, but it was too late.

You fool! Compare 11:40.

This very night. This is in the emphatic position; no time was available to amend his ways.

Your life will be demanded from you. Here the third person plural (literally *They are demanding your soul*) serves as a substitute for the divine passive (see comments on 16:9) and means *God is demanding your soul.* Compare Wis 15:8.

Then who will get what you have prepared for yourself? One should not introduce at this point a concern for children and family, for this is not a real story but a parable. In light of 12:19 the possessions were to be thought of as totally lost (cf. Ps 39:6). Thus like the millionaire's accountant when asked how much his employer left when he died, the reply is a succinct, "All!"

12:21 This is how it will be. Jesus applied the parable.

Who stores up things for himself. The fool hoards instead of being concerned for neighbors and for God (Luke 12:33).

Not rich toward God. This is a synonym for "treasure in heaven" (12:33; 18:22). Salvation is by grace alone, and human merit has no standing before God (17:7-10; 18:9-14); however, God grants rewards to those who serve him.

The Lukan Message

Ellis sums up well Luke's main point and entitles 12:13-34 "To Have or to Live?"[106] Two important themes in this section have come up

---

[105] Cf. 1 Cor 15:32/Isa 22:13; Eccl 8:15; Tob 7:9. Cf. Luke 16:19-31; Ps 49:16-20.
[106] Ellis, *Luke*, 177.

already and will come up again. These are the issues of priorities (9:23-25; 17:33) and attitude toward wealth (5:11,28; 12:33-34; 18:22). Here they are intimately associated. In the face of the arrival of God's kingdom, to be concerned about inheritance rights and goods is folly indeed. Better to focus on the kingdom and allow oneself to be wronged (1 Cor 6:7) than to allow greed (Luke 11:39) to control one's life. One cannot serve God and Money (16:13). Luke's remedy in such circumstances was simple. Give to those in need (11:41; 16:9-12; 19:8). One can avoid becoming a slave to possessions by recognizing their temporary quality. The rich fool did not realize that he "owned" nothing. All he had—even his life—was on loan and could be called in at any time. Luke was telling Theophilus: "Friend, order your life in accordance with the one thing that is eternal—God. Let not greed for that which is temporary keep you from eternal treasure!"

(16) Care and Anxiety (12:22-34)

[22] Then Jesus said to his disciples: "Therefore I tell you, do not worry about your life, what you will eat; or about your body, what you will wear. [23] Life is more than food, and the body more than clothes. [24] Consider the ravens: They do not sow or reap, they have no storeroom or barn; yet God feeds them. And how much more valuable you are than birds! [25] Who of you by worrying can add a single hour to his life? [26] Since you cannot do this very little thing, why do you worry about the rest?

[27] "Consider how the lilies grow. They do not labor or spin. Yet I tell you, not even Solomon in all his splendor was dressed like one of these. [28] If that is how God clothes the grass of the field, which is here today, and tomorrow is thrown into the fire, how much more will he clothe you, O you of little faith! [29] And do not set your heart on what you will eat or drink; do not worry about it. [30] For the pagan world runs after all such things, and your Father knows that you need them. [31] But seek his kingdom, and these things will be given to you as well.

[32] "Do not be afraid, little flock, for your Father has been pleased to give you the kingdom. [33] Sell your possessions and give to the poor. Provide purses for yourselves that will not wear out, a treasure in heaven that will not be exhausted, where no thief comes near and no moth destroys. [34] For where your treasure is, there your heart will be also.

Context

Having given a negative example of the principle in 12:15 in the parable of the rich fool (12:16-21), Luke provided a corrective to the believer's relationship to possessions. What follows is material for the disciples, not for the crowds (cf. the introduction to the parallel material in Matt 5:1-2), for they alone know God as their Father (12:30,32), are God's flock (12:32), and possess the kingdom (12:32). The catchword that unites this section is the word "worry," which occurs in 12:22,25-26. (The synonym in 12:29 is also translated "worry.") Two other sections on possessions will follow in 16:1-31 and 18:18-30.[107]

Jesus said the disciples need not worry about their need for daily bread or clothing. In his sovereign care of his creation, God feeds the ravens and clothes the lilies. Having established God's care of these lesser species, Jesus completed his *a fortiori* argument. How much more, then, will God provide for his children. If the ravens and lilies do not worry, how much less should the disciples who, unlike the ravens and lilies, are conscious of God's promises and loving care. Having prayed to their Father for daily bread (11:2-3), they need not fear. If evil parents take care of their children, how much more will God take care of his (11:11-13). Besides, who can change anything by worrying (12:25)? Unbelieving Gentiles might worry about such things, but believers need not, for they know that their Father realizes they need such things.

Rather than worry about "things," believers should concentrate on the concerns of the kingdom. Having focused their prayers on God's kingdom, disciples should with singleness of mind focus their wills upon it as well (12:31a). God will provide the basic needs (12:31b).

Luke then added a word of encouragement (12:32; cf. John 21:15-17): they are God's "little flock." Although insignificant to the world, they are nevertheless cherished by God. This is followed by a final exhortation to sell their possessions and give to the poor (Luke 12:33) and a proverb that summarizes the problem caused by the accumulation of possessions (12:34). Human desires and longings will be focused on the place where the person's possessions are concentrated. Death either unites people with their heavenly treasures, which can never be taken away, or deprives them of everything (12:20-21).

Comments

12:22   Then Jesus said to his disciples.   The following material consists of teachings addressed to believers. The non-Christian must first of all repent and believe.

Therefore.   "Therefore" calls attention to the rationale for the following command: "Do not worry about your life" because of what happened to the rich man in the preceding parable; i.e., "because it is folly to concentrate one's life on the accumulation of possessions."

Do not worry about your life.   "Life" is literally *soul*, but here it refers to the whole human being, including his or her eating capacity.

Or about your body.   "Body" refers to the human being as one who needs clothing. Note the synonymous parallelism in 12:22c,d and in the following verse.

---

[107] The Matthean parallels to this material are located elsewhere in his Gospel (6:25-34 and 6:19-21). The main difference between the two accounts is that Luke 12:32-33a is lacking in Matthew.

12:23 The first reason given for the exhortation in 12:22 is that there is more to life than eating. As Jesus stated in 4:4, "Man does not live on bread alone."

12:24 Consider. Compare 6:41; 12:27; 20:23.

Ravens. The Matthean parallel (Matt 6:26) has "birds of the air." Luke's ravens, who do not exhibit the rich man's folly and greed (Luke 12:18), bring God's care even more to mind because of Ps 147:9 and Job 38:41. In contrast to humans, "they do not sow and reap."

How much more. This introduces an *a fortiori* argument (see comments on 11:11) and the second reason for the exhortation of 12:22: the believing community is precious in God's sight, and "he will take care of you."

12:25 Who of you? Compare 11:5.

A single hour? Literally a *cubit*. As a measure of length, the cubit was about eighteen inches. The next expression, "life" or "span of life" (RSV), can have either a physical or temporal meaning. In 2:52 and 19:3 it refers to stature, but here it refers to length of life, for adding a cubit to one's height would be more than a "little thing" (12:26). "Cubit" must therefore refer not to a measure of length but to a measure of time. This verse asks whether believers can extend the length of their lives in any way by worrying. The assumed answer is, of course, no. This then is the third reason for the exhortation of 12:22. Due to human impotence, worry is pointless.

12:26 Worry cannot prolong life even in the slightest way. It cannot contribute anything positive to one's life. (The negative effect that worry and anxiety have upon the quality, health, and length of life is becoming more and more recognized.) Whereas the following verses teach that the believer need not worry, these teach that worry is futile.

12:27 Lilies. Although the exact flower designated by the Greek term is uncertain, the meaning is clear.

Labor or spin. Jesus' audience may have recognized an Aramaic pun/play between the words "labor" (*hamal*) and "spin" (*hazal*), but Luke's readers would not have understood it because the pun did not carry over to their Greek text.

Solomon in all his splendor. Compare 1 Kgs 10 and 2 Chr 9.

There is extensive parallelism between Luke 12:27-28 and 12:24: "Consider the ravens"—"Consider the lilies"; "They do not sow or reap"—"They do not labor or spin"; "Yet God feeds them"—"God clothes the grass"; "How much more valuable you are than birds!"—"How much more will he clothe you."

12:28 Grass ... which is here today. Grass frequently is used in the OT as a symbol for the transitory nature of life.[108]

Thrown into the fire. "Fire" is better translated "oven." Wood was relatively scarce in Israel, and grass was used for fuel to bake bread.

How much more. Jesus' downgrading of the lilies to "grass" increases the strength of his *a fortiori* argument.

O you of little faith! The expression "little faith" is found not only in the parallel in Matt 6:30 but also in Matt 8:26; 14:31; 16:8.

12:29 Do not set your heart on. Literally *Do not seek.* Matthew 6:31 reads, "Do not worry." "Seek" is used here to balance the "seek" in Luke 12:31, so that we have, "Do not seek . . . " (12:29) but instead "Seek . . . " (12:31).

---

[108]Isa 37:27; 40:6-8; Job 8:12; Pss 37:2; 90:5-6; 102:11; 103:15-17; cf. 1 Pet 1:24.

Do not worry. Compare 12:22,25-26. This is a synonym for the Greek word used in the three earlier references.

12:30   For the pagan world. "Pagan world" is literally *nations*, i.e., the unbelieving Gentiles who do not know God (cf. 1 Thess 4:5).

All such things. "All" can go with "nations" (RSV) or "these things" (NIV) but is best understood as modifying "things."[109]

Your Father. This address indicates that this teaching is for believers (see comments on 11:2). Believers who pray daily to their Father for food (11:3) need to be reassured that the Father will care for them even better than earthly fathers do (11:11-13). The word "your" is emphatic.

12:31   But seek his kingdom. Matthew 6:33 adds "and his righteousness," which is a strong emphasis in his Gospel.[110] The exhortation means to pursue those things involving the kingdom of God rather than material possessions. To "seek his kingdom" can be understood as: (1) desiring the consummation of the kingdom (Luke 11:2), which in turn may include the thought that believers can in some way advance the coming of the kingdom; (2) praying the Lord's prayer; (3) seeking the blessings of the kingdom, i.e., treasure in heaven, rather than earthly possessions; (4) submitting to God's rule. In the present context (12:21 and esp. 33) the third alternative makes the most sense.

12:32 Once again there is an exhortation followed by a word of assurance (see comments on 12:11).

Do not be afraid. Although this is literally a command (the verb is an imperative), it functions as a reassuring word (cf. Josh 1:9). Two reasons are given. The first is found in the address "little flock" (cf. Matt 26:31), which identifies the believer as part of the true people of God (Mic 2:12). Even if sent out as lambs among wolves (Luke 10:3; cf. Acts 20:29), they need not fear, for God is with them. The second reason is that God has been pleased to give them (note the past tense, an inceptive aorist) his kingdom (cf. Luke 22:29-30), i.e., has made them part of his kingdom.

12:33   Sell your possessions. Compare 18:22. See Introduction 8 (7) for a discussion of how to understand this Lukan teaching.

Give to the poor. Compare 3:11; 6:34-35,38; 11:41; 14:12-14; 19:8; cf. also Tob 4:7-11; Sir 3:30; 29:12; 35:2; 1 Tim 6:17-19.

Provide purses . . . that will not wear out. "Purses" is a metaphor for the contents contained in them. One should use one's purse, i.e., money, to lay up treasure in heaven so that it will not be wasted. How one's money can be lost is given in the next two examples and was also illustrated in the parable of the rich fool (Luke 12:20).

Treasure in heaven. Heavenly treasure is a reward on deposit with God (cf. 12:21; 18:22).

That will not be exhausted. Such treasure will not be exhausted when at death or the parousia, naked and without possessions, one confronts the eternal God (cf. 16:9). Such treasure cannot be affected by the dangers that earthly treasures encounter.

---

[109]This seems clear from Matt 6:32 and Luke 16:14; 18:21; 21:12,36; 24:9.
[110]Cf. Matt 3:15; 5:6,10,20; 6:1; 21:32.

Where no thief comes near. The sense of the verb is "gets to it and takes it." Luke lacks "where thieves break in" (Matt 6:19). Luke's omission, if deliberate, may have been because his readers lived in a different kind of house from Jesus' Palestinian audience, where a thief would "break in" (literally *dig through the walls*). Compare however, Luke 12:39.

And no moth destroys. In ancient times one common form of wealth was clothing, which could be ruined by moths.

12:34 The concluding proverb teaches that if one's treasure is invested in the kingdom, especially through helping the poor (12:33), one's heart will be focused on God's kingdom as well. On the other hand, if one concentrates on the accumulation of earthly wealth, one cannot focus attention upon God. These are mutually exclusive concerns. One cannot serve God and money (16:13), but one can serve God by the correct use of money.

The Lukan Message

Luke continued his teaching on possessions by including various teachings of Jesus concerning this subject.[111] Although most of the material is traditional, the Lukan emphasis is nonetheless clear. Why Luke emphasized this topic cannot be known with certainty. A "mirror reading" of the material might suggest that Luke's audience was particularly materialistic and that he was trying to change their orientation, but this is mere speculation. They might also have been practicing these principles already, and Luke might have been seeking to reinforce the practice (1:4) by reassuring them that this was in accordance with Jesus' teachings. Yet despite lack of agreement on why, we do know what Luke was saying to his readers.

The Lukan emphasis on stewardship has been shown earlier and need not be repeated here. See Introduction 8 (7). What is important in this passage is Luke's unique contribution to the traditional material found in 12:32-33. These teachings on stewardship must be understood in light of the coming of the kingdom and in the sharing in its blessings. Because of the kingdom's surpassing worth believers should practice such magnificent almsgiving as Luke proposed in 12:33 and recorded in Acts 2:44-47; 4:32-37; 5:1f. By so doing, the great reversal is even now taking place. The "poor" (Luke 6:20) have treasure in heaven, and the rich, like the fool in the parable (cf. 16:19-31), lose all: their possessions and their very lives (12:20; 9:24-25).

(17) The Watchful Servants (12:35-48)

[35] "Be dressed ready for service and keep your lamps burning, [36]like men waiting for their master to return from a wedding banquet, so that when he

---

[111] Cf. Luke 8:14; 9:57-58; 12:13-34; 14:33; 16:9,13,19-26; 18:18-30; 19:8-9; Acts 2:44-47; 4:32-37; 5:1-2.

comes and knocks they can immediately open the door for him. [37]It will be good for those servants whose master finds them watching when he comes. I tell you the truth, he will dress himself to serve, will have them recline at the table and will come and wait on them. [38]It will be good for those servants whose master finds them ready, even if he comes in the second or third watch of the night. [39]But understand this: If the owner of the house had known at what hour the thief was coming, he would not have let his house be broken into. [40]You also must be ready, because the Son of Man will come at an hour when you do not expect him."

[41]Peter asked, "Lord, are you telling this parable to us, or to everyone?"

[42]The Lord answered, "Who then is the faithful and wise manager, whom the master puts in charge of his servants to give them their food allowance at the proper time? [43]It will be good for that servant whom the master finds doing so when he returns. [44]I tell you the truth, he will put him in charge of all his possessions. [45]But suppose the servant says to himself, 'My master is taking a long time in coming,' and he then begins to beat the menservants and maidservants and to eat and drink and get drunk. [46]The master of that servant will come on a day when he does not expect him and at an hour he is not aware of. He will cut him to pieces and assign him a place with the unbelievers.

[47]"That servant who knows his master's will and does not get ready or does not do what his master wants will be beaten with many blows. [48]But the one who does not know and does things deserving punishment will be beaten with few blows. From everyone who has been given much, much will be demanded; and from the one who has been entrusted with much, much more will be asked.

Context

At this point Jesus' teaching changes focus from earthly possessions (12:13-34) to watchfulness with respect to the parousia. Three parables or similitudes on vigilance follow: the watching servants (12:36-38), the watchful householder (12:39-40), and the servant in authority (12:42-48).[112] Watchfulness and faithfulness with one's possessions were not unrelated for Luke, in that true watchfulness, or living in readiness for the parousia, consisted in laying up treasure in heaven rather than on earth. Tannehill observes: "Detachment from possessions [12:13-21] and from cares of daily life [12:22-34] is an important part of the readiness for the coming of the Son of Man which Jesus wishes to see in his disciples."[113] This is also seen in Luke's conclusion to Jesus' eschatological teaching in Luke 21:34a and in the eschatological warning in 17:27-28. The three similitudes function less as a single, carefully constructed theme on watchfulness than as three separate portraits of what it means to be ready.

---

[112]The second and the third are found together in Matt 24:45-51 in the same order and with very similar wording.

[113]Tannehill, *Narrative Unity of Luke-Acts*, 248-49.

The section begins simply with a command to be ready and to have a lamp already lit in preparation for the master's return. If the servants are thus prepared when their master comes, they will be blessed, for the master will actually wait on them and share with them the messianic banquet. The next similitude serves more as a warning. It involves a homeowner unaware that a burglar is seeking to break into his home. If he had expected a thief to come in the night, he would have been prepared. So too the believer who believes in and expects the coming of the Son of Man is to be prepared, for he will come at an unannounced time.

The third similitude is the longest and is addressed particularly to the disciples. It involves the role of those to whom the master has entrusted his household. Those who faithfully discharge their duties are blessed. On the other hand, those who abuse their trust and live as foolish unbelievers (cf. 12:20,45) will be punished and placed with the unbelieving. Another analogy follows whose relationship to the preceding one is uncertain. Whereas the evil servant of 12:45-46 seems to receive eternal punishment, the evil servant of 12:47 is given "many blows" but not, apparently, eternal punishment. He appears rather to be "saved, but only as through fire" (1 Cor 3:15, RSV). Although he knew better (was wise), he did not prepare himself (was not faithful) and so will be severely punished. The one who was unprepared due to ignorance of these teachings will be treated less severely, for the guiding principle is that judgment is dispensed according to the knowledge that one possesses.

Some have argued that these three similitudes refer to what happens at death (cf. 12:20). Although there is a sense in which these three parables are quite applicable with respect to death, Luke's main point involves the parousia or coming of the Son of Man. This is clear from the use of the image of the thief coming in the middle of the night, a well-known image for the parousia,[114] from the explicit reference to the coming of the Son of Man in 12:40, and from the placement of these materials in Matthew's great eschatological discourse (Matt 24:45-51). Whatever these similitudes meant in their original setting, in Luke's situation (and in Matthew's) they were clearly understood as references to the parousia.

Comments

12:35 Be dressed ready for service. Literally *Stand, your waist having been belted.* This image of a man who has tucked his long robe up under his belt in order to run is found frequently in the Bible.[115] The use of the perfect participle, "having your waist belted," portrays someone who, instead of waiting until the last moment, is always prepared to act.[116]

---

[114]Cf. 1 Thess 5:2-4; 2 Pet 3:10; Rev 3:3; 16:15.
[115]Cf. Luke 17:8; Exod 12:11; 1 Kgs 18:46; 2 Kgs 4:29; 9:1; Eph 6:14; 1 Pet 1:13; cf. also 1QM 15:14; 16:11.
[116]Marshall, *Luke*, 535.

Lamps burning. Compare 8:16; 11:33; cf. also Exod 27:20; Lev 24:2-3.

12:36 Waiting for their master. Whether one translates *kyrios* as "master" or "Lord" depends on whether one interprets the saying in light of the first or a later *Sitz im Leben* (situation in life). In the original setting Jesus' disciples would have interpreted this term (*Mar* in Aramaic) as "master," but in a later situation Luke and Theophilus, knowing that the returning "master" is the Son of Man, would have interpreted it as "Lord."

A wedding banquet. In this parable the banquet is not the wedding supper of the Lamb (Rev 19:7-9) because the "Master" returns to his servants *after* the feast.

Knocks. In Rev 3:20 the knocking symbolizes Jesus' desire to be present in the church at Laodicea (and any church today), but in this text it refers to the return of the Lord at the end of history.

12:37 It will be good. "Good" is literally *Blessed.* See comments on 6:20. Here the interpretation of the parable becomes part of the parable itself instead of coming at the end as in most parables.

Watching. Compare Rev 16:15. This term is frequently used in the context of the parousia.[117]

When he comes. Christ's coming at the parousia is in view, not his coming for believers at death.

I tell you the truth. The NIV's phrase gives the sense of the Greek (literally *Amen*). See comments on 4:24.

Recline at the table. This refers to the messianic banquet (Luke 13:29; 14:15-24; 22:27-30; cf. Rev 19:9).

And will come and wait on them. The image of the "Lord" serving his servants at the parousia is unexpected and powerful. How blessed indeed are those whom the Lord will serve when he returns!

12:38 It will be good. Again "good" is literally *blessed.* The repetition of the benediction emphasizes how truly blessed those faithful servants will be.

Second or third watch. Luke probably was thinking of the Roman practice of dividing the night into four watches.[118] The watches were 6–9, 9–12, 12–3, and 3–6. The time would therefore be around midnight. If he was referring instead to the Jewish system of three watches (6–10, 10–2, 2–6), then the time would be around 2:00 a.m.

12:39 The thief was coming. A thief's coming was a common image in the early church for the parousia (1 Thess 5:2-4; 2 Pet 3:10; Rev 3:3; 16:15).

House be broken into. "Broken into" is literally *dug through.* This suggests a mud brick Palestinian house. See comments on 12:33.

12:40 The parable is applied to the disciples ("you") mentioned in Luke 12:22. Son of Man. See comments on 5:24.

Will come. As Ellis notes: "The parable discloses that the 'coming' of the Son of Man is nothing else than the 'returning' of the 'Lord' . . . that is, Jesus himself."[119]

12:41 Peter asked. Peter acted both as a representative of the disciples and as their spokesman.

[117]Matthew 24:42-43; 25:13; Mark 13:34-35,37; 1 Thess 5:6,10; Rev 16:15; and probably also 1 Cor 16:13; Col 4:2.
[118]Note the four sets of guards in Acts 12:4; cf. also Matt 14:25; Mark 13:35.
[119]Ellis, *Luke,* 180-81.

Lord. See comments on 5:12; 12:36.

To us, or to everyone? Was "this parable" (12:39-40) for the disciples only or for the crowds as well? Compare 12:1, where a distinction is drawn. The disciples were the target of this parable and even more so of the following one. This is evident, because similar instructions are directed to the disciples in 17:22-30; 22:24-38.

12:42 The Lord answered. See previous verse.

Faithful and wise manager. The parable uses a picture of a manager placed in charge of his master's household and has as its corresponding reality Christian leaders placed over the church by the Lord.[120] By introducing the parable as he did (12:41) and by using the term "manager" instead of "servant," Luke underlined the application of this parable to leaders of the Christian community even more clearly than Matthew.[121]

Puts in charge. The tense in Greek is future. Luke may have intended this to refer to those who would be appointed over the church (cf. Acts 1:8; 20:28; and esp 6:1-6, where the same word is used).

To give them their food allowance. Although there may not have been a particular reality corresponding to this in the original setting in Jesus' life, Luke and his readers quite possibly would have understood this to refer to the responsibility of church leaders to "feed" the people of God. Compare John 21:15-17; 1 Pet 5:2-3.

12:43 It will be good. This "good" is the third "Blessed" in this section (cf. Luke 12:37-38).

That servant. The servant is the manager placed over the other servants.

12:44 I tell you the truth. Compare 9:27; 21:3. This may be a variant way of saying "*Amen*, I say." See comments on 4:24.

In charge of all his possessions. Compare 19:17. Luke used this metaphor to describe the coming reward of those who by faithfully serving the Lord are prepared for his coming. Compare "rich toward God" (12:21); "treasure in heaven" (12:33; 18:22); "receive many times as much" (18:30); "take charge of ten [five] cities" (19:17,19). Christian "managers" have the potential for great reward or great punishment (12:46). Compare Jas 3:1.

12:45 The negative outcome if the manager is not faithful or wise is now given. The person described fits the picture of the defiant sinner in Num 15:30-31.

The servant. "The servant" is literally *that servant*, i.e., the manager opposite to the one described in the preceding verse.

My master is taking a long time in coming. This may suggest that the delay of the parousia was a problem for Luke and/or his readers.[122] For a discussion of this issue, see Introduction 7 (3). The predominant idea in this passage is, nevertheless, being prepared for the parousia. There is no displacement of the parousia into the far distant future, nor is there a "demythologizing" of the event into something else. On the contrary the warning involves being prepared "because the Son of Man will come at an hour when you do not expect him" (12:40).

Eat and drink and get drunk. Such behavior recalls the fool of 12:19; cf. also 21:34; 1 Cor 15:32/Isa 22:13.

12:46 On a day . . . and at an hour. This parallelism adds emphasis.

---

[120]Cf. 1 Cor 4:1-2; Titus 1:7; 1 Pet 4:10.

[121]Matt 24:45 speaks of a faithful and wise "servant."

[122]Cf. also Luke 12:38; 18:1,7-8; 19:11; Acts 1:6-11; cf. also 2 Pet 3:4.

He will cut him to pieces. "Cut him to pieces" is literally *cut in two* (cf. Exod 29:17). In Jer 34:18 such was the punishment for those who had broken covenant with God by mistreating their Hebrew slaves, i.e., God's other servants. Here it is uncertain whether this serves simply as a picture of severe punishment or whether it also includes the idea of being cut off from God's people (cf. 1QS 2:16). The next statement appears to lend support to the latter idea.

A place with the unbelievers. This explains the preceding statement. The plight of the unbeliever will be described in Luke 13:28.[123] The parallel in Matt 24:51 makes clear that the servant receives an eternal punishment because he goes with the hypocrites to the place "where there will be weeping and gnashing of teeth." Compare also Matt 8:12; 22:13; 25:30, which add "darkness"; 13:42,50, which add "fiery furnace"; and Luke 13:28.

12:47 This verse, along with 12:48a,b, is an example of antithetical parallelism. It deals with two managers like those in 12:43-46.

That servant. "That servant" is the one described in the following words.

Knows his master's will. Compare Acts 22:14; Rom 2:18. This servant is not the same as those described in Num 15:27-31; Deut 17:12; Ps 19:13. Yet he is more guilty than the next man, for "anyone then, who knows the good he ought to do and doesn't do it, sins" (Jas 4:17).

Will be beaten with many blows. "Will be beaten" is a divine passive for *God will beat.*[124]

12:48 **But the one who does not know . . . few blows.** Punishment of the one who sinned in ignorance is less severe.

More will be asked. This proverb, an example of synonymous parallelism, provides the principle by which the punishments in Luke 12:47-48a are differentiated. The servant who knows what to do and does not do it is more culpable than the one who does not do it because of ignorance.[125] Fitzmyer notes, "The presupposition in the sayings is that servants entrusted with tasks have also been given the wherewithal to carry them out."[126] This statement contains two divine passives, "has been given [by God]" and "will be demanded [by God]," and two uses of the third person plural as a circumlocution for God: "has been entrusted [by God]" (literally *they entrust*) and "will be asked [by God]" (literally *they will ask*). See comments on 16:9.

The Lukan Message

This section brings up the issue of whether Luke was addressing the problem of the delay of the parousia.[127] If Luke wrote some fifty years after Jesus' death and resurrection, he and his readers might have encountered the problem found in 2 Pet 3:4, "Where is this 'coming' he prom-

[123] Cf. Matt 24:51 with Luke 13:42,49-50; 22:13; 25:30.
[124] The same verb is used in Luke 20:10-11; 22:63; Acts 5:40; 16:37; 22:19.
[125] This same principle occurs in different forms in John 9:41; 15:22,24; Rom 4:15; 5:13b,20; 7:7-13; Gal 3:19; Jas 3:1; Num 15:27-31; Ps 19:12-13; Amos 3:2; cf. also Wis 6:6.
[126] Fitzmyer, *Luke*, 2:992.
[127] So H. Conzelmann, *The Theology of St. Luke* (New York: Harper, 1960), 95-136 and many others.

ised?" There are hints of this in Luke 12:38,45. (See comments on 12:45 for additional references.) Yet Luke had not abandoned the hope of an imminent parousia.[128] It is also doubtful that Luke saw the parousia as "delayed," for his understanding of God's sovereign rule of history would have prohibited interpreting the long wait as a "delay" in God's program of redemption. Luke may have been trying to correct a misunderstanding on the part of some Christians who assumed that the parousia should have occurred already, but this does not mean that Luke shared that misunderstanding. For Luke there was no "delay" on God's part. Furthermore Luke did not demythologize the parousia into a euphemism for death or transform it into a distant future event. The blessed hope is still alive and imminent in Luke's Gospel. If this were not so, he would not have included this section. See Introduction 7 (3).

Another important theme in this passage involves the need for vigilance because the Lord will return at an unexpected hour (12:40). Luke was especially concerned with encouraging and warning the Christian leaders among his readers. Their responsibility is a serious one, for since they have been given much, even more will be demanded of them (12:48). Being a member of the visible Christian community (rather than the true body of Christ) does not guarantee reward; it does not even guarantee salvation. Not even being a leader in the Christian community guarantees salvation. As the parable of the soils illustrates, it is possible to believe for a while and still fall away (8:13). (See 8:4-15—"The Lukan Message.") In the same way one can be a leader over God's people and still wind up "cut to pieces," consigned to a place with unbelievers (12:46) "where there will be weeping and gnashing of teeth" (Matt 25:30).

(18) Jesus—The Great Divider (12:49-53)

49 "I have come to bring fire on the earth, and how I wish it were already kindled! 50But I have a baptism to undergo, and how distressed I am until it is completed! 51Do you think I came to bring peace on earth? No, I tell you, but division. 52From now on there will be five in one family divided against each other, three against two and two against three. 53They will be divided, father against son and son against father, mother against daughter and daughter against mother, mother-in-law against daughter-in-law and daughter-in-law against mother-in-law."

Context

It is unclear why Luke placed this material at this point in his narrative.[129] It has been suggested that either Luke or his underlying tradition

---

[128]Cf. Luke 3:9,17; 12:38-48; 18:8; 21:32.

[129]The material is found in several different documents. The majority (Luke 12:51-53) is found in Matt 10:34-36, but Luke 12:49-50 is also paralleled in Mark 10:38b. There is also a

may have connected these sayings to the preceding parables because of the common idea of Jesus' coming (cf. 12:49,51 with 12:36-40,43,45-46). However, the parables refer to Jesus' coming at the parousia, whereas the present passage deals with Jesus' coming in his earthly ministry.

This collection of material forms a unit centering around Jesus' longing for the fulfillment of certain events. The account opens with the saying concerning Jesus' coming to bring fire on the earth. It is then followed by one in which Jesus referred to his future baptism. This is followed by Jesus' saying that he had come not to bring peace but division. The last two verses give examples of this division.

Comments

12:49 I have come. Compare 5:32; 7:19-20,34; 13:35; 19:10,38; cf. also John 3:2; 5:43; 7:28; 12:27,47; 16:28; 18:37.

To bring fire. "Fire" is an emphatic position (literally *Fire I have come to bring*) and can be interpreted either negatively as a reference to the coming judgment or positively as a reference to the coming of the Spirit (Acts 2:3). Elsewhere in Luke it is clearly a negative metaphor.[130] This, plus the fact that the immediate context (12:51-53) is negative, indicates that it should be interpreted negatively here.[131] The judgment that this fire brings can also be viewed in two ways. First, it can refer to the final judgment at the end of history. The preceding passage (12:35-48) favors this reading. Second, fire can refer to how the coming of God's kingdom divides people into two camps. The latter interpretation is demanded by the context (12:51-53). This theme of division is also found elsewhere in Luke.[132]

How I wish it were already kindled! The grammatical construction for a contrary-to-fact condition indicates that Jesus longed for the completion of his mission, which was as yet incomplete. Yet if "fire" is negative, why would Jesus have longed to cast it on the earth? The reason is that Jesus' coming would bring the "falling and rising of many" (2:34), and this involved both the blessing of the poor and the accompanying condemnation of the rich (1:51-53). Jesus' coming brings a baptism of the Spirit and fire (see comments on 3:16). In the same way, the parousia will bring reward for the faithful but also judgment for the unrepentant.

12:50 I have a baptism. Whereas the metaphor of fire "sets forth the result of His coming as it affects the world . . . [the metaphor of baptism does so] as it affects Himself."[133] The term "baptism" is used in Greek literature to describe being overwhelmed with catastrophe. Yet the key for understanding this metaphor is

---

parallel to Luke 12:49 in GT 10,16 (cf. also GT 82). Luke may have collected material from Mark and the common source he shared with Matthew and brought it all together in the present form.

[130]Luke 3:9,17; 9:54; 17:29; cf. also Gen 19:24; Exod 9:24; Ps 66:12; Rev 8:5,7; 20:9-10.

[131]For the view that it is positive and refers to the coming of the Spirit, see Ellis, *Luke*, 182-83.

[132]Luke 1:52-53; 2:34; 3:5,16-17; 6:20-26; 8:4-15; cf. also 8:26-39; 14:26; 21:16-17.

[133]A. Plummer, *A Critical and Exegetical Commentary on the Gospel according to Luke*, ICC (Edinburgh: T & T Clark, 1896), 334.

found in the parallel in Mark 10:38-39. Here "baptism" forms a parallelism with the "cup" Jesus was to drink and refers to Jesus' passion and death.[134] That this image is found in two different Gospels indicates that it was well-known and that the early church would have understood both Jesus' baptism and drinking the cup as references to his death.

There is a close parallel between Jesus' statements in Luke 12:49 and 12:50 (cf. Ps 11:6 [10:6 in the LXX]). Both "fire" and "baptism" are in an emphatic position at the beginning of the sentence; the order is the same (noun/verb/infinitive); and there are the same number of words in the Greek text (three, followed by a similar thought, "and how I wish"/"and how distressed I am"). If we remove the first two words (*dokeite hoti*) from 12:51, we also have a noun/verb/infinitive, but there is nothing corresponding to Jesus' wishing. Luke 12:49-50 exemplifies synthetic, not synonymous, parallelism.[135]

How distressed I am! Jesus' commitment to God's will was total. He was completely governed by the desire to complete his baptism, even though it meant suffering death in Jerusalem (13:32-33). He longed for his baptism despite what it entailed because only through its completion would the fire be kindled. Jesus' death is seen here not as a tragedy or a terrible twist of fate but as the fulfillment of the divine plan. The divine "must" (see comments on 9:22) is expressed by Jesus' magnificent obsession with completing his baptism.

12:51 The purpose of Jesus' coming was to divide God's people from the unrepentant. In apocalyptic literature such a division formed an integral part of the coming of God's kingdom. Elsewhere in Luke, Jesus' coming is described as bringing peace,[136] but at the same time it brought the rise of some and the fall of others (2:34), as illustrated in the next two verses.[137] The Matthean parallel (10:34) reads "not . . . peace, but a sword" and is no doubt closer to Jesus' words, though Luke's "division" conveys his sense well.

12:52 From now on. Compare Luke 1:48; 5:10. This division did not occur after Jesus' death and resurrection but had already begun. The remainder of the verse gives a general description of the division. Luke was fond of groups of five.[138]

12:53 This verse alludes to Mic 7:6 and gives specific examples of the forthcoming division. No doubt Luke would have seen in this a fulfillment of Scripture. See Introduction 7 (1).

The Lukan Message

The implied Christology of this passage should not be overlooked. Once again Jesus was speaking of his divine mission. "I have come"; "I

---

[134]The image of the "cup" in Mark 14:36 and John 18:11 also clearly refers to Jesus' death.

[135]See R. H. Stein, *The Method and Message of Jesus' Teachings* (Philadelphia: Westminster, 1978), 29.

[136]Luke 1:79; 2:14 (note the qualification); 7:50; 8:48; 10:5-6; 19:38; Acts 10:36.

[137]Other examples of this division can be found in 9:57-62 (vv. 61-62 is L material); 11:27-28 (L material); 14:26 (note L additions); 18:28-30; 21:15-17 (cf. also Josh 24:15; 1 Kgs 18:21).

[138]Cf. Luke 1:24; 9:13,16; 12:6; 14:19; 16:28; 19:18-19; Acts 4:4; 20:6; 24:1.

have a baptism"; "I came to bring." Luke clearly understood Jesus as the one who has come in fulfillment of the OT. He was also the one over whom all humanity is divided. Not only did Jesus bring division in this life, but this division continues in eternity, for the final judgment is dependent upon one's attitude toward Jesus (Luke 12:8-9; 9:26). Again the question must be raised, Who is this who makes such claims? See 8:22-25—"The Lukan Message."

(19) Signs of the Time and Settling with One's Opponents (12:54-59)

[54]He said to the crowd: "When you see a cloud rising in the west, immediately you say, 'It's going to rain,' and it does. [55]And when the south wind blows, you say, 'It's going to be hot,' and it is. [56]Hypocrites! You know how to interpret the appearance of the earth and the sky. How is it that you don't know how to interpret this present time?

[57]"Why don't you judge for yourselves what is right? [58]As you are going with your adversary to the magistrate, try hard to be reconciled to him on the way, or he may drag you off to the judge, and the judge turn you over to the officer, and the officer throw you into prison. [59]I tell you, you will not get out until you have paid the last penny."

Context

Having addressed the disciples in 12:22-53, Luke now presented two sets of teachings directed to the crowds.[139] The first similitude involves the crowd's inability to recognize what God was doing in that day and in their presence. They did not discern the significance of the present. Jesus contrasted the crowd's ability to interpret various meteorological signs with their culpable inability to recognize either the fact or the meaning of the spiritual signs happening right in front of them. They were blind to the fact that "the blind receive their sight, the lame walk . . . the dead are raised, and the good news is preached to the poor" (7:22; cf. 4:18-21). Yet even Jesus' opponents knew that his exorcisms meant something and needed to be explained (11:15). If they had been open to the truth, they would have been able to interpret the present and recognize that God's kingdom had in fact arrived. (For similar parallels see comments on 7:31-35; 14:15-24.)

The second saying deals with the eschatological significance of the present and functions as a proverb on the wisdom of reconciliation (cf. 1 Cor 6:1-8). It is better to seek a settlement with one's accuser than to appear before a judge. A decision should be made while there is time.

---

[139]Luke 12:54-59 parallels Matt 16:2-3 and 5:25-26. How the two teachings relate to the preceding material is unclear. It has been suggested that they were linked together because common words and phrases such as "hypocrites" (Luke 12:56 and 12:1) and "I tell you" (12:59 with 12:4,8,22,27,37,44,51).

Because of the arrival of God's kingdom (12:53-56), it is time to get one's life in order and be reconciled to God (12:58).

Comments

12:54   He said to the crowd. It is assumed that the disciples understood the implications of the present time.

Cloud rising in the west. The moisture-laden air coming from the Mediterranean Sea condenses into rain as it rises up the cooler hills of Palestine (cf. 1 Kgs 18:44).

12:55   South wind blows. "South wind" is a sirocco blowing from the desert in the south southeast (cf. Hos 13:15; Jonah 4:8). Compare Matt 16:2-3.

It's going to be hot. Compare Matt 20:12; Jas 1:11.

12:56   Hypocrites! Compare Luke 6:42; 12:1; 13:15. This reveals that the crowd's sin was not due to simple ignorance (12:48a) but to willful ignorance, for "their problem is much more an unwillingness to interpret than an inability."[140]

To interpret the appearance. Although Jesus refused to perform "signs" for the crowds (11:29-32), his actions (4:18-21; 7:22) were nevertheless signs for those with open hearts (8:15).

This present time? "This present time" is literally *this time*. Luke may have sought to avoid Matthew's "signs of the times" (Matt 16:3) due to Jesus' refusal to give signs (Luke 11:29-31). "This present time" refers to the time in salvation history marked by the coming of God's kingdom in Jesus' ministry, not to events leading either to the war of A.D. 70 or to the parousia. For Luke and Theophilus, this time referred to the "Christ event," i.e., the time from the events of Luke 1:5 on. This verse is an example of antithetical parallelism.

12:57   What is right? Compare Acts 4:19.

12:58 If this is a "saying," Luke may have changed its setting from a Jewish dispute, which could have been settled by a scribe (cf. Luke 12:13-14), to a Hellenistic one, which would have been settled by a judge, in order better to reflect the kind of situation his readers might face. The point would be that Christians should avoid having to appear before legal authorities. If this is a "parable" (or a similitude), however, then the reality part would refer to the present eschatological situation. God's kingdom has come! Therefore make peace now with God, the Judge, while there is yet time. If you delay, it will be too late.[141] The adversary, magistrate, and officer in the picture part of the parable do not have a corresponding reality but are simply part of the story's local coloring. In light of the eschatological context given in 11:54-56, it is best to interpret this as a parable.

He may drag you. Compare Acts 8:3; 14:19; 17:6.

Judge. If Luke 12:58 is a parable, this is a metaphor for "the Judge" (Acts 10:42).

Officer. *Praktōr* was a technical term for the officer in the Roman judicial system who was in charge of the debtor's prison.

12:59 This verse gives the interpretation of the parable and is integrated into the parable's structure.

---

[140]Fitzmyer, *Luke* 2:1000.

[141]Jeremias, *Parables of Jesus*, 43-44.

You will not get out. This is a measure of the severity of the judgment and should not be interpreted as teaching that sometimes one can eventually "get out" (cf. Luke 16:26).

The last penny. The "penny" (*leptos*) was the smallest coin in use in Palestine (cf. 21:2).[142]

The Lukan Message

Luke's view of the realized dimension of God's kingdom was clear in this passage. The "signs" of the kingdom were present for all to see (12:56). They were not the "signs from heaven" Jesus' opponents demanded (11:16), but they were signs nonetheless and could have been seen by those with eyes to see. What the OT promised was coming to pass. A great reversal was taking place (4:18-21; 7:22-23). This passage builds on prior passages that speak of the kingdom having come and will be reinforced by those that follow.[143] More than any other Synoptic Gospel, Luke emphasized the "already now" of God's kingdom.

In light of the eschatological situation, Luke stressed the need for reconciliation with God. In the urgency of the present time it was dangerous to delay. The parable in 12:58 urges such reconciliation even more strongly than its parallel in Matthew. Although exactly how that reconciliation comes about is not described in this passage, one need not look hard in Luke's writings to discover what the required response is. One must repent, ridding oneself of anything that might be an encumbrance to following Jesus, and one must believe with a whole heart. See Introduction 8 (6).

(20) The Need to Repent (13:1-9)

[1]Now there were some present at that time who told Jesus about the Galileans whose blood Pilate had mixed with their sacrifices. [2]Jesus answered, "Do you think that these Galileans were worse sinners than all the other Galileans because they suffered this way? [3]I tell you, no! But unless you repent, you too will all perish. [4]Or those eighteen who died when the tower in Siloam fell on them—do you think they were more guilty than all the others living in Jerusalem? [5]I tell you, no! But unless you repent, you too will all perish."

[6]Then he told this parable: "A man had a fig tree, planted in his vineyard, and he went to look for fruit on it, but did not find any. [7]So he said to the man who took care of the vineyard, 'For three years now I've been coming to look for fruit on this fig tree and haven't found any. Cut it down! Why should it use up the soil?'

[8]"'Sir,' the man replied, 'leave it alone for one more year, and I'll dig around it and fertilize it. [9]If it bears fruit next year, fine! If not, then cut it down.'"

---

[142]Matthew used *kodrantēs*, which was a small copper coin worth two *lepta*.

[143]Luke 4:18-21,43; 7:22-23; 8:1; 10:18,23-24; 11:20; 16:16; 17:20-21; 19:44; Acts 13:32-33; 28:31.

Context

At this point Luke introduced two pericopes that continue the theme of 12:57-59 concerning the need to repent. The controversy story (13:1-5) and the parable (13:6-9) are unique to his Gospel. The first alludes to a recent incident in which Pontius Pilate had killed a number of Galileans while they were offering sacrifices in the temple. In addition Jesus recounted another tragedy, the collapse of the tower of Siloam that killed eighteen residents of Jerusalem. Neither of these events is recorded elsewhere. Jesus pointed out that in both incidents the victims of these tragedies were not especially evil. The lesson drawn from these examples is the audience's need to repent, but how these illustrations relate to repentance is less clear. One possibility is that the fate of these people was meant as a warning that sudden death was a real possibility and therefore his hearers (and Luke's readers) needed to prepare by repenting (cf. 12:20).[144] Another possibility is that these tragedies were meant to teach that unless Jesus' audience repented, they too would perish. That both groups were killed in Jerusalem may suggest to Luke's readers, who read this account after A.D. 70, that "you too will perish" (13:3,5) had been a call for Israel's repentance. As they knew, this warning went unheeded and resulted in Jerusalem's destruction. This interpretation is supported by the following parable, which alludes to the coming judgment, the hostility of the unrepentant synagogue ruler (13:10-17), and above all by the lament in 13:34-35 (cf. 3:9). A final possibility is that the two incidents are meant to teach that Jesus' audience would indeed also perish unless they repented but that the death spoken of was spiritual and eternal. It would be understood that Jesus was using a real incident to illustrate a spiritual reality. Luke probably intended a combination of the last two interpretations, for the temple's destruction in A.D. 70 was both a temporal judgment on the nation and a spiritual one. As for Luke's readers, only the latter spiritual judgment faced them.

The parable illustrates this theme. A tree that has received special treatment from its owner has not borne fruit. Now he seeks to rid the vineyard of this worthless tree and plant something else that will use the space more profitably. The vinedresser, however, intercedes to give the tree one last opportunity. If it does not bear fruit in the coming year after additional care and treatment, it will then be cut down. The interpretation of the parable goes hand in hand with that of the preceding controversy story. It is therefore best to interpret it as symbolizing a last opportunity for the nation of Israel to repent before becoming subject to divine judgment.

---

[144]Fitzmyer, *Luke* 2:1004-5.

Comments

13:1 Now. "Now" is literally *at that very time* (RSV). This word links the present material closely with the preceding incident.

Galileans. Elsewhere Peter (22:59) and Jesus (23:6) are called "Galileans."

Blood Pilate had mixed with their sacrifices. They were killed as they were sacrificing. Therefore this had to have taken place in the temple in Jerusalem, the only place sacrifices could be made. For "Pilate" see comments on 3:1. Attempts have been made to relate this incident to some other recorded event,[145] but it appears that Luke preserved an incident that was not recorded by Josephus or the other contemporary writers.

13:2 Jesus raised the question of whether this calamity occurred because the Galileans were especially evil, which fits the view of the day that such events were due to one's sins.[146]

13:3 I tell you, no! Jesus, however, rejected such a direct association of suffering and sin (13:3,5; John 9:3). Compare Luke 1:60; 13:5; 16:30.

Unless you repent. Although no doctrine of original sin is being formulated here, both Jesus and Luke assumed the universality of sin. For "repent" see comments on 3:3.

You too will all perish. Does the "too" suggest a tragic death, such as Jerusalem's destruction in A.D. 70, or perishing in the final judgment? Luke combined these two possibilities, as is indicated in the following parable and 13:34-35. The term "perish" is also found elsewhere (9:24-25; 17:27,29; 17:33; 20:16), referring to perishing under God's judgment, although a tragic physical death may also be involved. The latter is symbolic and may be part of the former, even as physical death is generally symbolic and may be part of spiritual death (cf. Rom 6:23).

13:4 Were more guilty. "More guilty" is literally *debtors above all*. The term "debtors" is used here in the sense of "sinners" as in Luke 11:4b; Matt 6:12.

Tower in Siloam. This was most probably part of Jerusalem's wall near the pool of Siloam.

13:5 The repetition of Luke 13:3 adds emphasis to this thought.

13:6 Fig tree. For the presence of a fig tree in a vineyard, cf. Mic 4:4 (cf. also Isa 5:1-7). Does the fig tree in the parable represent "Israel" (cf. Hos 9:10,16; Mic 7:1; Jer 8:13; 24:1-10), or does it refer only to the people in Jerusalem? The former seems likely in light of passages such as Luke 20:16; Acts 13:46; 18:6; 28:25-28. For Luke, Jerusalem represented Israel.

13:7 For three years. This should not be understood as an allegorical reference to Jesus' three-year ministry, for Luke did not explicitly teach that Jesus had a three-year ministry.[147] "Three" probably should be understood as a round number indicating a "sufficient time" (cf. 13:21 [RSV] for a "sufficient amount" of dough).

Cut it down! The corresponding reality involves God's eternal judgment (cf. 3:9; Matt 7:19).

---

[145]Fitzmyer, *Luke* 2:1006-7.

[146]Cf. John 9:2; Job 4:7; 8:4,20; 22:4-5.

[147]The idea of a three-year ministry comes from the mention of the various Passovers in John (2:13; 6:4; 11:55; cf. also 5:1).

13:8 For one more year. The period of mercy and opportunity is extended but only for a limited duration (cf. Luke 13:34; 19:41-44).

Dig around it. The digging serves to loosen the soil in order to allow water to sink down to its roots and allow room for the roots to grow. If no fruit appears after that, it is clearly a bad tree (cf. 6:43-45; cf. also 8:14-15).

13:9 The lack of judgment in the present should not be considered a sign that all was well in Israel. It was a sign of God's mercy, not approval. Judgment, however, would not be held in abeyance forever. As in the time of Jeremiah, the people of Israel had before them "the way of life and the way of death" (Jer 21:8).

The Lukan Message

In this passage Luke continued the theme of 12:57-59 on the need to be reconciled to God. The particular expression he used to describe how this comes about is a favorite, "repent." John the Baptist's message (3:8) and Jesus' earlier preaching (5:23) is repeated, and it would be at the heart of the church's preaching in Acts as well. See Introduction 8 (6). In 13:1-5 the universal need for repentance is emphasized. It was not only Galilean sinners or victims of tragedy in Jerusalem who needed to repent; all of Jesus' (and Luke's) audience must repent lest they come under the divine judgment.

A second and related Lukan emphasis in this passage is the coming of the divine judgment. As in Jeremiah's time, so now God sent a prophet, his Son (and John the Baptist before him), to preach a message of repentance and judgment. There was still time, but the time was short. If the listeners did not repent, then judgment would come; and like the Galileans killed by Pilate and the Jerusalemites upon whom the tower of Siloam fell, they too would perish. This warning, along with the reference to Jerusalem (13:4), could not help but remind Luke's readers of the city's tragic destruction in A.D. 70. The exclusion of most Jews from God's kingdom, a theme repeated continually in Acts (13:46-47; 18:6; 28:26-30), would also be understood. Despite the respite from judgment, Israel brought forth no "fruit in keeping with repentance" (Luke 3:8). Jesus foresaw that his preaching, like Jeremiah's, would also fall on deaf ears, and so he grieved over Israel (13:34-35; cf. 21:24). The axe, already at the root (3:9), would be swung and the fallen tree thrown into the fire. Clearly Luke understood the events of A.D. 70 as the fulfillment of this divine judgment. Yet Luke also wanted his readers to understand that what happened to Israel was also a warning to them. After hearing the word, they too had to bring forth fruit (8:12-15) lest their own repentance be in vain.

(21) The Healing of the Crippled Woman on the Sabbath (13:10-17)

[10]On a Sabbath Jesus was teaching in one of the synagogues, [11]and a woman was there who had been crippled by a spirit for eighteen years. She was bent

over and could not straighten up at all. [12]When Jesus saw her, he called her forward and said to her, "Woman, you are set free from your infirmity." [13]Then he put his hands on her, and immediately she straightened up and praised God.

[14]Indignant because Jesus had healed on the Sabbath, the synagogue ruler said to the people, "There are six days for work. So come and be healed on those days, not on the Sabbath."

[15]The Lord answered him, "You hypocrites! Doesn't each of you on the Sabbath untie his ox or donkey from the stall and lead it out to give it water? [16]Then should not this woman, a daughter of Abraham, whom Satan has kept bound for eighteen long years, be set free on the Sabbath day from what bound her?"

[17]When he said this, all his opponents were humiliated, but the people were delighted with all the wonderful things he was doing.

Context

The exact reason for connecting this passage to the preceding one is debated. Luke may have placed them together because he saw this incident as an example of God's visitation of salvation among the people of Israel (12:56) and the hypocrisy with which Israel's leaders responded (12:54-13:17). The first aspect is also present in the following two parables (13:18-21). On the other hand, Luke may have placed this account here because of word association (cf. 13:11 "eighteen years" with 13:4 "eighteen"). Luke may even have found this episode already connected to the parable of the unfruitful tree in the source he was using. Some combination of the first and second explanations seems most likely. The sayings are connected within the passage by the words "set free," "untie," and "set free" (13:12,15-16). Although there are similar incidents in the Gospels (cf. 6:6-11), the present account is unique to Luke.

In this incident Christology takes second place to the pronouncement of the meaning of the Sabbath.[148] Here Jesus used his authority and power to heal a crippled woman. Although she was healed, it was done on the Sabbath, and the synagogue ruler rebuked Jesus for it. Healings should have been performed on other days, not the Sabbath. Jesus harshly called the ruler a hypocrite, pointing out that if it was permissible for animals to receive help on the Sabbath, how much more ought one of Abraham's children to have been allowed to receive such help. As Ellis observes: "Thus whereas earlier Jesus' authority over the sabbath is the

---

[148]The classification of this passage has been much debated. Some define it as a miracle story; others, as a pronouncement story. The question about which form-critical description best fits this passage stumbles over the fact that neither history nor oral recitation of tradition falls into such neat categories. The value of this question, however, is that it forces the interpreter to wrestle with identifying the main emphasis of the account.

issue (6:1-11), here the issue involves the meaning of the sabbath."[149] The result is that while the people rejoiced in this display of God's glory and power, the ruler and Jesus' other adversaries were humiliated.

Comments

13:10 On a Sabbath Jesus was teaching. There is no necessary connection of this account with what precedes. Compare 4:31.

In one of the synagogues. This is the last incident in which Luke referred to Jesus' teaching in a synagogue.[150]

13:11 Crippled by a spirit. The woman is described as having an evil spirit that caused her crippled condition.[151] See comments on 4:39 and 7:21.

Eighteen years. Compare 13:4 (cf. the tie between the accounts in Mark 5:25 and 5:42 with respect to the number "twelve").

Bent over and could not straighten up at all. "At all" can be interpreted as modifying "could not" ("could not at all straighten up") or "straighten up" ("could not straighten up at all"). The latter (NIV, RSV, NASB) is more likely.

13:12 When Jesus saw her. Something like "he was moved with compassion" probably should be assumed (cf. Luke 7:13). No request was made to Jesus. His compassion instigated the healing.

You are set free from your infirmity. The clause is literally *you have been released from your infirmity.* This is not to be understood as a divine passive, however, because of 13:14. If God had healed the woman, then the ruler would not have been able to complain. He complained because Jesus healed her. Compare also 13:17, where "the wonderful things he [Jesus] was doing" refers to his healing of the woman. The deliverance of the woman is described more as a healing than an exorcism.

13:13 Then he put his hands on her. Is the pronouncement of the healing in 13:12 to be understood as having preceded the healing or as contemporaneous with it? Acts 6:6; 9:17; 28:8 (cf. also Matt 19:13; Mark 7:32-34; 8:23) favor the latter.

Immediately. See comments on 18:43. In contrast to eighteen years of sickness, the woman's healing was instantaneous.

And praised God. An inceptive imperfect ("began to praise"). Compare Luke 2:20; 5:25-26; 7:16; 17:15; 18:43; 23:47. See comments on 5:25-26.

13:14 A typical healing miracle would end at 13:13, but this one is part of a larger controversy story concerning the Sabbath. For similar controversies cf. 6:1-11; 14:1-6; cf. also John 5:1-18; 9:13-17. For the Jewish reverence toward the Sabbath, see comments on 6:2.

Indignant. Jesus was rebuked supposedly for profaning the Sabbath. The ruler rose up in "righteous indignation" against extending mercy on the Sabbath to someone who had needed it desperately for eighteen years.

---

[149]Ellis, *Luke*, 187.

[150]Earlier examples can be found in 4:16-30; 6:6-11; cf. also 4:15,44.

[151]Cf. Luke 4:38-39; 8:2; 11:14,18; cf. 2 Cor 12:7. Contrast Marshall (Luke, 557), who states, "Perhaps we should not try to give too definite a meaning to *pneuma* and think of it simply as an evil influence."

13:15 The Lord. See comments on 7:13.

Answered him. Jesus was not answering a question directed to him (cf. 14:3; 17:17; 22:51) but rather responding to the synagogue ruler's statement, which had been directed at him (13:14).

You hypocrites! Jesus' scathing denunciation was addressed not only to the ruler but to all who thought like him, to all who put their religious traditions before mercy and compassion. The lack of concern over Abraham's daughter's eighteen years of suffering was sufficient reason for Jesus to call his opponents "hypocrites." The kind of religious thinking that cares so little for people in their misery and need is indeed damnable.

Doesn't each of you. Jesus offered an *a fortiori* (see comments on 11:11) argument to show the hypocrisy of their criticism. If it is permissible to show mercy to animals on the Sabbath,[152] how much more should mercy be shown to one of God's covenant people.

13:16 Jesus, who already had displayed his authority over the Sabbath in 6:1-5, now clarified the Sabbath's meaning (cf. also 6:6-11). Jesus had come to do God's bidding (4:18-19). Doing God's will should not/cannot be limited to certain days. If it is right to perform God's will on the first six days of the week, how much more should God's will, mercy, and love be performed on the Sabbath.

Should not. Is it not divinely necessary? For *dei* see Introduction 8 (1).

A daughter of Abraham. The rare title "daughter of Abraham" points to the full inclusion of women in the covenant community Jesus gathered. For Luke's typical complementary male example, cf. 19:9.

Whom Satan has kept bound. If "bound" animals were led to water on the Sabbath, how much more should this woman, "bound" by Satan, have been allowed to experience the refreshment of healing. The woman's illness was traced to Satan (see comments on 13:11).

Eighteen long years. Compare 13:4.

13:17 The story's conclusion finds Jesus' opponents humiliated and the people rejoicing (see comments on 6:17) at his marvelous deeds (cf. 7:16).

The Lukan Message

Luke again revealed Jesus' miraculous powers, but the emphasis was not on this but on the hostility official Judaism displayed toward Jesus. The reasons for their hostility vary. At different times it was due to Jesus' violation of the oral traditions (5:33-39; 11:37-44), his association with tax collectors and sinners (5:27-32), his Christological claims and actions (5:21), or his denunciation of the rich and arrogant (6:24-26; 16:19-31). Here it was the freedom he claimed to do God's work on the Sabbath that provoked their animosity (6:1-11; 14:1-6). The conflict described in 13:1-9 now was given concrete form. When official Judaism chose to disregard

---

[152]Cf. Luke 14:5; Matt 12:11; cf. *Sabb.* 5:1-4; 53a, 155a; cf. also *Yoma* 8:6. Within the Dead Sea community, however, mercy was extended neither to man nor beast on the Sabbath (cf. CD 11:5-6).

God's mercy toward people as desperate as a woman crippled for eighteen
years, that religion was doomed; judgment would be forthcoming. Looking for the true fruits of OT piety—justice, mercy, and humility (Mic
6:8)—Jesus found instead the worst of all sins: hypocrisy. Therefore the
fig tree would be cut down (13:8).

On the other hand Luke's emphasis on God's love for the outcasts and
oppressed resonates throughout the passage.[153] Luke delighted in proclaiming that divine salvation was coming to the powerless. Widows, har-
lots, the grieving, lepers, and cripples found that "today" God was visiting
them with the salvation promised long ago (4:16-21; 7:22-23). For Theophilus and the other readers, once Gentile "dogs" without hope and outside of the covenant of promise (cf. Eph 2:12), God's salvation had at last
appeared. As a result they too could delight in the wonderful things God
had done (Luke 13:17). Jesus brought the divine blessing of God's kingdom to the truly "poor" of this world (6:22).

Several other Lukan themes are also found in this account. One is
Christological: Jesus' power over disease and the demonic world had been
displayed once again. See Introduction 8 (4). The positive attitude the
crowd had toward Jesus is another (13:17; see comments on 4:15). A final
theme is the joyous experience of the messianic salvation (13:17). In the
coming of God's kingdom there is joy indeed (see comments on 1:14).

(22) The Parables of the Mustard Seed and Leaven (13:18-21)

[18]Then Jesus asked, "What is the kingdom of God like? What shall I compare it to? [19]It is like a mustard seed, which a man took and planted in his garden. It grew and became a tree, and the birds of the air perched in its
branches."

[20]Again he asked, "What shall I compare the kingdom of God to? [21]It is like
yeast that a woman took and mixed into a large amount of flour until it worked
all through the dough."

Context

Luke concluded the first section of his travel narrative with the parables
of the mustard seed and leaven.[154] The parable of the mustard seed appears
in Mark 4:30-32. Both parables, the first involving a man sowing mustard
seed in his garden and the second involving a woman adding leaven to
flour, are analogies used to describe God's kingdom. How these parables
relate to the preceding material is unclear. Luke's intent may have been to
emphasize that since God's kingdom had already come (13:18-21), the call

[153]For outcasts cf. Luke 5:12-16,27-32; 7:36-50; 17:11-19; 18:9-14; 19:1-10. For the
oppressed cf. 7:11-17; 8:43-48; 16:19-31; see Introduction 8 (5).

[154]These parables also appear together in Matt 13:31-33 but separately in the GT 20,96.

to repent (13:3,5) should be heeded, for both Jesus' hearers and his readers were living in the last period of God's grace (13:6-9). Although the present realization of the kingdom may appear insignificant (like a mustard seed or a little yeast), its power is already manifest (13:10-13), and its consummation will be immeasurable. The contrast between the size of the mustard seed and the leaven at the start compared to their final state illustrates this point. It is this contrast between the beginning and the end, rather than the idea of growth, that is the point of the two parables. As Marshall notes: "The stress is not so much on the idea of growth in itself as on the certainty that what appears tiny and insignificant will prove to have been the beginning of a mighty kingdom."[155]

Comments

13:18   What is the kingdom of God like?   The basic point of the following analogies is not to be limited to one part of the picture such as the man, the seed, the tree, or the birds. The basic point is to be found in the total picture of a small mustard seed that becomes a tree. See comments on 7:31.

13:19   Mustard seed.   By use of overstatement ("the smallest of all your seeds"), Matt 13:32 describes the proverbial smallness of the mustard seed. In contrast a mustard plant can grow to a height of eight to twelve feet.

A man.   Since this stands in parallel with "woman" in 13:21, it should not be translated generically "someone" as in the NRSV. Note again Luke's balance in using one example with a man and one with a woman.[156]

Planted in his garden.   Matthew 13:31 has "field." According to rabbinic teaching (*Kil'ayim* 3:2), mustard was not to be grown in a garden.

Grew.   Nothing is made of this aspect of the parable. The use of the past tense (a culminative aorist) indicates that the point of the parable is not the growing process but the contrast between the beginning and the end.

And became a tree.   There is no hint of irony in calling the end product of the mustard seed a tree.[157] There is an amazing difference between the insignificant mustard seed and its final product. An alleged comparison with the cedars of Lebanon is nowhere suggested. The point Luke wanted Theophilus to get was that the consummation of God's kingdom would be as different from its inception as a mature mustard plant was from its seed.

The birds of the air perched in its branches.   Although it has been alleged that birds cannot nest in a mustard "tree," it is possible. The reference to "birds" is frequently interpreted allegorically as a reference to Gentiles.[158] If "all" had been added ("all the birds"), this interpretation would be more plausible. The reference to birds (cf. Dan 4:12,21; Ezek 17:23; 31:6) may be an allusion to the Gentiles, but Luke's primary purpose in mentioning them was to emphasize the size of the final product.

---

[155] Marshall, *Luke*, 561.
[156] Cf. Luke 1:5-25 with 1:26-38; 2:25-35 with 2:36-38; 4:31-36 with 4:37-39; 7:1-10 with 7:11-17; 8:26-39 with 8:40-56; 15:4-7 with 15:8-10.
[157] Contrast P. Perkins, *Hearing the Parables of Jesus* (New York: Paulist, 1981), 85-88.
[158] So Jeremias, *Parables of Jesus*, 147-48.

13:20   What shall I compare the kingdom of God to?   This is the equivalent of Luke 13:18 but combined into a single sentence.

Yeast.   See comments on 12:1. This would be sourdough.

A woman took.   Luke balanced the example of the "man" in 13:19.

A large amount of flour.   "Large amounts" is literally *three measures (sata)*. This would be slightly more than a bushel. "Three" probably is used as a round number (cf. 13:7; Gen 18:6).

Until.   One should not press this for allegorical significance.

It worked all through.   "Worked all through" is literally *leavened.* The past tense (a culminative aorist) again reveals that the point of the parable is not in the growth process of the sourdough but in the contrast between its small size at the beginning and its final condition.

The Lukan Message

These two parables fit well the Lukan teaching that with Jesus' coming the long-awaited kingdom had arrived. Luke emphasized this theme more than any other Synoptic writer. See Introduction 8 (2). Yet the kingdom's arrival, while evident to all whose hearts were right (Luke 8:15), had not been as expected. While the demonic powers had been shaken and defeated, this world's rulers were oblivious to its arrival. They did not see that in the person of Jesus (and for Luke's readers in the Spirit's work in the life of the church) the kingdom was "now." When the consummation comes, however, the kingdom will be obvious for all to see, for it will be "on earth as it is in heaven" (Matt 6:10). In that day what now appears to be as small as a mustard seed will be a great tree; what appears to be a little speck of yeast will be a large leavened mass. For Luke's readers these parables provided assurance that the already "now" had arrived as well as assurance that the "not yet" would soon come.

2. The Second Mention of the Journey to Jerusalem (13:22–17:10)

(1) The Narrow Door (13:22-30)

[22]Then Jesus went through the towns and villages, teaching as he made his way to Jerusalem. [23]Someone asked him, "Lord, are only a few people going to be saved?"

He said to them, [24]"Make every effort to enter through the narrow door, because many, I tell you, will try to enter and will not be able to. [25]Once the owner of the house gets up and closes the door, you will stand outside knocking and pleading, 'Sir, open the door for us.'

"But he will answer, 'I don't know you or where you come from.'

[26]"Then you will say, 'We ate and drank with you, and you taught in our streets.'

[27]"But he will reply, 'I don't know you or where you come from. Away from me, all you evildoers!'

[28] "There will be weeping there, and gnashing of teeth, when you see Abraham, Isaac and Jacob and all the prophets in the kingdom of God, but you yourselves thrown out. [29] People will come from east and west and north and south, and will take their places at the feast in the kingdom of God. [30] Indeed there are those who are last who will be first, and first who will be last."

Context

Luke began the second part of his travel narrative by mentioning, for the first time since 9:51,53, Jesus' journey toward Jerusalem (13:22). What follows is a loose collection of Jesus' sayings that deal with entrance into God's kingdom (13:18-21). This section begins with a Lukan summary of Jesus' journey to Jerusalem, and the theme for what follows is given by the question, "Lord, are only a few people going to be saved?" (13:23). Jesus' earlier teachings have implied this.[159] Jesus did not answer this question directly but instead followed it with a series of warnings. The first two (13:24 [cf. Matt 7:13-14] and 13:25-27 [cf. Matt 7:22-23]) are connected by the term "door," although the analogies are different. The first exhorts the hearer to enter through the narrow door which leads to the kingdom. The second changes the door imagery, pointing out that Jesus controls the door of the kingdom, and unless one commits to following him now, he will deny that person entrance (9:26; 12:8-9). The similarity between the second warning and the parable of the wise and foolish maidens is evident (Matt 25:1-13).

The third warning continues the judgment theme, indicating that many in Israel ("you yourselves," Luke 13:28) will be excluded from the messianic banquet with Abraham, Isaac, and Jacob, whereas others from east, west, north, and south (clearly Gentiles) will share in it. This illustrates that many who expected to enter God's kingdom (the "first") will be excluded ("last"), while outsiders who had expected to be excluded (the "last") will be included ("first"). The chagrin of those who are excluded is shown by their weeping and gnashing of teeth (13:28). Participation in the kingdom is described as taking one's place at the feast in God's kingdom (13:29; cf. Matt 8:11-12), i.e., sharing in the messianic banquet. The account concludes with a proverb describing the great reversal (Luke 13:30; cf. Matt 19:30).

Comments

13:22 Jesus went through. The imperfect is better translated *was going through*. Compare 9:51,53.

Teaching. Compare 4:15,31-32,43-44.

To Jerusalem. Compare 9:51,53.

13:23 Lord. "Lord" probably meant *Sir* in the original context, but Luke and Theophilus understood it as "Lord." See comments on 6:46.

---

[159] Luke 6:24-26; 7:31-35; 8:5-15; 9:23-26; 10:13-15; 11:23,29-32,42-54; 12:8-12,49-53; 13:3,5.

Are only a few people going to be saved? In *Sanhedrin* 10:1 it is stated that "all Israelites have a share in the world to come." Jesus' audience sensed that his teaching was quite different. See "Context" for references (cf. also 2 Esdr 7:47; 9:15). For the same Greek construction see Luke 22:49; Acts 1:6; 7:1; 19:2. As in Acts 1:6, Jesus did not speculate on the abstract question, which belongs in God's domain, but instead addressed the personal dimension of this issue, i.e., the individual's responsibility. Jesus' hearers (and Luke's) should concern themselves with their own areas of accountability, not God's. The question, however, does receive an implicit answer in the next verse. For "saved" see comments on 7:50.

13:24 Make every effort to enter. That is, repent (Luke 13:3,5). Compare 16:16.

Many . . . will try to enter and will not be able to. The analogy should not be pressed into the idea that the difficulty is due to one's inability to earn/acquire this right. The reason some are not able to enter does not have to do with being good enough but with the willingness to repent (cf. 13:3,5), which they refuse to do. The main point of the verse centers on the need to make sure one is part of the "few" who have through repentance and faith experienced God's mercy and grace.

13:25 A new analogy is given that also involves a door, but the emphasis is less on the individual seeking to enter and more on the Lord's control over who enters and that the time when it is possible to enter will come to an end. The parable of the barren fig tree (13:6-9) has already raised this issue. Matthew 25:1-13 is an expansion of this theme. The time for enrollment is limited. The period of grace will irrevocably end, and the time of judgment will begin.

The owner of the house. "Owner" evidently refers to Jesus rather than God because the owner ate in their presence and taught in their streets (Luke 13:26).

Sir. The NIV translates the Greek term *kyrios* from the standpoint of the picture, but from the understanding of Luke and his readers it would be translated better "Lord" (RSV). See comments on 6:46.

I don't know you. Compare Matt 7:21-23; 25:41-45; John 10:14,27; 1 Cor 8:3; 2 Tim 2:19.

13:26 We ate and drank with you. The mere fact of being physically in Jesus' presence or being acquainted with him is not sufficient for entrance into God's kingdom, any more than membership and participation in church is sufficient today. One must repent and believe. See Introduction 8 (6). For Luke's readers this served as a warning that partaking of baptism and the Lord's Supper did not guarantee entrance into God's kingdom (cf. 1 Cor 10:1-5).

13:27 I don't know you. The repetition (cf. 13:25) adds emphasis.

Away from me. Compare Ps 6:9 (LXX) and Matt 7:23. The scene is the final judgment (25:41).

Evildoers! "Evildoers" is literally *unrighteous.* Compare Luke 16:8-9; 18:6; Acts 1:18; 8:23. The term is not found in Matthew or Mark.

13:28 Weeping . . . and gnashing of teeth. This is a favorite expression in Matthew to describe the horrors of eternal punishment.[160]

Abraham, Isaac and Jacob. This threesome symbolizes Israel.[161]

---

[160] Matt 8:12; 13:42,50; 22:13; 24:51; 25:30.

[161] The threesome is also found in Luke 20:37; Matt 8:11; Acts 3:13; 7:32; Deut 1:8; 6:10; 9:5,27; 29:13; 1 Kgs 18:36; 2 Kgs 13:23.

All the prophets. Compare Luke 11:50; 24:27; Acts 3:18,24; 10:43; but else-where in the Gospels it is found only in Matt 11:13.

In the kingdom of God. "In the kingdom of God" means *at the consumma-tion of the kingdom of God.*

You yourselves. Matthew 8:12 uses the expression "subjects [literally *sons*] of the kingdom." For both Evangelists this meant Israelites, who are contrasted to the people from east, west, north, and south, i.e., Gentiles, who enter (Luke 13:29). Compare Acts 13:46; 18:6; 28:28. Jesus' unrepentant hearers are con-trasted with the faithful patriarchs and believing Gentiles.

Thrown out. This should be understood as exclusion, for they are not ex-pelled after entry but are not allowed to enter the consummated kingdom.

13:29 People. Matthew 8:11 has "many," but Luke used a different term, probably to contrast with the use of "many" in Luke 13:24. For Luke's readers this clearly meant Gentiles.

East and west and north and south. Compare Ps 107:3.

Take their places at the feast. The banquet metaphor is often used to de-scribe God's kingdom.[162]

13:30 Last ... first. Compare Matt 19:30; 20:16; Mark 10:31. The paral-lels in Matthew and Mark indicate that Jesus used this proverb primarily to signify the admission of Israel's outcasts (tax collectors, sinners, the poor, the maimed, the lame, the blind) and the exclusion of the religious elite (Pharisees, scribes, lawyers, priests). Luke and his readers, however, also would have understood this in terms of Acts 13:46; 18:6; and 28:28, i.e., the unbelief of much of Israel and the inclusion of the Gentiles. The lack of the article before "last" and "first" indicates that neither all the last nor all the first would experience this reversal. Some Jews (the disciples and the church of Acts 1–9) did believe. The saying contrasts not all the last and all the first but "last ones" kinds of people and "first ones" kinds of people. Both the NIV and the RSV seek to convey this in their translations. Com-pare Luke 1:51-53; 2:34; 6:20-26; 14:11,15-24.

The Lukan Message

This section centers around a key theme, if not the key theme, of Luke-Acts: salvation.[163] Who will be saved? This was not simply an abstract philosophical question for Luke. He wanted his readers to make every effort to enter the narrow gate (13:24) so they could share in the messi-anic banquet (13:29), i.e., be saved (13:23).[164] Thus, although written to Christians (see Introduction 3), through Luke-Acts he sought not only to assure his readers of the truth of what they had been taught (Luke 1:4) but also to have them make sure they truly were participants in this great sal-

---

[162] Cf. Luke 14:15; 22:16,29-30; Matt 22:2-14; 25:10; Mark 14:25; Rev 19:9; Isa 25:6-8; 65:13; 1 Enoch 62:14; *2 Apocalypse of Baruch* 29:4.

[163] See I. H. Marshall, *Luke: Historian and Theologian* (Grand Rapids: Zondervan, 1989), 77-102.

[164] Cf. the similar exhortations found in Heb 4:1-11; 5:11–6:8.

vation. Israel's example was a warning to them. The great reversal that had taken place (13:28-30) warned that they too could fall away after believing for a time (8:13). Ellis notes that "by his conclusion (30) Luke appears to broaden the application to all followers of Jesus who do not strive to enter 'the narrow door' " (13:24; 2 Pet 1:10).[165] Although "all" can be saved, for "God does not show favoritism but accepts people from every nation who fear him and do what is right" (Acts 10:34-35), not all people will be saved.

The implicit Christology found in this passage should not be missed. Jesus is the one who controls the destiny of humanity. He possesses the keys of God's kingdom and as a result also of death and Hades (Rev 1:18). One's ultimate destiny is determined by whether Jesus will say on the final day "I know you" (Luke 13:25-27). See comments on 7:23; 9:24-26. This theme is, of course, not unique to Luke (cf. Mark 8:35,38; Matt 7:21-23; John 3:36). A Christological emphasis is also found in the address "Lord" given Jesus in Luke 13:23. Another theme related to salvation is the theme of Israel's rejection by God. They are excluded from the future messianic banquet (13:28), for the great reversal has taken place (13:30). See Introduction 8 (5).

(2) Warning concerning Herod and the Lament over Jerusalem (13:31-35)

[31]At that time some Pharisees came to Jesus and said to him, "Leave this place and go somewhere else. Herod wants to kill you."
[32]He replied, "Go tell that fox, 'I will drive out demons and heal people today and tomorrow, and on the third day I will reach my goal.' [33]In any case, I must keep going today and tomorrow and the next day—for surely no prophet can die outside Jerusalem!
[34] "O Jerusalem, Jerusalem, you who kill the prophets and stone those sent to you, how often I have longed to gather your children together, as a hen gathers her chicks under her wings, but you were not willing! [35]Look, your house is left to you desolate. I tell you, you will not see me again until you say, 'Blessed is he who comes in the name of the Lord.' "

Context

After Jesus' teaching that many of his contemporaries would be "thrown out" and not share in God's kingdom, Luke recorded an incident that illustrates Israel's rejection of the Prophet/Messiah. In this incident, found only in Luke, some Pharisees who were friendly to Jesus reported Herod's desire to kill him (13:31). Jesus replied rhetorically that the "fox" Herod would have no effect on his plans. He would continue his ministry of exorcism and healing and on the third day achieve his goal (13:32). For

---

[165]Ellis, *Luke*, 188.

Luke and Theophilus the mention of the "third day" would bring to mind Jesus' resurrection. The following verse (13:33) is connected to the preceding by the repetition of "today and tomorrow" and serves as a commentary to 13:32. Jesus' destination was Jerusalem where, as Israel's Prophet/Messiah, he, by divine necessity (*dei*), would meet his death. He was to die both "in" and at the hands of Jerusalem.

This double pronouncement story is followed by Jesus' lament over Jerusalem.[166] Luke's arrangement may have been due to word association with "Jerusalem" in 13:33-34. Jesus lamented that he would often have gathered the people of Jerusalem together but that they continually refused. Instead they continued to kill the prophets and as a result would be forsaken and experience divine wrath. One day, however, they would welcome Jesus and bless him. Although Luke possibly was alluding to the triumphal entry (cf. 19:38), his primary focus was on the parousia, when the Lord returns in glory. The nature of this blessing may be understood positively, indicating either that Israel will by that time have turned in faith to the Lord, or negatively, indicating that they will be forced to acknowledge him in the day of judgment but that it will be too late for salvation.

Comments

13:31   At that time.   This ties the following material closely to what has preceded.

Some Pharisees.   For "Pharisee" see comments on 5:17. These Pharisees were genuinely interested in Jesus' welfare. Attempts to portray them as purposely giving false information in order to lure Jesus to his death in Jerusalem are based either on the view that all Pharisees were evil or that Luke sought to portray all Pharisees in an evil light. Both views are incorrect. Some Pharisees were sympathetic to Jesus and the Christian movement (cf. John 3:1; Acts 5:34-40; 15:5; 23:6-10), and in this incident Jesus did not rebuke them. These Pharisees were in fact friendly. Luke did, however, see the chief priests and Sadducees as irredeemable.

Herod.   This was Herod Antipas, the tetrarch of Galilee. See comments on 3:1. Herod already had killed John the Baptist (Luke 3:19-20; 9:9). He was curious about Jesus (9:9; 23:8), and although he was not directly responsible for Jesus' death, he made no attempt to save him (23:6-16).

Wants to kill you.   Some have speculated about whether it was Herod's desire to kill him that caused Jesus to leave for Jerusalem. Luke, however, saw Jesus' journey to Jerusalem as fulfillment of a divine necessity. It was the theological issue that concerned Luke, not a reconstructed rationalistic one.

13:32   Go tell.   This is not a command meant to be fulfilled but a rhetorical comment.

---

[166]This lament is found almost word for word in Matt 23:37-39 (forty-nine out of Luke's fifty-one words). Its location in Matthew is different.

Fox. "Fox" was a metaphor for deceitful craftiness then as well as now.
I will drive out demons and heal people. The present tense of the verbs
"drive out," "heal," and "reach" in this partial summary of Jesus' ministry (cf. also
9:1-2) emphasizes this continuing aspect of his ministry.
   Today and tomorrow. Compare Exod 19:10. This denotes a limited period
of time.
   On the third day. Compare Luke 9:22; 18:33; 24:7,21,46; Acts 10:40. The
number of times Luke referred to Jesus' being raised on the third day makes it difficult to avoid thinking that he intended Theophilus to see here a reference to
Jesus' resurrection (cf. 1 Cor 15:4).
   I will reach my goal. Compare the *dei* of Luke 13:33. For Luke, Jesus' goal
was not merely his arrival in Jerusalem but the completion of his redemptive work.
To those, such as Theophilus, who were familiar with the story of Jesus, the next
verse would have indicated that this goal involved Jesus' death and resurrection.
Some have suggested that the verb "will reach my goal" (*teleioumai*) is a divine
passive[167] and should be interpreted "I shall have my goal completed by God."
But *teleioumai* can also be a middle voice and can be interpreted "I shall surely
complete my goal." Because this verb is in the first person and the other two verbs
in the sentence are all active in meaning and in the first person, this favors the latter interpretation. Regardless of all human opposition, Jesus would complete his
work. God's plan would be fulfilled. In fact, God was already working through
Jesus' opponents to bring about his plan.
   13:33 In any case. This is emphatic.
   I must keep going. For the divine *dei*, see Introduction 8 (1). This underlines
not only Jesus' determination but even more the inexorable force of the divine will.
   Today and tomorrow. See the previous verse.
   And the next day. "The next day" is the third day (13:32).
   For surely. Herod could not interfere with God's sovereign plan.
   No prophet can die outside Jerusalem! This is the second passion pronouncement in the travel section begun in 9:51. No doubt this saying reflects such
passages as Jer 26:20-23; 38:4-6; 2 Chr 24:20-21 and such extrabiblical traditions
as those found in Josephus, *Antiquities* 10.3.1 (10.38) and Justin Martyr, *Dialogue
with Trypho* 120.14-15.
   13:34 O Jerusalem, Jerusalem. Jesus' lament, like Jeremiah's, bemoaned
the fate of the sacred city that refused to heed God's Prophet. (Compare Ps 137 for
a similar lament.) It was Jesus who spoke these words, not God or a personified
Wisdom. Jerusalem's negative reaction to Jesus is evident.[168] Jerusalem should
not be understood as referring simply to the twenty-five to thirty thousand people
who lived in the city but as representing Israel as well. See comments on 10:41.
   You who kill the prophets. Compare 13:33. The present participles in this verse
reveal that they continued to do so even in Luke's day. This accusation covers not only
the death of Jesus but also the deaths of Stephen (Acts 7) and James in A.D. 62.
   And stone those sent to you. Compare 1 Sam 30:6; 1 Kgs 12:18; 21:13;
2 Chr 24:21; Acts 7.

---

[167] Marshall, *Luke*, 572; Fitzmyer, *Luke* 2:1031.
[168] Cf. Luke 5:21,30; 6:2,7; 7:30; 11:37-54; 19:39-40,47; 20:19-20; 22:2.

How often. This does not require that Jesus had been in Jerusalem on numerous occasions, although it suggests it, and John explicitly stated that he had. We should instead understand it to mean the many times Jesus had yearned to gather the people of Jerusalem to himself.

As a hen gathers her chicks. The mother hen is a common metaphor for loving protection.[169]

But you were not willing! Note the contrasting "I willed" (*ēthelēsa*), but "you did not will (*ouk ēthelēsate*).

13:35 Your house. The term "house" may refer to the temple proper, the physical city itself, or the city's people. Probably the city and its people were meant. The city will be the focus of attention in 21:5-24.

Is left . . . desolate. Matthew followed this with the apocalyptic sayings of Matt 24–25, which refer to Jerusalem's destruction and the parousia. "Is left to you desolate" alludes to Jer 12:7; 22:5; Ps 69:25; 1 Kgs 9:7-8. Here the reference is to the Romans' destruction of Jerusalem. This is evident from 19:42-44 and 21:6, where the same verb is used to describe Jerusalem's fall in A.D. 70, as well as from the fact that Luke's readers knew from hindsight of this tragic event. The verb is a divine passive for *God has abandoned you* [*to judgment*]. There is no suggestion here that God was replacing the temple with the church. There is a sense in which God's judgment of Israel began to manifest itself even before A.D. 70 in that the kingdom had been given to the Gentiles.[170]

You will not see me again until you say, "Blessed." In Matt 23:39 this saying occurs after Palm Sunday and must therefore refer to a later event. Although there are terminological similarities with Palm Sunday (Luke 19:38), where the event follows this saying, Luke also intended this blessing to refer to the parousia. Any allusion to Palm Sunday is at most ironic for at least two reasons. First, it was not the people of Jerusalem who uttered this blessing in 19:38 but the disciples. Second, the blessing of 13:35c comes *after* the destruction of Jerusalem described in 13:35a.

The blessing, which comes from Ps 118:26, was chanted to incoming pilgrims on feast days. In the context of this Gospel it can be understood (1) negatively as Israel will not see Jesus again until the parousia, but, alas, it will be too late or (2) positively as Israel will be converted before the end time and will greet the parousia with faith (cf. Rom 11:26-27; cf. also Acts 3:19-21). The former interprets the "blessing" along the lines of Phil 2:10-11, i.e., a forced confession apart from conversion (cf. Luke 8:28). The lack of any clear Lukan teaching about a future conversion of Israel and unqualified statements such as are found in Acts 13:46-47; 18:6; 28:25-26 favor the first interpretation.

The Lukan Message

The Lukan theological emphasis in this pronouncement story is twofold, corresponding to the double nature of the story itself. The first theme is God's sovereign rule. Herod's desire to kill him did not worry Jesus, for no two-bit politician could frustrate the divine plan. Nothing could hinder its

[169] Cf. Deut 32:11; Pss 17:8; 36:7; Ruth 2:12; cf. also Ps 57:1.
[170] Cf. Luke 13:28-30; 20:16; Acts 13:46-47; 18:6; 28:25-28; cf. Rom 11:17-24.

fulfillment. Since Luke 9:51 Jerusalem had been the goal, and nothing could thwart the fulfillment of Jesus' destiny. Death clearly awaited him. He would die in Jerusalem like other prophets (13:33-34), but that would not be the end; for on the third day Jesus would complete his mission (13:32). Luke's readers would understand this to be a reference to the resurrection, due to 9:22 and their knowledge of the resurrection tradition. For a discussion of Luke's understanding of the divine necessity of Jesus' death and the sovereignty of God, see Introduction 8 (1).

The second emphasis in this pronouncement story is Jesus' rejection by Israel, here represented by Jerusalem. Jesus' ministry to the people had been a continual invitation for them to repent and enter the kingdom God had sent them. As their fathers had in earlier times, so Israel in the first century rejected God's Prophet/Messiah, even putting him to death. Furthermore, Jesus' death would not be the last one (cf. 11:47-51). Israel would put to death God's messengers in the early church as well, for they "always resist the Holy Spirit" (Acts 7:51). Such wrongdoing cannot go forever unpunished, as the parable of the barren fig tree (Luke 13:6-9) points out. Even as Judah's sin led to Jerusalem's destruction in 587 B.C., so it would lead to another even more tragic destruction in A.D. 70. Jerusalem had been forsaken by God. Like Jonah, Jesus preached divine judgment against a great city, but this judgment would not be rescinded because, unlike the Ninevites (Jonah 3:1-10), Jerusalem did not respond with repentance.

In this passage Luke explained to his readers once again that Israel's fate was understandable in light of the rejection of their Messiah and that readers need not be shaken by what had happened to Israel. See Introduction 7 (2). Whether Luke understood the final saying in 13:35 to mean that Israel one day would turn in faith to Jesus is unclear (see comments on 21:24). Paul, however, did have such a hope (Rom 11:26-27).

(3) Healing of the Man with Dropsy (14:1-6)

[1]One Sabbath, when Jesus went to eat in the house of a prominent Pharisee, he was being carefully watched. [2]There in front of him was a man suffering from dropsy. [3]Jesus asked the Pharisees and experts in the law, "Is it lawful to heal on the Sabbath or not?" [4]But they remained silent. So taking hold of the man, he healed him and sent him away.

[5]Then he asked them, "If one of you has a son or an ox that falls into a well on the Sabbath day, will you not immediately pull him out?" [6]And they had nothing to say.

Context

Luke brought together a block of three episodes critical of the Pharisees (14:1-24) that center around eating. They serve to illustrate the hostility

official Judaism displayed toward Jesus and his gospel (cf. 13:1-35). The
first, found only in Luke, is filled with favorite Lukan expressions such as
"when he went to eat" (14:1); "there . . . was a man" (14:2); "Jesus asked"
(literally *answering he said*, 14:3); "remained silent" (14:4); "he asked
them" (literally *he said to them*, 14:5); and "had nothing to say" (14:6). The
account has no link with what precedes ("One Sabbath"). It involves Jesus'
third and last Sabbath healing (cf. 6:6-11; 13:10-17) and by pointing the
readers' attention to his opponents' desire to trap him ("he was carefully
watched," 14:1) recalls the summary of 11:53-54 (cf. also 6:7). This incident illustrates the rejection of Jesus referred to in the preceding lament
(13:34-35). Once again Jesus raised the question "Is it lawful to heal on the
Sabbath or not?" (14:3; cf. 6:9; 13:16). When he rephrased the question
(14:5), the response, silence, was repeated as well. In 6:11 Jesus' opponents
"were furious." In 13:17 they "were humiliated." Here they "had nothing to
say" (14:6). Jesus' defense of his Sabbath healings could not be refuted, yet
the hostility remained. This pronouncement story (the emphasis is more on
the pronouncement than on the healing) demonstrates that once again Jerusalem refused to be gathered to their Messiah (13:34).

Comments

14:1   One Sabbath.   On some unspecified Sabbath, Jesus was invited to be a
guest in the home of a Pharisee. Visiting speakers were often invited to a Sabbath
meal after the synagogue service. For a Lukan introduction similar in form, cf.
5:1.

To eat.   Literally *to eat bread*. Compare 14:15. Luke often showed Jesus' participation in various meals.[171]

The house of a prominent Pharisee.   Compare 7:36; 11:37. Josephus, *Life*
21 speaks of leaders of the Pharisees.

He was being carefully watched.   Jesus' opponents were seeking to find
fault with him (cf. Luke 6:7; 11:53-54; 20:20). Luke did not say whether the ruler
himself was involved, perhaps even staging this opportunity in order to find fault
(cf. 14:3, where other Pharisees and lawyers were present). It was not relevant to
Luke's purpose.

14:2   There . . . was a man.   We are not told whether he was an intruder, a
guest, or a plant. That was not important for Luke, who frequently introduced parables in a form similar to this one. See 16:19-31, "Context." The addition of "in
front of him" (literally *behold*), however, makes this somewhat different.

Dropsy.   "Dropsy" is literally *hydrōpikos*, probably edema in which various
parts of the body become filled with fluid.

14:3   Jesus asked.   "Asked" is literally *answering said*. This can be understood idiomatically, i.e., *spoke*, or more literally *in response to their thoughts he
said*. Compare 13:2,15, where the same terminology is used to describe Jesus' response to his opponents' statements (not questions).

---

[171]Cf. Luke 5:29; 7:36; 9:13; 10:40; 11:37; 22:15; 24:30.

Is it lawful to heal on the Sabbath or not? Compare 6:9. This was not merely a rhetorical question, for Luke revealed that a response was expected in 14:4; "but they remained silent." Here, as in 6:9, the question preceded the healing, in contrast to 13:15-16, where it followed. The emphasis was less on Jesus' authority to perform miracles on the Sabbath than on his opponents' concern for rituals and traditions above their brothers and sisters.

14:4 But they remained silent. Compare 6:9; Mark 3:4. The silence was not due to uncertainty about whether this man's life was in danger but reveals that they had no answer to Jesus' argument. No matter how his opponents tried to catch him in his words and actions (Luke 11:54), Jesus was their Master (cf. 13:17; 14:6).

14:5 Jesus justified his healing by giving examples of less lofty Sabbath deeds that even his opponents would deem legitimate, such as rescuing a son (the best texts support the reading "son") or an ox from a well (cf. 13:15; Deut 22:4; Matt 12:11).[172]

Will you not? The "not" (*ouk*) assumes a positive answer. See comments on 13:16.

14:6 They had nothing to say. Luke used even stronger language here than in 14:4 in order to underline how irrefutable Jesus' wisdom was (cf. 13:17; 20:26; Acts 4:13-14; 11:18).

The Lukan Message

The hostility that official Judaism had toward Jesus and his teaching is illustrated once again in this Sabbath healing. Under the guise of piety, his opponents sought to censure him for his Sabbath behavior. A similar incident was related in 13:10-17. This incident gave Theophilus another reason for Jerusalem's desolation (13:35) and the giving of the gospel to Gentiles. Such hardness of heart (6:7; 11:53-54; 14:1; 20:20) revealed a resistance to the Spirit (Acts 7:51) that excluded the possibility of faith.

Two other themes can be seen in this account. One involves Jesus' greatness. His unparalleled wisdom became manifest once again, as the one greater than Solomon (Luke 11:31) continued to confound his adversaries (14:4,6). Jesus clearly was his opponents' master. A second theme involves the ethical implications of Jesus' teachings. As elsewhere (13:10-17), Theophilus saw that God's commandments were not about external conformity but about acting with love, justice, and mercy. What better way to honor the Sabbath than to do good and to heal. What the law requires is love in action (6:27-36; 10:25-37), not appearances (11:37-52).

(4) Sayings concerning Banquet Behavior (14:7-14)

[7]**When he noticed how the guests picked the places of honor at the table, he told them this parable:** [8]**"When someone invites you to a wedding feast, do not**

---

[172] In contrast the Qumran community would not allow even this much to be done on the Sabbath (see comments on 13:15).

take the place of honor, for a person more distinguished than you may have been invited. [9]If so, the host who invited both of you will come and say to you, 'Give this man your seat.' Then, humiliated, you will have to take the least important place. [10]But when you are invited, take the lowest place, so that when your host comes, he will say to you, 'Friend, move up to a better place.' Then you will be honored in the presence of all your fellow guests. [11]For everyone who exalts himself will be humbled, and he who humbles himself will be exalted."

[12]Then Jesus said to his host, "When you give a luncheon or dinner, do not invite your friends, your brothers or relatives, or your rich neighbors; if you do, they may invite you back and so you will be repaid. [13]But when you give a banquet, invite the poor, the crippled, the lame, the blind, [14]and you will be blessed. Although they cannot repay you, you will be repaid at the resurrection of the righteous."

Context

In the context of Jesus' dining with a Pharisee (14:1-6), Luke introduced two unique sets of ethical teachings illustrating Christian attitudes and behavior. The first set (14:7-11) was directed to partakers of a meal and the second (14:12-14) toward the hosts. The first set of teachings is called a "parable" (14:7), which is somewhat surprising, for what follows does not appear to be what is traditionally thought of as a parable. Luke intended for his readers to understand that the following ethical teachings involved more than just instructions about how to behave at a meal. That the instructions should be taken literally is, of course, true. However, they were also metaphorical and teach a general attitude toward self and others appropriate to members of God's kingdom (cf. 14:15). Meekness and humility are basic to the proper attitude believers should display in their relationship toward God, and service to the needy is characteristic of the proper attitude one should have toward others. It is in this manner that these sayings function as a parable. How one should behave among others at a banquet, whether as a guest or as the host, is how one should behave before God.[173]

Both sets of teachings are structurally quite similar. They are tied together by the common theme of an invitation to a meal. The key term "invite" is repeated five times (14:8,9,10,12,13). Both accounts also have "When[ever] you ... " followed by "do not ... " and a "lest ... " (14:8,12, RSV). They are then concluded by "but when[ever] you ... " (14:10,13) and a less exact "so that when ... " (14:10) and a "you will be ... " (14:14). The parallelism between these two sets of teachings is quite strong.

The teaching in these verses was inspired by Jesus' observation of how various guests maneuvered themselves at a dinner (cf. 14:1) in order to sit

---

[173]Goulder (*Luke: A New Paradigm*, 585) seeks unconvincingly to argue that nothing other than a pragmatic teaching concerning banquet behavior was intended in these teachings.

in the positions of greatest honor. Pragmatically, Jesus pointed out the risks of so doing. It was not worth the disgrace and loss of face that would result from having to give up a place to one more worthy in front of all the guests. Similarly, believers were not to seek status from others but should wait in humility before God, whose praise alone is important. The first set of teachings ends with a proverb (14:11) that appears again in 18:14. Similar teachings are found elsewhere (see "Comments" on 14:11).

The second set of sayings turns to the case of a host who was self-seeking in his selection of guests. Hosts were challenged not to invite guests who were able to reciprocate. Four groups were mentioned: friends, brothers, relatives, and rich neighbors (cf. 6:32-35). One should, instead, use the banquet as an opportunity to help those who cannot reciprocate. Again, four groups were mentioned: the poor, the crippled, the lame, and the blind. The one who did this would be rewarded not by the recipients (cf. 16:3-7, where a steward acted with this purpose in mind) but by God at the day of judgment.

Comments

14:7 When he noticed. Jesus was observant and perceptive about human nature.

The guests. "Guests" are literally *those invited.* This refers to the Pharisees and experts of the law mentioned in 14:3.

Picked the places of honor at the table. "Places of honor" are literally *first-seats,* which would be the equivalent today of the "speaker's table." The same term is used in 14:8; Matt 23:6; Mark 12:39 (cf. also Luke 11:43; 20:46). Precedence in seating was usually based on rank, reputation, or age.

Parable. See comments on 5:36. Compare 18:1,9; 19:11, where Luke, when introducing a parable, also gave Jesus' purpose in telling it.

14:8 Wedding feast. Compare 12:36. This may be an idiomatic term for a "banquet."

Do not take the place of honor. "Do not take" is literally *do not recline* in the place of honor. See comments on 7:36; cf. also 9:14-15; 24:30. In the picture part of this parable, the advice is not so much ethical as prudent, but the reality taught by the parable, i.e., humility, is ethical.

Invited. This key term helps tie these sections together (cf. 14:8-10,12-13, 16-17,24).

14:9 Humiliated. Humiliation is not the same as humility. The former frequently results from the lack of the latter.

14:10 So that. "So that" (*hina*) probably denotes the result more than the purpose of such behavior, although it is difficult to decide whether a clear distinction should be made in this instance (cf. 16:9).

Move up to a better place. Compare Prov 25:6-7; Sir 3:17-20.

You will be honored. In the parable the honor came from the host who publicly acknowledged the humble guest. In the reality part of the parable the honor came from God, for the passive "will be honored" is a divine passive.

14:11 This proverb is also found in Luke 18:14 and Matt 23:12 (cf. also Matt 18:4).[174] For Jesus' criticism of the Pharisees for not acting in this way, cf. Luke 11:43; 20:45-47. The proverb is an example of antithetical parallelism. **Will be humbled . . . exalted.** These divine passives mean *God will humble* (or *exalt*) *you at the final judgment.*

14:12 Luncheon or dinner. The RSV has "dinner or banquet." It is uncertain whether the primary difference between these two terms involves the time of day or the kind of meal. The latter is more likely in light of the use of the latter term for "banquet" in 14:16. **Do not invite your friends.** Jesus did not prohibit having friends over for a dinner/banquet. His words are better understood as reflecting the Semitic idiom "not so much (friends . . . neighbors) as rather (needy)."[175] The present tense of the verb is perhaps better translated, "Stop continually inviting." Compare 10:20; 12:4; 23:28.

They may invite you back and so you will be repaid. Compare Matt 6:2, where present recompense from one's contemporaries is also contrasted with future reward from God.

14:13 Poor, the crippled, the lame, the blind. This same grouping, although in a different order, appears again in Luke 14:21 (cf. also 4:18, where a comparable foursome is mentioned). Such people were excluded at Qumran from participation in the final war of the Sons of Light (1QM 7:4) and from the communal meal (1QSa 2:5-6), and among the Levites they were excluded from participation in sacrificing (Lev 21:17-23). Compare also 2 Sam 5:8. For Luke's love of "fours" see comments on 6:22.

14:14 You will be blessed. In contrast to Luke 6:20-22, which speaks of a present blessed state, this blessing occurs in the future at the resurrection. **You will be repaid.** Both this future passive and the one above are additional examples of the divine passive, meaning *God will bless/repay.* **At the resurrection.** Jesus' (and Luke's) belief in the resurrection coincided with that of the Pharisees as opposed to the Sadducees, who denied the resurrection (Acts 23:8). Compare Luke 20:35-39; Acts 23:6-9 for the Pharisaic hope of the resurrection. **Of the righteous.** From Acts 24:15 it is evident that this is short for "of the righteous and the unrighteous." Compare John 5:28-29; 2 Tim 4:1; cf. also Luke 10:12; 11:31-32; Rom 2:5-11.

The Lukan Message

These two sets of sayings serve a primarily hortatory function. The first, summarized in 14:11, emphasizes the need for humility both before others and especially before God. The theme is repeated in 16:15 and again word for word in 18:14. This goes along with the exaltation of the lowly in 1:48-50,52-53; 13:30. Pride and arrogance are abominations before God. The great reversal should be understood as a rejection of the

---

[174]For similar sayings, see Luke 16:15; cf. also Matt 11:23; Jas 4:10; 1 Pet 5:6; Ezek 17:24; 21:26; *Epistle of Aristeas* 263; for related teachings, note 22:24-27; Mark 10:35-45.
[175]Marshall, *Luke*, 588.

proud, who exalt themselves, in favor of those who humble themselves. To know God is to understand both his infinite greatness and our own impotence and sinfulness. Pride is not possible under such circumstances. Along with the teaching on humility comes concern for the unfortunate. Love of one's neighbor (10:27) is expressed as love for those who are in need (14:13,21). Elsewhere it is demonstrated in Jesus' acceptance of tax collectors and sinners (5:30; 15:1-2) and his teaching on loving one's enemies (6:27-32) and the needy (11:41; 12:33; Acts 2:44-45; 4:35).

The ethical behavior enjoined here, however, stands in sharp contrast to the arrogance of the Pharisees (Luke 11:43-44; 14:7,11; 20:46), who neglect justice and mercy (11:42; 13:15-16; 20:47). As a result this section also helped Theophilus and Luke's other readers understand why the Pharisees' lack of repentance led both to their exclusion from the people of God and to the events of A.D. 70 (13:5,9,25,28-30,34-35).

(5) The Parable of the Great Banquet (14:15-24)

[15]When one of those at the table with him heard this, he said to Jesus, "Blessed is the man who will eat at the feast in the kingdom of God."

[16]Jesus replied: "A certain man was preparing a great banquet and invited many guests. [17]At the time of the banquet he sent his servant to tell those who had been invited, 'Come, for everything is now ready.'

[18]"But they all alike began to make excuses. The first said, 'I have just bought a field, and I must go and see it. Please excuse me.'

[19]"Another said, 'I have just bought five yoke of oxen, and I'm on my way to try them out. Please excuse me.'

[20]"Still another said, 'I just got married, so I can't come.'

[21]"The servant came back and reported this to his master. Then the owner of the house became angry and ordered his servant, 'Go out quickly into the streets and alleys of the town and bring in the poor, the crippled, the blind and the lame.'

[22]"'Sir,' the servant said, 'what you ordered has been done, but there is still room.'

[23]"Then the master told his servant, 'Go out to the roads and country lanes and make them come in, so that my house will be full. [24]I tell you, not one of those men who were invited will get a taste of my banquet.'"

Context

The setting of this parable is a Sabbath meal in the home of a Pharisee (14:1).[176] The remark about the blessedness of sharing in the messianic

---

[176]A similar parable is found in Matt 22:1-10 and GT 64. It is uncertain whether these are variants of a single original parable (so E. Linnemann, *Jesus of the Parables: Introduction and Exposition* [New York: Harper, 1966], 166) or, as seems more likely, two different ones: Luke 14:15-24/GT 64 and Matt 22:1-10 (see Stein, *Parables of Jesus* [Philadelphia: Westminster, 1981], 83-84). The parable in GT 64 has some affinities to the Matthean parable in that

banquet (14:15) picks up the motif of the banquet and the resurrection in the last day from the previous parable (14:7-14). Other ties to the preceding material involve the term "invited" (14:8-10,12-13,16,18,24) and the expression "the poor, the crippled, the lame and the blind" (14:13,21). The parable culminates the series of lessons in 14:1-24.

There are several different views on the main point of the parable. Should the title of the parable be (1) the parable of the replacement guests (the main point being the giving of God's kingdom to the outcasts); (2) the parable of the disobedient guests (the main point being the rejection of God's kingdom by official Judaism); (3) the parable of the irate master (the main point being God's rejection of Israel); or (4) the parable of the great banquet (the main point being the arrival of God's kingdom and its consequences)? In favor of the first suggestion is the twofold sending of the servant in 14:21-23. The concluding verse argues in favor of the second. However, the fourth suggestion seems best because the use of the metaphor "banquet" in 14:15-16 focuses attention on the coming of the messianic banquet (cf. Matt 22:2). The picture (and reality) parts of the parable flow as follows: a great banquet was given (the messianic banquet/God's kingdom had now come); the invited guests refused to come (the Pharisees and religious elite of Israel rejected the Messiah and his teachings); the outcasts of society were brought in as guests to the banquet (the least in Israel entered God's kingdom instead of the religious elite); and even more distant outcasts were brought in as guests (the Gentiles entered God's kingdom instead of Israel). The two invitations (14:16-17) should not be allegorized (the first as the OT message; the second as Jesus' message), for they simply were part of the local coloring (see comments on 14:16 and 14:17).

Comments

14:15 Will eat at the feast in the kingdom of God. The metaphor (literally *eat bread*) speaks of the messianic banquet and refers to participating in the resurrection of the righteous (14:14). This is another way of describing salvation and the inheritance of eternal life (cf. 18:18,25-26). While sounding devout, the statement assumes that God's kingdom is a distant abstraction rather than, as Jesus had been teaching (see comments on 4:21; 11:20), a present reality brought about by his coming. To "eat bread" means to eat a meal (cf. 14:1).

---

the servant was sent only once to bring in guests from the streets, but it is actually much closer to the Lukan one since it was a banquet rather than a marriage feast and those who rejected the invitation were clearly excluded. An attempt has been made to see behind this parable a rabbinic story of a rich tax collector who held a banquet for city counselors. When they refused to come, the tax collector invited the poor to eat so as not to waste the food. For this God rewarded him (so Jeremias, *Parables of Jesus*, 178-79). This is not entirely convincing. In any case the parable came to Luke from the Christian tradition as a parable of Jesus. He was almost certainly unaware of a hypothetical connection with this rabbinic story.

14:16 A certain man. This was Luke's customary way to begin a parable. See comments on 16:19.

A great banquet. This is a clear allusion to the Jewish hope for the time when the Messiah would come and share a great feast with Israel's devout.[177]

Invited many guests. It was customary to extend two invitations. The first (as here) was to "make reservations" and the second to announce that the banquet was beginning.[178]

14:17 At the time of the banquet he sent his servant. This would have been the second invitation. Compare Matt 22:2-3 and GT 64, which refer to the guests (the first invitation) who are summoned (the second invitation).

Come, for everything is now ready. What the Pharisee relegated to the distant future Jesus proclaimed as having already come. See comments on 14:15.

14:18 But they all alike began to make excuses. While it was unlikely in real life that every guest invited would refuse to attend, this is a parable, i.e., fiction, and thus the unlikely can occur quite easily (cf. Matt 18:24; 25:5).

I have just bought a field. The hearers/readers may have assumed that the purchase was conditional, subject to a later inspection and approval. This may also have been their assumption regarding the five yoke of oxen in the next example.

14:20 I just got married. Compare Deut 20:7; 24:5. No explanation is given about why the groom was not free to attend the banquet. Was it to make sure that no opportunity to beget children would be missed? The attempt to explain the three excuses as referring to the right to be excluded from service in a holy war based on Deut 20:5-7[179] was far too obscure for Luke's Gentile readers. Luke did not comment on the validity of the three excuses. The fact that they made excuses was what mattered to him, not their validity or lack of validity. From Luke 14:26 it is clear that God's kingdom, which is now present, must take precedence over everything else. As a result no excuse is valid. What is a good excuse for forfeiting one's soul (9:25)? The attempt to interpret the excuses as apologies for arriving late rather than failure to come at all[180] is unconvincing because no tardy arrivals are recorded in the parable.

14:21 Streets and alleys of the town. Israel's outcasts were brought to the banquet.

The poor, the crippled, the blind, and the lame. These four names occur in a different order than in 14:13, but they witness to a typical Lukan fondness for "fours" (see comments on 6:22).

14:22 Sir. See comments on 6:46.

14:23 Roads and country lanes. This has no parallel in Matt 22:1-10 and GT 64. This detail would almost certainly have been interpreted allegorically by Luke's readers as an indication that Gentiles also were invited to partake of the messianic banquet.

---

[177]Cf. Isa 25:6; 65:13-14; Ps 81:16; 2 Esdr 2:38; Enoch 62:14; 1QSa 2:11-13; cf. also Luke 13:28-29; 22:15-20,30; 1 Cor 11:23-26; Rev 19:9.

[178]See Stein, *Parables of Jesus*, 84.

[179]See J. D. M. Derrett, *Law in the New Testament* (London: Darton, Longman & Todd, 1970), 126-55.

[180]Linnemann, *Jesus of the Parables*, 88-89, 159-62.

Make them come in. In the past the command *to make them* had been used to justify forced conversions to Christianity. This picture part of the parable portrays a persuasive insistence for the outcasts to enter. It was done in order to overcome their shyness and feelings of unworthiness. God's fervent desire to share salvation with humanity is the reality that corresponds to this part of the picture—not a specific evangelistic technique.

So that my house will be full. Luke emphasized the divine necessity of evangelism in order to fill up the kingdom as well as the assurance that such efforts would succeed. As Fitzmyer observes, "God's will is not foiled by the rejection of human beings; the places at the kingdom banquet will be filled."[181]

14:24 I tell you. Luke often used this same ending for his parables/sayings.[182]

The exclusion of the original guests is emphasized in this verse. Compare Acts 13:45-47; 18:6; 28:25-28; and see Introduction 8 (5). Compare also Matt 25:1-13. The exclusion had little meaning in the picture part of the parable since the excluded guests did not want to come anyway, but it was of great significance in the reality part, where persons foolishly declined God's gracious offer of salvation.

The Lukan Message

The parable fits well the Lukan emphasis on the realized nature of God's kingdom. When the Pharisee spoke of the kingdom as a future abstraction (Luke 14:15), he stood in direct contradiction to Jesus' preaching that God's kingdom had come. Jesus' central message (and John the Baptist's before him) was the arrival of that awaited kingdom.[183]

The Gospel of Luke proclaims the present reality of God's kingdom in Jesus' ministry, and to reject Jesus' announcement of the arrival of the kingdom is to miss sharing in both its present realization and its future consummation. Those who do not become part of the present kingdom will not share in its future consummation. Luke's particular emphasis is seen in the twofold sending out of the servant in 14:21-23. The second sending is unique to Luke and speaks of the entrance of the Gentiles into God's kingdom. The rejection of Jesus and the kingdom by official Judaism (14:24) precipitated the inclusion of Israel's outcasts (4:18; 7:22) and the Gentiles (Acts 13:47-48; 18:6; 28:25-28). The great reversal had taken place. Alas, Israel, however, was rejected (13:34-35). They ignored the day of their visitation, the "now" of Jesus' ministry (4:21; cf. 2 Cor 6:2). See comments on 21:24, however.

The parable also contains an emphasis on God's providential rule of history. The rejection of the gospel by Israel's leadership would not thwart God's plan. Those like the Pharisee in the account who believed they were

---

[181]Fitzmyer, *Luke* 2:1054.

[182]Cf. Luke 3:8; 10:24; 22:16,18; cf. also 11:8; 15:7; 16:9; 18:8,14; 19:26. All of these are unique to Luke.

[183]Cf. Luke 3:4-6; 4:18-21,43; 6:20; 13:18-19; 16:16; 17:21.

guaranteed a place in the kingdom had excluded themselves (14:18-20) and would not participate (Luke 14:24), but God's plan would be fulfilled nevertheless. The first were indeed last (13:30); those who exalted themselves had been humbled (14:11). In contrast the last had taken their place; the humble had been exalted (1:51-53). The kingdom has come, the banquet room will be filled, and God's plan will be accomplished.

(6) Conditions of Discipleship (14:25-35)

[25]Large crowds were traveling with Jesus, and turning to them he said: [26]"If anyone comes to me and does not hate his father and mother, his wife and children, his brothers and sisters—yes, even his own life—he cannot be my disciple. [27]And anyone who does not carry his cross and follow me cannot be my disciple.

[28]"Suppose one of you wants to build a tower. Will he not first sit down and estimate the cost to see if he has enough money to complete it? [29]For if he lays the foundation and is not able to finish it, everyone who sees it will ridicule him, [30]saying, 'This fellow began to build and was not able to finish.'

[31]"Or suppose a king is about to go to war against another king. Will he not first sit down and consider whether he is able with ten thousand men to oppose the one coming against him with twenty thousand? [32]If he is not able, he will send a delegation while the other is still a long way off and will ask for terms of peace. [33]In the same way, any of you who does not give up everything he has cannot be my disciple.

[34]"Salt is good, but if it loses its saltiness, how can it be made salty again? [35]It is fit neither for the soil nor for the manure pile; it is thrown out.

"He who has ears to hear, let him hear."

Context

After the parable of the great banquet, which emphasizes the presence of God's kingdom and the need to respond to its coming, Luke related a number of Jesus' teachings that describe the conditions for membership. He did so in order to avoid possible misinterpretation of the parable. (Cf. Matt 22:11-14, in which the conditions for attendance at the messianic banquet follow the parable in 22:1-10.) In this passage Luke gave Jesus' answer to the question "What must I do to be saved?" (Acts 16:30). Salvation (Luke 7:50), being a disciple (14:26), entering God's kingdom (18:24), having eternal life (18:18), eating bread in God's kingdom (14:15), being acknowledged before God's angels (12:8), and following Jesus (14:26) are different ways Luke expressed the same reality. After the introduction (14:25), there are two parallel sayings describing the cost of discipleship (14:26-27; cf. Matt 10:37-38), two parabolic illustrations found only in Luke (14:28-30, 31-32), a third saying on the cost of discipleship (14:33), and a parabolic conclusion (14:34-35; cf. Matt 5:13). This theme, the cost of discipleship, is also found in Luke 9:23-27,57-62; 18:24-30.

Following Jesus involves "hating" one's family and even one's life (14:26). Over the centuries this verse has caused great despair and confusion. Clearly Jesus, who summarized all God's commandments as loving God and one's neighbor (10:27-28), could not here have been demanding blind, raging hatred of one's family. The confusion is due to Jesus' use of a Semitic idiom. To love one person more than another is described in OT language as "loving one and hating another" (cf. Gen 29:30-31, RSV). In contrast to Luke's "word-for-word" translation of Jesus' words, Matthew gave a "thought-for-thought" translation in Matt 10:37, revealing that Jesus' demand is for his followers to love/obey him more than anyone else, even their own families. Being Jesus' disciple entails primary allegiance to him. No one and no thing can usurp his supreme position. Even as God is to be loved supremely, with no other god or thing taking priority over him, so too Jesus takes priority even over family. The absolute nature of this demand should not be overlooked. This demand is further described by the illustration of a commitment even to martyrdom, i.e., the cross (Luke 14:27).

In 14:28-32 two similitudes emphasize the need for serious and sober reflection on this commitment. Jesus does not solicit a hasty, emotional decision. Instead, he urges those who would follow him to think seriously, to "count the cost" (14:28; cf. 9:57-62). Perseverance (8:15; 21:19) will result only after sober consideration of the cost of following Jesus. The section concludes with another condition of discipleship. Along with willingness to place him above family and life, Jesus also calls his followers to surrender their possessions (14:33).

At this point Luke added a somewhat enigmatic analogy concerning salt, which is found at a different place in Matthew (Matt 5:13; cf. Mark 9:50). Coming after the two similitudes dealing with counting the cost of following Jesus, this saying is meant to remind Theophilus that Jesus' disciples must continue to be the "salt of the earth" (Matt 5:13). If the above three characteristics of discipleship (Luke 14:26-27,33) fade away, they, like "unsalty" salt, will be worse than useless (cf. Rev 3:15-17; Heb 6:1-8).

Comments
14:25   Large crowds.   Luke pointed out that the people were still attracted to Jesus. The conditions of discipleship that follow were not addressed to believers in order to make them apostles but to the crowds. They are therefore conditions for salvation, not conditions for Christians to become a spiritual elite or to reach a new level in their Christian lives.

Were traveling with Jesus.   This recalls the journey to Jerusalem begun in Luke 9:51.

14:26   If anyone comes to me.   "Comes to me" means *seeks salvation* or *makes a decision to follow Jesus* (cf. 18:26,28).

And does not.   The decision to follow Jesus must be accompanied by three conditions (14:26-27,33).

Hate. This is the first condition. From Matt 10:37 we know that this means to "love [one's family] less." This is evident from Gen 29:30-31, where Jacob's greater love for Rachel (29:30) is phrased as hating Leah (29:31, RSV). Compare also Deut 21:15-17, where the same love-hate dichotomy is used. (The KJV translated the Hebrew literally as love/hate, but the NIV and RSV have translated the Hebrew as loves/does not love and love/dislike.) Compare also 16:13, where a love-hate, devote-despise dichotomy describes preferring one master over another.[184] A person who commits himself or herself to Christ will develop a greater love for both neighbor and family, although at times loving and following Christ may be seen as renunciation, rejection, or hate if the family does not share the same commitment to Christ.

Father and mother. "Father and mother" is the first of three matching sets. The Matthean parallel lacks "wife" in the second set and in the last set "brothers and sisters." Compare 18:29 for a similar grouping.

Wife. Compare 14:20; 18:29.

Even his own life. Compare 9:23-24; 17:33; John 12:25. This is the fourth set in the series. For Luke's love of "fours," see comments on 6:22.

Cannot be my disciple. This refers to becoming a Christian, i.e., becoming a "disciple,"[185] not to becoming an apostle or one of the "twelve disciples."[186] Matthew 10:37-38 uses these words in the same way, for the person not fulfilling these conditions "will not be worthy of Jesus" (10:37), which is further described as "losing one's life" (10:39).

14:27 Does not carry his cross and follow me. This is the second condition for discipleship. Compare 9:23.

14:28 Suppose. The following similitudes illustrate the need to consider carefully what it means to become a Christian.

One of you. "One of you" is literally *Who out of you.* Compare 11:5,11; 12:25; 15:4; 17:7; cf. also 14:31.

Build a tower. Compare 13:4. This may have served as a protection for a house or vineyard or was perhaps some sort of farm building (cf. Mark 12:1).

Estimate the cost. This term was used both for counting votes and for adding up numbers in business ledgers.

14:29 Will ridicule him. Compare 18:32; 22:63; 23:11,36.

14:30 This is a derisive comment, a jeer, not a statement of fact.

This fellow. A derogatory use of the article "this." The point of the similitude was not made explicit because it was self-evident. Do not promise to follow Jesus unless you understand the "cost" and are willing to "pay" it. This does not imply that salvation must be earned. Rather the point being made is that God's grace can only be received by those who, in repenting, place him above everything else.

14:31 Or suppose a king. Whereas 14:28 has "one of you," here Luke omitted "of you" because Israel had no king in his/Jesus' day.

---

[184]Cf. also Prov 13:24; Isa 60:15; Mal 1:2-3; Rom 9:13; and the parallel to this saying in GT 55. For a fuller discussion see Stein, *Difficult Passages*, 201-2.

[185]In the sense used in Acts 6:1-2,7; 9:1,10,19,26,38.

[186]In the sense used in 5:30; 6:1,13.

14:32 A delegation. Compare 19:14.

14:33 The third condition is described. A disciple must relinquish everything. Similar teachings are found in 12:33; 18:22; cf. also 5:11; 11:41. See comments on 5:28.

Give up. Compare 9:61, where the same term is used. The present tense emphasizes that this renunciation must be continual (see comments on 9:23).

14:34 If it loses its saltiness. The question arises about how salt can lose its taste, i.e., become insipid. Since this is a parable, the idea of salt becoming "unsalty" need not cause difficulty, even if in actuality this were not possible. However, the thought here may reflect the fact that most salt came from the Dead Sea and contained carnallite or gypsum. If carelessly processed, it would become insipid or poor tasting. Such salt was of little or no use; in fact, it was a distinct liability because it now had to be discarded. Although salt was used in sacrifices (Lev 2:13), here the focus is on its function as a seasoning. The verb "loses its saltiness" is translated everywhere else in the NT as "to become foolish." Yet how can salt become "foolish"? It may be that the reality part of this analogy, which involves the "foolishness" of an unconsidered decision to follow Jesus, has intruded into the analogy itself, with the salt becoming equally worthless/foolish by losing its taste.

14:35 It is fit neither for the soil nor for the manure pile. Bad salt is worse than nothing. It has a negative value. It is a kind of environmental hazard, for it would ruin soil or even a manure pile. Sowing the earth with salt was the ultimate punishment for a defeated enemy.

He who has ears to hear. Compare Luke 8:8.

The Lukan Message

In this section Luke reiterated what is involved in becoming a Christian. The teaching, much like 9:23-27,57-62; 18:24-30, deals with the "cost" of discipleship. Neither Jesus nor Luke encouraged an unthinking, impulsive "leap of faith" into discipleship. They emphasized instead that one should reflect on what the act of commitment involves. The three conditions described in this passage (hating one's family, i.e., putting Jesus above all other relationships [14:26], bearing the cross and following Jesus [14:27], and renouncing possessions [14:33]) are repeated throughout Luke-Acts in a multitude of different images and terms. These include taking up the cross daily (9:23), leaving family (18:29), repenting (5:32; 10:13; 13:3,5; 15:7, 10), believing or having faith (7:50; 8:46; Acts 16:31), losing one's life (Luke 9:24), repentance and being baptized (Acts 2:38), hearing and doing God's will (Luke 8:21), acknowledging Christ (12:8), and entering the narrow door (13:24). These are all to be understood as complementary expressions of the same kind of commitment. None of them can be fulfilled without fulfilling the others. Luke made clear that the decision to follow Jesus must be made consciously, with full awareness of the implications (14:28-32; cf. 9:57-62). See Introduction 8 (6).

Since Luke was writing to Christian believers, however, (see Introduction 3), these teachings function somewhat differently than they did in Jesus' day. His purpose was to remind his Christian readers of what they had committed to Christ lest they minimize the scope of their obligation. Luke wanted his readers to know that Jesus provides no "cheap grace." It is cheap neither from the divine perspective nor from the human one. What it has cost, Jesus' death on the cross, was everything; and the response that enables us to receive that grace is likewise everything. Theophilus was to remember that it is not only the beginning of one's Christian life that is important but above all how one perseveres (8:14-15). A half-hearted discipleship is doomed.

This passage also contains a strong, if implicit, Christology. Jesus demands a position above all else in life. Even the basic sociological unit of society, the family, must not take priority over one's commitment to Jesus. Being a Christian is not primarily about adherence to a particular ethical teaching, although that is indeed involved; more than anything else it entails following Jesus (14:27). The absolute nature of this demand implies a high Christology indeed.[187]

(7) The Parables of the Lost Sheep, Lost Coin, and Gracious Father (15:1-32)

[1]Now the tax collectors and "sinners" were all gathering around to hear him. [2]But the Pharisees and the teachers of the law muttered, "This man welcomes sinners and eats with them."

[3]Then Jesus told them this parable: [4]"Suppose one of you has a hundred sheep and loses one of them. Does he not leave the ninety-nine in the open country and go after the lost sheep until he finds it? [5]And when he finds it, he joyfully puts it on his shoulders [6]and goes home. Then he calls his friends and neighbors together and says, 'Rejoice with me; I have found my lost sheep.' [7]I tell you that in the same way there will be more rejoicing in heaven over one sinner who repents than over ninety-nine righteous persons who do not need to repent.

[8]"Or suppose a woman has ten silver coins and loses one. Does she not light a lamp, sweep the house and search carefully until she finds it? [9]And when she finds it, she calls her friends and neighbors together and says, 'Rejoice with me; I have found my lost coin.' [10]In the same way, I tell you, there is rejoicing in the presence of the angels of God over one sinner who repents."

[11]Jesus continued: "There was a man who had two sons. [12]The younger one said to his father, 'Father, give me my share of the estate.' So he divided his property between them.

[13]"Not long after that, the younger son got together all he had, set off for a distant country and there squandered his wealth in wild living. [14]After he had spent everything, there was a severe famine in that whole country, and he began to be in need. [15]So he went and hired himself out to a citizen of that

---

[187]See Stein, *Method and Message of Jesus' Teachings*, 118-19.

country, who sent him to his fields to feed pigs. [16]He longed to fill his stomach with the pods that the pigs were eating, but no one gave him anything.

[17]"When he came to his senses, he said, 'How many of my father's hired men have food to spare, and here I am starving to death! [18]I will set out and go back to my father and say to him: Father, I have sinned against heaven and against you. [19]I am no longer worthy to be called your son; make me like one of your hired men.' [20]So he got up and went to his father.

"But while he was still a long way off, his father saw him and was filled with compassion for him; he ran to his son, threw his arms around him and kissed him.

[21]"The son said to him, 'Father, I have sinned against heaven and against you. I am no longer worthy to be called your son.'

[22]"But the father said to his servants, 'Quick! Bring the best robe and put it on him. Put a ring on his finger and sandals on his feet. [23]Bring the fattened calf and kill it. Let's have a feast and celebrate. [24]For this son of mine was dead and is alive again; he was lost and is found.' So they began to celebrate.

[25]"Meanwhile, the older son was in the field. When he came near the house, he heard music and dancing. [26]So he called one of the servants and asked him what was going on. [27]'Your brother has come,' he replied, 'and your father has killed the fattened calf because he has him back safe and sound.'

[28]"The older brother became angry and refused to go in. So his father went out and pleaded with him. [29]But he answered his father, 'Look! All these years I've been slaving for you and never disobeyed your orders. Yet you never gave me even a young goat so I could celebrate with my friends. [30]But when this son of yours who has squandered your property with prostitutes comes home, you kill the fattened calf for him!'

[31]"'My son,' the father said, 'you are always with me, and everything I have is yours. [32]But we had to celebrate and be glad, because this brother of yours was dead and is alive again; he was lost and is found.' "

Context

In this chapter we encounter a new scene in which the Pharisees and scribes complain of Jesus' association with publicans and sinners (15:1-2). We have already encountered this criticism in 5:27-32 (Matt 9:11; Mark 2:16), in Luke 7:39, and will encounter it again in 19:7. Three parables follow that serve both as a defense of Jesus' ministry to such outcasts (cf. 14:15-24) and an appeal to his opponents to join in celebrating their entrance into the kingdom (15:7,10,28,31-32). We find a similar collection of two short parables followed by a longer one in 13:1-9.

The parables are connected by theme (the joy of the lost being found) and by key words ("lost" and "found," 15:6,9,24,32; "rejoice" and "celebrate," 15:6,9,24,32). Together the three parables form a tightly knit unit with a single, strongly Lukan theme—God's love for outcasts and sinners. The arrangement of this unit is almost certainly due to Luke's hand. (Note how each parable contains a similar concluding application: 15:7,10,32.)

The tie to what precedes is not as clear.[188] Luke may have placed this material at this point because it further demonstrates the hostility of the Pharisees and scribes toward Jesus (cf. 15:2 with 14:1-6,15-24; cf. also 16:14-15,19-31) or because, like the parable of the great banquet (14:15-24), it speaks of the entrance of the outcasts into the kingdom and the exclusion of the religious elite. Luke may even have decided at 14:15 to bring together a collection of parables extending to 16:31.[189] Whereas it is difficult to know the exact reason Luke connected these three parables with the preceding material, they fit well the material found in chap. 14.

The first two parables, like the parables of the mustard seed and leaven (13:18-21), refer to a man (shepherd) and a woman in the same order. It is evident that Luke understood them as a matched pair from the "or" in 15:8 (cf. the "again" in 13:20).[190] In the first parable a shepherd seeks for his lost sheep until he finds it. Returning he rejoices that the lost sheep is found, i.e., returned to safety and the other sheep. The picture part of the parable clearly refers to Jesus' ministering to Israel's outcasts and to their entering God's kingdom. Through the parable Jesus both censured and appealed to his opponents: "The lost of Israel are finding forgiveness; sinners are finding salvation. It is time to rejoice. In heaven God rejoices over this. Why won't you enter into this joy?" The second parable makes this point using in its picture a woman who has lost a silver coin and finds it.

The third parable is perhaps the most famous of all Jesus' parables. The question has been raised about whether 15:11-32 originally consisted of two separate parables (15:11-24 and 15:25-32). The fact that 15:11-24 is frequently treated in isolation from 15:25-32 supports such a view. Furthermore, no one would think that the parable was incomplete if it ended in 15:24. Yet the parable is clearly a contrast parable (cf. 7:41-42; 18:9-14; Matt 21:28-31; 25:1-13) that contrasts *two* brothers (Luke 15:11). Without 15:25-32 this contrast would be lacking. Furthermore, whereas the first part of the parable can stand by itself, the second cannot. One need only read 15:25 and 15:27 to see how this part of the parable requires and builds upon the first part.

As one might expect, this parable has been extensively allegorized throughout history.[191] Such allegorization, of course, completely loses

---

[188] Although there is no chronological tie to the preceding chapter, this material possibly was connected in Luke's source. Matthew's placement of the parable of the lost sheep in 18:10-14 at a different place in his Gospel (cf. also GT 107) and the absence of the parable of the lost coin and the prodigal son in his Gospel argue against this.

[189] The material in 14:34-35; 16:9-18 interrupts the parable sequence but serves as commentaries to them.

[190] For other twin parables cf. Luke 5:36-39; 14:28-32.

[191] Frequently the details have been allegorized as follows: "squandered his wealth" means *lost his natural ability and wisdom as a descendant of Adam*; "citizen" is the devil; the pigs are

sight of the parable's context (15:1-3), the point of the former two parables, and the fact that Jesus' audience would never have been able to associate various parts of the parable, such as the ring and the feast, with the Christian ordinances.

In seeking to understand the main point of the parable, two important principles come into play. The first has been called "the rule of end stress."[192] This means that in a parable, as in most stories, the climax comes at the end. What comes at the end of this parable involves the antagonism of the older son toward his father. This fits well the context in 15:1-3. A second principle involves the importance of direct discourse in a parable. In 15:29-32 such a discourse is found between the father and the older son, and this focuses attention on the older son's protesting his father's love toward his outcast brother. There is no similar conversation between the father and the younger son. The end stress of the parable and the presence of a lengthy discourse at the end indicate that the parable's main point is to be found in the interaction of the father and the older brother.

As in the parable of the laborers in the vineyard (Matt 20:1-16), we have in the picture part of the parable (1) a "faithful" son (first-hour worker) (2) protesting the father's (vineyard owner's) (3) gracious reinstatement of his son (giving of a denarius to the worker who worked only one hour). Jesus used these parables both as a defense of his ministry to the outcasts and as an invitation to grumbling older brothers, such as the Pharisees and teachers of the law (Luke 15:2), to share in the joyous participation of outcasts in the kingdom (cf. also Matt 21:28-32). Thus this parable continues the same theme, God's love for the lost, found in Luke 15:4-10. Whereas in the first two parables the presence and hostility of Jesus' opponents is gleaned from the context (15:1-2), however, here it appears in the parable itself in the form of the older brother (15:25-32). In light of this, the parable should be named after the main character in both halves of the parable—the parable of the gracious father.

Comments

15:1 The tax collectors and "sinners." These are "the poor, the crippled, the blind, and the lame" of 14:21. The two groups are found together in 5:30 and 7:34. For "tax collector" see comments on 3:12.

Were all gathering. Note the hyperbolic use of "all."[193] The paraphrastic (literally *were . . . nearing*) indicates that this was a habitual experience in Jesus' ministry.

To hear. This connects the following material to the teachings in 14:26-35. The tax collectors and sinners have "ears to hear" (14:35).

---

demons; the robe is the sonship Adam lost due to sin; the ring is Christian baptism; feast is the Lord's Supper; the fattened calf is the Savior's presence in the Lord's Supper.

[192] See Stein, *Parables of Jesus*, 56, 123, 127.

[193] Cf. Luke 3:15-16; 4:15; 5:17; 6:17; 9:43.

15:2   The Pharisees and the teachers of the law. Compare 5:30 and 5:21; 6:7; 11:53, where in the Greek text the order is reversed. Compare also 5:17; 7:30; 14:3. **Muttered.** Compare 5:30; 19:7; Matt 20:11.

This man welcomes sinners and eats with them. Compare Luke 5:29-32; 7:39; 19:7. For the significance of such eating, see comments on 5:30. The OT warnings not to associate with sinful people were no doubt applied to Jesus' association with tax collectors and sinners.[194] Yet Jesus associated with such people to offer them salvation through repentance and faith, not to participate in their sin. Compare the derogatory "this man" with 14:30.

15:3 Compare the similar introduction in 5:36.

Parable. As in 5:36, the singular "parable" is followed by more than one parable. Here it may mean *a parabolic discourse.*

15:4   Suppose one of you. This was a common way for Luke to introduce a parable.[195]

The metaphor of a shepherd is used for God in Ps 23:1-4; Ezek 34:11-16. In the picture part of the parable a shepherd is counting his sheep at night and finds one missing.

Hundred sheep. "A hundred" is a round number.

Leave the ninety-nine. The question of who would take care of these sheep while the shepherd searched for the lost one would be relevant if this were a true story. In a parable, however, it is irrelevant. The story teller "takes care" of the ninety-nine.

Open country. Literally *desert.* Matthew 18:12 has "on the hills," but since most shepherding was done on "desert mountains" east of Bethlehem, either term could be used to describe this area.

Go after. Compare Ezek 34:11-12; John 10:11-15.

Lost. Compare 15:4,6,8-9,24,32; cf. also 13:3,5, where the same term is translated "perish." For the reality to which this word refers, cf. 19:10.

Until he finds it. This phrase reveals the persistence of the shepherd. Compare Matt 18:12-13, which leaves open the possibility of not finding the lost sheep.

15:5   Puts it on his shoulders. This aspect of the parable's picture expresses the shepherd's loving care and has been a favorite artistic theme through the centuries. Frequently a sheep that became lost was weak and could not keep up with the rest of the flock. Thus the shepherd needed to carry it on his shoulders.

15:6   Calls his friends and neighbors. Compare Luke 15:9. This detail is lacking in the Matthean parallel (cf. 18:13).

Rejoice with me. Compare 15:9,23-24.

Lost sheep. In Matt 18:10-14 the sheep are not "lost" but "wandering."[196] If Matthew and Luke are two versions of the same parable, Luke's version seems to fit Jesus' situation better.

15:7   In the same way. Compare 15:10.

---

[194]Prov 1:10-19; 2:1-15; 4:14-17; Ps 1:1; cf. also 1 Cor 15:33.

[195]Cf. Luke 11:5,11, 12:25; 14:28; 17:7; cf. also 14:5.

[196]The reality part in Matthew refers to believers who are straying (cf. 18:10, "little ones" and "their angels"). Matthew appears to have applied Jesus' teaching to the situation of the early church in his own day. If so, this indicates that Matthew believed he was not only a recorder of Jesus' words and acts but also an authoritative interpreter.

There will be more rejoicing. The future tense can refer to the time of the final judgment or may be a "proverbial" future referring to the present time. The latter seems more likely since the parallel in 15:10 uses the present tense "is rejoicing" (*ginetai chara*). The use of the third person "there will be" functions like a divine passive, for "God rejoices." See comments on 16:9. "More" does not translate a Greek term but must be supplied because of the "than" later in the verse.

In heaven. "In heaven" is a circumlocution for "God" (cf. 15:18,21; cf. also 6:23; 10:20).

Repents. Repentance is a strong Lukan emphasis (see comments on 3:3).[197] The verb occurs fourteen times in Luke-Acts and the noun eleven times.

Righteous persons who do not need to repent. Compare 5:31-32. From 10:13; 11:32; 13:3,5; Acts 2:38; 17:30 it is evident that for Luke everyone had need of repentance, whether Jew or Greek (Acts 11:18; 17:30). If the ninety-nine refer to the Pharisees and scribes, then these words must be understood ironically as *those who think they are righteous and have no need to repent.*[198] Less likely is the view that Jesus assumed for the sake of argument the claim of his opponents that they were righteous. In the context of Luke 15:1-3 the parable is in fact a call for "the righteous" to repent by sharing God's joy in the salvation of "sinners." Most probably one should not press this detail in the parable and seek meaning with respect to who the ninety-nine represent. The basic reality to which this parable points is God's great joy over the repentance of the lost as they receive life.

15:8 Or suppose a woman. Even as 14:28-32 contains two parables, the second of which begins "Or suppose a king," so we have again two parables involving a similar introduction for the second parable. For Luke's tendency to balance men and women in his examples, see comments on 13:19.

Silver coins. The exact value of such coins (literally *drachmas*), which are not mentioned anywhere else in the NT, is difficult to estimate. They may have been equal to a denarius. Speculation about whether these were part of the bridal headdress and dowry is unnecessary and irrelevant to the story, as is the exact value of a drachma. No comparison is intended between the hundred-to-one or ten-to-one ratios.

Light a lamp, sweep . . . search. These are necessary actions to find a lost coin in a dark, windowless house.

Until she finds it. Compare 15:4. This parable could well be called the parable of the seeking woman.

15:10 In the same way. Compare 15:7.

In the presence of the angels of God. Like "in heaven" (15:7), this is a circumlocution for God. See comments on 12:8.

15:11 There was a man. This is a typical Lukan introduction to a parable. See comments on 10:30; 16:19-31, "Context."

Two sons. This indicates that this parable does not find its completion after 15:24 but after 15:32. If 15:25-32 were not an integral part of the parable, the parable could begin "There was a man who had *a* son."

---

[197] Cf. Luke 3:8; 5:32; 10:13; 11:32; 13:3,5.
[198] For other examples of Jesus' use of irony, cf. Luke 5:32; 11:47-48; 12:54-56; 13:33; 18:9-14.

15:12 The younger one. Speculation concerning his age and marital and family status is irrelevant for the parable. Luke included in the present account all that was necessary for his readers to understand the meaning of the parable.

Give me my share of the estate. The older son would receive two thirds of the estate and the younger son one third (Deut 21:17). Actually the younger son would receive slightly less than a third if there were daughters, for money would be needed for their dowries. Usually such a division of the inheritance took place upon the death of the father, but it could occur earlier. Sirach 33:19-23, however, advises against the latter.

So he divided his property between them. The wisdom, or foolishness, of the father in doing this is an irrelevant issue. Jesus wanted the father to do so in order to tell the rest of the story. One should not allegorize this detail and search for meaning in it.

15:13 Not long after that. "Not long" is literally *not many days*.[199]

Got together all he had. "Got together all he had" means *converted to cash his inheritance*. The question of how this was done, whether a sale of land was involved and so forth, is unstated and therefore irrelevant.

Set off for a distant country. Compare Luke 19:12. The purpose of his doing so is not stated. It is not important.

Squandered his wealth. The next phrase explains how this took place. It was not due to a business failure.

In wild living. "In wild living" is literally *living recklessly*. Luke described this more fully in 15:30.

15:15 Hired himself out. Due to the circumstances described in 15:14, the younger son seeks to avoid starvation.

A citizen of that country. He is a Gentile, as his raising pigs reveals. Compare Acts 10:28.

Sent him . . . to feed pigs. These were "unclean" animals (Lev 11:7; Deut 14:8; cf. 1 Macc 1:47). This part of the parable gives a poignant picture of a Jewish man on "skid row." Compare *Baba Qammma* 82b, "Cursed be the man who would breed swine."

15:16 He longed to fill . . . that the pigs were eating. This may mean that he saw the pigs eating and being filled and he would have liked to have been full also. It was psychologically impossible, however, for him to eat such "pig-food."[200] It could also mean that he would have liked to have eaten the food the pigs ate, but it was physiologically impossible to do so since humans could not eat such food. Finally, it could mean that he would have liked to have eaten the food the pigs ate, but the "citizen" would not allow him to do so. It is uncertain which of these is more likely, but what is clear is that the younger son has fallen as far as he can. He is working for a Gentile, feeding pigs, and is in some way or other contemplating "breaking bread" with them. "Pods" are carob pods used to feed animals, and at times the poor were forced to eat them.

---

[199]Litotes, a figure a speech in which the negation ("not") of the opposite ("many days") expresses what is meant (*a few days after*) is a common Lukan device. Cf. Acts 1:5; 14:28; 15:2.

[200]So Fitzmyer, *Luke* 2:1088.

No one gave him anything. This is a further description of the younger son's desperate plight.

15:17 Came to his senses. This is a Hebrew/Aramaic expression for "repented."[201] This refers not only to a mental process that causes him to think more clearly about his situation but also to a moral renewal involving repentance. This is evident from Luke 15:7,10 and the younger son's confession in 15:18,21.

He said. "Said" means *thought to himself.* Compare 12:17.

Hired men. Compare Matt 20:1-16, where work is done by "hired servants" rather than slaves.

15:18 Father. For those who seek to make this parable into an allegory in which the Father is God, note that the "Father" in this verse ("you") is clearly distinguished from God ("heaven").

Sinned against heaven and against you. "Heaven" is a circumlocution for God. Note how Jesus' order "God and man" follows his teaching in 10:27 concerning "God and neighbor" (cf. Exod 10:16; Num 21:7; 1 Sam 15:24). See comments on 10:27. Jesus' theological orientation is apparent. The young man has first of all sinned against God (cf. Ps 51:4, which was commonly understood as describing David's repentance over his adultery with Bathsheba and murder of Uriah). The younger son has sinned against his father by dishonoring him (Luke 15:12). In so doing he above all has sinned against God who gave this, the Fifth, Commandment (Exod 20:12).

15:19 No longer worthy to be called your son. The issue does not involve the young man's legal status (I am not legally your son any longer) but his filial status (a father like you deserves better than a son like me).

Like one of your hired men. The younger son's attitude reveals his true repentance. He knows he has no grounds for being treated like a son.

15:20 While . . . a long way off, his father saw him. The question of how the father could have seen his son a long way off can be answered easily. Jesus, the teller of the parable, wanted him to.

Filled with compassion. Compare 7:13.

Ran to his son. Throwing aside Oriental behavioral conventions, Jesus has the father run to his son in order to show God's love, joy, and eagerness to receive outcasts. Compare Sir 19:30.[202]

Threw his arms around him. "Threw his arms around him" is literally *fell on his neck* (cf. Acts 20:37; Gen 33:4; 45:14-15). This action shows the father's loving acceptance of his son (cf. Gen 33:4 and 10).

Kissed him. Compare Acts 20:37; 2 Sam 14:33.

15:21 Compare Luke 15:18-19. The father is so eager to receive him that the young man cannot complete his prepared speech.

15:22 But the father said. The father is about to practice "usufruct," i.e., the right to exercise control over the property he has irrevocably given to his older son.

---

[201] Jeremias, *Parables of Jesus,* 130; K. E. Bailey, *Poet & Peasant/Through Peasant Eyes: A Literary Cultural Approach to the Parables in Luke* (Grand Rapids: Eerdmans, 1983), 173-75.
[202] See Bailey, *Poet & Peasant,* 181-82.

To his servants. These probably would be understood as household servants in contrast to the field workers, or hired men, in 15:17.

Best robe. The best, not the former robe he left behind. This refers to the robe reserved for notable guests.

Ring. Through the ring the father bestows his authority upon his son. Compare 1 Macc 6:15.

Sandals. Sandals were a luxury, and servants did not wear them. The son is not, however, to be treated as a servant. He is to wear sandals. These individual details in the parable are not to be allegorized in order to have them correspond to some spiritual reality but are only meant to reveal the father's full acceptance of his son. Compare Gen 41:42.

15:23   The fattened calf. Meat was not usually eaten at meals. The slaughter of the fattened calf, which was specially fed and kept for special occasions, indicates a great feast/banquet in celebration of the lost son. Compare Gen 18:7-8; Amos 6:4.

Let's have a feast and celebrate. At times such feasting and rejoicing is appropriate. In contrast to the rich fool in 12:19, thanksgiving is offered to God for bringing the prodigal son back from death unto life. In 12:19 what is condemned is a godless self-indulgence.

15:24   Dead. In the picture part of the parable this is a metaphor for "assumed physically dead" or "missing from the family unit," but in the reality part of the parable this refers to being "spiritually dead," i.e., dead in trespasses and sins.

Alive. In the picture part this is a metaphor for "present again in the family"; in the reality part, for "saved," i.e., possessing life in God's kingdom.

Lost and is found. This ties this parable to the preceding two (cf. 15:6,9) and to the conclusion of this parable (cf. 15:32).

15:25   Meanwhile, the older son. The second part of the parable is now introduced.

In the field. The question of why the brother was not at home but in the field is easily answered. For the sake of his parable, Jesus wanted him there.

15:26   Asked . . . what was going on. Compare 18:36; Acts 21:33.

15:27   Safe and sound. "Safe and sound" is literally *healthy*. More is implied than his physical health. In the picture part of the parable this would refer to his moral and spiritual health; but in the reality part, to his having received salvation.

15:28   Pleaded with him. Even as in this parable the father enjoins his son to share in the banquet, so Jesus was appealing to his opponents to join in and celebrate what God was doing in this acceptable year of the Lord (Luke 4:18-21).

15:29   The older brother refuses to join the banquet. He likens his relationship to his father as years of servitude ("I've been slaving for you") without any joyous recognition ("you never gave me even a young goat [and for this son of yours you killed the fattened calf]").

Never disobeyed your orders. Compare 17:9-10.

15:30   This son of yours. "This" is used derogatorily, as in 14:30; 15:2; 18:11; Acts 17:18.

The older brother's refusal in the picture part of the parable to acknowledge that the returned son is indeed his "brother" corresponds well in the reality part of the parable with the Pharisees' refusal to acknowledge the outcasts as brothers. Compare the lawyer's unwillingness to acknowledge that it was a "Samaritan" who proved to be a neighbor in 10:37.

Who has squandered your property with prostitutes. How did the older brother know this? Again the answer is that Jesus provided this knowledge to the older brother.

15:31 My son. Jesus was making an affectionate appeal to his opponents through the parable. In this instance there was still hope they would have a change of heart (cf. also Luke 7:40ff.). Elsewhere, however, there was no such hope (cf. 11:37-52; 13:15-17). The positive appeal to the Pharisees and teachers of the law indicates that the parable originated in the situation of Jesus rather than of the early church, for in the latter situation there was little of such hope.

Everything I have is yours. The assumption is that the division of 15:12 also involved the older brother, who possesses all that remains of the inheritance (over two thirds), even though the father still has usufruct of it.

15:32 We had to celebrate. Literally *it was necessary* (*edei*). The word indicates a divine necessity. See Introduction 8 (1). God requires his people to rejoice that salvation is coming to the outcasts.

This brother of yours. Through the parable Jesus taught the Pharisees and teachers of the law (15:2) that the outcasts, who were receiving life, were Abraham's children, i.e., their brothers.

Why did the older brother react this way? Jesus did not tell us. As a result it is illegitimate to question the thinking of this fictional character. Fictional characters do not exist and therefore cannot think. It is legitimate, however, to ask why Jesus' opponents reacted so negatively to Jesus' ministry to publicans and sinners. One reason is that this may have resulted from the view that godly people should not associate with the ungodly because they would be tempted to share in their evil deeds. This is an overreaction to such views as found in the references listed in 15:2. Another reason is that such behavior clashed head-on with their view of how righteousness is achieved. The full acceptance of repentant publicans and sinners, before they could achieve a holy life-style and track record, contradicted their understanding of piety. They believed in repentance and forgiveness, but the immediate acceptance of such people as "righteous" was difficult to accept. Perhaps also despite the claim that the law was a delight, many of Jesus' opponents saw it as a burden that all people should have to bear. To receive forgiveness freely, apart from bearing such a burden, made their own burdensome keeping of the law seem unnecessary and worthless (cf. 15:29; Matt 20:12). Rather than feeling sorry that the outcasts missed the joy of the life of obedient faith, they were angry that they could receive salvation without having to bear the burden of the obedient keeping of the law.

The question has often been raised about how the older brother responded to his father's words in Luke 15:31-32. This question loses sight of the fact that this is a parable, i.e., a work of fiction. There is no real older brother. Jesus did not want this character to respond, and he ceased to exist after 15:32. On the other hand the question of how the Pharisees and teachers of the law responded to Jesus' parable is a legitimate one. There is no indication of how this particular group of

Pharisees and scribes responded, but elsewhere it is clear that the majority of them responded negatively.[203]

The Lukan Message

These three parables fit well the Lukan emphasis on God's love and grace for outcasts (cf. 14:12-14,21-23). God's mercy (cf. 6:36) is now described poignantly by these parables. God has shown his mercy (1:50, 54,58,72,78) by visiting the needy (1:51-53). No doubt for Luke and Theophilus their own entrance as Gentiles into God's kingdom would have come to mind. Was Luke seeking to reassure his readers of God's love and acceptance of them in light of such opposition as found in Acts 11:2-3; 15:1 (cf. Gal 2:11-14)? Probably when Luke wrote, this was no longer an issue. Nevertheless, the parables found in this chapter would remind Luke's readers of what they once were (cf. Eph 2:1-3,12) and of God's great love for them. God accepts all repentant sinners, no matter how outcast they may be.

Several other theological themes appear in this chapter. We should not lose sight of the Christological claims found here. In Jesus' eating with tax collectors and sinners, God was at work offering his kingdom to outcasts. For Luke these parables had to be understood in light of 4:18-21. God's Son has come, bringing with him God's kingdom, and he is offering it to the lost. It is true that the eyewitnesses and ministers of the word also through their preaching offer the kingdom to sinners, but there is a difference. They offer the kingdom to sinners in Jesus' name. Jesus' eating with publicans and sinners *is* God's offering the kingdom to sinners. For Luke there was a distinct difference between those who go out and minister in Jesus' name and the One who goes out and ministers in his own name.

Another theme that appears frequently in this chapter involves the need for repentance. The aim and goal of such repentance is clearly the forgiveness of sins. The people represented by the lost sheep (15:7), the lost coin (15:10), and the "lost" son (15:17-21) repent in hope of the forgiveness of sins. See comments on 3:3; Introduction 8 (6). Although it is not expressly stated, Luke believed that the need to repent is universal (see comments on 15:7). This implies a doctrine of sin and depravity. And if repentance results in immediate entrance into the kingdom, then this also implies that salvation is by grace. Even though the parable of the gracious father was not given to teach the doctrine of justification by faith, the younger son's acceptance by his father rings true to this biblical teaching. His acceptance was entirely gracious.

---

[203] Luke 6:2,7; 11:53-56; 13:31-35; 14:1-6; 22:1-2.

The question has been raised about whether this parable teaches that God's forgiveness is "free." Did Luke believe there was thus no necessity of an "atonement." One cannot require in a parable such as this, which teaches God's love for the outcasts and the hostility this encounters, a complete doctrine of the atonement as well. A parable is not meant to serve as a shorter catechism of all Christian doctrine. Luke expected that this parable would be interpreted in light of what he had already said in his Gospel (cf. 9:22), what he would say shortly (cf. 19:10; 22:17-22), what he would write in Acts (4:12; 13:26-39; 20:28), and what they had already been taught (perhaps a tradition such as 1 Cor 15:3-8). The purpose of this parable is to teach essentially one basic point dealing with the situation described in 15:1-2. To ask more of it than this is unwarranted.

The church must continually examine the significance of this parable. Will we be the church of the elder brother or the church of the loving father?

(8) The Parable of the Dishonest Manager (16:1-8)

[1]Jesus told his disciples: "There was a rich man whose manager was accused of wasting his possessions. [2]So he called him in and asked him, 'What is this I hear about you? Give an account of your management, because you cannot be manager any longer.'

[3]"The manager said to himself, 'What shall I do now? My master is taking away my job. I'm not strong enough to dig, and I'm ashamed to beg— [4]I know what I'll do so that, when I lose my job here, people will welcome me into their houses.'

[5]"So he called in each one of his master's debtors. He asked the first, 'How much do you owe my master?'

[6]" 'Eight hundred gallons of olive oil,' he replied.

"The manager told him, 'Take your bill, sit down quickly, and make it four hundred.'

[7]"Then he asked the second, 'And how much do you owe?'

" 'A thousand bushels of wheat,' he replied.

"He told him, 'Take your bill and make it eight hundred.'

[8]"The master commended the dishonest manager because he had acted shrewdly. For the people of this world are more shrewd in dealing with their own kind than are the people of the light.

Context

The material in 16:1-31 centers around the theme of the proper use of possessions and wealth. It begins with the parable of the unjust steward (16:1-8) to which two sets of sayings concerning "Money" (16:9-13, esp. 16:9,11,13) and the Pharisaic love of money (16:14-15) have been added; it concludes with the parable of the rich man and Lazarus (16:19-31). In the middle of the chapter we find sayings concerning the law (16:16-17) and divorce (16:18), which appear to be unrelated to the main theme of the chapter. The material in the chapter is, for the most part, unique to Luke. Only 16:13 (Matt 6:24), 16:16-17 (Matt 11:12-13; 5:18), and 16:18 (Mark 10:11-12) have significant parallels. Luke may have brought this material together because it deals with the common theme of possessions. The chapter can be divided into two parts according to the two audiences in the chapter (Luke 16:1-13 is addressed to disciples; 16:14-31 is addressed to Pharisees) or into three parts (16:1-8; 16:9-15; 16:16-31) according to the form of the material in the chapter (parable; sayings; parable).

The relationship of this material to the preceding chapter is unclear. Both the audience (15:1-32, Pharisees; 16:1-13, disciples) and subject matter (15:1-32, God's love for the outcast; 16:1-31, possessions) are different. The material of this chapter may have been placed after 15:1-32 for one of the following reasons: (1) They deal with similar literary forms, i.e., both chapters consist primarily of parables. (2) Luke found them already together in his source. (3) Luke wanted to attach the material involving Pharisees in 16:14-15,19-31 with the three parables addressed to Pharisees in 15:3-32. (The last suggestion is weakened by the fact that 16:1-13 is not material addressed to Pharisees but material addressed to disciples [16:1].) (4) Luke brought the material together because of the key words "squandered/wasting" in 15:13 and 16:1, which are different translations of the same Greek verb (*diaskorpizein*). No really convincing solution has been brought forward as yet.

Few passages of Scripture have caused as much confusion as the opening parable. Questions raised by the parable include the following: (1) Where does the parable end? After 16:7, 16:8a, 16:8b, or 16:9? (2) Who is the "master" of 16:8? Is he the rich man (16:1) who is called "master" in 16:3,5, or is he Jesus? (3) Why was the manager called "dishonest"? (4) Were the manager's actions in 16:5-6 honest or dishonest? These are only some of the questions this parable elicits, and the interrelatedness of these questions makes them even more difficult to answer.

Probably the most fundamental question that determines how the parable should be interpreted involves the moral dimension of the manager's actions. The strongest argument in favor of their being viewed as honest and moral is the master's commendation in 16:8a. If these actions are commended, must they not therefore be morally good? As a result attempts have been made to justify the lowering of the master's bills in a number of ways: (1) The steward lowered the bills by removing his commission. Thus he won approval and favor from the debtors, and as a result of making his master look good, he received his favor also. (2) The steward lowered the bills by removing his master's high and illegal interest. Thus he protected his master from possible legal complications and by making him look good found favor from him.[204]

---

[204] See Stein, *Parables of Jesus*, 106-11.

Such attempts to justify the manager's behavior, however, encounter numerous difficulties. For one, how could Jesus and Luke have expected their audiences to supply such information to the parable. One does not find any suggestion of such explanations within the parable itself. Luke probably assumed that everything his readers needed for understanding the parable was contained in it. Second, how would the first explanation have helped the manager? Having the favor of the debtors and master would be far less helpful than having the moneys his commissions would bring. Third, the money owed by the debtors is specifically said to have been owed to the manager's master, not to the steward (16:5). Fourth, note that the manager is only called dishonest *after* his lowering of the bills. This eliminates any possibility of interpreting his actions as moral. The manager need only have been inept, uncreative, or a poor manager to have wasted his master's money (16:1). No interpretation should overlook that the manager is called dishonest not because of wasting his master's possessions (16:1) but because of "fixing" the accounts (16:5-7). Fifth, the manager's actions were purely selfish and egocentric (16:4). He was not the least concerned for his master. Finally, note that the master's praise was not directed to the manager's being moral but to his being "shrewd." This implies only that he was wise, crafty as a fox, and prepared himself for his being fired from his managerial position.

It is best to interpret the manager's actions as being dishonest. This traditional interpretation takes the parable at face value. The only serious criticism in understanding the behavior as being dishonest is a moral one. How can the master commend someone for his dishonesty? Yet the manager is not commended for his dishonesty but for his shrewdness. He is commended for acting and preparing himself for the judgment awaiting him. He is commended essentially for being a shrewd scoundrel and taking care of his future. Jesus in several other places drew lessons from the actions of less than noble characters. In the parable of the wise and foolish virgins (Matt 25:1-13), the wise virgins are in fact quite selfish (25:9). Compare also the behavior of the man who found treasure in his field (Matt 13:44) and how God can be likened to an unjust judge (Luke 18:1-8).

Luke found no difficulty in urging his readers to prepare themselves for the coming judgment, as the dishonest manager did, by acting "shrewdly." How that shrewdness is to be manifested is, of course, quite different. It is not through dishonesty but in the wise stewardship of possessions (16:9-13). If Theophilus, who knew that a day was coming in which he had to render an account to his Lord (2 Cor 5:10; Heb 9:27), was a faithful steward of his possessions, then he also would have been acting shrewdly and would have received a commendation from his Master.

Comments

16:1 Jesus told his disciples. There is no necessary connection between this material and what preceded. Note the change in audience between Luke 16:1 and 15:3.

There was a rich man. This is Luke's equivalent of saying "What follows is a parable." See comments on 10:30; 16:19-31, "Context."

Manager. The "manager" manages the rich man's estate.

Accused of wasting. There is nothing in this charge that implies dishonesty on the manager's part. Compare 15:13.

16:2 Give an account. Compare Matt 12:36; Acts 19:40; Heb 13:17; 1 Pet 4:5. The sense here is that of being dismissed and giving a final accounting report, *Turn in the books and ledgers of your stewardship.* Jesus and Luke expected their audiences to assume that the charges were correct.

16:3 Said to himself. Jesus shared the inner thinking of this fictional character with his audience in order to explain his actions in 16:5-7 (cf. 12:17; 15:17).

Not strong enough to dig. A physiological problem exists with respect to this option. The manager lacks strength for such manual work.

Ashamed to beg. A psychological problem exists with respect to this option. The manager has too much pride to beg.

16:4 I know. This is a "dramatic aorist" expressing the suddenness of the idea and decision.

What I'll do. In the last moments of his managerial role, he will do something to insure his future after he is fired from his job.

So that . . . people will welcome me into their houses. Literally *they will welcome me.* The manager anticipates that this last action will ingratiate his master's debtors toward him and obligate them in some way so that this will guarantee his future. Note that the steward acts not for the benefit of his master but purely for his own selfish ends. Thus it is impossible to see in his actions a noble and moral act.

16:6 Eight hundred gallons of olive oil. The NIV gives a modern equivalent of the ancient measure, literally *a hundred measures (batous) of olive oil.* The exact amount is uncertain, but it would have been around eight to nine hundred gallons.

Take your bill. There is not the slightest suggestion by Jesus or Luke that the manager is removing his commission or his master's illegal interest from the bill. What he is doing is "dishonest" (16:8).

16:7 A thousand bushels of wheat. The NIV again gives a modern equivalent of the ancient measure, literally *a hundred 'cors' of wheat.*[205]

16:8 Without the conclusion in 16:8 the parable would be incomplete.

The master commended the dishonest manager. This is a surprising and unexpected twist in the story. Jesus' skill as a storyteller is clearly shown here. "Master" here can refer either to the rich man in the parable (16:1-3,5) or to Jesus.[206] It is also possible to understand this verse as being Jesus' interpretation of the parable rather than part of the parable itself. Support for this is seen in the parable of the unjust judge (18:1-5). Here we find a similar literary pattern in which a concluding statement (18:6) is made by the *kyrios*, and in this instance the master/Lord must refer to Jesus. In 18:6, however, this sentence with its reference to the *kyrios* clearly is not part of the parable itself but rather its interpretation. It means *learn from what*

---

[205] Jeremias (*Parables of Jesus*, 181) points out that the reductions of the two debts were approximately the same—about five hundred denarii.

[206] The Greek term κύριος is usually translated "Lord," although it can mean "master." See comments on 6:46.

the unjust judge says. In 16:8, on the other hand, this sentence with its reference to the *kyrios* must be part of the parable because the parable is incomplete at 16:7. Also it would seem unusual for Jesus to commend a fictional character rather than that character's actions. It seems more reasonable therefore to translate all three references to *kyrios* in 16:3,5,8 consistently as "master" than to change the meaning in the last reference because the parable gives no indication of such a switch in meaning. In 16:3,5 the term *kyrios* must be translated "master" because it clearly refers to the master of the estate. Therefore the "master" in the picture part of the parable commends the dishonest manager. In the reality part of the parable, however, it is the "Lord" Jesus Christ who urges the reader to act shrewdly to prepare for the great meeting (2 Cor 5:10; Heb 9:27).

Only now is the manager described as "dishonest." This is due to his behavior in Luke 16:5-7 rather than to his wasting his manager's goods in 16:1. For "dishonest" cf. 16:9,11; 18:6.

Acted shrewdly. Shrewdness need not refer to a moral quality. Here it refers to the rapscallion behavior with which the manager prepared himself for being fired.

For the people of this world. "People of this world" is literally *sons of this age.* This comment picks up the "shrewdness" of 16:8a and urges believers to act as prudently with regard to divine things as unbelievers do with regard to earthly things. With this the parable proper ends.

People of the light. "People [literally *sons*] of the light" was a favorite designation for God's people in the Qumran community (1QS 1:9ff.; 1 QM 1:1ff.).

The Lukan Message

Jesus' parable presupposes a final judgment exists in which God will judge the world. Jesus, Luke, and their respective audiences readily acknowledged this (cf. Acts 17:31; Rom 2:2-11). The "blesseds" and above all the "woes" in Luke-Acts would make no sense without such a judgment. The basis for that judgment, however, is already decided. Persons will be judged on whether they accept Jesus and follow him (Luke 9:26; 12:8-9). In light of this one should act decisively and with shrewd self-interest (16:8) to prepare for that time when an accounting must be made before God (16:2). What ultimately does anything profit if in that day a person loses his or her very self (9:25)? The parable emphasizes the great need to be ready for that day. It leaves to the following section, as well as the entire context of Luke-Acts, how the reader is to practice this shrewdness and make ready. In the Lukan context the parable is addressed to believers (16:1) to instruct them "on the necessity of not forgetting the priority of values related to future life."[207]

At the end of this parable Luke also indicated that he worked out of a two-age eschatological understanding. In 16:8 "this world" or age stands over by implication "that age" or "the age to come" (cf. Matt 12:32).

---

[207] Sabourin, *Luke*, 293.

Luke shared this two-age scheme with Jesus and first-century Pharisaism, but for Luke (and Jesus) there was a significant difference. For him God's kingdom had already entered into this present evil age through Jesus' ministry and the Spirit's presence. For Luke the age to come was now already realized. See Introduction 8 (2).

(9) Sayings on Stewardship (16:9-18)

[9]I tell you, use worldly wealth to gain friends for yourselves, so that when it is gone, you will be welcomed into eternal dwellings.
[10]"Whoever can be trusted with very little can also be trusted with much, and whoever is dishonest with very little will also be dishonest with much. [11]So if you have not been trustworthy in handling worldly wealth, who will trust you with true riches? [12]And if you have not been trustworthy with someone else's property, who will give you property of your own?
[13]"No servant can serve two masters. Either he will hate the one and love the other, or he will be devoted to the one and despise the other. You cannot serve both God and Money."
[14]The Pharisees, who loved money, heard all this and were sneering at Jesus. [15]He said to them, "You are the ones who justify yourselves in the eyes of men, but God knows your hearts. What is highly valued among men is detestable in God's sight.
[16]"The Law and the Prophets were proclaimed until John. Since that time, the good news of the kingdom of God is being preached, and everyone is forcing his way into it. [17]It is easier for heaven and earth to disappear than for the least stroke of a pen to drop out of the Law.
[18]"Anyone who divorces his wife and marries another woman commits adultery, and the man who marries a divorced woman commits adultery.

Context

Between the parables of the unjust manager (16:1-8) and the rich man and Lazarus (16:19-31) Luke inserted a series of Jesus' teachings. The first set involves possessions (16:9-15) and fits neatly with the preceding parable. The teachings are also tied to the parable by the term "dishonest" (*adikias*) in 16:8 and "worldly" (*adikias*) in 16:9, "dishonest" (*adikos*) twice in 16:10, and "worldly" (*adikō*) in 16:11. This sayings collection is also tied together by the term "wealth/money" (*mamōna*) in 16:9,11,13. To these general statements concerning possession are appended two verses describing the Pharisees' reaction to Jesus' teaching on this subject. The tie between these early verses and the remaining ones (16:16-18), however, is unclear. It has been suggested that the last one dealing with divorce might be connected either to 16:16-17 as an example of how the law was not made void[208] or to 16:9-15 as an example of how to

---

[208]Marshall, *Luke*, 631.

handle possessions, since first-century wives were thought of more as possessions.[209] It has also been suggested that these verses may have been placed here in order to prepare for the following parable that refers to the law and the prophets (cf. 16:27-31). Quite likely Luke brought together various sayings of Jesus in this section that stood isolated in the tradition to help his readers understand what it means to act "shrewdly" in light of the final judgment.[210]

Comments

16:9 I tell you. This expression is found over thirty times in Luke and can introduce seams that tie accounts together or conclusions to accounts (11:9; 13:24; 15:7,10). It can, however, also be found within accounts as well (3:8; 7:9,26,28).

Worldly wealth. Literally *the mammon of unrighteousness. Mammon* is an Aramaic term that means *money* or *possessions.* This expression does not refer to wealth gained through dishonesty, for in 16:11 we are told to be trustworthy in our handling of the "mammon of unrighteousness," and one cannot be trustworthy with respect to wealth obtained dishonestly. The expression is idiomatic and refers to "filthy lucre" or as the NIV translates it "worldly wealth."

To gain friends. Even as the dishonest manager used his master's money to gain friends, so Luke exhorted his readers to use their money similarly. The text does not make clear who these friends are, but if "they" will welcome the believers when worldly wealth no longer exists, they may refer to the angels; the righteous poor who are in God's presence (16:22); Abraham, Isaac, and Jacob (13:28); or this may be a circumlocution for "God." The latter interpretation seems more likely. Regardless, the general sense is clear even if the meaning of "friends" is not. Believers should so conduct their lives that when this world and its wealth comes to an end, God will welcome them into his presence.

So that when it is gone. This refers to the final day when the possessions of this world and the world itself come to an end, not to when one goes broke like the prodigal son. "So that" indicates that what follows is the purpose of the preceding.[211]

You will be welcomed. This use of the third person plural, "You will be welcomed," is literally *they will welcome you* and is a circumlocution for *God will welcome you.*[212]

Eternal dwellings. This is a metaphor for believers' final destiny after the day of judgment. Elsewhere in Luke "eternal" is only used in conjunction with

---

[209] Fitzmyer, *Luke* 2:1119-21.

[210] The scattered nature of this parallel material in Matthew and GT supports this: Luke 16:13 (Matt 6:24; GT 47); Luke 16:16-17 (Matt 11:12-13; 5:18; GT 11); and Luke 16:18 (Matt 19:9; cf. also Mark 10:11-12).

[211] A. Plummer (*A Critical and Exegetical Commentary on the Gospel according to S. Luke,* ICC [Edinburgh: T & T Clark, 1896], 385) argues that "so that" (ἵνα) "if it indicates purpose and not result, refers to Christ's purpose in giving this advice rather than to that of the disciples following it." This, however, seems too subtle and is probably based more on the desire to defend the doctrine of justification by faith than on exegetical considerations. If the advice of Luke 16:9a, however, is understood as referring to the need to repent and to produce fruit in keeping with such repentance (3:8), the problem is negated.

[212] Cf. Luke 6:38; 12:20,48; 23:31; cf. also 15:7,10.

"life" (10:25; 18:18,30; Acts 13:46,48). The giving of alms to the poor does not bring about eternal life, but the life of repentance and faith that gives alms out of a love for God and neighbor does. The use of one's possessions described here does not bring about God's mercy and grace (to earn "grace" is a contradiction of terms) but is itself brought about by God's mercy and grace.

16:10 This is a proverb with two lines in antithetical parallelism. Being a proverb, it is a general truth and allows for exceptions without in any way affecting its truthfulness. For faithfulness as a quality of a manager, cf. 12:42; 19:17.

16:11 Worldly wealth. A slightly different expression is used here from 16:9, but the meaning is the same. Since it is the use of this worldly wealth, not the possession of it which is condemned, worldly wealth is in itself neutral. The rich fool in the next parable is not culpable because he was wealthy but because he did not use his wealth to love God and his neighbor, Lazarus.

Who will trust you? God will not trust the individual who trusts in worldly wealth.

True riches. Literally *the true* _____ . This probably is best understood as heavenly reward (12:33; 18:22) rather than the stewardship of the gospel.

16:12 This verse stands in synonymous parallelism with the preceding one.

Someone else's property. This phrase is a synonym for "worldly wealth" (16:11). Thus it refers to the wealth God has loaned members of his creation during their lifetime and over which they are to exercise faithful stewardship. Compare 19:11-27.

Property of your own. This stands in parallelism with "true riches" in 16:11 and likewise refers to heavenly reward. In contrast to the worldly wealth over which people exercise only temporary stewardship, what people truly possess, i.e., that which can never be taken away and which will be eternally theirs, results from the use of worldly wealth for the good of others. The irony of greed lies in the fact that the more people accumulate for themselves in this life, the less they truly possess "property of their own."

16:13 This and the parallel in Matt 6:24 agree almost exactly—twenty-seven out of the twenty-eight words are exactly the same. We have here an example of chiasmic parallelism: hate (*A*) love (*B*) devoted to (*b*) despise (*a*). The two lines or strophes (*A B* and *b a*) are also an example of synonymous parallelism. Examples of a saying being an example of both chiasmic and antithetical parallelism are far more numerous.[213]

Cannot serve God and Money. A person ought not accumulate money (Mammon), for in such instances a person is the servant of money, i.e., its slave. Only by making God one's Master can there be freedom from bondage to money. People can choose whose slave they will be. Money will either be in the service of the believer who is God's servant, or a person will be the servant of money. There are examples in Jesus' day of a slave working for two masters. What is stated here is that the exclusive loyalty Jesus demands cannot be shared. *Gospel of Thomas* 47 introduces this saying with "It is impossible for a man to ride two horses [and] to stretch two bows."

16:14 The Pharisees, who loved money. Luke used this as a narrative transition to change the audience. Compare Luke 11:39; 20:46-47.

---

[213] Cf. Luke 9:24; 14:11; Matt 7:6; Mark 9:43b,45b,47b; 10:31.

Were sneering. The term is more hostile than the "muttered" of 15:2.

16:15 Justify yourselves. This concern is mentioned in 10:29; 18:9,14. In the last reference the Pharisees sought to demonstrate their righteousness to others by their external behavior (cf. Matt 23:27-28). God, however, knew their hearts. This is a common OT as well as Lukan theme.[214]

What is highly valued . . . is detestable. This is a proverb that warns us not to conform to the way this world thinks (cf. Rom 12:2). Jesus was not saying that values of the world are not exactly the same as God's or that at times they are different or that frequently they are different. Rather the value system of this world is "detestable," i.e., an abomination to God (cf. 1 Cor 3:19). An example of this is found in Luke 18:9-14.

16:16 It is difficult to understand how this verse relates to what has preceded.

The Law and the Prophets. This cannot refer to the OT because for Jesus and Luke the OT did not cease with the coming of the kingdom as the next verse shows. See comments on 1:6; Introduction 7 (2). The contrast is also not between the OT and NT Scriptures. This expression must refer here to the OT period or age.[215]

Until John. The crux in interpreting this verse is the understanding of how "until" should be interpreted. It can be interpreted "up to but not including" or "up to and including" John. In the second instance John the Baptist is understood as not being part of the realized kingdom. According to this interpretation, he was a Jewish preacher of repentance before the coming of the kingdom. Contrary to Conzelmann and others who hold this view,[216] Luke understood John the Baptist as a bridge between the old age and the new age. Thus he was also part of God's kingdom. This finds support in the following: (1) John the Baptist preached the "good news" just as Jesus did (cf. Luke 1:19; 3:18). (2) John's mission was associated with the fulfillment of Scripture (3:4-6) just as was Jesus' (4:18-19), Peter's (Acts 2:17-21), and Paul's (13:47). (3) Luke 3:1-2 introduces the coming of the kingdom temporally with John's appearance. There is no such introduction for Jesus' coming because there is no need for one—the NT era began with John's appearance. (4) John's message was the same as that of Jesus and the early church.[217] (5) John's coming was associated with the Spirit's coming (1:15,17,41, 67,80). He thus fulfilled Elijah's role (1:17). (6) John's teachings are presented as normative for the church (3:8-14; see comments on 3:10). (7) Matthew 11:12, the parallel to Luke 16:16, portrays John as part of the NT age. It now is generally agreed that if Conzelmann had included Luke 1-2 as part of the Gospel, he would not have been able to argue so strongly for placing John in the OT era (see comments on 1:68).[218]

Since that time. "That time" is the time of John the Baptist's coming.

[214]Cf. 1 Sam 16:7; 1 Kgs 8:39; 1 Chr 28:9; Prov 21:2; 24:12; Acts 1:24; 15:8.

[215]The term "dispensation" could be used here if understood in the broad sense of *the OT period of salvation history.* The term *covenant* also could be used. Cf. Luke 16:31; 24:44; Acts 13:15; 24:14; 28:23; cf. also 1QS 1:3; 8:14ff.

[216]H. Conzelmann, *The Theology of St. Luke* (New York: Harper, 1960).

[217]Cf. Luke 1:77; 3:3,8; Acts 13:24; 19:4 with Luke 5:32; 24:47; Acts 2:38; 5:31; 11:18.

[218]See P. S. Minear, "Luke's Use of the Birth Stories" in *Studies in Luke-Acts,* ed. L. E. Keck and J. L. Martyn (New York: Abingdon, 1966), 120-25.

Good news of the kingdom of God is being preached. The Greek expression that this translates is awkward (the "kingdom of God 'is being evangelized' [*euangelizetai*]").

Everyone is forcing his way into it. The verb can be a middle ("everyone is forcing his way") or a passive ("everyone is being forced"). The parallel in Matt 11:12 (cf. also Luke 14:23) favors the passive. This view would emphasize the resistance the kingdom receives from Satan, the demons, and Jesus' opponents and how only through urgent, demanding preaching people enter the kingdom. The middle probably is better, however, and this emphasizes the "violent" decision one must make in order to enter the kingdom (cf. 13:24). Compare 14:25-35.

16:17 Luke placed this saying next to the preceding one (contrast Matt 5:18 and 11:12-13) to affirm the continuity of the OT and NT eras.

Easier for heaven and earth to disappear. It is easier for God's creation to pass away than for his word not to be fulfilled. God's word is eternal, and his promises will never come to naught, even if creation will (2 Pet 3:12).

Least stroke of a pen to drop out. This refers to the mark that differentiates two similar Hebrew letters. (It would be, for example, the mark that distinguishes an *E* and from an *F*.) Clearly this is an example of hyperbole in that only a proposition or statement can be fulfilled. Parts of letters, letters, even individual words cannot be fulfilled. Jesus' use of hyperbole here, however, indicates how strongly he felt that the OT Scriptures would be fulfilled. What does it mean to say that the smallest part of a letter in the OT will not become void? It can mean the following: (1) All the laws in the OT will remain. (2) All the moral but not the ceremonial and civil laws found in the OT will remain. (3) All the promises/prophecies in the OT will be fulfilled. (4) The OT is transformed and fulfilled in Jesus' teachings. (5) The OT in all its aspects, i.e., its law, promises, and prophecies, will be fulfilled. In light of the following verse it appears that the second interpretation probably was meant.[219]

16:18 Most Jewish debate on divorce centered on what the expression "something indecent" in Deut 24:1 meant. Hillel interpreted this broadly and permitted divorce in such cases as a wife burning supper or if a husband found another woman more attractive. Shammi interpreted this more narrowly and permitted divorce only in the case of sexual unchastity on the wife's part.

Divorces his wife. Neither Luke nor Matthew discussed the possibility of a wife's divorcing her husband, although Mark (10:12) did. In Israel a wife's divorcing her husband was either impossible or at least very unusual, and so nothing is said concerning this possibility. (Note, however, that John the Baptist lost his head for criticizing Herod Antipas for marrying a woman who had divorced her husband.)

And marries another woman. This is not seen as a second, separate act but as part of the act of "divorcing and remarrying" because one article is used for both participles ("the divorcing and marrying another person").

---

[219] See Stein, *Method and Message of Jesus' Teachings*, 108-9: "The Old Testament is not rejected by Jesus. It still remains as an expression of the will of God. By expressed statements certain aspects such as rules of purity and cleanliness are now removed, certain commands are seen as temporary concessions, and the principles and intention of the Law are expounded. But the commandments, especially the moral dimension of the commandments, are still valid."

The man who marries a divorced woman. This is a most difficult statement because it penalizes the woman divorced by her husband. In other words it seems to penalize the "innocent" party.

Through the centuries the church has struggled with the meaning of Jesus' sayings on divorce. The proper framework for understanding them may be that we take seriously such teachings on discipleship as 9:57-62; 13:24; 14:25-35. If we approach the divorce sayings believing in a "cheap grace," they will seem unusually harsh and out of step with the "modern day." But we must remember that the world's thinking on such matters is an abomination to God (16:15) and that such teaching as found in 16:18 is addressed to those who seek first the kingdom of God, who build their attitude toward marriage around their faith commitment and not their faith commitment around their attitude toward marriage. Clearly Jesus' statement indicates that God hates divorce (Mal 2:16).

In contrast to Matthew (5:32; 19:9) and Paul (1 Cor 7:15), Mark (10:11-12) and Luke knew of no "exception clauses." It appears that the Markan and Lukan accounts are closer to Jesus' actual words (the *ipsissima verba*) and that Matthew and Paul interpreted Jesus' teaching, which is somewhat hyperbolic, for their audiences.[220] Elsewhere the NT seems to permit divorce in the case of sexual immorality (Matt 5:32; 19:9) or desertion by the unbelieving partner (1 Cor 7:15). (Paul apparently could not conceive of a Christian's divorcing another Christian and advised against a Christian's divorcing an unbelieving partner; cf. 1 Cor 7:10-14.) If the church takes the NT teachings seriously, divorce will always be seen as an evil. In some cases it may be the lesser of two evils, but it will be an evil nonetheless, for it reveals a failure of God's intended purpose.

The Lukan Message

Luke's placement of this material after the parable of the unjust manager (16:1-8) and before the parable of the rich man and Lazarus (16:19-31) indicates that this material deals with how his readers will be able to face the final accounting (16:2,22-23,28). To prepare for that day one must today experience a repentance and faith that leads to renouncing the lordship exercised by possessions for the lordship exercised by Christ (16:13). Under Christ's leadership the believer can use worldly wealth to serve God by giving to the needy. The amount of material Luke devoted to this subject indicates its importance for him. See Introduction 8 (7). A person's eternal destiny (18:24-25) and felicity in eternity (12:33) are intimately associated with his or her relationship to worldly wealth. Life is to be lived with eternity's values in view. A believer's attitude toward marriage is also to be determined in light of this. Love for God and commitment toward his kingdom is to be such that marriage is not viewed from the perspective of "what should marriage do for me?" but rather "how

---

[220] See R. H. Stein, "Divorce" in *Dictionary of Jesus and the Gospels* (Downers Grove: InterVarsity, 1992), 192-99.

can I practice the love of God and my neighbor/mate in this marriage?" With such an attitude there is seldom need for contemplating divorce.

Luke also pointed out that the kingdom's value system stands diametrically opposed to that of the present age. With John's ministry God's kingdom has entered history. Entrance into the kingdom, however, is not easy and few enter (13:22-30), for it takes a violent repentance and rejection of this world's values to enter it (16:16b; cf. Matt 5:29-30). Two other Lukan themes found in this section involve the coming of the kingdom (see Introduction 8 [2]) and the fulfillment and binding nature of the OT. See Introduction 7 (1).

(10) The Parable of the Rich Man and Lazarus (16:19-31)

[19]"There was a rich man who was dressed in purple and fine linen and lived in luxury every day. [20]At his gate was laid a beggar named Lazarus, covered with sores [21]and longing to eat what fell from the rich man's table. Even the dogs came and licked his sores.

[22]"The time came when the beggar died and the angels carried him to Abraham's side. The rich man also died and was buried. [23]In hell, where he was in torment, he looked up and saw Abraham far away, with Lazarus by his side. [24]So he called to him, 'Father Abraham, have pity on me and send Lazarus to dip the tip of his finger in water and cool my tongue, because I am in agony in this fire.'

[25]"But Abraham replied, 'Son, remember that in your lifetime you received your good things, while Lazarus received bad things, but now he is comforted here and you are in agony. [26]And besides all this, between us and you a great chasm has been fixed, so that those who want to go from here to you cannot, nor can anyone cross over from there to us.'

[27]"He answered, 'Then I beg you, father, send Lazarus to my father's house, [28]for I have five brothers. Let him warn them, so that they will not also come to this place of torment.'

[29]"Abraham replied, 'They have Moses and the Prophets; let them listen to them.'

[30]"'No, father Abraham,' he said, 'but if someone from the dead goes to them, they will repent.'

[31]"He said to him, 'If they do not listen to Moses and the Prophets, they will not be convinced even if someone rises from the dead.'"

Context

The parable of the rich man and Lazarus is connected to the preceding as an example (Luke 16:19-26) both of a man who was a lover of money (16:14) and who foolishly made poor use of his possessions (16:9-13) as well as an example (16:27-31) of the continued validity of the law and the prophets (16:16-18). The audience envisioned by the parable fits well the Pharisee of 16:14, and 17:1 suggests this by changing the audience to the disciples.

This parable is unusual for at least two reasons. For one it is the only parable in which a character is named. Because of the name "Lazarus" (16:20,23-25), it has been suggested that 16:19-31 is not a parable but a historical account.[221] Luke, however, clearly thought this was a parable, for he introduced it with "There was a [certain] rich man" (see comments on 10:30). Within the Gospel are seven instances in which an account begins "a certain man" (*anthropos tis*). In all but one (14:2) this was used to introduce a parable (10:30; 14:16; 15:11; 16:1 ["rich" is added]; 16:19 ["rich" is added]; 19:12 ["of noble birth" is added]). The last six examples are furthermore all introduced by "he [Jesus] said/was saying" whereas 14:2 is clearly part of a narrative. This account also begins with the same introduction as the parable in 16:1, "There was a rich man," so that Luke intended for his readers to interpret this as a parable, not as a historical account.

The parable is also unusual in that it is a two-part parable (cf. 15:11-32). Some have argued therefore that originally this was not one parable but two (16:19-26 and 16:27-31). As in 15:11-32 there is no compelling reason why this could not have consisted from the beginning as a two-part parable.[222] Non-Lukan vocabulary throughout the parable indicates that the present two-part form is pre-Lukan, and there is no reason Jesus could not have spoken the parable essentially in its present form unless we claim that the parable explicitly refers to Jesus' resurrection (16:30-31) and that he could not have made such a reference.

The meaning of the parable is relatively clear. The first part (16:19-26) illustrates the blessedness of the poor believer (6:20) and the woe of the unbelieving rich (6:24). This reversal of roles between this life and the next was well-known in Egyptian and Jewish folklore, and Jesus may have borrowed some of the material for his parable from such folklore. Such a reversal fits well Jesus' teaching and Luke's emphasis concerning riches (cf. 12:13-21). See Introduction 8 (5). The second part of the parable (16:27-31) teaches that unbelief and the refusal to repent are not the results of lack of evidence (or lack of a sign) but due to a stony heart.

---

[221] The striking similarities between this parable and Lazarus's resurrection in John 11–12 include: the name "Lazarus," the death of Lazarus, the request to send him back from the dead (16:27)—Lazarus's return from the dead (John), and the lack of faith resulting from such an event (Luke 16:31; John 12:9-11). It has been suggested that the Johannine account is a "historization" of the parable. (See R. E. Brown, *The Gospel according to John*, AB [Garden City: Doubleday, 1966], 428-30.) It has also been suggested that the parable arose from the story. Others suggest that they were independent accounts but that the name "Lazarus" was added to the parable due to influence from the Johannine story (not the Gospel but the story during its oral period). The similarity between these two accounts is interesting and curious, but there is no solid evidence that the account in either Gospel caused or influenced the material in the other. The similarities while interesting remain unfortunately quite puzzling.

[222] See C. L. Blomberg, *Interpreting the Parables* (Downers Grove: InterVarsity, 1990), 204.

Comments

16:19 There was a rich man. By this introduction (literally *a certain rich man*), Luke indicated that what follows is a parable (see "Context" and comments on 10:30). Some manuscripts supply a name for the rich man, no doubt to parallel the name of the poor man. Various names are found, but the best known is "Dives," which is the word used to translate "rich" in the Latin Vulgate. The oldest recorded name is "Nives," which is found in the Bodmer Papyrus ($\mathfrak{P}^{75}$). The man's richness is described in two ways: his dress and his eating habits.

Dressed in purple and fine linen. Compare Prov 31:22. The "purple" indicates that he dressed "royally." Compare 1 Macc 8:14, where wearing purple is associated with kingship; cf. also Mark 15:17,20; Rev 18:12. He also wore a "linen," probably a fine Egyptian linen undergarment.

And lived in luxury every day. This phrase is literally *enjoying himself [by eating] sumptuously each day.* For "enjoying himself" cf. Luke 12:19; 15:23-24, 29,32. The extravagance of this feasting is indicated by the additions of "sumptuously" and even more so by "every day." This daily feasting is not to be compared with *the* occasion of feasting in the parable of the gracious father (15:23f.) but is more indicative of the attitude of the rich fool in 12:19. Compare 3:11; Jas 5:5.

16:20 At his gate. The rich man's home was large enough to have a gate (cf. Acts 10:17; 12:13; Matt 26:71).

Was laid. "Was laid" is literally *had been cast.* This expression is frequently used to describe the sick and the lame (Matt 8:6,14; 9:2; Mark 7:30).

Lazarus. Lazarus, a common name, is the Greek form of Eleazar and means *He (whom) God has helped.* This is the only instance in a parable where a character is named. Jesus may have named the poor beggar intentionally as a pun in order to help his hearers understand that this poor man ("whom God has helped") should be identified with such poor as referred to in 4:18; 6:20; 7:22 and later in 21:3, i.e., he was a poor believer. The name may also have been intended to facilitate the discussion in 16:24-31. If Jesus intended this pun, there is still the question of whether Luke recognized the play on the name and whether Luke's readers would have understood it. This is doubtful. Regardless, Luke did not call attention to the possible pun. Yet Luke continued the theme of reversal by giving the forgotten, poor man a name while the rich man went nameless. The plight of the poor man is now described by means of a fourfold contrast between the rich man and Lazarus: 16:19 (20-21), 22b (22a), 23a (23b), 24-25a (25b). For similar contrasts and reversals, cf. 1:51-53; 3:5; 6:20-26; etc.

Covered with sores. The sores were ulcers. Since he was begging in public and at the gate of this man's house, the poor man in the parable was not a leper.

16:21 Longing to eat. Compare Luke 15:16. This is an unfulfilled wish, as in the case of the prodigal son.

What fell. Whether this refers to the crumbs or scraps of the meal or the pieces of bread used as napkins to clean one's hands is uncertain and immaterial. The rich man's dogs were better fed than the poor Lazarus (cf. Matt 15:27).

Even the dogs came and licked. The Greek indicates this was the culmination of Lazarus's misery. In Jewish eyes dogs were not romanticized as "man's best friend" but were seen as impure, disgusting scavengers. Even the dogs tormented the poor man by licking his ulcerated sores. Luke wanted his readers to understand that the rich man's continual neglect of Lazarus, who lay at his gate and was known by name (Luke 16:24), while he himself feasted sumptuously was the reason he went to hades.

16:22   The beggar died and the angels carried him to Abraham's side. This introduces the second contrast. Lazarus was not even buried. Nevertheless he entered into God's presence. The expression and thought "angels carried him" is unusual. The expression "Abraham's bosom" (KJV) is unknown elsewhere in first-century Judaism, but such passages as 4 Macc 13:17; 1 Kgs 1:21; 2:10; 11:21 contain a similar idea. The exact meaning of "Abraham's side" is uncertain, but Lazarus clearly enjoyed close fellowship with Abraham in the afterlife (Luke 13:29). Although not a technical term for "heaven" in Jesus' day, through the parable it later became one.

The rich man also died and was buried.   Even in death he was treated differently in this world from Lazarus. He was buried.

16:23   In hell.   "Hell" is literally *hades*. In Greek thought this was the place of the dead, and in the LXX it was used to translate Sheol. In the OT it can mean *the place of the dead* or *the place where the unrighteous dead go*. It is contrasted with "heaven" in Ps 139:8 and Amos 9:2. In the present context it refers to the place of the unrighteous dead in contrast to "Abraham's side," or the place of the righteous dead. It probably is a synonym here for Gehenna, or hell.

In torment.   The parable does not see the wicked as being annihilated but continuing in a terrible conscious and irreversible condition after death. Although many aspects of the parable do not have a corresponding reality, the reality being taught by the parable would be meaningless unless this were true.[223] Compare 1 Enoch 103:5-7.

Looked up and saw.   This picture part of the parable should not be pressed to mean that those in hades are "below" Abraham's bosom or that those in hell can see into heaven[224] or that they can converse with those in heaven. These details are necessary to make the parable work, but there is no corresponding reality to which they refer.

Abraham far away.   There is a great, unbridgeable chasm between heaven and hell which, as Luke 16:26 makes clear, is uncrossable.

16:24   Father Abraham.   Compare 16:27,30. Abraham was the father of the Jewish people (3:8; 13:16; 19:9; Gen 12:1-3).

Have pity on me.   Compare Luke 17:13; 18:38-39. The merciless now desires mercy but will not receive it (6:24-25), for the time of grace is over (cf. 12:20,39-40,58; 13:8-9).

Send Lazarus.   Since the rich man knew the name of the beggar, readers should assume that he was aware of the continual misery and need of the beggar lying at his gate.

---

[223]Cf. Sabourin (*Luke*, 301): "No attempt should be made to gain from the parable any precise information on afterlife, except that a different situation awaits there the poor and the rich who had no concern for them."
[224]Cf. 2 Esdr 7:85,93; *2 Apoc. Bar.* 51:5-6; cf. also Luke 13:28.

Water and cool my tongue. Should this be understood as an actual or symbolic description of the torments of hell (cf. 2 Esdr 8:59; 1 Enoch 22:9)? Since this description is found in a parable, it would not be wise to assume that this is a literal portrayal of hell. Nevertheless, the reality of hell's horror is so terrible that in the picture even licking water from a fingertip would bring some welcome relief.

Agony in this fire. Flames are frequently associated with the final destiny of the unrighteous.[225]

16:25 Son. Compare Luke 15:31. Although the rich man was physically a "son of Abraham," apart from repentance Abraham's offspring, like the rest of humanity, will experience God's wrath (3:7-8; cf. John 8:39).

In your lifetime you received . . . good . . . but now . . . you are in agony. The rich man's posthumous fate illustrates the great reversal.[226]

While Lazarus received bad things, but now he is comforted. This illustrates the reversal of 6:20; 13:30. "Is comforted" is a divine passive meaning *God is comforting him.* The "blesseds" and "woes" of 6:20-26 are now fulfilled.

16:26 And besides all this. The phrase is literally *and in all these things.* Not only was the rich man's request of 16:24 not granted because of God's justice, in addition the situation in which he found himself was irreversible. Here lies the real horror of his situation. His punishment was eternal.

Great chasm has been fixed. This is a divine passive indicating that God has established this great chasm. Compare 1 Enoch 18:11-12.

So that. "So that" (*hopos*) indicates purpose here.[227] God has established this unbridgeable chasm for the twofold purpose of (1) keeping those in hades, such as the rich man, from coming to Abraham's bosom and (2) keeping those in Abraham's bosom, such as Lazarus, from crossing over to give aid as the rich man requested.

16:27 Send Lazarus to my father's house. The second part of the parable begins at this point. In the parable this request expresses the rich man's desire to warn his brothers of their need to act shrewdly as the dishonest manager (Luke 16:8), i.e., to prepare for their future and not wind up where he is. In 16:30 what they needed to do is explicitly stated. They needed to repent and produce fruit in keeping with repentance (3:8) such as using their worldly wealth (16:9) to help people like Lazarus.

16:28 Five brothers. This is simply a round number (cf. 14:19) and should not be allegorized. Speculation about whether the brothers were unmarried, still living with the father, or whether his parents were still alive is immaterial. If this were necessary to understand the parable, Luke would have included this information.

Warn them. "Warn them" means *warn/witness to them to repent* (16:30). The request asked that Lazarus be sent as a "sign" to verify the message of the law and the prophets. In all the other instances where Luke used this Greek term, "witness" tends to be a better translation.[228] To "warn" should therefore be understood in the

---

[225] Cf. Luke 3:17; Isa 66:24; Matt 18:8-9; 25:41; Mark 9:48; cf. also 1 Enoch 10:13.

[226] Cf. Luke 6:24-25; 12:13-21; 13:30; 16:11-12.

[227] As in Luke 2:35; 7:3; 10:2; 11:37; 16:28.

[228] Acts 2:40; 8:25; 10:42; 18:5; 20:21,23-24; 23:11; 28:23.

sense of witnessing to them, so that the five brothers would not experience the same fate as their brother. There is, of course, in all "witnessing" a negative side that "warns."

So that. This "so that" (*hina*) indicates the purpose of the warning. The thought here may be that additional information (of his brother's evil condition resulting from his way of life) would lead the brothers to repent. Or it may be that Lazarus's return from the dead would function as a sign that indicates this message of repentance should be obeyed. The latter interpretation is more likely in light of 16:31 (cf. also 11:16,29-30).

16:29   Moses and the Prophets. "Moses and the Prophets" means *the Law and the Prophets*, or *the OT*. See comments on 16:6.

Let them listen to them. "Listen" carries the sense of *heed*.[229] Abraham's reply was that the brothers already had the OT, which warned them of their need to repent (and which witnessed to Jesus). The OT also spoke of the need to be concerned for the poor.[230]

16:30   No . . . but if. This is best understood not as an additional witness, i.e., the OT and Lazarus, but as a sign confirming what the OT says. See comments on 16:28.

They will repent. This indicates that the rich man's fate was not due to his being rich but his lack of repentance. See comments on 3:3, Introduction 8 (6).

16:31   If they do not listen. See comments on 16:29.

They will not be convinced. The rich man saw Lazarus's return as a sign that would compel his brothers' belief and repentance. Abraham replied that a sign would not compel faith. Even if someone rises from the dead, this will not compel faith. This is confirmed in John when Lazarus's resurrection helps some to believe (John 11:45; 12:11) but does not compel faith from those who oppose Jesus (11:47; 12:10-11).

Even if someone rises from the dead. The wording of the request in Luke 16:27 has been changed at this point to fit more closely Jesus' resurrection (cf. 18:33; 24:7,46; Acts 2:24). In Jesus' situation such a statement would have been interpreted abstractly: If a person, any person, would come back from the dead. In Luke's situation this would have been understood as the fulfillment of the sign of Jonah (11:29-30), for even Jesus' resurrection from the dead (cf. 9:22; 13:32; 18:33; Acts 17:31) did not result in Israel's coming to faith. The Scriptures are a sufficient witness for faith (cf. Luke 24:27-32). As Marshall aptly notes, "Miracles will not convince those whose hearts are morally blind and unrepentant."[231]

The Lukan Message

Two strong Lukan themes are found in this parable. The first, which is found in the first part of the parable (16:19-26), involves the great reversal. See Introduction 8 (5). Tied to this are two related Lukan emphases involving the need for repentance (see comments on 3:3; Introduction 8

---

[229]Cf. Luke 8:8; 9:35; 10:16; 14:35; 16:31.
[230]Exod 22:21-24; Deut 24:10-15; Isa 58:7; Amos 6:1-7.
[231]Marshall, *Luke*, 639.

[6]) and the stewardship of one's possessions. See Introduction 8 (7). The rich man suffered reversal in the afterlife not because he was rich but because he was rich and lacked compassion for the needy. He could callously feast each day sumptuously and ignore the needs of poor Lazarus lying at his gate. He suffered irreversible damnation (16:26) because he lacked a repentance (16:31) that produced fruit (3:8). His actions reveal a heart never made tender by repentance and regeneration. God's love did not abide in him (1 John 3:17). As a result his attitude toward his possessions was one of self-serving greed. Like another rich fool (Luke 12:13-21), foolishly ignoring that his worldly wealth was only on loan, he possessed no true riches that would be eternally his (16:11-12) and lost his very self (9:25). Theophilus and the other readers were reminded once again that they needed to make certain they were "rich toward God" (12:21) and possessed "treasure in heaven" (12:33). Only by using their worldly wealth to serve God and others would they possess "true riches" (16:11).

The second part of the parable (16:27-31) involves Jesus' adamant rejection of a sign to satisfy his opponents. The parable argues that a refusal to repent is not due to the lack of a sign. If one is sincere, all that is necessary for faith is the Scriptures (16:31). A sign does not necessitate faith, as 11:14-23 has already shown (see comments on 11:16). Jesus at the very beginning of his ministry refused this way of fulfilling his messianic mission (4:1-13). "Jews demand miraculous signs" (1 Cor 1:22), but only the preaching of Christ crucified is necessary for those with a tender heart for God. For those with stony hearts even a witness returned from the dead will not convince them to believe. This is seen elsewhere in the Gospels, for when Lazarus was raised from the dead (John 11:38–12:9), instead of faith the result was a plot to kill him (12:10-11). There is little doubt that Jesus' original audience would have understood the rich man's request (Luke 16:27) and Jesus' concluding statement about "someone . . . from the dead" (16:31) as involving the sending of Lazarus to his brothers. In Luke's setting, however, his readers could not have helped thinking of Jesus' resurrection and applying 16:30-31 to him. The Lord had indeed risen from the dead (16:30), but even this did not result in Israel's repenting (16:31). It is on this point that the main emphasis of the parable falls. Compare Rom 10:5-17.

Another theme found in the second part of the parable involves the continued validity of the OT (Luke 16:29-31). Luke prepared his readers for this by what he already had said about the OT Scriptures in 1:1f., but in the immediate context he prepared them for this in 16:17. From the first chapter of the Gospel (cf. 1:6,45) to the last (cf. 24:25-27,32,44-48), from the first chapter of Acts (cf. 1:16-18) to the last (28:23,25-27), the eternal validity of the OT Scriptures is taught both explicitly and implicitly.

(11) Teachings Addressed to the Disciples (17:1-10)

[1]Jesus said to his disciples: "Things that cause people to sin are bound to come, but woe to that person through whom they come. [2]It would be better for him to be thrown into the sea with a millstone tied around his neck than for him to cause one of these little ones to sin. [3]So watch yourselves.

"If your brother sins, rebuke him, and if he repents, forgive him. [4]If he sins against you seven times in a day, and seven times comes back to you and says, 'I repent,' forgive him."

[5]The apostles said to the Lord, "Increase our faith!"

[6]He replied, "If you have faith as small as a mustard seed, you can say to this mulberry tree, 'Be uprooted and planted in the sea,' and it will obey you.

[7]"Suppose one of you had a servant plowing or looking after the sheep. Would he say to the servant when he comes in from the field, 'Come along now and sit down to eat'? [8]Would he not rather say, 'Prepare my supper, get yourself ready and wait on me while I eat and drink; after that you may eat and drink'? [9]Would he thank the servant because he did what he was told to do? [10]So you also, when you have done everything you were told to do, should say, 'We are unworthy servants; we have only done our duty.'"

Context

In this section we have a collection of four of Jesus' sayings whose relationship to what has preceded and to one another is unclear. They are only loosely connected in form (sayings of Jesus) and in general theme (discipleship). The first involves the need to avoid becoming a stumbling block to other believers and causing them to sin (Luke 17:1-3a). It is better to die prematurely (described as drowning by having a millstone tied to one's neck) than to be a scandal to God's "little ones," i.e., believers as the parallels in Matt 18:6; Mark 9:42 show (cf. also Matt 18:10).

The second deals with the continual need for believers to forgive repentant fellow believers (Luke 17:3b-4; cf. Matt 18:15, 21-22). When a believer is sinned against by another, he or she is to go and rebuke the offender. Implied, although not stated, is the purpose and manner of the rebuke. Since it seeks the offender's repentance, the rebuke is understood as being loving and caring rather than judgmental.

The third saying (Luke 17:5-6; cf. Matt 17:20, where the saying is attached to the disciples' inability to perform an exorcism) involves a request by the disciples for faith. Jesus' reply is somewhat frustrating, for he does not appear to have addressed the request. Instead, Jesus pointed out that what is needed is not a "quantity" of faith but a "quality" of faith. Even the smallest amount of true faith, a mustard seed's amount, could do mighty things.

The fourth and final saying (Luke 17:7-10) is a parable, unique to Luke, which illustrates a proper understanding of the believer's relationship to God. Believers are like servants who, even when they have done all that was demanded can at best confess that they are unworthy and have only fulfilled their obligations. Jesus may have originally addressed this parable to self-righteous Pharisees (cf. 18:9-14).

Comments

17:1 Jesus said to his disciples. The following sayings are addressed to a different audience from 16:14 (the Pharisees). The introduction picks up the "disciples" of 16:1, who are called "Apostles" in 17:5.

Things that cause people to sin. The term *skandala* has a broad semantic range that includes the meaning *things that cause people to sin.* This refers to anything that might cause believers (the "little ones" of 17:2) to lose or lessen their allegiance to Jesus Christ.[232]

Are bound to come. Jesus knew that due to the world, the flesh, and the devil such temptations would continue. Compare 17:23; 21:8; Acts 20:29-30.

But woe to that person. The "but" is emphatic and should perhaps be indicated by underlining or by putting in caps. Compare Luke 22:22, where the Son of Man's betrayal is described and these words are found.

17:2 It would be better. This phrase translates a Greek word used only here in the NT. The meaning is that it would be "less worse" to drown in the following manner than to cause a believer to stumble.

Millstone tied around his neck. This was a proverbial statement in NT times as well as today, although a reference to a millstone's use to drown a person has not been discovered before this. A millstone was used for grinding grain. It could vary in size from a small stone used by an individual to grind grain to a large round stone turned by an animal. The latter may have been meant here (cf. Matt 18:6; Mark 9:42).

Than for. The worse of the two evils is now described.

Little ones. This refers to believers in general as the parallels in Mark 9:42 and Matt 18:6 reveal (cf. also Matt 18:10).

17:3 So watch yourselves. This imperative can serve as a conclusion to what has preceded (NIV) or an introduction to what follows. The former is more likely.

If your brother sins. Envisioned here are individual acts of sin (the verb is an aorist) of one brother, i.e., a Christian,[233] against another. For "sin" cf. 15:18, 21; Acts 25:8.

Rebuke him. This refers to a loving admonition in which a believer tells an offending Christian of the wrong done.

And if he repents. Compare Luke 15:1-32. This is the goal of the rebuke. As a result the rebuke is aimed at persuasion rather than condemnation. Christians, even after "the" repentance that enabled them to enter God's kingdom, need on occasion to experience a similar kind of repentance. This saying concerns not so much the church's purity (cf. 1 Cor 5:1-13) but the brother's restoration.

---

[232] Cf. Rom 14:13-23; 1 Cor 8:9-13; 10:32; 1 John 2:10; Rev 2:14.
[233] Cf. Luke 8:21; Acts 1:15-16; 6:3; 9:17; 11:1.

17:4   Seven times. This is not to be taken as the "upper limit" of times one is to forgive, as the "in a day" indicates. Matthew 18:22 has seventy times seven (or seventy-seven), which again is not an upper limit but symbolic for "always." See comments on 11:26.

Forgive him. "Forgive him" is literally *you will forgive him.* The sense of the future tense, used here as an imperative, is perhaps better seen in the RSV, "You must forgive him."

17:5   The apostles. For Luke this meant the "twelve" (cf. Luke 6:13; Acts 1:26).

Lord. See comments on 7:13.

Increase our faith! This can mean (1) give to us a greater faith than we already have; (2) add to the gifts we already have "faith"; or (3) give us faith (with the possible implication that they do not possess faith). Since those asking probably would have had some faith already because they were apostles, the first possibility is to be preferred.

17:6   If you have faith . . . seed. This unusual Greek construction portrays a contrary-to-fact condition using a present rather than an imperfect tense. It is perhaps best translated, "If you have faith . . . (and you do), you could."[234] Compare Jas 1:6-8.

Mustard seed. The mustard seed's smallness was proverbial (cf. Luke 13:19).

Mulberry tree. There is confusion about exactly what kind of tree Jesus was referring to here. Discussion about whether he referred to a mulberry tree (NIV) or a sycamine tree (RSV), however, can lose sight of the point. For any tree to be uprooted and planted in the sea (which sea is irrelevant) is a mighty miracle indeed. And even a mustard-seed faith could do this. Why one would want to do this is beside the point. This is what a little faith could do. In practice such faith would not be directed to performing such manifestations of power but to preaching, healing, endurance,[235] and forgiving one's brother (17:3-5). In Matt 17:20 such faith removes a mountain (cf. 1 Cor 13:2; cf. also GT 48).

17:7   Suppose one of you. "Suppose one of you" is literally *Who out of you* as in 11:5.

A servant. This servant was a small farmer's only servant/slave, who worked both outside (plowing and shepherding) and inside the house.

Would he say? The assumed answer is, of course, no.

17:8   Would he not rather? The Greek implies a yes.

Prepare my supper. If only two possibilities exist, the servant and the master, the servant would have to prepare the meal. Contrast, however, 12:37.

Get yourself ready. Compare 12:35.

17:9   Would he thank? The Greek implies a no.

17:10   So you also. The reality to which the parable points is now given.

Unworthy servants. Believers are unworthy in the sense that at their very best all they have done is what they should have done, i.e., what the command-

---

[234] See N. Turner, *Grammatical Insights into the New Testament* (Edinburgh: T & T Clark, 1965), 51-52.

[235] Preaching (Acts 2:14-41; 3:11-26; 4:8-20; 7:1-53), healing (Acts 3:1-10; 4:22,30; 5:12-16; contrast Luke 9:37-43), endurance (Acts 4:21,23-30; 5:17-42; 7:54-60).

ments teach. They have not done more than that. On the contrary, usually they have done much less. Compare *'Abot* 2:8: "If you have learned much Torah, do not puff yourself up on that account, for it was for that purpose that you were created." Contrast, however, the Pharisee in Luke 18:12 and *Sukka* 45b; *Berakot* 28b.

The Lukan Message

In this account we have a collection of sayings on discipleship with respect to believers' relationships to their neighbors (brother) and their personal relationship with God. The first set of teachings involve a warning not to become a scandal to a fellow believer. How one can become such a scandal is not specified. This might include some of the following: offending someone by ridicule; lying to or cheating them; performing acts that might be harmless in themselves but cause a weaker believer to become troubled (1 Cor 10:14-33; Rom 14:1-23); teaching heresy (Acts 20:25-31; Gal 1:6-9; 2 Cor 11:1-4), seeking self-aggrandizement (Phil 2:21); persecuting believers (Acts 9:1-19). The warning against such behavior is severe indeed. It is better to die suddenly, for such a death has only physical consequences, whereas an offense against God's people has eternal repercussions. Luke's readers needed to beware that they must never outlive their love for Christ and become stumbling blocks to other believers and thus to Christ.

A second exhortation involves the need to seek reconciliation with other Christians and to forgive and accept their repentance. Although "repentance" for Luke usually referred to the conversion experience,[236] here it involves a subsequent experience of sincere sorrow over having offended a fellow believer. The resulting forgiveness is not to be limited to a single or several occasions but is to be unlimited. The Lord's Prayer comes to mind at this point: "Forgive us our sins, for we also forgive everyone who sins against us" (Luke 11:4). The saying does not deal with the question of what a believer should do if his brother does not repent.[237]

The last two sayings deal with the believer's personal relationship to God. The first involves an increasing of faith. A twofold example is given of what even the smallest amount of faith can do. It can uproot a tree and plant it in the sea. The Matthean parallel involves moving a mountain from one place to another (Matt 17:20; cf. 1 Cor 13:2; GT 48). These hyperbolic expressions describe what faith can do, but in practice Jesus was not speaking of a faith that stages wonders[238] but of a faith that facilitates healing,[239] that understands the need of Christ to suffer (24:25-26), that has confidence

---

[236]Cf. Luke 3:3; 5:32; 15:7; 24:47; Acts 2:38; 17:30.
[237]Cf., however, Luke 6:27-38; 23:34; Acts 7:60; and cf. also Matt 18:15-20.
[238]Cf. Luke 4:9; 11:16,29; 16:27-31.
[239]Luke 7:9; 8:48; 18:42; Acts 14:9.

in God's providential care (8:25), that will not fall away (8:13; 22:32) but will endure (Acts 14:22), and that will believe God and grow.[240]

The last saying is directed to the church (Luke 17:1,3,5,7) and reminds the readers that there is no place for boasting and that disciples must remember who is to serve whom. Luke may even have been warning the church leaders among his readers that their service did not merit them any special reward. There will always be a need to emphasize this, for at times some Christians tend to reverse these roles and see God as their servant. Whereas a sovereign God delights to bless his servants (12:35-37), the church must always remember that he is the Lord of all creation and that they are, even at their best, forgiven sinners. Believers are the apples of God's eye, and woe to those who would cause them to stumble; but believers who see clearly only confess, "We are unworthy servants." All too often they are not even able to say, "We have only done our duty." Believers have no claim on God. Their only hope is God's gracious character and promise.

3. The Third Mention of the Journey to Jerusalem (17:11–19:27)

(1) The Grateful Samaritan (17:11-19)

[11]Now on his way to Jerusalem, Jesus traveled along the border between Samaria and Galilee. [12]As he was going into a village, ten men who had leprosy met him. They stood at a distance [13]and called out in a loud voice, "Jesus, Master, have pity on us!"

[14]When he saw them, he said, "Go, show yourselves to the priests." And as they went, they were cleansed.

[15]One of them, when he saw he was healed, came back, praising God in a loud voice. [16]He threw himself at Jesus' feet and thanked him—and he was a Samaritan.

[17]Jesus asked, "Were not all ten cleansed? Where are the other nine? [18]Was no one found to return and give praise to God except this foreigner?" [19]Then he said to him, "Rise and go; your faith has made you well."

Context

The account of the grateful Samaritan, which is unique to Luke, introduces the third section of the travel account (cf. 17:11 with 9:51 and 13:22). Jesus continued toward Jerusalem, where he would die (9:22,31,44), for he must fulfill his passion in the holy city (13:33). The classification of this story is difficult, but its emphasis lies with the pronouncement in 17:17-19.[241]

---

[240] Acts 6:5; cf. Luke 1:45 with 1:20.

[241] The narrative does not fit neatly the normal form-critical categories. It possesses characteristics of a miracle story, a pronouncement story, as well as a story about Jesus. Probably it is best described as a pronouncement story.

The account begins with Jesus' healing ten lepers at a distance (17:12, 14; cf. 7:6-10). Lepers had to live apart from society (Lev 13:38-46; Num 5:2-4), and to reenter society they had to be declared clean by a priest (Lev 14:1-32). As they proceeded to the priests, they were healed. One of the lepers upon observing his healing returned to give thanks to Jesus. It is then pointed out that this leper was a Samaritan. This one had been not only physically healed but spiritually healed as well (17:19). Whereas the other nine received God's word and believed for a time, they fell short of the ultimate healing, i.e., experiencing the divine salvation. They had "been enlightened . . . [and] tasted the heavenly gift" (Heb 6:4) in their experience of divine healing, but they fell short of saving faith.

Comments

17:11 On his way to Jerusalem. This is the third mention of Jesus' traveling to Jerusalem (cf. 9:51; 13:22).

Along the border between Samaria and Galilee. The expression "along between" (dia meson) is difficult to interpret, and as a result there are several textual variants. Since Galilee lies north of Samaria, one would think that Jesus would have been going in a north-south direction, and "along between" suggests an east-west direction. Some scholars have suggested that Luke revealed here a great ignorance of Palestinian geography.[242] Luke may have meant, however, that Jesus and the disciples were traveling east-west along the Plain of Esdraelon (Valley of Jezreel). Although one might expect the reverse, Samaria is mentioned first because of the importance the Samaritan leper plays in the story. For "Samaria" see comments on 10:33.

17:12 Ten. "Ten" is a round number. Compare 2 Kgs 7:3, where a group of lepers are found together, probably for mutual aid and encouragement.

A village. The name is irrelevant. What happened, not where it happened, is important. Compare 9:52,56; 10:38.

Leprosy. See comments on 5:12.

They stood at a distance. The law required the segregation of lepers (cf. Lev 13:45-46; Num 5:2-4).

17:13 Jesus, Master. Elsewhere only Jesus' disciples used this term "Master" (epistata) to address him (see comments on 5:5), whereas nondisciples used the term "teacher" (didaskalos).[243]

Have pity on us! Compare Luke 16:24; 18:38-39. The particular mercy being sought is not mentioned. The lepers might have sought alms from others, but from the address "Master" Luke suggested they sought more, i.e., healing, from Jesus.

17:14 Go, show yourselves to the priests. Compare 5:14. "Priests" is plural because there were ten lepers. That Jesus anticipated that the Samaritan would go to a Samaritan priest is speculative. Luke was not concerned with this detail.

As they went, they were cleansed. In contrast to 5:12-16, where the healing took place before the command to show oneself to the priest, here the healing took place on the way (cf. 2 Kgs 5:10-14). The obedience to Jesus' word reveals a cer-

---

[242]Conzelmann, Theology of St. Luke, 68-70.
[243]Luke 7:40; 9:38; 10:25; 11:45; 12:13; 18:18; 19:39; 20:21,28,39; 21:7.

tain degree of faith on the part of all ten lepers (cf. John 9:7). "Cleansed" refers to healing from leprosy, as Luke 17:15 reveals.

17:15 One of them. The Samaritan in response to his healing did four things.

Praising God. Praise as the appropriate response to God's salvation is a favorite Lukan theme (see comments on 5:25).

In a loud voice. "A loud voice" is a favorite Lukan expression.[244]

17:16 Threw himself at Jesus' feet. See comments on 5:12.

And thanked him. Only here in the NT are thanks directed to Jesus rather than God.[245] Compare, however, where prayer is offered to Jesus in Acts.[246] Compare 2 Kgs 5:15 for a similar reaction from Naaman the leper.

And he. "He" is emphatic, "And *he* . . . "

Samaritan. Mention of this has been delayed in the story to dramatize this fact. This would remind Luke's readers of the parable of the good Samaritan and that it was a Samaritan, not the priest or Levite, who proved to be a neighbor (cf. 10:30-37). It would also affirm to them the subsequent history of the church and how Samaritans received the gospel and official Judaism did not. Even though they already knew this, they would later read about this in Luke's second work.[247]

17:17-18 Jesus asked three rhetorical questions.

Nine. The nine were the Jewish lepers who were healed, in contrast to the "foreigner." For Luke's Jewish readers the pathos of these questions would have been great (cf. Rom 9:2-5). Once again the last had become first and the first last (Luke 13:30).

Give praise to God. True faith and worship involves praising, i.e., glorifying, God. See comments on 5:25; contrast Acts 12:23.

17:19 Your faith. In the first situation in life, this no doubt referred to a faith in God and in Jesus as his representative. In the Lukan setting such faith would be more Christologically oriented and refer to faith in Jesus as the Lord Christ, God's Son, who rose from the dead, reigns, and will return.

Has made you well. "Made you well" is literally *saved you.* See comments on 7:50. For Luke true faith, which leads to salvation, was intimately connected with glorying God even as it is elsewhere connected with the forgiveness of sins (Luke 5:20), entering God's kingdom (18:24-25), and inheriting eternal life (18:18-30). Compare the connection between faith and glorifying God in 18:42-43 and in Acts 11:14,18.

The Lukan Message

A clear Christological emphasis is present, for the account provides another example of Jesus' power. He is able to heal lepers (Luke 4:14,18-21; 5:17). This emphasis is furthermore heightened by 17:17. Between

---

[244]Cf. Luke 4:33; 8:28; 19:37; 23:23,46; Acts 7:57,60; 8:7; 14:10; 16:28; 26:24.

[245]Cf. Luke 18:11; 22:17,19; Acts 27:35; 28:15, where God is thanked.

[246]Acts 9:5-6/22:7-10; 9:10-16 (esp. v. 17).

[247]Cf. Acts 1:8; 8:1-25; 9:31; 13:45-47; 15:3; 18:6; 28:25-28.

the praise of God offered by the believing Samaritan (17:15) and the praise of God referred to by Jesus (17:18), we find that the Samaritan threw himself at Jesus' feet and "thanked him" (17:16). Only here in all the NT are such thanks directed to Jesus. Elsewhere they are directed to God (18:11; 22:17,19; Acts 27:35; 28:15). Luke made clear in Acts 10:25-26 that such homage does not belong to humans, only to God (cf. also Acts 12:21-23). Yet such homage is also to be directed to Jesus. Thus Luke demonstrated once again Jesus' uniqueness. Earlier (Luke 5:20-21; 7:48-49) Luke portrayed Jesus as exercising the divine prerogative of forgiving sins.

A second emphasis involves a soteriological truth. Luke warned his readers that one can experience God's work of grace and yet fall short of receiving salvation. Ten lepers were healed. All experienced the beginning of faith, for all went out in faith to show themselves to the priests. Yet, like the seed that fell upon the rock, they received Jesus' "word with joy . . . but . . . only believe[d] for a while" (8:13). Only one soil retained the word and persevered in faith (8:15). Luke again warned his readers that one can experience God's work and even his healing but fall short of salvation, and this last state may in fact be worse than the first (cf. 11:24-26). Nine lepers were able to say: "We ate and drank with you, and you taught in our streets. [You even healed us!]." But they will be denied (13:26-27). Luke's readers were instructed to make certain they were identified with the leper who persevered.

Two other Lukan themes are also found here. The theme of the great reversal is once again seen. It was the outcast, the Samaritan, who truly believed. See Introduction 8 (5). His experience foreshadows the future inclusion of the Samaritans into the believing community, as well as the rejection of the gospel by mainstream Judaism.[248] A final theme involves the continued validity of the OT as God's Word. Jesus sent the lepers to the priests in order to receive certificates of cleansing, for this was what the law taught. See 2:21-40—"The Lukan Message."

(2) The Coming of the Kingdom of God (17:20-37)

[20]Once, having been asked by the Pharisees when the kingdom of God would come, Jesus replied, "The kingdom of God does not come with your careful observation, [21]nor will people say, 'Here it is,' or 'There it is,' because the kingdom of God is within you."

[22]Then he said to his disciples, "The time is coming when you will long to see one of the days of the Son of Man, but you will not see it. [23]Men will tell you, 'There he is!' or 'Here he is!' Do not go running off after them. [24]For the Son of Man in his day will be like the lightning, which flashes and lights up the sky

---

[248]For Samaritan acceptance cf. Acts 1:8; 8:1,4-25; 9:31; 15:3. For Jewish rejection cf. 13:45-47; 18:6; 28:25-28.

from one end to the other. [25]But first he must suffer many things and be rejected by this generation.

[26]"Just as it was in the days of Noah, so also will it be in the days of the Son of Man. [27]People were eating, drinking, marrying and being given in marriage up to the day Noah entered the ark. Then the flood came and destroyed them all.

[28]"It was the same in the days of Lot. People were eating and drinking, buying and selling, planting and building. [29]But the day Lot left Sodom, fire and sulfur rained down from heaven and destroyed them all.

[30]"It will be just like this on the day the Son of Man is revealed. [31]On that day no one who is on the roof of his house, with his goods inside, should go down to get them. Likewise, no one in the field should go back for anything. [32]Remember Lot's wife! [33]Whoever tries to keep his life will lose it, and whoever loses his life will preserve it. [34]I tell you, on that night two people will be in one bed; one will be taken and the other left. [35]Two women will be grinding grain together; one will be taken and the other left."

[37]"Where, Lord?" they asked.

He replied, "Where there is a dead body, there the vultures will gather."

Context

The setting of this material is unspecified, and as the introductory seam reveals, there is no necessary tie with the preceding material. Luke wove this section from various traditional materials[249] and placed it here for reasons other than chronology. Why he placed this material at this point, however, is unclear. The account consists of two different sets of material. The first speaks of the "already now" or realized aspect of God's kingdom (17:20-21). The second speaks of the "not yet" or future aspect of the kingdom (17:22-37). The two sets of teachings are connected by catchwords: "come" (17:20)—"is coming" (17:22); "here it is" or "there it is" (17:21)—"there he is!" or "here he is!" (17:23).

Similar material is found in 21:7-35. The authenticity of most of this material has been generally accepted, although 17:25, due its clear portrayal of the crucifixion, is considered by some as a prophecy after the fact (*vaticinia ex eventu*) since this involves the miraculous. Those who deny the authenticity of any of the Son of Man sayings, of course, deny the authenticity of 17:22,24,26,30.

---

[249] Although Luke 17:20-21 lacks any clear parallel in Matthew, we find a parallel to this material in GT 3,113. There are no clear Gospel parallels to Luke 17:22,25,28-29,32,34 (cf. however GT 61) or Luke 17:37a. The other material is paralleled as follows: Luke 17:23-24 (Matt 24:23,27); Luke 17:26-27 (Matt 24:37-38); Luke 17:30 (Matt 24:39); Luke 17:31 (Mark 13:15); Luke 17:33 (Matt 10:39); Luke 17:35 (Matt 24:40-41); Luke 17:37b (Matt 24:28). The scattered nature of the parallel material and the lack of clear parallels to some of this material in Matthew and Mark indicates that Luke arranged this material into its present form.

In this section Luke argued in the following manner: God's kingdom would not be preceded by signs that could be calculated and observed. On the contrary the kingdom was already present in the coming of Jesus Christ (17:20-21). As to the consummation of the kingdom brought about by the return of the Son of Man, this would not come in the disciples' lifetime (17:22). The Son of Man will furthermore not come in some secret fashion (17:23), for his coming will be observed by all (17:24). Yet before all this, the Son of Man in his present ministry faced rejection and death (17:25). As for the Son of Man's coming, it will be unexpected, and people will be unprepared (17:26-30). In that day the final separation will take place dividing even families (17:31-35). Just as one knows the presence of carrion by the attending vultures, so the return of the Son of Man will be clear to the whole world (17:37).

Comments

17:20 Once, having been asked. There is no tie between this material and what has preceded, and what follows has been placed here by Luke for other than chronological reasons.

By the Pharisees. For "Pharisee" see comments on 5:17.

When the kingdom of God would come. To interpret this as a question about how one knows that God's kingdom is already a present reality is too subtle and to be rejected.[250] There is no evidence that the question is an attempt to trap Jesus. No doubt the Pharisees brought with them certain popular ideas about what would happen "in that day." This involved such things as the resurrection of the dead, the destruction of Israel's enemies, and the appearance of a kingly Messiah.

Does not come with your careful observation. This does not mean that the messianic age will not come on the night of observation, i.e., the Passover night; neither does it mean the messianic age will not come by means of our religious observances (a la Qumran). It means rather that the messianic age will not be preceded by signs that will enable one to predict beforehand its arrival. The expression "careful observation" (*paratēreseōs*) is found only here in the NT and the LXX. It probably refers to watching for the premonitory signs of the coming of God's kingdom in order for those alert to such signs to predict its coming. It may involve the reckoning of the "times and seasons"[251] for the purpose of producing a chart of the last things—a temptation succumbed to all too easily and often. Acts 1:7 also rejects such an endeavor.

17:21 Here it is. This can be translated "here it is" or "here he is." Since the immediate context involves God's kingdom rather than the Son of Man's return, it is best to translate it "here it is." Yet the consummation of the kingdom takes place when the Son of Man returns so that in the new context provided by Luke 17:23 (cf. also Mark 13:21) the same expression can be translated "here he is."

---

[250] Cf. H. Riesenfeld, παρατήρησις, *TDNT* (Grand Rapids: Eerdmans, 1972), 8:150, n. 15: "When does one know the kingdom of God is there?"

[251] Cf. 1 Thess 5:1; Mark 13:3-4/Matt 24:36; Wis 8:8.

Because the kingdom of God is within you. The reason given for not looking for such premonitory signs can be either (1) that the (realized) kingdom had already come into their midst (17:21b) or (2) that the (consummated) kingdom will come suddenly and unexpectedly and when it comes all will know immediately (17:22-37). The first possibility is the correct one, for in 17:20-21 the emphasis is on the already realized dimension of God's kingdom. The expression "within you" (*entos hymōn*) can mean "in your hearts," "in your midst," or "in your reach." The first interpretation ("within you") was much in favor in theological liberalism, which saw God's kingdom as God's rule in the human heart. But nowhere else in the Scriptures is God's kingdom portrayed as an inner condition of the human heart or life. Furthermore the saying is addressed to the Pharisees, who were most unlikely candidates for Jesus' saying that God rules within their hearts. Even if one makes "you" indefinite and not limited to the Pharisees, the first argument is conclusive: "Jesus speaks of men entering the kingdom, not the kingdom entering men."[252] Since Jesus the "king" was present, God's reign had already begun. Thus the text should be translated "in your midst" or "in the midst of you," as in the RSV and not as in the NIV. The third interpretation, which sees God's kingdom as having come and at the disposal of Jesus' hearers if they only accept it ("in your reach"), is less likely than the second; but it is correct in understanding God's kingdom as having arrived.

17:22 Then he said to his disciples. Through a change in audience Luke applied these teachings more directly to his readers.[253]

The time is coming. See comments on 5:35.

When you will long to see. This same desire is expressed in "your kingdom come" (11:2) and in "*Maranatha*."[254] No major event of salvation history is seen as intervening between the disciples' time and the Son of Man's coming, though in the larger context of Luke-Acts the Spirit's coming at Pentecost and the preaching of the gospel to the whole world from Jerusalem to Rome are major events in salvation history. For Luke and his readers only the return of the Son of Man still lay in the future.

One of the days of. One would expect "the day of" (cf. 17:24,30), but the plural may be used to parallel "in the days of Noah/Lot" (17:26,28).[255] This expression probably means "the time when the Son of Man returns and reigns."[256] This does not refer to a desire to reexperience the time of Jesus' ministry.

But you will not see it. This can mean (1) *it will never come*; (2) *it cannot be seen*, i.e., *it is invisible*; (3) *you will no longer be alive*. The last interpretation is clearly the correct one and may suggest that Luke was seeking to help his readers resolve the problem of the delay of the parousia. See Introduction 7 (3).

17:23 This verse warns against believers' being misled into thinking that the Son of Man's coming will be concealed from the world or that the Son of Man (or some messianic pretender) has already come in some secret and mysterious way,

---

[252] Marshall, *Luke*, 655.

[253] Note the changes in audience in 15:2 (Pharisees); 16:1 (disciples); 16:14 (Pharisees); 17:1 (disciples); 17:20 (Pharisees); 17:22 (disciples); 18:9 (Pharisees).

[254] First Corinthians 16:22; cf. Rev 22:20; 6:10.

[255] For a discussion of some of the ways in which the term "one" can be understood, see Fitzmyer, *Luke* 2:1168-69.

[256] For a discussion of some of the ways in which "days of the Son of Man" can be understood, see Marshall, *Luke*, 658-59.

a warning all too frequently ignored in the church's history. This verse is essentially a conditional sentence, although the first part (the protasis) is lacking an "if." The sense is, "If they should say . . . , do not go running."

"There he is!" or "Here he is!"   Compare Mark 13:21; Matt 24:23,26. A textual problem exists involving the order of these sayings. In an apparent attempt to harmonize the order of these sayings with that in Luke 17:21, numerous early manuscripts reversed this order.[257] The present reading in the NIV supported by $\mathfrak{P}^{75}$ and B is more likely. The meaning of the verse is little affected by which variant one chooses. Compare Mark 13:21; Matt 24:23,26.

Do not go running off after them.   The reason for this is given in the following verses: there will be no mistaking the Son of Man's coming.

17:24   The Son of Man's coming will be as visible as lightning that lightens up the whole sky. Therefore exhortations to go somewhere to see a secret coming are deceitful and absurd and must be rejected.

In his day.   Three of the oldest and most important Greek manuscripts ($\mathfrak{P}^{45}$, B, D) lack this phrase, so there is some uncertainty about whether it should be included. The inclusion or omission of this phrase, however, has no effect on the meaning.

Like the lightning.   This may be an allusion to the Son of Man's glory (cf. 9:29). The main emphasis involves lightning's brightness, which lights up the whole sky, and thus the universal visibility of the Son of Man's coming rather than its suddenness.

17:25   But first he must suffer.   Compare 9:22. For the divine "must" (*dei*) of God's providential will, see Introduction 8 (1). Suffering must precede the Son of Man's glory (cf. 24:26). Luke and his tradition knew of no distinction between Jesus and the Son of Man or between the Son of Man who would suffer and the Son of Man who will return gloriously.

By this generation.   Compare 7:31 and 9:41, where this generation is portrayed as unwilling to accept the witness of John the Baptist and Jesus and is described as "unbelieving and perverse." The specific generation referred to was Jesus' contemporaries.

17:26   Luke 17:28 parallels 17:26-27a, and 17:29 parallels 17:27b.

In the days of Noah.   See comments on 17:22.

Days of the Son of Man.   The time immediately preceding his coming.

17:27   Eating, drinking, marrying.   This refers not so much to the evil of Noah's contemporaries (cf. Gen 6:11) but to how they were unsuspecting and unprepared for the judgment that came upon them. Life proceeded as usual when judgment came. For Luke's love of "fours," see comments on 6:22.

Then the flood came and destroyed them all.   God's judgment came swiftly, and there was no time to prepare. It was too late.

17:28   In the example of Lot, the issue again is not so much the evil of the residents of Sodom (or the righteousness of Noah and Lot[258]) but that the judgment came unexpectedly upon an unprepared people.

---

[257] See B. M. Metzger, *A Textual Commentary on the Greek New Testament* (London: United Bible Societies, 1971), 166-67.

[258] A number of examples in Jewish literature place Noah and Lot side by side as examples of the judgment of the wicked and the salvation of the righteous. Cf. *T. Naph.* 3:4-5; 3 Macc 2:4-5; Wis 10:4,6; *Sanh.* 10:3.

Eating and drinking, buying and selling, planting and building. God's judgment caught them totally by surprise, for they lived as though it would never come. The reference to "marrying and being given in marriage" in the previous verse is omitted because Sodom was not famous for its marrying.

17:29   Fire and sulfur. Judgment came differently in the days of Lot than in the days of Noah, but it came just as suddenly and was just as total for Sodom.[259]

17:30   It will be just like this. The main comparison is not that the Son of Man's coming brings certain and horrendous judgment. While this is true, the main point of comparison here is that it will catch people just as unprepared.

The Son of Man is revealed. This was Luke's way of expressing the "coming of the Son of Man" (Matt 24:39). Compare 1 Cor 1:7.

17:31   On the roof. A Palestinian home with a flat roof and exterior stairs leading up to the roof is envisioned.

Should go down. This picture part of the saying should not be interpreted as implying that there is a chance to escape the judgment when the Son of Man is revealed so long as one does not "tarry." The picture is a well-known image of war describing the swiftness of an approaching enemy army, which does not permit time to prepare. One can only flee.[260] The basic point of the analogy is that there will be no time to prepare oneself when the Son of Man returns. It will be too late then.

Go back. Lot's wife "turned back" (Gen 19:26) and became a pillar of salt.

17:32   Remember Lot's wife! This probably is a warning to Luke's readers to seek without reservation the escape from the future judgment that is available in following Jesus.

17:33 Luke interjected into this eschatological discourse a saying of Jesus that recalls 9:24. This may have been elicited by the exhortation in the previous verse. Since there is no opportunity to save one's life when the Son of Man returns, Luke's readers should remember what happened to Lot's wife because of her incomplete obedience. They should remember the saying of Jesus recorded earlier (9:24).

17:34   That night. "Night" does not designate a specific time of day but is used because of the following two illustrations. For the use of "night" to illustrate unexpectedness, cf. 1 Thess 5:2.

Two people. This could be a married couple or two men, but the following "the one" and "the other" are masculine, so that two men probably are envisioned. If Luke was seeking to pair the two in this verse with the two women in the next verse (see comments on 13:19), this also would argue for their being men; however, the masculine could have been used because the man could be taken or left behind. This would allow for the two to be a married couple.

Will be taken . . . left. These appear to be divine passives. If it is the Son of Man, however, who will "take" or "leave," then these "divine passives" are used to describe his actions.[261] This statement can be interpreted as being taken away from judgment (positive) and being left for judgment (negative) or being taken

---

[259] Cf. Rev 9:17-18; 14:10; 19:20; 20:10; 21:8.
[260] Cf. Jer 6:1; 48:6; 49:8,30; 51:6.
[261] Cf. Luke 9:26; John 14:3; 1 Thess 4:17; Matt 24:31; 25:31-46.

away for judgment (negative) and being left for salvation (positive). "Taken" is best understood as positive because both Noah and Lot were taken (into an ark/ away from the city) and not left for judgment (cf. John 14:3; 1 Thess 4:17). The meaning of the verse, however, remains the same regardless of which interpretation one chooses. The term "taken" does not mean *to disappear* but *to escape judgment*.[262]

17:35 This verse stands in synonymous parallelism with the previous verse. **Two women will be grinding.** Two people were normally involved in utilizing an ancient grinding mill.

17:36 This verse is omitted in the best Greek manuscripts and thus should not be included.

17:37 Where? Jesus' words in Luke 17:23 are ignored in the question. **Lord.** See comments on 6:46.

The following proverb is quite confusing, but it may mean that just as vultures know where carcasses are, so the world unmistakably will know when and where the Son of Man returns.[263]

The Lukan Message

Within this "little Lukan apocalypse" we find side-by-side teachings that demonstrate the twofold nature of God's kingdom. The realized nature of the kingdom is seen in Luke 17:20-21. In fulfillment of the OT promises God's kingdom is seen by Jesus and Luke as having already arrived so that the Pharisees' question in 17:20 reveals the same error as the statement in 14:15. Questions involving the future coming of God's kingdom must not lose sight of the already-now dimension of the kingdom.[264] Already now the kingdom has come, and the future not-yet dimension of God's kingdom will be shared only if one now enters the kingdom in its present manifestation.

In the remainder of this section the focus turns to the consummation of the kingdom. Several aspects of the kingdom, for which the believer continually yearns and prays (11:2), are revealed in this passage. For one there is present the clearest statement in all of Luke that the kingdom would not come in the disciples' lifetime (17:22).[265] Luke continued to assist his readers in understanding that Jesus did not promise that the kingdom would be consummated in the disciples' lifetime. In the parable of the unjust judge that follows (18:1-8), Luke picked up this theme (cf. also 12:35-48; 19:11). Whether Luke's audience was troubled by the

---

[262]There is an interesting parallel to this saying in GT 61: "Jesus said: Two will be resting on a bed; one will die, (and) the other will live." Here the eschatological element has been eliminated and the saying made into a bland proverb.

[263]Matthew placed the proverb after the saying found in Luke 17:24 (Matt 24:27-28).

[264]Cf. Luke 4:18-21; 7:20-23; 16:16; see Introduction 8 (2).

[265]Cf. John 21:22-23 for a similar clarification concerning one of the last apostles.

"delay" of the parousia (cf. 2 Pet 3:3-7) cannot be known with certainty, but it is possible. What is clear is that Luke was addressing this issue here. What is also clear is that Luke had not relegated the Son of Man's coming to the remote future. The exhortation in 17:33 is not directed to being ready for physical death but to the need for his readers to be ready for the consummation. See Introduction 7 (3).

Luke also pointed out that the coming of the kingdom, described as the days of the Son of Man, would not be secretive or hidden but clear for all to see. It would be as visible as lightning that lights up the whole sky (17:21a,22-24,37). The disciples (and thus Luke's readers) should not be misled by rumors of the Lord's return. There would be no mistaking his return. Luke took a number of the eschatological teachings Jesus addressed to the disciples and applied them specifically to his readers' needs. In so doing he did not change Jesus' original teachings so much as focus on their implications for his readers. It is tempting to assume by means of a "mirror reading" that Luke's audience was troubled with erroneous views concerning a secretive return of the Lord or some messianic figure. This may or may not have been a problem. Regardless, for his readers these teachings are most valuable. The return of the Son of Man will be evident to all. Whereas the presence of the realized dimension of God's kingdom is clear enough for those with eyes of faith and an open heart to see (7:20-23; 12:54-56), in its consummation it will be clear to all. In that day the mustard seed will have become a tree, and all will see it (13:19).

The kingdom's consummation also will be sudden and unexpected, and people will be unprepared (17:26-30). This reveals that even as the realized dimension of the kingdom is not preceded with signs that serve as precursors (11:29-30), so too will the consummation. There will be no warning, no opportunity to prepare oneself. Life among "this generation" will continue as normal (17:27-28) in ignorance of the oncoming judgment. As in the case of the rich fool (12:20), so in that day the world will be caught unprepared. And the result of this will be condemnation at the final judgment. There will be no respite or time to prepare (17:34-35; cf. 12:57-59), for the time of grace will have ended (13:6-9).

Within the little Lukan apocalypse are also several statements by which Luke reminded his readers of earlier themes. For one, the present mission of the Son of Man and the divine necessity of his death is again pointed out (17:25; cf. 9:22). Luke also inserted an exhortation to save life by losing it in 17:33 (cf. 9:24), which seems somewhat foreign to the section's main theme. This, however, may have been occasioned by the need for his audience to prepare for the coming of the kingdom and the fact that earlier (17:25) he referred to a passion prediction (9:22) and this may have brought to mind the exhortation found next to this (9:24). Regardless, Luke warned his readers to be prepared for the consummation so that they would not lose their lives.

Also present is a powerful Christological emphasis. The one who will exercise judgment in the final day is the Son of Man. The day of final judgment is "the day of the Son of Man" (17:26,30; cf. 9:26). The glorious appearing of the Son of Man (9:26; 21:27), like his coming through the virgin Mary, brings both blessing for the believer (6:21-23) and woe for the unbeliever (6:24-26). He brings both the Spirit and fire (see comments on 3:16), and as in his earthly ministry the Son of Man also brought division already in this life (12:49-53; 14:26), so in his appearing in glory will he bring by his judgment the final and ultimate division.

(3) The Parable of the Unjust Judge (18:1-8)

[1]**Then Jesus told his disciples a parable to show them that they should always pray and not give up.** [2]**He said: "In a certain town there was a judge who neither feared God nor cared about men.** [3]**And there was a widow in that town who kept coming to him with the plea, 'Grant me justice against my adversary.'**

[4]**"For some time he refused. But finally he said to himself, 'Even though I don't fear God or care about men,** [5]**yet because this widow keeps bothering me, I will see that she gets justice, so that she won't eventually wear me out with her coming!' "**

[6]**And the Lord said, "Listen to what the unjust judge says.** [7]**And will not God bring about justice for his chosen ones, who cry out to him day and night? Will he keep putting them off?** [8]**I tell you, he will see that they get justice, and quickly. However, when the Son of Man comes, will he find faith on the earth?"**

Context

This parable[266] is closely connected to the preceding material by theme and audience, even though the tie between them is not as intimate as the NIV's "then" suggests. The parable continues Jesus' teaching of the

---

[266]Although the parable's authenticity is granted by most scholars (E. Linnemann, *Parables of Jesus* [London: SPCK, 1966], 119-24, is an exception), the authenticity of certain parts is debated. For a helpful discussion see E. D. Freed, "The Parable of the Judge and the Widow (Luke 18:1-8)," *NTS* 33 (1987): 38-60.

The parable consists of 18:2-5 to which an introduction (18:1) and interpretation are added (18:6-8). The introduction is from Luke's hand. It is possible that 18:8b is either an isolated saying of Jesus that Luke added to this parable or Luke's editorial comment. There is no reason, unless it is presumed that Jesus never gave any interpretations to his parables (see 8:4-15, "Context"), to deny that the material in 18:6-8a, apart from "And the Lord said," came from Jesus.

disciples (18:1; literally *them*; cf. 17:22) and deals with the consummation of God's kingdom. By his introduction ("that they should always pray
and not give up," 18:1), Luke applied the parable to the issue of the delay
of the parousia. The concluding statement concerning the Son of Man's
return (18:8b) ties this parable even more closely to 17:22-37. Thus the
parable serves as a concluding illustration to 17:22-37 and teaches that
the day of the Son of Man will certainly come, even if there is an apparent
delay. A close analogy to the parable is found in 11:5-8.

In the parable two characters make up the picture part: a persistent
woman and an unjust judge. As in 16:1-8, Jesus used a less-than-noble
character as an illustration (cf. also Matt 13:44: 25:1-13). The corresponding reality to which the characters point involves an *a fortiori* argument. If the unjust judge finally granted the persistent widow's request,
how much more will a just God hear and grant the petitions of his followers who pray to him day and night. Thus in light of the "delay" in the
coming of the day of the Son of Man (Luke 17:22-37), the disciples—and,
in the Lukan setting, Theophilus—should not give up but continue to pray
"Your kingdom come" (11:2) and remain faithful (18:8).

Comments

18:1   Then Jesus told.   Literally *and he was saying* (cf. 5:36; 6:39; 21:29).

His disciples.   The NIV clarifies the addressees (literally *to them*).

That they should always pray.   For "prayer" as a Lukan emphasis and a pattern for the Christian life, see Introduction 8 (7). For "always" cf. 1 Thess 5:17.
The idea is of continual prayer, not continuous, nonstop prayer. In light of the
context in Luke 17:22-37, the content of this prayer is no doubt "Your kingdom
come" (11:2; cf. also 21:36). Because of the delay in the consummation of the
kingdom, it is especially important for persistent prayer to characterize the Christian life. This will insure that a community of faith will exist when the Son of Man
comes (18:8).

And not give up.   The thought is not to give up in light of the delay of the
consummation.[267] See Introduction 7 (3).

18:2   A judge.   He is depicted as indifferent to God or the wishes of other
people and therefore to the woman in 18:3.

Neither feared God.   This describes the judge's lack of the most fundamental
requirement in life, reverence toward God (cf. Prov 9:10).

Nor cared about men.   Compare Josephus, *Antiquities* 10.5.2 (10.83) for a
similar description. Jesus' and Luke's understanding of the law as summarized by
the two commands of love of God and neighbor is witnessed to here. See comments on 10:27.

18:3   There was a widow.   The widow represented the needy, helpless,
poor, and oppressed. She was the kind of person spoken of in 20:47. In this in-

---

[267]Cf. 2 Thess 3:13; Gal 6:9; 2 Cor 4:1,16; Eph 3:13.

stance her insignificance resulted in an injustice (18:5).[268] Luke showed great concern for widows.[269]

Who kept coming. The widow's only hope and weapon was her persistence ("kept coming" is an iterative imperfect) in coming to the judge. She would not stop until she was vindicated.

Grant me justice. This verb (*ekdikeō*) can mean *to avenge* (cf. Rom 12:19), but in the present judicial context it means *to render justice by upholding the innocent and punishing the guilty.*

18:4 For some time he refused. Speculation about why he refused (the judge was too lazy, or he did not want to side with the widow against her more influential opponent) is misguided, since this is a parable and not an actual incident. The judge refused because Jesus, the storyteller, wanted him to.

He said to himself. See comments on 15:17.

Even though. "Even though" introduces a concessive clause, i.e., not *because* but *despite the fact that.* The repetition of 18:2b emphasizes the character of the judge as one that ignores the two basic commandments (10:27).

18:5 The reason for the judge's granting justice to the widow is now given.

So that she won't eventually wear me out. Literally *hit me under the eye.* This must be interpreted metaphorically, for the widow would hardly have attacked the judge physically. There are two possible ways of interpreting the metaphor: she will wear me out (by her continual coming), or she will blacken my face, i.e., make me look bad by having ignored her and thus give me a bad reputation. The former is more likely since the judge did not care what other people thought (18:2,4). Ultimately, however, the exact reason for the judge's yielding to the widow's request has no corresponding reality. What the parable seeks to teach is not *why* God will bring justice for his people (18:8) but *that* he will.

18:6 This verse may be either a Lukan editorial comment calling attention to the following interpretation of the parable or, excluding "and the Lord said," be part of the parable itself.

Lord. See comments on 7:13.

The unjust judge. Just as in 16:1-8, where we read of the dishonest (*adikias*) manager, the parable uses a disreputable ("unjust," *adikias*) character as an example.

18:7 The basic argument of the parable involves an *a fortiori* reasoning that culminates in 18:7-8a. Although the conclusion of the argument is in the form of a question that expects a positive answer, it can be reworded as follows: "If the unjust judge yielded to the continuous cries of the widow, who was a stranger, and granted her the vindication she sought (the picture part of the parable), how much more will God, who is just and their loving Father (12:30; 11:2), hear the cries of his chosen ones who cry out to him day and night (the reality part)."

And will not God. Compare John 18:11 for a similar construction.

Bring about justice. This can mean *to rescue God's people* (Acts 7:24) or *to bring judgment upon those who abuse them* (cf. Rev 6:10; 19:2). The latter is

---

[268]The destitution of such people is illustrated by Exod 22:22-24; Deut 10:18; 24:17; Mal 3:5; Ruth 1:20-21; Lam 1:1; Isa 54:4; Ps 68:5; Jas 1:27; (cf. also Sir 35:12-20).

[269]Cf. Luke 2:37; 4:25-26; 7:12; 20:47; 21:2-4; Acts 6:1; 9:39,41. In contrast widows are mentioned only three times in the other Synoptic Gospels.

revenge/vengeance when people take the divine prerogative into their own hands (Rom 12:19), but it is justice when performed by a righteous God or by agents whom he has ordained (cf. Rom 13:4; Num 31:2). Without a specific context it is difficult to understand exactly how the expression should be interpreted.

Chosen ones. This is the only place in Luke-Acts where this OT expression is used to describe God's people (cf. Luke 23:35, where it is used of Christ). "Chosen ones" designates those who have responded to God in repentance and faith and are thus the recipients of his love and grace rather than to the elect by some kind of predestination.

Cry out. For the content of such prayer, cf. 11:2; Num 20:16. For the experience cf. Mark 15:34; Ps 22:2.

Day and night. "Day and night" means *continually* (cf. Luke 2:37; Acts 9:24; 20:31; 26:7). Compare Luke 18:1, where the analogy is praying "always."

Will he keep putting them off? This is a *crux interpretum* and can be interpreted in various ways. Some interpretations suggest that the present Greek text is a mistranslation of Jesus' words and seek to reconstruct what Jesus actually said. Others seek to interpret the saying in light of various possible meanings of the verb (*makrothymei*): God is patient and longsuffering with them, i.e., the wicked (2 Pet 3:9); will God be patient much longer as he sees his chosen suffer? (an implied no being understood); will not God vindicate his chosen? (an implied yes being understood).[270] For a similar thought see comments on 12:45.

18:8 Jesus answered his own question (Luke 18:7).

I tell you. This common Lukan introduction underscores the truthfulness of what follows.[271]

He will see . . . justice. God will, even more certainly than the unjust judge, bring the justice for which his people continually pray.

Quickly. The meaning is *soon*, i.e., *shortly*, rather than *suddenly*, i.e., *when people are unprepared.*[272] For Luke, as for Jesus, the consummation was a vibrant hope and expectation. Although it may appear to be delayed, Luke (and believers through the centuries) expected that the blessed hope (Titus 2:13) would take place soon. Although chronological time may seem to deny this, in God's understanding (cf. 2 Pet 3:8) and in faith's reckoning of time the consummation will always be "soon."

However, when the Son of Man comes. An abrupt shift at this point can be understood as Jesus' concluding words to the parable, a saying of Jesus said elsewhere but placed here by Luke, or a Lukan editorial comment. By this comment, as well as the introduction in Luke 18:1, the Evangelist applied the parable to the discussion of the delay of the parousia in 17:22-37.[273]

---

[270] For a discussion of the various ways in which this phrase can be interpreted, see Marshall, *Luke*, 674-75. It seems best in this context to translate the term "delay long" (RSV) or "keep putting them off" with no being understood. This interpretation fits best its use in 2 Pet 3:9 and Sir 35:18 (35:19, LXX). This provides a better parallel with the picture part of the parable than "even if he puts their patience to the test by not answering them immediately, God will hasten to rescue them."
Jeremias, *Parables of Jesus*, 155.

[271] Cf. Luke 7:9,26; 9:27; 10:12,24; 11:8,51; 12:4,8,27,37,44,51,59; 13:3,5,24.

[272] Contra Ellis, *Luke*, 213. Cf. Acts 12:7; 22:18; 25:4; cf. also Rom 16:20; Rev 1:1; 22:6.

[273] For other exhortations involving the return of the Son of Man, cf. Luke 12:35-40,42-48; 17:22-37; 21:34-36.

Will he find faith?   Persistent prayer and perseverance are necessary in order for God's chosen ones to remain true to the faith until the Son of Man returns. The use of the article before "faith," i.e., "the faith,"[274] suggests that this question should be translated "Will he find the faith?" rather than "Will he find faithfulness?" Another way of expressing this thought is found in 21:36.

The Lukan Message

By this parable Luke taught his readers the proper response to the delay of the parousia spoken of in 17:22-37. Luke revealed to his readers that Jesus foresaw an interval between his death and ascension and his glorious return. This is why he told this parable (18:1) and the parable of the pounds (19:11). During this interval, it was important for them, like the widow in the parable, to persevere in faith and bear fruit (cf. 8:15; 18:1,3-4). Such perseverance was possible by continuing in prayer. For only by so doing would they be able to keep from giving up (18:1) and not succumb to the temptations of the coming days (21:34-36).

Some suggest Luke may have had grave doubts concerning the reality of his readers' faith when he wrote.[275] It is doubtful, however, whether these exhortations must be due to an existing problem. A "mirror reading" of this exhortation need not be employed because Luke may simply have been seeking to prevent future problems, i.e., the exhortation was preventative. Good preaching and teaching frequently seek to avoid problems from arising. Again we are confronted with the fact that we can know *what* Luke was seeking to teach his readers through this passage even if we cannot climb into his mind in order to understand *why*.

(4) The Parable of the Pharisee and the Tax Collector (18:9-14)

[9]To some who were confident of their own righteousness and looked down on everybody else, Jesus told this parable: [10]"Two men went up to the temple to pray, one a Pharisee and the other a tax collector. [11]The Pharisee stood up and prayed about himself: 'God, I thank you that I am not like other men—robbers, evildoers, adulterers—or even like this tax collector. [12]I fast twice a week and give a tenth of all I get.'

[13]"But the tax collector stood at a distance. He would not even look up to heaven, but beat his breast and said, 'God, have mercy on me, a sinner.'

[14]"I tell you that this man, rather than the other, went home justified before God. For everyone who exalts himself will be humbled, and he who humbles himself will be exalted."

Context

This parable is connected to the preceding material due to its being a parable and its reference to prayer (cf. 18:1,7 with 18:10-13). Also Luke

---

[274]Cf. Acts 6:7; 13:8; 14:22; 16:5; cf. also 24:24; 26:18.
[275]So Freed, "Parable of the Judge and the Widow," 56.

perhaps placed this parable here to serve as an example of those who will
be found faithful when the Son of Man returns (18:8). Thus 18:9-14 and
the three following accounts all deal with what it means to have "the
faith" (18:8). The theme of the parable, God's mercy to tax collectors and
sinners, has been encountered earlier[276] as has the form, a parable in
which the behavior of two characters is contrasted.[277]

Within the parable we encounter a self-righteous Pharisee whose
prayer in the temple is essentially a self-eulogy. He thanked God that he
was not like others. In itself the prayer could be quite acceptable if the
Pharisee were thanking God for protecting him from circumstances that
might have led him to become a thief or an adulterer. However the Pharisee saw his not having succumbed to such sins as purely his own doing.
There was no thanks for what God had done but rather a long list of personal achievements. (Note all the *I's*!) He had no sense of being an
unworthy servant and having done only his duty (Luke 17:10). Actually
he believed he had done more than God required. He had not only kept
the law perfectly and thus did not need to pray for God's forgiveness, he
even fasted twice a week and tithed everything he bought (not just what
he earned). His attitude was clear. God was very fortunate to have someone like him. He knew nothing of God's perfection and holiness and his
own sinfulness! He possessed an unusually high self-worth and had
learned nothing from the penitential psalms[278] or such thoughts as Rom
3:10-20, which exclude all such boasting (Luke 17:10; Rom 3:27).

In contrast the tax collector demonstrated his attitude even by his physical stance. He stood "at a distance," "would not even look up to heaven,"
and "beat his breast" (Luke 18:13). Even apart from his prayer he exhibited humility and contrition. His prayer sought God's mercy and forgiveness just like the psalmist (Ps 51:1). The result, which would have been
shocking for many of Jesus' hearers, was that the sinner who sought
God's mercy left justified, not the Pharisee.

Comments

18:9   To some who were confident of their own righteousness. As in 18:1 and
19:11, Luke gave the reason/interpretation of the parable at the very beginning. This
can be translated "they trusted in themselves that they were righteous" or "they
trusted in themselves because they were righteous." The latter interpretation would
understand the reason for their confidence as being their (supposed) knowledge of
their righteousness. The former interpretation, however, is more likely because in every other instance in Luke where "that/because" (*hoti*) is used with a participle it is

---

[276]Luke 5:29-32; 7:36-50; 15:1-32; 16:19-31.
[277]Luke 7:36-50; 15:11-32; 16:19-31; cf. also Matt 20:1-16; 21:28-32.
[278]Pss 6; 32; 38; 51; 102; 130; 140.

best translated "that."[279] Luke did not specifically identify the "some" of this verse, but the earlier reference to the Pharisees as those who "justify yourselves in the eyes of men" (16:14-15; cf. 10:29) and the reference to the Pharisee in the parable suggest them as the audience both in his (and Jesus') mind.

Looked down at everybody else. Compare 23:11; Acts 4:11. Those who like the publican understand their sinful condition and know that they can only be saved by grace, find it difficult to despise others, for there is nothing of which they can boast. Only those who possess a false confidence in their own righteousness look down at others.

18:10 Two men. Compare Luke 15:11; 17:34-35; cf. 7:41-42.

Went up to the temple. Since the temple was on a hill, people went up to it even if they were already in Jerusalem (cf. 18:14, "went home," literally *went down to his house*, and Acts 3:1, *were going up to the temple*).

To pray. One could pray privately at any time in the temple, but the times for public prayer were 9:00 a.m. (Acts 2:15) and 3:00 p.m. (3:1).

A Pharisee. See comments on 5:17.

Tax collector. See comments on 5:30. This term is often used in combination with "sinners" (Luke 5:30; 7:34; 15:1; cf. Matt 9:10-11; 11:19; Mark 2:15-16) and even "prostitutes" (Matt 21:31-32).

18:11 The Pharisee stood up. This was the normal posture for prayer. Since the publican stood "at a distance" in the temple, the implication is that the Pharisee stood "at the front."

Prayed about himself. This can also be translated "prayed these things to himself" (*pros heauton*) and can mean that his prayer never went to God because he was only talking to himself or that he was praying silently and not aloud. The former is too subtle and the latter is too contrary to normal Jewish practice. It is best to interpret this as the NIV does.

God, I thank you. Note that there was no petition in the Pharisee's prayer. He really did not need God.

I am not like other men. If humility toward God and compassion for neighbor are excluded, the Pharisee possessed an impeccable life-style. But humility toward God and compassion for neighbor are the essence of true piety. See comments on 10:27.

Robbers, evildoers, adulterers. The first and third sins are forbidden in the Decalogue (Exod 20:14-15). The middle term (*adikoi, unrighteous, evildoers*) is more general and may be present to match the term "righteous" (*dikaioi*) in Luke 18:9.

This tax collector. For the deprecatory use of "this," see comments on 15:30.

18:12 I fast twice a week. A "fast" would generally involve going without food or drink from sunrise to sunset. This is the earliest reference to the Jewish practice of fasting twice a week (cf. *Did.* 8:1). The two days of fasting mentioned in the Talmud are Monday and Thursday (*Ta'an.* 12a).

Give a tenth of all I get. Compare Luke 11:42. The Pharisee did more than the law demanded in that he tithed everything that came into his possession, not

---

[279]Cf. Luke 1:45; 7:37; 8:47,53; 17:15; 23:7; cf. also 9:22; 14:30; 15:2; 19:7,42; 20:5; 21:5; 23:5; 24:7,34; contrast, however, 13:14.

simply what he earned. He may have done this in case the person who sold this to him had not tithed it. By these two acts the Pharisee boasted of his works of supererogation, i.e., he thought he did more than God required of him.

Needless to say, not all Pharisees trusted in their own righteousness like the one in this parable (see comments on 11:42). Yet unless we claim that the entire Gospel depiction of the Pharisees is incorrect, some Pharisees were like this.[280] That certain Pharisees did think this way is evident from the Talmudic materials.[281] Similarly, it should not be assumed that all tax collectors were like the one portrayed in the parable, but some were. Thus the parable is not a caricature.

18:13   But the tax collector stood at a distance. This indicates that he sensed a personal unworthiness to stand close to the sanctuary.

Would not even look up to heaven. Compare 1 Enoch 13:5. "For from thence forward they could not speak (with Him) nor lift up their eyes to heaven for shame of their sins for which they had been condemned." For looking up to heaven in prayer, cf. Mark 6:41; 7:34; John 11:41; 17:1; cf. also Ps 123:1.

Beat his breast. As a sign of contrition or grief (cf. Luke 23:48).

God, have mercy on me, a sinner. The verb used here (*hilasthēti*) is found elsewhere in the NT only in Heb 2:17. It means *to expiate* or *propitiate*. The noun (*hilastērion*) is used in this sense in Rom 3:25 (cf. also 1 John 2:2; 4:10), and in Heb 9:5 it designates the place where such expiation/propitiation takes place. The publican in his prayer sought God's mercy in order to have his sins covered and the divine wrath removed from him.[282]

18:14   I tell you. Note the Christological claim in these words. Jesus claimed to know the mind of God.

This man, rather than the other. Jesus gave a surprise ending to the parable (cf. Luke 16:8). His audience would have seen the Pharisee as a positive example of true piety and the publican as a negative one of what they should not be like. For Luke's readers, familiar with Jesus' teachings and perhaps even this parable, the ending is not unexpected. They already knew that "everyone who exalts himself will be humbled, and he who humbles himself will be exalted" (14:11).

Went home. "Went home" is literally *went down into his house*, i.e., left the temple for home.

Justified. This term means more than just being forgiven, for it also involves the gift of a new standing before God. This is evident from 18:9, where the noun is used to describe a "righteous" standing before God (cf. 16:15). The publican

---

[280]Cf. Luke 10:29; 11:39-52; 16:14-15; cf. also Phil 3:4-9.

[281]In *Berakot* 28b we have a close analogy to the Pharisee's prayer: "I give thanks to Thee, O Lord my God, that Thou hast set my portion with those who sit in the Beth ha-Midrash . . . and . . . not . . . with those who sit in [street] corners." Also in *Sukka* 45b one rabbi boasted: "I am able to exempt the whole world from judgment from the day that I was born until now, and were Eliezer, my son, to be with me [we could exempt it] from the day of creation of the world to the present time, and were Jotham the son of Uzziah with us, [we could exempt it] from the creation of the world to its final end." The same rabbi went on to boast: "I have seen the sons of heaven and they are but few. If there be a thousand, I and my son are among them; if a hundred, I and my son are among them; and if only two, they are I and my son."

[282]See L. Morris, *The Apostolic Preaching of the Cross* (Grand Rapids: Eerdmans, 1956), 125-223.

stood before God after his prayer possessing a new relationship (not a moral character) with God. He possessed a righteousness given him by grace (cf. Phil 3:8). **For everyone who exalts himself.** The proverb of Luke 14:11 (cf. Matt 23:12) is repeated. For Jesus and Luke, as well as for Paul, salvation was by grace through faith (cf. Eph 2:8). In justifying himself before God, the Pharisee rejected the possibility of receiving God's gift of justification that comes through faith (Phil 3:9). What happens after justification is not mentioned in the parable, but Luke would demonstrate this in the story of Zacchaeus (cf. Luke 19:8).

The Lukan Message

In reading this parable one is reminded of the Pauline teaching on justification by faith. Without reading into the parable the Pauline teaching, it is nevertheless evident that "justification" involves a standing before God rather than a moral perfection or even a moral character. The Pharisee clearly possessed a better moral character than the tax collector, at least from the perspective of his society. He was not a thief, an evildoer, or an adulterer (18:11). He kept the law outwardly far better than the tax collector. But he did not receive the pronouncement of being "justified." The tax collector did. Thus justification must involve a standing before God, for it is instantaneous. Like the Pauline teaching, it involves forgiveness (cf. 18:13 and Rom 4:6-8); but it also bestows a standing, i.e., a declared righteousness. This parable reveals that the Pauline teaching on justification is not an anomaly but is also found in Luke and is ultimately rooted in Jesus' teaching.

Whereas moral renewal (regeneration in John but the baptism of the Spirit in Luke-Acts) can be assumed to have been associated with the conversion of the tax collector, it is neither stressed nor mentioned in our account. A moral character will develop from the baptism of the Spirit that accompanies justification. Out of positional righteousness will develop a concomitant personal holiness. The latter must follow the former, for in the experience of conversion along with one's new standing, God also gives his Spirit (Acts 2:38), making the individual a new creation (2 Cor 5:17). Thus, although the metaphor of justification involves a standing before God and has no necessary tie with an obedient life of faith, the experience of conversion, through which justification comes, also bestows at the same time other benefits indicated by such metaphors as regeneration, forgiveness, the baptism of the Spirit, being "in Christ," reconciliation, and sanctification. And these metaphors do reveal a necessary tie between the experience of a new standing before God with an obedient life of faith.

Through this parable Luke sought to teach his readers that their justification was due to God's mercy alone and that they daily needed to pray, "Forgive us our sins" (Luke 11:4). There is no room for boasting (17:10).

One can only boast in the Lord (1 Cor 1:31; 2 Cor 10:17), who has exalted the lowly and brought down the haughty (Luke 1:38,52-53). Because justification comes when the humble repent and believe (15:7, 10), the great reversal is taking place. See Introduction 8 (5). Those who like the Pharisee in the parable exalt themselves are humbled, but those who like the tax collector humble themselves and seek God's mercy are exalted and justified by God (14:11; 18:14).

(5) Jesus' Blessing the Children (18:15-17)

[15]People were also bringing babies to Jesus to have him touch them. When the disciples saw this, they rebuked them. [16]But Jesus called the children to him and said, "Let the little children come to me, and do not hinder them, for the kingdom of God belongs to such as these. [17]I tell you the truth, anyone who will not receive the kingdom of God like a little child will never enter it."

Context

In 9:51 Luke left the Markan narrative at Mark 9:40 in order to insert his travel narrative material.[283] At this point he picked up the Markan narrative once again at Mark 10:13. The exact conclusion of the Lukan travel narrative is uncertain.[284] If this section in Luke is truly a "travel narrative," it is better to see this section as extending from 9:51 to either 19:10 or better still to 19:27, where Jesus enters Jerusalem (see comments on 9:51–19:27). This is supported by the fact that 18:15–19:10 continues the theme of what the "faith" (18:8) involves.

In 18:9-14 the kind of faith acceptable to God is described as being one of humility. In the present account Jesus taught that one must receive God's kingdom like a little child (18:17). Luke made several changes in his version of the account. He changed "little children" (Mark 10:13) to "babies" (Luke 18:15) and Mark's "was indignant" (10:14) to "called" (Luke 18:16), and he omitted the blessing of the children found in Mark 10:16. The latter two correspond with Luke's general tendency to avoid describing Jesus' emotions. The change of "little children" to "babies," however, is more difficult to understand, for the inability of children to have a conscious faith seems to weaken the application in 18:17. How can people receive God's kingdom unless they have the mental capacity to make a conscious act of commitment? Luke may have thought that

---

[283] It is impossible to be certain about why Luke did not reproduce Mark 9:41–10:12, but it is quite possible that this material was omitted because of his inclusion of similar material elsewhere (cf. Mark 9:42-50 with Luke 17:1-2; 14:34-35; Mark 10:1 with Luke 9:51; and Mark 10:2-12 with Luke 16:18).

[284] Should it be bounded by where he left the Markan narrative and where he resumed it? If so, the travel narrative extends from 9:51 to 18:14.

"babies" (*brephē*) fit the verb "being brought," i.e., were carried, better than "children."

Comments

18:15 People were also bringing. The imperfect tense of the verb implies that parents often were bringing, i.e., carrying, their babies/little children to Jesus.[285]

Babies. Luke, following the Markan account, used "little children" everywhere else in this account but here. Perhaps the verb "were bringing" caused him to use this term at this point, since babies would have been carried to Jesus where little children would have been led (cf. 2:27; 18:16).

To have him touch them. The purpose of people bringing their babies/little children to Jesus was for him to "touch," i.e., bless, them (cf. 5:13; 6:19; cf. Matt 19:13; Gen 48:14-15).

The disciples . . . rebuked them. The tense of the verb is best understood as a conative imperfect.[286] The disciples *attempted* unsuccessfully to rebuke them, i.e., keep the people from bringing their babies to Jesus.

18:16 But Jesus called the children to him. Luke omitted Mark's "Jesus . . . was indignant" (10:14).[287]

Let the little children come to me. Jesus' attitude toward children contrasts significantly with that of his day (see comments on 9:48). Luke followed Mark at this point and used the expression "little children" instead of "babies," for babies cannot "come" to Jesus.

For the kingdom of God belongs to such as these. Jesus did not say that God's kingdom belongs "to these" but "to *such as* these." Jesus was not saying that all children, simply because they are children, have received God's kingdom (Luke 18:17). Jesus was not attributing to children an innate goodness. Rather, he appealed to some quality possessed by little children that is essential for entering God's kingdom. Unfortunately neither Jesus nor the Gospel writers elucidated exactly what this quality is. Some suggestions are (1) the humility little children possess because they lack anything to boast of and can make no claim on God (cf. 18:9-14; Matt 18:4), (2) a simple faith free from doubt (Luke 17:5-6), and (3) a lack of attachment to possessions (18:18-30). In light of the preceding passage (18:9-14) and Matthew's specific application of "childlikeness" to humility (Matt 18:4), the first suggestion seems best.

18:17 I tell you the truth. See comments on 4:24.

Receive the kingdom of God. This is an unusual expression. Usually we read of "entering" God's kingdom.[288]

Will never enter it. Whereas "receiving the kingdom" refers to the acceptance of God's kingdom in its present manifestation in Jesus' ministry, entering it probably is best understood as entering into the consummated kingdom in the day of the Son of Man (17:22-37).

---

[285] In Luke 5:14; 23:36; Acts 7:42; 8:18; 21:26 the verb is used in the sense of "carry" rather than "lead." Only in Luke 23:14 is it used in the sense of "lead."

[286] Cf. Matt 3:14a for another example of a conative imperfect.

[287] Cf. also how he omitted the description of Jesus' emotion in Luke 18:22 (cf. Mark 10:21, "Jesus . . . loved him"). See Fitzmyer, *Luke* 1:95.

[288] Cf. Luke 18:17b,24-25; Acts 14:22; John 3:5; cf. also Luke 13:24.

The Lukan Message

Luke continued the theme of discipleship begun in 18:9-14 and described what is needed to enter God's kingdom. Luke described that basic needed response in various ways. See Introduction 8 (6). Here, if 18:16 has been interpreted correctly, the fundamental need of humility is emphasized. Access to the kingdom is given to childlike people such as the tax collector in the preceding account who boast of nothing but simply depend on God's mercy. Such humility is of course accompanied by repentance and faith, but the emphasis here is on humility. Only the last, who humble themselves, shall enter the kingdom. The first in their self-exaltation see no need to humble themselves and accept God's grace (13:30; 14:11; 18:14).

Although this passage later became a proof-text for infant baptism (Jesus' blessing the children has even been called a "baptism without water"), in the context of Jesus' ministry these words do not deal with the issue of infant baptism. It is furthermore difficult to believe that Luke understood this passage as a reference to children's baptism because for him baptism was intimately associated with repentance (cf. 3:8; Acts 2:38) and faith (Acts 8:12-13; 16:31-33).

(6) The Rich Ruler (18:18-30)

[18]A certain ruler asked him, "Good teacher, what must I do to inherit eternal life?"

[19]"Why do you call me good?" Jesus answered. "No one is good—except God alone. [20]You know the commandments: 'Do not commit adultery, do not murder, do not steal, do not give false testimony, honor your father and mother.' "

[21]"All these I have kept since I was a boy," he said.

[22]When Jesus heard this, he said to him, "You still lack one thing. Sell everything you have and give to the poor, and you will have treasure in heaven. Then come, follow me."

[23]When he heard this, he became very sad, because he was a man of great wealth. [24]Jesus looked at him and said, "How hard it is for the rich to enter the kingdom of God! [25]Indeed, it is easier for a camel to go through the eye of a needle than for a rich man to enter the kingdom of God."

[26]Those who heard this asked, "Who then can be saved?"

[27]Jesus replied, "What is impossible with men is possible with God."

[28]Peter said to him, "We have left all we had to follow you!"

[29]"I tell you the truth," Jesus said to them, "no one who has left home or wife or brothers or parents or children for the sake of the kingdom of God [30]will fail to receive many times as much in this age and, in the age to come, eternal life."

Context

The story of the rich young ruler is found in all three Synoptic accounts (cf. Matt 19:16-30; Mark 10:17-31). In all three he is described as "rich," but only Matthew stated that he was a "young man" (19:20); and only Luke, that he was a "ruler" (18:18). In the previous two accounts Luke taught how true righteousness (18:9-14) and entrance into God's kingdom (18:15-17) come through humility. In this account he dealt with the same subject: "What must I do to inherit eternal life?" (18:18). Another way of wording this is, "What must a person do to enter the kingdom of God?" (18:24-25). In the three accounts found in 18:9-30, Luke was dealing with the theme of salvation, even though three different metaphors were used to describe this: justification (18:14), entrance into the kingdom of God (18:17,24), and inheriting eternal life (18:18).

This passage contains a number of theological difficulties. The first is encountered in Jesus' statement in 18:19: "Why do you call me good? . . . No one is good—except God alone." The second involves Jesus' reply about how the rich ruler could inherit eternal life in 18:20. (Would Martin Luther have counseled a person in this way?) The third involves the ruler's reply that he had kept all these commandments since his age of accountability and Jesus' apparent acceptance of this statement (18:20-21). Finally, there is the issue of whether Jesus' command to sell all that he had and give to the poor is a requirement for salvation or whether it is "evangelical counsel" for Christians to enable them to enter a higher stage of discipleship. If it is to be understood as a requirement for salvation, did Luke then understand it as a universal requirement for all Christians or uniquely addressed to this one individual?

The main attempts to resolve the first question are (1) Jesus' question was intended to teach the ruler that he (Jesus) was divine; (2) Jesus was acknowledging his own "nongoodness" in contrast to God, i.e., he was acknowledging that he had sinned; (3) Jesus rejected the simplistic view of "goodness" implied in the ruler's statement; (4) Jesus, without in any way saying anything about his own person, wanted to direct the ruler's attention to God, in whom alone true goodness resides. Explanations (3) or (4) seem to fit the text best.

The second and third issues involve Jesus' first instructions to the ruler. They are essentially the same as found in 10:25-28, although in the present account Jesus concentrated on the second table of the law, which involves behavior toward one's neighbor. Does this, however, conflict with such teachings as, "Believe in the Lord Jesus, and you will be saved" (Acts 16:31)? It should be noted that Luke recorded both sets of these teachings so that for him they did not contradict each other. In his mind (unless it is assumed that he was grossly inconsistent) they were compatible. For Luke true faith involved loving God with all one's heart and one's neighbor as oneself (see comments on 10:25-37, "The Lukan Message"). Likewise loving God with all one's heart . . . and one's neighbor as oneself involves faith in Jesus. Jesus' command to the ruler to sell all that he had and give to the poor is a crystallization of the commandments found in 18:20. If the rich ruler truly kept these commandments as he claimed, he would neither have needed to be told to sell all that he had and give to the poor nor have had difficulty obeying this command. See Introduction 8 (6).

The fourth problem involves the universality of Jesus' command in 18:22. What essentially did the ruler lack? Was it reward in heaven or salvation itself? One of the earliest explanations of this and other related texts, such as 14:26, involved a two-level ethic. See Introduction 8 (7). This interpretation is not possible, however, for what the rich ruler was seeking was eternal life (18:18), and what he lacked upon leaving was entrance into God's kingdom (18:24-25). The ruler's address to Jesus ("Good teacher") is furthermore an address that nondisciples use in Luke. If Luke understood the ruler as a follower of Jesus, he would have indicated this by having him address Jesus as "Good Master" (see comments on 5:5). Finally, if the disciples received eternal life for following Jesus (18:28-30), we must assume the ruler, by not following Jesus (18:22-23), did not receive eternal life. For Luke the specific command to sell all one has (18:22; 13:33) was not necessary for salvation.[289] Nevertheless the commitment that such a command requires and illustrates is necessary. No one can serve two masters. One must choose between God and Money (16:13; 12:34). See Introduction 8 (7).

The account of the rich ruler is followed by a group of sayings concerning the difficulty of a rich person entering God's kingdom. This difficulty is described hyperbolically by a saying about a camel (the largest animal in Israel) going through the eye of a needle (the smallest opening). This in turn is followed by Peter's comment that the disciples indeed had left everything to follow Jesus. (Leaving family is singled out in 18:29.) To the disciples and others who had left everything, the promise was given that they would receive an even greater family in this life (the "church") and in the age to come the eternal life, which the ruler sought but did not receive.

Comments

18:18 A certain ruler asked him. He possibly was a "ruler of a synagogue" (8:41) or a member of the Sanhedrin (23:13,35; 24:20). He is presented as a religious leader whose moral and religious life was exemplary. Like the Pharisee (18:11), he was one of the first (13:30) and came with impeccable credentials.

Good teacher. The designation "good teacher" appears somewhat unusual, although humans can be called "good" (6:45; Prov 12:2; 14:14; Eccl 9:2). For "teacher" as a nondisciple designation for Jesus, see comments on 5:5; 17:13.

What must I do? See comments on 10:25.

To inherit eternal life? Compare Luke 18:30; Acts 13:46,48. From 18:24-25 it is clear that this is a synonym for entering God's kingdom (cf. John 3:3-5,16).

---

[289]Cf. Luke 8:3; 16:8-12; 19:8; Acts 5:4; 28:30.

18:19   Why do you call me good?   Jesus did not let the superficiality of the ruler's use of "good" pass by unanswered. For the meaning of Jesus' question, see "Context."

No one is good—except God alone.   Compare 1 Chr 16:34; 2 Chr 5:13; Pss 34:8; 106:1; 118:1,29; 136:1.

18:20   Do not.   The five following Commandments all come from the second table of the law and deal with love for one's neighbor. All three Synoptic Gospels contain these five Commandments, but Matthew and Luke excluded Mark's "do not defraud" (10:19) because it is not found in Exod 20:1-17. The Lukan order of the Commandments differs from Mark and Matthew in that the order of the first two Commandments (adultery, the seventh, and kill, the sixth in the law) are reversed. His order is found, however, in Rom 13:9 and Jas 2:11 and in the order of Exod 20:13-15 in the LXX. Although the first table of the law is not quoted, Luke assumed his readers would have understood it as being included because of the parallel in 10:25-28. Jesus probably focused on these Commandments because it would be easier to judge whether they were kept. Jesus' answer is in keeping with what any teacher of the law would have said.

18:21   All these I have kept since I was a boy.   Compare Acts 26:4. The ruler believed that he had kept all these Commandments since he became accountable.[290] (In Judaism today such accountability takes place at a boy's *Bar Mitzvah*, but this term was not used in this sense in Jesus' day.) Compare Paul's claim in Phil 3:6. Note the positive sense in which this thought appears in Luke 1:6 and the negative sense in 18:11. The ruler's reply was sincere but superficial as the next verses indicate. Both Matthew and Luke improved on Mark's grammar by changing his "kept," *ephylaksamēn* (Mark 10:20), to "kept," *ephylaksa*.

18:22   Luke omitted Mark's reference (10:21) to Jesus' loving the ruler. See comments on 18:16.

You still lack one thing.   This has been interpreted in several ways. (1) Jesus agreed with the ruler and offered an additional suggestion that would enable the ruler to enter a higher stage in his discipleship. This is refuted by 18:24-25. (2) Jesus sought to clarify the man's answer and show that he really had not kept the Commandments (cf. Rom 3:9-20). One must be careful not to read Pauline theology into Luke. Nevertheless without presuming the Pauline teaching, since the ruler lacked eternal life/entrance into the kingdom (18:24-25), he must not really have "kept" the Commandments; for the result of keeping the Commandments is eternal life (10:25-28). It seems best therefore to see this statement as a clarifying "commandment" intended to show the ruler that he had not really kept the Commandments.

Sell everything you have and give to the poor.   Luke heightened Jesus' teaching here by adding "everything" (cf. Matt 19:21; Mark 10:21). In so doing Luke both picked up the "everything" claim of the young ruler in Luke 18:21 (this is clearer in the RSV than the NIV) and introduced a strong Lukan theme on the stewardship of possessions. See Introduction 8 (7). By his clarification of the Commandments in 18:20, Jesus sought to help the ruler understand that he really did not love God with all his heart and his neighbor as himself: "Jesus always requires from one just that earthly security upon which one would lean."[291]

---

[290] Fitzmyer, *Luke* 2:1200.

[291] Ellis, *Luke*, 217.

You will have treasure in heaven. Compare 12:33 where, however, this teaching is addressed to believers (cf. 12:22, disciples; 12:32, "little flock"). "Treasure in heaven" is a synonym for eternal life (18:18,30) and entering God's kingdom (18:24-25).

Then come, follow me. Compare 9:23, where "following" is an invitation for salvation (cf. 9:24). See comments on 5:11. This was not a second command independent from the command to sell all. Selling and following were two aspects of the same command. The command to sell all was the ruler's first step in following Christ. See comments on 9:23.

18:23 When he heard this, he became very sad. Like the rich man in 16:19-31, he too lost his life, for the love of money is a terrible burden (cf. 6:24; 8:14). Jesus' commandment reveals that the ruler was an idolater and loved his possessions more than God and his neighbor.

Because he was a man of great wealth. We must add something like "and he loved his money too much" or "he loved his money more than God" or, to use the words of the rich man in 16:30, he would not "repent." Thus this man who appeared as an attractive candidate for God's kingdom, a "natural," one of the "first," failed to enter.

18:24 Jesus looked at him and said. Whereas the parallels (Matt 19:23; Mark 10:23) begin a new section of sayings attached to the story, in Luke what follows is part of the story itself.

How hard it is for the rich. Wealth was seen by Jesus and Luke as a great hindrance for salvation.[292]

To enter the kingdom of God! "How hard it is for the rich to enter the kingdom of God" is literally, *With what difficulty rich people enter the kingdom of God*. Whereas Matt 19:23 and Mark 10:23 have the future tense ("shall enter"), Luke used the present tense ("enter") and emphasized that one must enter now the already realized dimension of God's kingdom (cf. Luke 14:15-24; 18:17). This difference can be seen in the RSV but not the NIV.

18:25 Indeed, it is easier for a camel. Attempts to understand this saying as involving a camel going through a small city gate (no evidence exists of a gate named *Eye of a Needle*) or as a mistranslation (*camel* is a mistranslation of the word *cable*) lose sight of the hyperbolic nature of Jesus' words here. For other examples of Jesus' use of hyperbole, see comments on 6:41. There is a rabbinic analogy that speaks of an elephant going through the eye of a needle (cf. *Ber.* 55b; *B. Meṣ.* 38b). Its late date does not detract from its use as an example of the hyperbolic nature of the saying in Luke 18:25.

Than for a rich man to enter. The fact that the comparison Jesus gave above is hyperbolic should not lessen the impact of his words. On the contrary, wealth is so great a hindrance for a person's entering God's kingdom that Jesus emphasized this by his use of hyperbole.

18:26 Those who heard this asked. Luke "generalized" the audience at this point to demonstrate more clearly the applicability of this teaching for his readers.

Who then can be saved? If a rich person—whose wealth was understood as a sign of God's blessing and who could offer more alms and sacrifices due to this

---

[292]Cf. Luke 6:24; 8:14; 12:13-21; 16:9-15,19-31.

wealth can scarcely be saved, how could others—who lacked this sign of God's blessing and who could not be as generous in their alms and sacrifices—be saved? **18:27 What is impossible with men is possible with God.** Compare 1:37; Gen 18:14. For Luke salvation came from God, and God can break the hold that riches have on a person. By God's grace it is possible to give up all and follow Jesus as Luke 18:28-30 reveals, and it is even possible for a rich man to enter God's kingdom as 19:1-10 reveals.

18:28 Peter said to him, "We have." The "we" is emphatic and may refer to the disciples in general, but it refers at least to Peter, James, and John (cf. 5:10-11). For "Peter" see comments on 8:45.

Left all. "Left all" is literally *left our own things*. This can refer to their families (18:29; cf. 14:26) or everything they had (18:22). Probably both are meant (cf. Acts 21:6).

18:29 I tell you the truth. See comments on 4:24.

No one who has left. Compare Luke 14:26; 12:51-53.

Wife. Only Luke included "wife" in the list of relatives. He also did this in 14:26. This probably refers not so much to breaking up a present marriage as renouncing the possibility of marrying, as in Matt 19:10-12.[293]

For the sake of the kingdom of God. Mark 10:29 has "for me and the gospel" (cf. Matt 19:29, "for my sake"; cf. also Mark 8:35). In the setting of Jesus, the Lukan version may be more authentic, but the meaning of the Lukan expression can be translated "thought for thought" as Mark and Matthew have.

18:30 Will fail to receive many times. This is emphatic (a double negative in Greek). Following Jesus brings reward, but this reward is granted, not "merited."

In this age. In the present life believers may lose this family as a result of following Jesus, but they will receive a much larger family, the family of believers (cf. Luke 8:21; Mark 3:35). What a person gives to God is returned many times over not just in the age to come but even in this life.

Age to come. Compare Luke 20:34-35; 16:8; cf. also Matt 12:32; Eph 1:21; Heb 6:5.

Eternal life. See comments on 10:25; 18:18; cf. also Luke 16:9. The concluding proverb found in Mark 10:31 and Matt 19:30 is omitted. In so doing Luke ended the account with the words "eternal life." This forms an inclusio with Luke 18:18, where the opening question is, "What must I do to inherit eternal life?"

The Lukan Message

In the present account Luke sought again to teach his readers how one can obtain salvation and to warn them about the danger of riches. His concern for the relationship between these is evident from the material he devoted to it. We find throughout his writings the need to "sell everything,"[294] to "give up" or "leave everything" (5:11,28; 14:33), and to be generous.[295]

---

[293] Marshall, *Luke*, 688.

[294] Luke 12:33; 18:22; cf. Acts 2:44-45; 4:32; 5:1-11.

[295] Luke 3:11; 6:34-35,38; 7:5; 8:3; 10:34-35; 11:41; 14:12-14; 16:9-13; 19:8; Acts 9:36; 10:2,4,31; 20:35.

And warnings about riches appear to be almost omnipresent.[296] Luke heightened this teaching found in the tradition by his addition of the term "everything" (*panta*) in 18:22. Riches are a real liability with respect to salvation. The narcotic effect of the ruler's riches dulls his resolution, and instead of receiving the blessing of the poor (cf. 6:20 and 18:28) he receives the woe of the rich (cf. 6:24 and 18:23-25). For the relationship of salvation and selling one's possessions, see Introduction 8 (7).

Within this passage Luke also emphasized the arrival of God's kingdom in a way that Matthew and Mark did not. For all the Gospel writers the kingdom was both a present reality and a future hope. Yet Luke more than Matthew and Mark stressed the arrival of the kingdom. Whereas the rich man exemplifies one who because of his riches "*shall* not enter" the consummated kingdom in Matt 19:23 and Mark 10:23, in Luke he exemplifies one who "*does* not enter" the kingdom in its present manifestation (Luke 18:24; cf. 18:17). The kingdom has come, and those who want to share in the glorious messianic banquet "then" need to participate in the present manifestation of that banquet "now" (14:15-24). Those who want eternal life in the future (18:18) must begin to experience that life now (cf. John 3:16,36; 5:24). The Lukan emphasis on the realized dimension of God's kingdom is clearly seen in 16:16; 17:20-21. See Introduction 8 (2).

(7) The Third Passion Announcement (18:31-34)

[31]Jesus took the Twelve aside and told them, "We are going up to Jerusalem, and everything that is written by the prophets about the Son of Man will be fulfilled. [32]He will be handed over to the Gentiles. They will mock him, insult him, spit on him, flog him and kill him. [33]On the third day he will rise again."

[34]The disciples did not understand any of this. Its meaning was hidden from them, and they did not know what he was talking about.

Context

This account, like its parallels in Matt 20:17-19; Mark 10:32-34, involves Jesus' third passion prediction. Whereas Mark clearly arranged the three passion sayings into a carefully organized scheme,[297] Luke by his travel narrative separated this third passion prediction from the first two (9:22,43b-45) by nine chapters. Nevertheless, Luke gave a number of reminders throughout the travel narrative (12:50; 13:32-33; 17:25) that the way to Jerusalem was the way of the cross.

---

[296]Luke 6:24; 8:14; 12:13-21,34; 16:10-13,19-31.

[297]Mark's three-part pattern includes (1) a passion prediction (8:31-32a; 9:30-32; 10:32-34), (2) followed by misunderstanding (8:32b-33; 9:33-34; 10:35-41), (3) followed by teachings on discipleship (8:34–9:1; 9:35-37; 10:42-45).

Comments
18:31 Jesus took the Twelve aside. In each of the Synoptic Gospels the following passion announcement is addressed to the Twelve.
We are going up to Jerusalem. The NIV omits the introductory *Behold.*
This statement is found in all three Synoptic Gospels, but it fits especially well the
framework of the Lukan travel narrative (cf. 9:51-53; 13:33; 19:28).
Everything that is written by the prophets about the Son of Man. The
"prophets" refers to the entire OT, as 24:25,27,32 indicates. For "is written" see
comments on 2:22. It is uncertain whether "about the Son of Man" modifies the
participle, i.e., "written concerning the Son of Man," or the verb, i.e., "will be fulfilled for the Son of Man." The former is more likely than the latter[298] because the
phrase "about the Son of Man" is located after the participle and because of its
distance from the verb. For "Son of Man" see comments on 5:24.
Will be fulfilled. "Will be fulfilled" is a divine passive, i.e., *God will bring
about its fulfillment.* See Introduction 7 (1).
18:32 He will be handed over. Compare 9:44. This is another divine passive (cf. Acts 2:23) and explains how God will fulfill the things written by the
prophets. These things will be fulfilled because God's sovereign plan requires it.
See Introduction 8 (1).
To the Gentiles. This is fulfilled in Luke 23:1 (cf. 20:20; Acts 2:23; 13:28).
They will mock him, insult him, spit on him, flog him and kill him. For
"mocked" cf. Luke 22:63; 23:11,36. Only Luke has "insult." For "spit" cf. Mark
14:65; 15:19. For "flog" cf. Mark 15:15. Luke did not tell of the fulfillment of
"spit" and "flog," but he expected his readers to assume that these were fulfilled,
just as today's readers of Luke assume their fulfillment.
18:33 On the third day. See comments on 9:22.
He will rise again. See comments on 9:22. The middle voice (not the passive) is used here as in 1 Thess 4:14, indicating that Jesus would raise himself
from the dead (cf. 1 Thess 1:10, where God raised Jesus from the dead).
18:34 The disciples did not understand. Compare Luke 2:50, where Joseph and Mary did not understand.
Its meaning was hidden. The disciple's incomprehension is mentioned a
second time. Whether the verb should be understood as a divine passive is unclear.
See comments on 6:21.
And they did not know what he was talking about. The disciples' incomprehension is now mentioned a third time. Luke did not explain why the disciples
did not grasp Jesus' teaching. Some suggestions are (1) the idea of a suffering
Messiah was too difficult for them to accept; (2) they were not able to see how
such a death as Jesus spoke of would fulfill the OT; (3) they did not understand
why the Messiah had to die; or (4) God had chosen to veil this truth from them. It
is difficult to think that if asked, the disciples would have been unable to repeat
what Jesus had said about his forthcoming passion. If they could have said, "Jesus
said" and repeated 18:31-33 (and surely they could have), then probably what was
meant was that they could not mentally conceive that what Jesus had said would
take place. In other words the disciples did not believe that what Jesus said about

---

[298]Marshall (*Luke*, 690) favors the participle; Fitzmyer (*Luke* 2:1209), the verb.

himself would happen (1 and 3) or understand how this would fulfill the Scriptures (2). One need not deny a divine element (4) in this. In the pre-Easter situation Jesus' teachings of a dying Messiah were so contrary to contemporary Judaism's understanding of the messianic role that it is not difficult to accept 18:34 as an accurate description of the disciples' confused state.

The Lukan Message

Luke's theological emphases in this passage are seen in two areas. The first is found in 18:31c and involves the Son of Man's fate and the relationship of this to OT prophecy. Jesus' death in Jerusalem fulfills OT prophecy. The theme of fulfillment is encountered throughout Luke, from the opening verse of the Gospel to its conclusion (24:44-49; cf. also Acts 1:1-7; 28:25-29). Speculation about *why* we have this emphasis (for example that some readers questioned why if Jesus was the Christ he had to die) remains simply speculation. We know *that* Luke was emphasizing that Jesus had to die and that his death was due to the divine plan. The divine passives ("will be fulfilled," "will be handed over") strengthen this emphasis, but *why* Luke emphasized this alludes us. See Introduction 7 (1).

A second recurring emphasis is the Twelve's incomprehension (Luke 18:34).[299] This incomprehension about Jesus' death comes to a final resolution in 24:25-35,44-47 (cf. esp. 24:31). Only after the resurrection would the necessity of Jesus' death be understood and the scriptural teaching concerning this be made clear. Again it is unclear why Luke emphasized this incomprehension, but that he wanted to do so is clear from the fact that he repeated this same thought three times in 18:34.

(8) The Healing of the Blind Man at Jericho (18:35-43)

[35]As Jesus approached Jericho, a blind man was sitting by the roadside begging. [36]When he heard the crowd going by, he asked what was happening. [37]They told him, "Jesus of Nazareth is passing by."

[38]He called out, "Jesus, Son of David, have mercy on me!"

[39]Those who led the way rebuked him and told him to be quiet, but he shouted all the more, "Son of David, have mercy on me!"

[40]Jesus stopped and ordered the man to be brought to him. When he came near, Jesus asked him, [41]"What do you want me to do for you?"

"Lord, I want to see," he replied.

[42]Jesus said to him, "Receive your sight; your faith has healed you." [43]Immediately he received his sight and followed Jesus, praising God. When all the people saw it, they also praised God.

Context

As Jesus approached Jerusalem, his city of destiny, he came to Jericho, whose nearness to Jerusalem the reader already knows (see comments on

---

[299]Cf. Luke 2:50; 9:45; 24:16,25-26; cf. 19:11.

10:30). Luke would recount two incidents connected with this city: a miracle story in which Jesus healed a blind man (18:35-43) and a pronouncement story involving a tax collector (19:1-10). The first story[300] is the fourth and last miracle story in the travel narrative (cf. 13:10-17; 14:1-6; 17:11-19).

Comments

18:35 As Jesus approached Jericho. See comments on 10:30.

A blind man. Literally *a certain blind man.* Compare 18:18, "a certain ruler." In Mark 10:46 he is named "Bartimaeus"; in Matt 20:30 two blind men are mentioned.

Was sitting by the roadside. According to Mark, Jesus met blind Bartimaeus as he left Jericho.[301]

Begging. This was the blind man's means for obtaining the necessities of life.

18:37 They told him, "Jesus of Nazareth is passing by." We assume the blind man knew of Jesus' fame and healings. The spelling "Nazareth" (*Nazōraios*) is found also in Acts,[302] but "Nazarene" (*Nazarēnos*) is found in Luke 4:34; 24:19. These may simply be variant spellings, although the former may have some allusion to *Neṣer*, "the shoot" from the stump of Jesse, in Isa 11:1. This would fit well with the use of the title "Son of David" in Luke 18:38-39.

18:38 Jesus, Son of David. Luke followed his source here (cf. Mark 10:47). Why the blind man addressed Jesus this way probably would not have entered Luke's mind. Luke had already described Jesus as the Son of David[303] and was preparing the reader for 19:28-40. See comments on 1:27.

Have mercy on me! See comments on 17:13.

18:39 Those who led the way rebuked him and told him to be quiet. Society offers the outcast neither pity nor help.

But he shouted all the more. The "he" is emphatic. His persistence reveals faith. He believed that Jesus could help and like the widow (18:3-5) persisted until he received help. Nothing would keep him from the one who could help him.

Son of David. Luke's readers would not have understood this simply as a form of address but as a confession of faith.

18:40 Jesus stopped. Jesus' compassion and mercy, and thus God's compassion and mercy, are revealed.

---

[300] The narrative has a parallel in Mark 10:46-52; Matt 20:29-34. Significant variations in these accounts have not been resolved; however, Luke was reporting the same incident. He omitted the preceding account in Mark 10:35-45, which involves the request of James and John, perhaps because of his insertion of similar material in 12:50; 22:24-27. Or Luke may have believed that since he had already referred to a weakness in the disciples' understanding in 18:34, he could omit 10:35-45. Or Luke may have omitted the account because Mark 10:35-45 does not fit the theme of salvation begun in Luke 18:18 and which continues through 19:27.

[301] For attempts to harmonize the various accounts see Plummer, *Luke,* 429-30; Marshall, *Luke,* 692-93; G. L. Archer, *Encyclopedia of Bible Difficulties* (Grand Rapids: Zondervan, 1982), 332-33. No attempt to harmonize the diverse elements in the three accounts is convincing.

[302] Acts 2:22; 3:6; 4:10; 6:14; 22:8; 24:5; 26:9.

[303] Luke 1:27,32,69; 2:4,11; 3:31 (cf. Acts 13:34).

18:41   What do you want me to do for you?   Jesus' question did not seek to supply his lack of knowledge about what the blind man wanted: the blind man clearly wanted healing. Jesus' question sought rather to elicit faith from him.

Lord.   See comments on 6:46. In the present context, after having addressed Jesus as the "Son of David," this address by the blind man is more than simply "Sir."

I want to see.   He believed and had the faith spoken of in 17:5-6.

18:42   Receive your sight.   Literally *See*. It took but a single word for the Lord to work this miracle.

Your faith has healed you.   "Healed" is literally *saved*. See comments on 7:50; cf. 5:20. Although these words come from Luke's Markan source, they support his strong emphasis on faith. "Faith" saved the man (cf. Acts 16:31).

18:43   Immediately.   One   word   brings   instantaneous   healing.   This (*parachrēma*) is a favorite word of Luke.[304]

He . . . followed Jesus.   Even though this is found in Luke's source, this is nonetheless a strong Lukan emphasis. See comments on 9:23; 5:11.

Praising God.   Literally *glorifying God*. Luke added this strong Lukan emphasis to the Markan tradition. His repeating this in the next part of the verse heightens its importance. See comments on 5:25. The blind man stood in marked contrast to the rich ruler, for he followed Jesus praising God, whereas the ruler left Jesus very sad (18:23).

When all the people saw it, they also praised God.   For the positive attitude of the people toward Jesus, see comments on 4:15.

The Lukan Message

This particular healing miracle is replete with Lukan themes and emphases: the continuation of the travel narrative, which leads to Jerusalem (18:35); the praise of God, which Luke added to the account and repeated twice in the same verse (18:43), as a sign of faith; and the portrait of the people as being positive toward Jesus (18:43). The man's being healed from blindness is symbolic of passing from darkness into light (cf. Acts 26:18), and thus a soteriological emphasis. Through faith this salvation is appropriated (see comments on 7:50). Possessing true faith, the man now "follows" Jesus (see comments on 9:23). The gratuitous nature of salvation is clearly indicated because its reception is instantaneous and through faith.

We find a Christological emphasis in the account as well. Along with the description of Jesus as the Son of Man in 18:31, two additional titles are given. From the tradition comes the title "Son of David" (18:38-39). This underscores Jesus' messianic character. Jesus is David's Son, the hoped for Messiah. Luke's readers have been taught this from the very

---

[304] It is found sixteen times in Luke (1:64; 4:39; 5:25; 8:44,47,55; 13:13; 18:43; 19:11; 22:60) and Acts (3:7; 5:10; 12:23; 13:11; 16:26,33) and only two other times in the rest of the NT (Matt 21:19-20).

first chapter (see comments on 1:27), and this prepares them for the title
"King of the Jews" (23:38) at Jesus' crucifixion. In Luke's situation there
was little danger of Jesus' mission being misinterpreted, so that he had no
fear in pointing out this Christological dimension. Yet Jesus is even more
than the Son of David. He is also "Lord" (18:41). For the Christological
implications of this title, see comments on 1:43. Along with these explicit
titles we find in the account a portrait of Jesus as one who with a single
word can heal the blind (cf. John 9:32). Such power and might cannot
help but raise the question, "Who is this one who does such things?" And
the answer is given in the text: It is Jesus, the Son of David, the Lord!

A final Lukan emphasis in the account involves the great reversal. The
"first," as represented by the Pharisee (Luke 18:9-14) and the young ruler
(18:18-30), did not receive spiritual healing. They had been blinded by
their riches (18:24) and self-righteousness (18:11-12). Yet the "last," as
represented by tax collectors (18:9-14; 19:1-10) and the blind man (and
for Luke's readers, the Gentiles), entered the kingdom. The irony of iro-
nies is that the blind now see and the unrighteous become righteous,
whereas the seeing have become blind and the righteous have become
unrighteous because, boasting of their own self-righteousness, they will
not accept the only real righteousness, "the righteousness that comes from
God and is by faith" (Phil 3:9). This great reversal will be the theme of
the next account as well.[305]

(9) Zacchaeus, the Tax Collector (19:1-10)

**[1]Jesus entered Jericho and was passing through. [2]A man was there by the
name of Zacchaeus; he was a chief tax collector and was wealthy. [3]He wanted to
see who Jesus was, but being a short man he could not, because of the crowd.
[4]So he ran ahead and climbed a sycamore-fig tree to see him, since Jesus was
coming that way.**

**[5]When Jesus reached the spot, he looked up and said to him, "Zacchaeus,
come down immediately. I must stay at your house today." [6]So he came down at
once and welcomed him gladly.**

**[7]All the people saw this and began to mutter, "He has gone to be the guest of
a 'sinner.' "**

**[8]But Zacchaeus stood up and said to the Lord, "Look, Lord! Here and now
I give half of my possessions to the poor, and if I have cheated anybody out of
anything, I will pay back four times the amount."**

**[9]Jesus said to him, "Today salvation has come to this house, because this
man, too, is a son of Abraham. [10]For the Son of Man came to seek and to save
what was lost."**

---

[305]Goulder (*Luke: A New Paradigm*, 673), comparing the present account with that of
the rich ruler states, "Riches and poverty, refusal and discipleship, sorrow and joyful praise,
loss and salvation: the two stories could not stand in finer contrast."

Context

Closely associated with the healing of the blind beggar (Luke 18:35-43) is one of Jesus' most famous pronouncement stories—the story of Zacchaeus. Found only in Luke, it, along with the healing of the blind and lepers, illustrates the reception of the good news of the gospel by the outcasts (cf. 4:18; 7:22; 15:1-32). Its conclusion (19:10) functions as a summary of Jesus' ministry in the travel narrative. Jesus came to seek and save the lost. And, despite the difficulty (18:24), he can save even a rich man (19:9).

The key issue in this account involves the interpretation of the verbs found in 19:8. How should the present tense (in Greek) of the verbs "give" and "pay back" be interpreted? Are they "customary presents" that reveal what Zacchaeus had been doing for some time? Was Zacchaeus claiming "I have been in the habit of giving half my goods to the poor and paying back fourfold"? If so, Jesus' words in 19:9 serve more as a vindication of Zacchaeus's faith than as a statement of his conversion. On the other hand, the verbs can be translated as "futuristic presents," which reveal what Zacchaeus was about to do, because of his encounter with Jesus, i.e., due to his conversion. Then we should translate these verbs "[As a result of my coming to faith] I shall give half of all I own . . . and restore fourfold." The grammar permits either interpretation.

The latter interpretation fits the context best for several reasons: (1) if the two verbs in 19:8 are not interpreted as futuristic presents, they then tend to portray Zacchaeus as boasting (cf. 18:11-12; 15:29; note also 18:21). (2) "My goods" (*tōn hyparchontōn*) is better interpreted "what I have had all along"[306] rather than "my income." (3) "I pay back" is best understood as "I shall restore" than "I have always been restoring what I have been defrauding." (4) What wealthy man in Luke was not lost and in need of salvation when he met Jesus?[307] (5) The statement "Today, salvation has come to this house" when taken at face value suggests that something had just happened to Zacchaeus that had brought him salvation that day. If the verbs are futuristic presents, they serve as signs of Zacchaeus's repentance and conversion. If they are customary presents, there is no reason to understand why "today" salvation had come. (6) The previous pericopes (18:9-14,15-17,18-30,35-43) all deal with individuals being confronted with the offer of salvation. (7) The final argument involves 19:10. This serves as a summary for Luke not only of this account but of 18:9–19:10. Jesus' statements in 19:9-10 are therefore best understood as bearing witness to the conversion of this man. Jesus came to Jericho to

---

[306] As in Luke 8:3; 11:21; 12:15,33,44; 14:33; 16:1; Acts 4:32.
[307] Cf. Luke 6:24; 12:16-21; 16:19-31; 18:18-25.

save a lost Zacchaeus, not to vindicate a righteous Zacchaeus. Although Zacchaeus's repentance is not specifically mentioned, Luke intended his readers to understand his statement in 19:8 as witnessing to a fruit in keeping with repentance (3:8); and although faith is not specifically referred to, 19:4,6,8 implies its presence.[308]

Comments

19:1 Jesus entered Jericho and was passing through. Luke tied this account closely to the preceding (18:35) and to the whole travel narrative in which Jesus was passing through to Jerusalem (cf. 17:11).

19:2 Zacchaeus. "Zacchaeus" is the Greek form of the Hebrew *Zaccai* (cf. Ezra 2:9; Neh 7:14). Nothing else is known about this man. Although the name in Hebrew means *Righteous One*, nothing is made of the meaning of the name, and it is quite unlikely that its root meaning would have been known to Luke's readers.

A chief tax collector. This term (*architelōnēs*) is found nowhere else in contemporary literature. Jericho was a well-known toll place in Palestine, especially for goods passing east and west between Judea and Perea.

And was wealthy. Compare Luke 18:23.

19:3 He wanted to see who Jesus was. We are not explicitly told why. It was not for the sake of curiosity (cf. 9:9; 23:8) or to see him perform a sign (11:16,29; 23:8). Luke revealed to his readers what Zacchaeus sought by describing what he received in 19:9. Zacchaeus sought the salvation Jesus spoke of in 19:9-10. "Who Jesus was" is literally *who he is*. For this same thought in question form, see comments on 9:9.

But being a short man he could not. This refers to Zacchaeus, not Jesus. The crowds proved to be a hindrance for Zacchaeus both here and in 19:7.

19:4 So he ran ahead and climbed a sycamore-fig tree. Such undignified behavior, according to that culture, indicates that more than curiosity was at play here. For "sycamore" cf. 17:6, where *sykaminos* is used. *Sykomorea* is found only here in the NT. Herodian Jericho, unlike OT Jericho, had numerous parks and avenues in which trees grew.

Since Jesus was coming that way. The phrase is literally *because he was about to pass through [that way].* The same verb is used here as in 19:1.

19:5 Zacchaeus, come down immediately. How Jesus knew Zacchaeus's name is not stated. Was it due to supernatural knowledge (cf. John 1:47-48)? Was it due to Zacchaeus's being small of stature and well-known? Whatever the explanation of this in Jesus' setting in life, for Luke such a question was unimportant and probably irrelevant since he made nothing of this.

I must stay. The "must" (*dei*) implies a divine necessity to do so. See comments on 4:43; Introduction 8 (1). Just as Jesus' forthcoming passion in Jerusalem was divinely ordained, so Jesus' individual actions all fit into the divine plan, even his bringing salvation to Zacchaeus's home. Because of Luke 19:10, Jesus had to stay at Zacchaeus's home.

---

[308] Note how in Acts 2:38 "faith" is not mentioned but must be assumed, and how in Acts 16:31 "repentance" is not mentioned but must be assumed. For further discussion see D. Hamm, "Luke 19:8 Once Again: Does Zacchaeus Defend or Resolve?" *JBL* 107 (1988): 431-37.

Today. Besides the literal meaning, there may be a suggestion here of God's kingdom having come in Jesus' ministry with its offer of salvation to the outcasts (cf. 4:21). "Today" prepares the reader for the "today" in 19:9.

19:6 So he came down at once and welcomed him gladly. Luke may have intended to imply by this joyful reception faith on Zacchaeus's part. The use of the participle "gladly" (*chairōn*) seems to suggest this (cf. 19:37; Acts 5:41; 8:39; cf. also Luke 15:5).[309]

19:7 All the people . . . began to mutter. An example of the hyperbolic use of "all" (see comments on 2:1). The symbolic significance of Jesus' staying in Zacchaeus's home was clear to all (see comments on 5:30). For other examples of such muttering, see comments on 5:30; 15:1-2; cf. also 7:39; 13:14; 14:1. The people's negative attitude stands in contrast to Luke's usual portrayal of their being positive toward Jesus (see comments on 4:15).

19:8 But Zacchaeus stood up. We are not told if this took place after Zacchaeus came down from the tree, in Zacchaeus's home, or after dinner. For Luke such a question was unimportant.

And said to the Lord. See comments on 7:13.

Look, Lord! See comments on 6:46.

Here and now I give. "Here and now" is not found in the Greek text. The verbs "give" and "pay back" in this verse are in the present tense in Greek and may be translated "I am in the habit of giving" or "I shall now give." The latter is far more likely (see "Context"), but the NIV is somewhat misleading here in that it gives the impression that "here and now" is part of the Greek text. The RSV ("behold") is a more literal translation at this point.

Half of my possessions. This refers to half of his belongings (cf. 8:3; 12:33; Acts 4:32), not his earnings. As Ellis notes, "It is a thank offering expressive of a changed heart."[310] Zacchaeus provides an example that whereas the demand to sell all (Luke 12:33; 18:22) is not obligatory for all believers, generosity is. See Introduction 8 (7).

To the poor. Use of financial resources to aid the poor is a clear Lukan emphasis (cf. 11:41; 12:33; 18:22).

And if I have cheated anybody . . . four times the amount. Compare Exod 22:1; 2 Sam 12:6. In other less severe instances the OT requires only a 20 percent increase (Lev 6:5; Num 5:6-7). It is difficult to interpret this as a customary act of Zacchaeus in the past. It is best understood as a futuristic present, which along with his giving half of his goods to the poor reveals in Zacchaeus's actions what "I repent" says in words. See "Context." For "cheated" cf. 3:14; 2 Sam 12:6.

19:9 Jesus said to him. The statement was made to Zacchaeus, but it was directed to the people because of their reaction in Luke 19:7.

Today. Compare 19:5. The salvation brought by God's kingdom was now "realized" by Zacchaeus.

Salvation has come. This is not to be interpreted as meaning that the "Savior" had come to Zacchaeus's house but that salvation had occurred. The lost Zac-

---

[309] In a number of places this verb "rejoice" is used in a secular sense (Luke 22:5; 23:8; Acts 15:23; 23:26), but in all the other fourteen instances in Luke-Acts such rejoicing is associated with salvation.

[310] Ellis, *Luke*, 221.

469   LUKE 19:10

chaeus had been sought (19:5) and now saved (19:10). The promised salvation[311] had come to Zacchaeus and his family (cf. Acts 16:31). **Because this man, too, is a son of Abraham.** This was not due to his being racially a descendant of Abraham (cf. 3:8bc) but to his having brought forth fruit in keeping with repentance (3:8a) and having responded in faith and repentance to Abraham's Seed (Acts 3:25-26; cf. Gal 3:16). By this Zacchaeus bore witness to God's grace by which even a rich man can be saved (Luke 18:27). For the sense of being Abraham's seed due to physical descent, cf. 13:16.

19:10 For. What follows summarizes the preceding account.

Son of Man. See comments on 5:24. Here the title describes the earthly ministry of the Son of Man.[312]

Came to seek and to save what was lost. See comments on 5:32; cf. 4:18-19; 15:4-7; cf. also Ezek 34:16. This indicates that Zacchaeus had not experienced vindication but rather salvation (see "Context").

The Lukan Message

The present account alludes to various Lukan themes such as Jesus' journeying to Jerusalem (19:1,4), concern for the poor (19:8), the coming of the eschatological salvation (God's kingdom) into history (19:5,9), and the use of the title "Lord" to describe Jesus (19:8). But the main message of the incident involves the coming of salvation/God's kingdom to the outcasts and the proper use of money.[313] Jesus' parabolic teaching concerning the coming of salvation to the outcasts[314] receives concrete expression here, just as in 18:35-43, in the life of one such outcast. Despite the protests of Pharisees (5:30; 7:39; 15:2-3) or Pharisaic types (19:7), salvation came to the outcasts,[315] who responded in repentance and faith (or who by their actions [19:8] revealed their repentance and faith). Luke never tired of this theme of the great reversal. See Introduction 8 (5). With each example he sought to reassure his readers that salvation had come to them even though they were outcasts, i.e., Gentiles. The Son of Man did not come for the righteous but for lost people, like them. It is for sinners that Jesus has come, and there is no other way of salvation than the way of Zacchaeus, the prodigal son, and other sinners. Apart from the prayer of the tax collector

---

[311] Luke 1:69,71,77 (cf. also Acts 13:26,47; 16:17).

[312] Cf. 5:24; 6:5; 7:34; 9:58; 12:10; 22:48.

[313] For the journey to Jerusalem see comments on 9:51; for concern for the poor see Introduction 8 (5); for the coming of eschatological salvation (God's kingdom) into history, see Introduction 8 (2); for the use of the title "Lord" to describe Jesus, see comments on 6:46 and 7:13. J. O'Hanlon ("The Story of Zacchaeus and the Lukan Ethic," *JSNT* 12 [1981]: 11) states: "It is clear that the story of Zacchaeus provides Luke with an excellent summary of many of his major themes and that the Travel Narrative as a whole can be seen as its interpretative context but not exclusively so. The roots of this story run to the gospel's first pages."

[314] Luke 14:15-24; 15:3-32; 16:19-31; 18:9-14.

[315] Luke 5:32; 15:7,10,24,32; cf. 7:47-50.

("God, have mercy on me, a sinner," 18:13), there can be no salvation. If this offends the self-righteous, so be it. There is no other gospel, for "the Son of Man came to seek and to save what was lost" (19:10).

Closely related is another theme Luke never grew weary in emphasizing. This involves the correct use of possessions. See comments on 4:18. Luke had twice as many references to the poor in his Gospel than Matthew, Mark, or John. The believer cannot be indifferent to their need but should use possessions wisely to relieve their misery. For Luke one's possessions were simply a temporary loan by which one can alleviate the sufferings of the poor (contrast 16:19-31) and acquire true riches (16:10-12). Alongside his teachings about prayer, Luke probably emphasized the stewardship of one's possessions more than any other Christian responsibility. See Introduction 8 (7).

(10) The Parable of the Ten Minas (19:11-27)

[11]While they were listening to this, he went on to tell them a parable, because he was near Jerusalem and the people thought that the kingdom of God was going to appear at once. [12]He said: "A man of noble birth went to a distant country to have himself appointed king and then to return. [13]So he called ten of his servants and gave them ten minas. 'Put this money to work,' he said, 'until I come back.'

[14]"But his subjects hated him and sent a delegation after him to say, 'We don't want this man to be our king.'

[15]"He was made king, however, and returned home. Then he sent for the servants to whom he had given the money, in order to find out what they had gained with it.

[16]"The first one came and said, 'Sir, your mina has earned ten more.'

[17]" 'Well done, my good servant!' his master replied. 'Because you have been trustworthy in a very small matter, take charge of ten cities.'

[18]"The second came and said, 'Sir, your mina has earned five more.'

[19]"His master answered, 'You take charge of five cities.'

[20]"Then another servant came and said, 'Sir, here is your mina; I have kept it laid away in a piece of cloth. [21]I was afraid of you, because you are a hard man. You take out what you did not put in and reap what you did not sow.'

[22]"His master replied, 'I will judge you by your own words, you wicked servant! You knew, did you, that I am a hard man, taking out what I did not put in, and reaping what I did not sow? [23]Why then didn't you put my money on deposit, so that when I came back, I could have collected it with interest?'

[24]"Then he said to those standing by, 'Take his mina away from him and give it to the one who has ten minas.'

[25]" 'Sir,' they said, 'he already has ten!'

[26]"He replied, 'I tell you that to everyone who has, more will be given, but as for the one who has nothing, even what he has will be taken away. [27]But those enemies of mine who did not want me to be king over them—bring them here and kill them in front of me.' "

Context

The parable of the ten minas concludes the Lukan travel narrative that began in 9:51. It brings together several themes contained in that narrative (the proper use of possessions, the Jewish rejection of Jesus, the return of the Son of Man, the kingship of Jesus, the delay of the parousia) and prepares for the following account of the triumphal entry (cf. the nobleman receiving his kingship in 19:12 with 19:38). In his introduction to the parable, Luke provided his readers with the interpretative key for understanding it (cf. 18:1 and 18:9).

The relationship between this parable and Matthew's parable of the talents (25:14-30) has received considerable attention,[316] as has the attempt to reconstruct the original form (or forms if they represent two separate parables) of Jesus' parable(s).[317] As has been stated earlier, the purpose of this commentary is to ascertain what the author intended to teach his readers by his inclusion and interpretation of the Jesus traditions. See Introduction 9. As a result readers interested in such source and historical questions should read the helpful summaries found in Fitzmyer and Blomberg.[318] For the purpose of this commentary, the issue of whether Luke was repeating a version of the same parable that Matthew used or an entirely separate one is not of major importance. As an interpreter of the Jesus traditions, his editorial work in this parable is quite evident. All of 19:11-27 does not stem from Jesus. The opening verse is clearly from Luke's hand, and this reveals how he interpreted this parable. Other material in the parable also reveals his theological emphases.

In its present form in Luke, the parable contains a number of allegorical elements. The man of noble birth clearly represents Jesus, the Son of

---

[316]Do the differences in the parables (minas versus talents, ten servants versus three, the amounts trusted—one mina each versus five, three, and one talent, secular reward versus secular and spiritual, nobleman-king versus master, the hostility and judgment of certain citizens versus their omission, etc.) suggest that these were originally two separate parables? This is the view of most older scholars. On the other hand, do the similarities found in the two parables (cf. Luke 19:13 and Matt 25:14; Luke 19:16 and Matt 25:20; Luke 19:17 and Matt 25:21; Luke 19:21 and Matt 25:24; Luke 19:22 and Matt 25:26; Luke 19:23 and Matt 25:27; Luke 19:24 and Matt 25:28; Luke 19:26 and Matt 25:29) suggest that these were two variants of one original parable? This is the view of most modern scholars. If they were one parable originally, are the differences due to the redaction of Luke, of Matthew, of both, or due to the different sources they used?

[317]Here one's presuppositions play a decisive role. Could Jesus have known of his rejection in Jerusalem (Luke 19:14)? Could he have known of Jerusalem's coming destruction (19:27)? Did Jesus believe in his personal return as the Son of Man (19:12,15)? Did he teach such a harsh judgment as found in 19:27? Is it possible that the disciples thought that Jesus' entrance into Jerusalem would bring the coming of God's kingdom, or must this be purely an allusion to the church's experience of the delay of the parousia toward the end of the first century?

[318]Fitzmyer, *Luke* 2:1228-33; Blomberg, *Interpreting the Parables*, 214-21.

David, who departs into a far country to receive his "kingship."[319] During his absence he entrusted his servants with his possessions. At this point there is an aside concerning the citizens of the nobleman who request that the nobleman not be allowed to reign, i.e., not be granted the kingship. (See comments on 19:14 for the historical allusion.) When the nobleman returns as king (cf. Acts 1:11), he judges his servants (cf. 17:31). The faithful are rewarded most graciously. The unfaithful are judged. Clearly the parable in Luke refers to the return of the Son of Man at his parousia, for Luke's readers had already read such passages as Luke 12:35-40; 17:22-37 and would soon read 21:25-28,34-36. As to the aside concerning the protesting citizenry (19:14) and their judgment (19:27), Luke's readers would have thought of its fulfillment as having occurred, at least in part, in A.D. 70.

Comments

19:11 While they were listening to this. Luke tied this parable closely to the preceding incident.

He went on to tell them a parable. As in 18:1,9 the reason for the parable, and thus the key to its meaning, precedes the parable itself.

He was near Jerusalem and the people thought that the kingdom of God was going to appear at once. That this reason for the parable stems from Luke's pen is evident, but this does not mean that he created this from nothing in order to answer the question about the delay of the parousia in his own day. Several passages suggest that the disciples might have been led to think the consummation of the kingdom was imminent.[320] The same expectation is encountered in Acts 1:6. Such expectation among the disciples was perhaps further heightened as Jesus approached his final destination—Jerusalem. If this is true, then Jesus' parable, which was intended to teach that there would be a time of stewardship between the present time, i.e., the time of Jesus' ministry, and the end, was used by Luke to teach his readers that Jesus himself taught a "delay" in the consummation. The term "people" indicates that Luke had the same audience in mind as referred to in 19:7. "To appear" refers to the appearance of the kingdom in its consummated form. At that time the "thou petitions" of the Lord's Prayer (11:2-3) would find their fulfillment.

19:12 A man of noble birth. Literally *a certain nobleman* (see comments on 10:30). Unlike the man in Matt 25:14-30, the man in this parable was clearly a nobleman as revealed by his receiving kingly rule (Luke 19:12,15) and his ability to delegate cities (19:17,19).

To a distant country. Compare 15:13. In Matt 25:19 this dimension is supplied by stating that the man returned "after a long time." His departure, of course, necessitated stewardship of his belongings (cf. Mark 13:34).

---

[319]Cf. Acts 2:36; 5:31; cf. also Luke 24:26; Acts 7:56; 13:33-34; 17:31.

[320]Cf. Luke 9:27; 21:32; 24:21; note also the request of James and John with regard to the kingdom (Mark 10:37) to which one should not add "after we die," Matt 10:23.

To have himself appointed king. Literally *to receive for himself a kingdom.* This "kingdom" must be understood dynamically as "kingly authority" or "kingship" rather than statically as referring to territory, for what he brought back in Luke 19:15 was not territory but the right and power to rule (see comments on 4:43). Two interesting historical analogies may have provided background for this allusion. Both Herod the Great in 40 B.C. and his son Archelaus in 4 B.C. went to Rome to receive confirmation of their rule. Herod received the kingship of Judea, Samaria, and Idumea.[321] Archelaus received not "kingship" but only the title "Ethnarch."[322]

19:13 Ten minas. This is a much smaller amount than Matthew's talents. A mina was worth about a sixtieth of a talent or about one hundred drachmas, i.e., about three months' wages.

Until I come back. For Luke's readers this would be understood as referring to the time between the ascension and the parousia.

19:14 In the case of Archelaus (see comments on 19:12) a delegation was sent opposing his rule.[323] For Luke's readers, however, this would be interpreted as reflecting the Jewish rejection of Jesus.[324] See comments on 13:34.

19:15 He was made king. Literally *having received the kingdom.*[325] In the reality part of the parable Luke was thinking of Christ's resurrection/ascension as his accession to kingship.[326]

19:16 Sir. Literally *Lord.* See comments on 6:46.

Has earned ten more. In a parable 1,000 percent return is perfectly reasonable. Actually this was not impossible in the first century.

19:17 Because you have been trustworthy in a very small matter. Compare 16:10.

Take charge of ten cities. The disproportionate nature of reward to service should be noted. The reality part of this picture involves "treasure in heaven" (12:33; 18:22).

19:19 You take charge of five cities. Again the reward is disproportionate.

19:20 Then another servant came. Literally *and the other one came.*[327]

Sir, here is your mina. This servant did nothing with the mina given him.

I have kept it laid away in a piece of cloth. This "napkin" (RSV) probably refers to a scarf worn around one's face or neck for protection from the sun.

19:21 I was afraid of you, because. The wicked servant defended his behavior on the grounds of the nobleman's being a "hard man." This "hard" quality is then described as taking an unusually high margin of profit from his investments and reaping a harvest that others have produced. In his defense the wicked servant sought to paint a negative picture of the character of the nobleman. The

---

[321] Cf. Josephus, *Antiquities* 14.13.1-4 (14.370-85) and *Wars* 1.14.4 (1.284-85).

[322] Josephus, *Antiquities* 17.9.1-3; 17.11.4 (17.206-23,318) and *Wars* 2.2.2; 2.6.3 (2.18,94).

[323] Cf. Josephus, *Antiquities* 17.11.1-2 (17.299-314) and *Wars* 2.6.1-2 (2.80-92).

[324] Cf. Luke 23:2,18-25; Acts 2:23; 3:13-15; 13:27-29.

[325] Cf. Josephus, *Antiquities* 14.14.5 (14.389) and *Wars* 1.14.4 (1.285).

[326] Acts 2:36; 5:30-31; 7:55-56; 13:33-34; 17:31; Luke 24:26.

[327] This seems to ignore the other seven servants mentioned in 19:13. Some have therefore suggested that originally the parable spoke of only three servants as in Matt 25:14-30.

readers of the story know this is incorrect, however, because of his generosity in 19:17,19.

19:22 I will judge you by your own words. The nobleman judged the wicked servant on the basis of his own presuppositions. If his presuppositions about the nobleman's character are false and the hearers/readers of the parable know that they are, he is even more condemned. The term "judge" (*krinō*) can mean *to judge*, but here, since the servant would be judged unfavorably, it means *to condemn*.

19:23 The nobleman states, "If what you said about me is true, you should then at least have invested my money in a bank (literally *on the table of money changers*). In this way the master would at least have received interest.

19:24 Take his mina. In Matt 25:30 the wicked servant's condemnation is explained, and the reality of eternal judgment enters into the picture part of the parable itself.

Give it to the one who has ten minas. The one who served faithfully is rewarded with even more. The gift of a *mina* here is insignificant compared to the reward described in Luke 19:17,19. This may be the result of trying to show in these earlier references the surpassing generosity (bestowing "cities") of the king to his servants.

19:26 Compare 8:18, where the same proverb is found.

19:27 But those enemies of mine. Luke and his readers would have interpreted this picture part of the parable as referring to the reality of the events of A.D. 70.[328] This verse and certain others[329] have caused some commentators to speak of Luke as having been anti-Semitic. Yet in the parable the Jewish people were not condemned because the faithful servants in the parable were also Jews. Furthermore for Luke the "eyewitnesses and servants of the word" (1:2) were all Jews. That certain Jews are condemned is, of course, clear; but there is present no hatred of the Jewish people. The preachers in Acts and the followers of Jesus in Luke were all Jewish. Actually if one compares this passage with such intra-Jewish name-calling and animosity found in some of the rabbinic and Qumran materials, these NT passages appear at times quite mild.[330]

The Lukan Message

In this account Luke dealt with the issue of the "delay" of the parousia. The parable is clearly a parable of stewardship, but Luke sought to point out to his readers that stewardship necessitates that there be an interval between the time of the historical Jesus and the consummation. Stewardship has no meaning if the "king" is not absent for a time. Luke used this aspect of stewardship to tell Theophilus that Jesus by this parable taught

---

[328] Because of such references as Luke 13:35; 19:41-44; 21:6,20-24; 23:28-31.

[329] Cf. Luke 4:16-30; 10:30-35; 14:15-24; Acts 2:22-23,36; 3:12-15; 7:51-60.

[330] See L. T. Johnson, "The New Testament's Anti-Jewish Slander and the Conventions of Ancient Polemic," *JBL* 108 (1989): 419-41 and C. A. Evans, "Is Luke's View of the Jewish Rejection of Jesus Anti-Semitic?" in *Reimaging the Death of the Lukan Jesus*, ed. D. D. Silva (Frankfurt: Anton Hain, 1990), 29-56.

that he would be absent for a time. Jesus in fact taught this parable to allay a similar misunderstanding in his day that expected the consummation would occur immediately (19:11; cf. Acts 1:6). Luke did not seek to answer the question "Where is this 'coming' he promised?" (2 Pet 3:4) in the same way that 2 Pet 3:4-10 does. Rather he answered it by pointing out to his readers that Jesus himself taught a delay by means of this parable. Thus the present "delay" should not disturb them. Matthew has a similar understanding of his parable in 25:19 when he states, "After a long time the master . . . returned and settled accounts with them." Again Luke was not arguing that the return of the Lord had been delayed but rather that the expectation that he should have already returned is based upon a misunderstanding. Jesus never taught this but taught rather that his return would be "after a long time" (Matt 25:19). See Introduction 7 (3).[331]

This parable on stewardship fits well other teachings found elsewhere in Luke. We have a similar parable in 12:35-40 in which faithful stewardship is described as being "watchful" (12:37) and "ready" (12:38). In this parable faithful stewardship is also intimately connected to the parousia. An earlier parable described faithful stewardship as "producing a crop" (8:15). Whereas in the parable of the soils (8:5-15) only one soil represents faithful stewardship and all the rest exemplify unfaithful stewardship, in the present parable only one servant is unfaithful in his stewardship and the rest are faithful. Thus nothing should be made of the "ratios" found in these parables. For the Lukan emphasis concerning stewardship of one's possessions, see Introduction 8 (7).

Within the parable also are present two additional themes. One involves Jesus' kingship. Luke prepared his readers for this in the first chapter (see comments on 1:32-33), and this will be a main theme in the following account (cf. 19:35-38) and in the passion narrative (cf. 23:2-3, 11,37-38; cf. also 22:29). Also associated with this parable is an emphasis on Jesus' rejection by the Jewish nation. Luke's references to this in the parable (19:14,27) are not found in the Matthean parable but are unique to him. This theme has also been prepared for in the opening chapters (see comments on 2:34) and continues throughout Luke-Acts. Once again Luke pointed out that Israel was to blame for their exclusion from the kingdom. See Introduction 7 (2) and 8 (5).

---

[331] For a contrary view see L. T. Johnson, "The Lukan Kingship Parable" (Lk 19:11-27), *NovT* 24 (1982): 139-59.

———————————— *SECTION OUTLINE* ————————————

VI. JESUS' MINISTRY IN JERUSALEM (19:28–21:38)
   1. The Messianic Entry into Jerusalem (19:28-40)
   2. Lament over Jerusalem and the Cleansing of the Temple
      (19:41-48)
   3. A Question of Jesus' Authority (20:1-8)
   4. The Parable of the Wicked Tenants (20:9-19)
   5. A Question about Tribute to Caesar (20:20-26)
   6. A Question about the Resurrection (20:27-40)
   7. A Question about the Son of David (20:41-44)
   8. Warnings concerning the Scribes (20:45-47)
   9. The Widow's Offering (21:1-4)
  10. The Destruction of the Temple (21:5-6)
  11. Signs before the End (21:7-11)
  12. The Coming Persecution of the Disciples (21:12-19)
  13. The Desolation Coming upon Jerusalem (21:20-24)
  14. The Coming of the Son of Man (21:25-28)
  15. The Parable of the Fig Tree (21:29-33)
  16. Exhortation to Vigilance (21:34-36)
  17. The Ministry of Jesus in the Temple (21:37-38)

——— **VI. JESUS' MINISTRY IN JERUSALEM (19:28–21:38)** ———

The "triumphal" entry marks the beginning of the sixth section of Luke's Gospel. The travel narrative (9:51–19:27) has come to an end, and Jesus now enters Jerusalem, his city of destiny.[1] This new section devoted to Jesus' ministry in Jerusalem continues until 21:38. It is then followed by the passion narrative (22:1–23:56) and the resurrection account (24:1-53).

In the present section Luke paralleled the material in Mark 11:1–13:37 quite closely. The only significant differences are his addition of Jesus' lament over Jerusalem (19:41-44), which has no parallel in either Matthew or Mark; his omission of Jesus' cursing of the fig tree (Mark 11:12-14,20-26); his omission of the exhortation for vigilance (Mark 13:33-37), which has parallels to Luke's parable of the minas (19:11-27); his substitution of a different exhortation for vigilance (21:34-36); and the addition of his own concluding summary (21:37-38). Even as the travel narrative began with Jesus' rejection in Samaria (9:51-56), so this section begins with his rejection in Jerusalem (19:39-40).

---

[1] Cf. Luke 9:51,53; 13:22,33-34; 17:11; 18:31; 19:1,11.

1. The Messianic Entry into Jerusalem (19:28-40)

[28]After Jesus had said this, he went on ahead, going up to Jerusalem. [29]As he approached Bethphage and Bethany at the hill called the Mount of Olives, he sent two of his disciples, saying to them, [30]"Go to the village ahead of you, and as you enter it, you will find a colt tied there, which no one has ever ridden. Untie it and bring it here. [31]If anyone asks you, 'Why are you untying it?' tell him, 'The Lord needs it.' "

[32]Those who were sent ahead went and found it just as he had told them. [33]As they were untying the colt, its owners asked them, "Why are you untying the colt?"

[34]They replied, "The Lord needs it."

[35]They brought it to Jesus, threw their cloaks on the colt and put Jesus on it. [36]As he went along, people spread their cloaks on the road.

[37]When he came near the place where the road goes down the Mount of Olives, the whole crowd of disciples began joyfully to praise God in loud voices for all the miracles they had seen:

[38]"Blessed is the king who comes in the name of the Lord!"

"Peace in heaven and glory in the highest!"

[39]Some of the Pharisees in the crowd said to Jesus, "Teacher, rebuke your disciples!"

[40]"I tell you," he replied, "if they keep quiet, the stones will cry out."

Context

In this account the promised Son of David, spoken of in the opening chapters (1:27,32,69; 2:4,11; 3:31) and in the previous chapter (18:38-39), enters the holy city itself. The "coming one" (7:19; 19:38; cf. 3:16) has now arrived. In preparation for this Jesus sends two disciples to bring a colt upon which no one has ridden, for only such an animal was worthy of his royal entry. As the disciples scatter their garments in homage before him, the King of Israel comes (19:38; cf. 19:12,14-15), but he comes in meekness and humility, as Zechariah foretold (cf. Zech 9:9). Despite the joy and praise of the disciples, Jerusalem does not receive its King. Its leaders, represented by the Pharisees, seek instead to quench the joyful praise (Luke 19:39). Yet on this day nothing can stop this homage to Israel's King. The heavenly anthem (2:14) rings out again from Jesus' disciples (19:37), for this is God's day. If the disciples were to stop their praise, the stones themselves would break forth into song (19:40).

Numerous questions have been raised about the historicity of this account. How could such an open messianic demonstration have been tolerated by the Roman authorities? Why was this messianic display not mentioned at Jesus' trial when his opponents were desperately seeking evidence against him? Was Zech 9:9 later read into the incident or was it present in Jesus' mind from the beginning? It is quite possible that, as in the case of Peter's confession, the crowd's response was more correct than its understanding (cf. Mark 8:29 and 8:31-33; note also John 11:49-53). Perhaps something like the following took place: Jesus, conscious of his messiahship, chose (perhaps even arranged) to ride into Jerusalem on a young colt in fulfillment of Zech 9:9. He was welcomed by the crowds who greeted him, and the other pilgrims, with a typical pilgrim greeting: "Blessed is he who comes in the name of the Lord. From the house of the Lord we bless you" (Ps 118:26).[2] This was done with great enthusiasm, especially by Jesus' disciples, due to his popularity and fame. Thus, although the people did realize it, Jesus' self-conscious messianic act of entering into Jerusalem in fulfillment of Zech 9:9 was greeted with a response worthy of the messianic King. There was, however, no equivalent understanding by those extending this greeting. Later the church, reflecting upon this event and the OT Scriptures, came to a fuller understanding of what had transpired and highlighted certain aspects of this (cf. "king" in Luke 19:38).

Comments

19:28   After Jesus had said this.   By his introduction Luke linked the triumphal entry closely with the preceding parable dealing with Jesus' kingship (cf. 19:12,14-15).

He went on ahead, going up to Jerusalem.   For Luke a divine necessity lay behind this. See Introduction 8 (1).

19:29   He approached Bethphage and Bethany.   The exact location of Bethphage, even whether it lies east or west of Bethany, is uncertain. Luke most probably referred to it because it was found in his Markan source. Bethany lies on the eastern slope of the Mount of Olives two to three miles from Jerusalem. It is referred to again in 24:50.

At the hill called the Mount of Olives.   The Mount of Olives lies directly east of Jerusalem 2,660 feet above sea level. To reach Jerusalem one would proceed west down the Mount of Olives, through the Kidron Valley, and into the temple area through the eastern gate, later called the Golden Gate.

He sent two of his disciples.   The disciples are unnamed in all three Synoptic Gospels.

19:30   Go to the village ahead of you.   The village possibly was Bethphage.

As you enter it, you will find.   This can be interpreted as an example of Jesus' prescience or as due to his prearrangement. If Jesus prearranged this, then the messianic character of the triumphal entry is heightened, for this means that Jesus intentionally sought to fulfill Zech 9:9 by riding into Jerusalem on a colt that never had been ridden. This would explain from a historical perspective why the owners of the colt permitted the disciples to take it. Yet it is quite possible that Luke and his readers might not have interpreted this text in so historical a manner.

---

[2] See L. C. Allen (*Psalms 101–150*, WBC [Waco: Word, 1983], 124-25), who points out that this was originally a greeting addressed to the Davidic king as he approached the temple.

They might have thought that Jesus, the Lord (Luke 19:34), knew that a colt would be there because of his supernatural knowledge.[3]

A colt. Matthew 21:2 assumes that this was the colt of a donkey. The term (*pōlon*) simply means *colt* and can refer to a young horse or a young donkey. Luke's readers may very well have known this tradition, and if Matt 21:5 reflects a common association of this event to Zech 9:9, they would have assumed that the "colt" referred to a young donkey.

Which no one has ever ridden. Compare Luke 23:53. Such an animal was qualified to perform a sacred task (cf. Num 19:2; Deut 21:3; 1 Sam 6:7). This may also allude to the "young colt" of Zech 9:9.

19:31   If anyone asks. Jesus prepared the disciples for the future encounter with the owners.

The Lord needs it. "Lord" (*kyrios*) would be interpreted by Luke's readers as the Lord Jesus, not the owners (literally *lords* [*kyrioi*]) of the colt (19:33). This is evident because the owners/lords were told "the Lord needs it." Historically there is no reason why Jesus could not have arranged beforehand to have a colt ready. Only if we deny Jesus a messianic consciousness can we deny this possibility. The likelihood of the owners' accepting the commandeering or requisitioning of their animal by a stranger is quite low, as is the availability of a donkey that had never been ridden.

19:32   Those who were sent ahead. Compare 13:34.

Found it just as he had told them. Compare 19:30; 22:13.

19:33-34 Compare 19:31. The strongest argument favoring a prearrangement is the total compliance of the owners. Why would they permit the disciples to do this? To say "the Lord needs it" requires either a prearrangement or that the owners were believers who would do whatever Jesus asked.

19:35   Threw their cloaks on the colt. The disciples used their garments to serve as a kind of saddle.

Put Jesus on it. Luke changed his sources, "he [Jesus] sat on it" (Mark 11:7), and thus paralleled more closely Solomon's coronation (1 Kgs 1:33).

The space devoted to the colt (Luke 19:30-35) suggests its important role in the story. As a result Zech 9:9, even though not quoted, is a key to what is taking place. Luke therefore understood Jesus' entry into Jerusalem as a parabolic action.[4]

19:36   People spread their cloaks on the road. Spreading cloaks on the road is an act of homage as in 2 Kgs 9:13 (cf. also Josephus, *Antiquities* 9.6.2. [9.111]). Luke made no mention of the spreading of branches, perhaps due to the nationalistic overtones of such an act.[5]

19:37   Where the road goes down the Mount of Olives. What takes place, occurs as Jerusalem comes into sight.

The whole crowd of disciples. The following response of praise came from the disciples, not from Jerusalem. Jerusalem's response is found in Luke 19:39-40,

---

[3]Cf. Luke 22:13; cf. also 5:22; 6:8; 7:39-40; 22:21,34.

[4]For other parabolic actions of Jesus, see R. H. Stein, *The Method and Message of Jesus' Teachings* (Philadelphia: Westminster, 1978), 25-27.

[5]Cf. Mark 11:8; Matt 21:8. This is especially true of palm branches (John 12:13; cf. 1 Macc 13:51; 2 Macc 10:7; Rev 7:9), which appear in the coinage of Judas Maccabeus.

even though this occurs before Jesus enters the city. For the existence of a large group of disciples, see comments on 6:13.

Began joyfully. Luke may have added this in order to tie this episode more closely to Zech 9:9, which begins "Rejoice."

To praise God in loud voices. For praising (*aineō*) God, see comments on 2:13 (for a similar term [*doxazō*], see comments on 5:25). The praise of the angels and shepherds (Luke 2:13,20) at the birth of the Son of David now resumes as he enters Jerusalem. "In loud voices" echoes a favorite Lukan expression.[6]

For all the miracles they had seen. Compare 10:13; Acts 2:22; 8:13; 19:11. Luke wanted his readers to know that the four miracles listed in the travel narrative (Luke 13:10-17; 14:1-6; 17:11-19; 18:35-43) are only samples of Jesus' works.[7]

19:38 Blessed is the king who comes in the name of the Lord! This, minus the words "the king," comes from Ps 118:26. This psalm was used to greet pilgrims entering Jerusalem. At first glance this verse appears to be the fulfillment of Luke 13:35, but on closer examination it is evident that the prophecy of 13:35 was not fulfilled. Jerusalem was not yet forsaken (13:35a), and it was not Jerusalem that uttered this benediction but Jesus' disciples. As 13:32-33 foretold, Jerusalem's response would be quite different. Matthew's placement of this saying (Matt 23:39) after the events of Palm Sunday indicates that he did not think the events surrounding the triumphal entry fulfilled this prophecy. It is best to interpret Luke similarly. See comments on 13:35. Luke omitted from his source "Hosanna" and "Blessed is the coming kingdom of our father David" (cf. Mark 11:9-10). The first omission corresponds to his tendency to omit Aramaic terms (see comments on 8:54). The second may be due to what Luke said about the coming of the kingdom in 19:11.

The king. This is a clear Lukan addition to the tradition, as a comparison with Matt 21:9; Mark 11:10 reveals. Jesus' kingship has been alluded to in Luke 1:32 and in 18:38-39 (cf. also 23:3,37-38; Acts 17:7). In the preceding parable his kingship is seen as bestowed at his resurrection/ascension and exercised at his parousia. Thus the beatitude here is a proleptic announcement of Jesus' kingship, which like God's kingdom is already a present reality in Jesus' ministry but whose ultimate consummation awaits the parousia.

Who comes. See comments on 7:19.

Peace in heaven. This is a strange statement, whereas "peace on earth" (Luke 2:14) would be perfectly understandable. Luke may have changed the wording of 2:14 to "peace in heaven" because the peace Jesus sought to bring (10:5-6) does not find fulfillment in Jerusalem. On the contrary, as the next pericope reveals, Jerusalem would not experience peace (19:42) but war and destruction (19:43-44). Nevertheless peace reigns in heaven, for God's divine plan is being fulfilled. Only when the Son of Man returns will peace finally come to Jerusalem (13:35).

Glory in the highest! Literally the two expressions are *in heaven* (A) *peace* (B) and *glory* (b) *in the highest* (a) and form a chiasmus. Compare 2:14.

---

[6]Cf. Luke 4:33; 8:28; 23:46; Acts 7:57,60; 8:7; 14:10; 16:28; 26:24; cf. also Luke 17:15; 23:23.

[7]As Luke 4:14,36; 5:17; 6:17-19; 8:46; 9:1; 10:13,19 reveal.

19:39 Luke ended his account of the triumphal entry with a brief conversation between Jesus and the Pharisees found only in Luke. He added this to show the reality portrayed in the picture part of the preceding parable (cf. 19:14).
Some of the Pharisees in the crowd. This is the last reference to the Pharisees in Luke. It was for Luke a demonstration of the parabolic picture in 19:14 and in 20:9-18. Whereas in some instances the Pharisees are viewed positively, or at least neutrally (see comments on 13:31; cf. Acts 5:34-39; 15:5; 23:6-9), here, as in most instances, they are portrayed negatively. Luke's readers would not have interpreted this as a Pharisaic attempt to save Jesus from the consequences of this messianic excitement. They would have interpreted this as an attempt to squelch the disciples' praise of God (cf. Matt 21:14-16).
19:40 If they keep quiet, the stones will cry out. The Greek construction (*ean* with the future indicative) is rare, and the verse is capable of several interpretations. The most likely is, "If the disciples would stop their praising of God and his Son, then the stones would take their place and cry out praise in their stead." Nothing can detract from this day. There may be an allusion here to Hab 2:11. Whereas earlier Jesus had given a command to silence (see comments on 9:21), this day there was no silencing the welcoming of the Son of David, Israel's King.

The Lukan Message

Luke incorporated the tradition of the triumphal entry into the overall purpose and scheme of his "orderly account." Jesus' entry into Jerusalem brings the travel narrative (cf. Luke 9:51) to its consummation. Christologically, Jesus' Davidic sonship, his kingship, and his role as the Coming One are not only supported by this incident but reach a climax. His prearrangement or prescience (see comments on 19:30) also supports this Christological teaching as does the title "Lord" (19:31). Luke anticipated that his readers would see in this account a confirmation of much of the Christology of which they had been taught (1:4). Jesus is the promised Messiah. Born of Davidic lineage (1:27,32; 3:31), he entered Jerusalem as Israel's true King. He would die as King of the Jews (23:2-3,11,38,42), but he would also be raised and return as their King (Acts 2:33-36; 13:21-23,30-39). Luke in recounting this story wanted his readers to know that Jesus is indeed the fulfillment of all the OT promises. This Jesus, in whom they believed, is truly the Son of God.
Yet there is a dark cloud hanging over this whole incident, and Luke taught his readers once again that what had happened to Israel was the result of their rejection of the Christ. See Introduction 7 (2). The Pharisaic response (Luke 19:39) reveals that Israel had not received their King (cf. 19:14). The "triumphal" entry from a human perspective was not "triumphal." What had been true from the very beginning continues even now. The Son of God is rejected. This theme, the rejection of Jesus and the resulting judgment, will be brought to the forefront by Luke in 19:41-44, which is the climax of 19:28-40. Here the cry of 13:34-35 will be

repeated. Judgment will come. Tragedy would soon strike, for Israel had headed down a road that did not lead to peace (19:42) but, on the contrary, to destruction. Judgment would come upon the nation in the events of A.D. 70 but even more frightfully in its exclusion from the kingdom (cf. Acts 13:46-47; 18:6; 28:25-28). Finally, such characteristics as obedience, rejoicing, and praising God are also emphasized in the account.

2. Lament over Jerusalem and the Cleansing of the Temple (19:41-48)

[41]As he approached Jerusalem and saw the city, he wept over it [42]and said, "If you, even you, had only known on this day what would bring you peace— but now it is hidden from your eyes. [43]The days will come upon you when your enemies will build an embankment against you and encircle you and hem you in on every side. [44]They will dash you to the ground, you and the children within your walls. They will not leave one stone on another, because you did not recognize the time of God's coming to you."

[45]Then he entered the temple area and began driving out those who were selling. [46]"It is written," he said to them, " 'My house will be a house of prayer'; but you have made it 'a den of robbers.' "

[47]Every day he was teaching at the temple. But the chief priests, the teachers of the law and the leaders among the people were trying to kill him. [48]Yet they could not find any way to do it, because all the people hung on his words.

Context

Luke concluded Jesus' entrance into Jerusalem with three different and unrelated accounts. The first involves Jesus' lament over the city (Luke 19:41-44); the second is an abbreviated account of his cleansing of the temple (19:45-46); and the third is a summary of Jesus' teaching ministry in the temple and the plot by the religious leaders to kill him (19:47-48). The account of Jesus' weeping over Jerusalem is unique to Luke. Having entered Jerusalem as Israel's King (19:38), Jesus as its Prophet announced for the second time its judgment (cf. 13:34-35). He would do this a third time on the way to the cross (23:26-31). There is a parallel between Jesus' lament and the Benedictus (1:68-80). In both there is reference to "enemies" (cf. 19:43 and 1:71,74), "knowing" (cf. 19:42 "known" and 19:44 "recognize," the same Greek word as in 1:77), "coming" (cf. 19:44 and 1:68,78), and peace (cf. 19:42 and 1:79). Tannehill notes, "These links make it highly likely that the narrator intends to connect the arrival in Jerusalem with the birth narrative in order to highlight the tragic turn which the narrative is now taking."[8]

Luke drastically abbreviated the account of the cleansing of the temple.[9] In so doing he (1) omitted the cursing of the fig tree (Mark 11:12-14), due perhaps to his inclusion of similar material in Luke 13:6-9; (2) sharply cur-

---

[8]R. C. Tannehill, *The Narrative Unity of Luke-Acts* (Philadelphia: Fortress, 1986), 160.

[9]This is apparent as one compares the material: Matt 21:10-17; Mark 11:11,15-17; John 2:13-17; Luke 19:45-46.

tailed Jesus' actions in the temple and omitted any description of Jesus' violent action (cf. Mark 11:15; John 2:15-17); (3) eliminated Jesus' prohibition of using the temple as a shortcut (Mark 11:16); (4) eliminated the reference to Jesus' teaching (Mark 11:17), due to his referring to this later in Luke 19:47; and (5) eliminated "for all nations" (Mark 11:17) in the Isa 56:7 quotation, due perhaps to the temple's having been destroyed and being unable to fulfill that function.

The final account is a Lukan summary that focuses on Jesus' teaching and the plot to kill him (Luke 19:47-48). One of the results of Luke's abbreviation of the cleansing narrative is that whereas in Mark the plot to kill Jesus is associated with the cleansing of the temple (cf. Mark 11:18 with what has preceded), in Luke the plot (19:47b-48) is more closely associated with his teaching (19:48a).

The historicity of the lament and the cleansing of the temple has been questioned. The historicity of the former presents less of a difficulty than the latter, for we find similar prophetic material throughout the Gospels.[10] Any astute observer might well have been able to see that Jewish nationalism would one day lead to a confrontation that could only end in disaster. (Cf. how in 1QpHab 9:6f.; Hab 2:7-8 is interpreted as a prophecy of Jerusalem's future defeat by the Romans.) There is no reason to deny that Jesus spoke of Jerusalem's future destruction.[11] Such a depiction can be found in the OT descriptions of Jerusalem's destruction in 587 B.C.[12]

As for the temple cleansing, the classic question is whether there was one cleansing (as in the Synoptic Gospels and in John) or two (as reconstructed from the Synoptic Gospel with John). And if there was one, which dating and account is more authentic, the Synoptic Gospels' or John's? The question has also been raised whether any cleansing could have been possible in light of the presence of Roman soldiers in Jerusalem and the apparent messianic nature of such a cleansing. For the purpose of this commentary such questions while important cannot be dealt with. See Introduction 9. This tradition, however, already existed when Luke wrote his Gospel, and we will concentrate attention on what Luke sought to teach his readers through his reporting of this tradition.[13]

Comments

19:41 He wept. Compare Luke 13:34, where Jesus experiences a similar sorrow but there is no mention of weeping. Only here and in John 11:35 do we

[10]Cf. John 2:19-22; Mark 13:2 (Matt 24:2; Luke 21:6); Mark 14:58 (Matt 26:61).

[11]See E. P. Sanders, *Jesus and Judaism* (Philadelphia: Fortress, 1985), 61-76.

[12]Cf. Jer 6:6,8,14-15; 8:18; 9:1; Isa 29:3; Hos 10:14; Nah 3:10,14; Ps 137:9. See C. H. Dodd, "The Fall of Jerusalem and the 'Abomination of Desolation,'" *JRS* 37 (1947): 47-54, and J. A. T. Robinson, *Redating the New Testament* (Philadelphia: Westminster, 1976), 26-30.

[13]See J. A. Fitzmyer, *The Gospel according to Luke*, AB (Garden City: Doubleday, 1985), 1260-67, for a helpful discussion of the historical issues.

read of Jesus' weeping in the Gospels. Jesus wept, however, not for himself and his fate but rather for the fate of Jerusalem and the people of Israel (Luke 23:28-31). Compare the weeping of the OT prophets: 2 Kgs 8:11; Jer 8:18-21; 9:1; 14:17. The experience of Ps 137 after the destruction of Jerusalem in 587 B.C. will soon be relived.

19:42 If you, even you. The NIV in its translation reveals that the "you" is emphatic. The form of the sentence is that of a contrary-to-fact condition (second class condition), but it is never completed as the dash in the NIV text indicates, i.e., there is no apodosis. This breaking off of the sentence in the middle (called "aposiopesis") reveals the strong emotions present at the time. Compare Acts 23:9; John 6:62.

This day. This refers to "the time of God's coming to you" (Luke 19:44), which refers broadly to the coming of God's kingdom but more narrowly to the coming of Israel's King in 19:28-40.

Peace. The city, within whose name is the word "peace" (*salem*), rejected the messianic peace offered it and instead would experience war. Compare Pss 122:6-9; 147:14.

Is hidden. This could be a divine passive, i.e., *God has hidden*.[14] What the blind beggar saw (Luke 18:35-43) was not seen by the leaders of Jerusalem.

19:43 The days will come. Compare 23:29; see comments on 5:35.

Upon you. This refers primarily to Jerusalem's destruction in A.D. 70, but it also involves the gospel going to the Gentiles.[15] The forthcoming judgment can be seen as due to either (1) Israel's rejection of God's Anointed and a resultant divine judgment or (2) an attitude of heart that rejected God's Anointed and would lead Israel to revolt against Rome and experience the catastrophe of A.D. 70. The latter, however, is a "historical" explanation that would have been foreign to Luke's way of thinking. For him the events of A.D. 70 are God's judgment upon Israel because of the rejection of their King. This judgment is described as follows:

Enemies will build an embankment against you. Compare Isa 29:3; 37:33; Jer 6:6-21; Ezek 4:1-3. The Romans were not specifically mentioned, but the reference is to the palisade they built around Jerusalem.

And encircle you. This refers to the wall later built to surround the city to keep people within the city from escaping. Compare Luke 21:20; 2 Kgs 6:14; Isa 29:3.[16]

And hem you in on every side. This refers to the continual pressure of attacks against the city. Compare Ezek 4:2; 21:22; Jer 52:5; 2 Macc 9:2.

19:44 They will dash you to the ground, you and the children within your walls. This is a traditional feature in the description of sieges.[17] It describes the slaughter in war that often befell the defeated in a most literal way and to which Luke 23:28-31 refers.

---

[14] J. Jeremias, *New Testament Theology* (New York: Scribner's, 1971), 12.

[15] Acts 13:46-51; 18:6; 28:25-28; cf. also Rom 11:13-32.

[16] I. H. Marshall (*The Gospel of Luke*, TNIGTC [Grand Rapids: Eerdmans, 1978], 718) suggests that this palisade was burned down by the Jews and then replaced by a "stone siege-dyke" Luke may have been alluding to by the next expression "and encircle you."

[17] Cf. Ps 137:9; Hos 10:14; 13:16; Nah 3:10; 2 Kgs 8:12.

They will not leave one stone on another. Compare 21:6. This is the fifth and final description of the coming judgment. Compare 2 Sam 17:13; Mic 3:12; Ps 137:7. This describes Titus's attempt to raze the entire city. For a detailed description of what happened, see Josephus, *Wars* 7.1.1. (7.1-4) and 7.8.7 (7.375-77). The use of hyperbole in this instance is easily excused by anyone familiar with Jerusalem's destruction in A.D. 70.

Because. The reason is now given for this judgment. This favors the first view given in Luke 19:43. By their rejection of God's Son, the day of visitation that was meant to fulfill Israel's hopes and expectations (1:54-55,68-79) would instead bring God's judgment.[18]

19:45   Then he entered the temple area. As the "coming one" (19:38), Jesus immediately entered the temple (cf. Mal 3:1).

And began driving out those who were selling. Jesus' cleansing of the temple was a messianic act in the sense that he did this as the Messiah. It probably was not a messianic act in the sense that the Messiah was expected to do this. Luke minimized this particular incident in the tradition, perhaps due to his desire to avoid misinterpreting Jesus' actions as revolutionary (cf. Luke 12:51 with Matt 10:34). The incident took place in the court of the Gentiles (cf. "for all nations" in Mark 11:17), where one could purchase the necessary sacrifices or, at certain times during the year (*Seqal.* 1:3; cf. also *Ker.* 1:7), exchange money for the Tyrian silver coins that alone were acceptable for paying the half-shekal temple tax.[19] The latter are not mentioned in Luke's abbreviated account (cf. Mark 11:15).

19:46   It is written. As at the temptation, Jesus quoted Scripture to justify his behavior.

House of prayer. Luke omitted the reference "for all nations," which appears in his Markan source and in Isa 56:7. He may have done this because the temple now lay in ruins and as a result could not have become a house of prayer for all nations.

Den of robbers. Compare Jer 7:11.

19:47   Every day he was teaching at the temple. The temple, his "Father's house" (Luke 2:49), would serve as the classroom for Jesus' teaching (21:37) and for the teaching of the early church.[20] The periphrastic "was teaching" and "every day" emphasize the continual nature of Jesus' teaching in the temple.

Chief priests, the teachers of the law and the leaders among the people. Luke added "the leaders among the people" to the tradition (cf. Mark 11:18). This latter group is mentioned in Acts 25:2; 28:17 as rejecting the gospel message. The expression probably is a synonym for "elders," which also appears in Luke 9:22 together with "chief priests and teachers of the law."

Were trying to kill him. Judas later provided the means by which this could be accomplished (see comments on 22:3-6). This is the first clear reference to a deliberate intention of Jesus' opponents to do away with him. Allusions to this intent,

---

[18] Cf. Exod 32:34; Isa 29:6; Jer 6:15; 10:15; Wis 14:11; Sir 16:18; 18:20; 23:24; 1 Pet 2:12. Cf. also 1 QS 3:14,18; 4:11-14,18-19,26.

[19] See J. Jeremias, *Jerusalem in the Time of Jesus* (Philadelphia: Fortress, 1969), 48-49.

[20] Cf. Acts 2:1-47 (Luke probably understood the "place" of 2:1 as the temple); 3:1-4:2; 5:12,42.

however, can be found in 6:11; 11:53-54; cf. also 4:29; 13:33-35. The decision to do this had already been made, but the reader is not told when the decision was reached. What is clear is that Jesus' future trial would not determine his guilt or innocence but rather determine the basis for the death sentence.

19:48   Yet they could not . . . because all the people. The people are clearly distinguished here and in Mark 11:18 from Israel's leaders by their positive attitude toward Jesus (see comments on 4:15). The tension between these two groups, the people and the leadership of Israel, carries over into the Book of Acts. In light of the anti-Semitism over the centuries, one should take care to separate this attitude of the Jewish people from the attitude of their leaders with respect to Jesus.

The Lukan Message

The one unifying feature that ties these three accounts (Luke 19:41-44, 45-46,47-48) together is that they all witness to the failure on the part of official Israel to submit itself to God's rule and the horrible consequences of this. Official Israel, represented by the "chief priests, teachers of the law and the leaders among the people" (19:47), misunderstood the purpose of the temple and misused it (19:45-46). They not only sought to squelch the "heavenly" praise of their King in their day of visitation (19:39-40) and refused his rule over them (19:14), but they also increased their guilt by seeking their King's death (19:47-48). This can only result in a visitation of divine judgment (19:42-44), and knowing this, Jesus wept for Jerusalem (19:41). How could the blind have seen so clearly (18:35-43) but those whose eyes were supposedly open and seeking this great day, i.e., the religious elite, have been so blind (19:42) that they sought the death of their Messiah, the Son of David, the King of Israel, the Son of God? Jerusalem, the "foundation of peace," ironically rejected the visitation of the Prince of peace (2:14; 19:36; Acts 10:38) and would treat its Savior as it had the other prophets (Luke 13:34). Such blindness was willful and culpable and would bring judgment. This was why, Luke said, judgment came upon Israel. See Introduction 7 (2). The most explicit references to Jerusalem's destruction found in the Gospels occur in Luke (19:41-44; 21:20-24; 23:28-31; cf. 13:34-35).

Within this account several other Lukan themes appear. The arrival of God's kingdom is described by the expression "the time of God's coming to you" (19:44). In his summary (19:47) Luke referred to Jesus' continual ministry of teaching and thus explained to his readers the source of the material they had been taught (1:4). Luke also continued to emphasize the division within Israel between the people and the religious leadership (19:48). Jesus was not rejected by the Jewish people. He was rejected by Israel's leadership. The "first" chose to become last, but many of the people, especially the "last" among them, chose to follow Jesus (see comments on 4:15).

3. A Question of Jesus' Authority (20:1-8)

[1]One day as he was teaching the people in the temple courts and preaching the gospel, the chief priests and the teachers of the law, together with the elders, came up to him. [2]"Tell us by what authority you are doing these things," they said. "Who gave you this authority?"
[3]He replied, "I will also ask you a question. Tell me, [4]John's baptism—was it from heaven, or from men?"
[5]They discussed it among themselves and said, "If we say, 'From heaven,' he will ask, 'Why didn't you believe him?' [6]But if we say, 'From men,' all the people will stone us, because they are persuaded that John was a prophet."
[7]So they answered, "We don't know where it was from."
[8]Jesus said, "Neither will I tell you by what authority I am doing these things."

Context

Closely associated with the temple cleansing is the question of Jesus' opponents concerning his authority to do this.[21] While teaching in the temple, Jesus was challenged by a deputation of chief priests, scribes, and elders about his authority for cleansing the temple, as well as other activities. Jesus responded in this controversy story with a counterquestion about the source of John the Baptist's authority. Was it from God or not? The opponents were thus placed upon the horns of a dilemma, for if they answered that John's message came from God, Jesus was likely to say, "Then why did you not repent and be baptized by him?" (literally *believe in him*). On the other hand if they denied that John was a prophet, then the people, who acknowledged him as such, would be so angry they might stone them. In light of these unacceptable alternatives, Jesus' opponents refused to answer his question and feigned ignorance. In response to this hypocritical refusal, Jesus declined to answer their question, for any further discussion with them would have been useless.

Comments

20:1 One day. Compare 19:47.

He was teaching . . . and preaching the gospel. No difference in the content or substance should be seen in these two verbs. For their combination cf. Acts 5:42; 15:35; cf. also Luke 4:15,18. What Jesus was teaching and preaching is not stated, but Luke would have expected his readers to assume that it was the material found in Luke 4–19 and the subsequent chapters of Luke and Acts.

Chief priests and the teachers of the law, together with the elders. Compare 9:22; 22:66; see comments on 19:47. This looks like an official delegation representing the leadership of Israel, i.e., the Sanhedrin (see comments on 22:66). Their purpose in coming is clear from 19:47-48.

---

[21]This is not only true in Matthew (21:12-17,23-27), Mark (11:15-17,27-33), and Luke (19:45-46; 20:1-8), but also in John (2:13-22).

20:2   By what authority.   This is emphatic. The source of Jesus' authority is already known to Luke's readers. He manifested such authority (see comments on 4:32) because he is the Son of the Most High (1:32,35), the Christ (2:11,26), the Holy One of God (4:34), the Son of Man (5:24), the Son of David (18:38-39), and Israel's King (19:12,15,38).

These things.   Because of its proximity, the temple cleansing is clearly one of "these things," but the plural (*tauta*) includes more. No doubt for Luke's readers and for these religious leaders this included such things as Jesus' authority to forgive sins (5:24; 7:49), to heal on the Sabbath (6:6-11; 13:10-17), and to demand total allegiance (9:23-24,57-62; 14:26).

Who gave you this authority?   The same question is now worded more pointedly. Together with the previous question, this becomes an example of synonymous parallelism.

20:3   I will also ask you a question.   Jesus answered the hostile question with a counterquestion. See comments on 5:23.

20:4   John's baptism.   This reference to John's baptism includes not just his act of baptizing but his whole ministry and message.

From heaven.   "From heaven" is a circumlocution for *from God.* Compare 15:18,21; John 3:27; Dan 4:26.

From men.   This asks if John's ministry had simply a human point of origin, i.e., if it was not from "heaven." Compare Acts 5:38-39.

20:5   They discussed it among themselves.   This is better translated as an ingressive aorist, "They began to discuss this." The discussion is best understood as a whispering among themselves rather than an unspoken reflection within each of them. Compare Luke 20:14.

If we say, "From heaven."   The opponents recognized the first horn of the dilemma. If they answered affirmatively, they faced the charge that they did not believe in John, i.e., did not repent and submit to his baptism. Compare 7:28-30.

20:6   But if we say, "From men."   The second horn of the dilemma is not discussed. This opened them up to the hostility of "all" the people (note the hyperbole) because the people acknowledged John as a true prophet. The reader, of course, knows that John's authority was "from heaven" (1:76; 7:26,28-30).

Will stone us.   This threat of being stoned is unique to Luke. This probably should not be interpreted as an example of hyperbole, for the volatility of the people made something like this quite possible.[22] Another possible interpretation is that by claiming John the Baptist was not a true prophet, the Jewish leadership would have been liable to the penalty for false prophesy—"stoning" (Deut 13:1-11). On the other hand the implication might be that by claiming John the Baptist was not a true prophet, the Jewish leadership would be guilty of false witness and liable to that punishment the falsely accused would have received—in this case stoning as a false prophet. The latter two suggestions probably would have been too subtle for Luke's readers.

20:7   To avoid the dilemma, Jesus' opponents claimed ignorance. Even if their claim of ignorance was sincere, this would indicate that they, the religious leadership of Israel, were incompetent to decide such a basic religious issue as

[22]Cf. Acts 5:26; 7:54-60; 14:19; John 10:31-33.

whether a man was truly a prophet. Yet it was not ignorance but insincerity and hypocrisy that shaped their answer.

20:8   Neither will I tell you. Discussion with such biased and hostile people was worthless, so Jesus ended the conversation (cf. Luke 22:67-68). Compare Prov 9:7-8a.

The Lukan Message

Luke sought to remind his readers once again of the hostility of official Judaism toward Jesus. This leadership group of chief priests, teachers of the law, and elders has already been encountered in the first passion prediction in Luke 9:22 and in 19:47, where a synonymous term is used. As a result Luke's readers knew that this group was ultimately responsible for Jesus' death. They represented official Judaism, for they represented Jerusalem (cf. 13:33-34; 19:14). This reference also prepares the reader for their complicity in the trial (cf. 22:67-68; 23:10). Nevertheless the reader also knows that they were but instruments in God's sovereign plan. See Introduction 8 (1). It is clear, however, that the people (19:48b; 20:1, 6) opposed official Judaism. Luke wanted his readers to know that with regard to the general populace, "everyone praised him [Jesus]" (see comments on 4:15; cf. 20:6).

The present passage also teaches an important Christological truth. The importance of John the Baptist as a prophet and forerunner of the Messiah is evident in the opening chapters of Luke. Unlike the Fourth Gospel (cf. John 1:8,19-34, esp. v. 20), Luke did not minimize the importance of this great prophet (see comments on 7:28). Yet if John was a prophet with divine authority, how much more authority must Jesus have had (Luke 20:2) in that he was greater than John (3:16). As a result his teachings (20:1) are to be obeyed and kept no matter how difficult they may seem.

4. The Parable of the Wicked Tenants (20:9-19)

[9]He went on to tell the people this parable: "A man planted a vineyard, rented it to some farmers and went away for a long time. [10]At harvest time he sent a servant to the tenants so they would give him some of the fruit of the vineyard. But the tenants beat him and sent him away empty-handed. [11]He sent another servant, but that one also they beat and treated shamefully and sent away empty-handed. [12]He sent still a third, and they wounded him and threw him out.

[13]"Then the owner of the vineyard said, 'What shall I do? I will send my son, whom I love; perhaps they will respect him.'

[14]"But when the tenants saw him, they talked the matter over. 'This is the heir,' they said. 'Let's kill him, and the inheritance will be ours.' [15]So they threw him out of the vineyard and killed him.

"What then will the owner of the vineyard do to them? [16]He will come and kill those tenants and give the vineyard to others."

When the people heard this, they said, "May this never be!"
[17]Jesus looked directly at them and asked, "Then what is the meaning of that which is written:
" 'The stone the builders rejected
    has become the capstone'?
[18]Everyone who falls on that stone will be broken to pieces, but he on whom it falls will be crushed."
[19]The teachers of the law and the chief priests looked for a way to arrest him immediately, because they knew he had spoken this parable against them. But they were afraid of the people.

Context

The parable of the wicked tenants appears to have been addressed to the same audience ("the people," 19:9) as mentioned in 20:1. However, although spoken to the people in the temple, Luke clearly understood the parable as directed against Jesus' opponents, who were described as "teachers of the law and chief priests."[23]

The parable, which is found in all three Synoptic Gospels, contains several allegorical allusions to the fate of Jesus and Israel in God's salvific plan of history. A man planted a vineyard and leased it to tenants. The vineyard functioned as a symbol for Israel's privileged status as God's people (see comments on 20:9). The servants sent to obtain fruit from the tenants, i.e., Israel and in particular the rulers, represented the prophets whose treatment had already been described.[24] Yet the owner had one more hope for obtaining fruit from his vineyard, and so he sent his "beloved son." The evil tenants, however, took him outside the vineyard (the crucifixion took place outside the city of Jerusalem) and killed him, as had been foretold (cf. 9:22). Jesus asked rhetorically what the owner would do and then answered the question. Judgment would come upon the tenants (A.D. 70), and the vineyard would be given to others. These "others," for Luke's readers, would be understood as Gentiles (cf. Acts 13:45-47; 18:6; 28:25-28).

The parable concludes with a quotation from Ps 118:22 in which Jesus declared that he is God's foundation stone. God will establish his kingdom on him, and he will be the focal point of judgment. This is followed with a comment that the teachers of the law and chief priests sought to arrest Jesus because they knew the tenants in the parable represented them (cf. 19:47-48). They were kept, however, from carrying out their desire at the present time because of the people, who were supportive of Jesus (19:48; 20:6,16b). By means of the parable and concluding statement, Luke continued to prepare his readers for the crucifixion.

---

[23]Luke 20:19; cf. 19:47; 20:1; cf. also Matt 21:45 and Mark 11:27; 12:1,12.
[24]Luke 4:24; 6:23; 11:47-51; 13:33-34; cf. Acts 7:52.

The authenticity of this parable is frequently denied. The primary reasons are the clear presence of allegory in the parable; the precision of the future actions portrayed in the parable (Jesus' being put to death outside of Jerusalem; the success of the Gentile mission; and the destruction of Jerusalem in A.D. 70); the use of an OT quotation in the parable; and the presence of a more simplified form of this parable in GT 65-66. Yet the charge that Jesus could only have spoken "allegory-less" parables is now being discredited.[25] It is difficult to understand why, if the early church could have added allegorical details to a parable, Jesus could not have done so. Furthermore it would have been most strange if Jesus had not thought of the possibility of death in light of the martyrdom of John the Baptist and the hostility his ministry evoked. There is no reason this parable could not have come from Jesus. In it he spoke of his rejection by official Israel and his forthcoming death. The early church later interpreted, and expanded somewhat, the parable for the sake of clarification. In favor of the authenticity of the parable is the reference to the death of the son without an explicit reference to the resurrection. It is difficult to imagine that a church-created parable would have excluded a reference to this cardinal tenet of their faith. Examples of the clarification of the parable by Luke or the early church are the murder of the son taking place outside the vineyard (cf. 20:15 and Matt 21:39 with Mark 12:8) and the reference to the stone in Luke 20:18, which is lacking in the other Synoptic Gospels.

Comments

20:9 He went on to tell the people. This ties the parable with the preceding scene (20:1), but the parable is directed primarily to Israel's leaders (cf. 20:19).

A man planted. Literally *a certain man.* See comments on 10:30.

A vineyard. Even though Luke abbreviated the introduction by omitting the reference to a wall, the pit for the winepress, and the watchtower (cf. Mark 12:1; Matt 21:33), the use of "vineyard" as a metaphor for God's people is clear.[26] Here it refers to Israel's privileged position of being the covenant people and heirs of God's kingdom (cf. Matt 21:43).

Rented it to some farmers. The term farmers (*geōrgois*) can refer to farmers or vinedressers. The latter is more likely here due to the reference to a vineyard in Luke 20:10,13,15-16.

Went away for a long time. It has been suggested that this is an allusion to the delay of the parousia. See Introduction 7 (3). Yet since it is the "man," i.e., God, who went away for a long time and not the son, and since this took place in part during the OT period (the servants are the OT prophets), it is unlikely that

---

[25] See K. Snodgrass, *The Parable of the Wicked Tenants,* WUNT (Tübingen: Mohr, 1983), 12-26; C. L. Blomberg, "Interpreting the Parables of Jesus: Where Are We and Where Do We Go from Here?" *CBQ* 53 (1991): 50-78.

[26] Cf. Isa 5:1-7; 27:2; Jer 2:21; Ezek 19:10-14; Hos 10:1-4; Ps 80:8-13.

Luke was alluding here to the delay of the parousia. Likewise the judgment that was forthcoming was not the judgment the Son of Man brings at the parousia (cf. 17:22-37; 21:25-28) but the judgment of A.D. 70 and the gospel's being given to the Gentiles (20:16). Thus the "delay" appears to refer to God's long-suffering toward his people and the judgment that the rejection of his Son would bring upon disobedient Israel. Nevertheless the reference to "a long time" after which God brings judgment is unique to Luke. While this verse is not a direct reference to the parousia, God's patience in delaying judgment upon his people might have resulted in some of Luke's readers' thinking, *That's kind of like God's long delay in sending the Son of Man.*

20:10   At harvest time he sent a servant.   The servant represents the OT prophets. Three servants were sent. Luke may have chosen "three" to parallel the "three" in 19:16-23. The suggestion that the servant was beaten because he refused to go away without receiving what was owed his master loses sight of the fact that this is parable. The tenants beat the servant because the storyteller wanted them to do so. If there was a "reason" for a beating, it lies in the reality that the speaker wanted symbolized by this action. A more legitimate question would be, Does the beating symbolize Israel's abuse of the OT prophets? Almost certainly it does.

20:11   Beat and treated shamefully.   The abuse of the second servant is increased. The question about whether the second sending took place during the same year is again beside the point because of the parabolic nature of the material. If this were important for the message of the story, the storyteller would have mentioned it.

20:12   The third servant was abused even more. He suffered wounds. There is a clear crescendo of abuse heaped upon the servants that would reach its climax in the murder of the son.

20:13   What shall I do?   For similar soliloquies within a parable, cf. 12:17; 15:17-19; 16:3.

I will send my son, whom I love.   Because of 3:22; 9:35 the reader clearly understands this as a reference to Jesus. Luke furthermore had just spoken of the son's coming in 19:28-40. Compare the wording of the RSV, "my beloved son."

Perhaps they will respect him.   This is God's last and most gracious attempt to win over his people. The adverb "perhaps" (*isōs*) occurs only here in the NT. By this addition to the parable (cf. Mark 12:6; Matt 21:37), Luke may have been seeking to safeguard God's sovereign rule over history and his ultimate control of the events surrounding Jesus' passion.[27]

20:14   This is the heir.   Jesus in his parable gave the tenants the knowledge that this was the owner's son.

Let's kill him.   Compare 19:47; 20:19.

And the inheritance will be ours.   Exactly how the son's death would have resulted in the vineyard becoming the tenants' property is uncertain. In the parable this is not explained, but in the situation of first-century Galilee with absentee landlords, the death of the heir in the parable could have been understood as resulting in such a situation.[28]

---

[27] So C. E. Carlston, The *Parables of the Triple Tradition* (Philadelphia: Fortress, 1975), 79.

[28] See Snodgrass, *Parable of the Wicked Tenants*, 31-34.

20:15   So they threw him out of the vineyard and killed him.   Luke and
Matthew (21:39) reversed Mark's order (12:8) in order to correspond more precisely with the historical circumstances (cf. Heb 13:12-13; John 19:17). Although
this part of the parable requires that the vineyard refer to both Israel and Jerusalem, this is understandable, for Jerusalem represents Israel.
What then will the owner [literally *Lord*] . . . do to them.   This is best understood not as part of the parable itself, which ends in Luke 20:15a, but as the interpretation of the parable.
20:16   He will come and kill those tenants.   This judgment occurs within
history, for it is associated with the giving of the vineyard to others. Luke wanted
his readers to understand that this was fulfilled in Jerusalem's destruction in A.D.
70 (cf. 13:35; 19:43-44; 21:20-24; 23:29-31).
And give the vineyard to others.   Compare Acts 13:45-47; 18:6; 28:25-28.
Here the vineyard refers to God's kingdom, which would be offered to the Gentiles, whose time had now come (21:24). Matthew 21:43 elaborates on this,
"Therefore I tell you that the kingdom of God will be taken away from you and
given to a people who will produce its fruits."
When the people heard this, they said.   The people by their response stood
in sharp contrast to their leaders (cf. Luke 19:47-48; 20:6,19). They expressed
horror at the whole course of events in the parable, and their hearts furthermore
were favorably disposed to the preaching of Jesus (20:1).
May this never be!   This strong negative (*mē genoito*) occurs only here in the
Gospels but thirteen times in Paul's writings.
20:17   Then what is the meaning of that which is written?   The perfect
participle "written" (*gegrammenon*) is frequent in Luke-Acts.[29] For the sense of
the tense see comments on 2:23.
The stone the builders rejected has become the capstone?   The capstone
refers to the head cornerstone that bore the weight and stress of the two walls built
upon it. Its function and importance was like that of a capstone in a cathedral
without which the vaulted ceiling would collapse. Without the cornerstone the two
walls built upon it would collapse. Jesus, rejected by official Israel, is the key,
foundational element in God's building, the church. This verse found in all three
parallel accounts (and also immediately following the parable in GT 65-66) comes
from Ps 118:22 and was an important OT text in the early church.[30] For "rejected"
cf. 9:22.
20:18   Everyone who falls . . . broken to pieces.   The quotation from Isa
8:14-15 demonstrates that those who are offended by the gospel and reject the
stone will experience a disastrous judgment. Simeon in Luke 2:34 had already alluded to this. Jesus is the divine divider who separates the wheat from the tares,
the sheep from the goats, the blessed from the damned.
But he on whom it falls will be crushed.   The same thought of 20:18a is repeated, but the image now involves not the Jewish leaders' falling on the stone but
their being crushed by having the stone fall upon them. Compare Isa 8:14; Dan 2:34-
35,44-45 for the source of this imagery. Compare *Midr. Esth* 7.10 on 3:6, which

[29]Luke 18:31; 21:22; 22:37; 24:44; Acts 13:29; 24:14.
[30]It is also found in Acts 4:11; 1 Pet 2:7b. It is also connected with Isa 8:14 in 1 Pet 2:7-8.

quotes Isa 30:14 and follows with the proverb: "If a stone falls on a pot, woe to the pot! If a pot falls on a stone, woe to the pot! In either case, woe to the pot!"

20:19 The teachers of the law and the chief priests looked for a way. Luke revealed the audience to whom the parable was addressed was the same as that in the preceding pericope (Luke 20:1; cf. 19:47-48).

Immediately. "Immediately" is literally *in that hour.* The time for the judgment of the wicked tenants had not yet arrived, but it would arrive shortly (cf. 22:53).

Because they knew he had spoken this parable against them. The meaning of the parable is self-evident.

But they were afraid of the people. Compare 19:48b. The people again are portrayed as supportive of Jesus (cf. 18:43b), as they were of John the Baptist (20:6).

The Lukan Message

The Lukan emphases in this parable are evident from both his editorial work and the content of the parable itself. The theme of stewardship is seen in the parable, for the tenants are clear examples of how persons should not behave toward the things God has "let . . . out" (20:9, RSV) to them. The continuity of God's covenant is also revealed, for the son followed in the path of the prophets before him. Another possible Lukan theological emphasis in the parable is the delay of the parousia, but this allusion is far from certain (see comments on 20:9). Strongly emphasized in the account is Israel's rejection of the prophets sent to them and especially their rejection of God's Son. Israel's rejection of its Messiah, taught throughout the Gospel,[31] will soon climax in 22:66–23:25. The coming judgment about to fall upon Israel has also been taught throughout the Gospel[32] and will climax in the events of A.D. 70 and in the coming mission to the Gentiles when the vineyard will be given to others.[33] Although the "others" mentioned in 20:16 might have been understood in the original setting of the parable as referring to the poor, maimed, lame, and blind, for Luke's readers this would also have been understood as extending to them, i.e., to the Gentiles.

The most significant teaching found in this parable, however, is its Christology. Whereas the OT prophets are described as servants (20:11-13), Jesus is described as God's "beloved son" (20:13, RSV). He is not simply his favorite servant or his most beloved servant. He is sufficiently different from the OT prophets that a qualitative change of category must be used to

---

[31] Luke 4:16-30; 7:31-35; 11:29-32,49-54; 13:34-35; 19:14,39-40,47-48; cf. also Acts 4:1-23; 7:51-60.

[32] Luke 2:34-35; 3:8-9; 13:6-9,35; 19:27,43-44; 21:20-24; cf. also 23:29-31.

[33] Luke 21:24; cf. Acts 13:45-47; 18:6; 28:25-28.

describe him. He is not a servant but the Son. Without reading more out of the parable than is warranted, the question of an "ontological" uniqueness of the Son is raised here. Jesus' unique role as the "Church's One Foundation" (see 20:17; Acts 4:11-12; Eph 2:20; 1 Cor 3:11) is then shown by the quotation of Ps 118:22. Whether the judgmental role of the stone alludes to the role of the Son of Man in judgment[34] is uncertain, but that each individual will be judged on the basis of his or her attitude toward Jesus is clear (Luke 9:26; 12:8-9; Acts 4:12). The Lukan emphasis on this point is evident, for Luke alone added in 20:18 the allusion to Isa 8:14-15; Dan 2:34-35,44-45. The reference to the Son as Heir (20:14) also has Christological significance, for here Jesus is seen as the future Lord of the vineyard. This lordship over the church and creation is more clearly described elsewhere in the NT, but it is found in Luke-Acts as well.[35]

5. A Question about Tribute to Caesar (20:20-26)

[20]Keeping a close watch on him, they sent spies, who pretended to be honest. They hoped to catch Jesus in something he said so that they might hand him over to the power and authority of the governor. [21]So the spies questioned him: "Teacher, we know that you speak and teach what is right, and that you do not show partiality but teach the way of God in accordance with the truth. [22]Is it right for us to pay taxes to Caesar or not?"

[23]He saw through their duplicity and said to them, [24]"Show me a denarius. Whose portrait and inscription are on it?"

[25]"Caesar's," they replied.

He said to them, "Then give to Caesar what is Caesar's, and to God what is God's."

[26]They were unable to trap him in what he had said there in public. And astonished by his answer, they became silent.

Context

The frustrated attempt of Jesus' opponents to seize him (Luke 20:19) is followed by the well-known pronouncement story on paying tribute to Caesar. Luke followed his Markan source (Mark 12:13-17; cf. Matt 22:15-22). Jesus' opponents sought to entrap him in his words (cf. Luke 11:53-54) so that accusations could be brought against him before the Roman governor. A finely worked-out snare was laid. After flattering Jesus about his truthfulness and fidelity toward God, they raised a question that placed Jesus on the horns of a dilemma. The question involves whether one should pay taxes to Caesar. If Jesus said no, they could

---

[34]Luke 9:26; 12:8-9; 21:26-27,36; Acts 10:42; 17:31.

[35]Cf. Phil 2:9-11; Col 1:15-20; Heb 1:2; Luke 20:41-44; Acts 2:33-35; 5:31; 7:55-56.

report to the governor that he was teaching sedition, and Rome would immediately act and arrest him. If, on the other hand, he said yes, then he would lose the favor of the people; for they loathed paying this poll tax to their pagan oppressors. For many this tax was an insult to God, who alone was the true ruler of Israel. Whereas earlier Jesus had placed his opponents in a similar dilemma (cf. 20:3-4), now the situation was reversed. Yet Jesus brilliantly escaped the dilemma by asking about the image found on a denarius. When his opponents replied that it contained Caesar's image, he responded, "Then give to Caesar what is Caesar's and to God what is God's" (20:25). Jesus had gotten the better of them. His wisdom had overcome their plot, and his opponents, who reluctantly had to marvel at his answer, were reduced to silence.

The interpretation of this account is not without its problems. An attempt has been made to reconstruct the original form of the account and portray Jesus as advocating a Zealot-like refusal to pay tribute to Caesar.[36] According to this view, since God is the only King of Israel, Jesus meant that to give God what is God's required abstaining from giving tribute to Caesar, for such tribute belonged only to God, the true Ruler of Israel. The present text of all three Gospel accounts clearly teaches the opposite, however, and there are too many other teachings of Jesus (e.g., Matt 5:5,9,38-41) that refute such a reconstruction. Jesus' fellowship with tax collectors and above all the presence of a tax collector among his disciples further refutes such a view.[37]

Another popular interpretation of this passage sees Jesus' teachings as establishing two separate kingdoms: one civil and one religious (cf. 2 Chr 19:11). Caesar should have been obeyed in the one area and God in the other. The problem with this interpretation is that it places Caesar and God on almost equal levels. From our text it is evident that Jesus saw government, i.e., Caesar, as having a legitimate role in the divine governing of God's creation. Thus tribute was due him (cf. Rom 13:1-7; 1 Pet 2:13-17, which may reflect a knowledge of Jesus' teaching on the subject), but far more important is the fact that one must give God what belongs to him. This was affirmed by Luke, who recorded Peter's words in Acts 5:29 ("We must obey God rather than men!") when a conflict resulted between what government demanded and what God commanded. There are "things" within the life of the believer that fall within the legitimate concerns of government. Ultimately they are a subdivision of the things of God and must be in submission to divine concerns. Yet within the boundaries of the legitimate concerns of the state, the believer is to render to Caesar what is due him. Unfortunately it is not always

---

[36] So S. G. F. Brandon, *Jesus and the Zealots* (New York: Scribner's, 1967).

[37] See O. Cullmann, *Jesus and the Revolutionaries* (New York: Harper, 1970).

clear when the "things of Caesar" encroach upon the "things of God," but when this resulted, what to do was clear for Luke and the early church. And not only the early church but believers throughout history have repeated on such occasions, "We must obey God rather than men." But even as the example of Christian martyrs magnificently witnesses to this conviction, so must the church equally witness its love for God by submitting itself in those areas where the state has a legitimate role.

Comments

20:20 Keeping a close watch on him, they. "They" refers to the teachers of the law and chief priests referred to in 20:19. For "keeping a close watch," cf. 6:7; 14:1; cf. also 11:53-54.

Sent spies, who pretended to be honest. "Honest" is literally *righteous*. Probably the term "honest" (*dikaious*) should be translated "righteous" and understood in the sense of 1:6, "upright [i.e., righteous] in the sight of God, observing all the Lord's commandments and regulations blamelessly." Luke added this reference to their being "spies" and pretending to be "righteous." On the other hand he omitted naming the Pharisees as part of this plot (see comments on 13:31).

They hoped to catch Jesus in something he said. Compare 11:53-54. This and the following clause, not their being "righteous," give the reason for their coming to Jesus.

So that they might hand him over. By this statement, which is not found in either Mark or Matthew, Luke intensified the role of official Judaism in Jesus' death. This statement prepares the reader for 23:2-5 and has been predicted in more general terms in 18:32. From this incident (and other information) the reader knows that the charges against Jesus in 23:2 were false.

Governor. See comments on 3:1.

20:21 So the spies questioned him. The clause is literally *and they asked him.*

Teacher, we know that you speak and teach what is right. Jesus was flattered as orthodox in his teaching. Compare 7:43; 10:28. For "Teacher" see comments on 5:5.

You do not show partiality. The flattery of Jesus continued. Compare Acts 10:34; Gal 2:6. Jesus was no respecter of persons. Yet this very quality for which Jesus' opponents commended him is why Jesus ate with tax collectors and sinners and one of the reasons his opponents sought to kill him.

But teach the way of God in accordance with the truth. This is the third flattering statement. The "way" is a common description of the Christian faith in Luke-Acts.[38]

20:22 Is it right for us to pay taxes? "Us" refers to Jews, like these spies who were "righteous" (20:20) and kept the way of God.

Taxes. Luke used the more correct term for poll tax (*phoros*, 23:2; Rom 13:6) instead of Mark's less accurate *kēnson*. Josephus, *Wars* 1.7.6 (1.154) and

---

[38]Cf. Luke 3:4; Acts 9:2; 19:9,23; 22:4; 24:14,22; cf. also Acts 16:17; 18:25-26; Deut 8:6; 10:12-13; Pss 27:11; 119:15.

2.8.1 (2.118) refers to this tribute, and the latter example reveals how great the
Jewish hatred was toward paying it.

Caesar?   At that time the caesar was Tiberius (Luke 3:1).

20:23   He saw through their duplicity.   Compare 5:22; 6:8; 7:39-40.

20:24   Show me a denarius.   This Roman coin bore the emperor's head on
one side. Jesus may have explicitly asked for a denarius, the official coinage in
which the poll tax was to be paid, because he knew it contained the emperor's image. On the side with the image were the words "Tiberius Caesar, son of the divine
Augustus."

20:25   Then give to Caesar what is Caesar's.   It has been suggested that
since Jesus was arguing that the denarius bore Caesar's inscription, it was therefore "his" money and belonged to him. And since humans bear God's image, they
belong to God. The problem with this reasoning is that Jesus was not saying that
all money bearing Caesar's image belonged to him. Taxes belonged to him, but not
all money. The reasoning behind these words seems to have been: "This coin represents the tribute you are to give. Caesar demands this, and it is a rightful demand. Therefore give the taxes that should be given him." Jesus did not in this
pericope explain why Caesar had this authority and right, as Paul and Peter did in
Rom 13:1-5 and 1 Pet 2:13-14 (cf. Eccl 8:2).[39] The term "give" (*apodote*) is used
here in the sense of "pay," not "give back."

And to God what is God's.   Jesus added another concern, the most important
one. Give to God what belongs to him—faith, love, praise, glory, and obedience.
This command is not a second one parallel to the first, for God and Caesar were
not equals. This command stands above the other, even as the command to love
God stands before and is the ground for loving one's neighbor (10:27).

20:26   They were unable to trap him . . . in public.   For the people's positive attitude toward Jesus in contrast to that of official Judaism, see comments on
4:15.

And astonished by his answer.   Even Jesus' opponents marveled at his wisdom and how he had gotten the better of them. See comments on 4:22. For "astonished" see comments on 2:18.

They became silent.   See comments on 14:6.

The Lukan Message

This account contains a number of Lukan themes and emphases. The
truth of Jesus' teachings is attested to even by his opponents, who confessed that he truly taught God's way (20:21). As a result Luke's readers
can possess certainty about the truthfulness of Jesus' teachings they have
been taught (1:4). The divine wisdom of God's Son, and thus of his having come from God, is also seen by his escaping the two horns of the
dilemma facing him and by the fact that even his enemies as they were
silenced marveled at the wisdom of his answer (20:26). Once again

---

[39] For examples of similar reasoning in Jewish literature, see R. H. Stein, "The Argument
of Romans 13:1-7," *NovT* 31 (1989): 329-30.

Luke's readers see that Jesus of Nazareth is indeed greater than even Solomon, the wisest of men (11:31). The account also continues to describe the hostility building up against Jesus. This is heightened by Luke's editorial work in 20:20, where he spoke of "spies" coming, whose purpose was to turn him over to the Roman governor. The parallel accounts speak only of the attempt to "catch him in his words" (Mark 12:13). This crescendo of plotting hints at a time, of which the reader was already aware, when despite the people (Luke 19:48; 20:19; 22:2) Jesus' opponents would have their way and kill him.

Finally, within the parable Jesus and Luke teach that believers are to be good citizens both of God's kingdom and of the earthly rulers over them. This is a common theme in Luke-Acts.[40] Partially because of such obedience to the state, Theophilus and the other readers need not fear it. See Introduction 7 (4).

6. A Question about the Resurrection (20:27-40)

[27]Some of the Sadducees, who say there is no resurrection, came to Jesus with a question. [28]"Teacher," they said, "Moses wrote for us that if a man's brother dies and leaves a wife but no children, the man must marry the widow and have children for his brother. [29]Now there were seven brothers. The first one married a woman and died childless. [30]The second [31]and then the third married her, and in the same way the seven died, leaving no children. [32]Finally, the woman died too. [33]Now then, at the resurrection whose wife will she be, since the seven were married to her?"

[34]Jesus replied, "The people of this age marry and are given in marriage. [35]But those who are considered worthy of taking part in that age and in the resurrection from the dead will neither marry nor be given in marriage, [36]and they can no longer die; for they are like the angels. They are God's children, since they are children of the resurrection. [37]But in the account of the bush, even Moses showed that the dead rise, for he calls the Lord 'the God of Abraham, and the God of Isaac, and the God of Jacob.' [38]He is not the God of the dead, but of the living, for to him all are alive."

[39]Some of the teachers of the law responded, "Well said, teacher!" [40]And no one dared to ask him any more questions.

Context

Luke now reports a second and final attempt to confound Jesus in argument. This time the Sadducees, who are only mentioned here in the Gospel, raise a far-fetched example, in order to refute the belief in the resurrection held by both Jesus (14:14) and the Pharisees (Acts 23:8) but

---

[40]Cf. Luke 2:52; 5:14; 17:14; 23:14-15,22,40-41,47; Acts 23:29; 25:11; 26:32.

which they deny. Quoting Moses' command that a man should marry his brother's widow if no heir has been left (Deut 25:5) in order to provide an heir (Gen 38:8), they then describe the following conundrum: "There were seven brothers. The first married and died without leaving an heir. The second, following the levirate regulations, married this brother's wife and died without leaving an heir. The remaining brothers all fulfilled their levirate responsibility, but none left an heir. At the time of the resurrection, whose wife will she be?" The example has been carefully worked out, for since no brother left an heir, none has any real advantage over the other. The Sadducees knew that neither Jesus nor the Pharisees would have answered "All seven equally," so they felt confident that the whole doctrine of the resurrection had to be rejected as illogical.

Once again, however, Jesus in this pronouncement story refutes his opponents. He does so by refuting their premise that the situation and conditions governing this present age (Luke 20:34) will continue into and govern "that age" (20:35), i.e., the age to come. Since there is no longer death in the age to come, the need to procreate through marriage will have ceased (cf. Gen 1:28). Thus marriage as we know it will cease to exist. Having refuted the Sadducean attack on the resurrection, Jesus argues in favor of the resurrection based on the Pentateuch, which alone is the supreme authority for the Sadducees. He refers to Exod 3:6, where the Lord, i.e., YHWH, refers to himself as the God of Abraham, Isaac, and Jacob. If long after their death God still remains the God of Abraham, Isaac, and Jacob, then they must still be alive, for dead people cannot have a God. Only living people can. Jesus' refutation of the Sadducees is so masterful that even a group of Jesus' opponents commend his defense of the resurrection. The account ends with Jesus' complete mastery of his opponents (Luke 20:40).

Two important questions are raised by this passage. One involves the argument in 20:37-38. In what sense are Abraham, Isaac, and Jacob alive? Did Jesus (and Luke) mean that their "souls" were with God, i.e., they were immortal? Or did he mean that although they were not presently alive they would be on the day of resurrection and that because of God's covenant with the patriarchs a resurrection was necessary? The Sadducean attack on the resurrection was an attack on life after death in general, for they denied not only the resurrection but life after death as well. For both Jesus and Luke the resurrection of the dead was clearly a future event (14:14; Acts 23:6; 24:15,21). Nevertheless in some way they believed that the patriarchs were alive at the present time. Jesus and Luke believed both in a conscious life immediately after death (cf. 16:19-31; 23:39-43) as well as a final day of resurrection. Their thinking may have been very much like that of Paul in 2 Cor 5:1-5; Phil 1:21-23. Since Abraham, Isaac, and Jacob were alive now, the Sadducean disbelief in

life after death is refuted; and since the present bodiless existence of the
patriarchs was incomplete, it must find its fulfillment in a resurrection.[41]

The second question involves the practical concern of happily married
believers who do not want the God-given union with their mates simply to
end in death. Granted that marriage is "until death do us part," will the
intimacy, love, fellowship, and partnership between married Christians
end at death? The NT does not give a complete answer to this question. It
assumes that the need for love, fellowship, and whatever is necessary for
joy and blessedness will be provided in the age to come. The believer in
that age will lack nothing. Some things, however, will end. Like faith and
hope, some "lesser" things will come to an end in order that the "greater"
blessings of the kingdom may be even more intensified. So too will the
sexual experience as we now know it (cf. Gen 1:28). Yet the believer, in
faith, believes that if anything good in this age is not carried over in the
age to come, it is because it will be replaced by something far, far better.

Comments

20:27 Some of the Sadducees. Although this group is only mentioned here
in Luke, cf. Acts 4:1; 5:17; 23:6-8. The Sadducees originated as a priestly sect
claiming descent from Zadok, the high priest under David (1 Kgs 1:26). In Jesus'
day they were no longer exclusively priestly but were a party or circle of priestly
and lay aristocrats, hellenistic in orientation, who catered to the well-to-do. They
were bitter opponents of the Pharisees, who were a lay party with whom most
Jews were sympathetic. This hostility went back to the second century before
Christ (see Josephus, *Antiquities* 13.5.9 [13.171-73]; 13.10.6 [13.293-98]). After
Jerusalem's destruction in A.D. 70, the Sadducees disappeared from the scene.

Who say there is no resurrection. The Sadducees differed from the Pharisees doctrinally in that they denied the resurrection of the dead or life after death,
the existence of angels or demons, the validity of the oral traditions and in practice all the OT except the Pentateuch, and divine providence (Acts 23:6-8).[42]

20:28 Teacher. See comments on 5:5.

Moses wrote. Compare Deut 25:5.

And have children for his brother. Compare Gen 38:8. This levirate regulation is witnessed to in Ruth 4:1-12; cf. also Josephus, *Antiquities* 4.8.23 (4.254-
56); Tob 6:9-12; 7:12-15. (*Levirate* comes from the Latin *levir*, which means *husband's brother.*) Such a marriage would not conflict with the prohibitions of Lev
18:16 and 20:21, for in these references a brother has a sexual relationship with
his living brother's wife.

---

[41] See, however, E. E. Ellis, *The Gospel of Luke*, NCB (Grand Rapids: Eerdmans, 1981),
235, for the view that this passage assumes the "soul-sleep" of Abraham, Isaac, and Jacob
until the day of resurrection.

[42] Cf. Luke 4:2; Josephus, *Antiquities* 13.5.9 [13.173]; 18.1.4 [18.16]; *Wars* 2.8.14
[2.165]). By this statement Luke prepared his readers for the following narrative.

20:29 Now there were seven brothers. No special significance is to be seen in the number. "Seven" was simply a favorite number.[43]

20:30 The second and third brothers are mentioned, but for economy sake the expression "and died childless" is omitted.

20:31 In the same way the seven died, leaving no children. The hypothetical situation is well-crafted. It is, of course, true that if anyone had left a child, the levirate regulation would have come to an end at that point. But even the seventh brother did not leave a child, so that none of the seven have an advantage in claiming to be the husband.

20:33 Now then, at the resurrection whose wife will she be? The question is stated.

Since the seven were married to her? The Sadducees reminded Jesus of the basic problem. In their thinking this multiple husband-wife relationship made the idea of a resurrection preposterous.

20:34 The people of this age. Compare Luke 16:8b. This expression means *human beings in their present earthly life.* Jesus at the very beginning pointed out the flaw in the Sadducean thinking. They were equating behavior in "this age" with behavior in "that age."

Marry and are given in marriage. A few manuscripts headed by Codex Beza (D) read "beget and are begotten." The majority reading found in the NIV is clearly preferred.

20:35 But those who are considered worthy. "Those who are considered worthy" is a divine passive for *those God considers worthy.* Compare 4 Macc 18:3; 2 Thess 1:5. Luke expected his readers to understand that "those considered worthy" are those who through repentance and faith have entered God's kingdom, i.e., those who are saved (cf. Luke 18:25-26). Luke was not a universalist with respect to salvation.

In that age. In 18:30 "that age" is referred to as "the age to come." This is the time of the consummation when the "kingdom comes" (11:2).

And in the resurrection from the dead. Compare Acts 4:2; 1 Pet 1:3. This does not describe a second level of attainment, after first gaining entrance into the age to come, but another description of sharing in "that age," i.e., *in that age in which the dead are raised.*

Will neither marry nor be given in marriage. Marriage is not an eternal fixture in God's creative purpose. It came into being at a point in time, and it will cease when time as we know it ceases to be. The need of marriage to fill the earth (Gen 1:28) will be past and the need for procreation ended. The need for companionship, which marriage was meant to fill (Gen 2:18-25), will no longer be needed, for that need will be met by God himself and the family of believers.

20:36 And they can no longer die. The reason is now given why marriage as an institution is ended in the age to come.

For they are like the angels. This may explain either why there is no marriage (Luke 20:35) or why believers can no longer die (20:36a) in "that age." If it describes the former, then the asexual nature of angels is being cited. If, and this is more likely, it explains why they can no longer die, then the immortality of the

---

[43]Cf. Luke 2:36; 8:2; 11:26; 17:4; Acts 6:3; 13:19; 19:14; Tob 6:13; and above all Revelation, where the number appears thirty-four times.

angels is being cited. Compare 2 Bar 51:10-16; Enoch 104:4-6. Since the Sadducees did not believe in the existence of angels, there is present in this saying a rebuke of their unbelief in this matter.

They are God's children. Compare Luke 6:35, where the future tense ("your reward will be great, and you will be sons of the Most High") refers to this blessedness of the believer in the consummated kingdom. In this state death is no more (Rev 21:4), and the believers' sonship is completed by the resurrection, just as Jesus' sonship was (Acts 13:33; cf. Rom 1:4; Acts 2:32-36).

Since they are children of the resurrection. This clause is a causal participle (literally *being children*) that indicates why the full sonship of the believer has been realized. It is because the resurrection (the general resurrection, not Jesus' resurrection) has now taken place, and the mortal has been clothed with immortality (1 Cor 15:53-54).

20:37 But in the account of the bush. Since the OT was not versified or even divided into chapters at this time, Jesus referred in this manner (literally *at the bush*) to the place in Exodus he cited (cf. Rom 11:2). The clearest OT references to the resurrection are found in Job 19:26; Ps 16:9-11; Isa 26:19; and Dan 12:2. Because his opponents believed that the Pentateuch alone was the supreme authority, Jesus limited himself to this portion of the OT and used Exod 3:6 as his proof text for the resurrection.

That the dead rise. Literally a divine passive: *that the dead are raised by God.* See comments on 6:21.

For he calls. The present tense indicates that Moses still speaks, i.e., that as Scripture what Moses "said" continues to speak. For a similar use of the perfect tense, see comments on 2:23.

The God of Abraham, and the God of Isaac, and the God of Jacob. Even after their death, God still identifies himself as "being," not "having been," their God.[44]

20:38 He is not the God of the dead, but of the living. "God" is emphatic, so the sentence may be translated better, "God is not [a God] of the dead but of the living!" Jesus drew the conclusion from Luke 20:37 and completed his argument: "Only living people can have a God."[45]

For to him all are alive. Compare Acts 17:28; 4 Macc 7:19; 16:25. The thought in this statement, which is unique to Luke, appears to be that all the patriarchs (and those considered worthy of the resurrection, Luke 20:35) live because of their association with the God of life. For a similar argument, cf. *Sanh.* 90b. It is incorrect to interpret this as referring to a future resurrection from their present state of sleep or as a reference to being "in Christ" in the Pauline sense.[46]

20:39 Some of the teachers of the law responded. Compare Acts 23:6-10, where despite the common animosity toward Paul, the centuries-old animosity between the Pharisees and Sadducees arises over their differences concerning the resurrection. Since the teachers of the law tended to be Pharisaic in orientation, we may have another example of this here.

---

[44] Cf. Matt 22:32, where the Evangelist added the "I am" found in the LXX translation of Exod 3:6.

[45] Marshall, *Luke*, 743.

[46] See Fitzmyer, *Luke* 2:1307.

20:40   Luke omitted the next account in Mark 12:28-34 and Matt 22:34-40 concerning the great commandment since he included a similar passage in Luke 10:25-28. However, he used Mark's concluding sentence in 12:34 here because it serves as a good conclusion to Luke 20:27-39 and reinforces what has been said in 13:17; 19:48; 20:19,26.

The Lukan Message

As in the previous pericope Luke sought to demonstrate Jesus' surpassing wisdom and knowledge. Even as his opponents marveled at his wisdom and were driven to silence in the previous account (20:26; cf. also 13:17), so here they were forced to commend him and recognize that further attempts to catch him in his words would be useless (20:39-40). Jesus, God's Son, has a wisdom too great for them, for his wisdom is greater than that of the wisest of all men, King Solomon (cf. 11:31).

Another Lukan emphasis becomes evident when one compares his account with that of Mark and Matthew. Luke's editorial work is most clearly seen in 20:35a,36b,39. In 20:35a he pointed out that not all people will participate in the blessedness of the resurrection. On the contrary, only those "considered worthy" will experience the resurrection of that age. Luke did not define here what it means to be "considered worthy," but in 14:14 and Acts 24:15 he referred to the resurrection of the righteous; and in Luke 18:14 it was the humble and repentant tax collector who was justified, i.e., declared righteous. Luke did not think it necessary to describe how one is "considered worthy" because he assumed his readers would apply at this point the other teachings in this work that describe what is needed to enter God's kingdom. It is the humble, who repent and believe the good news, whom God pronounces righteous (18:14). Thus with respect to "that age," the last enter and share in the resurrection of the just, whereas the first experience the resurrection of the wicked (Acts 24:15; cf. Rev 20:11-15).

7. A Question about the Son of David (20:41-44)

[41]Then Jesus said to them, "How is it that they say the Christ is the Son of David? [42]David himself declares in the Book of Psalms:
   " 'The Lord said to my Lord:
   "Sit at my right hand
[43]until I make your enemies
   a footstool for your feet." '
[44]David calls him 'Lord.' How then can he be his son?"

Context

After two accounts in which Jesus was asked hostile questions (three in Mark and Matthew), Jesus now asked his opponents (literally *them*) a question concerning the Messiah's character.[47] Jesus raised a rhetorical question concerning the general view that the Messiah would be David's son, i.e., a descendant of David. This question (Luke 20:41) is then followed by a second question that focuses on a puzzling element in the first question. How, if the Messiah was David's son, did David (in Ps 110:1) call him his "Lord" by saying "the Lord [YHWH] said to my [David's] Lord [the Messiah] 'Sit at my right hand'" (Luke 20:42-43)? Since David referred to the Messiah as his Lord, how could he simply have been his son?

Some scholars have suggested that this passage must be interpreted as a rejection of the Messiah's Davidic origins. But Luke, and the other Gospel writers, did not understand it this way, as is clear from texts that refer to Jesus as the Messiah or Christ.[48] It is unlikely that Jesus or the early church sought to reject this established and accepted belief of Judaism. Rather for Luke and the other Evangelists, this incident taught that the Messiah was indeed the Son of David, but he was more. He was greater than David (cf. 11:31-32). He was David's Lord.

Comments

20:41 How is it that they say the Christ is the Son of David? The reason for this is obvious. The people ("they") assumed this on the basis of the OT teachings.[49]

20:42 David himself declares in the Book of Psalms. It is unclear why Luke, who emphasized the Spirit's role, changed Mark's "speaking by the Holy Spirit" (Mark 12:36; cf. Acts 1:16; 4:25). David was the second king of Israel, and his descendants ruled Judah until the fall of Jerusalem in 587 B.C. Some seventy-three psalms are attributed to him. See comments on 20:37 with respect to the present tense of "declares." Whether Ps 110 was considered a messianic psalm in Jesus' day is uncertain, but it was considered such by Luke and the early church.

The Lord said to my Lord. The quotation follows the LXX.[50] Since David was presumed to be the author of this psalm, the hearers of Jesus and the Gospel accounts would have understood this quotation as follows: "The Lord [YHWH] said to my [David's] Lord [the Messiah]." Thus the Messiah must be greater than David, Israel's greatest king.

Sit at my right hand. The "right hand" is the place of honor where the Lord shares YHWH's rule. Compare Mark 10:35-45.

---

[47]The form of this account is difficult to classify, but it probably is best described as a pronouncement story.

[48]Luke 1:27,32-33; 2:4,11; 3:23-38; 18:38-39; Acts 13:34.

[49]Cf. 2 Sam 7:8-16; Ps 89:20-37; Isa 9:6-7; 11:1-16; Jer 23:5-6; 30:8-9; 33:14-18; Ezek 34:23-24; 37:24; Mic 5:2.

[50]In the Masoretic text the Hebrew lacks the pun since the two terms for "Lord" are *YHWH* and *Adonai*, but in the reading of the Hebrew text the pun would have been present for *Adonai* and would have been substituted for *YHWH* in order to avoid pronouncing the sacred name. In Aramaic the pun could also be present, "The *Mar* (Lord) said to my *Mar* (Lord)."

20:43   Until I make your enemies a footstool for your feet.   Ancient reliefs portray this scene.[51]

20:44   David calls him "Lord."   David's future offspring is seen as possessing greater authority than his "father." Compare Acts 2:34-36.

How then can he be his son?   In the biblical setting a son would frequently address his father as "Lord." The reverse, which is described here, would be most unusual. Yet such is the Messiah's greatness that Israel's greatest king in this psalm calls his son "Lord."

The Lukan Message

The meaning of this pronouncement story for Luke and the other Evangelists involves the surpassing greatness of Jesus, the Christ. As the Christ he is greater than Israel's beloved King David. He is greater than David in two ways. First, he is David's Lord. Second, the Lord (YHWH) has granted him the privilege of sitting at his right hand, giving him the authority to judge the world. The former occurs at Jesus' resurrection and exaltation (Acts 2:32-36; 5:31; 7:56; cf. Phil 2:9-11). The latter will occur when he returns as the Son of Man.[52] This understanding of the incident would have been quite elusive to Jesus' audience, and it would have functioned no doubt like a parable or riddle. For Luke and his readers, however, the Christological teaching about the character of the Messiah, and thus of Jesus, would have been clear and self-evident. They would have interpreted this passage in light of their postresurrection understanding. Jesus is both Messiah and Lord, and God has given to him the prerogative to judge the world. Luke in this passage is telling Theophilus and his other readers that the Jesus in whom they believe is one in whom they can have confidence. He is the Messiah, the one before whom every nation and tongue will one day bow and confess "Jesus Christ is Lord" (Phil 2:11).

8. Warnings concerning the Scribes (20:45-47)

[45]While all the people were listening, Jesus said to his disciples, [46]"Beware of the teachers of the law. They like to walk around in flowing robes and love to be greeted in the marketplaces and have the most important seats in the synagogues and the places of honor at banquets. [47]They devour widows' houses and for a show make lengthy prayers. Such men will be punished most severely."

Context

Luke, following his Markan source (cf. Mark 12:38-40), concluded the preceding "debate" accounts with a warning concerning the teachers of

---

[51]See J. B. Pritchard, *The Ancient Near East in Pictures* (Princeton: University Press, 1954), 2:249.
[52]Luke 12:40-48; 19:27; 21:27,36; Acts 10:42; 17:31.

the law. Jesus warned the disciples of teachers who are ostentatious in their dress, self-aggrandizing in their social behavior, cheaters of the poor, and hypocritical in their religious behavior.

Comments

20:45 Jesus said to his disciples. The last reference to the disciples was in Luke 19:39.

20:46 Beware of the teachers of the law. Although not all the scribes fit the description that follows, enough did so that Jesus could use universal language. His unqualified use of "teachers of the law" makes a more powerful saying than "beware of some teachers of the law." For other examples of Jesus' use of exaggeration and hyperbole, see comments on 11:9. What follows in this verse is a description of how the teachers of the law liked to be seen and treated.

They like to walk around in flowing robes. These *stolai* were no doubt meant to be ostentatious. Compare Matt 23:5.

Love to be greeted ... seats in the synagogues ... places of honor. Compare Luke 11:43; 14:7-8; Matt 23:6-7.

20:47 They devour widows' houses. This statement may refer to the teachers' cheating widows of their houses and estates while serving as the executors of these properties. This is more likely than the view that they were abusing the hospitality of poor widows. Compare Luke 11:39.

And for a show make lengthy prayers. It was less the length of their prayers that Jesus was condemning than the motivation to "look devout." Compare Matt 6:5-6.

The Lukan Message

Luke used the teachers of the law as a negative portrait of what his readers should not be like. (Note that these sayings are addressed to the disciples.) Whether Luke sought to deal with a present problem among his readers (a mirror reading of the passage)[53] or to head off such behavior in the future (a preventative reading of the passage) is uncertain. Luke also explained why judgment had to come upon official Israel and the nation. The teachers of the law represent those who exalted themselves at marriage feasts and presumed to sit in places of honor (Luke 14:7-8) rather than humble themselves (14:10). The threefold reference to this behavior in 11:43; 14:7-8; 20:46 places added emphasis on this. Because of their self-seeking and lack of humility, they would be punished more severely (20:47) and humbled (14:11). They were like the Pharisees mentioned earlier, who loved the best seats in the synagogues and salutations in the marketplaces (11:43; 20:46). But "woe" to them (11:44), for they

---

[53] So Ellis, *Luke*, 238-39: "All of Jesus' judgments upon the religious Judaism of his day were, in the Gospels, not only read *in* the Church but *to* the Church. This is, therefore, a warning to the Church's own leaders who are in danger of falling into the pattern of the Jewish churchmen."

would be punished more severely (20:47). Instead of concern and compassion for the needy, they devoured the houses of poor widows. Such behavior represents the hypocrisy of the religious elite who were concerned only with external appearance and sought to look good in the eyes of others (16:15a). They would be judged (20:47) because God knew their hearts (16:15b). The day was coming when the Son of Man would vindicate their victims (18:2-8). Luke's readers needed to know this was why judgment had come upon official Israel and that they should avoid such behavior.

9. The Widow's Offering (21:1-4)

[1]As he looked up, Jesus saw the rich putting their gifts into the temple treasury. [2]He also saw a poor widow put in two very small copper coins. [3]"I tell you the truth," he said, "this poor widow has put in more than all the others. [4]All these people gave their gifts out of their wealth; but she out of her poverty put in all she had to live on."

Context

Having referred to widows in 20:46, Luke continued with a pronouncement story concerning a widow (cf. also Mark 12:41-44). By eliminating much of the Markan introduction to the account (Mark 12:41a), Luke sharpened the contrast found within the story between the rich and the poor widow. Whereas in Mark 12:41 the contrast is between the poor widow and the crowd, in Luke the contrast is between the rich and the poor. The exact point of the story, however, is not as clear as first appears. Several suggestions have been made: (1) the measure of one's gift does not involve how much one gives but how much remains, i.e., how much one keeps; (2) a gift is measured by the spirit in which it is given; (3) one's giving should be commensurate with one's means; and (4) true giving involves giving all one has.

The question has even been raised about whether or not Jesus was commending the widow for what she had done. Some have suggested that Jesus was not praising but lamenting what the widow had done. According to this interpretation, the widow had been so indoctrinated by the religious leaders that she brought about voluntarily the devouring of a widow's house, which is condemned in Luke 20:46.[54] This interpretation, however, does not explain the present form of the account, for 21:3 is clearly a commendation. The widow's having given more to God than the rich would have been interpreted as a positive action by Luke's readers.[55]

---

[54]So A. G. Wright, "The Widow's Mites: Praise or Lament?—A Matter of Context," *CBQ* 44 (1982): 256-65.

[55]This is clear in light of Luke 5:11,28; 12:33-34; 14:33; 16:9-13,19-31; 18:28.

His readers would have understood the widow as an example of one who was rich toward God (12:21), who was not anxious about this life, but who sought first God's kingdom (12:22-31). She, like Jesus' other followers, was willing to sell everything (12:22) and leave everything (5:11,28) in her love for God. Practical concerns for the widow (What reputable pastor or evangelist would recommend a parishioner to do so?) should not blind us to the point Jesus was making. Nothing is made of the inner spirit of the widow, and the widow's gift was clearly not commensurate with her means since she had nothing left. Thus the main point appears to be that God measures the gifts of his people not on the basis of their size but on the basis of how much remains.

Comments

21:1 The rich. Luke changed the Markan "crowd" (Mark 12:41) to "rich." In so doing he stressed one of the emphases in his Gospel. See Introduction 8 (5).

Into the temple treasury. This probably refers not to the treasure chambers of the temple itself[56] but to the thirteen collection boxes in the temple (*Seqal.* 6:5).

21:2 Two very small copper coins. These coins (*lepta*) were the smallest coins in use.

21:3 I tell you the truth. See comments on 9:27.

This poor widow has put in more than all the others. This does not mean *more than any of the others*. God's way of reckoning is overwhelmingly gracious. Compare Luke 19:17 and 19 and how generous the reward is for faithful service. Ten and five cities are given for faithfulness in the stewardship of ten and five minas. "More" must be understood as *more in God's eyes*, for by human standards the widow put in considerably less (cf. Jas 2:5). It is most difficult to see in Jesus' words anything other than a commendation. This saying envisions the blessedness of the poor spoken of in Luke 6:20.

21:4 All these people gave . . . but she. This is the reason for the statement in 21:3.

The Lukan Message

Luke reaffirmed to his readers what he had said on numerous occasions earlier in his Gospel. The account is an illustration of such teachings on stewardship found in 12:33; 14:33. See Introduction 8 (7). It also shows the great reversal taking place in Jesus' ministry. The poor, such as this widow, are blessed (6:20) and enter the kingdom, whereas the rich are excluded. See Introduction 8 (5). This Lukan emphasis is clearly seen in this contrast being portrayed as involving the rich and a poor widow (21:1), whereas his source portrayed the contrast as involving the crowd and the poor widow (cf. Mark 12:41).

---

[56]Cf. John 8:20; Neh 12:44; 1 Macc 14:49; 2 Macc 3:6,24,28,40; Josephus, *Wars* 5.5.2 (5.200) and 6.5.2 (6.282).

10. The Destruction of the Temple (21:5-6)

⁵Some of his disciples were remarking about how the temple was adorned with beautiful stones and with gifts dedicated to God. But Jesus said, ⁶"As for what you see here, the time will come when not one stone will be left on another; every one of them will be thrown down."

Context

Jesus' teaching in the temple, which began in Luke 19:45, concludes with a long eschatological discourse involving the destruction of the temple-Jerusalem and the end of the world. Although Luke already has presented various teachings of Jesus on this subject (12:35-48; 13:35; 17:20-37; 19:41-44), he, like Mark and Matthew, included these additional teachings on the subject because of their importance.[57] He used this opportunity to clarify several misconceptions concerning the destruction of Jerusalem and the end of the world. As the disciples called attention to the magnificent stones and offerings that adorned the temple, Jesus replied that the day would come when the temple would experience destruction, and that destruction would be so great that not one of these magnificent stones would remain standing upon another. What follows is the third and largest pronouncement of Jerusalem's destruction found in the Gospel (cf. 13:34-35; 19:41-44).

Comments

21:5 Some of his disciples were remarking. Literally *certain [ones] were saying*. Although Luke may have omitted referring to the disciples here and in 21:8 to shorten his account (cf. Mark 13:3; Matt 24:3), more likely he wanted to direct Jesus' words to a larger audience. As a result the NIV translation is misleading at this point.

How the temple was adorned. After Solomon's temple was destroyed by the Babylonians in 587 B.C., those returning from exile under Zerubbabel (Ezra 3–6) and Haggai (Hag 1–2) replaced it with a smaller temple built on the same site. This structure, which was clearly inferior to Solomon's temple (Hag 2:1-3), was completed around 515 B.C. Under Herod the Great the temple experienced massive reconstruction, which began in 20 B.C. (cf. John 2:20) and continued until A.D. 63. This new temple exceeded even Solomon's temple in beauty and size and justifiably could have been included among the seven wonders of the world.[58]

---

[57] Although Luke added additional material to the discourse (cf. 21:12,15,18,20-22,23b-26a,28), his main source appears to have been Mark. Whether his additional material came from another source or sources (L, proto-Luke, some apocalyptic source) is debated. For further discussion see M. D. Goulder, *Luke: A New Paradigm*, JSNT (Sheffield: JSOT, 1989), 701-4, and C. F. Evans, *Saint Luke*, TPI New Testament Commentaries (London: SCM, 1990), 731-33.

[58] For descriptions of the Herodian Temple, see Josephus, *Wars* 1.12.1 (1.40); 5.5.1-6 (5.184-227) and *Antiquities* 15.11.1-7 (15.380-425).

With beautiful stones. Josephus described the size of some of these stones as being forty-five cubits by five cubits by six cubits (*Wars* 5.5.6 [5.224]). Elsewhere, however, he described them as twenty-five cubits by eight cubits by twelve cubits (*Antiquities* 15.11.3 [15.392]). (A "cubit" probably was about eighteen inches.) Regardless of which dimension one chooses as correct and allowing for exaggeration on the part of Josephus, the temple clearly was adorned with "beautiful stones." Josephus (*Wars* 5.5.6 [5.223]) stated that the whiteness of the stones was such that from a distance the temple appeared to be a snow-clad mountain. Some of these stones can still be seen in the lower courses of the Wailing Wall.

With gifts dedicated to God. The ornaments of the temple, such as tapestries, golden and bronze doors, and golden grape clusters were given by people as offerings to the temple.[59]

21:6 As for what you see here. All too often one is enamored with the technical and artistic beauty of an object and is not aware of the spiritual poverty, blindness, and even evil that may underlie it. Jesus saw the latter and not so much the physical beauty of the temple (cf. Luke 13:33-35; 19:41-44), and in his understanding the widow's two very small copper coins were more precious to God than all this.[60]

The time will come. This expression refers to a future event within history (Luke 5:35; 17:22; 23:29; cf. also 19:43), and it is not used in Luke to describe the end of the world, i.e., the coming of the Son of Man (cf. "that day," 10:12; 17:31; 21:34).

Not one stone will be left on another. The saying is an example of Jesus' use of exaggeration, for some stones adorning the temple complex can still be seen.[61] This, however, does not in any way refute Jesus' prophecy or minimize the massive destruction the temple experienced in A.D. 70. Such use of exaggeration only reveals the intensity Jesus felt when he spoke these words. See comments on 11:9.

The Lukan Message

Writing after Jerusalem's destruction, Luke once again reminded his readers that Jesus had predicted all this. Thus this tragic event fits into the divine plan and rule of things (see Introduction 8 [1]) and must be understood as resulting from Israel's sin and rejection of the Messiah (see 20:9-19, "The Lukan Message").

11. Signs before the End (21:7-11)

[7]"**Teacher,**" **they asked,** "**when will these things happen? And what will be the sign that they are about to take place?**"

---

[59]Cf. 2 Macc 3:2-40; 9:16; Tacitus, *History* 5.8.1, who spoke of the enormous richness of the temple; Josephus, *Wars* 5.5.4 (5.210-12), *Antiquities* 15.11.3 (15.395).

[60]Cf. also how Paul was less impressed with the artistic and architectural beauty of Athens in his day than with the ignorance (Acts 17:23), idolatry (17:24,29), and need of repentance this revealed (17:30).

[61]For other predictions of the temple's destruction, cf. Luke 13:33-35; 19:41-44; Mark 14:58; 15:29; John 2:19; Acts 6:14. For a vivid description of the destruction of the temple, see Josephus, *Wars* 5-6.

[8]He replied: "Watch out that you are not deceived. For many will come in my name, claiming, 'I am he,' and, 'The time is near.' Do not follow them. [9]When you hear of wars and revolutions, do not be frightened. These things must happen first, but the end will not come right away." [10]Then he said to them: "Nation will rise against nation, and kingdom against kingdom. [11]There will be great earthquakes, famines and pestilences in various places, and fearful events and great signs from heaven.

Context

After the introductory scene in 21:5-6, the following discourse consists of six sections: 21:7-11,12-19,20-24,25-28,29-33,34-36. The meaning of this account is best understood when we compare it with the parallel in Mark. The question asked Jesus in 21:7 is sharpened by Luke. He was asked when "they [these things]" (not when "all [these things]," Mark 13:4) would take place. As a result of omitting Mark's "all," the question is narrowed down to a single event—the "these things" of Luke 21:6. Thus what follows involves the time when the beautiful stones and gifts adorning the temple would be "thrown down" (21:6). Luke also changed Mark's "about to be fulfilled" (Mark 13:4) to "about to take place" (Luke 21:7) because the Markan term has more apocalyptic connotations associated with it than its Lukan counterpart. Luke also omitted Mark's "these are the beginning of birth pains" (13:8) in Luke 21:11. By all this, Luke made clear to his readers that the "end" spoken of in 21:9 and the sayings in 21:8-24 refer not to signs preceding the world's end but rather to signs preceding Jerusalem's destruction in A.D. 70. In 21:25-36 the theme switches to Jesus' teachings concerning the end of the world. Luke also separated 21:25-36 from the preceding material by his omission of the phrase "but in those days" and "following that distress [or 'tribulation']" in Mark 13:24 and Matt 24:29 (cf. Luke 21:25). In so doing Luke separated the material in 21:25-28, which deals with the end of the world, from 21:5-24, which deals with the fall of Jerusalem.

Comments

21:7 Teacher. This title of address is usually used in Luke by unbelievers (see comments on 5:5). This may indicate Luke understood the teachings that follow as having been addressed to a Jewish audience for whom the warnings of Jerusalem's fall had been particularly applicable.

When will these things happen? The use of the same term "these things" (*tauta*) here as in 21:6 indicates that the question involves what was referred to in the previous verse, i.e., the destruction of the temple.

And what will be the sign that they [literally these things] are about to take place? The sign referred to concerns "these things" of 21:6. Luke also focused the question more clearly to A.D. 70 by changing Mark's "about to be fulfilled" (*synteleisthai*, 13:4) to "about to take place" (*ginesthai*). Contrast Matt 24:3, which seeks to show how Jerusalem's destruction is a type of Jesus' coming at the end of the age. The present clause stands in synonymous parallelism with the preceding one.

21:8 Watch out that you are not deceived. On Jesus' lips and, if Mark were written before A.D. 70 on his as well, this was a warning to the church not to be deceived by false prophets and messianic types who would flourish during the years before Jerusalem's destruction. Josephus (*Wars* 6.5.2-3 [6.285-88]) gave witness to such false prophets at this time.[62]

For many will come in my name. "In my name" can mean (1) *under my authority*, (2) *claiming to be me*, or (3) *claiming the title of messiah*.

Claiming, "I am he." Literally *I am*. This can mean (a) *I am the Messiah* or (b) *I am Jesus, risen from the dead*. Since the Jewish false prophets associated with Jerusalem's fall made no claim to be associated with or to be Jesus, for Luke the meaning of these phrases probably is (3) *they claim to be the messiah, [falsely] saying* (a) *I am the Messiah*.[63]

And "The time is near." In Luke's setting this looks back to the coming of false prophets before Jerusalem's destruction who proclaimed the world's end. Luke may have intended, however, for his readers to understand that those in their own day proclaiming "the time is near" were also false prophets. Compare Luke 7:22; Rev 1:3; 22:10.

Do not follow them. Why Luke replaced the parallel statements in Mark 13:6 and Matt 24:5 ("and will deceive many") with an imperative is unclear. This is especially puzzling, if, as maintained, the present description refers to what happened at the fall of Jerusalem, which is now past. A similar command is found in Luke 17:23. Perhaps Luke made this into a command because he expected his readers to understand that just as there was a rash of such false prophets before A.D. 70, so false prophets would be a continual problem for the church (cf. Acts 20:29-31). Jesus' two commands found in Luke 21:8-9, even though directed to a particular time and audience (the believers before A.D. 70), thus function as commands for Luke's present audience, even as the particular form of OT piety exhibited by Elizabeth and Zechariah (1:6,59), the baptism of John (3:3,16), and even certain teachings of Jesus (5:14; 17:14) directed to a particular time and audience are to be applied by his readers to their own situations.

21:9 When you hear of wars and revolutions. The revolutions referred to probably refer to the Jewish revolt in A.D. 68–70 because of the reference to "these things" in the latter part of this verse. War is a standard image in eschatological/apocalyptic imagery.[64] It has also been suggested that this may allude to the tumultuous period between the reigns of Nero and Vespasian (ca. A.D. 68–69).

Do not be frightened. Although directed by Jesus and Mark to believers before the destruction of Jerusalem, Luke saw this injunction as also applicable for his readers.

---

[62] Cf. also Acts 5:36-37; 21:38; Josephus, *Antiquities* 18.4.1. [18.85-87]; 20.5.1 [20.97-99]; 20.8.6. [20.169-72] for accounts of earlier false prophets in the first century; cf. also 2 Pet 2:1-3; 1 John 2:18; 4:1; 2 John 7; *Did.* 11:4-12; 16:3; Shepherd of Hermas 11:1-21.

[63] See Marshall, *Luke*, 763, for a discussion of issues involved in the interpretation of these last two phrases.

[64] Cf. Isa 19:2; Dan 11:25,44; Rev 6:3-4,8; 9:9; 12:7; 2 Esdr 13:31.

These things must happen first. Luke's readers could take heart at such a time, for God's sovereign rule requires this.[65] The reference to "these things" refers back to the destruction of Jerusalem in 21:7-8.

But the end will not come right away. In this section the "end" refers to the destruction of Jerusalem just mentioned and repudiates the claim of the false prophets in 21:8 that "the time is near." Other things must take place before this occurs. These other things are described in 21:10-18.

21:10 This verse repeats the thought of 21:9a. The imagery may come from 2 Chr 15:6 and Isa 19:2.

Kingdom against kingdom. Compare 2 Esdr 13:31.

21:11 There will be great earthquakes. Compare Ezek 38:19.[66] It is unlikely that Luke was thinking here of the events associated with the catastrophic eruption of Vesuvius in A.D. 79.

Famines and pestilences in various places. Compare Acts 11:28.

And fearful events and great signs from heaven. Reference to such signs is frequently made in eschatological/apocalyptic literature.[67] Such descriptions may be used to describe historical events in the future such as the destruction of Babylon (Isa), the destruction of Pharaoh's army (Ezek), the coming of the Spirit at Pentecost (Joel), and the destruction of the Northern Kingdom of Israel (Amos). Thus the description of "these things" given in these verses is best understood as referring to the destruction of Jerusalem. According to Josephus (*Wars* 6.5.3-4 (6.288-315), such signs occurred before Jerusalem's destruction.

The Lukan Message

Luke in this passage sought to alleviate some of the confusion associated with the prophetic pronouncements about Jerusalem's destruction in A.D. 70. The appearance of false Christs (Luke 21:8), wars (21:9-10), natural disasters (21:11), and even astronomical signs (21:11) are not to be interpreted as signs of the world's end. "The end will not come right away" (21:9) after "these things" (21:6-7,9) take place. What these things announced was not the world's end but Jerusalem's destruction. Yet even Jerusalem's destruction would not come immediately but would be preceded by these events. Theophilus and Luke's other readers should understand that Jesus clearly taught that there would be an interval of time not only between his ministry and the consummation of all things but between his ministry and the destruction of Jerusalem.

If this understanding of Luke is correct, the question can be raised not only with regard to *what* Luke was seeking to teach his readers through this passage but also *why* he was teaching this. The latter question is, however, more hypothetical than the first and must be based upon a correct understanding of the first. Luke wanted his readers to distinguish

---

[65]Cf. Luke 2:49; 4:43; 9:22; 13:33; 17:25; 22:37; 24:7,26,44; Acts 1:16; see Introduction 8 (1).

[66]Cf. also Acts 16:26; Rev 6:12; 8:5; 11:13,19; 16:18.

[67]Cf. Isa 13:9-10,13; Ezek 32:5-8; Joel 2:10,30-31; Amos 8:9; Rev 6:12-14.

between the events of A.D. 70 and the coming of the Son of Man, which will bring history to its conclusion. This fits well those instances where Luke seems to have emphasized that the end was not to be expected immediately (cf. 18:7-8; and see comments on 19:11). Luke may have been seeking to discourage an overly imminent expectation of the end on his readers' part. Perhaps Jerusalem's destruction had been interpreted by his readers as a sign that the end of all things was imminent. If so, the warnings in 21:8-9 would be relevant for them as well as for Jesus' original hearers. Or perhaps the destruction of Jerusalem may have discouraged his readers because the Son of Man had not returned and they were now despairing of this hope (cf. 2 Pet 3:3-6). Luke perhaps was seeking to show his readers that their experiences of suffering portrayed in this section, and even more in the next (21:12-18), had been predicted and that all this fits within the divine plan (21:9). Certainty with regard to the *why* of Luke's teaching is impossible, as the *may be* and the various *perhapses* indicate. Nevertheless *what* Luke was seeking to teach is reasonably clear. See Introduction 9. Luke was seeking to help his readers understand that they must separate the prophetic pronouncements of the destruction of Jerusalem from the prophetic pronouncements of the end of history. These are two distinct events.

12. The Coming Persecution of the Disciples (21:12-19)

[12]"But before all this, they will lay hands on you and persecute you. They will deliver you to synagogues and prisons, and you will be brought before kings and governors, and all on account of my name. [13]This will result in your being witnesses to them. [14]But make up your mind not to worry beforehand how you will defend yourselves. [15]For I will give you words and wisdom that none of your adversaries will be able to resist or contradict. [16]You will be betrayed even by parents, brothers, relatives and friends, and they will put some of you to death. [17]All men will hate you because of me. [18]But not a hair of your head will perish. [19]By standing firm you will gain life.

Context

Having warned about the danger of being misled by false prophets (21:7-9) and of a false interpretation of the events surrounding Jerusalem's fall (21:10-11), Luke then described the persecution that would come upon believers from government (21:12-15) and from family and friends (21:16-17).

Nevertheless he reminded his readers that in the midst of such persecution, Jesus has promised wisdom (21:14-15) and, to those who persevere, eternal life (21:18-19). Luke followed Mark in placing this material after 21:7-11 (cf. Mark 13:3-8 and 13:9-13). The present passage indicates Luke intended his readers to interpret 21:7-11 as referring to events surrounding

Jerusalem's fall and not events preceding the final consummation. This is seen not only by the opening words "but before all this" but in his depiction of these persecutions to fit the experience of the church in Acts.[68] Thus he omitted the reference to appearing before "councils" (literally *sanhedrins*) in Mark 13:9 since no account of this will be given in Acts. Luke also omitted Mark 13:10 because of its end-time association. His omission of "to the end" as a description of the endurance necessary (cf. Luke 21:19 with Mark 13:13) is also best understood as due to his desire to make clear that the persecutions described in Luke 21:12-19 involve not the end time but the fall of Jerusalem. (Cf. also 21:7 and how Luke changed Mark 13:4, "about to be fulfilled" [literally *to come to its end*], to "about to take place.")

The chronological designation with which this section begins indicates Luke's understanding of 21:7-11. If 21:7-11 referred to the end time, the statement "but before all this" (21:12) would be quite unnecessary, as is evident from Mark 13:9 and Matt 24:9, which lack this. Of course, persecution must come before the end time, if it is to come at all. It is self-evident that an event in history such as the persecution of the church must take place before the end, i.e., before history comes to its conclusion. However, if as maintained Luke 21:7-11 refers exclusively to the fall of Jerusalem in A.D. 70, then there could be a question if the following persecutions in 21:12-19 were to take place before or after "these things" associated with Jerusalem's fall.

Comments

21:12 But before all this. "All this" means *before the events of 21:7-11*, which involve Jerusalem's destruction in A.D. 70. Compare Acts 5:36; 21:38.

They will lay hands on you. Compare Luke 20:19 (the Greek text is much closer in these verses than the NIV translation's suggestions); cf. also Acts 4:3; 5:18; 12:1; 21:27.

And persecute you. Compare 11:49; Acts 7:52. As with Jesus, so it will be with his followers in the early church.[69]

They will deliver you to synagogues. What follows describes how the previous two statements will be fulfilled. Compare Acts 9:2; 22:19; 26:11; cf. also 2 Cor 11:24.

And prisons. Compare Luke 22:33; Acts 5:19,22,25; 8:3; 12:4-6,17; 16:16-40; 22:4; 26:10; cf. also 26:19.

And you will be brought. Compare Luke 22:66; 23:26; cf. also Acts 12:19.

Before kings. Compare Acts 12:1-11; 25:13–26:32; cf. also 4:26; 9:15.

And governors. Compare Acts 23:24–24:27; 25:1–26:32; cf. also Luke 23:1-25.

---

[68] Marshall (*Luke*, 767) states: "Luke may be now describing things that are already past history for his readers . . . ; he is thinking of the church's experience of persecution in the period before A.D. 70."

[69] Cf. Acts 4:5-21,29-30; 5:17-41; 6:8–8:3; 9:1-2,13-14,20-21,23-25; 12:1-5.

All on account of my name. Although this expression was a common one in the early church (cf. John 15:21; 1 Pet 4:14,16; 3 John 7; Rev 2:3), it occurs most frequently in Luke-Acts.[70]

21:13 This will result in your being witnesses to them. The clause is literally, *It shall be to you for a witness.* This can be interpreted, "This will be a witness on your behalf in the day of judgment" or "This will be (an opportunity) for you to witness" (to them). The latter is more likely in light of Luke 24:48 and Acts 1:8. This is how Mark 13:10 interprets the expression. Compare Acts 4:33.

21:14 But make up your mind. "Make up your mind" means *decide.* Compare Luke 9:44; Acts 5:4; 19:21.

Not to worry beforehand how you will defend yourselves. Compare Luke 12:11b. To "worry beforehand" may mean *to practice or memorize one's reply beforehand.*[71]

21:15 For I will give you words and wisdom. Compare Exod 4:11,15; Ezek 29:21. For examples of this wisdom, cf. Acts 4:8-12; 5:29-32; 6:10.

For Luke 21:14b-15a, cf. 12:11b-12. In Luke 12:11b-12 (as in the parallel in Mark 13:11), the Holy Spirit is the giver of this wisdom. Luke may have omitted the reference to the Holy Spirit here because of his reference to him in 12:11b-12 and because of a desire to emphasize the role of the risen Christ at such times. The "I" is emphatic in this verse, *I, myself, will give.*

That none of your adversaries will be able to resist or contradict. Compare Acts 6:10; cf. also 4:13-14; 13:8-12.

21:16 You will be betrayed even by parents. Although such opposition is not expressly described in Luke-Acts, cf. Luke 12:53; 14:26; 18:29.

And they will put some of you to death. Compare Acts 7:54-60; 12:1-2; 26:10.

Again as with Jesus, so it will be with his followers. The use of the term "some" suggests that this will not be the normal experience of the church.

21:17 All men will hate you. Literally, *You shall be hated by all.* This is another example of exaggeration in which Luke followed Mark 13:13.[72] That Luke understood this as hyperbolic is clear from Acts 2:47; 3:9; 4:21; 5:13. Yet such language is appropriate in expressing that Jesus' followers would experience persecution.

Compare the similar use of exaggeration for the sake of emphasis in Acts 4:26-28 (cf. also 28:22). For similar warnings cf. Luke 6:22,27-28.

Because of me. See comments on 21:12.

21:18 But not a hair of your head will perish. This proverbial statement[73] seems strange after such statements as found in 21:12-17. Note especially "they will put some of you to death" (21:16). Luke was certainly not unaware of these earlier statements when he added this proverb of Jesus to the account. Does this mean that in Luke's thinking, except for a few martyrs, the church would remain unharmed?

---

[70]Cf. Luke 9:48-49; 10:17; 21:17; 24:47; Acts 2:38; 3:6,16; 4:10,17,18,30; 5:28,40-41; 8:16; 9:15-16,21,27.

[71]See Marshall, *Luke,* 768.

[72]Note Luke's exaggerated use of "all" in 1:48; 2:1,3; 5:17; 6:17; 7:29; 12:7; 15:1; 19:7.

[73]Cf. Luke 12:7; Acts 27:34; 1 Sam 14:45; 2 Sam 14:11; 1 Kgs 1:52.

The whole flavor of 21:12-19 indicates that whereas martyrdom may be experienced by only a few, many will experience persecution. Furthermore, although Acts ends before the Neronian persecutions, Luke's readers must have known about them, and the martyrdoms at that time were more than a "few." Most probably this proverb is meant to contrast what humanity can do and what it cannot do to God's people. In 12:4-5 the reader is told not to fear those who kill the body and after that can do no more. Rather they are to fear him who has power to cast into hell.

After this warning of future persecution, there follows in 12:7a, as here, a similar statement ("the very hairs of your head are numbered"). These words are therefore meant to encourage Jesus' followers by reminding them that whatever may happen to them by way of persecution, nothing can ultimately harm them, not even death, for they possess eternal life (18:30; cf. John 10:28).

21:19 By standing firm you will gain life. Literally *gain your souls*. Here Luke described how not a hair of their heads would perish. By faithfully enduring (cf. Luke 8:15) in this time of persecution, the believer gains for himself or herself eternal life (cf. 9:24).[74] There is confusion among the manuscripts about whether the verb is an imperative (*ktēsasthe, Gain!*) or a future indicative (*ktēsesthe, you will gain*).

The manuscript evidence favors the former, and so we probably should interpret this as an exhortation (an imperative) rather than an encouraging word (an indicative).

The Lukan Message

One Lukan emphasis found in this passage can be seen in the opening words of 21:12, which are lacking in the parallel account in Mark 13:9. The persecutions of this section are not interpreted by Luke as the beginning of the end woes (contrast Mark 13:8 and Matt 24:8) but as persecutions believers would experience before Jerusalem's fall described in the previous section. This persecution and the testimony of Jesus' followers in the midst of such persecutions (Luke 21:13; cf. 24:46-49) will be described by Luke in detail later in his second work, for they find their fulfillment in the experience of the early church. The reason *why* Luke emphasized this is once again less certain than *what* he was emphasizing.

In 21:15 Jesus emphatically promised that as the risen Christ he would give the disciples wisdom about what to say in time of persecution. The close relationship of the activities of the risen Christ and the Spirit should be noted in this regard.[75] For similar promises of Christ's abiding presence, cf. Acts 18:10; 23:11; Matt 28:20. The Christological implications of Jesus' continual presence and guidance of his disciples are not devel-

---

[74] See S. Brown, *Apostasy and Perseverance in the Theology of Luke*, AnBib (Rome: Pontifical Biblical Institute, 1969), 48-50.
[75] Cf. Luke 24:49 with Acts 1:8; Acts 10:14 with Luke 10:19; Acts 9:5,17; 18:9; 23:11 with 20:23; Acts 13:47 with 13:2. See Evans, *Luke*, 743-44.

oped or explained by Luke. The ability of the risen Christ to do so would appear to go beyond categories of *function* and seem to suggest the need to describe Jesus as possessing an *essence* different from others.

A final Lukan theme is his emphasis on perseverance, i.e., "standing firm" (Luke 21:19). As in the parable of the soils (8:15), so here the need to persevere is stressed. In the parable such perseverance results in being "saved" (8:12). Here this same result is described somewhat differently as "gaining your lives" (21:19, RSV). Luke encouraged his readers, "By faithful endurance gain your lives." This ability to stand firm in times of persecution depends in part on counting from the start the cost of following Jesus (14:25-33). Additional dangers to standing firm involve the everyday cares of life (8:14; cf. also 14:15-24; 17:26-30), the concern for possessions,[76] and the desire for pleasure (8:14; cf. 12:19,45-46).

13. The Desolation Coming upon Jerusalem (21:20-24)

[20]"When you see Jerusalem being surrounded by armies, you will know that its desolation is near. [21]Then let those who are in Judea flee to the mountains, let those in the city get out, and let those in the country not enter the city. [22]For this is the time of punishment in fulfillment of all that has been written. [23]How dreadful it will be in those days for pregnant women and nursing mothers! There will be great distress in the land and wrath against this people. [24]They will fall by the sword and will be taken as prisoners to all the nations. Jerusalem will be trampled on by the Gentiles until the times of the Gentiles are fulfilled.

Context

Having described in 21:5-19 what must take place before the destruction of Jerusalem in 21:5-19, Luke then described the destruction itself.

A number of differences between the Lukan account and its parallels in Mark and Matthew help us understand Luke's particular interpretation. One involves the reference to the "abomination of desolation" found in Mark 13:14; Matt 24:15. Luke omitted this and referred instead to Jerusalem's being surrounded and its desolation having neared (21:20). He may have done this because his Gentile readers would not have understood this expression. More likely, however, is that he did this in order not to confuse Jerusalem's fall with the events associated with the end time. Similarly, he omitted Mark 13:20; Matt 24:22 in which Jesus speaks about the shortening of the days for the sake of the elect. Whereas Mark and Matthew used Jerusalem's fall as a type of the persecutions of the end time, Luke was referring in 21:20-24 only to Jerusalem's fall in A.D. 70, and the "elect" were not involved in this event. If Eusebius (*Eccl. Hist.* 3.5.3) was correct and the Christian church fled Jerusalem before its

---

[76]Luke 8:14; cf. 12:13-21; 16:10-13,19-31; 18:24-26.

destruction, and if Luke and his readers knew of this, then mention of the
elect being involved in the events of 21:20-24 would have caused confusion with respect to his argument. His omission of the expression "abomination of desolation" indicates once again that Luke understood 21:5-24
as referring to the events of A.D. 70 and not to the end time. This is further indicated by "you will know that its desolation is near" (21:20).
Whereas the cry of the false prophets, "The time [of the consummation]
is near" (21:8), was untrue, tragically Jesus' prophetic pronouncements
concerning Jerusalem (cf. 13:35; 19:42-44; 23:28-31) were coming true.
The time of Jerusalem's desolation had come.

Luke described Jerusalem's desolation poignantly. The city was about
to be surrounded by armies (21:20). Since disaster was at hand, none
should seek safety in hoping that its good defensive position and massive
walls would provide protection. Those in the area (in Judea) should flee
away to the relative safety of the mountains (21:21). Those in the city had
to leave, for this was the time of God's vengeance (21:22). As in the time
of Nebuchadnezzar, Jerusalem was doomed. The prophets sent to it (John
the Baptist and above all Jesus) should have been heeded, for like Jeremiah their message was prophetic. Woe to those who were most vulnerable, such as pregnant women and nursing mothers (21:23), for the
executioners of God's wrath and war did not discriminate. Death or captivity awaited Jerusalem's residents, and the city itself would be destroyed
and lose its centrality in God's plan of salvation history until the era of
the Gentiles comes to its conclusion (21:24).

Comments
21:20 When you see Jerusalem being surrounded by armies. Compare
19:43. "Armies" can also mean *camps*, and Josephus so used the word.[77] Josephus
also described Jerusalem's encirclement by the armies of Rome.[78] Luke may have
been reporting Jesus' words here from a post-A.D. 70 perspective. For "surrounded" cf. Tacitus, *Historiae* 5.11. For related OT imagery cf. Isa 29:3; 37:33;
Jer 34:1; 52:7. The present participle ("being surrounded") may refer to the time
when escape was still possible because the wall the Romans built around the city
had not been completed (cf. Josephus, *Wars* 7.8.5 [7.304]).
You will know. The "when" of Luke 21:7 is now realized.
That its desolation. Compare 13:35. Luke reworded "abomination of desolation" (Mark 13:14; Matt 24:15) in order to keep his readers from confusing the
fall of Jerusalem with the end time.[79]
Is near. What had arrived was not what the false prophets had been proclaiming, i.e., the final consummation that will bring history to its close (Luke

---

[77] *Wars* 5.2.1 (5.47); 5.2.2 (5.65); 5.2.3 (5.68).
[78] *Wars* 5.2.1-5 (5.47-97); 6.2.7 (6.149-56).
[79] Cf. 2 Chr 36:21; Jer 4:7; 7:34; 22:5; 25:18; 44:6,22.

21:8), but rather Jerusalem's destruction predicted by Jesus[80] and what was asked in 21:7 (see comments on 21:7).

21:21 Then. This refers to the "when" of 21:7. The following advice clearly involves behavior at Jerusalem's destruction and not at the consummation of all things, for such flight would be useless when the Son of Man returns.

Let those who are in Judea flee to the mountains. Those living in the villages and cities should flee to the more remote mountainous areas of Judah, which would provide a better chance for survival. Compare Gen 19:17-19; Ps 11:1; 1 Macc 2:28. Since the Roman armies marched slowly and methodically, there would be time for such flight.

Let those in the city get out. During the siege that would follow, Jerusalem would be the worst place to be.

And let those in the country not enter the city. Along with the first two commands in this verse, this forms a three-member example of synonymous parallelism.

21:22 For this is the time of punishment. *Ekdikēseōs* can refer to *punishment* or *vengeance*.[81] The latter is clearly meant in Rom 12:19 and here is so translated by the RSV, NASB, and NRSV. This refers not to Roman vengeance but to God's. Luke wanted his readers to understand that Jerusalem's desolation was not simply a tragedy or a wretched twist of fate. It is the result of God's wrath. The Roman army under Vespasian and Titus, like the Babylonian army under Nebuchadnezzar, was God's instrument to bring his judgment upon official Israel. Luke assumed that his readers would remember such earlier passages as 19:27 and 20:16.

In fulfillment of all that has been written. For the phraseology cf. 18:31; 24:44; Acts 13:29. Luke may have been thinking of such OT prophecies that speak of God's judgment upon Jerusalem due to its sins such as Jer 6:1-8; 26:1-6; Mic 3:12; cf. also 1 Kgs 9:6-9. Whereas the OT prophecies would speak of Jerusalem's judgment as due to its sins, what those sins entailed is found in Luke-Acts. They involve oppressing the poor (Luke 18:7; 20:47); rejecting its Messiah (13:33-34; 20:13-18); not recognizing the time when God visited and the kingdom was offered to it (19:44); rejecting the gospel message (Acts 13:46-48; 18:5-6; 28:25-28); but above all official Israel's involvement in the death of God's Son.[82] At this point Luke omitted Mark 13:15-16; Matt 24:17-18 because he referred to something similar in Luke 17:31.

21:23 How dreadful it will be in those days! "Those days" are the days of Jerusalem's destruction in A.D. 70. Compare 23:29.

Pregnant women and nursing mothers! Upon such people "total war" is always more severe. Whether their condition is a hindrance to their fleeing Jerusalem (21:21) or to survival in Jerusalem's siege is uncertain, but ultimately this makes little difference with respect to their unfortunate condition. What was normally seen as a blessing and joy (pregnancy and nursing one's children) was now a curse. Compare Josephus, *Wars* 6.3.4 (6.201-11) for a tragic example. At this point Luke

[80] Cf. Luke 13:35; 19:27,42-44; 20:16; 23:28-31.

[81] Cf. Hos 9:7; Jer 46:10,21; 51:6; cf. also Deut 32:35.

[82] Luke 9:22: 18:31-33; 19:47; 20:14-19; 22:1-2,52–23:25. See J. B. Chance, *Jerusalem, the Temple, and the New Age in Luke-Acts* (Macon: Mercer, 1988), 116-27.

omitted Mark 13:18; Matt 24:20, which refer to praying that this flight not be in the winter.[83] Luke probably omitted it, however, because he knew that Jerusalem's siege lasted from April to late August, and the reference to winter would not fit.

There will be great distress in the land and wrath against this people. The term "land" can be translated "earth" (cf. RSV), but in the present setting in Luke it refers to *the* land, i.e., Judea (Luke 21:21; cf. 4:25).[84] Compare Josephus, *Wars* 5.13.7 (5.571). Luke changed Mark 13:19; Matt 24:21 ("those will be days of distress unequaled from the beginning . . . until now") in order to avoid confusing Jerusalem's destruction, which he was describing, with the final tribulation that precedes the return of the Son of Man, which Mark and Matthew were describing.

21:24 They will fall by the sword. "The sword" is literally *the mouth of the sword.*[85] Compare Heb 11:34; Sir 28:18; Jer 21:7. Josephus gave the total of those killed in Jerusalem's destruction as 1,100,000.[86] Even allowing for exaggeration, the number is enormous.

And will be taken as prisoners to all the nations. Josephus numbered the captives at 97,000.[87] Compare Deut 28:64; Zech 7:14.

Jerusalem will be trampled on. Compare Zech 12:3 (LXX); Isa 63:18; Ps 79:1; Dan 8:10,13; Rev 11:2; cf. also Tacitus, *Historiae* 5.8-13.

Until the times of the Gentiles are fulfilled. "Until" may suggest that there is a time coming when Jerusalem/Israel will be restored.[88] Israel's judgment may not be final. There may even be a promise here.[89] From the time of the fall until "that" time, the time of Gentiles will take place.[90] At this point Luke omitted Mark 13:20; Matt 24:22 because the "elect" were not involved in Jerusalem's destruction in A.D. 70.

The Lukan Message

Again we find that Luke sought to assist his readers in sorting out the sayings of Jesus concerning Jerusalem's fall and the end time. Up to this point in the chapter, he intended for his readers to understand that these traditions did not talk about the final consummation when the Son of Man returns but rather about Jerusalem's fall and the events associated with it. Properly understood the return of the Son of Man had nothing to do with the events surrounding A.D. 70. Thus there should have been no disappointment or confusion concerning a "delay" and no following after false prophets. What would precede the final consummation Luke would

---

[83] In Mark and Matthew such a reference is acceptable because of its alluding to a situation at the final consummation.

[84] For the opposing view, see Evans, *Luke*, 751.

[85] For "edge [or mouth] of the sword," cf. Gen 34:26: Josh 19:47; cf. also Josh 8:24; 10:28,30; Judg 1:8.

[86] Cf. *Wars* 6.5.1 (6.271-73); 6.9.3 (6.420).

[87] *Wars* 6.9.3 (6.420); 7.5.3 (7.118); 7.5.5 (7.138); 7.5.6 (7.154).

[88] Cf. Rom 11:25-32; Acts 3:19-21; cf. also Luke 13:35; 22:30; Acts 1:6.

[89] Cf. Dan 8:13-14; 12:5-13; Zech 8:12-14; Rev 11:2; cf. also Tob 14:4-6.

[90] Cf. Acts 13:46-48; 18:5-6; 28:25-28; cf. also Mark 13:10; Rom 9:30-33; 11:11-16.

describe next, but first he wanted to distinguish those events associated with A.D. 70. See Introduction 7 (3).

In his presentation of the Jesus traditions concerning Jerusalem's fall, the Lukan theme of fulfillment appears in 21:22. Here the fulfillment of the divine plan in history and the authority and accuracy of the word of God is again emphasized by Luke. This has already been emphasized in the births and ministries of John the Baptist and Jesus. The fulfillment of the divine word about Jerusalem's destruction, whether in the OT (21:22) or in the sayings of Jesus, and the coming of the time of the Gentiles, are additional evidence of such fulfillment. The latter will be shown more clearly in Acts as the gospel, rejected for the most part by Judaism (13:46-48; 18:5-6; 28:25-28) meets great success in the mission to the Gentiles. Because of such fulfillment Luke's readers could have great certainty about the truthfulness of what they had been taught. See Introduction 7 (1).

Another Lukan theme appearing in this passage involves the issue of what had happened to Israel. God's vengeance had fallen upon it (see comments on 21:22). Numerous reasons have been given throughout Luke-Acts for this. As a result the rejection of Jesus by official Israel should not cause a misunderstanding. Such rebellion on the part of God's people is well known and not uncommon in the OT. See Introduction 7 (2). There may be hints in Luke about a future restoration of Israel in 13:35 and 21:24, but they are elusive, so that certainty on this issue is impossible.[91]

14. The Coming of the Son of Man (21:25-28)

[25]"There will be signs in the sun, moon and stars. On the earth, nations will be in anguish and perplexity at the roaring and tossing of the sea. [26]Men will faint from terror, apprehensive of what is coming on the world, for the heavenly bodies will be shaken. [27]At that time they will see the Son of Man coming in a cloud with power and great glory. [28]When these things begin to take place, stand up and lift up your heads, because your redemption is drawing near."

Context

From 21:5-24 Luke shared with his readers Jesus' teachings concerning Jerusalem's destruction in A.D. 70. Having distinguished between those events associated with Jerusalem's fall and the consummation of all things, he now introduced Jesus' teaching concerning the latter. The return of the Son of Man in power and glory (21:25-27,36) will bring about the final consummation (21:31).[92] In order not to confuse his readers, Luke omitted

---

[91] See Chance, *Jerusalem, Temple, and New Age*, 127-38. Chance's view that Luke clearly teaches such a restoration, however, goes beyond the evidence.

[92] Cf. also how the consummation of the kingdom of God is identified with the coming of the Son of Man in 17:20-37; 19:11,22-27; 21:31,27.

the parallel material in Mark 13:21-23; Matt 24:23-24 because he had dealt with this earlier (cf. Luke 17:23-24; 21:8). He also omitted Mark's "but in those days" (Mark 13:24) because he did not want to connect what follows (the consummation) with the preceding material (Jerusalem's fall). Whereas the portrayal of Jerusalem's fall involved historical-prophetic descriptions ("great signs from heaven [Luke 21:11]" are the one exception), the Son of Man's return involves cosmic-apocalyptic descriptions ("world" [21:26], "heavenly bodies" [21:26], "whole earth" [21:35]). This further helps to keep these two events separate. Preceded by apocalyptic events, the Son of Man will return in great glory and power to bring about his people's redemption.

Comments

21:25 There will be signs in the sun, moon and stars. This metaphorical imagery is frequently found in the OT.[93] Such impressionistic language reveals that God is about to enter world history either for blessing or woe or for both. Again the signs associated with the Son of Man's coming are cosmic, whereas those associated with Jerusalem's fall are terrestrial, so that Luke kept these two events distinct. For Luke these "signs" and the ones that follow do not provide a clock or timetable by which one is able to know the "times or dates" (Acts 1:7) of the Son of Man's coming.

On the earth, nations will be in anguish and perplexity. For similar imagery cf. Isa 3:24–4:1; 33:9; 34:1-15; Jer 4:23-26; Nah 1:4-5.

21:26 Men will faint from terror. By this addition to the tradition (cf. the parallels in Mark 13:25; Matt 24:29) Luke heightened the despair of the last days. The result of the anguish and perplexity of Luke 21:25 is terror.

Apprehensive of what is coming on the world. Luke now enlarged the scene to include not just the "land" (21:23) or "Jerusalem" (21:20) but the "world" (*oikoumenē*; cf. "ecumenical").

For the heavenly bodies will be shaken. Compare Isa 13:13; 34:4; Dan 8:10; Hag 2:21. All these passages refer to the overthrow in history of earthly nations and empires. The prophets frequently understood such cosmic imagery as metaphorical rather than literal.

21:27 At that time. This is the time of the Son of Man's coming, not "the time" referred to in Luke 21:6-7.

They will see. In light of Acts 1:11, it is clear that Luke envisioned a visible bodylike return of the Son of Man in which he will be seen returning in similar fashion as he was seen ascending into heaven.

The Son of Man coming. The parallel in Acts 1:11 prohibits an allegorical interpretation of this event as referring to Jerusalem's fall or the Spirit's coming in Acts 2. Luke understood this as the literal return of Jesus, the Son of Man.

In a cloud. Whereas Mark 13:26 and Matt 24:30 refer to "clouds," Luke used the singular (cf. also the singular in Acts 1:9). This may be due to the use of

---

[93]Cf. Isa 13:9-11; Ezek 32:7-8; Amos 8:9; Hab 3:11; Joel 2:10,30-31; 3:15; cf. Rev 6:12f.

the singular "cloud" in the transfiguration account (see comments on 9:34). There is a clear allusion here to the "one like a son of man, coming with the clouds of heaven" in Dan 7:13 (see comments on 5:24).

With power. "Power" is associated with Jesus' birth (Luke 1:35), his ministry (see comments on 4:14), his coming as the Son of Man, and the life of the church (Acts 1:8).

And great glory. The "glory" of Jesus as the Christ, the Son of Man is a Lukan emphasis. See comments on 9:26. For Luke's fondness for this word, see comments on 4:6. For the tie in Luke's thinking between the transfiguration and the parousia, see comments on 9:27 and 9:28-36, "The Lukan Message."

21:28 When these things begin to take place. "These things" are those associated with the Son of Man's coming (21:25-27), not the "things" associated with Jerusalem's fall in A.D. 70 (21:5-24).

Stand up and lift up your heads. For this as a sign of hope and confidence, cf. Judg 8:28; Job 10:15; Pss 24:7,9; 83:2. In the midst of crisis, when things are as bad as they can be (Luke 21:25-26), Christians can take heart. The Lord is at hand. It cannot be much longer. Even in the midst of lesser times of crisis (21:10-19), believers are assured that their Lord is near (21:14-15), for he has promised to be with them always (cf. Matt 28:20). In that day, however, they can be even more encouraged because the glorious consummation is at hand. Their "redemption" is coming.

Because your redemption is drawing near. This is the reason for being able to stand up and lift up their heads. "Redemption" (*apolytrōsis*) is found only this one time in Luke-Acts, but Luke probably meant *the consummation of the hopes and promises for God's people.*[94] Luke's readers would no doubt think of this redemption as involving salvation in its fullest sense.

The Lukan Message

With Jesus' coming, God's kingdom entered history in fulfillment of the OT promises. See Introduction 8 (2). Now at the consummation the firstfruits will give way to the harvest. The church's cries (Luke 18:7) and its fervent prayer (11:2) are answered. The Son of Man returns in glory as Luke both explicitly and implicitly taught and as the church has preached.[95] The mustard seed has become a tree (see comments on 13:19); the yeast has leavened the whole dough (see comments on 13:20). The longings of Luke's readers are now realized to the fullest.

15. The Parable of the Fig Tree (21:29-33)

²⁹**He told them this parable: "Look at the fig tree and all the trees. ³⁰When they sprout leaves, you can see for yourselves and know that summer is near. ³¹Even so, when you see these things happening, you know that the kingdom of God is near.**

---

[94]Luke 6:20-23; 9:24; 10:20; 11:2-3; 12:8,37-38; 14:14; 16:9,22; 18:7,29-30; 19:17,19, 26; 22:18,29-30.

[95]Luke 9:26; 12:40-48; 13:35; 17:22-37; 18:8; 19:11-27; Acts 3:20-21; 17:31.

[32]"I tell you the truth, this generation will certainly not pass away until all these things have happened. [33]Heaven and earth will pass away, but my words will never pass away.

Context

Luke, like Mark 13:28-32; Matt 24:32-36, now added a parable to illustrate how the "signs" of Luke 21:25-26 serve to indicate that the deliverance just mentioned in 21:28 is near. The account consists of a short parable, or similitude (21:29-30), involving an analogy of a fig tree. To this has been added an application (21:31) and two warnings (21:32-33). Just as a fig tree (and most other trees) gives certain signs that reveal summer is near, so there will be certain signs that will reveal that the redemption brought by the Son of Man is also near.

Two major interpretative difficulties are encountered in this passage. One deals with the reference to "this generation" not passing away until all has taken place. This expression has been interpreted as referring to (1) Jesus' own generation, (2) the Jewish people, (3) humans in general, (4) the last generation in history, and (5) Luke's contemporaries. (Compare how the Qumran community wrestled with the identity of the final generation in 1 QpHab 2.7; 7.2.7 and how the "final generation" referred to several generations.) Even though every other reference to "this generation" in Luke can include Jesus' own generation, it is quite unlikely that here Luke understood "this generation" in this manner because that generation had essentially passed from the scene, and the parousia still lay in the future. The fourth interpretation is so bland as to be meaningless. As long as humanity is present when the Son of Man returns, this by definition must be true; for unlike people in the nuclear generation who wonder if humanity may destroy itself in nuclear war, Luke and his contemporaries had no doubt that the return of the Son of Man would take place in the presence of people. The second suggestion fails to take into consideration that the scene of the coming of the Son of Man is not the "land" (Luke 21:23) of Judea but the "earth" and the "nations" (21:25), so that to restrict the audience here simply to the Jewish people would be to lose sight of the cosmic focus of 21:25-36. Furthermore why would Luke or his readers think that the Jewish people might be wiped from the face of the earth? The fifth suggestion is unattractive to many interpreters since it is obviously wrong. The Son of Man did not come in Luke's generation. However, in the pursuit of Luke's meaning one cannot rule out this possible interpretation simply because one does not like it. Nevertheless this interpretation would be strange if in his Gospel Luke was combatting a misunderstanding that the parousia already should have taken place. See Introduction 7 (3). Luke probably would have been hesitant to date the coming of the Son of Man in such a way.

The third suggestion appears to be the best option. Elsewhere in Luke this expression is used to describe sinful humanity unresponsive to God and oblivious to the possibility of immediately encountering him (cf. 12:16-21,35-40; 17:26-36). "This generation," which ignored the coming of the kingdom in Jesus' ministry, continues in its rejection of the gospel message until the very end. Thus "this generation" of 21:32 stands in continuity and solidarity with "this generation" of Jesus' day.[96]

The second major interpretative problem involves the "signs" that accompany the Son of Man's return and the fact that his coming will catch people unawares. How can these "signs" help one escape all that is about to happen (21:36)? The "signs" associated with the arrival of the kingdom in Jesus' ministry were perceived by those possessing eyes to see (cf. 4:16-30; 7:21-23). Yet the majority did not see or understand, and even the sign of Jonah was not recognized (11:29-30). If even one returning from the dead will not force people to see (16:31), neither will the "signs" preceding the end. Furthermore if we interpret the fulfillment of the signs of 21:25-26 in the same way Luke interpreted the fulfillment of the signs in Joel 2:28-32 (cf. Acts 2:16-21), then these signs may be more metaphorical and picturesque than literal. Over the centuries in times of crisis and war, Christians have frequently asked themselves if the present events might be precursors of the end. Such questions, as long as they remain hypothetical and deal with possibility and not certainty, are appropriate, for they help believers watch, i.e., be prepared, for their Master's coming. Thus believers, as they watch (Luke 21:36) and pray for the consummation (11:2), will not be caught unawares. Such believers may be surprised, but not unprepared.

It has been suggested that the parable found in our passage may have had a different meaning in Jesus' situation than in its present setting. Some have suggested that originally the parable functioned much like 12:54-56, i.e., as referring to the coming of God's kingdom in Jesus' ministry.[97] This is impossible to demonstrate; but if for the sake of argument such a view is correct, this would mean that a parable of Jesus that speaks of an event (summer) clearly following certain signs (leaves) was applied to two analogous situations: signs of Jesus' ministry indicating the coming of God's kingdom (by Jesus) and signs of the end time indicating the coming of the consummation by the Son of Man's return (by Luke). In either situation the analogy would still be valid.

Comments
21:29 For a similar parable involving a fig tree, cf. 13:6-9.

---

[96] For a helpful discussion that arrives at a different conclusion, see R. Maddox, *The Purpose of Luke-Acts* (Edinburgh: T & T Clark, 1982), 111-15.
[97] So J. Jeremias, *The Parables of Jesus* (New York: Scribner's, 1963), 121.

And all the trees. Luke may have added this to broaden the analogy for his non-Palestinian audience, who may not have been as familiar with fig trees as Jesus' audience.

21:30 When they sprout leaves. "When they sprout leaves" is literally *when they put out* (*probalōsin*). This absolute use of the verb without a noun such as "leaves" is unusual.

Summer is near. This is a conclusion all would acknowledge. This verse provides the picture part of the parable.

21:31 Even so. This introduces the reality part of the parable.

When you see these things happening. "These things" are those associated with the Son of Man's coming (21:25-26), not the things associated with Jerusalem's fall in A.D. 70 (21:5-24).

The kingdom of God is near. This is another way of saying the Son of Man's coming is near (21:27). Compare the parallels in Mark 13:29; Matt 24:33, "You know that he is near" (RSV). The similar wording in Luke 21:28 indicates that the consummation of God's kingdom brings the believers' redemption. The attempt to see in this a "de-eschatologizing" of the parousia by Luke is in error,[98] for Luke saw the coming of the kingdom and the coming of the Son of Man (21:27) as two ways of expressing the same event. The expressions are different and the emphases differ somewhat as well, but the same eschatological event is meant (see Luke 21:25-28, "Context").

21:32 I tell you the truth. This adds solemnity to what follows. See comments on 4:24.

This generation. "This generation" is often used pejoratively in Luke-Acts,[99] and in every instance cited it refers to (or at least can also refer to) Jesus' own generation. Here it is also pejorative and refers to the final generation that stands in solidarity both in descent and behavior with the generation of Jesus' day.

All these things. Literally *all*. The parallels in Mark 13:30; Matt 24:34 have "all these things." This is best understood as referring to the signs and coming of the Son of Man (Luke 21:25-28) and not the events surrounding A.D. 70 (21:5-24).

21:33 Heaven and earth will pass away. Compare 16:17. Compare Ps 102:25-27; Isa 51:6. This verse is tied to the preceding both by its content and by the verb "pass away."

My words. Compare Luke 9:26; Isa 40:6-8; 55:10-11; Ps 119:89. The particular aspect of Jesus' teachings referred to involves the Son of Man's coming (cf. 9:26; 12:40; 17:22-37; 18:8). At this point Luke omitted Mark 13:32; Matt 24:36, perhaps for Christological reasons or because he had something like this in Acts 1:7.

The Lukan Message

The present parable serves as a reassuring word for the preceding statement about the Son of Man's coming. Even as the leafing of a fig tree announces and guarantees the coming of summer, so the signs of 21:25-26 will announce and guarantee the Son of Man's parousia. Jesus' teach-

---

[98] Contrary to Carlston, *Parables of the Triple Tradition*, 82-83.
[99] Cf. Luke 7:31; 11:29-32,50,51; 16:8; 17:25; Acts 2:40.

ings concerning this (see comments on 21:33) will be fulfilled. The certainty of all this is assured by two emphatic elements: the "I tell you the
truth" of 21:32 and the fact that the coming of the Son of Man is a more
enduring promise than the existence of heaven and earth (21:33). The latter will pass away, but not Jesus' words. As a result "this generation" that
rejected Jesus will in the last day, due to its solidarity with its descendants, experience the fulfillment of Jesus' words and judgment as a result
of its rejection of him.

16. Exhortation to Vigilance (21:34-36)

[34]"Be careful, or your hearts will be weighed down with dissipation, drunkenness and the anxieties of life, and that day will close on you unexpectedly like
a trap. [35]For it will come upon all those who live on the face of the whole earth.
[36]Be always on the watch, and pray that you may be able to escape all that is
about to happen, and that you may be able to stand before the Son of Man."

Context

Luke ended his eschatological discourse with a practical appeal consisting of two warnings unique to his Gospel. The first involves a warning
to beware of being overcome with drunken revelry or worldly concerns
for this life, for these may cause one to be unprepared for "that day"
(21:34). The second is to be watchful and to pray in order to be prepared
for "that day." This is described as being able to stand before the Son of
Man (21:36). Only by heeding these warnings will Luke's readers be able
to escape the judgment that is coming in that day and which, despite the
signs of 21:25-26, will catch the rest of the world unawares (21:34b-35).

Comments

21:34 Be careful. See comments on 12:1.
Or your hearts will be weighed down. See comments on 6:45. Compare
Exod 7:14.
With dissipation, drunkenness. The first term can bring about the second,
i.e., revelry in drinking leads to drunkenness. Drunkenness that results from any
kind of behavior, however, is condemned.
And the anxieties of life. Compare how in Luke 8:13-14 these can choke
God's word so that it becomes unfruitful. Compare 10:41; 12:22-26.
That day. "That day" is the day when the Son of Man returns (21:27) and
these things take place (21:31).
Will close on you unexpectedly. Despite all warnings the world will be
caught unprepared like the rich fool (12:16-21) and like Noah's generation and
Sodom (17:22-37). Compare 12:35-48; 1 Thess 5:2-3.
Like a trap. It is uncertain textually whether this should go with what pre-
cedes ("will close upon you unexpectedly like a trap") or what follows ("for it

will come upon those . . . like a trap"). The former has slightly better textual support (ℵ, B, D, it, Cop).

21:35   For it will come. "It" refers to the Son of Man (21:27) or the kingdom of God (Luke 21:31).

On the face of the whole earth. As in 21:26 the cosmic scene extends to the whole earth and not just to the land of Judea (21:21,23).

21:36   Be always on the watch. This involves not so much having a correct chronological chart of the end events or physically looking and searching for the Son of Man's return but rather being prepared at all times for his coming. It involves a life of faithful perseverance (8:15) made possible through prayer. As a result that day will not "surprise them as a thief" (1 Thess 5:4).

And pray. "Prayer" is a favorite Lukan emphasis. See Introduction 8 (7). This injunction probably is best understood as an instrumental participle revealing the means by which one can be watchful: *Be always watchful by praying.*

That. "That" means *in order that.* The purpose of this continual prayer is now given.

You may be able to escape. The purpose of prayer is to escape (literally *be strong enough to escape*) the things that are about to take place. Only through such prayer will they be able to "not give up" (Luke 18:1) and "keep the faith" (cf. 18:8).

All that is about to happen. This alludes to the "messianic woes" suggested in the signs of 21:25-26. These circumstances, which come upon the believer from outside, along with those mentioned in 21:34-35, which come from within, pose a danger. Through prayer, however, the believer will be strengthened and able to escape from apostasy and sin.

And . . . stand before the Son of Man. This refers to escaping the wrath and judgment of the Son of Man.[100] It is to hear "well done" (19:17) rather than "I don't know you. . . . Away from me, all you evildoers" (13:25-27).

The Lukan Message

Within these last exhortations of the larger Lukan apocalypse we find a favorite theme of the Gospel: the importance of prayer. Along with two general exhortations, "Be careful" and "Be always on the watch," Luke gave one specific command. That one specific command chosen above all others by the Evangelist involves the need to "Pray!" Prayer is the means by which one is able to be watchful (see comments on 21:36) and careful. To cease praying is equivalent to giving up (18:1). Only by praying can one keep from falling into temptation (22:40,46) and have faith when the Son of Man returns (18:8). Thus Luke stressed that a key for persevering until the Son of Man's coming is prayer. Luke therefore urged his readers to continue in prayer so that they would be found faithful in that day (12:35-48).

The present passage also indicates that despite the signs spoken of in 21:25-26, Luke did not understand them as being so clear and distinct that

---

[100]Cf. Luke 9:26; 12:9; Acts 17:31; Matt 25:32; Rev 6:15-17.

they of necessity bring about a radical readjustment of thinking and behavior by all the residents of the earth. On the contrary, life continues to go on as if nothing is happening. The Son of Man's coming will catch people unprepared much like the flood did in Noah's day and Sodom's destruction in Abraham's day (17:22-37). This is even possible for believers, who are warned that they should not be caught unawares. Thus Luke quite possibly understood the "signs" of 21:25-26 as more metaphorical than literal in their imagery. See comments on 21:26.

17. The Ministry of Jesus in the Temple (21:37-38)

[37]Each day Jesus was teaching at the temple, and each evening he went out to spend the night on the hill called the Mount of Olives, [38]and all the people came early in the morning to hear him at the temple.

Context

These two verses form a concluding summary not only for Jesus' eschatological teaching (21:5-36) but also for the entire section devoted to Jesus' ministry in Jerusalem (19:28–21:38). The theme of Jesus' teaching found in 19:47; 20:1 is repeated here, and the material is uniquely Lukan.

Contents

21:37   Each day Jesus was teaching.   The imperfect periphrastic verb emphasizes Jesus' continual practice of teaching in the temple. That which began in 2:46-49 is now being fulfilled. For Jesus as a teacher, see comments on 4:15.

Hill called the Mount of Olives.   Luke portrayed Jesus as "tenting out" each night on the Mount of Olives. Compare 22:39. This would have been quite common during the celebration of the Passover and the Feast of Unleavened Bread. This does not exclude the possibility that, as Matt 21:17 states, Jesus also lodged in Bethany, which lies on the eastern slopes of the Mount of Olives.

21:38   And all the people came.   See comments on 4:15. Compare Luke 19:48.

To hear him.   This expresses the purpose of their coming.

The Lukan Message

Luke again pointed out that the people were positive toward Jesus. They sought eagerly to hear the word he spoke.[101] They, of course, stood in sharp contrast to Israel's leadership, who "were trying to kill him" (19:47) and to "trap him in what he . . . said . . . in public."[102] Luke's readers were thus reminded that it was not the people of Israel who

---

[101]Luke 19:48; 20:1,6,19,26,45.

[102]Luke 20:26; cf. also 20:1-8,19-40.

rejected the Son of God and the gospel message but rather official Israel. This, along with the statement that Jesus taught every day in the temple, indicates to the readers that Jesus was innocent of any wrongdoing. His ministry "was not done in a corner" (Acts 26:26). His teaching was open for all to hear. Because of this teaching ministry, Theophilus and the other readers could also be assured that the teachings they had received (Luke 1:4) were not imaginary or later creations but came from their Master Teacher who every day taught openly in the temple.

──────── *SECTION OUTLINE* ────────

VII. JESUS' PASSION (22:1–23:56)
  1. The Last Supper (22:1-38)
    (1) The Plot to Kill Jesus (22:1-6)
    (2) Preparation of the Passover Meal (22:7-13)
    (3) The Passover—Lord's Supper (22:14-20)
    (4) Jesus' Betrayal Foretold (22:21-23)
    (5) Greatness in the Kingdom of God (22:24-30)
    (6) Peter's Denial Foretold (22:31-34)
    (7) Two Swords (22:35-38)
  2. Arrest and Trial (22:39–23:56)
    (1) The Prayer of Jesus (22:39-46)
    (2) The Arrest of Jesus (22:47-53)
    (3) Peter's Denial (22:54-62)
    (4) The Mocking of Jesus (22:63-65)
    (5) Jesus before the Sanhedrin (22:66-71)
    (6) Jesus before Pilate (23:1-5)
    (7) Jesus before Herod (23:6-12)
    (8) Pilate's Sentence (23:13-16)
    (9) Jesus Delivered to Be Crucified (23:17-25)
    (10) The Way to the Cross (23:26-32)
    (11) The Crucifixion (23:33-38)
    (12) The Two Criminals (23:39-43)
    (13) The Death of Jesus 23:44-49)
    (14) The Burial of Jesus (23:50-56)

──────── **VII. JESUS' PASSION (22:1–23:56)** ────────

The shift in scene (from the temple to the city) and content (teachings of Jesus to stories about Jesus) indicates Luke began the seventh section of his Gospel at this point. The first part of the passion narrative is introduced by the plot to betray Jesus (22:1-6), centers on the last supper (22:7-23), and concludes with various teachings of Jesus (22:24-38). The second part of the passion narrative consists of Jesus' arrest (22:39-53), trial (22:54–23:25), crucifixion (23:26-49), and burial (23:50-56). This will then be followed by the eighth and final section of the Gospel—the resurrection and ascension of Jesus (24:1-53). Within the Lukan account of the passion narrative we find several unique Lukan additions.[1] Whether this material came

───────────────────────

[1] Cf. Luke 22:15-17,24-32,35-38; 23:2,4-16,27-32,39b-43.

from a non-Markan passion narrative such as L or Proto-Luke is much debated but impossible to demonstrate. What is clear is that Luke added other traditions concerning Jesus' passion to the Markan framework of these events.[2]

Of all the Gospel traditions the passion materials probably were the earliest to be placed in a continuous narrative. For one, the regular observation of the last supper recalls both the night in which Jesus was betrayed (1 Cor 11:23), Jesus' death (1 Cor 11:25-26), and his victory over death (1 Cor 11:26). As a result the celebration of the last supper would have continually raised the question of how these events were related. Second, whereas various forms of the Gospel traditions could easily have circulated as independent units because they were complete in themselves (healing miracles, pronouncement stories, parables), the material associated with the arrest, trial, and crucifixion are less easily broken into such independent units. Time and time again in the passion narrative one cannot help but raise the question, "And then what happened?" Third, the common elements in all four Gospel accounts of the passion[3] are best explained on the basis of an early passion narrative containing this material.[4]

1. The Last Supper (22:1-38)

(1) The Plot to Kill Jesus (22:1-6)

[1]Now the Feast of Unleavened Bread, called the Passover, was approaching, [2]and the chief priests and the teachers of the law were looking for some way to get rid of Jesus, for they were afraid of the people. [3]Then Satan entered Judas, called Iscariot, one of the Twelve. [4]And Judas went to the chief priests and the officers of the temple guard and discussed with them how he might betray Jesus. [5]They were delighted and agreed to give him money. [6]He consented, and watched for an opportunity to hand Jesus over to them when no crowd was present.

Context

The passion narrative is introduced by a statement concerning the plot of the chief priests and teachers of the law to kill Jesus at the Passover (22:1-2). The plot is made possible by Satan entering into Judas Iscariot,

---

[2]See J. B. Green ("Preparation for Passover [Luke 22:7-13]: A Question of Redactional Technique," *NovT* 29 [1987]: 317), who refers to the "near-consensus among NT scholars that Luke has made use of the Markan narrative and no other written source material."

[3]Despite their differences each Gospel refers to Judas's betrayal, a last supper with the disciples, the arrest across the Kidron Valley, Peter's denial, the questioning before the high priest, an appearance before Pontius Pilate, who sought to release Jesus, the journey to the cross, crucifixion between two others, a title on the cross, and so forth.

[4]For an opposing view, see W. H. Kelber (ed.), *The Passion in Mark* (Philadelphia: Fortress, 1976), 153-59.

one of the Twelve (22:3). He agreed to help the chief priests and the officers in charge of the temple guard get rid of Jesus (22:4; cf. 20:19) in the absence of the crowd (22:6) since the crowd was positive toward Jesus (20:19). Luke followed Mark 14:1-2,10-11 in this respect. He omitted, however, the anointing of Jesus found in Mark 14:3-9. He had included already a similar anointing story in Luke 7:36-50 and probably sought to avoid duplicating such a story here. Luke probably also saw the account in 23:55–24:1 as being more directly related to the anointing of Jesus' body for burial than that in Mark 14:3-9.

Comments
22:1   Now the Feast of Unleavened Bread. This feast was celebrated for seven days from 15–21 Nisan. Nisan, the first month in the Jewish sacred calendar, comes around the middle of March.[5]
Called the Passover. See comments on 2:41. It is clear from this explanation that Luke was addressing a non-Jewish audience. Originally the Passover was a one-day feast that preceded by a day the Feast of Unleavened Bread, i.e., it was celebrated on the 14th of Nisan. In NT times, however, in popular thinking, the Passover was the beginning of the Feast of Unleavened Bread.[6] In the Talmud Jesus' death is also associated with the Passover (*Sanh.* 43a; cf. 1 Cor 5:7).
22:2   And the chief priests and the teachers of the law. Compare Luke 19:47-48; 20:19. For their future role in the passion, cf. 22:52,54; 23:1,4,13,35, 50-51.
Were looking for some way. "Some way" is literally *how* (*pōs*). Tiede notes: "There is no longer any question whether Jesus should die. Only the question of *means* to that end is discussed."[7]
For they were afraid of the people. Compare 20:19; see comments on 4:15. For the generally positive attitude of the people during the passion, cf. 23:27,35a, 48. Whereas Luke referred to the cause of Jesus' opponents' fear (the people's support of Jesus), Mark 14:2 refers to the possible result ("the people may riot").
22:3   Then Satan entered Judas. Although Satan/devil has been mentioned in Luke 8:12; 10:18; 11:18; 13:16, he has been comparatively inactive since 4:13. In fact he has been on the defensive and under attack, but now is his hour (cf. 22:53), and his frontal attack on Jesus begins again via Judas. For Satan "entering" or "departing," cf. 8:30-32; Acts 5:3. Compare John 13:2 and especially 13:27.
Called Iscariot. See comments on 6:16.
One of the Twelve. See comments on 6:13.
22:4   And Judas went to the chief priests. See comments on 9:22.
And the officers of the temple guard. This group, referred to once again in 22:52, probably were the leaders of the temple police.[8]

---

[5] Cf. Exod 12:17-20; 23:15; 34:18; Deut 16:1-8, where the month is called Abib.
[6] Cf. Acts 12:3-4; Josephus, *Antiquities* 3.10.5 (3.249); 14.2.1 (14.21); 17.9.3 (17.213); 18.2.2 (18.29); *Wars* 2.1.3 (2.10); *Pesah.* 9:5.
[7] D. L. Tiede, *Luke*, ACNT (Minneapolis: Augsburg, 1988), 376.
[8] Cf. Acts 4:1; 5:24; Josephus, *Wars* 6.5.3 (6.294); *Antiquities* 20.6.2 (20.131).

How he might betray Jesus. For "betray" cf. 9:44; 18:32; 22:6,21-22,48; 23:25; 24:7,20. We are not explicitly told *why*, from a human point of view, Judas betrayed Jesus. Was it for money? Yet in Mark 14:11 and here (Luke 22:5) money seems to have been after the fact, i.e., Judas was given money after he decided to betray Jesus (contrast Matt 26:15). Clearer is the *what* of Judas's betrayal. *What* he betrayed was how (22:2) the chief priests and officers might seize Jesus quietly apart from the people. Judas provided this information. (That Judas betrayed the "messianic secret," i.e., that Jesus was claiming to be the Messiah, is refuted by his absence at Jesus' trial. When charges against Jesus were sought, Judas did not provide evidence that he was claiming to be the Messiah. After Jesus' arrest Judas was no longer needed, for he had delivered Jesus into the hands of the chief priests.)

22:5 They were delighted. Judas provided the needed information on how they could arrest Jesus apart from the people (20:19). Thus he "simplified matters enormously."[9]

Agreed to give him money. This does not appear to have been the main reason for Judas's actions because it came after Judas already had agreed to betray Jesus (22:4). Matthew 26:15 specifies the amount—thirty pieces of silver. Luke may have mentioned money here to illustrate for his readers how money can destroy a person (cf. Luke 12:13-21; 16:19-31; 18:18-25).

22:6 Watched for an opportunity . . . when no crowd was present. "Watched" is literally *was watching* (a durative imperfect). Once again Luke mentioned the positive attitude of the crowd toward Jesus (cf. 19:48; 20:6,19).

The Lukan Message

Several editorial modifications within this account reveal Lukan emphases. His addition of "when no crowd was present" in 22:6 is in a sense redundant, for he already had stated this in 22:2 (cf. Mark 14:2; Matt 26:5). By repeating this, he sought to make clear that the people in general were positive toward Jesus (and later in Acts toward the preaching of the gospel). Luke emphasized this throughout the Gospel (see comments on 4:15), but he did so especially in the preceding section (cf. Luke 19:37,48; 20:16,19; 21:38). In contrast the leadership of Israel continually resisted Jesus (19:39; 20:1-8,20-40) and sought to kill him (19:47; 20:14-15,19; 22:2-6). Luke's readers should know that the people were not responsible for Jesus' death. On the contrary they were a hindrance to any attempt to kill Jesus. The responsibility for Jesus' death lies with official Israel.

Another Lukan emphasis can be seen in his addition of "then Satan entered into Judas" (22:3; cf. Mark 14:10; Matt 26:14; but note John 13:27). In 4:13 Luke told his readers that the devil left Jesus "until an opportune time." Now the opportune time had come. Jesus' death was thus not just due to human evil on the part of official Israel. More was

---

[9] A. Plummer, *A Critical and Exegetical Commentary on the Gospel according to S. Luke*, ICC (Edinburgh: T & T Clark, 1896), 491.

involved than this. The supreme evil one was also involved, for Satan was arrayed against God's Son. Having failed at the temptation (4:1-13), he aggressively resumed his attack on God's Son. Yet the reader knows that ultimately Jesus' death was not due to the triumph of Satan and the chief priests. It was not because of official Judaism or even Satan that God's Son had to die. Jesus went willingly to his death because God had ordained it (22:39-46). There is a divine necessity in this. See comments on 9:22; Introduction 8 (1).

At least one other Lukan emphasis can be seen in his mention of the tradition of the money to be given Judas (23:5; cf. Mark 14:11; Matt 26:15). Later Satan entered into another "disciple," Ananias, because of money (Acts 5:3), and this also resulted in sin and tragedy. Luke wanted his readers to remember what had already been said with regard to the danger of possessions and to heed Jesus' teachings in this respect. See Introduction 8 (7).

(2) Preparation of the Passover Meal (22:7-13)

[7]Then came the day of Unleavened Bread on which the Passover lamb had to be sacrificed. [8]Jesus sent Peter and John, saying, "Go and make preparations for us to eat the Passover."

[9]"Where do you want us to prepare for it?" they asked.

[10]He replied, "As you enter the city, a man carrying a jar of water will meet you. Follow him to the house that he enters, [11]and say to the owner of the house, 'The Teacher asks: Where is the guest room, where I may eat the Passover with my disciples?' [12]He will show you a large upper room, all furnished. Make preparations there."

[13]They left and found things just as Jesus had told them. So they prepared the Passover.

Context

In following the Markan narrative (Mark 14:12-17), Luke told of Jesus' arrangements for the Passover. While the preceding account tells of the preparation by Jesus' opponents for his death, this account tells of the preparation of Jesus and the Twelve to celebrate the Passover and to inaugurate the "Lord's Supper." Unique to the Lukan account we find that Jesus took the initiative in sending the disciples (Luke 22:8, note Luke's omission of Mark 14:12c,d); the two disciples were named (Peter and John, 22:8); and reference is made to "the hour" having come (22:14).

Comments

22:7 The day of Unleavened Bread on which the Passover lamb had to be sacrificed. See comments on 22:1. Luke followed Mark 14:12 at this point and gave a popular, although inexact, dating of the Passover. (A similar example would be for those whose celebration of Christmas begins on Christmas Eve rather than Christmas morning.) Compare Josephus, *Wars* 5.3.1 (5.99) for the same dating of the Passover.[10] Matthew 26:17 omits the reference to the sacrifice of the Passover lamb.

22:8 Since the Passover meal had to be eaten within the walled city of Jerusalem (Luke 2:41; 2 Chr 35:16-19; Jub. 49:15-16), Jesus prepared to eat the meal within the city.

Jesus sent Peter and John. Only Luke made explicit who the two disciples were (cf. Mark 14:13). Luke may have mentioned them here to reveal the leadership role of these two church leaders.[11] Sending representatives in pairs is an ancient custom (see comments on 10:1).

Go and make preparations. This involved overseeing the sacrifice of the lambs in the temple, seeing that the lamb was roasted, preparing the place, and preparing all the side dishes and wine. For the ritual slaughtering of the Passover lamb, cf. *Pesaḥim* 64a-65b.

To eat the Passover. In the Synoptic Gospels the meal eaten on the night of Jesus' betrayal was clearly the Passover. See 22:14-20, "Context."

22:10 As you enter the city, a man carrying a jar of water. From the following verse this appears to be less an example of Jesus' foreknowledge than a prearrangement on his part (cf. Matt 26:18). See comments on 19:30. A man carrying a jar of water would have been most unusual, for in the first century this was considered a task for women. Jesus may not have openly told the location of the upper room due to the presence of Judas,[12] but this is speculative.

22:11 The Teacher asks. Since the owner knew of the prearrangement, this designation is sufficient. Compare Luke 19:31.

Where is the guest room, where I may eat the Passover with my disciples? That the same Greek word is used here for "guest room" as in 2:7 for "inn" probably is not significant.

22:12 He will show you a large upper room, all furnished. This presupposes that Jesus prearranged to celebrate the Passover there. The owner had furnished the room with cushions and other furniture needed for eating the Passover. There is no reason to assume that the room upstairs (*hyperōon*) in Acts 1:13 and this upper room (*anagaion*) were the same.

Make preparations there. Whereas the owner supplied the place and furniture for the celebration of the Passover, the two disciples were to prepare what was needed for the eating of Passover.

22:13 Found things just as Jesus had told them. Compare Luke 19:32.

So they prepared the Passover. See comments on 22:9.

The Lukan Message

Jesus is portrayed as an obedient Jew who kept the law and celebrated the Passover. The importance of such behavior has been pointed out in

---

[10] See R. H. Stein, "Last Supper" in *Dictionary of Jesus and the Gospels* (Downers Grove: InterVarsity, 1992), 444-50.

[11] Cf. Acts 3:1,3-4,11; 4:13,19; 8:14; cf. 1:13.

[12] So I. H. Marshall, *The Gospel of Luke*, TNIGTC (Grand Rapids: Eerdmans, 1978), 792.

2:41-52 (see "The Lukan Message"; comments on 1:6). Thus Theophilus and the other readers were reminded once again that their Christian faith stood in continuity with OT religion. See Introduction 7 (2). Yet shortly they would also be reminded that their faith represented a "new covenant" (22:20) that revealed they shared in the faith of Abraham, Isaac, and Jacob in its fulfilled form.

(3) The Passover—Lord's Supper (22:14-20)

[14]When the hour came, Jesus and his apostles reclined at the table. [15]And he said to them, "I have eagerly desired to eat this Passover with you before I suffer. [16]For I tell you, I will not eat it again until it finds fulfillment in the kingdom of God."

[17]After taking the cup, he gave thanks and said, "Take this and divide it among you. [18]For I tell you I will not drink again of the fruit of the vine until the kingdom of God comes."

[19]And he took bread, gave thanks and broke it, and gave it to them, saying, "This is my body given for you; do this in remembrance of me."

[20]In the same way, after the supper he took the cup, saying, "This cup is the new covenant in my blood, which is poured out for you.

Context

The account of the Lord's Supper is the seventh meal scene found in Luke.[13] The Lukan version of the Lord's Supper differs from the parallel accounts in Mark and Matthew in two major ways. First, he placed Jesus' statement about his betrayal after rather than before the supper (cf. 22:21-23 with Mark 14:18-21; Matt 26:21-25). He may have done this for literary reasons in order to give a more orderly account of the events surrounding Jesus' passion. Thus it is placed along with the accounts of who is the greatest (Luke 22:24-30), Peter's denial (22:31-34), and the account of the two swords (22:35-38). Second, he had a tradition of an earlier cup (22:15-18) that gives the unusual order of cup-bread-cup.

A classic problem with regard to this account involves the issue of whether the Lord's Supper was associated with a Passover meal or whether it preceded the Passover. In the Synoptic Gospels it is clearly associated with the Passover (22:7-15; Mark 14:12-16; Matt 26:17-19). According to John, however, Jesus was arrested and crucified before the Passover.[14] Numerous attempts have been made to reconcile these two different traditions. These involve understanding John's "Passover" as referring not to the Passover meal itself but to later meals and feasts associated with the Feast of Unleavened Bread; claiming that Jesus anticipated the Passover meal a

---

[13]Cf. Luke 5:29-32; 7:36-50; 9:12-17; 10:38-42; 11:37-44; 14:1-24; cf. also 24:28-32.
[14]John 13:1,29; 18:28; 19:31; cf. *Sanh.* 43a.

day or so earlier, since he knew that he would not be alive at the time when
the Passover was to be celebrated; and claiming that different groups celebrated the Passover on different days.[15] Unfortunately none of these
attempts is truly convincing, and the problem of how to reconcile the two
traditions remains unresolved.

It seems reasonably certain that the Lord's Supper was associated with
a Passover meal for the following reasons: the Passover had to be eaten
within the walled city of Jerusalem, and the Lord's Supper was also eaten
within the walled city; the Passover evening had to be spent in "greater
Jerusalem," which included the Mount of Olives, but not Bethany, and
Jesus and the disciples spent that evening in the garden of Gethsemane on
the Mount of Olives; Jesus and the disciples reclined at the Lord's Supper
(Luke 22:14; Mark 14:18), and this was required at the Passover, whereas
at most meals one sat; the Lord's Supper, like the Passover, was eaten in
the evening, whereas most meals were eaten in the late afternoon; the
Lord's Supper ended with hymn (see Mark 14:26), and it was customary
to conclude the Passover with Hallel Psalms (Pss 111–117).[16]

The Passover was a carefully ordered ritual in which each element of
the meal reminded the participants of their redemption from Egypt.[17] At
the end of the meal someone (usually the youngest son) was designated to
ask, "Why is this night different from other nights?" The host of the meal,
in this instance Jesus, would recount the exodus story. The story tells of
God's remembering his covenant (cf. "new covenant" in Luke 22:20);
deliverance from slavery in Egypt (cf. "for the forgiveness of sins" in
Matt 26:28); the blood of the Passover lamb (cf. "my blood" in Luke
22:20; "Christ, our Passover lamb, has been sacrificed," 1 Cor 5:7); the
interpretation of the elements of the Passover meal (cf. "This is my
body. . . . This cup is" in Luke 22:19-20); and a call for the continual celebration of the Passover (cf. 1 Cor 11:24).

Comments
22:14 There is a question about whether this verse is best understood as concluding 22:7-13[18] or as introducing 22:15-20.[19] The issue is of no great impor-

---

[15] For further discussion see Stein, "Last Supper," 444-50.

[16] See J. Jeremias, *The Eucharistic Words of Jesus* (London: SCM, 1966), 41-62.

[17] The Passover lamb reminded them of the blood of the lamb smeared on the door lintels
in order to escape the visitation of the angel of death. The unleavened bread reminded them
of the swiftness of their redemption in that there was no time to bake bread. The bowl of salt
water reminded them of the tears of their captivity; the bitter herbs, of the bitterness of their
slavery; the paste or *Charosheth*, of the clay used to make bricks during their bondage; and
the four cups of wine reminded them of the four promises of Exod 6:6-7a.

[18] So J. A. Fitzmyer, *The Gospel according to Luke*, AB (Garden City: Doubleday, 1985),
2:1376 and 2:1384.

[19] So Marshall, *Luke*, 794.

tance, however, and following the NIV it is treated here as an introduction to the following material. **When the hour came.** Compare John 13:1; 17:1. In Jesus' setting this referred to the hour to celebrate the Passover, but for Luke's readers this could mean the "hour" in which Jesus would bring his mission to completion. Compare Luke 22:53. **Jesus and his apostles reclined at the table.** The last supper, as all celebrations of the Lord's Supper, was meant for those who professed to be Jesus' followers (cf. 1 Cor 11:26-34). "Jesus and his apostles reclined" is literally *he reclined, and his disciples with him.* The wording emphasizes Jesus' initiative. The Passover was eaten in a reclining position, i.e., lying on the side facing a short table with cushions under the arm. Compare *Pesaḥim* 99b, "Even the poorest man in Israel must not eat [on the night of Passover] until he reclines." Other festive meals also were eaten in a reclining position (cf. Luke 11:37; 14:10; 17:7). The famous painting of the Last Supper by Leonardo da Vinci in which Jesus and the disciples are portrayed as sitting at a table is a beautiful sixteenth-century rendition of the event. It is not true, however, to the biblical account, in which the meal was eaten reclining.

22:15 I have eagerly desired. The construction found here (*with desire I have desired*) is also found in Acts.[20] It can be understood in several ways: (1) as an unfulfilled wish, i.e., *I have desired but unfortunately will not be able to eat this Passover.* This interpretation frequently is due to an attempt to harmonize this account with John 18:28, where the Passover is still future. In Luke, Jesus clearly eats the Passover (Luke 22:11,15), so that this interpretation must be rejected. (2) *I have looked forward to sharing the joy of eating the Passover with you, to teach you of the new covenant in my blood and to bring my work to a conclusion.* (3) *I have desired to participate in this (or possibly a future) Passover with you but will not.* The third interpretation, that Jesus could not or intentionally refrained from participating in the Passover, is unlikely in light of 22:11,15, so that the second interpretation is to be preferred.

This Passover. This can mean the Passover lamb or the Passover meal. If it refers to the former, this is an example of synecdoche, in which a part of the meal is being used to describe the whole meal so that there is little difference.

Before I suffer. For Luke the whole scene of the Lord's Supper centered around Jesus' suffering (cf. 9:22; 24:46; Acts 1:3; 3:18).

22:16 I will not eat it again. This is the strongest negation possible in Greek (the subjunctive of emphatic negation) and refers not to abstinence from the present Passover but to the fact that his forthcoming death would prohibit him from sharing future Passovers with the disciples.

Until it finds fulfillment in the kingdom of God. This refers to the time of the messianic banquet at the end of history, i.e., when the kingdom is consummated (cf. Mark 14:25; Matt 26:29; 1 Cor 11:26). This same thought is repeated in Luke 22:18. What the "it" refers to is unclear. It cannot be the "kingdom of God" because the "it" is distinguished from the kingdom. Probably "it" is best understood as referring to the Passover as a type of the messianic banquet. Jesus would not share again in such a banquet meal with the disciples until God's kingdom has been consummated. Since a Passover meal is specifically referred to here, the references to Jesus' eating with

[20] Acts 2:17; 5:28; 16:28; 23:14; 28:10.

the disciples in 24:30,41-43; Acts 10:41 do not contradict this saying. The divine passive found in this phrase should be noted. See comments on 6:21.

22:17 After taking a cup. The cup is one of the earlier cups associated with the Passover meal (cf. Exod 6:6-7a). **He gave thanks.** See comments on 22:19. **Take this and divide it among you.** A single cup probably was shared by the disciples. Whether Jesus himself partook of this cup is unclear.

22:18 For I tell you. Compare Luke 22:16. **I will not drink again . . . until the kingdom of God comes.** Once again we have a subjunctive of emphatic negation. See comments on 22:16. No distinction should be made between the drinking mentioned here and the eating mentioned in 22:16. They simply are descriptive of eating a meal and in particular the messianic banquet. It is reading too much into the present text to see it as demonstrating an established practice of fasting in the early church.[21]

22:19 For the parallels with the feeding of the five thousand, see comments on 9:16.

And he took bread. "Bread" (*arton*) refers to a "loaf" of bread whether leavened or unleavened. It is used of unleavened bread in Exod 29:2; Lev 2:4; 8:26; Num 6:19.

Gave thanks. Like 1 Cor 11:24, Luke used "thanks" (*eucharistēsas*), from which we get *Eucharist*, rather than "thanks" (*eulogēsas*) or "bless" as in Mark 14:22 and Matt 26:26. There is little difference in meaning between these two Greek terms.

This is my body. As Jesus earlier interpreted the unleavened bread in the Passover ritual (see "Context"), so in the Lord's Supper he also interpreted the bread. "This" refers to the bread just mentioned. The fact that "this" is neuter whereas "bread" is masculine does not refute this, for the change in gender is due to the assimilation of "this" to the predicate "body." Thus the change is due to literary reasons (to have the pronoun agree in gender with the noun in this sentence with which it goes), not theological ones (to show that the bread had been transformed into the body of Christ). The "bread" represents the "body of Jesus" in the sense that it represents Jesus. The bread thus represents, using Johannine terminology, the "Word [which] became flesh," not the "flesh" alone but the person who tabernacled in flesh (John 1:14).

At this point we encounter an important textual problem. An important manuscript D (Codex Beza) and the Old Latin omit the rest of this verse and all of the next. This results in the following: a word about a cup (Luke 22:17-18) concluded by a short word about the bread (22:19a). In favor of this textual reading are both the age of these textual witnesses and the difficulty of the reading. (It is more difficult to understand why a scribe might willingly omit the concluding word about the cup than to understand why one might want to add the final word about the cup in order to make it conform to the parallel accounts.) Yet the textual support in favor of including 22:19b-20 is overwhelming: $\mathfrak{P}^{75}$, ℵ, A, B, W, Vg, Cop.[22]

[21] Contra E. E. Ellis, *The Gospel of Luke*, NCB (Grand Rapids: Eerdmans, 1981), 253-54.
[22] For further discussion see B. M. Metzger, *A Textual Commentary on the Greek New Testament* (New York: UBS, 1971), 173-77; J. B. Green, *The Death of Jesus*, WUNT (Tübingen: Mohr, 1988), 35-42.

Given. "Given" is literally *being given*, a present participle used for a future event. It is unclear whether the "Giver" is understood as Jesus or God. Probably the latter is meant, but there would be little difference in Luke's understanding, for Jesus is God's Son. The verb "given" is used of sacrifice in 2:24; Mark 10:45: Gal 1:4.

This is. "This is" is best understood metaphorically in the Zwinglian sense of "symbolizes/represents" rather than "this has now become/been transformed into" in the Roman Catholic sense of transubstantiation or "In, with, and around the bread there is actually present my body" in the Lutheran sense of consubstantiation. (It is interesting to note that even after the supposed transformation of the bread and cup, the elements are still called the bread and cup [cf. 1 Cor 11:26].) John Calvin's position, emphasizing the spiritual presence of the Lord (see 1 Cor 10:16), also has been an important perspective for many in the Puritan and Free Church tradition.

For you. Compare 1 Cor 11:24. This preposition often has a vicarious sense.[23] "Given for you" explains how the bread, i.e., the self-giving of Jesus, relates to the believer.

Do this in remembrance of me. Compare 1 Cor 11:24. The authenticity of these words is frequently questioned because they are not found in the parallel accounts in Mark and Matthew. Yet the parallels between the Lord's Supper and the Passover make such a statement quite understandable since the Passover was to be continually celebrated (Deut 16:1-3) and its meaning remembered. Another argument against their authenticity is that "since" Jesus expected the immediate end of the age during his lifetime, he could not have instituted any rite or ordinance to be continually remembered in the future. It has been argued elsewhere that Jesus in fact did expect and teach that there would be a period of time requiring stewardship and faithfulness (see 19:11-27, "The Lukan Message"). "Do" is frequently used for the repeating of rites.[24] This is not to be interpreted *Do this in order that God might remember me*[25] but rather *Do this, i.e., share the bread and the cup, in your celebration of the Lord's Supper remembering me, my work, and my presence among you.*

22:20 After the supper. The Lord's Supper comes at the end of the Passover and builds on its imagery. See "Context."

This cup is. As in the case of the bread, it is better to understand "is" metaphorically in the sense of symbolizes/represents. The fact that drinking blood was forbidden by the law (Lev 3:17; 7:26-27; 17:14) makes it most difficult to think the disciples and early Jewish Christians thought that in drinking the cup they were actually drinking real blood. (One need only remember Peter's hesitation in Acts 10:6-16 to eating unkosher meat to see how difficult it would have been for the disciples to have drunk the cup if they believed that in so doing they were in fact drinking the blood of Jesus.)

The new covenant in my blood. Compare Jer 31:31 and how the Qumran community thought of itself as the community of the new covenant.[26] For the expression "blood of the covenant," cf. Exod 24:8; Lev 17:11-14. The cup is understood as representing sacrificial blood that inaugurates and seals a new covenant

---

[23] Cf. Isa 53:12; Rom 5:6; 8:32; 2 Cor 5:14; Gal 3:13; 1 Pet 2:21.
[24] Exod 29:35; Num 15:11-13; Deut 25:9; 1 QS 2:19; 1 QSa 2:21.
[25] This is the view of Jeremias, *Eucharistic Words of Jesus*, 237-55.
[26] 1QpHab 2:4-6; CD 6:19; cf. also Ezek 36:26-27; cf. also 2 Cor 3:3,6.

(cf. Gen 15:8-21). In *Tg. Onq.* and *Tg. Ps.-J.* on Exod 24:8 the expression "blood of the covenant" is clearly seen as atoning for sins because they add "to atone [*kopher*] for the people." Matthew 26:28 indicates a similar understanding and adds "for the forgiveness of sins" (cf. Heb 9:25-28).[27]

Which is poured out. This clause "is as vicarious and soteriological in its thrust as is v. 19c. Indeed, 'poured out' is even more connotative of death than 'given.' "[28] Compare Gen 9:6; Ezek 18:10; Isa 59:7; cf. Luke 11:50; Acts 22:20. This clause balances liturgically "given for you" in Luke 22:19.[29]

For you. This makes more explicit the "for many" of Mark 14:24 and parallels the "for you" in Luke 22:19.

The Lukan Message

Several Lukan emphases appear in this passage. One involves the understanding that Jesus' death lies within God's providential rule and plan. Jesus both knew of his coming death and saw it as involving a divine necessity. Jesus would die because God had given him over to death. See Introduction 8 (1). Thus his death was not a surprise or tragedy but the fulfillment of God's purpose and plan. Luke by repeating this tradition may also have been seeking to assure his readers that their practice of celebrating the Lord's Supper stemmed from Jesus himself. Thus they could know the "certainty" of this practice that they had been taught (1:4).

Within the present account we also have a strong eschatological emphasis concerning the future consummation of God's kingdom. Jesus will not return and share the messianic banquet until the final consummation when the events of 21:25-36 take place. Of all the Synoptic writers, Luke most clearly portrayed the arrival of God's kingdom in Jesus' ministry. See Introduction 8 (2). Although Satan already had fallen from heaven (10:18), the promised Spirit was present among them (Acts 2:1f.), and a new covenant had been established (Luke 22:20), Luke reminded his readers that their celebration of the Lord's Supper revealed that the final consummation was still in the future. Even as among their Jewish contemporaries the Passover awakened hopes and longings for the coming of the messianic banquet, so even more should the Lord's Supper cause Luke's readers to look not only backward to their Lord's death but forward to his return.[30]

One final theological teaching found in this passage can be mentioned, even if it is not a particular theological emphasis of Luke. From this passage it is evident that Luke understood Jesus' death as being both sacrificial

---

[27]For further discussion see Green, *Death of Jesus*, 194-97.

[28]Fitzmyer, *Luke* 2:1391.

[29]The rhythmic balance is closer in the Greek text than in the NIV: τὸ ὑπὲρ ὑμῶν διδόμενον in 22:19 and τὸ ὑπὲρ ὑμῶν ἐκχυννόμενον in 22:20.

[30]Luke 22:16,18; cf. Mark 14:25; Matt 26:29; 1 Cor 11:26.

and vicarious. Jesus' death is understood as sacrificial blood poured out to establish a new covenant (22:20). His death is vicarious because it is "for you" (22:19-20). To say that Luke was quoting the tradition in no way eliminates the fact that Luke believed and accepted what the tradition taught on this subject. If Luke disagreed with this teaching of the tradition, he easily could have eliminated it. He did not do this, however. Later in Acts 20:28 he once again revealed that he was in agreement with the tradition's teaching of the vicarious and sacrificial nature of Jesus' death. Thus, although Luke may not have emphasized this understanding of Jesus' death in Luke-Acts, it certainly is present. See Introduction 8 (8).

(4) Jesus' Betrayal Foretold (22:21-23)

[21]But the hand of him who is going to betray me is with mine on the table. [22]The Son of Man will go as it has been decreed, but woe to that man who betrays him." [23]They began to question among themselves which of them it might be who would do this.

Context

Unlike Mark and Matthew, where the scene switches immediately to the Mount of Olives, in Luke after the Lord's Supper Jesus gives a "farewell discourse" to his disciples. In this Luke resembles John, who has a lengthy discourse (chaps. 14–17) after the supper. There is, however, little resemblance between the content of the Lukan and Johannine discourses. The Lukan discourse consists of four parts loosely joined together.[31] How this material fits into the present context is not clear. It has been suggested that Luke sought to have a collection of four disciple failures: Judas's betrayal (Luke 22:21-23), the selfish desire for greatness (22:24-30), Peter's denial (22:31-34), and the misunderstanding concerning the nature of the kingdom (22:35-38). Another suggestion is that Luke sought to create a parallelism between Jesus' promise of a new covenant (22:14-20) and Judas's failure/betrayal (22:21-23) and between Jesus' promise of sharing his reign (22:28-30) and Peter's failure/denial (22:31-34). But what then of 22:24-27? The attempt to see 22:1-23 as a unit consisting of betrayal (22:1-6), Passover (22:7-20), and an inclusio of betrayal (22:21-23) is not convincing.[32]

Probably this section is best understood as a four-part farewell discourse. Frequently found in such a farewell discourse are a meal, prediction of death, warnings and final instructions, prayer for the followers,

---

[31] At times the material found in Luke's discourse comes from Mark (Luke 22:21-23 [Mark 14:20-21]; Luke 22:25-26 [Mark 10:42-44]; Luke 22:33-34 [Mark 14:29-31]), from Q (Luke 22:28-30 [cf. Matt 19:28]), and from Luke's special source L (Luke 22:27,31-32,35-38).

[32] Contra M. D. Goulder, *Luke: A New Paradigm* (Sheffield: JSOT, 1989), 727.

and the appointing of a leader.[33] No doubt Peter's denial was well-known in the church, and since he plays a decisive role in Luke's second work, Luke had to include this account in his work. Jesus' foreknowledge of his betrayal and the subsequent reinstatement of Peter (22:32) are therefore essential in Jesus' farewell discourse (22:14-38). It is, of course, apparent that Jesus' farewell discourse is somewhat unique from other such discourses in that he rose from the dead and gave further instruction to his disciples (Luke 24; Acts 1).

Comments

22:21 But. Literally *But behold*. The foretelling of the Judas's betrayal is closely tied to the Lord's Supper.

The hand of him. This expression is a synecdoche, a figure of speech in which a part (the hand) is used to represent the whole (Judas).[34]

Who is going to betray me. Literally *who is in the process of betraying* [a present participle] *me*. The betrayal had already begun (22:3-6).

With mine on the table. This is better translated "with me at the table." Compare 22:30, where the expression is translated "*at* the table."[35] By referring to Judas's betrayal after the Lord's Supper rather than before (cf. Mark 14:18-21; Matt 26:21-25), Luke revealed that participation in the Lord's Supper does not guarantee membership in God's kingdom. Compare John 13:26 and 13:27-30. Luke presented similar teachings elsewhere (see comments on 8:4-15; 13:22-30, "The Lukan Message").

22:22 The Son of Man. See comments on 5:24.

Will go. Literally *proceeds*. The certainty of this future event is so great it can be spoken of in the present tense. What Jesus had begun in 9:51 (cf. also 13:33) was about to be accomplished.

As it has been decreed. The divine passive should be noted. What was about to happen would occur because God had ordained it. This will be affirmed again in 24:25-27. See Introduction 8 (1). In Acts 2:23 this same verb ("set purpose") is used with respect to the passion and in Acts 10:42; 17:26,31 describes God's providential rule in and over history. The use of "decreed" instead of "written" (Mark 14:21; Matt 26:24) reveals Luke's interest in emphasizing that Jesus' death fulfills the divine plan and purpose.[36]

But woe to that man who betrays him. Any attempt to romanticize Judas's role in fulfilling the divine plan[37] is shipwrecked on this statement. Compare Mark 14:21 and Matt 26:24, which add, "It would be better for him if he had not been born." The Evangelists understood Judas as damning himself by his action

[33] See E. Stauffer, *New Testament Theology* (New York: Macmillan, 1955), 344-47 and J. Neyrey, *The Passion according to Luke* (New York: Paulist, 1985), 5-48.

[34] For other examples of this literary form, cf. 11:21; 22:15; 1 Sam 18:21; 22:17; 24:12-15; 2 Sam 14:19.

[35] Cf. also 20:37, "*at* the passage concerning the bush," and Acts 5:23, "*at* the doors."

[36] Cf. Acts 1:16-17, where Judas's betrayal is described as the fulfillment of Scripture.

[37] For such an attempt see N. Kazantzakis, *The Last Temptation of Christ* (New York: Bantam, 1960).

(cf. Acts 1:18-20).[38] The present verse is a good example of how divine sovereignty and human responsibility exist alongside each other.

22:23   They began to question among themselves. The horror of betrayal by a friend was far greater in biblical times than today. One catches a glimpse of this in Ps 41:9. Compare in 1 Cor 11:29-30 how Christians' sitting at table with the risen Lord and "betraying him" is also seen as resulting in judgment and even death.

Which of them it might be who would do this. Judas was still present with the disciples (Luke 22:21).

The Lukan Message

After the Lord's Supper, Luke pointed out Jesus' knowledge of the future and his awareness of what was about to take place. He was even aware that one of the Twelve was in the process of betraying him. As a prophet and as the Son of God, he was not caught unawares as to what was about to happen. What he began in 9:51 by proceeding to Jerusalem he would continue to do in order to fulfill the divine plan. Luke expected his readers to understand the Christological implications of this. He also expected they would see God's sovereign rule and control in this as well. Even the betrayal is in accord with the divine plan. The desire of the chief priests, teachers of the law, the decision of Judas, and even the role of Satan were seen by Luke as serving the divine purpose. God is in control. Luke did not explain how individual responsibility, in the case of Judas and the Jewish leadership, and the divine foreknowledge and ordination of what was to take place fit together. He simply stated that they did.[39] What is clear is that Luke wanted his readers to know that Jesus' death was not a "tragedy" but determined and foreknown and that Jesus and his Father were in complete control throughout. It was God who "decreed" what took place (22:22). See Introduction 8 (1).

It may also be that Luke, like Paul, was seeking to teach his readers that participation in the Lord's Supper (and by implication, baptism) does not guarantee one a place in God's kingdom (cf. 1 Cor 10:1-5). More certain, however, is that he wanted his readers to ask themselves whether as they share the Lord's table they are faithful disciples.[40]

(5) Greatness in the Kingdom of God (22:24-30)

[24]**Also a dispute arose among them as to which of them was considered to be greatest. [25]Jesus said to them, "The kings of the Gentiles lord it over them; and**

---

[38]Cf. the "woes" of Luke 6:24-26; 10:13-14; 11:42-44; 17:1-2; cf. also Acts 1:18-20.

[39]Cf. C. F. Evans, *Saint Luke*, TPINTC (London: SCM, 1990), 794: "The juxtaposition of the divine necessity for something to happen and the human culpability for its happening is simply made without any resolution of the logical problem."

[40]X. Léon-Dufour, *Sharing the Eucharistic Bread* (New York: Paulist, 1987), 235.

those who exercise authority over them call themselves Benefactors. [26]But you are not to be like that. Instead, the greatest among you should be like the youngest, and the one who rules like the one who serves. [27]For who is greater, the one who is at the table or the one who serves? Is it not the one who is at the table? But I am among you as one who serves. [28]You are those who have stood by me in my trials. [29]And I confer on you a kingdom, just as my Father conferred one on me, [30]so that you may eat and drink at my table in my kingdom and sit on thrones, judging the twelve tribes of Israel.

Context

After telling of the worst of the disciples, i.e., of Judas and his betrayal, Luke included materials that involve what it means to be the greatest (Luke 22:24) of the disciples. Whether this section should be treated as one or two sections (22:24-27,28-30) is debated.[41] For Luke, however, this material is brought together and made into a single section. This is clear from the repetition of "you" in 20:26,27,28,29,30 and the lack of any break in 22:28.

A dispute over who was to be considered the greatest among the disciples became an occasion for Jesus to teach about true greatness in God's kingdom. Elsewhere in Luke (9:46-48; cf. 20:45-47) we find such teaching.[42] Jesus contrasted the attitude and values of the world with what it means to be great in God's kingdom. Even as membership in the kingdom is the reverse of how the world thinks, for the last have become first and the first last (13:30), so too greatness within the kingdom is the reverse of how the world thinks. In this world the first (kings) rule and exercise their authority over the last (their subjects). Great people in this world are served by others under them. But Jesus had not come to be served but rather to serve. He came to pour out his blood in order to establish a new covenant (22:20). Thus to be great in the kingdom means to follow Jesus and to become one who serves, to think of oneself as having the least "rights," i.e., to be the youngest.

Comments

22:24 Also a dispute arose among them. The "also" (literally *and it came to pass*) ties what follows closely to what precedes in 22:21-23.

As to which of them was considered to be greatest. "Greatest" is literally *greater*, but the comparative ("greater") frequently was used for the superlative

---

[41] Similar material is found in two separate places in the other Synoptic Gospels (cf. Mark 10:42-45 [parallel, Matt 20:25-28]; Matt 19:28).

[42] In Mark 10:35-45; Matt 20:20-28 we find an account in which James and John requested the privilege of sitting at Jesus' right and left side when he entered his glory/kingdom. The exact relationship of Luke 22:24-27 to the parallel passages in Mark and Matthew is debated.

("greatest"). The play on words is lost, however, if we do not note that the terms "greatest" (22:24), "greatest" (22:26), and "greater" (22:27) all translate the same Greek word (*meidzōn*). Compare 9:46-48; cf. also 12:37.

22:25 The kings of the Gentiles lord it over them. For "Gentiles" cf. 12:30; 18:32; 24:47. The same verb is also used negatively in 2 Cor 1:24; cf. also 1 Pet 5:3.

And those who exercise authority over them call themselves Benefactors. The form of the verb can be passive, "are called" (RSV, NASB, NEB), or middle, "call themselves" (NIV). The term "benefactor" was frequently used to describe gods, heroes, and kings who were in fact at times quite despotic, so that there may be some irony in this statement.

22:26 But you are not to be like that. The "you" is emphatic.

Instead, the greatest among you. Jesus' words are addressed to church leaders. The following words do not deny that there are leaders of the church. What they do is describe how such leaders are to lead. The greatest in the church are not to behave as the greatest in the world. For "greatest" see comments on 22:24. The implications for Luke's readers of Jesus' instructions to the apostles are sufficiently self-evident that no direct application needed to be made by the Evangelist.

Should be like the youngest. "Youngest" is literally *younger*. See comments on 22:24. The "youngest" does not refer to an established group in the church. Rather the youngest represent people who possess the least claim for "ruling over" others.

And the one who rules like the one who serves. "The one who rules" may be a semitechnical term for an officer in the church (cf. Acts 15:22; Heb 13:7,17, 24). The Greek word for "serves" is *diakonōn*, from which the word *deacon* comes. Compare Acts 6:1-6. The terms "serves," "servant," and "service" occur over ninety times in the NT. Elsewhere Jesus described himself as one who came to "serve" (Mark 10:45). Compare 1 Pet 5:2.

22:27 For who is greater, the one who. Jesus introduced two rhetorical questions that describe the world's thinking and value system. Greatness in the world's eyes involves being served by others. There may be a possible allusion here to the office of deacon, whose responsibility it is to serve (cf. Acts 6:1, "daily distribution" [literally *service*]; 6:2, "wait on tables" [literally *to serve tables*]).

But I am among you as one who serves. Although Jesus is clearly "greater" than the disciples, his behavior during his earthly ministry was one of serving them (cf. John 13:3-17; Phil 2:6-11). Thus one who would follow Jesus also should be servant of all.

22:28 You are those who have stood by me in my trials. It is false to think that the time of Jesus between Luke 4:13 and 22:3 was completely free from Satanic temptation (see comments on 4:13). The disciples had continued (a perfect participle in Greek) with Jesus during his times of trial. This can only mean that throughout Jesus' past trials (not just the recent ones in Jerusalem) they were with him. Yet they only joined him after the temptation (cf. 5:1f.). Thus, whereas Jesus may in his ministry have been spared from a direct frontal attack of Satan such as 4:1-13, this does not mean that Satan was not active in seeking to undermine and thwart his ministry. During all this time, the disciples were with him. (Compare Acts 1:21-22, where the only requirement listed for being the twelfth apostle was to "have been with us the whole time.") Although the disciples would themselves face trials in the future (Luke 12:4-12; 22:36; Acts 20:19), the trials in this verse look backward, not forward, and are associated with Jesus, not them.

22:29   And I confer on you a kingdom, just as my Father conferred one on me.   For the description of Jesus as King, cf. Luke 1:32-33; 2:4,11; 19:11-40 (esp. 19:12,15); 23:42. For the parallel between the relationship of the disciples to Jesus and Jesus to the Father, cf. John 15:9; 20:21 (cf. also Luke 9:48; 10:16). The term "confer" (*diatithemai*) can also mean *make a covenant with* and thus brings to mind the new "covenant" (*diathēkē*) of 22:20. The covenant established with the apostles in 22:20 ultimately involves the promise of sharing in the future consummation of the kingdom when the Son of Man returns to reign. Whereas in 12:32 the Father confers the kingdom, here Jesus himself does this.

22:30   So that you might eat and drink at my table in my kingdom.   The difference in wording between this and the parallel in Matt 19:28 reveals that Luke was consciously tying this saying to Luke 22:16,18, where Jesus spoke of his not eating or drinking with the apostles again until he does so with them in God's kingdom. Compare also 13:29; 14:15. Note "*my* table" and "*my* kingdom."

And sit on thrones, judging the twelve tribes of Israel.   Compare Matt 19:28, where Matthew mentioned sitting on the "twelve" thrones and judging the twelve tribes. Luke may have omitted the reference to the twelve thrones because due to Judas's betrayal (Luke 22:3-6,21-23) there were only eleven apostles at the time. This would be remedied in Acts 1:15-26. Exactly what was meant by this verse is debated. Does this refer to a future restoration and rule over Israel (cf. Luke 13:35; 21:24);[43] the future judgment of the literal Israel, which rejected Jesus (cf. 11:31-32); a glorious reward in heaven; or the disciples' future rule over the church as seen in Acts? In light of the future dimension of the parallel sayings in 22:16,18, it is best to understand this promise as referring to that time when the believer will share in the benefits of Jesus' kingly rule (cf. 22:29-30a). Like the first promise in 22:30a, this one is best understood metaphorically as referring to participating in the consummated kingdom where believers experience the blessings of their Lord's reign. Although there is a sense in which Jesus already at his resurrection reigned as King (22:69; Acts 2:33; 5:31), the kingly rule referred to here will take place in the consummation at the redemption brought by the Son of Man (21:28). Matthew understood it in this manner, for he spoke of this taking place "at the renewal of all things" (Matt 19:28). Compare 1 Cor 6:2-3; 2 Tim 2:12; Rev 2:26-29; 3:21.

The Lukan Message

Luke reminded his readers, and especially the leaders among them, that greatness in God's kingdom is contrary to the world's values, for it involves serving rather than being served. If there were "deacons" among Luke's readers, they might have been reminded that their "office" was one of service (cf. Acts 6:1-6). The rich were reminded that they should serve the poor (cf. Acts 4:34-37). Luke, like Jesus, was well aware that even

---

[43] See J. B. Chance, *Jerusalem, the Temple, and the New Age in Luke-Acts* (Macon: Mercer, 1988).

within the fellowship of the believing community a this-world attitude toward power and greatness could still be present.[44] Greatness, however, means service; it means to live as if one were the youngest or least. Such faithfulness, however, will not go unrewarded. Jesus in his reign (Luke 22:29) promises his followers that they will share in the benefits of that rule. The degree to which the language of 22:30 is metaphorical is uncertain, but the reality to which it refers is concrete. What awaits Jesus will be shared with his followers. Luke's readers are encouraged to seek a role of servanthood because Jesus has promised that such faithfulness, endurance (8:15; 21:19), and following (9:23-24) will result in "treasure in heaven (18:22,30; 19:17-19). Such people will "dine" with Jesus in God's kingdom (13:28-20; 14:14; 22:16,18,30).

Associated with the pericope's teaching concerning true greatness are several important Christological assertions concerning Jesus' kingship and unique relationship to God. He who announced the coming of God's kingdom is its King and will in the consummation reign as king (22:29; cf. 19:12,15,27; 23:42). Already at his entry into Jerusalem, Luke has shown that Jesus entered as the awaited King (19:28-40; cf. Mark 11:9-11; Matt 21:4-9). Luke added a comment about Jesus' kingship in 23:2 and included traditional material in 23:3,37-38,42-43. This kingship will also be witnessed to indirectly in Acts 17:7. Luke wanted Theophilus and his other readers to remember that the Jesus in whom they believe is Lord and that the consummation of history brings with it the reign of their Lord as King.

(6) Peter's Denial Foretold (22:31-34)

[31] "Simon, Simon, Satan has asked to sift you as wheat. [32]But I have prayed for you, Simon, that your faith may not fail. And when you have turned back, strengthen your brothers."

[33]But he replied, "Lord, I am ready to go with you to prison and to death."

[34]Jesus answered, "I tell you, Peter, before the rooster crows today, you will deny three times that you know me."

Context

The third part of Jesus' farewell discourse[45] begins with his statement that Satan, whose activity has intensified since 22:3, had sought to separate

---

[44]Cf. L. Sabourin, *The Gospel according to St. Luke* (Bombay: St. Paul Society, 1984), 363: "That the warning against seeking honours finds such varied expression in the gospels and elsewhere in the NT, shows it was needed already in the early Church."

[45]The material is a mixture of Lukan (L) material (22:31-32) and traditional material found in the other Gospels (cf. Mark 14:29-30; Matt 26:33-34; John 13:37-38). The much debated relationship of Luke's account to these other accounts is unresolved. Luke may have been influenced not only by the Markan account (see Introduction 5) but also by other forms of the tradition, both oral and written, such as witnessed to in John 13:37-38.

the disciples (the "you" in 22:31 is plural) from Jesus. He would not be successful, however, for Jesus had prayed on their behalf. As a result, although Peter (and the other disciples also) would fall, he would return and find restoration. Jesus then commanded Peter to strengthen the church after his restoration. Peter protested that he was prepared to suffer imprisonment and even death for Jesus, but he was told that before the cock crowed he would in fact deny three times that he knew Jesus.

Comments

22:31 Simon, Simon. See comments on 10:41. The use of Peter's "pre-Christian" name (see comments on 6:14) instead of "Peter," the name he was called as one of the great leaders of the church, is probably intentional. Peter shortly would revert back to an earlier life-style and behavior, predating his following Jesus (6:13-14).

[Behold.] The NIV leaves this Greek term (*idou*) untranslated and loses the dramatic intensification placed upon the following words.

Satan has asked to sift you as wheat. The meaning of this verse is uncertain. Its interpretation is further complicated by the fact that the word translated "asked" (NIV) or "demanded" (RSV) is found nowhere else in the NT or LXX. The nearest analogy is found in Job 1–2, where Satan is permitted to test Job. This and the vocabulary in Amos 9:9 suggests the following interpretation: "Satan is seeking [a dramatic aorist] to shake you disciples violently as one sifts wheat and to cause you to fall." The metaphor of sifting wheat should not be pressed in order to determine what is "wheat" and what is "chaff," for this contrast is not mentioned. The use of this metaphor is simply intended to indicate the coming time of testing (cf. Luke 3:17; Amos 9:9). One should not interpret this as God's granting a request by Satan for permission to test the disciples as in Job 1–2. The saying speaks primarily of Satan's trying to unsettle the disciples and cause them to become unfaithful. Although Luke tended to avoid emphasizing the disciples' failures (note his omission of Mark 8:32-33; 14:27-28,50), he was aware of their faults and was not averse to mentioning them. The "you" here (*hymas*) is plural and refers to Peter and the other disciples (not Peter and Judas). By mentioning the role of Satan in Peter's denial, Luke may have been seeking to increase his readers' empathy toward the apostle.

22:32 I have prayed. The "I" is emphatic. Jesus' prayer would prove greater than Satan's attempt to undo his disciples' allegiance. Jesus prayed as their advocate against Satan ("the accuser"). Compare John 17:6-26; 10:27-29. For the importance of prayer and Jesus' practice of prayer, see Introduction 8 (7). Compare 1 John 2:1, where the risen Christ continues to intercede before the Father for his followers.

For you, Simon. The "you" (*sou*) here is singular, and Jesus' attention turned from the disciples in general to Peter in particular.

That your faith may not fail. The "that" (*hina*) reveals the purpose of Jesus' prayer as well as its content. "Faith" here refers not to correct doctrinal belief but to "faithfulness." Jesus prayed that Peter (and the other apostles) would not lose their faithfulness, i.e., their loyalty to him (cf. Luke 18:8; Acts 14:22) during this sifting period. Jesus, as well as Luke's readers, knew that Peter would deny the Lord (Luke 22:34,54-62). Thus the content of this prayer should not be understood as a prayer that Peter would not deny Jesus. If this were so, then Jesus' prayer failed completely. Rather the prayer was that Peter would not disavow his allegiance and loyalty to Jesus. This Peter did not do; and the reader, who is aware of Peter's leadership role in the early church, knows that Jesus' prayer for Peter was answered.

When you have turned back. The "you" is emphatic. The issue was not whether Peter would repent but what he would do after he repented. Jesus foreknew that Peter's faith would not fail but that after his denial he would repent because he prayed for him. Although the verb (*epistrephas*) can mean "having physically returned" (back to Jerusalem), it must be understood here as referring to Peter's repenting.[46] Note how it is used together with "repent" (*metanoein*) in Acts 3:19; 26:20. Although *turn back* is not used in the parable of the prodigal son (Luke 15:11-32), what *turning back* means is described metaphorically in the action of the prodigal son (re)turning back to his father. Peter's true faith and perseverance would be revealed in his repentance, not in his sinlessness.

Strengthen your brothers. In the NT this verb frequently describes the process of helping someone grow in the Christian faith.[47] How Peter fulfilled this is seen in Acts by his leadership in completing the number of the disciples to twelve (1:15-26), his preaching at Pentecost (2:14-40), his early preaching and leadership in Jerusalem (chaps. 3–5), and his role in the expansion of the church to Samaria (8:14-25) and to the Gentiles (chaps. 10–11; 15:7-11). "Brothers" therefore refers to more than just the other apostles and is essentially a synonym for "believers" (cf. Acts 1:15; 15:23). For the Johannine parallel to this, cf. John 21:15-19.

22:33 Lord, I am ready. Compare John 13:37. For the fulfillment of the first part of Peter's confession, cf. Acts 5:17-42; 12:1-11. The fulfillment of the latter part of his confession is not recorded in Acts but was no doubt known both to Luke and his readers. Note the parallels in Acts 21:13; 23:29.

22:34 You will deny . . . that you know me. The Lukan account differs here slightly from Mark 14:30 and Matt 26:34. In Mark and Matthew, Peter would "disown" Jesus, whereas in Luke he would "deny knowing" Jesus. Luke may have been seeking to avoid a misconception that Peter by his denial disowned Jesus in the sense of Luke 12:9 (cf. 9:26). The fulfillment of Jesus' prophecy will be recounted in 22:54-62.

The Lukan Message

A familiar Lukan emphasis is seen most clearly in 22:32. The importance of prayer in the life of Jesus and in the early church has been referred to on several occasions. See Introduction 8 (7). Luke in this account revealed to his readers that prayer was the means by which Peter and the disciples were kept from falling away from the faith. Because Jesus prayed, Peter's failure did not result in apostasy. Luke by this incident also

[46]The term "turn back" is also used in this sense of "repent" in Luke 17:4; Acts 9:35; 11:21; 14:15; 15:19; 26:18,20.

[47]Cf. Rom 1:11; 16:25; 1 Thess 3:2,13; 2 Thess 2:17; 2 Pet 1:12; cf. Acts 18:23.

foreshadowed the future role of the great apostle, which was well-known to his readers. He revealed how Peter, despite his denial (22:34c), was able to be restored (22:32b) and how he was commissioned by Jesus for the leadership role he played in the early church. Whether Luke's readers were troubled with this issue is impossible to know. What is clear is that by this account Luke helped them understand how, despite his denial, Peter was able to play such an important role in the early church. Apart from Jesus' prayer, however, this would not have been possible. Thus Luke's readers needed to continue in prayer (18:1; 22:40,46).

Another theme involves Jesus' foreknowledge. Once again Luke wanted his reader to see Jesus as one who knows the future. He knew the future exactly, for he knew that Peter would deny him three times before the cock crowed. Like the prophets of old, Jesus knew what would take place, but unlike the OT prophets who received their knowledge from God, nothing is said of the Father's revealing this to Jesus. He knew because of who he is. Luke did not develop the Christological implications of this, but just as he could speak of the future messianic banquet as Jesus' table and of God's kingdom as his kingdom (22:30), so he could speak of Jesus himself knowing the future.

(7) Two Swords (22:35-38)

[35]Then Jesus asked them, "When I sent you without purse, bag or sandals, did you lack anything?"

"Nothing," they answered.

[36]He said to them, "But now if you have a purse, take it, and also a bag; and if you don't have a sword, sell your cloak and buy one. [37]It is written: 'And he was numbered with the transgressors'; and I tell you that this must be fulfilled in me. Yes, what is written about me is reaching its fulfillment."

[38]The disciples said, "See, Lord, here are two swords."

"That is enough," he replied.

Context

The last account in Jesus' farewell discourse is not found in any of the other Gospels. In it Jesus contrasts the past mission of the disciples in 9:1-6 (and the seventy disciples of 10:4) with the changed situation that was about to take place. On their early mission the disciples went out without provisions and depended entirely on the hospitality of their hearers. In the new situation brought about by Jesus' death (22:37), they must go equipped and be prepared to face hostility and persecution. This involved their purchasing a "sword" because what the Scriptures said about the death of God's Son was about to be fulfilled. The opposition to Jesus that had been mounting[48] was

---

[48]Luke 6:11; 11:53-54; 19:47; 20:19; 22:2.

about to come to its culmination, and the end was very near. To Jesus' frustration, however, the disciples failed to grasp his meaning in the use of the sword metaphor, and he concluded the conversation.

Comments

22:35 When I sent you without purse, bag or sandals. This describes the mission of the seventy (cf. 10:4) better than the mission of the Twelve (cf. 9:3). However, since the Twelve are being addressed here, Luke probably had both passages in mind.

Did you lack anything? The question expects a negative response. Earlier they could count on the people's hospitality (cf. 9:4; 10:5-9).

"Nothing," they answered. As 10:17 indicates, the disciples did not lack anything. On the contrary in their ministries they experienced great spiritual victories.

22:36 But now. The "but" is emphatic. A new situation was arising. *What* that situation was is explained in 22:37, but first Jesus explained *how* to prepare for this new situation. The "now" did not take place immediately at this point but looked forward to the postresurrection period.

If you have a purse, take it, and also a bag. For "purse" and "bag" see comments on 10:4 and 9:3.

And if you don't have a sword, sell your cloak and buy one. Even if the exact interpretation of this verse is uncertain,[49] it is clear that a new situation is envisioned. The disciples would soon encounter greater opposition and even persecution (cf. Acts 8:1-3; 9:1-2; 12:1-5). The reference to the purchase of a sword is strange. Attempts to interpret this literally as a Zealot-like call to arms, however, are misguided and come to grief over the saying's very "strangeness." Understood as a call to arms, this saying not only does not fit Jesus' other teachings but radically conflicts with them. Also if two swords are "enough" (22:38), war with the legions of Rome was certainly not envisioned. See 20:20-26, "Context." The "sword" is best understood in some metaphorical sense as indicating being spiritually armed and prepared for battle against the spiritual foes. The desperate need to be "armed" for these future events is evident by the command to sell one's mantle, for this garment was essential to keep warm at night (see comments on 6:29).

22:37 It is written ... must be fulfilled in me. For a more literal translation of this verse see the RSV. Once again the divine "must" (*dei*) appears. Jesus' forthcoming death had been foretold in Scripture, so that it was not fate or tragedy that awaited him but the fulfillment of the divine will and plan. See Introduction 8 (1). The divine passive is present in the infinitive "be fulfilled," i.e., *God will fulfill it in me.*

---

[49] There are several ways of interpreting this difficult clause: (1) *Let the person with a purse and bag and let the one not having a purse and bag sell his cloak, and let them both go and buy a sword.* (2) *Let the person with a purse and bag take them now (whereas before he did not), and let the person not having a sword, let him sell his cloak and buy one.* This interpretation is followed by the NIV, RSV, NASB, NEB. (3) *Let the person having a sword also take a purse and bag, and the one who does not have a sword, let him sell his cloak and buy one.* The second interpretation is the most probable. See Fitzmyer, *Luke,* 2:1431-32.

He was numbered with the transgressors. Compare Isa 53:12. This finds its fulfillment for Luke in 23:32-33,39-43. This is the only place in the Gospels where Isa 53 is quoted.

What is written about me is reaching its fulfillment. This last clause in the Greek text can mean either (1) *What is written about me is now to be fulfilled* or (2) *What has been written about me now comes to its climax.* The difference is not so much one of substance as nuance. Each interpretation reinforces the first part of the verse, which emphasizes the central place of Jesus' death in Scripture and God's sovereign rule in all that was about to take place. The purpose of this verse is to explain the "but now" of Luke 22:36. Whereas their union of destinies will one day lead to the apostles' sharing in the Son of Man's reign (22:29-30), in the more immediate future the treatment facing Jesus also awaited them. Thus they must arm themselves with a similar resolve to fulfill God's plan for them despite prison, persecution, and even death.

22:38 See, Lord, here are two swords. The disciples misunderstood Jesus' words in 22:36 by interpreting them literally, and their lack of understanding is most evident at this point. That they were armed is evident from 22:49-50. The wearing of a sword for protection against thieves was common (*Sabb.* 6:4).

"That is enough," he replied. Clearly two swords were not enough for any planned armed resistance. Jesus' words are best understood as breaking off further conversation as in Deut 3:26, i.e., "Enough of this [foolish] conversation." Compare also 1 Kgs 19:4; 1 Chr 21:15.

The Lukan Message

Like the previous account, this passage reveals both Jesus' knowledge of the future and how the divine plan concerning Jesus' death must be fulfilled. Since the Scriptures reveal God's will, what they say concerning Jesus' death "must" be fulfilled because God's sovereign will cannot be frustrated. This Lukan emphasis is especially evident in Luke 22:37, which speaks of "what is written" and its "fulfillment" and refers to the divine "must." Luke wanted his readers to have no doubt concerning Jesus' death. The death of God's Son was divinely decreed from the beginning.

Luke may also have sought through this passage to show his readers why Jesus' earlier teachings concerning missionary work were no longer followed by the church. Whether the instructions of 9:3 and 10:4 had caused a problem among his readers, because the church's present practice was somewhat different, is impossible to know. What is clear is that Luke recognized a clear difference between the preaching of the gospel during Jesus' ministry and the new situation, the "but now" of the post-Pentecost church. Much of Jesus' teachings to the twelve and the seventy remained applicable, but some things had changed. Nevertheless these changes, Luke argued, were taught by Jesus himself. See 9:1-6, "The Lukan Message."

2. Arrest and Trial (22:39–23:56)

With 22:39 we have a clear transition from the first part of the passion
narrative, dealing with the Lord's Supper (22:1-38), to the second part,
which involves the events surrounding Jesus' trial and crucifixion (22:39–
23:56). After the Lord's Supper and Jesus' farewell discourse, the scene
changes to the Mount of Olives (cf. Mark 14:26; Matt 26:30,36; John 18:1).
Thereafter Jerusalem is center stage. This section contains fourteen
accounts beginning with Jesus' prayer (22:39-46) and proceeding to
Jesus' arrest (22:47-53), trial (22:54–23:49), and burial (23:50-56).

(1) The Prayer of Jesus (22:39-46)

[39]Jesus went out as usual to the Mount of Olives, and his disciples followed
him.
[40]On reaching the place, he said to them, "Pray that you will not fall into
temptation." [41]He withdrew about a stone's throw beyond them, knelt down and
prayed,
[42]"Father, if you are willing, take this cup from me; yet not my will, but
yours be done." [43]An angel from heaven appeared to him and strengthened him.
[44]And being in anguish, he prayed more earnestly, and his sweat was like drops
of blood falling to the ground.
[45]When he rose from prayer and went back to the disciples, he found them
asleep, exhausted from sorrow. [46]"Why are you sleeping?" he asked them. "Get
up and pray so that you will not fall into temptation."

Context

The opening account in this new section involves Jesus' prayer on the
Mount of Olives. Luke's abbreviated account (seven verses to eleven in
Mark and Matthew) has eliminated a number of details.[50] Along with various omissions Luke also made a significant modification in 22:40b,46c by
wrapping the entire discourse around an inclusio of the words "pray that
you will not fall into temptation." Thus Luke shifted the focus of attention
from Jesus' own struggle and temptation (22:28) to the disciples' need to
pray in order to be victorious in their own struggles and temptations. With
the twofold command to pray and the omission of the textually doubtful
22:43-44 (see comments on 22:43-44) we have the following chiastic structure: A (22:40) B (22:41) C (22:42) b (22:45) a (22:46).

---

[50]These include the omission of the name "Gethsemane"; the separation of Peter, James,
and John from the main body of disciples; the threefold return of Jesus to the sleeping disciples; Jesus' rebuke of the disciples for not praying; the description of Jesus' distress and
sorrow; and the concluding statement that the "hour" had come and that the Son of Man was
betrayed into the hands of sinners.

Comments

22:39   Jesus went out as usual to the Mount of Olives. Literally, *Going out he proceeded.* Jesus proceeded on the way to the cross just as predicted.[51] For the expression "as usual" cf. 1:9; 2:42; for Jesus' practice of going to the Mount of Olives and spending the night there with his disciples, cf. 21:37. This was the needed information that Judas supplied to the chief priests and teachers of the law by which he betrayed Jesus. Compare 22:2,4 with 20:19 and 19:47-48. For the "Mount of Olives" see comments on 19:29.[52]

And his disciples followed him. In 22:14 the Twelve are called apostles. Here they are called "disciples" as in Luke's source (cf. Mark 14:32). Judas has left the group and will only appear again in 22:47. As in 5:11,27-28; 9:23,49 the disciples "follow" Jesus. Even as they followed him in this time of suffering, so some of them would follow him in death (cf. Acts 7:54–8:1; 12:1-5).

22:40   On reaching the place, he said to them. Although Luke did not mention the garden of Gethsemane, his readers may be aware of "the place" where Jesus was betrayed. Compare John 18:2.

Pray that you will not. As in Luke 14:7; 18:1,9; 19:11 the theme of what follows is made clear at the beginning. Its repetition in 22:46 forms an inclusio. For similar teachings cf. 1 Cor 16:13; Eph 6:18; 1 Thess 5:6; 1 Pet 5:8.

Fall into temptation. Literally *enter not into temptation.* For the meaning of this phrase, see comments on 11:4. As in 11:4 the lack of the article before "temptation" should be noted. The prayer involves not so much a concern not to fall in the time of "The Temptation" at the end of history (cf. Matt 24:15-31; Rev 3:10) but rather not to fall in the daily encounters with temptation. This is made even clearer by the context, for Luke had in mind Peter's temptation in the immediate future (22:31-34,54-62).

22:41   He withdrew about a stone's throw. Compare "going a little farther" (Mark 14:35; Matt 26:39).

Knelt down. Compare Acts 7:60; 9:40; 20:36; 21:5.

And prayed. For the importance of prayer for Jesus, see Introduction 8 (7).

22:42   Father. See comments on 11:2. Luke omitted the Aramaic "Abba" found in Mark 14:36.

If you are willing. The substance of Jesus' prayer for Luke is the same as Mark 14:36; Matt 26:39, but here Jesus appealed first to God's will.

Take this cup from me. For "cup" as a metaphor for Jesus' suffering, cf. Mark 10:38-39; Matt 20:22-23.[53] It is a metaphor here not for physical death in general[54] but for the particular death Jesus would suffer.

Yet not my will, but yours be done. For similar examples of Jesus' struggle in prayer, cf. John 12:27; 18:11; Heb 5:7. For similar experiences in the early church, cf. Acts 21:14.

---

[51] Luke 9:51,53; 13:33; 17:11; 19:28.

[52] For camping on the Mount of Olives during the Passover, see J. Jeremias, *Jerusalem in the Time of Jesus* (Philadelphia: Fortress, 1969), 61.

[53] Cf. also Isa 51:17,22; Jer 25:15; 49:12; Lam 4:21; Ps 75:8.

[54] Contra O. Cullmann, *Immortality of the Soul or Resurrection of the Dead* (London: Epworth, 1958), 19-27.

22:43-44 Whether these verses were part of the original text of Luke is debated. They are found in several significant manuscripts: ‫א‬, D, Vg, and many of the early church fathers. Yet they are not found in the best manuscript tradition: $\mathfrak{P}^{69}$, $\mathfrak{P}^{75}$, B, A, W, it, Cop, various early church fathers, etc. Because these verses do not fit particularly well the present context and are lacking in the best manuscript tradition, they should not be regarded as part of the original Gospel of Luke.[55]

22:45   When he rose . . . asleep. Compare Luke 9:32.

Exhausted from sorrow. This is found only in Luke. As in 9:33e, where Luke explained Peter's foolish remark in the earlier part of the verse, so here he sought to explain the disciples' failure. No explanation is given for why the disciples were sorrowful. However, Luke's readers knew why, for they were familiar with the passion story and knew what was about to take place. As for the disciples, such sayings of Jesus as 22:14-23,31-34 are sufficient to explain their grief (cf. John 16:6,20-22).

22:46   Get up and pray so that you will not fall into temptation. The reiteration of this command (cf. 22:40) closes the account and shows that Luke considered this its dominant theme. Compare 18:1.

The Lukan Message

Now, as the disciples face Satan's sifting (22:31), they need to pray so that their faith will not fail. Now that the hour has come, they especially need to arm themselves with prayer. Only then will they be able to persevere (8:15) and be found faithful (18:8). As in the prayer Jesus taught them as disciples, they need to pray "Lead us not into temptation" (11:4). Their lack of prayer at this crucial time would help Luke's readers understand Peter's failure in the temptation that was to follow (22:54-62). For prayer as a Lukan emphasis, see Introduction 8 (7).

Luke's readers were again reminded that Jesus' suffering was due to God's plan. Jesus' prayer (22:42) clearly reveals that despite his own personal desire, he submitted himself to the divine will, which involved the necessity of his death (cf. 22:37). His prayer also serves as a pattern for Luke's readers who might have to walk in the footsteps of their Lord.

(2) The Arrest of Jesus (22:47-53)

[47]While he was still speaking a crowd came up, and the man who was called Judas, one of the Twelve, was leading them. He approached Jesus to kiss him, [48]but Jesus asked him, "Judas, are you betraying the Son of Man with a kiss?"

---

[55]For some believers who have been raised on the *King James Version* of the Bible, to speak of "omitting" certain verses from the Bible seems heretical, and the warning of Rev 22:19 comes to mind. What is at issue here, however, is not "omitting" something from the sacred text but rather not allowing something that was never in the sacred text to be added to it. It is just as wrong to add something to the Scriptures as it is to take away something from them. When we therefore speak of "omitting" Luke 22:43-44 from the text, we mean that we should not include what some later scribe added to the original Gospel penned by the Evangelist Luke.

⁴⁹**When Jesus' followers saw what was going to happen, they said, "Lord, should we strike with our swords?"** ⁵⁰**And one of them struck the servant of the high priest, cutting off his right ear.**

⁵¹**But Jesus answered, "No more of this!" And he touched the man's ear and healed him.**

⁵²**Then Jesus said to the chief priests, the officers of the temple guard, and the elders, who had come for him, "Am I leading a rebellion, that you have come with swords and clubs?** ⁵³**Every day I was with you in the temple courts, and you did not lay a hand on me. But this is your hour—when darkness reigns."**

Context

The continuous nature of the passion narrative is evident by the interconnectedness of this account with both the preceding ("while he was still speaking," 22:47) and the following ("then seizing him," 22:54).[56] The story of Jesus' arrest and betrayal is found in all four Gospels. Luke's account is the shortest. Yet it omits nothing essential to the story and even contains additional materials not found elsewhere, such as the healing of the servant's ear (22:51) and the statement about "your hour—when darkness reigns" (22:53). The account in Luke consists of three "acts." In the first (22:47-48) Judas leads a crowd—later described as consisting of the chief priests, officers of the temple guard, and elders (22:52)—to Jesus. As he draws near, Jesus reveals that he knows Judas will betray him with a kiss. In the second act (22:49-51) the disciples ask Jesus whether they should fight, and before Jesus can answer, a disciple takes a sword and cuts off the ear of a servant of the high priest. Jesus then rebukes his disciples and heals the servant. In the third act (22:52-53) Jesus rebukes his opponents for their cowardice in not arresting him openly while he taught in the temple. He also points out that this is the last desperate attempt of the power of darkness to thwart God's plan.

Comments

22:47   While he was still speaking.   The present account is tied closely to the preceding.

A crowd came.   Literally, *Behold a crowd.* The make-up of this crowd is described in 22:52. According to John 18:3,12, Roman soldiers were also part of this crowd. Usually the "crowd" (*ochlos*) is seen as positive in their attitude toward Jesus (see comments on 4:15). The term may appear in this verse, however, because of its use in Luke's source (cf. Mark 14:43; cf. also Matt 26:47).

The man who was called Judas, one of the Twelve.   The historicity of Jesus' betrayal by a disciple is undeniable. No one in the church would have created a story in which one of Jesus' own disciples betrayed him.

---

[56]This same interconnectedness is found in the following accounts as well: "The men who were guarding Jesus," 22:63; "At daybreak the council," 22:66; "Then the whole assembly rose," 23:1; "On hearing this, Pilate," 23:6; "Pilate called together the chief priests," 23:13.

Was leading them. In the sense of "going before" the crowd. Judas was not the actual "leader" of the group.

He approached Jesus to kiss him. A kiss was frequently given when greeting someone.[57] Perhaps here we have a customary kiss of greeting from a disciple to his teacher. Luke omitted the Markan explanation that a kiss by Judas was the means by which he revealed which person in the darkness was Jesus (Mark 14:44).

22:48 Judas, are you betraying the Son of Man with a kiss? This is perhaps better translated *by means of a kiss.* In Mark 14:45; Matt 26:49, Judas actually kisses Jesus. Luke did not explicitly state this, but he may have assumed that his readers were familiar with the account (cf. Luke 1:4) and knew this. This was likely the means by which Judas identified Jesus on the Mount of Olives. The horror of betraying a friend is heightened by his use of a kiss to do this. The seriousness of this act is shown by Luke's pointing out that Judas was in fact betraying the Son of Man. For Son of Man see comments on 5:24.

22:49 When Jesus' followers saw what was going to happen. Literally *seeing the about to take place thing.* In the original situation this referred to Jesus' arrest, but Luke and his readers may have thought more along the lines of the fulfillment of God's plan, i.e., the Son of Man was now being betrayed into the hands of men as he said (9:44), and Peter was about to deny Jesus (22:34).

Lord, should we strike with our swords? This, asked by one of the two who possessed a sword (22:38), was a rhetorical question in the original setting in life as their actions showed, but for Luke and his readers the question may have been more deliberative in nature. Luke may have wanted his readers to reflect on whether force fits into the Christian life. For "Lord" see comments on 6:46.

22:50 One of them struck the servant of the high priest. John 18:10 states that this was Simon Peter and that the name of the servant was Malchus.

Cutting off his right ear. Compare John 18:10.

22:51 No more of this! Literally *permit as far as this.* This can be addressed to the disciples and mean "Stop, no more [of this]" (NIV, RSV) or "Let them [my opponents] have their way" (NEB). Or it can be addressed to Jesus' opponents, "Tolerate this much violence on the part of My followers."[58] The first interpretation is more likely: Jesus was rebuking the action of the disciples. As in 22:38 they did not understand Jesus' teachings. They did not pray (22:40,46), and thus they neither knew nor were able to act correctly in this time of trial.

He touched the man's ear and healed him. Only Luke recorded the healing. Thus he showed that even in his time of trial Jesus modeled his teachings (cf. 6:27-31,35-36). For the use of touch in healing, cf. 5:13; 7:14; 8:43-47.

22:52 Chief priests, the officers of the temple guard, and the elders. In Mark 14:43 instead of officers of the temple (cf. Luke 22:4) the third member of this group are the teachers of the law.

Am I leading a rebellion, that you have come with swords and clubs? This question is literally, *Have you come out against a robber?* The word "robber" (*lēstēn*) can also refer to a revolutionary.[59] Luke 22:37 may find partial fulfillment here, even though its primary fulfillment occurs in 23:32-34,39-43.

---

[57] Cf. Luke 7:45; 15:20; Rom 16:16; 1 Cor 16:20; 2 Cor 13:12; 1 Pet 5:14.

[58] See Plummer, *Luke,* 512.

[59] Cf. Luke 23:19 and Mark 15:7 with John 18:40; Josephus, *Wars* 2.13.2-3 (2.253-54).

22:53   Every day I was with you . . . and you did not lay a hand on me.
Jesus rebuked his opponents for their cowardice. They were afraid to arrest him in
the openness of the temple. The reason was clear to Luke's readers—the people
would have opposed them (19:47-48; 20:19; 22:2; cf. also John 18:20). The very
fact that Jesus taught daily and openly in the temple distinguishes his activity
from that of the revolutionaries, who operated in the mountains and had to be
hunted down. Jesus did not operate in the darkness, as his opponents were presently doing, but in the light.

But this is your hour.   Compare Luke 22:36; cf. also John 7:30; 8:20. Mark
14:49 states, "The Scriptures must be fulfilled," which is another way of pointing
to the arrival of the time in which God's redemptive plan would take place and
find its fulfillment.

When darkness reigns.   That which was taking place involved a far deeper
opposition than that between the Jewish leadership and Jesus. It involved the cosmic opposition between Satan, the ruler of this age, and God (cf. Acts 26:18; cf.
also Luke 22:3,31). The darkness of the present moment is symbolic of the reign
of darkness at this time. Compare John 13:30.

We do not read of the fleeing (literally *leaving* in the sense of "forsaking") of
the disciples as in Mark 14:50; Matt 26:56. In so doing Luke may have been seeking both to play down the disciples' failure at this time (cf. Luke 8:11; 9:33e;
22:45,53; and parallels), as well as to emphasize the cosmic nature of what was
taking place. Luke probably assumed that his readers knew this and would supply
this information to the story from the traditions they had been taught (1:4).[60]

The Lukan Message

Luke tied this account closely with the preceding one. Because of his
omission of Jesus' threefold prayer and the disciples' threefold failure in
favor of a single telling of each and because of the inclusio formed by the
twofold "pray that you will not fall into temptation" (22:40,46), the
present account exemplifies the disciples' failure in this, their first major
trial (22:49-51). As a result of their failure to watch and pray, they erred
in their response to Jesus' betrayal and arrest. In the context of Luke's
teaching on prayer (see Introduction 8 [7]) the readers were not only to
understand why the disciples failed in this time of trial but to resolve to
pray lest they too fail in their own time of trial.

Luke also wanted his readers to note the portrait of Jesus in this
account. As he had foretold, his betrayal by one of the Twelve was taking
place. Yet his healing ministry continued. Jesus revealed by his words in
22:53 and his actions in 22:51 that he was anything but a revolutionary.
He rebuked the use of force by the disciples and healed his enemies, for

---

[60]Cf. Evans (*Luke*, 815), who quotes LaGrange: "He seems to presume the facts as well
known, and his literary revision has as its aim to given [*sic*] them their meaning and to complete them."

his kingship was not of this present world. He furthermore is a perfect model of his teachings concerning love for enemies (6:27-28,35-36).

Nevertheless God's sovereign will must be done. God had permitted the opponents of his Son this hour. The power of darkness would be allowed to do what it wanted with Jesus. Yet what took place was not their will but God's, for "this hour [was] Satan's only because it [was] granted to him, for in the last resort even he [was] only an instrument in God's plan of which the passion forms a part."[61] The opponents of Jesus had been granted this hour in order to fulfill God's plan as foretold in Scripture. All that Jesus foretold his disciples was beginning to take place, and this was God's design, not that of Jesus' opponents. The Son of Man went as God had decreed (22:22). As Jesus foretold, Judas had now betrayed him (22:22). Next Peter would deny him (22:31-34).

(3) Peter's Denial (22:54-62)

[54]Then seizing him, they led him away and took him into the house of the high priest. Peter followed at a distance. [55]But when they had kindled a fire in the middle of the courtyard and had sat down together, Peter sat down with them. [56]A servant girl saw him seated there in the firelight. She looked closely at him and said, "This man was with him."

[57]But he denied it. "Woman, I don't know him," he said.

[58]A little later someone else saw him and said, "You also are one of them."

"Man, I am not!" Peter replied.

[59]About an hour later another asserted, "Certainly this fellow was with him, for he is a Galilean."

[60]Peter replied, "Man, I don't know what you're talking about!" Just as he was speaking, the rooster crowed. [61]The Lord turned and looked straight at Peter. Then Peter remembered the word the Lord had spoken to him: "Before the rooster crows today, you will disown me three times." [62]And he went outside and wept bitterly.

Context

The three events in Luke following Jesus' arrest are Peter's denial (22:54-62), the mocking of Jesus (22:63-65), and Jesus' appearance before the high priest (22:66-71). In this he differed from Mark and Matthew, who placed the denial of Peter later. In John the denial of Peter is associated with Jesus' appearance before the high priest Annas. Luke chose to deal with Peter's denial first, however, so that he could present this material in a more logical order (cf. 1:3). Since 22:21 he has dealt with Jesus' instructions to the disciples and their future failures. He dealt with Judas's betrayal (22:21-22,47-53), and now he sought to complete this section by telling of Peter's denial (22:31-34,40,46,54-62). Whereas

---

[61] H. Conzelmann, *The Theology of St. Luke* (New York: Harper, 1960), 182.

this may not have been the exact chronological order of events, it makes Luke's presentation of the events more orderly both by completing the description of the disciples' failures and by not requiring various changes in scene such as we find in Mark and Matthew.

Peter's denial is recorded in all four Gospels. Differences within these accounts[62] should not detract from their great unanimity. All four point out that Peter denied his Lord three times on the night of Jesus' betrayal in the courtyard of the high priest, that a maid questioned Peter, and that a cock crowed "immediately" after the third denial.

Comments

22:54 Then seizing him. Since this term (*syllabontes*) is a technical term for making an arrest,[63] it is best to translate this, *Then arresting him*. We know, however, that Jesus allowed himself to be arrested. Jesus' arrest is also referred to in Acts (1:16), where Luke showed how Peter (12:3) and Paul (23:27) followed in their Lord's footsteps and also were arrested.

Took him into the house of the high priest. Matthew 26:57 names the high priest—Caiaphas. He would not have been present among the chief priests at the arrest (Luke 22:52). In John 18:13-27 Jesus is brought to the house of Annas, the high priest, before he is brought to the house of Caiaphas, the high priest. The meeting at Annas's home may have been to allow time for the Sanhedrin to meet at the home of Caiaphas. For the existence of more than one high priest, see comments on 3:2. Whereas Mark 14:53,55; Matt 26:57,59 mention the presence of the Sanhedrin, Luke did not.

Peter followed. Luke did not say "why" Peter followed, only "that" he did. Compare Matt 26:58, where Peter's actions were due to his desire to see the "outcome" (NIV) or "end" (RSV).

22:55 Kindled a fire in the middle of the courtyard. Mark 14:67 and John 18:18 state that Peter sought to warm himself by the fire.

22:56 A servant girl. The Synoptic Gospels all state that the first person questioning Peter was a maid. John (18:25) did not specify.

This man was with him. In what way (on the Mount of Olives when Jesus was arrested? during his ministry? in the temple?) was not specified.

22:57 He denied it. That is, Peter denied he was with Jesus.

Woman, I don't know him. Peter refused to acknowledge his association with Jesus and thus fulfilled Jesus' prophecy (see comments on 22:34).

22:58 Someone else saw him. In Mark 14:69; Matt 26:71 it is another maid, but in Luke it is a "man."

You also are one of them. Here the charge is that Peter belonged to the group of Jesus' disciples. The "you" is emphatic.

---

[62] Differences within these accounts involve such things as: exactly where and when the three denials took place, who the people were who questioned Peter, the exact wording of Peter's denials, and the number of cock crows (one or two).

[63] Cf. Acts 1:16; 12:3; 23:27; 26:21; John 18:12.

Man, I am not!   Peter denied his association with the disciples. Luke dropped
the reference to Peter's "denying" Jesus as found in Mark 14:70 and especially
Matt 26:72.

22:59   About an hour later.   In John 18:26 the third accusation comes from
a servant of the high priest who was a relative of Malchus, the servant whose ear
was cut off.

Certainly this fellow was with him.   This man was sure of Peter's association with Jesus and the disciples.

For he is a Galilean.   The NIV omits *also*: literally *for he also is a Galilean*
(just like Jesus [23:6] and the other disciples). Matthew 27:73 states that Peter's
accent gave him away.

22:60   Man, I don't know what you're talking about!   Luke omitted the
reference to Peter's cursing and swearing found in Mark and Matthew.

Just as he was speaking, the rooster crowed.   As Jesus predicted in 22:34,
the rooster crowed.

**22:61   The Lord turned and looked straight at Peter. Then Peter
remembered.**   Ellis notes, "No phrase in the Gospels is more charged with feeling than [this]."[64] For "Lord" see comments on 7:13. See comments on 22:34.

22:62   He went outside and wept bitterly.   Luke agreed with Matt 26:75 in
his wording against Mark 14:72. Possibly both were completing the story with traditional material with which they were familiar and which they preferred over
Mark. Luke expected his readers to see in this not just remorse but Peter's "turning back" to the Lord (Luke 22:32).

The Lukan Message

The account of Peter's denial again exemplifies Jesus' knowledge of
the future. God's Son had known all the time what would happen. Nothing had caught him unprepared. All was taking place as he foretold
(22:31-34). This should have given Luke's readers confidence in the truth
both of Jesus' Christological claims as well as his teachings.

Although Luke did not record Peter's swearing and cursing, he did
record Peter's threefold failure in his temptation. Satan indeed has violently sifted him (22:31). Because Peter did not arm himself with prayer
(22:40,46), he found himself denying his Lord. Yet Luke wanted his readers to know that Jesus had prayed for Peter (22:32), and because of this
his failure would not lead to a complete disavowal of Jesus. He did not
"deny Jesus," but rather he denied "knowing Jesus."[65] His bitter weeping
(22:62), however, revealed that Jesus' prayer for him would lead to his
turning and strengthening his brothers (22:32). Luke's readers should
have resolved not to be caught as unprepared as Peter but by prayer and
endurance to bring forth fruit (8:15; 21:19).

---

[64]Ellis, *Luke*, 260.

[65]D. M. Stanley, *Jesus in Gethsemane* (New York: Paulist, 1980), 195.

(4) The Mocking of Jesus (22:63-65)

[63]The men who were guarding Jesus began mocking and beating him. [64]They blindfolded him and demanded, "Prophesy! Who hit you?" [65]And they said many other insulting things to him.

Context

After his arrest Jesus was mocked (18:32; cf. also 23:11,36) and suffered (9:22; 17:25; 18:32-33) just as he predicted. Because of being acknowledged as a prophet by the people (7:16,39; 9:8,19; 24:19), he was blindfolded and asked to prophesy who beat him. The account ends with Jesus' being further insulted by his captors. Throughout this scene, however, we sense that he who predicted that all these things would take place was in charge and was allowing this to take place in order to fulfill the divine plan. Matthew made this most evident by his addition of 26:53-54. Luke 22:53 (cf. also John 18:11) also clearly implies that what was taking place in this hour of darkness had clearly been permitted by Jesus and not forced upon him.

Comments

22:63   Jesus . . . him.   The name "Jesus" does not appear in the sentence but only the pronoun "him." The name is supplied in the translation (cf. NIV and RSV) to indicate that the subject has switched from Peter in the previous verse to Jesus. Luke took for granted that his readers knew the passion narrative well enough (cf. Luke 1:4) that he need not use the proper name "Jesus" and simply used "him." The "men" referred to were less likely the members of the Sanhedrin (22:66) than the guards or servants of the Sanhedrin. Compare Isa 50:5-6; 53:3-5.

22:64   Blindfolded him . . . "Prophesy! Who hit you?"   Matthew 26:68 and Luke agree in their wording against Mark. This may be due to their inclusion of a well-known part of the passion tradition that Mark omitted. The guards' behavior assumes a well-established tradition of Jesus' being a prophet (cf. 7:16,39; 9:8,19; 24:19). What was transpiring here was more likely a kind of blind man's bluff based on Jesus' reputation as a prophet than an official Jewish test to see if Jesus was really a prophet or the Messiah.[66]

22:65   Said . . . insulting things to him.   Literally *blaspheming him.* Whereas in Mark 14:64; Matt 26:65 Jesus was accused of blasphemy, Luke portrayed Jesus rather as the object of blasphemy. Compare also Luke 12:10; 23:39. In Acts 13:45; 18:6 the apostles were recipients of such blasphemy.

The Lukan Message

Luke continued to reveal both Jesus' foreknowledge of all that would take place as well as the fulfillment of the divine plan in all that was taking place. Whether Luke's readers had difficulties understanding why

---

[66]The last interpretation is suggested by J. D. M. Derrett, *Law in the New Testament* (London: Darton, 1970), 407-8.

God's Son was mocked and beaten is unknown, but Luke's teaching continued to point out that all that he experienced was known and prophesied beforehand. The passion took place because it was foretold in Scripture, and it was foretold in Scripture because it was the divine plan from the beginning. Christologically this passage points to Jesus' role as a prophet both by the fulfillment of his predictions (9:22; 17:25; 18:32-33) and in his being taunted as such by his captors (22:64).

(5) Jesus before the Sanhedrin (22:66-71)

⁶⁶At daybreak the council of the elders of the people, both the chief priests and teachers of the law, met together, and Jesus was led before them. ⁶⁷"If you are the Christ," they said, "tell us."

Jesus answered, "If I tell you, you will not believe me, ⁶⁸and if I asked you, you would not answer. ⁶⁹But from now on, the Son of Man will be seated at the right hand of the mighty God."

⁷⁰They all asked, "Are you then the Son of God?"

He replied, "You are right in saying I am."

⁷¹Then they said, "Why do we need any more testimony? We have heard it from his own lips."

Context

As one reads through the various passion accounts in the Gospels, one is confronted with two fundamental questions that are somewhat interrelated. The first is chronological and seeks to establish the order of the events described in the various accounts. The second is primarily historical and seeks to ascertain exactly what happened. The particular historical issue that tends to dominate the latter question is the extent of Sanhedrin involvement in Jesus' trial and crucifixion. This is a very sensitive issue among Jews today.

Luke's account of Jesus' appearance before the Sanhedrin (22:66-71; 23:1) is the shortest of the three Synoptic accounts. It consists of seven verses compared to thirteen in Mark (14:53,55-65; 15:1) and Matthew (26:57,59-68; 27:1-2).[67] Luke combined activities involved in two Sanhedrin meetings (Mark 14:53-65; 15:1) to abbreviate the material and to concentrate on the key issue of the trial—Christology. Who is Jesus? Luke followed Mark and Matthew in pointing out that the key determining factor for what took place at the Sanhedrin meeting was Jesus' claim that he is the Christ, the Son of God.

---

[67] In his abbreviated account Luke omitted: the summoning of witnesses (Mark 14:55-60); Jesus' saying about the destruction of the temple, which appears later in Acts 6:14 (Mark 14:57-58); Jesus' silence (Mark 14:61a); the ceremonial tearing of the high priest's garment as an act of condemnation (14:63); Jesus' being condemned for blasphemy (14:64a); the official verdict (14:64b,c); and the second meeting of the Sanhedrin (15:1a).

Regarding establishment of a chronological order of the main events, the biblical data consists of essentially three accounts: Mark-Matthew; Luke; and John. In Mark-Matthew we find the following:
1. Jesus is arrested.
2. He is brought before the Sanhedrin (Mark 14:53), which is led by Caiaphas (Matt 26:57), the high priest (Mark 14:60). There he is questioned concerning his messianic claims (Mark 14:61-62) and found guilty (14:63-65).
3. The Sanhedrin meets again in the morning (15:1).
4. Jesus is led to Pilate (15:1).
In John we find:
I. Jesus is arrested (18:1-11).
II. He is brought before Annas, the high priest (18:13), and questioned in general about his teachings (18:19-23).
III. He is brought before Caiaphas, the high priest (18:24,28).
IV. He is led to Pilate (18:28-29).
In Luke we find:
A. Jesus is arrested (22:47-53);
B. He is brought before the Sanhedrin (22:66), where he is questioned about his messiahship (22:67-70) and found guilty (22:71).
C. He is led to Pilate (23:1).
The most common attempt to reconstruct these events is as follows:
• Jesus is arrested (1-I-A).
• Jesus appears before Annas (II).
• Jesus is "tried" by the Sanhedrin led by Caiaphas (2-III-B).
• The Sanhedrin meets a second time to draw up official charges against Jesus to be presented before Pilate (3).
• Jesus is led to Pilate (4-IV-C).
The preceding reconstruction is not without problems. The historical problems involved in the trial have been much discussed.[68] The most significant is that the account of Jesus' trial violates a number of rules for such trials found in the Mishnaic tractate *Sanhedrin.*

It has also been claimed that if the Jewish leadership had wanted to put Jesus to death, they did not have to go to Pilate, for they could have done this on their own authority. The right to put a Gentile to death for entering the temple area and the stoning of Stephen (Acts 7) are frequently given as examples.

With regard to the legal prescriptions found in the tractate *Sanhedrin* it needs to be pointed out that these rules were written down after A.D. 200,

[68] See D. R. Catchpole, *The Trial of Jesus,* SPB (Leiden: Brill, 1971), esp. 261-71, and P. Winter, *On the Trial of Jesus,* Studia Judaica (Berlin: Gruyter, 1961) for a discussion of the issues involved.

and it is unclear whether they reflect rules that actually existed in Jesus' day or whether they reflect an idealized description of what such laws should have been like.[69] Second, some of the rules found in this tractate conflict with Josephus's description of how things were in the first century. Third, the mere existence of rules and laws does not guarantee that they will be carried out fairly. One need only think of judicial procedures in Nazi Germany and how little protection written laws gave opponents of Nazism. Almost every country has had its own sorrowful history of "kangaroo courts."

Finally, if there is a conflict between the Gospel accounts and the tractate *Sanhedrin*, it is unclear why the latter, which was written well over a century after the Gospel accounts, should be given greater credibility. Certainly the tractate *Sanhedrin* is no more neutral or objective and has just as much an apologetic purpose as the Gospels. As for whether Judaism possessed the right of capital punishment in the time of Jesus, this is expressly denied in John 18:31 and in some of the rabbinic material. Compare "forty years before the destruction of the Temple the Sanhedrin went into exile. . . . They did not adjudicate in capital cases" (*Sabb.* 15a; cf. also *y. Sanh.* 1.18a, 34; 7.24b,41; Josephus, *Antiquities* 20.9.1. [20.197-203]).[70] Christians must be sympathetic and supportive of attempts to alleviate and undo anti-Semitism. The evil of such behavior, often done in the name of Christianity, is a terrible blemish in the history of the Christian church.

Yet Christian anti-Semitism is ultimately a contradiction of terms, for the Object of Christian faith was born a Jew. Furthermore the leaders of the early church were all Jews, and Gentiles entering into the church knew they were now sharing in the covenant God made with Abraham. For evangelicals, however, opposition to anti-Semitism does not allow them to repudiate the teachings of Scripture. In Luke the Jewish *leadership* was clearly at fault in Jesus' death, but Luke pointed out unceasingly that the Jewish *people* were positive toward him (see comments on 4:15). For Luke (as well as all the NT writers) the hatred revealed in anti-Semitism is precluded from Christian behavior, for it is diametrically opposed to Jesus' teachings of love for one's neighbor (see comments on 10:27) and even for one's enemies (Luke 6:27-31).

Comments

22:66 At daybreak. Luke combined the material of the first Sanhedrin meeting (Mark 14:53-65) at this point with the second (Mark 15:1).

---

[69] See J. Blinzler, *The Trial of Jesus* (Westminster: Newman, 1959), 149-57.

[70] A. N. Sherwin-White (*Roman Society and Roman Law in the New Testament* [Oxford: Clarendon, 1963], 36) states that "the capital power was the most jealously guarded of all the attributes of government, not even entrusted to the principal assistants of the governors." For an overall view concerning the historicity of the trial, see Catchpole, "The Problem of the Historicity of the Sanhedrin Trial," *Trial of Jesus*, 47-65.

The council of the elders of the people, both the chief priests and teachers of the law. The "council of the elders of the people" probably is a synonym for the Sanhedrin, whose meeting place is mentioned in the latter part of this verse. The term "council" is also found in Acts 22:5. "Chief priests and teachers of the law" stands in apposition to "council of the elders of the people" and describes the general make-up of the Sanhedrin. The third group of "elders" (cf. Luke 9:22; 20:1) probably is omitted due to the similarity between the noun "council of elders" (*presbyterion*) and the noun "elders" (*presbyteroi*). The Sanhedrin was the highest Jewish ruling body in Israel and was granted control by Rome over virtually all internal Jewish matters. It contained seventy members and a president, who was the high priest. The Sanhedrin membership consisted primarily of two groups: (1) the Sadducees, who were the leading priestly families and lay aristocrats, and (2) the Pharisees, who were teachers of the law and middle-class laity, made up the "elders" mentioned in 20:1.

Jesus was led before them. Literally *they led him into their council* (*synedrion*). The term "council" may mean here the place where the Sanhedrin met, i.e., the council chamber rather than the council members themselves.

22:67 If you are the Christ. Luke's omission of the summoning of witnesses and the saying about the destruction and rebuilding of the temple in three days (Mark 14:55-60) enabled him to focus on his key concern in this passage, which was Christological in nature. The actual question of the Sanhedrin was, *Are you claiming to be the Christ whom Israel is awaiting?* Jesus' answer was both yes and no. He is the Messiah foretold in Scripture, but not the kind of Messiah most of Israel was awaiting. Whereas Mark 14:62 witnesses that Jesus answered this question affirmatively, Luke 22:67–23:3 and Matt 26:64 indicate that although Jesus' affirmation was clear, it was also qualified. According to Mark 14:61, the high priest asked the question; and according to Matt 26:63, only after Jesus was placed under an oath in which silence would have been a confession of guilt (cf. Lev 5:1; 1 Kgs 22:16; Prov 29:24) did he respond.

They said. The plural may "stress the corporate responsibility of Israel for what is to follow."[71]

You will not believe me. Jesus understood that answering their question was ultimately useless, for there was no desire to learn or interact with him but only to condemn him.[72]

22:68 And if I asked you, you would not answer. Compare Luke 20:3-8.

22:69 But from now on. Compare 12:52; 22:18,36; cf. also 1:48; 5:10; 2 Cor 5:16.

The Son of Man will be seated at the right hand of the mighty God. The Son of Man was about to end his earthly ministry and suffer death, but he would through this exodus (Luke 9:31) enter into his glory (24:26; Acts 3:13; cf. also Phil 2:9-11). The present imagery combines Ps 110:1 ("right hand") and Dan 7:13 ("Son of Man"). Luke may have omitted "you will see" (Mark 14:62; Matt 26:64) to avoid the misconception that Jesus' prophecy was not fulfilled since the Sanhedrin did not see this.[73] Stephen, however, did see this (cf. Acts 7:54), for Jesus'

[71] Evans, *Luke*, 835.
[72] Cf. Luke 11:53-54; 20:20,26; cf. also 20:1-8 and John 10:24-26.
[73] See P. Benoit, *The Passion and Resurrection of Jesus* (New York: Herder, 1969), 110.

enthronement takes place not at the parousia but immediately after his resurrection and ascension.

Luke also omitted the reference to the Son of Man's "coming on the clouds of heaven" (cf. Mark 14:62; Matt 26:64) possibly because it might have been interpreted as a prediction of the parousia in the lifetime of the Sanhedrin members, who now either because of age or Jerusalem's destruction were dead. That coming, mentioned in Luke 21:27, finds its fulfillment at the end of history. See Introduction 7 (3). "Mighty God" is literally *the power of God*. Luke substituted this phrase for Mark's "right hand of Power" (14:62) since the use of "Power" as a circumlocution for God might not have been clear to his Gentile readers. Seated at the right hand of God, Jesus is the believer's advocate (Luke 12:8) but the unbeliever's prosecutor (12:9).

22:70 Son of God? Although the titles Son of Man, Christ, and Son of God are not synonyms but portray separate functions and roles, they are related in the sense that they refer to the same person. For Luke and his readers this question is a logical deduction from the previous statement as the "then" (literally *therefore*) indicates.[74]

You are right in saying I am. This Greek clause possesses a reservation which the NIV misses (cf. 23:3). The "you" is emphatic. Jesus' opponents clearly took this as an affirmation as 22:71–23:2 indicates. It is probably to be interpreted, *You have worded the question, and I will not deny that I am, but I would have worded it somewhat differently*[75] (cf. Matt 26:64). For Luke, Jesus' answer was an affirmation, for elsewhere he taught that Jesus is the Son of God.[76]

22:71 Why do we need any more testimony? Jesus' answer is understood as an affirmation and a claim to be the Christ, the Son of God. Since Jesus' own words are all that really matter, Luke omitted the testimony of the false witnesses (cf. Mark 14:55-61). As far as Jesus' opponents were concerned, their purpose (cf. Luke 11:54; 20:20,26) had now been achieved. Exactly "what" it was in Jesus' answer that the Sanhedrin considered worthy of death is unclear. For Pilate, Jesus' claim to be the Christ was the issue, for this title had political implications. This therefore is how the accusation was presented to him (see comments on 23:2-3). Yet the Sanhedrin's condemnation of Jesus is less political than religious, for Jesus was found guilty after accepting the title "Son of God." Compare John 19:7.

In the original setting in life, the reason for Jesus' condemnation by the Jewish leadership is unclear. Their motivation in part was due to his accusing them of hypocrisy, his being a threat to their leadership of the people, and possibly their concern that Jesus might bring the Jewish nation in conflict with Rome (cf. John 11:49-50; 18:14). The legal reason for having condemned him is more difficult to assess. Was it Jesus' claim that he would sit at the right hand of God? Was it the

---

[74]Cf. Luke 1:32-33, where "Son of the Most High," i.e., Son of God, and "throne of his father David," i.e., the Christ, are interchangeable and complementary titles in that they all describe Jesus (cf. also 4:41; Acts 9:20-22; Mark 14:61; Matt 16:16; John 20:31).

[75]See D. R. Catchpole ("The Answer of Jesus to Caiaphas" [Matt xxvi.64], *NTS* 17 [1970]: 226), who after his study concludes that Jesus' reply is "affirmative in content, and reluctant or circumlocutory in formulation."

[76]Cf. Luke 1:32-35; 3:22; 4:3,9,41; 8:28; 9:35; Acts 9:20; 13:33.

claim to be the Messiah? (But later Bar Kochba in A.D. 132–35 claimed to be the messiah, and the claim itself was not thought worthy of death.) Was it the claim to be the Son of God (cf. John 10:33-36)? Was it due to his speaking against the temple (cf. Mark 14:58)? The Gospel presents Jesus' "trial" as unjust and in essence a kangaroo court. As a result the question of whether Jesus was legally worthy of death was less an issue for the Sanhedrin than what the grounds would have been for carrying out the death sentence. The Jewish leadership's role in Jesus' death would be a recurring theme in Luke-Acts.[77]

We have heard it from his own lips.   Compare 4:22; 11:54; 19:22; Acts 22:14.

The Lukan Message

Here Luke effectively brought together the Christological teachings found throughout the Gospel. For Luke the main point involved, "Who is Jesus?" (22:67). The answer came from Jesus' own lips. Jesus is the Christ. His answer in 22:70 is understood as a clear affirmation by the Sanhedrin, as both the condemnation (22:71) and the charge (23:2) reveal. What was foretold in 1:32-33, came about by a virgin birth (2:11), received a divine commissioning at the baptism (3:21-22), was proclaimed in Jesus' first sermon (4:18-19), was confessed by the disciples (9:20-21) was now openly confessed to Israel's leaders (22:67-70) and would become more and more apparent in the subsequent events.[78] Jesus of Nazareth is the Christ. Yet he is also more. He is the Son of Man who will soon share the divine rule (22:69). And he is even more. He is the Son of God. What had been known to Luke's readers[79] was now made known to the Jewish leadership. And Jesus' glorification does not await the future parousia but has already begun with his ascension to God's right hand (22:69). Jesus' bearing throughout this scene furthermore reveals that he was indeed in control of the events taking place.

Israel's rejection of its Messiah has come up several times already and will reappear time and time again in Acts (2:23; 3:14-15; 7:52; 13:27-28) as the preaching of Jesus as the Christ is rejected and becomes a stumbling block for Israel (13:44-47; 18:5-6; 28:25-28). See Introduction 7 (2); 8 (5). This rejection may have been an experience that Luke and his readers had themselves witnessed. Also found in this account is the movement of salvation history. "From now on" (22:69) the Son of Man would be exalted to reign with God on high. He, who emptied himself and became obedient unto death, was soon to be highly exalted (Acts 2:31-36; 13:32-37; cf. also Phil 2:9-11). Luke may also have intended his readers to note that already the crucified one had begun his reign at God's

---

[77]Cf. Luke 24:20; Acts 2:23; 3:14-15; 7:52; 13:27-28.

[78]Luke 23:2,35,39; 24:26,46; cf. also 23:3. Note the frequent use of the title "Christ" in these last references.

[79]Luke 1:32,35; 3:22; 4:3,9,41; 8:28; 9:35; etc.

right hand. Their Lord was not therefore to be conceived as a helpless idealist who died in weakness but rather as the Lord of glory.

(6) Jesus before Pilate (23:1-5)

¹Then the whole assembly rose and led him off to Pilate. ²And they began to accuse him, saying, "We have found this man subverting our nation. He opposes payment of taxes to Caesar and claims to be Christ, a king."
³So Pilate asked Jesus, "Are you the king of the Jews?"
"Yes, it is as you say," Jesus replied.
⁴Then Pilate announced to the chief priests and the crowd, "I find no basis for a charge against this man."
⁵But they insisted, "He stirs up the people all over Judea by his teaching. He started in Galilee and has come all the way here."

Context

After his condemnation by the Sanhedrin, Jesus is brought before Pontius Pilate, who alone possessed authority in Judea to exercise capital punishment (see 22:66-71, "Context"). Although the seat of the Roman government was located in Caesarea, Pilate was in Jerusalem during the Passover festivities. This was wise policy because Passover was a time of heightened nationalistic hopes and memories. If trouble were to arise, the odds were that it would take place during the Passover and in Jerusalem. At this point Jesus, having been "rejected by the elders, chief priests and teachers of the law" (Luke 9:22), was "betrayed into the hands of men" (9:44) and "handed over to the Gentiles" (18:32). Soon he would be mocked and ridiculed (cf. 23:11; 18:32).

The charges brought by the Sanhedrin against Jesus were transferred from the religious grounds, for which Jesus was condemned, to political ones, for which Pilate might condemn him. (We find a similar example in Acts, where the religious grounds of Paul's condemnation by the Jewish leaders [Acts 21:28] were changed to political ones when they were presented before Felix, the Roman governor [24:2b-6].) The general charge found in Mark 15:3 is spelled out in Luke 23:2. Jesus was accused of (1) subverting the nation, (2) opposing the payment of taxes to Caesar, and (3) claiming to be the Messiah, i.e., a king. The first charge is a subjective judgment that Jesus could just as well have leveled against his accusers. The second, the reader already knew, was false because of 20:20-26. The third is partly true. Jesus is indeed a king, and the *titulus* on his cross would proclaim this (23:38; Mark 15:26; Matt 27:37; John 19:19), but he was not a political threat as king, as Luke 20:20-26 reveals (cf. John 18:36-37). Nevertheless it is clear from the crucifixion and the *titulus* that Jesus was crucified on the political charge of claiming to be Christ, a king.

Thereupon Pilate asked Jesus directly if he was the "king of the Jews." Jesus replied with the same guarded affirmation as found in Luke 22:70. Luke then added that Pilate pronounced Jesus' innocence to the chief priests and crowd. They, however, insisted that Jesus was unsettling the entire nation by his teachings.

Comments

23:1 The whole assembly arose. Literally *all the multitude* (cf. 19:37; Acts; 4:32; 6:2; 15:12,30). This refers to the members of the Sanhedrin mentioned in Luke 22:66 (cf. Acts 23:7).

Led him off to Pilate. The reason for this is not stated by Luke, but we know from John 18:31 that only Pilate had the authority to exercise capital punishment.[80] Luke omitted the description of Jesus' being bound (Mark 15:1; Matt 27:2). By placing Peter's denial after the arrest of Jesus, Luke was able to proceed from Jesus' condemnation by the Sanhedrin immediately to his trial before Pilate. For Pilate see comments on 3:1.

23:2 Began to accuse him. The term "accuse" probably means *brought charges* as in Acts 22:30; 24:2-21; 25:5-22.

We have found this man. "This man" is emphatic and derogatory. Compare 22:56,59, where "this man/fellow" also is emphatic (cf. also Acts 23:9; 26:31). What follows are the Sanhedrin's charges against Jesus, reworded to appeal to Pilate's political concerns.

Subverting our nation. For "subverting" cf. Luke 9:41; Acts 13:8,10; 20:30. In the last three references it means *to seduce from the true faith*; but since these charges were brought before the Roman governor, it means here "to seduce from loyalty to the empire."[81] This thought is repeated in Luke 23:5 (cf. *Sanh.* 43a: Jesus "has practiced sorcery and enticed Israel to apostasy") and recalls Jesus' popularity with the people. It also reveals that his teachings conflicted in important ways with those espoused by the Jewish leadership.

Opposes payment of taxes. This was clearly incorrect (20:20-26), but the charge was intended to mark Jesus as a revolutionary. For "taxes" see comments on 20:22.

Claims to be Christ, a king. This can be translated "an anointed king"[82] or "Christ, a king."[83] The latter is more likely, but regardless, the emphasis here and in what follows is on the last term. By the term "king" Jesus' opponents explained to Pilate and Luke explained to his non-Jewish audience that "Christ" means *king*. The expression "claims to be" is best understood contemptuously as in Acts 5:36; 8:9. Compare the threefold charge directed against Paul in Acts 17:6-7; 24:5-6 and his threefold defense in 24:12; 25:8.

23:3 So Pilate asked Jesus, "Are you the king of the Jews?" Pilate ignored the first two accusations (perhaps because the first was too ambiguous and the second he knew was incorrect) and focused on the third. Luke was interested in the third

---

[80]Cf. Josephus, *Wars* 2.8.1. (2.117); see 22:66-71, "Context."
[81]Evans, *Luke*, 845.
[82]So Fitzmyer, *Luke* 2:1475.
[83]So Marshall, *Luke*, 853.

accusation because of its Christological implications. All four Gospels contain this question and the title "King of the Jews," i.e., Christ/Messiah, in the *titulus* (Luke 23:38; Mark 15:26; Matt 27:37; John 19:19).

Yes, it is as you say. Jesus' answer is identical in all four Gospels—"You say" (*su egeis*, Mark 15:2; Matt 27:11; John 18:37). Each Gospel writer understood the reply as an affirmation. The title "King of the Jews" recorded on the *titulus* in each Gospel also assumed that Jesus' reply was affirmative. See comments on 22:70.

23:4 This and the next verse are unique to Luke and serve his purpose in seeking to demonstrate Jesus' innocence.

Chief priests and the crowd. Probably this refers to the Sanhedrin members of 23:1; 22:66 and the "people." Luke may have included the reference to the "crowd" because of its appearance in Mark 15:8,11,15. For Luke's usual view of the people, see comments on 4:15.

I find no basis for a charge against this man. This is Pilate's first proclamation of Jesus' innocence. Compare 23:14-16,22-24; cf. also 23:20.[84] Luke's purpose here is clear, for "the reader of the Lukan Gospel recognizes the truth of Pilate's conclusion: Jesus and his disciples constitute no threat to Roman authority."[85] Compare also Introduction 7 (4). The similarity between this verse and John 18:34 is striking, and some have argued for a literary dependence between Luke and John. However, it probably is best to see in this agreement the use of similar traditions rather than the direct use of one Gospel by the writer of the other.[86] The "I find" stands in contrast to the "we have found" of Luke 23:2.

23:5 But they insisted. The "they" refers to the chief priests and the crowd of 23:4 who stand in contrast to the people in the next statement.

He stirs up the people all over Judea by his teaching. This is a repetition of the first charge in 23:2 (cf. Acts 24:5a,b), although different words ("subvert" and "stirs up") are used. A distinction is made between the "crowd" of 23:4 and the "people." What this supposed teaching entails is not stated. Probably it was not necessary, for Luke's readers both knew Jesus' teachings (1:4) and had just read them (1:1–22:4). "Judea" refers to the land of Israel (including Galilee), not just the Roman province by that name. See comments on 1:5.

He started in Galilee and has come all the way here. This illustrates well Luke's orderly presentation of his Gospel: 1:1–4:15, antecedents and birth; 4:16–9:50, Jesus' ministry in Galilee; 9:51–19:27, Jesus on the way to Jerusalem; 19:28–24:53, Jesus in Jerusalem. Compare Acts 10:38-39.

The Lukan Message

One clear Lukan theme involves his desire to demonstrate that Jesus was innocent and wrongly put to death. This is seen in the declaration of his innocence by Pontius Pilate, the Roman governor (Luke 23:4). This declaration will be repeated twice (23:14,22), along with Luke's comment that Pilate wanted to release Jesus (23:20). The Lukan case for Jesus' innocence would

---

[84]Note also the threefold declaration of Jesus' innocence by Pilate in John 18:38; 19:4,6.
[85]Fitzmyer, *Luke* 2:1476.
[86]See R. H. Stein, "The Matthew-Luke Agreements Against Mark: Insight from John," *CBQ* 54 (1992): 486-88.

be further supported by the words of Herod Antipas (23:15), a thief (23:39-43), and a centurion (23:47). Each of these will also testify to Jesus' innocence.[87] Jesus' innocence was quite evident to Luke's readers because of the weakness of the accusations against Jesus.[88] The readers knew that Jesus did not subvert the nation by his teachings. How could a nation be subverted by the teaching of love for neighbor (10:27) and enemies (6:27-31)? As to the second charge, they knew from 20:20-26 that this was blatantly false. And even the third charge they also knew was false, in that Jesus' kingship was not of this world. Thus even if the view that "both the gospel and the Acts of the Apostles were written as an apologia, to show the Romans that they had nothing to fear from Christianity, either from Paul or from Jesus"[89] goes further than the evidence warrants, Luke obviously sought to demonstrate in this account Jesus' innocence.

A second theme found in this passage involves the understanding of who Jesus is. Jesus reaffirmed the Christology of 22:66-71, but whereas the claim that he was the Christ, the king of Israel, was directed in 22:66-71 to the Jewish Sanhedrin, here it is directed to the Roman governor. Jesus confessed that he was the king of the Jews. Thus, although wrongly condemned and put to death, his regal position and authority was acknowledged by Jesus himself and would be proclaimed on his *titulus*. Jesus is the Christ, the King of the Jews.[90] See comments on 1:33.

Another theme involves the guilt and persistent role of official Judaism in Jesus' death. Having been condemned by the Sanhedrin, Jesus was brought before a Gentile governor. And ironically, whereas the governor acknowledged his innocence and sought his release (23:20), the persistence of the Jewish leadership (23:23-25; Acts 2:23; 13:28) ultimately led Rome to put the King of the Jews to death. A final theme involves the fulfillment of prophecy. Jesus' rejection (Luke 9:22), mockery and ridicule (18:32), and betrayal into the hands of Gentiles (18:32) have all taken place exactly according to Jesus' foreknowledge and exactly in accordance with God's plan. See Introduction 8 (1).

(7) Jesus before Herod (23:6-12)

[6]On hearing this, Pilate asked if the man was a Galilean. [7]When he learned that Jesus was under Herod's jurisdiction, he sent him to Herod, who was also in Jerusalem at that time.

[8]When Herod saw Jesus, he was greatly pleased, because for a long time he had been wanting to see him. From what he had heard about him, he hoped to

---

[87]Cf. the parallels in the case of Paul in Acts 23:29; 25:25; 26:30-32; 28:21.

[88]Cf. Goulder (*Luke: A New Paradigm*, 756), who points out that Luke "formulates . . . [the accusations] in such a way that the listener is struck by their unfairness."

[89]Benoit, *Passion and Resurrection*, 143.

[90]Cf. Luke 1:32-33,69; 2:4,11; 19:38-39; 23:38; Acts 17:7.

see him perform some miracle. [9]He plied him with many questions, but Jesus gave him no answer. [10]The chief priests and the teachers of the law were standing there, vehemently accusing him. [11]Then Herod and his soldiers ridiculed and mocked him. Dressing him in an elegant robe, they sent him back to Pilate. [12]That day Herod and Pilate became friends—before this they had been enemies.

Context

The account of Jesus' appearance before Herod Antipas is unique to Luke. It is mentioned only here and in Acts 4:27-28. It has been suggested that Luke created this entire account in order to provide an example of the fulfillment of Ps 2:1-2: "Why do the nations conspire and the peoples plot in vain? The kings of the earth [Herod] take their stand and the rulers [Pontius Pilate] gather together against the Lord [God] and against his Anointed One [Jesus]." This seems unlikely, however, for several reasons. For one, the reference in Ps 2:1-2 seems too vague to have caused the creation of such an account. Second, if Luke did create such an account in order to fulfill Ps 2:1-2, why did he not mention this passage in the account. To create an account in order to fulfill a prophecy of Scripture and not to mention the passage it fulfills until Acts 4:25-26 would be quite strange. Third, Herod was a well-known historical figure, and whether Jesus actually appeared before him would have been known and could easily have been checked out. More likely the actual event of Jesus' appearance before Herod was later seen by the church as a fulfillment of Ps 2:1-2 than that this verse prompted the creation of a fictional account. Perhaps Luke had access to information concerning this incident through such people as Joanna (see comments on 8:3) and Manaen (Acts 13:1).[91]

There is no need to deny the historicity of the present account. It is quite feasible that Pilate could have sought Herod's counsel in this instance. Exactly why he sent Jesus to Herod, however, is unclear. Was it to "pass the buck" in that he believed Jesus was innocent and did not want to order his execution (cf. 23:4,14-15,20,22; Matt 27:19)? Was it to bring about a reconciliation with Herod by honoring him with the opportunity to make this decision or by seeking his counsel (Luke 23:12)?[92] Was it to seek Herod's aid in making a decision due to his familiarity with Jewish issues (23:15)?[93] Luke's purpose in recording this account is much clearer. Herod would provide a second ruler's testimony to Jesus' innocence (cf. 23:15).

[91]For the question of the historicity of this event, see H. W. Hoehner, *Herod Antipas* (Cambridge: University Press, 1972), 224-50.

[92]Does Luke 13:1 perhaps provide the reason for the hostility?

[93]Cf. how Festus enlisted the aid of Herod Agrippa in Acts 25:13–26:32, and esp. 25:26; 26:3,31-32. For a discussion of this question, see H. W. Hoehner, "Why did Pilate Hand Jesus over to Antipas?" *Trial of Jesus*, 84-90.

Comments

23:6   Pilate asked if the man was a Galilean.   The reader knows this from
1:26; 2:4; 4:16.

23:7   Jesus was under Herod's jurisdiction.   See comments on 3:1 (also cf.
Josephus, *Antiquities* 14.15.2 [14.403]).

He sent him to Herod, who was also in Jerusalem at that time.   Herod probably resided in the Hasmonean palace, which lay just west of the temple. The term
"sent" is not used here as a technical term for *to send to a higher authority* as in Acts
25:21, for Herod was not a higher authority over Pilate. Actually the reverse was true.

23:8   He had been wanting to see him.   Compare 9:9c.

Perform some miracle.   For the desire for signs, cf. 11:16,29. Herod's desire
to see Jesus was not to kill Jesus as in 13:31, for he returned him to Pilate with the
conclusion that he was innocent (23:15). Rather Herod was curious and wanted to
see if some of the stories of Jesus' miracles were true.

23:9   Jesus gave him no answer.   Luke revealed through Jesus' behavior
that Jesus, not Herod or Pilate, was in control of the situation (cf. Mark 14:61).
This silence was broken before the Sanhedrin only because the high priest placed
Jesus under an oath (see comments on 22:67). Although Jesus' behavior brings Isa
53:7 to mind, no Gospel writer directly quoted or alluded to this verse. In fact nowhere in the NT is this passage directly quoted. Thus rather than understand the
story of Jesus' silence as being created from Isa 53:7, since this verse is never
quoted in these accounts,[94] it is easier to believe that the early church later saw in
Jesus' silence the fulfillment of Isa 53:7. Whether Jesus himself consciously
sought by his silence to pattern his behavior along the lines of the suffering servant of Isa 53:7 is impossible to know. Compare Jesus' refusal to answer his opponents' hostile question in Luke 20:1-8.

23:10   The chief priests and the teachers of the law.   In sending Jesus to
Herod, Pilate also sent those who were accusing him. Luke did not repeat the accusation of Jesus' opponents. He expected his readers to assume they were the
same ones mentioned in 23:2.

23:11   Then Herod and his soldiers.   These were probably Herod's bodyguards.

Ridiculed and mocked.   Compare 18:32.

Dressing him in an elegant robe.   It is possible to interpret the Greek text as
saying that Herod himself put on an elegant robe, but in light of Mark 15:16-17;
Matt 27:28; John 19:2 it is best to interpret these words as "dressing Jesus in an
elegant robe." In Mark 15:17-20 this was done in apparent mockery of Jesus' alleged kingship.[95]

23:12   That day Herod and Pilate became friends.   Luke did not explain
why, but their cooperation as "king" and "ruler" is referred to in Acts 4:26-27. The
irony here should not be lost. Jesus' passion brings reconciliation even between
such people as Herod and Pilate.

---

[94] Cf. Matt 26:63; 27:12,14; Mark 14:60-61; 15:4-5; Luke 23:9; 1 Pet 2:23.

[95] Fitzmyer (*Luke*, 2:1482) argues that "there is no suggestion in this Lukan episode that
the gorgeous robe has anything to do with Jesus' alleged kingship." Yet the very question of
why Herod clothed him with this robe and why Luke told his readers about this makes one
look for some answer, and the one nearest at hand is that this was done in mockery of Jesus'
alleged kingship.

Before this they had been enemies. Once again Luke did not explain why. Possibly this may have been due to the incident recorded in Luke 13:1. Perhaps Pilate was seeking to alleviate the hard feelings caused by this incident by asking Herod if he would like to handle the case of the present Galilean in his jurisdiction. This, however, is only speculation.

The Lukan Message

Luke used this story to demonstrate further Jesus' innocence. Not only the Roman governor, Pontius Pilate (cf. 23:4,14-15,22), but also the tetrarch, Herod Antipas (23:15), declared Jesus' innocence. Here, as in the previous and succeeding accounts, Luke emphasized the innocence of God's "holy servant Jesus" (Acts 4:27). The reason for Jesus' crucifixion therefore must lie elsewhere. In human terms it is explained by the animosity of the Jewish leadership who used Pilate to bring about their opponent's death. But Luke wanted his readers to understand that on the cosmic and divine level Jesus' death was due to God's will and plan.

(8) Pilate's Sentence (23:13-16)

[13]**Pilate called together the chief priests, the rulers and the people,** [14]**and said to them, "You brought me this man as one who was inciting the people to rebellion. I have examined him in your presence and have found no basis for your charges against him.** [15]**Neither has Herod, for he sent him back to us; as you can see, he has done nothing to deserve death.** [16]**Therefore, I will punish him and then release him."**

Context

Luke resumed the account of Jesus' trial before Pilate. Pilate continued to declare Jesus' innocence (23:14) and decided to punish and then release him. In keeping with his tendency to eliminate or minimize violence in his sources,[96] Luke made only oblique reference to Jesus' scourging (23:16,22, 25). The final scenario of the trial consists of three parts: (1) the sentence by Pilate (23:13-16), (2) the insistence of the Jewish leadership and the people on Jesus' death (23:18-23), and (3) Pilate's succumbing to the wishes of Jesus' opponents (23:24-25).

Comments

23:13   Chief priests, the rulers and the people.   The chief priests were expected opponents.[97] The mention of the "people" is strange, for usually Luke portrayed them

---

[96]Cf. Luke 3:19-20; 19:45; 22:70, and parallels and note his omission of the account of Jesus' being crowned with thorns in Mark 15:16-20.

[97]Cf. Luke 22:66, where we find "elders, chief priests and teachers of the law"; Acts 4:5, where we find "rulers, elders and teachers of the law"; and Acts 4:8, where we find "rulers and elders of the people." The "rulers" are also mentioned in Luke 23:35; 24:20; Acts 3:17; 13:27, where they probably refer to other members of the Sanhedrin.

as having a positive attitude toward Jesus (see comments on 4:15). Tannehill notes, "This represents a drastic shift from the favor which Jesus previously enjoyed with the people."[98] They are not mentioned here and in 23:4 simply serve as witnesses to Pilate's statement concerning Jesus' innocence, for together with the chief priests and rulers they cried out against Jesus.[99] Thus here Luke pointed out the people's culpability. Perhaps Luke's loyalty to the tradition caused him to refer to the people's involvement in the trial.[100]

23:14 As one who was inciting the people to rebellion. Here, as in 23:5, only one of the three charges of 23:2 is mentioned.

I have examined. The term is used in the technical sense of having gone through a legal examination (cf. Acts 4:9; 12:19; 24:8; 28:18).

Found no basis for your charges against him. This is the second of Pilate's three declarations concerning Jesus' innocence (cf. 23:4,22).

23:15 Neither has Herod. This is emphatic. It can mean *Also Herod did not* or *But not even Herod [who understands Jewish matters better than I]*. Here for the first time the reader learns of Herod's verdict in the incident recorded in 23:6-12.

Sent him back to us. This implies that if Herod had found Jesus guilty, he would not have sent him back but would have tried and punished him in some way. "To us" may indicate that the chief priests and teachers of the law sent to Herod (23:10) had returned and were present. Or it may indicate that some of them had remained at the governor's tribunal all the time and only a delegation of them had been sent to Herod to testify against Jesus. A number of manuscripts (A, D, W, $\mathfrak{P}^1$) read here "for I sent you to him," but the best attested reading ($\mathfrak{P}^{75}$, $\aleph$, B) is "for he sent him back to us" and makes much more sense.

He has done nothing to deserve death. The goal of the accusations from Jesus' opponents was now made apparent. This can be interpreted *Herod has done nothing to Jesus that would make us conclude that Jesus is deserving of death* or *Jesus has done nothing to deserve death*. The latter interpretation is to be preferred and is chosen by the NIV, RSV, NEB.

23:16 Therefore, I will punish him and then release him. The intended "punishing" of Jesus would involve a beating or whipping, but not the more severe "scourging" that preceded crucifixion.[101] Luke revealed to his readers that Pilate clearly wanted to release Jesus (23:20,22).

The Lukan Message

Theophilus and his other readers were clearly told that two rulers—the Roman governor Pontius Pilate and the tetrarch of Galilee, Herod Antipas—both found Jesus innocent and wanted to release him. Jesus' crucifixion therefore had nothing to do with personal guilt or culpability (cf. Deut 19:15).

---

[98] R. C. Tannehill, *The Narrative Unity of Luke-Acts* (Philadelphia: Fortress, 1986), 164.
[99] Luke 23:13,21,23; cf. also Acts 3:13-15,17; 13:27-28.
[100] Cf. Mark 15:11,13,15; cf. John 18:38-40; 19:12.
[101] Cf. Mark 15:15; Matt 27:26; cf. also John 19:1, where a different term is used.

(9) Jesus Delivered to Be Crucified (23:18-25)

[18] With one voice they cried out, "Away with this man! Release Barabbas to us!" [19] (Barabbas had been thrown into prison for an insurrection in the city, and for murder.)
[20] Wanting to release Jesus, Pilate appealed to them again. [21] But they kept shouting, "Crucify him! Crucify him!"
[22] For the third time he spoke to them: "Why? What crime has this man committed? I have found in him no grounds for the death penalty. Therefore I will have him punished and then release him."
[23] But with loud shouts they insistently demanded that he be crucified, and their shouts prevailed. [24] So Pilate decided to grant their demand. [25] He released the man who had been thrown into prison for insurrection and murder, the one they asked for, and surrendered Jesus to their will.

Context

Pilate continued to seek Jesus' release. This time he sought to do so by allowing the people to chose, according to the custom, which "criminal" they wanted released. Pilate assumed the choice would be clear-cut. The people would certainly prefer to have Jesus of Nazareth released instead of the murderer Barabbas. To Pilate's dismay the Jewish leadership and the people cried instead for the release of Barabbas. For the third time Pilate pronounced Jesus innocent and sought to release him, but the cries for Jesus' crucifixion continued. Finally he released Barabbas to the people and handed Jesus over to their will.[102]

Comments

23:17 This verse has little textual support. It is omitted by $\mathfrak{P}^{75}$, A, B, it, Cop and should not be included in the text. It probably was added by a scribe from the parallel account in Mark 15:6-8 to explain the practice of releasing a prisoner at the festival.

23:18 With one voice they cried. Literally, *But all together cried out.* "All" refers to the chief priests, rulers, and the people of Luke 23:13. Why Luke did not include the reference to the chief priests' inciting the crowd at this point (cf. Mark 15:11) is unclear, for this would have supported his overall portrayal of the Jewish leadership's opposition to Jesus. Its omission probably is due to Luke's desire to abbreviate the account. That Luke included the "people" in the demand for Jesus' death is surprising.

Away with this man! "Away with" him means *execute* him (cf. Acts 21:36; 22:22; John 19:15) by means of crucifixion (Luke 23:21). "This man" is used contemptuously as in 23:2.

---

[102] Luke abbreviated this account. In so doing he omitted the chief priests' role in inciting the crowd to choose Barabbas (Mark 15:11), Pilate's reference to Jesus as King of the Jews (Mark 15:9,12; cf. Matt 27:17,22, which use the title "Christ"), and the explanation of the custom of releasing a prisoner to the people (Mark 15:6-8). The latter custom was presumed but not mentioned by Luke. Probably he expected his first readers to know this tradition (cf. Luke 1:4) and interpret the account accordingly, much like Luke's modern reader does.

Release Barabbas to us! Luke assumed that his readers knew the tradition regarding release of a prisoner at a festival.[103] The word "Barabbas" is not a personal name but a family name—*Son of Abbas*. In Matt 27:16 several manuscripts (primarily the Caesarean text family) give his name as "Jesus Barabbas." The possible omission of the name "Jesus" from the text, out of reverence for Jesus Christ, would be understandable, but manuscript support for the reading "Jesus Barabbas" is quite limited.

23:19 Insurrection . . . and for murder. Luke explained here that Barabbas was the very kind of person the chief priests, rulers, and people claimed Jesus to be, i.e., a revolutionary. See comments on 22:52. There is a tragic irony here. Jesus came offering peace (Luke 2:14; 19:41-44) but was rejected in favor of a revolutionary who promoted murder. This verse foreshadows the tragedy of the Jewish revolt in A.D. 70. Luke portrays the choice available for Jesus' opponents as a clear decision between good and evil; a holy, righteous man and a murderer; Jesus and Barabbas.

23:20 Pilate again sought to release Jesus (cf. 23:16,22).

23:21 They kept shouting. The verb tense (a durative imperfect) reveals the continued, unending nature of their cry. Compare 23:18,23.

Crucify him! Crucify him! Since crucifixion was *the* method of execution in Jesus' day, this describes the means by which the cry of 23:18 would be carried out. Luke emphasized the evil cry by doubling it. Contrast Mark 15:13; Matt 27:22. See comments on 10:41.

23:22 For the third time he spoke to them. Luke pointed out to his readers that Pilate declared Jesus innocent not just once but three times.

What crime has this man committed? This reveals that Pilate saw the charges brought against Jesus as spurious.

I have found in him no grounds for the death penalty. This is Pilate's third declaration of Jesus' innocence (cf. 23:4,14).

Therefore I . . . release him. Compare 23:16,20. Pilate may have been seeking to appease the crowd by offering to chastise Jesus before releasing him, but this did not satisfy Jesus' opponents.

23:23 They insistently demanded. Literally, *They kept on pressing him* (a durative imperfect).

Their shouts prevailed. Again Luke emphasized that Pilate personally saw no guilt in Jesus but was intimidated by the Jewish leadership and the crowd. Their animosity toward Jesus was so great that it would be satisfied with nothing less than his crucifixion.

23:24 Pilate decided to grant their demand. Compare the RSV, which is more literal, "So Pilate gave sentence that their demand should be granted." In 2 Macc 4:47 and 3 Macc 4:2 the term "gave sentence" (*epekrinen*) is a technical term for giving a judicial sentence. Pilate did not declare Jesus guilty. He declared only that what Jesus' opponents desired should be granted.

23:25 He released the man who had been thrown into prison. Compare Acts 3:14. Luke, by repeating who Barabbas was (contrast Mark 15:15; Matt 27:26), showed the horrible irony of this situation. Jesus' opponents preferred the release of a revolutionary and a murderer rather than the one who "went around

---

[103] Mark 15:6-8; Matt 27:15-16; John 18:39-40; cf. Acts 3:13-15.

doing good and healing" (Acts 10:38). Luke perhaps suggested that Israel, by rejecting "what would bring . . . peace" (Luke 19:41), chose instead the path that would lead to Jerusalem's destruction.

Surrendered Jesus to their will. The term "surrendered" (*paredōken*) also appears in the passion predictions.[104] As in the previous verse, Jesus was not found guilty or handed over to a sentence of death. Rather he was handed over to the will of his opponents. No mention is made in Luke of Jesus' scourging (cf. Mark 15:15; Matt 27:26; John 19:1). Numerous attempts have been made to absolve Pontius Pilate from the part he played in Jesus' crucifixion.[105] He is understood by some as a man caught in tragic circumstances and pressed into doing something he really did not want to do. No sympathy, however, should be lost over a man who willingly executed someone he knew to be innocent. The one human being who had the most to do with Jesus' crucifixion was Pontius Pilate. He had the authority to release an innocent man or crucify him. He chose the latter to preserve his political career. As a result history and the church will always confess that Jesus "was crucified under Pontius Pilate."

The Lukan Message

Jesus was innocent of all charges and wrongly put to death. Furthermore he was declared innocent by the leading Roman authorities (Pilate and Herod Antipas).[106] Due to the Jewish leadership, however, he was put to death. This theme, which already was in the tradition of Jesus' trial used by Luke, has been heightened by the Evangelist in several ways. For one he had Pilate declare Jesus' innocence three times (23:4,14-15,22, none of which have parallels in Mark or Matthew; cf. however, John 18:38; 19:4,6). He also emphasized that Pilate sought three times to release Jesus (23:16, 20,22). Luke emphasized this again in 23:23-25. In Mark 15:15; Matt 27:26 Pilate delivered Jesus to be crucified. This, however, might be misinterpreted to mean that Pilate had found him guilty. As a result Luke stated instead that Pilate delivered Jesus "to their will." In so doing Luke emphasized the culpability of the Jewish leadership for the crucifixion. While Rome was in no way guiltless in the death of Jesus, it is nevertheless seen as sympathetic toward Jesus, and in Acts the empire frequently is portrayed as a defender of Christians against Jewish hostility.

(10) The Way to the Cross (23:26-32)

26As they led him away, they seized Simon from Cyrene, who was on his way in from the country, and put the cross on him and made him carry it behind

---

[104] Luke 9:44, "The Son of Man is going to be betrayed"; 18:32, "He will be handed over to the Gentiles"; and 24:7, "The Son of Man must be delivered." Cf. 20:20; 22:21-22,48; 24:20; cf. also Acts 3:13.

[105] Cf. the Gospel of Peter 1:1-2 and P. L. Maier, *Pontius Pilate* (Wheaton: Tyndale, 1970).

[106] Just like Paul would later be (cf. Acts 18:14-16; 23:26-30; 25:24-27; 26:30-32).

Jesus. [27]A large number of people followed him, including women who mourned and wailed for him. [28]Jesus turned and said to them, "Daughters of Jerusalem, do not weep for me; weep for yourselves and for your children. [29]For the time will come when you will say, 'Blessed are the barren women, the wombs that never bore and the breasts that never nursed!' [30]Then

" 'they will say to the mountains, "Fall on us!"

and to the hills, "Cover us!" ' "

[31]For if men do these things when the tree is green, what will happen when it is dry?"

[32]Two other men, both criminals, were also led out with him to be executed.

Context

Jesus is now led from the presence of Pilate to the place of execution. On the way Simon of Cyrene is commandeered to carry Jesus' cross. As they proceed, a great multitude of people follow. Among them are women, mourning and weeping over what is happening. Jesus uses this opportunity to pronounce that such mourning should not be directed toward him but reserved for themselves. A most terrible time of tribulation is coming upon them. The pronouncement ends with a riddlelike proverb. If what is happening to him (a green piece of wood) appears terrible, what will happen to them (a dry piece of wood)? The account ends with two criminals being led away with Jesus to experience a similar fate.

Once again Luke abbreviated the material he shares with Mark and Matthew.[107] Luke, however, added a number of things to the narrative not found elsewhere. As a result his parallel account is actually longer than Mark's or Matthew's. He also added to Simon's bearing of the cross the reference to his "carrying it behind Jesus" (23:26). Luke's hand is most clearly seen in 23:27-31, which is unique to his Gospel. In this poignant scene Jesus uttered a final prophetic warning of the judgment coming upon Israel.

Comments

23:26 They seized Simon of Cyrene. "They" refers to the Roman soldiers whom Pilate placed in charge of the crucifixion (23:26,47). Luke, however, wanted his readers to understand that the real culprits responsible for the crucifixion were the "they" of 23:13,18,21,22,25 (cf. John 19:16), i.e., the opponents of Jesus who demanded his crucifixion. "They" were the ones responsible for what followed. The Roman soldiers were only their servants in this. Luke, like Mark and Matthew, provided no explanation about why Simon was seized and pressed into carrying Jesus' cross. Possibly this was due to Jesus' physical condition. The

---

[107]He omitted their leading Jesus out "to crucify him" (Mark 15:20) and, like Matthew, he omitted the reference to Simon of Cyrene's being the father of Alexander and Rufus (Mark 15:21). Whereas the latter was meaningful for Mark's audience, who knew Alexander and Rufus, it was not for Luke's (and Matthew's).

scourging that preceded crucifixion[108] was in itself so severe that it could cause
death. Generally the condemned man was to carry his own cross: "Every criminal
who goes to execution must carry his own cross on his back."[109] Indeed "the definition of the disciple as one who takes up his own cross (9:23) depends on
this."[110] Cyrene is modern Libya. Simon was almost certainly Jewish.[111]

Who was on his way in from the country. Since Simon was not coming in
from "work" (it was too early in the day and it was the Passover), he, like Jesus
and the disciples who had spent the night on the Mount of Olives, may have resided outside the city wall. Thus his coming in from the country on the day of the
Passover causes no historical difficulty.

And put the cross on him. We probably should understand this along the
lines of Matt 5:41 and the Roman right to requisition citizens for certain duties.
The "cross" refers to the crossbeam or *patibulum*. "Put" may mean here *placed on
him the obligation to carry the cross behind Jesus.*[112]

And made him carry it behind Jesus. Compare Luke 9:23; 14:27. It is uncertain whether Luke implied that Simon was a believer. It is also speculative to
raise the question of whether Luke personally knew Simon and his sons, Alexander and Rufus. By his wording (contrast Mark 15:21; Matt 27:32), Luke used
this scene as a pictorial portrayal of what it means to "follow Jesus" even though
different wording is used in both Luke 9:23 and 14:27.

23:27 A large number of people followed him. The latter part of this
verse indicates that, for Luke, their following was due to sympathy, not curiosity.
Once again the people's positive attitude toward Jesus came to the forefront. The
term "followed" should be understood in a physical, not spiritual, sense here.

Including women who mourned and wailed for him. Compare 7:32; Matt
11:17; John 16:20 for the wording. Compare Josephus, *Antiquities* 6.14.8 (16.377)
for the combination of these two verbs. Compare Zech 12:10-14. There apparently
existed a band of women who sought to give condemned victims a drugged drink
(wine and frankincense) as an act of mercy and compassion (cf. *Sanh.* 43a; Matt
27:34).[113] Possibly these women belonged to this group.

23:28 Daughters of Jerusalem. The following prophecy concerning Jerusalem was directed to those who would suffer most in the coming tribulation—the
women of Jerusalem.[114]

Do not weep for me; weep for yourselves and for your children. This is an
example of chiasmic parallelism: A "[do not] weep"; B "for me"; b "for yourselves

[108]Mark 15:15; Matt 27:26; John 19:1, but not mentioned in Luke. Mark 15:22 may
imply that Jesus needed help to reach the place of execution.
[109]Cf. Plutarch, *De sera num. vind.* (*The Divine Vengeance*), 554 A-B.
[110]Evans, *Luke*, 861.
[111]Josephus, *Antiquities* 16.6.1-5 (16.160-70); 1 Macc 15:23; 2 Macc 2:23; and Acts
2:10; 11:20 (cf. also 6:9) refer to Jews living in Cyrene.
[112]See Evans, *Luke*, 861.
[113]For further discussion see D. A. Carson, *Matthew*, EBC (Grand Rapids: Zondervan,
1984), 575.
[114]For "daughters of Jerusalem" cf. Song 1:5; 2:7; 3:5,11; 5:8,16; 8:4; Isa 37:22; Zeph
3:14; Zech 9:9.

and your children"; *a* "weep." For a similar pattern cf. Luke 10:20. For a secular parallel cf. Seneca, *Agamemnon* 659-61: "Restrain your tears [for me] . . . ye Trojan women, and . . . you yourselves grieve for your own dead with groans and lamentations." Both Jesus' entrance into Jerusalem (19:41-44) and his leaving were marked by weeping.

23:29   For the time will come.   What follows is the reason for Jesus' lamentation in 23:28. It is a pronouncement of judgment and doom, not a call to repentance.[115] Compare 19:43; 21:6,22-24, where the same temporal designation is used to describe Jerusalem's coming destruction.[116] Luke may have been emphasizing to his readers by these passages that Jesus had predicted Jerusalem's fall and that it was a divine judgment. Even now at his crucifixion Luke portrayed Jesus not so much as the judged but the Judge (cf. Acts 10:42; 17:31) who was fully in control of the situation.

Blessed are the barren women.   To appreciate the horror envisioned in Jesus' saying, one must remember that childlessness was considered a shame and a disgrace in Israel (cf. Luke 1:25; Gen 30:23; Isa 4:1). Contrast the usual joy of childbirth.[117] Compare 21:23.

23:30   They will say to the mountains.   As in Hosea 10:8 the cry was to be spared further punishment and an appeal to be put out of their misery. It was not a cry to be spared and escape the coming tribulation, for there is no "escape" for those on which a mountain falls. Compare also Rev 6:16.

And to the hills.   This phrase stands in synonymous parallelism with the preceding.

23:31   For if men do these things when the tree is green, what will happen when it is dry?   The saying is based on an *a fortiori* argument, but its riddlelike quality makes its interpretation difficult. The picture part of the saying involves the fact that dry wood burns much more readily than green wood. The main issue involves to whom the "they" refers. Is it a circumlocution for God? Does it refer to the Romans? (If the Romans are doing this to me, whom they acknowledge as innocent, what will they do to you in A.D. 70 when you are truly guilty of rebellion?) The Jews? (If the Jews do this to their Anointed One who has come for their salvation, what will God do to them for having killed his Son?)[118] Human beings in general? In light of the use of the third person plural as a circumlocution for God in 6:38; 12:20,48; 16:9, the most likely interpretation is *If God has not spared his innocent Son from such tribulation* [by permitting his crucifixion], *how much worse will it be for a sinful nation when God unleashes his righteous wrath upon it* [by permitting the Romans to destroy Jerusalem].

23:32   Two other men, both criminals, were also led out with him.   This prepares us for 23:33,39-43 and fulfills the prophecy of 22:37. Although technically this verse can be translated *two other criminals were*, there is no doubt that Luke

[115]J. H. Neyrey, "Jesus' Address to the Women of Jerusalem (Lk 23.27-31)—A Prophetic Judgment Oracle," *NTS* 29 (1983): 74-86.

[116]The frequent references to this in Luke should be noted: 11:49-51; 13:1-9,34-35; 19:41-44; 20:15-16; 21:6,20-24, 23:29-31; Acts 6:14.

[117]Luke 1:57-58; 11:27; Gen 21:6-7; Isa 54:1.

[118]See Neyrey, *The Passion according to Luke*, 114.

meant *two others, criminals, were.* It is uncertain whether this verse is best understood as a conclusion of what has preceded or as an introduction of what follows.

The Lukan Message

The people once again are portrayed as sympathetic toward Jesus by their mourning (23:27). The negative portrayal of them found in 23:4-26 is now ended. In 23:35 they will be distinguished from the mocking rulers, and in 23:48 they express grief over what has happened. There is also an allusion in 23:26 to what it means to be a disciple. Being a disciple means to take up a cross and follow Jesus. Simon is, so to speak, the first person to take up his cross and follow Jesus. All is proceeding precisely in accordance with what the Son of God has prophesied. Jesus knows exactly what will take place. He knows the future like no other. Once again Luke wanted his readers to understand Jesus' death was not a tragic mistake but the fulfillment of the divine plan and will. See Introduction 8 (1).

The judgment about to come upon Jerusalem is a strong emphasis here.[119] The sins of the Jewish leadership had condemned Jerusalem irrevocably to judgment; and just like dry, aged wood is ready for burning, so Jerusalem was ripe for destruction. The days of this judgment would be so terrible that women would have preferred to bear the reproach of childlessness than to experience those days. Jerusalem's terrible destruction was a divine judgment, for a divine judgment awaits all who reject God's Son (cf. 9:23-26; 12:9). For Luke's readers there was also present in such a recounting of divine judgment a warning and exhortation to faithfulness and perseverance.[120]

(11) The Crucifixion (23:33-38)

[33]**When they came to the place called the Skull, there they crucified him, along with the criminals—one on his right, the other on his left.** [34]**Jesus said, "Father, forgive them, for they do not know what they are doing." And they divided up his clothes by casting lots.**

[35]**The people stood watching, and the rulers even sneered at him. They said, "He saved others; let him save himself if he is the Christ of God, the Chosen One."**

[36]**The soldiers also came up and mocked him. They offered him wine vinegar** [37]**and said, "If you are the king of the Jews, save yourself."**

[38]**There was a written notice above him, which read:** THIS IS THE KING OF THE JEWS.

---

[119]Cf. Luke 11:49-51; 13:1-9,34-35; 19:41-44; 20:15-16; 21:6,20-24, 23:29-31; Acts 6:14.

[120]Cf. M. L. Soards ("Tradition, Composition, and Theology in Jesus' Speech to the 'Daughters of Jerusalem' (Luke 23,26-32)," *Bib* 68 [1987]: 244), who states: "Thus the words of Jesus to the Daughters of Jerusalem cause the reader to look to and through the destruction of Jerusalem and the difficult period of the last days at the coming of the Son of Man, which for the believer is the day of redemption."

Context

After Jesus arrives at the place of the skull, he is crucified between two thieves. As he is crucified, he prays for the forgiveness of his opponents. Lots are cast and Jesus' garments are divided. While the people watch, the rulers taunt Jesus, repeating some of his Christological claims. The soldiers also taunt him over his claim to be king of the Jews and offer him sour wine. The account concludes with the inscription of the *titulus* "THIS IS THE KING OF THE JEWS" (23:38).

The account in Luke differs from the parallels in Mark and Matthew in several ways. Besides changing the order somewhat, Luke abbreviated his Markan source.[121] On the other hand he probably added the saying concerning Jesus' prayer of forgiveness (Luke 23:34, see discussion of verse), added the title "Chosen One" (23:35), added the taunt by the soldiers (23:36—he added another, the third taunt, in 23:39), and added a second reference to Jesus' being the king of the Jews (23:37).

Comments

23:33   The place called the Skull.   As usual Luke omitted the Aramaic term found in his Markan source (cf. 22:39; see Introduction 3). The word for *skull* in Greek is *Kranion*; in Aramaic, *Golgotha* (Mark 15:22; Matt 27:33; John 19:17); and in Latin, *Calvariae*, i.e., Calvary. The place probably was so-called because it looked like a skull. This is most likely the site of the Church of the Holy Sepulchre in Jerusalem. In Jesus' day this site was outside the walled city.

There they crucified him.   The brevity of the Gospel accounts (cf. also Mark 15:25; Matt 27:35; John 19:18) should warn against overdramatizing and making a melodrama of Jesus' sufferings. Although crucifixion could be performed without nails, John 20:25 (cf. Col 2:14) states that nails were used. Luke 24:39 may suggest that both Jesus' hands and feet were nailed to the cross. Crucifixion was a common form of capital punishment from the sixth century B.C. until it was banned by Constantine in 337.[122]

Along with the criminals.   Mark 15:27 and Matt 27:38 refer to these as *lēstai*. This term can refer to robbers or revolutionaries (see comments on 22:52). Luke as a result may have chosen the term "criminals" (*katourgoi*; literally *evildoers*) to avoid Jesus' being associated with revolutionaries in his crucifixion. This is a clear fulfillment of Luke 22:37; Isa 53:12.

23:34   There is a major textual problem associated with Jesus' prayer in this verse. Some very good Greek manuscripts (א, A, C, $\mathfrak{P}^1$, $\mathfrak{P}^{13}$, it [most], vg syr [most],

---

[121] Luke omitted the mocking referred to in Mark 15:20, the Aramaic name "Golgotha" (15:22), the offer of a drugged drink (15:23), a reference to the time of day (15:25), the taunting and blaspheming of the crowd (15:29-30), the reference to destroying and rebuilding the temple in three days (15:29), and the first taunt directed at Jesus to save himself (15:30).

[122] For a discussion of the history and a description of this "cruel and disgusting penalty" (Cicero, *Against Verres* 2.5.64), see M. Hengel, *Crucifixion* (Philadelphia: Fortress, 1977).

many early church fathers, and even Marcion) include "Jesus said, 'Father, forgive them, for they do not know what they are doing.' " On the other hand this is not found in $\mathfrak{P}^{75}$, B, D, W. Internal arguments as to its authenticity are fairly evenly divided. The appearance of a similar saying in Acts 7:60, however, favors its authenticity, since Luke frequently showed how the disciples in Acts followed in Jesus' footsteps in the Gospel. It is impossible to be dogmatic with regard to whether this verse was originally part of Luke's Gospel or whether it was perhaps an authentic saying of Jesus inserted into the text by a copyist. If the prayer is Lukan, Jesus was asking his Father to forgive "them"[123]—not just those who nailed him to the cross but all those involved in his death. Jesus' prayer clearly makes any attempt to justify anti-Semitism on the basis of his crucifixion impossible.

Father. Compare Luke 10:21; 11:2; 22:42; 23:46.

Forgive them, for they do not know. For forgiveness due to ignorance, cf. Acts 3:17; 13:27; 17:30 (cf. also 1 Tim 1:13). For a similar prayer on the lips of one of Jesus' followers, cf. Acts 7:60 (cf. also 1 Pet 2:21). Compare Luke 11:4. Ellis notes, "The prayer is answered by his death, which brings the forgiveness of sins (Acts 2:38)."[124]

They divided up his clothes by casting lots. That is, they cast lots to see who would receive what. This is another example of the fulfillment of Scripture (cf. Ps 22:18). Whether Jesus was crucified naked or was permitted some sort of "loin-cloth" is uncertain. The clothes of the victim were the executioners' perquisites.

23:35 The people stood watching. Luke contrasted the people's behavior with the rulers' (cf. Mark 15:29). This contrast is further developed in Luke 23:48. "Watching" may be an allusion to Ps 22:7. Compare also John 19:37; Zech 12:10.

The rulers even sneered at him. In contrast to the people the members of the Sanhedrin (see comments on 23:13) are portrayed as responsible for Jesus' death and agony. This is a further allusion to Ps 22:7 and is the first mocking.

He saved others. For examples of this, cf. Luke 7:50; 8:36,48,50; 17:19; 18:42.

Let him save himself. This is the first of three taunts directed at Jesus to save himself (cf. 23:36-37,39; Mark and Matthew have only one). Luke's readers would have realized the irony in this taunt, for Jesus in coming to save others could only do so by not saving himself. It is precisely because Jesus is the Savior of Israel (Luke 2:11; Acts 5:31; 13:23) that he must suffer and fulfill what the Scriptures said.[125] For similar taunts cf. Luke 4:3,9,23. Jesus had settled the issue of being a miracle-working, sign-giving Messiah at the very beginning of his ministry, i.e., at the temptation. See 4:1-15, "The Lukan Message."

If he is the Christ of God. This clause is literally *if this one is the Christ of God.* "This one" is again used contemptuously. See comments on 23:2. Luke's readers of course knew that Jesus is the Christ of God (i.e., God's Messiah) because of what Luke said previously (see comments on 9:20). "Of God" describes "Christ" (see comments on 9:20).

The Chosen One. A similar title is used of Jesus in 9:35.[126]

---

[123] I.e., the "they" of Luke 23:13-14,18,20-21,23-25; cf. Acts 2:36.

[124] Ellis, *Luke*, 267.

[125] Luke 9:22; 17:25; 18:31-33; 24:26; Acts 3:18; 4:25-28; 26:23.

[126] Cf. 1 Pet 2:4; Isa 42:1; cf. also 1 Enoch 39:6; 40:5; 45:3; 46:3; 49:2; 51:3; 52:6,9.

23:36 The soldiers also came up and mocked him. This is Luke's first mention of the role of the Roman military in the crucifixion. They produce the second mocking of Jesus (cf. 23:35,39).

They offered him wine vinegar. This act is mentioned in all four Gospels (Mark 15:36; Matt 27:48; John 19:29-30). "Wine vinegar" was the ordinary wine drunk by soldiers. Whether this was an act of kindness giving a dying victim something to drink or mockery meant to prolong the victim's agony by giving him strength and delaying his death is unclear. The mocking that preceded and followed this (23:36a,37) suggests Luke saw this as a negative gesture. A possible allusion to Ps 69:21 also argues for its being negative (cf. also 1QH 4:11).

23:37 If you are king of the Jews, save yourself. This basically repeats Luke 23:35. For Luke this title was essentially a synonym for "Christ" because of 23:2 ("Christ, a king") and especially because of Pilate's question in the following verse in which "king of the Jews" substitutes for "Christ." This is also evident from the chiasmic-like collection of titles in 23:35-39: A—Christ, 23:35; B—King of the Jews, 23:37; b—King of the Jews, 23:38; a—Christ, 23:39.

23:38 There was a written notice above him. It was customary to have the charge of the victim present at his execution (cf. Suetonius, *Caligula* 32 and *Domitian* 10; Eusebius, *Eccl. Hist.* 5.1.44). Whereas in the situation of Jesus the inscription of the *titulus* was one of condemnation, i.e., his "crime," in Luke's situation it confesses who Jesus really is.

THIS IS THE KING OF THE JEWS. Despite some differences, all four Gospels record this title (Matt 27:37; Mark 15:26; John 19:19). As far as Rome was concerned Jesus was crucified on political grounds. He confessed (or at least acknowledged) he was the King of the Jews, the Christ.

The Lukan Message

The Lukan Christological emphasis and teaching in this passage is apparent. In the space of five verses (23:35-39) Jesus is referred to as "the Christ of God, the Chosen One," "the King of the Jews" (twice), and "the Christ." While it is true that three "confessions" come from mockers and one from the Roman governor, Luke expected his readers to understand that they were correct because they confirmed the Christology that he had taught, i.e., that Jesus is the Christ (1:32-33; 2:11,26; 4:41; 9:20), the King of the Jews (1:32-33; 19:38; cf. 2:4; 18:38-39). Thus, ironically enough, even Jesus' mockers witnessed to who Jesus is. For Luke and his readers the political connotations of the title "Christ," which caused Jesus to avoid its use in public, were no longer a problem. By then the nonrevolutionary nature of Jesus' life and teachings and the behavior of his followers allowed the use of this title without fear of political misconceptions. A soteriological emphasis is also associated with the Christology of this account in that Jesus' work as "Savior" is also mentioned. The saving nature of Jesus' ministry is referred to four times in the space of five verses (23:35 [twice],37, 39). Again, although the reference to Jesus' saving activity came in the form of mockery from his opponents, Luke's readers knew that Jesus is indeed the Savior because of Luke's earlier teachings on the subject. Luke wanted his readers to know that Jesus of Nazareth even in his death, no especially in his death, was the promised Christ, the King of the Jews, and Savior of the world.

If the prayer of 23:34 is authentic, Jesus modeled his own teachings on love for enemies, forgiveness, and nonviolence.[127] For Luke's readers it should be easier to love their enemies possessing this example of how the Christ, the King of the Jews, forgave his enemies. Who had ever been more wronged than God's Chosen One? Yet he forgave his enemies. The love of one's enemies, to which Luke's readers are called, would always pale in comparison to this.

As in the entire passion narrative, Luke emphasized the fulfillment of Scripture. Jesus died between two criminals in fulfillment of Scripture. His garments were divided by lot in fulfillment of Scripture. He was mocked in fulfillment of Scripture. Rather than see all this as the creation of stories by the church in order to fulfill OT texts that were thought to refer to the coming of the Messiah, it is more reasonable to understand the process as having occurred in reverse. In other words the events of the passion caused the church to discover in their reading of the Scriptures prophecies that spoke of these events.

Finally, Luke again pointed out that whereas the Jewish leadership by their mockery still actively opposed Jesus, the people were no longer part of this opposition. This is seen both by Luke's omission of the description of the people's mocking Jesus found in his source (Mark 15:29-30) and by his description of them as only watching (Luke 22:35). Later Luke described them as expressing sorrow and contrition over what had happened (23:48).

(12) The Two Criminals (23:39-43)

[39]One of the criminals who hung there hurled insults at him: "Aren't you the Christ? Save yourself and us!"

[40]But the other criminal rebuked him. "Don't you fear God," he said, "since you are under the same sentence? [41]We are punished justly, for we are getting what our deeds deserve. But this man has done nothing wrong."

[42]Then he said, "Jesus, remember me when you come into your kingdom."

[43]Jesus answered him, "I tell you the truth, today you will be with me in paradise."

Context

Luke now introduces an account unique to his Gospel. Whereas Mark 15:32; Matt 27:44 refer only to the criminals insulting Jesus, Luke adds

---

[127]Found in Luke 6:27-29 (esp. 6:28b),31-33,35; 10:30-37; 11:4; 22:49-51; cf. Acts 7:60.

that one also gives a taunt (the third taunt in Luke) that if Jesus were in fact the Messiah he should save himself and them. The other criminal promptly rebukes him and contrasts their just suffering and guilt with Jesus' unjust suffering and innocence. Then turning to Jesus he asks to be remembered when Jesus enters into his reign. The account ends with Jesus' pronouncement that the "repentant" criminal will enjoy paradise with him that day.

Comments

23:39 One of the criminals. Luke used the same term here as in 23:32-33.

Who hung. "Hung" is a synonym for "was crucified" (Acts 5:30; 10:39; cf. also Gal 3:13).

Hurled insults. Literally *was blaspheming* (see comments on 22:65).

Aren't you the Christ? This is "a more bitter taunt than 'If thou art?' "[128]

Save yourself and us! This taunt is repeated for the third time. This criminal repeated the taunt of Jesus' opponents but also of his and Jesus' executioners.

23:40 But the other criminal rebuked him. In the Acts of Pilate 10:2, this criminal is given the name "Dysmas."

Don't you fear God? The reply assumes the two criminals justly faced death due to their guilt. It was therefore not the time for hurling insults at one who was innocent but rather for seeking God's mercy. "Fearing God" is a proper attitude toward God in Luke-Acts.[129]

23:41 We are punished justly. This criminal confessed his sins and acknowledged that he deserved to be punished. Such a confession is an integral part of repentance. In rebuking the other criminal, this one rejected the view that if Jesus were the Christ, he would save himself. As Tannehill notes, "The criminal recognizes that Jesus' death is not a refutation of messianic claims but a prelude to messianic power."[130]

This man. The use of this phrase here contrasts with its contemptuous use in 23:2,18 (cf. also its more neutral use in 23:14,22).

Has done nothing wrong. Compare Acts 25:5. Along with Pilate's threefold witness to Jesus' innocence (23:4,14,22) and Herod's witness (23:15), we now have the witness of this criminal. Shortly we will have the witness of a centurion (23:47).

23:42 Jesus, remember me when you come into your kingdom. Some manuscripts ($\aleph$, A, W, f^1, f^{13}, syr, the Byzantine texts) read "*in* [or "with"] your kingdom," i.e., when you come at the parousia to reign. The NIV (following $\mathfrak{P}^{75}$, B, it) is more likely to be correct. In the original setting the criminal, believing that Jesus would have been better off than he due to his innocence, gave an implicit Christological confession and asked Jesus to remember him when he entered into his reign. In the setting of Luke the readers would have understood this as a request to Jesus that when he entered into his reign through his death-resurrection-

---

[128] Plummer, *Luke*, 534.

[129] Cf. Luke 1:50; 12:4-5; 18:4; Acts 10:2,22,35; cf. also Acts 13:16,26. See comments on 1:65.

[130] Tannehill, *Narrative Unity of Luke-Acts*, 126.

ascension, he should remember him, i.e., act to save him. Compare Gen 40:14; Pss 74:2; 106:4; *Did.* 10:5 for "Remember."

23:43 I tell you the truth. See comments on 4:24.

Today. To the criminal's vague "when" Jesus responded with a precise "today," referring less to *within the next twenty-four hours* or *before the sun goes down* than to *the realization of Jesus' reign through his death, resurrection, and ascension.* This day through Jesus' death, salvation was being achieved, and the criminal would share in it. As a result even though this took place temporally that day, "Luke's 'today' belongs . . . more to theology than to chronology."[131] For "today" see comments on 2:11; 4:21.

You will be with me in paradise. Once again the last had become first. The "first" mocked and sought Jesus' death; this condemned criminal, surely the "last," sought the Lord's mercy and amazingly found salvation. In the OT the term "paradise" can refer to a park with trees (Song 4:13; Eccl 2:5; Neh 2:8), a "garden of the Lord" (Gen 13:10), a "garden . . . in Eden" (2:8), or can be understood in a future eschatological sense (Ezek 31:8). In the intertestamental literature[132] and in the NT (2 Cor 12:4; Rev 2:7) the expression is used more and more to describe the final abode of the righteous. It is used in this sense here. The criminal would experience salvation. He would not "today" experience the resurrection, for the resurrection of the dead will only occur at the parousia. Whatever the temporary state may have been, however, he would have a conscious experience with Jesus in paradise (cf. 16:19-31). This same thought is found in different terminology in 1 Thess 4:17; and Phil 1:21-23.

The Lukan Message

The theme of Jesus' innocence is continued here. Whereas earlier the governor, Pontius Pilate, and the tetrarch, Herod, witnessed to the innocence of Jesus, now a criminal does as well. In the next account they will be joined in their witness by a centurion. Luke's readers should have had no doubt therefore that even though Jesus was crucified between criminals, he was innocent. His death was an unjust one. Yet his death is salvific. How Jesus' death is able to save was not developed by Luke (see Introduction 8 [8]), but that he died as a "Savior" is clear (23:35-37,39). The criminal was able to be saved precisely because Jesus did not save himself. Jesus' cross is intimately involved in his being able to "seek and to save what was lost" (19:10) and to forgive sins (5:20-26; 7:36-50; Acts 10:39-43); in this account he is able to save even the "most lost." Tax collectors, prostitutes, the poor, the blind, and even criminals being executed for their crimes are able in the eleventh hour to find in Jesus an all-sufficient Savior.

In the great reversal the chief priests and teachers of the law[133] rejected God's Son and as a result experienced judgment (23:28-31; 20:9-19). Those

---

[131] Sabourin, *Luke,* 390.

[132] *T. Levi* 18:10-11; *Pss. Sol.* 14:2; 2 Esdr 8:52; cf. also the imagery in 1 Enoch 61.

[133] Luke 22:66–23:2,10,13-18,21,23-25.

who were first are again shown to be last, i.e., excluded from the kingdom and subject to the divine judgment. The last, who are helpless and without hope, however, can turn to Jesus and find life everlasting. The last thus become first. The supreme irony is that the criminal rightfully being executed for his crime(s) was infinitely better off than Israel's high priest, who by his rejection of God's Son was eternally damned. What a reversal indeed. See Introduction 8 (5). Luke wanted his readers to remember that the kingdom is for the poor, the hungry, the sorrowful, the despised.

Luke's readers should also be aware that the Jesus in whom they believe is already reigning at God's right hand. Already, today, he is Lord and King. Fitzmyer notes: "In a sense this episode becomes the peak of the Lukan scene of crucifixion, for it not only presents the third taunt against Jesus, yet another (implicit) declaration of his innocence, but a manifestation of his salvific mercy to one of the dregs of humanity." [134]

(13) The Death of Jesus (23:44-49)

[44]It was now about the sixth hour, and darkness came over the whole land until the ninth hour, [45]for the sun stopped shining. And the curtain of the temple was torn in two. [46]Jesus called out with a loud voice, "Father, into your hands I commit my spirit." When he had said this, he breathed his last.

[47]The centurion, seeing what had happened, praised God and said, "Surely this was a righteous man." [48]When all the people who had gathered to witness this sight saw what took place, they beat their breasts and went away. [49]But all those who knew him, including the women who had followed him from Galilee, stood at a distance, watching these things.

Context

The passion narrative continues with the account of Jesus' death. Along with Mark 15:33 and Matt 27:45, Luke recorded the coming of darkness upon the land from noon until Jesus' death at 3:00 p.m. He also recorded the tearing of the temple curtain (23:45b), but he placed this earlier in the account right after the coming of darkness (22:44-45a). In so doing he heightened the eschatological nature of what was taking place. The account's high point is found in the centurion's words, which serve as the final witness to Jesus' innocence (22:47). Luke then concluded the account like Mark by stating that "the women" and Jesus' acquaintances witnessed these things.

Luke, however, omitted several things found in the parallel accounts. He omitted Jesus' cry of dereliction from Ps 22:1 (cf. Mark 15:34, which some of Luke's readers might have interpreted as a confession of guilt) and Mark's reference to Elijah (15:35-36), which Luke replaced with

---

[134]Fitzmyer, *Luke* 2:1508.

Jesus' prayer (cf. Ps 31:5) of commitment to his Father (Luke 23:46). Luke also omitted at this point mention of the soldiers' offering Jesus a drink of wine vinegar (23:36), since he had told this earlier (cf. Mark 15:36). He added, however, that the darkness was due to the sun's having stopped shining (Luke 23:45) and that all the people beat their breasts in remorse and contrition for what happened (23:48).

Comments

23:44 It was now about the sixth hour. This would be noon. Compare Mark 15:33; Matt 27:45; cf. also John 19:14.

Darkness came over the whole land until the ninth hour. "The ninth hour" was 3:00 p.m. All three Synoptic Gospels record this. The coming of darkness is frequently a portent of an eschatological event.[135] Apocalyptic imagery such as we find in this verse is at times symbolic rather than literal. For Luke, however, the present imagery was understood literally as well as figuratively because of the following explanation (23:45a). The darkness and the tearing of the curtain in the temple have been understood as portents of God's displeasure over what happened.[136] They can also be understood as portents of the eschatological significance of what was happening, for what was taking place was not simply the death of an innocent Jew by crucifixion. It was not just the death of a righteous prophet. It was far, far more. This was the death of God's Son by which he is able "today" (23:43) to be the Savior of the world.

23:45 For the sun stopped shining. Luke explained the darkness as due to the sunlight's failing. This is, of course, a "prescientific" description. Attempts to explain this as due to an eclipse of the sun stumble over the fact that Passover took place at full moon, when an eclipse would have been impossible. Compare Acts 2:20.

The curtain of the temple was torn in two. According to rabbinic tradition (*Yoma* 54a) there were thirteen different curtains used in the temple. It has been suggested that this refers to the curtain at the entry to the holy place, i.e., the inner temple, because this could be more easily seen. It is best, however, to understand this as referring to the curtain at the entrance of the holy of holies, i.e., the place where once a year on the day of atonement the high priest would enter and offer sacrifice for the sins of the people.[137] Matthew 27:51 explains this as having taken place due to an earthquake. The tearing of the curtain has been interpreted as (1) a portent of the judgment of Jerusalem in A.D. 70 (Luke 23:28-29; eclipses were frequently interpreted in the ancient world as portents of destruction and doom);[138] (2) the opening of salvation to all through the death of God's Son (cf. Heb 9:6-28; 10:19-22; Matt 27:51-53); (3) the ending of the ceremonial and ritual

---

[135] Cf. Deut 28:28-29; Isa 13:9-11; Jer 15:9; Joel 2:30-31; Amos 8:9; Mark 13:24-25; Acts 2:19-20.

[136] Cf. Fitzmyer (*Luke* 2:1519) and D. C. Allison, Jr. (*The End of the Ages Has Come* [Philadelphia: Fortress, 1985], 74-75), who see the imagery as emphasizing that this was the hour of darkness (22:53).

[137] Cf. Heb 6:19; 9:3,6-28; 10:20; cf. also *T. Levi* 10:3 and *T. Benj.* 9:4 which, however, may be Christian interpolations into the text.

[138] See Evans, *Luke*, 876.

laws of the old covenant; (4) the replacement of the temple by the body of Christ. (The latter does not appear to be correct, however, for in Acts the early church continues to worship in the temple.) Exactly how Luke understood this event is uncertain, but either the first or second interpretation seems more likely.

23:46 Jesus called out with a loud voice. Compare Acts 16:28; Mark 1:26; Rev 14:18.

Father. See comments on 10:21. Compare how Jesus' prayers in Luke 10:21; 22:42; 23:34 also begin with "Father."

Into your hands I commit my spirit. Compare Ps 31:5; Acts 7:59; cf. 1 Pet 4:19. Jesus, knowing that he had completed his departure/exodus (Luke 9:31), committed his spirit, i.e., his life, into his Father's hands in order to enter into his glory (24:26). In so doing Jesus is a model for his followers (cf. Acts 7:59).

When he had said this, he breathed his last. Mark 15:37 has the same expression; Matt 27:50 reads, "He gave up his spirit"; John 19:30 has, "With that, he bowed his head and gave up [a different word from Matthew] his spirit." Even in his death Jesus was in control. He was not killed. He did not die. Rather he voluntarily gave up his life to death. Jesus was Master even in his death.

23:47 The centurion. See comments on 7:2.

Seeing what had happened. Although "what had happened" is singular (cf. Luke 23:48, where it is plural), this involves such things as the darkness, Jesus' behavior against his enemies (23:34), his words to the criminal (23:43), his prayer to the Father (23:46), and his giving up of his life (23:46). The centurion would not have been able to "see" the tearing of the curtain in the temple, so Luke probably was not thinking of this.

Praised God. See comments on 5:25-26. He did this is by confessing Jesus' innocence. There is no need to interpret this as meaning that he had become a believer.

Surely this was a righteous man. In Mark 15:39; Matt 27:54 the centurion confessed, "Surely this man/he was the Son of God." For Luke the centurion's confession concerning Jesus' innocence was more important than the Christological confession he found in Mark. Being the Son of God would imply, of course, that Jesus was righteous, for an "unrighteous Son of God/Christ" would be a contradiction of terms. In the present context provided by Luke 23:4,14-15,22, "righteous" (*dikaios*) means *innocent* (cf. Acts 3:14; 7:52; 22:14; Matt 27:19).

23:48 When all the people. Luke now tells of the people and their response to this. "All" is used hyperbolically (see comments on 21:17).

Saw what took place. Compare Luke 23:47.

They beat their breasts and went away. This involves not only a sadness over what had happened[139] but, due to the parallel in 18:13, remorse and the assumption of guilt.

23:49 But all those who knew him. This probably refers to relatives and friends from Galilee and the disciples.

Including the women who had followed him from Galilee. These were referred to in 8:1-3 and are distinguished from the "daughters of Jerusalem" mentioned in 23:28. The women will play an important role in the next two stories (23:55-56; 24:1-12). Compare John 19:25-27.

---

[139] So Sabourin, *Luke*, 392.

Stood at a distance, watching these things. It is uncertain whether Luke alluded here to Ps 38:11 or 88:8.

The Lukan Message

The present account is the culmination of the Lukan emphasis concerning Jesus' innocence. Jesus was unjustly crucified and killed by wicked men (Acts 2:23; 7:52). Yet he was holy and righteous (3:14), God's holy Servant (4:27,30), the Righteous One (22:14). He was totally innocent as Pontius Pilate confessed three times before all (Luke 23:4,14,22). Herod Antipas, who was familiar with Jewish customs, also confessed his innocence (23:15). But others who were in a position to know also confessed this. A criminal crucified with Jesus admitted that although he himself was guilty and deserving of death, Jesus was innocent (23:41). Finally the centurion who witnessed all that took place also confessed Jesus' innocence (23:47). Luke's readers therefore need not be embarrassed or confused because the Object of their faith died a criminal's death, for all who were in a position to know witnessed to his innocence. Why Luke emphasized this theme is not clear, even if the fact that he did so is.

This account also stresses the eschatological nature of Jesus' death. This was not just a prophet's death, although it was that. This was the death of God's Anointed, the Messiah/Christ, the King of the Jews, the Son of God, the Lord, the Son of Man. The eschatological nature of this death is seen by darkness coming upon the land, for this was a sign of God's entrance into history to fulfill his purpose (see comments on 23:44). Added to this is the report of the tearing of the temple curtain in two. These portray Jesus' death as the eschatological event that inaugurates a new covenant (22:20). Luke did not describe fully how Jesus' death brings all this about. He presented no developed theory of the atonement. What he did say was that Jesus came for the lost (19:10) and that because of his death he was able to forgive sins.

Even in his crucifixion Jesus was in control of all that was taking place. All that was taking place was in accordance with and the fulfillment of his teachings and plans. He resolutely set out for this goal (9:51), for this was the departure or "exodus" the Scriptures had prophesied for him (9:31). Thus after finishing his mission, Jesus committed himself into his Father's hands and breathed his last. No one took his life from him. He gave it freely (cf. John 10:18).

The account also distinguishes the attitude of the Jewish leaders and the people toward Jesus. The leaders unceasingly demanded his death (23:2,5, 10,18-25), and they showed no remorse for his death. The eschatological signs of darkness and the tearing of the temple curtain (23:44-45) reveal God's judgment against "official" Israel. The people, however, despite their involvement in the crucifixion (23:4-5,13,18), were now portrayed quite differently. They mourned and wailed over Jesus' fate (23:27-28), did not participate in the mocking but stood apart (23:35), and now in the present account showed remorse and contrition (23:48). Thus there was hope for them, and in Acts they would respond positively to the gospel proclamation. Luke wanted his readers to make a clear distinction between the attitude of the Jewish people and that of the Jewish leadership.

(14) The Burial of Jesus (23:50-56)

[50]Now there was a man named Joseph, a member of the Council, a good and upright man, [51]who had not consented to their decision and action. He came from the Judean town of Arimathea and he was waiting for the kingdom of God. [52]Going to Pilate, he asked for Jesus' body. [53]Then he took it down, wrapped it in linen cloth and placed it in a tomb cut in the rock, one in which no one had yet been laid. [54]It was Preparation Day, and the Sabbath was about to begin.

[55]The women who had come with Jesus from Galilee followed Joseph and saw the tomb and how his body was laid in it. [56]Then they went home and prepared spices and perfumes. But they rested on the Sabbath in obedience to the commandment.

Context

The passion is now concluded. Joseph of Arimathea, a Sanhedrin member, requests and obtains Pilate's permission to bury Jesus. Joseph is described as a good and upright man, who looked for the coming of God's kingdom. Luke also points out that he had not consented to the Sanhedrin's plans and actions. He takes the body of Jesus down from the cross, prepares it for burial by wrapping it in a shroud, and then lays it in a tomb cut out of the rocks. The tomb, Luke points out, had never been used. It is late Friday afternoon, and the Sabbath is about to begin. The women, who had come with Jesus from Galilee, follow and observe the tomb, and, upon returning to where they were staying, prepare spices and ointments in order to return to the tomb and better prepare Jesus' body for burial after the Sabbath.

Luke omitted several details in the story that are found in the Markan parallel.[140] He did, however, add a number of unique details to his account. These involve a lengthy description of Joseph as good and upright (23:50) and as not having consented to the Sanhedrin's plot and actions (23:51). He also added that Jesus' death and burial took place on the Sabbath eve (23:54) and that the women, although preparing spices and ointments, rested on the Sabbath because of the OT Commandment (23:56).

---

[140]The most significant is his omission of Pilate's verifying Jesus' death in Mark 15:44-46. Two other omissions involve the references to Joseph's courage in approaching Pilate (Mark 15:43) and to the stone rolled against the door of the tomb.

Comments

23:50 There was a man named Joseph. This man, otherwise unknown, is referred to in all four Gospels (Mark 15:43; Matt 27:57; John 19:38). The fourfold reference to him in the Gospels and the fact that he played no known role in the life of the early church assures the historicity of his part in Jesus' burial.

A member of the Council. This refers to his being a member of the Sanhedrin as the next verse shows. We know nothing about whether he was a priestly or a lay member. That we find some positive comments in Luke-Acts concerning the Pharisees (see comments on 5:17) but none concerning the Sadducees may suggest he was more likely Pharisaic in his sympathies. He might very well have been a source of information for the early church of what occurred at the trial of Jesus.

A good and upright man. "Upright" (*dikaios*) possesses a richer and more religious sense here than in 23:47, where it means "innocent."[141] Luke's description implies that he was a believer, and Matt 27:57 and John 19:38 expressly state this.

23:51 Who had not consented to their decision and action. Having stated that Joseph was a Sanhedrin member, Luke felt compelled to add this qualification. (This reveals that 23:18 is hyperbolic.) In so doing he witnessed to Joseph's innocence even as he witnessed to Jesus' innocence earlier. The Sanhedrin's "decision" probably refers to their plot to get rid of Jesus (22:2-5) and their "action" of turning him over to Pilate (23:1).

He came from the Judean town of Arimathea. Compare 4:31 for a similar kind of qualification. The reference to Arimathea's being a Judean town suggests the majority of Luke's readers were Gentiles. See Introduction 3. The exact location of this town is debated, but it may have been the modern city of Remphis, some ten miles northeast of Lydda (present-day Lod).

Waiting [*prosedecheto*] **for the kingdom of God.** This description is also found in Mark 15:43. Luke has a similar description of Simeon in 2:25, who was "waiting [*prosdechomenos*] for the consolation of Israel," and of Anna in 2:38, who was "looking forward [*prosdechomenois*] to the redemption of Jerusalem." For Luke these expressions essentially were synonyms. He expected his readers, like these models of faith, to pray for the kingdom to come (11:2), expect the return of the Son of Man (12:40), watch (12:36-37; 21:36), and faithfully look for the coming of the Son of Man (18:7). For "kingdom of God" see Introduction 8 (2).

23:52 Going to Pilate, he asked for Jesus' body. As a member of the Sanhedrin he would have had greater access to Pilate's ear than Jesus' family and friends. That Pilate granted the request is assumed (cf. Mark 15:45).

23:53 Then he took it down. As in Mark 15:46, Joseph is described as personally having removed Jesus' body from the cross. (The "they" of Acts 13:29 does not contradict this in that Joseph of Arimathea was a Jew.) According to Jewish law (Deut 21:22-23) a body could not remain hanging after sundown, and the Romans apparently accommodated their practice in Judea accordingly. In 11Q Temple 64:11-13 the need for removing a crucified person before sundown is expressly

---

[141] Cf. Luke 2:25 for a similar description of the prophet Simeon ("righteous" [same Greek word as "upright"] and devout"); 1:6, where Zechariah and Elizabeth are also called "upright"; Acts 10:22, where Cornelius is described as "a righteous [same Greek word as "upright"] and God-fearing man"; cf. also Acts 11:24.

stated (cf. also Josephus, *War* 4.5.2 [4.317]). Thus we read of the breaking of the criminals' legs to hasten death in John 19:31-33 and a spear wound to verify death in 19:34.

Wrapped it in linen cloth. No mention is made here of any preparation of the body for burial, although some such preparation was normal and could not have been postponed for twenty-four to thirty-six hours due to the warm climate. John 19:39-40 expressly states that Nicodemus, who helped in the preparation of the body, brought along a significant amount of the needed spices. The women, however, intended to remedy any lack of preparation (Luke 23:55-56). With the negative results from carbon 14 testing, all speculation about the authenticity of the Shroud of Turin should now cease. This was not the linen cloth spoken of in this verse.

Placed it in a tomb cut in the rock. For the Jewish concern that the dead be buried, see Josephus, *Against Apion* 2:29 (2.111); Tob 1:17-18. The tomb is specifically identified in Matt 27:60 as Joseph's own tomb. The other accounts probably assume this. (How else would Joseph find a tomb, and especially a rich man's tomb cut out of the rock, so quickly?) The identification of the tomb as Joseph's and the women's observation of Jesus' burial in this private tomb prepares for the following story of the empty tomb. The Church of the Holy Sepulchre is a far more probable site of the tomb than the so-called Gordon's Tomb. The record of the burial is quite important in the pre-Pauline confession found in 1 Cor 15:4. It is difficult not to see in Paul's reference in 1 Corinthians the same kind of understanding found in the Gospel accounts, i.e., that this rock-hewn tomb containing the body of Jesus on Good Friday was empty on Easter Sunday (cf. Acts 2:29-31; 13:29-30, which must be understood in light of Luke 24:1-12,22-23). Luke alone commented that the tomb was cut out of the rock. Usually victims of crucifixion were buried in a common pit. Jesus, however, although he was crucified between two criminals, was not buried as a criminal.

In which no one had yet been laid. As in 19:30, where Israel's king deserves and receives an unused colt, so here he receives an unused tomb. Compare John 19:41 and Matt 27:60, which state that the tomb was "new."

23:54 It was Preparation Day. This refers to the day before the Sabbath, as the rest of the verse makes clear, rather than the day before the Passover. Since the Sabbath began at sunset Friday, this refers to late Friday afternoon.

Sabbath was about to begin. The verb "about to begin" (*epephōsken*) usually means *begin to shine*. Some have suggested therefore that Luke confused a non-Semitic reckoning of time in which day began at daybreak with the Semitic reckoning in which day began at nightfall. It is quite possible, however, that the verb has a broader meaning here and should be interpreted "was about to begin."

23:55 The women. Compare Luke 23:49. This refers primarily to the women of 8:2-3 and 24:10—Mary Magdalene, Joanna, Susanna, and Mary, the mother of James.

Followed Joseph. Compare Acts 16:17.

Saw the tomb. Thus they were able to return to this place in Luke 24:1. This makes it impossible to think of the resurrection as a myth based upon the women's having come to a wrong, empty tomb.

And how his body was laid in it. Seeing how the body was prepared, the women went home and prepared spices and perfumes (23:56a). Apparently in their minds the body was not prepared adequately.

23:56   Spices and perfumes. Although not stated, it is assumed that the reader will understand that these would be used in preparing Jesus' body more adequately for burial (cf. Mark 16:1). This was why they brought these to the tomb in Luke 24:1. According to *Sabbat* 23:5, the activities necessary for preparing the dead for burial were permitted on the Sabbath.

But they rested on the Sabbath in obedience to the commandment. It is uncertain whether this is the conclusion of the present account or the beginning of the next one. Because each of the other resurrection accounts begins with a temporal designation concerning the first day of the week (Mark 16:1-2; Matt 28:1; John 20:1), it seems better to place it with what precedes than with what follows. Just as Zechariah and Elizabeth observed all the Lord's commandments and regulations blamelessly (see comments on 1:6), so the women also rested on the Sabbath according to the Commandment found in Exod 20:10; Deut 5:14.

The Lukan Message

Luke used the present tradition to provide a model of Christian behavior for his readers. This is why "Luke likes to emphasize moral and spiritual qualities."[142] He combined the character and actions of Joseph of Arimathea and the women for this purpose. Joseph is described as good and upright (Luke 23:50) like Simeon (2:25), Zechariah and Elizabeth (1:6), and Cornelius (Acts 10:22). A similar description is given to Barnabas (11:24). Joseph is also described, like Simeon (Luke 2:25) and Anna (2:38), as one who was waiting for God's kingdom. As for the women, they continued to keep the Commandment(s), like Zechariah and Elizabeth did (1:6). For Luke the ethical character prescribed before Jesus' coming is the same as God prescribed now (see comments on 1:6). Whatever God's activity in salvation history, the ethical character God approves and seeks has not changed. For Luke's readers this meant that although they may call themselves "Christians" (Acts 11:26), they follow in the steps of Abraham, Isaac, and Jacob and the saints of the OT, who were good and upright, looking for the kingdom, and keeping the Commandments. See Introduction 7 (2). See comments on 1:6; 2:21-40, "The Lukan Message."

Finally, Luke's addition that Jesus' tomb was "one in which no one had yet been laid" emphasizes Jesus' character as King. Even as only a virgin colt was worthy for the King of Israel as he entered into Jerusalem, so only a "virgin" tomb was worthy for the burial of the King of the Jews.

---

[142] Benoit, *Passion and Resurrection*, 216.

—————— *SECTION OUTLINE* ——————

VIII. THE RESURRECTION AND ASCENSION OF JESUS (24:1-53)
1. The Women at the Empty Tomb (24:1-12)
2. Jesus' Appearance on the Road to Emmaus (24:13-35)
3. Jesus' Appearance to the Disciples in Jerusalem (24:36-43)
4. Jesus' Commission to the Disciples (24:44-49)
5. The Ascension (24:50-53)

———— **VIII. THE RESURRECTION AND ASCENSION** ————
OF JESUS (24:1-53)

The seventh and last section of Luke's Gospel deals with Jesus' resurrection and ascension. With Jesus' predicted suffering (9:22,44; 17:25) and departure/exodus (9:31) over, Luke recounts the Son of Man's appearance to his followers and his entering into glory (9:32). This section is the culmination of all that precedes and contains numerous Lukan themes. The literary unity of this chapter can be seen chronologically in that all the events are placed within the framework of the same day, geographically in that all takes place in or around Jerusalem, and thematically in that all the accounts involve Jesus' resurrection and the apostles' qualification as eyewitnesses of the risen Christ (cf. 1:2). The section consists of five accounts. The first involves the story of the empty tomb in which Mary Magdalene and the other women play a predominant role (24:1-12). This is the first story in every Gospel resurrection account. The second involves Jesus' appearance to two disciples on the road to Emmaus (24:13-35). The third involves Jesus' appearance to the Eleven and the other disciples (24:36-43). The fourth involves Jesus' commissioning the disciples to a worldwide ministry and his equipping them with the Spirit (24:44-49). The fifth tells of Jesus' ascension into heaven. The last provides an inclusio to the entire work, for the Gospel began with Zechariah serving in the temple in Jerusalem (1:5-25) and concludes with the disciples praising God in the temple. Although Luke did not tell his readers that a second work will follow, he prepared them for this, for Acts picks up where the Gospel ends.[1] Luke 24:1-53 therefore not only concludes the story of what Jesus "began to do and to teach" (Acts 1:1) but also serves as a bridge for the continuance of that story. In Acts, Luke tells of what Jesus continues to do and teach through his chosen witnesses.

---

[1]Cf. Acts 1:2 with Luke 24:50-51; Acts 1:3 with Luke 24:1-53; Acts 1:4-5 with Luke 24:49b; Acts 1:8 with Luke 24:49; Acts 1:9-11 with Luke 24:50-51; Acts 1:12 with 24:52; Acts 2:1f. with Luke 24:49b.

1. The Women at the Empty Tomb (24:1-12)

[1]On the first day of the week, very early in the morning, the women took the spices they had prepared and went to the tomb. [2]They found the stone rolled away from the tomb, [3]but when they entered, they did not find the body of the Lord Jesus. [4]While they were wondering about this, suddenly two men in clothes that gleamed like lightning stood beside them. [5]In their fright the women bowed down with their faces to the ground, but the men said to them, "Why do you look for the living among the dead? [6]He is not here; he has risen! Remember how he told you, while he was still with you in Galilee: [7]'The Son of Man must be delivered into the hands of sinful men, be crucified and on the third day be raised again.'" [8]Then they remembered his words.

[9]When they came back from the tomb, they told all these things to the Eleven and to all the others. [10]It was Mary Magdalene, Joanna, Mary the mother of James, and the others with them who told this to the apostles. [11]But they did not believe the women, because their words seemed to them like nonsense. [12]Peter, however, got up and ran to the tomb. Bending over, he saw the strips of linen lying by themselves, and he went away, wondering to himself what had happened.

Context

On the first day of the week, having observed the burial (Luke 23:55), the women come to the tomb bringing the spices they had prepared (23:56). Finding the stone rolled away, they enter the tomb and find it empty. In their perplexity they meet two angels (24:4-8,23) who announce that Jesus is not dead but alive and recall to them Jesus' earlier prophecies concerning his death and resurrection. The women return and tell the apostles, but their witness is met with skepticism. Peter then runs to the tomb and finds it empty, except for the linen strips. He leaves, marveling over what had taken place.

All four Gospels possess accounts of the women's coming to the empty tomb. All four refer to the first day of the week, women as the chief characters in the story, Mary Magdalene's being one of the women, the stone's being rolled away, the women's finding the tomb empty, and an angelic message. Yet several differences in the accounts make it difficult to harmonize them.[2] Apparently in the early church there existed several separate traditions concerning the empty tomb. Although the differences within them may at times be frustrating, they serve as multiple witnesses to the existence of the empty tomb.[3]

---

[2]For a recent attempt at such harmonization, see J. Wenham, *Easter Enigma* (Grand Rapids: Zondervan, 1984).

[3]This is the argument of multiple attestation. See R. H. Stein, "The 'Criteria' for Authenticity," *Gospel Perspectives*, ed. R. T. France and D. Wenham (Sheffield: JSOT, 1980), 1:229-32.

The Lukan account contains several unique features. Although Luke omitted the women's questioning of how the stone would be rolled away (Mark 16:3), he added a reference to their bringing the spices they had prepared (Luke 24:1; cf. 23:56). He also recalled Jesus' earlier prophecies concerning his betrayal, death, and resurrection (24:7) and transposed the names of the women from the beginning of the account (cf. Mark 16:1; Matt 28:1) to the end (Luke 24:10).

Comments
24:1 On the first day of the week. In all four Gospels the day of the resurrection is Sunday, the first day of the week. Shortly the first day of the week replaced the Sabbath as the main day of worship for the church (cf. Acts 20:7; 1 Cor 16:2; Rev 1:10).[4]
The women. Literally *they*. Compare Luke 23:56. The "they" is not explained until 24:10.
24:2 They found the stone rolled away from the tomb. Luke, unlike Mark 15:46; 16:3; Matt 27:60,66; 28:2, has not mentioned the stone up to this point. He may have assumed that his readers knew this information. The situation envisioned in the Gospels involves a cavelike tomb with a large wheel-like stone that was rolled down a channel to cover the tomb opening.
24:3 But when they entered, they did not find the body of the Lord Jesus. The phrase "of the Lord Jesus" is not found in D and it (Itala). The manuscript support for its inclusion is strong, however, so that it should be accepted as part of the text. "Lord" is here used of the earthly Jesus (see comments on 7:13), for they were not seeking the body of the risen Lord. In Acts 1:21; 4:33; 8:16 it is used of the risen Lord.
24:4 Two men in clothes that gleamed like lightning. In Matt 28:2,4 the men are explicitly called angels, and Luke referred to them as angels in 24:23. For a similar description of "divine messengers," cf. 9:30-31; Acts 1:10; 10:30. The number of the angelic visitors has always been a problem (cf. Mark 16:5-7; Matt 28:2-7; John 20:12). Whereas the women wondered about why the tomb was empty, for Luke and his readers the empty tomb was a proof that Jesus rose from the dead.
24:5 In their fright. For a similar reaction on the part of the disciples in the presence of the risen Christ, cf. Luke 24:37 (cf. also Acts 10:4; 24:25, where the same term appears). This fear probably should be understood more in the sense of reverential awe such as we find in Luke 1:12 (see comments); 1:30; 2:9-10 rather than in the sense of their experiencing stark terror.
The women bowed down with their faces to the ground. Compare 5:8,12; 17:16; Acts 9:4.
Why do you look for the living among the dead? Although in the form of a question, the angelic response is even more positive in Luke than in Mark 16:6;

---

[4]For the thesis that this change of worship from the seventh day to the first is due to the resurrection having occurred on the first day of the week, see E. L. Bode, *The First Easter Morning*, AnBib (Rome: Pontifical Biblical Institute, 1970).

Matt 28:6. Jesus was not in the tomb because he lives. Tombs are for dead people. The women should not have been looking for the living Jesus here. If Luke 20:38 was true of the patriarchs, how much more would it be true of the Son of God, who prophesied that he would rise from the dead. This emphasis on Jesus as "living" is found again in 24:23; Acts 1:3; 3:15; cf. Rom 14:9.

24:6 He is not here; he has risen! These words are not found in D and it (Itala) but are present in $\mathfrak{P}^{75}$, $\aleph$, A, B, and the vast majority of manuscripts. They should be understood as part of Luke's Gospel. "Risen" probably should be interpreted actively ("has risen" rather than *has been raised*) as in Luke 11:8; 13:25 because in 24:7 "be raised" is active (see comments on 24:7).

Remember how he told you. Although Jesus' teaching on his passion and resurrection were primarily directed to the disciples,[5] it is assumed that the women knew this teaching. It is possible that the women were present when Jesus said these things or that they heard them from the disciples. For similar wording, cf. 22:61; Acts 11:16; 20:35.

While he was still with you in Galilee. Since Luke did not list any accounts of Galilean resurrection appearances, he omitted the references to Jesus' future meeting of his disciples in Galilee found in Mark 14:28 (Matt 26:32) and Mark 16:7 (Matt 28:7). Such appearances are described in Matt 28:16-20; John 21:1-23. Luke did this because all the events of the chapter took place on the same day and in or around Jerusalem.

24:7 The Son of Man must be delivered. This is a collage of such passages as Luke 9:22 ("the Son of Man must . . . and on the third day"); 9:44 ("the Son of Man is going to be betrayed into the hands of men"); and 18:32-33 ("he will rise again"). The reference to being "crucified" is not found until 23:21, but it is essentially a clarification of being "killed" (9:22; 18:32) and of Jesus' "exodus" (9:31). The reference to "sinful" men is not found earlier but probably is an interpretation of "Gentiles" mentioned in 18:32. Once again the divine necessity ("must be") of Jesus' death is stressed. See Introduction 8 (1).

On the third day. See comments on 9:22.

Be raised again. It is unclear why the NIV interpreted this verb (*anastēnai*) as passive. Although in some instances it is passive (cf. John 11:24; 1 Thess 4:16, where believers are said to "rise," and the sense must be "are raised"), it is best to interpret this verb actively here as "rise" (RSV, NEB). Jesus' resurrection was his own doing (cf. Luke 18:33; 24:46; Matt 17:9,23; Mark 8:31; 9:31; 10:34).

24:8 Then they remembered his words. "His words" are Jesus' prophecies lying behind Luke 24:7 (cf. 9:22,44; 18:32).

24:9 From the tomb. This is omitted by D and Itala, but it is included by the vast majority of witnesses and is best understood as part of the Lukan text.

They told . . . the Eleven. Since Judas no longer was part of the Twelve and a replacement had not yet been found (cf. Acts 1:15-26), the Twelve were now the Eleven. Compare Luke 24:33; Acts 1:26; cf. also Acts 2:14.

All the others. These are not specified but probably would have included the 120 of Acts 1:15. They must have included the two disciples on the road to Emmaus due to Luke 24:14,22-24.

---

[5]Cf. Luke 9:18,21-22,43-44; 17:22,25; 18:31-32.

24:10   It was Mary Magdalene, Joanna, Mary the mother of James. The
first two women were mentioned in 8:2-3. The grammar permits Mary to have been
either the mother, wife, or daughter of James (literally "Mary the [____] of James").
The first possibility is the correct one because the same expression is found in Mark
16:1 and 15:40, where this Mary is described as the mother of James.
   Others with them. In the Greek text "others" is feminine, so this refers to
the women mentioned in 23:49,55, excluding those just mentioned by name.
   Told. Literally "were telling." Some confusion exists about what the subject
of this verb is. The verse could be translated: "It was Mary Magdalene, Joanna,
Mary the mother of James. And the others with them told." The verse is better
translated, however, as having the women named as well as "the others" as the
subjects of the verb (so NIV, RSV).[6]
   The apostles. See comments on 6:13. This prepares us for the future role of
the apostles as witnesses to the resurrection (see "The Lukan Message").
   24:11   They did not believe the women. Even the angelic message repeated
by the women and the fact of the empty tomb were insufficient to produce faith in the
disciples. This, however, does not imply that the women did not believe.[7] Later we
read that the disciples would "not believe it because of joy" (24:41; cf. Matt 28:17;
John 20:25,27). Psychologically this is understandable, for opening their hearts to
this possibility would have made them susceptible to additional disappointment if
this were not true. All rationalistic explanations based on the psychological predis-
position of the disciples and the women for "resurrection experiences" flounder in
that Jesus' followers were anything but ready to believe. (Note that the women came
to the tomb to make sure that Jesus' body had been adequately prepared for burial,
not to welcome the risen Lord with a rendition of the "Hallelujah Chorus.") Luke
possibly was seeking to reassure his readers of the truth/certainty of the things they
had been taught (Luke 1:4) by showing that the disciples only believed in the resurrection because of the overwhelming evidence they encountered in the appearance of
the risen Christ. Thus the disciples' unbelief becomes an aid to belief for Luke's
readers. By magnifying the disciples' incredulity, Luke magnified the miracle. Only
the clear and unmistakable appearance of the risen Christ could have overcome such
doubt and replaced it with unshakable faith.
   24:12   We encounter here the same textual problem as in 24:3,6,9, i.e., Codex
Beza (D) and the Old Latin manuscripts (it) omit this verse. Yet the strength of the
manuscript tradition that includes this verse is much too strong to be rejected.
Even the fact that we find a very close parallel in John 20:3-5 should not negate
the strong manuscript evidence in its favor.[8] Luke 24:24 assumes the existence of
this verse.

---

[6] See I. H. Marshall, *The Gospel of Luke*, TNIGTC (Grand Rapids: Eerdmans, 1978), 887.
[7] See J. Plevnik, "The Eyewitnesses of the Risen Jesus in Luke 24," *CBQ* 49 (1987): 92.
[8] Cf. M. D. Goulder (*Luke: A New Paradigm* [Sheffield: JSOT, 1989], 776-77), who
argues that the repeated pattern of appearance (angels to women, 24:4-7; Christ on the
Emmaus road, 24:15-31; Christ to disciples, 24:36-51), disbelief (the eleven, 24:11; Cleopas
and the other disciple, 24:25; disbelief for joy, 24:41), and faith (Peter marveling, 24:12; the
breaking of bread leading to faith, 24:30-33; the commissioning of the disciples, 24:45-59)
requires that 24:12 be understood as authentic.

Peter, however, got up and ran to the tomb. Compare John 20:3-4.
He saw the strips of linen lying by themselves. Compare John 20:5. The
"strips of linen" refer to the linen cloth of Luke 23:53. The strips of linen witness
to the resurrection by revealing the absence of Jesus' body.

He went away, wondering to himself what had happened. Whereas "wondering" can be associated with doubt and unbelief (11:38; Acts 13:41), it is usually seen as a positive response to what has happened or is taking place.[9] As a
result Peter's wondering should not be interpreted negatively, even if the empty
tomb does not in itself produce faith. (For the disciples, however, an unempty
tomb would preclude faith.) The resurrection appearances would change all this.
This verse prepares us for Luke 24:34 and Peter's future role in the church
(22:32).

The Lukan Message

As has been seen on numerous occasions, this account emphasizes the
necessity of Jesus' death. The various resurrection accounts are replete with
references to the necessity of Jesus' death (cf. 24:7,18-21,25-27,44-46).
There is clearly some reason why Luke emphasized this. Yet *why* Luke so
strongly emphasized this divine necessity and what the situation was that
called for it is uncertain. Nevertheless *that* he emphasized this is clear.

Closely associated with this theme is the fulfillment of Scripture.
Although such fulfillment is not directly referred to in this account, Jesus'
suffering, death, and resurrection was for Luke a fulfillment not just of
Jesus' prophecies but, as he pointed out in 24:26-27, the fulfillment of OT
prophecy as well. The repeated references to Jesus' and the OT's prophecies concerning his death and resurrection tie the entire chapter together.
As a result this chapter becomes in essence a continuous commentary on
both the significance and necessity of Jesus' death and resurrection.

The resurrection is of cardinal importance for Lukan Christology. The
resurrection is the theme of this entire chapter and will occupy a central
position in Acts. There the proclamation of Jesus' resurrection is the chief
task of the apostolic witness[10] and the heart of their preaching.[11] As Evans
notes, "Luke-Acts is thus more responsible than any other NT writing for
the presentation of Christianity as a religion of resurrection."[12]

---

[9]Cf. Luke 1:21,63; 2:18,33; 4:22; 7:9; 8:25; 9:43; 11:14; 20:26; 24:41; Acts 2:7; 3:12;
4:13; 7:31. The terms "amazed" (*existēmai*) appears eleven times in Luke-Acts and is always
positive, as is the term "astonished" (*ekplēssomai*), which occurs three times. See Plevnik,
"Eyewitness of the Risen Jesus," 92.

[10]Acts 1:21-22; 2:32; 3:15; 4:33; 5:30-32; 10:39-42; 13:29-31.

[11]Acts 2:24-26; 3:14-15; 5:30-32; 10:39-42; 13:28-31,35-37; 17:18,31; 23:6; 24:15;
26:8,23; cf. also 8:35; 13:5; 16:31.

[12]C. F. Evans, *Saint Luke*, TPINTC (London: SCM, 1990), 888.

The fulfillment of Jesus' teaching concerning his death and resurrection indicates that his other teachings could also be accepted as truthful by Luke's readers. Such difficult teachings on wealth and the love of enemies have the stamp of approval of the risen Lord. They, like the OT Scriptures, can now be preceded by "Thus says the [risen and glorified] Lord."

Jesus' power over death and the grave is seen in 24:7. Whereas the NT speaks of Jesus' being raised from the dead by the Father (9:22; Acts 3:15; 4:10; 5:30; 10:40; 13:30,37), the resurrection was also Jesus' own doing, i.e., a self-activity (see comments on 24:7).

With his resurrection Jesus passed from his time of humiliation to his time of exaltation as Lord and Christ (Acts 2:33-35; 5:30-31). That he was Lord and Christ before his resurrection is, of course, clear from Luke's use of these titles to describe the earthly Jesus. See Introduction 8 (4). Now, however, he is Lord and Christ with power (cf. Rom 1:4). Such passages as Acts 2:33-35; 5:30-31 probably are best understood along the lines of Phil 2:9-11.

Finally, only Luke, of all the Gospel writers, referred to the "apostles" in the account of the empty tomb (Luke 24:10). In so doing he indicated that the apostles, whom Jesus sent out (24:49; Acts 1:25-26), were eyewitnesses of the resurrected Christ (Luke 24:48; Acts 1:22). Thus the message of the resurrection, which Luke's readers had heard and trusted, could be believed with certainty because it ultimately came from the apostles who "from the first were eyewitnesses and servants of the word" (Luke 1:2).

2. Jesus' Appearance on the Road to Emmaus (24:13-35)

[13]Now that same day two of them were going to a village called Emmaus, about seven miles from Jerusalem. [14]They were talking with each other about everything that had happened. [15]As they talked and discussed these things with each other, Jesus himself came up and walked along with them; [16]but they were kept from recognizing him.

[17]He asked them, "What are you discussing together as you walk along?"

They stood still, their faces downcast. [18]One of them, named Cleopas, asked him, "Are you only a visitor to Jerusalem and do not know the things that have happened there in these days?"

[19]"What things?" he asked.

"About Jesus of Nazareth," they replied. "He was a prophet, powerful in word and deed before God and all the people. [20]The chief priests and our rulers handed him over to be sentenced to death, and they crucified him; [21]but we had hoped that he was the one who was going to redeem Israel. And what is more, it is the third day since all this took place. [22]In addition, some of our women amazed us. They went to the tomb early this morning [23]but didn't find his body. They came and told us that they had seen a vision of angels, who said he was alive. [24]Then some of our companions went to the tomb and found it just as the women had said, but him they did not see."

[25]He said to them, "How foolish you are, and how slow of heart to believe all that the prophets have spoken! [26]Did not the Christ have to suffer these things and then enter his glory?" [27]And beginning with Moses and all the Prophets, he explained to them what was said in all the Scriptures concerning himself.

[28]As they approached the village to which they were going, Jesus acted as if he were going farther. [29]But they urged him strongly, "Stay with us, for it is nearly evening; the day is almost over." So he went in to stay with them.

[30]When he was at the table with them, he took bread, gave thanks, broke it and began to give it to them. [31]Then their eyes were opened and they recognized him, and he disappeared from their sight. [32]They asked each other, "Were not our hearts burning within us while he talked with us on the road and opened the Scriptures to us?"

[33]They got up and returned at once to Jerusalem. There they found the Eleven and those with them, assembled together [34]and saying, "It is true! The Lord has risen and has appeared to Simon." [35]Then the two told what had happened on the way, and how Jesus was recognized by them when he broke the bread.

Context

The story of Jesus' appearance on the road to Emmaus is the first of three resurrection appearances reported in Luke and is unique to his Gospel.[13] The second, the appearance to Peter, is also reported within this account (24:34). The story is one of the longest in Luke and consists of four parts. The first involves Jesus' encounter with the two disciples traveling from Jerusalem to Emmaus (24:13-16). The second (24:17-27) concerns (1) the ensuing conversation in which one disciple, Cleopas, explains to the stranger about Jesus' death at the hands of the Jewish leadership; (2) the women's report concerning the empty tomb, which had been confirmed by others; and (3) the report of the angelic visit to the women. At this point the stranger explains from the Scriptures the necessity of the Messiah's death and resurrection. The third part tells of the two disciples inviting the stranger to stay at their home and of the subsequent meal. When the stranger (as in the Lord's Supper) takes bread, blesses it, breaks it, and begins to distribute it, their eyes are opened. They recognize that the stranger is Jesus, and his teachings concerning the divine necessity of the passion are confirmed. Jesus then disappears (24:28-32).

---

[13]Interesting parallels exist between this account and the conversion of the Ethiopian Eunuch (Acts 8:26-40). We find characters: traveling and confused (Luke 24:13-24; Acts 8:30-31); going from Jerusalem (Luke 24:13,33; Acts 8:27-28); met by a messenger (Luke 24:15-19; Acts 8:29-30), who explains the Scriptures (Luke 24:27; Acts 8:32-35), showing the necessity of Jesus' death (Luke 24:25-26; Acts 8:32). We find a sacrament—the Lord's Supper or baptism (Luke 8:30; Acts 8:36,38); the disappearance of the messenger (Luke 24:31; Acts 8:39); and people rejoicing (Luke 24:32; Acts 8:39). These similarities are helpful in pointing out Luke's theological emphases in the two accounts.

The final part involves the return of the two disciples to Jerusalem, where they are informed that the Lord has risen and appeared to Simon (24:33-35). In turn they share their experience of the risen Christ and how he was revealed to them in the breaking of the bread.

Comments

24:13 Now that same day. That is, the first day of the week (24:1) when the empty tomb was discovered.

Two of them were going to a village called Emmaus. The "two" belong to the "others" of 24:9. Possibly they were returning home after the Passover festivities since the Sabbath was over. The exact location of Emmaus is uncertain.[14]

About seven miles from Jerusalem. "Seven miles" is literally *sixty stadious* from Jerusalem. A *stadion* is about 607 feet; therefore the distance is approximately 6.8 miles. Some manuscripts, however, read 160 *stadious* or 18.4 miles. The latter probably was an attempt to correct Luke's sixty *stadious* by later scribes who identified Emmaus with the village of Amwas about twenty miles from Jerusalem.

24:14 About everything that had happened. This is explained in 24:20-24.

24:16 But they were kept from recognizing him. For a similar motif, cf. 9:45 and 18:34, although the terminology is different. As in John 20:14-15; 21:4 Jesus' followers did not recognize the risen Christ. The passive "were kept from recognizing" is a divine passive, i.e., *God kept them from recognizing Jesus.* This lack of recognition allowed Jesus to teach the necessity of his death and resurrection and to show how this was the fulfillment of Scripture (Luke 24:25-27).

24:18 One of them, named Cleopas. Cleopas is not the Clopas of John 19:25, for Cleopas is a shortened form of the Greek name Cleopatros (masculine form of Cleopatria), whereas Clopas is a Hebrew/Aramaic name. Some have suggested that perhaps Cleopas was known to Luke's readers in the same way that Alexander and Rufus were known to Mark's (cf. Mark 15:21). This is purely speculation, and even more speculative is discussion about who the other person was.

Are you only a visitor to Jerusalem and do not know? This is a better translation than, "Are you the only resident of Jerusalem who does not know." Clearly these things, according to Luke, did not happen in a corner (cf. Acts 26:26).

24:19 "What things?" he asked. Jesus led the disciples into the discussion that followed.

About Jesus of Nazareth. Literally, Jesus, the Nazarene.[15]

He was a prophet. This should not be interpreted negatively as being incorrect but positively in light of 7:16,39; 9:8,19. This is also evident from Jesus' use of this title as a self-designation in 4:24; 13:33 (cf. also Acts 3:22-23; 7:37). See comments on 7:16.

Powerful in word and deed. Compare Luke 4:14; Acts 2:22; cf. also 7:22. The combination "word and deed" is also found in Rom 15:18; Col 3:17; 2 Thess 2:17; cf. also 1 John 3:18. Compare Acts 1:1, "All that Jesus began to do and to teach."

---

[14]See J. A. Fitzmyer, *The Gospel according to Luke*, AB (Garden City: Doubleday, 1985), 2:1561-62, for a brief discussion.

[15]For the use of this title elsewhere in Luke-Acts, cf. Luke 4:34; 18:37; Acts 2:22; 3:6; 4:10; 6:14; 10:38; 22:8; 26:9.

Before God. That is, Jesus was approved by God. Compare Luke 1:6, where Zechariah and Elizabeth are referred to as righteous "before God."

All the people. Jesus was approved by the people. Here Luke repeated this familiar theme.[16] See comments on 4:15.

24:20 The chief priests and our rulers. The responsibility for Jesus' death was placed upon the Jewish leadership. They are mentioned in 23:13 (where the "people" are also mentioned, but in 24:19 the people side with Jesus). "The chief priests and our rulers" probably is used as a synonym for similar expressions in Luke-Acts.[17]

Handed him over to be sentenced to death. This refers to the events of 22:71–23:2; 23:25; cf. Acts 3:13; 13:27-28. For an earlier prediction of this, cf. Luke 9:44; 18:32. For the earlier resolve of the Jewish leadership to put Jesus to death, cf. 20:20.

They crucified him. Although it is clear from 23:1f. that the Romans officially crucified Jesus, here Luke placed the ultimate responsibility on the Jewish leadership.[18] Compare 23:21,25; Acts 5:30.

24:21 We had hoped that he was the one who was going to redeem Israel. Compare Acts 1:6. The two disciples expressed their disappointment in the course of events. Undoubtedly they possessed a more political than religious understanding of how the Christ would redeem Israel. For them the redemption of Israel meant Israel's liberation from their enemies, i.e., the Romans. For Luke, however, Jesus did in fact redeem Israel[19] and brought the kingdom of God. Yet it was by his death that Jesus accomplished this redemption and sealed this new covenant (Luke 22:20).

And what is more. In addition to not understanding that the redemption of Israel had in fact taken place, there was an additional "thing" that caused their sadness (24:17).

It is the third day since all this took place. This is not an allusion to the Jewish view that on the fourth day the soul left the body,[20] for no allusion is made to this, and Luke's Gentile readers would not have known this. It was rather for Luke a reference to Jesus' resurrection predictions found in 9:22; 13:32; 18:33.

24:22-23 In addition, some of our women amazed us ... said he was alive. These two verses give a short summary of 24:1-12. The summary includes the empty tomb (24:3), the angelic appearance (24:4), and the message that Jesus was alive (24:5; cf. Acts 3:15). For "early" cf. Luke 24:1.

24:24 Then some of our companions went to the tomb. This verse assumes the authenticity of 24:12. There only Peter is mentioned, although John 20:2-10 also mentions the "other" disciple. This implies that after Peter's visit, other disciples also went to the tomb.

Found it just as the women had said, but him they did not see. The fact of the empty tomb, prepared for by Luke 23:55, was important for Luke (cf. 24:3,

---

[16]Cf. Luke 7:29; 18:43; 19:48; 20:19; 21:38; 22:2; 23:5,27,35; Acts 2:47.

[17]Luke 9:22; 19:47; 20:1,19; 22:2,4,52,66; 23:4,10,13,35; Acts 3:17; 4:26; 13:27.

[18]In Acts 3:17; 13:27-29 both the rulers and residents of Jerusalem were blamed, and in Acts 2:23,36; 3:13-15; 4:10; 7:52; 10:39, it is the people of Israel who are blamed.

[19]See comments on 1:66-74; 2:25,30; cf. also 2:38; 23:51; Acts 28:20.

[20]Contra Marshall, *Luke*, 895.

24). He did not portray these and the other disciples as psychologically disposed to faith.

24:25   How foolish you are, and how slow of heart to believe all that the prophets have spoken! Compare 18:31. This verse is a thematic summary of 24:26-27 and leads to one of the main emphases of the chapter, as the parallels in 24:6-7 and 24:44-46 demonstrate. Jesus himself explained his passion and entrance into glory as the fulfillment of the OT prophecies. If the disciples believed the Scriptures (cf. 16:31; Acts 26:27), they would not have been sad (Luke 24:17) or confused (24:19-24). Jesus did not designate which prophets or where these prophets spoke of him. For Jesus and the Evangelists "all" the prophets "everywhere" spoke of him.

24:26   Did not the Christ have to suffer these things? Once again the "must" (*edei*) of divine necessity is emphasized. See Introduction 8 (1). This teaching is encountered again in 24:44-48 (cf. 1 Cor 15:3-5). Whether there existed in the Judaism of Jesus' day the concept of a "suffering Messiah/Christ" is greatly debated. For Luke and the early church, however, this was not an issue because for them God's Son, the Son of Man, the Christ, the Savior, the Servant of Isaiah 53, and the Prophet were one person, Jesus of Nazareth. Any allusion of suffering associated with any of these figures in the OT therefore referred to the suffering of Jesus Christ.

And then enter his glory? Luke referred earlier to Jesus' entering into his glory (Luke 9:26; 21:27), and the transfiguration provided a proleptic glimpse of this (9:32). The tense of the verb indicates that with the resurrection Jesus has now entered into his glory (cf. 22:69; Acts 2:33; 7:55; 22:11). The question of why the Christ had to suffer is answered by, Because the Scriptures said this. The next question, Why did the Scriptures say this? is not asked in Luke-Acts. Elsewhere in the NT, however, this is explained (cf. Mark 10:45; Rom 3:25-26; 2 Cor 5:21; Gal 3:10-14; etc.).

24:27   What was said in all the Scriptures. "In all the Scriptures" can be interpreted in two ways: *the third section of the OT called the Writings* (cf. Luke 24:44) or *the Law and the Prophets*, i.e., *the whole of Scripture* (cf. 16:16). The second interpretation, which understands the word "Scriptures" as a synonym for "Moses and all the Prophets," is to be preferred. The term "all" is another example of Luke's fondness for exaggeration, for time would not have permitted Jesus to refer to "all" the Scriptures that referred to him. See comments on 21:17.

24:28   As they approached the village . . . Jesus acted as if he were going farther. Jesus gave the two disciples the opportunity to practice hospitality to "a herald" of the gospel message. Luke may have intended for this to serve as a model of such hospitality.[21]

24:29   But they urged him strongly. The same verb is used in Acts 16:15.

Stay with us. This invitation to spend that night in their (or one of their) homes, which was seven miles from Jerusalem, implies that they were Judeans, not Galileans.

24:30   When he was at the table with them. A number of the resurrection appearances are associated with meals.[22]

---

[21]Cf. Luke 9:1-6,52; 10:1-12; Acts 16:15; cf. also 3 John 5-8; Heb 13:2.

[22]Luke 24:41-43; Acts 1:4; 10:41; John 21:9-15; cf. also the noncanonical Mark 16:14.

He took bread, gave thanks, broke it and began to give it to them. The
similarity between this and the Lord's Supper (22:19) is striking. There is also a
similarity with the account of the feeding of the five thousand (see comments on
9:16). Luke purposely portrayed this meal as a kind of Lord's Supper.[23]

24:31 Then their eyes were opened and they recognized him. In the fellowship of the Lord's Supper the two disciples recognized Jesus. The verb "were
opened" is a divine passive much like "were kept from recognizing him" in 24:16
(cf. 2 Kgs 6:17). Through the explanation Jesus gave in Luke 24:25-27 and in the
sharing of the sacred meal, the two disciples came with divine help to understand.
Attempts to explain this recognition as due to their identification of Jesus' voice,
his unique blessing, his special way of breaking bread, seeing the holes in his
hands, seeing a gesture of some sort peculiar to Jesus should be rejected. Luke
gave no hint of this. On the contrary he stated that Jesus was recognized in the
"breaking of bread" (24:35), which for Luke meant the breaking of bread in the
Lord's Supper.[24] Luke sought to convey to Theophilus and his readers that as certainty came to the disciples in the sharing of Scripture and the "breaking of bread,"
so too could they experience this certainty as they heard the Scriptures in the context of the church's breaking of bread (cf. Acts 2:42-47). The term "recognized
[*epegnōsan*]" is the same word Luke used in 1:4 with respect to "knowing [*epi-
gnōs*]" the certainty of the things they had been taught.

Disappeared from their sight. Compare John 20:19,26, where the body of
the risen Christ also appeared and disappeared miraculously (cf. also Luke 24:36).

**24:32 Were not our hearts burning within us while he . . . opened the
Scriptures to us?** The two disciples recalled that even before they recognized
Jesus his interpretations of the Scriptures (24:27) were already at work convincing
them of his resurrection. For "opening the Scriptures," cf. Acts 17:3, where the
word "explaining" translates the same Greek word. This word is also used in Luke
24:31, "eyes were opened." Luke's readers were to understand that through the
opening of the Scriptures, i.e., their correct interpretation (24:27), one comes to
know the certainty of the Gospel traditions (1:4). Compare the part the Scriptures
play in the early church confession found in 1 Cor 15:3-8.

24:33 They got up and returned at once to Jerusalem. The distance of
sixty *stadious* (Luke 24:13) makes more sense here than 160 *stadious*.

There they found the Eleven and those with them. Compare 24:9.

24:34 And saying. The Eleven and those with them shared the news.

It is true! The Lord has risen and has appeared to Simon. Since the departure of the two disciples from Jerusalem, the Eleven and the others had come to
believe. They now knew with certainty that the Lord had arisen because he had appeared to Simon. The reference to Jesus' appearance to Simon is firmly established in the early church confession found in 1 Cor 15:4, even though it is
nowhere described. This is not to be confused with John 21:15-23, which took
place later and in Galilee. Because of the reference to "Simon" rather than "Peter,"
this verse recalls Luke 22:32. This appearance together with his remorse in 22:61

---

[23] Probably the various references to the "breaking of bread" in Acts 2:42,46; 20:7,11;
27:35 are also to be understood in this manner.

[24] Cf. Luke 9:16; 22:19; 24:35; Acts 2:42,46; 20:7,11; 27:35.

results in the "turning back" of Simon so that from henceforth he was able to "strengthen" his Christian brothers (22:32).[25]

24:35 Then the two told what had happened on the way. The Emmaus disciples now recounted their experience of the risen Lord, which affirmed that "the Lord has risen" (23:34a).

How Jesus was recognized by them when he broke the bread. Once again Luke emphasized that Jesus was known in the breaking of bread, for he wanted his readers to experience this as they participated in the "breaking of bread." Marshall notes, "In the reading of Scripture and at the breaking of bread the risen Lord will continue to be present, though unseen."[26] Luke believed that the fellowship of faith with believers around the Lord's table builds faith.

The Lukan Message

This account provides an interpretative key for much of Luke's theology, for a number of important theological emphases appear. It is the most important passage in the Gospel for understanding how Luke interpreted Jesus' death. On the human level Jesus' death was caused by the Jewish leadership. Luke in fact went so far as to say the Jewish leadership crucified him (24:20; cf. Acts 5:30). Yet Jesus' death must be understood as ordained by God, for only through death could he enter his glory (Luke 24:26). Jesus' death was therefore not a tragic accident but a divine necessity taught in Scripture (24:26-27; see 24:1-12—"The Lukan Message"; Introduction 8 [1]). Jesus' death was not the end, for the tomb was empty (24:22-23). The angels had declared that he lives (24:23). Two disciples on the Emmaus road had seen him (24:31), and so had Simon (24:34). This emphasis will appear again in the next account (24:44-45).

Luke revealed how his readers could come to know the certainty of the things they had been taught (1:4). One way was by the reading of this Gospel. Having laid out before his readers his credentials (1:1-3), Luke anticipated that his record of the events surrounding the life and death of Jesus would support what his readers already had been taught and thus would confirm this earlier teaching. Luke did not expect this account to be treated with the historical skepticism of those who argue that everything in the Gospels is to be disbelieved unless it can be proven true. Luke expected that the "burden of proof" lies with those who would deny his Gospel.[27] Thus the very reading of his "orderly account" (1:3) should confirm what the readers had been taught.

---

[25] The attempt by F. W. Danker (*Jesus and the New Age* [Philadelphia: Fortress, 1988], 395) to interpret this verse as a question is unconvincing.

[26] Marshall, *Luke*, 900.

[27] For a discussion of the "burden of proof," see C. Blomberg, *The Historical Reliability of the Gospels* (Downers Grove: InterVarsity, 1987), 240-54.

A second aid to such certainty is the proof from prophecy. All that Jesus taught and did, all that he experienced, was prophesied beforehand. Thus the Scriptures witness to the truthfulness of what Luke's readers had been taught. This involves not only the facts about Jesus but also the interpretation of those facts.

A third support involves the various witnesses to the resurrection. These include an empty tomb, an angelic message, a resurrection appearance to the two disciples on the way to Emmaus, and an appearance to Peter. The doubt and unbelief of the disciples lends support to the overwhelming nature of these witnesses. Brown notes: "The slowness of the disciples to accept the corporeality of Jesus' resurrection [24:41], just as their refusal to accept the story of the empty tomb, guarantees the *asphaleia* [certainty] which is the author's purpose to establish." [28]

A fourth aid to faith for Luke's readers involves the reading of Scripture and breaking of bread within the community of faith. Through such participation they could come to assurance of the truth. They too could experience their hearts burning within them in the context of "devot[ing] themselves to the apostles' teaching and to the fellowship, to the breaking of bread and to prayer" (Acts 2:42). The applicability of the experience of the Emmaus disciples to the situation of his readers caused Luke to deal with it at great length. The lack of such applicability in the case of Peter's experience (24:34) may be why Luke dealt so briefly with it.

3. Jesus' Appearance to the Disciples in Jerusalem (24:36-43)

[36]While they were still talking about this, Jesus himself stood among them and said to them, "Peace be with you."

[37]They were startled and frightened, thinking they saw a ghost. [38]He said to them, "Why are you troubled, and why do doubts rise in your minds? [39]Look at my hands and my feet. It is I myself! Touch me and see; a ghost does not have flesh and bones, as you see I have."

[40]When he had said this, he showed them his hands and feet. [41]And while they still did not believe it because of joy and amazement, he asked them, "Do you have anything here to eat?" [42]They gave him a piece of broiled fish, [43]and he took it and ate it in their presence.

Context

Although the next three accounts (24:36-43,44-49,50-53) will be treated separately, they are all part of the final scene in the Gospel. There is no clear literary break between them. They are all part of the last resurrection appearance in Luke and build up to the conclusion in 24:50-53. They are

---

[28] S. Brown, *Apostasy and Perseverance in the Theology of Luke*, AnBib (Rome: Pontifical Biblical Institute, 1969), 79.

treated separately, however, in order to focus individually on each of the three acts that make up this last scene of the Gospel. A parallel exists between this scene and the preceding one that should be noted. Both involve a resurrection appearance of Jesus in which he is not recognized (cf. 24:16,37), a scriptural explanation of the necessity of Jesus' death and resurrection (24:25-27,32,44-47), a meal or the eating of food (24:30-35,42-43), and a supernatural disappearance of Jesus from the scene (24:31,51).

There is also a close parallel between this account and John 20:19-23 (cf. in addition 1 Cor 15:5 and the longer ending of Mark 16:14-16). Some of the parallels between these two accounts and other resurrection accounts in John are: "stood among them" (Luke 24:36; John 20:19); "and he said to them, 'Peace be with you'" (Luke 24:36; John 20:19); Jesus' showing the disciples his "hands and feet/side" (Luke 24:40; John 20:20); a reference to "joy" (Luke 24:44; John 20:20); the invitation to touch him (Luke 24:39; John 20:27); and Jesus' eating a piece of fish (Luke 24:42; John 21:13). Attempts to explain this as due to the use of one Gospel by the other are less convincing than to understand them as having used similar traditions.[29]

Immediately following the report of the Emmaus disciples, Jesus appears in the midst of the believing community. (Note how in Matt 28:9-10,16-20; John 20:11-18,19-23 a resurrection appearance to individuals is followed by an appearance to a larger group.) Startled, they think they are seeing a ghost. Jesus, however, assuages their doubts and fears by providing two proofs. The first is by demonstrating his physical nature. He has real hands and feet, whereas ghosts do not have flesh and bones. Second, he shows that his resurrection body is not simply an apparition by eating a piece of fish in their presence.

Comments

24:36 While they were still talking about this. That is, recalling their experience with the risen Christ. This indicates that this appearance took place on the same day as the other two, the first day of the week (24:1).

Jesus himself stood among them. "Jesus" is literally "he." For Jesus' ability to appear and disappear supernaturally, cf. John 20:19,26.

And said to them, "Peace be with you." In a number of places in Luke 24 Codex Beza (D) and the old Latin manuscripts (it) omit passages found in the vast majority of manuscripts, such as 24:6a,12,36b,c,40,51b,52a. Although several of these "Western Noninterpolations" have parallels in John, the manuscript evidence in favor of including them is so great that they must be accepted as part of the text. Rather than being understood as later scribal additions from the Gospel of John, the Luke-John parallels are best understood as common elements in related traditions of Jesus' resurrection appearances.

---

[29] See R. H. Stein, "The Matthew-Luke Agreements Against Mark," *CBQ* 54 (1992): 486-88.

For "peace," compare John 20:19. See comments on 2:14. Compare also Luke 7:50; 8:48; 10:5; 19:38; Acts 10:36.

24:37 They were startled and frightened. Compare Luke 24:5, where the women were also "frightened" and the same word is used (cf. also Acts 10:4; 24:25). **Thinking they saw a ghost.** That is, a bodiless Jesus (cf. Luke 24:39; cf. also Acts 23:9).

24:38 Why are you troubled? For a similar "troubling" of devout people in the presence of the supernatural, see comments on 1:12.

Why do doubts rise in your minds? These "doubts" have been understood as (1) the fact of the resurrection, i.e., whether Jesus had actually risen from the dead; (2) the identity of the "ghost," i.e., whether the person they were encountering was actually Jesus; and (3) the corporeal nature of Jesus, i.e., whether the Jesus they were encountering was a ghost or possessed a real body. It is even possible that all these are involved, but foremost in Luke's mind was (3) as the following verses make clear. Jesus again knew the thoughts of the disciples.

24:39 Look at my hands and my feet. If Luke assumed his readers would interpret these words in light of John 20:25,27—i.e., that Jesus' hands and feet were nailed to the cross—then Luke, like John, sought to answer (2) above—i.e., the identity of the person they encountered. However, if we should not assume this—and this seems best because Luke made no reference to the nail marks—then the answer involves (3) above, i.e., the corporeal nature of the risen Jesus.

It is I myself! The risen Christ is the same person as Jesus of Nazareth.

Touch me and see. This confirms that the basic point of Luke was the physical reality of the risen Jesus (cf. Acts 2:31). For a similar concern in Luke-Acts with regard to the resurrection, cf. Acts 17:18,31-32; 23:6-10; 24:15,21; cf. also Matt 28:9.

A ghost does not have flesh and bones, as you see I have. The NIV omits the introductory "for" (cf. RSV). This causal clause explains why the disciples should have touched Jesus, i.e., because in so doing they would have known that Jesus was not a ghost. Thus any misconception that the preceding appearances involved only a "spiritual presence" of Jesus is resolved.

24:40 He showed them his hands and feet. For the textual problem associated with this verse, see comments on 24:36.

24:41 And while they still did not believe it because of joy and amazement. The disciples were hesitant to believe, to accept what they now knew was true, for it was too good to be true. From a psychological perspective such a hesitancy is thoroughly credible (see comments on 24:11). Compare Acts 12:14. For a similar explanation cf. Luke 22:45. Benoit observes, "This psychological note is very characteristic of Luke."[30] For "joy" cf. 24:52. The "it" which they disbelieved involves the corporeal nature of Jesus.[31]

Do you have anything here to eat? Jesus planned to give additional evidence of his resurrection; for ghosts, spirits, and disembodied souls do not eat.

---

[30] P. Benoit, *The Passion and Resurrection of Jesus Christ* (New York: Herder, 1969), 283.

[31] See Plevnik, "Eyewitnesses of the Risen Jesus," 99, and Brown, *Apostasy and Perseverance*, 79, who states: "It must be evident that the object of *apistountōn* ["disbelieved"] in v. 41 is not the resurrection itself but the *corporeal nature* of the resurrection."

24:42   They gave him a piece of broiled fish.   Some have argued that this story must have originally been located in Galilee because of the reference to fish. One of the gates into Jerusalem, however, was called the Fish Gate (Neh 3:3; 12:39), and fish were certainly sold and eaten in Jerusalem (Neh 13:16).

24:43   And he took it and ate it in their presence.   Compare John 21:13-15; Acts 10:41. This shows again that the risen Jesus was not a disembodied spirit or angel, for they do not eat (cf. Tob 12:19; Josephus, *Antiquities* 1.11.2 [1.197], Philo, *On Abraham* 118). This was not the eating Jesus referred to in Luke 22:16 (see comments on 22:16).

The Lukan Message

Luke's purpose in this account was twofold. One point Luke wanted to make was that Jesus had indeed risen from the dead. The present account is further proof of Jesus' resurrection. Jesus appeared not only to Peter and the two Emmaus disciples. He also appeared to all the disciples at once. (Compare 1 Cor 15:5 and note the same order: "he appeared to Peter, and then to the Twelve.") As Jesus' witnesses they had to verify for themselves the reality of the resurrection. Thus what was delivered to Luke and what he subsequently passed on to his readers in this "orderly account" (Luke 1:3) came ultimately from the eyewitnesses (1:2) who had personally witnessed the risen Christ (cf. also Acts 1:21-22). Their experience was of such a nature that it could not be doubted but led to certainty (cf. Luke 1:4).

Another purpose was to demonstrate the physical reality of the risen Christ. What the disciples experienced was not the immortal soul of Jesus or some ghostlike apparition from the nether world. Rather they experienced the resurrected Christ, and this involved the resurrection of the *body*. True, Jesus' body was in a sense different. He could disappear and appear at will, but he did possess flesh and bones. For Luke the resurrection was furthermore not simply a resuscitation of a corpse but the transformation of Jesus into his eternal state, and this transformed state involved a real body.[32] Whereas Paul in 1 Cor 15:35-50 sought to emphasize the difference between Jesus of Nazareth before the resurrection and the Lord Jesus after the resurrection, Luke sought here to emphasize the similarity. The difference between 1 Cor 15:50 and Luke 24:39 may be more apparent than real. The risen Lord of Luke's Gospel was, like the risen Christ of 1 Cor 15, different from the Jesus of history and did not possess the flesh and blood of which Paul spoke (1 Cor 15:50). Yet Paul's risen Lord was, like the risen Lord of Luke 24, also corporeal, for a Pharisee would have regarded a spiritual resurrection of Jesus' "soul" as a

---

[32] Although Ignatius (*Smyrneans* 2-3) used this passage to refute the docetism of certain Gnostics, it is uncertain "why" Luke emphasized the corporeal nature of the risen Christ.

contradiction of terms. The resurrection involved the transformation of the body to its final, eternal state. For both Luke and Paul the resurrection of Jesus was truly a resurrection of the "body."

4. Jesus' Commission to the Disciples (24:44-49)

[44]He said to them, "This is what I told you while I was still with you: Everything must be fulfilled that is written about me in the Law of Moses, the Prophets and the Psalms."
[45]Then he opened their minds so they could understand the Scriptures. [46]He told them, "This is what is written: The Christ will suffer and rise from the dead on the third day, [47]and repentance and forgiveness of sins will be preached in his name to all nations, beginning at Jerusalem. [48]You are witnesses of these things. [49]I am going to send you what my Father has promised; but stay in the city until you have been clothed with power from on high."

Context

Having assured the disciples of his physical resurrection (24:36-43), Jesus now gives them his final instructions. As with the two disciples on the road to Emmaus, he explains to them that what is written in the three sections that make up the Scriptures (the Law, the Prophets, and the Psalms, i.e., the Writings) had to be fulfilled. Thus the Christ had to die and rise from the dead. To fulfill the Scriptures something else must also be accomplished, however, and this will be the theme of the second part of Luke's work, i.e., the Book of Acts. This involves the preaching in Jesus' name of repentance for the forgiveness of sins to all the world, beginning in Jerusalem. The disciples are Jesus' witnesses, and they are to proclaim what they themselves have seen and heard. First, however, they are to wait in Jerusalem until Jesus sends the promise of his Father (the promise of Joel 2:28-32) so they will be divinely empowered to fulfill this mission. In two other Gospels, as well as in the longer ending of Mark, there exists some form of a final commissioning scene (cf. Matt 28:19-20; John 20:21-23; Mark 16:15-16).

Comments

24:44   This is what I told you. What is referred to here is not so much Jesus' general teachings but his teachings concerning his death and resurrection (cf. Luke 9:22,44; 17:25; 18:31-33; 22:37).

While I was still with you. This indicates that the risen Christ is the same person as the "historical Jesus" (cf. 24:39). It also reveals that a new period had been inaugurated in which Jesus would no longer be "with them."

Everything must be fulfilled that is written about me. The content of "what" (24:44) Jesus had told the disciples is introduced. As in 24:25 the central message of the OT is seen as focusing on Jesus (cf. John 5:39; 20:9). For Luke the OT was a Christian book from beginning to end. This was not grasped by the disciples during

Jesus' ministry. Now, however, due to Jesus' interpreting of the Scriptures, they saw this clearly (cf. Luke 24:27,45; Acts 17:3; cf. also John 12:16).

In the Law of Moses. That is, the first major section of the OT, consisting of the first five books.[33]

The Prophets. That is, the second major section of the OT consisting of the "former prophets" (Joshua through 2 Kings) and the "latter prophets" (the major prophets: Isaiah, Jeremiah, Ezekiel; and the minor prophets: Hosea through Malachi).[34] In Acts 13:15; 24:14; 28:23 the Law and the Prophets appear together and refer to the entire OT.

And the Psalms. This probably refers to the third major section of the OT called the "Writings," which contains the rest of the books in the OT. The first (in the Hebrew arrangement) and largest book in this section is the Psalms. We find the same threefold division of the OT in the prologue of Sirach, where we read twice of the law, the prophets, and the other books (the writings).

24:45 Then he opened their minds so they could understand the Scriptures. Through Jesus' interpretation of the Scriptures (Luke 24:27), the disciples came to understand its teaching concerning his death and resurrection. This new understanding contrasts with their earlier lack of understanding (9:45; 18:34). The disciples' new understanding of the necessity of Jesus' death and resurrection was not achieved through their own study of the Scriptures. What was involved was not a new hermeneutic or method of interpretation. Rather this understanding was given them by Jesus. Paul was later commissioned to open people's eyes (Acts 26:17-18) through preaching and interpreting the Scriptures (17:2-3). Benoit notes: "The missionary's two instruments are witness and Scripture."[35]

24:46 This is what is written. "This" refers to the content that follows.

The Christ will suffer. See comments on 24:26, where this refers not so much to specific OT passages, which teach that the "Christ" would suffer, but to the entire OT teaching on this. (The early church frequently referred to Ps 22 and Isa 53 [cf. Acts 8:26-40] as proof that the Christ must suffer.) The "Christ" is, as the reader of the Gospel knows, Jesus of Nazareth. Compare the earlier passages in Luke that speak of the Son of Man suffering: 9:22,44; 17:25; 18:32.

And rise from the dead on the third day. Compare 9:22; 18:33; 24:7,21; Acts 10:40; cf. also 1 Cor 15:3-4. The Lukan Jesus did not specify where these references are to be found. (Cf., however, Ps 16:10; Acts 2:3; 13:35.) Since the prophecies concerning the Messiah were fulfilled in Jesus' passion and resurrection, this serves as a proof for Luke that Jesus is the Messiah. See Introduction 7 (1).

24:47 And repentance and forgiveness of sins will be preached. The commission found in this and the next two verses is also seen as having taken place to fulfill "what is written" (Luke 24:46). For the association of repentance and forgiveness, see comments on 3:3.

In his name. While in Luke there is one other reference to preaching and ministering in Jesus' name (9:48), in Acts this expression is found frequently.[36]

---

[33]Cf. Luke 2:22-24,39; 5:14; 10:26; 16:16,29; 20:28,37; 24:27; Acts 3:22; 6:11-14; 13:15; 24:14.

[34]Cf. Luke 1:70; 16:16,29; 18:31; 24:25,27; Acts 3:18,21,24; 10:43; 13:15; 24:14.

[35]Benoit, *Passion and Resurrection*, 327.

[36]E.g., Acts 2:38; 3:6,16; 4:10,12,17-18,30; 5:28,40; 8:12,16; 9:27-28; 10:43,48; 16:18; 19:5.

To all nations. Compare Acts 1:8; 15:17; 26:23 (cf. Matt 28:19). In Acts 15:14-18 the entrance of the Gentiles into God's people is seen as the fulfillment of Scripture. Whereas Peter introduced this mission by the conversion of Cornelius (10:43-48; 11:15-18), it was Paul above all whom God used to bring this about (9:15; 22:21; 26:16-18).

Beginning at Jerusalem. Compare Acts 1:8; 2:1f.

24:48 You are witnesses. Luke saw the role of the disciples as witnesses as assuring the veracity of the message.[37] The disciples were not just proclaimers of Jesus' message but eyewitnesses who were to share their personal experience of the risen Christ. The earlier mission of the Twelve (Luke 9:1-6) and the seventy (10:1-12) were a proleptic foretaste of the future mission of Jesus' witnesses after the resurrection.

Of these things. That is, the message of 24:46-47.

24:49 I am going to send you what my Father has promised. The verb is a futuristic present (literally "I am sending") that emphasizes the certainty of what God was about to do. This promise was the coming of the Spirit (Acts 1:4-5; cf. also 2:33; Gal 3:14; Eph 1:13) and refers to the OT promise of the Spirit's coming (cf. also Luke 3:16). Luke thought above all of Joel 2:28-32 (Acts 2:16-21). As in John 16:7, Jesus himself sends the Spirit. In John 14:16,26 the Father sends the Spirit.

But stay in the city. This command is repeated in Acts 1:4. The city is, of course, Jerusalem.

Until you have been clothed with power from on high. The tie between power for God's ministry and the gift of the Spirit has been alluded to already in 1:17,35; 4:14; 5:17 (cf. also 6:19) and will be even clearer in Acts 1:8; 10:38 (cf. also 4:31). See comments on 1:17.

The Lukan Message

Even as the commissioning scenes in Matt 28:19-20 and John 20:21-23 contain important theological emphases found in those Gospels (teaching and making disciples in Matthew and the sending of the Spirit in John), so the commissioning scene in Luke is replete with Lukan emphases. One such emphasis involves the fulfillment of Scripture, and, associated with this, the necessity of Jesus' death. Jesus' ministry, death, and resurrection are all the fulfillment of Scripture (Luke 24:47). The church's worldwide mission and the Spirit's coming to empower them for that ministry is also the fulfillment of Scripture. This theme's importance for Luke is evident in that this theme has already been stated earlier in this chapter (24:25-27). See Introduction 7 (1).

Another Lukan emphasis found in this passage involves the Spirit's coming. Even as the Spirit was present in Jesus' conception (1:35,41), earliest years (2:25-38), baptism (3:21-22), and ministry (4:1,14,18; 5:17), so the Spirit would come upon the disciples. Shortly the "baptism of the Spirit" promised by John the Baptist (3:16; Acts 1:5) would take

---

[37]Cf. Luke 1:2; Acts 1:8,21-22; 2:32; 3:15; 4:33; 5:32; 10:39-41; 13:31; 22:15; 26:16,22.

---

place as they became "filled with the Holy Spirit" (2:4). In the second part of his work Luke would begin with a twofold affirmation of this promise (1:4,8) and describe its fulfillment with respect to the disciples at Pentecost (2:2-4,16-21) and subsequently to all who follow Jesus (2:38-39). The Spirit's coming was so central to Luke's theology that in Acts the possession of the Spirit is "the" decisive mark of being a Christian (cf. Acts 10:44-48; 11:15-18; 15:8; 19:2-7).

Because of the numerous other Lukan emphases found in this passage, we simply list them:

1. The message of repentance associated with John the Baptist (Luke 3:3,8; Acts 13:24; 19:4) and Jesus[38] was continued by the early church.[39] The gospel message of Luke-Acts can be summarized just as easily by the command to repent as by the command to believe (16:31). Note how Paul's ministry is summarized in 20:21 as proclaiming "repentance to God and . . . faith in our Lord Jesus Christ" (RSV). See Introduction 8 (6).
2. Salvation can be equated with the forgiveness of sins.[40] See comments on 1:77.
3. Jerusalem's centrality in the redemptive plan of God is once again emphasized.[41] See Introduction 7 (2).
4. The worldwide and universal nature of the gospel message is emphasized.[42]
5. Salvation comes only in the name of Jesus.[43]
6. The disciples' role as eyewitnesses of the gospel message assures its truthfulness.[44] The entire chapter has focused on their role as eyewitnesses of Jesus' ministry, death, and resurrection. See Introduction 7 (1).

5. The Ascension (24:50-53)

[50]When he had led them out to the vicinity of Bethany, he lifted up his hands and blessed them. [51]While he was blessing them, he left them and was taken up into heaven. [52]Then they worshiped him and returned to Jerusalem with great joy. [53]And they stayed continually at the temple, praising God.

Context

The resurrection appearance that began in Luke 24:36 continues but with a change in scene. Leaving Jerusalem, Jesus leads the disciples to

---

[38]Luke 5:32; 10:13; 11:32; 13:3,5; 15:7,10; 16:30.

[39]Luke 24:47; Acts 2:38; 3:19; 5:31; 11:18; 17:30; 20:21; 26:20.

[40]Luke 1:77; 3:3; 24:47; Acts 2:38; 5:31; 10:43; 13:38; 26:18.

[41]Luke 24:47; Acts 1:4,8; 2:5-6; 3:1-2; 8:1,14-17; 9:26; 11:2-18; 15:1-29; 18:22; 21:15-16.

[42]Luke 24:47; 2:31-32; Acts 1:8; 2:5; 8:1,5-8,14-17,26-40; 9:15,31; 10:1–11:24; 13:1-2,44-50; 15:1-29; 18:6; 22:13-15; 26:16-18, 23; 27:24; 28:28.

[43]Luke 24:47; Acts 2:38; 3:6,16; 4:10,12,30; 8:12,16; 10:48; 16:18; 19:5.

[44]Luke 1:2; 24:48; Acts 1:8,21-22; 2:32; 3:15; 4:33; 5:32; 10:39-41; 13:31; 22:15; 26:16,22.

Bethany on the Mount of Olives. After bestowing upon them his parting
blessing, he is taken up into heaven. Having worshiped Jesus, the disciples return with great joy to Jerusalem. There, while waiting for the promised Spirit, they are continually in the temple blessing God. Thus the
Gospel ends as it has begun with God's people praising and blessing him
in the temple (cf. 1:5-23). Luke has carefully prepared his readers for
Jesus' ascension. At the transfiguration Moses and Elijah spoke of Jesus'
future "departure/exodus" (9:31). Jesus' trip to Jerusalem had as its goal
his being "taken up" (9:51). At his trial Jesus refers to his being seated
soon at God's right hand (22:69), and his death is seen as necessary for
his entering into his glory (24:26). With Jesus' ascension, Luke concludes
his Gospel, and at this place he will begin his second work.

The care with which Luke tied together Acts and his Gospel should be
noted. Yet in Luke the ascension and all the Easter appearances take place
on Sunday, whereas in Acts the ascension takes place forty days after the
resurrection (Acts 1:3). It is quite unlikely that Luke was unaware of this
difference. Rather it is more probable that Luke intended for his readers
to understand this chapter as telescoping the events of the forty days without temporal distinction, whereas Acts seeks not to correct the previous
account but to indicate the temporal dimension of these events. This
would then be another example of how the Evangelist facilitated his purpose by presenting his readers with an "orderly account" (Luke 1:3) of the
things accomplished among them. Two other examples of this can be seen
in Acts. Whereas in the first two accounts of Paul's conversion the commission to be a witness is delivered to Paul via Ananias (Acts 9:15-19;
22:12-16), in the third account the conversion experience is telescoped
and Ananias's role is omitted, as is Paul's blindness and recovering of
sight (26:9-18). A second example of this can be found in the conversion
of Cornelius. In the first account Peter speaks to Cornelius and while still
speaking (note the *eti* with a present participle) the Spirit comes (10:44).
In the second account the Spirit comes as Peter began to speak (11:15).
See comments on 1:4.

The story of the ascension is recorded only by Luke. However, he
recorded it twice, as the conclusion of his first work and as the beginning
of his second (Acts 1:6-11). References to the ascension, however, are
found elsewhere in the biblical tradition. The clearest NT reference outside of Luke-Acts is found in John 20:17 ("I am not yet ascended . . . I
ascend," KJV) from which the term "ascension" comes. Another reference
is found in the longer ending of Mark (cf. Mark 16:19).[45]

---

[45] Other allusions may be Acts 2:33; 1 Tim 3:16; Eph 4:8-10; 1 Pet 3:22; Heb 4:14; 6:19-20; 9:24.

Comments

24:50 When he had led them out to the vicinity of Bethany. Acts 1:12 states that the ascension took place on the Mount of Olives. Bethany is on the Mount of Olives (see comments on 19:29).

He lifted up his hands. Compare Lev 9:22; cf. also Sir 50:20-21; 1 Tim 2:8.

And blessed them. Compare Luke 1:28,42; 2:34; 6:28; 13:35; 19:38; Acts 3:25,26 for people's being blessed and 9:16; 24:30 for things being blessed. Before departing Jesus pronounced a final blessing upon his followers. Compare Gen 27:27; 49:28; 2 Enoch 56:1; 57:2; 64:4.

24:51 While he was blessing them. This indicates that the blessing of Luke 24:50 lasted for a period of time.

He left them. For the departing of supernatural visitors, cf. 1:38; 2:15; 9:33; Acts 10:7; 12:10; cf. also Gen 17:22; 35:13; Judg 6:21; 13:20.

And was taken up into heaven. This should be retained in the text. See comments on 24:36. Compare Acts 1:9,11,22, where the same verb is used. John 20:17 speaks of Jesus' "ascending."[46] This marks the end of the resurrection appearances and of Jesus' physical presence with his disciples.

24:52 Then they worshiped him. Compare Matt 28:17. This should be retained in the text. See comments on 24:36. In light of Luke 4:7-8 the disciples' worship of Jesus demonstrates that Luke's Christology is a high one indeed. Compare 5:20-26; 7:47-50.

To Jerusalem. Thus Luke returned his readers to where his orderly account began (1:5-6).

With great joy. Compare 2:10. All doubt, questions, and fear have been removed (24:11,19-25,37-38,41), and the result is great joy.

24:53 And they stayed continually at the temple. Luke returned his readers to where the Gospel began (1:8-9). That the early church continued worshiping in the temple after Easter is evident from Acts.[47]

Praising God. See comments on 1:64; 5:25-26.

The Lukan Message

In the concluding account of the Gospel, Luke emphasized the duty of believers to live for the praise of God. The Gospel began with the devout of Israel praying and worshiping in the temple (1:9-10), and the praise of God is at the center of the birth accounts.[48] It is found throughout the Gospel (see comments on 1:64; 5:25-26) and is perhaps best illustrated in the account of the healing of the ten lepers, where only one fulfilled what was most important and returned to praise God (17:15-18). Luke could think of no better way to end his Gospel, and he expected his readers, knowing the certainty of the things they had been taught, to join in blessing God.

---

[46]There are similar ascensions found in Gen 5:24; Sir 44:16; 48:9; 2 Kgs 2:11; 1 Macc 2:58; 2 Esdr 14:9; *As. Mos.* 10:12.

[47]Acts 2:46; 3:1; 5:42; 21:23-36; 22:17; 24:11-12,18; 26:21.

[48]Luke 1:46-55,64,68-79; 2:13-14,20,28.

A second emphasis is Christological. He who was heralded before his birth as Son of God and Christ (1:32-33)—who referred to himself as the Son of Man, is called "Lord," Son of God, prophet, and king[49]—has finished his earthly ministry and entered his glory. He now sits at God's right hand (22:69; Acts 7:55-56). What the disciples believed and confessed in faith, that Jesus was "Lord," is now a reality. Jesus ascended to his rightful place at God's right hand. When he returns, it will be as Lord, King, and Judge over creation. The days of his humiliation have ceased. His physical presence with his church has come to an end. The period of salvation history inaugurated in Christ's coming has now entered a new stage. The exalted Christ will send ("has sent" for Luke's readers) his Spirit upon his church. In this sense it was better for his disciples to have him depart, for now he could send the promise of the Father upon them (cf. John 17:7). Thus, although Jesus had physically departed from his disciples, he would be present with them through his Spirit and in the breaking of bread (Luke 24:35). God's kingdom, which was manifested in Jesus' ministry, would come in a new way as his disciples experienced the baptism of the Spirit and tasted the firstfruits of God's kingdom (cf. 2 Cor 1:22; Eph 1:13). The worship of Jesus in Luke 24:52 brings the Christology of the Gospel to its culmination. "Who is this Jesus?" is now fully answered. Plevnik notes: "In the temptation accounts, Luke 4:8, Jesus answers Satan's request for worship by quoting Deut 6:13: 'You shall worship the Lord your God, and him only shall you serve.' We find a confirmation of this in Acts 10:25-26. Accordingly, worship is not to be given to Satan or to any man, but only to God. The disciples' worshiping Jesus is thus their acknowledgment of his divinity."[50]

---

[49] For the significance of these titles, see comments on 5:24; 6:46; 7:13; 1:35; 7:16; and 23:1-5—"The Lukan Message."

[50] Plevnik, "Eyewitnesses of the Risen Jesus," 102.

Selected Subject Index[1]

Angel of the Lord/Angels   69–70, 74–75,
    84–86, 108, 110–11, 113, 148, 160,
    277, 348, 416, 502, 604–7, 609
Anxiety   353–56
Ascension   622–25
Atonement   54–57
Audience of Luke   26–27
Authorship   19–24
Baptism   132–35, 137, 139–45, 149, 160,
    183, 364–65, 379, 398, 454, 488
Beatitudes   200–203, 206, 209, 225
Betrayal   545–47, 560–62
Birth of Jesus   69–70, 81, 84, 85, 102–10
Birth of John the Baptist   73–81, 96–103
Blasphemy   177
Christian life   51–54
Christological titles/Christology   23–24,
    38, 46, 48–49, 67, 79, 83, 85–87, 90,
    95, 99, 108, 111, 115, 124, 137, 143,
    162, 165–66, 171, 178–80, 187–89,
    203, 215–16, 221–23, 225–26, 238–
    39, 252, 256, 259, 264, 277, 280–81,
    283, 287, 289–90, 294, 313, 348, 359,
    365–66, 372, 377, 381, 399, 409, 434,
    437, 439, 446, 448, 463–65, 470, 481,
    486, 489, 429, 494, 504–7, 522, 523–
    25, 546–47, 551, 554, 565, 567, 570–
    72, 574–76, 588–90, 607, 625
Date of Luke   24–26
Death of Christ   276, 278, 291–92, 382–
    83, 385, 476, 489, 558, 573, 581–98,
    609, 611, 614, 620, 623
Devil/Demons   144–49, 164, 240–41,
    246, 252, 254–59, 267, 272, 288–90,
    293, 309–11, 329–33, 336, 374, 377,
    544, 549, 552, 559, 562, 625
Disciples/Discipleship   191–96, 200, 206,
    213, 216, 225, 245, 265–68, 275–81,
    286, 291–92, 298, 300–307, 311–14,
    320, 345, 349, 354, 380, 395–98, 412,
    421, 428–31, 438, 444, 453, 455, 461,
    472, 478, 510, 515–19, 537, 559, 563–
    65, 589, 613–18, 625
Eschatology   23, 42–43, 131, 137, 162,
    184, 198, 280, 283, 358–63, 366, 368,
    392–93, 414, 417, 424–26, 437–39,
    442, 444, 446, 456, 460, 469, 492,
    511–14, 519–36, 554, 595, 597
Faith, Forgiveness/Repentance   99, 101,
    103, 128, 130, 132, 138, 170, 174–83,
    202, 210–12, 217, 233–36, 238, 240,
    250, 326, 348, 368–71, 379, 387, 391,
    398, 404, 408, 410, 417, 420, 429–31,
    434–35, 447, 452, 467, 469, 589, 592–
    94, 619–20, 622
Genealogy   139–43
Healings   152, 161–67, 172, 175, 179,
    196, 224, 240, 272, 288–89, 386–87,
    462–65
Humility   389–91, 452, 454, 507
Hymns   70, 88–95, 540
Hypocrisy   345–46
Infancy Narratives   69–124
Joy   51, 75, 90, 186, 309, 311, 375, 400,
    404, 408, 435, 480, 617
Judging, Judgment   94, 132, 134, 210–12,
    214–16, 279, 281, 335–37, 359, 366,
    371, 378–79, 382, 384–85, 389, 390,
    414, 416, 440–44, 485–86, 492–94,
    495, 521, 524–25, 550, 586–87, 593
Justification   23, 281, 409, 447–51
Kingdom of God   46–47, 78, 102, 145,
    160, 162, 165, 178, 184, 199–201,
    205, 216, 221, 223, 230, 233, 240,
    242, 245, 249, 272, 275, 280, 300,
    306, 308, 313, 325, 330–31, 353–56,

[1]Indexes were prepared by Lanese Dockery.

365, 368, 375–81, 385, 392, 394–95, 409, 418–19, 435–42, 444, 453, 456, 458, 460, 465, 472–74, 496, 499, 509, 514, 527–28, 541–42, 547–50, 554, 594, 599, 601
Kingship   84, 200, 397, 472–73, 475
Law/teachers of the law   23, 115, 119–20, 175, 180, 184, 189–90, 209, 316, 320, 338–44, 387, 390, 392, 408, 410–11, 417, 435, 449, 481, 503, 507–8, 570, 578
Lord's Supper   273, 292, 379, 537–44, 609, 614
Marriage   82, 418–20, 500, 502
Miracles   77, 161–68, 175, 179, 221, 223, 252, 261, 271–74, 277, 335–37, 374
Natural theology   23
New Covenant   187
Parable   185, 212, 232, 239–52, 314, 327–29, 350–52, 358–60, 376–78, 388, 392–94, 398, 400–414, 421–26, 443–51, 454–59, 470–75, 489–95
Passover   121, 536–40
Persecution   205, 207
Pneumatology   47–48, 79, 89, 95, 98, 115, 134, 140, 145–46, 156, 160, 180, 196, 280, 328, 348–49, 364, 505, 621–22, 625
Prayer   74–75, 173, 184, 192, 194, 284, 322–29, 448–50, 530, 552–53, 557–60, 565, 624
Priests   73, 77, 117, 127, 173, 433, 485, 489, 494, 560, 564, 575, 594, 611
Prologue   62–68
Promises   74, 78, 95, 160, 186, 525
Prophet/Prophecy   38–39, 41, 64, 70, 78, 98, 100, 110, 117–18, 128, 130, 137, 155–57, 160, 223–24, 230, 236, 270–

71, 287, 292, 342, 383, 461–62, 484, 523, 525, 553–55, 563, 567, 570, 576–77, 591, 605, 607, 612, 615, 620–21
Purification   113–14
Purpose of Luke   35–45
Resurrection   184, 249, 279, 292, 304, 335–37, 382–83, 385, 390, 422, 476, 480, 499–503, 518–19, 592–93, 602–15
Salvation   50–51, 79, 99–100, 103, 116, 119, 129, 137, 160, 171, 178, 319, 351, 380, 382, 394, 396, 408, 409, 435, 458–59, 466, 469, 601, 622
Shepherds   108, 110–12
Sin/sinners   116, 119, 137, 171, 174–82, 234, 236–37, 290, 326, 328, 409, 432, 450
Sources of Luke   28–30
Sovereignty   45–46, 107, 115, 432, 563, 576
Stewardship   415–21, 423–27, 457, 470, 474, 498, 508–10
Synagogue   154–59, 219, 261, 341, 349, 373
Synoptic Problem   28–29
Teaching/Preaching   152, 154–59, 163, 167, 177, 183, 197–216, 240, 250, 267, 269, 272, 292, 371, 373, 376, 378, 381, 387–89, 487, 496, 512, 532, 538
Temple   73, 117–24, 483, 485, 510–12, 531–32, 595, 624
Temptations   144–49, 447, 557–59, 562
Tradition   21, 62, 67, 205
Transfiguration   281–87, 292, 623
Trial of Jesus   567–80
Wine   76, 186

Person Index

Allen, L. C. 478
Allison, D. C., Jr. 595
Archelaus 473
Archer, G. L. 463
Augustine 318
Augustus (Gaius Octavius) 105

Badia, L. F. 129
Bailey, J. A. 167, 406
Barr, J. 312
Barrett, C. K. 22, 203
Bauckham, R. J. 44
Behm, J. 284
Benoit, P. 570, 576, 601, 617, 620
Billerbeck, P. 147, 222
Blass, F. 293
Blinzler, J. 569
Blomberg, C. L. 79, 119, 136, 422, 471, 491, 614
Bock, D. L. 39
Bode, E. L. 604
Boslooper, T. D. 81
Bovon, F. 35
Brandon, S. G. F. 496
Brooks, J. A. 189
Brown, R. E. 70, 81, 89, 96, 113, 120, 123, 141, 167, 422
Brown, S. 148, 247, 518, 615, 617
Bultmann, R. 175, 303

Cadbury, H. J. 20, 62
Calvin, John 543
Carlston, C. E. 493, 528
Carson, D. A. 585
Carter, W. 103
Catchpole, D. R. 568, 569, 571
Cerokee, C. P. 177

Chance, J. B. 521, 523, 550
Childs, B. S. 39
Cicero 588
Clement of Alexandria 21
Conzelmann, H. 42, 43, 71, 99, 102, 125, 148, 362, 418, 433, 563
Cullmann, O. 496, 558
Culpepper, R. A. 57
Cyrus 105

Danker, F. W. 614
Daube, D. 202
Davies, W. D. 203
Debrunner, A. 293
Derrett, J. D. M. 393, 566
Dillon, R. J. 63
Dioscorides 20
Dodd, C. H. 166, 483

Edwards, R. A. 335
Ellis, E. E. 299, 308, 352, 360, 364, 372, 373, 381, 446, 457, 468, 501, 507, 542, 565, 589
Euripides 158
Eusebius 21, 141, 159, 519, 590
Evans, C. A. 159, 251, 270, 474
Evans, C. F. 133, 510, 518, 522, 547, 562, 570, 574, 585, 607

Farris, S. 71, 89, 96
Fitzmyer, J. A. 22, 30, 45, 51, 56, 60, 64, 70, 75, 84, 85, 90, 102, 104, 107, 127, 141, 154, 172–73, 219, 226, 228, 233, 235, 251, 255,

267, 270–71, 288–89, 297, 303, 323, 330, 340, 347–48, 358, 362, 367, 369, 370, 383, 394, 405, 416, 438, 453, 457, 461, 471, 483, 503, 540, 544, 555, 574–75, 578, 594–95, 610
Foakes-Jackson, F. J. 62
France, R. T. 603
Freed, E. D. 443, 447
Furnish, V. P. 208, 316

Good, R. S. 186
Gooding, D. 335
Goppelt, L. 201
Goulder, M. D. 202, 294, 327, 351, 388, 465, 510, 545, 576, 606
Green, J. B. 534, 542, 544
Griesbach 28
Guelich, R. A. 201

Hamm, D. 467
Hemer, C. J. 22
Hengel, M. 588
Hennecke, E. 136
Herod Agrippa 193, 577
Herod Antipas 127, 134, 136, 218, 241, 382, 419, 579, 583, 597
Herod the Great 70, 80, 127, 473, 510
Hiers, R. H. 44
Higgins, A. J. B. 83
Hillel 419
Hippocrates 20
Hobart, W. K. 20
Hoehner, H. W. 106, 577
Horbury, W. 203
Hurst, L. D. 282

Ignatius 25
Irenaeus 21

Jeremias, J. 73, 176, 192,
  215, 243, 318, 327,
  367, 376, 392, 406,
  413, 446, 484, 485,
  527, 540, 543, 558
Jerome 21, 138, 251
Jervell, J. 79
Johnson, L. T. 53, 474–75
Jones, P. R. 317
Josephus 20, 62–63, 75,
  105, 127–28, 134, 136,
  142, 146, 175, 226,
  298, 331, 342–43, 370,
  383, 386, 444, 473,
  479, 497, 501, 509–11,
  513–14, 520–22, 535,
  538, 561, 569, 574,
  578, 585, 600
Justin Martyr 207, 316,
  383

Kazantzakis, N. 546
Keck, L. E. 71, 418
Kelber, W. H. 534
Kodell, J. 296
Kümmel, W. G. 125, 225,
  309

LaGrange 562
Lake, K. 62
Laurentim, R. 108, 141
Leon-Dufour, X. 547
Lewis, C. S. 183
Linnemann, E. 391, 393,
  443
Lucian 20
Luther, Martin 455

Macabbeus, Judas 479
Machen, J. G. 81
Maddox, R. 42, 527
Maier, P. L. 583
Manson, T. W. 315
Marshall, I. H. 35, 43, 50,
  62–63, 77, 83, 117,
  176, 211, 219, 226,
  237, 244, 258, 264,
  288, 321, 330–31, 334,
  340, 346, 348, 359,

373, 376, 380, 383,
  390, 415, 426, 438,
  459, 461, 463, 484,
  503, 513, 516–17, 538,
  540, 574, 606, 611,
  614
Martyn, J. L. 71, 418
Mattill, A. J., Jr. 44
Maximus, G. Vibius 105
Metzger, B. M. 439, 542
Minear, P. S. 71, 418
Mohr, J. C. B. 22
Morris, L. 450

Nebuchadnezzar 105
Nero 25
Neyrey 586
Nolland, J. 60, 71, 90,
  106, 135, 169, 176–77,
  191, 206, 221, 223,
  240, 257, 263, 276

Oelke, A. 241, 322
Ogg, G. 106
O'Hanlon, J. 469
Origen 21, 256
O'Toole, R. F. 35, 50, 51

Payne, P. B. 244
Perkins, P. 376
Philo 143, 316, 618
Pilgrim, W. 53
Plevnik, J. 606–7, 617,
  625
Pliny the Elder 236
Plumacher, E. 22
Plummer, A. 167, 257,
  364, 416, 463, 536,
  561, 592
Plutarch 20, 585
Polycarp 25
Powell, M. A. 35
Pritchard, J. B. 506

Quirinius 105–6

Riesenfeld, H. 437
Robbins, V. K. 22, 262
Robinson, J. A. T. 483

Sabourin, L. 196, 226,
  280, 327, 414, 424,

551, 593, 596
Sanders, E. P. 132, 483
Schneemelcher, W. 121
Seccombe, D. P. 53, 200
Sherwin-White, A. N. 569
Smith, M. 194
Snodgrass, K. 491, 493
Soards, M. L. 587
Stanley, D. M. 565
Stauffer, E. 546
Stein, R. H. 25, 28, 47, 53,
  57, 64, 67, 76, 135,
  165, 177, 178, 213,
  218, 229, 245, 266,
  271, 283, 319, 328,
  365, 391, 393, 397,
  399, 402, 411, 419,
  420, 498, 538, 540,
  575, 603, 616
Strack, H. L. 147, 222
Stuhlmacher, P. 62

Tacitus 520
Talbert, C. H. 22, 63, 81,
  85, 152, 155, 162, 191,
  201, 271, 297, 337,
  345
Tannehill, R. C. 46, 92,
  157, 164, 186, 253,
  277, 298, 304, 330,
  344, 358, 482, 580,
  592
Tertullian 21
Thrall, M. E. 333
Thompson, B. P. 22
Tiede, D. L. 535
Tolbert, M. O. 67
Trites, A. A. 52, 282
Turner, N. 430

van Unnik, W. C. 83

Wachsmann, S. 169
Wenham, D. 603
Wenham, J. 23, 603
Wilson, S. G. 35
Winter, P. 586
Witherington, B., III 240
Wright, A. G. 508
Wright, N. T. 282

Selected Scripture Index

Genesis
1:28. . . 500-502
2:18-25. . . .502
2:24. 113
3:1-15 310
4:1 . . . . 84, 97
4:17. 84
4:25. 84
5:1-32 140
6:3 91
6:8 83
9:5 343
9:6 544
11:10-26 . . .140
11:30 74
12:1-3 424
12:3. . . .38, 207
12:18 122
14:19-20 . . . 90
15:1. 75
15:2. 116
15:8. 77
15:8-21. . . .544
15:15 116
16:4. 74
16:7-13 . . 74-75
16:11 . . . 74, 83
17:1-21. . . . 75
17:4. 100
17:12-14 . . . 97
18:1-15. . . . 75
18:4. 237
18:6. 377
18:11 74
18:14 . . .86, 459
18:18 38
19:8. 84
19:17-19 . . .521
19:24-28 . . .306
19:26 440
19:29 94
20:9. 122
21:1. 99
21:3. 97
21:4. 97
21:6. . . .78, 202
21:8. . . 102, 181
21:12 83
21:15 186
21:17-18 . . . 74
22:10-18 . . . 74

22:16-17 . . 100
22:18 38
25:21 . . . 74, 75
25:22 89
25:24 . . 97, 107
25:25-26 . . . 97
26:4. 38
26:5. 73
26:10 122
26:30 181
27:4. 91
27:25 91
27:29 207
29:30-31 .396-97
29:31 74
29:32 . . 74, 91
30:1. 74
30:2. 90
30:13 . . . 83, 92
30:22 75
30:22-23 . . . 74
30:23 . . 78, 586
31:11-13 . . . 74
33:4. 406
37:11 110
38:8. . . 500-501
40:14 593
41:42 407
41:46 142
42:22 343
45:14-15 . . 406
48:14-15 . . 453
49:10 114
49:25 333
Exodus
2:24 . . . 94, 100
3:2-4 74
3:4-6 168
3:6 500
4:1-17. 77
4:11. 517
4:15. 517
4:31. 99
6:6 93
6:6-7 . .540, 542
6:14-25 . . . 140
7:3 312
7:14. 529
10:16 406
12:17-20 . . 535
13:1-2. . . . 113

13:2 114
13:12 114
13:15 114
14:19-20 . . . 74
15:16 93
15:20 117
15:26 73
16:7 108
16:10 108
18:21, 25 . . 273
19:3 . . 84, 282
20:1-17 . . . 457
20:7 201
20:10 601
20:12 406
20:13-15 . . 457
22:1 468
22:25 209
22:26-27 . . 207
23:4-5 206
23:15 535
23:16 285
24:5-8 55
24:8 . . 55, 543
24:15-18 . . 286
24:16 282
24:17 108
27:20 360
29:2 542
29:17 362
30:7-8 74
30:14 56
32:13 94
34:18 535
34:22 285
34:28 146
34:29 282
34:29-35 . . 284
40:34 108
40:34-38 . . 286
Leviticus
2:4. 542
2:13 398
3:17 543
5:1. 570
6:5. 468
7:26-27 . . . 543
8:26 542
10:9 76
10:7 . . .257, 405
12:3 97

12:3-4 113
12:6 114
12:6-8 113
12:8 114
13:38-46. . . 433
13:45-46. . . 433
14:1-32 . . . 433
14:2-32 . . . 173
15:19-27. . . 262
16:10 333
17:11 57
17:11-14. . . 543
17:14 543
18:5 316
19:2 209
19:18 208, 315-16
20:20-21. . . .74
21:1-4. . . . 341
21:10-11. . 301-2
21:11 341
21:17-23. . . 390
22:14 56
23:5-6 . . . 121
23:33-43. . . 285
23:36 283
24:2-3 360
25:5-9 189
25:8-55 . . . 157
25:35-37. . . 209
26:42 100
27:30-33. . . 340
Numbers
3:13 114
3:47-48 . . . 113
4:3. 142
5:2-3. 172
5:2-4 433
5:6-7. 468
6:2-5. 76
6:6-7. . . .301-2
6:19 542
6:23 117
6:24-26 77
9:6-10 341
10:35 93
11:26-30. . . 292
12:9-15 . . . 172
15:27-31. . . 362
15:30-31. . . 361
18:15-16. . . 114
19:2 479

19:11 223
19:16 223
20:16 446
20:29 116
21:7. 406
24:17 101
27:1-11 351
31:2. 446
32:41 261
35:30 304
36:7-9 351
Deuteronomy
3:14. 261
3:24. 93
3:26. 556
4:29. 327
4:34. 93
4:40. 73
5:14. 601
6:1-2 73
6:4-9 155
6:5 315-16
6:10-16. . . .142
6:13. . . 147, 625
7:13. 90
7:14. 90
8:1-3 146
8:1-9:22 . . .142
9:9 146
9:27. 94
10:21 92
11:13-21 . . .155
13:1-11. . . .488
14:8. . . 257, 405
14:22-29 . . .340
16:1-3 543
16:1-8 535
16:13-16 . . .285
16:16 121
17:12 362
18:15-18 223, 226
18:15-19 . . . 38
19:15 . . 225, 304
20:5-7 393
20:7. 393
21:3. 479
21:15-17 114, 351, 397
21:17 405
21:22-23 . . .599
21:23 56
22:4. 387
23:24-25 . . .188
24:5. 393
25:5. . . 500-501
25:5-10. . . .141
26:7. 91
27:15-28:6 . .199
28:4. 90
28:34 283
28:67 283
32:5. 289
32:20 289
33:17 99
Joshua
1:9 356

9:4 186
9:13. 186
13:30 261
24:3. 100
Judges
2:1-5 74
2:9 74
3:10. 139
4:4 117
4:19. 186
5:24. 90
6:12. 83
6:17. 83
6:22-23 . . . 168
6:23. 75
6:34. 13
6:36-40. . . . 77
8:28. 525
11:12 163
11:29 139
11:39 84
13:2-3. 74
13:3. 83
13:3-5. 76
13:3-20 75
13:4-5. 76
13:5. 83
13:22-23 . . 168
13:24 83
13:24-25 . . 102
16:17 76
18:6. . .238, 262
17:2. 207
21:12 84
Ruth
1:6 99
2:4 83
2:20. 90
1 Samuel
1:1 89
1:3 121
1:5 74
1:5-6 74
1:7 121
1:10-17 75
1:11 174, 76, 91-92, 113
1:17. 262
1:18. . . . 83, 86
1:19. 84
1:20. 83
1:21. 121
1:22. 113
1:22-24 . . . 113
1:24-28 . . . 113
1:28. 113
2:1-10. . . 89, 91
2:2 91
2:4-5 94
2:5 93
2:5-8 74
2:7 93
2:7-8 94
2:10. 99
2:19. 121
2:20. 117

2:21 102, 118, 123
2:26 102, 118, 123
3:19 118
6:7. 479
9:16 91
10:2-7. 77
15:24 406
16:1 106
17:12 106
17:15 106
17:58 106
21:1-6. . . . 188
21:13-14 . . . 98
24:6. 115
24:10 115
25:32 99
25:41 237
26:9. 115
26:11 115
26:16 115
26:23 115
30:6. 383
30:12 278
30:13 278
2 Samuel
4:11 343
5:4. 142
5:7. 106
5:8. 390
5:9. 106
6:10 106
6:12 106
6:16 . . . 89, 106
6:23 74
7:8-16 505
7:12-13 84
7:12-16 . . . 100
7:13 84
7:16 84
11:15 98
12:6. 468
15:25 83
16:10 163
17:13 485
22:3 99
22:18 100
22:50 312
1 Kings
1:21 424
1:26 501
1:33 479
1:48 99
2:10 424
8:15 99
8:61 73
9:7-8 384
10:1-4. . . . 336
10:1-13 . . . 335
10:7 . . .282, 336
11:21 424
12:18 383
17:10 222
17:17-24 222, 227
17:18 163
17:21-22 . . 263
17:23 223

18:1 159
18:46 98
19:4 556
19:7-18 . . . 282
19:19-21. . . 301
21:13 383
22:16 570
22:17 238
22:19 109
2 Kings
1:10 299
1:12 299
2:9-10 76
3:13 163
4:8-37 222
4:29 305
4:31-37 . . . 288
4:36 223
4:42-44 . . . 273
5:10-14 . . . 434
5:15 434
6:14 484
6:17 613
7:3-9. 172
8:11 484
9:13 479
9:28 106
10:6 98
12:21 106
15:5 172
20:5 75
20:8-9 77
22:14 117
1 Chronicles
16:34 457
20:5 261
21:15 556
29:18 93
2 Chronicles
5:13 457
9:1-12 335
15:1 139
19:11 496
20:14 139
24:20-21. . . 383
24:20-22. . . 342
24:21 383
31:5-12 . . . 340
33:3 109
33:5 109
35:16-19. . . 538
36:22 100
Ezra
2:9. 467
Nehemiah
2:8. 593
7:14 467
9:6. 109
9:30 139
10:35-36. . . 114
Esther
1:3 181
5:4 181
5:8 181
Job
1:6-12 309

2:1-7 309
2:8 307
8:21. 202
10:15 525
12:10 91
12:19 . . . 93-94
14:1. 230
15:14 230
19:26 503
31:16-20 . . .133
38:41 355
42:2. 86
42:5-6 169
Psalms
1:3 132
2:1-2 577
2:7 . . . .38, 140
6:9 379
11:1. 521
11:6. 365
16:8-11 38
16:9-11 503
16:10 . . .38, 620
18:16-19 . . .254
19:13 362
22:1. 594
22:2. 446
22:7. 589
22:10 76
23:1-4 403
24:5. 91
24:8. 92
25:5. 91
31:5. 596
31:7. 91
34:2. 91
38:11 597
41:9. . . 326, 547
51:1. 448
51:4. 406
63:2. 108
65:7. 259
69:25 384
69:30 91
77:2-3 91
78:70 106
80:8-13 492
80:17 98
88:8. 597
88:20-21 . . .286
89:4. 84
89:10 93
89:20-37 . . .505
89:48 115
91:11-12 . . .148
91:13 310
95:1. 91
97:10 100
102:25-27 . .528
103:17 92
105:7-11 . . . 94
105:26 286
105:42 94
106:10 101
106:23 286
107:3-9 201

107:20 . . . 220
110:138, 505, 570
111:9 92
118:22 . 38, 490,
    493, 495
118:26   226, 384,
    478, 480
119:1 73
119:166 . . . 114
123:1 450
126:1-2 . . . 202
132:12 84
132:17 99
133:1 351
137:7 485
139:8 . .307, 424
143:4 91
145:8-9 . . . 209
147:9 355
148:1-2 . . . 109
Proverbs
1:20-33 . . . 342
3:13. 198
3:34. 200
8:1-36. . . . 342
9:7-8 489
9:10. 444
12:2. 456
13:24 397
14:14 456
16:19 200
25:6-7. . . . 389
28:6. 204
28:11 204
29:24 570
31:22 423
Ecclesiastes
2:5 593
3:4 185
8:2 498
9:2 456
10:16 199
10:17 198
Song of Solomon
4:13. 593
Isaiah
1:3 107
2:5-6 84
3:10. 199
3:24-4:1 . . 524
4:1 586
5:1-7 492
6:1-13. . . . 171
6:4 139
6:5 168-69
6:8 139
6:8-13. . . . 171
6:9 245
6:9-10. 38
7:11. 77
7:14 . .82-84, 117
8:14. . .117, 494
8:14-15 . . . 495
8:17. 84
8:18. 117
9:2 101

9:6. 84
9:7. 84
10:33-34 . . 133
11:1 463
11:2 . . .135, 139
13:13 524
13:21 145
14:12 309
14:13 307
14:15 307
22:13 361
25:6 275
25:6-7. . . . 201
25:9 114
26:9 91
26:1938, 227, 503
27:2 492
28:16 38
28:16-17 . . 117
29:3 . . .484, 520
29:18 . . 38, 227
29:19 199
30:9-11 . . . 204
30:14 494
30:27-28 . . 132
32:15 134
33:9 524
34:1-15 . . . 524
34:4 524
34:13-14 . . 333
34:14 145
35:5 227
35:5-6. 38
37:33 . .484, 520
38:17 101
40:1 114
40:3 101, 128-30,
    229
40:3-5 . . 38, 76
40:4 129
40:5 . 116, 129-30
40:6-8 528
40:10 93
41:8-9 94
42:1 . 56, 94, 135,
    139,
    140, 286
42:7 101
42:18 . . 38, 227
42:19 94
44:1 94
44:2 76
44:3 134
44:21 94
45:4 94
46:4 289
48:1 84
48:6 337
48:8 76
49:1 76
49:5 76
49:6 . . . 56, 116
49:9 101
49:10-13 . . 201
49:13 199
50:5-6. . . . 566

51:2 100
51:5 93
51:6 528
51:9 93
52:10 116
52:13-53:12 . .56
53:1 93
53:3-5 566
53:7 . . . 56, 578
53:7-8 56
53:11 56
53:12 38, 56, 117,
    139
55:3 38
55:6 327
55:10-11. . . 528
56:7 483
58:6 . 38, 155-56
58:7 133
58:8 116
59:7 544
60:1 116
60:15 397
60:19 116
60:20 202
61:1 38, 135, 139,
    140, 227
61:1-2 . .38, 155,
    199
61:2 299
61:3 202
65:1 327
65:13 199
65:13-14 204, 275
66:13 114
66:14 98
Jeremiah
1:2 128
1:2-3 73
1:5 . . . 76, 313
2:21 492
3:14 246
5:26-29 54
5:31 204
6:1-8. . . . 521
6:6-21 . . . 484
8:13 370
8:18-21 . . 484
12:7 384
12:15 38
14:8 107
15:15 99
17:8 132
19:13 109
21:7 522
21:8 371
22:5 384
22:30 74
23:5 101
23:16-22. . 204
24:1-10 . . 370
26:1-6 . . . 521
26:20-23. . 383
31:13 . . . 202
31:31 . . . 543
31:31-33. . . 186

31:34 101
33:15 101
34:1. 520
36:30 74
38:4-6 383
52:5. 484
52:7. 520
Lamentations
2:20. 90
4:20. 108
Ezekiel
1:1 139
1:3 98
1:25. 139
1:28. 139
1:28-2:2 . . .168
3:14. 98
3:22. 98
3:26. 77
4:1-3 484
16:4. 107
17:23 376
18:7. 133
18:10 544
19:10-14 . . .492
20:33-38 . . .129
21:22 484
24:27 77
29:21 . . .99, 517
31:6. 376
31:8. 593
31:12 133
32:5-8 514
34:11-16 . . .403
34:16 469
36:17 262
36:27 134
37:14 134
38:19 514
39:29 134
Daniel
2:21. 103
2:34-35 . . 494-95
2:44-45. . 494-95
4:12. 376
4:14. 133
4:15. 103
4:21. 376
4:25. 103
4:26. 488
4:28. 110
4:34-35 103
5:21. 103
7:13. . .226, 233,
      525, 570
7:13-14 . 84, 178-
      79
8:10. . .109, 522
8:13. 522
8:16. 77
9:3 307
9:21. 77
10:12 75
10:19 75
12:2. 503
12:7. 159

Hosea
1:1 128
2:14-15 . . . 145
2:14-23 . . . 129
9:10. 370
9:16. 370
10:1-4 . . . 492
10:8. 586
13:4. 109
13:15 367
Joel
2:10. 514
2:28. 134
2:28-32 . .38, 48,
      619, 621
2:30-31 . . . 514
Amos
1:1 73
3:2 313
6:1 204
8:4-6 54
8:9 514
9:2 . . .307, 424
9:9 552
9:11-12 38
Jonah
1:4-5 253
3:1-10. . . . 385
3:6 307
4:8 367
Micah
1:1 128
2:1-5 54
2:11. 204
2:12. 356
3:12. . .485, 521
4:4 370
4:8 104
5:2 104, 107, 111
6:8 316, 341, 375
7:1 370
7:6 365
7:7 91
Habakkuk
2:7-8 483
2:11. 481
3:18. 91
Zephaniah
2:2 132
3:17. 92
Haggai
1:1 128
2:1-3 510
2:21. 524
Zechariah
1:15. 89
3:8 101
6:12. 101
7:14. 522
8:6 86
9:9 477-80
12:3. 522
12:10 589
12:10-14 . . 585
12:12-13 . . 141
14:5. 226

Malachi
1:2-3 397
2:2. 98
2:16 420
3:1. 38, 101, 128,
     225, 226,
     229-31, 288,
     298, 485
4:2. 89
4:5. 226, 231, 270
4:6. 77
Matthew
1:1. . . . .71, 82
1:1-17. . . . 140
1:2-17. 82
1:3. 141
1:5-6 141
1:11-12 . . . 141
1:16 . . . 71, 141
1:16-17 . . . 141
1:18 . . . .70, 71
1:19 82
1:19-20 82
1:20. 71
1:20-21 71
1:21 . 71, 75, 83,
     113
1:23 71
1:24. 82
1:24-25 71
1:25 . .71, 83-85,
     107,
     251
1:26 430
2:1. . . 70-71, 73
2:1-18. . . . 105
2:1-19. . . . 142
2:6. 111
2:7. 114
2:11 114
2:13-22 . . . 118
2:16 114
2:18 232
2:22-23 71
3:1. 128
3:11 135
3:12 135
3:13 139
3:14-15 . . . 138
3:15 139
3:15-17 . . . 130
3:17 143
4:1. 149
4:1-11. . . . 145
4:12-17 . . . 160
4:13-17 . . . 145
4:14-16 28
4:16 101
4:17 165
4:18-22 . . . 170
5:1. 196
5:1-2 200
5:1-7:29. 197-98
5:3-12. . . . 197
5:5. 496
5:9. . . 83, 496

5:11 198
5:12 203
5:13 . . . 395-96
5:15 337
5:15-16 . . . 338
5:17-20 . . . 319
5:18 . . 411, 419
5:29-30 . . . 421
5:32 420
5:33-37 27
5:33-42 20
5:38-41 . . . 496
5:38-42 27
5:38-48 . . . 206
5:45 209
5:46-47 . . . 208
5:48 209
6:1-6. . . .20, 27
6:10 92, 325, 377
6:12 . . 237, 370
6:14-15 . . . 326
6:16 307
6:16-18 . .20, 27
6:17-18 . . . 184
6:22-23 . . . 337
6:24 . . 411, 417
6:26 355
6:30 . . 136, 355
6:33 356
7:1. 211
7:1-5. 213
7:2. . . 211, 212
7:3-5. 213
7:13-14 . . . 378
7:16-18 . . . 214
7:21-23 . . . 379
7:22-23 . . . 378
7:25-27 . . . 215
7:51-52 . . . 342
8:5-13 217
8:6. 423
8:11-12 . . . 378
8:12 . . 362, 380
8:14 423
8:16 220
8:17 28
8:19 300
8:19-22 . . . 300
8:24 253
8:26 355
8:29 256
9:1. 175
9:2. 423
9:8. 149
9:2. 423
9:8. 149
9:9. 181
9:10-11 . . . 449
9:11 400
9:15 185
9:37-38 . . . 304
10:1 192
10:2 193
10:2-4 191
10:3 194
10:5 308

10:10 306
10:11-15 . . .306
10:24-25 . . .213
10:26-27 . . .249
10:32 348
10:33 348
10:34 485
10:37 397
10:37-38 . . .395
10:40-42 . . .304
11:2 226
11:2-19 229
11:7-19 217
11:10 . . 128, 225
11:12 418
11:12-13 411, 419
11:13 380
11:14 231
11:17 585
11:25-27 . . .311
12:11 387
12:24 330
12:28 28
12:32 . . 414, 459
12:33-37 . . .214
12:34 132
12:36 413
12:39 . . 289, 335
12:40-42 . . .335
12:43-45 . . .333
12:50 251
13:10-17 . . .242
13:16 313
13:16-17 . . .311
13:17 313
13:18 247
13:24-30 304, 305
13:31 376
13:32 376
13:35 28
13:44 444
14:3-4 136
14:9 270
14:13 272
14:15 273
14:31 355
14:34 30
14:36 261
15:1-2 340
15:1-9 339
15:14 212
15:27 423
16:2-3 367
16:3 367
16:4 289
16:8 355
16:9-12 271
16:13 277
16:17 245
16:21 . . 276-78
16:22-23 . . .276
17:1 284
17:9 283
17:15 288
17:20 . . .430-31
17:22 290

17:23 278
17:24-27 . 20, 27
18:2-6 312
18:4 . . .390, 453
18:6 428
18:8 135
18:10 428
18:10-14 . . 403
18:15 428
18:21-22 . . 428
18:22 430
18:23-35 . . 326
18:24 393
19:3-12 . . . 53
19:9 420
19:10-12 . . 459
19:13 453
19:16-30 . . 454
19:19 97
19:23 . .458, 460
19:26 86
19:28 . 192, 280,
    550
19:30 . 378, 380,
    459
20:1-16 .402, 406
20:2 318
20:9 318
20:11 403
20:12 . .367, 408
20:13 318
20:16 380
20:17-19 . . 460
20:22-23 . . 558
20:29-34 . . 463
20:30 463
21:2 479
21:4-5 28
21:4-9 551
21:5 479
21:9 480
21:14-16 . . 481
21:17 . . . 531
21:28-31 . . 401
21:28-32 . . 402
21:31-32 . . 449
21:37 492
21:39 . .491, 493
21:43 491
22:1-10 .391, 393
22:2-3 393
22:11-14 . . 395
22:13 362
22:15-22 . . 495
22:35 315
23:2 157
23:3 342
23:5 507
23:6 389
23:6-7 507
23:12 . .390, 451
23:13 343
23:27-28 341, 418
23:31 157
23:32 343
23:33 132

23:34 342
23:39 . .384, 480
24:3 . . .510, 512
24:8 518
24:9 516
24:15 . .519, 520
24:15-31 . . 558
24:20 522
24:21 522
24:22 . .519, 522
24:23 439
24:23-24 . . 524
24:26 439
24:29 512
24:30 286
24:32-36 . . 526
24:33 528
24:39 440
24:51 362
25:1-13 . 378-79,
    401,
    412, 444
25:5 393
25:14-30 471-72
25:19 . .472, 475
25:30 . 362, 363,
    474
25:31-46 . . 293
25:40 293
25:41 . .135, 257
25:41-45 . . 379
25:45 293
26:5 536
26:14 536
26:15 . . 536-37
26:17-19 . . 539
26:21-25 539, 546
26:24 546
26:26 . .273, 542
26:28 . . 55, 540
26:29 541
26:32 605
26:34 553
26:47 560
26:49 561
26:55 157
26:56 562
26:57 . .564, 568
26:57-58 . . 65
26:59 564
26:63 570
26:64 570
26:65 566
26:68 566
26:69-75 . . 65
26:71 . .423, 564
26:75 565
27:2 574
27:9 28
27:11 575
27:19 577
27:22 582
27:26 . . 582-83
27:32 585
27:33 588
27:34 585

27:35 588
27:37 . 573, 590
27:38 588
27:44 591
27:45 594
27:48 590
27:50 596
27:51 595
27:51-53 . . 595
27:54 596
27:57 599
27:60 600
27:73 565
28:1 . . 601, 604
28:2 604
28:4 604
28:7 605
28:9-10 . . . 616
28:16-20 . . . 605
28:19-20 619, 621
28:20 . 518, 525
Mark
1:2 225
1:2-3 128
1:2-11 126
1:3 90
1:4 128
1:6 233
1:8 135
1:9 139
1:10 140
1:11 143
1:14 136
1:14-15 145, 160
1:14-3:19 . . 239
1:15 165
1:16 . . 168, 193
1:16-20 . . . 167
1:20 170
1:21-39 . . . 161
1:21-45 . . . 152
1:24 154
1:29-31 218, 236
1:34 165
1:34-39 . . . 161
1:40-3:12 . . 171
1:41 172
1:44 173
1:45 . . 172, 243
2:1-3:6 . . . 174
2:2 243
2:6 175
2:12 149
2:13-17 . . . 184
2:15-16 . . . 449
2:16 400
2:18-22 . . . 184
2:21 186
2:28 . . 90, 189
3:4 387
3:7-12 . . 65, 195
3:8 196
3:11 165
3:13 192
3:13-19 65
3:14 . . 192, 193

3:16-19 191
3:17. . . 193, 298
3:18. 194
3:21. 110
3:22. 330
3:28-30 349
3:31. 91
3:35. 251
4:1 . . . 242, 253
4:1-2 167
4:1-20 242
4:1-6:44 . . .239
4:2 244
4:10-12 . 242, 312
4:11. 245
4:12. 246
4:13. 54, 242, 245
4:14. . . 243, 247
4:15. 246
4:24. 212
4:24-25 213
4:33. 243
4:35. 253
4:35-5:20 . . .152
4:35-5:43 . . .252
4:36. 253
4:37-38 . .65, 253
4:40. . . .54, 253
5:2 256
5:7 256
5:8 255
5:12. 255
5:20. . . 258, 259
5:21-43 260
5:23. 260
5:25. 373
5:26. . . .20, 260
5:28. . . 260-62
5:30. 262
5:31. 262
5:32. 261
5:42. 65
6:1-6 . . 153, 264
6:3 107, 158, 250-51
6:4 . . . .91, 158
6:6-13 267
6:6-16 264
6:7 . . . 192, 267
6:8 268
6:12. 268
6:13. 268
6:14. 136
6:17. 136
6:17-18 . 65, 130, 136
6:17-19 136
6:17-29 270
6:25. 270
6:29. 184
6:30. 272
6:30-44 271
6:31. 272
6:34. 170
6:36. 273
6:41. 450

6:44 65
6:45 29
6:45-52 . 29, 265
6:45-8:26 . 29-30, 59, 161, 265, 275-76
6:53 29-30
6:53-56 29
6:56 261
7:1-23 . . . 20, 30
7:2-5 341
7:2-8 342
7:13 . . . 64, 168
7:14-17 . . . 185
7:24 29
7:24-37 . 30, 265
7:28 90
7:30 423
7:31 29
7:32 97
7:32-34 . . . 373
7:34 450
7:37 97
8:1-10 271
8:1-21 30
8:11-12 . . . 335
8:15 346
8:19-20 . . . 271
8:22 29
8:22-26 30
8:23 373
8:27 276
8:29 478
8:31 . . .276, 278
8:31-33 . . . 478
8:32-33 276, 285, 552
8:33 291
8:34 279
8:35 . . .279, 381
8:38 381
9:1 . . . 43, 280
9:2 . . .282, 284
9:9 286
9:9-13 . .230, 231
9:11-13 .270, 288
9:12-17 30
9:24 90
9:25 97
9:28-29 54
9:30 292
9:31 . . .278, 290
9:32 291
9:33 292
9:35 293
9:38 331
9:39 294
9:40 452
9:41-10:12 . 452
9:42 429
9:43 135
9:47-48 . . . 347
9:48 135
9:50 396
10:1-12 20, 27, 30

10:11-12 411, 420
10:12 419
10:13 452
10:16 452
10:17-31 . . 454
10:20 457
10:21 . . 53, 457
10:23 458
10:31 380
10:34 278
10:35-44 . . . 54
10:35-45 54, 505
10:38-39139, 364, 558
10:45 54-56, 543, 549
10:46-52 . . 463
10:47 463
11:1-13:37 . 476
11:3 90
11:9-10 . . . 480
11:9-11 . . . 551
11:10 480
11:12-14 476, 482
11:15 .483, 485
11:16 483
11:17 .483, 485
11:18 .483, 485
11:20-26 . . 476
11:25 326
12:1 491
12:6 492
12:8 491
12:13-17 . . 495
12:28 315
12:36 505
12:36-37 . . .90
12:38-40 . . 506
12:41 . . . 508-9
12:41-44 . . 508
13:3 510
13:3-8 515
13:4 512
13:6 513
13:8 518
13:9 . . .516, 518
13:9-13 . . . 515
13:10 516
13:13 516
13:14 178, 519-20
13:19 522
13:20 .519, 522
13:21 437, 439, 524
13:24 .512, 524
13:26 524
13:28-32 . . 526
13:29 528
13:30 528
13:32 313
13:34 472
14:1-2 535
14:2 . . . 535-36
14:3 236
14:3-9 . .235, 535
14:5 236

14:10 536
14:10-11. . . 535
14:11 . . 536-37
14:12-16 . . . 539
14:12-17 . . . 537
14:18 540
14:18-21 539, 546
14:21 546
14:22 542
14:22-25 56
14:24 . . 55, 544
14:25 . . . 541
14:26 540
14:27-28 . . . 552
14:30 553
14:32 . . . 558
14:36 324
14:40 285
14:43 . . 560-61
14:44 561
14:45 561
14:49 562
14:50 . 552, 562
14:53 564, 567-68
14:53-54. . . .65
14:53-65. . . 569
14:55 564
14:55-60 567, 570
14:55-61. . . 571
14:55-65. . . 567
14:58 572
14:60 568
14:61 578
14:61-62. . . 568
14:62 43, 570-71
14:64 177
14:66-72. . . .65
14:67 564
14:69 564
14:72 565
15:1567, 569, 574
15:2 575
15:3 573
15:6-8 581
15:11 581
15:13 582
15:15 . 461, 582, 583
15:16-17. . . 578
15:17 423
15:17-20. . . 578
15:20 423
15:21 . 585, 610
15:22 588
15:25 588
15:26 . 573, 590
15:27 588
15:29 589
15:32 591
15:33 594
15:34 . 446, 594
15:36 590
15:37 596
15:39 596
15:40 . 193, 606
15:41 241

15:43 . . .598-99
15:44-46 . . .598
15:45 599
15:46 599
16:1601, 604, 606
16:1-2 601
16:3. 604
16:5-7 604
16:15-16 . . .619
16:18 147
16:19 623
16:20 39
Luke
1:1 25, 28, 36, 37,
   62-65, 67,
   69, 79, 266
1:1-2 62
1:1-3 614
1:1-4 . 21-23, 27-
   28, 59, 62-64
1:1-2:52 . . . 71
1:1-4:42 . . .165
1:1-9:20 . . . 60
1:1-24:53 . 30, 58,
   71
1:1-24:55. . . 60
1:2 20, 24, 28, 35,
   37, 63-65,
   67, 195, 205,
   242, 266,
   281, 474,
   608
1:3 21, 24, 26, 29,
   36, 63-64,
   67, 152, 198,
   253, 614,
   623
1:3-4 . . . . 36, 63
1:4 24, 27, 36, 40,
   59,
   63, 66, 76,
   79, 357, 380,
   486, 498,
   532, 561,
   562, 606,
   614, 622
1:5 27, 31, 36, 65,
   70, 79, 89,
   104, 110,
   115, 142
1:5-7 . . . 73, 81
1:5-23 . 120, 623
1:5-25 71, 80, 84,
   86, 87, 96,
   100, 126
1:5-38 89
1:5-67 99
1:5-80 102
1:5-2:32 . 21, 41,
   73
1:5-2:52 . 30, 69,
   112, 120
1:6 73, 78-79, 83,
   86, 90, 99,
   114, 118,
   119, 137,

150, 176,
   513, 611
1:6-26. 21
1:7 50, 70, 74-75
1:8 . . . 74, 622
1:8-20. 73
1:8-23. 69
1:9 74, 115, 121,
   176
1:9-10. . 52, 624
1:9-11. . . . 139
1:9-23. . . . 112
1:10 79
1:11 . 74-75, 108,
   176
1:11-13 81
1:12 . .75, 83, 98,
   617
1:13 . .75, 78, 83,
   97, 108
1:13-1770, 75, 81,
   126
1:13-20 . 75, 108
1:14 . .70, 75, 76,
   79,
   82, 90, 97,
   108, 246
1:14-17 . . 38, 70
1:15 . .48, 70, 76,
   78-79,
   81, 83, 85,
   87, 99-100,
   102, 128,
   139, 176
1:15-16 . 76, 101
1:15-17 76
1:16 .76, 111, 176
1:16-17 70
1:17 . .48, 70, 73,
   76,
   78-79, 81,
   85, 87, 89,
   100, 109,
   111, 140,
   230, 288
1:18 . .75, 77, 81,
   85-86
1:18-20 74
1:19 . .71, 74, 77,
   87,
   108
1:19-2075, 81, 86
1:19-23 85
1:2038, 77, 91, 98
1:21 . 74, 77, 110,
   115,
   116
1:21-23 73
1:21-24 81
1:22 . .38, 77, 97,
   115
1:23 . .78, 86, 89,
   113, 298
1:24 . . . . 70, 78
1:24-2538, 70, 73,
   88

1:24-28 . . . 114
1:25 . 50, 74, 78,
   97, 586
1:26 . 27, 81, 82,
   86, 104, 108,
   162
1:26-27 81
1:26-3871, 75, 80,
   84, 86, 122,
   230
1:27 . .49-50, 70-
   71, 82,
   84, 100, 106,
   109, 111,
   141, 143,
   477, 481
1:28 82
1:28-30 81
1:28-37 . . . 108
1:29 83
1:30 . .75, 83, 98
1:30-37 70
1:31 . 71, 82, 83,
   113
1:31-3338, 70, 81,
   89
1:31-35 . 39, 138
1:32 . 49, 71, 76,
   81, 83,
   85-87, 122,
   144, 256,
   477, 481
1:32-3346, 49, 70,
   82, 86, 87,
   109, 111,
   590, 625
1:32-35 . . . 140
1:33 . .46, 84, 87
1:3470-71, 81, 84,
   86
1:34-35 . . 82, 86
1:3548-49, 70-71,
   77-79, 81-
   87, 89, 100,
   102, 115,
   122, 144,
   525
1:35-37 . . 81, 87
1:36 . 78, 82, 86,
   89, 124
1:36-37 . . 81, 88
1:37 . 70, 78, 86,
   459
1:37-38 . . . 126
1:38 . 81, 86, 87,
   89, 92
1:39 . 73, 78, 89,
   104, 109
1:39-41 88
1:39-45 89
1:39-55 . . . 112
1:39-56 87
1:40 89
1:41 . 70, 76, 79,
   89, 95,
   98, 102, 115,

174
1:41-44 . 94, 203
1:41-4538, 70, 87
1:4283, 90-92, 95,
   98,
   334
1:42-45 . .70, 88
1:42-55 88
1:43 . 76, 90, 95,
   101,
   109, 124
1:44 . 79, 89, 90,
   95, 128
1:45 . 90-91, 95,
   313, 334
1:46 . 70, 89-91
1:46-47 . 91, 93,
   99
1:46-55 . 70, 88,
   95
1:46-56 . . . 89
1:47 . 79, 90-91,
   99,
   108, 130
1:47-48 . . . 70
1:48 .50, 89, 91-
   93,
   111, 114,
   130, 365
1:48-49 . . . 94
1:48-50 . 91-92
1:48-55 . . . 95
1:49 92
1:50 . 92-93, 99,
   209, 228
1:50-55 . . . 92
1:51 . . . 93-94
1:51-52 92, 130,
   317
1:51-53 . 50, 91,
   93, 314,
   380, 394
1:51-54 . . . 94
1:51-55 . 46, 92
1:52 . 50, 92-94,
   108, 111,
   114, 129
1:52-53 . 47, 93,
   199-
   200, 228
1:52-55 . . . 70
1:53 .50, 70, 93-
   94, 111,
   114, 204
1:53-55 . . . 92
1:54 . 93-94, 115
1:54-55 . 70, 91,
   94-95
1:55 94
1:56 . 86, 88-89,
   94, 112
1:57 . . 97, 107,

112-13
1:57-58 .94, 96,
   102-3
1:57-80 .38, 95,
   126
1:58 .79, 91, 97,
   110
1:58-80 . . 112
1:59 97, 113, 513
1:59-66 96, 112
1:59-79 . . 103
1:59-80 . . 112
1:60 .97-98, 370
1:62 . . . 77, 97
1:63 97-98, 110,
   116
1:63-64 . . . 38
1:64 97-98, 109,
   464,
   624
1:65 .73, 75, 98,
   126
1:65-66 . . 110
1:66 98, 102, 123
1:67 .76, 79, 96,
   98, 102,
   103, 115
1:67-79 70, 112
1:67-80 . 95-96
1:68 .47, 69, 78,
   96,
   98-100,
   102, 118,
   228, 482
1:68-70 . . . 70
1:68-71 . . . 47
1:68-75 .46, 70,
   96, 99,
   102
1:68-79 96, 102-
   3,
   115, 117
1:69 .49, 84, 91,
   99,
   100, 102-3,
   108-9, 111,
   115-16, 130
1:70 100
1:71 91, 99-100,
   130
1:72 94, 100-101
1:72-73 . . 103
1:72-74 . . . 70
1:73 100
1:74 100
1:75 100
1:76 .76, 83, 87,
   89-90, 96,
   100-102,
   109, 111,
   128, 230,
   288

1:76-77 76, 101-2
1:76-79 .87, 96,
   119
1:77 .47, 50, 71,
   91,
   99-101,
   103, 128,
   130, 179,
   329, 482
1:77-79 . . 238
1:78 99, 101, 482
1:78-79 . . 101
1:79 . . 96, 101,
   228, 482
1:80 70, 96, 102-
   3,
   112, 118,
   123, 126,
   128-29
2:1 .73, 104, 126
2:1-2 .59, 63, 73,
   79, 130
2:1-3 . . 36, 111
2:1-5 104
2:1-7 38
2:1-19 . . . 112
2:1-20 . . 102-3,
   112, 122
2:1-39 . . . 113
2:1-52 . . . 103
2:2 105
2:3 106
2:4 49, 70-71, 73,
   82,
   84, 106,
   109, 111,
   123, 477,
   622
2:4-7 71
2:5 . . . 70, 106
2:6 97, 107, 111,
   113
2:6-7 . . 49, 104
2:7 106-7
2:7-14 50
2:8 . . . 108, 114
2:8-20 . 70, 104
2:9 108
2:10 .70, 75, 77,
   97-98, 108
2:10-12 . . . 70
2:11 .49, 70, 76,
   84,
   90-91, 95,
   99, 106,
   108, 109,
   111, 129-
   30, 138,
   477, 488,
   590
2:11-12 . . . 38
2:12 . . .108-10

2:13 109
2:13-14 . . .110
2:14 . 109, 116,
   582
2:15 . . 109, 126
2:15-18 . . . 38
2:16 . . .109-10
2:17 109-10, 126
2:17-18 . . . 98
2:18 . 110, 116,
   122
2:18-20 . . . 98
2:19 98, 109-10,
   123, 126
2:20 86, 98, 109-
   13, 373
2:21 .51, 83, 97,
   112-13, 119
2:21-40 . . 103,
   111, 120,
   122, 435
2:22 . . 41, 106,
   113, 119
2:22-24 70, 107,
   112-13,
   119, 137
2:22-38 69, 112
2:23 85, 113-14,
   119, 128
2:24 . . 55, 113,
   114, 130
2:25 73, 76, 106,
   114-16,
   118-19,
   202, 599
2:25-26 95, 119
2:25-27 .48, 70,
   119
2:25-38 . . 112,
   114, 139
2:26 .38, 49, 70,
   76,
   109, 113-
   16, 119, 488
2:26-32 . . . 70
2:27 . . 74, 110,
   113,
   115, 116,
   119, 121,
   122, 137
2:27-32 . . . 38
2:28 98
2:28-32 . . . 56
2:29 . 113, 115,
   119, 126
2:29-32 .70, 95,
   119
2:30 .47, 84, 91,
   99,
   115-16,
   118-19

2:30-32 . . .130
2:31 116
2:31-32 . . .116
2:32 . . 50, 116,
   119, 129
2:33 . 110, 115-
   16, 122
2:34 70, 98, 116,
   119, 493
2:35 38, 116, 117
2:36 . . 109, 117
2:37 74, 114-15,
   117-18, 446
2:37-38 119, 139
2:38 . 51, 70, 95,
   99, 115,
   118, 119
2:38-39 . . .622
2:39 . . 71, 106,
   118-19,
   137, 150
2:39-40 . . .112
2:39-51 . . .154
2:40 . . 70, 102,
   118, 120,
   123, 144
2:41 . .115, 121,
   124,
   150, 538
2:41-45 . . . 41
2:41-51 .69, 112
2:41-52 103, 118-
   19, 538
2:42 . . 121, 615
2:43 115
2:44 . . 114, 121
2:46 74, 114-15,
   122-24
2:46-47 . . 118,
   120, 122,
   124
2:47 . 114, 122-
   23, 202
2:48 . . 115, 122
2:49 46, 86, 120,
   122,
   124, 140
2:49-50 . . . 70
2:50 . . 123, 461
2:50-51 . . .126
2:51 71, 98, 110,
   123-24
2:52 . . 70, 102,
   118,
   122-24, 144
3:1 . . 30-31, 73,
   105, 121,
   125, 127,
   136, 139,
   142, 178
3:1-2 30, 43, 59,
   62-63, 73,

79, 104,
125, 130
3:1-3 36
3:1-6 . . 46, 126
3:1-2075, 125-26
3:1-22 77
3:1-4:15 . . 125
3:2 . 102, 126-27
3:3 51, 101, 128,
132, 138,
329, 513
3:4 . 76, 90, 100,
101,
126, 128,
136, 225
3:4-6 38
3:5 129-30
3:6 . 47, 99, 116,
129
3:7 . 132, 137-39
3:7-9 131
3:7-14 . . . 100
3:7-20 . . . 131
3:8 . . . 51, 132
3:8-9 248
3:9 44, 133, 135-
37
3:10 133
3:10-14 .131-32
3:11 . . 53, 133
3:12 . 132, 133,
138
3:12-13 . . . 50
3:13 134
3:14 . .132, 134
3:15 49, 98, 134
3:15-17 . . 131
3:15-18 .227-28
3:16 .38, 47-48,
76, 79,
81, 126,
134-35,
138, 140,
228, 513
3:17 . . 44, 135
3:18 . . 77, 125,
128,
131, 136
3:18-20 . . 130
3:19 . .127, 136
3:19-20 65, 131,
139,
265, 382
3:20 136
3:21 . 108, 138,
194
3:21-22 .39, 47,
65,
118, 138
3:21-38 . . 137
3:21-4:15 . 125,
137

3:22 . 48-49, 86,
123-24,
138-39,
144, 156
3:23 104, 140-41
3:23-27 . . 140
3:23-38 . 30, 82
3:24 142
3:27 142
3:27-28 . . 140
3:28-31 . . 142
3:31 49
3:31-34 . . 142
3:33 140
3:3827, 138, 142
4:1 48, 115, 138,
140,
143, 145
4:1-15 . . . 143
4:2 . . .104, 146
4:3 . 49, 86, 138,
146
4:4 146
4:5 147
4:6 147
4:7 147
4:8 . . .147, 625
4:9 . 49, 86, 115,
138, 148
4:9-13 41
4:10 148
4:12 148
4:13 . . 148, 175
4:14 48, 77, 140,
143,
149, 178,
190, 210
4:14-15 125, 144
4:14-30 . . . 22
4:15 . 109, 124,
149,
487, 569
4:16 . . 154, 200
4:16-20 . . 155
4:16-21 .46, 47,
78, 375
4:16-22 . . 154
4:16-30 .44, 50,
65,
197, 221,
297, 527
4:16-44 . . 167
4:16-5:16 . 152
4:16-9:50 . 125,
152,
153, 296
4:17 155
4:17-21 38, 153
4:18 .48, 50, 77,
101,
125, 128,
138, 140,

155, 183,
186, 221,
227
4:18-19 . . 128,
140, 143,
150, 166,
221
4:18-20 . . .130
4:18-21 . . 140,
227, 368,
407, 409
4:19 . . 157, 299
4:20 157
4:20-27 . . .124
4:21 . . 52, 108,
156,
157, 178
4:22 . . 98, 110,
116, 118,
123, 153,
157, 498
4:23 . . 65, 153,
158,
161, 218
4:23-27 . . .153
4:23-30 40, 154
4:24 . 38, 49, 91,
137,
153, 158,
160, 205,
277, 453
4:25 . . 73, 159
4:25-26 . . .118
4:25-27 . . .161
4:25-30 . . .153
4:26 159
4:27 159
4:2846, 136, 159
4:28-30 . . . 38
4:29 . .117, 159
4:30 . . 39, 160
4:3127, 162, 599
4:31-37 162, 175
4:31-44 . . .161
4:31-6:19 . . 28
4:32 . 162, 173,
178,
488
4:33 . 140, 163,
256
4:33-36 . . .166
4:34 49, 86, 102,
163,
166, 488
4:35 163
4:36 . . 49, 163,
166, 173,
178, 190
4:37 . . 20, 164
4:38-39 50, 162,
167
4:38-40 . . . 49

4:39 164
4:40 . . .98, 164
4:40-41 .39, 240
4:41 49, 86, 140,
162,
164, 166
4:43 . 46, 47, 77
4:43-44 . . .154
4:44 . 20, 27, 73,
128, 166
5:1 . 30, 64, 168
5:1-11 . 167, 171
5:2 167
5:3 . . 124, 169
5:3-9 168
5:4 . . . .38, 169
5:5 169
5:5-7 38
5:5-10 174
5:6 169
5:7 169
5:8 . 49, 90, 168-
69, 171
5:9-10 170
5:1038, 170, 365
5:11 53, 170-71,
200,
207, 509
5:12 . 20, 49, 90,
172, 174
5:12-16 . . 171,
182, 433
5:13 172
5:13-14 . . .101
5:14 . . 172, 513
5:15 173
5:16 173
5:17 . 48, 73, 77,
143,
175, 179,
190, 339
5:17-26 174, 180
5:17-32 . . .128
5:17-6:11 . .174
5:18 . . .20, 176
5:19 . . .27, 176
5:20 . . 176, 183
5:20-21 . . .238
5:20-26 . . . 50
5:21 . . 49, 102,
177, 179
5:2298, 158, 177
5:23 177
5:24 . 20, 28, 49,
176-77, 488
5:24-25 . . .179
5:2586, 178, 180
5:25-26 98, 109,
373
5:26 . . 98, 108,
178, 253
5:27 133, 180-81

5:27-32 50, 180, 374
5:27-6:11 . 180
5:28 180-81, 183, 200, 207, 509
5:29 181
5:29-30 . . 133
5:29-32 . . . 50
5:30 180-81, 233, 449, 468-69
5:31 . . 20, 182
5:31-32 . . 404
5:32 50-51, 125, 180, 182-83, 185
5:33 . . 75, 134, 184, 232
5:33-39 184, 374
5:34 185
5:35 . . 73, 104, 185, 187, 438, 511
5:36 185
5:36-39 . . 184
5:37 186
5:38 186
5:39 186
6:1 188
6:1-5 . . 49, 187, 190
6:1-11 187, 191, 373
6:2 188
6:3 188
6:4 . . . 123, 188
6:5 . 49, 90, 189
6:6 189
6:6-11 187, 190, 372, 374
6:7 174, 189, 386
6:8 . . . 158, 189
6:9 . . . 190, 387
6:10 190
6:11 . 174, 190, 386
6:12 . 52, 73, 89, 139, 192, 194
6:12-16 65, 162, 191
6:12-49 . . 191
6:13 . 192, 266, 430
6:13-16 . . . 64
6:14 20, 27, 164, 193
6:15 194
6:16 194
6:17 27, 73, 196, 374
6:17-18 . . 197

6:17-19 65, 168
6:17-49 . . 196
6:18 . . 20, 196
6:19 . . 98, 196
6:20 . 46, 50, 54, 183, 197, 200, 213-14, 216, 357, 509
6:20-21 . . . 91
6:20-22 91, 225, 390
6:20-26 . 93-94, 114, 130, 197
6:20-49 . . 198
6:21 47, 93, 201, 211
6:21-23 . . 443
6:22 45, 49, 198, 202, 206, 216
6:23 41, 79, 203
6:24 . . 54, 204
6:24-25 . . 424
6:24-26 . 50, 94, 374, 443
6:25 . . 202, 204
6:26 204
6:27 . . 206, 214
6:27-28 . . 203, 210, 563
6:27-31 . . 569
6:27-36 . . 205
6:27-42 . 213-14
6:28 . 98, 206-7
6:29 . 133, 207, 208
6:30 . 133, 201, 208, 210
6:31 . . 208, 212
6:32 208
6:32-34 . . 209
6:32-35 . . 389
6:32-36 318, 320
6:33 208
6:34 208
6:34-35 53, 206, 208
6:35 . . 83, 201, 209, 256, 503
6:35-36 . . 563
6:36 . . 209, 211
6:37 211
6:37-42 . . 210
6:38 . 53, 211-12
6:39 212
6:40 213
6:41-42 . . 213
6:43 214
6:43-44 . . 248

6:43-45 132, 137
6:43-49 . . . 213
6:44 . . 137, 214
6:45 215
6:46 49, 90, 215-16, 473
6:47 215
6:47-49 . . . 228
6:48-49 27, 215
7:1 . . . 218, 223
7:1-10 . . 20, 50, 216-17, 224, 235, 239, 259
7:1-50 . 216, 221
7:2 218
7:3 . . . 27, 218
7:4 219
7:5 . 53, 207, 219
7:6 90, 169, 219, 222
7:7 220
7:8 220
7:9 . . . 110, 220
7:10 220
7:11 222
7:11-17 . 20, 50, 118, 216, 221, 222, 224, 235, 239, 260
7:12 222
7:13 90, 222, 373
7:16 . 47, 49, 98-99, 222-24, 234, 374
7:17 27, 73, 223
7:18 225
7:18-19 . . 184
7:18-23 39, 110, 216-17, 224
7:18-24 . . . 134
7:18-28 . . . 131
7:18-35 235, 239
7:19 . . 90, 226
7:19-20 217, 228
7:20 50, 221-22, 226
7:20-23 . . . 224
7:21 226
7:22 . 47, 49-50, 77, 108, 226, 228, 233, 366, 513
7:22-23 . 38, 47, 221, 225, 368
7:23 . . 49, 225
7:24 229
7:24-28 . . . 128

7:24-30 224, 228
7:25 229
7:26 . . 100, 111, 229, 488
7:26-27 . . . 76
7:27 . . 38, 100-101, 128, 225, 230-31, 288
7:28 76, 187, 230
7:28-30 . . . 488
7:29 . . 50, 108, 133, 230, 231, 233
7:29-30 129, 229
7:30 46, 231, 343
7:31 . . 232, 439
7:31-35 . . 129, 224, 231, 366
7:32 232
7:33 . . 232, 326
7:34 49-50, 133, 233, 234, 236, 449
7:34-50 . . . 50
7:35 233
7:36 235
7:36-50 50, 175, 217, 234, 239
7:37 236
7:38 236
7:39 . . 49, 236, 400, 469
7:40 . . 158, 236, 408
7:41 236
7:42 237
7:43 . . 237, 497
7:44 237
7:45 237
7:46 237
7:47 . . . 236-38
7:47-48 . . . 236
7:48 238
7:48-49 50, 179, 239
7:49 49, 102, 238
7:50 51, 99, 238, 239, 319, 589
8:1 . 47, 77, 240-42, 244, 447
8:1-3 . . 50, 239
8:1-21 . 239, 250
8:2 . . . 240-41
8:3 53, 127, 241, 322, 468
8:3-4 447
8:4 244

8:4-15 .241, 363
8:4-17 . . . 249
8:4-9:17 . . 239
8:5 244
8:5-15 . . . 475
8:6 244
8:8 244, 247, 398
8:9 245
8:9-10 . . . 242
8:10 . .245, 250
8:11 54, 64, 245
8:11-12 . . 220
8:11-15 243-44,
    247
8:12 .51, 64, 99,
    242, 246
8:12-15 . . 371
8:13 . . 64, 243,
    246-48,
    253, 363,
    432
8:13-14 . . 529
8:14 . . 53, 243,
    246,
    248, 321
8:14-15 . . 399
8:15 . . 64, 137,
    243,
    247-48,
    250, 253,
    322, 334,
    338, 377,
    447, 551
8:16 . . 27, 249
8:16-17 . . 250
8:16-18 . . 248
8:17 . .249, 346
8:18 . 244, 248-
    50, 474
8:19 91
8:19-21 . . 107,
    117, 250,
    334
8:20 251
8:21 . 117, 251-
    52, 322
8:22 . . 73, 252
8:22-25 .29, 39,
    252,
    332, 366
8:22-39 . . 152
8:22-56 . . 252,
    264, 273
8:23 .65, 252-53
8:24 . . .252-53
8:25 .49, 54, 98,
    110,
    116, 179,
    252-53,
    266, 269
8:25-26 . . 432
8:26 255

8:26-27 . . 254
8:26-39 254, 332
8:27 . .254, 256
8:28 49, 86, 255-
    56, 259
8:29 . . 28, 140,
    254, 256,
    258-59
8:30 . .257, 259
8:30-32 . . 255
8:31 257
8:32 257
8:33 . .255, 257
8:34-37 255, 261
8:35 . . .257-58
8:36 . .258, 589
8:37 . . 98, 258
8:38 258
8:38-39 . . 255
8:39 49, 86, 258,
    264
8:40 . . 98, 260
8:40-48 . . 222
8:40-56 50, 259,
    332
8:41 261
8:42 . . 65, 261
8:43 .20, 260-61
8:43-48 . . 260
8:44 . . 20, 261
8:45 . .253, 261
8:46 262
8:47 . .108, 262
8:48 51, 99, 262,
    319, 589
8:49 . .219, 262
8:50 .38, 75, 99,
    254,
    263, 589
8:51 263
8:52 263
8:53 263
8:54 20, 27, 263
8:54-56 . . . 38
8:55 263
8:56 . .122, 264
9:1 . . .267, 272
9:1-2 . .195, 272
9:1-6. 266, 303,
    308-9, 556
9:1-50 . .264-65
9:2 .46, 267, 272
9:3 . . . 49, 556
9:3-5. . . . 200
9:4 268, 308, 555
9:5 268
9:6 .77, 268, 270
9:7 127, 266, 270
9:7-8. . . . 277
9:7-9. . 75, 136,
    265, 269,
    271, 276

9:8 . . . 49, 270
9:9 49, 102, 127,
    179,
    270, 275,
    281-82, 467
9:10 272
9:10-16 . . . 49
9:10-17 . 29, 39,
    93,
    265, 271
9:11 268, 272-73
9:12 273
9:13 273
9:14 . . 65, 273
9:15 273
9:16 . . 98, 273
9:17 274
9:18 52, 139, 277
9:18-20 . . . 49
9:18-21 . . .282
9:18-27 . . .275
9:18-50 . . . 28
9:19 . . 49, 277
9:20 49, 86, 115,
    272,
    275, 277,
    281, 287
9:21 277
9:21-22 . . .290
9:22 . 38, 46, 49,
    56,
    122, 218,
    278, 281,
    287, 291,
    297, 383,
    426, 485,
    487, 489,
    490, 541,
    567, 570,
    573, 576,
    602, 605
9:23 45, 51, 279,
    281,
    464, 398,
    458, 585
9:23-24 . . .551
9:23-25 . . .353
9:23-26 49, 587
9:23-27 . . .282
9:24 .99, 279-81
9:25 . 279, 281,
    319, 393
9:26 49, 51, 109,
    279, 281,
    287, 366,
    414, 443
9:27 . 38, 42-44,
    280, 287
9:28-29 52, 139
9:28-36 38, 281
9:29 . .284, 439
9:30 284

9:31 . . 41, 284,
    287,
    290, 297,
    299, 623
9:31-32 . . .287
9:32 . . 109, 285
9:33 285
9:34 . . .85, 286
9:35 49, 86, 286-
    87, 589
9:36 73, 104, 286
9:36-43 . . .222
9:37 . . .73, 288
9:37-43 . . .287
9:38 288
9:39 . . 140, 288
9:40 288
9:41 289-90, 439
9:42 . .140, 289,
    291
9:43 . 49, 54, 98,
    110,
    116, 289-
    90, 294
9:43-45 278, 290
9:44 38, 56, 290-
    91, 294,
    297, 602
9:44-45 . . .122
9:45 . .123, 291,
    299
9:46 293
9:46-48 . . 247,
    296, 311
9:46-50 . . .292
9:47 . . 158, 293
9:48 230, 292-93
9:49 . . . 292-93
9:50 294
9:51 31, 41, 285,
    296,
    298, 303,
    385, 432,
    471, 547
9:51-53 . . .461
9:51-56 . . 297,
    301, 320,
    476
9:51-13:21 .297
9:51-18:14 .296
9:51-19:27 . 41,
    296
9:51-19:28 .120
9:52 . . 298, 303
9:52-55 . . . 50
9:53 . . .41, 298
9:54 49, 90, 135,
    294, 298
9:55 299
9:56 299
9:57 300
9:57-58 . . .200

9:57-62 51, 183,
    300,
    398, 420
9:58 . . 300-301
9:59 90, 300-302
9:60 . . 46, 300-
    301, 303
9:61 90, 300-302
9:62 . . 300-301
10:1 . 90, 303-4
10:1-12 64, 267
10:1-16 302, 308
10:2 52, 304, 308
10:3 305
10:4 . 304, 308,
    555-56
10:5 304
10:5-9 . . . 555
10:6 . . 200, 304
10:7 305
10:7-8 . . . 308
10:8 306
10:9 . . 44, 306
10:10 . . . 306
10:10-11 . . 303
10:10-15 . . 306
10:11 . 44, 303,
    306
10:11-15 . . 304
10:12 306, 308,
    390
10:12-15 . . 304,
    336
10:13 . . . 306
10:13-14 . . 196
10:13-15 . . . 93
10:14 . . . 308
10:15 . . . 307
10:16 293, 303,
    307, 311
10:17 47, 75, 79,
    90, 309,
    310, 555
10:17-20 49, 308
10:18 . . 44, 47
10:18-19 . . 309
10:19 . . . 310
10:20 . 309-11,
    350, 586
10:20-21 . . . 79
10:21 109, 311,
    314,
    317, 589
10:21-22 28, 311
10:21-23 . . 324
10:21-24 . . 311
10:22 . 86, 123,
    312
10:23 . . . 313
10:23-24 . 44, 47,
    311
10:24 . . . 313

10:25 . . 27, 50,
    132,
    231, 315,
    317, 417
10:25-28 . 51, 73,
    118,
    150, 455
10:25-37 50, 302,
    314, 341,
    455
10:26 . 316, 319
10:27 . 314-16,
    341, 569
10:27-28 . . 319
10:28 . 316, 497
10:29 . 314-15,
    317, 319,
    418, 449
10:29-37 . . 320
10:30 106, 317,
    422
10:31 . . . 317
10:32 . . . 317
10:33 . . . 317
10:34 . . . 318
10:34-35 . 20, 53
10:35 . . . 318
10:36 314, 317,
    318, 320
10:37 . 318, 408
10:38 . . . 320
10:38-42 50, 320
10:39 . . 64, 90,
    321-22
10:40 . 90, 321
10:41 . 90, 321,
    552
10:42 . 241, 321
11:1 75, 90, 134,
    139,
    184, 323
11:1-4 . 52, 323
11:1-13 . . 322
11:1-18 . . 344
11:2 47, 92, 324,
    326,
    438, 445,
    527, 589
11:2-3 . . . 354
11:2-4 36
11:3 325
11:4 . 212, 237,
    326, 431,
    451, 589
11:5 327
11:5-8 . . . 323
11:5-13 . . . 93
11:6 327
11:7 327
11:8 . . 327, 605
11:9 . 327, 416,
    507

11:10 328
11:11 328
11:11-13 . . .354
11:13 323
11:14 . 110, 330
11:14-23 . . .329
11:14-36 . . .330
11:14-54 . . .330
11:15 330
11:16 . 77, 331,
    467
11:17 . 158, 331
11:18 51, 330-31
11:19 331
11:20 44, 46-47,
    160, 167,
    328, 330-31
11:21-22 . . .47,
    310, 330
11:22 . 134, 332
11:23 . 294, 332
11:24 . 140, 333
11:24-26 . . 334,
    435
11:24-28 . . .332
11:25 333
11:26 333
11:27 . 90, 333
11:27-28 . . 117,
    230, 334
11:28 . . 51, 64,
    168,
    251, 333
11:29 . 77, 335,
    467
11:29-30 . 38-39,
    442
11:29-32 . . 232,
    331, 334
11:30 . 117, 335
11:31 . 335, 499
11:31-32 . . .505
11:32 . 125, 336
11:33 . 249, 337
11:33-35 . . .337
11:33-36 . . .336
11:34 . 337, 339
11:35 338
11:36 . . .337-38
11:37 . 235, 541
11:37-38 . . .339
11:37-52 . . .408
11:37-54 . . 338,
    349, 351
11:38 . 110, 340
11:39 . 90, 340,
    351, 353,
    417, 507
11:39-40 . . .339
11:39-48 . . .342
11:40 340
11:41 . 53, 340

11:42 . 340-42,
    391, 450
11:42-44 . . .339
11:43 . 341, 507
11:43-44 . . .391
11:44 . 341, 507
11:45 341
11:45-46 . . .231
11:46 341
11:46-52 . . .339
11:47 342
11:47-48 . . 41
11:47-51 . . 205,
    344, 385
11:49 . 342, 345
11:49-51 . . .137
11:50 . 41, 343,
    380, 544
11:50-51 . . 232,
    343
11:51 343
11:52 . 27, 231,
    245, 343
11:53 344
11:53-54 . . 339,
    345, 386,
    495, 497
11:54 . 344, 387
12:1 . . 345-46,
    349-50,
    377
12:1-12 . . .345
12:2 . . 249, 346
12:3 347
12:4 . . .347-48
12:4-5 . 45, 346,
    349,
    518
12:4-12 . . .550
12:5 347
12:6 347
12:6-7 . . .346
12:6-8 . . .350
12:7 . . 347, 518
12:8 348
12:8-9 . 49, 51,
    279, 349,
    366, 414
12:8-10 . . .346
12:9 . 348, 553,
    587
12:10 348
12:11 349
12:11-12 . 38, 350
12:12 349
12:13 . 350-51,
    499
12:13-14 . . .367
12:13-21 53-54,
    94,
    350, 358,
    422, 427

12:13-34. . 352,
 358
12:14 . . . 351
12:15 .351, 353
12:16 . . . 352
12:16-21. . 353,
 527
12:17 352, 413,
 492
12:17-19. . 351
12:18 .352, 355
12:19 352, 407,
 423
12:20 352, 359,
 369,
 424
12:20-21. . 354
12:21 352, 361,
 427,
 509
12:22 .354, 509
12:22-31. . 268,
 509
12:22-34. . 246,
 353, 358
12:22-53. . 366
12:23 . . . 355
12:24 . . . 355
12:25 . . . 355
12:25-26. . 354
12:26 . . . 355
12:27 . . . 355
12:28 . . . 355
12:29 . .354-55
12:30 353, 356,
 445
12:31 .354, 356
12:32 .353, 356
12:32-33. . 357
12:33 . . 52-54,
 133, 137,
 352, 354,
 356, 357,
 427, 468,
 473, 509
12:33-34. . . 53
12:34 .354, 357
12:35 . . . 359
12:35-37. . 432
12:35-40. . 472,
 475, 527
12:35-48.27, 44,
 357, 442,
 510, 530
12:36 .115, 360
12:36-38. . 358
12:36-40. . 364
12:37 274, 360,
 475
12:38 360, 363,
 475
12:38-40. . . 44
12:39 .357, 360

12:39-40. . 358,
 361, 424
12:40 49, 359-60
12:41 90, 360-61
12:41-48. . . 44
12:42 . 90, 361
12:42-48. . 358
12:43 .361, 364
12:44 . . . 361
12:45 359, 361,
 363
12:45-46. . 359,
 364
12:46 . . . 361
12:47 . . . 362
12:48 . .362-63
12:49 135, 364-
 65
12:49-53. . 363,
 443
12:50 .139, 365
12:50-53. . . 45
12:51 . 364-65,
 485
12:51-53. . 117,
 350
12:52 . 92, 365
12:53 .302, 365
12:54 . . . 367
12:54-56. . 527
12:54-13:17 372
12:55 . . . 367
12:56 233, 367-
 68, 372
12:57 . . . 367
12:57-59. . 369,
 371, 442
12:58 . 367-68,
 424
12:59 . . . 367
13:1 . .127, 370
13:1-5 114, 369,
 371
13:1-9 . . . 368
13:1-35 . . 386
13:2 . .237, 370
13:3 369-70, 376
13:4 . 237, 370,
 372
13:5 369-70, 376
13:6 370
13:6-9 133, 369,
 376,
 385, 442
13:7 . .370, 377
13:8 . .371, 375
13:8-9 . . . 424
13:9 . .133, 371
13:10 . . . 373
13:10-13. . 376
13:10-17.20, 50,
 369,
 371, 480

13:11 . 20, 140,
 372-74
13:11-13. . .129
13:12 . .372-73
13:13 373
13:14 . 189, 373
13:15 . 90, 374
13:15-16. . 372,
 387
13:15-17. . .408
13:16 . 374, 386
13:17 . 79, 374-
 75, 504
13:18 . .376-77
13:18-21. . 372,
 375,
 378, 401
13:19 . 82, 118,
 376-77,
 430, 440
13:20 377, 401,
 525
13:21 345
13:22 . 41, 378
13:22-30. . 377,
 421
13:22-17:10 .297
13:23 . .46, 90,
 378, 380
13:24 . 379-81,
 416, 420
13:25 . 90, 379
13:25-27. . 378,
 530
13:26 379
13:26-27. . .435
13:27 379
13:28 . 378-79,
 416
13:28-29. 46-47,
 274
13:38-30. . 381,
 551
13:29 182, 380,
 381,
 424, 548
13:30 . . 50, 94,
 133,
 380-81,
 454, 548
13:31 127, 381-
 82
13:32 . 20, 381-
 82, 385,
 426
13:32-33. . 108,
 365
13:32-34. . . 38
13:33 41, 46, 49,
 56,
 86, 137,
 478, 383,
 461

13:33-34. . 205,
 382,
 385, 489
13:33-35. . 117,
 511
13:34 . 41, 383,
 473, 486
13:34-3528, 369-
 70
13:35 . . 25, 98,
 384,
 386, 480-
 81, 510
14:1 . .235, 386,
 388, 391
14:1-6 . 20, 374,
 385, 388,
 401, 480
14:1-24 385, 392
14:2 386
14:3 . .374, 386
14:4 387
14:5 387
14:6 387
14:7 . . .388-89
14:7-8 507
14:7-11 . . .388
14:7-14 387, 392
14:8 . . .388-89
14:8-10 . . .392
14:9 389
14:10 340, 388-
 89, 541
14:11 . 93, 129,
 389-90,
 395, 450-
 51, 454
14:12 390
14:12-1453, 133,
 294, 388
14:13 50, 390-91
14:14 . 91, 388,
 390,
 392, 499-
 500
14:15 .388, 392,
 394,
 441
14:15-24. . 133,
 181,
 391, 400-
 401, 458,
 460, 519
14:16 . 392-93,
 422
14:16-17. . .392
14:17 . .392-93
14:18 393
14:18-20. . .395
14:19 425
14:20 393
14:21 . 50, 391,
 393

14:21-23 . . 392,
  394
14:22 . . . 393
14:23 .393, 419
14:24 137, 394-
  95
14:25 . . . 396
14:25-33 . . 519
14:25-35 . . 394,
  419-20
14:26 . 53, 240,
  251,
  302, 396,
  443, 459
14:26-27 45, 396
14:26-35 . . 402
14:27 . 51, 279,
  397,
  399, 585
14:28 . .396-97
14:28-32 . . 396,
  404
14:29 . . . 397
14:30 . . . 397
14:31 . . . 397
14:32 . . . 398
14:33 . 52, 181,
  183,
  398, 509
14:34 . . . 398
14:35 . . . 398
15:1 . . 73, 133,
  233, 402,
  449, 568
15:1-2 181, 258,
  400, 402
15:1-3 .402, 404
15:1-29 . . 344
15:1-32 . . . 50
15:2 . 401, 403,
  408
15:2-3 . . . 469
15:3 403
15:3-32 . . 258
15:4 403
15:4-10 114, 402
15:5 . .403, 468
15:6 . .400, 403
15:6-7 79
15:7 51, 93, 125,
  183,
  400, 403,
  406, 409
15:8 404
15:9 . .400, 403
15:9-10 . . . 79
15:10 . .51, 93,
  125, 348,
  400, 404,
  406, 409
15:11 401, 404,
  422, 449

15:11-24. . 401
15:11-32. . 422,
  553
15:12 . . . 405
15:13 .405, 413
15:15 . . . 405
15:16 . . . 405
15:17 406-7, 413
15:17-21. . 409
15:18 . . . 406
15:19 . . . 406
15:20 . . . 406
15:21 . . . 406
15:22 . . . 407
15:23 . . . 407
15:24 .400, 407
15:25 . . . 407
15:25-32. 401-2,
  404
15:26 . . . 407
15:27 . . . 407
15:28 .400, 407
15:29 . . 407-8
15:29-32. . 402
15:30 405, 407,
  449
15:31 . . . 425
15:31-32. . 408
15:32 . 79, 400,
  407
16:1 . . .411-14
16:1-8 . 410-11,
  415,
  420, 445
16:1-9 27
16:1-13 . . 411
16:1-31 354, 410
16:2 . .413, 420
16:3 413
16:3-7 . . . 389
16:4 . . .412-13
16:5 . . .412-13
16:5-7 . . . 414
16:7 . .411, 413
16:8 . 232, 411,
  413,
  425, 502
16:8-9 27
16:9 . . 53, 133,
  411,
  414-16, 459
16:9-12 . . 344
16:9-13 . . 412
16:9-15 411, 415
16:9-18 . . 415
16:10 . . . 417
16:10-12. . 470
16:10-13. 53-54
16:11 . 414-15,
  417
16:11-12. . 427
16:12 . . . 417

16:13 . . 28, 54,
  357, 417,
  420, 456
16:14 . 417, 421
16:14-15. . 401,
  410, 449
16:14-31. . .411
16:15 . 418, 508
16:16 43-44, 47,
  75,
  77, 100,
  125, 160,
  184, 187,
  328, 418,
  421, 460
16:16-17. . 410,
  415
16:16-18. . .421
16:16-31. . .411
16:17 . 73, 118,
  419
16:18 419
16:19 423
16:19-26. . 421,
  426
16:19-31. 50, 53,
  54, 93, 357,
  374, 401,
  410, 415,
  420-22, 470
16:20 423
16:21 423
16:22 . 416, 424
16:22-23. . .420
16:22-39. . . 44
16:23 424
16:24 424, 425,
  433
16:25 . 94, 425
16:26 . 425, 427
16:27 425
16:27-31. . . 77,
  416, 421,
  427
16:28 . 420, 425
16:29 426
16:29-31. . .427
16:30 . .425-26
16:30-31. . . 51
16:31 . . 38-39,
  258, 270,
  336, 401,
  426-27
17:1 . . 429, 432
17:1-3 428
17:2 429
17:3 . 346, 429,
  432
17:3-4 428
17:4 430
17:5 429-30, 432
17:5-6 . 90, 428,

  453
17:6 . . 430, 467
17:7 . .340, 430,
  432
17:7-10 .27, 428
17:7-35 . . .436
17:8 430
17:9 430
17:10 .203, 430,
  448, 451
17:11 41
17:11-19. 20, 50,
  164, 172,
  299, 432
17:11-19:27 432-
  33, 467
17:12 433
17:13 .424, 433,
  463
17:14 .173, 433,
  513
17:15 . 434, 435
17:15-18. . .624
17:16 . 434, 435
17:17-18. . .434
17:17-19. . .432
17:18 435
17:19 51, 99, 434
17:20 . 436-37,
  441
17:20-21. 44, 47,
  160,
  328, 436-
  38, 441, 460
17:20-37. . 435,
  510
17:21 . 436-37,
  439
17:22 . 42, 436-
  38, 441,
  511
17:22-37. . 436,
  438, 444,
  446, 447,
  453, 472,
  492, 531
17:22-18:8 . 44
17:23 . .436-38
17:24 287, 436-
  39
17:25 38, 46, 56,
  278,
  436-37,
  439, 567
17:26 . . 49, 73,
  436,
  438, 439
17:26-30. . 437,
  442
17:27 439
17:27-28. . 358,
  442

17:28 . .438-39
17:29 .135, 440
17:30 . 49, 436,
     438, 440
17:31 . . . 440
17:31-35. . 437
17:32 . . . 440
17:33 353, 440,
     442
17:34 . . . 440
17:34-35. . 442,
     449
17:35 . . . 441
17:36 . . . 441
17:37 . 90, 437,
     441
18:1 . . 52, 444,
     446-48,
     471, 530,
     554, 559
18:1-5 . . . 413
18:1-8 . .47, 50,
     412,
     442-43
18:1-11 . . 568
18:2 . . .444-45
18:2-5 . . . 118
18:2-8 . . . 508
18:3 444
18:3-5 . . . 463
18:4 445
18:5 445
18:6 90, 413, 445
18:7 . 445, 446,
     525
18:7-8 100, 445,
     515
18:8 44, 49, 445,
     446,
     448, 530
18:9 . 418, 448,
     450, 471
18:9-14 50, 233,
     429,
     447-48,
     452-54,
     455, 465-66
18:9-30 . . 455
18:10 . . . 449
18:10-13. . 133,
     447
18:11 435, 449,
     451
18:11-12.465-66
18:12 . . . 449
18:13 448, 450-
     51,
     470, 568
18:13-14. . . 23
18:14 . .54, 93,
     129,
     390, 418,

450, 454-
     55, 504
18:15 297, 447,
     452-53
18:15-1728, 296,
     452, 455,
     466
18:15-43. . . 28
18:15-19:10 452
18:15-21:38 296
18:16 . .452-54
18:17 . 50, 314,
     452,
     455, 458
18:18 50-51, 53,
     132,
     315, 392,
     417, 455-
     56, 459, 463
18:18-20. 51, 73
18:18-22. . 150
18:18-23. . 316
18:18-30. . 118,
     354,
     453-54,
     465-66
18:19 .455, 457
18:19-20. . . 46
18:19-23. . 568
18:20 .455, 457
18:21 .457, 466
18:22 50, 53-54,
     133,
     183, 456,
     457, 460,
     473
18:23 458, 464,
     467
18:23-25. . 460
18:24 455, 458,
     460,
     466
18:24-25. 46, 50,
     53,
     434, 455-57
18:25 . . . 458
18:25-26. . .51,
     392, 502
18:2651, 53, 458
18:27 . 92, 459,
     469
18:28 .200, 459
18:28-30. . 240,
     456
18:29 .456, 459
18:29-30. . 251
18:30 315, 417,
     459,
     502
18:31 38, 41, 55,
     106,
     461-62,

464, 566,
     573
18:31-33. . .461
18:31-34. . 122,
     460
18:32 . .38, 56,
     461, 576
18:32-33. . .567
18:33 . 38, 122,
     383,
     461, 605
18:34 . 54, 123,
     291,
     461, 462
18:35 . 55, 463-
     64, 467
18:35-43 . 156,
     462, 466,
     469, 484
18:37 463
18:38 463
18:38-39. . 424,
     433,
     463-64, 477
18:39 463
18:40 463
18:41 90, 464-65
18:4251, 99, 464
18:42-43 . .434
18:43 . 98, 108,
     464
19:155, 467, 469
19:1-10 50, 459,
     465
19:2 . . 133, 467
19:3 . . 102, 467
19:4 . . 467, 499
19:5 46, 50, 467,
     469
19:6 .79, 467-68
19:7 .50, 468-69
19:8 .50, 53, 90,
     134, 344,
     451, 466-69
19:9 . . 99, 108,
     466, 468,
     490
19:9-10 . . . 47
19:10 31, 49-50,
     93, 99, 115,
     183, 466,
     469-70,
     593, 597
19:11 41-43, 55,
     442, 447,
     472, 475,
     515
19:11-27. . 471,
     476, 543
19:12 405, 471-
     73, 477
19:13 473

19:14 . 84, 472-
     73, 475,
     481
19:14-15. . .477
19:15 473
19:16 473
19:16-23. . .492
19:17 31, 473-74
19:18 473
19:19 . .473-74
19:20 473
19:21 473
19:22 474
19:23 474
19:24 474
19:26 . 249, 474
19:27 . 84, 472,
     474-75
19:28 . 55, 106,
     478
19:28-40 . .492
19:28-21:38 . 31,
     531
19:29 478
19:29-31. . . 38
19:29-24:53 . 41
19:30 . 478-79,
     538
19:30-35. . .479
19:31 . 90, 479,
     538
19:32 . 479, 538
19:32-34. . . 38
19:33-34. . .479
19:34 90
19:35 479
19:35-38. . .475
19:36 479
19:37 . .79, 98,
     109,
     196, 477,
     479, 536
19:38 . .49, 84,
     109,
     382, 471,
     478, 480,
     482, 590
19:38-39. . . 49
19:39 .477, 481,
     507
19:39-40 . .476
19:40 . 477, 481
19:41 . 483, 583
19:41-44 42-43,
     117, 137,
     476, 481,
     482, 486,
     510, 511,
     582, 586
19:41-48 . .482
19:42 484
19:42-44 . .486

19:43 . . . 484
19:43-44. . . 25
19:44 31, 47, 484
19:45 . 485, 510
19:45-46. . 482, 486
19:46 . 123, 485
19:47 122, 485-87, 531
19:47-48. . 108, 117, 482-83, 486-87, 493, 494
19:48 486, 491, 499, 536
20:1 73, 77, 166, 487, 490, 494, 570
20:1-8 . 49, 129, 487, 578
20:2 488
20:3 488
20:3-4 . . . 496
20:3-8 . . . 570
20:4-6 75
20:4-7 . . . 139
20:5 488
20:6 . 488, 491, 493
20:7 488
20:8 489
20:9 . 490, 491, 494
20:9-18 . . 481
20:9-19 489, 511
20:10 . .491-92
20:11 . . . 492
20:11-13. . 494
20:12 . . . 492
20:13 . 49, 140, 491-92
20:14 . 117, 492
20:15 . 491, 493
20:15-16. . 491
20:16 137, 491-93, 536
20:17 . 38, 493
20:17-19. . 117
20:18 491, 493-95
20:19 136, 493-95, 499, 536
20:20 461, 497, 499
20:20-24 . . . 43
20:20-26. . .44, 495, 555, 573-74, 576
20:21 51, 497-98
20:22 . . . 497
20:23 . . . 498

20:24 . . . 498
20:25 . 51, 496, 498
20:26 110, 498, 504
20:27 . 175, 501
20:27-38. . . 47
20:27-40 28, 499
20:28 . . . 501
20:29 . . . 502
20:30 . . . 502
20:31 . . . 502
20:33 . . . 502
20:34 . 500, 502
20:35 500, 502-4
20:36 . . . 502
20:37 . . . 503
20:37-38. . 500
20:38 . . . 503
20:39 . . . 503
20:39-40. . 504
20:40 . 500, 504
20:41 . . . 505
20:41-44. . 504
20:42 . . . 505
20:42-44. . . 90
20:43 . . . 506
20:44 . . . 506
20:45 . . . 507
20:45-47. . 506
20:46 . . 507-8
20:46-47. . 417
20:47 118, 160, 507-8
21:1 509
21:1-4 . . .50, 94, 118, 508
21:2 509
21:3 . . . 508-9
21:4 509
21:5 510
21:5-6 . . . 510
21:5-19 . . 519
21:5-24 . . 137, 384, 520, 523
21:6 511
21:6-7 . . . 514
21:7 . . 512, 521
21:7-8 . . . 514
21:7-11 28, 511-12, 516
21:8 513-14, 520
21:8-9 . . . 513
21:8-24 . . 512
21:9 .46, 513-15
21:9-10 . . 514
21:10 . . . 514
21:10-19. . 525
21:11 512, 514, 524
21:12 . 516, 518

21:12-17. . .517
21:12-18. . .515
21:12-19. . 512, 515-16, 518
21:13 . . 517-18
21:14 517
21:14-15. . 349, 525
21:15 38, 517-18
21:16 517
21:16-17. . . 45
21:17 517
21:18 517
21:19 516, 518-19
21:20 25, 519-20
21:20-24 42, 512, 519-20
21:21 73, 520-22
21:22 . 520-51, 523
21:23 104, 132, 520-51, 526
21:24 520, 522-23
21:25 512, 524, 528
21:25-26. 525-31
21:25-27. . .523
21:25-28. . 492, 512, 523
21:25-36. . .44, 512, 526
21:26 524
21:27 109, 129, 524, 530
21:27-28 47, 100
21:28 . 99, 525
21:29 527
21:29-30. . .526
21:29-33. . .525
21:30 528
21:31 528
21:32 44, 528-29
21:32-33. . .526
21:33 . . 528-29
21:34 358
21:34-35. 529-30
21:34-36. . 447, 476, 529
21:35 . 524, 530
21:36 . 52, 447, 527, 529-30
21:37 . 531, 558
21:37-38. . 122, 476, 531
21:38 . 98, 108, 476, 531
22:1 27, 121, 535
22:1-2 534
22:1-6 . .533-34

22:1-38 . . .534
22:1-23:56 . 31, 476, 533
22:2 499, 535-36
22:3 . .148, 535, 551
22:3-6 38
22:4 . . .535-36
22:5 536
22:6 536
22:6-16 . . . 42
22:7 . . .27, 537
22:7-13 537, 540
22:7-23 . . .533
22:8 . . .537-38
22:10 538
22:10-12. . . 38
22:11 . 538, 541
22:12 538
22:13 . .38, 538
22:14 46, 49, 56, 537, 540
22:14-20.93, 539
22:14-38. . .546
22:15 541
22:15-18. . .539
22:15-20. . .540
22:16 51, 541-42
22:17 542
22:17-18. . .542
22:18 47, 92, 542
22:19 . 55, 542, 544
22:19-20. . 540, 545
22:20 55-57, 187, 539-40, 543-45, 548, 611
22:21 . 546-47, 563
22:21-22.38, 563
22:21-23. . 539, 545
22:22 . 46, 546-47, 563
22:23 547
22:24 548
22:24-27. . . 54, 247, 548
22:24-30. . 545, 547
22:24-38. . .533
22:25 549
22:26 549
22:27 . .45, 549
22:28 . 55, 548, 549, 557
22:28-30. . 545, 548
22:29 123, 550-51

22:29-30. . 356
22:30 160, 550-
    51, 554
22:31 148, 552,
    559, 565
22:31-34. . . 38,
    545, 551,
    563, 565
22:32 . .52, 76,
    546,
    552-54, 565
22:33 . 90, 553
22:34 348, 553-
    54, 561
22:35 303, 555,
    591
22:35-36. . 269
22:35-38. . 267,
    539, 545,
    554
22:36 550, 555-
    56, 562
22:37 38, 46, 56,
    554-56,
    559, 561
22:38 . 90, 556
22:39 121, 557-
    58
22:39-46. . 537
22:39-53. . 533
22:39-23-56 557
22:40 . 52, 329,
    530, 554,
    558, 562
22:40-41. . 139
22:41 . . . 558
22:42 20, 27, 46,
    558-59
22:43 . . . 121
22:43-44. . 557,
    559
22:44-45. . 594
22:45 285, 559,
    617
22:46 . 52, 326,
    530,
    554, 557,
    559, 562
22:47 .560, 594
22:47-48. . .38,
    237, 560
22:47-53. . 557,
    559,
    563, 568
22:48 . . . 561
22:49 . 90, 379,
    561
22:49-50. . 556
22:49-51. . 560,
    562
22:50 . . . 561
22:51 20, 560-62

22:52 . .560-61
22:52-53. . 560
22:53 560, 562,
    566
22:54 .560, 564
22:54-55. . . 65
22:54-6238, 553,
    559, 563
22:54-23:25 533
22:54-23:49 557
22:55 . . . 564
22:56 . . . 564
22:56-62. . . 65
22:57 . . . 564
22:58 . . . 564
22:59 . . . 565
22:60 . . . 565
22:61 . 90, 565
22:62 . . . 565
22:63 .461, 566
22:63-65. . 563,
    566
22:63-23:38 . 38
22:64 . .566-67
22:65 . 566, 592
22:66 . 568-69,
    574
22:66-71. . 563,
    573, 576
22:66-23:25 344,
    489,
    494, 567
22:67 . 49, 140,
    570,
    572, 578
22:67-68. . 489
22:67-70. . .49,
    568, 572
22:68 . . . 570
22:69 42-43, 92,
    570, 572,
    625
22:70 . .49, 86,
    140, 571,
    572, 574
22:71 568, 571-
    72
22:71-23:2. 571
23:1 . . 461, 574
23:1-5 . . . 573
23:1-12 . . 114
23:1-56 . . 127
23:2 49, 84, 574,
    580, 597
23:2-3 . 49, 475
23:3 . . 84, 574
23:4 44, 56, 575,
    579, 580,
    583, 592
23:4-26 . . 587
23:5 573, 575, 580
23:5-7 73

23:6 578
23:6-10 . . .503
23:6-12 . . 271,
    576, 580
23:7 578
23:7-12 . . .127
23:8 578
23:9 . . 56, 578
23:10 .578, 580
23:11 449, 566,
    573, 578
23:12 .577, 578
23:13 . 579-80,
    584, 611
23:13-16. . .579
23:14 . 579-80,
    592
23:14-15. . . 56,
    579, 583
23:14-16 44, 575
23:15 . 44, 577,
    579, 580,
    592, 597
23:16 . 579-80,
    583
23:17 581
23:18 581, 584,
    599
23:18-20. . . 27
23:18-23. . .579
23:18-25. . .581
23:19 582
23:20 575, 580,
    582-83
23:21 .582, 584
23:22 . .44, 56,
    579-80,
    582-84, 592
23:22-24. . .575
23:23 582
23:23-25. . .576
23:24 582
23:24-25. . .579
23:25 .582, 584
23:26 .584, 587
23:26-32. . .583
23:26-49 . .533
23:27 .585, 587
23:27-28. . .598
23:27-31. . .584
23:28 585
23:28-29. . .595
23:28-31 25, 484
23:29 . 44, 586
23:30 586
23:31 586
23:32 586
23:32-33. . .556
23:33 588
23:34 210, 299,
    588, 591
23:35 . .49, 56,

115,
    587-90, 598
23:35-37.49, 593
23:35-39. . .590
23:36 .566, 588,
    590
23:37 . 84, 588,
    590
23:37-38. . . 49
23:38 . 84, 465,
    588, 590
23:39 . 49, 588,
    592, 593
23:39-43 . 556,
    591
23:40 75, 92, 98,
    592
23:40-43 . . 50
23:41 . 592, 597
23:42 592
23:43 .108, 593,
    595
23:44 595
23:44-49 . .594
23:45 . . 20, 27,
    115,
    594-95
23:46 . . 595-96
23:47 44, 56, 73,
    584,
    592, 596-97
23:48 .587, 591,
    595-96, 598
23:49 596
23:50 73, 598-99
23:50-51. . .114
23:50-56. . 533,
    557, 598
23:51 . . 20, 27,
    115, 598-99
23:52 599
23:53 . 599, 607
23:54 . 598, 600
23:55 .600, 603,
    611
23:55-56.50, 600
23:56 . 73, 118,
    598, 600,
    601, 603
24:1 . . 604, 610
24:1-11 . . . 50
24:1-12 . 602-3
24:1-53 31, 476,
    533, 602
24:2 604
24:3 . . .90, 604
24:4 108
24:4-8 603
24:5 . . 604, 617
24:5-6 574
24:5-7 123
24:6 605

24:6-7 . . . 292
24:7 .38, 46, 56,
    122, 383,
    605, 607
24:8 605
24:9 . .605, 610
24:10 .604, 606
24:11 . . . 606
24:12 . 86, 110,
    574, 606
24:13 . . . 610
24:13-16. . 609
24:13-35. . .93,
    292, 602,
    608
24:14 . . . 610
24:16 . . . 610
24:17-27. . 609
24:18 . 36, 610
24:18-21. . 607
24:19 . .49, 92,
    108,
    463, 610
24:20 . . . 611
24:20-24. . 610
24:21 . 99, 122,
    611
24:22 . . . 122
24:22-23. . 611,
    614
24:23 .603, 614
24:24 .607, 611
24:25 . . . 612
24:25-2623, 122-
    23
24:25-27. . 607,
    613
24:26 . .49, 56,
    109, 612
24:26-27. . .46,
    607, 614
24:27 . . . 612
24:27-32. . 426
24:28 . . . 612
24:28-32. . 609
24:29 . . . 612
24:29-30. . 274
24:30 . 98, 612
24:30-35. . 616
24:31 . . . 613
24:3237-38, 613-
    14
24:33 . . . 613
24:33-35. . 610
24:34 . .74, 90,
    607,
    609, 613-15
24:35 .614, 625
24:36 .616, 622
24:36-43. . 602,
    615, 619
24:37 .604, 617

24:38 . . . 617
24:39 . .617-18
24:40 . . . 617
24:41 . .75, 79,
    110, 606,
    615, 617
24:42 . . . 618
24:43 . . . 618
24:44 . 46, 619
24:44-46. . 607
24:44-47. . 292
24:44-49. . 462,
    602,
    615, 619
24:45 . 123, 620
24:44-51. . 359
24:46 . .49, 56,
    122, 620
24:46-47. . . 56
24:46-48. . 269
24:46-49. . 195,
    518
24:47 50-51,101,
    125,
    128, 130,
    183, 620
24:47-49. . 307
24:48 . 37, 248,
    621
24:49 21, 38, 47-
    48, 77,
    123, 135,
    140, 621
24:49-53. . . 41
24:50 . 478, 624
24:50-51. . . 98
24:50-53. . 615,
    622
24:51 . . . 624
24:5250, 75, 624
24:52-53. . . 21
24:53 . .74, 98,
    109,
    118, 624
John
1:1-3. 85
1:4. 116
1:5. 116
1:6-8. . . . 184
1:8. 489
1:9. 116
1:11 117
1:13 250
1:14 542
1:15 . . 90, 184
1:19-34 . . 489
1:20 . .134, 489
1:31-33 . . 139
1:33 135
1:34 143
1:35 129
1:47-48 . . 467

1:51 139
2:4. 163
2:16 123
2:18 336
2:20 510
3:1 382
3:2. . . 126, 364
3:3-5. 456
3:16 . 456, 460,
    489
3:22-23 . . .136
3:27 488
3:29 90
3:35-36 . . .313
3:36 . . 381, 460
4:1-2. 136
4:9. 318
4:19 309
4:20-21 . . .318
4:35 305
4:42 99
4:44 158
4:46-53 . . .217
4:48 336
5:1-18 . 188, 373
5:18 . . .176-77
5:19-30 . . .313
5:24 460
5:24-25 . . .301
5:28-29 . . .390
6:2. 272
6:9. 274
6:14 226
6:25 321
7:7. 157
7:15 158
7:20 233
7:23-24 . . .188
7:28 90
7:30 . .160, 562
7:37 90
8:12 116
8:20 562
8:37 133
8:39 . . 133, 425
8:44 132
8:46 139
8:48 318
8:48-49 . . .233
8:51 115
8:52 280
8:53 133
8:59 159
9:3. 370
9:5. 116
9:13 373
9:13-16 . . .188
9:32 465
10:11-15. . .403
10:14 379
10:18 597
10:20 233

10:27 379
10:27-29. . .552
10:28 518
10:33 177
10:35 168
10:36 177
10:41 77
11:1 321
11:1-2:11 . .336
11:16 194
11:31-33. . .232
11:35 483
11:41 450
11:45 426
11:49-50. . .571
11:49-53. . .473
11:52 332
12:1-8. . . .235
12:5 236
12:9-11 .39, 335
12:11 426
12:16 620
12:19 309
12:25 . 279, 397
12:46 116
13:1 . . 121, 541
13:2 535
13:3-17 . . .549
13:13-14. . .237
13:16 213
13:18 326
13:27 . . 535-36
13:37 553
14:3 441
15:9 550
15:13-15. . .347
15:14 216
15:21 517
16:6 559
16:20 202
16:20-22. . .559
16:25 245
16:29 245
17:1 . . 450, 541
17:6-26 . . .552
17:7 625
18:3 560
18:10 561
18:11 566
18:12 560
18:13 127
18:13-27. . .564
18:14 571
18:19 127
18:23 157
18:24 127
18:25 564
18:26 565
18:31 574
18:36-37. . .573
18:37 575
18:38 583

19:1 583
19:2 578
19:4 583
19:6 583
19:7 571
19:15 . . . 581
19:16 . . . 584
19:17 .493, 588
19:18 . . . 588
19:19 .573, 590
19:25 . . . 117
19:25-27. . 596
19:29-30. . 590
19:30 . . . 596
19:31-33. . 600
19:37 . . . 589
19:38 . . . 599
20:1 601
20:3-4 . . . 607
20:5 607
20:11-18. . 616
20:14-15. . 610
20:17 .324, 623
20:19 .613, 616
20:20 . . . 616
20:21 . . . 550
20:21-23. . 619,
   621
20:24 . . . 194
20:25 .588, 606
20:26 . . . 613
20:27 . . . 606
20:30-31. . 178
20:1-23 . . 605
21:2 194
21:4 610
21:15-17. . 354,
   361
21:15-19. . 553
Acts
1:121, 25-26, 66,
   602
1:1-2. 62
1:1-5. 21
1:1-7. . . . 462
1:2 .191-92, 298,
   342
1:3 .46, 541, 623
1:4 . . . 41, 298
1:4-5 .21, 38, 48,
   79, 135
1:4-8. . . . 140
1:5 . 47, 76, 102,
   134,
   135
1:6 . . .379, 475
1:6-8. 42
1:6-9. 43
1:7 524
1:821, 26, 37-38,
   42, 47-48,
   50, 63, 77,

85, 135,
   191, 248,
   250, 267,
   269, 272,
   304, 307,
   328, 525,
   621
1:9 . . .286, 624
1:9-10 21
1:1074, 157, 604
1:11 .43, 44, 47,
   52, 298,
   472, 524
1:12 624
1:13 191
1:14 .50, 52, 91,
   107, 139,
   240, 251
1:15 . . . 39, 89
1:15-26 550, 605
1:16 . . 46, 100,
   505, 564
1:16-18 . . 427
1:16-21 . 38, 46
1:21 . . 77, 604
1:21-22 . 37, 64,
   549, 618
1:21-26 . . . 64
1:22 . . 77, 126,
   193, 608
1:24 . . 195, 344
1:24-25 . . . 74
1:24-26 . . . 52
1:25-26 . . 608
1:26 . . 74, 191
2:1 . .38, 48, 74,
   76, 79,
   102, 135,
   544
2:1-2. 47
2:1-4 . . . 139
2:3 74, 135, 364,
   620
2:5 50
2:7 . . .110, 122
2:12 122
2:14 191
2:14-36 . . . 48
2:14-40 22, 154
2:14-42 . . 195
2:15 449
2:16-21 .38, 41,
   44, 78, 157,
   527
2:17 218
2:17-21 42, 130,
   418
2:18 104
2:20 595
2:2199, 116, 139
2:2239, 272, 480
2:22-25 . . . 46

2:22-36 . . . 48
2:23 . . 46, 343,
   461, 546,
   572, 597
2:24-36 . . . 39
2:25-28 . . . 38
2:25-36 . . . 78
2:27 115
2:30-31 . . . 49
2:31 617
2:32 . . . 37, 63
2:32-36 503, 506
2:33 . .550, 612
2:33-35 224, 608
2:33-36 . . .481
2:34-35 . . . 38
2:36 49, 90, 278
2:37 . 132, 315,
   319
2:37-41 . . .100
2:38 . . 51, 101,
   125, 128,
   130, 183,
   404, 451
2:38-39 . . . 48
2:40 . 129, 183,
   232
2:41 39
2:42 52, 93, 274
2:42-47 . . .613
2:43 39, 98, 258
2:44-45 53, 391
2:44-47 . . .357
2:46 . . 93, 274
2:4739, 109, 517
3:1 52
3:1-10 50
3:6 293
3:7 20
3:8-9 109
3:9 517
3:12 110
3:12-16 . . . 39
3:12-18 . . . 78
3:12-26 . . . 48
3:13 .41, 49, 56,
   611
3:13-14 . . . 56
3:13-23 . . . 48
3:14 .49, 56, 73,
   85-86, 226,
   596
3:14-15 . . .572
3:15 .37, 49, 63,
   608
3:16 51
3:17 589
3:18 .38, 46, 49,
   56,
   100, 115,
   278, 541
3:19 51, 76, 125,

553
3:21 . . .44, 100
3:22-23 . . . 38
3:22-26 . . . 78
3:24 65
3:24-26 . . . 41
3:25 . . .38, 342
3:25-26 .41, 469
3:26 . . . 49, 56
4:1 501
4:1-22 44
4:2 . . . 122, 502
4:4 . . 39, 51, 64,
   243, 246
4:5 218
4:5-22 38
4:6 127
4:8 . 76, 79, 218
4:8-12 48
4:8-13 328
4:9 580
4:10 608
4:10-12 . . . 48
4:11 449
4:11-12 . . .495
4:12 . . 99, 111,
   113, 410
4:13 110
4:17-20 . . .309
4:23 218
4:23-31 . . .139
4:24 115
4:25 . .100, 116,
   505
4:25-26 .38, 577
4:26 115
4:26-27 . . 140,
   143, 156,
   578
4:26-28 . . .517
4:27 .49, 56, 86,
   116, 127
4:27-28 . . .577
4:29 64
4:30 . 49, 56, 86
4:31 .52, 64, 76,
   79, 328
4:32 . . .53, 466
4:33 . . 195, 517
4:34-35 . . . 50
4:34-37 . . .550
4:35 391
5:1-11 53
5:3 535
5:4 53
5:5 . 20, 98, 258
5:10 20
5:11 . . .98, 258
5:12 39
5:13 91
5:14 39
5:17 . . .77, 501

5:17-40 . . . 44
5:19-20 . . . 74
5:25 122
5:29 496
5:30 . . 56, 592,
    608, 611
5:31 49, 99, 101,
    108, 125,
    128, 130,
    506, 550
5:31-32 . . . 51
5:32 37
5:33-39 . . . 40
5:34-39 . . 481
5:34-40 . . 382
5:35 346
5:36 36
5:36-37 . . 114
5:38 46
5:38-39 . . . 40
5:41 79, 203, 468
5:42 77, 109, 166
6:1 . 39, 50, 118
6:1-2 50
6:1-6 . . 241, 550
6:3 118
6:4 . 52, 64, 246
6:5 76
6:6 . 52, 195, 373
6:7 39
6:8 39
6:9 159
6:14 64
6:15 157
6:20-26 . . . 93
7:1 379
7:1-8:3 44
7:2 74
7:2-53 . . 41, 78
7:2-60 38
7:12 346
7:18-35 . . . 75
7:25 99
7:30 74
7:31 110
7:35 74
7:41 104
7:48 83
7:51 387
7:51-52 . . 342
7:52 56, 73, 137,
    205,
    572, 597
7:54 136
7:55 75, 76, 612
7:55-56 . . 625
7:56 . . 139, 506
7:58 159
7:59 596
7:59-60 . . 210
7:60 299
8:1 . 42, 50, 299

8:1-3 555
8:3 367
8:4 243
8:4-25 50
8:5 . . . 42, 128
8:8 79
8:12 . . . 46, 51
8:12-13 128, 454
8:13 . . 39, 480
8:15 52
8:15-17 . . 139
8:18-19 . . 294
8:21 163
8:22 . . 52, 128
8:24 52
8:26 74
8:26-40 50, 620
8:27-40 . . . 38
8:32-33 . . . 56
8:33 92
8:35 77
8:36-37 . . . 51
8:39 . . 79, 468
9:1-2 . . 44, 555
9:1-19 . . . 431
9:2 42
9:3-19 42
9:4-5 293
9:11-12 . . 139
9:15-16 . . . 38
9:15-19 . . 623
9:17 . 74, 76, 79,
    373
9:18 51
9:20 . . 86, 140
9:20-25 . . . 38
9:21 122
9:22 . . 86, 140
9:23-25 . . . 44
9:24 446
9:29 63
9:31 . 40, 42, 50
9:33 20
9:35 76
9:36 53
9:37 . . 73, 104
9:39-43 . . 118
9:40 . . 52, 223
9:43 73
10:1 42
10:1-2 50
10:2 . 52-53, 219
10:2-6 . . . 139
10:4 . . . 52-53
10:6-16 . . 543
10:9 52
10:9-16 . . 139
10:11 . . . 139
10:12 . . . 244
10:20 . . . 219
10:22 . 73, 114,
    219, 601

10:23 219
10:25-26 . . .625
10:28 220
10:30 604
10:30-31 . . . 52
10:31 53
10:34-35 . . .381
10:34-43 . . 48
10:34-48 . . 42
10:35 51
10:36 102, 109,
    126, 238
10:36-43 . . 48
10:37 . 73, 126,
    128
10:37-38 . . 140,
    143
10:38 . 77, 140,
    156, 267,
    486, 583
10:38-39 . . .575
10:39 20, 27, 56,
    276,
    592
10:39-41 37, 263
10:40 . 122, 383
10:41 279
10:42 . 49, 312,
    367,
    546, 586
10:43 . . 38, 51,
    101, 130
10:44-45 . . 65
10:44-48 48, 622
10:46 91
10:47-48 . . 51
11:1-17 . . .330
11:1-18 . . . 42
11:2 106
11:2-3 187
11:3 . . 182, 306
11:4 65
11:4-18 . . .182
11:5 52
11:6 244
11:13 139
11:14 434
11:15 65
11:15-16 . 76, 79
11:15-18 . . .622
11:16 38, 134-35
11:17-18 . . 48
11:18 . 51, 125,
    182,
    404, 434
11:19 42
11:19-20 . . 21
11:20 77
11:21 . . 40, 76
11:24 . . 40, 76
11:26 . 49, 286,
    601

11:27 106
11:27-28 . . . 38
11:28 . 36, 105,
    514
11:28-30 . . . 38
11:49-51 . . . 38
12:1-5 . .44, 555
12:1-23 . . .127
12:7 108
12:7-11 . . . 74
12:12 52
12:14 617
12:19 580
12:23 20, 23, 434
12:24 40
13:1 . . 42, 127,
    269, 577
13:1-3 308
13:1-4 21
13:2-3 .139, 184,
    195
13:3 . . .52, 187
13:4-5 22
13:5 . 20, 27, 38
13:9 . . . 76, 79
13:13 22
13:15 . 155, 620
13:16 219
13:16-37 . . . 78
13:16-41 41, 48
13:17 45
13:17-23 . . 45
13:18 45
13:19 45
13:20 45
13:21 45
13:21-23 . . .481
13:22 45
13:23 45, 49, 99,
    108
13:23-40 . . 48
13:24 .125, 128,
    304
13:24-25 . . .126
13:26 . 99, 219
13:26-39 . . .410
13:27 . 38, 589
13:27-28 . . 572,
    611
13:29 . .56, 599
13:31 37, 64, 75,
    106
13:32-33 . 41, 47,
    157
13:33 503
13:33-38 . . . 39
13:34 38
13:35 38
13:36 46
13:38 . 101, 130
13:38-39 . . .319
13:41 . 110, 607

13:45 . . . 566
13:45-47. . .40,
    394, 470,
    493
13:46 . 42, 137,
    249,
    315, 380,
    417, 456
13:46-47.26, 38,
    371
13:46-48. . .27,
    521, 523
13:4756, 99, 130
13:47-48. . 394
13:48 315, 417,
    456
13:50 44
13:51 . . . 268
13:52 . . 76, 79
14:1 . 20, 27, 40
14:3 . . 39, 158
14:9 99
14:11 . . . 284
14:14 73
14:15 76
14:16 46
14:19 44
14:21 40
14:22 . 46, 432
14:23 . 52, 184,
    187
14:25-26. . . 22
14:26-28. . . 21
15:1 99
15:1-3 21
15:1-5 . . . 187
15:1-29 22, 108
15:2 106
15:3 50
15:5 . .382, 481
15:6 163
15:7-11 . . . 42
15:8 . . . 344
15:9 51
15:11 . . 51, 99
15:12 39
15:12-21. . . 48
15:13-21. . . 42
15:13-40. . . 21
15:1447, 99, 223
15:16-17. . . 38
15:19 76
15:21 . . . 128
15:22 . . . 549
15:24-26. . . 62
15:28 65
15:35 . . . 166
15:39 26
16:5 40
16:9 . . . 51, 74
16:10-17. . . 21
16:13-17. . . 22

16:15 .269, 331
16:17 . 99, 256,
    600
16:25 . . . 203
16:26 52
16:28 . . . 596
16:3050-51, 132,
    248, 319,
    395
16:31 51, 79, 99,
    263, 469
16:31-33. . 128
16:33-34. . 293
16:34 . 79, 269
16:36 . . . 238
16:40 . . . 251
17:1 . . . 20, 27
17:2 38
17:3 46, 109, 279
17:6-7 . . . 574
17:7 49, 85, 105,
    480
17:11 . . . 150
17:14-15. . . 22
17:17 . . . 551
17:18 . 77, 407,
    617
17:24 . . . 312
17:26 . . . 546
17:26-27. . . 46
17:28 . . . 503
17:30 . 51, 404,
    589, 426,
    546, 586
17:31 46-47, 49,
    160, 414
17:31-32. . 617
18:2 36
18:5-6 . 26, 523
18:6 .27, 38, 42,
    92,
    137, 249,
    371, 380,
    394, 490,
    493, 566
18:8 128
18:9-10 . . . 38
18:10 .108, 518
18:11-18. . . 38
18:12 36
18:12-17. . . 44
18:14 . . . 454
18:18 22
18:18-30. . 454
18:21 22
18:22 51
18:22-23. . . 21
18:23 65
18:25 . . . 134
18:25-26 66, 184
19:1 69
19:1-7 .134, 184

19:2 48
19:4 128
19:4-5 128
19:8 46
19:8-10 . . . 51
19:13 . 63, 309
19:13-14. . .331
19:13-16. . 292,
    294
19:17 . . 91, 98
19:20 40
19:23-41 . . 44
19:27 38
19:35-37. . . 44
19:40 . 44, 413
19:43-44 . . 38
19:47-48 . .490
20:1-2 22
20:4-5 23
20:5-21:18. . 21
20:7 . . 93, 604
20:7-12 . . . 22
20:11 93
20:18-38. . . 22
20:19 550
20:20 73
20:21 51
20:25 46
20:25-31. . .431
20:27 46
20:28 49, 55, 57,
    289, 346,
    410, 545
20:28-31. . . 36
20:29-30. . .429
20:29-31. . .513
20:31 .118, 446
20:32 158
20:35 53
20:37 406
21:5 52
21:5-24 . . . 38
21:6 459
21:7-27:1 . . 29
21:9 117
21:10-11. . . 38
21:11 . . 20, 27
21:12 106
21:13 .203, 553
21:15 106
21:20 73
21:21 66
21:24 . . 66, 73
21:28 . . .573
21:33 38
21:36 581
22:3 . .258, 321
22:10 132
22:12 . 73, 118
22:12-16. . .623
22:14 . 73, 362
22:16 128

22:17-21. . .139
22:20 544
22:21 38
22:22 581
22:30 574
23:1-10 . . . 38
23:3 49
23:6 500
23:6-8 501
23:6-9 175
23:6-10 . . .503
23:7 574
23:8 499
23:9 177
23:11 . 108, 518
23:26 . . 26, 65
23:28-31. . . 38
23:29 . .56, 553
23:35 . .49, 127
23:39 49
24:2 26
24:2-21 . . .574
24:3 65
24:5 575
24:5-6 574
24:8 580
24:10-23. . . 38
24:15 . 73, 115,
    500, 504
24:21 500
24:23 44
24:25-35. . .462
24:26 49
24:26-27. . . 44
24:31 462
24:44-47 . .462
25:136, 106, 122
25:2 485
25:5 592
25:5-22 . . .574
25:7 106
25:8 . . 118, 429
25:9 106
25:11 . .56, 226
25:16 226
25:18-19. . . 44
25:21 105
25:25 . .56, 105
26:1-32 . . . 38
26:4-5 65
26:6 41
26:7 . . 118, 446
26:12 346
26:12-18. . . 42
26:16 63-64, 74
26:16-18. . . 38
26:17 116
26:18 . . 51, 76,
    101, 130,
    156, 250,
    580
26:18-20. . .130

26:20 . .51, 76,
125, 132,
553
26:22-23 . 38, 46
26:23 . . . 116
26:25 . . 26, 65
26:26 . 36, 130,
149,
532, 610
26:31 56
26:32 44
27:1-38 . . 184
27:1-28:16. . 21
27:23-24. . . 38
27:24 . . . 226
27:25 91
27:34 99
27:35 . . . 435
27:44 38
28:2-10 . . . 22
28:7 122
28:8 . . . 20, 52
28:15 . . . 435
28:16-31. . . 42
28:17 . 73, 485
28:20 41
28:23 46
28:24-28. . . 27
28:25-28 . 26, 38,
137, 394,
490, 493,
523
28:25-29. . 462
28:26-27. 38, 42
28:26-30. . 371
28:27 76
28:28 42, 46, 99,
116, 380
23:31 46-47, 71,
166
Romans
1:3 82
1:3-4. 86
1:4 .49, 503, 608
1:16 280
2:2-11 . . . 414
2:5-11 . . . 390
2:13 216
2:18 362
3:9-20 . . . 457
3:10-20 . . 448
3:10-23 . . 182
3:25 450
3:25-26 . . 612
3:27 448
4:6-8 451
4:25 56
5:8-10 . . . 208
6:13 301
6:23 370
8:9-11 23
8:14-17 . . 324

8:15 90
8:15-16 . . 324
8:23 . . 47, 325
8:31-34 . . 326
8:35-39 . . 347
9:2-5. . . . 434
9:7. 83
9:13 397
9:20 333
9:27 90
9:31 331
9:33 117
10:5-17 . . 427
10:9 51
10:18 . . . 333
11:17 . . . 133
11:25 . . . 245
11:26-27. 384-85
12:1 114
12:2 418
12:19 . 445-46,
521
13:1-5 . . . 498
13:1-7 . . . 496
13:4 446
13:6 497
13:9 . .316, 457
14:1-23 . . 431
14:9 605
14:13-23. . 305
15:3 203
1 Corinthians
1:7. 440
1:19-25 . . 312
1:22 . .331, 336
1:31 . .311, 452
2:4 77
3:11 495
3:15 359
3:19 418
5:1-13 . . . 429
5:6 346
5:7 540
6:1-8. . . . 366
6:2-3. . . . 550
7:15 420
7:28-35 . . 322
7:32-35 . . 321
8:3 379
9:1 193
9:5 . . .164, 251
10:1-5 . . . 547
10:14-33. . 431
10:16 . . . 543
10:25-31. . 305
11:2 64
11:5 117
11:23 . 64, 273,
534
11:24 540, 542-
43
11:25-26. . 534

11:26 534, 541,
543
11:26-34. . .541
11:29-30. . .547
12:12-31. . .293
12:13 . 23, 135
13:2 . . .430-31
15:3 64
15:3-5 612
15:3-8 . 410, 613
15:4 600
15:5 . 192, 616,
618
15:35-50. . .618
15:50 618
15:58 199
16:22 325
2 Corinthians
1:3-4 99
1:22 . . 47, 625
1:24 549
3:16 76
4:16 205
4:17 205
5:1-5. 500
5:5 47
5:10 . . 211, 412
5:17 451
5:21 56, 139, 612
6:2 394
10:14 331
10:17 452
11:3 310
11:30 311
12:4 593
12:12 39
Galatians
1:4. . . 56, 543
1:14 341
1:15 76
1:19 251
2:1-10 22
2:6 497
2:11-14 . . .409
2:12 306
2:12-13 . . .182
2:15 182
3:10-14 . . .612
3:13 . . 56, 592
3:16 469
4:4 . . . 113, 230
4:4-7. . 209, 324
4:6 . . . 90, 324
5:6. . . 252, 316
5:14 316
6:6 . . . 66, 306
Ephesians
1:3 621
1:3-10 99
1:13 625
1:14 47
1:21 459

2:1. 301
2:1-3 409
2:8. 451
2:20 495
3:20 . . 274, 332
5:14 301
5:18 76
6:18 558
Philippians
1:21-23 500, 593
2:6-7 107
2:6-9 283
2:9-11 . 49, 506,
570, 572,
608
2:10-11 325, 384
2:11 506
2:15 289
2:21 431
3:4-9 450
3:5. 97
3:8. . . 333, 451
3:9. . . 451, 465
3:16 331
3:20 109
3:21 92
Colossians
2:14 588
2:15 310
4:10-14 . . . 20
4:14 . . . 20, 23
1 Thessalonians
1:9. 76
1:10 461
2:13 246
2:15 343
2:16 331
4:5. 356
4:13-18 . . .325
4:14 461
4:17 . .286, 441,
593
5:2. 440
5:2-3 529
5:2-4 360
5:6. 558
5:17 444
2 Thessalonians
1:5. 502
3:6-13 208
3:8. 326
1 Timothy
1:13 589
2:6. 56
4:1. 246
5:8. 302
5:19 225
6:6-10 351
6:17-19 . . .356
2 Timothy
2:4. 301
2:8. 82

2:12 550
2:15 349
2:19 379
4:1 390
4:11 23
Titus
2:13 446
2:14 56
Philemon
24 23
Hebrews
2:4 39
2:9 . . .280, 283
2:14-18 . . 123
3:12 246
4:15 139
5:8 144
5:8-9 123
6:1-8 396
6:4 433
6:5 459
7:26 139
9:6-28 . . . 595
9:14 139
9:20-22 . . . 55
9:25-28 544
9:27 412
10:28 . . . 225
10:29 . . . 244
11:5 115
11:18 83
11:26 . . . 203
11:34 . . . 522
13:7 549
13:12-13 . . 493
13:17 .413, 549
James
1:6-8 430
1:10 92
1:11 367

1:12 327
1:22 216
1:22-25 . . 216
2:5 201
2:11 457
2:16 238
2:17 252
2:25 321
3:1 361
3:11-12 . . 137
4:3 328
4:7 347
4:9 202
5:5 423
5:17 159
1 Peter
1:3 502
1:3-5 99
1:10-12 . . 313
1:21 283
2:6-8 117
2:13-14 . . 498
2:13-17 . . 496
2:19-20 . . 208
2:21 589
2:23 578
2:24 56
2:25 76
3:18 56
4:5 413
4:12-13 . . 327
4:14 . .203, 517
4:16 517
4:19 596
5:2 549
5:2-3 361
5:3 549
5:8 558
5:9 347

2 Peter
1:10 381
1:15 284
1:16-18 . . .283
2:4 257
2:21 64
3:3-7 442
3:4 . . .362, 475
3:4-10 475
3:8 446
3:10 360
3:12 419
1 John
1:1-3 37
1:1-4 227
1:9 . . .326, 329
2:1 552
2:2 450
2:16 144
3:5 56
3:17 427
4:10 450
4:19 237
3 John
7 517
Jude
3 64
7 135
Revelation
1:3 513
1:10 . . 115, 604
1:17-18 . . .264
1:18 381
2:3 517
2:7 593
2:10 327
2:13 348
2:26-29 . . .550
3:3 360
3:10 558

3:15-17 . . .396
3:20 360
3:21 550
4:1 139
6:10 445
6:12-14 . . .514
6:16 586
7:17 202
10:4 139
10:8 139
11:2 . . 159, 522
11:12 . 139, 286
12:6 159
12:9 310
12:14 159
12:14-15 . . .310
14:10-11 . . .135
14:13 139
14:15-16 . . .305
14:18 596
16:15 360
18:11 202
18:12 423
18:15 202
18:19 202
19:1-2 109
19:2 445
19:6-8 109
19:7-9 360
19:11 139
19:19 360
20:2 310
20:3 . . 163, 257
20:9-10 . . .163
20:11-15 . . 335,
        504
21:4 . . 202, 503
22:10 513
22:20 . 215, 325
22:19 559

Selected Bibliography

Books and Commentaries

Badia, L. F. *The Qumran Baptism and John the Baptist's Baptism.* Lanham, Md.: University Press of America, 1980.

Bailey, J. A. *The Traditions Common to the Gospels of Luke and John.* NovTSup 7. Leiden: Brill, 1963.

Benoit, P. *The Passion and Resurrection of Jesus.* New York: Herder, 1969.

Blomberg, C. L. *The Historical Reliability of the Gospels.* Downers Grove: InterVarsity, 1987.

———. *Interpreting the Parables.* Downers Grove: InterVarsity, 1990.

———. *Jesus and the Gospels.* Nashville: Broadman & Holman, 1998.

Bock, D. L. *Luke.* Baker Exegetical Commentary on the New Testament. 2 vols. Grand Rapids: Baker, 1994–96.

———. *Luke.* IVP New Testament Commentary. Downers Grove: InterVarsity, 1994.

———. *Luke.* NIV Application Commentary. Grand Rapids: Zondervan, 1996.

———. *Proclamation from Prophecy and Pattern: Lucan Old Testament Christology.* JSNTSup 12. Sheffield: Sheffield Academic Press, 1987.

Bovon, F. *Luke the Theologian: Thirty-Three Years of Research (1950–1983).* Princeton Theological Monograph Series, No. 12. Allison Park: Pickwick, 1987.

Brown, R. E. *The Birth of the Messiah.* Garden City: Doubleday, 1979.

———. *The Death of the Messiah.* New York: Doubleday, 1994.

———. *The Virginal Conception and Bodily Resurrection of Jesus.* New York: Paulist, 1973.

Brown, S. *Apostasy and Perseverance in the Theology of Luke.* AnBib. Rome: Pontifical Biblical Institute, 1969.

Bultmann, R. *The History of the Synoptic Tradition.* New York: Harper, 1968.

Cadbury, H. J. *The Style and Literary Method of Luke.* Cambridge: Harvard University Press, 1920.

———. *The Making of Luke-Acts.* London: SPCK, 1958.

———. "Commentary on the Preface of Luke." In *The Beginnings of Christianity.* Edited by F. J. Foakes-Jackson and K. Lake. London: Macmillan, 1922.

Catchpole, D. R. *The Trial of Jesus.* SPB. Leiden: Brill, 1971.

Chance, J. B. *Jerusalem, the Temple, and the New Age in Luke-Acts.* Macon: Mercer, 1988.

Childs, B. S. *The New Testament as Canon: An Introduction.* Philadelphia: Fortress, 1984.

Conzelmann, H. *The Theology of St. Luke.* New York: Harper, 1960.

Danker, F. *Jesus and the New Age.* Philadelphia: Fortress, 1988.

Daube, D. *The New Testament and Rabbinic Judaism.* London: Athlone, 1956.

Dibelius, M. *Studies in the Acts of the Apostles.* New York: Scribner, 1956.

Drury, J. *Tradition and Design in Luke's Gospel.* London: Darton, Longman & Todd, 1976.

Ellis, E. E. *The Gospel of Luke*. NCB. Grand Rapids: Eerdmans, 1981.

Esler, P. F. *Community and Gospel in Luke-Acts*. Cambridge: University Press, 1987.

Evans, C. A. *Luke*. Peabody, MA: Hendrickson, 1990.

Evans, C. F. *Saint Luke*. TPINTC. London: SCM, 1990.

Farmer, W. *Luke the Theologian: Aspects of His Teaching*. London: Geoffrey Chapman, 1989.

Farris, S. *The Hymns of Luke's Infancy Narratives*. JSNTSup. Sheffield: JSOT, 1985.

Fitzmyer, J. A. *The Gospel according to Luke*. AB. 2 vols. Garden City: Doubleday, 1979–85.

———. *Luke the Theologian*. Mahweh, N.J.: Paulist, 1989.

Flender, H. *St. Luke: Theologian of Redemptive History*. SNTMS 57. London: SPCK, 1967.

Gasque, W. W. *A History of the Criticism of the Acts of the Apostles*. Grand Rapids: Eerdmans, 1975.

Goulder, M. D. *Luke: A New Paradigm*. Sheffield: JSOT, 1989.

Green, J. B. *The Theology of the Gospel of Luke*. Cambridge: University Press, 1995.

———. *The Death of Jesus*. WUNT. Tübingen: Mohr, 1988.

Guelich, R. A. *The Sermon on the Mount: A Foundation for Understanding*. Waco: Word, 1982.

Hemer, C. J. *The Book of Acts in the Setting of Hellenistic History*. Tübingen: Mohr, 1989.

———. *The Book of Acts in the Setting of Hellenistic History*. WUNT 49. Edited by C. Gempf. Tübingen: Mohr, 1989.

Hoehner, H. W. *Chronological Aspects of the Life of Christ*. Grand Rapids: Zondervan, 1977.

Jeremias, J. *Jerusalem in the Time of Jesus*. Philadelphia: Fortress, 1969.

Jervell, J. "The Law in Luke-Acts." In *Luke and the People of God*. Minneapolis: Augsburg, 1972.

Johnson, L. T. *The Gospel of Luke*. Sacra Pagina. Collegeville, MN: Liturgical, 1991.

———. *The Literary Function of Possessions in Luke–Acts*. SBLDS 39. Missoula: Scholars, 1977.

Juel, D. *Luke-Acts: The Promise of History*. Atlanta: John Knox, 1983.

Kingsbury, J. D. *Conflict in Luke: Jesus, Authorities, Disciples*. Minneapolis: Fortress, 1991.

Kümmel, W. G. *Introduction to the New Testament*. Nashville: Abingdon, 1975.

———. *Promise and Fulfillment*. London: SCM, 1961.

Laurentim, R. *The Truth of Christmas*. Petersham: St. Bede's, 1986.

Machen, J. G. *The Virgin Birth of Christ*. New York: Harper, 1930.

Maddox, R. *The Purpose of Luke-Acts*. Edinburgh: T & T Clark, 1982.

Marshall, I. H. *The Gospel of Luke*. NIGTC. Grand Rapids: Eerdmans, 1978.

———. *Luke: Historian and Theologian*. Grand Rapids: Zondervan, 1989.

Mattill, A. J., Jr. *Luke and the Last Things*. Dillsboro: Western N.C. University Press, 1979.

Minear, P. S. "Luke's Use of the Birth Stories." In *Studies in Luke–Acts*. Edited by L. E. Keck and J. L. Martyn. New York: Abingdon, 1966.

Nolland, J. *Luke 1–9:20, 9:21–18:34, 18:35–24:53*. WBC. 3 vols. Waco/Dallas: Word, 1989–93.

O'Toole, R. F. *The Unity of Luke's Theology: An Analysis of Luke-Acts*. GNS 9. Wilmington: Glazier, 1984.

Pilgrim, W. *Good News to the Poor.* Minneapolis: Augsburg, 1981.

Plummer, A. *A Critical and Exegetical Commentary on the Gospel according to St. Luke.* ICC. Edinburgh: T & T Clark, 1896.

Powell, M. A. *What Are They Saying about Luke?* New York: Paulist, 1989.

Sabourin, L. *The Gospel according to St. Luke.* Bandra, Bombay: St. Paul Publications, 1984.

————. *The Divine Miracles Discussed and Defended.* Rome: Catholic Book Agency, 1977.

Sanders, E. P. *Jesus and Judaism.* Philadelphia: Fortress, 1985.

————. *Paul and Palestinian Judaism.* Philadelphia: Fortress, 1977.

Sanders, J. T. *The Jews in Luke-Acts.* Philadelphia: Fortress, 1987.

Schweizer, E. *The Good News according to Luke.* Atlanta: John Knox, 1984.

Seccombe, D. P. *Possessions and the Poor in Luke-Acts.* Studien zum Neuen Testament und seiner Umwelt. Freistadt: Plochl, 1982.

Stein, R. H. *Difficult Passages in the New Testament.* (Grand Rapids: Baker, 1990).

————. *Gospels and Tradition.* Grand Rapids: Baker, 1991.

————. *An Introduction to the Parables of Jesus.* (Philadelphia: Westminster, 1981).

————. *The Method and Message of Jesus' Teachings.* Rev. ed. (Philadelphia: Westminster, 1994).

————. *The Synoptic Problem.* Grand Rapids: Baker, 1987.

Strack, H. L. and P. Billerbeck. *Kommentar zum Neuen Testament.* München: C. H. Beck'sche, 1956.

Talbert, C. H. *Reading Luke.* New York: Crossroad, 1982.

Tannehill, R. C. *The Narrative Unity of Luke–Acts.* Philadelphia: Fortress, 1986.

Tiede, D. *Prophecy and History in Luke-Acts.* Philadelphia: Fortress, 1980.

Tolbert, M. O. "Luke." BBC. Vol. 9. Nashville: Broadman, 1970.

van Unnik, W. C. "*Dominus Vobiscum*: The Background of a Liturgical Formula." In *New Testament Essays.* Edited by A. J. B. Higgins. Manchester: University Press, 1959.

Wilson, S. G. *The Gentiles and the Gentile Mission in Luke–Acts.* Cambridge: University Press, 1973.

————. *Luke and the Law.* SNTSMS 50. Cambridge: University Press, 1983.

Witherington, B., III. *Women in the Earliest Churches.* SNTSMS. Cambridge: University Press, 1988.

————. *Women and the Genesis of Christianity.* Cambridge: University Press, 1990.

Articles and Journals

Bauckham, R. J. "The Delay of the Parousia." *TynBul* 31 (1980): 3–36.

Blomberg, C. L. "Interpreting the Parables of Jesus: Where Are We and Where Do We Go from Here?" *CBQ* 53 (1991): 50–78.

————. "The Law in Luke-Acts." *JSNT* 22 (1984): 53–80.

Carter, W. "Zechariah and the Benedictus (Luke 1,68–79): Practicing What He Preaches." *Bib* 69 (1988).

————. "Luke's Use of the Elijah/Elisha Narratives and the Ethic of Election. *JBL* 106 (1987): 75–83.

Catchpole, D. R. "The Answer of Jesus to Caiaphas. *NTS* 17 (1970).

Evans, C. A. "Luke's Use of the Elijah/Elisha Narratives and the Ethic of Election." *JBL* 106 (1987): 75–83.

———. "Is Luke's View of the Jewish Rejection of Jesus Anti-Semitic?" In *Reimaging the Death of the Lukan Jesus*. Edited by D. D. Silva. Frankfurt: Anton Hain, 1990.

Good, R. S. "Jesus, Protagonist of the Old, in Luke 5:33–39." *NovT* 25 (1983): 19–36.

Green, J. B. "'The Message of Salvation' in Luke-Acts." *ExAuditu* 5 (1989): 21–34.

Hiers, R. H. "The Problem of the Delay of the Parousia in Luke-Acts." *NTS* 20 (1974): 145–55.

Johnson, L. T. "The New Testament's Anti-Jewish Slander and the Conventions of Ancient Polemic." *JBL* 108 (1989): 419–41.

Kodell, J. "Luke and the Children: The Beginning and End of the Great Interpolation (Luke 9:46–56; 18:9–23)." *CBQ* 49 (1987): 415–30.

Payne, P. B. "The Authenticity of the Parable of the Sower and Its Interpretation." In *Gospel Perspectives*. Edited by R. T. France and D. Wenham. Sheffield: JSOT, 1980.

Robbins, V. K. "The Woman Who Touched Jesus' Garment." *NTS* 33 (1987): 506–7.

Smith, M. "Zealots and Sicarii, Their Origins and Relation." *HTR* 64 (1971): 1–19.

Stein, R. H. "The 'Criteria' for Authenticity." In *Gospel Perspectives*. Edited by R. T. France and D. Wenham. Sheffield: JSOT, 1980.

———. "Is the Transfiguration (Mark 9:2–8) a Misplaced Resurrection-Account?" *JBL* 95 (1976): 79–96.

———. "What Is Redaktionsgeschichte?" *JBL* 88 (1969): 45–56.

Trites, A. A. "The Prayer Motif in Luke-Acts." In *Perspectives on Luke-Acts*. Edited by C. H. Talbert. Danville, VA: Association of Baptist Professors of Religion, 1978.

———. "The Transfiguration in the Theology of Luke: Some Redactional Links." In *The Glory of Christ in the New Testament*. Edited by L. D. Hurst and N. T. Wright. Oxford: Clarendon, 1987.

Wachsmann, S. "The Galilee Boat—2,000-Year-Old Hull Recovered Intact." *BAR* 14.5 (1988): 18–33.

Wenham, J. "The Identification of Luke." *EvQ* 63 (1991): 3–44.